The Lion
Handbook
to the
Bible

Consultants and Advisers

The Rev. Dr G. Mike Butterworth
Principal of the St Albans and Oxford Ministry Course;
specialist in Old Testament history and Prophets

Dr David Instone Brewer
Research Fellow, Tyndale House and Library for Biblical
Research, Cambridge

The Rev. Dr R.T. France
Former Principal of Wycliffe Hall, Oxford; New Testament
scholar and writer

Dr Sue Gillingham
Fellow and Tutor in Theology, Worcester College, Oxford
and University Lecturer in Theology (Old Testament);
specialist in Psalmody

Alan R. Millard
Rankin Professor of Hebrew and Ancient Semitic
Languages, University of Liverpool; Fellow of the Society
of Antiquaries and international lecturer on biblical
archaeology

The Rt Rev. John B. Taylor
Old Testament scholar and former Bishop of St Albans

Dr Stephen Travis
Vice-Principal and Director of Research, St John's
College, Nottingham; New Testament specialist

Dr Ben Witherington
Professor of New Testament Interpretation, Asbury
Theological Seminary, Wilmore, Kentucky; adviser of
doctoral students, University of St Andrews; sometime
Fellow of Robinson College, Cambridge

The Lion
Handbook
to the
Bible

THIRD EDITION
Completely revised and expanded

Edited by
PAT AND DAVID ALEXANDER

A LION BOOK

Copyright © 1999 Pat and David Alexander

The authors assert the moral right
to be identified as the authors of this work

Published by
Lion Publishing plc
Sandy Lane West, Oxford, England
www.lion-publishing.co.uk
ISBN 0 7459 3870 1

First edition 1973
Second edition 1983
Third edition 1999
10 9 8 7 6 5

All rights reserved

Design, maps and graphics
by Tony Cantale Graphics

A catalogue record for this book
is available from the British Library

Printed and bound in Slovenia

PREFACE

The Bible is the world's most widely-distributed and widely-read book. Some read it out of curiosity, some as part of a spiritual search, others because of its rich cultural heritage.

This Handbook is designed for use with the Bible; to stand alongside it. It is not just for reference, telling the reader *about* the Bible. The intention is to bring together on-page, where it happens, information that would otherwise have to be gathered from a number of different reference books. This is provided visually as well as through the written word. The pictures, maps and graphics are there, not to decorate the text but to illuminate its meaning. The Handbook can be used with any version of the Bible.

As well as being a book to have alongside the Bible, the Handbook also aims to be alongside the reader, to be inviting and approachable. In editing the Handbook we have had especially in mind those who may be new to the Bible. So no background knowledge is assumed. The many expert contributors communicate in a simple – not simplistic – way. Technical terms are kept to a minimum. Where they need to be used, they are explained.

The first aim is to help readers understand the actual text of the Bible. The 'Bible-guide' sections – Part 2 on the Old Testament, Part 3 on the New – go through each Bible book, section by section, summarizing and providing notes where explanation is needed. Short feature articles, written by specialists, allow particular interests to be followed up in more detail.

The next steps are to interpret what is read and to appreciate what the Bible may be saying to us today. That means discovering whether a particular book is written as poetry or prose, as story or letter – and its historical setting. The charts and feature articles in Part 1 are designed to help with this. And Part 4, the Rapid Factfinder, makes it quick and easy to locate information about people, places and subjects, and to find pictures.

Opening the Bible at Genesis and reading right through to Revelation is not usually the best way to begin! 'Reading the Bible' (in Part 1) offers a number of helpful alternatives. The Handbook is ready to hand wherever you decide to begin: with a Bible book, a Bible character, a particular issue, biblical archaeology, culture, literature. For some the fun lies in dipping in; for others in working through.

Why a completely new edition?

The Handbook was first published in 1973. In 1983 it was revised to take account of the important new translations which had appeared in the interval. Over 25 years, sales have approached the three million mark and the Handbook has been published in 28 languages around the world. In the words of an Asian publisher, it proved to be a 'seminal work'.

The aim of this major revision is to serve readers in the new millennium. The opportunity to do a complete re-write and re-design fired our imagination. We have many new pictures to help bring the past to life, and the book has all-new maps and graphics. It has taken account of develop-ments in biblical scholarship, and roots the Bible firmly in history. It also reflects the more recent concerns of readers. We have invited many new contributors, women and men, to share their expertise. A poet writes on Psalms, a gifted author with many years' experience in the Middle East has written character studies of the women of the Bible. We have reflected people's interests – in care for the creation, in story (which plays such a major part in the Bible narrative), in justice, in the role of women,

in a multi-faith society, in the place of the Bible in the world today...

As in the previous editions, the Bible text has been taken largely as it stands, in sympathy with its different types of literature. The major concern is the content and meaning of the Bible, rather than matters of purely technical interest. Where scholars disagree, we have tried to say so, without necessarily going into the debate.

We are grateful to the scholars for sharing the fruits of their labour with a wide audience. The standard reference works at a more academic level have been a vital source of information. We thank all who have contributed to this book directly or indirectly, by sharing insights into the Bible's teaching, making their own material readily available, or simply by their own delight in the study of the Bible and their conviction of its relevance and power to transform life.

We are also grateful to those who have helped in many other ways. Some are listed under 'Acknowledgments', though this hardly does justice to the enthusiastic assistance received from a wide variety of sources – from directors of specialist museums and collections to those who provided hospitality, help, information and above all encouragement.

On a personal note, no other book has played such a significant role in our own lives as the Bible. We hope that the Handbook in its new form will help future generations of readers to understand the Bible afresh.

Pat and David Alexander
Oxford

Contents

INTRODUCING THE BIBLE

THE OLD TESTAMENT

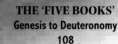

3

THE NEW TESTAMENT
Full contents listing on page 525

Introduction
527

THE GOSPELS AND ACTS
Matthew to Acts
538

THE LETTERS
Romans to Revelation
674

4

RAPID FACTFINDER
Page 779

Authors and Contributors

David and Pat Alexander, editors of the original Handbook; until 1994 respectively Publishing Director and Editorial Director of Lion Publishing, Oxford:
- *All photographs (except those listed in Acknowledgments) especially taken by David Alexander*
- *Outline-guide to the Bible in Parts 2 and 3, with notes and articles not otherwise attributed, by Pat Alexander*

The Rev. David Barton, Head of Advisory Services, Diocese of Oxford Schools Department:
- *Jacob, Joseph, David, Portrait of Jeremiah*

The Rev. Dr Craig Bartholomew, Research Fellow in the School of Theology and Religious Studies, Cheltenham and Gloucester College of Higher Education:
- *The text and the message*

Dr Richard Bauckham, Professor of New Testament Studies, University of St Andrews:
- *A story through women's eyes (Ruth), Women's perspectives in the Gospels, Understanding Revelation*

R.J. Berry, Professor of Genetics, University College London:
- *A geneticist comments on the virgin birth*

Dr John Bimson, Director of Studies and Lecturer in Old Testament, Trinity College, Bristol; author of *The World of the Old Testament*; consulting editor, *Illustrated Encyclopedia of Bible Places*:
- *Bringing the past to life, Nomadic life, Settled life*

The late **E.M. Blaiklock**, sometime Emeritus Professor of Classics, University of Auckland, New Zealand:
- *The Herod family, A historian looks at the New Testament*

The Rev. Dr Gerald L. Bray, Anglican Professor of Divinity, Beeson Divinity School, Samford University, Alabama; author of *Biblical interpretation, past and present*:
- *Interpreting the Bible down the ages*

The Rev. Dr Richard A. Burridge, Dean of King's College, London, and Hon. Lecturer in Theology; author of *What are the Gospels?, Four Gospels, One Jesus?* and *John* in the People's Bible Commentary series:
- *Studying the Gospels*

The Rev. Dr Mike Butterworth, Principal of St Albans and Oxford Ministry Course; specialist in Old Testament history and Prophets:
- *The Prophets*

The late **George Cansdale**, sometime Superintendent, Zoological Society of London:
- *The quail, Fishing in Lake Galilee*

The Rev. Colin Chapman, Lecturer in Islamic Studies, Near East School of Theology, Beirut; writer on the Arab-Israeli conflict and Christian-Muslim relations:
- *The promised land, 'Holy War'*

Rabbi Dan Cohn-Sherbok, Professor of Judaism, Department of Theology and Religious Studies, University of Wales, Lampeter:
- *The Hebrew Bible*

The Rev. A.E. Cundall, former Principal, Bible College of Victoria, Australia; author of various books and studies related to the Old Testament:
- *Unravelling the chronology of the kings*

Dr Katharine Dell, Lecturer in Divinity, Cambridge University; Fellow, Tutor and Director of Studies at St Catherine's College; specialist on Job and Wisdom literature:
- *Understanding Job, Wisdom in Proverbs and Job*

John H. Eaton, former Reader in Old Testament Studies, University of Birmingham; author of studies on the Psalms and Prophets:
- *The Psalms in their setting*

Dr Mark Elliott, Lecturer in Historical and Systematic Theology, Nottingham University:
- with Dr Stephen Travis: *An approved list – the 'canon' of Scripture, Deuterocanonical books*

Dr Grace I. Emmerson, formerly of the Department of Theology, University of Birmingham:
- *Understanding Hosea*

Mary J. Evans, Course Director in Christian Life and Ministry and Lecturer in Old Testament, London Bible College:
- *Prophets and prophecy*

The Rev. David Field, former Vice-Principal, Oak Hill Theological College, London:
- *The kingdom of God*

The Rev. Dr R.T. (Dick) France, former Principal of Wycliffe Hall, Oxford; New Testament scholar and writer:
- *Jewish religion in New Testament times, Jesus and the Old Testament, 'God with us' – the incarnation, The Old Testament in the New Testament, The Jewish Dispersion*

Frances Fuller, writer, editor and former Director of Baptist Publications, Beirut; resident for many years in the Middle East:
- *Sarah, Hagar, Portrait of Ruth, Hannah, Portrait of Esther, Mary, Martha and Mary, Mary Magdalene*

Dr David Gill, Sub-Dean, Faculty of Arts and Social Studies, Department of Classics and Ancient History, University of Wales Swansea:
- *The Roman province of Judea, The city of Athens, Roman rule, Greek culture, The city of Rome, The city of Corinth, The city of Ephesus*

Dr John Goldingay, Professor of Old Testament, Fuller Theological Seminary, Pasadena, California; author of *Models for Scripture* and *Models for Interpretation of Scripture*:
- *Keys to understanding (the Bible)*

Paula Gooder, Lecturer in Biblical Studies, Ripon College, Cuddesdon, Oxford; specialist studies: evidence for belief in Jewish mysticism in the New Testament, feminist theology, biblical interpretation:
- *Understanding Colossians*

The Rev. Dr Michael Green, New Testament scholar, author and lecturer; Adviser in Evangelism to the Archbishops of Canterbury and York:
- *'Good News!' – from the first Christians, Spiritual gifts*

The Rev. Geoffrey W. Grogan, former Principal, Bible Training Institute, Glasgow:
- *The Holy Spirit in Acts*

Dr P. Deryn Guest, Lecturer in Hebrew Bible studies, Birmingham University, Westhill College:
- *Understanding Judges*

Michele Guinness, Jewish Christian freelance journalist and writer:
- *Passover and the Last Supper*

The late **Dr Donald Guthrie**, sometime Vice-Principal, London Bible College:
- *The Letters* (revised for this edition by The Rev. Dr Stephen Motyer)

Richard S. Hess, Professor of Old Testament, Denver Seminary, Colorado; specialist in the Bible and the ancient Near East:
- *Personal names in Genesis 1 – 11*

Colin Humphreys, Goldsmiths' Professor of Materials Science, Cambridge University:
- *The star of Bethlehem, The census*

Dr David Instone Brewer, Research Fellow, Tyndale House and Library for Biblical Research, Cambridge:
- *Jesus and money, Jesus and the cities, Jesus and women*

The Rev. Philip Jenson, Lecturer in Old Testament Studies, Trinity College, Bristol:
- *A way of life – The Ten Commandments, Old Testament priesthood*

Dr Philip Johnston, Tutor in Old Testament, Wycliffe Hall, Oxford:
- *Old Testament views of the afterlife*

The Rev. F.D. Kidner, former Warden of Tyndale House and Library for Biblical Research, Cambridge:
- *Poetry and Wisdom*

Dr K.A. Kitchen, former Reader in Egyptian and Coptic, School of Archaeology and Oriental Studies, University of Liverpool:
- *Egypt*

Dr Nobuyoshi Kiuchi, Associate Professor of Old Testament, Tokyo Christian University:
■ *Sacrifice*

Dr Todd E. Klutz, Dallas Theological Seminary and Wheaton College Graduate School; doctorate in ancient demonology and exorcism, Sheffield University; Lecturer in New Testament Studies, Manchester University:
■ *Magic in the Old Testament*

J. Nelson Kraybill, President of Associated Mennonite Biblical Seminary, Elkhart, Indiana; author of *Imperial Cult and Commerce in John's Apocalypse*:
■ *Emperor worship and Revelation*

Dr Melba Padilla Maggay, President of the Institute for Studies in Asian Church and Culture, Manila, Philippines:
■ *Cultural perspectives: East and West*

Dr I. Howard Marshall, Honorary Research Professor of New Testament, University of Aberdeen; specialist studies – Luke-Acts, the Letters of John, and the Pastoral Letters (Timothy and Titus):
■ *The Gospels and Jesus Christ, The New Testament miracles*

The Rev. Dr Andrew McGowan, Principal, Highland Theological College, Dingwall, Scotland; Adjunct Professor of Theology, Reformed Theological Seminary, USA:
■ *The twelve disciples of Jesus*

Alan R. Millard, Rankin Professor of Hebrew and Ancient Semitic Languages, University of Liverpool; Fellow of the Society of Antiquaries and international lecturer on biblical archaeology:
■ *The Old Testament and the ancient Near East, Creation stories, Flood stories, Abraham, Where were Sodom and Gomorrah?, Moses, Cities of the conquest, Canaanites and Philistines, The lost Ark, Solomon's Temple and its successors, The scribe, The Assyrians, The Babylonians, The Persians*

Evelyn Miranda-Feliciano, writer and Lecturer, Institute for Studies in Asian Church and Culture, Manila, Philippines:
■ *Justice and the poor*

The Rev. J.A. Motyer, former Lecturer in Old Testament:
■ *The names of God, The significance of the Tabernacle, The Prophets* (with Dr Mike Butterworth)

The Rev. Dr Stephen Motyer, Lecturer in New Testament and Hermeneutics, London Bible College:
■ *The Letters, Paul*

Rt Rev. Dr Michael Nazir-Ali, Bishop of Rochester, former head of the Church Mission Society and formerly Bishop of Raiwind, Pakistan:
■ *The Qur'an and the Bible*

Dr Stephen Noll, Professor of Biblical Studies at Trinity Episcopal School for Ministry, Ambridge, Pennsylvania; author of *Angels of Light, Powers of Darkness: thinking biblically about angels, Satan and principalities*:
■ *Angels in the Bible*

Meic Pearse, Course Leader, London Bible College; visiting Professor of Church History, Evangelical Theological Seminary, Osijek, Croatia:
■ *Our world – their world*

The Rev. Dr John Polkinghorne, former Professor of Mathematical Physics, University of Cambridge; Fellow of the Royal Society:
■ *A scientist looks at the Bible*

Claire Powell, Tutor in New Testament, lecturing in New Testament, Greek, Christology, Hermeneutics and Gender at All Nations Christian College, Ware, Herts:
■ *Women of faith, The Bible through women's eyes*

Professor Sir Ghillean Prance, Director, Royal Botanic Gardens, Kew, England:
■ *People as God's caretakers*

Dr Vinoth Ramachandra, Regional Secretary for South Asia, International Fellowship of Evangelical Students, Colombo, Sri Lanka; author of *The Recovery of Mission, Faiths in Conflict?*:
■ *Jesus in a plural society*

Dr Harold Rowdon, former Lecturer and Resident Tutor, London Bible College; General Editor and International Secretary of Partnership, a network of independent churches:
■ *Roman soldiers in the New Testament, Pilate*

The Very Rev. J.A. Simpson, Dean of Canterbury:
■ *The virgin birth*

The Rev. Vera Sinton, former Director of Pastoral Studies, Wycliffe Hall, Oxford:
■ *Sexual issues in the church at Corinth*

The Rt Rev. John B. Taylor, Old Testament scholar and former Bishop of St Albans:
■ *Introducing the Old Testament, The 'Five Books', Israel's History*

Dr Joy Tetley, Principal of the East Anglian Ministerial Training Course, Cambridge:
■ *Understanding Hebrews*

Dr Stephen Travis, Vice-Principal and Director of Research, St John's College, Nottingham; New Testament specialist:
■ *Reading the Bible*; with Dr Mark Elliott: *An approved list – the 'canon' of Scripture, Deuterocanonical books*

Steve Turner, performance poet, journalist and author of a number of books of poetry and biography:
■ *A poet looks at Psalms*

The Rev. Dr Peter Walker, Tutor in New Testament, Wycliffe Hall, Oxford; author of *Jesus and the Holy City*:
■ *Jerusalem in New Testament times*

The Rev. Dr Steve Walton, Lecturer in Greek and New Testament Studies, and Academic Secretary, London Bible College; specialist on Luke-Acts.
■ *What is the Bible?, Spreading the word – the task of translation*

Walter Wangerin Jr, holder of the Jochum Chair at Valparaiso University, Indiana; teacher on literature and creative writing; theologian and writer; author of *The Book of God: the Bible as a novel*:
■ *The Bible as story*

The Rev. Dr Jo Bailey Wells, Dean, Clare College, Cambridge:
■ *Storykeepers – the oral tradition, The scribes, Editors at work*

Dr Gordon Wenham, Professor of Old Testament Studies, Cheltenham and Gloucester College of Higher Education:
■ *Covenants and ancient Near Eastern treaties*

The Rev. David Wheaton, Canon Emeritus of St Alban's Cathedral; former Principal of Oak Hill Theological College, London; Honorary Chaplain to Her Majesty The Queen:
■ *Jesus' resurrection*

The Rev. Dr D. Wilkinson, Fellow in Christian Apologetics and Associate Director of the Centre for Christian Communication, St John's College, Durham University; theoretical astrophysicist and Fellow of the Royal Astronomical, Society; lecturer and broadcaster on issues related to science and religion; author of *God, the Big Bang and Stephen Hawking* and *Alone in the Universe?*
■ *God and the universe*

Hugh G.M. Williamson, Regius Professor of Hebrew, Oxford University:
■ *Understanding Isaiah*

Robert Willoughby, Lecturer in New Testament, London Bible College; specialist in the Gospels and political theology:
■ *The peace of God, Love*

INTRODUCING THE BIBLE

'Your word is a lamp to my feet and a light to my path.'
Psalm 119:105

STARTING WITH THE BIBLE

The books of the Bible

OLD TESTAMENT (39 books)

THE 'FIVE BOOKS'

■ Genesis
■ Exodus
■ Leviticus
■ Numbers
■ Deuteronomy

These books contain stories of the creation of the world, the great flood and the founding fathers (and mothers!) of the nation of Israel (Genesis); enslavement in Egypt and the exodus (Exodus); and 40 years spent wandering the Sinai 'wilderness'(Numbers; Deuteronomy).

They also record the gift of God's law for his people summed up in the Ten Commandments (Exodus; Deuteronomy) and detailed regulations for sacrifice and worship, centred on the Tabernacle (God's special Tent) (Exodus; Leviticus).

Horus, symbolized by this eye, was one of the gods of Egypt, where the Israelites were enslaved.

ISRAEL'S HISTORY

- Joshua
- Judges
- Ruth
- 1 & 2 Samuel
- 1 & 2 Kings
- 1 & 2 Chronicles
- Ezra
- Nehemiah
- Esther

POETRY AND WISDOM

- Job
- Psalms
- Proverbs
- Ecclesiastes
- Song of Solomon

The ram's horn *shofar* was blown to call the Israelites to war.

THE PROPHETS

- Isaiah
- Jeremiah
- Lamentations
- Ezekiel
- Daniel

- 12 'minor prophets':
  Hosea, Joel, Amos, Obadiah, Jonah, Micah, Nahum, Habakkuk, Zephaniah, Haggai, Zechariah, Malachi

Starting with the conquest of the land God had promised to his people (Joshua), these books continue the story of the nation, its heroes and those who failed the nation by leading them astray from God. The period of rule by 'judges' (Gideon, Samson and the rest) ends with Samuel, Israel's king-maker. After kings Saul, David, and Solomon who built a Temple for God in Jerusalem (1 and 2 Samuel; 1 Kings), ten northern tribes break away to form the kingdom of Israel, while David's line continues in Judah. The fall of Samaria to Assyria marks the end of Israel. But a remnant from Judah survives the destruction of Jerusalem and exile to Babylon, returning home. Renewing their obedience to God's law, they rebuild the Temple and city walls (Ezra; Nehemiah).

These books contain most of the Bible's poetry, and the 'wisdom' (much of it in the form of proverbs: Proverbs, Ecclesiastes) which was particularly popular in the ancient Near East around the time of King Solomon. Job is a poetic drama about suffering. The Psalms are Israel's hymn-book. The Song of Solomon is lyric love-poetry.

God's people often deserted him for other gods. This is a figure of the Canaanite Baal.

The prophets brought God's word to his people: warning of judgment (when they were straying from God and breaking his laws) and encouraging with hope and promises (when times were bleak). Most lived in the 8th and 7th centuries BC, when the nation was under threat, first from the Assyrians, then from the Babylonians. Amos was one who spoke out for justice on behalf of the poor. A few belong to the time of the return from exile. A number of prophecies (the best-known are in Isaiah) look forward to a coming 'Messiah', whom God will send to set his people free and to rule in peace and justice.

DEUTEROCANONICAL BOOKS/APOCRYPHA

A statuette of Artemis (Diana) of Ephesus, the city where Paul's teaching caused a riot.

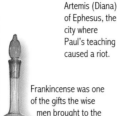

Frankincense was one of the gifts the wise men brought to the infant Jesus.

The earliest surviving fragment of John's Gospel dates from AD125-150.

- Tobit
- Judith
- Additions to Esther
- Wisdom of Solomon
- Ecclesiasticus
- Baruch
- 1 & 2 Esdras
- Letter of Jeremiah

- Prayer of Azariah/Song of the three Jews
- Susanna
- Bel and the Dragon
- 1, 2, 3 & 4 Maccabees
- Prayer of Manasseh

Judea was under Roman military rule in New Testament times.

Much of this additional material, included in Roman Catholic and Common Version Bibles but not generally in Protestant ones, comes from the Greek (Septuagint) translation of the Hebrew Bible. Maccabees recounts the Jewish struggle for independence in the time 'between the Testaments'. See further, 'Deuterocanonical books'.

Pens, ink and pencase from the New Testament period.

John's Gospel records how Jesus turned the water in storage jars like this to wine.

Pontius Pilate, the Roman governor who issued this coin, gave his consent to Jesus' crucifixion

NEW TESTAMENT (27 books)

THE GOSPELS AND ACTS

- Matthew
- Mark
- Luke
- John
- Acts

The four Gospels record the life of Jesus, majoring on his three years as a travelling teacher and healer, and the final week when he was crucified. His resurrection is seen as confirming his claim to be the promised Messiah/'Son of God'. All draw on the eye-witness evidence of his closest followers; each writer has his own particular purpose in telling the story.

Acts is the sequel to Luke's Gospel, the story of how the first Christians, particularly Peter and the convert, Paul, spread the 'good news' of Jesus in the Jewish and Gentile worlds, as far as Rome itself.

Codex Sinaiticus, dating from the 4th century AD, contains the whole New Testament.

THE LETTERS AND REVELATION

- Romans
- 1 & 2 Corinthians
- Galatians
- Ephesians
- Philippians
- Colossians
- 1 & 2 Thessalonians
- 1 & 2 Timothy
- Titus
- Philemon
- Hebrews
- James
- 1 & 2 Peter
- 1, 2 & 3 John
- Jude
- Revelation

The first 13 of these letters – written to newly-formed 'young churches' – deal with particular situations, questions the Christians were raising, and the needs of leaders. All are under the name of Paul, the 'apostle to the Gentiles', whose dramatic conversion is recorded in Acts.

Hebrews (more of a sermon than a letter) is anonymous.

The other, 'general' letters, speak to wider groups of Christians.

Revelation, although a circular letter, is the only New Testament example of 'apocalyptic' writing. Addressed to persecuted Christians, it reassures them that God's purposes are being and will be carried out, until history itself is wound up, evil is finally destroyed, and God's people enjoy his presence for ever in 'a new heaven and a new earth'.

What is the Bible?

Steve Walton

For many people the Bible is an unknown book.

What does it contain?

What is it all about?

It is helpful to see the 'big picture' of what the Bible is about, so that we don't get lost in the detail.

Two ways of looking at the Bible are particularly useful:

■ seeing it as a story

■ and hearing it as a witness.

The big story

The Bible is a superb story-book, full of exciting tales well told. But it is more than just a collection of stories – there is one big story told by the whole collection of individual stories.

At the centre of the big story is God and what he is doing with the world and the human race.

The Bible begins with God creating the heavens and the earth, and tells the story of his dealings with humankind through to the day, yet to come, when he will wrap history up, and war, disease, death and pain will be no more. This big story has six key parts.

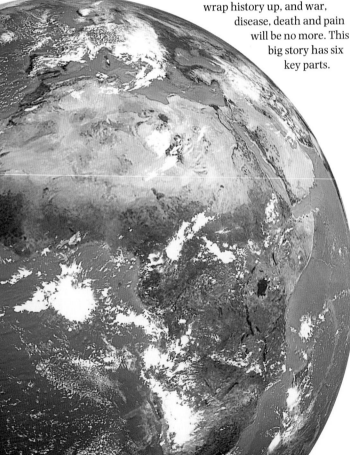

1. Creation

God brought the universe into being out of nothing, by simply speaking. Genesis 1 records six occasions when God spoke and adds, 'And it was so.'

God was pleased with the universe he had created, so that he called it 'very good' (Genesis 1:31). He placed people in his world to care for it and bring out its full potential, giving them responsibility for the animals, birds, trees and plants.

2. 'Fall'

God gave to the first people freedom to explore the garden in which he had placed them, but forbade them to eat the fruit from one particular tree (Genesis 2:15-17). Pressed by a talking serpent (the embodiment of evil), they chose not to do as God wished (Genesis 3:1-7), and God responded by ejecting them from the garden (Genesis 3:22-24).

This story (often called the 'fall' of humankind) is vital for understanding much of the Bible, for it explains that the human race is out of relationship with God – and the whole of creation has been affected by that break of relationship.

3. Israel

Next comes the time of Israel. God chose one man, and his descendants after him, to be the means of undoing the damage which human rebellion against God had produced – a man called Abra(ha)m living in the city of Ur.

God gave Abraham a threefold promise:
- a family to follow after him
- a land which God would give to his descendants
- and that through Abraham's family God would do good to all humanity (Genesis 12:1-3).

God's intention was that the whole world would be 'blessed' through the nation of Israel (Abraham's family).

Having chosen this nation, God guarded and cared for them.

They became slaves in Egypt, but God acted to deliver them through Moses, bringing them out of Egypt, through a 40-year wandering around the deserts of the Sinai Peninsula, and into the land where Abraham had lived before them.

This mighty act, called the exodus, became a defining moment for the nation of Israel and, ever afterwards, they looked back on it as the time when God saved them and adopted them as his own. To this day, Jewish people celebrate the exodus in the annual Passover festival.

While they were in the desert, God did something else for them which was to be central to the life of the nation: he gave them his law. The nation was his because of his kindness in taking them out of Egypt: hence the 'Ten Commandments', a summary of the heart of the law, begin:

'I am the Lord your God, who brought you out of the land of Egypt, out of the house of slavery' (Exodus 20:2).

The commandments then go on to speak of how God's people are to live (Exodus 20:3-17).

But the people were unable to live consistently as God wanted, and so another crucial part of the law was the sacrificial system.

When the people failed to keep the law, God provided a way to 'cover' their failure and restore the relationship with him which had been broken. This was by killing an animal in the place of the one who broke the law. The guilty person laid a hand on the head of the animal, to show it was being killed for them, so that God would overlook their law-breaking.

This was costly, for animals were a major measure of wealth in ancient rural society. In later times the sacrifices were offered in the Temple in Jerusalem, the capital city of the nation.

The life of Israel went on through many ups and downs over more than 1,000 years.

The nation divided after the death of King Solomon, and the northern half of the kingdom (Israel) fell to the Assyrians in the 8th century BC, because they compromised their belief and trust in God by taking up with other faiths.

The people of the southern kingdom (Judah) were taken into exile in Babylon about 150 years later, for similar reasons.

But God wasn't finished with his people. Amazingly he restored the people of Judah to their own land about a half-century later. Prophets – who spoke from God to the people – interpreted this homecoming as a 'new exodus', like the escape from Egypt in the time of Moses (see, for example, Isaiah 40:3-5; 43:1-7). The prophets had also announced a coming deliverer, whom God would send to free his people, a person the Jews called 'Messiah'. Different groups of Jews had different beliefs about the Messiah, but all looked forward to him bringing God's rule of justice.

4. Jesus

The prophets promised more than just restoration to the land. They spoke of other good things which God would do for his people, including freedom to worship and live as God's people, and the chance to grow old without fear. That made it doubly hard when the people found themselves prisoners in their own land and oppressed by pagan political powers. In the 1st century AD they saw themselves as still in exile, still being punished by God, even though they were physically back in the land. The Romans governed them and they were not free to live in the way the people of God were called to live. But the key stories which defined them as a people were stories of God acting to rescue them – he had done it in the exodus and in bringing them back from Babylon, and so they believed God would do it again.

Into this scene stepped Jesus, a Jewish teacher and healer who spoke of God's 'kingdom' – affirming that God was still in charge, in spite of the fact that his people were suffering and oppressed.

For three years Jesus taught, healed and freed people from oppressive forces, announcing that God's power could be seen in what he was doing and saying (Luke 11:16-20).

Jesus cared for the poor and outcasts of society – he would even help the despised aliens who came to him (e.g. Matthew 8:5-13). Jesus saw himself as offering renewal to the nation, bringing news of God's forgiving love. He spoke of the Temple in ways which suggested that it would be destroyed and replaced in some sense by himself (John 2:18-22; Mark 13:1-2).

5. Christ's followers

Such a message was not welcome to the Jewish leaders, who had invested their lives in the Temple. Many of them were collaborating with the Roman rulers, and did not want the instability that Jesus seemed to bring.

That led to a plot to put Jesus to death (John 11:47-53). Amazingly, Jesus did not resist this. He seemed to know what was going on and spoke of it in coded terms (Mark 12:1-12). More than that, Jesus saw his coming death as achieving the reality to which the sacrifices had pointed: forgiveness and renewal for the people.

On the night he was arrested and tried he spent time with his friends, celebrating the Passover meal that commemorated the exodus from Egypt. Jesus gave that meal a new significance. He interpreted the bread and wine of the meal as symbols of his body and blood, given up in death (Luke 22:14-20).

Shortly afterwards Jesus was arrested, tried and condemned to death by the Jewish leaders, and then by the Romans (for the Jews could not carry out a death sentence in those days). He was executed by being hung on a wooden cross. Darkness covered the land while he hung there. Jesus died.

Within three days his followers were totally amazed and overjoyed to see him alive again: death had not been able to defeat him. He was the same Jesus they had known for three years, but somehow more alive than ever before. He was truly the Messiah!

After Jesus rose from the dead he gave his followers the responsibility of telling others about him. Before he left them to return to God his Father, he promised them the power to carry out this huge task, a personal power he called the Holy Spirit.

At the Jewish festival of Pentecost, shortly afterwards, the small group of Jesus' followers were overwhelmed by a powerful wind and given the ability to speak new languages, so that a large crowd was attracted to hear them speak about Jesus. This was the power which would enable them to spread the message!

The early Christians began as a small group, but rapidly spread the message about Jesus all over the countries around the Mediterranean Sea. Small groups of Christians began to form, initially amongst Jewish people, but later also including non-Jews: the promise to Abraham that the whole of humanity would be blessed through his descendants was beginning to be fulfilled! These groups met in homes, usually belonging to a more wealthy member of the group.

And the early Christian groups had their problems! The letters of the early Christian leaders show the kinds of difficulties they had, coming to terms with a new way of living which meant that the old barriers between people were broken down – barriers of gender, slavery and race (Galatians 3:28).

They had to learn that being a follower of Jesus meant you could not simply live as you liked. Care for others, particularly other Christians, came before your own needs. More than that, they had to be

ready to suffer for their faith in Jesus – many were excluded socially, others died because they were committed to following him.

6. The end-time

How did the early Christians handle this suffering? How did they understand what God was doing now that Jesus had departed from the earth?

The last book of the Bible, Revelation, offers a vision of God in control of the processes of history which would lift the spirits of persecuted Christians to the great God they served. More than that, the early Christians looked forward to a day when Jesus would return to this earth to complete, finally, the work which he began in his life, death and resurrection.

In that day, Christians look forward to the whole universe being renewed and restored to God's original intention in creation (Revelation 21:1-8).

It will also be a day in which evil and wrong are removed from the world, in which those who reject God will be judged, and those who trust in Jesus will see God face to face.

The Bible as a witness

The Bible does not simply tell this story in a detached way, as a historian might. It is written to invite those who hear its message to respond to Jesus too. It is a testimony to what God has done in history and what God will yet do. It is written to persuade its readers to become followers of Jesus, and to help them understand how to follow him in company with others. Reading the Bible is like receiving an invitation to a party – it seeks our response!

A Christian young people's group in Asia represents the millions down the ages who have heard the Bible's story and responded to become followers of Jesus.

Bible versions

The Bible has been translated into many languages over the last 2,000 years since the Christian faith began.

Many different English versions have been produced, especially in the 20th century. Today those who read in English have several to choose from.

Some people love the older translations (most famously the Authorized or King James' Version). But many find them difficult because they are using a form of English that is no longer current.

It is worth trying two or three versions out. You might like to try the following modern versions:

- New Revised Standard Version
- New International Version
- Good News Bible
- Revised English Bible.

Each of the versions has been produced for a particular reason or reader. See 'English Versions', p.77.

How Bible references work

Sections of the Bible are referred to using a system which began in the 13th century AD.

- Each book within the Bible has a name. This comes first in a reference.
- Each book is sub-divided into 'chapters' (sections between half a page and a page or so long). The chapter comes next in the reference.
- Each chapter is then divided into numbered 'verses' (a sentence or two).

So a typical Bible reference gives the book, chapter and verse(s). For example:

Romans 3:21-26
Genesis 12:1-3.

That makes it easier to find.

Use the references to find your way around the Bible, but don't let chapters and verses dictate how you read a particular passage! They were not there in the original Hebrew and Greek, and sometimes there is a chapter break in the middle of an important story, or argument, spoiling the flow.

Reading the Bible

Stephen Travis

Reading the Bible can be difficult. Sometimes it is exciting, life-giving. But sometimes we find it puzzling.

So how do we get into it and stay with it?

It helps to be clear why we are reading. People read the Bible for many different reasons.

- You can read it as literature. The Psalms, for example, and the book of Isaiah are rated among the greatest books of the world.
- You can read it to discover the history of the ancient world.
- You can read the Bible to study the foundations of Jewish and Christian beliefs and ethical standards.
- Or you can read the Bible to discover the themes and stories which inspired the work of many of the world's artists, musicians and writers.

All these are positive reasons for studying the Bible. But we get to the heart of the matter only if we ask why the biblical books were written.

What motivated the people who told the stories, composed the psalms, wrote the letters, prophesied the future?

> **66** *When... an individual humbly takes this book written by ordinary people, with the marks of time and the difficulties caused by transmission evidently upon it, the Holy Spirit gets to work and conveys Christ through it to the mind and heart and conscience of the reader.* **99**
>
> Donald Coggan

How did they see God impacting on human lives?

We may summarize their purpose under four headings.

Story

First, they tell the story of how God invited a particular group of people to get to know him, so that in the long run the whole world may learn to know and love him. Despite the variety of books within the Bible,

The Bible is like a compass, giving direction to our lives.

and the long time-span over which it was written, there is a thread running through the whole which gives perspective to the different parts.

Relationship

Secondly, they speak about our relationship with God. There are stories about people aiming to obey God, messages of prophets and apostles urging people to rediscover God's way for them, prayers of people longing to know God's blessing.

Community

Thirdly, they speak about our relationship to God's people, the church. The books of the Bible were written mainly for a community, not for individuals. So we may find that their message addresses us more clearly when we study the Bible with others rather than on our own.

Society

Fourthly, they speak – especially in the Old Testament – about our relationship to society and to the world. The Bible is not a book about private religion. It shows how God's people are meant to reflect in their own lives God's character and his concern for the whole world. It gives thousands of instances of what it means to 'love the Lord your God... and your neighbour as yourself'.

If, then, we want to hear the Bible's message, how do we set about reading it?

- **Recognize the variety in the Bible.** There is story and parable, prayer and love song, prophecy and proverb, visions of heaven and practical guidance for everyday life.

There are many different aspects to our lives and God has an interest in all of them. For this reason, it is not normally a good idea to try to read the Bible through from Genesis to the end. It is better, for example, to move from time to time between Old and New Testaments.

A good plan might be to begin with a Gospel, then to read a few psalms, then one of the shorter letters of the New Testament, and then the first section of Genesis (chapters 1 – 11).

▪ **Ask, 'What kind of a book am I reading?'** We read a history book in a different way from a car maintenance manual. And different kinds of biblical books need different approaches. When I read the Sermon on the Mount (Matthew 5 – 7) I pause over each phrase, because every word of Jesus is a vital clue to Christian living. When I read the Old Testament book of Ecclesiastes I take a more relaxed approach, smiling at its wry insights into human nature.

▪ **Try sometimes to read large sections at one go**, especially if you are studying a narrative book. We wouldn't read just a couple of pages of a novel and then put it aside until tomorrow.

Read a Gospel as a whole and you will notice things about Jesus you never thought of before.

Read through the story of David in 1 and 2 Samuel and you will gain a sense of God's involvement in all the ups and downs of his life which you could never grasp by reading only a few verses at a time.

▪ **As you read, ask what insights the passage offers** about the four aspects of the

Reading the Bible together, in a small group, can be a stimulating way to study it, as members share their understanding.

Bible's purpose described above: What do I learn about God's plan for the world; about my relationship with God, with God's people, and with society and the world?

Of course, not every passage will shed light on each of those four areas of our life. But there will always be something to help you reflect on your life with God.

▪ We need also to **allow the Bible to ask questions** of us – to allow it to challenge our assumptions, our behaviour and our priorities.

We shall hear its message if we come to it with a proper reverence – not a reverence for print on paper, but for the God who addresses us through the Bible.

▪ **Don't be put off** by the feeling that you ought to do a crash course in biblical interpretation before you are qualified to read.

No one learns to play football or any other game by sitting in an armchair reading coaching manuals! Use the guides that are available to you, starting with this Handbook. But don't let them stand between you and getting onto the pitch!

▪ **The Bible isn't a cook-book** with a recipe for every circumstance of modern life. It acts more like a compass to guide us in the right direction, than a map with every detail marked in. The Bible's message gradually makes us the people we are meant to be.

The Bible makes the Christian, and the Christian responds to God and to the issues of life in a Christ-like way.

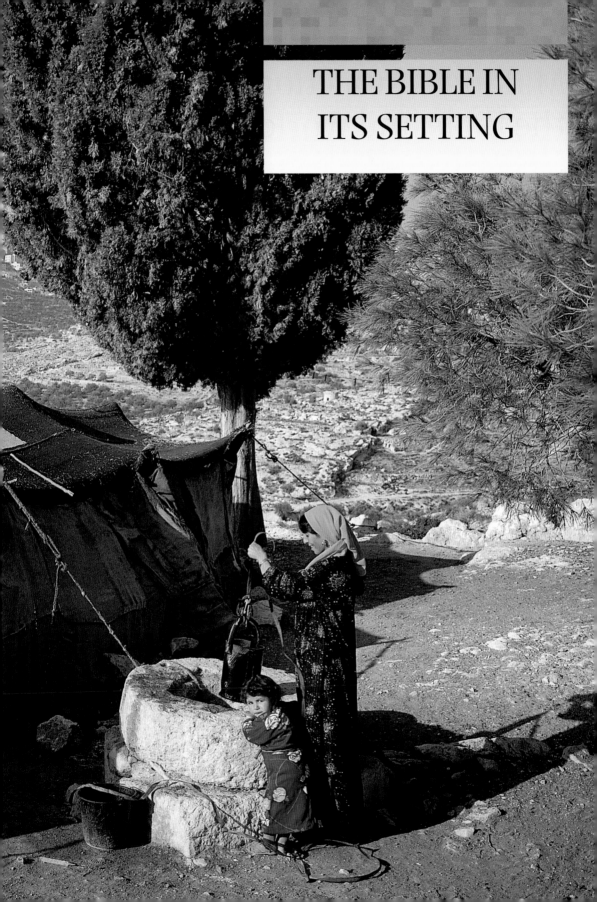

THE BIBLE IN
ITS SETTING

Making connections – the Bible and world history

2000 BC – AD 2000

	2000 BC	1600	1200	800	400	0
Judaism					Synagogues developed; Maccabean revolt	First Jewish revolt; Jerusalem Temple destroyed; Josephus, Jewish historian; Second Jewish revolt under Bar Kokhba
Bible period	Abraham and patriarchs	Israelites in Egypt; The Exodus; Ten Commandments	Kings David and Solomon; Jerusalem Temple	The Prophets; Jerusalem and Temple destroyed; exile begins; Jews return, Temple rebuilt	Greek Septuagint translation of Hebrew Bible	**Jesus**; Paul
Christianity						Churches established in Roman Empire, India; Emperor Constantine adopts Christianity; Sunday made day of rest; Council of Nicea establishes creed; Hymn-singing developed by Ambrose

The Bible period since Abraham overlaps with about half of our history to the present day. How do Bible events relate to what was going on elsewhere? Making connections can be fascinating. Did the Israelites bring monotheism to Egypt, which was later suppressed? The new faiths in Asia came at the same time as the prophets of Israel. The message of Jesus came at a unique time, when Roman communications and a common Greek language made it possible for it to spread rapidly both in the Roman Empire and to the East. This chart suggests only a few of the people, events and ideologies which help show the development of ideas since 2000 BC.

Buddhism, Hinduism, Asian religions	Siddhartha, Gautama Buddha; Rig-Veda, Upanishads: Hindu poetry and teaching; Jainism founded in India; Confucius in China; Taoism

	2000 BC	1600	1200	800	400	0
Ideologies, beliefs, ideas	Polytheism, ethnic religions, primal religions; Stonehenge, Britain: Druids	Period of monotheistic sun-worship in Egypt	Classic paganism in Greece; Pantheistic religion develops in India; Baal worship	Lao-Tse, Chinese philosopher; Zoroaster, founder of Persian religion; Aeschylus, Sophocles, Herodotus, Euripides; Socrates, moral philosopher	Greek philosophy: Aristotle, Plato; Stoicism; Epicurus and 'Epicurean' philosophy	Neo-Platonism, Greek philosophy

	2000 BC	1600	1200	800	400	0
Civilizations, people, events	Ancient Egypt; Mesopotamia; Hammurabi of Babylon's law-codes; First seven periods of Chinese literature; Minoan culture in Crete	Bronze Age; Hittites in Anatolia; Canaanites	Iron Age; Etruscan civilization	Celtic people spread from central and western Europe; Assyrian Empire; First recorded Olympic Games; Babylonian Empire; Persian Empire; Greek civilization; Homer's *Iliad* and *Odyssey*; Acropolis in Athens built; Democracy adopted in Athens; Beginning of Indian Empire	Alexander the Great conquers Persia, invades India; Great Wall of China; Greece under Roman control; Roman Empire; Pompey captures Jerusalem; Julius Caesar; Chinese ships reach India; Horace, Ovid, Seneca	Pacific colonization by Polynesians; Roman rule, Hellenistic culture; Emperor Constantine reunites East and West empires, with capital at Constantinople; Huns invade Europe

	800	1200	1600	1800	AD 1900
	Jews settle in Germany, develop Yiddish language	Ibn Ezra, scholar Maimonides, philosopher Cabbalistic Jewish mysticism Persecution of Jews in Europe		Theodor Herzl and Zionism	Jewish Holocaust Jewish state of Israel
Augustine Desert hermits Monasticism Benedictine order founded Celtic missions in Britain: Patrick, Columba, David Caedmon, earliest English Christian poet	Split between Roman and Eastern churches becomes permanent Cathedral building in Europe Scholastic theology Bernard of Clairvaux, hymn-writer Waldensians Francis of Assissi, Franciscans Albigensians	Dominican order founded Thomas Aquinas, theologian John Wycliffe, English reformer Jan Hus, reformer in Bohemia Anabaptists Reformation (Luther, Calvin) William Tyndale translates the New Testament into English Ignatius Loyola and the Jesuits Council of Trent: Roman Catholic Counter-Reformation	King James/Authorized Version of the Bible Presbyterians and Puritans Pilgrim Fathers sail in Mayflower to America Congregationalists Baptists: first London church Pietists John Wesley and the Methodists	Missionary and Bible societies founded Sunday schools started Pentecostalism First Vatican Council and papal infallibility Revivalism in the US: Moody and Sankey Biblical criticism	Ecumenical movement to unite churches 'The Fundamentals' published in US, coining the word 'fundamentalism' Existentialism in theology Billy Graham, evangelist Second Vatican Council, Catholic reforms Charismatic movement
Islam Muhammad Muslim empire from Spain to China	Sufi mystics Cairo world's first university Development of Shari'a, Islamic law	Many new mosques built in Iran and Ottoman Empire	Islamic empire in India	Impact of Western culture and law in many Muslim areas	Islamists promote Muslim states
Spread of Hindu empire and writings First Shinto shrines in Japan				Ranjit Singh and the Sikhs Ramakrishna, Hindu teacher	
	Golden era of Arabic learning	Renaissance in art and learning Rise of science; scientific societies founded Copernicus claims the earth goes round the sun	Galileo The Enlightenment: rationalism, humanism Philosophers: Hobbes, Descartes, Spinoza, Locke, Hume, Rousseau, Kant Boyle, Newton, Linnaeus, scientists	Development of science: Pasteur, Faraday Charles Darwin, 'On the Origin of Species by Natural Selection' Marx and Engels, Communist Manifesto Nietzsche, philosopher	Psychology (Freud, Jung) Albert Einstein and relativity Communism Quantum theory in physics Logical positivism Existentialism Feminism Microbiology, genetics Environmental movement New Age movement
Maya civilization, Mexico Golden age of Byzantine art First printed newspaper – in Peking Arabs conquer Syria, Mesopotamia, Egypt, Jerusalem Lindisfarne Gospels	Otto founds Holy Roman Empire of the German nation New Maya empire in Mexico Charlemagne first Holy Roman Emperor The Crusades begin	Mongol invasion of Asia and Europe Aztecs in Central America Ottoman Empire founded Inca culture in Peru Printing (Gutenberg) Leonardo da Vinci Christopher Columbus sails to the New World William Shakespeare	Baroque period Rembrandt, artist J.S.Bach, Handel, composers Classicism in theatre, architecture, literature Mozart, Beethoven and Classical music	The Industrial Revolution Romantic movement The railway age Exploration and colonialism Anti-slavery movements Telephone, electricity Development of medicine Coca-Cola introduced First modern Olympic Games Automobiles	First World War Splitting of the atom Television invented Second World War The Electronic Revolution Martin Luther King Pop and Rock culture First landing on the moon AIDS epidemic The Internet

0	800	1200	1600	1800	AD 1900

The Bible in its time

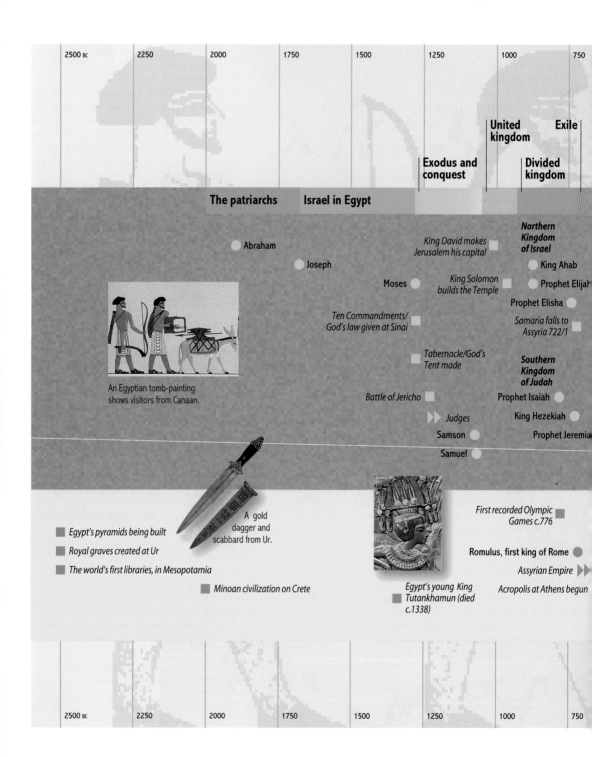

| 2500 BC | 2250 | 2000 | 1750 | 1500 | 1250 | 1000 | 750 |

United kingdom   **Exile**

Exodus and conquest   **Divided kingdom**

The patriarchs   **Israel in Egypt**

Northern Kingdom of Israel

Abraham

Joseph

King David makes Jerusalem his capital

King Ahab

Moses   *King Solomon builds the Temple*   Prophet Elijah

Prophet Elisha

Ten Commandments/ God's law given at Sinai   *Samaria falls to Assyria 722/1*

Tabernacle/God's Tent made   *Southern Kingdom of Judah*

An Egyptian tomb-painting shows visitors from Canaan.

Battle of Jericho   Prophet Isaiah

Judges   King Hezekiah

Samson   Prophet Jeremiah

Samuel

First recorded Olympic Games c.776

Egypt's pyramids being built

Royal graves created at Ur   A gold dagger and scabbard from Ur.

The world's first libraries, in Mesopotamia

Minoan civilization on Crete   Romulus, first king of Rome

Assyrian Empire

Egypt's young King Tutankhamun (died c.1338)   Acropolis at Athens begun

| 2500 BC | 2250 | 2000 | 1750 | 1500 | 1250 | 1000 | 750 |

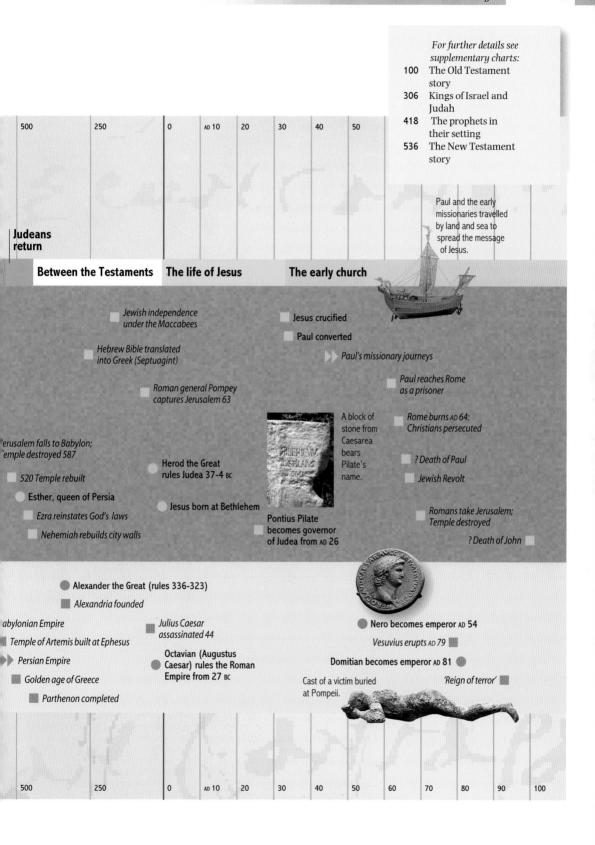

For further details see
supplementary charts:
100   The Old Testament
      story
306   Kings of Israel and
      Judah
418   The prophets in
      their setting
536   The New Testament
      story

| 500 | 250 | 0 | AD 10 | 20 | 30 | 40 | 50 |

Paul and the early
missionaries travelled
by land and sea to
spread the message
of Jesus.

**Judeans
return**

Between the Testaments   The life of Jesus   The early church

Jewish independence
under the Maccabees

Jesus crucified

Paul converted

Hebrew Bible translated
into Greek (Septuagint)

▶▶ Paul's missionary journeys

Roman general Pompey
captures Jerusalem 63

Paul reaches Rome
as a prisoner

A block of
stone from
Caesarea
bears
Pilate's
name.

Rome burns AD 64:
Christians persecuted

*erusalem falls to Babylon;
*emple destroyed 587

Herod the Great
rules Judea 37-4 BC

? Death of Paul

520 Temple rebuilt

Jewish Revolt

Esther, queen of Persia

Jesus born at Bethlehem

Ezra reinstates God's laws

Romans take Jerusalem;
Temple destroyed

Pontius Pilate
becomes governor
of Judea from AD 26

Nehemiah rebuilds city walls

? Death of John

Alexander the Great (rules 336-323)

Alexandria founded

abylonian Empire

Julius Caesar
assassinated 44

Nero becomes emperor AD 54

Temple of Artemis built at Ephesus

Vesuvius erupts AD 79

▶▶ Persian Empire

Octavian (Augustus
Caesar) rules the Roman
Empire from 27 BC

Domitian becomes emperor AD 81

Golden age of Greece

Cast of a victim buried
at Pompeii.

'Reign of terror'

Parthenon completed

| 500 | 250 | 0 | AD 10 | 20 | 30 | 40 | 50 | 60 | 70 | 80 | 90 | 100 |

Bringing the past to life

John Bimson

The *tell* (ruin-mound) of the ancient biblical city of Lachish. *inset*: Archaeologist's tools.

'Does archaeology prove the Bible is true?'

This is a question frequently put to archaeologists who also work with the Bible. The questioner usually wants to know whether there is archaeological evidence that particular events happened.

In fact archaeology can rarely provide evidence of that kind. More often it provides a background against which the Bible can be better understood.

New approaches

Today, archaeology involves much more than the excavation of *tells*. Regional surveys can help us to see how cities, villages and nomad encampments related to each other, and to understand the ancient environment, food production and changing patterns of settlement.

These approaches may seem to have little to do with the Bible (and some archaeologists dislike the term 'biblical archaeology'), but if they enable us to understand how society worked in biblical times they can indirectly bring the Bible to life for the modern reader.

UNCOVERING ANCIENT CITIES
Until recently a great deal of biblical archaeology involved the excavation of *tells*, the ruin-mounds of ancient cities. Cities in biblical times were often rebuilt many times on the same spot, usually following destruction by enemies, fires or earthquakes. A city which is frequently rebuilt on top of its own ruins will eventually form a sizeable mound, and such a mound is a *tell* in Arabic (or *tel* in Hebrew). Excavating a tell means digging into many layers (or strata), each layer representing a period of occupation. Careful excavation and recording enables archaeologists to piece together the history of a city, to see changes in its status and culture.

A CAUTIONARY TALE
Early attempts to link archaeological discoveries with the Bible led to some misleading conclusions. A series of long, rectangular buildings discovered at Megiddo in 1928 (*above*) were interpreted as stables and dated to the time of Solomon. The find was soon linked with a reference in 1 Kings 9:15 to Solomon rebuilding Megiddo, and with the 'chariot-cities' mentioned three verses later.

Subsequently the buildings were redated to the reign of Ahab, a full century after Solomon. Now it is suggested that these buildings may be later still, and some archaeologists doubt whether they were stables at all. This should caution us against making hasty connections. Archaeological evidence is not always easy to interpret.

POTTERY HELPS WITH DATING
The dates of a tell's strata are usually established by its pottery. Pottery styles were always changing, so fragments of pottery (always plentiful in occupation layers) are a good clue to the date when a particular stratum was a flourishing city. Ultimately, the dates of the pottery styles depend on connections with Egypt or Mesopotamia, regions where long periods of ancient history have been reconstructed from lists of kings.

Light on the Old Testament

Often archaeology illuminates the cultural, rather than the historical setting of an event in the Bible, as these Old Testament examples show.

SOLOMON'S TEMPLE

The plan of Solomon's Temple, with its three-fold division, has parallels from Canaanite temples of the Late Bronze Age, as well as a later temple from north Syria. Inside, Solomon's Temple had wooden panels carved with cherubim, palm trees, gourds and flowers. Carved ivory plaques of Phoenician style, found at Samaria (palms picture, *left*) and in Syria and Assyria, provide parallels to these designs.

Solomon's practice of covering much of the interior decoration of the Temple with gold can be illustrated from Egyptian temples.

These examples help us to picture the Jerusalem Temple. They also show that the details of the description are completely plausible in their proper context.

The Rosetta Stone was found by Napoleon's men near Rosetta on the River Nile. It records a decree of King Ptolemy V of Egypt, in Greek (bottom), Egyptian demotic script (middle) and hieroglyphs (top). It was the key to understanding ancient Egyptian writing.

A seal inscribed 'Abdi, servant of Hoshea' (Israel's last king: 2 Kings 17).

The victories of Pharaoh Merneptah (about 1208 bc) are recorded on this stele (over 2m/7ft high). It contains the earliest reference outside the Bible to a people called Israel.

INSCRIPTIONS

There is now plenty of archaeological evidence that some level of literacy was widespread in ancient Israel, as the Bible suggests (see, for example, Judges 8:14; Isaiah 10:19). Inscriptions on pottery and stone vessels, on tombs, weights, ivories and seals have turned up at many localities. Some of these throw further, indirect light on Israelite society.

This ring, bearing the owner's name in Hebrew, dates from the 8th-7th centuries BC.

A collection of ostraca (inscribed pottery fragments) from Samaria, dating from the 8th century BC, record the payment of taxes in kind (wine and oil) to the city's storehouses. They reveal that a few individuals supplied great quantities – evidence that they were the owners of large estates. The accumulation of land by the rich was widely condemned by the 8th-century prophets, because it was usually at the expense of the poor (Amos 8:4; Micah 2:2; Isaiah 5:8).

Fragments of broken pottery (potsherds), ready to hand, were often used for short records and letters in ancient times.

OLIVE OIL PRODUCTION

Olive oil was one of the most important products of biblical times (Hosea 2:8, etc.). It was used for cooking, lighting, cosmetics and in various rituals.

Excavations at Ekron (Tel Miqne, on the coastal plain west of Jerusalem) have thrown light on olive oil production from the 7th century BC.

Rectangular basins and stone rollers were used for crushing the olives to a pulp, and each basin was flanked by two vats for pressing the pulp to produce liquid (20-30% oil). Several 77kg/170lb stone weights were used in the pressing process. It is calculated that Ekron's 115 oil presses could have produced 500 tons, or 145,000 gallons in a season.

The above two pictures show different methods of extracting olive oil: oldest is the beam and weight; then the heavy stone roller, and latest the crusher.

right: These pots were for storing olive oil.

Light on the New Testament

RELIGIOUS LIFE

The discovery of the Dead Sea Scrolls in 1947 transformed our view of Jesus' world.

The Scrolls revealed a branch of Judaism (probably that of the Essenes) with many distinctive features, and opened our eyes to the fact that Judaism in the 1st century was not one, static faith; it was changing and contained great variety within it.

The Dead Sea Scrolls were put in storage jars like these and hidden in local caves by the Qumran community when it was overrun by the Romans at the time of the Jewish Revolt.

A Dead Sea Scroll, before the delicate work of separating the tightly rolled layers.

Among the scrolls relating to the community itself were texts of the Hebrew scriptures 1,000 years older than any previously known. This is part of the Isaiah scroll.

Excavation at Qumran has uncovered the scriptorium where the scrolls were written and carefully copied.

KING HEROD'S BUILDINGS

In many respects the world Jesus knew had been given its character by Herod the Great (37-4 BC). Herod was responsible for many building schemes which transformed Jerusalem and other cities of his kingdom, such as Hebron, Jericho and Samaria (renamed Sebaste, a Greek name honouring Augustus Caesar).

At Caesarea (also named in honour of the emperor), Herod transformed a small anchorage into a major port, setting his engineers to create an artificial harbour

big enough for the largest trading vessels of the time.

The city was built on a matching scale, with a theatre, amphitheatre, public baths, a stadium and a temple to Augustus.

Herod's own palace in Caesarea later became the residence of the Roman governors of Judea, including Pontius Pilate.

Part of a monument bearing Pilate's name and title was discovered at Caesarea in 1961 (see 'Jews under Roman rule: the province of Judea').

A present-day aerial view of ancient Caesarea shows part of the archaeological site. The walls are from Crusader times.

King Herod's new theatre at Caesarea.

FIRST-CENTURY JERUSALEM

Excavations in the Jewish Quarter of Jerusalem in the 1970s uncovered examples of palatial houses, occupied by upper-class (perhaps priestly) families in the 1st century AD.

One of these, now known simply as the mansion, was built on two levels on a

slope. The main living areas were on the ground floor, and the basement level contained cisterns and baths for ritual cleansing. One of the ground floor rooms had an upper storey.

Walls were plastered inside and out and the interiors were elaborately ornamented. Some of the floors were decorated with mosaics. Luxury glassware and pottery, and stone tables of high quality were found in these houses, which had been destroyed in AD 70 when Jerusalem fell to Roman armies.

These finds give a glimpse of the life enjoyed by the wealthy of Jesus' day, such as the ruler in Luke 18:18-23.

CAPERNAUM

By contrast, clusters of houses excavated at Capernaum illustrate the much more basic homes of people living in the provinces.

The walls were of unshaped basalt stones, with smaller stones and plaster to fill the gaps. Some floors were cobbled, and small objects could easily have been lost between the stones, as in Jesus' parable of the lost coin (Luke 15:8). Some houses had an upper storey. Roofs consisted of beams supporting branches or reeds, covered with baked clay.

Rooms and objects uncovered by excavations in Jerusalem's Upper City, opposite Herod's Temple. These houses had been burned down when the Romans took Jerusalem in AD 70, after the Jewish Revolt.

EVERYDAY LIFE

In the very dry climate of the Dead Sea basin, sandals, baskets, mats and clothing have survived from the 1st and 2nd centuries at Masada and Engedi. These provide unique glimpses into everyday life in ancient Judea.

Bronze jugs, plates and household objects have been recovered from Masada.

Cosmetic jars, a comb and other items recovered from Masada.

Sandals, too, have survived the centuries almost intact.

For more information
on daily life see:
Nomadic life **198**
Settled life **242**

Partial reconstruction of one of the Jerusalem houses destroyed in AD 70. Its furnishings and mosaic floor give an idea of the lifestyle of wealthy people, only 40 years after Jesus was put to death.

inset: Sometimes beautiful examples of skilled craftsmanship come to light, like this glass vase, dated close to the lifetime of Jesus.

A reconstructed well helps us to understand an important aspect of daily life in Bible times.

The land of Israel

Israel has never been a large or particularly powerful country. The distance from Dan in the north to Beersheba in the south is less than 230km/150 miles. But its position on the narrow strip of land between sea and desert at the eastern end of the Mediterranean Sea has given it a special importance. From early times to the present day the land and its people have been caught in a succession of power struggles. In Bible times this was mostly between the great civilizations of Mesopotamia to the north-east and Egypt to the south.

Pomegranates are one of the many fruits of the land the Old Testament describes as 'flowing with milk and honey'. The shape was copied around the edge of the High Priest's robe, and carved on the pillars in Solomon's Temple.

Produce and resources

Israel produces a wide variety of crops. Cereals and pulses, green vegetables, grapes, figs, pomegranates, olives and dates have been grown since Bible times.

From the days of Abraham and before, sheep and goats have grazed the rough and stony hills, providing milk, meat and wool. Richer pastures support cattle. Fish are plentiful in Lake Galilee.

The Dead Sea supplies salt and minerals. Further south, copper has been mined, and the desert has a wealth of minerals.

CROSS-SECTION OF THE LAND
The geographical regions of Israel run roughly north to south, parallel to the coast. Inland, the coastal plain gives way to low hills, then the main central highland forms the 'backbone' of the whole country. Beyond these mountains the land drops steeply to the Jordan Valley, with more mountain ranges to the east.

Ashdod
+42m/140ft

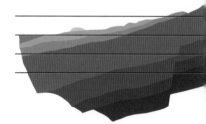

THE COASTAL PLAIN
The southern end of the coastal plain was once the land of the Philistines. Near Haifa, in the north, the plain is broken by the Carmel range of hills which runs inland to join the central highlands.

THE CENTRAL HIGHLANDS
The hills of Samaria, and the Judean hills to the south, are part of this 'backbone' region of rough, rocky hills.

For further information see:
Animals and birds **38**
Trees and plants **40**

RAINFALL

Israel has two seasons: winter, cold and wet; summer, hot and dry. The temperature varies a great deal from region to region. In winter Jerusalem may have snow, Galilee freezing rain, while Jericho enjoys an average temperature of 15°C/59°F. In summer, 22-25°C/71-77°F is average for the coast and hills; the Dead Sea has a constant daytime 40°C/104°F. The rains begin in October, are heaviest in December/January and end about April.

Average annual rainfall

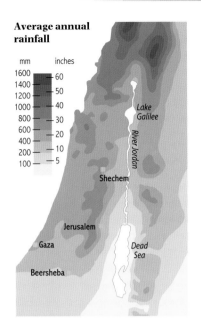

mm	inches
1600	60
1400	50
1200	
1000	40
800	30
600	20
400	10
200	5
100	

Lake Galilee

River Jordan

Shechem

Jerusalem

Gaza

Dead Sea

Beersheba

Regions of Israel

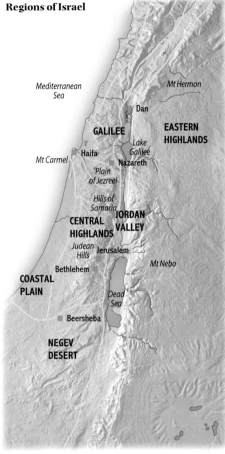

Mediterranean Sea

Mt Hermon

Dan

GALILEE

EASTERN HIGHLANDS

Mt Carmel   Haifa   Lake Galilee

Nazareth

'Plain of Jezreel'

Hills of Samaria

CENTRAL HIGHLANDS

JORDAN VALLEY

Judean Hills   Jerusalem

Bethlehem

Mt Nebo

COASTAL PLAIN

Dead Sea

Beersheba

NEGEV DESERT

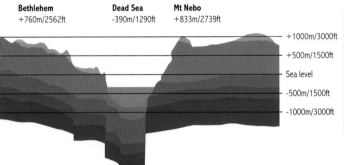

Bethlehem	Dead Sea	Mt Nebo
+760m/2562ft	-390m/1290ft	+833m/2739ft

+1000m/3000ft

+500m/1500ft

Sea level

-500m/1500ft

-1000m/3000ft

THE JORDAN VALLEY

The Jordan rises close to the foot of Mt Hermon and flows south, descending about 1000m/3000ft by the time it reaches the Dead Sea (the lowest place on earth, at its deepest, more than 800m/2600 ft below sea level). The valley is a deep trough, created by geological faults in this unstable area. It has a hot and humid climate all its own.

GALILEE

North of Carmel the land opens out into the broad, fertile plain of Esdraelon/Jezreel. Beyond lie the hills and valleys surrounding Lake Galilee. The town of Dan and snow-capped Mt Hermon (2840m/9232ft) mark the northern boundary.

THE DESERT

South of Beersheba lies the Negev Desert. Here rainfall is low, with only tiny patches of green and the occasional acacia tree among the bare brown hills. These get higher, more rugged and dramatic, towards Sinai in the south.

Animals and birds

Animals

From before Abraham's time, sheep and goats have grazed the rough and stony hills of Israel, providing milk, cheese and meat. Wool for clothing has always been especially valuable.

The richer pastures of Gilead and Bashan, east of the River Jordan made these regions famous for their cattle.

Camels and donkeys have been beasts of burden and people-carriers in Middle Eastern countries from very early times. Mules are a cross between donkey and horse. There were horses in Egypt by Joseph's time. They drew chariots and were ridden into battle.

Many more wild animals inhabited Israel in Bible times than live there today – wolves, lions and bears, fox and jackal, the wild ass (onager), ibex, deer and gazelle,

mouse, rat and other small creatures as well as the shy rock hyrax.

There were many snakes, most of them harmless, but a few that could be deadly, including the desert carpet viper, perhaps the one which struck the people during their journey through the wilderness.

There were also grasshoppers and occasional disastrous swarms of the desert locust.

Lake Galilee was well stocked with a variety of fish (see 'Fishing in Lake Galilee').

Camels were especially important in regions in and around desert. The Midianites rode in on camels to raid Israel (Judges 6:5). The Queen of Sheba used them to transport goods (1 Kings 10:2).

*For more pictures
and information see:*
Sheep and goats 144, 269, etc
Locusts 165, 489
Quail 196
Donkeys 248, 259, etc
Raven 291
Hyrax 383
Dove 405, 599
Gazelle 405

There are snakes in every region of Israel. It is not easy to identify those mentioned in the Bible. The deadly snake of Numbers 21 is probably a carpet viper, similar to the horned viper (*above*). Many, like Clifford's snake (*below*), are harmless.

There are more than 40 varieties of lizard in Israel. This is the ornate Dabb lizard.

God said that Ishmael, the son Hagar bore to Abraham, would be at odds with everyone, like the wild ass (onager).

For most ordinary people, donkeys were the main means of transport for themselves and for loads of all kinds throughout Bible times. It was on a humble donkey that Jesus made his triumphal entry to Jerusalem.

The fat desert rat is one of many small rodents that live in Israel's varied habitats.

The 'wild goat' of older versions of the Bible is the Nubian ibex. Although in the valley here, the ibex is a great climber, still to be seen today in the rocky area around Engedi.

Birds

A range of habitats, from semi-tropical to desert, makes Israel rich in birds. In addition to the residents, many birds pass through in spring and autumn on a main migratory route from Africa to Europe and West Asia.

The Bible mentions many birds we cannot now clearly identify. Those we can, include the eagle, vulture, owl, stork, crane, swallow, sparrow, quail, partridge, dove, pigeon, crow and raven.

The (desert) oryx is now almost extinct in the wild.

Trees and plants

Trees

Although Israel was probably never densely forested, some areas bare today were tree-clad in Bible times.

The tree of the desert is the acacia, used by the Israelites to build the Ark of the Covenant and parts of the Tabernacle.

Oaks, firs, the upright cypress and pines grew on the hills.

Poplars, willows, tamarisk and oleander formed dense thickets along the banks of the River Jordan.

Most important were the fruiting trees: vine and olive, fig, pomegranate, date palm and almond.

The cedar used for King David's palace and Solomon's Temple was imported from Lebanon.

Grapes ripen on the vine.

Pines are common in Israel.

Date palms grow in a sub-tropical climate.

A tamarisk in flower.

Figs form on a shady tree close to a house.

Olives are an important crop in Israel.

For more pictures and information see:
Desert acacia 174
Poppies 391
Pomegranate 405
Vine 427, 638
Fig 623
Olive 640, 688

Plants and herbs

The contrasts in climate result in an unusual variety of wild plants and flowers.

A riot of wild flowers jewel the hillsides of Galilee in the spring – Jesus' 'lilies of the field' – crocus, anemone, narcissus, cyclamen, poppy, yellow crown daisies and many others.

Herbs and spices have always been valued, some for their use as medicines, others for the flavour they add to a rather dull diet. Amongst the common herbs are cummin, dill, garlic, anise, hyssop, rue, mint and mustard.

There are also more than 120 kinds of thistle and thorn in Israel!

The Bible uses over 20 words for thistle!

The horned poppy flowers in the wild.

Crown daisies may be among Jesus' 'lilies of the field'.

Poppies bloom even in the rockiest places.

Brightest of spring flowers is the red anemone.

The yellow iris is a marsh plant.

In ancient times writing-paper was made from stems of the papyrus.

A caper flourishes among the rocks.

Wormwood has a bitter taste.

Both leaf and flower of the myrtle are scented.

Among many herbs used for medicine and in cooking are (*clockwise from top left*): sage, mint, rue, black mustard and dill.

Israel's calendar

A calendar is one of those essentials we all take for granted. The earliest calendars, including that of ancient Israel, evolved around the seasons of the farmer's year, and the religious rites associated with them. Because of this, and because it was all so complex, the priests became the experts in managing the calendar. Trade and government made their own demands for accurate dating. So the great empires of Mesopotamia and the Nile Valley developed their varying systems to a high degree of accuracy.

We know little about the old Israelite calendar, apart from the festivals. But the Mishnah (the collection of Jewish law at the end of the 2nd century AD) fully describes the system the Jews had worked out under Babylonian influence. This carried on alongside the Roman calendar reformed so well by Julius Caesar that it survives almost intact after 2,000 years.

When the Israelites first settled in Canaan they used the local Canaanite names for the months. During the exile these names were replaced by the Babylonian names used in the columns below.

MARCH	APRIL	MAY	JUNE	JULY	AUGUST	SEP
Nisan MONTH 1 *early name: Abib*	**Iyyar** MONTH 2 *early name: Ziv*	**Sivan** MONTH 3	**Tammuz** MONTH 4	**Ab** MONTH 5	**Elul** MONTH 6	
Flax harvest	Flax and barley harvest	Grain harvest	Vines tended	Summer fruit harvest	Grape and olive harves	
Festivals: 14-21 Passover and Unleavened Bread		*Festivals: Harvest/Weeks (Pentecost)*				

Harvest/ Weeks (called Pentecost in the New Testament) seven weeks after Passover.

14-21: Passover and Unleavened Bread

21: Firstfruits of harvest

1: Trumpets /New Year

A PROBLEM

The weekly sabbath (rest-day) presented its own problems, because the year does not contain a whole number of weeks, any more than a whole number of months. In early times the sabbath may have been adjusted to coincide with major festivals, or even with new moons (see Leviticus 23). After the exile, the seventh-day sabbath was more strictly observed and became independent of the lunisolar calendar, so the orthodox Jews had problems over the relationship of the sabbaths and festivals.

IN THE NEW TESTAMENT

Most New Testament writers pinpoint events in relation to the current Jewish calendar. Occasionally they reckon dates by reference to non-Jewish rulers. Luke, for example, refers to the Roman Emperor Tiberius in his Gospel. The accounts are punctuated by the great annual festivals: Passover, Tabernacles, Pentecost. But even in this there was not absolute uniformity. There were minor differences between the calendar followed by the Pharisees and that of the Sadducees.

For further information see:

The great festivals **190**

The picture shows a simple aid for remembering the seasons of the farmer's year. The notes were scratched in Hebrew on limestone in about 900 BC. Found at Gezer, it is known as the 'Gezer Calendar'.

...MBER	OCTOBER	NOVEMBER	DECEMBER	JANUARY	FEBRUARY	MARCH
Tishri MONTH 7 *...rly name: Ethanim*	**Marchesvan** MONTH 8 *early name: Bul*	**Kislev** MONTH 9	**Tebet** MONTH 10	**Shebat** MONTH 11	**Adar** MONTH 12	
...Grape and ...live harvest *Festivals: ...mpets (New Year) ...bernacles/Shelters*	Ploughing and planting *Autumn rains*	Ploughing and planting *Autumn rains Festivals: Lights (Temple dedication)*	Ploughing and planting	Late planting *Spring rains*	Late planting *Spring rains Festivals: Purim*	

10: Day of Atonement

15-21: Tabernacles/Shelters

25: Dedication/ Lights

13-15: Purim

UNDERSTANDING
THE BIBLE

Keys to understanding

John Goldingay

The Bible is not what most of us would expect a religious book or a sacred text to be.

In the first place, it is more a library than a single volume. Inside its covers are histories, stories, laws, prayers, poems, letters, visions, prophecies, and other kinds of writing. These are not the work of a single author, but a range of human authors writing in more than one continent, living in more than one millennium, and speaking more than one language.

So this 'message from God' – which is what the Bible claims to be – is different from that which some other religions believe they have.

Most of the Bible does not claim to have been 'dictated' by God. It is not always God speaking to people. It can be people speaking to God, as in the Psalms. Or it can be people speaking to people, as in the New Testament letters written by Paul.

God speaks through people
Throughout the Bible God speaks through people. This means that understanding people can help us to understand the Bible,

If, for example, you know what it is like to be in pain, to be angry, to be depressed, to be joyful, to love, or to worship, you will understand and empathize with many of the psalms.

If you can put yourself in the shoes of a church leader fretting about a congregation, or of a church member being taken to task by the pastor, that will contribute to your understanding of the New Testament letters, written to the early churches.

When we open a Bible book, we need to ask what we are reading. It may be a story. It may be a letter.

> 66 *More than anything, Christianity is a narrative religion, and narrative is what makes it strong. The stories are eloquent. Even for non-Christians, or atheists, they enter into our being.* 99
>
> Jim Crace

What kind of book is this?
To understand a particular Bible book, we also need to discover what kind of material we are reading.

If we receive four items of mail in the morning, we will read each one in the light of what it is – an advertising promotion, a bill, a love letter, or a prayer letter.

If the mail comes to us from within our own culture, we know instinctively how to read it. If it comes from another culture, we are more likely to misunderstand. We may actually *believe* the

promotional brochure when it says: 'this is a special offer just for you personally'!

The Bible books all come from cultures different from our own, so how do we go about understanding them?

Different guidelines apply to different kinds of writing, but more than half the Bible is history or story, so that is where we begin.

The nature of Bible history
We need to keep three things in mind if we are to understand the Bible's books of history and story.

■ First, most of them have **an interest in facts**. This makes them more like history than fiction.

The Christian faith is fundamentally a 'gospel' – a 'good news' message from God. It tells people, through the story of Israel and the accounts of the life of Jesus, what God has done for them, in the conviction that these things are decisive for the way they relate to God. If God never did anything for Israel or in Jesus, there is no gospel. So *facts matter* in understanding the Bible.

But we must not impose on the Bible our own expectations about its historical nature. Biblical history is a divinely-inspired combination of facts and literary creativity.

The fact that the Bible story links with the nature of the Christian faith as a 'gospel' has another implication.

People are often tempted to read the Bible story primarily for examples of how to live their lives. But if the Bible's story had been designed simply to inspire us in this way, it would have been a different kind of story. The characters of the Bible seem as often to be showing us how *not* to be people of God as modelling how to live faithful and committed lives.

That in itself reflects the fact that the Bible story is more about what God has done with people than about what people have done. Events come about despite them as often as through them.

So in reading the Bible story, a question we have in the front of our minds is:

'What is God doing here, and how, and why?'

■ A second feature of a Bible story, like any story, is that it is **written for an audience**.

We do not always know who the audience was, but often we do, and this can help our understanding.

For instance, Samuel/Kings and Chronicles give us two versions of the story of Israel in the period of the kings. They are different versions of the same story, because they are designed for audiences in different situations:

– Israel under God's punishment after the fall of Jerusalem
– and Israel a century later, when God has in some measure restored them.

These two communities needed to have different insights brought home to them. If we understand who the book was written for, we will appreciate why the story is told the way it is and understand more of what it is designed to convey.

■ A third feature of a Bible story is that **it is story**, with all the characteristics that make for a good story.

It has a beginning, a middle,

The New Testament books are addressed to a number of different audiences, using words and ideas familiar to them:

■ People 'out in the market-place', as the Gospel stories of Jesus and the Christian message spread.

■ Religious Jews, typified by the two men reading the Torah at Jerusalem's Western Wall.

■ Romans, like those reading scrolls in this relief.

■ People in the Greek-speaking culture of the Hellenistic world which had colonized so much of the area – as in the city of Jerash in modern Jordan.

■ Thinkers and philosophers, like those who debated with Paul at Athens.

and an end, and a *plot* with twists and turns (take the Joseph story, or Jesus' story, for example).

It has *characters*: some rounded characters as complex as we know ourselves and those close to us to be, and other flatter characters we do not get to know as well (the Ruth story is an example).

It has a *theme* (Judges, for example, is about the interwovenness of sex and violence). An interesting story may have more than one theme (Jonah is about how not to be a prophet, and also about how God cares for the Gentiles, and also maybe about how God invites Israel to repentance).

So it needs appreciating and understanding as a story. That implies a number of things:
– A story needs to be read as a whole, not only in small episodes, as often happens in church services and daily Bible-reading schemes.
– We need to allow ourselves to be drawn into the story. Interpreting the Bible requires us to exercise our imagination.

This does not mean we should read things into the Bible, though we all do that unconsciously. Sometimes this does not matter; the story may even invite us to do so. After all, a storyteller does not (cannot) tell us everything, and knows that we learn by making the story our own. But it is important not to read alien meanings into the story.

Reading in the company of other people is a safeguard against this, as well as being a positive help in other ways. When we read the Bible with a group of people and discuss it with them, we are nearer to what its writers would have had in mind, for the practice of silent

Much of the Hebrew Bible, the Torah this rabbi is reading, is instruction – the 'dos and dont's' with which God safeguards his people's freedom.

> **❝** *One word of truth outweighs the world.* **❞**
>
> Alexander Solzhenitsyn

reading and study by individuals is a rather modern one.

'Dos and Don'ts'

Inside the big Old and New Testament stories are substantial sections of instructions about how to live.

Neither the Old Testament nor the New is interested in mindless obedience, so we need to understand the reasons for these instructions. In fact the Bible often gives them, though they are sometimes taken for granted or only half-explained because they would be readily understood in the culture they come from (for instance, the reason why Old Testament Israelites should not cook a kid goat in its mother's milk, or why women at Corinth in the New Testament should have their heads covered in church).

We need to work at understanding the issues behind God's instructions, in order to see how we can take the equivalent action in our own context.

We can ask, for example, what these instructions were meant to achieve. What situation did they presuppose? What problem were they seeking to solve, or what danger were they trying to avert? What theological and moral convictions underlay them?

We can then try to work out whether there are equivalent problems and dangers that we need to address in equivalent ways.

In ancient Israel, for instance, people had to build a wall round the (flat) roof of their houses to stop people falling off. In parts of some large cities today, speed retarders might be a comparable way of protecting people's lives.

Another sort of question arises out of the varying standards of the instructions in different parts of the Bible. Some seem very liberating for women and slaves, for instance; others seem to accept their oppression.

Here we can see God's ideals confronting real situations in a practical way.

Jesus, in speaking about marriage and divorce, talked of the tension between what God wanted at the creation and what Moses allowed for because of people's stubbornness (Mark 10).

The point he makes about that particular issue can be applied more widely. The question then is, what is the nearest we can get to God's ideal while allowing for the fact of human stubbornness in *this* context with regard to *this* question?

Looking at the context

We have looked at the Bible's stories and instructions. But in addition to these we have the Prophets in the Old Testament and the Letters in the New. These, even more than the other books, need to be understood in terms of their historical context. The opening verses of a prophecy or a letter usually makes that point, by telling us about the context.

So we need to discover what we can about (say) life in Judah in the 7th century BC, or life in Ephesus in the 1st century AD, if we are to understand prophecies and letters written to communities there.

The prophets' introductions remind us that they are not speaking about Middle Eastern events in our own day. They *are* still relevant to the present day, but we discover *how* by looking to see how God was speaking through the prophets to their immediate audiences.

Asking questions: hearing God speak

From what we have said about the Prophets and the Letters, it is clearly appropriate for us to ask questions. We are thus involved in 'biblical criticism' (see 'The text and the message' and 'Studying the Gospels'), but asking questions does not have to mean being critical of the Bible or imposing human evaluations upon it (as some scholars have done). Asking questions means taking nothing for granted – seeking to understand the Bible on its own terms and allowing it to say what it wants to say.

When we do that, we find that the Bible speaks to us. It is itself, in the phrase Christians so often use, 'the word of God'.

There are two key implications of that:
- We find that God says amazing things. God, after all, *is* amazing; so when God speaks, God is never boring. God constantly surprises and astonishes us.
Those who want to

understand the Bible must be prepared to be astonished, mind-blown, offended, puzzled, and ultimately turned upside down in the way they look at the world.
- God's word is effective. When God speaks, things *happen*. At God's word (in Genesis 1) the world gets created!

When people read the Bible, things happen, too. They see themselves in new ways, they find themselves forgiven and healed, and they are driven to go and do new things.

Understanding the Bible

The Bible was written centuries ago to people in a very different culture from our own.

These stages in understanding and applying it will help avoid:

- picking a bit out of context. The Bible is *not* a magic box!
- building a doctrine on a verse which has been misunderstood – as frequently done by cults and deviations.
- saying it's too remote and difficult for ordinary people: it's not!
- reading it just as literature or geography or history: it *is* these things, but *more*: it's the message that matters.
- reading it as magic, or fables, or fairy stories ... the Bible was written by people in real situations as they were inspired by God.

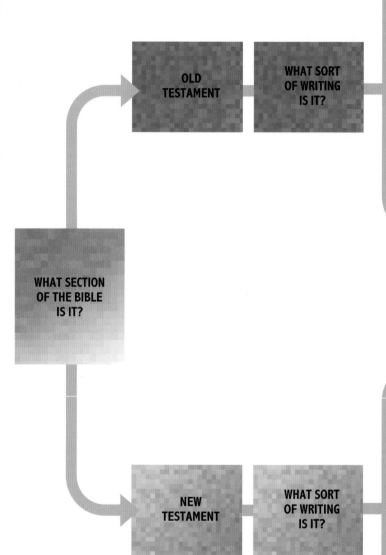

OLD TESTAMENT

WHAT SORT OF WRITING IS IT?

WHAT SECTION OF THE BIBLE IS IT?

NEW TESTAMENT

WHAT SORT OF WRITING IS IT?

| **LAW** | Is this moral law, for all time? Or matters of social or ceremonial law? If the latter, what point was being expressed, or general principle? |

| **HISTORY** | What happened? Where? To whom? Why was the story told? Is this a story-with-a-point? |

| **POETRY/WISDOM** | Don't read poetry as if it's prose! Expect imagery, picture language. Instead of rhyme, Hebrew poetry said things twice in different words. |

| **PROPHECY** | What was the historical setting, the story behind the passage? Is the writing poetic, symbolic? What was the original purpose of the prophecy? |

WHAT DID THE PASSAGE MEAN TO THE ORIGINAL READERS OR HEARERS?

HOW DOES THE SAME MESSAGE APPLY TO US TODAY?

| **GOSPEL** | Four accounts of the teaching and events of the life of Jesus. Is the passage narrative or a story-with-a-point? |

| **HISTORY (ACTS)** | What happened? Was the story included to make a special point? |

| **LETTER** | Who was writing to whom — and why? (See e.g. beginning of letter.) What is the main point or argument of the letter as a whole? How does the passage fit into this? |

| **APOCALYPTIC (REVELATION)** | Set against Roman persecution, John used 'apocalyptic' literary style: Old Testament and poetic imagery. Read with imagination, emotion, to get the universal point. |

The Bible as story

Walter Wangerin Jr

The Bible is at its core a story. Creation is accounted for in story. Israel, the nation's ancestors, history, judges, kings and prophets, is chronicled in story. And Jesus Christ appears not so much in systematic propositions as in a moving narrative.

The thing about story is its ambiguity. It does not, as doctrine does, corral people in a single, explicable thought, defining unanimity, proscribing the maverick wanderings of the individual. It admits of as many varieties of interpretation as it has hearers.

Preachers – when they use a story whole – often make it serve their own ends. It becomes an illustration, something less than the point they intend to teach. The one thing preachers often fail to do with a story is, simply, to tell it – to give it life and breath.

'Holy Truth', the goal of any religion, is a living thing. It desires *relationship* with the people, who seek relationship with it. And story is the meeting-place in which relationships begin, mature, may be experienced whole, may be named, are certainly remembered, and live.

Religions have existed and do exist without theologies. But no religion has existed without story. And story is not story until it is told. And that telling is one critical duty of religion's leaders.

What are the stories that the leaders of the Christian faith are constrained to tell? In which stories does the encounter with God find its opportunity? And why stories, after all?

'Encounter' itself implies dramatic action. Characters with

> 66 *(The creation story) is at once the best known and the worst known of all the stories in the Old Testament. What most people know is not the text, but the vast structure of doctrine which past theologians have built upon it. The story lies hidden in the foundations and all we see is the building above it.* 99
>
> Trevor Dennis

characters move through an evolving relationship in which certain events stand out as significant and signifying. These are moments of intensest interaction, when God's presence, for good or ill, is felt so strongly that every other thing, every detail or gesture, is defined by that presence.

These moments, strung together, form the history of the religion; and they are both remembered and retold as stories, for they were, at first, events. They are significant; they testify, each time they are told, a timeless relationship with God.

But these same foundational stories also make sense of the experiences which people suffer in the present, common knock of their lives. They are signs which name and contain a storm of immediate feelings, helpless impulses, shifting human relationships, spiritual yearnings.

It is not as though people's lives were explained to them intellectually and they understood, but rather as though a loving and powerful parent came and put arms around them and they were comforted.

Story brings order out of chaos.

Because the story form is itself orderly, because it acknowledges and uses the elements of this existence as elements of itself, and because it invites the hearer into its world, it beds that hearer consolingly, with all of his and her experiences, in an orderly and meaningful world.

Story comforts.

Teaching may engage the understanding mind; but story engages the whole person – body, senses, reason, emotion, memory, laughter, tears – so that the one who was fragmented is put together again.

Moreover, story knits people into a community – in time and across the times.

This is what happens when Jews retell and relive the story of the Exodus at Passover, when Christians retell and relive the story of the Passion at Communion, when Martin Luther King cries a story to thousands in the civil rights movement – 'I've been to the mountaintop! I've looked over, and I've seen the Promised Land! I may not get there with you' – evoking for thousands the image of old Moses on Mt Nebo while all Israel stood ready on the plains to cross.

This is what happens: peoples fragmented are put together again feelingly, in the very hearing of their common story told.

Story is as old as religion itself because it is in the nature of religions to story the world.

Interpreting the Bible down the ages

Gerald L. Bray

Down the ages, in the history of the church, the Bible has been read in many different ways. Some of these were inherited from Judaism, but many more grew up later, often under the impact of missionary work among previously pagan peoples.

Two main types of biblical interpretation predominate.

■ The first emphasizes the straightforward, literary-historical meaning of the text.

■ The second concentrates more on its spiritual meaning.

Both have existed since New Testament times, though their relative importance has varied from one century to another.

Literary-historical interpretation

This is the oldest kind, and goes back to Judaism, which placed enormous emphasis on the exact spelling and meaning of every individual word in the Old Testament. Christians took this over and applied it to the Greek translation of the Old Testament (the 'Septuagint') and to the New Testament as well.

Early Christian commentaries

Many early commentaries consist mainly of explanations of unusual words, biblical names and so on. Some of them are correct, but many are fanciful, like the once popular English belief that the word 'Saxon' was a corruption of 'Isaac's son'.

By the 4th century AD there were continuous commentaries on the substance of the biblical texts, especially of the Gospels and the letters of Paul. One school, based in Antioch, concentrated heavily on theological themes, for instance, proving the divinity of Christ. Another, in the Latin-speaking western part of the Roman Empire, was more concerned to develop the social and ethical implications of biblical teaching, and focussed on the Old Testament to a degree unusual elsewhere at that time.

The early centuries of the church saw different emphases and philosophies brought to the interpretation of the Bible. The strongest influence came from the Greeks, producing the creeds still used by the church today. But they also introduced ideas (of the soul, for example) which took Christian faith and practice away from its Hebrew roots. Origen (born about 185) represented both the influence of Greek philosophy on Christian thinking and the use of allegory as a way of understanding the Old Testament.

In the Middle Ages the 'scholastic' tradition built a doctrinal edifice on the creeds, organizing Christian teaching into a 'systematic' theology. It was only too easy for the Bible to be reduced to proof texts, out of context or divorced from their original meaning. Despite the Reformers, the same tendency re-surfaced in the Reformed churches, with church teaching being read back into Bible texts.

Decline and revival During the Middle Ages, this kind of interpretation declined in importance, not least because few people could read Greek or Hebrew. But it did not disappear, and for a long time the church insisted that its doctrine should be based on the plain statements of Scripture. This helped to keep a sense of the importance of the text's literary-historical meaning alive in people's minds, and encouraged them to study it more carefully.

From about 1200, there was a revival of interest in it, and some monks even learned Hebrew in order to be able to comment on the Old Testament more accurately. The great revival of learning in the 15th and 16th centuries brought it to the fore again.

Martin Luther (1483-1546) insisted that this was the only method of interpretation that could be relied on to convey the 'Word of God' to us, though he did not always follow this principle in practice.

John Calvin (1509-1564) adopted Luther's views and systematized them in a series of commentaries which remain classics of their kind.

Calvin believed that a text should be read in its historical context and as a connected narrative. He also placed great emphasis on the dictionary meaning of the words, and decried attempts to alter this merely to help make some theological point or other.

'Covenant' interpretation From this belief, there developed a much closer study of the historical parts of the Bible, which eventually led to what is called 'covenant' interpretation. This regards the Bible as the historical record of God's saving relationship with his people, enshrined in the 'covenant' God made with them. This relationship grew and developed over time, until it was fulfilled in Christ.

Covenant interpretation is a very good way of demonstrating how the Old Testament can remain the 'Word of God', even if parts of it are no longer applicable to us today. ('Testament' is the same as 'covenant' in both Hebrew and Greek.)

The food laws of Leviticus, for example, were given as part of the covenant which God made with Israel through Moses, but when Christ came they were no longer

relevant and so could be discarded.

This does not mean the laws did not come from God in the first place. But, as circumstances altered, a new application of the ancient teaching became necessary. This application was provided by Jesus, who reinterpreted the covenant in a radical way.

Historical-critical thinking
Historical interpretation of the covenant type continued to dominate the field of biblical studies until the beginning of the 19th century, when it was supplemented and partly replaced by what we now call the 'historical-critical' way of thinking.

This takes over Calvin's historical emphasis, but regards the Bible primarily as the record of the covenant community and its understanding of God, not as God's revelation to it. This approach has detected many different theological opinions in the Bible, with the result that it has become more difficult to read it as a single book.

Canonical interpretation More recently there has been a reaction to this kind of analysis, and a new proposal, 'canonical interpretation',

All too often, the Bible has been used as a 'magic book', with texts lifted out of context to spook the reader or to support mystery religions understood only by the initiated.

Alongside the scholastic emphasis of Catholic faith was the devotional tradition. This illustration is from a 1689 edition of Loyola's 'Spiritual Exercises'. It is of the Seven Deadly Sins, quoting Job 2 and Revelation 9.

has been put forward.

This accepts that the Bible may have many different sources, but says that what matters is the fact that these have come down to us as a single message in a single book. Therefore what holds the Bible together is more important than what reminds us of the very diverse origins of some of the material it contains.

In the modern world it is safe to say that almost every academic interpreter of the Bible follows a form of literary-historical interpretation, and that most of them can be classified as 'historical critics'.

Spiritual meaning

There have always been those who have thought that the Bible is not a straightforward message from God, but a hidden riddle which has to be deciphered, usually in some highly complex and mysterious way.

A secret code of numbers? For example, in Hebrew and in Greek each letter also stands for a number, and so theories developed according to which the Bible was a secret numerical code.

Numerology, as this is called, was very popular in certain Jewish circles, and it has resurfaced from time to time among Christians, although nowadays no reputable scholar or theologian takes it seriously.

Allegory? Around the time of Jesus, Philo of Alexandria (died AD 50) developed the belief that the Old Testament was in large measure an allegory of divine things. Allegory

is a literary form in which one thing stands for another, even though there is no real connection between the two.

It became very popular as a way of interpreting the Song of Solomon, which many Christians regarded as a picture of the relationship between Christ and his bride the church, or between Christ and the individual believer.

As a method of interpretation, allegory came into the Christian church through Clement of Alexandria (died about AD 215), who took it over from Philo. Clement's pupil Origen (about 185-254) developed it into a systematic form of biblical interpretation.

According to Origen there were three levels of meaning in Scripture: the literal, the moral and the spiritual. These paralleled the three 'parts' of a human being: body, soul and spirit. Later on, the 4th-century monk John Cassian added another spiritual sense, the 'anagogical',

The Dutch scholar Desiderius Erasmus (1466-1536) applied his understanding of Hebrew and Greek to the interpretation of the Bible. William Tyndale (1494-1536) also went back to the original languages to produce his groundbreaking translation into English. This was the basis for the King James or Authorized Version, which brought the plain meaning of Scripture to all. The advent of the printing press brought the Bible out from the study and into the market-place.

which is similar to the spiritual but concentrates on the future life of the Christian in heaven.

Allegory was very popular in the Middle Ages, especially among monks, though serious scholars did their best to keep it under control. However, it seemed to offer a very attractive way of interpreting the Old Testament, which no longer had to be taken literally. The events it describes – the slaying of the Amalekites, for example – were not to be understood as models for Christian behaviour but rather as signs, pointing to the fact that we have to put sin to death in our lives.

People who adopted this approach often accused Jews of being 'literalists' in their reading of the Old Testament, which was supposed to be why they failed to see Jesus in it.

At its best, allegory was a means of finding references to the Saviour in places which at first sight looked highly unlikely (as in the example of the Song of Solomon), and of applying obscure biblical passages to everyday life.

After the Reformation, allegory died out among academic interpreters, but it remained popular in other places. Many hymns used it. In 'Guide me O thou great Jehovah', for example, the wilderness journey of the people of Israel stands for the Christian life. This is a favourite allegorical theme going back to ancient times. Negro spirituals, in which the River Jordan stands for death, the Promised Land for heaven, and so on, make great use of allegory. In the 19th century, especially, preachers loved to use allegory.

Different levels of meaning In recent years, increasing attention among scholars to the literary genres used in the Bible has made many people aware of different levels of meaning within the text, and this in turn has given the ancient spiritual interpretation a new lease of life.

Much allegorical interpretation is crude or obviously wrong, but it does at least make us aware that there may be more to the meaning of a passage than meets the eye.

Some modern theories have much in common with allegory, and many attempts to make the Bible 'relevant' to women, to people in the developing world, and to other contemporary concerns must obviously go beyond what the actual words of the text say.

Those who study the Bible do not have to choose between the two main types of interpretation: they can borrow ideas from both of them. But it is best to determine the straightforward literary-historical interpretation first.

Christians believe that the Old

Key figures in bringing the understanding of the Bible back to its literary-historical tradition were Martin Luther (1483-1546) and John Calvin (1509-1564).

Alongside the literary-historical interpretation, the spiritual and devotional use of the Bible was continued, for instance, by the Pietists. Hymn-writer Paul Gerhardt (1607-1676) used Bible imagery in the hymns which were used in Bach's cantatas and are still sung in churches today.

The development of scientific method produced various ways of approaching the Bible. Some, like Blaise Pascal (1623-1662), made positive use of scientific 'proofs', showing, for example, how Old Testament prophecy was fulfilled in the New. Other scientists, particularly in the 19th century, used a 'reductionist' approach (if science showed human origins as evolutionary, the Bible's account must be wrong). More recently, as people have come to appreciate the different forms of literature in the Bible, many understand the biblical account and the scientific view as complementing one another. They are different ways of looking at the same thing, and answer different questions.

Testament covenant between God and his people finds its fulfilment, and therefore its true meaning, in Christ. That has to be born in mind when we try to apply a particular Old Testament passage to the present day.

Has the coming of Christ altered the conditions in which a particular Old Testament text was originally applicable? If so, the chances are that it must be used differently today. For example, what the Old Testament says about the ancient Temple sacrifices (which are no longer carried out) can throw light on the meaning of Christ's death on the cross, as a sacrifice on our behalf.

Even in the New Testament, it is important to distinguish what the text teaches as an abiding theological principle from what it simply records as historical fact (the two are not identical). For instance, Christians are called to follow the example – to 'imitate' – both Christ and the apostle Paul. That means sharing their attitudes and beliefs, and living in a way they would approve – not taking up carpentry or tent-making!

The Bible is the most important book in the history of Western civilization. It has been taken up in many cultures and communities, influencing faith and practice. It is crucial that it be read in a way which appreciates the different kinds of writing it contains (see further, 'Keys to understanding').

In the 20th century, concern for justice for the poor in Latin America produced Liberation Theology. Elsewhere there has been an emphasis on Feminist Theology, or on Black Theology. Each applies Scripture to different areas of life. The danger lies in reinterpreting Scripture to suit the cause. Meanings may be read back into the Bible that are not in line with the original text.

A choir from Soweto, South Africa. Gospel songs and spirituals use a rich tradition of Bible imagery to express the hopes and fears and spiritual yearning of Christians up against the harsh realities of life.

The sun 'goes down'. No one now thinks those words describe what actually happens. They simply describe what the observer sees. Equally, the language of poetry is not to be taken literally: yet this does not make it less 'true'. One of the challenges of our time has been to use our understanding of the different forms of writing in the Bible to determine whether a text is meant 'literally' or not.

The text and the message

Craig Bartholomew

Academic study of the Bible ('biblical criticism') has been dominated by a number of different emphases, each in turn coming to the fore.

The first is a *historical* emphasis. The *historical-critical* method, developed in Germany in the 19th century, was taken up by scholars in Britain and the United States early in the 20th century.

This method was *critical*, in the sense that it read and evaluated the biblical text from the perspective of the modern worldview. It was *historical*, in the sense that it used the historical tools that emerged out of modern philosophy of history. It was also historical in its concern, not so much with the text in its present form as with the history of the text and the events it referred to.

The main types of analysis of biblical texts that emerged out of this approach were:

- **textual criticism**, concerned with the establishment of the most reliable Hebrew and Greek texts of the Old and New Testaments
- **source criticism**, concerned with the sources underlying the text
- **form criticism**, concerned with the form or genre of small units of text and the origin of their genre in the societal life of Israel
- **tradition criticism**, concerned with the origin and development of biblical themes in the life of Israel
- **redaction criticism** (from the German word for editor: *redaktor*), concerned with the way in which the text has been edited into its final shape.

Scholars study the text in many different ways to help people understand and interpret the message.

A serious weakness of the historical-critical method is its failure to focus on the books of the Bible in their present form.

Not surprisingly, in the 1970s, a *literary* emphasis developed in response to this failure. This new emphasis focussed on the biblical books as literary texts and explored them from this angle. The narrative shape of much of the Bible received fresh attention and questions such as the role of the narrator, the shape of the plot and the portrayal and development of characters were explored.

By the late 1970s some radical new developments were taking place in literary theory. Movements such as 'post-structuralism' and 'deconstruction' raised questions such as, 'Do texts have meanings that we can discover, or do readers construct these meanings, so that there are as many meanings for a text as there are readers?'

Because of the literary emphasis in biblical studies it was inevitable that these new movements in the theory of literature would soon have an effect. And in the last few years these new questions have been applied to the Bible.

Because they represent a reaction to modern theories these new approaches are often known as *postmodernism*. Postmodernism has raised complex questions about texts, authors, readers, and the world, suggesting that texts do not have single meanings and that their meaning largely depends upon the reader/s.

Under the general category of postmodernism it has become commonplace for scholars to make deconstructionist, feminist, and other readings of biblical texts. A deconstructionist reading will, for example, look for places in a text where there are tensions between the overall message and what a small section of the text may be saying. In this way deconstruction exposes contradictions that it looks for and expects to find in all texts. A feminist reading will examine how women are or are not portrayed in biblical texts.

The effect of postmodernism on biblical studies has been to undermine the dominant historical criticism, leaving no one main method in its place. The impression often given nowadays is of a *smorgasbord* of interpretive approaches which we can choose from and enjoy, simply as a matter of personal preference. In the broader scholarly community there is no agreement about how to read the Bible or how to move forward in biblical studies.

Biblical interpretation is in crisis!

Most recently, there are signs of a *theological* emphasis coming to the fore, with some scholars arguing that biblical studies require a Christian theory of interpretation. This means our approach to the Bible should be rooted in a biblical understanding of the world, and that we ought to read the Bible above all to hear what God is saying to us through it.

Two points in particular should be noted about this history of different emphases:
- The Christian story or view of the world relates to the whole of life: so a biblical theory of interpretation *ought* to be shaped by the Christian story. In this sense the theological emphasis is right.
- We need an integrated approach to biblical interpretation. The historical, the literary and the theological are all important aspects of biblical texts. A proper understanding of the Bible means being alert to all of these, and how they relate to one another – drawing on their different insights, and integrating them within a Christian theory of interpretation.

In my opinion this is best developed by taking what may be called a *communication model* and understanding the biblical texts in terms of:

SENDER
MESSAGE
RECEIVER

If Scripture is primarily God's Word to us, that should be the framework within which we read it.

However we hear God's Word through the message of the original sender and it is here that the hard interpretive work has to be done.

A communication model of biblical interpretation will focus attention on the text in its final form, employing all its energies to help us understand the message.

Analysis of the sources of the text is an important element in this process. The biblical texts were written in very different times and cultures from today and knowledge of Hebrew, Aramaic, Greek and

> **"** *For many decades Old Testament scholarship has been largely preoccupied with looking through the text to what may or may not lie behind it. Scholars have come to treat the text as a window...*
>
> *Exciting things are happening, however. Since the mid-1970s... many books have appeared which have approached the text not as a window but as a picture. They have been concerned to look at the text, at what it says and how it says it. They have encouraged... an engagement with it, an enjoyment of it. The exercise of interpretation they have promoted... has brought the imagination into play, and the emotions... It has asked readers to pay attention to the text.*
>
> *One great advantage of the approach is that it does not demand an enormous amount of background knowledge before we begin. The 'ordinary' reader can have a go.* **"**
>
> Trevor Dennis

associated languages, knowledge of the cultural context in which the text was written, and so on, are vital elements in interpretation.

The examination of sources must, however, be subsidiary to helping us understand the message of the text. And study of sources must be related to understanding the text as we have it.

Knowledge of the context also plays an important role in assessing the type of the text we are dealing with – whether it is wisdom, narrative or prophecy, for example. But this too must help us focus on the particular text and its individual structure.

The rest of the Bible is also an important part of the context of each book: exploration of this, too, must help in explaining the message of the individual book.

The aim of a communication model of interpretation is to hear the message of each book of the Bible in the context of the whole of Scripture. If we understand aspects of the history of a text and something about its literary shape but fail to hear the message, our interpretation will be faulty. Our efforts at interpretation must aim to discern the message of the text, first to its original hearers and then to readers today.

There is, rightly, a growing recognition of the role of the reader/s in interpretation. It is recognized that readers inevitably bring their own views with them in the reading process. A key question is whether or not there are right views to bring.

In my opinion there are! Scripture is most appropriately read out of a deep conviction that it is God's Word, and readers best approach it in this way. That does not mean there are no difficult issues in interpretation: clearly there are. But analysis of the Bible out of a biblical view of the world will allow the real problems to emerge, without creating problems where none exist.

PASSING ON
THE STORY

Storykeepers – the oral tradition

Jo Bailey Wells

The story of the people of God in the Old Testament begins with Abraham in Genesis 12. Yet the stories about Abraham and the other patriarchs who followed him – Isaac and Jacob – are told in Genesis from the perspective of hindsight. We read of Abraham's call to *set out* in faith for the promised land from the settled position of Israel's *arrival* in the promised land. The stories are told as if – through the eyes of Moses – Israel is looking back over its pre-history.

This raises the question of how Moses – or whoever wrote Genesis – knew about events that happened at least 600 years before his lifetime. Without denying that Moses was inspired by God, we might imagine he had some written sources from which to build the account. However, we have no evidence of these. Indeed, it is unlikely that a nomadic people was concerned with reading and writing and preserving records. The matter of survival would be more immediate.

It is now recognized, rather, that the stories in Genesis stem from oral sources circulating among the people. That is, stories about the patriarchs were passed by word-of-mouth from one generation to another, in the manner of folktales, until the point where this living tradition developed also into a written tradition.

Scholars in the field of form criticism (see 'The text and the message') have identified the influence of oral tradition behind many parts of the Bible. In the Old Testament these include particularly the books of Genesis, Exodus, Joshua, Judges and the books of Samuel. In the New Testament, oral tradition has especially influenced the Gospels.

Travellers' tales

Stories which have come to be written down from oral sources have a particular character, and this is important for the way they are to be understood.

■ **We cannot tell where or when they originated** The form and content of a story is liable to change as it is told and retold. Therefore these stories are not suitable material from which to reconstruct a detailed and accurate history.

■ **The stories are adapted to the needs or situation of the hearers** The patriarchal stories are concerned with promises of land, family rivalries, the longing for descendants and the associated need to protect the patriarch's wife – important concerns for a migrant people. It is therefore relevant for us to ask, 'How might this story be adapted to my situation?', which may be very different.

■ **The stories are told to make a particular point**, often a moral point, to enliven or inspire. For example, the story of Abraham's obedience in offering Isaac for sacrifice (Genesis 22) is told in such a way as to inspire the people of Israel to live with the same single-minded faithfulness to God.

■ **The themes of oral stories follow typical patterns and motifs** Just as each culture has characteristic genres of folktales (the English tell jokes about Irishmen, Germans recount romances between royal princes and lowly maidens, Kenyans explain how the leopard gained its spots), so there are specific genres of biblical folktales.

An Orthodox Jew in Jerusalem follows God's instruction to pass the story on to his children, as they look at a model of the Temple.

Previous pages: An African storyteller holds an audience spellbound in this painting by Tony Hudson.

One recurring motif is that of the hero who leaves home and later returns having found fortune:
– Jacob flees his brother Esau and returns with wives and wealth (Genesis 27 – 35).
– Joseph is banished by his brothers yet later rules over them (Genesis 37 – 45).

The significance of these stories does not lie with the motif itself, but in the subtle way in which the motif is used and varied to make a point. For Jacob, it is hard to return because he must first make peace with Esau. In the story of Joseph, the homecoming takes place in reverse, with the brothers unwittingly encountering Joseph.

The art of the storyteller

Stories which are told (parables, for example) are different from stories intended to be read (such as novels). They must hold the hearers' attention to gain effect. We can identify some storytelling techniques in the parables of Jesus:

- **Reversal** The motif of the hero leaving home and returning with a fortune is reversed in the parable of the prodigal son (Luke 15:11-32). This provides a surprise twist-in-the-tail.
- **Repetition** In the parable of the tenants (Luke 20:9-16) there is a three-fold repetition of the sending of a servant to the vineyard for the harvest. This serves to build tension and anticipate the climax when – *finally* – the owner sends his son.
- **Brevity** The narrative detail of an oral story is terse, leaving much to the listeners' imagination. That which is given, therefore – the name of a character or the colour of a garment (the rich man, in purple, and Lazarus, Luke 16:19-20) – carries great moment.
- **Direct speech** The plot of a

parable frequently unfolds through the use of direct speech. In the parable of the persistent widow, we hear not only the pleas of the widow but also the private mutterings of the unjust judge (Luke 18:1-8).
- **Language** If stories are to be striking, their language must be colourful and concrete, even to the point of exaggeration. It is not necessarily intended to be taken literally. Consider the scale of the debt in the parable of the unmerciful servant (Matthew 18:21-35). Ten thousand talents is an unimaginable amount of money, so as to emphasize the limitless scope of God's forgiveness.

Can we rely on oral tradition?

Understanding the likely origins of biblical material helps us to be wise in the way we read and use it. For example, although it might be unwise to seek to reconstruct Israel's earliest history from the stories in Genesis, it is highly appropriate to use the same stories as examples of faithful (and un-faithful) living. They express truths which have proved revelatory and instructive in the experience of countless generations who have

Many of the Bible's stories were told before they were written down to be read. Here a storyteller in modern Iran retells tales of Alexander the Great for his audience.

lived by them, treasured them and passed them on.

Furthermore, inhabitants of oral cultures have more reliable memories than those of us who depend upon filing-cabinets and computers. The Israelites, especially, worked hard at story-keeping. They valued the gift of memory – developing sophisticated memorization techniques – and undertook to recount the stories of God's faithful deeds to succeeding generations:

'Take care: keep careful watch on yourselves so that you do not forget the things that you have seen with your own eyes; do not let them pass from your minds as long as you live, but teach them to your children and to your children's children' (Deuteronomy 4:9; see also 5:1; 6:7, and so on).

The scribes

Jo Bailey Wells

Ancient Israel did not live in a world dependent on oral tradition alone. Our inheritance of the Bible, and of the Old Testament in particular, owes its existence entirely to generations of Jewish scribes, who copied and recopied portions of scripture for more than 1,500 years.

The alphabet was already established in Canaan when Israel became a nation. This provided a simple means for recording accounts of divine revelations, oral traditions and historical events.

The oldest Hebrew texts which have been found date from the 9th century BC, though it is quite likely that previous generations of Israelite scribes were also writing with the alphabet.

In the pre-exilic period Hebrew shared a script with the Canaanites and Phoenicians, based on a 22-letter alphabet. This made reading and writing relatively simple, compared with the cuneiform writing systems in Mesopotamia and Egypt. After the exile, under the influence of the Aramaic script, Hebrew came to be written with fuller block-shaped letters in a 'square' script, as above.

The written word

While much was told by word of mouth and passed on that way from generation to generation (for example, Exodus 13:14-15), the existence of writing meant there was something to check against.

Consider, for example, the giving of the law on Mount Sinai. It is highly significant that the story says Moses was given the commandments, not just verbally, but also written down on tablets of stone. According to the accounts in Exodus and Deuteronomy, Moses carried these down the mountain and placed them in the Ark for safe-keeping (Deuteronomy 10:4-5).

Writing carries significant impact within a predominantly oral culture:

- **It lends authority** Writing gives power to words in a way that makes them different from the spoken word. Once written, the law could be preserved and remain unchanged for centuries. Thus it became an authoritative source.
- **It allows accessibility** A piece of writing can be copied any number of times – even onto every doorpost (Deuteronomy 6:9; 11:20). While the original texts of the law were kept safely in the Ark (eventually, in the sanctuary of the Temple in Jerusalem), copies could be made that anyone with questions or doubts might consult.
- **It provides for accuracy** The words of a prophet might be written the day they were spoken and kept for verification (compare Deuteronomy 18:22). Records about kings, their policies and related events could be maintained and updated, and later used as sources by the biblical historians (for example, 1 Kings 11:41; 2 Kings 23:28).

Scribes as writers

Understood literally, a scribe – in Hebrew, *sopher* – is any person who writes . Although anyone who was determined could learn to read and perhaps also write Hebrew without enormous effort, the term is normally used to describe a designated guild of people who fulfilled the special task of writing – and copying – Israel's sacred and historical accounts.

Before the exile, these people probably formed administrative centres in the royal court. Later on, around the 2nd century BC, 'the Scribes' became a distinct political party made up of a highly-educated class of people, affiliated with the Pharisees.

Ezra is depicted as the archetypal scribe (see also 'The scribe'). That is to say, he was a member of a learned class of people who devoted himself to copying, guarding and interpreting the law. This work demanded care and training over several years (see Psalm 45:1; Ezra 7:6) and was taken very seriously (Jeremiah 8:8). It operated in close relation with the work of the priesthood. According to the tradition, Ezra performed several roles. These are probably idealized in the writing of Ben Sira (Ecclesiasticus 38:24 – 39:11):

- preacher: assembling the people every year in order to read out the law, explain it and urge people to keep it
- judge: listening to those with complaints and giving rulings on particular matters of Jewish law
- teacher: running schools in writing and for the training of apprentice scribes
- academic: studying the law, and producing writing and theory in response.

Copying The copyist's task was to reproduce the text as accurately as possible. So we cannot tell how many times a portion of the Old Testament has been copied, as long as it has been done well. We can only identify the occasions where mistakes were made, based on the variations between texts.

Differences between texts can be understood to stem from:
- the omission or addition of a word
- misspellings, which later result in misreadings
- the inclusion within the main text of an interpretative note originally intended for the margin
- damage to a scroll, leaving us to guess illegible or missing words
- a scribal alteration, made to soften ideas perceived as offensive.

Ben Sira's portrait of the ideal scribe, from Ecclesiasticus 39

'He seeks out the wisdom of all the ancients, and is concerned with prophecies;
he preserves the sayings of the famous and penetrates the subtleties of parables;
he seeks out the hidden meanings of proverbs and is at home with the obscurities of parables.
He serves among the great and appears before rulers…
If the great Lord is willing, he will be filled with the spirit of understanding…
The Lord will direct his counsel and knowledge…
He will show the wisdom of what he has learned, and will glory in the law of the Lord's covenant.'

In days long before printing, Hebrew scribes made copies of the scriptures with a care and accuracy which seems extraordinary to readers today, living in a world which generally cares less for truth. Jewish scribes still work with the same scrupulous attention to detail.

Though minor errors were committed by copyists which have passed into the printed text, the process of copying included careful checking and correction.

The close similarity between different copies of the text, transmitted through different channels, originating from different eras and even received in different languages, is remarkable.

The discovery of the Dead Sea Scrolls in 1947 – manuscripts over 1,000 years older than anything previously known – has highlighted the extraordinary accuracy of this process.

Editors at work

Jo Bailey Wells

The Hebrew scriptures, as we know them, are likely to have come into existence gradually. The original sources make up the raw materials, from which it is supposed that generations of editors worked to compile these 'ingredients' until the books reached their final form in the 'canon' (the official agreed list).

This process of editing – or 'redaction', to use the technical term – probably took place from some time before the exile through to the 2nd century BC. The New Testament became 'fixed' much more quickly, and the work of editors is less significant.

The importance of the editors

Study of the work of the editors is known as 'redaction criticism' (see 'The text and the message'). This attempts to uncover the theological purposes behind the arrangement of material in a book, since the form of the books as we now have them reflects the editors' work as well as the authors' and translators'.

If we can understand how a book came to be written as it is, we are more likely to understand its particular message and perspective. For example:

- In the books of Samuel, the Song of Hannah is placed at the beginning of the story. This tells the alert reader at an early stage that the story is going to focus on the identification of a 'king', or 'anointed one', in Israel (1 Samuel 2:10), and about God's faithfulness to him. The arrangement of texts within a book affects our broad understanding of the meaning of the whole book.
- In Kings and Chronicles there are different portrayals of King Manasseh. According to the editor of Kings, judgment and exile came to Judah because of an accumulation of sin, especially that of Manasseh (2 Kings 23:26). In contrast, the Chronicler tells of the *repentance* of Manasseh, to show how God is always ready to respond to a penitent (2 Chronicles 33:12-17). In the history books, especially, the editors selected their stories to bring out a particular interpretation of events.

Without the work of editors who gathered and arranged material, there would be no Bible. These scrolls of the scriptures in a synagogue at Tsefat in northern Israel stand as a testimony to their work.

COLLECTING AND ARRANGING THE OLD TESTAMENT SECTIONS

The Pentateuch: Genesis to Deuteronomy

The first five books of the Bible appear as a single coherent story — as if produced by a single author with no need for an editor. Yet there are many different styles of writing, and some stories are repeated from different perspectives. It is commonly supposed, therefore, that this represents the final work of compilers who wove together several sources.

The 19th-century German scholar, Wellhausen, suggested there were four, known as J, E, D and P, which originated from different periods and places. Each treated the origins of Israel in its own distinctive way. If this is actually so (and it remains a theory), the story we now have represents not only the work of 'weaving' by the final editors — during or after the exile — but also that of earlier 'sub-editors' on the individual sources.

The Deuteronomic history: Joshua, Judges, 1 & 2 Samuel, 1 & 2 Kings

These historical books take their section title from Deuteronomy, the book they follow, since they continue the same themes and theology of covenant.

Their composition is complicated, because they contain traditions from Israel's early period as a tribal organization in the promised land, as well as the stories of royal administrations from David through to the exile.

So the books bring together work done by different generations of historians. The reports of past events are also given the benefit of hindsight: the editors reflect on the past in the light of current events (around the time of exile). These 'editors' were, therefore, sophisticated scholars and writers too.

The later histories: Chronicles – Ezra – Nehemiah

Whether or not these books originated from the same author, or are by different authors, they have been brought together by an editor (known as 'the Chronicler') to form a continuous narrative, emphasized by the repetition at the beginning of Ezra of the last two verses of 2 Chronicles.

This narrative, dated around 400 BC (though sometimes later), is told so as to encourage the small restored community to believe that they really are the inheritors of God's ancient promises to Israel.

It is possible that 'the Chronicler' had a major influence in gathering and arranging other Old Testament books to form the canon.

The Psalms

These derive from the worship of ancient Israel. It is likely that these 'hymns' were assembled during the exile, when the people were deprived of normal worship at the Temple. The process of editing has gathered the collection so as to create a book for study (Psalm 1 sets out this idea at the very beginning). So the psalms are arranged into five 'books', which include smaller collections as whole units (e.g. the Psalms of Asaph, 73-83; the Songs of Ascent, 120-134). Furthermore, each psalm is given a heading to aid meditation (see e.g. Psalm 51).

The Prophets: Isaiah, Jeremiah, Ezekiel, the 12 'minor prophets'

It is possible that Jeremiah was responsible for the formation of the book bearing his name (see Jeremiah 36:32). But, in general, it is likely that the records of the pre-exilic and exilic prophets were preserved through the exile and edited afterwards.

As with the Deuteronomic history, the material is re-assessed in the light of the experience, and post-exilic books (Haggai, Zechariah, Malachi) are added.

The Hebrew Bible

Dan Cohn-Sherbok

The basis of the Jewish faith is the Bible. For the Jews, Scripture is referred to as the *Tanakh*: this term is an abbreviation of the principal letters of the words which stand for its three divisions: *Torah* (teaching); *Neviim* (prophets); *Ketuvim* (writings).

An agreed list of books

The Torah consists of the Five Books of Moses: Genesis, Exodus, Leviticus, Numbers and Deuteronomy. According to tradition, these books were revealed by God to Moses on Mt Sinai.

The second division of the Hebrew Bible – Prophets – is divided into two parts.

■ Former Prophets – contains the books of Joshua, Judges, 1 and 2 Samuel and 1 and 2 Kings.
■ Latter Prophets – is composed of the major prophets (Isaiah, Jeremiah and Ezekiel) and the minor prophets (Hosea, Joel, Amos, Obadiah, Jonah, Micah, Nahum, Habakkuk, Zephaniah, Haggai, Zechariah and Malachi).

The third division consists of a variety of divinely inspired books: Psalms, Proverbs, Job, Song of Songs (Solomon), Ruth, Lamentations, Ecclesiastes, Esther, Daniel, Ezra, Nehemiah and 1 and 2 Chronicles.

During the Second Temple period (after the Jews returned from exile in Babylonia), a large number of other books were written by Jews in Hebrew, Aramaic and Greek, which were not included in the official list (canon) of Scripture.

Nonetheless, these texts did gain official status in the Roman Catholic and Eastern Orthodox Churches. Known as the Deutero-canonical books or Apocrypha, they had an important impact on Christian thought. The most substantial is the Wisdom of Jesus Son of Sirah (also know as Ben Sira or Ecclesiasticus). Other works include: the Wisdom of Solomon, 1 and 2 Maccabees, Tobit and Judith.

Additional literary sources of the Second Temple period are known as the Pseudepigrapha. These non-canonical books consist of such works as the *Testament of the Twelve Patriarchs, 1* and *2 Enoch* and *Jubilees*.

In rabbinic sources, a distinction is drawn between the revelation of the Pentateuch (Torah in the narrow sense) and the prophetic writings. This is frequently expressed by saying that the Torah was given directly by God, whereas the prophetic books were given by means of prophecy.

The remaining books of Scripture – the Hagiographa – were conveyed by means of the Holy Spirit rather than through prophecy. Nonetheless all these writings constitute the canon of Scripture.

Interpretation

According to the rabbis, the expositions and elaborations of the written law were also revealed by God to Moses on Mt Sinai. Subsequently they were passed from generation to generation, and through this process additional legislation was incorporated. Thus traditional Judaism affirms that God's revelation is twofold and binding for all time.

In the Middle Ages this traditional belief was continually affirmed. The 12th-century Jewish philosopher, Moses Maimonides, for example, declared that the belief in Torah MiSinai (Torah from Sinai) is a fundamental belief in Judaism:

'The Torah was revealed from heaven. This implies our belief that the whole of the Torah found in our hands this day is the Torah that was handed down by Moses, and that it is all of divine origin. By this I mean that the whole of the Torah came unto him from before God in a manner which is metaphorically called "speaking"; but the real nature of that communication is unknown to everybody except to Moses to whom it came.'

Like Maimonides, the 13th-century philosopher Nahmanides in his *Commentary to the Pentateuch* argued that Moses wrote the Five Books of Moses at God's dictation. It is likely, he argued, that Moses wrote Genesis and part of Exodus when he descended from Mt Sinai. At the end of 40 years in the wilderness he completed the rest of the Pentateuch.

Nahmanides observed that this view follows the rabbinic tradition that the Torah was given scroll by scroll. For Nahmanides Moses was like a scribe who copied an older work.

Underlying this conception is the mystical idea of a primordial Torah which contains the words describing events long before they happened. This entire record was in heaven before the creation of the world.

In addition, Nahmanides maintained that the secrets of the Torah were revealed to Moses and are referred to in the Torah by the use of special letters, the numerical values of words and letters, and the adornment of Hebrew characters.

Paralleling Nahmanides' mystical interpretation of the Torah, the medieval mystical work, the *Zohar*, asserts that the Torah contains mysteries beyond human comprehension. As the *Zohar* explains:

'Said R. Simeon: "Alas for the man who regards the Torah as a book of mere tales and everyday matters! If that were so, even we could compose a Torah dealing with everyday affairs, and of even greater excellence. Nay, even the princes of the world possess books of greater worth which we could use as a model for composing such Torah. The Torah, however, contains in all its words supernal truths and sublime mysteries... Thus had the Torah not clothed herself in garments of this world, the world could not endure it. The stories of the Torah are thus only her outer garments, and whoever looks upon that garment as being the Torah itself, woe to that man – such a one has no portion in the next world."'

The impact of modern scholarship

In the modern period, however, it has become increasingly difficult to sustain the traditional Jewish concept of divine revelation in the light of scholarly investigation and discovery.

As early as the 16th century, scholars pointed out that the Five Books of Moses appear to be composed from different sources.

In the middle of the 19th century two German scholars, Karl Heinrich Graf and Julius Wellhausen, concluded that the Five Books of Moses are composed of four main documents which once existed separately but were later combined by a series of editors or 'redactors'.

Other scholars rejected the

A scroll of the Hebrew Bible is held high in a Jewish synagogue. The law is honoured as God's gift to his people.

theory of separate sources; instead they maintain that oral traditions were modified throughout the history of ancient Israel and only eventually were compiled into a single narrative.

Yet despite these different theories, there is a general recognition among modern biblical critics, including Reform, Conservative, and Reconstructionist Jews, that the Pentateuch was not written by Moses. Rather, it is now seen as a collection of traditions originating at different times in ancient Israel.

For Orthodox Jews, however, such a modern view is irrelevant. Orthodox Judaism remains committed to the view that the written as well as the oral Torah was imparted by God to Moses on Mt Sinai. This act of revelation serves as the basis for the entire legal system as well as doctrinal beliefs about God.

Within the non-Orthodox branches of Judaism, on the other hand, there is a general acceptance of the findings of biblical scholarship. Such a non-fundamentalist approach, which takes account of recent scholarly developments in the field of biblical studies, rules out the traditional belief in the infallibility of Scripture and thereby provides a rationale for changing the law and reinterpreting the theology of the Hebrew scriptures in the light of contemporary knowledge.

In the modern period, therefore, there has been a shift away from the fundamentalism of the past. Nonetheless, non-Orthodox Jews join ranks with the Orthodox in continuing to regard the Jewish Bible as fundamental to the faith.

An approved list – the 'canon' of Scripture

Stephen Travis with Mark Elliott

The Bible consists of 66 books. But why these particular books?

Why is a Jewish book such as the Wisdom of Solomon not included in the Old Testament?

Why were four Gospels included, no more and no less?

And why do the Jewish and Christian communities attach unique significance to these books?

These are questions about 'canon'.

The word 'canon' in Greek meant a stick or measuring-rod, hence a standard or rule. Christians came to use it to refer to a list of the books inspired by God which they acknowledge as authoritative Scripture.

The Jewish scriptures

By the time of Jesus the Jews categorized their scriptures into three sections – the Law, the Prophets and the Writings. These three collections came together in stages.

- **The Law** or Torah (Genesis to Deuteronomy) was the first to be acknowledged as the foundation document of Israel because of its association with Moses. In the 5th century BC Ezra brought it back in its written form from Babylonia to Jerusalem, and the whole community recognized it as 'the book of the law of Moses' (Nehemiah 8:1).
- **The Prophets** consisted of the Former Prophets (the narrative sequence from Joshua to 2 Kings, which interpreted history from a prophetic perspective) and the Latter Prophets (Isaiah, Jeremiah, Ezekiel and the 12 'minor prophets', known by Jews as 'the Book of the Twelve' and collected together into a single scroll).

It is likely that these also were a recognized collection by the time of Ezra or soon afterwards. Certainly Ecclesiasticus 44 – 49 (2nd century BC) shows familiarity with the Law and the Prophets as we know them. New Testament writers use the phrase 'the Law and the Prophets' as a designation of these scriptures (Matthew 5:17; John 1:45; Acts 13:15; Romans 3:21).

- **The Writings** consisted mostly of later documents, and their general acceptance as a definitive collection came probably in the 1st century AD. But 200 years earlier the prologue to Ecclesiasticus already referred to 'the Law, the Prophets and the other books of our ancestors'. And the Dead Sea Scrolls include copies, or at least fragments, of every book of the Jewish Bible except Esther, indicating that the community which produced them (about 150 BC to AD 68) valued all these books.

Other books from the period 300 BC – AD 100 were treasured by various groups of Jews. The Greek translation of the Hebrew Scriptures, known as the Septuagint, included several of them (see 'Deuterocanonical books'). But after the catastrophe of Jerusalem's destruction by the Romans in AD 70 the Jews, under the leadership of the Pharisees, opted for a leaner canon of 24 books. They excluded literature which they deemed too recent, or too risky in its theology, or which was associated with groups within Judaism rather than the whole Jewish community.

The resulting list is identical with the 39 books of what Christians call the Old Testament. The Jewish method of counting reckons 1 and 2 Samuel, 1 and 2 Kings, 1 and 2 Chronicles, Ezra – Nehemiah and the 12 minor prophets each as a single book.

Christians have endorsed the canon as defined by 1st-century Jews mainly because Jesus and the New Testament writers refer to a wide range of Old Testament books as having the authority of God. Quotations are frequently introduced with a formula such as 'It is written', or even 'God says'.

According to Luke 24:44, the risen Jesus said, 'Everything must be fulfilled that is written of me in the Law of Moses, the Prophets and the Psalms'. 'Psalms' here may refer to the Writings as a whole, among which the Psalms were normally placed first.

Probably the first Christian to consider critically which Jewish documents should be regarded as holy scripture was Melito, bishop of Sardis around AD 170. His list was identical with the 24 books of the Hebrew canon, which he called 'the books of the Old Covenant' (Eusebius, *Church History* 4.26.13-14).

The New Testament

The story of the New Testament canon is the story not so much of a collection of individual documents as of a collection of collections.

The first documents to be collected together were **Paul's letters**. The heretic Marcion provides evidence that before his time (about AD 140) there was already a fixed collection of Paul's ten major letters. By AD 200 there were collections which also included 1 and 2 Timothy and Titus. Christian writers of this period cited them often as having scriptural authority.

Although there was frequent doubt about the authorship of the Letter to the Hebrews, by AD 200 Egyptian Christians included it in their collection of Paul's letters But it was not firmly established in the Western church until the 4th century.

■ **The Gospels** As Christians became familiar with more than one Gospel they became aware of their different perspectives on the story of Jesus. Since they believed firmly that there was a single, coherent gospel message this became something of a problem. But the advantages of affirming the distinctive contributions of four Gospels eventually prevailed.

Around AD 150 Justin had described how Christians gathered for worship read from the 'memoirs' of the apostles 'which are called Gospels' (*Apology* 1.66).

John's Gospel was slower to gain acceptance than the other three – perhaps because it was being used by Gnostics to promote their own version of Christian faith, perhaps simply because it was so different from the others. But before AD 200 Irenaeus was arguing that it is just as natural that there should be four Gospels as that there are four winds and four corners of the earth (*Against Heresies* 3.11.8).

Other Gospel-like documents such as the *Gospel of Peter* and the *Gospel of the Egyptians* continued to be used in Eastern churches, but eventually fell out of favour because they expressed doctrine which had more in

From scroll to book

The approved list of scriptures which make up the Hebrew Bible were collected in scroll form. Scrolls were originally made from sheets of papyrus about 30cm/11ins high by 20cm/8ins wide glued side by side to make rolls of variable length, though it was unusual to paste more than 20 sheets together. The Temple Scroll (largest of the Dead Sea Scrolls) is

8.2m/27ft long. Scrolls were written on leather as well as papyrus, and this was the norm for Hebrew biblical scrolls.

The text was read column by column and the handles at either end enabled readers to unroll one side and roll up the other as they read.

By New Testament times, most scrolls (including New Testament documents) were made of papyrus rather than of leather. But scrolls were cumbersome to carry about. Christians may in fact have been pioneers of the early book form – the 'codex' – with pages folded and fastened together at one side. This began

to replace the scroll during the 2nd century AD. Covers were later added to protect it.

left: A Hebrew scroll.

right: A page of Codex Sinaiticus, the earliest surviving complete manuscript of the New Testament (plus part of the Old). Written in Greek on parchment, it was discovered in the 19th century at St Catherine's Monastery at the foot of Mt Sinai. The Codex dates from the 4th century AD.

The spine shows the book-form of Codex Sinaiticus.

Codex Alexandrinus was a present from the Patriarch of Constantinople (who seems to have taken it with him from Alexandria in Egypt) to the king of England (Charles I, by the time the gift arrived in 1627). One of the oldest copies of the Bible, hand-written in Greek, it dates from between AD 400 and 450.

common with Gnostic heresy than with the tradition received by the church.

■ **The Catholic Letters** (James-Jude) formed the latest collection to come together. Because there was no unambiguous acknowledgment of their apostolic authorship, all except 1 Peter and 1 John were little used before the 4th century. Soon after AD 300,

Eusebius referred to a collection of seven 'catholic letters'. Probably the collection arose from a desire to demonstrate a common witness of the 'pillar apostles' (Galatians 2:9) alongside the letters of Paul.

■ **Acts and Revelation** fell outside these three collections. Though from the same author as Luke's Gospel, Acts was early separated from it and is not cited by Christian writers before Justin. But by 200 its significance was recognized as evidence that Paul and the other apostles preached the same gospel, in contrast to the efforts of Marcion and other heretics to claim Paul for themselves and reject the others.

Revelation was accepted more readily in the West than in the East, but even in the West it was under suspicion because of its use by Montanists with their excessive enthusiasm for end-of-the-world speculation. In the 4th century its scriptural status was recognized in the East – on the understanding that the millennium of Revelation 20 was not to be interpreted literally.

After three centuries of usage the churches began to confirm formally which books commanded the authority to determine their life and teaching. Lists of authoritative books were drawn up in various parts of the Christian world. Particularly interesting among these is Eusebius' categorization of documents into three groups:

■ those accepted in the churches without qualification – four Gospels, Acts, 14 letters of Paul, 1 John, 1 Peter, and also Revelation 'if it seems desirable'

■ disputed books, i.e. those not yet universally accepted – James, Jude, 2 Peter, 2 and 3 John, the *Acts of Paul, the Shepherd of*

Hermas, the *Apocalypse of Peter*, the *Letter of Barnabas*, and the *Didache*

■ those firmly rejected, including the *Gospels of Peter*, of *Thomas* and of *Matthias*, and the *Acts of Andrew* and of *John*.

In his Easter Letter of AD 367, Athanasius offered for the first time a list of authoritative books identical with the New Testament as we know it, and this was widely approved in the East. The same conclusion was endorsed in the West by a papal declaration in 405, and in North Africa at the Synods of Hippo (393) and Carthage (397).

But the extent of the canon was never formally defined by an ecumenical council of the whole church. So even today, while Orthodox, Roman Catholic and Protestant churches share the same New Testament canon, the Ethiopian church has a canon of 38 books.

If we review the criteria by which the 27 books attained canonical status, we can see that four key questions were being asked of each document under consideration.

■ **Is it apostolic?** In many cases this was simply a question about authorship. Paul's letters, for example, were readily accepted on this ground, whereas Hebrews remained in doubt for longer because its authorship was uncertain.

Other documents were included because they came from someone closely associated with an apostle if not from the apostle himself. Thus the Gospels of Mark and Luke were recognized as having equal authority with Matthew and John.

It was crucial that each document was known to come from the earliest period of the church's existence. However, the test of apostolicity was not rigidly applied. For instance, despite the doubt about the authorship of Hebrews, it came to be accepted because it met the following criteria.

■ **Is it orthodox?** Does it conform to the understanding of the faith which has come to us through the living tradition of the church?

On this basis many documents with authentic-sounding titles like the *Gospel of Thomas* and the *Acts of John* were rejected because their teaching was Gnostic in character.

■ **Is it catholic?** Does it communicate God's word to the church at large, not merely to a select group? Letters originally addressed to a specific church were accepted if their message could speak to a wider audience.

Thus even the seemingly insignificant 2 John became canonical because of its stress on defending the truth against 'those who deny that Jesus Christ has come in the flesh' (verses 7-11).

■ **Has it nurtured the life of the churches over time?** In the long run the most important test of a document was whether it had proved its God-given value by its ability to renew, sustain and guide the church.

So we should not imagine that the process of defining the canon was a matter of committees sitting in judgment on Christian writings and deciding whether they should be in or out. It would be truer to say that the documents which eventually made up the canon demonstrated their intrinsic authority through constant usage.

In modern times suggestions have sometimes been made that the contents of the canon should be reviewed.

Some have suggested that

scholarly scepticism about the apostolic authorship of certain books should throw their canonicity in doubt. Others have asked why the New Testament canon should be rigidly limited to these 27 books. Why not include other early Christian documents such as the *Gospel of Thomas* or the *Acts of Paul?*

But, as we have seen, doubts about authorship are not a sufficient reason for excluding a document. The books concerned have for too long proved their worth in Christian experience. And although readers may profit from reading a wider range of early Christian literature, the New Testament documents remain special.

Probably none of the documents occasionally proposed for inclusion is as early as any New Testament document. Their message is derived – and sometimes deviates – from the well-spring that is the New Testament.

The books of the New Testament canon are distinctive in providing first-hand witness to the story of Jesus Christ and his impact in the formative period of the church's life. The canon is a case of the survival of the fittest.

Early on, church leaders had to decide which of the writings in circulation were genuine and would be of benefit to the whole church. The four Gospels with which our New Testament opens stood out from the rest. These pages from an unknown Gospel are very early – from the first half of the 2nd century.

Spreading the word – the task of translation

Steve Walton

Most modern people do not read the Bible itself, but versions of the Bible in their own language, for the books of the Bible were written in three ancient languages: Hebrew, Aramaic and Greek.

Most of the Old Testament is written in Hebrew, the language of the Israelites; a few parts of the Old Testament are in Aramaic, a language which was common in Israel/Palestine at the time of Jesus and which is related to Hebrew.

The New Testament is written in 'common' Greek – the language spoken by many people all around the Roman Empire at the time of Jesus.

The authors of the biblical books wrote to communicate, and therefore used the language of their target audience. However, it was not long before the message began to be spread beyond people who knew those languages – the work of translating the scriptures began even before the time of Jesus.

The Old Testament in Greek

The Jewish people of the 3rd century BC produced a version of the Old Testament in Greek known as the **Septuagint**. The Septuagint was used for reading aloud in many synagogues of the Roman Empire in Greek-speaking cities, such as Corinth, Antioch or Rome. The Jews in these cities often could not understand the Hebrew Old Testament, and so they needed their Bible in their own language.

Something similar happened in Israel/Palestine around the same period, for most people spoke Aramaic rather than Hebrew, and so they did not understand much of the Old Testament. The 'Targums' are an Aramaic version of the Old Testament in use before and during the time of Jesus – often expanding and paraphrasing the original quite a lot.

The first New Testament translations

These versions of the Old Testament were written mainly to help those who were already Jews to understand their faith. Within 300 years of the death of Jesus, the early

One of the earliest languages into which the New Testament was translated was Coptic (for Egypt), in the 3rd century AD. This is a page of John's Gospel.

Christians produced versions of the New Testament in a variety of languages – so that people who knew no Greek could read about Jesus and believe in him.

They started with **Latin**, the language of the Romans (about AD 150-220), **Syriac**, spoken in ancient Syria (about AD 160), and **Coptic**, a language from Egypt (about 3rd century AD), and expanded into the languages of the Middle East, North Africa and Europe.

These early translators were motivated by two factors: they believed the New Testament books to be inspired by God, and they had grasped Jesus' call to 'make disciples of all nations' (Matthew 28:19). These twin beliefs spurred them to make the books of the New Testament accessible to as many people as possible in their own languages – so that their lives could be changed by the message of Jesus too.

At this point Christianity contrasts in an interesting way with Islam, for Muslims speak of producing commentaries on the Qur'an and interpretations of it, but not translations – for they regard the original (in Arabic) as strictly untranslatable.

Because Christianity is a missionary faith, committed to helping others meet with God through Jesus Christ, the New Testament was first written in the common language of its day, and then translated into the languages of many peoples.

An explosion of translations

In the 16th century AD there was a great revival of Bible translation in Europe, as Christians recovered the importance of spreading the message of Jesus to others, particularly those who did not know Latin, the language of highly educated people. The Dutch scholar Erasmus wrote:

'Christ wishes his mysteries to be published as widely as possible... I wish they were translated into all languages of all Christian people, that they might be read and known, not merely by the Scotch and the Irish, but even by the Turks and the Saracens. I wish that the husbandman may sing parts of them at his plough, that the weaver may warble them at his shuttle, that the traveller may with their narratives beguile the weariness of the way.'

For a time this belief was opposed by the traditionally-minded church of that day, which feared that people would produce their own interpretations of the Bible if they read it in their own language. That would mean the church would lose control of what people believed.

But those who wanted the Bible in the language of ordinary people did not think that this would lead to anarchy – they wanted the life-changing power of the Bible to be open to all, and not just to scholars.

The invention of printing shortly before this meant that there was a cheap method of making these new translations available to many people.

Today, the United Bible Societies and Wycliffe Bible Translators carry on the work of producing versions of the Bible in different languages.

Of the 6,701 known languages worldwide just 5% have the full Bible, a further 13% have the full New or Old Testament, and a further 14% have at least one Bible book translated. Added together, these figures mean that over 95% of the world's population have at least some of the Bible in a language they know – there is still some way to go!

Translators today use the tools of modern technology to help them in their task.

How translation works

Modern Bible versions are usually the work of a group and go through four stages before being published.

- A draft translation of each book is produced, by one translator per book, leading to a discussion with the group of translators. Some languages do not have a written form – so many years of hard work can precede this step, to reduce the language to writing, working in co-operation with native speakers.

  This step involves a decision about which Greek, Hebrew and Aramaic texts to use.

  We do not have the original manuscripts of the biblical books written by the first authors; we have a large number of ancient copies of the biblical texts (5,000+ for the New Testament alone) – but the copies don't always agree. No major item of Christian belief depends on a difference between these ancient copies, but the translation of a particular passage can depend on which ancient copy is closest to the original.

  The science of textual criticism (see 'The text and the message') is used to decide which copy is closest to the original, by considering the age of the different copies and the spread of a particular wording across the range of copies.

- A panel of specialists will advise on particular questions, including textual criticism, issues in the original languages, archaeological questions, or style and particular expressions in the target language.

- Church and other representatives will review the draft translation, sometimes by using Bible study groups to try out sections or whole books.

- Finally, the original translators will 'polish' the draft into its final form for publication, sometimes going back to the specialists to check individual points as they work on it.

Different versions

Different groups of translators produce different versions – sometimes very different from one another.

Why are they so different?

■ **Focussing on the original language** In the first place, the focus language can be different. If the translators focus on the original (or source) language, they produce a word-for-word

if the translators focus on the target language, they can produce a version which reads very well, but which isn't quite so literally accurate. At the extreme of this approach are paraphrases, which re-write the original very freely in the target language, often using startling or interesting phrases.

In practice most versions fall somewhere between the extremes

'inclusive' language is important – for example, in English that means using 'people' rather than 'men' when the original clearly includes women as well. Other languages do not have this difficulty, since there is a term for 'men and women' used for mixed-sex groups.

All of this means it is helpful to own and use more than one Bible version. Different versions will give different nuances on the original, and for someone who doesn't read Hebrew, Aramaic and Greek, that will enrich their understanding of the message of the Bible.

And there will be situations where one version or another is more useful – such as reading aloud in church, personal study, a Bible discussion group, or teaching children about the Christian faith.

Good news is for sharing. 'Go into all the world and tell everyone about me,' Jesus instructed his disciples. That has been the task of Christians from the very beginning until now: by the spoken word, through love and care, and by the written word – the gospel translated into local languages. The joy of that good news touches an African mother and child, as it reaches people in every continent today.

version which is written using the way the source language organizes words and sentences.

This can sound a little strange or stilted to someone who does not know the source language – but it can be an advantage (for example) in translating Hebrew poetry (such as the Psalms), where the reader can see the way the original was structured.

■ **Focussing on the target language** On the other hand,

of very literal and paraphrase.

■ **Focussing on the target readership** A second factor in the variety of versions is the target readership.

For example, if a version is produced particularly with children in mind, its language will be simpler, and sentences will be shorter, than in one for adults.

If a version is for those for whom the target language is not their mother tongue, the translators will avoid rarer words or particular phrases which are unusual.

A version for use by scholars and students can be more technical.

For some modern versions in some languages, using

ENGLISH VERSIONS

There are many versions of the Bible in English today. Here is a brief summary of their characteristics.

THE AUTHORIZED (KING JAMES') VERSION AND ITS DESCENDANTS

These are more 'literal' versions, in increasingly modern styles of English. This family of versions has developed as knowledge of the original languages has grown and better (more ancient) copies of the original texts have been found.

- **Revised Version**

- **Revised Standard (American Standard) Version**

- **New American Standard Bible**
  An attempt to translate each Greek and Hebrew word consistently, quite word-for-word literal.

- **New King James' Version**
  An American version which updates the language of the AV/KJV while retaining its sentence structures.

- **New Revised Standard Version**
  Adopts 'inclusive language', and tries to show where the original includes both women and men by using 'people' and other equivalent words.

Other versions towards the 'more literal' end include:

- **New International Version**
  Aims to combine dignity of language with faithfulness to the original. There is an Anglicized version and an 'inclusive language' British edition as well as the (American-produced) original.

- **New International Reader's Version (NIV's companion)**
  Uses simplified sentences and a smaller vocabulary.

NEW TRANSLATIONS

- **New English Bible**
  A modern language version by a team of British scholars in the 1960s. The language and style are rather formal and intellectual, reflecting the fact that most of the team were academics.

- **Revised English Bible**
  A thorough revision of NEB, using inclusive language, producing a version which is more readable and accessible, while still being dignified, flowing and suitable for public reading. It offers some striking and thought-provoking renderings.

  NEB is not to be confused with the **New English Translation**, a version available on the Internet (http://www.bible.org/netbible/index.htm) in draft form, as well as in a printed edition (New Testament plus parts of the Old Testament). NET is a word-for-word version which provides many footnotes explaining the translators' choices.

- **Jerusalem Bible**
  The first Roman Catholic version to use the original Greek and Hebrew texts. It uses quite an elegant English style.

- **New Jerusalem Bible**
  A revision of JB which is a little freer, and is notable for its poetic language; it features inclusive language. Both JB and NJB use 'Yahweh' as the name of God in the Old Testament – an unusual feature.

FREER TRANSLATIONS

- **J.B. Phillips**
  New Testament and some of the Old Testament prophets available. One of the earliest freer versions. Phillips worked at providing accessible English for the 1940s and 1950s for those who did not know the language of AV/KJV.

- **Good News Bible (Today's English Version)**
  Modern, readable English in a form that is particularly suitable for those reading English as a second language. It attempts to use 'common language' – words known by the majority of readers of English worldwide – and avoids colloquial or specialist language. GNB translates sentence by sentence, looking for a 'dynamic equivalent' of the original. Has used inclusive language since 1994.

- **Contemporary English Version**
  A free version designed to be used for reading aloud as well as reading personally. It aims to be accessible to those who have little English and works with quite a limited vocabulary. It minimizes the repetitions of Hebrew poetry, changing the way it reads quite markedly.

- **New Century Version**
  Particularly suitable for young people and children. It simplifies the language and ideas in the Bible quite imaginatively.

- **Living Bible and New Living Translation**
  Paraphrases. LB was originally produced by Kenneth Taylor for his children, and is in colloquial American English. NLT is the work of a team, aiming to provide explanations and modern equivalents to ideas not known by modern westerners.

- **The Message**
  A one-person version by Eugene Peterson, and more of an interpretation than a paraphrase. Peterson uses modern metaphors, ideas and word-plays in place of those in the original language.

The title page of the Authorized (King James') Version of the Bible, 1611.

THE BIBLE
TODAY

Cultural perspectives – East and West

Melba Maggay

Until recently, those from the West most closely involved in communicating the Christian message to other cultures have been largely unconscious of the cultural assumptions behind their own reading of Scripture. They have assumed that their reading of the gospel as recorded in the Bible is more or less objective.

So the same 'package' is taken from culture to culture, regardless of whether the social context is Third or First World, and whether the people being addressed are immersed in an animist or Buddhist or Hindu worldview.

In reaction, Christian voices from the Third World have raised the issue of context, challenging Western theologies and methods of communication and stirring awareness of culture in the reading and teaching of the Bible.

The Western theological tradition is an important part of the heritage of the church the world over, but it is only one of the readings possible, and what one culture perceives as the 'barest essentials' can certainly differ from what another culture considers an important focus.

Filipinos live in a culture still awed by 'the power that can be clearly perceived in things that have been made', yet Western Christianity speaks to them as if they were long past the age of the mythical, and needed to be laboriously convinced of the existence of a supernatural God. Our people have yet to see nature 'demythologized', stripped of the wondrous and the magical. Yet the

West defends the Bible in our culture as if we were all scientific rationalists.

What's wrong?

Many scholars have observed that Christianity as it has developed theologically in the West has mostly centred on the complex of ideas surrounding sin and guilt. The question that most concerns the 'introspective conscience of the West' is whether we can find assurance of really making it to heaven.

This question, while not entirely irrelevant, is somewhat unimportant and off the track to Filipinos, where what counts most is access to the centre of power that rules their life and the universe.

Each culture has an internalized sense of what it deems as 'wrong', occasioning some soul-searching or reflection. In the Philippines, disruption of harmony in our relationship with society or with the cosmos is an important failure.

The Western bent towards individualizing and personalizing 'sin' – seeing it primarily as a matter of cheating and lying and engaging in unlawful sex, or in general things that have to do with infractions of inward integrity and encroachments on other people's rights – needs to grow towards an appreciation of its social and cosmic dimension.

Split personality

Filipino wholism counters the Western tendency to compartmentalize reality. Filipinos make no sharp distinction between the

natural and the supernatural, the sacred and the secular, public and private realms. They see reality as seamless.

Greek-based Western cultures tend to split a person into body and soul, sharply distinguishing between 'spirit' and 'matter'.

The Western sense that religion has to do with matters of the 'spirit' and not with material things like food and drink has led to the sharp separation between spirituality and involvement in the world. The sharp divide between the 'saving of souls' and the 'feeding of bodies' is a far cry from the justice and nationalist dimensions of indigenous religious movements.

Thinking and feeling

People in a largely oral society such as the Philippines experience life as a primary reality – passing events stored in memory and reinterpreted over time; hence the sense that the world is unfixed, a dynamic interpersonal system of encounters with people and other beings.

Thought and expression are often highly organized, but in ways that are imaginative and intuitive rather than analytical and abstract. Concrete human experiences are distilled in proverbs, riddles, myths and parables – hence the preference for stories rather than propositions, for the power of images rather than abstract words.

Here, in the Filipino pre-Hispanic culture, writing was used mainly as a form of social intercourse rather than as a repository of ancient wisdom and tradition.

Expressions of faith

Protestantism's emphasis on the cognitive, propositional and verbal expressions of faith as against Catholicism's emphasis on the affective, ritual and image, dates back to the historical connection between the Reformation and the invention of the printing press.

Gutenberg's invention made possible the printing and distribution of Bibles, democratizing the reading of Scripture which in turn led to widespread literacy. The liturgical centre shifted from the altar to the pulpit, from Image to the Word.

With 400 years of literacy behind it, the West evolved a religious culture heavily on the side of abstract intellectualism,

assuming that whatever it is that God is doing, he must be doing it in the head.

Consequently, faith is mainly defined in terms of acquisition of biblical information, rather than discipleship; the ability to signify mental assent to certain faith formulations, rather than the capacity to apply such knowledge to everyday life. This ethos is far removed from the indigenous culture which prizes wisdom, or the ability to integrate life and knowledge, wise sayings and effective handling of people and situations.

A matter of time

Time as a dominant value in organizing life in Western societies

We are all conditioned by our culture. Both East and West can contribute to the understanding of the Bible and its message. This market scene is from Manila, Philippines: the author's own cultural background.

is another instance of culture clash. The sense of time as linear – of a single, absolute clock time, where there are always 60 minutes to an hour which can be lost or saved or given monetary value, is very different from the indigenous sense of time as organic, tied up to the seasons and lunar movements.

A farmer wakes at dawn to work, and stops when the sun gets too hot. A fisherman watches the tide and waits for moonless nights. Festivals occur in seasons of harvest and ritual, and measures of time range from weather cycles to the length of time it takes to consume one cigarette.

Because time in this culture is tied to the flow of events, rather than to the clock, things begin when we are ready and end when we are finished. What we call 'Filipino time' is really synchronicity with the flow of events as they happen. This can be seen when events begin only as seats get filled up and organizers get themselves ready, or when a flurry of preparations happen all at once at the last minute because the event is now at hand.

The Filipino is interested, not in when something happens but in whether an action is finished or belongs to the 'not yet'. This in a way is closer to the Hebrew sense of time as 'appointed' or as 'opportunity'; a moment ripens into whether it is the appointed time to build or to plant, or to uproot and destroy. People discern the seasons, and ascertain if it is *kairos* (opportune) time or merely *chronos* (passing) time, and act accordingly.

The emphasis on time as a living present has been misunderstood in such terms as 'mañana habit', when it is actually more accurate to see it as a lack of futurism or of anxiety about tomorrow. 'Sufficient unto the day is the evil thereof,' says Jesus. There is no use in fretting about a tomorrow that we cannot control anyway, contrary to the Western illusion that by sheer planning and management we can buttress ourselves against the uncertainties of the future.

While there is a sense in which time is linear – the Bible speaks of time as having a beginning and an end, of history as going somewhere, not an endless cycle of birthing and dying, of the rise and fall of empires – there is a sense in which we experience time as a cycle.

These are, of course, not the only examples of the differences between Western and Eastern thinking. It is hard really to communicate across cultural barriers. But to become aware of our own cultural conditioning and to recognize it is a move in the right direction. We begin then to be open to other cultural insights. And the combined perspectives of both East and West will bring a richer understanding of the Bible and its message.

Jesus in a plural society

Vinoth Ramachandra

The biblical writers lived in a social environment as pluralistic in religion as our own. Israel was called to 'walk in the ways of God' before a watching world. The uniqueness of Israel's social ethos sprang from the unique revelation God had entrusted to Israel.

God, as the world's creator and sovereign, was at work in the histories of all nations and cultures. But in no nation other than Israel was God at work *for the sake of* all nations.

Whenever Israel thought of God as simply another tribal deity or sought to worship God in the manner of Canaanite fertility rituals, they were betraying their vocation in the world.

The Gospel writers see in Jesus of Nazareth the story of Israel coming to its true completion. He embodies God's purposes for the nations in living as God's faithful Son. He is the one of whom Moses wrote, the one whose day Abraham rejoiced to see, the one who is even David's Lord. On him converge the Old Testament imagery of Isaiah's 'Servant of God', bearing the wrath of God for the healing of the nations, and Daniel's 'Son of Man', receiving an everlasting kingdom which embraces all peoples.

But Jesus also brings the story of God to its true climax. Very early on, the Christian church, also living in a religiously plural world, thought it fitting to speak of Jesus in language used of God in the Hebrew scriptures. They even worshipped Jesus. Some of the earliest 'christologies' first found expression as hymns of collective worship.

> **❝** *The claim is not so much that Jesus is like God, but that God is like Jesus.* **❞**

A fragment from one of these early hymns probably lies behind the following words, written about 25 years after the crucifixion. It is part of a letter by Paul, a Jewish Christian leader, to one of the churches he had founded in the Roman colony of Philippi. He writes of 'Christ Jesus' (Philippians 2:6-11):

'who, though he was in the form
    of God,
    did not regard equality with God
    as something to be exploited,
but emptied himself,
    taking the form of a slave,
    being born in human likeness.
And being found in human form,
    he humbled himself
    and became obedient to the
      point of death –
even death on a cross.
Therefore God also highly exalted
    him
    and gave him the name
    that is above every name,
so that at the name of Jesus
    every knee should bend...
and every tongue should confess
    that Jesus Christ is Lord,
    to the glory of God the Father.'

In this passage, 'the name that is above every name' is a clear allusion to Isaiah 45:22-24 in the Hebrew Bible, where God declares himself the unique and universal Saviour. He summons all the nations of the earth to bend the knee only to him. But here, it is at the name of *Jesus* that, at the end of human history, all will bend the knee. The whole world will come to acknowledge that Jesus is the true Lord. And this staggering claim is made of a recently executed Jewish state criminal!

Equally remarkable is the literary context in which it appears – an exhortation to imitate this pre-incarnate person in his humble mentality and servant lifestyle!

Here again, as in ancient Israel, the covenant people of God (in this case, the Jewish/Gentile church) proclaims the uniqueness of God/Christ by walking in the ways of God/Christ.

This exalted view of Jesus surely arose from the way Jesus himself understood his relation to God and to Israel. Both Jesus' teaching and

Palestine at the time of Jesus was a plural society much like our own. There was a shrine to the Greek god Pan at Caesarea Philippi, the place where Peter acknowledged Jesus as the Messiah sent from God. Niches which once held statues of the gods can still be seen in the rock-cliff.

his lifestyle imply a profound self-understanding. For Jesus, the 'kingdom of God' – the great hope of Israel for God's saving presence – was breaking into the world, and taking shape in and through his words and deeds.

In his presence, men and women were offered unconditional forgiveness for their sins. Moral failures and social outcasts were given new identities and relationships. In declaring such forgiveness Jesus bypassed the Temple with its

divinely-instituted priesthood and sacrificial system. Since the Temple in Jerusalem represented the very identity of Israel as a nation, Jesus' action was truly radical.

Jesus presented himself as also the one to whom *all nations* will give account at the end of history. In the remarkable story of the final judgment in Matthew 25:31ff., the basis of judgment will be the nations' response to *him* – expressed in their response to those with whom he has identified

himself. The matter-of-fact way in which Jesus often assumed the rights and prerogatives of God startled his contemporaries and provoked the indignation of the religious authorities.

At the heart of the first disciples' faith and preaching lies the claim that Jesus was *resurrected* by God: that over a period of 40 days after his crucifixion he encountered them in a physical body, and afterwards he continued to communicate with them, 'indwell'

The Jewish hope of resurrection now becomes faith in Jesus who declares himself in John 11:25 'the resurrection and the life'. In raising Jesus, God has given him his own life-giving power to raise the dead. He is the 'author of life' (Acts 3:15), 'the living one' (Revelation 1:18; compare its use as a divine title in Deuteronomy 5:26; Joshua 3:10;

> **"** *At the name of Jesus,*
> *at the end of human history,*
> *all will bend the knee.* **"**

Psalm 42:2, etc.), the 'life-giving spirit' (1 Corinthians 15:45), the one to whom the Father has granted 'life in himself' so that he may give life to others (John 5:21-26).

By speaking of Jesus, Spirit and God in the same breath, they not only make remarkable claims about Jesus but, at the same time, make staggering claims about God. The claim is not so much that Jesus is like God, but that God is like Jesus. Jesus, and especially Jesus in his crucifixion, is in some way the fullness of deity in human personhood. With this conviction the early Christians refused to think of themselves as simply members of one 'religion' among many: they were witnesses among the nations to what God in Jesus had done for all humankind.

them and empower them in a new mode of Spirit.

In contemporary Jewish belief 'resurrection' marked the conquest of evil, the dawn of a new world order. This language was applied to Jesus after his appearance on the other side of the cross because it gave meaning to his words and works before the crucifixion. Through Jesus, the Creator God would bring his creation out of its bondage to evil and death and lift it to share in his own life.

The Qur'an and the Bible

Michael Nazir-Ali

The sacred book of the Muslims, the Qur'an, repeatedly claims continuity with the revelation given in the Judeo-Christian tradition and is itself seen by Muslims as the last of a line of scriptures given to the prophets:

'We believe in Allah and that which was sent down on us, on Abraham, Ishmael, Isaac, Jacob and the Tribes of Israel and that which was given to Moses and to Jesus and that which was given to all the Prophets from their Lord. We make no difference between any of them for it is to Allah that we have submitted' (Q2:136).

The other scriptures are mentioned quite often, in particular the *Tawrat* (or Torah), the *Zabur* (Psalms) and the *Injil* (or Gospel). Jews and Christians are exhorted, moreover, to live by the will of God as it has been revealed in their books:

'Let the people of the Gospel judge according to that which Allah has revealed therein and whoever judges not by that which Allah has revealed is of the rebellious' (QS:50).

A few verses earlier, the Jews too are challenged to live by the light and guidance of the Torah.

Where the Qur'an and Bible differ

Already during the Prophet of Islam's lifetime, however, it was becoming clear that the scriptures of the Jews and Christians differed markedly from the revelation which the Prophet claimed to have received. How could this be so if they were all the Word of God?

The difficulty is countered in different ways but mainly by the claim that the Qur'an 'fulfils' the other, more partial, revelations; that, in certain cases, it 'reminds' its readers of what has been forgotten and that it 'relaxes' or abrogates certain parts of the older scriptures:

'Whatever revelation we abrogate or cause to be forgotten, we bring a better or similar one in its place' (2:106).

People in a mosque in Istanbul listen to the imam.

This verse has often been used not only to evaluate the other scriptures in relation to the Qur'an but also to determine how certain fundamental passages in the Qur'an relate to other parts of the book.

As far as the Mosaic law is concerned, the Qur'anic view is that at least some of its provisions were enacted as a punishment for rebellion. Jesus is supposed to have relaxed some of these and the Prophet of Islam relaxed others

(3:50; 4:160; 5:90). The Qur'an, then, in the Muslim view, is the final and definitive revelation which 'fulfils' the other scriptures and, where these contradict the Qur'an, they stand abrogated.

A corrupted text?

Another way in which Islam has sought to address the discrepancies between its Scripture and those of the Jews and Christians has been through the charge of *Tahrif*. This is

the belief that the older 'People of the Book' have 'changed' or corrupted their books in such a way that they do not now agree with the Qur'an. The 'People of the Book' are charged with altering the scriptures for their own purposes (2:75-79; 4:46; 5:14). It may be, however, that Christians are not charged, in the Qur'an at any rate, with altering the scriptures but simply of 'forgetting' what they had received (cf. 5:15).

The earliest Muslim commentators, such as Tabari and Razi, were of the view that the alteration was *tahrif bi'l ma'ni*, a corruption of the *meaning* of the text without necessarily involving corruption of the text itself.

Gradually, however, a consensus emerged that the 'People of the Book' were guilty of *tahrif bi'l lafz*, that is, of corrupting the text itself. The Spanish theologian Ibn Hazm and the traveller in India, the scientist Al-Biruni, did most to propagate this view. Many scholars, however, continue to hold that the Qur'an does not assert general corruption of the Judeo-Christian scriptures but only that texts have been misused and certain passages concealed.

Use of the Bible

Although Muslims believe that the contents of their holy book have been directly received from God and do not, therefore, depend on any other literary or historical document, many Muslim scholars do, nevertheless, refer to the Bible as they seek to comment on the meaning of the Qur'an.

Nor are such scholars only from a more 'liberal' school of thought. Conservatives too use the Bible extensively as a background to the study of their own book. In doing so, they have to come to a view regarding the extent to which the *text* has altered, irrespective of the

interpretations which Jews and Christians may have put upon it.

Many come to surprising conclusions; agreeing, for instance, that narrative and commentary in the Bible can suffer alteration but not the inspired words of the prophets themselves. This, of course, leaves intact the integrity of large parts of the Bible!

How Muslims see revelation

For Christians to understand the Muslim view of the Bible, it is crucial for them to have some knowledge of how Muslims see *revelation*. The idea of a pre-determined corpus descending from heaven, for which the prophet is only a medium, is hardly congruent with the way most Christians understand revelation.

In dialogue it is very important to explain how Christians see revelation as mediated, not only through the limitations of culture and language but also through a process of accretion in traditions, of reflection and of editing by communities and individuals.

The way in which manuscript evidence is treated in the two traditions is a case in point. All present editions of the Qur'an are descendants from a single recension (the variants having been destroyed during the course of history). For Muslims this is a sign of the book's integrity and reliability.

Where the Judeo-Christian scriptures are concerned, on the other hand, there are a number of manuscripts, sometimes in different languages, which are used to establish the critical edition of a text. Reliability is achieved not by depending on a single line of manuscript evidence but by comparing different manuscript traditions with one another.

These are very different ways of arriving at what the community sees as a reliable text.

Books outside the official 'canon'

Sometimes Muslims produce books like the so-called *Gospel of Barnabas* which they claim is the authentic Gospel. However, neither the Qur'an itself, nor early Muslim tradition, ever refer to such works. 'Barnabas' is, in fact, a fairly modern work, written in Muslim Spain, which disagrees with the Qur'an in certain important respects!

Attempts to produce such works show, however, the extent of the difficulties which Muslims have with Christian understandings of how different books of the Bible were written and how the approved list came to exist in its present form.

Mutual understanding

Patient dialogue between Muslims and Christians on the scriptures of each faith has, in fact, deepened understanding of the other side's position. Christians have come to see the extent of the Qur'an's continuity with their own scriptures, while Muslims have been able better to appreciate some of the scriptures to which the Qur'an refers.

This is greatly to be welcomed as it can only lead to a better under-standing of what is in common and to the provision of a base for tackling the serious differences which remain.

The Bible through women's eyes

Claire Powell

The 20th century saw great changes world-wide in attitudes to the status and role of women. Education of women was one of the keys to opening new spheres of opportunity in the workplace, and in giving greater respect to work traditionally done by women.

A change of perspective on the Bible was also needed, not because women relate to God or see the Bible differently from men, or that all women think the same way, but because, until recently, almost all biblical interpretation has been by men.

In secular culture and in the church, masculinity had become the norm of what it means to be human, and it was an easy step to marginalize, however unconsciously, the contribution and significance of women. Theologians had focussed mainly on God's dealings with men, including as of most importance in theology and Christian history the things which men do, while women, their roles, faith, experience and interests took a back seat. Both women and men grew used to learning about faith from biblical examples of men like Peter, while examples of women like Mary were subconsciously labelled 'for women only'!

It therefore benefits the whole church, women and men, to value the experience of faith through women in scripture, to recover the forgotten importance of women in the history of the church's mission, and to redress an imbalance where women and the feminine have tended in the past to be marginalized in translations of the Bible, in theology, and in the church.

Equal partners

Genesis begins with the fact that men and women are created equal in the sight of God and of each other. The creation of both is pronounced 'very good' (Genesis 1:31). Woman is created out of man, not to show subordination, but to show that she is like him rather than like the other created beings, and to show the interdependence which Paul in 1 Corinthians 11:11-12 says is forever characteristic of the human race:

'In our life in the Lord, woman is not independent of man, nor is man independent of woman. For as woman was made from man, in the same way man is born of woman.'

Rivalry and competition

Trouble between man and woman does not begin until disobedience brings about humanity's 'fall' in Genesis 3. Then, instead of the mutuality and complementarity of Eden, rivalry and competition begins. From Genesis 4 onwards, it is played out in fulfilment of the prediction that the man would rule over the woman (Genesis 3:16). This was not God's ideal, but part of the inevitable consequences of the fall.

If Genesis sets the scene, the drama is played out in the story of salvation in the rest of the Bible. There is no unequivocal command in the Old Testament about the position of women, yet men are seen to prevail, assume power even in religious life, and the women seem rarely to be seen or heard. What is recorded is most often in the form of descriptive narrative. The question posed by this is whether the narrative asserts God's will for the roles and status of men and women in every culture for evermore, or simply describes what was happening at the time (in the same way as, for example, polygamy or slavery), which is for us to learn from, by emulating what was good, but correcting what was not. Scripture records many things that it does not advocate!

Are God and the Bible biased?

Is the Bible itself more biased towards men than women? And is patriarchy (in its widest sense, the system of men in power) justified by the very text itself? Is God treating women this way? Much more likely, what we find described is how women's status, function and experience fall short of God's ideal of equality. There are sufficient indications in the text itself that this is so.

Although much of the history focusses on the activities of men, even so, the women are there and play important parts. Leadership is not restricted to men. Both Deborah the judge (Judges 4) and Huldah the prophet (2 Kings 22) take responsible roles of leadership which are not commented on in the text as exceptional in any way. Instead they are respected.

From the Old to the New

The fact that most leaders were men represents the developed patriarchal culture of the time. There is no divine mandate for it. Women were excluded from the Old Testament priesthood, but so were many of the men! And the New Testament presents us with a

priesthood of all believers, male and female.

In the Old Testament, circumcision was the sign of belonging to God's covenant people – a sign physically performed exclusively on men. But with the birth of the church came a new sign of belonging. Baptism was physically inclusive of men and women, Jew and Gentile.

In the New Testament Letters there is every indication that any restrictions on women apply within a specific culture and context. Where the particular details of a 1st-century situation differ from ours, it is the principle behind the teaching which is properly binding for all time. Thus, when Paul indicates in 1 Timothy 2 that women should not teach or have authority over men, he is addressing a particular problem of false teaching and wrongful authority in Ephesus. In such a context the women were to stop

what they were doing wrong.

The abiding principle for today is that women are forbidden to teach what is wrong, but not therefore forbidden to teach what is right! In this they may function as an object lesson for men, too, just as examples of men are usually understood as applicable to women.

We know from Acts and the Letters that women were prominent among the leaders in almost all the earliest house-church groups. Lydia was a leader in Philippi; Phoebe was a deacon in Cenchrea (Romans 16:1); Junia (the majority manuscript evidence points to Junia as a woman) was an apostle (Romans 16:7).

Believers are told by Paul to teach one another (e.g. Colossians 3:16) and no caveat here bars women from teaching men. Priscilla is on record as teaching Apollos (Acts 18:26).

The New Testament lists of

A group of women at Tacloban, Philippines, meet to study the Bible.

giftings (e.g. Romans 12; 1 Corinthians 12; Ephesians 4) do not specify gender at all. Given the patriarchal culture of the time, it is not surprising that men in leadership outnumbered women, but this is a description, not a blueprint.

One indication of this may be seen in 1 Timothy 3:2, where someone must be the 'husband of one wife' to qualify as a bishop. This could point to a necessity of being married, to monogamous marriage or, most probably, to purity and faithfulness within marriage. Where the likelihood is that most leaders would have been men, and almost certainly married, this functions as a regulation for the known situation in Ephesus, not a future prohibition for all women or single men! 1 Timothy 3:12 uses exactly the same stipulation about deacons, yet cannot mean that all deacons are to be men, since Paul calls Phoebe a deacon in Romans 16:1. Biblical leadership and responsibilities in the church are to be based on character, calling and Christian commitment, not gender.

God as male or female?

Many people hold a mental image of God as male, or at least somehow more male than female. This is largely due to the images of God in early art, and to the description of God as 'he' and 'father'.

Deuteronomy 4:15-16 reminds Israel that God is without form. They were not to make graven images (or presumably to form mental images) of God as either male or female. Male and female are biological differences in created humanity. Both sexes equally reflect an image of the Creator.

In languages which do not have an inclusive pronoun, either masculine or feminine must be used to reflect the fact that God's nature is personal, not impersonal. 'It' will not do. The use of 'he' for God points to God as a person. It is nothing to do with sex (that which is biologically determined) or gender (that which is socially determined).

In recent years the female images for God in Scripture (such as birthing, or providing food) have been rediscovered. So too has the use of feminine terms for God, e.g. the Holy Spirit and wisdom in the Old Testament. Both masculine and feminine grammatical labels are used, but do not necessarily thereby convey being or essence.

There has also been progress in recognizing the social masculine bias inherent in many languages and the consequent margin-alization of women – pushing them to the side, ignoring them, or regarding them as atypical of human experience. This is not the biblical view. In the past, where God was seen as male, the fallacy lay in seeing male as more like God.

The example of Jesus

Jesus brought in no revolutionary movement to overturn the male-dominated Jewish culture of his time. Yet he clearly broke with the norms of his day. He taught women; discussed theology with them; accepted worship from them; elevated their position in debates on divorce; and touched ritually 'unclean' women. These are not major by today's standards, but they were noticeable then, and they pushed out the boundaries of what was acceptable. This paved the way for his followers to do the same.

In the past, the fact that Jesus was born as a man was seen as giving greater status to men. If the point of the incarnation is 'God made male', then redemption of women is in doubt, or at least secondary, and Jesus is better rep-resented in the priesthood by men than by women.

But the Bible nowhere makes the maleness of Jesus a point of comparison, only his humanity, which is common to both women and men. And the New Testament clearly teaches a priesthood of all believers; all are able to approach Jesus and all are able to represent him on earth.

In the incarnation Jesus represents a model of humanity, not of masculinity. Women, as much as men, may find their pattern in him and follow his example in every respect.

A scientist looks at the Bible

John Polkinghorne

The search for religious truth is similar to the search for scientific truth. If we want to know what God is like we shall have to find out what he has done and how he has made himself known.

The Bible is the most important record of religious experience that we have to help us in that search for truth.

The Bible as a source of evidence

The Hebrew Bible – what Christians call the Old Testament – is concerned with how God encountered some wandering shepherd chiefs, like Abraham; how God brought their descendants out of slavery in Egypt; how God was involved with the history of the people of Israel, both in judgment and deliverance.

In the New Testament we read how God has acted to make himself known in a new and clearer way. The Gospels tell us about the life and death and resurrection of Jesus, whilst the other writings (such as Paul's letters) – many of which are earlier than the Gospels – tell us how the first Christians were overwhelmed by the new life they had found in Christ.

When we read the Bible as the record of spiritual experience from which we can learn about God's ways with humanity – as *evidence* in our search for truth – we are necessarily to some extent subjecting it to our judgment. We have to decide whether we are reading a historical account or a story, whether what is said reflects God's will or human custom.

I think we need to read the Bible in this way, but we certainly need

❝ We shall never have God neatly packaged up. He will always exceed our expectations. ❞

also to read it in other ways as well. In particular, we are not only to judge it but we must allow it to judge us.

A scientist's approach

Whatever it is that we do in life, the experiences we have will colour our thoughts and mould our ways of thinking. I have spent 30 years of my life working as a theoretical physicist, trying to use mathematics to understand some of the beautiful patterns and order of the physical world. For good or ill (and no doubt it is a mixture of both) this affects how I think about all sorts of things.

I like to start with the phenomena, with things that have happened, and then try to build up an explanation and an understanding from there. 'Start with particular cases and only then try to go on to understand what's happening in general,' is my motto.

This kind of 'bottom-up' thinking is natural for a scientist for two reasons.
- We are looking for ideas which have reasons backing them up; these reasons will lie in the evidence we consider, the events that motivate our belief.
- We have learnt that the world is full of surprises. That means it is very hard to guess beforehand what the right *general* ideas will turn out to be. Only experience can tell us that. In fact, this element of surprise is one of the

things that makes scientific research worthwhile and exciting. You never know what you will find round the next corner.

Take just one example. Every day of my working life as a theoretical physicist I used the ideas of quantum mechanics. This theory describes how things behave on a very small scale, the size of atoms or even smaller. It turns out that the behaviour of the very small is totally different from the way we experience the world on the 'normal' scale of everyday life.

We seem to live in a world which is reliable and picturable. We know where things are and what they are doing. All this changes when you get down to the level of atoms.

Take an electron, one of the constituents of an atom. If you know where it is, you cannot know what it is doing; if you know what it is doing, you cannot know where it is! (This is called Heisenburg's uncertainty principle.)

The quantum world is fuzzy and unpicturable. We cannot imagine in everyday terms what it is like. Nevertheless we can *understand* it, using mathematics and the special set of quantum ideas which we have learnt from a bottom-up approach to atomic phenomena.

No one could have guessed beforehand that matter would behave in this very odd way when looked at subatomically. In fact it took many extremely clever people 25 years to figure out what was happening.

A scientific research worker uses an electron microscope.

If you want to understand nature, you have to let the physical world tell you what it is like. You have to start at the bottom, with actual behaviour, and work your way up to an adequate theory.

Now, if the *physical* world is so full of surprises, it would be strange if God did not also exceed our expectations in quite unexpected ways.

Commonsense thinking by itself won't be adequate to tell us what God is like. We will have to try to find out from how he has actually made himself known. To see the Bible as a source of evidence about how God has acted in history and, above all, in Jesus Christ, is a natural strategy for a bottom-up thinker to pursue.

In fact, I find there is a lot in common between the way I search for truth in science and the way I search for truth in religion. People are sometimes surprised that I am both a physicist and a priest. They think there is something odd, or maybe dishonest, in the combination. Their surprise arises because they don't realize that truth matters quite as much in religion as it does in science.

There is an odd view around that faith is a matter of shutting one's eyes, gritting one's teeth and believing impossible things because some unquestionable authority tells you that you have to.

Not at all!

The leap of faith is a leap into the light and not into the dark. It involves commitment to what we understand *in order that we may learn and understand more*. You have to do that in science. You have to trust that the physical world makes sense and that your present theory gives you some sort of idea of what it's like, if you are to make progress and gain more understanding and a better theory. You will never see anything if you don't stick your neck out a bit!

You have to do the same in the religious quest for truth. We shall never have God neatly packaged up. He will always exceed our expectations and prove himself to be a God of surprises. There is always more to learn.

Reader beware!

There is one important difference, however, between scientific belief and religious belief. The latter is much more demanding and dangerous. I believe passionately in quantum theory, but the belief does not threaten to change my life in any significant way. I cannot believe in God, however, without knowing that I must be obedient to his will for me as it becomes known to me. God is not there just to satisfy my intellectual curiosity; he's there to be honoured and respected and loved as my Creator and Saviour.

So beware! Reading the Bible can change your life.

Our world – their world

Meic Pearse

To say that the Bible is a collection of historical documents is to state the obvious. Yet we can easily overlook the implications of this as we try to understand what we are reading.

The 'baggage' we carry

We need to be aware that, whether we are Christians or not, we have all sorts of ideas about the world and about the Bible itself before ever we come to open its pages.

What is more, 2,000 years of reflection, of theologizing, and of development of doctrine, stand between even New Testament times and our own.

We can all too easily come to the Bible assuming that it will simply reflect the ideas we have absorbed in our own time or within our own church tradition.

Those who come to the Bible confident that it will back their own political or other opinions can take a salutary lesson from the experience of people in the past who were (wrongly) sure it backed theirs!

The very building-blocks of the Western worldview – objectivity and subjectivity, human rights, feminism, free-market economics, socialism – would have meant nothing to people in Bible times (or indeed, to anyone else living before the 18th century).

We need to allow the Bible to speak into *our* situation – but on *its* own terms. We will not properly understand the Bible if we read our

A multi-racial crowd in a city street represents the world of many Bible readers today – far removed from the traditional life of Bible times, illustrated by a Bedouin woman at a well near Bethlehem. There are boundaries to cross in understanding the Bible's timeless message.

modern ideas back into the mind of Abraham – or of Ruth, or Amos, or the elders in the Jerusalem church.

A different lifestyle

In the Bible we come face to face with people and cultures utterly different from those of modern 'developed' countries: overwhelmingly agricultural and hierarchical, in which high infant mortality, the ever-present threat of famine due to crop failure, and the likelihood of a relatively early death for most people could be taken for granted.

In a word, they *lived* as most people in human history have lived, with the exception of a few generations of modern Westerners.

They accepted arranged marriages and even slavery. A word like 'freedom' meant, not some moral principle, but a condition of not being a slave or, perhaps, of not being hungry or in want.

A different mind-set

They seldom thought of God (or, in the case of pagan nations, the gods), angels and evil forces as subjects whose existences were

open questions. Rather, they were the greatest realities to be faced, in the light of which all of life was to be lived.

In a word, they *thought* as most people in human history have thought, with the exception of a few generations of modern people today.

It is clear, then, that for many of us reading the Bible, a considerable effort of mind is necessary if we are to step out of our own skins and meet the people of the Bible on their own terms. But that effort is so much worth making! At the very least, it will put us in 'touch' with the rest of the human race. At best, we will touch – or be touched by – not the god of this age, but the God of the ages.

THE OLD TESTAMENT

2

All through Old Testament times – from the making of the covenant-agreement, when the people persuaded Aaron to make them a bull-calf to worship like the ones which represented the god Apis in Egypt, to the times of the prophets – God's people struggled to keep their promise to worship only him.

Introducing the Old Testament

Christians have long grown accustomed to calling the first part of the Bible, from Genesis to Malachi, the Old Testament. But it dates back to before the time of Christ and before ever there was a New Testament, so it is important to remember that it once had a life of its own, and that it was, and still is, the complete Bible of the Jewish people.

Understandably, Jews do not like the name 'Old Testament', because that implies it is incomplete without the Christian 'New Testament'. To them it is the whole revelation of God, the Hebrew Bible, and they treat it with the utmost reverence and respect.

They call it the Tannakh, which is an acronym for its three parts:
- the Torah, or the Law of Moses
- the Nebi'im, which consists of the Prophets
- and the Kethubim, or the Writings.

In the Hebrew Bible the order of the 39 books is somewhat different from what Christians are used to, but this is where we need to begin.

Scribes copied out the Old Testament writings by hand. They wrote column by column on lengths of parchment which, like this scroll, were rolled up and kept in the synagogues.

The Torah

The Law, the Five Books of Moses – Genesis, Exodus, Leviticus, Numbers and Deuteronomy – is the foundation-stone of the Hebrew Scriptures, the most important part. Frequently the whole of the Bible is described by Jews as 'The Torah'.

The Nebi'im

This is a plural word meaning Prophets. No less than 21 books are included in this part of the Tannakh, and for simplicity they are divided into Former Prophets and Latter Prophets.

The Former Prophets are what we would regard as histories: Joshua, Judges, 1 and 2 Samuel and 1 and 2 Kings. See the Introduction to the Historical Books to understand more fully why they are described as Prophets. Very briefly it is because these books are not pure, factual history or dull annals. Instead they tell the stories of Israel's developing life as a kind of working out of God's word and promises through Abraham, Moses and David. They are more than just history, they point to the God of Israel and illustrate his word and his ways.

The Latter Prophets bring us to more familiar ground: Isaiah, Jeremiah, Ezekiel and the 'Book of the Twelve', or 'Minor Prophets': Hosea to Malachi.

The Writings

The Kethubim includes all the rest in the following order: Psalms, Job, Proverbs, the Five Megilloth (see below), Daniel, Ezra, Nehemiah, 1 and 2 Chronicles.

It is interesting to note that Daniel is not included in the Prophets where our Old Testament order puts him. That is quite right, in a way, because Daniel is a different kind of writing, apocalyptic (see Revelation introduction and features) rather than prophecy.

Also, Ezra and Nehemiah come before 1 and 2 Chronicles which historically precede them. The Old Testament rightly reverses the order. The Hebrew may, however, reflect the sequence in which the various books were accepted into the canon of authorized Scripture. The only other thing to note is the Five Megilloth (literally, 'little scrolls'), the short books of

Ruth, Song of Solomon (often called Canticles), Ecclesiastes, Lamentations and Esther. These were collected together and were used in association with five Jewish festivals: the feast of Weeks (Ruth), Passover (Canticles), Tabernacles (Ecclesiastes), the fast commemorating the fall of Jerusalem in 587 BC (Lamentations), and Purim (Esther).

These then were the three subdivisions of the Hebrew Bible and they go back to early times, certainly to the first century AD, and echoes are found in Jesus' teaching. For instance, we have already noted that the Jews often referred to their scriptures as the Torah, the law. But there were also times when they were called 'the law and the prophets', reflecting the first two major subdivisions of the Tannakh.

Jesus often referred to the Old Testament in those terms. The most interesting reference is Luke 24:44 when, after he had risen from the dead, Jesus told his followers in the upper room that 'everything written about me in the law of Moses and the prophets and the psalms must be fulfilled'. As if to show that the whole of the Hebrew Scriptures pointed to himself as the Messiah of Israel he specifically mentioned all three sections of the Tannakh. This completely justifies the Christian renaming of the Hebrew Bible as the 'Old Testament' – preparing the way for the New Testament which was yet to come.

■ See also 'The Hebrew Bible' and 'Jesus and the Old Testament.

God's people learned hard lessons during their desert wanderings, where the harsh physical conditions underlined their dependence on God for even the basic necessities of life.

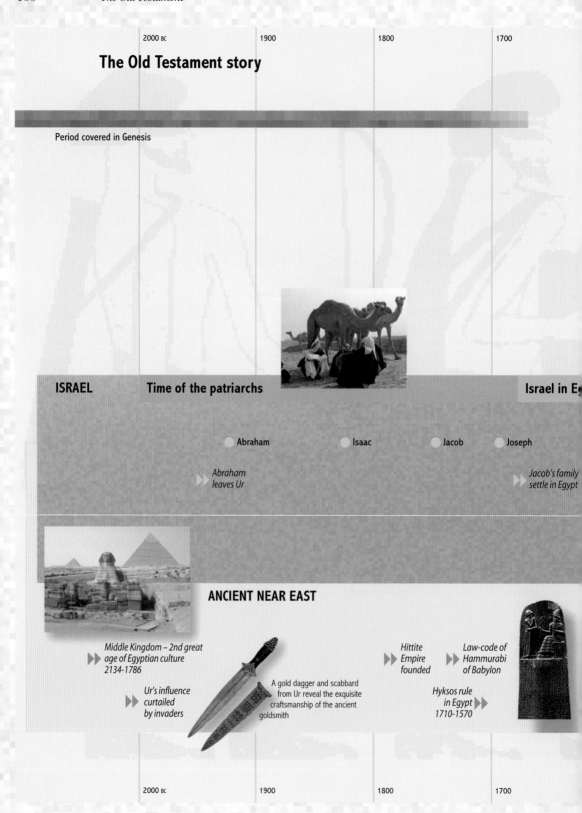

The Old Testament story

2000 BC   1900   1800   1700

Period covered in Genesis

ISRAEL   **Time of the patriarchs**   **Israel in E**

Abraham   Isaac   Jacob   Joseph

Abraham
leaves Ur

Jacob's family
settle in Egypt

ANCIENT NEAR EAST

Middle Kingdom – 2nd great
age of Egyptian culture
2134-1786

Hittite
Empire
founded

Law-code of
Hammurabi
of Babylon

Ur's influence
curtailed
by invaders

A gold dagger and scabbard
from Ur reveal the exquisite
craftsmanship of the ancient
goldsmith

Hyksos rule
in Egypt
1710-1570

2000 BC   1900   1800   1700

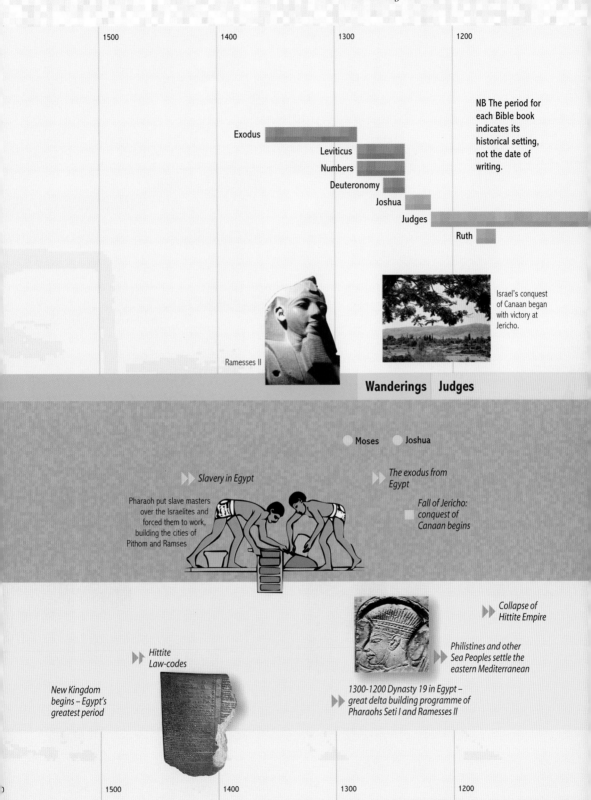

1500   1400   1300   1200

NB The period for each Bible book indicates its historical setting, not the date of writing.

Exodus

Leviticus

Numbers

Deuteronomy

Joshua

Judges

Ruth

Ramesses II

Israel's conquest of Canaan began with victory at Jericho.

Wanderings | Judges

Moses   Joshua

Slavery in Egypt

The exodus from Egypt

Pharaoh put slave masters over the Israelites and forced them to work, building the cities of Pithom and Ramses

Fall of Jericho: conquest of Canaan begins

Collapse of Hittite Empire

Hittite Law-codes

Philistines and other Sea Peoples settle the eastern Mediterranean

New Kingdom begins – Egypt's greatest period

1300-1200 Dynasty 19 in Egypt – great delta building programme of Pharaohs Seti I and Ramesses II

1500   1400   1300   1200

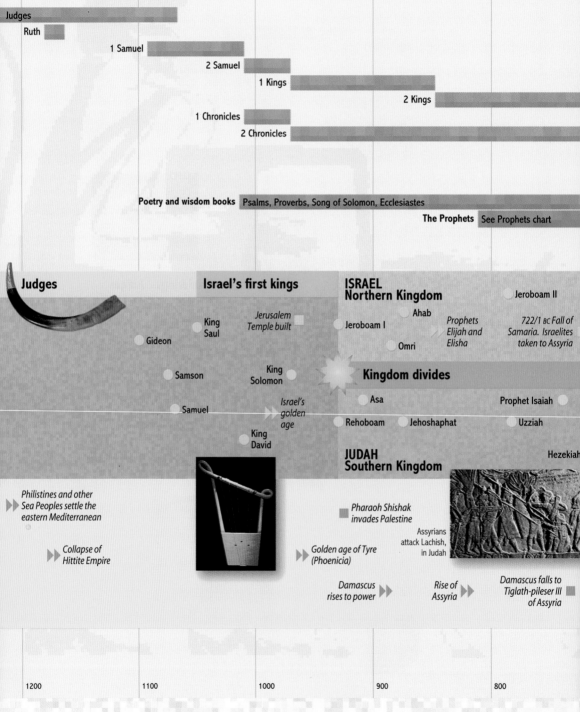

1200	1100	1000	900	800

Judges

Ruth

1 Samuel

2 Samuel

1 Kings

2 Kings

1 Chronicles

2 Chronicles

Poetry and wisdom books Psalms, Proverbs, Song of Solomon, Ecclesiastes

The Prophets See Prophets chart

Judges

Israel's first kings

ISRAEL Northern Kingdom

Gideon

Samson

Samuel

King Saul

King David

King Solomon

Jerusalem Temple built

Israel's golden age

Jeroboam I

Omri

Ahab

Prophets Elijah and Elisha

Jeroboam II

722/1 BC Fall of Samaria. Israelites taken to Assyria

Kingdom divides

Asa

Rehoboam   Jehoshaphat

Prophet Isaiah

Uzziah

JUDAH Southern Kingdom

Hezekiah

Philistines and other Sea Peoples settle the eastern Mediterranean

Collapse of Hittite Empire

Pharaoh Shishak invades Palestine

Golden age of Tyre (Phoenicia)

Damascus rises to power

Assyrians attack Lachish, in Judah

Rise of Assyria

Damascus falls to Tiglath-pileser III of Assyria

1200	1100	1000	900	800

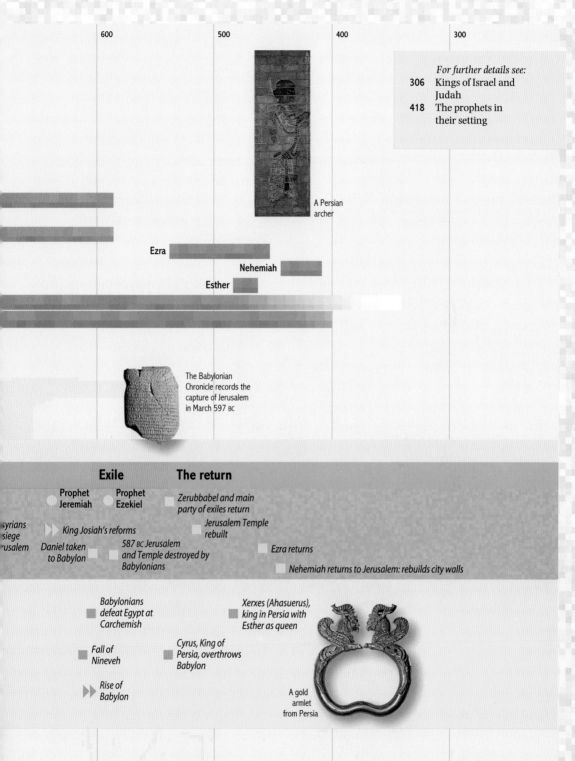

600   500   400   300

For further details see:
306   Kings of Israel and Judah
418   The prophets in their setting

A Persian archer

Ezra

Nehemiah

Esther

The Babylonian Chronicle records the capture of Jerusalem in March 597 BC

Exile   **The return**

Prophet Jeremiah   Prophet Ezekiel   Zerubbabel and main party of exiles return

syrians siege rusalem   King Josiah's reforms   Jerusalem Temple rebuilt

Daniel taken to Babylon   587 BC Jerusalem and Temple destroyed by Babylonians   Ezra returns

Nehemiah returns to Jerusalem: rebuilds city walls

Babylonians defeat Egypt at Carchemish   Xerxes (Ahasuerus), king in Persia with Esther as queen

Fall of Nineveh   Cyrus, King of Persia, overthrows Babylon

Rise of Babylon   A gold armlet from Persia

600   500   400   300

Israel in
Old Testament
times

A   B   C   D

1

Tyre
Abel-beth-maacah
Dan
Kedesh

2
Hazor
Merom
BASHAN
River Jordan
Chinnereth
The Great Sea
River Kishon
GALILEE
Sea of Chinnereth
Ashtaroth

Gath-hepher
△ Mt Carmel
Plain of Jezreel
△ Mt Tabor
Edrei
Endor
Dor
△ *Hill of Moreh*
Lo-debar
Ramoth-gilead

3
Megiddo
Shunem
Jezreel
GILEAD
Taanach
△ Mt Gilboa
Beth-shan
Cherith Brook
Sharon
Ibleam
Tishbe
Dothan
Jabesh-gilead

Samaria
Tirzah
Plain of Sharon
Succoth
Penuel
Shechem △ Mt Ebal
△ Mt Gerizim
R. Jabbok

4
Aphek
ISRAEL
River Jordan
Adam
AMMON
Shiloh
Joppa
Timnath
Bethel   Ai
Rabbah
Lower Beth-horon
Michmash
Shittim
Upper Beth-horon
Mizpah
Gilgal
Gibeon
Geba
Heshbon
Gezer
Gibeah
Jericho
Ekron
Anathoth
△ Mt Nebo
Timnah
Sorek   Aijalon
Kiriath-jearim
Jerusalem

5
Eshtaol
Ashdod
Beth-shemesh
Bethlehem
Makkedah
Wilderness of Judea
Libnah
Azekah
Ashkelon
Valley of Elah
Adullam
Tekoa
Ataroth
Keilah
Kiriathaim
Lachish
Mareshah
Beth-zur
Dibon
Gaza
Eglon
Hebron
Aroer
PHILISTIA
Salt Sea (Sea of the Arabah)
River Arnon
Engedi
JUDAH

6
Maon
Ziklag
MOAB
Gerar
Arad
Beersheba
Ar
Hormah

Negev Desert
Kir-hareseth

7
AMALEKITES

EDOM

The Old Testament and the ancient Near East

Alan Millard

The Bible is an ancient text, a historical record. As such it is very helpful to study it in the light of our knowledge of the world in which it was written. This is important because Christian faith depends on historical events, things which actually happened.

Testing, testing...

The events recorded and explained in the Bible can be set alongside other events known from other historical sources. The Bible itself consists of documents as ancient and as historically verifiable as any others.

The Bible's accuracy can also be tested and checked against other known historical sources. However, this is not always as simple as it may seem. Documents are often damaged or incomplete. Archaeological evidence is in many cases open to more than one interpretation. We possess very few ancient writings which describe the same events that the Bible describes, and in any case two observers will rarely describe the same event from an identical standpoint.

The Hebrews were a relatively insignificant people. Their career made little impact on the major powers whose records we possess. Hardly any of the biblical characters appear in other writings, apart from some of the later kings of Israel and Judah. None the less, where we are able to make comparisons, the accuracy of the biblical writers is impressive. Although we seldom find parallel accounts of the same events, we often find examples of customs and occurrences very like those described in the Old Testament, even though they are in no way connected. A superficial similarity can of course be misleading, so we have to be cautious. And a knowledge of the ancient Near East can help, even when it provides neither direct nor circumstantial evidence of the Bible's historical accuracy: the study of Israel's neighbours – customs, culture, literature, history – gives us an idea of what to expect in the case of the Hebrew nation.

These three types of evidence:
- direct evidence
- circumstantial evidence
- and the evidence of analogy

must be taken in turn to show how they shed light on the Bible.

Direct evidence

As we have seen, direct references to Israel are rare, and almost solely limited to royal names.

Amongst those we do have is the record of an invasion by Shishak, king of Egypt from about 945 to 924 BC (1 Kings 14:25f.). His inscription at Thebes, badly preserved, lists many towns conquered in Palestine – evidence of his campaign there.

Assyria's power first touched Israel about 853 BC, when forces of 'Ahab the Israelite', allied with Damascus and other cities, fought Shalmaneser III (858-824 BC) and a few years later 'Jehu son of Omri' paid him tribute.

Tiglath-pileser III (745-727 BC) re-established Assyrian rule over Syria and Palestine following some decades of weakness, when Jeroboam II had made Israel prosperous and Uzziah had built up Judah. The Assyrian records the tribute paid by Menahem of Samaria and claims to have been responsible for replacing Pekah by Hosea (2 Kings 15:19-20, 30). In 2 Kings 15:19 (see also 1 Chronicles 5:26) Tiglath-pileser is called Pul and he was known by that name to Babylonian chroniclers of the 6th century BC, when it is believed 1 and 2 Kings were finally compiled.

After this, Assyrian rule in Samaria involved Judah as a vassal, but her kings preferred to struggle for independence, seeking Egypt's aid. So Hezekiah rebelled, and Sennacherib brought his forces to overwhelm Judah and lay siege to Jerusalem. The Assyrian tells of this in many inscriptions. He relates how Hezekiah sent tribute to him in Nineveh (the amounts seem to differ slightly from 2 Kings 18:14ff.), yet lays no claim to the capture of Jerusalem, nor, naturally enough, does he mention his army's fate. The Babylonian Chronicle reports Nebuchadnezzar's first capture of Jerusalem (2 Kings 24:8-17), dating it precisely to 15/16 March 597 BC.

Circumstantial evidence

Most of the discoveries which feature in books of archaeology and the Bible fall into the class of circumstantial evidence – matters which make no direct reference to biblical events, but supply examples of practices or incidents apparently comparable with passages in the Bible.

In this way we learn that Abraham's marriage to the slave-girl Hagar because of Sarah's childlessness, and his later refusal – ▶▶

▶▶ until reassured by God – to send her from his household, agree with requirements in the contemporary Laws of Hammurabi of Babylon.

The names of the patriarchs of Israel also accord with names generally used in the first half of the 2nd millennium BC, now known from thousands of contemporary documents.

Solomon's glory gains credence from Egyptian sources. According to 1 Kings 9:16, he married the pharaoh's daughter. Yet two or three centuries earlier, in Egypt's heyday, the princesses of Egypt did not leave the court, and when an important foreign king requested one as his bride he was refused. In the 10th century BC however, under the less glorious 21st dynasty and its successor, this rule was broken. So it was that Solomon received his bride.

Solomon's lavish use of gold to plate the interior of the Temple (1 Kings 6:21-22) is consistent with splendid decoration in Egyptian and also in Babylonian and Assyrian temples.

A little before Solomon's time, the hero Gideon called on a boy to write down the names of trading men in Succoth – apparently just a boy who happened to be available (Judges 8:14). That names could be easily written and recognized then is shown by copper arrowheads found near Bethlehem and in other places, inscribed with their owners' names and dated to the 12th and 11th centuries BC.

The evidence of analogy

The fact that we have virtually no written record of ancient Hebrew life, thought and history apart from the Old Testament means that many aspects of life can hardly be known at all. Normal processes of decay have destroyed any

documents on leather or papyrus buried in the cities of Palestine along with furniture and clothing.

Where such items are preserved in neighbouring cultures, it is possible sometimes to attribute similar usages to ancient Israel. Each case needs thorough testing to ensure that the circumstances

An Egyptian tomb-painting of brick-making helps us to visualize the labour of the Israelite slaves in Egypt.

really are parallel, but some are sufficiently clear to help us evaluate the Old Testament. No literature has survived from Israelite towns, but there is no doubt it existed. The Old Testament itself is witness to that, although scholars debate just how old its written form is.

In Egypt and Babylonia the complicated writing-systems gave the scribes a monopoly. In Israel (and adjacent states) the simple 22-letter alphabet was learnt easily by any who wanted, so writing was more widespread amongst the population, although professional scribes still had an important role. Evidence from various minor written documents demonstrates this fact for ancient Israel. If writing was used for daily affairs,

this implies it could be used for works of literature, too.

The written word was treated with respect. Valuable old books were copied with great care. They could be revised or edited, but the way this has been done is seldom detectable unless the older copies survive for comparison.

Egypt, Assyria and Babylonia, the Hittites and Canaanites all had elaborately arranged religious rites, sacrifices, and priestly orders. Their temples were finely built and lavishly furnished, especially by successful kings. If Israel had been different in this they would have been the odd ones out, but in fact they were not. These analogies show that the Tabernacle, Solomon's Temple, and the Levitical regulations were Israel's counterparts.

As in neighbouring nations, moreover, the mass of the people toiled and suffered to provide for the magnificence demanded by the king.

We would expect Israel, as a nation among nations of related stock, to share similar modes of thought and expression. When Babylonian or Egyptian literature shows features strange to modern thought, we take great pains to understand them – to account for inconsistencies, paradoxes, and apparent contradictions without impugning the accuracy of the texts which are our only sources of information (unless there are firmly founded objective reasons for doing so).

Israel's literature may be expected to contain similar quirks, and they too should be treated with respect. Some are clear, for instance narration of events out of chronological order, or the collecting of items without evident relation to the context.

Similarities and differences

These examples are sufficient to show the value of gathering, studying and applying whatever the ancient Near East affords by way of background to the Bible. The direct and indirect evidence agrees so strikingly with the Old Testament that it makes attempts to discredit its picture of Israel's culture and career very dubious indeed.

No discovery has been proved to contradict the Hebrew records. There may be discrepancies, uncertainties, unanswered questions. The incomplete nature of all our evidence makes this inevitable. New discoveries solve old problems, frequently revealing false premises in modern theories. At the same time they may raise fresh questions and stimulate deeper study, new approaches, and better understanding.

If the similarities between Israel and the neighbouring nations form the bulk of the contribution made by biblical archaeology, the differences merit attention as well. The Old Testament proclaims an unbridgeable gap between them. Although sharing so much in language and culture, in faith Israel stood apart from the rest. To find material traces of Israel's monotheistic faith, imageless worship, centralized cult, is difficult. Israel's neighbours reckoned her God as no more than a national god like their own (Chemosh of Moab, or Milcom of Ammon), unaware of his unique place. To make things more complicated, Israel never remained entirely faithful, so pagan religious objects can be found in the ruins of her cities.

It is in comparing biblical teaching with contemporary texts that the distinctions are best seen.

A Canaanite ivory plaque from Megiddo shows us the kind of harp that David played. Solomon's throne and the furniture in King Ahab's palace were richly decorated with carved ivory.

The absolute demands of the Ten Commandments, the people's exclusive devotion to the God who had chosen them, the equality of individuals balancing their corporate responsibility, the altruism of the prophets – all these, and many others, find no true echo elsewhere in the world of the Old Testament.

Some may find them incredible, yet we possess actually preserved manuscripts which guarantee them an antiquity of well over 2,000 years.

Some may find them unacceptable, but although so old they still speak sense in today's world.

If the historical and cultural aspects harmonize with our knowledge of ancient times, as in fact is the case, the ethical and religious distinctions need explanation. The Old Testament gives one: God spoke.

The Five Books

GENESIS TO DEUTERONOMY

John Taylor

The name given to the first five books of the Bible is 'Pentateuch'. It comes from two Greek words meaning 'five scrolls'. But it is better to think of the Pentateuch as one book divided into five sections, rather than as five books rolled into one. In this way justice is done both to its Hebrew origin – the Jews call it the 'Torah' (Law) or the 'Five fifths of Moses' – and also to its own inherent unity.

This does not mean to say that the Pentateuch consists of an extended piece of narrative writing in strict chronological order. It is immediately obvious to the reader that it contains a wide variety of literary material – narratives, laws, ritual instructions, sermons, genealogies, poetry – which have been drawn together from different sources. It does mean, however, that the material has been carefully constructed within a narrative framework, with a clear purpose in mind and with identifiable objectives on the part of the author or editor.

The Prologue

The story begins with the call of Abraham in Genesis 12, but first there is a Prologue consisting of ancient records and traditions which serve not only to introduce the main themes of the narrative but also to relate them to God's purposes in the world of fallen human beings, of divided nations and of a created order which was originally good.

These chapters are still a source of puzzlement to modern readers, thanks to their pre-scientific language, the astonishing life-span of their characters and the intense difficulty of placing them in an identifiable historical setting. And of course they differ so markedly from the scientific descriptions of the origins of the universe and of life that are taught in our schools today. Genesis 1 – 11 has material written in a variety of styles, which many scholars attribute to different sources, woven together by a thoughtful author/editor. Regardless of its origin, its chief focus is not to provide a scientific

treatise on how things began and how life originated, but to provide the reader with the religious, social and geographical setting for the story that begins with Genesis 12.

Some of the material has been described as 'myth', but this can be a misleading term, even when 'myth' is understood in its technical sense of a 'religious text designed to account for a custom, institution or other phenomenon'. It gives the impression that what is written is totally unhistorical and untrue. But in fact these early chapters of Genesis bear witness to religious realities –

■ that the world as we know it came into being by the will of God

■ that men and women were made in God's image

■ that sin entered human life through moral disobedience

■ and that the whole human race is caught up in the consequences of sin.

Inevitably there is much symbolical language and expression used in describing these features and events, but they contain some of the most profound truths in the whole of the Bible and must not be dismissed too readily, through inadequate appreciation of what the texts are saying.

It is to these chapters that we turn for biblical guidance on the fundamental questions concerning God, humanity and the world. At every stage God is present – not simply presupposed, but constantly and actively at work. This world is God's world. Human history is the outworking of God's plan. He is totally responsible for the world and all that is in it. All people are God's creation, made in his image, with spiritual capacities for goodness, worship and fellowship with God. There is no place whatsoever for other gods. Genesis 1 is all-embracing: sun, moon and stars are God's handiwork, with duties to perform in an ordered universe, even the sea-monsters (the *tanninim* of ancient mythology) were created by God (Genesis 1:21).

Human beings are the climax of creation, superior to all else but subordinate and accountable to their Creator. Only when they aspire above their station and want to be like God do they fall to a lowlier status and discover that all their relationships are soured.

■ From being a good, companionable, shame-free relationship, sex becomes secretive, lustful, anomalous.

■ Child-bearing is painful and hazardous.

■ The care of the land becomes a drudgery.

■ Even the ground itself is affected, and instead of producing food plentifully it has to be tamed and coaxed and sweated over.

There is nothing that sin has not blighted. Its taint reaches out to family life, where religion soon breeds rivalry, brotherly affection turns to murder, and justice degenerates into blood-lust (Genesis 4).

God's response to sin is, consistently, a blend of judgment and mercy. From the provision of clothing for Adam and Eve, and the guarding of the way to the tree of life, to the confusion of tongues at Babel, God tempers his justice with generosity. Beyond the immediate punishment of casting Adam out from the garden of Eden or Cain from human society, beyond the destruction of the flood and the scattering of the nations, there is always God's ultimate intention for humanity's wellbeing and blessing.

Thus, in a world of disorder and corruption, it is seen to be totally in keeping with God's nature that he should call out one man, Abraham, and through him his descendants the Jews, to be the channel of grace and revelation to all the world. It is this story which the Pentateuch goes on to tell.

The story is in two sections:
■ The first half (Genesis 12 – 50) is dominated by the four generations of the patriarchs – Abraham, Isaac, Jacob and Joseph.
■ The second half (Exodus – Deuteronomy) is dominated by the towering figure of Moses.

While it is notoriously difficult to be sure of dates at this early stage of Israel's history, a reasonable estimate allows a period of about 600 years for these events, i.e. from about 1900 BC to about 1250 BC. Before we read the story, as it is told in the Five Books, it is as well to notice that it majors on four important themes.

God's chosen people

The Old Testament was written for the people of Israel – the people who looked back to Jacob (= Israel) as their common ancestor and to Abraham as the founder of their nation. Christians, too, look to Abraham as the father of all those who depend in faith on God rather than on anything they can do for themselves (see Romans 4:16). We therefore read the story of Abraham's call by God to become the ancestor of God's chosen people, not simply as an event in the distant past, but as something of present-day significance to us all.

The idea of God's special choosing (election) of individuals carries with it two subsidiary features: promise and responsibility. Genesis 12 – 22 is interspersed with words of promise spoken by God to Abraham.
■ Abraham is promised descendants as countless as the stars of heaven.
■ He is given the land of Canaan as his children's inheritance.
■ He is promised a great name in days to come.
And the Lord God's special favour was to be shown not only to Abraham and his family but to all people through him.

So God's promises to Abraham were not just for the selfish enjoyment of a chosen few. They were to be used responsibly so that others might share in the benefits. Right at the heart of God's choice of Israel it is made plain that God has a missionary purpose. Israel's history must be read as the long story of their attempts to fulfil their responsibilities – with some successes, but with many conspicuous failures.

God's covenant

The English word 'covenant' suggests legal restrictions, documents tied with pink tapes and sealing wax. But to the Hebrew mind the covenant idea covered all kinds of human relationships. It was the bond which united people in mutual obligations, whether through a marriage contract, a commercial enterprise or a verbal undertaking. It was only natural that people's relationship to God should also have been expressed in terms of a covenant.

On three separate occasions in the Pentateuch, these covenant terms are used:
■ when God promises Noah that he will

never again send a flood upon the earth
(Genesis 9:9).
- when God makes his promises to
  Abraham (Genesis 15:18; 17:4).
- when the Sinai covenant is established
  with Moses and summarized in the
  'book of the covenant' (Exodus 24:7).

Although in everyday use covenants
were made between equals, the religious
use of the term always referred to a
relationship between a greater and a lesser
partner. The form of the covenant between
God and Israel in Exodus and Deuteronomy has been helpfully illuminated by
the discoveries of Hittite suzerainty treaties
made between a king and his vassal. They
consisted of
- a historical introduction
- a list of stipulations
- curses and blessings invoked on the
  parties
- a solemn oath
- and a religious ceremony to ratify the
  covenant.

Most of these features can be found in
the Old Testament pattern of covenants.
(See 'Covenants and Near Eastern
treaties'.)

More important than the form of the
covenant, however, was its theological
significance.

It was based on the initiative of God.
God acted in mercy and with sovereignty,
making an unconditional promise never to
judge humanity with another flood
(Genesis 9:11). God chose Abraham and
his descendants to be the channels of his
mercy to a fallen world. He cemented this
choice by committing himself to the
Israelite nation with the words, 'I will take
you for my people, and I will be your God'
(Exodus 6:7).

It implied a new revelation of God. God
appeared to Abraham as his shield (Genesis
15:1) and as God Almighty ('El Shaddai',
Genesis 17:1). He appeared to Moses as
'Yahweh' ('I am who I am', Exodus 3:14),
and later on as 'Yahweh your God, who
brought you out of the land of Egypt'
(Exodus 20:2). (See 'The names of God'.)

The Five Books
relate to God's
creation and his
law. A weaver,
at work on an
upright loom,
expresses the gift
of creativity and
reminds us that
God's law relates
to everyday life.

**It made moral and ritual demands
upon the people.** The stipulations of the
covenant included both these features.
Ritual was represented by the rite of
circumcision given to Abraham (Genesis
17:10), by the keeping of the sabbath, the
day of rest (Exodus 20:8ff.) and by all the
detailed requirements relating to worship
and sacrifice found in the Pentateuch. At
the same time the ethical requirements
were spelt out in the Ten Commandments
and other laws.

Though at first sight these two demands
seem strangely unrelated, they do in fact
meet in the idea of God's holiness. A holy
God requires his people to reflect his
character both in worship and in
behaviour.

The Law of God
The idea of law is central to the Five Books
and, as we have seen, it gave its name
(Torah) to the book as a whole. At its
simplest, it covered the Ten Commandments (Exodus 20; Deuteronomy 5) but
associated with these were various
collections of laws which have been
classified as:
- the book of the covenant (Exodus
  21 – 23)

The exodus speaks of God's rescue: how he took his people from Egypt, across the inhospitable Sinai 'wilderness' to a new land of their own.

■ the holiness code (Leviticus 17 – 26)
■ the law of Deuteronomy (Deuteronomy 12 – 26).

Comparisons have been made with other ancient Near Eastern law-codes, especially the Code of Hammurabi, and many similarities noted. These are to be expected, since Israel was a part of Eastern Mediterranean culture and shared in the ideas and experience of their neighbours. What is so significant is not the similarities but the differences which made Israel's laws distinctive. These may be summarized as:

■ their uncompromising monotheism (everything is related to the one God)
■ their remarkable concern for the underprivileged: slaves, strangers, women, orphans
■ their community spirit, based on the covenant relationship shared by all Israel with the Lord God.

It has also been pointed out that the laws in the Old Testament are expressed in two forms. They are set out either as 'thou shalt...'/ 'thou shalt not...' (*apodictic*) or 'when a person..., he/she shall...' (*casuistic*). As most ancient law-codes consisted of the casuistic type, it may be that the apodictic was a peculiarly Israelite form, in which case the Ten Command-ments were unique to Israel.

Didn't Jesus reject the Law? Some Christians have mistakenly seen Jesus'

teaching in the Sermon on the Mount as a rejection of the Jewish law in favour of his new law of love. But Jesus' criticisms were in fact directed not at the laws, but at the way the rabbis had interpreted them. ('You have heard that it was said' was the traditional rabbinic formula for introducing their interpretation.) He was uncovering the inner motivation behind the commandments, which interpreters had failed to appreciate.

A list of 'don'ts'? Some too have criticized the Ten Commandments for being negative. But they follow a positive assertion: 'I am the Lord your God...' Those who have experienced deliverance by the hand of God, and who live under God's sovereignty, must show it by distinctive behaviour. The Ten Commandments therefore began as God's charter for his liberated people. They consisted not of generalities but of specific commands for specific situations: worship, work, home life, marriage, respect for life and property, elementary justice and the personal realm of the will. To all these areas of human experience God had a word that was explicit and inescapable. Christ did not destroy it: he fulfilled and enlarged it.

What about the other rules? Much of Leviticus and other parts of the Pentateuch is taken up with ceremonial and ritual laws. The purpose of these laws was to provide guidance for the day-to-day running of the Israelite community, and also to teach how a holy God was to be worshipped by a holy people. So, in addition to regulations for worship (festivals, sacrifices, etc.), detailed guidance was given for the preservation of ritual purity. The Israelite people had to be kept free of contamination from outside sources, especially the corrupting influence of Canaanite religion. They must approach God with a due sense of his moral and ritual distinctiveness.

These regulations no longer apply to the Christian church, though the underlying principles still have much to teach. And the elaborate sacrificial system has found its fulfilment in the one sacrifice of Christ –

the perfect Lamb of God – through whom sins are forgiven and atonement is made for all people for ever (see Hebrews 10:1-18).

Exodus: God to the rescue

The fourth major theme found in the Five Books, and recurring throughout the Bible, is the exodus from Egypt described in Exodus 1 – 12. For all Jews this was and is the great saving act of God to which all later generations look back with thankfulness.

- It was a miraculous intervention by God in response to the cries of his enslaved people (Exodus 3:7).
- It was essentially God's act – 'with mighty hand and outstretched arm'.
- It was a great victory over the gods of Egypt which demonstrated God's total supremacy.
- It was a moment in history recalled every year in the Feast of the Passover.

Later generations were frequently reminded that they were once members of a slave community whom God had mercifully redeemed from bondage. They were encouraged to remember the past and warned of the danger of forgetting what God had done for them (e.g. Deuteronomy 6:12).

As a historical event the exodus was definitive. The fact that God had done it once meant that God could do it again. When Israel was in exile in Babylon the nation looked for a second exodus (Isaiah 51:9-11). And when Christ came, his work of deliverance was described in the language of the exodus (e.g. Luke 9:31).

These, then, are the four themes which are never far below the surface, the constant preoccupation of these five books. The only other theme which recurs with depressing regularity is the persistent sinfulness of the people of Israel. They were slow to accept Moses as their deliverer. They grumbled about the hardships of the journey. They even hankered after the old life in Egypt (suitably glamorized, Numbers 11:5).

They were daunted by the prospect of moving into the land of Canaan. And they wandered for 40 years in the wilderness of indecision. Not even Moses was immune, and he was punished by not being allowed to lead the people into their promised land. But sin was no new problem. Those introductory chapters of Genesis 1 – 11 made that clear, as we saw earlier. In a remarkable way, God's overruling providence was able to deal with human disobedience and to find a way through it and beyond it.

Genesis

Summary

The creation of
the world and its spoiling.
The call and promise of
God to Abraham and
his descendants.

Chapters 1 – 11
The creation
Human downfall
The great flood

•

Chapters 12 – 50
Stories of Abraham,
Isaac, Jacob, Joseph

Genesis is an epic, a collection of momentous stories. The title means 'beginning' and this is the Bible's book of beginnings – the beginning of the world and the beginning of a nation. It is important to appreciate the early chapters especially as *story*: concerned with truth and meaning at the deepest level; delighting in pictures and patterns. Story has to be taken whole, not piecemeal. If we appreciate the nature of the material, many 'problems' simply disappear.

The making of the book

Genesis has no named author or date of writing. Its stories were told orally long before they were collected together and written down. Many scholars think that the earliest collections of Old Testament material were probably made in King David's or King Solomon's time, with some further editing perhaps as late as 400 BC.

Many ancient peoples had their own creation stories, and we can imagine these stories being told and retold, around the camp fire, down the generations. Did Moses, with his Egyptian court education, begin the process of writing them down? A long tradition links his name with the Bible's first five books. How the books reached their present form may be a matter of debate, but what is clear is that these stories express the deepest convictions of God's people that this world is the work of the one Creator-God, who is utterly good and who loves and cares for his creation. They had no need to argue for God's existence: they knew him for themselves.

Content

The 'prologue' (chapters 1 – 11) moves swiftly from the world as God made it to the world as we know it. God's good creation is progressively soured as a result of human sin in turning away from the Creator and ignoring his warnings. From the very first, people have chosen to go their own way, with calamitous results.

Then comes the great flood, sweeping everything away. God acts in judgment and also in saving. Noah and his family are rescued. There is a new beginning. Yet these chapters end in the folly of Babel: the nations are divided and dispersed.

In chapter 12 the emphasis shifts from the big canvas of the human story to focus on a single individual, Abraham, and his descendants. The world is no better after Noah, but God will not destroy it. Instead God begins, through a particular person and nation, to carry out his purpose of 'redeeming' the world and mending broken relationships.

Genesis takes the story on through Isaac and Jacob to the death of Joseph in Egypt. And still the story of God's great purpose for humanity is scarcely begun. It continues through the Bible's pages to the very last words of the book of Revelation.

1:1 – 2:3
A good creation

The great drama of the beginning of all things starts with God. The language is simple but vivid. It evokes the wonder and richness of creation from formlessness to teeming life.

More than this, it offers us the key to understanding ourselves and the world around us. The story, styled and shaped to a conscious pattern, makes it clear that
■ the origin of the world and of life was no accident; there is a Creator – God;
■ God made everything there is;

> 66 *In the beginning God created the heavens and the earth. Now the earth was formless and empty, darkness was over the surface of the deep ... And God said, 'Let there be light.'* 99
>
> 1:1-3

- all that God made was good;
- of all God's marvellous creation, people are special: they alone are made in God's 'likeness' and given charge over everything;
- God's six 'days' of creative activity, followed by a 'day' of rest, sets the pattern for working life.

Creation is described as taking place in six days. Eight times God speaks, and there is something new:

Day 1 Light is separated from darkness: there is day and night
Day 2 The separation of 'the heavens' (Earth's atmosphere)
Day 3 Land and seas are separated, and the 'making' begins:
Plants and trees
Day 4 Sun, moon and stars
Day 5 Sea creatures and birds
Day 6 Land animals
People
Day 7 Creation completed, God rests

This is not a chronological account. The 'separations' of the first three days create the 'spaces' which God then fills. We are not told *when* creation took place. Nor are we given details as to *how* God brought the earth and life into being – nor how long it all took. The storyteller does not share the preoccupations of a scientific age. He is concerned with more important things.

▶ **Days** These are best understood as a pattern chosen as the most vivid means of expressing the creative energy and satisfaction of God, the orderliness and simple majesty of the way he created all things. They are used to point a lesson: 2:3.

▶ **The 'image' or 'likeness' of God (1:27)** Of all creation, only man and woman are described as being made in God's likeness. It is a phrase that sets people apart from the animals. It establishes them in a special relationship with God. God gives them control over the newly-made world and all its creatures. The 'likeness' is so basic to human nature that even humanity's subsequent downfall – the 'Fall' – did not destroy it. Sin has certainly spoiled and blurred it, but people are still reasoning, morally responsible, and creative in a way that animals are not: we can imagine, we can dream, plan and shape our future. We can take responsibility for our environment and care properly for it. We

can enjoy a variety of relationships. We are also still free to choose, though that freedom now has a false bias.

2:4 – 3:24
The spoiling

2:4-25 Man and woman
If the world God made was good, how did it get to be the way it is now?

This second story, after the creation, accounts for the bad as well as the good in our world. It focusses on the first two human beings and their relationship with God. Significantly, God now has a different name. In the first story he was *Elohim*, God the Creator, the one High God. Now he is *Yahweh* (Jehovah) *Elohim*, the *personal* name by which he can be known (see 'The names of God').

'Adam' in Hebrew is both a personal name and a word for 'mankind'. God forms the first human being and plants for him a garden in Eden in the east. But neither birds nor animals provide the companionship man needs, and he is not made for a solitary, self-sufficient life. So God creates woman, who shares man's own nature. Here is the ideal partner. 'This one at last is bone from my bones, flesh from my flesh' cries Adam in delight, giving us the first lines of poetry in the Bible. These two are literally 'made for one another'. They are naked, totally open to one another. And this is right. It will never be quite the same again.

In 2:24 the editor reinforces the point: true marriage is a unique and exclusive relationship.

▶ **The two trees** What does this powerful picture-language mean? Does one tree stand for life and the other for forbidden knowledge? Is the phrase 'good and evil' a Hebrew idiom for 'everything' — all knowledge? Or does the real importance of the trees lie in the opportunity they present for the man and the woman to say 'Yes' or 'No' to God? Their fatal choice will cut them off from the 'tree of life'. They will leave God's presence. They will experience death. Yet hope remains. In the last book of the Bible, the tree stands beside the river in the 'new Jerusalem', where God and his people live

Creation stories

Alan Millard

How did the world begin? That is a question most people ask. And many peoples around the world have their own creation stories, told and retold down the years, in an attempt to provide an answer. Are the Genesis stories, then, simply another version, adapted to suit Hebrew beliefs?

One source for all?

Genesis 1 and 2 consist of a general account of the creation of the heavens and the earth, followed by a more detailed description of the making of humankind. These stories have several points in common with other stories of cosmic and of human creation:

■ pre-existent deity;
■ creation by divine command;
■ human beings as the ultimate creature, formed from the earth as a pot is made, yet in some way a reflection of deity.

   Almost all polytheistic faiths possess family-trees of their gods which can figure in creation stories. A primal pair or even a single self-created and self-propagating god heads the divine family, all of whose members represent or control natural elements and forces.

   For some peoples, the physical universe or a basic element such as water or earth always existed, and the gods arose from it. For others it was the handiwork of a god or gods. These are simple concepts based on observation and elementary logic. For example, the concept of humans as 'dust' is easily deduced from the cycle of death and decay.

   Common ideas, however, do not necessarily mean a common origin. It is misleading to reduce differing stories from all over the world to their common factors in order to claim that they do. A single source for all, or large numbers, of different stories is improbable.

Long before stories like those in the early chapters of Genesis were written down, they were told and retold around the camp fires of nomadic peoples and within the family.

The Babylonian Genesis

The famous Babylonian Genesis, usually linked with the Hebrew creation story, is one of several, and was neither the oldest nor the most popular. Written late in the 2nd millennium BC to honour Marduk, god of Babylon, who is its hero, it begins with a watery mother-figure, Tiamat, from whom the gods are born. (The name is related to the Hebrew word for 'the deep' – Genesis 1:2 – through the prehistoric linguistic connections between Babylonian and Hebrew.) She is killed by Marduk in a battle with her children whose noise had angered her, and her corpse is formed into the world. People are made to relieve the gods of the toil of keeping the earth in order, so the gods have rest.

There are clear indications that this story was made up from older ones, and earlier compositions have been found which contain some of these features. Only one theme recurs often, the relief of the gods from their labour by the making of mankind with a divine ingredient. The battle of the gods in the Babylonian Genesis has no Old Testament equivalent, despite attempts by many scholars to discover underlying references to it in the text of Genesis 1:2 and other passages which speak of God's power over the waters.

This clay tablet is inscribed with a part of the Babylonian account of the creation. It was copied in about the 7th century BC but is dependent on other stories going right back to the 3rd millennium BC.

▶▶ Genesis and other ancient Near Eastern stories

It is more interesting, and more to the point, to set Genesis beside other accounts from the ancient Near East, the world of the Old Testament. When we do so, we find that few of the ancient creation stories share more than one or two basic concepts – such as the separation of heaven and earth, and the creation of human beings from clay.

The Babylonian stories, however, have some striking resemblances to the Hebrew. In the century since the first of the Babylonian accounts was translated into English, they have frequently been cited as the ultimate source of the Hebrews' beliefs. Recently,

however, the recovery of more texts and the re-assessment of those long known have shown that many of the accepted similarities are in fact illusory. For example, the seven days of creation in Genesis and the fact that the Babylonian Genesis is written on seven tablets are completely unrelated: the division of the Babylonian story bears no relation to its contents, or to stages in the poem.

The factual similarities only serve to emphasize the wide difference in moral and spiritual outlook between the Hebrew Genesis and its closest counterparts. There is no need to argue, as many have done, that Genesis was derived from the others. The differ-

ences of standpoint and content are in fact so marked that they serve to highlight the 'revelation' aspect of Genesis, which sets it so clearly apart from simple folk tale.

The Atrakhasis Epic

One particular Babylonian poem, the *Atrakhasis Epic*, invites comparison with Genesis. This is concerned with the infancy of mankind and the beginning of society, and hints at the order of the world without describing its creation. It starts with the minor gods working to irrigate the land, then rebelling at their lot, from which they are relieved by the creation of people who are to do the work instead. Human beings are a satisfactory substitute until their noise causes disturbance and leads to their destruction in the flood.

In outline, *Atrakhasis* (known from copies made about 1600 BC) has some similarity to parts of Genesis 2 – 8.
- People are made from clay and a divine part ('breath' in Genesis, the flesh and blood of a god in *Atrakhasis*).
- Their task is to keep the earth in order (arduous labour in *Atrakhasis*, control of a paradise in Genesis).

- The whole human race is eventually destroyed by flood, except one family.

On the other hand, *Atrakhasis* has people toiling from the first, has no single 'Adam', no separate making of woman, no Eden, and no Fall – in fact no moral teaching at all. The sense is rather that this is how our lot came to be and we should accept it.

A Sumerian version names five important cities in the time before the flood, and they link with separately preserved lists of pre-flood kings whose ages far exceeded those of the patriarchs in Genesis 5. Babylonian writers looked upon the flood as a major interruption in their country's history. (See 'Flood stories'.)

In their over-all coverage, therefore, Genesis and the tradition represented by *Atrakhasis* look back to the same events.

Some of the themes in the Babylonian story – in particular,

people's place as substitute workers – can be traced in a Sumerian poem, 'Enki and Ninmakh', written before 2000 BC.

together once more – and its leaves are for 'the healing of the nations' (Revelation 22:2).

▶ **A river (2:10)** This is a real, geographical location. Although Pishon and Gihon are not known, the Tigris and Euphrates rivers flow into the Persian Gulf. The name Cush (a descendant of Noah) is linked with Babylon in 10:8,10. So the description may be of four rivers, all flowing into the Gulf, with 'Eden' somewhere above it.

3 A fatal choice

Enter the serpent – a creature made by God and yet a rebel. Where does the bad come from in this good world? The story does not say. But clearly God has taken an enormous risk in giving his creatures the freedom to choose. What follows is a brilliant insight into the psychology of temptation and sin: the attempt to shift the

People as God's caretakers
Ghillean Prance

The Genesis text leaves us in no doubt that people were created to be caretakers and not destroyers of the Earth.

Amidst the terrifying environmental destruction, pollution and loss of species that is happening today it is salutary to look at the remit given by God to the first people: 'Then the Lord God took the man and put him in the Garden to till it and keep it' (Genesis 2:15).

The Hebrew word *abad* translated 'till' also means to serve and *shamar*, translated 'keep', means to watch or preserve. The instruction to the first people was to serve and preserve the land. Humankind was given dominion or 'lordship' over the rest of creation to look after it and not to destroy it and all the other creatures which God also created.

It follows that care for creation is a Christian responsibility today since those who know the Creator should really be the first to give a lead in the protection of his creation.

Genesis 2:9 says: 'And out of the ground the Lord God caused to grow every tree that is pleasing to sight and good for food.'

It is significant that the utilitarian is not placed first in this text. The purpose of the trees was

to be aesthetically pleasing as well as useful, yet we show little respect for trees today as large acres of rainforest are felled every minute. However, the text also indicates that the trees were intended for use as food, which we can fairly take to include the timber they yield, rubber latex and many other products. We are not to overuse these resources but also to leave trees standing for pleasure and for shade.

The responsibility human beings have for all creatures is re-emphasized in the 'covenant' God made with Noah after the flood. This agreement was not just between humans and God, it encompassed 'every living creature

that is with you for all successive generations' (Genesis 9:12). 'Now behold I myself do establish my covenant with you and with your descendants after you and with every living creature that is with you, the birds, the cattle, and every beast of the earth with you: of all that comes out of the ark, even every beast of the Earth' (Genesis 9: 9-10). Since the covenant was with all creatures we have a responsibility to look after them, not cause species to go into extinction because of overuse and destruction of their habitat.

We must take care of creation because it belongs to God, not to us. 'The Earth is the Lord's and all it contains' are the opening words of Psalm 24. We must also be caretakers of creation because Christ is 'the first-born of all creation' (Colossians 1:15) and 'by him (Christ) all things were created, both in the heavens and on earth... all things have been created by him and for him.' We today are called to be his caretakers or stewards of creation until he returns.

This giant fern, in Fiji, is just one example of the extraordinary and lush growth of plant life since the beginning.

blame, and eventual shame.

The serpent questions what God has said, then calls God a liar. The woman has to set the enticing fruit, the desire to have knowledge like God's, against God's plain command. Eve exaggerates God's strictness and plays with temptation. Does she want simply to know as God knows, or to be God's equal (in contrast to the Son of God, willing to humble himself: Philippians 2:6ff.). The decision is deliberate, and fatal. The silent Adam makes no protest. He too eats. Man and woman have chosen to go their own way, to disregard the God who gave them life.

But the goodness of God and human sin are like oil and water. Separation is inevitable. The relationship of God with people, and people with one another, is wrecked. Man and woman are no longer at ease together. The serpent is now at enmity with human beings. The woman will experience suffering – in childbirth, the most fundamental human process. Desire and domination will hurt relations between the sexes. Adam's work will be sweat and toil.

Because of their deliberate wrongdoing, access to the 'tree of life' is now denied them. They are to leave the garden, for ever. They are on their own, apart from God, alive yet only half alive without him. Death is only a matter of time. God's word was true. Yet still he shows them tender, parent care (3:21).

▶ **Adam** In the rest of the Old Testament the word means mankind. It is also very like the Hebrew word for 'ground' (a play on words like 'human' and 'humus'). In the New Testament

Adam is our ancestor, the founder of the race to which we all belong. Paul contrasts Adam with Christ: as descendants of Adam we all die, separated from God, but Christ restores us to eternal life, reuniting us with God (Romans 5; 1 Corinthians 15).

▶ **Adam and Eve** Competition and domination come in with the Fall. In the beginning the two were created equally 'in God's image'. They were independent and co-dependent, jointly responsible for the welfare of the world and of their children. The curse of Genesis 3:16-19 is a description of how the closest human relationship is spoiled because of disobedience to God: we see this played out in male/female relationships throughout the rest of Scripture and the world's history from then till now. In Genesis 1, Adam and Eve are described as being created together. In Genesis 2, Adam is created first, but no particular significance is attached to this. Eve is described as a 'helper' for Adam in compatible relationship and marriage, not in a sense of inferiority, since the word is used mostly of God in the Old Testament.

4 – 5
From Adam to Noah

4 Cain and Abel

Adam and Eve, after their expulsion from the garden, have two sons: Cain, the farmer, and Abel, the shepherd. In due course each brings his offering to God. Abel's is accepted, but not Cain's. It was not *what* Abel offered, but his faith (Hebrews 11:4) which made his gift acceptable. Cain's bitter resentment shows a very different spirit. As the prophets will say again and again, God is not bought off by sacrifices. He wants the offerer also to 'do well'(verse 7). True faith cannot be divorced from right behaviour.

Cain kills Abel – it is a short step from rebellion to bloodshed – and God condemns him to a nomadic life, but provides protection against death. Verses 17-24 list some of Cain's descendants, and show the beginnings of civilized life. Enoch builds the first city. His successors learn to play and enjoy music – also to forge iron and bronze. But creative skills are not

Personal names in Genesis 1 – 11

Richard S. Hess

Personal names in the biblical world often have a meaning or etymology that tells us something about the character or beliefs of the person named. In Genesis, as elsewhere in the Bible, the names of many of the main characters in the stories have a meaning and significance.

The name means...

The name **Adam** means 'humanity' and appropriately describes the first person and representative of the human race. It is used with this meaning in 1:26-28 and with the related meaning 'man' in chapters 2, 3 and most of 4. Only in 4:25 is the name Adam used for the first time.

The name **Eve** could be understood as 'Giver of life'. It describes her role as suggested in Genesis 3. Her name is given only at the end of this chapter.

Cain may have something to do with metal smithery and this is developed among his descendants, especially Tubal-Cain.

Abel is a Hebrew word used to describe something that is fleeting. It is translated 'vanity' in Ecclesiastes. It suggests the brief life of the man who was killed by his brother. It also suggests that Abel had no descendants, nothing to continue his name or to make it permanent.

Seth, on the other hand, can mean 'to set/place' or, in Genesis 1 – 11, 'to act as a substitute'. This of course fits the figure who substitutes for Abel as the one through whom the hope of Eve and Adam would be fulfilled.

Among other figures, **Enoch** means 'dedication' and may describe his devotion to God. **Nimrod**, 'we will rebel, let us rebel', describes the character in Genesis 10, especially if he is also associated with the Tower of Babel in Genesis 11.

Shem is 'the name', the one through whom comes Abram, whose name God would make great.

The name sounds like...

In addition to the straightforward meaning of the Hebrew word(s) which we find in the personal names in these early chapters of Genesis, there is also wordplay. Similar sounding words tie together the personal names and some of the events in the stories.

Adam sounds like the 'ground', the *adamah* from which God created him.

Cain sounds like the verb *qanah*, 'to create; to acquire', which Eve uses in 4:1 to describe God's involvement in his birth.

Noah resembles *nacham*, the 'comforting' that Lamech predicts he will provide.

Similar names

There are similar sounding names in the genealogies of Cain and Seth (in the cases of Enoch and Lamech they are exactly the same names). But that does not necessarily mean we have two variations of a single original genealogy. It may show that despite their outward likeness (similar names) people may be radically different in terms of their true character. These two lines lead in opposite directions: Cain's to murder and pride, Seth's to righteousness and the saving of Noah from the flood. This similarity in names is a feature of other genealogies from the ancient Near East.

The figure of Enoch (the good man God removes from this world in Genesis) occurs in ancient Near Eastern lists of sages who lived before the flood.

More interesting are the occurrences in the ancient Near East of names similar to those in these early chapters of Genesis. Some names and their elements occur in personal names at many times throughout the history of the ancient Near East. For example, the Semitic roots behind the names Eve and Shem occur frequently in personal names. Other roots, such as Lamech and Arpachshad, never occur. Some, such as Adam and the first part of Methuselah and Methushael, occur at specific times and places only in or before the 2nd millennium BC. They are not present in the personal names of the 1st millennium, the period of the Israelite kings, which suggests they date from an earlier period, not a later one.

matched by moral progress. Lamech takes two wives. The pain and problems this brings is all too evident in later stories. And he *boasts* of the murder he has committed, outdoing Cain.

The last two verses give a glimmer of hope. Seth is born to Adam and Eve, and people begin 'to call on the name of the Lord'.

▶ **Cain's wife** Verse 17 and verses 14-15 give the impression of an earth already, to some extent, populated. The simplest way of accounting for this is to assume other, unnamed, children of Adam and Eve. Others would argue from the fact that the word adam=man, or mankind, that a race was created, not a single pair.

5 Family tree

The Bible often provides family trees (genealogies) similar to this one to define an important line of descent. Many of them are selective, sometimes in order to create a pattern of a certain number of names (e.g. Matthew 1). We are not meant to add up all the figures and work out the length of time covered. (Ussher did this, arriving at 4004 BC for the date of Adam. Yet we know, from Jericho and other cities, of a civilization going back to 7000 BC, and that is not the beginning of human history.)

In the ancient Near East numbers were often used to signify importance, rather than actual quantity. The reducing ages from Methuselah to Joseph may be meant to suggest the cumulative effects of sin. Enoch's life of 365 years, a complete year's cycle of days, is worth special note.

The life-span assigned to these early ancestors is remarkable. It ranges from 777 years for Lamech to Methuselah's 969 years. Each of the ten records follows the same formula:

When A was x years old he had a son B. He lived another y years and had other sons and daughters. He lived z years, and then he died.

The sombre note of the final phrase 'and then he died' is varied only in the case of Enoch, the man who 'walked with God'. For him God had other plans. Noah, the last of the ten, in his turn also 'walked with God' (6:9). And he too, though in a different way, was saved from death.

❝ *As long as earth endures: seedtime and harvest, cold and heat, summer and winter, day and night will never cease.* **❞**

God's promise after the flood: 8:22

6 – 11
The flood and Babel

6:1-8 A lost race
The human race, lost in violence and corruption, is bringing destruction upon itself. God reduces the life-span to 120 years. But that alone will not answer. Only an act of judgment will rid the world of sin.

▶ **6:2** Different versions give 'sons of the gods' or 'sons of God' (i.e. angels) or 'supernatural beings'.

▶ **6:4** 'Nephilim' or 'giants': the 'mighty men' (heroes) of old.

6:9 – 9:29 Noah's story
As with creation, we should approach this account as *story*, expecting picture and symbol and pattern, looking for why it is being told, the 'big message(s)'.

In the beginning, God set the bounds of land and water, bringing order out of chaos. Now, as a result of human sin, the forces of destruction are let loose. But all is not lost.

Against a background of judgment, the story focusses on God's saving act. Noah, 'the only good man of his time', the one human being who 'lived in fellowship' with God, will not go down with the rest. God has a detailed rescue plan. He will provide a place of safety and refuge. A lifetime of knowing and trusting God has prepared Noah for this moment. And he does *exactly* as God tells him.

Sadly, even a completely fresh start does not restore Eden or change human nature. Though the 'image of God' (9:6) remains, so too does the dysfunction in creation. Animals are now food for humans. And Noah's own story ends on a low note. (Significantly, the Bible shows us the flaws in even its greatest figures.) Noah gets drunk, Ham dishonours his father, and the old man curses Canaan, Ham's younger (youngest?) son. Did Canaan in some way compound the disrespect? We do not know. But the Canaanites later became subject to Shem's descendants, the Israelites.

Flood stories have been handed down in many languages from most parts of the world. The Babylonian (Sumerian, and

Flood stories
Alan Millard

Memories of a great flood or floods are worldwide. As we would expect, they have such common features as escape by boat, animals taken aboard, and grounding on a high peak. Babylonia (alone amongst the ancient stories) has given us an account so close to Genesis that it has raised questions of borrowing or direct influence.

For a century this story has been known from *The Epic of Gilgamesh*, Tablet 11. The epic's theme is that human beings cannot hope for immortality, the only man who gained it being the Babylonian Noah, whose story it tells. That was taken into the Gilgamesh series from an older work the *Atrakhasis Epic* (see 'Creation stories'). Here it forms part of a longer account of human history from the creation, as in Genesis.

Drawing a moral

The flood story in Babylonia is also known from a Sumerian text telling virtually the same tale, though more briefly, and many Sumerian compositions refer to the distant days of the flood or before.

The Genesis flood story has a recognizable background in Mesopotamia, and the numerous similarities suggest it is a record of the same event as the Babylonian. They represent a common folk memory of a great disaster. But the moral and theological content are obviously very different. God's 'revelation' is to be found, not simply in the narrative of events but also in their interpretation.

The Babylonian Noah

After the first human beings were made, the Babylonian flood story relates, the noise of their many children was so great that the god of the earth could not sleep. His schemes for noise-reduction were thwarted when the pious Atrakhasis won the help of the god responsible for creating people. Finally, the gods decided upon a catastrophic flood, all swearing to keep the plan secret. Again, Atrakhasis was warned, the god instructing him in a dream to build a boat, take on board his family and animals, and explain his action to his fellow humans as a punishment inflicted upon him which would bring benefit to them. When all were aboard, the storm broke, and all mankind was swept away.

The gods themselves were also affected. With no people left to serve them, they lost the food and drink supplied in sacrificial offerings, and sat miserably in heaven until the seven days' tempest had ended. Then Atrakhasis sent out birds to learn whether the land was habitable again (an episode preserved only in the Gilgamesh version), and offered sacrifice on the mountain where his boat had come to rest. Eagerly, the gods gathered 'like flies', smelling the savour of the offering, swearing not to cause such destruction again. The mother-goddess swore by a necklace of blue stones. But the god whose sleep had been disturbed was not yet appeased, and after the unfairness of indiscriminate punishment had been discussed, a system was set up in which some women avoided childbirth by entering religious orders, while others lost infants through disease, thus limiting the population. (The terms used make it clear that this was an explanation of the social system of the author's time.)

This 7th-century BC inscribed clay tablet from Nineveh, the 11th tablet of *The Epic of Gilgamesh*, contains the Babylonian account of the flood.

▶▶

▶▶

The end of the flood:
Babylonian account

I made a libation on the peak of the
*   mountain,*
The gods smelled the savour,
The gods smelled the sweet savour,
The gods clustered like flies around the
*   sacrificer.*
When at last the great goddess
*   (Ishtar) arrived (she said):*
'All you gods here, as I shall never
*   forget my lapis lazuli necklace,*
I shall remember these days, and
*   never forget them.'*

The end of the flood:
Genesis account

Noah built an altar to the Lord; he
took one of each kind of ritually clean
animal and bird and burnt them as a
whole sacrifice on the altar. The odour
of the sacrifice pleased the Lord, and
he said to himself, 'Never again will I
put the earth under a curse because of
what people do; I know that from the
time they are young their thoughts
are evil. Never again will I destroy all
living beings, as I have done this
time.'

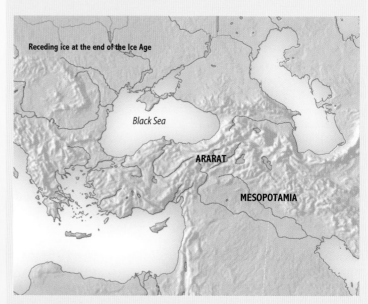

New light on Noah's flood?

Receding ice at the end of the Ice Age

Black Sea

ARARAT

MESOPOTAMIA

It is not surprising that there are a number of stories from folk memory of great floods. Marine geologists Dr William Ryan and Dr Walter Pitman found the biblical and Babylonian stories particularly intriguing. 'If, as the description suggested, it caused whole communities to move,' Dr Ryan says, 'then it was likely that the story of the flood would be passed down to future generations.'

The geologists found that the Black Sea was once a freshwater lake, but suddenly changed to salt water about 9,000 years ago. Other research revealed an estimated 60 metre water-level rise. More evidence came from a seismic profile of the seabed. Samples subjected to carbon-14 testing brought the flood-date forward to 7,550 years ago.

They speculated that the end of an Ice Age would lead sea levels to rise dramatically, and concluded that the most likely site for a catastrophic flow would be a bottle-shaped basin connected to the ocean by a narrow

neck. The Black Sea was a perfect candidate.

Could this be the origin of the flood stories? Were they brought to Mesopotamia by people migrating from the shores of the Black Sea, and then from Mesopotamia to Canaan by Abraham? It would explain the reference to Ararat as the highest mountain in the area.

Dr Ryan says: 'We have convincing evidence that a flood took place in the Black Sea. The evidence that it is the same one in the Bible and in *The Epic of Gilgamesh* is circumstantial, and that has led to a friendly dispute between us and the archaeologists.'

Babylonian tradition, however, clearly locates the impact of the flood in Babylonia, floating the ark northwards.

particularly Akkadian) accounts have considerable similarity with the story recorded here. This is not surprising, if both reflect memories of an actual event in the same general area. There is no need to assume the writer of Genesis must have drawn on the Babylonian stories for his information. Indeed, the crudeness of these (with their many bickering, capricious gods) makes it unlikely. The Genesis story may have been woven together from more than one source into its present unity.

▶ **Where and when?** From the language used in chapter 7 we are clearly intended to see the flood as a cosmic event, an act of judgment which reverses creation. What follows is a new beginning. But the writer does not share our concept of the global world. His 'whole world' is that of early human history as recounted in Genesis 2ff. (Compare Genesis 41:57; also Acts 2:5.)

We can only guess when the great flood which gave rise to these stories actually happened. The list of nations descended from Noah's sons (Genesis 10) would place it very early indeed – some thousands of years before the South Mesopotamian floods of about 4000 BC, traces of which have been found in the course of excavation. It may be that this story looks back to the end of the Ice Age, around 10,000 BC.

▶ **The covenant (6:18)** is an important, recurring theme. It is a formal agreement between God and his people, established successively with Noah, Abraham, the nation of Israel (through Moses), and King David. At each stage the covenant grows richer in promise, until the coming of Christ ushers in the 'new covenant'. (The word 'testament', as used in the titles Old and New Testament, has the same meaning.)

In every instance God takes the initiative. God draws up the terms and makes them known. And God alone guarantees their keeping. People enjoy the blessings of the covenant in so far as they obey God's commands.

See 'Covenants and Near Eastern treaties'.

▶ **Forty days** The Bible regularly attaches special significance to certain numbers. 'Forty' is used again and again to flag something important, a new development, an act of God, or simply to indicate 'a long time'.

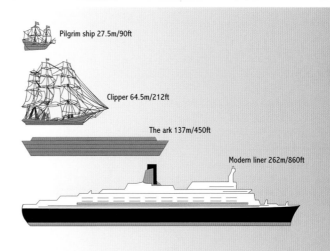

Pilgrim ship 27.5m/90ft

Clipper 64.5m/212ft

The ark 137m/450ft

Modern liner 262m/860ft

10 Noah's descendants

The nations of the Bible world are all traced back to Noah's three sons, Shem, Ham and Japheth. The family tree is arranged in the following pattern:

Heading (1)
Japheth's descendants (2-4)
Extra detail on Javan (5a)
Summary (5b)

Ham's descendants (6-7,13-18a)
Extra detail on Nimrod (8-12)
and Canaan (18b-19)
Summary (20)

Shem's descendants (22-29a)
Extra detail on Shem (21)
and Joktan (29b-30)
Summary (31)

Summary to the whole list (32)

Shem's family comes last: these are the nations around which the next stage of the narrative develops. 'Eber' is the same as the name 'Hebrew'.

11:1-9 The tower of Babel

Here is another ancient story, accounting for the way things are. Why are we divided? Why are there so many different languages? The tale of humanity's downfall does not tell it all. This story attempts an explanation.

In Shinar (= Sumer, ancient Babylonia),

The ark
The Hebrew word for the 'ark' means 'box' or 'chest', so the shape is simple. The measurements make it vast: an 18-inch cubit translates into 133 x 22 x 13m/450 x 75 x 45ft. It was designed to float, not sail – and there were no launching problems! The word is used elsewhere only for the 'ark of Moses', the watertight ' basket' in which the baby floated on the Nile – and was saved.

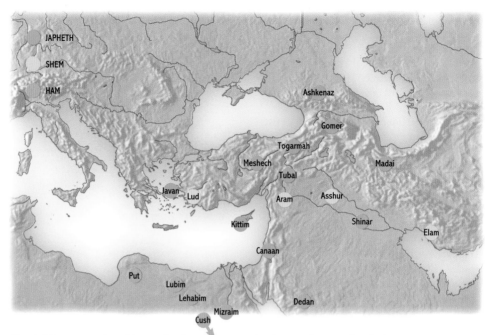

JAPHETH

SHEM

HAM

Ashkenaz

Gomer

Togarmah

Meshech   Madai

Tubal

Javan
Lud   Aram   Asshur

Kittim   Shinar

Elam

Canaan

Put

Lubim

Lehabim   Dedan

Mizraim

Cush

Nations descended from Noah's sons

Genesis 10 presents a view of the peoples of the world ancient Israel knew, stretching from the Sudan to the Caucasus mountains and from the Greek islands to Iran. Many of the names are found in other ancient writings and can be placed on a map, but others are still unknown. Names at first given to individuals then became the names by which all their descendants were known (like Israel). Relationships history records between some of the peoples differ from Genesis, but migrations, conquests and intermarriage may hide true origins.

kingdom of Nimrod the hunter (10:10), people get together on a great building project – a city and a tower with its top in the heavens. God looks down at this co-operative effort, and sees it as the beginning of worse rebellion against him. So he divides people by language (contrast Acts 2, where these barriers begin to be broken), and scatters them abroad – the very thing they were trying to insure against. The great tower remains for ever unfinished.

A reconstruction of the temple-tower (ziggurat) at Ur.

The tower of Babel (Babylon) was in all likelihood a multi-storeyed temple-tower, or ziggurat, similar to those developed in Babylonia in the 3rd millennium BC. There is a play on words between Babel and *balal*, 'confusion' or 'mixing'. An inscription relating to a much later ziggurat at Babylon describes it as 'the building whose top is in heaven'. The temple which crowned it was the place for the god to come down and meet those who served him.

11:10-32 Shem to Abraham

Here again the list of names is selective, probably abbreviating the total length of time involved. Noah's ancestors were considerably longer-lived than Terah's, and the age of parenthood is now much younger.

When Terah's name is reached the list becomes more detailed. This is the family we are to concentrate on. Terah's three sons are named, and their home-town given as Ur of the Chaldeans. After the death of Haran, Terah sets out for Canaan, with his grandson Lot, Abram and Sarai. The journey takes them 900km/560 miles north-west, following the River Euphrates, to Harran – like Ur, a centre of moon-worship. (Joshua 24:2 records that Terah 'served other gods'.) Here they settle. Terah dies, and the stage is set for the story of Abraham, who according to Acts 7:2-4 had heard God's call before they set out. His new name records God's promise to make this man the father of many nations, 17:5.

▶ **Ur** See 'Abraham'.

▶ **Harran** The route from Ur to Canaan via Harran was quite usual for travellers at this time. Harran was an important city at the meeting-place of caravan routes between Mesopotamia and the west. The name means 'crossroads' or 'highway'.

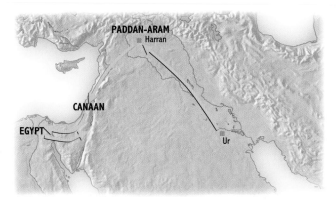

Abraham's
journey
from Ur to
Canaan

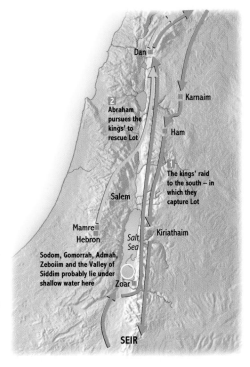

Abraham
and the
battle of the
kings:
Genesis 14

12 – 25:18
Abraham's story

12:1-9 The summons to move
12:1-4 records God's command and promise to one man, Abram, and his obedient response. Yet the consequences of this simple act were to spread like ripples on a pond, leading to the birth of a new nation and in course of time benefits for the whole world.

'So Abram went...' He had already left Ur, a prosperous city with security and a high standard of living. Now he sets out on the second stage of the journey, travelling another 700km/450 miles south-west to Canaan (Palestine), with Sarai, his child-less wife, his nephew Lot and their flocks and herds.

At Shechem, in the midst of Canaanite country, God speaks again in response to Abraham's call. 'This land' is to be the heritage of Abram's descendants. Yet the journey continues, down towards the Negeb, a region stretching south from Beersheba to the Sinai highlands – today semi-desert, but more hospitable in Abraham's time.

Abraham's lifestyle represents the life of

pilgrimage: the altar and the tent bear witness to his faith and his lack of a settled home.

▶ **Nomads** The stories of Abraham, Isaac and Jacob give us a picture of semi-nomadic life in ancient Palestine, of people who spent part of their time moving from pasture to pasture with their flocks and herds, and part of their time as settlers, farming the land. Groups like these could travel freely from one country to another at this time, without great language problems. See 'Nomadic life'.

▶ **'Be blessed'/'bless themselves' (12:3)** Both meanings are possible, but the New

> **66** *Go
> from your
> country and
> your kindred
> and your father's
> house to the land
> I will show you.
> I will make of
> you a great
> nation.* **99**
>
> God speaks to
> Abraham:
> 12:1-2

Testament, following the Greek version of the
Old Testament (the Septuagint) favours 'be
blessed'.

12:10-20 Famine

Hunger drives Abram into Egypt. Under
stress of fear and insecurity, this man of
faith defends himself with a dangerous
half-truth (see 20:12) which puts God's
whole plan at risk. God intervenes with
plagues, Sarai is saved and Abram is
ignominiously deported.

▶ **Sarai's age** It seems surprising to find Sarai,
at 65, described as 'very beautiful' (12:14).
She is, however, said to have lived to 127, so
maybe her 60s equate to our 30s or 40s.

13 Lot's choice

Increasing flocks and herds precipitate the
last break in family ties. Lot, generously
given the choice by his uncle, selects the
fertile pasture of the Jordan Valley.

14 Mysterious Melchizedek

In Abram's day, although a semi-nomadic
existence was common, there was also
settled life in villages and walled 'cities'
(small towns; see 'Settled life'). These were
ruled over by local 'sheiks', who in turn
were often vassals of more powerful kings.

The overlords (verse 1) of the five Dead
Sea towns (verse 2) came from distant
Elam and Babylonia (Shinar), and from
Anatolia (King Tidal). Trade-routes made

Abraham's war
with the tribal
kings was
followed by
the fellowship
meal with
Melchizedek,
king of Salem.
This 'standard'
buried in a royal
tomb at Ur some
centuries before
Abraham's time,
shows scenes of
war on one side,
and here the
victory feast and
parade of booty.
The standard is a
mosaic of shell,
red limestone
and lapis lazuli.

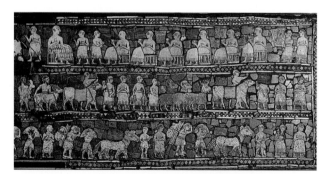

travel and communication between the
land of Abram's birth and Canaan
relatively easy. (The Elamites had considerable power in Babylonia. Ur was one of
the cities they conquered and sacked at
this time.)

▶ **Amorites (7)** Abram's allies belonged to a
tribe sharing the land with the Canaanites. They
had good reason to support Abram, since their
own people had been victims of the attack.
Speed of pursuit and a surprise attack give
Abram victory.

▶ **Melchizedek (18)** This is the only
appearance of the rather mysterious king/priest
of Salem (probably Jerusalem; the name means
'peace' – *shalom*, *salaam*). Melchizedek's
authority (a tenth – the 'tithe' – was God's
portion, so Abram treats this man as God's
representative), his lack of any named ancestors or descendants (extremely important for
any man claiming kingship or priesthood), and
his dual role as priest and king, led later writers
to see in him a foreshadowing of the Messiah
(see Psalm 110:4; Hebrews 7:1-10). 'God Most
High', see 'The names of God'.

15 The covenant confirmed

This time the covenant is not prefaced by a
command. God listens to Abram's doubts
and fears – 'I am childless' (verse 2); 'How
can I be sure...?' (verse 8) – and God's
response is full of reassurance as he repeats
his promises.

▶ **The heir** It was not uncommon practice at the
time for childless couples to adopt an heir,
sometimes, as here, a slave. The adoption
contract might contain a proviso that if a natural
son was born he would take precedence as the
legal heir.

▶ **Verse 6** 'Abram believed (put his faith/trust
in) the Lord, and he credited it to him as
righteousness (was pleased with him and
accepted him).' This is one of the most
significant verses of Scripture, and in the
circumstances a response of remarkable faith.
Paul (in Galatians 3:6ff.) argues from this that
Jews and non-Jews alike are put right with God
through faith, not through keeping God's rules
(since none of us can live perfect lives).
'Abraham believed and was blessed; so all who
believe are blessed as he was' (Good News
Bible).

▶ **The covenant ritual** This is the way treaties
were confirmed at that time (see Jeremiah
34:18). The penalty for breaking the agreement
was death – symbolized by killing and dividing
the animals. Here, significantly, it is only God
who puts himself on oath by passing between
the pieces. Darkness, smoke and fire mark

Hagar
Frances Fuller

Hagar was a slave. When Sarah gave her to Abraham to make a child for them, Hagar had no choice, but being pregnant with Abraham's child gave her an advantage. She had become valuable, able to do what Sarah could not. She became insolent, smugness showing in her looks and actions, but Sarah responded so severely that Hagar fled. Probably she intended to try to walk the long desert road back to Egypt. An angel of the Lord 'found her' at a spring on this road.

The angel called her by name and told Hagar astounding things. She would have descendants too numerous to count – the same promise made to Abraham and Sarah! God was aware of her oppression and promised that her child would be a 'wild ass of a man', hard to tame, hostile, independent, hard to oppress. The angel told her to go back to her mistress, and she obeyed.

The encounter must have been a profound spiritual experience. Hagar said about it, 'Now I have seen the God who sees me.' (The reader who remembers Sarah's discovery that God heard her laugh, though she laughed silently, may wonder what would have happened if Hagar and Sarah had shared with one another their spiritual journeys.)

For 13 more years Hagar served Sarah. When God spoke again, insisting that it was Sarah who would bear the son of the covenant, and Sarah conceived, life became tough again for Hagar. On the day Isaac was weaned, Sarah asked Abraham to send Hagar and her son away, and he did.

They trudged off across the desert, carrying a little food and an animal skin of water.

The water ran out, Hagar despaired and left Ishmael under a bush to die, but God called from heaven to remind her that he was going to make Ishmael into a great nation. They survived, living in the mountainous desert now called the Sinai. God watched over Ishmael as he grew and kept his promises to Hagar.

Their story speaks still of God's concern for powerless people, the outcasts, the poor, the mistreated, those outside the covenant, even those who may be far from faith.

Hagar's story is told in Genesis 16:1-16; 21:9-21; 25:12. See also Galatians 4:21-31.

God's presence, as at Mt Sinai (see Exodus 19:18; Hebrews 12:18).

▶ **Four hundred years (13)... the fourth generation (16)** The word 'generation' may also mean 'lifetime'. Abram is said to have lived for well over a century.

▶ **Verse 16b** Revised English Bible 'for till then the Amorites will not be ripe for punishment'. This helps a little with the order to destroy the Canaanite nations at the time of the conquest. God gave them more than four centuries to show a change of heart. By Joshua's time they had reached the point of no return. As with Sodom and Gomorrah, judgment could no longer be delayed.

16 Compromise
Sarai devises her own way of making God's promise come true. Childless herself, she falls back on custom, giving her slave-girl to Abram. (This provision could be written into the marriage contract: the resulting child becoming the wife's.) But human emotions in such a situation are complex, and the unhappy sequel is not surprising.

▶ **Angel of the Lord (16:7)** See on Judges 2:1.

17 The sign of circumcision
God confirms the covenant once again, giving new names to Abram and Sarai. Most ancient peoples, including the Hebrews, attached great significance to the names of people and places. People's

❝ *'Look towards heaven and count the stars, if you are able to count them... So shall your descendants be...' And Abraham believed the Lord.* ❞

15:5-6

Abraham

Alan Millard

Jews in Jesus' time were proud to claim, 'We have Abraham as our ancestor', a claim echoed by Jews and Muslims today.

Abraham is important as the man to whom God promised the land of Canaan and as the pattern of faith: he believed God and took him at his word. In effect, Abraham was the original holder of the title-deeds to a physical property and to spiritual security.

People of every era want their own identity and often try to find it in their past, through family trees

or national history. Land-owning families kept records of descent in order to prove their titles to their properties. In the same way, ancient Israel traced the title to their land from Abraham, although he had never taken possession of it himself.

Man of faith

Abraham's father moved the family from Ur in Babylonia to Harran in southern Turkey. It was there that God called Abraham and he responded obediently. How

This Sumerian document with its envelope, from Abraham's birthplace, the city of Ur, and the cuneiform multiplication table (*right*) illustrate the literate civilization he left in answer to God's call.

Abraham recognized God is not explained, for his family worshipped 'other gods' (Joshua 24:2), perhaps including the moon-god, patron of both Ur and Harran. In a world which adored many gods

Ur

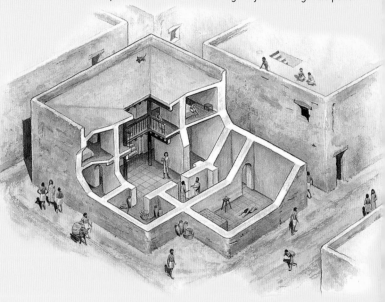

The city of Ur was already very ancient by the time Abram was born. Excavation of the 'Royal Cemetery' dating from about 2500 BC has revealed all kinds of treasures: decorated cups and tools

made of gold and the 'Royal Standard of Ur', inlaid with pictures of peace and war (see page 130).

At its height, around 2100 BC, Ur was a large city whose kings had power

The people of Ur delighted in music and art. This reconstructed harp is one of the treasures recovered from the Royal Graves.

and goddesses, to believe in only one who could meet every need was a commitment which set Abraham apart from his contemporaries. Yet that was clearly his conviction. Although various terms for God occur in relation to Abraham, the usual ones are Jehovah ('the Lord'), and God. Others appear once: God Almighty (El Shaddai, Genesis 17:1; cf. Exodus 6:3), Jehovah, Eternal God (Genesis 21:33), God Most High (Genesis 14:18-22). It is clear they all refer to the same Deity. Abraham could also identify him with 'the Creator of heaven and earth' whom Melchizedek, king of Salem served (Genesis 14:18-22). At various places in Canaan Abraham made sacrifices and prayed without rituals or priestly intermediaries in a simple, personal form of religion.

As soon as he arrived in the centre of Canaan, Abraham received God's promise that the land would belong to his descendants (Genesis 12: 7), a promise repeated in 13:15-17, solemnly in chapter 15 and in 17: 8. On this promise Israel's history was founded. Without expecting to possess the land himself, Abraham needed such reassurance, as he made clear to God (Genesis 15: 2,3). The altars he built and the trees he planted were, perhaps, a token of his aim to stay in the land, but they were primarily signs of his devotion to God. The sites did not become sacred shrines for ever. The only piece of the land he ever owned was the burial-place he bought near Hebron.

To leave his home, the society he knew, and travel to an unknown land at his God's command was an act of faith. His knowledge that he would never own the land extended his faith. The 25-year wait for the birth of his heir was a further test, one which he and Sarah tried to overcome through his connection with Hagar.

The ultimate test

Ultimately Abraham's faith was stretched by the command to sacrifice his heir to God, a command he obeyed, convinced that 'God himself will provide the lamb for the burnt offering' (Genesis 22:8; compare Hebrews 11:17-19). Human sacrifice was rare in the biblical world, so God's request would have carried unusual weight.

According to later tradition, Solomon built the Temple on the site where Isaac was bound. That this is not mentioned may be a sign of the greater age of the Genesis narrative, emphasizing simply that God provides.

When Isaac was ready to be married and father a son to whom the promise of the land might be bequeathed, Abraham, convinced that God would guide him, sent his servant back to Harran to find a bride in the family circle, a story

Beautiful vessels of gold were amongst the treasures found in the Royal Graves at Ur.

extending westward to the Mediterranean coast. During this period the great temple-tower ('ziggurat') was built in honour of Sin, the moon-god worshipped by the people of Ur.

The city was a centre for international trade, and had two busy harbours joined to the River Euphrates by canals. Most of the inhabitants lived in single-storey houses made from bricks of baked mud, although some two-storey houses existed. Many of the homes were quite large, with a number of rooms grouped round a central courtyard (reconstructed *left*).

The power of Ur was broken by invaders from Elam to the east in about 2000 BC, but the remains of the great ziggurat survive to this day.

▶▶

A bedouin sheik near Beersheba illustrates the life of a desert chieftain. Living in spacious tents, they are free to take their flocks to the best grazing-grounds.

ten righteous men could be found in it. Sadly, they could not, and the cities and their evil inhabitants were destroyed.

An historical figure?

From the Bible, we can place Abraham at about 2000 BC. Not surprisingly, no trace of him can be found in records outside the Bible. Abraham's lifestyle and the names of members of his family reflect well the culture of those semi-nomadic herdsmen modern scholars call Amorites (common across the Near East from about 2000 to 1600 BC). Although some episodes in his story (using a slave-girl as a surrogate mother, for example) could have occurred later in Israelite history, the overall picture corresponds best with the Amorite age.

The portrait of God and his relationship with Abraham is vital, challenging readers to measure up to his faith.

▶▶ beautifully told in Genesis 24.

A single family unit would have been easy prey for hostile forces. But Abraham was a wealthy man, with a strong band of men around him. So he could rescue his nephew Lot when raiders carried him off, and at the same time help the local people who had suffered the raid. Abraham's relationship with the Canaanite rulers in this case was positive. On other occasions, however, he created bad situations by passing off Sarah, his wife, as merely his sister (she was a half-sister), to protect his own life (Genesis 12, 20).

In the Sodom and Gomorrah story (Genesis 18 – 19), Abraham appears compassionate towards his fellow-men, even when God had condemned them for their sin. In his famous dialogue with God, he established the principle that God would not destroy the city if even

Abraham's story is told in Genesis, from 11:26 to 25:11. See also John 8:33-59; Romans 4; Hebrews 11:8-19.

KEY EVENTS

God's call **12:1-5**
The Covenant **15**
Prayer for Sodom **18**
Birth of Isaac **21**
'Sacrifice' of Isaac **22**

names often said something about their origins, or expressed a prayer ('May God...'). The change of name here indicates a new beginning. So Abram ('exalted father') is changed to Abraham ('father of many'). And Sarai becomes Sarah.

The physical sign of circumcision gathers not only Abraham but also Ishmael and the whole multi-racial household into the covenant.

Twenty-four years after the departure from Harran the birth of Sarah's son Isaac is announced.

▶ **Circumcision** was no new rite. In the nations around it marked admission to adult status in the tribe. Distinctively for Israel it was the outward sign – from birth – of a special relationship with God; not simply a mark of ownership, but a token of the reality of all God's promises expressed in the repeated 'I shalls' of these verses. Circumcision also signified obedience to God on the part of his people.

18:1-15 The messengers
Abraham welcomed a stranger and, all unknowingly, took the Lord himself into his home. The lavish welcome and provision (despite the inconvenience of the visitors' arrival during the midday siesta) are typical of hospitality amongst nomadic desert people even today. The 'morsel of bread' offered to the guests turns out to be a meal of fresh cakes, curds and milk, and the best veal. The words 'Is anything too hard for the Lord?' reveal the visitor's true identity, and Sarah's incredulous laughter changes to fear.

18:16-33 A plea for Sodom
Abraham's prayer gives an insight into the quality of his relationship with God. No wonder 2 Chronicles 20:7 describes him as God's 'friend'. God must know for himself (verse 21) the truth about Sodom and Gomorrah: hearsay will not do. Abraham leaps to the conclusion that judgment is inevitable, yet he knows it is against God's nature to condemn the innocent. He feels his way forward, not changing God's mind, but growing ever more certain that 'the judge of all the earth' will 'do what is just'. In the event, though Sodom could not produce even ten 'innocent' people, God

saved four – Lot, his wife and two daughters.

19 Destruction and rescue
'Where are the men who came to you tonight? Bring them out to us so that we can have sex with them' (verse 5). Every man in the city is implicated in this terrible intended gang-rape – not one supports Lot's protest against the infringement of the most sacred laws of hospitality, not to say humanity. God had clear evidence that the outcry against Sodom was justified (18:20-21).

▶ **What happened?** The catastrophe was probably an earthquake and explosion of gases in this volatile section of the Great Rift Valley. God's judgment takes the form of a 'natural' disaster, yet for Lot's sake God spares Zoar. 'I won't destroy that town. Hurry! Run! I can't do anything until you get there' (19:22). Even so, Lot's wife drags behind, stopping to look, and dies – becoming a 'pillar of salt' not by magic but by being engulfed in the suffocating rain of debris.

▶ **Moab and Ammon (37-38)** Close kin to Israel, these two tribes occupying land to the east of the Jordan and Dead Sea worshipped other gods (see Numbers 25) and were frequently denounced by the prophets. Despite their sordid beginnings, alienation was not inevitable, as the story of Ruth makes gloriously clear.

20 Shamed by a pagan king
Many take this story as a duplicate of 12:10-20, though Abraham would not be the first to repeat a sin in testing circumstances. Nor is he the only person to have been put to shame twice before those with 'no fear of God' to guide their actions. Abimelech (see 26:1) comes out of this more honourably than the man of faith. Once again we are held in suspense. Will God allow Abraham's folly to wreck his plan at the eleventh hour?

▶ **Gerar** An ancient city near the coast, to the south of Gaza.

21:1-21 Isaac and Ishmael
Twenty-five years have passed since the promise was first made. Isaac's elderly parents are naturally overjoyed at his

Where were Sodom and Gomorrah?

Alan Millard

The Dead Sea is so far below sea level that it has no outlet; the water evaporates, leaving a high concentration of salts which kill all life.

It is commonly believed that Sodom and Gomorrah were submerged after the cataclysm that destroyed them and now lie under the southern end of the Dead Sea, where there are strange salt formations. Bitumen, too is found there, which fits with the 'bitumen (slime) pits' mentioned in Genesis 14:10. But no ruins have been recovered to identify them, so the location is not proven. The cities could in fact have stood anywhere in the Dead Sea Valley.

Geologists have suggested that one of the earthquakes common in this volatile region 'could have caused an inferno and liquefaction of the bitumen on a scale big enough to have swallowed both Sodom and Gomorrah'.

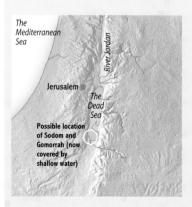

The Mediterranean Sea

River Jordan

Jerusalem

The Dead Sea

Possible location of Sodom and Gomorrah (now covered by shallow water)

birth. Sarah's demand that Hagar and Ishmael be sent away runs counter to custom, and Abraham needs a word from God before he will agree. Galatians 4:22ff. shows why the rift was inevitable. God's care for Ishmael, although he was not the child of the promise, once more shines through. Outcast by Sarah and Abraham, he is not cast out by God. On the contrary, 'God was with the child as he grew up' (20). (See also 25:9, 12-18; 28:9; 36:3, 10, and Paul's allegory in Galatians 4.)

▶ **Verses 6 and 9** 'Isaac' is the Hebrew word for laughter (see 17:17 and 18:12-15). The word comes again in verse 9: 'playing with'/'teasing'.

▶ **The child (14)** Ishmael must by now be 14 or more.

21:22-34 A dispute over wells

Water has always been precious to the herdsmen in the dry climate of southern Palestine. Monthly rainfall in this area drops from 100mm/4 ins in January to nothing at all in the four summer months. So Abraham's dispute over the well at Beersheba is not surprising (see Isaac's troubles, and the renewal of the pact, 26:17-33). 'Abimelech' may be a Philistine title for 'king' (like the Egyptian 'Pharaoh'), rather than a personal name.

▶ **Philistines** Abimelech and the people of Gerar may have been early Philistine settlers. By the time the Israelites left Egypt, the whole southern coastal area was in Philistine hands. And from the time of the Judges there was trouble between the two peoples.

22 A shocking test of faith

There is surely nothing in Abraham's previous experience of God to make him think that God would want child-sacrifice. For him, as for every reader from then to now, the devastating words with which the story begins come as a most dreadful shock: 'Take your son, your only son, whom you love so much'. What kind of God is this God we thought we knew? The instruction is more puzzling still, since all God's promises are vested in Isaac. How could God require his death?

The end of the story enables us to breathe again. God does *not* want child-sacrifice. God provides, and the two return together (verse 5). The issue is clearly presented as one of trust (see Hebrews 11:17-19). Is Abraham *willing* to offer up the one who is more precious to him than all the world? Will he trust God with Isaac? He has previously failed to trust God for his own safety: twice we have seen him selfishly put Sarah's life at risk. But now he trusts where he cannot understand. And in the offering of his only son, he mirrors the far more costly self-offering of God in Jesus.

And what of Isaac? Did he struggle or argue? In the telling, his role is passive, not active: an acceptance of suffering – like that of the servant of the Lord in Isaiah 53; like Jesus who went willingly to death.

▶ **'God tested Abraham' (1)** The older 'tempt' has this same meaning of proving or trying. Elsewhere in the Bible it is Satan who tests, or human beings who (wrongly) put God to the test. 'Do not put us to the test,' Jesus taught his followers to ask God in the Lord's Prayer. But the words of verse 1 are clear: this is how the

God's testing of Abraham ended with the provision of a ram for sacrifice. This portrayal of a ram's head, dates from about the time of Abraham.

There has been conflict over water rights in Palestine from Abraham's time to the present day. Here flocks are watered at a well in the hills of Judea.

Sarah
Frances Fuller

In Mesopotamia she was Sarai, half-sister of Abram and also his wife. God sent Abram looking for a land which God would give him, so Sarai became a nomad with him, moving frequently, living in tents, always an alien in strange cultures.

She was beautiful, so beautiful that her husband felt insecure.

Sarah shared her husband's life as a wandering nomad, living in tents like these women.

Someone might kill him to get her. So he told her, 'This is how you can show your love to me: everywhere we go, say of me, He is my brother.' This protected Abram but left Sarai vulnerable in a world in which a woman had no power over her destiny. Twice she was taken into the harem of a ruler, first by the Pharaoh of Egypt and then by King Abimelech of Gerar. The scripture does not mention how Sarai felt: betrayed? used? violated? Both times God intervened on her behalf, sending plagues on the Pharaoh and bad dreams to Abimelech, so that they asked Abram to come and take her away.

Sarai was barren. God had promised Abram descendants numerous as the stars, and month after month Sarai was disappointed and told Abram, 'Not yet.' Finally, Sarah took matters into her own hands. According to the custom, the child of Abram and Sarai's maidservant would be Sarai's child and a recognized heir. So Sarai gave Hagar to Abram, only to discover that the pregnant Hagar despised her, and she was herself angry at Abram. So she mistreated Hagar, and when Hagar gave them a son, Ishmael, Sarai was neither fulfilled nor happy.

Apparently, neither was God. When God spoke again, giving Abram the new name Abraham, he also changed her name to Sarah, meaning 'princess', and he promised to give her a son and make her the mother of nations and kings. Abraham fell on his face and laughed at the thought of Sarah bearing a child at the age of 90. Then two messengers came to tell him that in a year's time Sarah would give birth. Listening at the door of her tent, Sarah laughed from disbelief. Could a woman conceive long after menopause? Could a camel fly?

When at last Sarah held her baby in her arms, she believed that God could do anything and laughed for joy and triumph and amusement. 'God has brought me laughter,' she said and imagined that everyone who heard her story would laugh with her. They named the boy 'Laughter', as God, knowing all of Sarah's reasons for laughing, had instructed.

Afterwards, there was jealousy between Sarah and Hagar over their sons, and Sarah asked Abraham to send Hagar and Ishmael away. Sarah lived to be 127 and died in Hebron. Abraham wept for her and bought the cave of Machpelah for her burial place. For three years Isaac could not be comforted.

A document among the Dead Sea Scrolls, centuries later, focusses in detail on her physical beauty. But Jesus' disciple Peter, remembering Sarah's faithfulness to Abraham, ignoring her faults, wrote that she modelled the inner beauty of godly women.

Sarah's story is told in Genesis, chapters 12 – 23. See also 1 Peter 3:3-6; Hebrews 11:11.

writer saw it; this is, presumably, how it appeared to Abraham himself. (1 Corinthians 10:13 offers a further comment on testing, and God's provision.)

▶ **The land of Moriah (2)** Abraham's offering took place on one of the hills on which Jerusalem now stands (possibly the Temple hill itself – see 2 Chronicles 3:1). The journey of about 80km/ 50 miles took the little group three days.

▶ **Nahor's family (20ff.)** This quick catch-up on the other branch of Abraham's family introduces Rebecca, who will be the focus of attention in chapter 24.

23 A grave for Sarah

Abraham, as a resident alien, has no rights to land. He 'has not received the things promised' (Hebrews 11:13), and must bargain even for a place to bury his wife. This chapter and chapter 21 record the first *legal rights* of Abraham's family in Canaan.

The Hittites occupying the Hebron area may have been early settlers drawn south by trade from the Hittite Empire in Turkey (founded about 1800 BC). The deal is vividly described, conforming in detail to Hittite law (the mention of the trees, the weighing of the silver by current standards, and the proclamation in the presence of witnesses at the city gate).

Family tombs, often caves or cut from rock, were also customary. The traditional site of the burial-cave at Hebron is today covered by a mosque, for Islam holds Abraham in high regard.

24 Rebecca

Abraham is an old man. Isaac is unmarried. The fulfilment of the promise depends on a wife, and children, for Isaac: a wife essentially of God's choosing, from within the family of God's people. The story that follows is one of the loveliest in the Old Testament. It reflects the traditional Eastern arranged marriage. (Isaac is once again cast in a passive role.) The characters of the faithful steward and of Rebecca herself shine through the narrative. The steward's gifts in verse 53 seal the betrothal. It is a fitting conclusion that God, who has so clearly guided at every stage, should set his seal on the marriage

Rebecca was given silver and gold ornaments: a traditional silver necklace and headress are worn here by a Yemenite Jewish girl in present-day Israel.

in the deep love of Isaac for this remarkable young woman.

25:1-11 Abraham's last days

Keturah's sons are the ancestors of a number of north Arabian peoples. All were provided for by Abraham. But Isaac remained his father's sole heir, and on Abraham's death both possessions and promises become his: God 'blessed' Isaac.

▶ **Verse 11** Beer-lahai-roi, in the Negeb, is Hagar's well (16:14).

25:12-18 Ishmael's descendants

The tribes occupied Sinai and north-west Arabia – 'Havilah to Shur' (verse 18).

Important agreements could be put into writing from early times. Abraham's deal with the Hittites of Hebron could have been recorded in cuneiform on a clay tablet like this one.

Hebron, site of the traditional burial-place of the patriarchs, is high in the hills of Judea. The building over the burial-cave goes back to the time of Herod, with additions in Byzantine and Crusader times.

25:19 – 26:35
The story of Isaac

Once again the line is continued by the direct action of God. After 20 years' waiting, Esau and Jacob are born. Never were twins less alike in character.

The story in chapter 26 parallels incidents in Abraham's life, yet is distinct and different from the earlier accounts. Famine uproots Isaac from the Negeb, but he goes north to Gerar, not south to Egypt. He adopts the same ruse over Rebecca that his father had done (more truthfully) with Sarah: but Rebecca is not taken from him. Like most of us, Isaac vacillates between faith and fear, needing God's repeated reassurance: 'I am with you... do not be afraid. I shall bless you.'

Abimelech offers peace with honour, but there is bitter grief at home. In marrying Judith, the Hittite, Esau makes another wrong choice.

▶ **The birthright (25:31)** As firstborn son, Esau will succeed Isaac as head of the family and inherit a double share of the estate. When he sells his birthright he forfeits all title to the inheritance and to the blessing that goes with it. (In the Old Testament the father's spoken blessing conveys material prosperity on his son – the words have power. The New Testament adds a spiritual dimension to the concept of blessing.)

Jacob's cool calculation is described without comment – but Hebrews 12:16-17 censures Esau's attitude: he was 'worldly minded'; 'he sold his birthright for a single meal'; 'thus Esau showed how little he valued his birthright'.

▶ **Abimelech/Philistines (26:1)** See on 21:22-34.

27 – 35
Jacob's story

27 Jacob and Esau

No one comes out of this story well. Isaac's plan goes against what God revealed before the boys were born (25:23). Esau, in agreeing to the plan, is breaking his oath (25:33): the blessing goes with the birthright. Jacob and Rebecca, although in the right, make no reference to God, but cheat and lie to achieve their ends.

Isaac relies completely on his senses, each of which lets him down – even the sense of taste on which he prided himself. When his ears tell him the truth, he will not listen. The blessing is Jacob's, as God always intended – but at a heavy price. Esau is ready to do murder. The relationship between Isaac and Rebecca is spoilt. And Rebecca will never again see her favourite son. Jacob, the home-lover, goes into exile.

28 The dream

Isaac's parting blessing, this time genuinely given, recognizes Jacob at last as the true heir to God's promise. Jacob leaves, and at Bethel ('house of God'; 100km/60 miles north of Beersheba), as darkness falls, in a moment of unutterable loneliness, God stands beside him. God repeats to this unpromising man the promise made to Abraham and Isaac, adding a personal guarantee: 'I shall be with you to protect you... and I shall bring you back.' Scarcely daring to believe, Jacob responds with a promise of his own.

▶ **Verse 2** Paddan-aram ('plain of Aram') is the same region as Aram-naharaim, 'Aram of the rivers', the Greek Mesopotamia (modern east Syria – northern Iraq). Rebecca's homeland lay between the upper Euphrates and Habur rivers. We meet the Aramaeans later

settled further south, in Syria, and away to the east.

▶ **The dream (12ff.)** Much was made of dreams in ancient Egypt (see on Genesis 40 – 41) and in Babylon. There are significant dreams in the Old Testament, too – like this one. But there is no need for a special interpreter: God speaks clearly. The meaning comes with the dream.

The 'ladder' of some translations is a stairway (were tales of the great ziggurat of Ur passed down to Jacob?), with angels going up and down it (see too John 1:51).

The 'pillar' – not very large – consecrated by the oil is set up to commemorate the vision. Single stones and cairns are often used in this way (see 31:51f.)

29 – 31 Jacob meets his match

These three chapters cover the 20 years of Jacob's exile: 14 years' service for his two wives, six for flocks of his own. The years hold little joy for Jacob, who meets a crooked dealer after his own kind in his uncle Laban. The deceit over Leah leads to an intolerable home life. The unloved wife hopes with each new son to win her husband's affection. Rachel, lovely and loved, is embittered by continuing childlessness. And Jacob finds himself traded between the two. (The law would later rule out taking 'a woman who is your wife's sister to make her a rival wife': Leviticus 18:18.)

▶ **29:18** Jacob offers service in place of the usual marriage gift. Laban is not slow to exploit the generosity of the offer. The gift of a slave-girl to his daughter (verse 24) may have been part of the dowry.

▶ **29:28** After the week's festivities Rachel was given to Jacob, on condition he served another seven years for her.

▶ **29:31** Although Jacob may have despised Leah, God did not. She became the mother of Levi (the family line of the priests), and of Judah (the royal line).

▶ **30:3** This reflects the same custom as Sarah observed (16:1-2).

Abraham's servant had a train of ten camels when he set out to find a wife for Isaac, and Rebecca rode a camel on the return journey. By the time of Solomon, camels had become a major means of transport in peace and war.

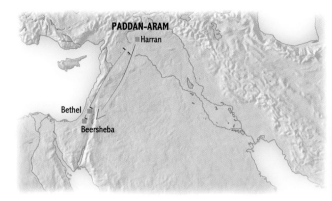

PADDAN-ARAM
Harran

Bethel

Beersheba

Jacob's journey and return

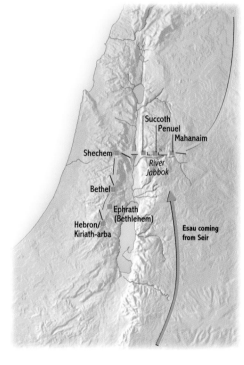

Succoth
Penuel
Mahanaim

Shechem

River Jabbok

Bethel

Ephrath
(Bethlehem)

Hebron/
Kiriath-arba

Esau coming from Seir

Standing stones or cairns were often set up as 'markers' of important events like the treaty between Jacob and Laban (31:45). This stone stands in the ruins of ancient Shechem.

▶ **30:14** Mandrakes were thought to induce fertility – which makes Leah's subsequent pregnancy ironic.

▶ **30:21** The story of Dinah's tragic rape is told in chapter 34.

▶ **30:37ff.** Jacob thought the sight of the rods during gestation would affect the unborn lambs. In fact he owed his flocks to the overruling of God, and to the practice of selective breeding which the dream revealed.

▶ **31:14** Leah and Rachel were entitled to part of the wealth their marriage-gifts brought Laban.

▶ **31:19** Rachel acts, as she thinks, in Jacob's interest. The possession of household gods

could help his claim to the inheritance.

▶ **31:44** The non-aggression pact made by Laban and Jacob has many contemporary parallels. The covenant meal seals it.

32 Jacob wrestles with God

Although Esau has settled in Seir in the far south, the meeting between the two brothers is inevitable. The news that Esau is coming at speed, and with a force, strikes terror into Jacob. This time, though, he plans *and* prays.

Alone, and sleepless, Jacob's lifetime struggle against God culminates in this strange wrestling-bout. He is neither the first nor the last, in some crisis, first to fight God, then to hold to God with new faith. Jacob emerges from the encounter crippled, but a new man. The next altar he erects will not be to the God of his fathers, but to 'God, the God of Israel' (*El Elohe Israel*, 33:20).

33 The brothers meet again

Esau's welcome to the brother who had wronged him is amazingly generous. Jacob's gift, and Esau's acceptance of it, seal the reconciliation.

▶ **Verse 14** Jacob has no intention of going to Seir, as the next stage of the journey shows. Even now he cannot be straightforward about it.

Women of faith
Claire Powell

For centuries the interpretation of Genesis has been connected with the lives of the great men of faith, the fathers or patriarchs of Jewish history. But in more recent times there has been a rediscovery of the stories of the women of faith and their centrality in God's unfolding history of salvation. There are more stories about the men, but in past interpretations, the women were often marginalized or ignored, even when they were there in the biblical text. So the ancient cultural prejudice towards women was continued.

Today women's experiences and opportunities seem to be very different from the world of Genesis. Of course, the Bible itself comes to us in and through culture and history, so there is a constant need to evaluate whether the patriarchal stories are describing the culture then, or prescribing what should be our culture now; whether the Old Testament is recounting attitudes to the roles of women then, or actively advocating them for all time.

Time and again there are hints in the patriarchal stories that God had a higher view of women than the way they were treated by people. For example, in Genesis 16:5, Sarah and Abraham maltreat Hagar. She is only a slave-girl to them, whereas the angel of the Lord calls her by name! Recent biblical studies have tended to notice such things and to discover, within the texts themselves, a higher status for women. Women's experiences as well as men's are seen to function as models of faith for all believers.

God's covenant
The account of God's covenant (Genesis 15 – 17) was pivotal to the promise of salvation, both to Abraham's descendants and, in terms of world mission, to all the nations.

But the covenant was not merely with Abraham. It was also with Sarah, who was blessed by God, given a new name just as Abraham was, and without whom Abraham could not have had Isaac, the son of promise (Isaiah 51:2). The sign of that covenant was (male) circumcision.

> **❝** *Women's experiences as well as men's are seen to function as models of faith...* **❞**

Nevertheless, although women were not circumcised, there is no hint that they were to be inferior members of the covenant because of this. And the New Testament recognizes faith, not circumcision, as having always been the biblical basis of acceptance with God. The new rite of baptism includes both men and women in the Christian church.

Childlessness
In the Old Testament a large family was seen as a great blessing from God. But in the patriarchal stories of Sarah, Rebecca and Rachel there is a pattern of the disappointment of childlessness (Genesis 16:1–2; 25:21; 30:1, 2).

In many cultures the women are wrongly blamed for this, and the three matriarchs would have felt the stigma keenly. In the case of Sarah and Rachel it is the wives who cannot conceive, although the case of Rebecca and Isaac is more ambiguous. However, the text makes it clear that it is God who gives or withholds the gift of children, even if the husband or wife is technically unable to have them.

Marginalization
Genesis 46:7, 27 says that Jacob took with him to Egypt his sons and grandsons, daughters and granddaughters, yet the final count of 'seventy in all' (the number is probably not literal, but means the idea of totality) specifically names the men, but possibly only two women, Dinah and Serah. The actual number of Jacob's family would have been much greater than 70 if all the women had been named, but in ancient Near Eastern culture often the women literally did not count. This may tell us about the silent and marginalized place of women in the culture of biblical times, but does not suggest this is the way they should be treated.

Jacob
David Barton

Jacob is the son of Isaac and Rebecca, the grandchild of Abraham. But where Abraham is the faithful servant of God, ready to respond whatever the personal cost, Jacob is a different character.

The story of his birth is typical of the later man. Second of a pair of twins who had evidently struggled much during the pregnancy, Jacob emerged from the womb with a firm hold on the heel of his first-born brother Esau.

Con-man
Astute and always concerned to advance his position, Jacob appears from the start to be the typical con-man. At an early stage he succeeds in extracting from a hungry and exhausted Esau the surrender of his birthright in exchange for a bowl of food.

Where Esau was a man of action and a hunter, Jacob was quiet and thoughtful, preferring the homelife of the family encampment. Father Isaac favoured his firstborn, but Jacob

Jacob became rich by careful management of his father-in-law's flocks.

was the favourite of his capable, manipulative mother Rebecca. It was her watchfulness that gave Jacob his advantage.

Isaac, blind and old, and sensing the approach of death, asks Esau to find him his favourite meal, as a prelude to the blessing that will confer on him the family inheritance. Rebecca overhears and suggests the trick of covering Jacob's smooth hands and neck with goat's hair to imitate the rough-skinned Esau, at the same time overcoming Jacob's fear of a punishing curse. It is a crucial moment. A blessing once given cannot be taken back, no matter how much Esau might complain. So, Jacob comes to stand in the line of Abraham and Isaac and God's promise to establish a great nation (all of which is implicit in God's words to Rebecca at the boys' birth).

Fresh fields to conquer
Jacob shrewdly judges it prudent to move as far as possible from his outraged brother, and travels to see his mother's brother in Harran. Laban is quite different from the

gentle Isaac and luckless Esau; in him Jacob finds his match. Falling in love with Laban's youngest daughter, Jacob is required to work seven years to win her hand. But, at the last moment, the wily Laban substitutes his oldest daughter Leah instead, and only then offers Rachel in marriage.

In all, Jacob works 14 years for Laban. But they are not wasted. He grows in substance and know-ledge, becoming a match for Laban himself. The story of the sheep and the goats (30:25-43) suggests that Jacob understands animal breeding in a way that his uncle does not. And he uses this knowledge to his considerable advantage. During this time too his family grows. The constant discord between his two wives, and his own favouritism of Rachel, however, sow the seeds of a family feud which will later prove highly dangerous to Joseph.

Nevertheless, having so many children, and his success in shepherding, ensures that Jacob is now someone to be reckoned with. Not surprisingly Laban cools in his regard for his nephew and former dependant. So, taking advantage of

Laban's temporary absence, Jacob returns to the land of his ancestors. Laban is furious, but it is a mark of Jacob's new status as an independent man of some wealth, that the outcome of their dispute is a pact to respect one another's territory.

Turning-point

At this point in the story another side of Jacob, his responsiveness to God, begins to emerge. Earlier, fleeing from his brother's anger, Jacob had an extraordinary dream of a ladder reaching to heaven (28:10-22), a vision later taken up by Jesus (John 1:51). He marked the spot and named it, for this was a meeting-place between God and humankind. But, though a sense of destiny may have shaped his dealings in Harran, the moral implications of the vision seem to have touched him very little. Now, travelling back to his home territory to face the possible wrath of his brother, Jacob is literally stopped in his tracks by the mystery of God.

He has made arrangements to impress Esau with the extent of his wealth, and buy peace with him if need be. On the evening before the meeting is to take place Jacob fords the Jabbok, and there he encounters a stranger. This night-long struggle marks the turning-point in the story of Jacob. It is certainly the old, wily Jacob who, sensing an advantage from one so strong, first demands not the man's name, as we might expect, but his blessing before he will let him go. But when the mysterious stranger has given the blessing (withholding his name), Jacob limps as he walks up from the water into the rising sunshine. The encounter has wounded him. He is frail as we have never seen him before. But at the same time he is greater than he

A turning-point in Jacob's life was the night he wrestled with a mysterious stranger, at the ford across the River Jabbok, pictured here.

was before, for now he has a new name, Israel, because he has 'struggled with God and with men' and prevailed. For once Jacob is awed, 'I have seen God face to face and have survived.'

Home again

The encounter with Esau goes well: he too has prospered. The two embrace, though from respect rather than affection, and eventually part to go different ways. Jacob purchases land at Shechem and there erects an altar to El, the God of Israel. Later he moves to Bethel, the place of his original, long-neglected dream. And there his status as patriarch is completed with a further appearance by God. The promises to Abraham and Isaac are now firmly established on him.

At this point the story of Jacob shades into that of his children: above all into that of his highly successful favourite son Joseph, child in their old age of his beloved Rachel. But God appears to him once more, this time as he prepares to move into Egypt to the home prepared for him by Joseph (46:3-4). Still the promise holds, from Jacob to the following generations.

God at work

That is perhaps the underlying thread of this narrative: the purpose of God is at work, not just

through the extraordinary faithfulness of Abraham, but through the devious areas of self-interest and personal ambition. Jacob has his good side. He genuinely loved Rachel, and his grief at Joseph's supposed death is profound. But most of his life was lived for the main chance, and he was ready to trample on others to get his way. Yet, the story implies, God takes us as we are. Even a scheming rogue like Jacob has his place in establishing God's will, and can in the end be changed by an encounter with the divine mystery.

The story of Jacob begins at Genesis 25, with Jacob as the central character to the end of 35. Genesis 50 records his death.

KEY EVENTS

The promise **25:22, 23**
The birthright **25:29-34**
The blessing **27**
The dream **28:12-22**
Marriage **29, 30**
Encounter with God **32:22-32**

34 Rape and revenge

Dinah is raped by Shechem, leading to the worse crime of murder by Dinah's brothers. The story shows Dinah as silent and powerless, where a modern, Western account might well focus on the victim and her feelings. But the issue that concerns the writer/editor here is one of tribal and national survival. The terrible vengeance exacted by Dinah's brothers for the insult to their sister shows the need for the law to limit revenge ('an eye for an eye' – *and no more*).

Did Hamor's people accept the terms out of greed (verse 23)? Or did they suspect nothing because the rite of circumcision was linked to marriageable status?

Chapter 49:5-7 goes some way to make up for the absence of moral comment here on Simeon and Levi. Their behaviour was wrong, and this was not forgotten.

▶ **Verse 30** If Jacob wanted appeasement, why did he do nothing (verse 5)? Once again the writer tells the story 'warts and all', with no attempt to whitewash the characters of the nation's forebears. They are sinners all.

35 Return to Bethel

As Jacob returns to the place of God's promise, the story comes full circle. This chapter is a rounding off, before Joseph's story begins. Foreign gods are put aside. God reaffirms his covenant. Rachel dies near Bethlehem (Ephrath), giving birth to Benjamin, the last of Jacob's 12 sons. The curtains close on the two brothers, Esau and Jacob, laying their aged father Isaac to rest in the family burial-place (see chapter 23).

36
Esau's family line

Once again, before starting a new chapter in the story, we catch up on the other branch of the family. Esau/Edom the Red (from the red broth for which he gave up his birthright) gave his name to the land of Seir which he took over from the Horites (20ff.)

▶ **Edom (8)** Esau's territory lies east of the Dead Sea, the valley of the Arabah extending south to the Gulf of Aqaba and the mountainous land on both sides. The king's highway, an important trade route, ran down the eastern plateau. In later days there was enmity between Edom and Israel.

▶ **Eliphaz and Teman (11)** Compare Job 4:1. Is Edom the setting for the story of Job?

▶ **Verse 31** This section seems to have been written at the time of Israel's kings.

37 – 50
Joseph's story

37 From favourite to slave

The final section of Genesis, centring on Joseph, now begins. This is the last of the family stories. Exodus to Deuteronomy will tell the story of a nation.

▶ **The special robe (3)** Whether this is long-sleeved (and so for leisure not work) or multi-coloured (like the Egyptian paintings of Asiatic dress), Joseph's brothers saw it as a sign that Jacob intended to make Joseph his heir (see 48:21-22 and 49:22ff.).

▶ **Shechem (12)** Was Jacob specially concerned for his sons' welfare, at the place of Dinah's rape and what followed (chapter 34)?

▶ **Verse 21** Reuben, the eldest – with most to lose if his father favoured Joseph – dissents from the violence, taking responsibility for his young brother.

▶ **Verse 24** The 'pit' of some versions is a dry well or cistern.

▶ **Ishmaelite/Midianite merchants (25, 28)** Both these groups of desert-dwellers were descended from Abraham. Some take the use of the two names to indicate different sources used by the editor. But the use of alternative names is a characteristic feature of Near Eastern writing, and the names here are interchangeable (compare verses 28 and 36; Judges 8:24).

The 'balm' of Gilead (an area roughly east of the Jordan and north of the Jabbok) was famous, and the spice-trade an important one from earliest times. Spices had many uses – in food preparation and the manufacture of incense and cosmetics. The trade-route from Damascus to the coast ran past Dothan.

▶ **Verse 26** Judah, from whose line come Israel's kings, scores a black mark here and in the next chapter. Yet in chapters 43 and 44 he

Beersheba, an oasis on the edge of the Negev 'wilderness', is often mentioned in the Genesis stories. Here vegetables are sold in Beersheba's Bedouin market.

shows up in a much better light. And in 49:8ff. Judah wins his father's blessing.

▶ **Verse 28** New English Bible and Revised English Bible take 'they' (from the Hebrew) to mean Midianites. But verse 27 and 45:4 make it far more likely that other versions are right: Joseph was sold by his brothers.

38 Judah's line

This extraordinary story is probably included because it forms part of the family tree of the (later) royal house, from which the Messiah himself was descended (Matthew 1:3; Luke 3:33 – and compare the story of Ruth). In placing it here, the editor points the contrast with Joseph's behaviour in chapter 39.

If a man died childless, his brother was duty bound to raise heirs to him by his

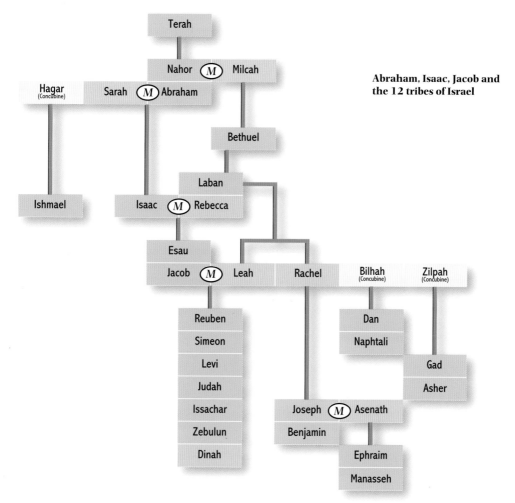

Abraham, Isaac, Jacob and the 12 tribes of Israel

widow (the Levirate law, Deuteronomy 25:5, from *Levir*=brother-in-law). Onan's action (and punishment) has nothing at all to do with contraception or masturbation: it has everything to do with rightful inheritance.

▶ **Verse 9** 'When' should be 'whenever'.

▶ **Verse 14** Tamar's veil disguises her as a (married) temple-prostitute. Festive times were linked with fertility rites in Canaanite religion – and by his marriage Judah was mixed up with all this.

▶ **Perez (29)** It was his line that led to David and so to Christ.

39 Joseph: success and disgrace

The account of Joseph's life in Egypt given in chapters 39 – 50 fits perfectly into the background of Egypt under the Semitic Hyksos pharaohs. They ruled from about 1710 to 1570 BC, from a capital (Avaris) in the eastern part of the Nile delta. Goshen was also somewhere in this region.

This story of seduction, refusal and false accusation, has been compared with the Egyptian *Tale of Two Brothers*, which begins in a similar way. But the magic and miracle that follow there are markedly different from the Joseph story and there is no real reason to connect the two. The key thing here is that Joseph keeps faith with God and, more important still, God keeps faith with Joseph, in success and in disgrace.

40 The prisoners' dreams

Great significance was given to dreams in Egypt at this time. Professional interpreters had manuals that listed dreams and their meanings. But Pharaoh's wine steward (the 'butler' of some versions) and his baker had no one to turn to. 'Interpretation belongs to God,' says Joseph – and God makes the meaning clear.

▶ **Verse 17** The Egyptian language had terms for 38 kinds of cakes and 57 kinds of bread.

41 From prison to palace

Two years later Pharaoh himself has a dream which defeats his magicians and wise men, despite all their training and a whole library of reference books. When the wine steward at last remembers him, Joseph not only proves able to explain

God's message, but comes up with a clear-cut plan of action.

'Not I, but God...' says Joseph. And Pharaoh sees this man 'as endowed with the spirit of God'.

▶ **Verse 14** Egyptian custom dictates that Joseph must be shaven and dressed in linen for an appearance at court.

▶ **Verses 40-43** Joseph's investiture follows Egyptian tradition – the ring (his badge of authority), fine linen (court dress) and a gold chain or collar in reward for his services. Horses and chariots had helped the Hyksos pharaohs to gain ascendancy in Egypt. After 13 years as a slave, Joseph becomes governor of all Egypt, second only to Pharaoh.

▶ **Verse 45** On = Heliopolis, ten miles north-east of Cairo, the centre of Egyptian sun-worship.

▶ **Verse 46** Joseph was 17 when the story began (37:2), and nine more years will pass before the family is brought together.

▶ **Verses 51, 52** 'Manasseh' and 'Ephraim' are Hebrew names.

▶ **Verse 54** Severe famine was not unknown in Egypt. But it was rare for famine to hit Egypt and Palestine simultaneously.

42 – 45 Famine leads to reunion

These chapters give a moving account of Joseph's meeting, testing and eventual reunion with his brothers. Behind his apparent harshness lies complete and generous forgiveness of the wrong done him, and a real understanding of the way God controls human destiny (45:5ff.). Joseph is clearly a man of deep feeling, moved to tears of sorrow and joy.

Under each new stress the brothers show a genuine change of attitude from the old days. Twenty years have not obliterated their sense of guilt (42:21-22). They will not behave towards the new favourite (Benjamin) as they did towards the old.

▶ **42:37/43:3** Judah succeeds where Reuben had failed. He now takes the lead.

▶ **43:32** The Egyptians probably considered that the presence of foreigners at the table defiled their food. For the same reason, later, Jews would not eat with non-Jews.

▶ **44:2,5** Joseph may have used his silver cup for divination (interpreting events by the

Joseph
David Barton

Joseph is the son of Jacob and Rachel, Jacob's first love, after long years of childlessness and the birth of ten step-brothers.

At Joseph's birth Rachel longed for another son. She got her wish, but the birth of Benjamin cost Rachel her life. This left Joseph deeply bound to Benjamin and specially loved by his father. As a mark of this favour, Jacob gives Joseph a fine woven coat.

The dreamer
Joseph is a dreamer, and the two dreams about his own significance, recorded in Genesis 37:5-11, hold the key to his whole life. At 17, the child of a remote shepherd, he has an inner sense of his own powerful

destiny. His father ponders this. But for his brothers it only breeds hatred for someone so different from themselves.

In the circumstances, it was therefore naïve, or wilfully blind, of Jacob to send Joseph to see his brothers as they pastured the flocks in the remote hills. Rabbinic comment suggests that the man Joseph meets on his way (37:15) is an angel, guarding over the young man. At all events, the sight of Joseph alone in the distance gives the brothers the opportunity to plan their revenge.

The slave
Their first thought was to kill him, but Reuben (the eldest) prevents that, and in the end Joseph is stripped of his coat, thrown down a well, and then sold into slavery to a passing merchant caravan. His distress is not mentioned until later (42:21). But we can guess at the emotions of someone with such a strong sense of his own future, who is thrown down a dark well and apparently left to die.

Meanwhile Jacob is told that his son is dead, and pours out his grief (37:31-36).

Canaan, the land of the patriarchs, was on the trading route between the nations to the north and east, and Egypt to the south. The caravan to which Joseph was now attached knew the value of a strong and articulate young slave. Potiphar, the Egyptian official to whom he is

Joseph as the king's governor in Egypt would have dressed like the Egyptian official portrayed by this statuette. It dates from the time when Israel was in Egypt.

sold, had a large household, and Joseph exploits the opportunity this offers for the advancement of his dreams. Before too long he is in charge of everything, second only to Potiphar himself.

The prisoner
But his progress is brought to a sudden halt by the intervention of Potiphar's wife. The relationship between the two of them in the attempted seduction is graphically told, though there is more than a touch of arrogance in the manner of Joseph's refusal (39:7-20). Was this the same conceit that had so enraged his brothers? At all events, Joseph discovers that a slave has no rights, not even the right of reply. He is thrown into gaol.

He looks again to his own inner resources. 'God was with Joseph' the story says, and this inner strength clearly impresses the chief gaoler. At the request of two of Pharaoh's former servants Joseph is brought again to the world of dreams. His interpretations are accurate: one is to die, the other to be reinstated. And so it happens. Joseph's hopes run high. But there is no escape from prison yet. The fickle cup-bearer forgets him in the pleasure of his own freedom.

Escape eventually comes in the most dramatic form. Pharaoh has a series of dreams that no one can interpret. Then, at last, the cup-bearer remembers. Joseph is hauled from prison to stand in the royal court. There he not only interprets the dream, he goes on to tell Pharaoh exactly what should be done in the light of it (41:1-36). It is a breathtaking performance.

▶▶

Pharaoh's right-hand man

As a result Joseph not only walks from the court a free man, he is given total responsibility for averting the famine foretold by Pharaoh's nightmare.

Dreamers are not always people of action. But Joseph combines remarkable insight with practical measures for storing grain in the years of plenty. As a result, when the lean years do come there is food to go round. Now Joseph is at the height of his power. He marries the daughter of a priest, and Pharaoh delegates the whole process of rationing to him.

The famine is hard and long. It afflicts not only Egypt, but the surrounding lands, and soon hungry traders from far and wide come to Joseph's palace. Among them are his brothers.

Balancing the scales

As the story is told, the rich ironies of the situation unfold. Joseph recognizes his brothers, but they see only a man of power to whom they come as supplicants. Joseph acts harshly, accusing the brothers of spying. Once he has ascertained that Jacob and Benjamin are well he demands the youngest brother's presence as proof of their innocence. The brothers for their part remember what they did to Joseph, and see their plight as retribution. Now Simeon is put in prison while the others return to collect Benjamin.

When Benjamin arrives Joseph secretly weeps to see his closest brother. But he has one further move to make. The brothers are feasted and then given grain. But Joseph's personal cup is hidden in Benjamin's sack, to be discovered by Joseph's servants as they all journey back to Canaan. It may be an obvious trick, but the brothers

know they are now totally in the power of this Egyptian lord. Only when Simeon begs for mercy and offers himself in Benjamin's place is Joseph satisfied that the scales of justice are now balanced. The dreams are fulfilled. Now he can reveal himself and forgive.

So the family is reconciled. Jacob, in his old age, is brought

Dreams were reckoned to be highly significant in ancient Egypt. This is part of an Egyptian dream-manual probably composed about the time of Joseph. Good and bad dreams are listed in columns, with their interpretations.

from Canaan to Egypt to greet his mighty son, and there they stay, on land granted by Pharaoh, protected by Joseph from the remaining years of famine.

The heart of the story

The Joseph story differs from those that precede it. It is a continuous narrative in a way that the stories of Abraham, Isaac and Jacob are not. In the earlier stories God reveals himself to each of the patriarchs, but Joseph is only the dreamer of dreams. God is always the God of Abraham, Isaac and Jacob. Despite his stature Joseph is never added to the list.

But with Joseph a new understanding of God's dealing with people is introduced: one that grows in significance as the Bible story develops. Joseph is vulnerable and rejected, yet he trusts God and through him God succeeds in saving, not only his own people, but other nations too. Forgiveness is the turning-point in Joseph's story. These are themes we meet again with Job, with the latter Isaiah, and supremely with Christ himself.

Joseph's story is told in Genesis 37 – 50.

KEY EVENTS

Birth 30:22-24
The coat, the dreams, and his brothers' treachery 37
Slave to Potiphar 39
In prison – the baker's and cup-bearer's dreams 40
Pharaoh's dream and Joseph's new status 41
The brothers – testing and reunion 42 – 45

movement of drops of oil on water), as some versions bring out. Or the steward may imply that it is impossible to escape detection by his wise and powerful master.

▶ **45:5, 8** 'Not you... but God.' There is no resentment in Joseph's heart: all that has happened has been part of God's providential plan. The slavery he suffered was to save lives.

▶ **45:10** In times of famine, nomads from Palestine are known to have been allowed pasturage in the eastern delta.

46 – 47 Down to Egypt

The people of Israel, Jacob's household, set out for Egypt with God's reassuring promise that he will accompany them and bring them back – by then a nation.

▶ **46:34** The Egyptian dislike of the nomadic shepherds is probably no different from the feelings of many settled people towards wandering gypsies. Here the dislike serves a useful purpose in keeping the family as an isolated unit. Otherwise the group's identity might quickly have been lost.

▶ **47:16-19** Under Joseph's economic policy Pharaoh gains ownership of the land, and the people become his tenants. Only the priests keep their estates.

48 – 49 Jacob's blessing

Once again a cycle is completed: from the blessing of Jacob by his blind old father to the blessing of Joseph's sons (singled out in Hebrews 11:21 as an act of faith). How simply Jacob's hands cross over to convey God's blessing to the younger son, in contrast to the Jacob and Esau story in chapter 27. Ephraim and Manasseh are counted as Jacob's own sons, so Joseph enjoys a double inheritance.

The spoken blessing looks to the distant future, when the descendants of these

Joseph ordered the measuring and storing of grain in Egypt. This painting from the Tomb of Menna, west Thebes, about 1400 BC, shows officials measuring grain for tax.

Joseph and his family go to Egypt

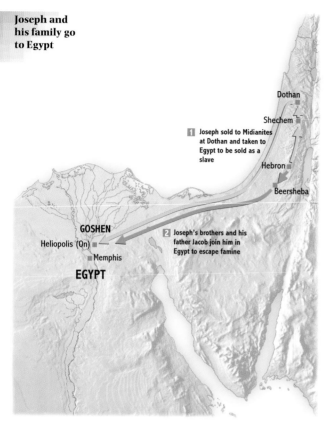

Dothan

Shechem

1 Joseph sold to Midianites at Dothan and taken to Egypt to be sold as a slave

Hebron

Beersheba

GOSHEN

Heliopolis (On)

2 Joseph's brothers and his father Jacob join him in Egypt to escape famine

Memphis

EGYPT

twelve will occupy the promised land. For the territories, see Joshua chapters 13ff. and map.

▶ **49:4** The outrage recorded in 35:22 costs Reuben his birthright as firstborn son.

▶ **49:5-7** Jacob's judgment of Simeon's and Levi's conduct at Shechem (34:13ff.) is clear. Both tribes will be scattered (but Levi's as the nation's priests).

▶ **49:10** From Judah comes the royal line of Israel, a coming golden age, and the Messiah.

▶ **49:13** Although near enough to acquire wealth from maritime trade, Zebulun's territory did not in fact stretch to the sea.

▶ **49:19** Such raids are recorded on the 9th-century Moabite Stone.

50 End of an era

Joseph returns to Canaan at last, but only to lay his father to rest in the family tomb at Hebron – still their sole possession in the promised land.

The huge canvas of Genesis, begun with the great strokes of creation and pulsating life in Eden, continued through destruction, promise, and the birth of a new nation in Canaan, closes with the death of Joseph in Egypt. Yet there will be more to

Joseph's family, moving to Egypt, may have looked very like this earlier group of visitors from southern Canaan, introduced to the Egyptian court. A nobleman had the scene painted on the walls of his tomb at Beni Hasan.

tell. 'God will not fail to... take you from here to the land which he promised,' Joseph says, full of trust and hope to the last.

▶ **Verses 2-3** It was normal to employ professional embalmers, but perhaps Joseph wanted to avoid religious entanglements. Two centuries later the normal embalming period was 70 days. The mourning observed for Jacob was only two days shorter than that for a pharaoh.

▶ **Verse 22** Joseph's life-span of 110 years was the Egyptian ideal, a token of God's blessing. His dying request sums up the faith of a lifetime.

▶ **Verse 26** The coffin would be of wood, with a painted head.

Joseph was given the burial rights of an important Egyptian. In Egyptian religion elaborate preparations were made for the afterlife. This model of a funeral boat comes from an Egyptian tomb.

Egypt

K. A. Kitchen

Egypt's history, like that of Sumer and Babylon, is a rich panorama covering 30 centuries. It began about 3000 BC, when the valley and delta were united under a single king. Hieroglyphs, the partly-pictorial writing system, had recently been invented. The long line of Egyptian kings or 'pharaohs' formed 30 royal families or 'dynasties'. But the whole period from 3000 down to 300 BC is more easily viewed in seven epochs: a beginning ('Archaic' age), three ages of greatness (Old, Middle, New Kingdoms) separated by 1st and 2nd 'intermediate' periods of dissension, and the Late Period of final decline. (See diagram.)

In recent years attempts have been made to lower the Egyptian dates by up to 300 years (identifying Pharaoh Ramesses II with biblical Shishak, and so on). However, the full evidence from both Egypt and Mespotamia supports the established dating.

Throughout most of Egyptian history, the real capital was at the junction of valley and delta, usually Memphis. In the New Kingdom, Thebes – 300 miles further south – became the southern capital; it long remained a religious centre as the city of the god Amun. In the Late Period, Memphis shared its role with various delta cities. Throughout, the pharaoh was the keystone of society, as the intermediary between gods and men. The gods were often embodiments of the powers of nature, or its phenomena (sun, moon), or of concepts (just order). The great temples maintained the official cult (the daily ritual of offerings) to which only pharaoh, the priest and higher dignitaries had access. Only at the spectacular processional festivals did the people share in honouring the great gods whose blessing on Egypt was sought through the temple-rites. Ordinary people worshipped their household gods, at lesser shrines of forms of the great gods, and at 'oratories' by gateways to the great temples. Magic flourished as an aspect of

A favourite form of jewellery in ancient Egypt was a collared necklace. This one is in blue faience.

The land

The real Egypt is not the blank square of modern political maps. It is the 600 miles of narrow valley north from Aswan culminating in the broad delta where the River Nile reaches the Mediterranean Sea. On a landmap, the delta and valley appear like a lotus-flower on a curving stem; the small 'bud' is the Fayum lake-province.

The sole source of life is the annual flooding of the Nile. Before the modern high dams, a 'good Nile' meant prosperity, leaving a new layer of silt and abundant water for crops. But a low Nile spelt doom by starvation and an excessive Nile widespread destruction. Wherever its waters reach, there is lush green plant-life; all else is dry, dead, tawny-yellow desert.

Flanked by deserts, inhabited Egypt, on the ribbon of valley cultivation and broad delta plains, was isolated but not insulated from her neighbours. Internally, the Nile was a major highway. Beyond, routes across north Sinai led to Palestine, and through the eastern desert valleys to the Red Sea. The Nile provided an agricultural economy, and the deserts yielded stone and metal.

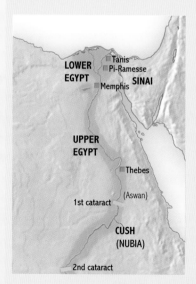

The history of ancient Egypt

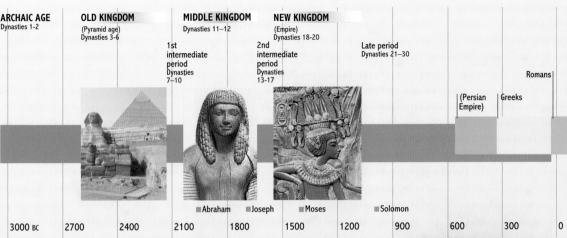

| ARCHAIC AGE | OLD KINGDOM | MIDDLE KINGDOM | NEW KINGDOM | | |
| Dynasties 1-2 | (Pyramid age) Dynasties 3-6 | Dynasties 11–12 | (Empire) Dynasties 18-20 | | |

1st intermediate period
Dynasties 7–10

2nd intermediate period
Dynasties 13-17

Late period
Dynasties 21–30

(Persian Empire) Greeks

Romans

■ Abraham ■ Joseph ■ Moses ■ Solomon

3000 BC   2700   2400   2100   1800   1500   1200   900   600   300   0

The sacred eye of the Egyptian god Horus was painted on boats to ward off evil.

religion. On the positive side it was, to use the terms of King Merikare's teacher, an arm to ward off life's blows. But 'black' magic was a punishable crime.

The secular side of pharaoh's rule was in practice shared with high officers of state: grand viziers for south and north, chief treasurers, superintendents of granaries, even chief taxation-masters! These departments were supported by a central and local bureaucracy of scribes in the capital and the provinces. The great priesthoods had their own estates and administrations. From the New Kingdom onward, pharaoh also led and maintained a standing army of chariotry and infantry. Education was based on scribal training in the civil administration and temple schools. Egypt developed a rich literature of stories, wisdom-books (similar to Proverbs), religious and lyric poetry, some of which became classics and 'set texts' for students.

The base and foundation of the social pyramid was the toil of the peasant farmers. The magnificence of its monuments – from giant pyramid-tombs and temples to delicate frescoes and tiny signet-rings – came from a large body of artists and craftsmen who served pharaoh, the temples and the leading men of each major epoch.

Egypt and the Bible
From Abraham to Joseph

Egypt's first major role in the Bible is as a haven from famine for the patriarchs (Genesis 12:10ff; 42 – 47). Since Egypt has the Nile, she could prosper independently of the Mediterranean rains which were vital to Syria-Palestine. Many others besides the Hebrew founding fathers sought famine relief in Egypt. Back in the Old Kingdom, starving foreigners appear in sculptured scenes, while a thousand years later (about 1210 BC) Edomite tribesmen are admitted to the pools of Pithom, 'to

keep them alive, and to keep their cattle alive, through the great provision of pharaoh'. Egypt maintained frontier guards and officials on her eastern border, visitors sometimes being escorted into the land (like Sinuhe in the *Story of Sinuhe*) or out of it (like Abraham in Genesis 12:20).

The pharaohs of Abraham's and Joseph's time probably belonged to the 12th and 13th/15th dynasties respectively (Middle Kingdom and after), when many foreigners found employment in Egypt at various levels, from slaves to high stewards

▶▶

(like Joseph under Potiphar, Genesis 39:1-4). And like Joseph (Genesis 41:45), many of his non-Egyptian contemporaries were given Egyptian second names. In all walks of life, amongst high and low, dreams were considered meaningful – so much so, that learned scribes wrote textbooks to help interpret them. The motif of seven cows occurs not only in Pharaoh's dream (Genesis 41:18ff.) but also in Spell 148 of the *Book of the Dead*, which is concerned with food in the hereafter.

On the economic plane, the Egyptian authorities kept detailed registers of land-holdings, and measured off standing crops on the eve of harvest for tax purposes. With such a system, the measures Joseph proposed could readily have been carried out (Genesis 41:34-35, 48-49; 47:23ff.). Also, the delta was a preferred area for pasturing cattle (Genesis 46:34), a fact evident from an inscription of about 1600 BC.

The fine linen garments worn by Joseph as a high official (Genesis 41:42) are familiar from countless Egyptian paintings, while the mummification and coffins of Egypt (Genesis 50:2-3, 26) as well as her tombs (Exodus 14:11) have been proverbial from those days till now.

Moses and the exodus

Four centuries later, many Hebrews had become slaves in the brickfields of New Kingdom Egypt for the great building-projects of that era. Their labours culminated in work on the cities Pithom and Raamses (Exodus 1:11), the latter being the famous east-delta residence of Pi-Ramesse, built by Ramesses II. In contemporary papyri, we read of Apiru (peoples who include the Hebrews) 'who drag stone for the great pylon-gateway of... (a temple of) Ramesses II'; of men 'making their quota of bricks daily'; and of officials having neither men nor straw for producing bricks (see Exodus 5:7). Conditions in Exodus 5 are echoed in Egyptian documents of that day. In western

The great pillared hall in the Temple of Amun at Karnak displays the power of Egypt's pharaohs.

Thebes the village of the workmen who cut the royal tombs has yielded up 'work sheets' scribbled on potsherds (pottery fragments which were the ancient equivalent of memo-pads). These record in detail days worked and days 'idle', sometimes giving specific reasons for the absenteeism of individuals: 'his wife is ill', or 'brewing beer with the boss', or (very sad!) 'stung by a scorpion'. Most interesting are the entries for a man 'offering to his god', or for the whole gang having several days off for a local religious festival. (Compare Exodus 5:1-5, where Moses seeks leave for the Hebrews, but Pharaoh is unwilling to concede further public holidays or to recognize Moses' God.)

That a princess in an east-delta harem should care about a foreign child, as in Exodus 2, is not surprising in the cosmopolitan society of New Kingdom Egypt. We know that youngsters from Canaan were brought up in harems elsewhere. Foreigners featured at every level of society from the most insignificant slave to the cup-bearer at pharaoh's right hand; a Moses was no anomaly here. The magicians and wise men of Exodus (7:11; 8:7, 18; 9:11) were the chief lector-priests and learned scribes. The Egyptians themselves told entertaining stories of the reputed exploits of such men.

When Israel left Egypt, the pharaoh – probably Ramesses II – sent his chariotry in pursuit. Six hundred chariots (Exodus 14:7) was a sizeable force but perfectly feasible, as much larger musters are known at that period. In the wilderness period, the Tabernacle – in essence, a prefabricated building – utilized techniques long-established in Egypt for structures needing to be readily erected and dismantled for secular and religious purposes. That Israel was out of Egypt and into western Palestine by the late 13th century BC is confirmed by the only known Egyptian mention of Israel (in context with Gezer and Ascalon), in the Libyan victory-poem of Merneptah (about 1210 BC), successor of Ramesses II.

Later periods

Egypt reappears in biblical history at the time of David and Solomon. Solomon married a daughter of a pharaoh who conquered Gezer and gave it him as a dowry (1 Kings 9:16). That pharaoh was most likely to have been Siamun (about

The mummies of ancient Egypt are world famous. This painting shows mummification in progress. Joseph's body was preserved like this.

rebuked their kings for relying on Egyptian support (see Isaiah 30 – 31; Jeremiah 46). Egypt was no match for Assyria or Babylon, and with the rise of the Persian Empire indeed became a 'lowly kingdom' (Ezekiel 29:15), losing her real national independence for ages to come.

970 BC), who probably raided the Philistines and south-west Palestine, to judge from a broken triumphal relief found at Tanis, the capital of his dynasty (biblical Zoan).

The literary layout of Proverbs – largely a 'wisdom-book' of Solomon – shows affinity with other such works of the biblical Near East, a number of them being Egyptian. However, the oft-repeated statement that Proverbs in part derives directly from the Egyptian work by Amenemope is without adequate foundation.

Siamun's line was soon replaced by a new king and line: Sheshonq I, founder of the 22nd dynasty, the biblical 'Shishak' (1 Kings 11:40; 14:25). He saw Solomon's Israel as a political and commercial rival. And when Rehoboam succeeded Solomon, by using Jeroboam he successfully broke that kingdom up into two warring factions, and briefly subdued the divided Hebrew monarchy to his own material profit. A vast triumph-scene in the Karnak Temple of Amun at Thebes commemorates his campaign,

besides inscriptions set up at Karnak and at Megiddo, in Palestine itself.

Thereafter, Egypt's real power swiftly sank. The Hebrew prophets

The dress of an Egyptian princess (as in Moses' story) is shown in this wall-painting of Queen Ahmes-Nefertari (about 1500 BC) from Thebes.

overleaf: One of Egypt's richest treasures: King Tutankhamun with his wife, portrayed in gleaming gold, silver and blue faience on the back of the king's throne.

Exodus

Summary

How God rescued
the Israelites from slavery
in Egypt and made them
his people.

Chapters 1 – 11
Israel in Egypt
Moses

•

Chapters 12 – 18
The exodus
Passover
Egypt to Sinai

•

Chapters 19 – 40
The people of God
The Ten Commandments
Law and Covenant
God's Tent and worship

The book of Exodus is the story of the birth of Israel as a nation. It is an epic dominated by the central figure of Moses. It was he who led the people out from Egypt, the 'exodus' (exit) which gives the book its name. Through him God gave his people their rule of life – the law – giving himself to them and making them his in a lasting contract (covenant). Exodus shows God in control of history. It reveals a God who can be known: one who rescues the oppressed; a 'holy' God whose goodness and justice are awesome.

Egyptian history does not mention the exodus, but according to 1 Kings 6:1 it was 480 years before Solomon's Temple (founded about 970 BC): that is 1450, if we add the dates together. A recent proposed recalculation of dates for Israel's history, based on Egyptian king-lists supports this as the actual date. But most scholars still favour a later, 13th-century date, for which there is good supporting evidence. The round figure of 480 (12 x 40) is probably meant to signify 12 'generations'. Calculating this, as we would now, at 25 years per 'generation' adds up to a 13th-century date. The historical comment that follows is based on this view.

1 – 12:36
Israel in Egypt

1 A slave nation
Nearly 300 years have elapsed since the death of Joseph, and the end of Genesis. Jacob's people have been in Egypt some 370 years. Their old privileged status is gone. Now they are a slave nation under a new pharaoh, of a dynasty which has long forgotten Egypt's debt to Joseph (see Genesis 41).

Things have changed in Egypt. The power of the Hyksos pharaohs has been broken and the Upper and Lower kingdoms once again united. The nation is at the height of its military power, ruled from Thebes and Memphis by a new dynasty of pharaohs. But with the accession of Seti I (probably the 'new king' of verse 8) attention once again focusses on the fertile delta region. A great building programme is begun, including store-cities for Pharaoh. One is named after Seti's successor, Ramesses II (who was mainly responsible for building it). And there is a ready-made, economic labour-force – the Israelites – resident in the area.

The existence of such a large (see 12: 37) alien group in his borderlands has for some time made Pharaoh uneasy. Here is his chance to ensure they keep out of mischief. The people are organized into gangs, under taskmasters, to dig out mud and make the bricks for building the new cities.

But despite increasing oppression the population explosion continues. Pharaoh decides on direct action (15-22). But the Hebrew midwives stand between the king and his intention to kill every male child. His power is no match for their faith and courage.

2 Moses, prince of Egypt
So now all Hebrew boy-babies are to be thrown into the Nile. That is Pharaoh's decree. But the water which drowns can also be used to float a watertight basket (the Hebrew word here is the same as in Noah's 'ark') – and Moses' life is saved by his mother's resourceful action.

Moses was 40 when he tried to strike his first blow for freedom (2:11-12), which

66 No book will more repay careful study, if we wish to understand the central message of the New Testament, than this book. 99

R.A. Cole

Moses was adopted by an Egyptian princess, and brought up, like a prince, in the royal household. A relief carving from Carchemish, 8th century BC, shows Queen Tawarisas holding her baby prince.

❝ God said to Moses, 'I am who I am.' ❞

3:14

ended in disaster. A further 40 years passed before the events of chapter 3 (Acts 7:23 and Exodus 7:7).

▶ **Pharaoh's daughter** was probably his child by a concubine, not a princess of blood-royal. (Ramesses II had about 60 daughters!) She would have taken Moses back to the harem to be brought up with others, learning to read and write the Egyptian hieroglyphic and 'cursive' scripts, studying laws and gaining expertise in various skills and sports (see Acts 7:22). It was not unknown at the time for foreigners to be brought up in this way, and trained for responsible posts in the army, priesthood or civil service.

▶ **Midian (15)** The Midianites were descendants of Abraham through his second wife, Keturah. They were desert-dwellers, so Moses could scarcely have had better preparation for the wilderness journeys with Israel than these years of nomadic life.

3 – 4 The burning bush

opposite: After killing a cruel Egyptian slave-driver, Moses fled into the desert. Here he was met by God in the dramatic experience of the burning bush.

Moses is actually at Sinai (Horeb), the very place where he will later receive the law, when God calls to him. Born a Hebrew, brought up an Egyptian, Moses is facing his own crisis of identity, made worse by his people's rejection. As he wanders the desert, he is halted by the sight of a blazing bush. Is it real? Is it a vision? He turns aside – and God meets him with an astounding commission: 'Be my messenger to

Pharaoh: lead my people to freedom.' But the emissary is most reluctant. He raises one objection after another, and each is countered by God:

■ 3:11: 'Who am I?' This is Moses' dilemma. It goes deeper than 'I am not up to the job.' And God's response is not 'you are uniquely qualified' – not 'you are' anything – but 'I am.' What gives us identity, what will give Moses authority, is God's identity, his presence. 'I will be with you.'

■ 3:13: 'How am I to explain to people who you are?' Moses cannot go back simply with a subjective experience. God describes himself more clearly: 'I am' is the living God, from whom all existence derives. And God connects himself to what the people already know: he is no stranger to his people. He is the God of Abraham and the rest, whose stories they know.

■ 4:1: 'The people won't believe me.' God gives Moses three signs – demonstrations of God's power – with which to convince them that he really has met with God. This is the kind of magic they are familiar with: the kind that went with the religion of Egypt (chapter 7).

■ 4:10: 'I am no speaker.' But God who made him will enable Moses to speak.

■ 4:13: 'Please send someone else.' This God will not do, but Moses is allowed his brother Aaron as spokesman.

▶ **Mt Horeb (3:1)** The precise location is uncertain, but long tradition identifies it with Gebel Musa (2,244m/7,363ft) in the southern part of the Sinai peninsula.

▶ **Angel of the Lord (3:2)** Virtually identified with God; see note on Judges 2:1.

▶ **The LORD (3:15)** The capital letters used in most English Bibles indicate the 'personal name' of God, in Hebrew 'YHWH', probably pronounced 'Yahweh', traditionally read as 'Jehovah'. (See 'The names of God'.)

▶ **Miracles (3:20)** In Hebrew thinking this is not a reversal of the natural order but a marvellous use of it by the God who made the world. The distinction often made today between 'natural' and 'supernatural' ways of working is quite foreign to the writer.

▶ **The spoil from Egypt (3:21ff.)** See 11:2-3;

The names of God

Alec Motyer

Two Hebrew words are translated 'God':

■ **El** 'The Deity', God in the power and distinctiveness of his divine nature.

■ **Elohim** Plural in form, signifying not 'gods' but the One who completely possesses all the divine attributes.

In distinction from these, there is also the personal name **Yahweh**. To avoid using this divine name Jewish tradition, out of reverence, substituted **Adonai**, 'LORD', in public reading. English Bibles for the most part still follow this convention, using 'LORD' to represent Yahweh or, where the Hebrew has Adonai Yahweh ('the Sovereign Yahweh'), as 'LORD God'. Much is lost if we forget to look beyond the substitute word (printed in capitals) to the personal, intimate name of God himself.

By telling his people his name, God intended to reveal to them his inmost character. As a word, Yahweh is related to the Hebrew verb 'to be'. This verb goes beyond 'to exist'; it means rather 'to be actively present'. Yahweh (Exodus 3:13-16) is the God actively present with his people – but the moment God chose to make this known was when they, as doomed slaves, needed to be redeemed.

In other words, the idea of 'active presence' tells us that God is with us but not what sort of God he is. In choosing the time of the exodus to reveal the meaning of his name, he identifies himself as the God who saves his people and overthrows his adversaries.

The holiness of God lies at the root of his self-revelation as Yahweh (Exodus 3:5). This works out in the holy redemption and holy wrath of the Passover (Exodus 12).

The Old Testament's under-standing of the character which the name reveals is well seen in passages such as Exodus 34:6ff; Psalms 103, 111, 146; Micah 7:18-20.

The progress of revelation

The name Yahweh appears in the Bible from the earliest times (Genesis 4:1) and in such ways as to imply that it was both known and used (e.g. Genesis 4:26; 14:22). How then can God say to Moses (Exodus 6:2-3) that 'by my name the LORD I did not make myself known to them' (i.e. to Abraham, etc.)?

Specialist Old Testament study has long answered this question by saying that we have differing traditions of the early history of the people of God: one tradition in which the divine name was known from the earliest times, and another – contradictory – tradition that it was first revealed to Moses.

Influential as this theory has proved, it is neither inescapable nor necessary. 'To know' in the Old Testament goes beyond the mere possession of information, to the active enjoyment of fellowship with the person known. For instance, the sons of Eli certainly knew the name as a divine 'label' but they 'had no regard for (literally, "did not know") the Lord' (1 Samuel 2:12; compare 1 Samuel 3:7; Exodus 33:12-13). So Exodus 6:2-3 is telling us that what had hitherto possessed only the significance of a 'label', a way of addressing God, now became significant as a statement of the character possessed by the God who was so named – that he is the holy Redeemer and Judge, ever present with his people.

This view of the meaning of Exodus 6:2-3 is borne out by the evidence of Genesis. If Abraham had been asked 'Who is Yahweh?' he would undoubtedly have replied 'God Almighty' or one of the other titles of God used by the patriarchs – 'God Most High', 'The Everlasting God', 'God, the God of Israel'...

So when Yahweh is said to be 'the God of your fathers' in Exodus 3 (verses 6, 13, 15, 16), all this richness of meaning is added to the revelation of the holy Redeemer.

God of all the world

But the God who specially reveals himself to one people, the God who is 'my God' to individuals within that chosen nation, 'The Holy One of Israel', cannot be confined to them. He is the 'Creator' (Isaiah 40:28), 'Judge' (Genesis 18:25) and 'King' (Jeremiah 10:7) – the God of all the world (Numbers 16:22; Jeremiah 32:27).

12:35-36. It was from this that God's Tent was furnished (35:20ff.).

▶ **4:19** Pharaoh's death was recorded in 2:23.

▶ **4:21** The Bible says God hardens Pharaoh's heart, Pharaoh hardens his own heart, and Pharaoh's heart was hardened: three different verbs with no real difference of meaning. For the Hebrew writer, the fact that God is the first cause of everything does not conflict with human responsibility.

▶ **Aaron (4:14)** Three years older than Moses (7:7), he was presumably born before Pharaoh's edict. Miriam was older sister to them both.

▶ **4:24-26** The 'him' in verse 24 may be Gershom rather than Moses. Either way, 'The Lord met... and would have killed' may be another example of God as first cause – perhaps through accident or sudden illness. Moses' family is now linked to Israel's forebears – the people of God – by the covenant-sign of circumcision.

5 – 6:13 First round to Pharaoh

The first request to Pharaoh merely aggravates the situation. The people turn against their 'deliverer'. Moses in his frustration turns once again to God. And God renews his calling, reminding Moses of who God is and telling him what he intends to do.

▶ **The request (5:1)** This seems less than the whole truth; but it is in the nature of a test-case. Israel had to leave Egypt in order to sacrifice because the nature of their sacrifice was offensive to the Egyptians (8:26). Pharaoh's reaction reveals his implacable hostility, already predicted by God (3:19).

▶ **Access to Pharaoh** If Ramesses II is the pharaoh in question, he is known to have made himself available even to ordinary petitioners (compare 5:15ff.). Moses, brought up in the harem, knew how to attract Pharaoh's attention.

▶ **6:3** The name YHWH is used in Genesis from 2:4 on, but of course it was known to those who later wrote the stories down.

6:14-27 Family line

Who are Moses and Aaron? The genealogy identifies them as the descendants of Jacob through the line of his son Levi. The list is an extract from the longer one in Numbers 26.

A mix of Nile mud and straw is placed in wooden brick-moulds and baked hard by the sun. Sun-dried mudbrick is widely used as a good, cheap building material in Africa and Asia. Chopped straw reinforces it.

6:28 – 10:29 Plagues hit Egypt

Pharaoh has heard and rejected Moses' request. He has shown the sort of man he is: 'Who is the Lord...? I do not know the Lord and I will not let Israel go' (5:2).

Now God begins a series of judgments which will teach Pharaoh and his people who the Lord is, and show them the extent of God's power over all creation (7:5, 17; 8:10, 22; 9:14). Nine times God acts, and Pharaoh, his magicians and all the gods of Egypt are powerless to reverse God's judgments. The magicians may counterfeit, but they cannot countermand.

1. The Nile, heart of the nation's economy and worship – its life-blood – 'turns to blood': the fish cannot live in the thick, red water (7:14-24).

2. Seven days later, frogs, driven from the river banks by the rotting fish, seek shelter in the houses (7:25 – 8:15).

3, 4. First gnats and then flies, breeding amongst the carcasses of fish and frogs, plague the land (8:16-32).

5, 6. Disease strikes the cattle, and skin infections break out on humans and beasts, carried by the frogs and insects (9:1-12).

7. Hail and thunderstorms ruin the flax and barley crops – but not wheat and spelt, which have not yet grown. And those Egyptians who take note of God's warning remain safe (9:13-35).

8. The wind blows in a plague of locusts

> *I have heard the groaning of the Israelites, whom the Egyptians are enslaving, and I have remembered my covenant. Therefore say to the Israelites: 'I am the Lord and I will bring you out from under the yoke of the Egyptians. I will free you... I will take you as my own people, and I will be your God.'*
>
> God's words to Moses, 6:5-7

from Ethiopia which strip the country bare of greenstuff (10:1-20).

9. For three days the light of the sun is blotted out by 'thick darkness' (probably a *khamsin* duststorm) (10:21-29).

The plagues occurred over a period of six months to a year. In each case God chose to use natural disorders to confound Pharaoh and the gods of Egypt (12:12). He caused the 'Nile-god' to bring ruin, not prosperity; the frogs (associated with Egypt's gods of fertility) to bring disease instead of fruitfulness; and the power of Re, the sun-god, was blotted out. The whole sequence of events follows a logical pattern which could have started with unusually high flooding of the Nile, bringing down thick red clay from Ethiopia or red algae which polluted the water.

A colossal statue of Pharaoh Ramesses II (the likely pharaoh of Exodus) is one of many monuments and buildings which still tell of his power in ancient Egypt.

However it happened, this was no mere 'chance' – God was demonstrating his absolute control. He distinguished between his people and the Egyptians. He controlled the extent and the areas affected by each plague. He announced the timing of each, and could call a halt at any time in answer to prayer.

▶ **7:24** The sandy soil filters the water.

▶ **7:25** Before the building of the Aswan high dam, the annual flood took place between June and October.

▶ **8:16,17** 'Gnats', 'mosquitos', 'lice', 'maggots': the word occurs only here. 'All the dust' is how it appeared.

▶ **The hardness of Pharaoh's heart** See on 4:21. God lets him be, lets him have his own way – so that in the end God's power is plain for all to see.

▶ **9:31** This is vivid local detail. Flax was vital for Egypt's important linen industry. Wheat – a major export – does indeed crop a month or two later than barley.

11 – 12:36 Death stalks the land

Preliminaries are over: God's warning of 4:22-23 is about to be realized. This is the end of the road for Pharaoh and his people. But for Israel it is the beginning. This is a day to remember down the ages: when God dealt death to the firstborn sons of Egypt, but spared and freed his own people. (Was it literally 'all' the firstborn, or the best of the young, including Pharaoh's own son? Was the bubonic plague or poliomyelitis God's instrument? We do not know. But the Egyptians were devastated.)

A new feast is instituted, and a new (religious) year begun. (The time is March/April.) The Passover lamb or kid, barbecued over an open fire in a pit, speaks of God's protection and provision for his people – Israel is God's firstborn. The bitter herbs remind them of all their suffering in Egypt. The flat unleavened bread recalls the haste of their departure (no time to use yeast, 'leaven', and wait for the bread to rise). See 'Passover and the Last Supper'.

But they do not go empty-handed. The years of slavery are in some measure paid for by the clothes and jewellery heaped upon them by the Egyptians, now only too anxious to see them go.

12:37 – 19:25
The exodus from Egypt

12:37 – 13:22 Night escape
Just as God foretold (Genesis 15:13-14), after four centuries in a foreign land Israel is free. The precise length of time may be in debate (Genesis 15:16 has 'generations'): the great, indisputable fact is God's deliverance. The journey to the border begins.

But first there are further instructions about how the Passover is to be celebrated, who may join in, and where it is to take place. The events are to be further commemorated in two ways:

▪ For a seven-day period after Passover the people are to eat unleavened bread as a reminder of the hasty departure from Egypt.

▪ As Israel's freedom has been purchased by the death of the firstborn of Egypt, the nation's firstborn belong in a special sense to God and are to be 'bought back'.

▸ **600,000 men (12:37)** Numbers 11:21 gives the same figure. Counting the women and children this would amount to a total of 2-3 million people – a very high figure. There may be a scribal error; the figures may come from a later census; the word for 'thousand' may have had the meaning 'clan' in early days – we do not know for certain. Even today, someone may use a large number simply to mean 'a lot', rather than a literal head-count. Subsequent chapters make it plain that their number was certainly too great for the wilderness to support – hence God's special provision of manna. They were also at times short of water, although they no doubt learnt to manage on very little, and their encampments would have been spread out to take advantage of several watercourses at each halt in the journey.

▸ **13:15** It is clear from Genesis 22, where God provides a ram in place of Isaac, that God never wanted the sacrifice of a child, no matter what went on in Canaan. And in Numbers 3:11-13 God chooses the Levites to represent all of Israel's firstborn: 'they are mine'.

▸ **13:16** See text and picture for Deuteronomy 6:8.

▸ **13:18** The 'wilderness' is steppe country where animals can graze. 'Red Sea', exactly

translated, is 'Sea of Reeds' – see note on 'The route of the exodus'. They are moving east of the Nile delta.

▸ **Joseph's bones (13:19)** See Genesis 50:24-25.

▸ **13:21** Was the column of cloud a desert whirlwind? Were cloud and fire supernatural phenomena? Both are symbols associated with God in the Bible.

14 Pursuit and disaster
Hemmed in between sea and mountains, with water before them and Pharaoh's forces at their backs, the people of Israel meet their first big test of faith – and they panic, crying out to God and accusing Moses of betrayal. But God drives back the waters so that they can cross in safety, sending a wall of water rushing down upon Pharaoh's forces, and Israel learns the truth of Moses' words: 'The Lord will fight for you; there is no need for you to do anything' (14:14).

▸ **Verses 17,18** Pharaoh is not said to have drowned, nor are all Egypt's chariots lost. Victory is won at Pharaoh's expense, and the detachment which pursues the runaway slaves into the water is swept away – a bad enough blow.

15:1-21 Victory song
If ever a victory deserves to be recorded for posterity this one does. First Moses leads the people in a great paean of triumph: God has saved Israel; he has destroyed their enemy. Then Miriam and all the women take up the refrain, and dance for joy. The

Plague 8 was a swarm of locusts, that ate the country bare.

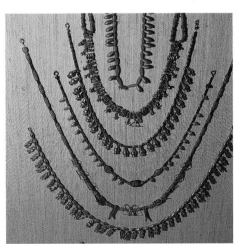

When the Israelites left Egypt, their 'plunder' included 'jewellery of silver and gold'. These Egyptian neck-laces date from the time of Moses.

Miriam took her tambourine and led the dancing after the triumphant crossing of the 'Red' Sea.

song is a fine example of ancient Semitic poetry (see 'Poetry and Wisdom', introduction).

▶ **The prophetess (20)** Miriam certainly claims to have been God's spokeswoman (Numbers 12:2), like the later prophetess, Deborah (Judges 4:4).

15:22 – 17:7 Harsh conditions

In the desert the people are soon thirsty and hungry – and mutinous. It is not long before the complaints start. There had been plenty of fish to eat in Egypt, and fruit and vegetables – and no shortage of water. Here God will provide in a way that teaches his people obedience and daily dependence on him.

▶ **Quails (16:13)** See 'Quail' in Numbers.

▶ **Omer (16:16)** A bowl holding about 2 litres/ approx. 4 pints.

▶ **Daily bread (16:31)** We cannot be sure what the 'manna' was, though various natural phenomena have been suggested. This

substance was Israel's staple food for 40 years, ceasing abruptly when they entered Canaan. It is described again in Numbers 11:7-9.

▶ **16:33** See also Hebrews 9:4. 'Testimony' (Revised English Bible)=Ark/Covenant Box.

▶ **Water from the rock (17:6)** God shows Moses the place. Sinai limestone is known to retain moisture. This incident, and the names Massah and Meribah, became a byword for rebelliousness (see Hebrews 3:7ff.). 'Test' is a neutral word in Hebrew, unlike English 'tempt'.

17:8-16 Attacked!

Joshua (the man who will be Moses' successor) leads a picked force against the Amalekites, a nomadic tribe descended from Esau. But it is God who gives the victory, as Moses lifts his hands in prayer.

The Amalekites may have been driving the Israelites away from a fertile oasis.

▶ **17:14, 16** The record may have been in the lost Book of the Wars of the Lord (Numbers 21:14). After Saul's 'holy war' (1 Samuel 15) the Amalekites are hardly heard of.

18 Sound advice

The burden of leadership is heavy, and Jethro's practical suggestion for reorganization and delegation is a sound one. Jethro, although a non-Israelite, is reckoned a godly man. He is welcomed and his advice taken. In religious matters, however, he learns from Moses (8-11). It is not clear when Zipporah returned home – perhaps soon after the incident recorded in 4:24-26.

▶ **18:13** Moses, as judge, sits; the petitioners stand.

19 The camp at Sinai

As God promised (3:12), Moses brings God's people to him at Mt Sinai. Here God will establish his covenant with the nation. Thunder, fire, earthquake and lightning herald God's presence and demonstrate his power (20:20 explains why; compare Elijah's experience in the same place – 1 Kings 19:8ff. – and the contrast drawn in Hebrews 12:18-25). The Lord God, holy, awesome, unapproachable, speaks.

▶ **19:15** 'Be ready... do not go near a woman' – see note on clean and unclean, Leviticus 15.

▶ **19:22** The priests did not exist as an order until after Sinai.

Out of Egypt: The desert wanderings

There is no certainty about the places mentioned and therefore the route. The Israelites did not take the direct coastal road (13:17) because they were not ready to encounter the Philistine forces. Instead they journeyed south to Succoth, turned north before the crossing, and then south again down the west of the Sinai peninsula. Progress would have been slow: a maximum of 15-25km/10-15 miles in a day, with flocks and herds. The 'Red (Reed) Sea' can refer to the Bitter Lakes region or to the Gulf of Suez. The actual crossing probably took place somewhere between Qantara (48km/30 miles south of Port Said) and just north of Suez – over the papyrus marshes.

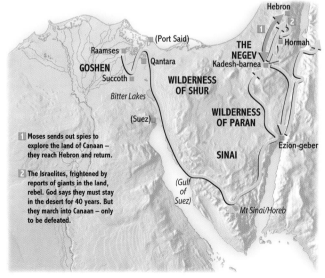

1 Moses sends out spies to explore the land of Canaan – they reach Hebron and return.

2 The Israelites, frightened by reports of giants in the land, rebel. God says they must stay in the desert for 40 years. But they march into Canaan – only to be defeated.

The Israelites halted their journey through the desert at the foot of awesome Mt Sinai, where God would own this people as his, and give them his law.

20 – 40
Laws – and a tent for God

20:1-21 The Ten Commandments

In the beginning, God spoke the words of life. Now God speaks the words for living.

> ❝ *And God spoke all these words: 'I am the Lord your God, who brought you out of Egypt, out of the land of slavery. You shall have no other gods before me...'* ❞
>
> The opening words of the Ten Commandments, 20:1-3

This summary and climax of God's covenant-agreement with his people sets out a basic ethical norm applicable to all people in all ages (since these are the 'Maker's' instructions). The first four 'words' concern people's relationship to God, the remaining six their relationship to one another. As Jesus summarized them, the commandments are all about loving God and loving our 'neighbour'(Matthew 22:37-40).

They show God's concern for the whole of life. God sets the standards in family relationships, regard for human life, sex, property, speech and thought. God made us: who else can lay down the best way to live?

Written on stone tablets, preserved in the Ark of the Covenant, these ten 'words' were the basis of Israel's law. In form they follow the standard pattern of Near Eastern treaties current in the 13th century BC, particularly those between vassals and their overlords (see 'Covenants and Near Eastern treaties'):

This is the site of the Israelite encampment beneath Mt Sinai.

- Title: identifying the author of the covenant (2a).
- Historical prologue: describing past relations of the two parties (2b).
- Obligations imposed on the vassal (3-17), accompanied by 'blessings' (e.g. 6, 12b) and 'cursings' (5, 7b).

20:22 – 23:33 The code of laws

This section, known as 'the book of the covenant', is the oldest record we have of Jewish law. It consists of 'judgments' – i.e. case-laws – and 'statutes', straightforward commands. Although similar in form to other ancient law-codes of Western Asia, the Jewish code has several distinctive features:

- The whole code rests on the authority of God, not of a king.
- There is no division between civil and religious law. Most oriental codes deal with legal matters only: morals and religion belong elsewhere. In the Bible legal, moral and religious laws are inseparable, showing God's concern for life as a whole.
- There is one law for all, whatever a person's status. Regulations protecting the weak and helpless (slaves, orphans, widows, foreigners) are particularly striking.

■ A high view of human life is demonstrated by fixed, limited penalties – one crime, one punishment.

These are the rulings of a God who cares: who is 'full of compassion' (22:27).

The legislation looks forward to the settled agricultural life of Canaan – Israel's rebelliousness had not yet condemned the people to 40 years in the Sinai peninsula. The section may be summarized as follows:

■ General instructions about worship (20:22-26).

■ Civil laws (21:1 – 23:13): the rights of slaves (21:1-11); manslaughter and injury to human life (21:12-32); injury, theft and damage to property (21:33 – 22:15); social and religious obligations (22:16-31); justice and human rights (23:1-13).

■ Laws for the three main feasts – Unleavened Bread, Firstfruits and Harvest (23:14-19).

■ God's undertakings for his obedient people (23:20-33).

These regulations fill out in detail the summary of 20:1-17.

▶ **She shall not go free (21:7)** Her master still has responsibility for his slave-wife.

▶ **21:23-24** Revenge/retaliation has strict limits: a life for a life, not an ongoing blood-feud. This is the famous *lex talionis*; a ruling for judges. In the area of personal relationships, Jesus ruled out vengeance altogether (Matthew 5:38ff.).

▶ **22:18** Witchcraft is condemned in the New Testament too (Acts 13:10; 19:19) but the death penalty was a ruling for these early times.

▶ **22:19** Bestiality (a feature of Canaanite religion) and homosexual acts (see Leviticus 20:13 and note on Leviticus 18:22) were both capital crimes in early Israel.

▶ **23:11** The land is entitled to a rest of its own: God preserves and provides for the creatures of the wild as well as humankind.

▶ **23:31** The 'Red (Reed) Sea' here is clearly the Gulf of Aqaba. These 'ideal' boundaries – the Gulf of Aqaba to the Mediterranean; Sinai to the Euphrates – were briefly realized under David and Solomon.

24 Sealing the covenant

The people's assent to the covenant is formally sealed by a special sacrifice, and by the covenant meal eaten by their representatives in the presence of God. The blood sprinkled on the people and on the altar unites the two parties to the agreement. In effect, each is swearing to keep it on pain of death.

▶ **Nadab and Abihu (1)** Two of Aaron's sons who later died, disgraced (Leviticus 10:1-2).

▶ **They saw the God of Israel (9-11)** Having a meal with someone is the essence of fellowship in the Near East. The writer is almost lost for words to describe the indescribable communion which followed the sacrifice and fulfilled the covenant.

▶ **Hur (14)** Obviously a man of standing in Israel. He and Aaron held up Moses' hands in prayer during the battle with the Amalekites (17:12).

▶ **Forty days and nights (18)** Certain numbers have special significance in the Bible. The round number 40 occurs at almost every new stage in Israel's history: e.g. at the flood, the time of the spies in Canaan, Elijah's journey to Horeb, Jesus' time in the wilderness, and the time between his resurrection and ascension.

25 – 27 The Tent for God

God has brought the nation out of Egypt. He has set out the terms of his covenant and they have been agreed. Now, as a visible sign that these are his people, he gives Moses instructions to make him a special tent: God is to have a home like theirs and live among them. God will guide and be with them wherever they go – and they will know that God is no local deity whose power is limited to Sinai.

Portable, prefabricated tent-shrines similar to God's Tent (the Tabernacle) were constructed in Egypt even earlier than this. Here, although the description is detailed, some practical points are missing – it is not a complete blueprint. The roof of the tent, for example, may have been flat or raised with a ridge-pole.

Page 177 shows the basic structure and the position of the furnishings. The framework of the actual tent was hung with linked curtains of linen, over which was a cover of cloth made from goat-hair, topped by two weatherproof coverings (of rams' skins dyed red, and of fine hide).

Many of the materials used were

> *All that Israel needed initially for salvation from Egypt was acceptance of God's deliverance. Now the thought is introduced that obedience is needed as well as faith.*
>
> R.A. Cole

> *The Decalogue... gave life a shape, a purpose, a plan. Though previous Eastern cultures had struggled upward temporarily to some knowledge that justice pleased the gods, it is on the thunderstone of the Tablets that Western civilization has built its house.*
>
> Joy Davidman

A way of life: the Ten Commandments

Philip Jenson

After the exodus from Egypt, the Israelites arrived at Mt Sinai and made a covenant with God. There God gave the Ten Commandments set out in Exodus 20:1-17, to enable the people to keep their side of the agreement (Exodus 19:5). The only other place they are found in full is Deuteronomy 5:6-21, where their completeness and finality is stressed (5:22). There are minor variations between the Exodus and Deuteronomy versions, but this only reflects the flexible approach to law found in the Bible as a whole.

In the Old Testament the Ten Commandments are literally the

The law God gave his people was a way of life, not simply a set of rules. In the Psalmist's words it is a lamp to the feet and a light on the path for all who study to follow it.

What is 'Torah'?

This is often translated 'law'. But law is often regarded as being impersonal and universal. Torah is more accurately 'instruction' or 'teaching.' It is God's personal word to his people about how they are to live. Later it was used as a title for the Pentateuch, since the stories as well as the laws there instructed the people about what God was like and how they were to live.

> **❝ The Torah is truth, and the purpose of knowing it is to live by it. ❞**
>
> Maimonides

'ten words', the Decalogue (Exodus 34:28; Deuteronomy 4:13; 10:4). Their importance is indicated by the fact that only these 'words' are spoken directly by God. All other laws are mediated by Moses (Exodus 20:1, 19).

God's gift to his people

'I am the LORD your God who brought you out of the land of Egypt' (Exodus 20:2) is the essential foundation for all that follows. First God graciously saves, then he summons the people to obey out of gratitude. Individual commandments are found in other ethical statements and law codes, but the Pentateuch sets

them in a unique historical and theological context. Because of what God has done for them, the people gladly commit themselves to the law. It was possible to exclude oneself through disobedience (20:5), but this was not their primary purpose. Eight of the ten are negative ('you shall not'), but these define the boundary within which the Israelites could live safely.

The New Testament demonstrates the same pattern; new life through Christ is freely available to all, but God's people are then required to live in a way which pleases him. 'If you obey my commandments, you will remain in my love,' Jesus said to his disciples.

Different kinds of law

Some laws are more general and universal than others. Deuteronomy distinguishes 'the commandment' from 'the statutes and the ordinances' (6:1). The positive form of 'the commandment' is the Shema, 'Hear, O Israel: The LORD our God, the LORD is one. You shall love the LORD your God with all your heart ...' (6:4-9). This is the positive form of the first of the Ten Commandments, 'You shall have no other gods before me' (5:7).

Other laws are very specific; they can be found in Exodus 21–23 and Deuteronomy 12–26.

The Ten Commandments are in-between in generality. They are written on stone to indicate their permanent validity in principle. There are also ten of them, the symbolic number of completeness. They were intended to be a comprehensive portrait of the obedient life. However, they also had to be selective since the portrait could only be sketched in outline. They invited interpretation and application, and we can already see this happening in the longer commandments. The reason for the sabbath commandment is traced back both to creation (Exodus 20:10) and to the exodus (Deuteronomy 5:15).

Right priorities

The order of the commandments is very significant.

- The first four deal with the decisive issue of Israel's attitude to God. These lead on to the laws that concern behaviour in the community.
- The sabbath commandment has already linked attitude to God and attitude to neighbour, since not even a slave was allowed to work on the day holy to God. Jesus reaffirmed this link in his double summary of the law (Matthew 22:36-40).

Ancient law-codes

There are various parallels between the individual commandments and laws found in law codes drawn up by Israel's neighbours. However, nowhere do we find such a concentrated summary. There are also often significant differences in detail. For example, the laws of the Babylonian king Hammurabi (pictured here) has the following:

> 'If a citizen has stolen an ox, or a sheep, or an ass, or a pig, or a boat, if it is the property of the temple or of the crown, he shall give thirty-fold, but, if it is the property of a vassal, he shall restore ten-fold, whereas if the thief has nothing to give, he shall die. (Law 8)'

In Israel there were no distinctions between classes of people, and the death penalty was not exacted for theft (Exodus 22:1).

Interpreting the commandments

What does 'do not murder' mean?

The meaning of a commandment is not always clear. The detailed laws explore difficult cases and set out different degrees of disobedience and punishment. For example, man-slaughter differs from murder (see Exodus 21:12-14). In Israel's context, the necessity for killing in war was so evident that it did not even need to be discussed! From time to time different conclusions could be reached due to different circumstances, but everyone accepted the overarching authority of the commandments.

There are different ways of numbering the ten. The reformed tradition (followed in this article) takes Exodus 20:2 as the prologue, the 'no graven images' as a separate commandment, and the double 'you shall not covet' as one commandment. Some alternatives are:

Jewish	Catholic/Lutheran	Reformed
1. introduction	1. no other gods	1. no other gods
2. no other gods no graven image	no graven image	2. no graven image
3. Lord's name	2. Lord's name	3. Lord's name
4. sabbath	3. sabbath	4. sabbath
5. honour parents	4. honour parents	5. honour parents
6. not kill	5. not kill	6. not kill
7. no adultery	6. no adultery	7. no adultery
8. not steal	7. not steal	8. not steal
9. no false witness	8. no false witness	9. no false witness
10. not covet	9. not covet house	10. not covet
	10. not covet wife	

▶▶

- The sabbath commandment is followed by the only other positive one, the call to honour parents. This points to the central value in the outworking of the law, family stability and harmony. It is the only commandment accompanied by a promise (Ephesians 6:2), for without honour society would collapse and God's purposes for the family of Abraham would be frustrated (Exodus 19:5-6).

- The tenth concludes by going beyond outward action to inward motivation, an emphasis that Jesus extended to other commandments (Matthew 5:21-48).

Letter and spirit

The context, content and tone of the Ten Commandments reflect an awareness that the spirit as well as the letter of the law was crucial. The prophets fiercely criticized those who tried to subvert or side-step them (Amos 8:5).

66 *The Law is given* **after God** *has saved his people, not before... Israel did not try to keep the Law in order to win salvation. Christians do not try to be good in order to get to heaven. God has already acted to bring salvation. The Red Sea has been crossed. Christ has died and risen. Obedience to God is the* response *to salvation, not a qualification for it.* 99

Marcus Maxwell

Similarly, Jesus criticized his contemporaries for interpreting the commandments narrowly (Matthew 23:23).

In line with other biblical writings, biblical law in general and the Ten Commandments in particular seek to establish a just and peaceable kingdom founded on the love of God and neighbour.

brought by the Israelites from Egypt (11:2-3) and willingly given, so that God's Tent might be as worthy of him as they could make it. Where there are no banks it is practical to convert wealth into jewellery, which can be worn and carried round easily. Wood is scarce in the Sinai desert: the acacia is one of the few trees which grow there. Their own herds provided skins.

The peoples of the ancient Near East were skilled in spinning, weaving and using natural dyes (scarlet from the cochineal insect; purple, for the wealthy, from the murex shellfish). Fine embroidery was also produced. Precious and semi-precious stones were rounded, polished and engraved (as those for Aaron). Gold and silver were beaten and worked into elaborate designs. All these skills God called into play for the construction of his Tent.

▶ **'Ephod' (25:1)** See 28:6ff, and the high priest picture and caption in 'Priesthood in the Old Testament'.

▶ **'Ark of the Covenant (Testimony)'/ 'Covenant Box'** This is a wooden chest with carrying poles, covered with gold and measuring about 1.22m x 76cm x 76cm/4 x 2.5 x 2.5ft. 'Testimony' conveys the underlying idea of witness, and the Ark contained the two small stone writing-tablets on which the 'ten words' were recorded; also a pot of manna, and later Aaron's staff. The 'cherubim' were most likely human-faced winged sphinxes representing God's messenger-spirits. The Ark was the visible symbol of God's presence.

The Ark of the Covenant was made of acacia wood. The acacia is one of the few trees which will grow in the harsh climate of the Sinai 'wilderness'.

▶ **25:37** The lamps on the lampstand were the only source of light in the Tent: the inner room was completely dark.

28 – 30 Priests and their duties

If God's Tent is to be a place of beauty and splendour, his priest must also be fittingly robed. His garments are intended 'to give him dignity and honour' (28:2) – not on his own account, but as befits the One he serves and represents. The precious stones engraved with the names of the twelve tribes point to his other function, as representative of his people, making atonement for their sin.

▶ **Urim and Thummim (28:30)** Two objects which stood for 'yes' and 'no'. Just how they were used to discover God's will is not known.

▶ **The bells on the hem of Aaron's robe (28:33-34)** Perhaps to ensure he does not enter God's presence unannounced.

▶ **28:42** The stipulation about underwear for the priests contrasts with ritual nakedness in other religions.

▶ **29:20** The ear for hearing and obeying God; the hand and foot to work for him.

▶ **30:13** The tax is a small silver piece (6gm/0.2oz). The half-shekel later became the annual Temple-tax (Matthew 17:24).

▶ **The consecration** Everything about this elaborate ceremonial points to the 'otherness' of God. He will be with his people, but there can be no familiarity. God is to be approached only in the ways he lays down. Sin disqualifies everyone from entering God's presence. The priests and every item of equipment must be specially set apart for God's service. So Aaron and his sons must be cleansed, robed and their sins expiated by sacrifice before they may take office. The living God is no impotent image to be worshipped as human beings think fit. God lays down the only terms on which it is possible for him to take up residence with his people.

31:1-11 Special skills

When God chooses people for a particular work he also equips them to do it. Verse 3 is one of the earliest references to the 'Spirit of God'. These craftsmen's skills are spiritual gifts for the service of God, and the names of the two go down in history.

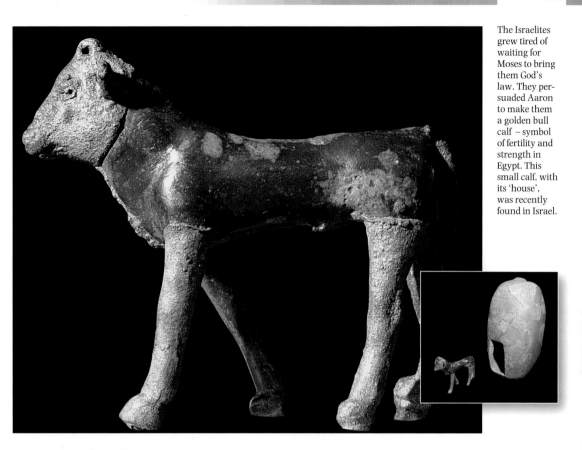

The Israelites grew tired of waiting for Moses to bring them God's law. They persuaded Aaron to make them a golden bull calf – symbol of fertility and strength in Egypt. This small calf, with its 'house', was recently found in Israel.

31:12-18 A day of rest

The way the sabbath day of rest is kept is an index of the nation's spiritual health. Obedience in this is a test of their obedience to God in other ways too.

32 A golden calf to worship

Only six weeks after making their solemn covenant-pledge with God the people are clamouring for a replica of the old gods of Egypt. 'They were a slave people, still with the minds of slaves, even if God had set them free' (R.A. Cole). And Aaron, God's high priest, not only makes the bull-calf, but identifies it with God.

Death is the penalty for those who break covenant – but Israel is saved by the selfless prayer of Moses. The broken tablets dramatically proclaim the broken covenant. Such sin cannot go wholly unpunished.

▶ **32:14** God takes account of human response, not so much 'changing his mind' as acting in a different way.

▶ **32:26ff**. 'Who is for God?' Moses' own tribe, the Levites, rally to him. What follows is 'holy war': an example is made of a few — maybe ringleaders, more likely worshippers caught by chance. 'Brother' means fellow-Israelite. But even family ties are less important than loyalty to God (see Jesus' words: Matthew 12:46-50).

33 The glory of God

God will not go back on his promise, but Israel has forfeited his presence. And without that, the promised land is nothing. Again Moses pleads for the people at a time of crisis. God's answer encourages him to press a personal plea for a revelation of God in all his splendour.

▶ **Face to face (33:11)** Numbers 12:8 adds by way of explanation 'clearly and not in riddles'.

▶ **Show me your glory (33:18)** Moses wants to see God as he is, but human beings can witness God only in his passing, can see God only in what he has done.

The significance of the Tabernacle

Alec Motyer

The people of God were encamped at Mt Sinai. Every day they gazed with trembling at the cloud covering the mountain (Exodus 19:16-22), for it signified God's coming down to speak with them. But during their stay, at Moses' instruction, they provided materials for the construction of the very complex tent which has come to be called the 'Tabernacle'. On the day when it was finally completed and erected, as they watched, 'the cloud covered the tent of meeting, and the glory of the Lord filled the Tabernacle' (Exodus 40:34). The Lord in his glory had actually come to dwell amongst his people. This is the supreme significance of the Tabernacle.

The ceremony

The ceremony described in Exodus 24 places the Sinai law-giving in its correct context. It included the following elements:

■ The altar with its 12 pillars (verse 4) stands for the bringing of the whole people of God into his presence (for there were 12 tribes of Israel). This truth is represented in stone: the relationship is a permanent one.

■ Dashing half the blood of sacrifice (verse 6) against the altar signifies that it is by means of shed blood that the people can come into the presence of God. Sin inevitably means death, being cut off from God. But when the death penalty has been satisfied, the people can be brought to God and established permanently in his presence.

■ Next, Moses goes through the law of God, the pattern of obedience which God requires from his blood-bought people (verse 7).

■ The people commit themselves to a life of obedience, and Moses sprinkles the remainder of the blood over them (verse 8) – identifying them with the sacrifice made on their behalf both initially and for the failures and sins of everyday life.

So Mt Sinai stands for the fulfilment of one half of the covenant promise of Exodus 6:7: 'I will take you for my people.' God has brought them to himself, and in the shed blood has provided a way for them to live and walk with him.

God in residence

But what about the other half of the covenant promise? God had also said 'and I will be your God' (Exodus 6:7). By taking up residence amongst them, pitching his Tent in the midst of their tents, the Lord makes this second sort of identification with his people. He is indeed their God. The Tabernacle represents the completion and climax of God's redemption of his people. Everything he had done was for this final purpose, 'that I might dwell among them' (Exodus 29:43-46).

There is great emphasis on this fact of God-in-residence – God's presence in and amongst his people – throughout the Tabernacle narrative. It is stressed in two specific ways:

■ A whole series of verses have this as their topic (e.g. 25:8, 22; 29:42ff.; 40:34-38). It was

The Tabernacle was a two-roomed tent for God, set within a large enclosed space where the sacrifices took place. Here priests and Levites were in charge.

The basic idea of a portable pavilion is attested in Egypt from before 2000 BC. Surviving examples have a framework of

Lamps were kept burning all night on the seven-branched lampstand.

Twelve loaves of bread, one for each of the tribes, were set out on a special table, 'sabbath by sabbath'.

Incense was burnt on the altar. The carrying poles are a reminder that the whole Tabernacle was designed to be portable.

wooden beams and rods, plated with precious metal and made with joints and sockets for easy erection. Ancient pictures show how they were once hung with curtains. Israelite craftsmen, trained in Egypt, would have known how to make such a structure, and all the materials used were obtainable in Sinai, or already in their possession (the gold and silver, for example).

After the conquest of Canaan, the Tabernacle was moved from one place to another until Solomon laid it up in the Temple.

God's intention that his people should always carry with them the values learnt at Mt Sinai. There God dwelt among them and they saw the visible manifestation of his presence.

■ But God was not just providing a memory to cling to. He is determined to live amongst his people, to travel with them. The Tabernacle represents something even more intense than the experience at Sinai (compare 24:18 with 40:35). They are not left with the diminishing glow of a receding experience. Instead, by living among them, God will himself guarantee the unabated reality of his personal presence.

The story of the Tabernacle is interrupted and marred by the incident of the golden calf (Exodus 32 – 34). On the one side of this act of rebellion lie the details of the plan for the Tabernacle (Exodus 25 – 31), and on the other side the details of the execution of that plan, point by point (Exodus 35 – 40). Why are we taken through the process of construction in such detail? Why is the summary statement of 40:16ff. not sufficient? Why must each separate moment of the work be dwelt upon? It is surely to emphasize this great truth: that not even the most audacious acts of human wilfulness and rebellion can deflect the Lord from his chosen purpose to dwell among his people. He has set his hand to it along lines dictated by his own will, and nothing can deter him. We may impatiently rebel but God will patiently continue.

God-centred religion

The general truth expressed by the Tabernacle, then, is that the Lord determined to live among his people and the will of God – what he wants – governs the whole plan of the great Tent and its construction.

From 25:10 onwards the description moves from the inside to the outside: first the furnishings, the Ark, table and lampstand (25:10-40), then the tent-covering (26:1-37), then beyond it to the altar and the court (27:1-19).

It is an ordered story, but on reflection the order is striking and unexpected. One might reasonably have expected that the 'building' would come first and then the things it housed. But this would have been to start from the visible, and the whole Tabernacle exists as the necessary 'wrapping' for the invisible God when he comes down to be with his people. God and his nature, not human beings and their needs, determines all.

In this way the Tabernacle sums up a basic biblical truth about religion: it must conform to the will and nature of God. Time and again the Bible exposes the human tendency to make religion suit our own needs and expectations. But if religion does not match the will of God it is ultimately futile (see, for example, Isaiah 29:13).

The Ark of the Covenant

At the very centre of this whole divinely-dictated religion was the Ark. Everything pointed to it. Three matching entrances (26:31, 32, 36, 37; 27:16, 17) led to it – for the purpose of entering the court of the Tabernacle was to enter the presence of God himself. Along the path leading to the Ark lay the altar of burnt-offering (27:1-8), the altar of incense (30:1-6), and the mercy-seat (the cover or lid of the Ark) where the blood of sacrifice was finally sprinkled (25:17ff.; Leviticus

16:14) – showing that it was only by sacrifice, prayer and the effectiveness of the shed blood that people could come to God.

Inside the Ark were the tablets of the law – the supreme verbal statement of God's holiness (25:16); at one and the same time the reason why God dwelt alone (for none can match his holiness), and why by means of blood a sinner might enter his presence (for the blood speaks of life laid down in payment for sin).

The whole structure of the Tabernacle therefore, speaks clear and splendid truths. It provides a visible summary of the central affirmations of the Bible: that God indwells his people (see 1 Corinthians 3:16; Ephesians 2:19-22); that he intends his people to worship him according to his will and not their own whim (see Mark 7:6-13); and that only by means of sacrifice and shed blood can sinners ever come to live with the Holy One (see Ephesians 2:11-18; Hebrews 10:19-25).

34 The covenant renewed

The tablets are engraved afresh in token of God's renewal of the covenant. This particular selection of laws is influenced by Israel's recent idol-worship, also by the coming temptations of Canaanite religion. Israel's firstborn belong to God, but are 'bought back' from him – there is to be no child-sacrifice as in Canaan. They must not forget sabbath law in the coming busy seasons of sowing and harvest. The firstfruits are to be brought to God, since it is he who makes the land fruitful. Israel is not to resort to the Canaanite practice of boiling a kid in its mother's milk to increase fertility.

Moses' long communion with God shows in his face when he returns to the people: he begins to reflect something of God's own glory (see 2 Corinthians 3:18).

35 – 40 Setting up God's Tent

These chapters record how the instructions given in chapters 25 – 31 are carried out to the letter. The craftsmen set to work, the people pour in their gifts, and the Tabernacle, its fittings and the priests' robes are all completed exactly as God has laid down.

When the work is finished, God gives

Moses his instructions for setting up and arranging the Tent, and for its consecration. Aaron and his sons are anointed for service.

When all is done, God signifies his satisfaction. The cloud, the visible token of God's presence, rests on the Tent, and the place is filled with the dazzling light of God's glory.

For 300 years, until it is replaced by the Temple in Solomon's day, God's Tent will remain the focal centre of the nation's worship.

God led his people out of Egypt, directing their way through the mountainous semi-desert of the Sinai peninsula, to the promised land.

Leviticus

Summary

The book of God's laws for his people.

Chapters 1 – 15
Sacrifices to remove sin and renew fellowship with God
The Priests
Clean and unclean
•
Chapters 16 – 27
Matters of conduct, morality and holiness
The Day of Atonement

Leviticus is the book of laws which springs directly out of God's covenant with his people at Sinai. It is essentially for the priests, who are to instruct the people.

Leviticus is presented as God's instructions to Moses. Again and again comes the refrain: 'The Lord told Moses...' And until medieval times both Jewish and Christian tradition saw Moses as the author of the book. There is, however no named author, and it is equally possible that a later writer set the material in its present order.

Israel entered into a special relationship with God at Sinai, one closely patterned on contemporary agreements between a great king and a smaller nation (Exodus 20 – 23). The detailed rules for life and worship set out in Leviticus find their focus in a single statement:

'You must be holy, because I, the Lord your God, am holy.'

This is why sins must be dealt with – the reason for the rules on purity and cleanness, health and hygiene. God's people are to be distinct and different from the nations around, whose religion did not require morality and holiness. A close relationship with God means a life of obedience and faith.

Leviticus is not much read by Christians today. A rule-book for the priests of ancient Israel would seem to have little more than curiosity value, and the very idea of blood-sacrifice is repulsive to many. The 'new covenant' has superseded the old.

Yet God is holy still, and requires his people to be holy. Jesus' famous 'love your neighbour' saying comes from this book. Leviticus has much to say about proper care for the poor, the foreigner, the land. And, most important, the New Testament understanding of the death of Christ – dealing with our sins, standing in our place – draws deeply on concepts set out in Leviticus.

But how much of Leviticus still applies? Here the Letter to Hebrews provides help (and a useful 'commentary'). Clearly not the rules and rituals of the Tabernacle – the 'one sacrifice of Christ once offered' is sufficient for 'the sins of the world'. Nor, for Christians, the ancient food laws. The apostles settled that question, as the good news spread to the non-Jewish world. Many of the detailed rules for health and hygiene also belong largely to a bygone age and lifestyle.

What remains are the underlying principles, the unchanging character of God, the need of human beings for forgiveness, atonement and a restored relationship which will find fulfillment in Christ.

1 – 7
The sacrifices

Instructions are given, from the standpoint first of the individual offerer (1:1– 6:7) then of the priest (6:8 – 7:6), for five different offerings:

1. The burnt-offering (chapter 1 and 6:8-13): the only one in which the whole animal was burnt; a token of dedication.
2. The cereal- or grain-offering (chapter 2 and 6:14-18): often an accompaniment to burnt- and peace-offerings.
3. The peace- or fellowship-offering (chapter 3 and 7:11-36): re-establishing fellowship between the offerer and God, and binding the offerers together as a family and/or community as they feast

together; or it could be a thank-offering.

4. The offering for unwitting sin (4:1 – 5:13 and 6:24-30): made in order to obtain forgiveness. The relationship between this and the guilt-offering is not clear. Generally speaking the sin-offering seems to have referred to offences against God, and the guilt-offering to social offences. (But even sin against others is seen as sin against God, as 6:2 plainly states.)

5. The guilt- or repayment-offering (5:14 – 6:7 and 7:1-10).

There was a standard pattern of ritual. Worshippers brought their offerings (physically perfect animals from the herd or flock, or, in the case of the poor, doves or pigeons) to the forecourt of God's Tent. They laid their hand on their offering, indicating that it was their property and substitute, and slaughtered it. (If it was a public offering the priest did this.) The priest took the basin of blood and spattered it against the altar. He burnt a specified part with certain portions of fat (or the entire animal in the case of the burnt-offering). The remainder was then eaten by the priests, or by the priests and their families, or (in the case of the peace-offering) by priests and worshippers together.

Sacrifice of some sort was almost universal practice amongst ancient peoples, and Israel's sacrifices have some similarities with those of their neighbours. Nonetheless, certain features are unique:

■ Israel's absolute monotheism – belief in the one true God – and the ritual as God's direct instruction.

■ The emphasis on ethics and morality, stemming from God's own absolute moral holiness; sin as a bar to communion; the need for repentance and atonement; the insistence on obedience to God's law (moral as well as ceremonial).

■ The complete absence (and prohibition) of associated practices in other religions; no magic or sorcery (see 'Magic in the Old Testament').

■ The high tone of the sacrificial system: no frenzy, or prostitution, orgies, fertility rites, human sacrifice, etc.

▶ **An aroma pleasing to the Lord (1:9)** This is a human way of expressing God's satisfaction with the offering. The people knew God did not need to be fed by them – he was feeding them with manna.

▶ **No leaven (yeast) nor honey... you shall offer salt (2:11ff.)** Yeast or honey caused fermentation. Perhaps the part played by wine in the excesses of Canaanite religion lay behind this ruling. Salt, on the other hand, is a preservative and a reminder of the solemn covenant meal.

▶ **You must not eat the fat (7:23)** This 'choice' part of the animal was offered to God.

▶ **You must not eat the blood (7:26)** The reason is given in 17:10-14 (see note).

8 – 10
Consecrating the priests

8 The ceremony

Now that the priest's sacrificial duties have been listed, Moses implements the instructions given in Exodus 29. In an elaborate and impressive ritual Aaron and his sons are instituted to the priesthood. Moses performs the priestly duties on their

The Tabernacle had an altar for sacrifice and an altar for incense. This limestone altar with a horn at each corner dates from about the time the Israelites conquered Canaan. It was found at Megiddo and is probably an incense altar.

Sacrifice
Nobuyoshi Kiuchi

Sacrifice was the central act of worship in Bible times, and was therefore understood by everyone. But it baffles modern readers. How can this crude and barbaric practice bring a person into relationship with God, let alone atone for sin? Yet both Testaments assert that this was so. Indeed the New Testament sees the death of Jesus on the cross as the culmination of all the animal sacrifices in the Old Testament. So we need a real act of creative imagination to enter the minds of ancient worshippers and see the function of sacrifice in their culture.

Context
We need to imagine life in a small village where practically everyone had some land of their own to grow food for their family. It was a hand-to-mouth existence and you thought yourself lucky to reach the end of the year with enough grain left over to sow for next year.

Your most valuable possessions were your animals. Many villagers would have had a flock of sheep and goats, and the more wealthy some cattle prized as much for their usefulness in ploughing and pulling carts as for their meat and milk.

Most people were near-vegetarians, not out of principle, but because they could not afford to slaughter their valuable animals. Only when a guest came to stay (for example, 2 Samuel 12:1-6), or at weddings or the great religious festivals, such as Passover, would meat be eaten. Even present-day affluent societies have echoes of this attitude in what they consider appropriate to eat for

special occasions, such as Christmas. Killing an animal and eating its meat therefore marked occasions of great celebration and involved real cost.

In offering a sacrifice you were, so to speak, entertaining the most important guest you could ever have: God himself. The materials offered in sacrifice corresponded to the foodstuffs you would give to an honoured guest. Though the Bible spends most time prescribing how the different animal sacrifices had to be offered, each of these had to be accompanied by a cereal offering, either grain itself, flour or bread, and by a libation of wine, which was poured out on the ground beside the altar (Numbers 15:1-12). A sacrifice was therefore a special meal prepared in honour of your creator.

Only the best
Within this context we can understand why all sacrificial animals had to be unblemished (e.g. Leviticus 1:3). It would show great disrespect to fob God off with second best (2 Samuel 24:24).

This is what Cain tried to do, merely offering some of the fruit of the ground, whereas Abel offered the firstlings from his flock and their fat pieces (Genesis 4:3-5). It was no wonder God rejected Cain's offering. The placing of this story so near the beginning of the Bible shows the importance of right attitudes and deeds in sacrifice.

This message is reinforced in Genesis 8 where, although mankind is seen as just as sinful as before the flood (compare 8:21-22 with 6:5-7), Noah's sacrifice

transforms God's attitude towards creation from an anger that would annihilate it into a promise that he would sustain it for ever.

Making peace
This brings us into the concept of atonement that is central to views of sacrifice in the Bible. Sacrifice is the means of dealing with the problems created by sin in disturbing the peace that should exist between God and humanity. Whereas other peoples saw sacrifice as a means of feeding the gods, this idea is emphatically denied by the Bible. God is the creator: he has no need of being fed by his creature, rather he supplies mankind with food (Genesis 1:29-30; Psalm 50:8-13). What then is the point of sacrifice?

Why sacrifice?
Sacrifice is first mentioned immediately after the expulsion of Adam and Eve from Eden and next straight after the flood. These stories illustrate the nature of sin and its consequences. Adam and Eve suffer a spiritual death by being separated from God. In Noah's day most of the human race dies in the flood. Only the soothing aroma of Noah's sacrifice changes God's attitude so that he promises never to destroy creation again.

In the passages about sacrifice this 'soothing aroma' is often mentioned, and the offerings are said to 'make atonement': worshippers sins are forgiven and they are 'at one' with God.

But why is it that God's attitude to sinners is transformed by sacrifice?

Various 'models' are used to interpret the sacrifices, and most have certain ideas in common.

■ All sacrificial animals, and the wine and wheat of vegetable offerings, represent the most precious things the offerer possesses: they are essential to life. In giving them up, the offerer returns to God his most valuable gifts.

■ The sacrificial victim represents the offerer. In placing his hand on the animal's head the worshipper is saying 'This is me.' The one making the sacrifice is either dedicating him or herself to God (probably central in the burnt-offering) or acknowledging that his sins mean that he deserves to die and that the animal is dying in his place (e.g. in the guilt offering). The animal's life is forfeit instead of the offerer's.

■ This leads to the idea that it is the blood which makes atonement. The blood represents life and it is the life of the animal poured out in death that makes peace between God and people (Leviticus 17:11). Sometimes this blood is viewed as a ransom payment, the animal's life taking the place of the sinner's life (e.g. in the burnt-offering). Sometimes it seen as making good a debt (the guilt-offering). At others (the sin-offering) it is seen as purifying both humans and sacred places and furniture, making it possible for God, the perfectly pure and holy, to dwell with mankind.

The death of Christ

All these images are brought together in the New Testament's interpretation of the death of Christ.

■ He is the true lamb of God who takes away the sin of the world (John 1:29).

■ He gave his life as a ransom for many (Mark 10:45).

The Jews ceased to offer sacrifices when their Temple fell to the Romans in AD 70 but the Samaritans still continue the sacrificial system of the old covenant.

■ His blood purifies us from all sin (1 John 1:7).

Finally the book of Hebrews (chapters 8, 10) insists that Christ is both the perfect priest who offers sacrifice and the ultimate sacrificial victim, whose death makes all further animal sacrifice unnecessary.

behalf. The blood on Aaron's ear, hand and toe indicate the dedication of the whole man to God's service, to hear and carry out God's instructions.

9 Aaron and sons take office

The order of their first sacrifices is significant:

1. A sin-offering: obtaining cleansing and forgiveness.
2. A burnt-offering of dedication to God.
3. A peace-offering: fellowship and communion with God is restored and enjoyed.

10 Fire!

The rejoicing is short-lived. In no time Aaron's sons Nadab and Abihu are deciding to do things their way: and God meets fire with fire, reducing the priesthood to three. Perhaps they were under the influence of drink (10:9). Whatever the reason, God's holiness requires absolute respect from those who serve him. His commands are meant to be obeyed, not tailored to suit anyone's fancy.

▶ **Verse 6** The uncombed hair and torn clothes are signs of mourning.
▶ **Verse 9** God's priests are to avoid the excesses of Canaan, where drunkenness went along with religious rites.
▶ **Verse 16** The people's sin-offering should have been eaten by the priests in the sanctuary area as a sign that God accepted the offering – Aaron's excuse is not clear, but Moses accepts it.

11 – 15
Clean and unclean

Today we can see past the detail of some of these laws to appreciate the sound principles of diet, hygiene and medicine which many of them express. God works in and through the processes he has built into the natural world.

11 Food laws

The rules for the nation's diet are clearly framed: borderline cases are excluded. Israel may eat:

■ Animals which chew the cud and have cloven hoofs.
■ Sea creatures with both fins and scales.
■ Birds not listed as forbidden.
■ Insects belonging to four classes of the locust family.

Amongst those banned are:

■ Carnivorous animals (these readily transmit infection in a warm climate where flesh decays rapidly).
■ Pork (especially dangerous in this respect; this is the reason for the old British saying, 'Only eat pork when there's an "r" in the month' – i.e. when it's cold). Pigs are also hosts to various parasites.
■ Vermin and predatory birds (likely disease-carriers).
■ Shellfish (these are still a common cause of food-poisoning and enteritis).

Verses 32-40 set out measures to prevent contamination of food and water

---

Strictly kosher

These are the food rules (*kashrut*) which strict Jewish households still observe:

■ Only animals that chew the cud and have cloven hooves can be eaten. Blood is forbidden, so the animal must be slaughtered by cutting the throat and allowing as much blood as possible to drain away.
■ Only fish that have fins and scales can be eaten. All shellfish are forbidden.

■ At a meal and in its preparation, there must be a complete separation of meat and milk. Separate sets of crockery and cutlery are used for meat and milk products. Dairy products may not be eaten after a meat meal for some hours.
■ Neutral foods, such as fish, eggs, grain, vegetables and fruit can be eaten with either meat or milk products.

The effect of these food laws has been to preserve a distinctive Jewish community down the long centuries. For 'if your meat has to be slaughtered in a certain way and you cannot eat numerous foods or mix many others, you are prevented from eating outside your own home and community. *Kashrut* is thus a weapon against the threat of assimilation' (Stanley Price).

Priesthood in the Old Testament
Philip Jenson

All religions have leaders who play a special role in relation to God. The quality of people's experience of God, and the very health of society, will depend on how well and how honestly the leaders do their job. Israel is no different, though there are also some significant differences.

Israel's religious leaders were called priests and Levites. They were religious experts with responsibility for making sure that there were good relations between God and the people.

The tasks of the priests

Priests were called by God to fulfil a number of important jobs. An early description of these is found in Deuteronomy 33:8-10. This text refers to the tribe of Levi, which had shown a particular zeal for God (compare Exodus 32:26-29). Because of this God had asked them to be an example and become religious leaders:

■ They were to teach other Israelites the law of God. This included not only general ethical instruction (Hosea 4:1-6), but also decisions about difficult ritual and legal cases (Deuteronomy 17:8-12).

■ They also took care of the shrines and sanctuaries. At these, incense and sacrifices were offered on behalf of the people.

■ A further responsibility was the Urim and the Thummim, the official means for casting lots, leading to a 'yes' or 'no' from God. They were carried in the priestly ephod (Exodus 28:30) and used at the request of

individuals or the king (1 Samuel 23:9-12; 28:6).

Developments through history

The story of how the priesthood developed through Israel's history is a complex one. Dating and interpreting the texts we have is often very difficult. Various texts provide us with snapshots of the priesthood throughout the Old Testament. They include:

■ The patriarchs themselves performing the priestly role of sacrifice (Genesis 31:54).

■ The tribe of Levi being given a special priestly role (Exodus 32:26-29).

■ Aaron and his sons being consecrated and made priests, with the other Levitical clans as their helpers (see below).

■ A tense conflict between Levites who wanted the same status as the priests (Numbers 16 – 17).

■ A wandering Levite of dubious character being appointed as a religious specialist (Judges 17 – 18).

■ Eli and sons: a small family business looking after the temple at Shiloh (1 Samuel 1 – 2).

■ A priesthood of growing size and prestige along with the growth of the monarchy. The high priest could be an important political as well as religious leader (2 Kings 11).

■ A group of Levites busy composing psalms for use by the people (psalms 50 and 73 – 83 are psalms of Asaph, a Levitical figure). The priests and Levites were responsible for the

This drawing of the high priest is based on the description in Exodus 28. It shows his blue robe fringed with bells and pomegranates; the shorter tunic ('ephod') tied with a girdle; and the breastplate with its 12 precious stones, one for each of the 12 tribes. In the high priest's hand is Aaron's rod of almond (Numbers 17).

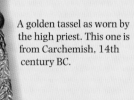

A golden tassel as worn by the high priest. This one is from Carchemish, 14th century BC.

personal as well as the ritual relationship of the people and God.

- Varied Levitical clans of singers, instrumentalists and gate-keepers enriching the Temple worship (1 Chronicles 15).

A key vision for worship

The most detailed description of the priesthood is found in Exodus, Leviticus and Numbers. These texts are often assigned to a priestly source (P), which many scholars regard as written down late in the history of Israel. However, it is possible for a late text to include early material, and other scholars hold that the essential core of these priestly instructions is indeed ancient, although they allow for the possibility that editors shaped and interpreted the texts throughout the generations.

Be that as it may, the priestly texts provide a key vision for how the worship of God was to be ordered in the life of the nation. Aaron and his family were consecrated by God to serve in the sanctuary, and so had to maintain the highest standards of purity and holiness. The Levites were to help the priests in their tasks and guard the Tabernacle (Numbers 8).

Aaron and his sons ministered in splendid clothes that reflected their holiness and special role. On the people's behalf they brought sacrifices to God that would deal with sin and impurity, thus enabling God to dwell in the midst of the people (Leviticus 15:31, and see 'Sacrifice'). Other sacrifices, the peace offerings, strengthened the bonds within the community and God. On God's behalf they instructed the people on ritual matters (Leviticus 10:10). The high priest had to maintain the highest standards of holiness, for it

was he who drew closest to God. On the Day of Atonement he offered sacrifices for the sins and impurities of all the people (Leviticus 16; see too 'The great festivals').

A substandard priesthood

In earlier times priests served God in local shrines and high places (e.g. 1 Samuel 21). However, other gods were often worshipped at these places rather than the LORD. One solution was to centralize everything in Jerusalem, the site of the national Temple. This was one of the purposes of the reform of Josiah (2 Kings 23).

Even here priests were not immune to the temptations that went with their God-given privilege. The priests could begin to care so much about maintaining the existing order that they were concerned only for their own comfort and ignored the desperate spiritual state of the people. The prophets often condemned them for leading the people astray and not teaching the Torah (Jeremiah 18:18).

This was not always the case, as we see in the writings of Ezekiel, who is both prophet and priest. He criticizes the negligent and apostate priests (Ezekiel 8; 22:26), but he uses priestly language and images to make his points. After Jerusalem fell, his promises of salvation and vision of the future were bound up with the re-establishment of the Temple and the priesthood (40 – 48).

A kingdom of priests

The priesthood as a separate class may have begun with the birth of the nation, but all Israel was called to be 'a priestly kingdom and a holy nation' (Exodus 19:6). The people were to behave as the priests

did, mediating the knowledge of God to other nations. It is this ideal of corporate witness and mission that is taken up in the New Testament (1 Peter 2:9).

The Pharisees wished to extend priestly levels of holiness and purity to a wider class, but this tended to be worked out primarily at a ritual level and they were condemned by Jesus for neglect of the weightier matters of the Torah (Matthew 23).

The Letter to the Hebrews powerfully explores the significance of the person and work of Christ by relating the Old Testament portrait of the high priesthood to the person and work of Jesus. The specific priestly work of sacrificial offering for sin was made unnecessary by the death of Christ. Because of this the earliest church avoided the language of priesthood in describing its leaders. But the New Testament also describes how specialists took up the other priestly functions, such as teaching, leadership and guidance. In the Old Testament, the priests were to enable the people of God to grow in knowledge and holiness. For all the discontinuity brought about by the death and resurrection of Christ, this remained an ideal for the church and its leadership.

supplies. Similar principles govern present-day public health regulations.

12 Childbirth

In Canaan, prostitution and fertility rites were all mixed up with worship. In Israel, by sharp contrast, anything suggesting the sexual or sensual is strictly banned from the worship of God – as this chapter and chapter 15 make plain. The intention is not to write off this side of life as 'dirty', as is plain elsewhere in Scripture. The purpose is to ensure its separation from the worship of God. The rule of strict cleanliness in all sexual matters was also a positive safeguard to health.

▶ **Uncleanness after childbirth** These laws are puzzling, especially since birth is a necessary part of life which God himself had created and commanded. The difference in time for a son (40 days) and a daughter (80 days) is probably due to the belief that there was a longer discharge of blood after a daughter. The children themselves are not unclean. And it is not the birth but the discharge which makes the woman 'unclean' in terms of offering purity of worship to God with no pollutants. (Chapter 15 has similar rules relating to male discharge and seminal fluid.) In Christ such disqualifications no longer signify: his perfect sacrifice renders the believing man and woman forgiven and fit to stand in his presence at any time.

▶ **Verse 6** See Luke 2:22-24.

13 – 14 Suspected skin disease

Although the word 'leprosy' is used throughout in many versions, true leprosy is only one of the skin diseases mentioned here. Chapter 13 is written in technical jargon – a professional textbook on diagnosis for the priest-physician, enabling him to distinguish between 'acute' and 'chronic' forms of the various diseases. This is the earliest formulation of quarantine regulations and preventive medicine relating to these diseases so far recovered from the ancient Near East.

As far as clothing and buildings are concerned, the 'disease' is a mildew, or fungus.

▶ **14:34ff.** We have a similar system of house inspection and treatment for dry rot today.

▶ **Cedarwood (14:49)** contains a substance used in medicine for skin diseases.

▶ **Hyssop (14:49)** A herb, possibly marjoram, containing a mild antiseptic.

15 Bodily discharge

See under chapter 12. Regulations are given for both normal (seminal and menstrual) and abnormal, possibly malignant, discharges. Washing is prescribed both to prevent infection and to sterilize.

▶ **Clean and unclean** The male ejection of semen, and female menstruation (or contact with either), rendered a man or woman ritually unclean. Neither was sinful in itself and there was no need for sacrifice. In later Judaism, only the rules concerning menstruation continued, effectively barring women from worship or contact with men at that time. In Christ, these restrictions no longer apply: no woman should be afraid to read the Bible and join in worship at such a time.

16
The Day of Atonement

The tenth day of the seventh month (Tishri – September/October) was to be the annual Day of Atonement ('at-one-ment') for the nation. Only on this occasion was Aaron allowed into the innermost part of God's Tent, where the Ark of the Covenant was housed. He had first to obtain forgiveness and cleansing for his own sin. Only then could he cleanse the Tabernacle and offer on behalf of the people's sins.

So, year after year, Israel was reminded of the sin which cut them off from God's presence – of the need for atonement to bring forgiveness and restore relations.

The New Testament Letter to the Hebrews sees Leviticus fulfilled in Christ. The trappings of the first covenant are 'symbolic, pointing to the present time' (9:9). Christ, the high priest of the 'new covenant', has entered, not a 'sanctuary made by human hands', but 'heaven itself, to appear before God on our behalf' (10:24), appearing 'once for all at the climax of history to abolish sin by the sacrifice of himself' (26).

▶ **Azazel (8, 10)** A place in the wilderness to

which the scapegoat was sent, symbolically carrying away the sins of Israel. The meaning is uncertain, but it cannot refer to an offering to a demon, as some suggest, for this was strictly forbidden (see, e.g., 17:7).

▶ **Outside the camp (27)** Neither offering might be eaten, since no one was to eat any of his own sin-offering, and Aaron identifies himself with the people in their sin-offering. Compare Hebrews 13:11-14.

17 – 26
Laws for life and worship

66 You must be holy, because I, the Lord your God, am holy. 99

19:1

66 You must love your neigbour as yourself. 99

19:18

66 When an alien resides with you... love him as yourself. 99

19:33-34

17 Blood is sacred
The context is one in which the killing of domestic animals is thought of as a kind of sacrifice. So, as a safeguard against sacrificing to the demons of desert places (17:7), all sacrifice must be offered in the proper place, and to the proper Person. (In New Testament Corinth, most of the meat on sale had been 'offered to the gods'. Paul deals with the problem this raises for Christians there in 1 Corinthians 8.)

▶ **17:10ff.** It is 'the blood' – that is the life laid down/poured out in death – which makes reparation: the animal 'stands in' as substitute for the offender. One precious life, forfeit, pays the price of another's freedom. For Christians, the connection with the atoning death of Christ is inescapable. Compare Romans 5:8-9; Ephesians 1:7.

18 Sexual taboos
18:3 provides a key to these chapters. From what we know of Canaanite and Egyptian religions it is clear that many of these laws are directed against the specific practices of Israel's neighbours.

6-18: marriage between those closely related by blood or by marriage is forbidden in Israel. In Egypt, which had no marriage-laws, such marriages were common.

19-30: adultery, child-sacrifice, homosexual relations, bestiality (perhaps a hangover from animal cults) were all part of the indescribably debased religions of Canaan. Israel is to shun behaviour which is bringing God's judgment on the land (compare Genesis 15:16).

▶ **Verse 18** Jacob had done just this, and it led to great unhappiness (Genesis 29ff.)
▶ **Verse 21** Child sacrifice, or the burning of a child while still alive, seems to have been associated with Molech, the god worshipped by the Ammonites and others.
▶ **Verse 22** Among the ancient Egyptians and Canaanites sexual activity was almost deified: cultic prostitutes were called 'holy ones' and homosexual practice and female prostitution were bound up with religious worship. The law here does not relate to predisposition but to practice. In Leviticus 20:13, the penalty is death. Both texts occur within the context of being holy and as part of a whole list of prohibitions. No one would argue that the death penalty should still apply for these offences. But is the principle binding, in a way that food laws clearly are not (as the New Testament makes plain)? Paul clearly thinks so (Romans 1:24-27): he sees homosexual and lesbian practice as against God's purpose in creation. The body, and what we do with our bodies – sexually and in every other way – matters to God. It is 'in the body' that we are to glorify God and to know his indwelling Spirit.

19 Holiness and justice
This chapter echoes the Ten Commandments. Verse 2 stands at the heart of the moral law for Jew and Christian alike (see 1 Peter 1:15-16). God's holiness, the holiness we are to reflect, shows itself in concern for the underprivileged (9-10, 14, 20): God cares about the poor, the foreigner, the disabled. God wants to see honesty, fair dealing, impartial justice (11, 13, 15): God cares if wages are delayed. He calls his people to respect life and reputation (16-18).

God is also concerned for the natural world, how we care for his creation. Patience while a tree is immature means better long-term yields (23-25). (Chapter 25 will expand the theme in terms of care for the land.)

▶ **Verses 26b-31** These are all heathen practices.

20 Penalties
Verses 6-21 list the penalties for disobedience to laws in chapters 18 and 19 (compare, e.g., 6 with 19:31; 9 with 19:3;

10 with 18:20). That such a wide range of offences should be punishable by death seems incredibly harsh to the modern reader. (Where we remove wrongdoers from the community by putting them in prison, these laws remove them by death: a kind of moral/judicial surgery.) All – it is worth noting – are in deliberate defiance of God's holy law, or offences against people: none relate to property.

▶ **20:13** See on 18:22.

21 – 22 Rules for priests

Because of their position and duties the priests are subject to particularly stringent regulations on ritual purity. Anything which makes them 'unclean' means they may not touch anything in God's holy sanctuary. The rules for the high priest (21:10-15) are even stricter (compare 11 with 1-2; 13-14 with 7). No one with any physical defect may serve as priest, though he may eat the holy bread.

Only the very best we can give – whether in the priesthood or sacrificial offerings – is in any measure worthy of God.

23 Feasts and celebrations

The seasons of the year, seedtime and harvest are marked with special festivals. Like the weekly sabbath, they reflect a pattern of sevens – pointing back to God setting the seventh day apart as a special day at creation.

1. The sabbath: one day of rest in seven.
2. Passover, followed by the seven-day **Feast of Unleavened Bread** (March/April).
3. Firstfruits (April), followed seven weeks later by
4. The Feast of Weeks (Pentecost): the harvest festival (June).
5. The Feast of Trumpets: the New Year Festival and first of three festivals in the seventh month (September/October); the others being
6. The Day of Atonement; and
7. The Feast of Tabernacles or **Shelters**: a perpetual reminder of the nation's tent-dwelling days following the deliverance from Egypt. (This feast was later associated with the grape harvest, the vintage.)

24 The lamp for the Tent; the holy bread; blasphemy

Chapter 24 turns from special festivals to two regular duties: the lamps which must be kept burning in God's Tent, and the weekly offering of twelve loaves. The loaves remind the tribes of their complete dependence on God's provision. They are not put there for God to eat (as in pagan religions). Aaron and the priests are openly instructed to eat the bread themselves.

Verses 10-23 record the ruling about a breach of the third commandment. The emphasis is on one law for Israelite and resident foreigner alike.

▶ **Eye for eye (20)** The principle is one of exact and limited public justice: it outlawed individual revenge and blood-feud. The fact that literal retaliation by bodily mutilation was legally allowed does not necessarily mean it was practised. Compensation for injury often took the form of a fine (as the exception made in the case of murder implies – Numbers 35:31ff.).

25 Sabbath and Jubilee

This chapter looks forward to the time when the nation will occupy the 'promised land'. The pattern of sevens reflected in the festivals (chapter 23) is extended to the land. One year in seven it is to lie fallow: a year in which the people, freed from much of their ordinary work, are to be taught and trained in God's law (Deuteronomy 31:10ff.).

The fiftieth year, following the seventh seven, is an extra fallow year for the land, which reverts to its original owner. It is a time when those who have fallen on bad times have their freedom and property restored. Jubilee, the year of restoration, serves a dual purpose. It reminds the people that the land belongs to God; and it prevents the wealthy from amassing land.

> *❝ The land is mine, and you come to it as aliens and tenants of mine. ❞*
> 25:23

26 Blessings and punishments

The reward of obedience is pictured as an idyll of peace and plenty. Best of all, God will walk amongst his people, as he walked in the garden with the first man and woman. This is Eden restored.

The great festivals

Israel's main religious festivals were closely linked with the seasons and the farmer's year. (See 'Israel's calendar' in Part One), reminding God's people of his provision for them. Some commemorated the great events of their history, when God had come to their rescue in a remarkable way. So they combined joyful celebration and enjoyment with more sober thoughts of their need for God's help and forgiveness.

There were three big occasions each year when all the 'men of Israel' were required to attend the national celebrations: Passover, Harvest, and 'Tabernacles'.

Passover and Unleavened Bread
Exodus 12:1-20; 23:15

In the first month of the year (March/April) came Passover. This joyful festival celebrates the nation's escape from Egypt under Moses' leadership.

In Old and New Testament times every family sacrificed a lamb on Passover Eve. As many as could make the journey came to the Temple in Jerusalem for this festival. But the Passover meal itself has been – and still is – a family celebration. The foods eaten symbolize different aspects of slavery in Egypt and of the escape. And the story is repeated of how God's angel 'passed over' the houses of the Israelites, sparing them, on the night that death came to

Egypt's firstborn (see New Testament feature, 'Passover and the Last Supper').

At the Passover feast and all through the following week only 'unleavened bread' (made without yeast) is eaten, because the women had no time to let the bread rise when they left Egypt.

Today only the Samaritans sacrifice lambs at Passover in the old way. The Jews have not done so since the Romans destroyed the Temple in AD 70.

Today the Passover is essentially a family celebration in Jewish homes.

Dancers celebrate harvest at a kibbutz (communal village) in Israel.

Harvest
Exodus 23:16; Leviticus 23:15-21

At the end of the grain harvest, 50 days (seven weeks) after Passover came the Feast of Weeks, later called Pentecost. As the people brought their offerings to God they were reminded that the land and everything it produced was God's gift to them. It was a time of great thanksgiving.

'Tabernacles'

Exodus 23:16; Leviticus 23:33-43

In the seventh month of the Jewish calendar (September/October) came the second great group of festivals.

On the first day of the month (after the exile, the **New Year festival**) a blast of trumpets sounded to mark the start of the most important month of Israel's year. A food offering was presented to God and no work was done that day (**Feast of Trumpets**; Numbers 29:1).

The **Day of Atonement** (Leviticus 16), on the 10th, was the time when the whole nation confessed their sin and asked God's forgiveness and cleansing. They fasted from sunset on the 9th to sunset on the 10th. The high priest put on his special robes. He sacrificed a bull as a sin-offering for himself and his family, and sprinkled some of the blood in front of the Ark of the Covenant. This was the only time in the year when he was allowed to go into the sacred inner room of the Tabernacle (later Temple). He killed a goat for the sins of the people and a second goat was driven into the desert to show that their sins had been carried away.

The **Feast of Tabernacles (Shelters)** took place on the 15th. It was a seven-day feast to celebrate the end of the fruit harvest, when the grapes and olives had been gathered in (its other name was **Ingathering**). The people made themselves shelters of branches. They became a reminder of the time when the nation lived in tents in the desert.

Sabbath and New Moon

There were other festivals beside the 'big three'.

On the seventh day of the week, all work stopped by law. The pattern for this was seen in God's six 'days' of creation, followed by rest on the seventh. It met the universal human need for regular rest and refreshment. Sabbath rules were strictly enforced after the exile (Jesus and his disciples found themselves in trouble over this) and sabbath observance became a lasting feature of Judaism.

From early times there were special meals and family sacrifices to mark each new moon, and trumpets were blown to announce the festival.

Purim and Dedication (Lights)

These two festivals were not laid down in the law.

Purim (Esther 9) commemorated the deliverance of the Jews from extermination at the hands of Haman in the time of the Persian Empire.

Dedication (John 10:22) celebrated the cleansing of the Temple after its desecration by Antiochus Epiphanes in 168 BC (the time of the Greek Empire).

top left: Children enjoy re-enacting the Esther story at Purim.
left: Dedication, in December, is a festival of light.

The lighting of the candle marks the start of the sabbath.

Disobedience, on the other hand, will bring calamity on the nation: fatal disease, famine, wild beasts ravaging the land, and war leading to exile (as indeed happened later in Israel's history). The cursings are more detailed than the blessings: human nature being what it is, fear brings a readier response than love. Yet even after all the disobedience, God still promises to respond to the call of genuine repentance.

27 Vows and tithes

Firstborn sons, the firstlings of flocks and herds, and firstfruits of the field are God's by right (he accepts part for the whole).

One-tenth of all cattle and produce are also God's due. Over and above this, people might vow individuals or possessions to God as a dedication or thank-offering. Normally these would be redeemed for their set valuation, plus one-fifth.

▶ **'Devoted' to the Lord (28)** Deliberately dedicated and set apart for God and therefore no longer available to the worshipper. Verse 29 presumably refers to someone 'set apart' under a death sentence.

▶ **Verse 34** brings us back to the source of authority for these and all the laws in Leviticus. The commands are God's, given through Moses, at Sinai.

Numbers

Summary

The travelogue of Israel's journey from Mt Sinai to the River Jordan.

Best-known stories
The twelve spies
(*chapter 13*)
The bronze serpent
(*chapter 21*)
Balaam and the angel
(*chapter 22*)
A new leader: Joshua
(*chapter 27*)

This is the fourth of the 'Five Books of Moses', containing God's instructions (*torah*) for his people.

Numbers covers 38 years in the history of Israel: the period of desert wandering in the Sinai peninsula. It begins two years after the escape from Egypt. It ends on the eve of entry into Canaan. The title comes from the 'numbering' (census) of Israel in the early chapters and chapter 26.

The book might have been called 'The grumblings of a nation'. The trust in God which took them out of Egypt evaporated as they began to experience the hardship of desert life. Numbers is one long sad story of complaining and discontent.

Because of the people's disobedience, a distance of about 350km/220 miles becomes a lifetime's journey. Only Moses, Joshua and Caleb, of the entire generation that had experienced God's marvellous deliverance from Egypt, survive the 40 years of wandering, to the end of the book and the point of entry to the promised land. Not even Moses will go in to enjoy it.

But God remains constant, present always with his people; and the hard lessons learned will enable Joshua to lead the new generation home.

1 – 9
Preparing to leave

1 Census
The purpose of the census is to list all men over 20 fit for military service. The Levites, by virtue of their other duties, were exempt. Moses and Aaron, the civic and religious heads, are in charge of the count, assisted by one representative from each tribe. In the second census (chapter 26), taken 38 years later, after Aaron's death, his son Eleazar takes his place.

▶ **603,550 (verse 46)** This is a very high figure: see on Exodus 12:37. A total population of some 2-3 million would equal the entire population of Canaan, yet other passages imply that the Canaanites were more numerous than the Israelites (Deuteronomy 7:7, 17, 22).

2 The camp
The arrangement of four groups of three tribes is the same for camping and for marching. When the nation moved, the three eastern tribes, headed by Judah, led the way. 10:17 gives a slightly different order for the middle section – Gershonites and Merarites carrying God's Tent, then Reuben, Simeon and Gad, followed by the Kohathites with the furnishings. The northern tribes, Dan, Asher and Naphtali bring up the rear. The tribal leaders are the same as those who helped in the census.

Ramesses II of Egypt (Moses' contemporary) used this same hollow rectangular formation in his Syrian campaign, so perhaps Moses was making

Dan | Manasseh | Levites carrying
Asher | Ephraim | God's Tent
ali | Benjamin |

Reuben | Judah
Simeon | Issachar
Gad | Zebulun

good use of earlier Egyptian military training.

▶ **The 12 tribes** These are Jacob's sons – Judah, Issachar, Zebulun, Reuben, Simeon, Gad, Dan, Asher, Naphtali, Benjamin – and Joseph's two sons, Ephraim and Manasseh. The Levites, the tribe of Israel's priests, are separate, as belonging to God.

▶ **The standards/flags (2:2)** Jewish tradition supplies the symbols: a lion for Judah, a human head for Reuben, an ox for Ephraim, an eagle for Dan.

3 On special assignment

God's claim on the firstborn goes back to the night of the Passover (Exodus 12). Now the Levites replace the firstborn of all Israel on special assignment to assist the priests in the service of God. But the census showed that the firstborn of Israel outnumbered the Levites by 273 and to redeem these a payment must be made.

▶ **Shekel of the sanctuary (3:47)** Silver weighing 12g/0.4oz, not a coin at this time.

4 The role of the Levites

The second census of Levites lists those between 30 and 50, eligible to take care of God's Tent. (The age-limits varied at different times: see 8:24; 1 Chronicles 23:24.)

Verses 1-20: the **Kohathites** are responsible for carrying the sacred objects of the sanctuary after

In the barren and inhospitable Sinai desert the Israelites thought longingly of fertile Egypt with its green vegetables, fish and fowl. An Eyptian tomb-painting shows men fowling in the marshes. The two fish on a spear come from 2nd millennium BC Egypt.

the priests have dismantled and covered them.

Verses 21-28: the **Gershonites** are in charge of transporting the curtains and coverings of the Tent and forecourt under Ithamar's supervision.

Verses 29-33: the **Merarites** are to look after and transport the framework – pillars, pegs, cords – also under Ithamar's supervision. Wagons drawn by a yoke of oxen are provided for the Gershonites and Merarites (7:7-8).

5 Trial by ordeal

Verses 1-4: those who are 'unclean' (see Leviticus 13, 15, 21) are sent into quarantine.

Verses 5-10 provide for compensation when one person wrongs another.

Verses 11-31 concern wives suspected of unfaithfulness. In the absence of evidence there is to be trial by ordeal. Trials of this kind were not uncommon in ancient times, and are well known today in parts of

Silver trumpets were sounded to summon the people and to break camp.

Africa and India. This one is mild by some standards – and also less heavily weighted than many towards a verdict of guilty. It is not clear whether the water contained some herb which would induce miscarriage if the woman were guilty and pregnant, or whether it worked simply by psychological suggestion.

6:1-21 The Nazirite
A special vow gives the Nazirite (not to be confused with Nazarene, someone from Nazareth) his or her spiritual status. The outward marks of consecration to God are:
- no wine or strong drink (the priests were forbidden this too, as part of fitting themselves to approach God; it may also reflect a commitment to nomadic simplicity, over against the 'corrupting' influences of civilization);
- uncut hair;
- special care to avoid defilement through contact with a dead body (see chapter 19).

The vow was usually for a limited time, but Samson (a somewhat unorthodox Nazirite) had a lifelong vow (Judges 13 – 16). Samuel may also have been a Nazirite.

It is not known how or when these practices originated, but Nazirites continued to feature on through the exile to New Testament times (see Acts 21:23ff. and Paul's own vow in Acts 18:18).

6:22-27 Aaron's blessing
This blessing has been used by both Jews and Christians in their worship. It acknowledges that it is God who gives all good things, and particularly asks for the gift of God's peace.

7 The tribes bring offerings
The dedication of the altar preceded the events of Numbers 1 by a month. Each day for 12 days a leader of one of the tribes brings a silver plate and silver basin filled with a cereal offering, a golden dish of incense, and animals for burnt-offering, sin-offering and peace-offering (see Leviticus 1 – 7).

8 Dedication of the Levites
Verses 1-4 concern the lamps for the outer room of God's Tent (see Exodus 27:20-21; Leviticus 24:1-4). The remainder of the chapter concerns the Levites.

Those who serve God must be clean through and through. Washing and shaving ensure outward cleanliness. The blood of sacrifice cleans the inward stain of sin.

9:1-14 The second Passover
No one may opt out of celebrating the Passover (see Exodus 12). But the absentee and anyone ritually unclean at the time may observe the feast one month later.
▶ **No bone broken (9:12)** Compare John 19:36. 1 Corinthians 5:7 describes Christ as 'our Passover lamb'.

9:15-23 The signal to move
God's guidance in the wilderness was a clear and visible reality. Cloud by day and fire by night covering the Tent at the centre of their camp marked God's presence in their midst. When the cloud lifted they moved on. Where it settled again, they camped: no movement of the cloud, no movement of the people.

10 – 21
On the move: from Sinai to Moab

10:1-10 At the trumpet-call
Two special silver trumpets sounded the alarm, summoned the assembly, and announced the feasts and new months. Long trumpets like these were common in Egypt about 1400-1300 BC. Some were

❝ The Lord bless you and keep you; the Lord make his face shine upon you and be gracious to you; the Lord turn his face toward you and give you peace. ❞

Aaron's blessing on Israel, 6:24-26

buried with the Pharaoh Tutankhamun
(about 1350 BC).

10:11-36 The journey begins

About three weeks after the census they
strike camp and leave Mt Sinai, in the
order described in chapter 2.

Moses' brother-in-law goes with them
as guide. The direction and company of the
Lord is a very real thing (33-36).

11 Complaints about food

The first delicious taste of manna (see
Exodus 16) was like wafers made with
honey. Now sheer monotony makes it stick
in the gullet like sawdust. Mouth-watering
thoughts of all the fish and vegetables that
abounded in the Nile delta soon produce
an irresistible craving: 'If only...' God gives
them what they want, till they are sick of
it! And with the surfeit comes judgment for
the attitude which lay behind the outcry.

Does God recognize the
exhaustion behind Moses'

The quail

The common quail, smallest of
the game birds, breeds in many
parts of West Asia and Europe. It
flies south in winter, and twice a
year its migration route takes it
across the region through which
the Israelites journeyed at the time
of the exodus. Some six weeks after
the Israelites left Egypt, in the latter
half of April, when the birds were
flying north, they answered the people's cry to
God for meat. A year later Numbers 11 records the same thing
happening. Exhausted by their long flight the birds flew in on the
evening wind and settled to rest: so for two days the people collected
them. The numbers involved are large, and figures are difficult. But in
Egypt, where the birds were cleaned and dried in the sun (compare
Numbers 11:32) and then exported, the annual kill was often 2-3
million. By 1924 this had reduced breeding-stocks to the point where
the annual migration which had been going on since the time of
Moses, stopped altogether.

own complaint (11-15)? His response is to
give a supporting leadership of 70 some of
the 'spirit' (a word that also means 'wind':
verse 31) given to Moses. The effect of this
is dramatic. Saul experiences something
similar after his anointing (1 Samuel 10:6,
9-13).

▸ **Verse 29** Moses displays a remarkable
attitude in a leader – power without a streak of
corruption (see 12:3).

▸ **Homer (32)** 'A donkey load'; 10 homers
(Good News Bible, 'a thousand kilogrammes')
is the measure of their gluttony.

12 A challenge to the leadership

Miriam and Aaron, Moses' sister and
brother, are the next to complain. The real
bone of contention is not Moses' wife (1),
but his position. As Miriam is the one to be
punished, presumably she was the
instigator. Moses is silent, but God's
answer is a remarkable tribute to the man
(6-8).

▸ **Cushite (1)** may be Midianite or Sudanese.

13 – 14 The spies report; Israel's mutiny

The Israelites are camped at Kadesh-
barnea.

From Deuteronomy 1:19-25 it seems
plain that Moses intended to go straight on
into the promised land at this point; it was
the people's suggestion that they should
send spies ahead. No doubt Moses
afterwards wished he had not listened. The
two men of faith put the true interpretation
on the facts (Numbers 13:30), but the
people listened to the ten prophets of doom,
with their tales of giants and grasshoppers.
God, and the good land, was forgotten.
Within sight of the goal, a whole
generation cut itself off from all that was
promised.

Moses' prayer at this point is staggering.
Only God's intervention has saved him
from death by stoning. Yet here he is,
pleading for the life of the stubborn nation
that caused him nothing but trouble! He
calls on God to remember who he is,
turning God's own words to good effect
(18). Time and time again Moses stands
between Israel and utter destruction
(Exodus 32:7-14; Numbers 11:1-2;

16:41-48; 21:5-9). Now his plea involves him in sharing their sentence with them. Instead of going north into Canaan God commands them to go east to Aqaba (the 'Red Sea', 25). But it takes a crushing defeat to make the people take notice (39-45).

▸ **The Anakim (13:22)... the Nephilim (13:33)** See Genesis 6:4. Nothing is known of them outside the Bible, but they were evidently a race of 'Goliaths'.

▸ **Caleb** never lost his whole-hearted trust in God. Forty-five years later, at the age of 85, he chooses Anakim territory to conquer as his possession (Joshua 14:6-15).

15 Various laws

The first verse of this chapter stands in total contrast to what has just passed. The instructions that follow are for 'when you enter the land'. It may be delayed, but it will surely happen!

Verses 1-31: offerings to be made after the conquest of Canaan.

Verses 32-36: the seriousness of sabbath-breaking. It was not just the man's disobedience but his arrogance which put him outside the community of God's covenant people.

Verses 37-41: the border of tassels is to remind forgetful Israel of God and his commands.

16 Korah's rebellion

The unholy alliance of Korah, Dathan and Abiram has a two-pronged attack. Not just Moses, this time, but Aaron too.

Korah's grievance (and that of his company of 250 Levites, 11) is Aaron's monopoly of the priesthood. 'Is it not enough' to serve as Levites? (9). 'Do you seek the priesthood as well?'(10b).

Dathan and Abiram (the Reubenites) challenge Moses on the grounds of high-handedness and his failure to bring them into the promised land (13-14). But at root the attack is on God (11), and it is God who puts the rebellion down.

God accepts the truth of Moses' and Aaron's plea (22), sparing the people. Yet the very next day the whole community opposes the leadership and is subject to God's judgment, to be saved once again by Moses and Aaron.

After their journey through the desert, the fertile valley found by the spies, with its grapes, pomegranates and figs, must have seemed a luxuriant foretaste of the promised land. The picture here is of Ein Avdat, on the northern side of the Negev Desert.

Nomadic life

John Bimson

Nomads wander from one area to another, sometimes on a seasonal pattern, to find grazing for their flocks. Typically they live in tents. It was once thought that nomads and settled farmers had conflicting lifestyles and never mixed with each other. We now know that things are more complex than this. Nomadic life can take many forms, from the camel nomadism of the Arabian desert to a semi-nomadic lifestyle with periods of settled existence. The lives of nomads are often enmeshed with those of the permanently settled population.

The stories of Abraham, Isaac and Jacob and their families

Nomads move from place to place, finding fresh grazing for their flocks. Here two modern Bedouin girls herd the flocks.

portray them as pastoral semi-nomads, moving around the country with their flocks and herds, and having regular contact with the settled population. Lot moved his flocks, herds and tents to live near Sodom (Genesis 13:12; 14:12); Abraham was often near Hebron, and bought land from its people (13:18; 14:13; 18:1; 23:17-18); Abraham and Isaac both made treaties with the king of Gerar (21:27; 26:31); Jacob bought land from the city of Shechem (33:18-19). These incidents fit well with what we know of how pastoral nomads lived.

During winter (the rainy season), pastoral nomads could find good grazing for their animals in the hilly regions of Palestine, but

in the long dry summer they had to find water and pasturage in the lowlands. In the Old Testament period, most cities were in the plains and valleys where crops could be grown relatively easily, so the summer movements of the nomads brought them into contact with the settled population. They grazed their animals in the harvested fields, which were fertilized in the process. The arrangement was mutually beneficial in other ways as well; the two communities traded their different products (Genesis 34:10). Grazing rights and water rights had to be negotiated, and the latter were often a bone of contention in a land of marginal rainfall (21:25; 26:20).

Recent studies show that nomadic lifestyles are often flexible, and changes in the economy, climate or politics of an area can cause a shift towards settlement. So it is not surprising to find Lot becoming an inhabitant of Sodom

The tents of today's Bedouin are thought to have developed thousands of years ago, so they are probably similar to those in which the patriarchs and their families lived. They are made of woven panels of hand-spun goat hair, sewn together to make long strips. Interior panels are hung to divide a long tent into rooms. One of these is a reception room for guests, with its side panels left open. Other side panels can also be raised in hot weather. The tents are waterproof, so are equally comfortable in the rainy season.

(14:12; 19:1), or Isaac settling near Gerar long enough to harvest his own crops (26:12).

▶ **Flowing with milk and honey (13,14)** A vivid depiction of a fertile land.
▶ **Gouge out the eyes (14)** Perhaps make slaves of, but more likely 'hoodwink' (Revised English Bible). The English equivalent of the Hebrew idiom is 'to pull wool over the eyes'.
▶ **The earth split open and swallowed them (32)** God makes use of natural forces to execute judgment (as in the plagues of Egypt). The phenomenon here may be the breaking up (perhaps by storm) of the hard crusty surface which forms over deep lakes of liquid mud in the Arabah rift valley where this incident occurred.

17 God chooses Aaron

Like all biblical miracles, the budding, blossoming and fruiting of Aaron's staff has a very practical point. Everyone can see where God's choice falls. There is no more room for dispute. The staff is kept in God's sanctuary as a permanent warning.

18 – 19 Duties, dues and ritual

Neither priests nor Levites share in the inheritance of the land: God is their share. Instead, God gives the priests the remainder of all the sacrificial offerings, firstfruits and firstlings. The Levites are given the nation's tithes (the tenth of all flocks, herds and produce, given to God). They in turn give one-tenth to the priests, as their gift to God. What they give must be the best.

The ritual with the red heifer (19:1-10) is the remedy for defilement by contact with a dead body, described in verses 11-22. To minimize the risk of accidental defilement, tombs were later painted white (see Matthew 23:27).

20:1-13 Miriam's death; Moses' failure

The best part of 38 years has passed since 13:1. At Kadesh, on the borders of Edom, Miriam dies. Miriam, Aaron (20:25ff.; 33:38ff.) and Moses (Deuteronomy 34:5-8) will all die in the same year – on the brink of entry into Canaan.

Nothing seems to cure the people's grumbles. They were moaning when they first left Egypt. They are moaning still, after

previous page:
The Israelites were faced with a circuitous journey through inhospitable country when Edom barred their way to the promised land.

all the years of God's providing.

The incident in verses 2-13 recalls the similar one at Mt Sinai (Exodus 17:1-7). Moses' sin seems to lie in the words 'Must *we* get water...?', as if he and Aaron, not God, brought the water from the rock. How often words spoken in haste (see Psalm 106:33) are repented at leisure. Because of this, Moses will not lead the people into the land he so longs to enter. Even the greatest of God's servants, after a long lifetime of trust and obedience, can fall.

▶ **Water out of the rock** Sinai limestone is known to retain water (see Exodus 17:6). Moses struck the rock in the place God indicated.

20:14-21 Safe-conduct refused
The Israelites had tried going north, directly into Canaan, against God's orders, and had suffered a punishing defeat

On Mt Hor, near the border of Edom, Aaron died. A monument called Aaron's tomb stands on the mountain-top today.

(14:25, 39-45). Now they must go east in order to travel north on the far side of the Dead Sea. But Edom stands in the way, deaf to Moses' sweet-talk.

▶ **Your brother Israel (14)** This is not just a manner of speaking: the Edomites were descendants of Esau, Jacob's brother.

▶ **King's highway/main road (17)** This runs directly north from the Gulf of Aqaba to Syria, leaving the Dead Sea to the west. Edom's refusal to let Israel pass involves them in a long detour south and round.

20:22 – 21:35 Avoiding Edom
20:22-29 records the death of Aaron. Mt Hor may be Jebel Madeira, north-east of Kadesh, on the north-west border of Edom. The traditional site (see picture), favoured by Josephus, is close to Petra and a long way from Kadesh.

Victory over King Arad is swiftly followed by complaints, as they trek south to the Gulf of Aqaba (the 'Red Sea' here) to clear Edom's territory. The venomous snakes are seen as punishment: but a remedy is provided. The people had only to look at the bronze snake to be healed.

Jesus reminds Nicodemus of this incident, saying that he too must be lifted up, so that everyone who has faith in him may have eternal life (John 3:14-15).

21:21-25: once again Israel requests safe-passage and is refused, but this time they fight and win. The Amorite King Sihon has taken the lands of Moab and rules from the Arnon in the south to the Jabbok in the north, from his capital city of Heshbon. Continuing north the Israelites defeat Og of Bashan (north-east of Lake Galilee) at Edrei.

▶ **Atharim (21:1)** The location of this place is not known.

▶ **21:13** The River Arnon carves a huge east-west gorge, a formidable frontier, on its way to the Dead Sea.

▶ **The well (21:16)** Water lies close to the surface in some parts of the Sinai peninsula and southern Jordan. The Israelites often had only to dig shallow pits to find it.

22 – 36
In the plains of Moab

22 – 24 Balak and Balaam
The victorious Israelites return to camp on the doorstep of Balak king of Moab, who, with Midianite support, sends post-haste to Pethor (probably Pitru, near Carchemish) on the Euphrates for Balaam the diviner to come and curse his enemies. It was a routine business arrangement for the prophet, in a day when everyone believed in the power of words (especially formal 'blessings' and 'cursings') to influence events. What is surprising is the disclosure that the source of Balaam's knowledge is God himself. And neither bribe nor threat will budge him from the truth as God reveals it to him.

Three times they go through the same ritual (22:41 – 23:10; 23:13-24; 23:27 – 24:9). Three times Balaam blesses

Israel, to the increasing anger of Balak. The fourth oracle tops all. 24:15-19 predicts a victorious future king who will defeat all Israel's enemies.

▶ **The incident of the ass** God's purpose seems to be so to impress Balaam, that no matter how hard Balak works on him, the prophet will stick to the truth.

▶ **The origin of these oracles** It is not known how these oracles came to be included in Numbers. But linguistic and other factors indicate that the oracles were written down by the 12th century BC.

25 Idolatry at Peor
It was at Balaam's instruction (31:16) that the Midianite women brought Israel low at Peor. And he paid for it with his life (31:8).

With the death of those who worshipped Baal, the last of the generation who had come out of Egypt (all but Moses, Joshua and Caleb) perished (26:65).

▶ **Verse 1** Sexual relations with the Moabite women led the men of Israel to break faith with God and worship Baal.

▶ **Baal of Peor (3)** The local deity of the place. 'Baal' (meaning 'master') gradually became a proper name for the great fertility god of the Canaanites. The events described here already show a blend of sexual and religious practices.

▶ **Moabite… Midianite** The interchange of terms sounds confused, but from late patriarchal times there was a good deal of overlap in the use of the terms 'Midianite', 'Ishmaelite', 'Medanite', 'Moabite'.

26 The second census
The numbers are slightly fewer than in the first census (one whole generation has been replaced by another, 64-65). The reason for the census, this time, was so that the land could be shared out fairly, according to the size of the different groups (verses 52ff.).

27:1-11 Daughters' right to inherit
The law said that land passed from father to eldest son, keeping it in the tribe. But Zelophehad left only daughters. Women could not normally inherit in other ancient Near Eastern countries, but in Israel the ruling is given that, failing sons, daughters may inherit. But they must marry within

their own tribe to safeguard the tribal inheritance (see chapter 36).

27:12-23 Joshua for leader
Moses' life is almost over, as he looks out over the promised land. Joshua, his right-hand man (Exodus 17:9ff.; 24:13; 33:11; Numbers 11:28) and one of the two faithful spies (14:6ff.), is God's choice of successor. He is now invested with authority to lead the nation in Moses' place.

▶ **Mt Abarim (12)** This is the name of the mountain range. Mt Nebo, overlooking Jericho, was the actual summit from which Moses viewed the land.

▶ **You disobeyed my command (14)** See 20:2-13.

28 – 30 Rules for public worship; vows
28:1-8, daily offerings; 9-10, sabbath offerings; 11-15, offerings for each new month; 16-25, offerings for Passover and Unleavened Bread; 26-31, the Feast of Weeks (Firstfruits).

Chapter 29: the feasts of the seventh month. Verses 1-6, offerings for the Feast of Trumpets; 7-11, for the Day of Atonement; 12-38, for the Feast of Tabernacles/Shelters.

For feasts, see Leviticus 23, and 'The great festivals'. For offerings see Leviticus 1 – 7 and 'Sacrifice'.

Chapter 30: vows. Promises made to God must be kept. Men in Israel are unconditionally bound by vows of any

The rebellious Israelites were bitten by poisonous snakes and many died. But any who looked to the bronze snake God told Moses to make were saved. John 3:14-15 likens this to Jesus' saving work on the cross. A modern bronze on Mt Nebo shows a snake entwining the cross.

The Israelites asked the Edomites' permission to take the King's Highway (pictured here), the main route north, but they refused.

kind (2). Verses 3-15 set out the terms under which vows made by women are binding. This is a patriarchal society in which men ensure their control over women.

31 Holy war against Midian
The Midianites are punished for their sin in inducing Israel to worship false gods (see chapter 25 and notes). Army and nation divide the spoil fifty-fifty. One five-hundredth of the army's share goes to the priests; one-fiftieth of the nation's share to the Levites. Verses 48-54 record the army's special offering given in gratitude for their safe return. This generation obeys God, and he gives them victory. But we will hear more of the Midianites (see Judges 6 – 8).

32 Tribes east of the Jordan
The tribes of Reuben and Gad want to settle the good grazing lands east of the Jordan. Their request is allowed, but only on condition that they help in the conquest of Canaan first. So they work out a practical plan to enable the fighting force to leave the livestock and their dependents behind, safe and secure. Part of the tribe of Manasseh conquers Gilead, and Moses gives them this land for their own.

33 Stages of the journey
This chapter is a resumé of the whole journey, from Egypt to the plains of Moab. See 'Out of Egypt: the desert wanderings' map in Exodus. Forty camping places are listed, most of them now unknown.

▶ **Verse 52b** The intention is to wipe out everything associated with idolatrous religions – the carved images and places of worship ('high places' where shrines were built).

34 Boundaries of the land
See also Joshua 13 – 19.

35 Provision for the Levites; cities of refuge
See also Joshua 20 – 21.

36 A test case
See on 27:1-11.

Deuteronomy

Summary

Moses addresses the people of Israel as they are about to enter the promised land. He reviews the journey and reminds them of their covenant with God.

Chapters 1 – 4:43
Reviewing the desert journey
•
Chapters 4:44 – 28:68
The Ten Commandments
God's law
Instructions for the new land
•
Chapters 29 – 30
Choose life!
•
Chapters 31 – 34
Moses' last words

In its opening verse Deuteronomy tells us 'These are the words that Moses addressed to all Israel': they were camped in the plains of Moab and about to enter the promised land (about 1260 BC).

The title, which comes from the Greek translation, implies a second law-giving, but in fact the book contains a restatement and reaffirmation of the Sinai covenant. It is an 'exposition' of the law, the heart of the old covenant. It is also quoted more than 80 times in the New Testament, an indication of its importance for the first Christians.

The structure of Deuteronomy (the Old Testament covenant form) is very like that of a contemporary treaty (see 'Covenants and Near Eastern treaties'):

1. Historical prologue 1:6 – 3:29
2. Basic stipulations 4 – 11
3. Detailed stipulations 12 – 26
4. Document clause 27
5. Blessings 28:1-14
6. Curses 28:15-68
7. Recapitulation 29 – 30

Many, but not all, of the laws recorded in Exodus 20:22 – 23:19 are paralleled in Deuteronomy. The Ten Commandments of Exodus 20 are repeated in Deuteronomy 5, with some slight variations. The focus throughout is on the settled life in a new land.

Until the critical studies of the 18th and 19th centuries, which led to a very fragmented view of the Pentateuch, Jews and Christians generally took Deutero-nomy at face value as the words of Moses. Scholars today would want to acknow-ledge the contribution of later editors and there is no agreed date for final composition, but the book remains firmly rooted in this great historical figure.

The land and God's covenant with his people are the great themes of Deutero-nomy. 'Remember that once you were slaves'; 'Remember God's love,' Moses urges the people. For it is to God that they owe their freedom and all the good things promised to them. This calls for a response: 'Remember to do...' – keep faith, obey. This is the key to God's blessings. To forget God in the new life is to court disaster.

1 – 4:43
First address: review of the journey

1:1-5 Introduction
Time and place are carefully specified. Forty years after the exodus from Egypt, at the end of the desert wanderings, in the plains of Moab east of the River Jordan, Moses gives God's message to Israel.
▸ **Verse 2** Horeb is another name for Mt Sinai.

1:6-46 Sinai to Kadesh
Verses 9-18 (see Numbers 11:14ff.): Moses recalls how he found relief from the solitary burden of leadership in delegating responsibility. The wise advice to do so came from his father-in-law, Jethro (see Exodus 18:13-26).

Verses 19-46, the spies and their report: see on Numbers 13 – 14.
▸ **Verse 7** The land God promised to Abraham: see Genesis 15:18-21.
▸ **Verse 19** 'Wilderness'/ 'desert' simply means uninhabited land. North of Sinai the land is barren and desolate, with rugged peaks and stony, flinty ground. But there are oases, with a surprising amount of vegetation after the winter rains.
▸ **Amorites (44)** Numbers 14:43 uses the wider term 'Canaanites'.

66 *The purpose of the covenant, in the Hebrew Bible... was never simply that the creator wanted to have Israel as a special people, irrespective of the fate of the rest of the world. The purpose of the covenant was that, through this means, the creator would address and save his entire world. The call of Abraham was designed to undo the sin of Adam.* 99

Tom Wright

Moses
Alan Millard

The family of the Hebrew Jacob which had joined Joseph in Egypt grew over time until the Egyptians found them a threat. Accordingly the king decreed all Hebrew male babies should be killed.

Moses' life-story

At this point Moses was born, then hidden by his mother in a rush basket in the Nile, rescued by a princess, reared by his mother and trained in the royal household (Exodus 2:1-10; cf. Acts 7:22).

Aware of his ancestry, he intervened to help another Hebrew and had to flee Egypt.

Living as a nomadic shepherd in the desert, with a local bride, he faced God at the 'burning bush' and reluctantly returned to lead his people to freedom from forced labour in Egypt (Exodus 3 – 4).

The king's obstinate refusal to let the people go provoked the ten plagues, the final one bringing the institution of the Passover and precipitating the Exodus (Exodus 5 – 14).

Moses led the people across the Red Sea into the Sinai region where, at Mount Sinai, he mediated to them the covenant God offered, making them into the nation of Israel. From God he received the religious and moral laws which formed Israel's constitution.

Despite rebellions and rejections, Moses led the nation through 40 years' quarantine until they were ready to enter the land God had promised to Abraham (Genesis 15).

After viewing the land from Mount Nebo in Transjordan, Moses died (Deuteronomy 32: 48 – 52; 34).

Man or superman?

Moses is portrayed as a great man, but not a superman, in the Bible's customary honest way. One text describes him as 'very humble' (Numbers 12:3) and his attempts to avoid God's commission and his need to have his brother Aaron as his spokesman suggest a shy nature (Exodus 4).

Moses' marriage to the Midianite Zipporah and his failure to circumcise his son (Exodus 4: 24-26) may indicate uncertainty about his identity while in exile, a matter that had to be put right before he could become Israel's leader.

On the wilderness journey the people's frequent complaints drove him back again and again to the God who promised to be with him (Exodus 15:23-25, etc.). Yet when God offered to make him the founder of a new nation after Israel's apostasy with the golden calf, Moses volunteered to bear God's punishment himself in place of Israel (Exodus 32, note verses

30-33; Deuteronomy 9:7-29).

His involvement in God's acts of power, all the way from Egypt to Canaan, showed God's approval of him, and helped mould the people to respect and accept him.

One God: the law for Israel

Moses dispensed justice before reaching Mount Sinai (Exodus 18: 13-26), but on the mountain he received from God the Torah, the law for Israel, including the Ten Commandments which became the basis of Jewish and Western society.

Moses was God's spokesman, his prophet (Deuteronomy 18:15-18), who presented God's Word to the people and interpreted it. The laws include some which Israel's neighbours who lived in similar ways already observed and endorsed as right (e.g. Exodus 21: 35,36). Others were similar to the customs of other people, but suited especially to Israel. The absolute demands the Ten Commandments make are not found in other ancient societies and it is hard to perceive how any polytheistic society could reach definite laws like these, for they presuppose a single ultimate authority.

Under Moses' hand the laws shaped Israel into a nation, teaching the previously disorganized tribes to live in unity, to share in the support of their communal shrine, the Tabernacle, and fight in defence of the whole people. Over all was reverence for the same single God.

The monotheism which Moses proclaimed (Exodus 20:1,2; Deuteronomy 6:4) is so different from all the other religious ideas of the ancient Near East that many scholars believe it cannot have developed before the 7th/6th centuries BC.

There is no direct evidence from Moses' own time. However, the Egyptian King Akhenaten imposed the worship of one god (the sun's disk, Aten), throughout Egypt in about 1340 BC, outlawing all other deities. This became known in modern times with the discovery of his capital, abandoned soon after his death when references to him and his god were erased from Egyptian records. Without that discovery, little would be known of his revolution. The possibility of the existence of Moses and the teaching he gave, although far superior in every way to Akhenaten's, may be argued through this analogy.

Historical setting

The historical and archaeological evidence strongly favours placing Moses' career in the 13th century BC when Ramesses II ruled Egypt (about 1279-1213 BC) and controlled Canaan. His successor Merneptah (about 1213-1203 BC) claimed the defeat of a people called Israel in Canaan, conceivably some of the tribes then taking over the land. The pharaohs gradually lost control there, leaving Philistines and others to settle.

This was a period of widespread change, with iron-working beginning to spread its new technology, and the city-states (as in Joshua 9 – 12) giving way to national states like Edom, Moab and, eventually, Israel.

The absence of any Egyptian

Beneath Mt Nebo, where Moses died within sight of the promised land, is a spring which still bears his name.

record of Israel's time in Egypt or of the exodus leaves the precise dates uncertain. Egyptian kings did not report disasters or defeats on their monuments and next to no administrative documents have survived.

The Israelites lived by the Nile delta and any papyrus reports about brick-making which might have been left in ruined cities there would have rotted long ago.

Despite various claims, nothing has been found relating to the deaths of the firstborn sons or the loss of Egyptian troops in the Red Sea.

The biblical narratives may have been completed some time after the events took place, but it is certainly possible that Moses kept some account of them and that the laws were preserved in writing, either in Egyptian, in Babylonian or in Canaanite (early Hebrew). They stand as records of the remarkable career of a very human man, the founder of Israel.

2:1 – 4:43 From Aqaba to the plains of Moab

2:1-8: see Numbers 20:14-21. Although the Edomites refused Israel passage along the main road, the King's Highway, it seems that some were willing to sell them food. The friendliness shown to Edom (Esau's descendants), Moab and Ammon (Lot's descendants, see Genesis 19:36-38) on grounds of kinship is characteristic of patriarchal and Mosaic times. God keeps his word down the ages, and expects his people to keep theirs.

2:26-37: see Numbers 21:21-35.

3:1-20: war against King Og; land east of the River Jordan settled by the tribes (see Numbers 21:33-35; and 32). Og's land was part of the Amorite kingdom. Bashan, famed for its cattle, with the area around was naturally attractive to the stockmen of Reuben, Gad, and Manasseh.

3:21-29: a new leader; Moses' punishment (see 4:21ff. and Numbers 20). The price of disobedience was a heavy one. Moses longed above all to lead his people into the promised land. 'Because of you' is not merely an attempt to shift the blame. It was the people's provocation which stung him to anger.

4:1-40: Moses calls the nation to obedience and warns against idolatry. Moses has recounted the history of God's dealings with Israel over the past 40 years. Now he reminds them of God's character as shown in his acts, and warns of the inevitable consequences of disobedience: 'The Lord is God in heaven above and on the earth below. There is no other... Keep his decrees and commands... so that it may go well with you.'

4:41-43: three cities of refuge east of the Jordan. See Numbers 35:6-29.

▶ **Seir (2:8)** The mountains of 'Seir' (Edom), rise to the south and east of the Dead Sea.

▶ **Made stubborn/obstinate (2:30)** The Old Testament sees no conflict between God's sovereignty and human freedom. See on Exodus 4:21. God is never described as 'hardening the heart' of a good person.

▶ **His bed (3:11)** is probably a coffin. The 'common cubit'/standard measure was about 450mm/18 inches – so the coffin is 4m x 2m.

▶ **The Arabah (3:17)** is the rift valley which

runs from the Sea of Galilee south to the Gulf of Aqaba. 'Kinnereth' is Galilee: the word comes from the harp shape of the lake. The 'Salt Sea' is the Dead Sea.

▶ **Pisgah (3:17 and 27)** A ridge of Mt Nebo, about 15km/9 miles east of the northern end of the Dead Sea.

▶ **Baal-peor (4:3)** See Numbers 25.

▶ **4:8** Permanent rules of conduct; case-laws and judicial decisions.

4:44 – 28:68
Second address: the law

4:44-49 Introduction
These verses introduce the restating of the covenant which Moses gave to the people before the crossing of the Jordan, in order to remind them of God's faithfulness to them as well as their covenant responsibilities.

5 – 11 The Ten Commandments
Chapter 5: see also Exodus 19:16 – 20:21, notes on Exodus 20 and 'A way of life: the Ten Commandments'.

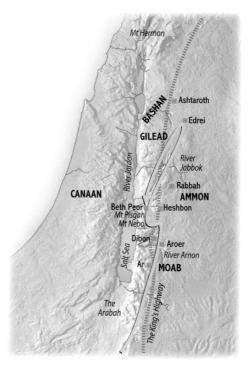

Israel east of the Jordan: defeat of Sihon and Og

There are some interesting minor changes here. Under the sabbath law, Moses adds 'so that your manservant and your maidservant may rest, as you do', and 'Remember that you were slaves in Egypt...' (instead of basing this law on God's rest after the creation). Under respect for parents, after 'that you may live long' he adds 'and that it may go well with you'. And the tenth commandment here places the wife first, setting her apart from possessions.

Chapter 6: the great commandment and instructions to teach future generations. Jesus said that the whole law could be summed up in the words of verse 5 and Leviticus 19:18 (see Matthew 22:37-40).

Chapters 7 – 11: Moses calls the nation to faith and obedience. Here Moses turns from the past to the present and future. Israel will soon be right in amongst the pagan nations. They will taste the heady glory of victory (chapter 7). Prosperity will bring an unprecedented rise in the

Covenants and Near Eastern treaties
Gordon Wenham

The Hittite code of laws inscribed on this tablet followed the familiar treaty pattern we can see in the record of God's covenant with Israel.

Hebrew uses the same word for an international treaty and a covenant between God and his people. Study has shown that similarities between ancient Near Eastern treaties and Old Testament covenants extend much further than this, and considerable light has been shed on the characteristics of Old Testament covenants, and our understanding of the Old Testament generally, by comparing them with treaties.

Most of the ancient treaties discovered this century date from about 1500 to 600 BC, a period in which much of the Old Testament was composed. It therefore seems likely that the writers would have been familiar with the way in which treaties were drafted. Furthermore their use of treaty terms and ideas shows that they found the relationship between treaty-partners an apt picture of that between God and his people.

The earliest covenant recorded in Scripture was made with Noah (Genesis 9). Covenants were also made with Abraham (Genesis 15, 17). But by far the most important covenant in the Old Testament is the covenant of Sinai (Exodus 19ff.). Though Sinai is commonly thought of as the occasion when God's law was made known to Israel, in fact the law-giving was only one part of a much larger event, the call of Israel to be a holy nation owing exclusive allegiance to the Lord. The new relationship was termed a covenant.

The covenant made at Sinai was the decisive step in the creation of Israel as a nation; all subsequent covenants looked back to Sinai as their model, and in a sense were regarded as renewals of it.

Covenants resemble treaties in three principal respects: language, form and ideology.

Covenant language
The purpose of a treaty is to secure the entire allegiance of a vassal-king or state to the other partner in the treaty, whether it be a king or an empire. To this end florid and rhetorical language is used in the treaties to stir the emotions of the vassal and impress on him the importance of obedience.

Rhetorical style has long been regarded as characteristic of Deuteronomy, a work that in other respects bears a close resemblance to a vassal treaty. Certain terms are used in treaties to describe an obedient vassal's behaviour. A good vassal should 'go after', 'fear', 'love', 'hearken to the voice of his lord. A rebellious vassal 'sins'. This phraseology is often echoed in the Old Testament.

The covenant form
The most striking similarity between treaties and Old

standard of living. There will be much to enjoy (chapter 8). And all these things bring dangers: the danger of losing their identity as God's people; the danger of false pride (chapter 9), of patting themselves on the back for all they have achieved; the danger of leaving God out of account.

But if they will let it, the past can keep them on the right lines for the future. So Moses urges them: 'Remember'; 'Do not forget.' Remember Egypt (7:18). Remember the desert years (8:2). God is driving the nations out because of their wickedness, not your righteousness (9:4): remember your own failings (9:7). Remember God's love, his power, his provision, his law, his judgments. And let that memory keep you humble, faithful, obedient (chapters 10 – 11).

▶ **Tie them... bind them... write them (6:9; 11:18-20)** Ordinary people possessed no copy of the law, so it was to be taught by word of mouth, and important parts written down where they could not fail to see it. The whole law was

> *Hear, O Israel: The Lord our God, the Lord is one. Love the Lord your God with all your heart and with all your soul and with all your strength.*
>
> 6:4-5

Testament covenants is in their form, in their basic outline structure. The classical Near Eastern treaty used by the Hittites had six parts:

1. A preamble naming the author of the treaty.
2. A historical prologue setting out the relations between the parties prior to signing the treaty.
3. Stipulations explaining the mutual responsibilities of the partners.
4. A document clause describing the treaty document and arranging for the vassal to read it at regular intervals.
5. A list of gods witnessing the treaty.
6. Curses and blessings, threatening the vassal with illness, death, deportation, etc. if he breaks the treaty, but promising him prosperity and blessing if he remains faithful.

Old Testament covenants have a similar though not identical structure. For instance, believing in one God, they omitted the list of gods as witnesses.

Deuteronomy contains most elements of the treaty form:

1 – 3	Historical prologue
4 – 26	Stipulations
27	Document clause
28	Blessings and curses.

Exodus 19 – 24, Joshua 24, and 1 Samuel 12 are other shorter examples of the treaty form in the Old Testament, though here the form is modified a little by its incorporation into narrative.

Covenant ideology

Treaties and covenants both begin with history and both insist on the grace and mercy of the author of the covenant. The Hittite king can remind his vassal of his kindness in allowing him to continue as king of the vassal state in spite of his recent rebellion. God in similar tones reminds Israel of his mercy, 'I am the Lord your God, who brought you out of the land of Egypt' (Exodus 20:2).

In both treaties and covenants, the basis of the stipulations is the undeserved favour of the overlord. Stipulations or laws come after the vassal has been reminded of what the treaty-lord has done for him. He is expected to obey the stipulations out of gratitude. Similarly in the Old Testament, law follows grace. Because of the way God has saved them, Israel is encouraged to obey.

Blessing and prosperity are promised if the vassal remains obedient, but curses are invoked on him if he rebels. Drafters of treaties and the authors of the Old Testament, well knowing the human heart, tend to dwell much more on the curses than the blessings. Appalling pictures are drawn of the sufferings the people will endure if they disregard the demands of the covenant (see Deuteronomy 28:15-68). Prophetic threats of coming judgment often echo these covenant curses. The prophets remind the people that the covenant relationship involves responsibility as well as privilege (e.g. Amos 3:2).

The Dead Sea Scrolls show that covenant ideas continued to be important in Jewish theology up to the New Testament era. Jesus himself clearly assumed that his disciples were familiar with covenant thinking, when he referred to his death as inaugurating the new covenant (Mark 14:24).

> **❝** *These commandments that I give you today are to be upon your hearts. Impress them on your children. Talk about them when you sit at home and when you walk along the road, when you lie down and when you get up.* **❞**

6:6-7

> **❝** *The Lord did not set his affection on you and choose you because you were more numerous than other peoples... it was because the Lord loved you.* **❞**

7:7-8

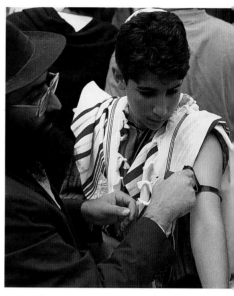

'Tie these commandments as symbols on your hands and bind them on your foreheads,' God instructed – and Jews today obey this to the letter. The 'phylactery' an Orthodox Jew wears on his forehead contains key verses of the law. At a boy's Bar Mitzvah (his 'coming of age' as a Jew) the law is bound to his arm. Both thoughts and actions are subject to God's will.

also engraved on plastered stones and set up in public places (see 27:1-10; Joshua 8:32).

Orthodox Jews literally bind miniature copies of verses from Exodus and Deuteronomy in small boxes called tefillin/ 'phylacteries' to right arm and forehead. Those discovered from New Testament times were much smaller than present-day ones. They also fasten small cylinders containing the verses to the doorposts of their houses.

▶ **Cisterns/wells (6:11)** Pits for storing water collected from rainfall or from a spring. The inside was coated with waterproof mortar. The pits narrowed at the top to reduce evaporation.

▶ **Massah (6:16)** See Exodus 17:6-7.

▶ **7:2ff.** 'Make no treaty... show no mercy'. Since God was responsible for victory in a holy war, the captives and all the spoil were God's to save or to destroy. Not everyone can have been slain, since Israel is warned not to intermarry with these peoples. As Lord of history, God brings judgment on the Canaanites — as he will later bring judgment on his own people. See 8:19, 20 and 'Holy War'.

▶ **Anakim (9:2)** See on Numbers 13:22.

▶ **10:6-9** The change to the third person here

points to a later insertion of text. The source is not known.

▶ **Seventy (10:22)** See Genesis 46:26, 27. This number did not include the wives and daughters of Jacob's sons.

▶ **Dathan and Abiram (11:6)** See Numbers 16.

▶ **Not like the land of Egypt (11:10)** There the vegetable crops depended on irrigation, using water from the Nile.

▶ **Blessing and curse: Gerizim... Ebal (11:26ff.)** See chapters 27 – 28.

12 – 26 Detailed laws

Chapters 12 – 13: idols, offerings, offenders.

12:1-14: all the places where the Canaanites practised their depraved rites are to be wiped out. Israel is not to use them. When the nation is settled God will select one specific place for the sacrifices. Shiloh was the nation's first religious centre, under Eli and Samuel. From David and Solomon's time Jerusalem, with its Temple, was God's holy city, though after Solomon's death the breakaway tribes set up two rival shrines for the northern kingdom.

12:15-28: meat was not a staple food for the ordinary Israelite, but all enjoyed it at feasts and sacrifices. On the matter of the blood, see Leviticus 17:10ff. and 'Sacrifice'.

12:29 – 13:18: the danger of being enticed away to false religions was very real. Anyone found on investigation (13:14) to have encouraged this must be made an example of and destroyed. It would be fatal for God's people to adopt the religious practices which had brought destruction on Canaan.

Chapter 14: mourning; clean and unclean food; animals; tithes.

Verses 1-2: pagan mourning practices are forbidden.

Verses 3-21: see Leviticus 11.

Verses 22-29: the tithe – see also Leviticus 27 and Numbers 18. As a reminder that all wealth is God's gift a proportion is to be regularly set aside. Jewish writers generally see the tithe (one-tenth) here as a 'second tithe', the first being given to the Levites. It provides an occasion for people to enjoy the results of their labour, and to share generously with others.

Chapter 15: the seventh year. Every seventh year the debts of fellow-Israelites must be cancelled and all fellow-Israelite slaves must be set free. See on Leviticus 25.

Verses 19-23: see on Leviticus 27.

16:1-17: the three main feasts.

See the full list, Leviticus 23, and 'The great festivals'. Three times each year – Passover, Weeks (Pentecost), Tabernacles (Shelters) – all Israelite men were required to come with a gift to the national place of worship. But these are not men-only festivals. They are to be enjoyed 'with your children, your servants, and the Levites, foreigners, orphans and widows who live in your towns'.

16:18 – 17:20: justice and judgments (16:18 – 17:13); the future king (14 – 20).

God requires a just, fair and impartial judiciary. No bribes are to be accepted, 'for gifts blind the eyes even of wise and honest men'. Sacrifice is not a way to get rid of defective animals. A death sentence may be carried out only on the clear testimony of two or more witnesses (which throws doubt on the legality of the trial of Jesus). Local judges must refer hard cases to higher authority at the nation's place of worship: that judgment is final.

Verses 14-20: God permits the monarchy, but does not set it up. The dangers foreseen here – military aggression, and sensuality leading to idolatry – became an uncomfortable reality later in Israel's history. God's law is the king's unfailing guide.

Chapter 18: revenue for priests and Levites (1-8); pagan rites (9-13); the future prophet (14-22).

Verses 1-8: see also Numbers 18.

Verses 9-14: compare Leviticus 18:3, 24-30; 20:1-6.

Verses 14-22: the true prophet is one like Moses; his words are proved true by events.

Chapter 19: cities of refuge (1-13); boundaries (14); witnesses (15-21).

Three cities of refuge in Canaan are added to the three east of the Jordan (4:41-43). Joshua 20 lists them as: Kedesh, Shechem, Kiriath-arba (Hebron), Bezer, Ramoth and Golan.

Chapter 20: rules for war. The text envisages a holy war (see article in Joshua). God goes with the army and gives the victory.

Those who have built a new house or planted a new vineyard, the newly married, and the fainthearted are excused military service.

Verses 10-18 make a distinction between the treatment of Canaanite nations and those further afield.

Verse 19: even under siege the fruit trees must not be cut down – 'they are not your enemies'.

Chapter 21: murder by an unknown hand (1-9); women captives (10-14); right of the

'Do not remove your neighbour's boundary stone,' says God's law. This boundary stone records a gift of land.

firstborn (15-17); sons beyond parental control (18-21); execution by hanging (22-23).

1-9 and 10-14: God sets a basic value and dignity on every human life. He is the advocate for those with no voice or power. The meaning of the ritual in 1-8 is uncertain, but corporate guilt and responsibility are real. The elders swear that their city is blameless.

10-14: the treatment of women captives here is in marked contrast to the cruel practices of neighbouring nations. Their pagan background is no barrier to marriage. (Interestingly in terms of the salvation story, Joseph's marriage to the daughter of an Egyptian priest, and Moses' marriage to the daughter of a Midianite priest are recorded as a matter of fact, with no hint of censure.)

15-17: the normal risk of favouritism within the family is made worse by polygamy (see Jacob's story). The rights of the firstborn need protection.

The promised land

Colin Chapman

If God is to put right any of the things that have gone wrong in the human race, how is he to do it? The book of Genesis explains how God begins his plan by calling Abraham to move from his home country (in the present Iraq) and to settle in a new land (the area now known as Israel/Palestine).

God commits himself through a special 'covenant' to do four things:
- to make Abraham's descendants into 'a great nation' (12:2);
- to give them the land of Canaan 'as an everlasting possession' (17:8);
- to enter into a special relationship to be their God (17:7);
- and to bring blessing to 'all peoples on earth' (12:2-3).

The book of Genesis goes on to describe how one obstacle after another to the fulfilment of the plan has to be overcome.

A famine in the land, for example, forces Abraham to migrate for a time to Egypt (12:10-20). Then a quarrel between the families of Abraham and his nephew Lot makes it look as if both families will not be able to settle in the land together (13:1-18).

Abraham for many years owns no land until he buys a plot of land in Hebron to bury his wife Sarah (23:1-20).

Later, when there is another famine in the land, Jacob takes his whole family down to Egypt to join Joseph. But he is determined that the family's connection with the land will not be broken, and makes his sons promise that they will bury him in the family grave in the land (49:29-33).

And the book of Genesis ends with Joseph, just before his death, making his brothers promise that they will bury him too in the land of their fathers (50:24-26).

In the rest of the Old Testament four major themes are developed concerning the land:
- The land *belongs to God*, because '... the land is mine...' (Leviticus 25:23).
- The gift of the land is *conditional*. If the people consistently fail to live up to the moral standards that God has set, they lose the right to live there and will be thrown out of the land (Deuteronomy 4:27).

- If the people during a time of exile turn back to God in repentance, they will *return to the land* (Deuteronomy 30:1-5).
- God holds out the promise that one day *the land will be transformed* as part of 'new heavens and a new earth' (Isaiah 65:17-25).

Some today interpret the promise of the land as an 'everlasting possession' very literally, and believe that the Jewish people today as the descendants of Abraham have a divine right to claim ownership of the land.

The majority of Christian scholars, however, believe that all the different promises contained in the original covenant God made with Abraham – concerning the nation, the land, the covenant relationship between God and his people, and the blessing for all humankind – find their fulfilment in the coming of the kingdom of God through Jesus.

Paul describes all believers in Jesus – whatever their nationality – as 'Abraham's seed and heirs according to the promise'

The disobedient son of verses 18-21 is in deliberate and repeated breach of the fifth commandment (5:16). The community is responsible for dealing with him. (There is no mention in the Old Testament of this sentence being carried out.)

Chapter 22: lost animals and lost property (1-4); keeping the sexes distinct (5); birds'-nesting (6-7); building, farming, clothing (8-12); sexual relations (13-30).

These are rules which encourage attitudes of mutual help and care, and a concern for sexual purity.

Chapter 23: membership of the congregation (1-8); social rules (9-25).

The Lord's community is both inclusive (7-8) and exclusive (1-6). It is marked by purity and holiness (10-14, 17-18) and practical humanity (15-16, 19-20).

Chapter 24: divorce and remarriage (1-4); humanitarian laws (5-22).

Children view the land God promised his people, from the top of Mt Nebo, where Moses died.

(Galatians 3:29). Christians therefore think of themselves as members of a worldwide family of faith, and their 'inheritance' as members of that family consists of everything that is offered to them by Jesus Christ.

When interpreted in this light, 'the promised land' of the Old Testament period is the scene of God's gradual revelation of himself – a revelation which would eventually lead to its climax in the coming of Jesus. It also points forward to the hope of 'new heavens and a new earth, where righteousness is at home' (2 Peter 3:13).

The Israelites camped in places like this on their wilderness journey.

Verses 1-4: Moses is not instituting divorce (that was probably taken for granted), though there must be genuine grounds and the rejected wife must be give a 'certificate'. The issue is remarriage and, perhaps, the protection of the second marriage. Contrast Jesus' teaching on divorce: Matthew 5:31,32; 19:1-12.

Verses 5-22: even in exercising their rights, God's people are to be thoughtful of others. To take away one millstone, for example, left the other useless for grinding flour to make the day's bread. No one may be punished for another's offences: not parents for their children nor children for their parents (16). Ruth and Naomi were just two of the widows and foreigners who benefited from the harvesting rules spelt out in verses 19-22.

Chapter 25: corporal punishment (1-3); compassion for working animals (4); the Levirate marriage law (5-10); fights (11-12); fair weights (13-16); punishment of the Amalekites (17-19).

Verses 1-3: the lash is to punish guilt, not extract confession. It must never take away human dignity or self-respect. The 40 lashes later became 39, for fear of inadvertently overstepping the limit (see 2 Corinthians 11:24).

Verses 5-10: the Levirate (from Latin *levir*, 'husband's brother') law was intended to prevent the calamity of a man

dying without an heir. It was not unique to Israel. See Ruth (and, for the sandal custom, Ruth 4:7).

Conflict with the Amalekites (17ff.) is repeatedly recorded, from 1 Samuel 14 to 2 Samuel 8.

Chapter 26: firstfruits and tithes (1-15); the summing up (16-19).

The instructions are for 'after you come into the land', when the good things promised come to fruition. The firstfruits ceremony includes the recital of a lovely prayer of remembrance and praise summarizing Israel's career.

Verses 16-19: blessing comes through obedience. Israel's is a high destiny, to bring God praise and fame and glory.

▶ **Do not cook...** (14:21) This may relate to a Canaanite fertility rite.

▶ **Asherah... pillar** (16:21-22) Wooden images, and symbols of pagan deities.

▶ **A prophet like me** (18:15) God raised up many prophets in succeeding centuries, but none measured up to the expectations aroused by this prediction. The New Testament sees in this a reference to the prophet par excellence, Jesus himself (John 5:46; Acts 3:22-26).

▶ **Avenger of blood** (19:6) The dead man's next of kin, whose duty it was to avenge his death. The regulations here are designed to prevent the development of a blood-feud.

▶ **Landmark** (19:14) A stone inscribed with the boundaries of the property.

▶ **Retaliation (19:21)** See Leviticus 24.

▶ **Completely destroy (20:17)** In contrast to the compassion and humanity of verses 1-11 and the spirit of conservation in verses 19-20 this ruling seems incredibly harsh. The concern is the danger to Israel of the evil and corrupt religious practices of the Canaanite nations. Genesis 15:16 indicates that God gave the people of Canaan four centuries, all the time Israel was in Egypt, to change their ways.

▶ **Shave her head (21:12)** A sign of purification from heathenism, or of mourning.

▶ **Under God's curse (21:23)** Paul applies this to Jesus' crucifixion (Galatians 3:13-14).

▶ **22:5** A rule intended to protect against perversion and immorality, perhaps related to a reversal of sexual roles in some Canaanite religious rites.

▶ **22:8** These were houses with flat roofs which served as extra space for work and relaxation — hence the risk.

▶ **22:9-11** People should not obliterate the clear distinctions God has made in nature.

▶ **Tassels (22:12)** See Numbers 15:37-41.

▶ **Proof of virginity (22:14)** The bloodstained cloth from the wedding-night is the innocent woman's protection against false charges. Alternatively, the evidence may relate to eligibility for marriage — proof that she was menstruating, and not pregnant at the time.

▶ **Assembly of the Lord (23:1)** This is more precise than 'the Lord's people' (Good News Bible). The assembly was called together, among other things, to take part in worship with its strict rules for ritual 'cleanness'.

▶ **23:1 and 17-18** Eunuchs and prostitutes are excluded as a protest and safeguard against Canaanite cultic practices. Contrast verse 1 with Isaiah 56:3-5.

▶ **23:2** A condemnation, not of the individuals concerned, but of the illicit sexual relationship in which they were conceived.

▶ **Balaam (23:4)** See Numbers 22 – 24.

▶ **23:15,16** This humane ruling contrasts with the earlier Near Eastern Hammurabi Code, which makes the harbouring of a runaway slave punishable by death. Paul's letter to Philemon provides an interesting New Testament comment.

▶ **Interest (23:19-20)** In the absence of security, ancient interest rates might be as high as 50 per cent.

▶ **23:24** The generous rules of hospitality to strangers are not to be abused.

▶ **Leprosy (24:8)** The term includes various skin diseases, as recent translations make clear. See Leviticus 13 – 14.

▶ **Miriam (24:9)** See Numbers 12.

▶ **Muzzling the ox (25:4)** The New Testament extends this principle — see 1 Corinthians 9:3-14.

▶ **A wandering Aramaean (26:5)** After leaving Ur, Abraham stayed in Aram-naharaim, where some of his family settled (to be known as Aramaeans) while he journeyed on to Canaan. Isaac's wife Rebecca came from this branch of the family, and the ties were strengthened in Jacob's years of exile and through his wives.

27 On entering Canaan

These are the instructions for the people when they enter the land. First and foremost is the renewing of the covenant. The curses and blessings are an integral part of this (see 'Covenants and Near Eastern treaties').

27:1-10: the law is recorded. See on 6:9.

27:11-26: the ceremony on Mt Ebal.

Moses points to the two distant mountains either side of Shechem in the hills of Samaria. From Gerizim the blessings are to be pronounced, from Ebal the curses.

With six tribes on either side, the Levites are to pronounce God's curse on 12 infringements of the law, the people adding their 'Amen' – 'So be it'. Four of these (five if moving a boundary mark is seen as theft of land) relate to the Ten Commandments: idolatry, respect for parents, murder (in secret or as a paid hit-man). Four concern forbidden sexual relations. Two are humanitarian. And the final one is a catch-all.

See Joshua 8:30-35 for an account of the actual event.

▶ **Verse 15** The second commandment: see 5:8; Exodus 20:4.

▶ **Verse 16** The fifth commandment: see 5:16; Exodus 20:12.

▶ **Verse 17** See 19:14.

▶ **Verse18** See Leviticus 19:14.

▶ **Verse 19** See 24:17-18; Exodus 22:21; 23:9; Leviticus 19:33-34.

▶ **Verse 20** See 22:30; Leviticus 18:8; 20:11.

▶ **Verse 21** See Exodus 22:19; Leviticus 18:23; 20:15.

▶ **Verse 22** See Leviticus 19:19; 20:17.

▶ **Verse 23** Leviticus 18:17; 20:14.
▶ **Verses 24-25** The sixth commandment: see 5:17; Exodus 20:13.
▶ **Verse 26** 'Law' (*torah*) means teaching: here it is probably the whole teaching of Deuteronomy that is meant. Paul quotes this verse in Galatians 3:10, arguing that 'no one is ever justified before God by means of the law'... 'Christ bought us freedom from the curse of the law'.

❝ *I have set before you life and death, blessings and curses. Choose life so that you and your descendants may live, loving the Lord your God, obeying him, and holding fast to him; for that means life to you.* **❞**

Moses' words to Israel, 30:19-20

28 Covenant blessings and curses

These are the formal 'covenant sanctions' of the treaty.

28:1-14: six blessings, 'if you obey', are pronounced. These are the material blessings of peace, prosperity, a fruitful land, children, victory in war. Above all, God 'will make you his own people'.

28:15-68: the remainder of the chapter spells out the consequences of disobedience. Verses 15-19 have the same rythmic pattern in the Hebrew as 3-6. The curses are opposites of the blessings: disease, famine, defeat, subservience, and ultimately exile, loss of homeland and all the joys of life.

Some of this catalogue of horror was later to befall the people, even to the obscenities of siege (52-57: see 2 Kings 6:24-30; Lamentations 2).

Israel's whole peace and well-being, their life, rests on right relationship with God; to be cut off from this is death – as Moses is about to spell out in his final address.

29 – 30
Third address: the call to commitment

Moses' life is fast drawing to a close. He puts his whole heart into this final appeal. He pleads (29:2-15). He warns (16-28). He encourages (30:1-14; God is ready to forgive and restore even those who have forsaken him). He confronts them with the choice: life (loving God and keeping his commands) or death (forsaking God), blessing or curse (15-20).

▶ **29:1** In the Hebrew Bible this is the last verse of chapter 28.

▶ **29:5-6** The voice of God breaks into the narrative, speaking directlly to the people. Is there any care like God's care? Was there ever a more dependent people?
▶ **29:14,15** The covenant is not with this generation alone, but with future generations as yet unborn.
▶ **29:23** Four cities at the southern end of the Dead Sea (Genesis 10:19) which met a catastrophic end. See Genesis 19:24ff. and Hosea 11:8.
▶ **Secret things (29:29)** Some things about God and his plans are known only to him (see Acts 1:7). The important thing here is not what is hidden: God's people have all they need to know in the law.
▶ **30:11-14** Moses speaks of the accessibility of God's word. Paul, in Romans 10:5-8, takes the thought and applies it to Christ, the Word made flesh.

31 – 34
Last words, and death, of Moses

31 The succession

Joshua is formally appointed and commissioned by God (14ff.) as the people's new leader (see Numbers 27:12-23). 'Be strong', 'Don't be discouraged', Moses tells him, 'God himself will be with you.'

The law is safely deposited with the Levites, and provision made for regular public reading. Throughout their subsequent history, Israel prospered in so far as they listened to God's word and obeyed it.

32:1-47 Moses' song

The literary form behind this song is that o a covenant lawsuit: it is an indictment and accusation (15-18), with heaven and earth called to witness.

God instructs Moses to warn his people of their future treacherous disloyalty in song (31:19), to be learned and remembered. And as Moses had sung the song of victory at the escape from Egypt (Exodus 15) so now he sings a last song – a record of disobedience. By contrast 'the song of Moses, the servant of God, and the song of the Lamb' in Revelation 15 is the song of the faithful who have withstood the forces of evil.

▶ **Apple of his eye (10)** The pupil, on which sight depends.

▶ **Jeshurun (15)** A poetic name for Israel.

32:48-52 One last look

God tells Moses to climb Mt Nebo in order to see the promised land. He cannot enter it because he failed to honour God in the matter of water from the rock at Meribah (Numbers 20:1-13) – an incident that became an example for ever of the stubbornness of God's people (Psalm 95:8).

33 Moses blesses the tribes

After all the warnings, this last blessing (although difficult to interpret) looks forward to a great and glorious future for Israel. From the historical allusions to the different tribes, it seems to focus on a time when the tribes had settled, maybe the 11th century. Simeon is not mentioned: his people were later absorbed by Judah. The blessing begins and ends with praise to God, the source of all security and prosperity for his people. (Compare Moses' blessing with Jacob's blessing in Genesis 49.)

▶ **Verses 2-5** The law-giving at Sinai is pictured as an eastern sunrise.

▶ **Let Reuben live (6)** The tribe's numbers were reduced through the rebellion of Dathan and Abiram (Numbers 16).

▶ **Thummim and Urim (8)** Two objects kept in the high priest's breastplate by which he ascertained God's will (see Exodus 28:30).

▶ **Massah, Meribah (8)** See Exodus 17 and Numbers 20.

▶ **Between his shoulders (12)** Either a picture of God as Shepherd, carrying his lamb, or a reference to God's house at Jerusalem, which would be built on Benjamite territory.

▶ **Joseph (13)** No tribe carried Joseph's name: the tribes of Ephraim and Manasseh were named after Joseph's sons.

▶ **Choicest fruits (14)** The valleys of Ephraim and Manasseh were laden with fruit, year by year.

▶ **Verse 18** Zebulun's success was in commerce, Issachar's in agriculture and domestic life.

▶ **Verse 23** The fertile land south and west of the Sea of Galilee.

▶ **Oil (24)** Asher's territory was famous for its olives.

34:1-8 The death of Moses

Numbers 27:12-14 and Deuteronomy 3:23-28; 32:48-52 also tell of Moses' last days. At last he sees the land he has for 40 years longed to enter. Israel sees Moses no more. But he appears once again in Scripture – on a mountain, talking to the Lord (Mark 9:2-4).

▶ **Sight undimmed... vigour unimpaired (7)** This is intended to be a figure of speech.

34:9-12 Conclusion

The action now passes to Joshua – but the book closes with a simple and moving tribute to the greatest of all Israel's leaders. Remember, remember Moses. There is none like him.

Israel's History

JOSHUA TO ESTHER

John Taylor

In the Hebrew Bible the account of Israel's history was in two separate sections:

- *The Prophets* included Joshua, Judges, 1 and 2 Samuel, 1 and 2 Kings;
- *The Writings* included 1 and 2 Chronicles, Ezra and Nehemiah. (Ruth and Esther are also included here, among 'the five scrolls', the Megilloth, grouped together because they were used at Jewish festivals: Ruth at Pentecost; Esther at Purim.)

Prophetic history

The historical narrative from Joshua to 2 Kings was in fact given the title 'The Former Prophets' in Hebrew. This was to distinguish the books from the Latter Prophets – Isaiah, Jeremiah, Ezekiel – and the twelve minor prophets. They may have been classed as prophecy because the main aim of the books was to teach rather than merely to chronicle; or else because they are the history not so much of the nation as of the way God's word was being fulfilled in the nation's life.

This group of six books (not counting Ruth) has been regarded by many scholars as one complete historical work. Some call it the 'Deuteronomic history', because the theological viewpoint expressed is similar to that of Deuteronomy.

Compiling the 'prophetic history'

If the books are treated as a basic unity in this way, the earliest date that could be given to the entire work would be shortly after the last event in 2 Kings – the release of King Jehoiachin from prison in 561 BC. However, this would apply only to the latest editorial work. Most of the material is much earlier and contemporary sources were often used.

Sources quoted in the text include the *Book of Jashar* (perhaps an ancient national song-book of Israel), the *Book of the Acts of Solomon* and the *Chronicles of the Kings of*

Judah and Israel (unconnected with the books of Chronicles in our Bible). These were court archives, or popular histories based on them. They illustrate two things:

- the amount of historical writing that had gone on in Israel during the monarchy;
- and the number of written sources which were available to the biblical authors. It is fair to assume that the sources quoted were not the only ones used, and that other writings – such as a Court History of David and a collection of Elijah-Elisha stories – were also freely drawn upon.

The books and their content

The period covered by these books extends from Joshua's entry into the land of Canaan until the middle of the exile. Most scholars prefer the late 13th-century date for the conquest to an earlier one in the 15th century. They would see the events of Joshua and Judges as taking place between 1240 and 1050 BC. Recently the early date (which appears to accord with 1 Kings 6:1) has received strong support from David Rohl's revised chronology of the pharaohs (see 'Egypt' for comment).

Joshua covers the life-span of Moses' successor and describes the conquest of Canaan from the crossing of the River Jordan to the covenant-renewal ceremony at Shechem which established the tribes in a united allegiance to the Lord God. Space is also given to a detailed description of the apportionment of Canaan among the twelve tribes (Joshua 13 – 21).

Judges begins with a reminder that the conquest under Joshua was by no means complete and that the territory assigned to almost every tribe still contained pockets of enemy resistance. In fact, this was the setting for the whole book, for throughout the period of the Judges individual tribes suffered from the incursions of hostile neighbours (or former residents!) and the judges, or 'liberators', were raised up to lead the tribes against them in open battle or guerrilla warfare.

Chief among these were:

- *Deborah and Barak* who led the combined forces of Zebulun and Naphtali against the Canaanites under Sisera
- *Gideon* of Manasseh who defeated the Midianites and Amalekites
- *Jephthah* the Gileadite who subdued the Ammonites

The historical books relate the story of Israel in the land God promised to give them.

■ and *Samson* the Danite who was the scourge of the Philistines.

The book ends with two bizarre episodes. The first describes the establishment of a new sanctuary for the tribe of Dan (Judges 17 – 18). The second deals with the punishment of the Benjamites for an outrage committed by the people of Gibeah (Judges 19 – 21).

So far the historical element in the writings has been relatively small: the style has been episodic, occasionally moralistic, and owing a good deal to the art of storytelling.

With **1 and 2 Samuel** (the division between them is artificial and probably due only to the limited length of a single scroll) we begin to have a more chronological record of events, and this is particularly true of the story of David.

Samuel is an important figure at the start, being judge and prophet combined, but the interest is really focussed on the question of whether or not to have a king, and Samuel fades into the background as first *Saul* and then *David* dominate the scene. Saul probably reigned from shortly after the defeat at Aphek in 1050 BC, when the Ark of the Covenant was captured by the Philistines, until about 1011 BC. David reigned from then until 971 (from Hebron for the first seven years and then from Jerusalem).

1 and 2 Kings continue the record, from the accession of Solomon to his father's throne, through the break-up of the kingdom 40 years later, and the continuing rivalry between the northern and southern kingdoms of Israel and Judah. This lasted until Israel became absorbed into the Assyrian Empire after the fall of Samaria in 722/1 BC. After that, Judah survived precariously for over a century, experiencing a miraculous deliverance from an Assyrian siege in the reign of Hezekiah and enjoying the extensive reforms of Josiah's reign (640-609). Then came the collapse before the Babylonian forces under Nebuchadnezzar, culminating in the fall of Jerusalem and exile in Babylon. The gloom of defeat is alleviated only by the concluding words of 2 Kings which tell of the release of King Jehoiachin from his Babylonian prison-cell. The hope of a survivor to keep alive David's line had not been totally extinguished.

Key themes

Kingship One of the main points of interest in this prophetic or 'deuteronomic' history, as we have seen, is kingship: in particular King David's dynasty.

In Judges 9 there was the abortive attempt of Gideon's son, Abimelech, to establish himself as a hereditary monarch in Shechem.

In Judges 17 – 21, the evils of the day were attributed to the fact that 'there was no king in Israel; every man did what was right in his own eyes'.

In 1 Samuel, five chapters (8 – 12) are devoted to the setting up of a monarchy, though it was done rather grudgingly, since Israel was thought to be a theocracy and the Lord God was their only rightful King. But with the rise of David all such hesitations disappear, even though his personal morality left much to be desired. The high point of his reign was God's promise of a lasting succession (2 Samuel 7). The fulfilment of this word can be traced in the lives of all the subsequent kings of Judah.

Prophecy A second main interest was prophecy and the word of the Lord. The writer's treatment of Deborah and Samuel, Nathan and Gad, Ahijah and Micaiah, Elijah and Elisha, to say nothing of a number of unnamed prophets and men of God who briefly figure in his narrative, bears witness to the importance he accorded to the office of prophet. These men could make and break kings. They acted as court advisers and political watchdogs. They were the men of power because they in turn were controlled by the word of God. And, in the view of the writer, it was the word of God which controlled history. A word once spoken – the curse on the house of Ahab, for instance – inexorably worked its way to fulfilment.

Temple A third interest of the writer was the Temple at Jerusalem. From the beginning of 1 Samuel we can trace a special concern about the welfare of the Ark of the Covenant as it moved from Shiloh to Philistia, back to Kiriath-jearim and eventually was brought to Jerusalem. It was David's desire to build it a more permanent home that provided the occasion for Nathan's prophecy of the hereditary kingship. And in Solomon's time the Temple was finally erected as a permanent house for it.

Worship Finally there was the fixed standard against which all kings, good and bad, were assessed. This was primarily a matter of worship. Was Yahweh, the true God, worshipped in purity at Jerusalem during their reigns, or were foreign idolatrous influences allowed in? Were the high places (the old pagan cult-centres which had been more or less taken over for the worship of Yahweh) stamped out or allowed to continue?

By the nature of the evaluation, all the kings of Israel (the northern kingdom) fell short because they perpetuated worship at the Bethel and Dan sanctuaries which Jeroboam had set up in competition with Jerusalem.

Kings of Judah also were found wanting when for political reasons they incorporated the religious practices of a foreign overlord as a mark of submission to him. Although a number were credited with 'doing right', only Hezekiah and Josiah received unqualified commendation.

The work of the Chronicler

The second part of the account of the history of Israel, included in 'The Writings' in the Hebrew Bible, was thought to have been originally one book. The author or compiler is often called the Chronicler, though it does not necessarily follow that only one man was involved. The period before the exile was covered by 1 and 2 Chronicles, and the first 100 years after the exile by Ezra and Nehemiah. At first only the second section was incorporated into the Hebrew Bible, probably because of the overlap between Chronicles and Samuel-Kings, but subsequently 1 and 2 Chronicles were admitted. That is why in the Hebrew

Bible Ezra-Nehemiah precedes Chronicles. In order to make their original continuity apparent, the opening verses of Ezra were tacked on to the end of 2 Chronicles.

The period covered

A summary of contents clearly shows the Chronicler's particular interests and the ground covered in these four books:

- *1 Chronicles 1 – 9*: genealogies from Adam to Saul.
- *1 Chronicles 10 – 29*: the reign of David.
- *2 Chronicles 1 – 9*: the reign of Solomon.
- *2 Chronicles 10 – 36*: the history of Judah from Rehoboam to the exile.
- *Ezra 1 – 6*: the rebuilding of the Temple after the exile.
- *Ezra 7 – 10*: Ezra's arrival in Jerusalem and reforms.
- *Nehemiah 1 – 7*: Nehemiah's rebuilding of the walls of Jerusalem.
- *Nehemiah 8 – 13*: Ezra's reading of the law and Nehemiah's reforms.

From this it can be seen that the northern kingdom, Israel, is ignored, and that most space is given to David and Solomon and matters to do with the Jerusalem Temple. To this extent the author was following in the same steps as the deuteronomic historian. He was a strong advocate of David's dynasty and did not regard the northern kingdom after its secession from Judah as belonging any more to the true people of God. Similarly, when rebuilding operations were in progress on both the Temple and the city walls, he was careful to note that the Samaritans – descendants of the mixed Israelite/Assyrian population – were debarred from participating in the work, or were actively hostile to it.

Megiddo, sited on the edge of the Plain of Jezreel by the entrance to the pass through the Mt Carmel range, was the scene of countless battles in Israel's history. This model, in the museum there, shows its massive fortifications.

The first great victory in the conquest of Canaan was at Jericho. The 'city of palms' is a green, sub-tropical oasis on the edge of barren hills.

The Chronicler's concerns

The Chronicler was also an admirer of David as the chief architect and genius behind the Temple, its worship and its organization. Even though Solomon was the actual builder, the ideas all came from David's mind. This resulted in what some have regarded as an idealized picture of David, far removed from the fallible guerrilla leader-turned-monarch of the Samuel-Kings version.

There is no doubt that the Chronicler paints a different portrait, as two artists might of the same subject, but that is because his primary concern was to record those features and events which had a bearing on the Temple and its earliest origins. In keeping with this emphasis, the Chronicler was fascinated by the part played by priests and Levites, and their unique position as cultic officials. He made particular mention of King Uzziah's leprosy, brought about through his entering the Temple unlawfully to burn incense; and he took care not to involve any but priests and Levites in the dethroning of Athaliah, which also took place in the Temple.

His evaluation of the individual kings of Judah tallies with the assessment given in 1 and 2 Kings, but he was keen to give reasons for unusual features where a strict law of retribution did not appear to work out – for instance, in the tragic death of a good king such as Josiah, or the long reign of a bad king like Manasseh. Always remember that he was writing as an ecclesiastical, not a political, historian.

His interest in things priestly did not cut him off from the world of prophecy. For in addition to his extensive use of the annals – e.g. 'the book of the kings of Israel and Judah' and many similar records that no longer survive – he also made use of many collections of the sayings of the prophets, such as Samuel, Nathan, Gad and Iddo.

This encourages us to respect the painstaking care with which he assembled and selected his material.

In the Ezra-Nehemiah period the compiler was able to use memoirs of both these men (notice the use of the first person singular in Ezra 7:27 – 9:15 and Nehemiah 1: 1 – 7:5; 13:6-31). Indeed, Jewish tradition has held that Ezra was himself the Chronicler, and this is not impossible. What we can say with confidence is that the Chronicler, if there was only one, was almost certainly on the Temple staff, that he was a man of deep piety (witness the many fine prayers that his work contains), and that he wrote in the late 5th century or early 4th century BC.

Joshua

Summary

The Israelites, led by Joshua, conquer the land God has promised to them.

Chapters 1 – 12
The conquest of Canaan

•

Chapters 13 – 22
Dividing the land among the tribes

•

Chapters 23 – 24
Joshua's call to the nation

Best-known stories
Rahab and the spies
(chapter 2)
Battle of Jericho
(chapters 5 – 6)

The book of Joshua takes the story of Israel's history on from the death of Moses, through the conquest of Canaan, to the death of Joshua. Chapters 1 – 12 cover the first five or six years after Moses' death. The events recounted in the last two chapters probably took place about 20 years later.

Many of these stories were told and retold long before they were collected and arranged in their present form. The editor repeatedly adds 'to this day' for the readers of his own time (4:9 for example).

The conquest probably began somewhere about 1240 BC, according to archaeological and other evidence. It seems likely that this account was written down at the time of Israel's first kings (1045 BC), during Samuel's lifetime, and before David captured Jerusalem (see Joshua 15:63). The book of Joshua gives the impression of a swift and complete conquest of the land. Judges paints a rather different picture of ongoing struggle. Both books emphasize the importance of keeping faith with God. Obeying God is the key to the people's success under Joshua.

Joshua himself was born in Egypt. He became Moses' right-hand man during the exodus and desert wanderings. He was a fine military commander (Exodus 17:8ff.). In the law-giving at Sinai he was Moses' companion (Exodus 24:13). Joshua was one of the 12 spies sent by Moses to reconnoitre the land. He and Caleb alone had the faith and courage to recommend advance (Numbers 14:6ff.) – and in consequence were the only ones to survive the 40 years of wandering. Joshua had long been marked out as Moses' successor. The formal commission to lead the nation came directly from God as Moses' life drew to a close (Deuteronomy 31:14-15, 23).

1 – 12
Israel takes the land of Canaan

1 A new leader: Joshua

This account of Joshua's accession is one of the great chapters of the Bible. Moses is dead: but God's purpose for the nation continues. The keynote of this prelude to the conquest is the repeated call to be strong and take heart (6, 7, 9, 18).

▶ **Verse 3** See Deuteronomy 11:24-25.

▶ **This book of the law (8)** See Deuteronomy 31:24-26. Joshua was with Moses when the law was given at Sinai.

▶ **Three days (11)** Either the events of chapter 2 have already taken place, or the meaning is simply 'soon'.

▶ **Verses 12ff.** See Numbers 32:28ff.; Deuteronomy 3:18-20. Joshua 22 sees the two and a half tribes sent home.

2 Prostitute Rahab saves spies

Jericho, the 'city of palm trees', lies just west of the River Jordan. Joshua's intention was to make his first thrust into the centre of the land, driving a wedge between north and south. Jericho stood directly in his path, an obvious first target. See 'Cities of the conquest'.

Rahab's action in harbouring the spies stemmed not from fear, but from belief that Israel's God is the true God (see Hebrews 11:31, which commends her faith). The storyteller makes no attempt to 'clean up' Rahab's reputation. The tale is simply told. As Rahab saves the lives of the spies, so she and her family come under God's protection – to find a permanent home among God's people and become part of the

> *As I was with Moses, so I will be with you; I will never leave you or forsake you. Be strong and courageous.*
>
> 1:5-6

Smaller towns and villages, with mud-brick houses, would have offered little resistance to Joshua's army.

great salvation story. Rahab was naturalized, married Salmon, and through her son Boaz (see Ruth 2 – 4) became an ancestress not only of David but of Jesus himself (Matthew 1:5). It is an outstanding example of God's grace.

Rahab's house was built on or into the city wall (maybe bridging the double-walled fortifications which Jericho is known to have had some centuries before), with a flat roof on which produce could be spread out to dry – in this case flax, from which she would spin linen thread. The house of a prostitute was somewhere two men might go with no questions asked; and no doubt a good place to pick up information. The Israelites kept their promise to her (6:22ff.).

▶ **2:1** 'Shittim' means 'acacias'.
▶ **Red Sea (2:10)** See Exodus 14.
▶ **Sihon and Og (2:10)** See Numbers 21:21-35 and Joshua 12:1-6.

3 Advance across the Jordan
It was spring – the first month of the Hebrew calendar (4:19), 'Nisan', which is

March/April (see 'Israel's calendar'), approaching the time of the barley harvest. The river was swollen with Mt Hermon's melted snows, not the best time for a crossing. Yet, as the priests stepped into the flood-water, a blockage at Adam, about 29km/18 miles upstream, dammed the river, leaving the river-bed dry. (In 1927 earth tremors caused a collapse of the high clay river-banks at the same spot, and the Jordan was dammed for over 21 hours.) As with the Red Sea crossing, 40 years earlier, natural forces are employed to clear the way in a miracle of timing.

▶ **The Ark of the Covenant/Covenant Box (3)** which contained the tablets inscribed with the law was a visible symbol of God's presence, his leading and guidance.
▶ **Sanctify/consecrate/purify (5)** I.e. 'prepare yourselves before God', by ritual purification and self-examination in the light of what God requires.

4 Marking the place
To commemorate the crossing for ever after, stones are taken from the river-bed,

12 to mark the place where the priests had stood, and 12 to mark the Israelites' first base-camp in the new land, at Gilgal. (This is the same stretch of the Jordan where John the Baptist's ministry and Jesus' baptism took place.)

▶ **The men of Reuben and Gad... (12)** See on 1:12.

▶ **Verse 14** Joshua's action in leading the people across the Jordan parallels Moses' crossing of the Red Sea: his position is established, and the nation honours him.

▶ **For you... for us (23)** None of the adults who had made the Red Sea crossing, apart from Joshua and Caleb, lived to cross the Jordan. Everyone else — all those over 20 at the time of the spies' report to Moses, died in the desert for their disobedience.

5:1-12 Gilgal: Israel circumcised
The rite of circumcision had not been practised because the covenant itself had been neglected for 40 years as a result of the people's disbelief and disobedience (Numbers 14). Now the sign of circumcision marks the new generation as

God's own people. There is no fear of attack – the story of the Jordan crossing has stolen all courage from their enemies.

It is the 14th day of the first month (Nisan) – the annual date of the Passover. There will never be a Passover like this one: the first taste of the produce in their own land.

▶ **Flint knives (2)** Bronze tools had superseded stone by this time, but the traditional tools are used for the religious rite.

▶ **The manna stopped (12)** See Exodus 16:13ff. This special provision of God had never failed through all the years in the wilderness. Now it is no longer needed.

▶ **Remove your sandals (15)** The instruction echoes God's words to Moses (Exodus 3:5). Sandals were always removed before going into a house — how much more for 'holy ground'.

5:13 – 6:27 Jericho taken
The conquest of Canaan was a holy war (see 'Holy War'). God was at the head of the army. No one knew this better than Joshua, after his encounter with 'the captain of the army of the Lord' (5:13ff.).

Cities of the conquest
Alan Millard

The Bible's accounts of Israel's entry into Canaan record the actual destruction of only a few cities. Throughout, they emphasize that Israel drove out the former inhabitants and took over (inherited) their property. A desolate land with its towns in ruins would be of little benefit to the Israelites, just emerging from 40 years of semi-nomadic life. What had to be destroyed were the pagan shrines of the Canaanites with their cultic paraphernalia.

Jericho was a special case. The city was an offering to God, a 'firstfruit' of the conquest. Ai and Hazor were also sacked. But again they were exceptional cases, perhaps as focal points of opposition. If the biblical record is to be believed, then, we shall not expect to find much physical evidence of the Israelite conquest. The change of ownership probably left few recognizable marks except in the religious sphere. More cities may have been sacked at that time than Joshua and Judges indicate, but the Hebrew accounts do not demand it.

So it is misleading to try to link all signs of destruction in Canaanite cities of the Late Bronze Age with the Israelite invasion. Excavations at the sites of Bethel, Beth-shemesh, Hazor and others have all revealed signs of violent destruction during the 13th century BC, but the dates are only approximate and the cities may not all have been destroyed at the same time. After their destruction the cities were deserted, or else reoccupied on a less elaborate scale.

Invasions from Egypt and Peoples of the Sea

Israel was only one of the Canaanites' enemies, although ultimately the worst. The history of the 13th century BC includes major military actions, invasions, and a general decline in cultural standards.

Egypt's pharaoh was lord of Canaan, and of Lebanon and Damascus. His governors and officials resided in major cities (e.g. Gaza, Megiddo), and other places served as garrison towns. There were periodic rebellions which were quelled by loyal neighbours or by Egyptian forces. Following a period of Egyptian weakness, Pharaoh Seti I campaigned in Canaan and east of the Jordan about 1290 BC. Archaeologists often identify his invasion with destruction levels in ruined cities, as at Hazor. Shortly afterwards, his son, Ramesses II, had to curb a revolt following an unsuccessful battle with the Hittites in Syria. He penetrated as far as Moab at this time (about 1275 BC).

Perhaps as a result of these firm measures, once Ramesses had made peace with the Hittite king (in about 1259 BC), there was no further invasion from Egypt for over half a century.

Trouble came again in the reign of Merneptah, Ramesses' son. Little is known beyond the fact of Egyptian intervention in Canaan, and indirect evidence of continuing Egyptian control there. One record supplies the oldest non-biblical reference to Israel, as one of a number of defeated foes. Merneptah had halted a wave of invaders from the north-west, the 'Peoples of the Sea'. Egypt was safe until another wave repeated the threat, marching through Syria and Canaan as well as coming against Egypt by sea.

Sea Peoples invade ◄

This wave was stemmed by Ramesses III (about 1184-1153 BC) who destroyed the fleet and stopped the advance before it reached the frontier, re-establishing his control of Canaan for a while. But many of the invaders remained, some seizing certain cities. The Philistines, for example, took over Ashdod, Ashkelon, Ekron, Gath and Gaza; and another group took control of Dor.

All these events, and others unknown to us, brought pillage and destruction to the towns of Canaan around the time of the conquest. Neighbouring princes could create as much devastation as an invading force.

1. HAZOR

We are told that three cities — Jericho, Ai and Hazor — were set on fire by Israel.

At Hazor in Galilee, there is evidence that the last city of the Late Bronze Age was violently destroyed at some time in the 13th century BC. The ruins of the last Canaanite city were not well preserved, partly because of exposure to the elements and damage by ploughing. But enough remained to show a city of importance, even if past its zenith. Other towns of the same date are closely similar. All were well-fortified, although the city walls often incorporated (or were renovations of) earlier defences.

Cities on the main roads — Megiddo, for example — tended to be far wealthier. On the other hand the relative poverty of such sites as Tell Beit Mirsim concentrated the excavators' attention on details of pottery styles, on which Palestinian archaeology depends for its comparative chronology.

2. AI

Ai, like Hazor, presents a problem. Excavations have revealed that the city was derelict from about 2500 BC until after 1200 BC, although it was important in the earlier period.

The name Ai means 'ruin', and many see the Joshua story simply as an attempt to explain the very impressive ruins. But even accepting the archaeological evidence, it is still possible that a group of Canaanites made use of the old fortifications of this strategic stronghold in their fight against the Israelites. Such a brief occupation would have left little or no trace.

3. JERICHO

At Jericho, the site where the clearest evidence of Israel's attack might have been expected, nothing has been found to show the existence of a city there in the middle of the 13th century BC. Severe erosion of the mudbrick ruins has left little trace of some earlier periods in the city's life. For this reason, the possibility of a fortified city standing there later in the century cannot be discounted. Its ruins would have disappeared during the long desertion of the site from Joshua's time to Ahab's (about 400 years; see 1 Kings 16:34).

The city walls, thought at one time to be evidence of Joshua's attack, in fact date from a much earlier period; the excavations show a city which had already been frequently destroyed and rebuilt before the time of Joshua.

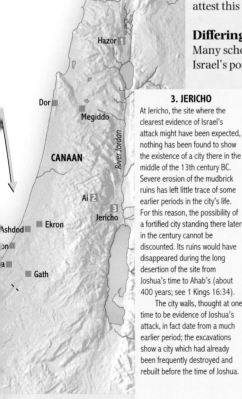

In short, we need not expect to find widespread and unmistakable signs of a specifically Israelite conquest in the ruins of Canaan. Israel's mission was in any case not totally destructive. And there were other causes of destruction. Towns may have lain deserted as a result of general turmoil, or have been only partially inhabited, until the Israelites were established in the land and able to exploit it. This they could not do fully while they were menaced by the Philistines and enemies from across the Jordan. The poor remains in several post-Canaanite (early Iron Age) sites attest this situation.

Differing views and theories

Many scholars have explained Israel's possession of the promised land in terms of a gradual infiltration by nomadic herdsmen. Or they see it as a combination of infiltration and a movement of a few tribal groups from Egypt, perhaps on more than one occasion and over several generations. Or they even envisage a general revolt of the people of the land.

These widely varying opinions are all connected with theories involving the documentary analy-

sis of the Pentateuch. These assign stories to a number of different sources, so proposing separate origins for them, and fostering views of unrelated tribal histories. Closely linked with this is a theory that the concept of Israel as a nation was formed long after the 'conquest', and read back into early times by later Israelite historians.

The idea of a gradual process is supported by analogy with other invasions and movements with peoples. It is emphasized that the occupation was limited. (Judges 1 for example lists the main Canaanite cities on the major roads as unconquered, or only occupied jointly with the native citizens.) The stories in Joshua are attributed to tribal or cultic sources. They are thought to describe what were really small, local events, or to relate folk-tales woven around the origin of ruined cities whose real history was forgotten.

It always pays to be cautious in arguing from analogies, and this is certainly so in the case of the 'conquest'. The analogies of nomadic infiltration are used in order to fit Israel into a known pattern. But all the nation's records claim that Israel was different. At best such approaches should be regarded as experimental, not factual. To rule out the account actually given in the Bible on the grounds that it is unusual is prejudiced and unscientific.

Entry into the promised land

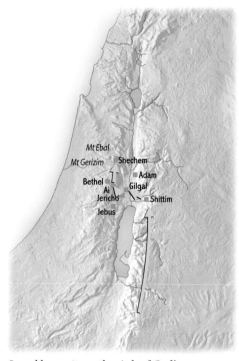

Mt Ebal
Mt Gerizim   Shechem
Bethel   ■Adam
Ai   Gilgal
Jericho   ■Shittim
Jebus

Weapons from early Israelite times.

Israel knew it, as the Ark of God's presence led the forces. And Israel's enemies knew it, and quaked (2:9-11; 5:1). It was a war of nerves for the men of Jericho; day after day the encircling troops, the trumpet-blasts, the silent army, building up to the great climax of the seventh day.

The city of Jericho has an incredibly long history of building and destruction (see 'Cities of the conquest' for the archaeological story).

▶ **Devoted things/under a ban (6:18)** The city and all its contents are dedicated utterly to God. It becomes sacrilege then, for anyone to take anything for themselves.

▶ **Outside the camp (23)** Until such time as they were 'cleansed' by a period of purification.

▶ **The curse (26)** The mound lay in ruins for 400 years, until Ahab's reign. Then Hiel rebuilt Jericho – and fell heir to the curse (see 1 Kings 16:34).

7 Achan defies God's ban

Because Achan defied God's ban (see on 6:18) 36 men died at Ai, and the whole nation was shamed before their Canaanite enemies. The disobedience of one individual touches the whole community: where wrong has been done there is corporate, as well as individual, accountability.

▶ **Ai (2)** 'The Ruin'. See 'Cities of the conquest'.

▶ **Consecrate/sanctify (13)** See on 3:5.

▶ **That I take/pick out (14)** The guilty man was discovered by means of the sacred lot, the two stones kept in the high priest's breastplate. It is not now known exactly how this was done.

▶ **Verse 24** Achor means 'Trouble'.

▶ **Verse 25** It would seem that Achan's family were also in the know and therefore to blame (see Deuteronomy 24:16).

8 Ai conquered

The evidence of the mound at Et-Tell is difficult to accord with the biblical record here – which suggests that this may not in fact be the correct site of Ai. But see 'Cities of the conquest'. Joshua's flight and ambush strategy makes capital out of Israel's previous defeat (7:2-5).

From Ai, Joshua moves 32km/20 miles north to establish himself at Shechem, in the valley between Mts Ebal and Gerizim. In God's name he takes possession of the land. And the covenant is sworn as Moses had commanded (Deuteronomy 27).

▶ **30,000 (3)** This may refer to the total force, unless there were two ambushes (12). But high numbers in the Old Testament present a real problem. See on Numbers 1.

▶ **Bethel (9)** is the place where Jacob had his vision. A well-fortified and prosperous city during Israel's early days in Egypt it had somewhat declined by Joshua's day. Either on this campaign (Bethel and Ai were only a short distance apart) or later, the king of Bethel was defeated (12:16).

9 – 10 Joshua defeats the kings of the south

Chapter 9: Gibeon was an important city about 8km/5 miles north of Jerusalem. The Israelites had been forewarned against any alliance with local people (Exodus 23:32). But the Gibeonites employ such cunning (even to the pretence that news of the recent victories at Jericho and Ai has not reached them, 9:10) that they not only get their treaty but include three other cities too (17). God is not consulted (14). And Israel cannot draw back from a treaty sealed in friendship (the meal eaten together). The worst they can do is reduce the Gibeonites to slave status (21). (King

Canaanites and Philistines
Alan Millard

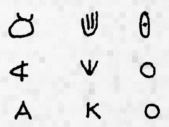

Some of the letters of the Roman alphabet, used today, with their Canaanite ancestors, about 1600 BC (top line), and Phoenician parents, about 1000 BC (middle line).

CANAANITES

'Canaan' was the name given to the coast of modern Lebanon and Israel after 2000 BC, eventually stretching inland to the River Jordan. The inhabitants included other peoples (Hivites, Jebusites...), often collectively known as Canaanites. By the time of the Israelite invasion under Joshua, Canaan consisted of a number of small towns each ruled by its own prince, nominally subject to Egypt.

Traders

The Canaanites who lived on the coast were great traders – so much so that the word 'Canaanite' came to mean 'merchant' in Hebrew. After 1000 BC, the Canaanites who had remained independent were called 'Phoenicians' by the Greeks. Their main ports were Tyre, Sidon, Beirut and Byblos in modern Lebanon. Ships from these ports carried cedar wood, oil, wine and other goods to Egypt, Crete and Greece. They brought back (for example) linen from Egypt and fine pottery from Cyprus and Greece. Papyrus was carried from Egypt to Byblos, so when the Greeks first saw papyrus scrolls they called them *biblia* ,'Byblos things', giving us the word 'Bible'.

This bronze plaque of a Canaanite was found at Hazor.

Skilled craftsmen

By the time of King Solomon the work of the Canaanite/Phoenician craftsmen was famous. Lebanese cedar was shipped down the coast from Tyre to build the Temple at Jerusalem. And Huram of Tyre could design and make the decorated bronze columns and Temple furnishings (1 Kings 5; 7:13).

The alphabet

The Babylonian cuneiform and Egyptian hieroglyphic writing systems dominated the Near East between 3000 and 1000 BC, but scribes invented other systems for different languages. In Canaan one scribe began to use a system where a picture of, for example, a door stood for its initial letter – 'd'. And so the alphabet was born.

By 1000 BC the alphabet was coming into general use in Phoenicia, Israel and other lands. The Greeks adopted it by 800 BC. Signs for sounds they did not need were used for vowels: so aleph (ox) became A.

Religion

The Canaanites worshipped Baal, god of weather and fertility, and Ashtoreth, his wife, goddess of love and war, with a host of other gods. El was the chief. Each town had its patron god or goddess. These gods did not set laws (like the Ten Commandments), although they might make cruel demands like child sacrifice – so people could behave much as they pleased. This, and its close link with good crops and fertility, made Canaanite religion easy and attractive. This is why the Israelites were told to avoid all contact (see e.g. Deuteronomy 7:1-6). Their failure to obey brought all kinds of trouble.

The furnished living-room of a typical Canaanite house.

PHILISTINES

Although some had come earlier, it was around 1200 BC that the 'Peoples of the Sea' (as the Egyptians called them), invaded the eastern Mediterranean coasts. When Egypt finally defeated them in 1175 BC they tried to take over Canaan, and fought the Israelites for the land. Eventually the Philistines kept control of five cities, each of which had its own ruler. The Philistines were subject to King David and some of his successors, remaining a distinct group into Persian times. Ultimately they gave the land its name: Palestine.

A Philistine warship.

Pottery, origins and iron

Pottery found in the Philistine region shows strong links with 'Mycenean' pottery from Greece, Crete and Cyprus. Other objects, too, point to the Philistines as foreigners from the north. The name Goliath and the word for ruler may show they spoke an Indo-European language. Iron-working was beginning to spread and the Philistines had some control of the skill. The Israelites had to take iron tools to Philistine smiths for repair and sharpening and were prevented from getting (more effective) iron weapons (1 Samuel 13:19-22).

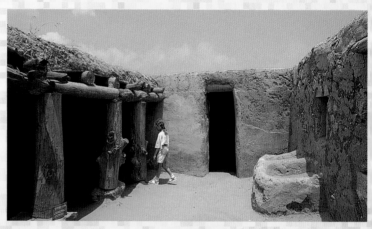

A courtyard-style Philistine house.

A soldier wears the characteristic Philistine headdress in this carving from Egypt.

The Philistine jug, with its distinctive decoration, connects these people to their north Mediterranean 'homeland'.

(Joppa)
Ashdod Ekron
Ashkelon   (Jerusalem)
                (Hebron)
Gaza   Gath
PHILISTIA

The five cities of the Philistines are marked in yellow.

Saul, 200 years later, tried to destroy the Gibeonites and God punished the nation for breaking their word. King David allowed the Gibeonites to kill seven of Saul's sons to set the matter right.)

Chapter 10: the treaty with the Gibeonites promptly involves Israel in war. All five Amorite kings are killed at Makkedah and their city-states (all except Jerusalem) destroyed in the campaign following the rout at Beth-horon. All the strategic cities of the south fall before Joshua's army. Israel now controls the land from Kadesh-barnea in the south to Gaza on the west, and as far north as Gibeon.

▶ **9:27** 'The place the Lord chose' – that is, Jerusalem.

▶ **The long day (10:12-14)** is usually taken as an extension of daylight, but it may be a prolongation of darkness. An eclipse of the sun has been suggested. Joshua's surprise attack was at dawn (as the positions of sun and moon in verse 12 also indicate) and the hailstorm increased the gloom and consequent confusion. People then believed that the earth stood still, with sun and moon moving around it – hence, Joshua's 'Sun, stand still'.

▶ **The Valley of Aijalon (12)**, on an important east-west trade route, has seen numerous battles down the centuries.

▶ **Book of Jasher (13)** A book of songs praising national heroes, referred to again in 2 Samuel 1:18. It has not survived.

▶ **Feet on the necks (24)** A customary gesture of total subjection.

▶ **Goshen (41)** A town south of Hebron, not Goshen in Egypt.

11 Joshua defeats the kings of the north

The powerful king of Hazor, commanding his vassals, assembles an even more formidable alliance than that of the south. But with no more success. Although the strategic cities were in Israel's hands within a short time of their entry into Canaan, mopping-up operations took a great deal longer (18).

▶ **Hazor (1)** A vast metropolis of 40,000 people (many times the size of Jerusalem in David's day), 16km/10 miles north of Lake Galilee. The lower city which Joshua destroyed was never rebuilt. See 'Cities of the conquest'.

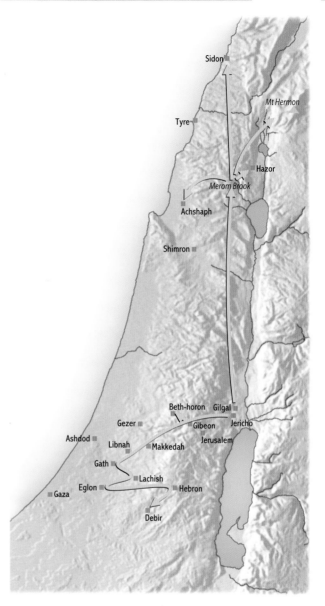

Joshua's campaigns

▶ **As far as Greater Sidon (8)** Tyre had evidently not yet risen to prominence.

▶ **The Lord made them (20)** The Bible's writers habitually attribute things directly to God as first cause with no sense that the humans involved have been robbed of their freedom to choose (see on Exodus 4:21).

▶ **The Anakim (21)** The colossal race who struck fear into the hearts of Moses' spies (Numbers 13:33).

▶ **Gaza, Gath, Ashdod (22)** All Philistine strongholds. Gigantic Goliath came from Gath (1 Samuel 17:4).

'Holy War'

Colin Chapman

Any group of people who engage in 'holy war' believe that the cause for which they are fighting is just and 'holy', and that their God will fight with them and for them in battle. Such ideas were widespread in the ancient Near East, and while the term itself is not found in the Old Testament, there are many indications that the Israelites had similar ideas:

- Yahweh, the God of Israel, is frequently described as 'the Lord of hosts' (i.e. 'the Lord of armies'). Before Joshua began the conquest of the land he came face to face with a man who described himself as 'commander of the Lord's army' (Joshua 5:14). Some years later the young David challenged the giant Goliath for daring to 'defy the armies of the living God' (1 Samuel 17:45).
- Defeat for the Canaanites during the conquest of the land under Joshua was seen as God's judgement on people whose religion and culture had become thoroughly corrupt.
- War was undertaken as a religious act and accompanied by religious rituals, like seeking guidance from God about strategy, offering sacrifices and taking religious symbols into battle.
- After victory in battle the Israelites would sometimes dedicate a whole town with its inhabitants and property to total destruction, to demonstrate that the fruit of the victory belonged to God and not to themselves.

It seems, however, that over a period of centuries popular ideas about 'holy war' were being challenged and gradually transformed:

- Although Yahweh was thought of as the God of Israel, the Israelites began to recognize that he cannot be a purely tribal God because he is also the God of the whole human race.
- War is not given blanket approval. Clear rules for engaging in war are laid down, and unnecessary acts of violence are condemned.
- The prophets frequently had to explain that the Israelites could not assume that God would automatically be on their side in every conflict with their enemies. When they failed to live up to God's moral standards, he could turn against them and defeat them in the same way that he had earlier defeated their enemies. He would judge their shortcomings even more harshly than those of their enemies.
- When the kingdoms of Israel and Judah were defeated and lost their independence, the prophets began very radically to rethink popular ideas about the relationship between God and the nation state. They came to see that the rule of God in the universe cannot be identified with the fortunes of any one particular people or state.
- These same prophets dreamed of the day when all war would be abolished. When God defeated all the forces of evil in one great final battle, nations would 'beat their swords into ploughshares

and their spears into pruning hooks' (Isaiah 2:4).
- New Testament writers never think of military conquest as a way of furthering the cause of God. They think instead of the peaceful spread of the good news about Jesus Christ.

Christians have traditionally spoken of their struggle against 'the world, the flesh (i.e. fallen human nature), and the Devil'. When faced with questions about conflict and war between peoples and nations, they have often turned to the concept of the 'just war' rather than of 'holy war' to guide them in their thinking.

What we witness in the pages of the Bible, therefore, is the gradual process by which God works in the history of a particular people for whom war is an essential part of the religion and culture. By doing so he transforms these ideas to enable all humankind to understand more clearly the nature of the world we live in.

12 Defeated Canaanite kings

Verses 1-6 rehearse the earlier victories east of the Jordan under Moses.

Verses 7-24 list 31 kings of south, central and northern Canaan defeated under Joshua. The list rounds off the section on the conquest.

13 – 21
Dividing the land

Not all the land allocated had been completely subdued – and not every tribe realized its ideal by conquering all its allotted territory. In several places, as in the previous chapters, the writer comments on the situation in his own day (13:13; 14:14; 15:63; 16:10).

13:1-7: the land still unconquered includes the Mediterranean coastlands (Philistine city-states) and land in the north (Phoenicia and Lebanon). Compare Judges 3:1-6. King David eventually subdued the Philistines, and the Syrians in the north. But Israel never controlled Phoenicia (Tyre and Sidon).

13:8-33 concerns the land east of Jordan already allotted to Reuben (15-23), Gad (24-28) and (half) Manasseh (29-33) in Moses' time. See Numbers 32:33-42; Deuteronomy 3:12-17.

14:1-5 concerns the dividing of the land west of Jordan among the remaining nine and a half tribes (excluding the Levites, who receive cities to live in, but not land). The inheritance of each tribe is decided by lot, by the high priest.

14:6-15: Caleb claims Hebron. Forty-five years after the spy episode (Numbers 13 – 14) Caleb remains a man of unwavering faith. Despite 10:21ff. there are still Anakim survivors to deal with (15:14; Judges 1:10, 20). Hebron became Levite property (21:11-13), but Caleb retained the surrounding land and villages.

Chapter 15: Judah's cities included those of Caleb – and also Jerusalem, or part of it (18:28). But the city was still unconquered much later, at the time of writing (63).

Chapters 16 – 17: the territory of

Division of the land among the tribes

Ephraim (16) and (west) Manasseh (17). These tribes were to have extended their territory by clearance and conquest. But the horses and chariots of the Canaanites holding the plains deterred them.

Chapters 18 – 19: the Israelites gather at Shiloh, the land is surveyed and Joshua distributes the land among the seven remaining tribes.

18:11-28: Benjamin's land. Jerusalem seems to have been partly on Judah's land, partly on Benjamin's (15:63; Judges 1:8, 21).

19:1-9: Simeon's land, furthest south, overlapped with Judah's, and Simeon became absorbed into the larger tribe.

19:10-16: Zebulun's land.

19:17-23: Issachar's land.

19:24-31: Asher's land.

19:32-39: Naphtali's land.

19:40-48: Dan, assigned land which brought them up against the Philistines and other tough enemies in the south, failed to conquer it and eventually settled in the far north. See also Judges 1:34; 13 (Samson belonged to the tribe of Dan); 18.

19:49-51: the division is completed with

> **❝** Not one of all the good promises the Lord your God gave you has failed. **❞**
>
> 23:14

The king of Hazor, a strong, walled city in the north, headed an alliance which Joshua's army defeated. The picture shows the city's 'high place' where the Canaanite gods were worshipped.

the gift of Timnath-serah (called Timnath-heres in Judges 2:9) to Joshua.

Chapter 20: six cities, three to the east of the Jordan, three to the west – all belonging to the Levites – are designated 'cities of refuge' (see Numbers 35:6-34; Deuteronomy 19:1-13), to protect those who caused accidental death from subsequent vengeance and blood-feud.

Chapter 21: the Levites receive no tribal inheritance: God is their inheritance. But they are given 48 cities, with pasture, by the other tribes. This provision ensures that the leaders of the nation's faith and worship are dispersed throughout the land.
▶ **Not one of all their enemies (21:44)** This

must be a generalization (the 'big picture') in view of earlier comments (and Judges 1).

22
Eastern tribes go home

Reuben, Gad and Manasseh have fulfilled their obligations to help in the conquest. Now they return home, with Joshua's blessing and a share of the spoil.

The fear that, once they are across the Jordan, Israel may at some future time disown them prompts the building of the altar which caused such misunderstanding. This was neither a sign of idolatry, nor a second sanctuary. It was a token of solidarity with the rest of Israel to whom they were bound by faith and worship of the one God.
▶ **Your own altar (16)** God had said he would choose the one place where they must worship him (Deuteronomy 12:13-14).
▶ **The sin at Peor (17)** When Israel worshipped Baal (Numbers 25).
▶ **Achan (20)** For his sin 36 men died (chapter 7).
▶ **Verse 22** A solemn oath, twice repeated, and using all three names of God: El, Elohim, Yahweh (see 'The names of God').

23 – 24
Joshua's last days

23 A call to the nation
Some years have elapsed since the division of the land. Joshua has reached the end of a long life, and is appointing no single successor. It is therefore vital to ensure that the leaders keep the law and remain faithful to God – the God who keeps his promises (23:14; see 21:45). It is God who has given them the land, God who has driven out great and powerful nations: 'You must hold fast to the Lord your God', keeping covenant with him.

24 A loyal pledge
Joshua assembles the people at Shechem to renew the covenant sworn there after their first victories in the land (8:30ff.). Here, as in Deuteronomy, the covenant pattern

follows that of contemporary treaties (see 'Covenants and Near Eastern treaties'). The King's title (2a) is followed by a rehearsal of his past favours (2b-13). The stipulations are made in 14-15, with warnings about the consequences of disobedience (19-20).

Joshua's own readiness to commit himself wholly to God remains unwavering at the end of a long life. The eagerness of the people to follow him in renewing the covenant is in itself sufficient tribute to his leadership. His 'we shall serve the Lord' is echoed and re-echoed by the voice of the people: 'We too shall serve the Lord; he is our God.' It is a high note on which to conclude the book, and verse 31 indicates the strength of Joshua's influence for good. The contrast between this and the book of Judges, which follows, is marked. Verse 32 rounds off the history of the patriarchs as Joseph's bones are buried in the promised land.

▶ **Balak... Balaam (9)** See Numbers 22 – 24.

▶ **I sent the hornet (12)** Recent versions translate this vivid image as panic.

▶ **110 (29)** This may be an ideal, symbolic age, especially since it matches that of Joseph (see

Tablets from El-Amarna, in Egypt, written by Canaanite kings to the Egyptian pharaoh, mention the problem of attack from roving bands of foreigners – the Habiru. Were these the Hebrews?

Genesis 50:22). The link is reinforced by verse 32. The promise to Joseph is kept. He is laid to rest on the only piece of land that belonged to his father, Jacob (see Genesis 33:19). The family which for long years had only burial-places purchased from the local people (see Genesis 23 for Abraham's purchase) now possesses the whole land of Canaan.

> ❝ *As for me and my household, we will serve the Lord.* ❞
>
> 24:15

Judges

Summary

The troubles which befell Israel after Joshua's death: a repeated pattern of disobedience to God, a turning back – and deliverance from enemies.

Chapters 1 – 3:6
After Joshua

•

Chapters 3:7 – 16:31
Stories of the nation's leaders, raised up to deliver them from their enemies

•

Chapters 17 – 21
The troubled times before there was a king

Best-known stories
Deborah and Barak
(chapters 4 – 5)
Gideon *(chapters 6 – 8)*
Samson *(chapters 13 – 16)*

Judges covers the period in Israel's history between Joshua's death and the rise of Samuel – roughly 1220 to 1050 BC. It was a difficult, unsettled time, when the scattered tribes were without central leadership, held together only by their common faith.

Loyalty to God meant a strong united nation: turning to the gods around brought weakness and division. That is the author's central theme as he arranges and brings together these stories of local heroes which have been told and retold down the years. He writes after the destruction of the sanctuary at Shiloh (18:31) but before David captured Jerusalem (1:21), looking back to the time when Israel had no king. (Though there were later editorial changes, as is clear from the sentence added to 1:7.) Deborah's song, celebrating the defeat of Sisera, is one of the oldest pieces of writing in the Old Testament.

Six of the 12 judges mentioned are described in some detail: Othniel, Ehud, Deborah/Barak, Gideon, Jephthah, Samson. These 'judges' of Israel were not simply legal advisers. They delivered tribe or nation from enemy oppression, winning their laurels in active service. Hebrews 11 includes four – Gideon, Barak, Samson and Jephthah – in its list of 'all-time great' examples of faith.

The human scene in Judges is a depressing one. The nation's fortunes follow a monotonous, repetitive cycle.

Israel deserts God for the local gods.
They suffer at the hands of the
Canaanites and cry out to God for help.
God sends a deliverer. All is well for a
while: then the old pattern of infidelity reasserts itself. There is no more graphic portrayal in Scripture of the tendency humans have to go their own way – even those who know God.

The wonder is God's constant love and

concern. Despite Israel's past unfaithfulness, and what God knows will happen again, as soon as they turn to him God answers. And he chooses to work with the most unpromising people: Jael, who breaks all the sacred laws of hospitality; Ehud, who stoops to assassination; Samson, who leads a life of sexual promiscuity; a nation that gloats over acts of cruel revenge against the enemy. They are examples to follow only in terms of their faith. The stories neither whitewash nor commend their behaviour. The moral questions this book raises, and particularly God's part in the action, create a real problem for readers today (see 'Understanding Judges' and the note on Jephthah's vow).

Dates and times

The compiler of Judges, in common with many ancient writers, does not always consider exact time-order to be important in the way that modern Western historians do. Added together, the figures in Judges total 390 years. Yet, with the most probable date for the conquest at about 1240, the period covered must be under 200 years. One of the reasons for this seeming discrepancy is the overlap between the periods of the different judges. We know, for example, from 10:7 that the Ammonite oppression in the east and the Philistine oppression in the west occurred at the same time. It is likely there is considerable

A figure of the Canaanite Baal, god of weather, war and fertility.

overlap elsewhere. A further factor is the frequent use of '40 years' as a round figure for 'a generation' rather than a precise length of time.

A.E. Cundall suggests the following approximate chronology:

1200	Othniel
1170	Ehud
1150	Shamgar
1125	Deborah and Barak
1100	Gideon
1070	Jephthah
1070	Samson

1 – 2:5
After Joshua's death

1 Successes and failures
Judah, the tribe from which David and his line of kings would come, is first to continue the conquest after Joshua's death, with notable success. The Benjamite failure to drive out the Jebusites from Jerusalem qualifies the victory of verse 8. The stronghold would not fall until King David took it (2 Samuel 5). Verses 10-15: see Joshua 15:13-19.

The capture of Bethel (22-25) by the 'men of Joseph' – Ephraim and Manasseh – is followed by a catalogue of failures, relieved only by a further success of the Joseph tribes in verse 35.

▶ **Verse 1** Yes-no questions were put to God through the use of the sacred lot by the high priest.

▶ **Thumbs, toes (7)** So that they could not grip a sword or stand steady.

▶ **City of palms (16)** Jericho.

▶ **Verse 19** This was the beginning of the Iron Age. The Philistines introduced and controlled the iron industry in Palestine and guarded it jealously (see 1 Samuel 13:19-22). Until David's time, Israel was at a disadvantage against the superior iron weapons and iron-clad chariots of their enemies.

2:1-5 Disobedience brings defeat
These verses serve as a comment on the failures recounted in chapter 1. Gilgal was where the people first camped and built an altar after crossing the Jordan. Bochim/Bokim is unknown.

▶ **The angel of the Lord (1)** Mentioned a

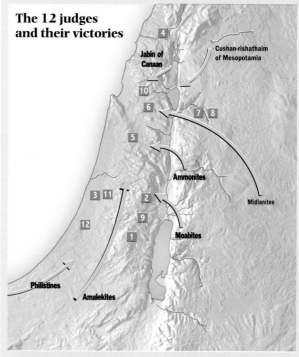

The 12 judges and their victories

Cushan-rishathaim of Mesopotamia
Jabin of Canaan
Ammonites
Midianites
Moabites
Philistines
Amalekites

1. **Othniel** of Judah (3:9): victory against Cushan-rishathaim.
2. **Ehud** of Benjamin (3:15): victory against Eglon of Moab.
3. **Shamgar** (3:31): victory against the Philistines.
4. **Deborah** (Ephraim) and **Barak** (Naphthali) (4:4-6): victory over Jabin and Sisera.
5. **Gideon** of Manasseh (6:11): victory over the Midianites and Amalekites.
6. **Tola** of Issachar (10:1).
7. **Jair** of Gilead (10:3).
8. **Jephthah** of Gilead (11:11): victory over the Ammonites.
9. **Ibzan** of Bethlehem (12:8).
10. **Elon** of Zebulun (12:11).
11. **Abdon** of Ephraim (12:13).
12. **Samson** of Dan (15:20): victory against the Philistines.

number of times in Judges (here and in the stories of Gideon and Samson) as well as in other Bible passages (the Hagar story and the 'sacrifice' of Isaac in Genesis; Moses and the burning bush in Exodus 3), the angel always comes as God's representative, with a special message from God. He speaks in God's name, often in the first person as God, and is virtually identified with God by those to whom he appears (see e.g. 13:22). Sometimes he shows himself as an ordinary person, sometimes as an awesome heavenly being (see chapter 13). But no one who sees him is left in any doubt of his authority.

The Israelites were constantly tempted to join the Canaanites in their worship of Baal, believing this local god to be in control of the weather and the fertility of the land.

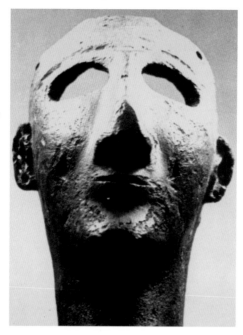

2:6 – 16:31
Israel under the Judges

2:6 – 3:6 Introduction
2:6-9 brings us back to the point at which the book of Joshua concluded. Verses 11-23 set out the repeated pattern of events which began once the conquest generation had died out (10). As a result of disobedience, of abandoning God in favour of the local gods, the surrounding nations are not driven out. They remain as a thorn in Israel's side, to test the nation and keep Israel's fighting men well trained in the skills of war (2:20 – 3:6).
▸ **Baals and the Ashtaroth/Astartes (2:13)** Local male and female gods of fertility and a fruitful land.
▸ **3:3** The five Philistine city-states were Ashdod, Ashkelon, Ekron, Gaza, Gath (see 'Canaanites and Philistines', the Samson story, chapters 13 – 16, and 1 Samuel 17:1-54). Judah did not hold their three cities for long (1:18).

3:7-11 Othniel's victory
If Cushan-rishathaim was indeed king of 'Mesopotamia' (8: i.e. modern east Syria, north Iraq) the attack must have come from the north – which makes his defeat at the

hands of a southern champion surprising. But some would emend the name to 'Cushan chief of Teman' (in Edom).
▸ **Anger... sold (8)** The writer ascribes human feelings to God and, since God is in charge of human affairs, expresses that in direct terms ('sold them') which often make modern readers uncomfortable. This is the style of the whole book, and we see it in many other parts of the Old Testament.
▸ **The Spirit of the Lord came upon him (10)** The same phrase is used of Gideon, Jephthah and Samson. The might of these champions was a special gift from God.
▸ **40 years (11)** is frequently used in the Old Testament as a round number meaning 'a generation' or 'for a long time'.

3:12-30 Ehud kills King Eglon
Eglon of Moab headed an eastern alliance which included Ammonites and Amalekites. They not only overran the land east of Jordan, but crossed the river to set up an outpost at Jericho.

Like Ehud, many of the Benjamites were left-handed or ambidextrous – the tribe's left-handed slingers had a formidable reputation (see 20:16; 1 Chronicles 12:2). On this occasion it meant that the movement aroused no suspicion.
▸ **80 years (30)** Twice 40 – an even longer time!

3:31 Shamgar's slaughter
This one-off feat with an 2.5m/8ft metal-tipped pole (the ox-goad) wiped out 600 men but did not restrain the Philistines for long. See chapters 13 – 16.

4 – 5 Prophetess Deborah leads Barak into battle
This powerful story is dominated by two extraordinary women – Deborah the prophetess and Jael, wife of tent-dwelling Heber the Kenite.

Deborah is a judge in the judicial sense (4:5), a woman of authority. Not only does she send for the military leader, Barak, and give him God's instruction, she is also perfectly ready to make an 80km/50 mile journey north to go with him into battle. Barak gets no glory from the action, for it is another woman, the resourceful Jael, who

Barak charged down the steep slopes of Mt Tabor to attack the armies of Sisera.

slays the mighty Sisera with a handy tent-peg and mallet.

The song that celebrates the battle provides the clue to the victory. A cloud-burst turned the Kishon into a raging torrent (5:21). Many of the chariots were swept away, the rest completely bogged down in the mud.

'The stars fought from heaven,
the stars in their courses fought against Sisera.
The torrent of Kishon swept him away,
the torrent barred his flight, the torrent of Kishon.
March on in might, my soul!
Then hammered the hoofs of his horses,
his chargers galloped, galloped away.'

5:20-22

The 'battle-hymn' has an eye-witness freshness and sheer exultation about it that comes through despite some problems arising from the age of the text. The poet-composer uses all the devices of sound, beat and repetition to depict scenes as swift and vivid as a film – finally cutting with dramatic effect from Jael, hammer raised, straight to Sisera's mother, waiting in vain for her son's return.

▶ **Mt Tabor (6)** A good choice for the muster.

Barak defeats Sisera and the Canaanites

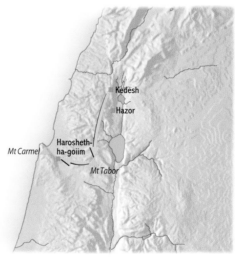

The distinctive rounded shape of this 400m/1300ft hill is visible from a long way off.
▶ **Hazor (4:2)** Joshua defeated an earlier Jabin, and destroyed the city. The lower part was never rebuilt, but the mound (tell) was re-fortified by the Canaanites, and later by Solomon.
▶ **5:19** Taanach is only 8km/5 miles from Megiddo (where trade routes passed through the Carmel hills), the scene of so many battles that it gave its name to the ultimate battle-place 'Armageddon'. The waters or stream of Megiddo is the River Kishon.

Settled life

John Bimson

After the Exodus from Egypt and Israel's conquest of the promised land, the shift to a settled existence was probably slow and piecemeal. 'To your tents, O Israel!' was still a catch-phrase in the early days of the monarchy (2 Samuel 20:1; 1 Kings 12:16), and the clan of the Rechabites made a permanent vow against settlement (Jeremiah 35:6-7).

Israelites in the lowlands were probably the first to settle. The hill-country was more difficult to cultivate, and settlement there required the terracing of the slopes and the creation of cisterns to store water. Most hill-country settlements were very small, unwalled villages.

Political and economic arrangements are never described in the Bible, and we can only guess at them from incidental details, helped by studies of similar societies. It seems that a number of farming villages were often exploited by a larger, fortified city. References to a city 'and all its daughters' (e.g. Numbers 21:25)

A communal granary at Megiddo, dating from the time of King Jeroboam II, 793-753 BC.

reflect this arrangement. Israelite cities generally had strong walls and gates, a palace/governmental building, a protected water supply (e.g. reached by a tunnel), and storehouses for such staple products as grain, wine and olive oil. In the 8th-7th centuries BC the communal granary at Megiddo was a large underground silo.

Oil and grain and other vital commodities were stored in pottery jars inside the houses.

Every home had its simple pottery lamp filled with olive oil.

In cities and villages the typical Israelite house was much the same. The main living area was a rectangular, open courtyard. This usually had narrow rooms on both sides and a third room running the width of the building – an arrangement sometimes known as a 'four-room house'. One of the side rooms was probably a shelter for animals, and sometimes a second storey provided a sleeping-loft. It was common for two or three small houses to be grouped together, probably reflecting a multiple family of up to three generations.

Hill-country settlements were small. It was tough work terracing the hillsides for cultivation.

In return for supplying grain and other produce to a fortified city, the surrounding villages probably received protection in times of war. Nomads who had a relationship with a city would also seek protection within its walls in a time of crisis – as the Rechabites did in Jerusalem when Babylonian armies invaded the land (Jeremiah 35:11).

Walled cities were a refuge for the people living in the villages close by in times of danger.

6 – 8:28 Gideon

Bedouin from the east – the Midianites who were descendants of Abraham by his second wife, Keturah (Genesis 25:1-4) – swept through southern Israel as far as the Philistine city of Gaza. The terror spread by these fierce camel-riders is vividly pictured in 6:11. Gideon is forced to thresh his meagre grain harvest secretly, in the confines of the wine press.

The faith of this man (see also Hebrews 11:32-33), for all his initial caution, is seen in his readiness to face the Midianite hordes with a force of only 300 men. Gideon uses his wits in the surprise attack, but the victory in the ensuing rout is God's.

Though he had risen to the occasion in a time of testing, sadly, prosperity 'became a snare for Gideon' (8:27).

> **6:11** The site of Ophrah is unknown (this is not the Benjamite Ophrah). See note on 2:1 above for the 'angel of the Lord'.

> **Asherah (6:25)** Sacred pole – symbol of the Canaanite mother-goddess.

> **7:5-6** Those who scoop up the water and lap it from their hands are more alert to danger than those who kneel.

> **7:13** The barley loaf stands for Israel (the settlers), the tent for the nomadic Midianites.

> **8:21** Crescent-moon-shaped ornaments are still popular among Arab peoples today. The Bible mentions them only here and in Isaiah 3:18.

> **Ephod (8:27)** Probably an image of God, which the law forbade, though Good News Bible translates 'idol'. The place then became a rival to Israel's official sanctuary.

66 A sword for the Lord and for Gideon! 99

7:20

8:29-35 Gideon's later years

On the death of Gideon, the Israelites once again began to worship the Baals. God was fine in a crisis, but when that was forgotten the pull of gods who would bind Israel to their neighbours (Baal of the covenant/ Baal-berith) and give good crops was too strong.

9 Rise and fall of Abimelech

Gideon, with some claim to kingship, firmly rejected it. Abimelech, his brutal and ambitious son, shows no such scruples. But Abimelech is not God's choice as his father was, and the writer plainly sees the dangers of inherited (dynastic) leadership. God –

and justice – has the last word, even if it is presented in a rather tit-for-tat fashion (56-57).

> **Shechem (1)** was the central sanctuary of Israel in Joshua's day. But now it has a temple/house to Baal. The city's history goes back a very long way, to Jacob and earlier.

> **Verses 7-21** This is an early example of a parable or story-with-a-point. Compare Nathan's parable in 2 Samuel 12:1-4.

> **Scattered salt (45)** Symbolically consigning the city to permanent desolation. It was in fact rebuilt 150 years later in the time of Jeroboam I.

> **Upper millstone (53)** Grain was ground between two heavy circular stone slabs about 45cm/18 inches across.

10:1-5 Tola and Jair

These two were not military leaders. They 'judged' Israel, respectively, for 23 and 22 uneventful years

> **Verse 4** 'Donkeys' and 'cities' sound alike in Hebrew: there is a play on words here.

10:6 – 12:7 Jephthah

Southern Israel is now caught in a vice between the Philistines on the west and the Ammonites on the east. Against Ammon, the new champion is the brigand-chief, Jephthah. Numbers 20 – 21 describes the events referred to in the parley of 11:12-28. Moab in fact had the better claim to the land, as part of it had been theirs until Sihon dispossessed them.

After the victory and its tragic aftermath (see below), Jephthah has to deal with the jealousy of powerful Ephraim. Where Gideon used soft words to placate these touchy tribesmen (8:1-3), Jephthah takes up the sword. At the fords the men's dialect pronunciation of 'Shibboleth' gives them away.

> **Three hundred years (11:26)** I.e. it was now the 3rd century since the events described (in fact about 160 years).

> **Jephthah's vow** is an indication of how little the Israelites understood God at this time. Human sacrifice might please the heathen gods, but never the God of Israel (Abraham had learnt this long before, and God's law forbade it: Deuteronomy 12:31). Yet, though ignorant and mistaken, the vow was made in good faith: Jephthah would forfeit 'whatever' (person or

animal) came out of the house first. And he kept his word, though it cost him his only child, and his daughter her life. (Since Jephthah comes onto the scene as an illegitimate outcast, he is not one to take home or family for granted. His heartbreak is genuine. And his daughter's response is astonishing: she will not have him break faith with God on her account.)

But how can a moral God associate himself with actions like this – with people like Jephthah, Samson and the rest? ('Understanding Judges' looks at some possible answers.) We certainly cannot discount the fact that the 'heroes' of Judges are people of their age – an age which the Bible plainly shows was one of religious decline, falling far short of the standards set out in God's law. God acts through men and women, by definition imperfect. These people are not set up as models: their failures, weaknesses and immorality are simply recorded, not glorified, condoned or glossed over. Only their faith and courage are commended. God does not remove himself or turn a deaf ear to a cry for help, even in an age of seemingly hopeless decadence. He

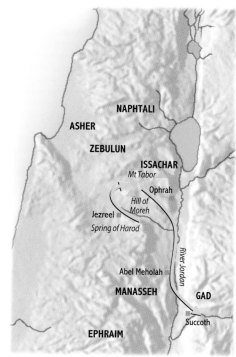

Gideon's defeat of the Midianites

Gideon's victory was won with just 300 men.

Coming over the hill (not up the valley) and at night, at the given signal his three divisions made enough noise to wake the dead! The Midianites thought themselves surrounded, and fled in confusion.

1 Spring of Harod: Gideon's base

2 Hill of Moreh

3 Gideon splits his forces into three

4 Gideon's men spring their surprise

5 Midianites flee

Delilah wove Samson's hair into the warp of her loom, seeking to rob him of his strength. Looms were upright, like this one, and also horizontal.

Remains of Ashkelon, the Philistine city where Samson slew 30 men, can still be seen (*right*). The statue and columns date mainly from Roman times.

acts, despite the lack of 'suitable' people. And because he acts, a 'dark age' like that of the Judges may be followed by a time of real spiritual advance.

The exploits of Samson

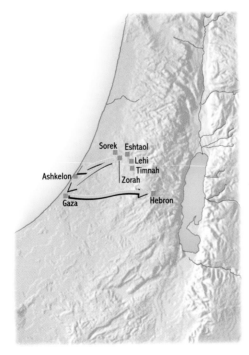

▶ **42,000 (12:6)** There is a question over the meaning of the Hebrew for 'thousand' which may account for the abnormally high figures we find in parts of the Old Testament.

12:8-15 Ibzan, Elon and Abdon
Two of these judges are remarkable for their families, but there is little else to note. They serve as an interlude before the next big story.

13:1 – 16:31 Samson
The champion against the enemy in the west (see 10:7) is set apart for the task from the moment of his conception. For Samson, the Nazirite vow (see Numbers 6) was lifelong. Yet he treats it with a casualness amounting to contempt, eventually enabling Delilah to shave off the long hair which was the sign of his dedication to God. Moral weakness robs the strong man of both spiritual stature and physical prowess – since his strength is God-given for a specific purpose.

Samson's was a one-man war, unlike the campaigns of other judges. Even his own people sided against him (15:11). But the Philistines were pushing inland (they

Understanding Judges

P. Deryn Guest

Judges contains some of the best-known stories of the Hebrew Bible. As an action-packed book, replete with gory assassinations, tales of treachery and violence, it demands attention, but leaves the reader uncomfortable with its contents. What is one to make of the gang-raped woman subsequently hacked to pieces (chapter 19) or the community burned to death whilst locked in a tower (9:42-49)? Perhaps more disturbing is the role of a God who is often involved in the various slaughters. Certainly, the book presents an ethical and theological challenge to any would-be interpreter.

A common response explains that these events happened at a time when the Israelites were experiencing a political, social and religious time of crisis. Having only recently gained their foothold in the promised land, they are struggling to maintain Israelite control, tribal unity and religious purity. In these turbulent times, there were inevitably land battles, tribal conflicts and lapses into paganism, and this goes some way towards excusing the macabre acts which occurred. It was unfortunate but

an unavoidable feature of the age.

However, accounting for the dubious elements of the text by locating them in a 'difficult settling-in time' for Israel no longer convinces some readers. It is too simplistic, and does not take account of the date of composition (much later than the events described), and its agenda for a later audience. Yet when we consider the text from this later viewpoint, a number of interesting points emerge.

■ The text has a clear *interest in leadership*. For success, leadership should rest on the initiative of God. Self-elected leaders such as Abimelech, or opportunist leaders like Jephthah, are portrayed negatively.

Some also find in the book and its progression a strong bias against the northern leadership. Chapter 19 particularly mentions places and events associated with Saul – Gibeah (his home town), Benjamites (Saul's tribe), the butchered concubine (Saul's butchered oxen). The writer tells his stories in a way which discredits the northern tribes and particularly Saul's dynasty.

It may be construed from this that the writer has a political interest in upholding Davidic kingship and a theological interest in upholding a kingship that acknowledges the overall sovereignty of God.

■ The narratives *warn against assimilation*. The book is set in a time when Israel lived in a land bordered by foreigners; the threat being that co-existence will lead to loss of identity. Judges shows how this threat turned to reality. By the closing chapters the reversal is complete, as an idolatrous cult site is set up within Israel, complete with forbidden images and mercenary priest. Judges thus functions as a kind of history lesson to the later audience, warning against such errors.

■ The book charts the *disintegration of tribal unity*. It begins with Deborah's chastisement of certain tribes for not entering into the coalition and dissolves finally into civil war. Tribal disunity is thereby identified as an integral feature of this period's failure. The writer thus shows his own ▶

---

would be a major threat to Israel until David finally dealt with them). Many of the Danites had probably moved north by this time (18:1ff.), Samson being among the few who remained in the territory the tribe was originally given. The Philistines were advancing by infiltration rather than outright war. Samson, by marrying a Philistine woman, seems to go along with this. But his subsequent exploits bring the danger into the open and the enmity to a head.

▶ **14:3** The Philistines were the only ones among Israel's neighbours not to practise circumcision (usually at puberty).

▶ **14:4** The editor's comment makes God responsible, since God is sovereign. But this does not make it right for Samson to break God's law and marry someone who worships other gods (Exodus 34:16) or to be disrespectful to his parents (Exodus 20:12). God did not take away his freedom of choice.

▶ **Samson's marriage** is formally arranged by his parents, but instead of the bride returning to

generation how not to progress if they are to live successfully in the land.

- The writer upholds the *sovereign freedom of God*. This is seen in the control he exerts over the weak and sometimes unworthy judges in order to achieve his own ends. It is also expressed in his ability to act ambiguously; for example in sending over 40,000 tribesmen to their slaughter in chapter 20.

It is unnerving to see God involved in such an act, and it raises significant moral questions. However, such ambiguous behaviour demonstrates that God cannot be relied upon to comply automatically with human demands and expectations. The writer shows how Israel tried to use God for their own ends, and how it was only when they acknowledged God's choice in the matter that his word proved faithful. Trying to 'get God to work for you' is a folly well exposed throughout Judges.

There are other features of course, but the overriding concern in all these matters is *the issue of identity*. Through the individual narratives the writer impresses upon his contemporary generation his ideals of how Israel should uphold and preserve a particular national identity. Interpreting Judges in this way may lessen the impact of the various outrages.

However, one cannot ignore the cultural influence the Bible has exerted, and even if we should be dealing with literary rape or murder, the practices and prejudices (against the foreigner, against women) within the text remain a problem. In attempting to deal with such issues, a number of different reading strategies have emerged.

One is a feminist approach, which does not share in, or condone, the events described and the ideologies transmitted. For example, the character of Delilah lives on in the cultural imagination as a *femme fatale*. The story carries the message that the sexually independent, foreign woman is a snare to good men. As Cheryl Exum has pointed out, the paintings of Moreau, Rubens and Solomon have built on this shared prejudice against the temptress figure by adding to the biblical narrative such details as Delilah's fleshy seductiveness, her prostitute-status, her feelings of triumph when Samson is captured. So the negative message of the story itself is continued and strengthened. The feminist view resists the tendency to 'agree with' the text and opens other questions, other possibilities for the reader.

There are other approaches emerging which fully recognize the repugnant acts and take seriously the ethical challenge the modern interpreter faces. Some studies consider the ancient dynamics of honour and shame. Others articulate a masculinist response.

The problematic issues raised by reading the book of Judges are being aired in new and creative ways, and this is a welcome and stimulating development as interpretation of this daunting text is reconsidered today.

The Philistines put out Samson's eyes and set him the task of a beast, turning the mill in his prison at Gaza.

Samson's home, as she would normally do, she stays with her family and her husband visits her, bringing gifts. Because of the deceit over the riddle there is no consummation at the end of the seven-day feast. A hasty second marriage to the best man is an attempt to lessen the bride's disgrace.

▶ **Three hundred foxes (15:4)** Jackals, who hunt in packs and would be easier to catch in large numbers, are more likely than the solitary fox.

▶ **Delilah (16:4)** Like Samson's other loves, Delilah was probably a Philistine. Fairly or unfairly, just as 'Samson' has come to stand for a 'strong man', so 'Delilah' has given her name to the *femme fatale* (see 'Understanding Judges'). Both are equally unscrupulous in the way they use others.

17 – 21
A time of do-as-you-please

This closing section differs from the rest of Judges. The writer turns from Israel's heroes to two incidents which illustrate the low state of religion and morality in the lawless days when Israel had no central government and everyone 'did as they saw fit'.

17 – 18 Micah's image; the tribe of Dan moves north

This story relates to the time when Philistine pressure on their southern territory led to the mass migration of the Danites to the far north of Israel. The image set up by Micah was strictly forbidden by the law that the Levites were supposed to administer (Exodus 20:4). To use an 'ephod' (see on 8:27) and 'teraphim' (household gods) for divination, was equally strictly prohibited. Nor has Micah any right to appoint the young Levite as priest.

This story, and the one that follows, shows that the Levites, specially chosen to serve God, had become as lawless and self-serving as the rest. They too did as they pleased.

The Levites were given cities to live in, yet here is one 'looking for somewhere to live'. He sells his services to Micah, then robs him of his sacred objects and transfers to the tribe of Dan, who set up a new shrine in the north, to rival Shiloh, the true religious centre of Israel at this time.

▶ **18:30** 'The exile' is presumably a later editor's reference to the Assyrian destruction of the northern kingdom of Israel.

19 – 21 Rape at Gibeah; Benjamin punished

The warm traditional hospitality of the concubine's father contrasts with the lack of it at Gibeah. The eventual kindness of the old man and what follows is very like the story of Lot and the men of Sodom (Genesis 19). There too, weighed against duty to an honoured guest, a woman counted for little. But in this case no angelic presence saves the concubine from horrible gang-rape. So, in a second terrible atrocity, her husband uses the pieces of her body to summon the 12 tribes to avenge her (chapter 20).

When the Benjamites refuse to hand over their fellow tribesmen (the men of Gibeah) civil war results. The outcome is the near-extinction of Benjamin, and great national grief.

Chapter 21 relates the lengths to which the tribes go to circumvent the rash oath made at Mizpah (21:1).

The writer has no need to point a moral. The simple statement of verse 25 is sufficient. The whole book makes plain the disastrous consequences of breakdown of authority, when people become a law unto themselves, setting their own standards of permissiveness.

▶ **19:28** The assumption is that the concubine was dead, though the story does not say so (an addition makes this clear in the Greek Septuagint text).
▶ **20:1** The phrase 'Dan to Beersheba' (furthest north to furthest south) came to stand for the whole land.
▶ **20:17** See the earlier note on large numbers.
▶ **20:36ff.** The details of the battle recall the strategy at Ai (Joshua 8).

Ruth

Summary

The story of a foreign girl whose courage and devotion won her a place in Israel's history in the family line of King David.

This quiet tale of ordinary life stands in strong contrast to the war and strife of Judges, which relates to the same general period. No doubt many people lived just such a normal peaceful life during this age. And although religion generally was at a low ebb, the book of Ruth makes it clear that the personal faith of many in Israel remained strong.

Of all the books of the Bible, Ruth is special in giving us the woman's perspective. In the society of the time women were wholly dependent on their fathers and husbands for provision. They could inherit property only in exceptional circumstances and under strict rules (Numbers 36). So the tale begins with three women who, in human terms, are objects of pity, dependent on charity. What it goes on to reveal, astonishingly in a context where religion meant power, is God's special concern for 'the helpless'.

Here God is intimately concerned in humble affairs. He is the One who orders all the circumstances of daily life, even for the most unimportant people. And so the new-found faith of a Moabite girl, and her sacrificial love for her mother-in-law are woven into the great tapestry of God's plan of salvation. For descended from Ruth is King David, and from the line of David comes the Messiah himself.

1:1-5 'Family flees famine!'

Give this story a modern headline, and we quickly feel the impact of the chilling facts spelt out in these verses. Approaching starvation drives this family of refugees from their homeland. Far from home, the man of the house and his two sons all die – leaving three widows unsupported. It is an appalling situation, especially for Naomi.

▶ **Verses 1-2** The journey from Bethlehem to Moab, on the far side of the Dead Sea, was about 80km/50 miles.

1:6-22 Setting out for home

News comes that the famine is over. Naomi's daughters-in-law see her on her way. Then the time comes to say goodbye. Orpah, sorrowfully, yields to Naomi's pressure to go home and hopefully marry again. But Ruth will not leave Naomi to a lonely old age. Her choice is Naomi's people and, significantly, Naomi's God. The two reach Bethlehem in April. The barley harvest is looking good, but they have no fields to reap.

2 Ruth finds a protector

There were not many ways for widows to earn a living, and Ruth and Naomi were poor. But the law (Leviticus 19:9-10) laid down that the gleanings of the harvest must be left for the needy. By 'chance' in the common open field Ruth gleans in the

❝ Where you go I will go, and where you stay I will stay. Your people will be my people and your God my God. Where you die, I will die, and there I will be buried. ❞

1:16-17

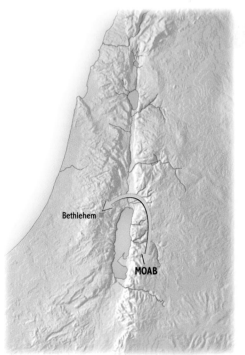

The journeys from Bethlehem to Moab, and back again

Bethlehem

MOAB

facing page: As the barley was cut, Ruth gleaned the grain that was left.

A portrait of Ruth

Frances Fuller

Ruth, heroine of a story loved by multitudes, began life as a Moabite. Moab was the son of Lot and his daughter, so Ruth's lineage was a shameful one in the eyes of the Hebrews. Her story could have been a sad one, but Ruth took charge of her own life and turned it into one of the happiest stories in the Old Testament.

Ruth married Mahlon, a Hebrew who came to the land of Moab with his father Elimelech, his mother Naomi and brother Chilion during a time of famine in Judah. Then the three men died leaving three widows. Naomi now had no way to survive in Moab and decided to return to her home in Bethlehem. Ruth and Orpah loved Naomi deeply and both determined to go home with her.

As they travelled, Naomi urged them to go back to their own mothers where they might find husbands and new lives. At last Orpah kissed her mother-in-law and turned back in tears, but Ruth clung to Naomi and vowed to stay with her for ever. Her beautiful words to Naomi are unmatched in Jewish or Christian literature as a commitment to another person.

She promised to live wherever Naomi lived, to worship Naomi's God and to be buried near Naomi.

The emotion in these words reveals that Ruth understood the risk she was taking. She would be an alien in Judah; without husbands she and Naomi would have no security or social status; she must adapt to new customs; and surely she would be homesick. Ruth had no reason to face these hardships except her treasured relationship with Naomi. She loved deeply and knew she could be loyal to what mattered most to her.

In Bethlehem Ruth became a scavenger to bring home food for herself and Naomi, picking up grain dropped in the fields by harvesters. As a strange woman alone she had to be careful. She must stay close to other women and never look at the young men who worked nearby.

Naomi had friends in Bethlehem, and she told about her wonderful daughter-in-law. These good words reached Boaz, a relative, and he extended protection to Ruth and ordered his workers to drop grain in front of her. Hearing this, Naomi schemed. Then Ruth,

with humility and courage, followed Naomi's plan, culturally correct but risky, and offered herself as wife to Boaz. The plan worked, because the honourable Boaz did what was right as next of kin to the husband of a widow.

The entire community approved this match and pronounced a blessing on them, evoking the names of the matriarchs Rachel and Leah, linking Ruth to their own people. When a boy was born to them, her women friends rejoiced with Naomi and praised Ruth as better for her than seven sons. These women named the child, calling him Obed. Obed became the father of Jesse and Jesse the father of David, and thus Ruth, a Moabite, became an ancestor of Jesus the Messiah.

part belonging to Boaz, Elimelech's kinsman. His kindness goes far beyond the law's demands (9, 14-16) and from April to June, through first the barley then the wheat harvest, Ruth gathers the grain she needs to make bread.

▶ **An ephah of barley (17)** The ephah was a large container holding about 22 litres. Ruth had gleaned about 10kg/a half cwt of barley by her own hard work and Boaz' generosity.

3 A husband for Ruth

Under the Levirate law (referred to by Naomi in 1:11-13), when a man died childless his brother was bound to raise an heir to him by the widow. This law extended to the next of kin, hence Naomi's plan. Ruth, by her action in verse 7, was claiming this right. It is complicated by the fact that Boaz is not in fact Elimelech's closest kinsman, but he promises to take up her case.

Verse 9 The 'covering' symbolized commitment to marriage (see Ezekiel 16:8).

4:1-12 The settlement

The city gate was the place for important assembly. It was also the place where legal business could be publicly transacted, as here. Ten 'elders' (2) made up a proper 'court' which could decide legal matters.

In addition to his obligation to raise an heir to carry on the dead man's name, the next of kin also had to buy his land, to keep it in the family. Boaz discusses the land first, then the widow. The kinsman would have bought the land to add to his own inheritance. But when he hears it will in fact go to Ruth and her son, and that he will have Ruth to provide for, he declares himself unable to purchase.

▶ **In those days (verse 7)** This old custom no longer applied at the time of writing.
▶ **Perez (12)** This ancestor of Boaz was the son of Tamar by her father-in-law, Judah. Tamar, a foreigner like Ruth, took this course because Judah denied her remarriage by refusing to honour the custom later formalized as the Levirate law (Genesis 28).

Ruth and Naomi reached Bethlehem at the time of the barley harvest, when Ruth could glean the fields. She made her approach to Boaz as he slept beside the heap of barley on the threshing-floor.

4:13-22 Ruth's son; the royal line

This is a real happy-ever-after ending to the story which began so bleakly. Boaz fulfils his own prayer of 2:12. The good wishes of the elders (4:12) are realized. God rewards Ruth with the gift of a husband and a son. And Naomi finds solace for her grief in this grandson.

When God steps in, the ordinary events of life take on extraordinary significance. The child Obed became grandfather to the founder of the royal line of Israel from which Christ himself took human flesh, in another birth at Bethlehem.

A story through women's eyes

Richard Bauckham

Recent feminist interpretation of the Bible has highlighted the extent to which the Bible is written from a male perspective. In Old Testament narratives, for example, most characters are male, and activities which were largely a male preserve in ancient Israel, such as war and politics, take up much space. The reader sees events – and the women who appear in the stories – through the eyes of Israelite men.

Men and women played different social roles in ancient Israel, and the structures of authority were male-dominated. So we cannot assume that the concerns and interests of women were identical with those of men. We have for the most part a one-sided view of things. But there are points where this dominantly male perspective is interrupted by an authentically female one.

The clearest example is the book of Ruth. It tells the story of two widows, Naomi and her devoted daughter-in-law Ruth, who find themselves, as widows often did, without any secure means of economic support. It is a story of two women's solidarity and resourcefulness in securing their future against the odds.

Their loyalty to each other, their independence and their initiative within the restricted options allowed them by their society come through clearly. It is Ruth, acting on Naomi's suggestion, who in effect proposes marriage to Boaz. He willingly responds, but it is the initiative of the women that leads to the event which secures their future: the birth of a son to Ruth.

The story illustrates how God's covenant society, Israel, ought to operate for the benefit of those most in need. The laws intended to assist widows and resident aliens (Ruth is both a widow and a non-Israelite) are shown operating as they should. They do so because the three main characters, acting with caring responsibility for each other, make them work for Naomi's and Ruth's advantage.

At only one point does the dominantly female perspective evident in the whole book change.

The legal transaction which enables Boaz to marry Ruth and provide an heir for Naomi's dead husband Elimelech who can inherit the family smallholding takes place among the men of Bethlehem (4:1-12). Legal affairs were a male responsibility, and the transaction reflects typically male concerns: to provide a male heir for Elimelech, to ensure the inheritance of land through the male line, and to provide sons for Boaz himself.

But this male-dominated scene is followed by a female-dominated one (4:13-17), where the birth of a son to Ruth is viewed not in legal but in practical terms, full of feeling. Ruth's devotion to Naomi ('your daughter-in-law who loves you, who is more to you than seven sons') has secured a son who will be Naomi's support in her old age.

This juxtaposition of the two perspectives on the same event shows how differently men and women view things, and highlights the fact that the story as a whole has adopted the women's viewpoint.

The story of Ruth shows us a society in which the formal structures of authority are male, but in which women exercise considerable power within the sphere of the household – the main social and economic unit of society.

We begin to realize that a story told from the male perspective, featuring mainly those aspects of society in which men took the lead, tends to make the society itself look more male-dominated than it really was. Only from the women's perspective can we appreciate the extent to which in their own eyes women were the real actors in significant events.

The book of Ruth gives us a new angle on ancient Israel which complements, even corrects, the mainly male angle provided by other Old Testament stories. But from this starting-point we can see the rest of the Old Testament story through the eyes of the women as well as of the men. We can identify passages in Genesis where the perspective of the matriarchs replaces that of the patriarchs (16; 21:6-21; 29:31 – 30:24). Even where the male perspective is dominant, we can supply the female perspective by reading between the lines and filling in the gaps. So Ruth can play an important role for us – men and women alike – in opening up fresh ways of reading the rest of the biblical story.

1 & 2 Samuel

Summary
The change from judges to kings: the reigns of Saul and David.

1 Samuel 1 – 7
Samuel, the last of the Judges, makes way for the kings.
•
1 Samuel 8 – 31
The reign of King Saul

Best-known stories
Hannah's baby
(chapters 1 – 2)
The boy Samuel *(chapter 3)*
David is chosen *(chapter 16)*
David v. Goliath
(chapter 17)
•
2 Samuel
The reign of King David

Best-known passages and stories
David's lament *(chapter 1)*
God's promise of a dynasty
for ever *(chapter 7)*
Bathsheba *(chapter 11)*

These two books were originally one volume in the Hebrew Bible. They provide a history of Israel from the end of the Judges period to the last years of David, the nation's second and greatest king – roughly 100 years (about 1075-975 BC). This is essentially religious history: the story of God and the nation – particularly God and the nation's leaders. Faithfulness to God is seen as the key to success: to disobey spells disaster.

Samuel gives his name to the books, not as author, but as the dominating figure of the early chapters, and Israel's 'king-maker' under God's direction. It was he who anointed first Saul and then David as king.

The author-editors may well have drawn material from Samuel's own writings (1 Samuel 10:25) and those of the prophets who followed him (1 Chronicles 29:29). David's poems are quoted in 2 Samuel 1:19-27; 22:2-51; 23:2-7. The books of Samuel are full of drama and display great storytelling skills. They must have been written and compiled some time after the division of the kingdom (there are several references to the separate kingdom of Judah, but the nation was not yet in exile: see, e.g. 1 Samuel 27:6). 900 BC is therefore the earliest likely date for the books as we know them. There appears to be some duplication – different accounts of the same event (e.g. the two sparings of Saul's life; the two occasions when Samuel announced God's rejection of Saul). Or they may be separate but similar events, recounted in order to emphasize certain points – repetition being used as a literary technique.

The Hebrew (Masoretic) and Greek (Septuagint) texts do not always agree. There are differences particularly over numbers. A Hebrew manuscript of parts of 1 Samuel, 1,000 years older than the existing Masoretic text, was discovered amongst the Dead Sea Scrolls. The fact that this sometimes agrees with the Greek rather than the previous Hebrew text may indicate that the Greek text is closer at some points to the original Hebrew.

1 Samuel 1 – 7
The prophet Samuel

1 Hannah's grief
In the Bible, when God has a special purpose for someone there is often something special about the birth. Hannah is not alone in the bitter experience of childlessness. Sarah and Rebecca in the Old Testament and Elizabeth in the New share her pain. Isaac, Jacob and John the Baptist – like Samuel – were born as God's answer to many years of prayer. Each had a special role to play in the great plan of God. When

The site of Shiloh is now no more than a ruin of fallen stones. At the time of Eli, the Shiloh sanctuary had become a regular structure for Israel's worship, not simply the Tent of Israel's travelling days, but a building that could be called a 'temple' (long before the Jerusalem Temple was built).

Hannah expressed her longing and her misery in prayer, in God's sanctuary. A lone woman stands in the Temple area of Jerusalem.

Hannah sees reflected all the wonder of God's character. God has reversed her fortunes (1). Peninnah's taunts have been silenced (3, 5). Emptiness, misery, shame are gone: in their place is life, joy, honour. And what God can do for one, he can and will do for all his people.

▶ **Sheol (6)** The shadowy land of the dead.
▶ **His king (10)** This is either inspired prophecy on Hannah's part, or verses 2-10 are part of a psalm added by the narrator, as being singularly appropriate to her experience.

2:11-36 The scandal of Eli's sons

The priests were entitled to a share in the sacrificial offerings (see Numbers 18:8-20; Deuteronomy 18:1-5). But what is going on here is a travesty of the law. Eli's sons seize the best bits before the offering has even been given to God (15). What is more, they are bringing prostitution into the worship of God, in the worst traditions of Canaanite religion (22). On his death these two will be the nation's 'archbishops' – and all Eli can do is reason with them!

Verses 27-36: the prophet's prediction is fulfilled in the death of Eli's sons in battle at Aphek (4:11). The priesthood passed from Eli's family to the line of Zadok in David's day (2 Samuel 8:17).

▶ **A linen ephod (18)** A tunic worn by the priests (see verse 28).
▶ **It was the will of the Lord to slay them (25)** The writer puts it this way because God is sovereign in every circumstance. It is equally true that their death is a direct outcome of their own free choice to disobey God. The Bible sees no conflict between God's sovereignty and our free will. See on Exodus 4:21.
▶ **Verse 26** Compare Luke 2:40, 52.

3 Samuel answers God's call

In the early hours (before the oil for the lamp ran out, as it would at dawn), when he is on duty near the Ark of the Covenant, inside God's Tent, Samuel hears God speak to him for the first time. It is a message of judgment for Eli.

From this time on, Samuel is God's messenger, and the whole nation knows it, from Dan in the far north to Beersheba on the edge of the southern desert.

▶ **Boy (1)** Samuel is not yet grown-up, but the

God gave Hannah the son she longed for he also gave Israel the last and greatest of the judges, and the first great prophet after Moses – the man who was to usher in the kings.

▶ **Verse 3** Shiloh, the place where Joshua had set up God's Tent (Joshua 18:1), was the centre of worship in the Judges period. The 'Temple' proper (9, 10) was not built till Solomon's day.
▶ **Hannah's vow (11)** The child is dedicated to God for life under a Nazirite vow (see Numbers 6, and compare the edict for Samson's parents in Judges 13).
▶ **Only her lips moved (13)** It was usual to pray aloud. Eli is quick to jump to the wrong conclusion. Religious life must have been at a low ebb if worshippers came drunk to God's Tent. Compare the conduct of Eli's own sons, 2:12ff.
▶ **Verse 24** A child was weaned at 2-3 years old.

2:1-10 Hannah's song

Hannah's song is echoed by Mary in the New Testament (Luke 1:46-55). In the small mirror of her own experience

Hannah
Frances Fuller

Hannah's desire for a child intruded upon and spoiled her opportunities to worship. Especially at those times, she would feel that God had withheld from her a basic need. Peninnah, who had children, knew this and taunted her. Elkanah, their husband, would show his love for Hannah in front of Peninnah and make matters worse by arousing jealousy. They were there at the Tabernacle in Shiloh to sacrifice to God and to eat a meal of celebration, but Hannah would weep and not eat.

Once, after this had happened, Hannah removed herself to a place where she could pour out her bitterness to God. She prayed with great emotion, weeping and moving her lips. Silently, she begged God, not for a miracle, but simply for nature to work, for her husband's seed to give her a child, and she promised that she would give this child back to God. Her behaviour was such that Eli the priest, observing her, rebuked her for being drunk. Hannah defended herself and told Eli about her anguish, and Eli added a prayer to hers. Hannah found peace then, and could eat.

When God answered Hannah's prayer, Elkanah must have recognized that the child was Hannah's in a unique way. He let her make all the decisions concerning him. She named him Samuel, which means, 'God hears', and explained: 'because I asked the Lord for him'. And she told Elkanah that when she weaned the boy she would take him to Shiloh and leave him to live there always. Elkanah was a Levite (1 Chronicles 6:25-26), so at some point his son would serve in the priesthood, but this was not required until the age of 25. Hannah wanted him to live in the place of worship at a tender age to become aware of God's presence and belong totally to him.

So when Samuel was about three years old, Elkanah went with her, and she took the child, along with a bull which would be sacrificed in the service dedicating Samuel to God. She explained to Eli that this was the child she had asked of God and that she was giving him back, not for a period of time but for his whole life, not later but now. And she left him there in the care of the old priest, perhaps helped by the women who served at the Tabernacle.

Having dedicated, with joy, the dearest thing in her life, Hannah was able to pray and to worship. Now she poured out, not bitterness, but elation and praise. Regularly she returned to the house of the Lord, and each time she took her growing son a new linen robe, which she had made. And though Hannah asked nothing more of God, he gave her three more sons and two daughters. And the child whom she had set on a spiritual path, became a great prophet, bringing God's word to his people and anointing kings.

Hebrew word gives no indication of his actual age.

▶ **Verse 10** So close is God that he can be described in human terms as 'standing there'. Clearly, though, Samuel did not literally see him.

4:1-11 Philistines seize the Ark

The Philistines may have transported the Ark on a wooden-wheeled wagon like this.

The Ark or Covenant Box (see Exodus 25 – 27) was Israel's most precious possession, kept in the inner room of God's Tent. Inside it was a copy of the law. Its lid was the mercy seat, symbol of the presence of God.

But now the nation wants to use it as a talisman, the ultimate protection against the enemy. The result is total disaster: the army defeated, the Ark in Philistine hands.

▶ **Philistines (1)** See 'Canaanites and Philistines'.

4:12-22 Shock news kills Eli

The Ark never returned to Shiloh. Although there is no mention of it here, the Philistines probably followed up their victory by destroying this city (see Jeremiah 26:6). These verses record the fulfilment of God's judgment on Eli's family (2:27-36; 3:11-14). It falls to the widow of Phinehas, dying in labour, to spell out the full measure of the tragedy: with the loss of the Ark 'God's glory has departed'. The nation is bereft.

▶ **Verse 12** The distance is about 32km/20 miles.

▶ **Verse 18** The (city) gate was where the 'court' sat to make judgments.

Samuel's early years: loss and return of the Ark

Most of Israel's judges were warrior-leaders (see Judges). But the last two, Eli and Samuel, were religious leaders and administrators of justice.

5 A dangerous trophy

To the Philistines' way of thinking, Dagon, their god, has given them victory. So they place the Ark as a war-trophy at his feet. But Dagon is not in the same class as the God of Israel. God is no inanimate object. After one night, Dagon is found face-down as if in worship. A second night, and the figure is dismembered, as they might have treated a captive king. Next, God's power breaks out of the temple to fall upon the people in an outbreak of plague (bubonic plague, carried by the rat-flea – verse 6 and 6:4, Revised English Bible). Moving the Ark simply spreads the disease.

6 – 7:1 Return of the Ark

After seven months of this, the Philistines have had enough. The religious leaders advise the Ark's return – but in a way which will show, once for all, whether or not Israel's God is responsible for the disasters. The cows, not trained for the yoke, are unlikely to pull together. In the nature of things they would also be expected to stay near their calves. Yet they respond to the yoke like a team of oxen, and head straight for the border.

6:19, with 70 men killed 'because they looked into the Ark', sounds a sombre note in all the rejoicing. Even Israel must learn not to overstep the mark. It is not safe to treat God as an object of idle curiosity.

▶ **Beth-shemesh** was one of the cities of the Levites.

7:2-17 Samuel rules as judge

Twenty years pass, and there is a genuine turning to God in national revival (verse 2). The images of Baal and Ashtoreth, the Canaanite fertility gods, are destroyed. And Samuel, judge and religious leader in Eli's place (see 15-17), leads the nation in an act of repentance and cleansing.

Immediately the test comes. The Philistines are advancing, and God uses the occasion to show Israel just what he will do for a people who keep faith with him. Israel is needed only for the mopping-up operation. The name of the place of a former defeat (4:1) is chosen to mark the present victory (12). It is God's help which makes such a dramatic reversal possible.

▸ **Verse 12** Ebenezer means 'Stone of Help'.

▸ **As long as Samuel lived (13)** This includes most of Saul's reign. War continued, but Saul and David kept the Philistines at bay until the great battle of Gilboa when Saul and Jonathan lost their lives.

▸ **From Ekron to Gath (14)** The two inland Philistine city-states. Israel won back their border towns.

▸ **Bethel, Gilgal, Mizpah, Ramah (16-17)** Samuel did an annual circuit of the four sanctuary towns.

1 Samuel 8 – 31
Saul: Israel's first king

8 'We want a king!'

History repeats itself, and Samuel's sons turn out little better than Eli's (2:12). Their bribery and corruption provide the people with a ready-made excuse to lobby the ageing Samuel for a king, like the nations around.

Samuel feels rejected and resists. But God advises Samuel to hear them out. In truth, it is not the prophet who is rejected but the whole concept of theocracy. And they must be warned of the consequences. Samuel spares them nothing. They have only to look at their neighbour states to see that having a king means conscription, forced labour, taxation, and loss of personal liberty. But even this does not deter them.

'Appoint them a king,' God says.

9 – 10:16 Saul is chosen

A search for lost donkeys, of all things, brings Israel's future king from Gibeah to Ramah and the meeting with Samuel. All Israel knows the prophet, but not, apparently, this young provincial. The oil (10:1) sets Saul apart for his high office. The detailed fulfilment of Samuel's predictions assures Saul of the prophet's authority. Saul goes home a new man (10:9).

▸ **The high place/altar on the hill (9:12)** The phrase has not yet acquired the idolatrous associations of later times.

▸ **A bed... on the roof (9:25)** The flat roof was a pleasantly cool place on a hot summer's night.

▸ **To Gilgal (10:8)** The instruction seems to relate to mustering for battle. When this took place (chapter 13) Saul disobeyed.

▸ **When they came to Gibeah (10:10)** Saul's ecstatic experience took place in his own home town.

10:17-27 'Long live the king!'

The casting of lots, tribe by tribe, makes it quite clear that God is choosing Israel's king; it is not left to the people. And when it

The Ark remained for 20 years at Kiriath-jearim, usually identified with the village of Abu Ghosh, about 16km/10 miles from Jerusalem.

Saul's search for his father's lost donkeys led him to the prophet Samuel and his destiny as Israel's first king.

comes to it Saul fights shy (like Moses before him) and has to be dragged from hiding. He need not have been afraid. A king who stands a head taller than the rest meets with the people's instant approval.

▶ **Verse 25** Samuel's briefing is carefully recorded. Was it brought out again at the crowning of Joash (2 Kings 11:12)?

11 Saul's first victory

God moves Saul to make his appeal (6) and the people to respond (7). For perhaps the first time since Joshua the nation is united: a good beginning to the new king's reign.

▶ **Jabesh (1)** Saul's timely help won lasting gratitude. See 31:11-13.

▶ **300,000 (8)** The problem of extraordinarily large numbers has been mentioned before.

Some take this as exaggeration for effect; some think that 'thousand' is actually a military unit — so here, '300 units' (number unknown).

12 Stern words from Samuel

This farewell speech marks the end of the rule of the judges. Samuel has always been alert to the dangers of monarchy (8; 10:17ff.). Politically the move to choose a king was no doubt wise. Religiously, it was a step in the wrong direction, a step away from the ideal of God alone as Israel's King. And Samuel does not mince his words: if God ceases to be King for his people, both nation and monarchy will be swept away (25). But, come what may, this old man of God will do as he has always done: pray for the people and teach them what is right.

▶ **Verse 9** Sisera was defeated by Deborah and Barak (Judges 4 – 5); 'the king of Moab' is Eglon, who was assassinated by Ehud (Judges 3:12-30).

▶ **Verse 11** Jerubbaal is another name for Gideon (Judges 6 – 8); for Jephthah see Judges 11 – 12. In place of the final reference to Samuel himself, some versions have Samson (Judges 13 – 16).

13 – 14 War with the Philistines

Saul musters his troops and waits seven days, during which time the army steadily dwindles. But he fails to see the seventh day out. And his disobedience and arrogance in taking over the function of the prophet costs him his dynasty.

Chapter 14: Jonathan and his armour-bearer seem to have been taken for deserters, so they were able to catch the Philistines unawares. Earth tremors add to the panic and confusion. And Israelite deserters change sides to help Saul to victory. Jonathan is seen as a man of outstanding faith and courage. (God does not need numbers to win a victory, as the writer makes clear from this story.) By contrast, the narrative begins to bring out those flaws in Saul's make-up which later developed into serious mental disorder.

▶ **13:1** The text is incomplete. Acts 13:21 puts Saul's reign in round figures at 40 years. Possibly a tens-unit has dropped out here (22 or 32 years). We know from 9:2 that Saul was a young man when he came to the throne. By this time he must be in his 30s, since he has a son

Saul's campaigns

1 Campaign against the Ammonites

2 Campaign against the Philistines

3 Saul's last campaign against the Philistines

old enough to fight. When he died, a younger son, Ishbosheth, was himself 40 (2 Samuel 2:10).

▶ **13:2** To hold Michmash and Gibeah (set on opposite slopes) meant control of the whole valley.

▶ **30,000 (13:5)** More probably 3,000 (see on 11:8 above).

▶ **The Israelites hid (13:6)** The atmosphere is much the same as it was in Gideon's day, when the people went in fear of the Midianites (Judges 6:2).

▶ **13:19** The Philistines jealously guard the means of working iron, the new metal which gives them such an advantage compared with bronze.

▶ **Bring the Ark (14:18)** Perhaps in view of Saul's command to the priest in 14:19, some versions have 'ephod' rather than 'Ark'. This was the tunic with the breastpiece containing the Urim and Thummim (14:41), the lots which were cast to discover God's will.

▶ **14:33** Eating meat with the blood in it is forbidden in Leviticus 17:10ff.

▶ **14:39ff.** The people intervene to save Jonathan from the consequences of his father's rash oath (contrast Judges 11).

▶ **Ishvi (14:49)** The short form of Ishbosheth.

▶ **Abner (14:50)** later set up Ishbosheth as king in opposition to David (2 Samuel 2:8 – 3:39).

15 Saul disobeys orders

This time Saul's disobedience is deliberate (9). He is rejected by God as king, and Samuel pays him no more official visits. The prophet had foreseen trouble. He might well have relished Saul's downfall. Instead he went home grieving.

▶ **Amalek (2)** The Amalekites were old enemies whose punishment had long been forecast (Exodus 17:8-16; Deuteronomy 25:17-19). Even so, we find it hard to accept the order to destroy them completely — notwithstanding the unparalleled atrocities of our own time. In the more realistic, less individualistic world of Saul's day, the whole community was held responsible for the misdeeds of its members, and suffered the consequences. Saul's disobedience (for the lowest of motives) left his people open to continued harassment from the Amalekites.

▶ **Verse 3** Everything was under a ban, not to be touched because it was dedicated to God for destruction. See 'Holy War'.

▶ **Kenites (6)** A nomadic Midianite tribe into which Moses had married. The Kenites acted as Israel's guides in the desert (Numbers 10:29-32).

▶ **Verses 22-23** Samuel's declaration became a major theme of later prophets.

16:1-13 An unlikely choice

On the basis of the first choice of king, Samuel might well have been looking for someone tall and handsome. But this time God makes it plain that he looks deeper. David may have sparkling eyes and the glow of health, but he is the least of his family: yet his heart is right. With the anointing, as in Saul's case, comes spiritual power (13). Again God chooses his man and prepares him long before he becomes a national figure. Learning to care for a wayward flock is no bad preparation for a leader! Ezekiel 34, with its shepherd imagery, looks back to David, the shepherd-king.

16:14-23 David in the king's court

When the Spirit of God leaves Saul, evil forces take charge. Saul is at the mercy of his own ungovernable temperament. His disordered mind plunges him into black depression and violence. But music can push back the shadows, and so Saul's need becomes David's opportunity.

▶ **An evil spirit from God (15)** To the observer, Saul is 'possessed' by a spirit sent by God in punishment. Since God is sovereign, both good and evil are directly attributed to him.

17 David and Goliath

The Philistine champion is 10ft (over 3m) tall, fully armed and clad in protective armour. Saul, who has fought valiantly against the Philistines, is as terrified as his men to answer the giant's challenge. But David's time in the hills alone with the sheep has added faith to courage – and given him deadly accuracy

A shepherd boy whirls his sling to release the stone, just as David did when he fought Goliath.

Jonathan used target practice with his bow and arrows to pass David the message that his life was in danger.

with the sling. The giant doesn't stand a chance. Once again God is shown as his people's protector: all he requires from them is trust and the courage to obey.

▶ **Verse 50** See on 2 Samuel 21:19.
▶ **Verses 55-58** This is difficult to tie in with 16:18ff. The events of chapter 17 may have taken place while David was still attending court only occasionally, when Saul's black moods came on him. 16:21-22 then refer to a later time. Or possibly the enquiry is a purely formal one concerning David's family background. The victor had, after all, been promised the king's daughter in marriage (17:25).

18 Saul grows jealous of David

Jonathan's instant liking deepens into lasting friendship with David, who will look back on this as one of the best things in his life (2 Samuel 1:26). Nothing could shake the amazing bond between the king's son and the man who, humanly speaking, was to rob him of the throne.

As David's prestige grows, Saul's jealous suspicion increases, and he plots David's death. David's poverty gives Saul the chance to suggest a bride-price which is likely to cost him his life. Such a toll could be exacted only from the Philistines, Israel's chief enemy: the other nations practised circumcision. David doubles Saul's demand and returns unharmed to claim his royal bride.

19 – 20 David flees Saul's court

Jonathan's first attempt at reconciliation succeeds (19:1-7). But one of Saul's black moods follows and only Michal's deception saves David's life (19:8-17). For a time he joins Samuel and his school of prophets at Ramah (19:18-24). Jonathan tries to secure David's safe return, but his father turns on him (20:30-33), and the two friends are forced to part (20:35-42).

▶ **Has Saul become a prophet? (19:24)** Compare 10:10-13. So irresistible is the power of the Spirit of God that not only is Saul's evil plan frustrated, but the king himself becomes 'infected'. Like his messengers, he too – for the time at least – turns prophet.
▶ **Tomorrow is the new moon (20:5)** The first day of each new month was a feast day.
▶ **20:8** refers to 18:3.

21 Priest aids David's escape

Ahimelech pays dearly for David's deception (22:11-19). But David is fed and armed, and makes good his escape to the Philistine city of Gath. In danger of recognition, he feigns madness, playing the part so effectively that Achish is completely convinced (see also 27:5-12).

▶ **Nob (1)** Israel's central shrine at that time.
▶ **Sacred bread (4)** Each sabbath 12 fresh loaves were placed on the altar and the 12 stale ones removed. Only the priests were entitled to eat them.
▶ **Verse 5** Israelite soldiers abstained from sexual intercourse during campaigns: a holy war required ritual purity. If Uriah had not steadfastly stuck to the rules, David would have had no occasion to resort to murder (2 Samuel 11:11).
▶ **Verses 12ff.** According to their Hebrew titles Psalms 34 and 56 reflect David's thoughts at this time.

22 King Saul's revenge

David and his whole family are outlawed or in exile. But still Saul is not satisfied. There seems to be more than a touch of paranoia in his outburst (7-8). Ignoring the voice of truth and reason (14-15) he orders first the slaughter of God's priests and then the death of all the inhabitants of Nob. When David hears the news, it is with an awful sense of responsibility.

▶ **Verse 1** The Hebrew titles of Psalms 57 and 142 connect them with this time.

▶ **Verse 4** David had Moabite blood in his veins (see Ruth). He leaves his parents with the king for safety.

▶ **Doeg (9ff.)** The Hebrew title of Psalm 52 relates it to this episode.

23 'I will hunt him down!'
David welds his band of outlaws into an effective military force. But Saul's relentless pursuit keeps them continually on the move. The encouragement of a friend in such a situation is comfort indeed. Jonathan, remarkably, acknowledges David's title to be king, humbly accepting a lesser role for himself (16-18).

▶ **The ephod (6)** See on 14:18.

24 David spares Saul's life
In the cave near Engedi Saul is completely at David's mercy. His refusal to take a short-cut to the throne brings the king to his senses. But Saul's word is as changeable as his mood. It is not to be relied on.

The Hebrew titles of Psalms 57 and 142 – two prayers for help – connect them with this time.

25 Abigail intervenes
The chapter opens with the death of Samuel. Not until Elijah will there be another religious leader to equal him. The old prophet had anointed Israel's greatest king, but did not live to see him reign. It is the end of an era.

David's request to Nabal (8; the name means 'fool') is not unreasonable. He is not demanding protection money, but asking some return on past services (15-16). After all, the man was rich and it was sheep-shearing, a feast time.

Abigail is as clever as she is beautiful. Her quick action saves the lives of her husband and household (22). She evidently made a good impression on David (see verse 39). The writer sees Nabal's death of a double stroke as God's punishment.

26 David again spares Saul
The pro-Saul Ziphites again lay information against David. And for a second time Saul finds himself at David's mercy and is shamed into repentance. No doubt Macbeth would have seen this as a heaven-sent opportunity for advancement! David knew that God did not need his help to put him on the throne. The Hebrew title of Psalm 54 connects it with this time.

▶ **Verse 6** Zeruiah, the mother of Abishai, Joab, and Asahel, was David's step-sister. Though brave, these military leaders caused David a great deal of trouble when he was king (2 Samuel 3:39; 18:14; 20:10).

27:1 – 28:2 Safe in enemy country
David takes refuge a second time amongst the Philistines. Achish is once again completely fooled (see 21:10-15). Pretending to raid Israel and her allies (10), David in fact wipes out enemy cities (8), leaving no one alive to tell the tale (11).

This helmet from Assyria is an example of contemporary armour.

66 The Lord forbid that I should ... raise my hand against ... the Lord's anointed. 99

David refuses to harm King Saul 24:6

In the hills and caves around Engedi there were plenty of hiding-places for a man like David, on the run from King Saul. Fresh water from the spring flows down a gorge to the Dead Sea, producing luxuriant vegetation in an otherwise barren, desert region.

David on the run from Saul

1 David flees from Saul.

2 David takes his parents to Moab for safety.

3 In hiding in the hill country.

4 David escapes to Philistia.

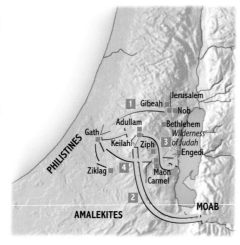

28:3-25 Saul consults a medium

Saul can get no reply from God (6). In desperation he does what has always been forbidden in Israel (Leviticus 19:31) and seeks out a fortune-teller, though he had once driven them from his land. He sets out at night and in disguise on a dangerous journey, close to the enemy camp at Shunem, to consult the medium at Endor. However, he finds Samuel no more reassuring in death than he had been in life. Saul's fate is sealed.

29 The break with the Philistines

The other Philistine overlords are less gullible than Achish, so David is spared the awkward predicament of facing his fellow countrymen in battle. This chapter refers to earlier events than chapter 28. The Philistines muster at Aphek. They have not yet moved north to Shunem.

30 Amalekite raiders caught

David's return is well-timed, and the slave's information more than a stroke of luck. All is recovered. And Judah and the Calebites, also victims of the raid (14), share in the spoil.

31 Saul's last battle

See also 1 Chronicles 10. The writer of Chronicles found this account of Saul's death more credible than the Amalekite's story (2 Samuel 1:4-10). The latter may well have adjusted the facts to suit his own

> **66** *Saul and Jonathan... together in life, together in death; swifter than eagles, stronger than lions ... I grieve for you, my brother Jonathan.* **99**
>
> David's lament
> 2 Samuel 1:23, 25

ends. Fittingly, it is the men of Jabesh who rescue the bodies. They have not forgotten what they owe to Saul's first great victory (chapter 11).

2 Samuel 1 – 20
The reign of King David

King David's reign is also recorded in 1 Chronicles 11 – 29.

1 David's lament

The Amalekite's story differs from the account of Saul's death in 1 Samuel 31. If he twisted the facts hoping for a reward, he did not know David. After the Amalekite raid on Ziklag (1 Samuel 30) David had no cause to love this race. Nonetheless it was not racial discrimination but his strong conviction that the king's life was sacred (14; and see 1 Samuel 24 and 26) that led to the death sentence.

The lament for Saul and Jonathan is one of the most moving and beautiful of all David's poems. His regret for the king seems wholly sincere; his distress at the loss of Jonathan, deep and genuine.

▸ **On the third day (2)** It was 100 miles from Gilboa to Ziklag.

▸ **The book of Jashar (18)** A lost anthology (see Joshua 10:13).

▸ **The shield... rubbed with oil (21)** The shield was leather; oil prevented it drying and cracking.

▸ **Verse 26** This was a unique friendship which David valued more highly even than the love of women, which he was never short of. The words do not imply more: homosexual practices were in any case forbidden in Israel (Leviticus 18:22). We know that Jonathan had a son (chapter 9) even though there is no mention of a wife.

2 Civil war; Abner kills Asahel

Only Judah (by this time probably including Simeon) acclaims David as king. The other ten tribes follow the lead of Abner, Saul's army commander, and give allegiance to Ishbosheth, Saul's son. For two years the nation is divided.

An attempt to settle the issue by representative single combat (14) at Gibeon is inconclusive, and full-scale

Magic in the Old Testament
Todd Klutz

Concerns about health, finances, reputation, relationships, and protection against misfortune have been common throughout history and among all known societies of the world. Unfortunately, these concerns are sometimes allowed to evolve into unhealthy obsessions, which can lead to anxious attempts to alter reality by means of magical formulas, rituals, or occult practices. This way of responding to difficulties is pictured in several passages of the Old Testament, where such efforts are given a wholly negative evaluation.

For example, although the word 'magic' is not used in Deuteronomy 18:9-13, there is a complete ban on anyone who engages in activities that are essentially magical in character: 'No one shall be found among you who makes a son or daughter pass through fire, or who practises divination, or is a soothsayer, or an augur, or a sorcerer, or one who casts spells, or who consults ghosts or spirits, or who seeks oracles from the dead' (10-11).

In addition to being rooted in egocentric desires to control reality, the practices described here are said to be routine behaviour among Israel's ancient enemies, and are taboo on this account. Their unreliability distinguishes them from authentic prophecy (14-22).

In this light, then, magic can be seen as an illegitimate way to fulfill a legitimate need – the almost universal human need to experience communion with a world beyond that which constrains everyday existence.

Magic is not only prohibited by Israelite legal statutes, it is also discouraged by examples found in a variety of biblical narratives.

In the book of Exodus, for instance, where the God of Israel liberates his chosen people from slavery in Egypt, God's human agents (Moses and Aaron) are opposed by the 'magicians' of Egypt, in a contest between the power of Israel's God and the magic of the Egyptian sorcerers (Exodus 7 – 9). Although the precise difference between the techniques

The liver of an animal was inspected by ancient seers endeavouring to predict future events.

of the Egyptian magicians and those of God's servants may not be obvious, two features of this story's context are revealing:

- whereas the Egyptian magicians serve a regime that is oppressive to God's people, Moses and Aaron serve a God whose ultimate aim is to accomplish deliverance and salvation;
- the power and purposes of the God of Moses and Aaron clearly emerge as victorious in the contest.

Thus, magic is represented in these narratives not only as contrary to the will of God, but also

Bound female spirits or daimones (often called 'Liliths' in Aramaic texts) were thought to cause troubles for both men and women. The drawing comes from ancient Mesopotamia.

as inferior in strength to the highest spiritual power available, namely that given by God to those who worship and serve him.

Attitudes very similar to those conveyed in Exodus 7 – 9 can be found in several other Old Testament stories involving magic. The most instructive of these are:

- the account of King Saul's use of a witch, to obtain information from the dead (1 Samuel 28:3-25)
- and the narratives portraying the biblical heroes Joseph and Daniel as superior to their pagan opponents in providing trustworthy knowledge of the spiritual realm (Genesis 41:1-57; and Daniel 1:17-20; 2:1-49; 4:4-33).

Outside the Old Testament and among the ancient Israelites' neighbours, a large portion of what we might call magic consisted of formulas and rituals for removing ill-health and protecting against evil influences. In some cases, however, magical purifications were performed in order to achieve success in war; and a large number of cursing tablets and binding spells in Greek from various parts of the ancient Mediterranean seem, at least on a superficial reading, to have been designed to injure or harm one's opponents.

Saul and Jonathan lost their lives to the Philistines in the mountains of Gilboa (in the far distance in this picture). Their bodies were brought here to Beth-shan, and hung on the walls. Remains of temples found in the course of extensive excavation could have been those where Saul's armour was displayed.

civil war follows.

▶ **Verse 13** The 'pool' collected precious rainwater: excavation has revealed a shaft 11.3m/37ft across and 10.6m/35ft deep.

▶ **Sons of Zeruiah (18)** See 1 Samuel 26:6.

▶ **The butt of his spear (23)** Abner did not intend to kill Asahel. But the butt was sharp so that it would stick in the ground, and the blow proved fatal.

▶ **The Arabah (29)** The long rift valley from Galilee to the Dead Sea and beyond; here, the Jordan Valley.

3 Abner makes terms; Joab's revenge

Ishbosheth is not the man his father was. Abner is the real power. If he transfers his support to David, he carries the nation with him. But he reckons without the implacable hatred of Joab, David's nephew and army commander. David leads the nation's mourning for Abner. Despite a public declaration of innocence, the taint of the murder remains with him all his life (1 Kings 2:5). Abner's death is to David's advantage, just as the death of Ishbosheth will be (chapter 4): both weaken the support for Saul's family.

▶ **Saul had a concubine (7)** A king's harem normally passed to his heir, which makes Abner's action tantamount to a claim to the throne. Compare Absalom's action, 16:20ff. Rizpah appears again in chapter 21.

▶ **A dog's head of Judah (8)** I.e. 'one of

Hebron was David's capital before he took Jerusalem. This aerial view shows the 'tomb of Abraham'.

David's contemptible supporters'.

▶ **Verse 9** The reason why God took Saul's throne from him is made plain in1 Samuel 13:13-14 and 15:22-28.

▶ **Dan to Beersheba (10)** The whole country, north to south.

▶ **My wife Michal... (14)** See 1 Samuel 18:20-27. Saul had given David's wife to another man.

Verse 29 A discharge, or 'running sore' disqualified a man from religious service. 'Hold a spindle/ply the distaff' means fit only for women's work.

4 Ishbosheth assassinated

Once again (see 1:1-16) David's supporters completely fail to understand his attitude to Saul and the royal family. Ishbosheth is given honourable burial, the two murderers are publicly disgraced.

5 David rules from Jerusalem

See also 1 Chronicles 11:1-9; 14. The writer makes it clear that David is no usurper. God has given him his title to the throne: a fact recognized by Saul (1 Samuel 24:18-20), by Abner (3:9-10) and finally by the whole nation (5:2).

Although part of Jerusalem fell to Judah at the conquest (Judges 1:8), the fortress itself had never been taken (Joshua 15:63; Judges 1:21). The Jebusites had some

David's family tree

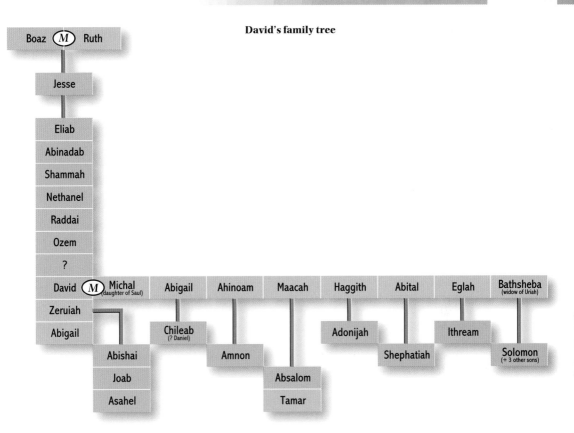

ground for their boast that a garrison of blind men and cripples could hold it (6). But they underestimated David.

Jerusalem was a first-rate choice of capital. It was centrally situated, tribally neutral, had a distinguished pre-history from Abraham's time and could therefore provide the 12 tribes with a unifying centre. It was held by Judah until Nebuchadnezzar destroyed it 400 years later.

▶ **Zion (7)** The name later became interchangeable with Jerusalem.

▶ **The Millo (9)** Part of the fortifications.

▶ **Hiram, king of Tyre (11)** A contemporary of David and Solomon (1 Kings 5), Hiram reigned about 979-945 BC. The sea-port of Tyre was capital of the Phoenician kingdom. Hiram's reign was a golden age of political expansion and commercial prosperity, when arts and crafts flourished. His craftsmen helped to build the Temple.

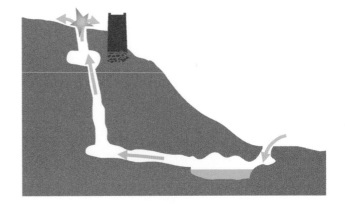

▶ **Verse 13** The polygamy of David and Solomon is noted but not condemned. The consequences for family life make their own point.

▶ **Verses 17ff.** Consulting God seems to have become second nature to David (see 2:1), though how David asked and God answered is not made clear.

David's men took the Jerusalem citadel by means of a tunnel which brought water into the city from an outside spring.

6 The Ark comes to Jerusalem

See also 1 Chronicles 13; 15 – 16.

After the Philistines returned the Ark (1 Samuel 4 - 6), it remained at Kiriath-jearim (Baalah in Judah; see 1 Chronicles 13:6). Now David brings it to his new capital. The occasion is marked with all the exuberance of Jewish worship. Even the king dances for joy. Only Michal stands aloof and outside it all, cold and unmoved by the presence of God.

▶ **Uzzah took hold of the Ark (6)** It is sacred: not even the Levites were allowed to touch it. This is the reason for the severe punishment. David blames himself for not following the instructions Moses laid down (1 Chronicles 15:2-15). At the next attempt the Levites carried the Ark on poles.

▶ **Verse 23** seems to indicate a severance of the relationship. Consequently there will be no grandchild of Saul through Michal to lay claim to the kingdom.

7 God's covenant with David

See also 1 Chronicles 17.

God will not allow David to fulfil his dream of building the Temple – that is for his son, a man of peace, not a warrior (1 Chronicles 22:7ff.). But the disappointment is followed by a promise that goes way beyond anything David could have asked: no wonder his response is a great outpouring of love and praise (18ff.). He may not build a house for God, but God will build *him* a house – a dynasty – which will be 'for ever' (16).

On this promise rests a hope which runs right through the remainder of the Old Testament, the hope of a Messiah. And when Christ came, the promise was fulfilled. He was born in David's birthplace, Bethlehem, and 'of the house and lineage of David' (Luke 2:4). The angel tells Mary: 'The Lord God will give to him the throne of his father David, and he will reign over the house of Jacob for ever; and of his kingdom there will be no end' (Luke 1:32-33).

▶ **Your son... shall build (12-13)** Solomon did build (1 Kings 5 – 7). But David contributed a great deal: he drew up the plans, provided materials, and organized and assigned Temple duties including music and worship (1 Chronicles 28:11ff.; 22:2ff.).

8 David's victories

See also 1 Chronicles 18.

This chapter pre-dates the events of chapter 7 (see 7:1).

▶ **Verse 2** Previously David was on good terms with the Moabites (1 Samuel 22:3-4), so this is hard to understand. Much later, a view was put forward that they had killed his parents.

▶ **Verse 9** Hamath is Hama, in Syria, north of Damascus.

▶ **Valley of Salt (13)** Probably in the barren section of the great rift valley south of the Dead Sea.

▶ **Verse 17** It was Zadok who anointed Solomon king (1 Kings 1).

▶ **Kerethites... Pelethites (18)** Philistine mercenaries.

▶ **David's sons were priests (18)** Although not from a priestly family, David was himself something of a priest-king (see chapter 6), like Melchizedek, a much earlier king of Jerusalem (Genesis 14:18).

9 David seeks out Jonathan's crippled son

The events of chapter 21 may pre-date this chapter. If so, no doubt the king's

David's wars

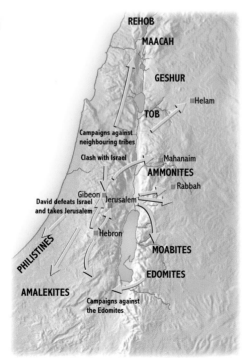

REHOB
MAACAH
GESHUR
■Helam
TOB
Campaigns against neighbouring tribes
Clash with Israel
Mahanaim
AMMONITES
■Rabbah
Gibeon
David defeats Israel and takes Jerusalem
Jerusalem
■Hebron
MOABITES
EDOMITES
PHILISTINES
AMALEKITES
Campaigns against the Edomites

summons terrified Mephibosheth. But David's motives are wholly good, 'for Jonathan's sake' (see 1 Samuel 20:42). He restores the family estates (7) and treats the young man as his own son (11).

Lo-debar (4) In north Gilead, not far from Jabesh.

▶ **Verse 10** This sounds contradictory, but being at court would mean an increase in general expenses, even if meals were provided.

10 Defeat of the Ammonite/Syrian alliance

See also 1 Chronicles 19.

Hanun provoked the war by his outrageous treatment of the ambassadors. But no doubt neighbouring nations were suspicious and afraid of Israel's powerful king.

The campaign in verses 16-18 may be the one mentioned in 8:3ff.

This victory marks another big

David

David Barton

David was Israel's second king. Under the surface of the biblical story are many different currents:

- the rise of the monarchy in the face of pressure from the Philistines
- the rivalry of two kingdoms, Israel and Judah
- the establishment of Jerusalem and David's dynasty.

All this is held together in an extensive and wonderfully crafted narrative from which David emerges as a living character.

Early days

At the start, we are brought in on the secret anointing of the king-to-be. David's qualities, unknown to his family, were recognized by God and made known to his prophet, Samuel.

David's public life begins with his battle with the Philistine champion, Goliath. The impulsive courage and trust in God he shows here never desert him. Brave, attractive and talented, the young David moves in and out of Saul's court, winning battles against the Philistines and playing the harp to

soothe the king's increasingly irritable moods.

He establishes a strong friendship with Saul's son Jonathan and marries his daughter Michal. But in the end Saul's jealousy makes it impossible for him to stay, so he becomes an outlaw in his own land, living in the cave of Adullam.

Hard times

There follow difficult times. For a while David even throws in his lot with the hated Philistines. But it is part of the greatness of David's character that, even though Saul seeks his life, he will not return the

hatred. The cat and mouse games of 1 Samuel 24 and 26 show David's loyalty to his king and father-in-law. They also suggest someone with an eye to his own future. Saul is sacred because he is king. One day David may need the same veneration.

When Saul and Jonathan die at Gilboa, David is settling his own scores with the Amalekites at Ziklag. There is a rich irony in the fact that it is an Amalekite who brings the news to David, lying about his part in it. That gives two reasons for killing the messenger. But David's grief is instant and

David was a shepherd boy, guarding his father's flocks in the pastures around Bethlehem, when he was chosen to be king.

▶▶

extension of the kingdom and David's power over neighbouring nations.

▶ **Rabbah (8)** is Amman, present capital of Jordan.

11 David sleeps with Uriah's wife

His army is fighting the Ammonites, but this spring the king is not with them. He is taking an after-siesta stroll in the cool, on the palace roof. And from his vantage-point he can see down into the open inner courtyard of a nearby house, where the lovely Bathsheba is going through the monthly purification ritual following menstruation. The events that follow – adultery and murder – are the watershed in David's life. From this point on he reaps the bitter harvest of his sin. Although all seemed to be going according to plan (27), 'The Lord was not pleased with what David had done.'

(Significantly, the Chronicler omits this

The beautiful cascade at Engedi, in the region where David was outlawed, is still called 'David's waterfall'.

genuine. Often we are drawn to him by his tears, and his lament for Saul and Jonathan is one of the great poems of the Old Testament.

King David

The years of Saul's decline brought chaos to Israel. When David first becomes king, it is of the small southern tribe of Judah. Only later does he become king of Israel.

In a shrewd political move to give himself independent power, David takes the Jebusite city of Jerusalem and makes it his capital. He can afford now to be even-handed between the two halves of his kingdom.

By moving the Ark there he ensures that Jerusalem will become both a religious and a political centre. His own palace reflects his new power. But when he wants to build a Temple to house the Ark, Nathan the prophet stops him. Instead, God will establish David's 'house' – his dynasty. David, awed by the extraordinary authority he has now acquired, turns to God in grateful prayer.

But the story from now on is in marked contrast to what has gone before. Against a background of war, David begins acting like a tyrant. He sees Bathsheba, and

whole episode from his account of David's life.)

▶ **Joab (1)** David had taken no action over Joab's murder of Abner (chapter 2). Now Joab must bring about the death of Uriah on the king's orders.

▶ **Uriah the Hittite (3)** Uriah was one of David's special guard (23:39), away on the king's war.

▶ **Verse 11** The army is on campaign, under canvas, and the rule is that the men abstain from sexual intercourse. Had Uriah been a man of less principle he would have gone home to his wife. The child might then have been passed off as his, and he would not have been killed. But maybe he already suspected the truth.

▶ **Jerubbesheth (21,** some versions) I.e. Jerubbaal/Gideon (Judges 9). 'Baal' being a pagan name, the scribes later substituted the word 'bosheth'/ 'besheth', 'shame'. So Jerubbaal became Jerubbesheth; Eshbaal became Ishbosheth; Meribbaal, Mephibosheth, and so on.

---

longs for her. After their adultery he plots to have her husband killed in battle, and then takes Bathsheba as his wife. What redeems David here is that in the face of prophet Nathan's rebuke he is prepared to admit his double sin. There are no excuses, and in the following sad verses we see again the greatness of the man.

Bitter harvest

David has repented, and Solomon his successor is born to Bathsheba, but the disarming boldness and sureness of touch of the younger David are for ever lost. From now on he begins to reap a bitter harvest. The gifted statesman, who can establish political and religious unity over disparate tribes, cannot bring peace and order to his own family.

2 Samuel 13 – 18 record the schemes and rebellions of his indulged son Absalom, a story with complex plots and sub-plots. Part of the intrigue of these chapters lies in the ambiguous character of David's henchman, Joab. It is never quite clear if his actions spring from blind loyalty or personal ambition. The family feud amounts to a civil war, and David's life is under threat. David weeps, this time for himself, as he walks up Mount Olivet, escaping his son.

Yet, when Absalom dies, David is once more torn with anguish. We sense his anxiety as he awaits news of the battle, and as he struggles to find the truth in the elaborate language of the messenger. Then, just a few simple words of grief, 'O my son Absalom', tell us that his family matters more to him than his throne, that his victory has become a bitter loss. The great commander whose first thought had always been for his men, must now be told that his grief is an insult to the soldiers who gave him victory and saved him from certain death.

After this, the last chapters of 2 Samuel are something of a relief, reminding us of David the poet, David the commander, and David the one who longed to build the Temple.

In the final scene in 1 Kings 1, David is old, unable to keep the cold from his bones, despite the warmth of the beautiful Abishag. About him the court schemes, sensing the end. Yet, feeble as he is, David asserts himself for one last time. He summons Solomon and has him publicly anointed king, and settles some old scores, including that with Joab, the killer of Absalom. The circle is closed.

Flawed hero

Fittingly, the king dies of old age in his own bed, like a true patriarch. For, flawed hero though he is, David ranks with Abraham and Moses as one of the great architects of Israel. From him begin ideas that still resonate. Part of the strength of his story is that it is told, without judgment, in all its disparate elements. The thread that holds everything together is David's trust in God. Through sin, crime and repentance, he never falters. For that reason God remains with him, and forgives. But though there is forgiveness, there is no escape from the consequences of his wrong-doing. David lives in the paradox of forgiven sin and a world of suffering. Perhaps that is why his tears touch us so deeply.

David's story runs from 1 Samuel 16 to 1 Kings 2. See also 1 Chronicles 11 – 29. The titles of many of the psalms link them to David: best-known of all, Psalm 23, the shepherd psalm.

KEY EVENTS

The anointing **1 Samuel 16**
David and Goliath **1 Samuel 17**
Lament for Saul **2 Samuel 1**
God's promise **2 Samuel 7**
Bathsheba **2 Samuel 11 – 12**
Absalom's rebellion
2 Samuel 15 – 18
Solomon's succession and
David's death **1 Kings 1 – 2**

12 Nathan's telling tale

Uriah is dead; the wedding over; the child born. It all seems to have blown over very nicely – until Nathan arrives. And then, by means of a simple little story with a sting in its tail, the whole sordid episode is exposed. The prophet's tale slips under David's guard, in the way of stories, and suddenly David sees himself as God sees him: a humbling experience for a king (see Psalm 51). God forgives him, but he is punished, and despite David's anguished prayer the child dies. Nor is there yet any resurrection hope to comfort him in his loss.

But this is not the end of the relationship with Bathsheba, nor is she rejected: for out of the grief and the comforting comes another life, and 'the Lord loved the boy (Solomon)' (24-25).

All this time David's army has been campaigning against the Ammonites. Joab has set things up for David to come in at the head of his troops and capture Rabbah/Amman (26-31). (See also 1 Chronicles 20:1-3.)

▶ **Pay four times over (6)** See Exodus 22:1.
▶ **Verses 10-11** The prophecy was fulfilled. Three of David's sons were murdered, two by their own brothers. And in the rebellion Absalom took over his father's harem (16:22).
▶ **Sent a message (25)** Presumably to reassure David that this child would not die.
▶ **A talent of gold (30)** About 30kg/66lb.

13 Rape in King David's family

Faced with the appalling rape of his daughter Tamar by her half-brother Amnon, David, though angry, does nothing at all. The strong king is a fatally weak father (see 1 Kings 1:6). Had David taken action he might have prevented both the murder and the later rebellion.

The story of the rape of Dinah in Genesis 34 gave her no voice. Here the writer lets us feel the agony of Tamar. Her voice is clearly heard, for its own sake and/or to explain Absalom's hatred, revenge and eventual rebellion against the king.

(The Chronicler's account omits both the rape and Absalom's rebellion, moving straight to the census of chapter 24.)

▶ **Verse 13** Tamar does not think marriage out of the question (though in view of Leviticus

18:11 they would have needed a special dispensation). The 'impossibility' of verse 2 lies in her careful seclusion – Amnon had no thought of marriage, he only wanted to satisfy his lust.
▶ **Geshur (37)** Absalom went to his mother's home (2 Samuel 3:3).

14 David allows Absalom home

Joab pierces the king's defences much as Nathan had done (chapter 12), but with a fake law-suit. This time the appeal is to waive the next-of-kin's duty to avenge his murdered relative. The message for David is obvious. He is willing to overrule in the case of one of his subjects; why not for his heir?

Joab wins his point, and Absalom returns from exile. But two long, frustrating years pass before he is admitted to his father's presence, and the relationship is deeply damaged.

▶ **Verses 17, 20** Knowing right from wrong/good from evil may equally mean knowing everything (compare Genesis 3:5).
▶ **Verse 26** It was Absalom's hair which eventually brought about his death (18:9). The weight is about 2.3kg/5lbs.

15 The king flees Jerusalem

With Amnon out of the way, and Abigail's son dead, Absalom is next in line to the throne. But Solomon is David's chosen heir. For four years Absalom lays his plans (1-6), gradually winning the people over. When he does come into the open (7-12) the challenge to David is extremely serious.

The king is caught unprepared. To save the city, and gain time, he leaves Jerusalem. But he organizes a spy-ring. And Hushai is sent back to outwit Ahithophel, whose far-sighted counsel is otherwise likely to win the day for Absalom.

▶ **The gate (2)** Where the city's business and legal transactions took place (see Ruth 4:1ff.).
▶ **Hebron (7)** David's former capital, in Judah.
▶ **Verses 25-26** Is this simply submission to God's will, or a crisis of conscience/confidence on David's part?
▶ **Verse 30** Jesus, betrayed like David, would spend his night of anguish on the Mount of Olives (Luke 22:39ff.)
▶ **Ahithophel (31)** Bathsheba's grandfather; wisest of all David's advisers.

16:1-14 Aid for the king – and a curse

Obsequious Ziba (1-4) clearly has an eye to the main chance. Mephibosheth later denies the charges made against him (19:24-30).

Shimei (5-8) takes a vindictive pleasure in the downfall of the man who robbed his family of the throne.

David has never thought less of himself (9-14). As he makes for the Jordan, on the run from his own son as he had once been from Saul, he is at an all-time low. What happens now will rest with God.

16:15-23 Absalom sleeps with David's women

Back in Jerusalem (15-19) David's agent Hushai succeeds in convincing Absalom of his loyalty.

Verses 20-23 provide an example of Ahithophel's political strategy. By taking over David's harem, Absalom will convince his followers that reconciliation with his father is impossible. No king could forgive such a public insult. So it happened as Nathan had predicted (2 Samuel 12:11-12).

17 Counsellor's suicide

Ahithophel's advice is to strike quickly, and only against the person of the king – so avoiding civil war. But Hushai gains time for David by a scheme which appeals to Absalom's vanity (11ff.). Ahithophel has the foresight to realize the probable consequences – hence his suicide (23).

Meantime, in an episode that recalls Joshua 2 and Rahab's saving of the two spies, Jonathan and Ahimaaz (on their way to David with the information) escape discovery through a woman's protective action (17-20). Their warning gives the king just enough time to escape: to a warm welcome and a good meal, at last, for his famished men.

▶ **Verse 14b** The writer points the message. The will of God works through human beings in the detail: David will be restored.

▶ **Amasa (25)** His mother Abigail was David's half-sister. Joab was his cousin.

▶ **Mahanaim (27)** A city belonging to Gad, east of the Jordan, in Gilead.

18 – 19:8 Victory for the king

David's defeat of Absalom is God's victory (18:28, 31). Joab's orders are to spare David's son, but he is shrewd enough to see that only the death of the pretender – or the king – can settle the issue. David did not forgive Joab for Absalom's death (see 19:13). It was ironic that the young man's beautiful hair (14:26) should tangle in the oak and leave him a helpless prey.

18:33 – 19:8: terrible grief and remorse (see 12:10) blind the king to the effect of his conduct on the people. Joab's harsh words bring him to his senses and save him from political disaster.

▶ **Pile of stones (18:17)** A cairn marked the grave of a criminal.

▶ **No son (18:18)** appears to contradict 14:27. Did they die young?

▶ **Ahimaaz and the Cushite (18:19-32)** Joab chooses the Sudanese/Ethiopian slave to take the bad news. The king would naturally have assumed (as he does in 27) that the priest's son brought good news. Joab may also have been thinking of the fate of earlier messengers (1:11-16; 4:9-12). But the direct hill-route proved slower than the route Ahimaaz took along the Jordan Valley (23).

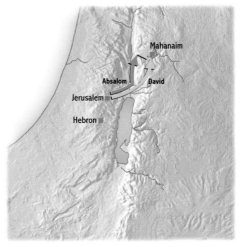

Absalom's rebellion

19:9-43 Aftermath of rebellion

Judah had backed Absalom. David's attempt to win them back, and his appointment of Amasa (Absalom's army commander, and his own nephew) in Joab's place leads to further trouble (41-43 and chapter 20). David is in effect punishing loyalty and rewarding rebellion. Now that the king is back in power, there are some who are anxious to find favour (Shimei, 16-22, see 16:5-14; Mephibosheth, 24-30, see 16:1-4; on Shimei and Barzillai, see also 1 Kings 2).

Verses 40-43: the dispute between the men of Judah and the ten tribes begins a rift which widens in chapter 20 and will split the kingdom after Solomon's death.

Jerusalem: City of David

The original settlement occupied a ridge of hill down towards the Gihon Spring. The hilltop 'platform' then made a natural defensive position and, later, the Temple area. Here, by tradition, Abraham's faith was tested when he heard God's call to sacrifice his son. Today it is the location of the Dome of the Rock mosque, shown in the picture below (which is a view from the south-west).

Present wall of the Old City

Later extension of the city and Temple area under Solomon

C

D

Fortified area

Gihon Spring

David's city

A

B

Jerusalem

A/C

David's city

B/D

1km/1,100yds

▶ **Verse 23** Although David extends mercy to Shimei here, he will order Solomon to kill him (1 Kings 2:8-9).

20 Sheba divides the tribes
Despite the statement in verse 2, those who actively support Sheba in his revolt, when it comes to it, are few (14ff.).

Joab is as quick to kill Amasa (a member of his own family) for his loss of command as he was to kill Abner, when his own position was threatened before. In both cases his treachery is despicable. The kiss and the sword-thrust bring to mind Judas' betrayal of Jesus. David did not forget, or forgive (see 1 Kings 2:5-6).

▶ **Verse 3** These are the concubines Absalom had made his own. The consequence for them is dire.

▶ **Adoram (24)** In a post not likely to win friends, he was stoned to death in the reign of Solomon's son.

▶ **Verses 23-26** Note the smallness of the king's inner cabinet: this is a monarchy without a bureaucracy. Contrast Solomon's vast array of officials (1 Kings 4).

2 Samuel 21 – 24
Records of David's reign

21 Gibeon appeased
Verses 1-14 probably precede Mephibosheth's welcome at court (chapter 9). The story of Israel's pact with Gibeon is told in Joshua 9:3-27. Saul had apparently broken the treaty (though this is not mentioned elsewhere), despite close family connections with the city (1 Chronicles 8:29ff.).

Verses 15-22 belong to the time of the events in 2 Samuel 5:17ff.

▶ **That you may bless (3)** And so remove the curse that brought the famine.

▶ **Verse 6** The Hebrew does not specify the manner of death, despite some translations.

▶ **Merab (8)** The daughter who had been promised to David as wife.

▶ **Used sackcloth to make a shelter (10)** Rizpah may have been there as long as six months. The coming of rain brought an end to the famine, and to the curse, leaving David free to act.

▶ **Elhanan... killed Goliath (19)** This seems to conflict with 1 Samuel 17. The text here may be confused. R. K. Harrison suggests it should read, 'Elhanan, the son of Jairi the Bethlehemite, slew the brother of Goliath', which ties in with 1 Chronicles 20:5. Another possibility is that a new champion took the name of the one killed by David.

22 David's victory song

This is virtually identical with Psalm 18, and can be compared with Moses' song in Deuteronomy 32. It belongs to the period of David's great early victories. Verses 21-25 contrast with the deeper self-knowledge which followed the Bathsheba/Uriah episode, expressed in Psalm 51.

23:1-7 David's 'last words'

These may be the last words 'the singer of Israel's psalms' set down in poetry (see 1 Kings 2 for his final charge to Solomon). His thoughts centre on what makes a good ruler, on his own standing before God, and on the promised dynasty – a fitting close to the life of the king who for all his faults was 'a man after God's own heart'.

23:8-39 David's special guard

The exploits of 'The Three' against the Philistines (8-12) are followed by an incident from the campaign described in 5:17-25 (13-17; Bethlehem was David's home town). Then come the exploits of two leaders (Abishai, leader of 'The Thirty', and Benaiah, leader of the Philistine mercenaries), followed by a list of the special guard. The group was probably formed at Ziklag, and helped to put David on the throne (1 Chronicles 12:1; 11:10). More than 30 are listed – those killed (e.g. Asahel, Uriah) were replaced by others.

24 The census and the plague

See also 1 Chronicles 21.

It is not clear why it was wrong to take the census. Perhaps it indicated reliance on numbers, instead of on God. The Chronicler (1 Chronicles 21:1) – perhaps conscious that his readers may have a problem with God first inciting David to take the census, then punishing him for doing so – has Satan doing the inciting.

Verses 8-25: the first readers did not need to be told the tremendous significance of David's purchase, explicitly mentioned in 1 Chronicles 21:18 – 22:1. On this threshing-floor the Temple was built, close to the place where Abraham prepared to offer up Isaac (2 Chronicles 3:1; Genesis 22:2).

▶ **Verse 16** The Old Testament writers in a number of places speak of God repenting, regretting doing something, or changing his mind (usually to adopt a more merciful course of action).

1 & 2 Kings

Summary

The history of the nation from King Solomon to the exile.

1 Kings 3 – 11
Solomon's reign
•
1 Kings 12 – 2 Kings 25
Kings of Israel and Judah

Best-known stories; key passages
The Temple
(1 Kings 5 – 8)
The Queen of Sheba
(1 Kings 10)
The kingdom splits
(1 Kings 12 – 14)
Elijah *(1 Kings17ff.)*
Elisha *(2 Kings 2 ff.)*

Kings (originally one book, not two) continues the story of Israel, picking up from the point where Samuel ended and covering the next four centuries. It takes us from the end of David's reign and the golden age of Solomon when the Temple was built, through the rift between the northern and southern tribes which divided the nation into two separate kingdoms – Israel and Judah – and on to the fall of Samaria (722/1 BC) and the destruction of Jerusalem (587 BC).

The account begins with a stable, united kingdom under a strong king and ends with total collapse and mass deportation to Babylon. It is a sombre story, and one in which the writer sees a clear moral. God is the Lord of history, actively involved in human affairs. When the nation and its leaders look to him and obey his laws, peace and prosperity follow. Political and economic disaster overtake Israel and Judah as a direct consequence of the weakening of the nation's moral and religious fibre.

An important element in the story is the emergence of the prophets, most notably Elijah and Elisha, to call the nation back to God.

The writer/compiler of this collection of stories is unknown. He was probably a prophet in Babylon during the exile, about 550 BC. He mentions a number of his sources (e.g. 1 Kings 11:41; 15:31): court and official records and cycles of stories about the prophets. He wrote his account as one volume, to be read through from beginning to end. Much of the material is paralleled in Chronicles.

There are problems with dates and chronology throughout. The issues are discussed in 'Unravelling the chronology of the kings'.

1 Kings 1 – 2
Who will succeed King David?

1 Rivals for the throne
King David is now an old man. Thoughts turn to his successor. With his three elder brothers dead, Adonijah is heir apparent. He has the backing of Joab, the army commander, and Abiathar, one of the two chief priests. But the throne has been promised to Adonijah's half-brother, Solomon (1:13, and see 1 Chronicles 22:9). And thanks to some quick thinking by the prophet Nathan, and even quicker action by the old king, Adonijah is out-manoeuvred. Solomon is made king, initially co-regent with David.

▶ **Abishag (3)** from Shunem near Nazareth, is sometimes identified with the heroine of the Song of Solomon, but there are no real grounds for this.

▶ **Verse 4** Older versions have 'knew her not',

Gezer was one of the cities rebuilt and fortified by King Solomon, after it had been destroyed by the Egyptians. The stone pillars were part of a Canaanite 'high place' of worship.

meaning 'did not have sexual intercourse'.

▶ **Verse 5** See 2 Samuel 18.

▶ **Verses 7-8** Zadok and Abiathar, see 2 Samuel 15:24ff.; Benaiah, 2 Samuel 23:20-23; Nathan, 2 Samuel 12. The mighty men were David's special guard: 2 Samuel 23:8-39.

▶ **Enrogel (9)** was on the boundary between Benjamin and Judah.

▶ **Verse 13** This promise is not recorded elsewhere.

▶ **Gihon (33)** A spring just outside the eastern wall of Jerusalem, in the Kidron Valley.

▶ **Kerethites and Pelethites (38)** Foreign (Philistine) mercenaries.

▶ **The tent (39)** in which the Ark was kept.

▶ **Horns of the altar (50)** Horn-like 'handles' on top, at the four corners.

2:1-12 The old king dies

As death approaches, David gives Solomon his final instructions. High-toned advice (1-4) is abruptly followed by worldly wisdom of doubtful morality (5-9).

▶ **Joab (5)** See 2 Samuel 3:26-30; 20:8-10. Solomon obeyed his father's instructions: see 2:28-34.

▶ **Barzillai (7)** See 2 Samuel 17:27-29; 19:31-39.

▶ **Shimei (8)** David did not regard his pledge to Shimei as binding on Solomon. See 2 Samuel 16:5-14 and 19:16-23.

2:13-46 Opposition purged

Adonijah, supported by Abiathar the priest and army commander Joab, has already laid claim to the throne (chapter 1). This time he pays dearly for what may have been an unthinking request. Solomon sees it as a second bid for kingship, since possession of his predecessor's harem was part of the eastern king's title to the throne (compare Absalom's action, 2 Samuel 16). Abiathar is dismissed (though he appears to have been reinstated, 4:4). And Joab dies the violent death he has meted out to others.

Shimei, another potential trouble-maker, is put on parole in Jerusalem to keep him away from fellow-Benjamites. When he breaks parole, even though for an innocent reason, Solomon has him killed.

▶ **Anathoth (26)** This town to the north of Jerusalem belonged to the Levites. It was the home of a later prophet, Jeremiah. Abiathar's disgrace would have left a lasting sense of shame.

▶ **The word... about Eli (27)** See 1 Samuel 2:27-36.

1 Kings 3 – 11
Solomon's glorious reign

3:1-15 'Give me wisdom'

See also 2 Chronicles 1:3-12.

Solomon is at Gibeon, a town 10km/ 6 miles north-west of Jerusalem making his sacrifice, when God appears to him in a dream offering a gift which is his to choose. He asks for wisdom to rule his people justly. It is the choice of a man whose heart is right before God and so he is given more than he asks for. Solomon will be renowned for wise judgment. His fame will spread far and wide. And his kingdom will enjoy economic prosperity as never before.

▶ **Verse 1** 'The city', i.e. the citadel on Mt Zion. See also article, 'Egypt'.

▶ **Verse 2** For shrines/altars older versions have 'high places', meaning the old Canaanite shrines (often, but not always, on hill-tops) which the Israelites took over. It was not long before the worship of God in these places became mixed with crude pagan practices. The later prophets condemn them.

▶ **The dream (5)** Dreams were reckoned to have real significance in the ancient world and the Old Testament records a number of dreams in which God reveals his will (see e.g. the message to Abraham in Genesis 20:6ff.; Jacob's dream, Genesis 28:12ff.; Joseph's dreams and God's gift of interpretation).

▶ **Burnt-offerings (4)** For sacrifice generally, see Leviticus 1 – 7.

3:16-28 'Cut the child in two!'

A particularly hard case serves to illustrate Solomon's God-given gift of wise judgment. Where it is one woman's word against another, special insight into human nature (wisdom from God, 28) is needed to uncover the true facts. The incident also shows the king's accessibility to ordinary folk, even two prostitutes.

Solomon's 12 administrative districts

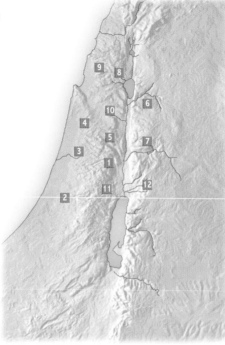

Deep below the old city of Jerusalem these great quarries extend 65m/ 200yds into the rock. The marks of the picks can still be seen. See on 1 Kings 6:7.

4 Serving King Solomon the wise

In contrast to the simple regime of King David, Solomon introduces a vast bureaucracy to adminster his kingdom. The court included not only the royal family (11:3 gives the size of the harem) but ministers, civil servants and domestics, and must have numbered several thousand. No wonder elaborate arrangements are necessary for their maintenance (7-28).

The king outshone his greatest contemporaries in wisdom, which he expressed, as they did, in proverbs and songs and sayings based on natural and animal life (see, for example, Psalms 72 and 127, both of whose titles ascribe them to Solomon, and Proverbs 10:1 – 22:16).

▶ **Verses 1-6** Azariah was head of inland revenue, in charge of those who collected taxes (in kind). 'King's friend' (some versions) = king's councillor.

▶ **Vine/fig-tree (25)** A proverbial phrase indicating idyllic conditions of peace and plenty.

5 Preparing for the Temple

See also 2 Chronicles 2.
Friendship with the Phoenician kingdom of Tyre, to the north (see 2 Samuel 5:11) is further cemented by a trade-pact: Hiram will supply raw materials for the Temple in return for foodstuffs.

▶ **Cedars from Lebanon (6)** 'Lebanon' is the mountain range and these cedars are the finest timber available. Just a few of these mighty trees remain today where once there was a great forest.

▶ **Cor/Kor (11)** A measurement of capacity. A cor of wheat = a donkey-load. A cor of oil = 48 gallons. Good News Bible reads '2,000 tonnes of wheat and 400,000 litres of pure olive oil'.

▶ **Byblos (18)** About 32km/20 miles up the coast from Beirut, Byblos was famous for its craftsmen. The Greek word *biblos* = book (hence English 'Bible') comes from 'Byblos', the city that made paper from Egyptian papyrus.

6 Building the Temple

See also 2 Chronicles 3.
In size the Temple was a chapel rather than a cathedral. It was intended as a house for God, not a building to hold vast gatherings of people. (The climate allowed the people to gather outdoors in the courtyards around the building at festival times.) It measured about 27 x 9 x 13.5m/ 90 x 30 x 45ft, divided into two sections, with part of the inner section curtained off to form the sanctuary. In front was a 4.5 x 9 m/15 x 30ft entrance porch, and along the sides were store-rooms.

Verses 11-13 highlight the point of it all: God with his people.

Verses 15-36 picture for us the beautiful

Solomon's Temple and its successors
Alan Millard

It was David's great ambition to build God a Temple, though this was only realized by his son, Solomon. It was natural for a powerful king to honour his God in this way, and the existing Tabernacle provided the pattern for a simple central sanctuary. The hilltop David bought is the site now covered by the 'Haram es-Sherif', the Mosque of Omar, in Jerusalem. The central rocky crust was perhaps the site of the altar of burnt-offering.

Solomon's Temple

The detailed descriptions in 1 Kings 6 – 7, and 2 Chronicles 3 – 4, give a fairly complete picture of the Temple. This is supplemented by evidence from archaeological discovery. The Tabernacle plan was extended by an entry porch, the resulting three rooms forming a scheme similar to some Canaanite temples (e.g. at

The Temple was built of stone and cedarwood from the forests of Lebanon. This grove of cedars is one of the few remaining in Lebanon today.

Hazor and Ras Shamra). This may have been the work of the Phoenician builders whose skill Solomon utilized. A series of storage chambers three storeys high ran round the outside of the holiest place and the middle room (the 'holy place'). The doorway was flanked by two giant free-standing pillars whose function is uncertain.

Comparison with Ezekiel's Temple suggests that the whole building stood on a platform above the level of the courtyard.

Solomon's craftsmen, decorating the Temple, used motifs similar to this ivory carving of a slightly later period.

An officiating priest would have crossed the courtyard, passing the great bronze altar for the sacrifices (about 10m/33ft square, 3m/10ft high) and the enormous bronze basin for water supported by twelve bronze bulls, before climbing the steps to the shrine.

Apparently the porch had no doors; gates may have closed the passage, but he would have faced a pair of folding doors at the entrance to the 'holy place'. These were made of cypress wood, carved with flowers, palm-trees, and cherubim, and plated all over with gold, as was all the woodwork.

In this room he would see the golden incense altar, the table for the sacred bread, and five pairs of lampstands. Additional light came from a row of windows high in the wall. Beneath his feet was a golden floor. And if he could see into the 'holiest place' the whole room would have shone a dim gold in the light admitted through the doorway. But these doors were opened rarely, perhaps only for the annual Atonement ceremony. The decorative motifs are well known from Phoenician ivory-carvings

▶▶

and bronze-work of the centuries around Solomon's time. And Egyptian and Babylonian kings boast of ornamenting their temples with gold wall-coverings, gold-plated doors and furnishings.

Solomon's Temple was destroyed by Nebuchadnezzar in 587 BC. Much of its glory had already been torn away and paid as tribute when foreign conquerors menaced Judah.

Timber for the Temple was transported down the coast in Phoenician vessels.

The rebuilt Temple

The disconsolate exiles in Babylonia were heartened by Ezekiel's vision of a new Temple (Ezekiel 40 – 44), described with minute attention, and including facts about the courtyard which hardly occur in the account of Solomon's work.

This sanctuary was never built, but the exiles who returned about 537 BC, after some delay, completed the rebuilding of the old one in 515 BC. The little we know about it shows it followed the old design closely, however inferior its appearance. Nothing has survived from the first Temple. But a length of stone walling above the Kidron Valley, on the east of the site, may be a part of the platform on which this rebuilt Temple was erected, and which King Herod incorporated into his walls.

The cosmopolitan nature of Jerusalem after the exile caused trouble to Nehemiah by bringing non-Jews into the sacred precinct (Nehemiah 13:4-9). It probably resulted in dividing off an outer courtyard from an inner one which only Jews could enter. This was certainly true of Herod's Temple. Two stone blocks have been found inscribed with a warning to non-Jews that they passed in at their own risk (see also Acts 21:17ff.).

The incense server on wheels may have resembled this bronze stand from 1200-1100 BC.

King Hiram of Tyre provided King Solomon with materials and craftsmen for building the Temple. The Phoenicians, in the city-states of Tyre (pictured here) and Sidon, to the north of Israel, were seafarers with an important role in international trade.

furnishings, the carved and decorated cedar panels, the walls gleaming with gold, the creatures whose great golden wings spanned the sanctuary (see Exodus 25:18-20). Seven years, and all was finished exactly to plan.

▶ **480th year (1)** The exodus probably took place something over 300 years before Solomon built the Temple. The round figure here (12 x 40) may indicate 12 generations rather than a precise number of years.

▶ **No noise (7)** Even at this stage the place was regarded as holy. The stone was quarried close to the site, but so deep underground that no sound would carry.

7 Fine buildings for Solomon; bronze for the Temple

Verses 1-12: Solomon builds the House of the Forest of Lebanon – a great hall panelled in cedar where weapons and golden vessels were stored (see 10:17, 21; Isaiah 22:8) – the Hall of Pillars, Hall of Judgment, and palaces for himself and for pharaoh's daughter (his queen). This may also have housed the rest of the harem.

Verses 13-51: Huram, the craftsman Solomon brought from Tyre, supervises the casting in bronze of two ornate pillars for the entrance to the Temple (15-22; see also 2 Chronicles 3:15-17); a huge bowl able to hold nearly 10,000 gallons (Good News Bible, 40,000 litres) of water (23-26; 2 Chronicles 4:2-6); ten wheeled stands to support more bowls (27-39), and numerous smaller items of equipment (40-50; 2 Chronicles 4:11ff.).

8 God's glory fills the Temple

See also 2 Chronicles 5:2 – 7:10.
Work complete, the Ark is brought from the citadel and installed in the inner sanctuary. And the whole Temple building shines with the light of God's presence – the same bright cloud that once rested on God's Tent in the desert (Exodus 40:34-38).

Solomon's prayer, for the royal house (23-26) and for the nation (27-53), echoes the language of Moses. He asks that God will hear the prayers and forgive the sin of his people when they focus on the Temple – even though no building on earth could ever contain the God of heaven.

Prayer is followed by blessing (54-61); blessing by sacrifice (62-64); sacrifice by feasting and rejoicing throughout the land

King Solomon's fortified cities

Excavating the lost city of Hazor, archaeologist Yigael Yadin used the biblical texts to help him recover its history. At the foot of the great mound, Yadin uncovered the lower city, a built-up area of 170 acres; the largest city in the Holy Land dating from Canaanite times; the city the Bible describes as 'the head of all those kingdoms' (Joshua 11:10). A thick layer of ash remained, probable evidence of Joshua's destruction of the city in the latter half of the 13th century BC.

❝ *The lower city was never rebuilt. The fields of today just cover the ruins of the last Canaanite city. But the Bible tells us that Solomon rebuilt the city. So where was that... ?*

In fact we did find Solomon's city – on the tell proper. When we dug under the later strata we discovered Solomon's fortifications. This was what we call a casemate wall: a double wall with an outer and inner wall divided into rooms. Nearby we found Solomon's city gate. We were struck by the fact that it was very similar in plan to a gate discovered many years ago in Megiddo, and also attributed to Solomon. The reason was, of course, that Solomon rebuilt three cities: Gezer, near Jerusalem, Megiddo and Hazor. So we copied the plan of the Megiddo gate just before proceeding with the excavation. We marked it on the ground and said to our workers:

'Dig here and you will find a wall. Dig here and you will find a room.'

Of course, when things turned out exactly as we'd said they thought we were wizards! However, the workers who knew their Bible – when I re-read the Bible passage to them – realized

how we arrived at this solution. Our prestige went down tremendously; that of the Bible was never higher.

So in Megiddo and Hazor gates were found of exactly the same plan, the same dimensions. What about the third city – Gezer – mentioned in that passage in the book of Kings... ?

Because of the biblical passage I decided to unearth the three-volume report of Macalister's much earlier excavations there. To my great surprise and delight, in the first volume I found what Macalister called a plan of the Maccabean castle, which looked identical to our gate and casemate wall. He had excavated only half the gate, and because of that it was not visible. But I published an article suggesting that this was in fact Solomon's gate and fortifications ...

An American expedition from the Hebrew Union College went to Gezer, and one of their aims was to test my theory. They were very cautious. But they did find the second half of the gate and, what is more important, on the floor of the gate they found pottery from the 10th century – Solomon's time. So in all three cities mentioned

The excavated remains of Solomon's city gate at Hazor and the common plan found also at Megiddo and Gezer confirm the historical accuracy of the Bible text.

in the Bible as rebuilt by Solomon, identical fortifications and gates were found. ❞

(65; see 2 Chronicles 7).

▶ **Clouds/darkness (12)** The inner sanctuary had no windows or lights.

▶ **My name (16)** God himself is present in a special sense in the Temple, as he was in the Tent of God. But Israel's Temple, unlike pagan temples, held no statue to represent their God.

▶ **An oath (31)** In which he solemnly swears his innocence.

Winged creatures, something like those which decorate the border of this gold epaulette from the 7th century BC, stood in the inner sanctuary of the Temple and decorated the panels on Huram's bronze carts.

9:1-9 God speaks to Solomon again

See also 2 Chronicles 7:11-22.

'If… if not' – God repeats the promise made to David (3-5), with a warning (6-9). Solomon ignored this and suffered the consequences (chapter 11), though God did not break his promise of a lasting family line.

▶ **As… at Gibeon (2)** I.e. when Solomon was given the gift of wisdom: 3:3-14.

9:10-28 Trade and forced labour

See also 2 Chronicles 8.

For all his wealth, Solomon has his balance of trade problems. On this occasion (10-14) he makes 20 cities over to Hiram of Tyre as security against a loan.

Verses 15-22: the vast labour force needed for new building and defence works is raised from two sources. Native Canaanites provide permanent slave-labour. And the Israelites are pressed into short-term forced labour.

Verses 26-28: Solomon is the first of Israel's kings to create a merchant navy. His ships traded with Arabia and beyond.

See trade map in 2 Chronicles.

▶ **Hazor, Megiddo, Gezer (15)** Solomon fortified these cities. See 'King Solomon's fortified cities'.

▶ **Verse 25** Exodus 23:17 says that all Jewish men must come together for worship at Passover/Unleavened Bread, Harvest/Weeks (Pentecost) and Ingathering/Shelters (Booths). These are the three 'pilgrim-feasts'.

▶ **Ophir (28)** Suggestions include South Arabia, East Africa, and even India.

10:1-13 Sheba's queen visits Solomon

See also 2 Chronicles 9:1-12.

Intriguing reports of Solomon's wisdom and splendour bring the queen from the Yemen to Jerusalem. Unlike the people of Christ's day (Matthew 12:42) this woman was prepared to undertake a long journey to find out for herself the truth of what she had heard.

▶ **Verse 11** Hiram's fleet: see 9:27-28.

▶ **Almug wood (11-12)** is possibly the red sandalwood of Ceylon and India. Good News Bible has 'juniper'.

10:14-29 Fabulous wealth

See also 2 Chronicles 9:13-28.

Solomon's revenue through trade and taxes (including a lucrative tourist trade, 24-25) is enormous. But consumer spending more than keeps pace. The country's position made him a convenient middleman for chariots from Egypt and horses from Turkey (Kue = Cilicia; see trade map in 2 Chronicles).

▶ **Verse 14** Good News Bible gives 23,000kg. The purchasing-power of the bullion is not known.

▶ **600 shekels (16)** 'Almost 7 kilogrammes'.

▶ **3 minas (17)** 'Almost 2 kilogrammes'.

▶ **Verse 22** Monkeys, or peacocks.

11 The king's downfall

Verses 1-13: Solomon's political marriage-alliances no doubt contribute to the country's peace and security. But foreign wives bring with them foreign gods (as Exodus 34:16 had warned). And Solomon in his old age turns from God to worship idols – a sin which will cost his son the greater part of his kingdom and divide the nation.

Solomon's reign is not wholly problem-free. In the south there is trouble from Hadad of Edom (14-22; a story reminiscent of Joseph's); in the north from Rezon of Damascus (23-25); and within his own nation there is Jeroboam (26-40), the man destined by God to rule over the ten breakaway tribes after the king's death.

Significantly, the Chronicler omits the negative aspects of Solomon's reign from his account (see 2 Chronicles 9:29-31).

▶ **Ashtoreth/Astarte, Molech/Milcom, Chemosh (5, 7)** 'Loathsome' because worship of these gods involved child sacrifice, fertility rites, prostitution and sexual practices forbidden in Israel.

▶ **One tribe (13)** The southern state of Judah also included the much smaller tribe of Benjamin (12:21). The other ten tribes broke away to form the northern kingdom of Israel.

▶ **House of Joseph (28)** The tribes of Ephraim and Manasseh.

▶ **Book of the annals of Solomon (41)** Otherwise unknown; presumably official court records.

▶ **Verses 41-43** This formula, with slight variations, is repeated throughout Kings, at the end of each reign.

1 Kings 12 – 14
The kingdom splits in two

It was never easy to hold the 12 tribes together. Ephraim, in particular, envied Judah's power. A split had threatened in David's day (2 Samuel 20). The secret of national unity and strength always lay in the bond of common worship of the one God. The monarchy in itself was no substitute. Without the religious tie, king and people would go down together, as Samuel so clearly foresaw at Saul's coronation. 'If both you and the king... will follow the Lord your God, it will be well; but if you... rebel against the commandment of the Lord, then the hand of the Lord will be against you and your king' (1 Samuel 12:14-15).

The nation's history as recounted in Kings fully bears this out. In 11:13 God reduces the kingdom because Solomon has broken covenant and disobeyed his

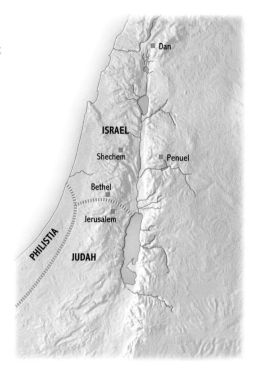

The division of the kingdom

commands (though mismanagement – especially in imposing forced labour on his own people – also played a part). And as Israel strays further and further from the law and worship of God, things go from bad to worse. Internal strife weakens both kingdoms. The nation becomes prey to stronger neighbours, and is eventually devoured by the great powers.

12:1-24 'I shall flay you!' says Solomon's son

See 2 Chronicles 10 – 11:4.
Solomon is dead. Rehoboam is king. And the people bring their complaints. The northern tribes find a leader and spokesman in Jeroboam. But negotiations break down in face of Rehoboam's strong-arm tactics. The rebel tribes declare independence and set Jeroboam up as king of Israel, though the northern kingdom will never (like Judah) enjoy the stability of a single dynasty.

The division is permanent, with a constant state of hot or cold war between the kingdoms. Only in the reigns of Ahab-Ahaziah-Joram in Israel and Jehoshaphat-

The 'Seal of Shema', who served King Jeroboam II of Israel. The inscription reads: 'belonging to Shema, servant of Jeroboam.' This is a bronze cast of the jasper original.

One of the sanctuaries King Jeroboam of Israel set up to keep his people from going to Jerusalem was at Dan in the far north.

The old prophet of Bethel was killed by a lion. This 9th-century Assyrian ivory from the palace at Nimrud (ancient Kalah) shows just such a grisly scene.

Jehoram-Ahaziah in Judah was the breach temporarily healed through a marriage alliance. And that resulted in the near-extinction of the royal house of Judah at the hands of Queen Athaliah.

▶ **Verse 11** The 'scorpions' of some versions are barbed whips used on slaves.

▶ **Verse 15** The writer comments.

▶ **Adoram (18)** The Adoniram of 4:6; 5:14.

▶ **Verse 20** See on 11:13.

▶ **180,000 (21)** The figure seems too high.

12:25-33 Jeroboam breaks with the Temple

Jerusalem had been the religious centre of the united kingdom. Jeroboam, fearful that visiting Jerusalem for the pilgrim-feasts will

This bracelet may have been made from gold plundered from the Temple. It belonged to Nemoreth, son of Pharaoh Shishak who conquered King Rehoboam and stripped the Temple of its gold.

lead his people to defect, creates two new sanctuaries for the northern kingdom. He also creates an unlawful priesthood (they were not Levites). And he makes bull-calves, the symbols of fertility, for the people to worship (as Aaron had done so disastrously after the exodus from Egypt). His actions encouraged idolatry and, as time went by, Israelite worship became more and more degenerate. The writers of Kings see him always as 'bad king Jeroboam', the one who set Israel on the downward path of sin against God.

▶ **Verse 32** This is a substitute for the pilgrim-feast of Tabernacles/Shelters which began on the 15th day of the seventh month.

13 The voice of the prophet

In this critical time for Israel and Judah, the role of the prophets is vital. The need to discern what is true from what is false is most acute in the case of those who claim to speak for God. But even a lying prophet (18) may sometimes speak (21-22) and recognize the truth (32). The prophet from Judah is wrong to accept the old prophet's word when it contradicts God's own word to him. The point the writer makes is that God must be obeyed. The prophet's death is a sign to Jeroboam and Israel of the severity with which God deals with disobedience. But there are none so blind as those who

Unravelling the chronology of the kings

Arthur Cundall

At first glance there seems to be enough data on the kings of Israel and Judah to construct an accurate chronology.

The reign of each king, except for Saul, is clearly given and after the split between Israel and Judah, the accession of each king is related to the reign of the king in the other kingdom.

There are also 'check-points', where one event simultaneously affected both kingdoms, such as Jehu's slaying of Joram of Israel and Ahaziah of Judah (2 Kings 9:21-28). The historian has integrated the chronologies of both kingdoms by dealing with the whole reign of one king from his accession until his death, and then returning to deal with the kings of the other kingdom whose reigns *began* during this period. An exception is in 2 Kings 8 – 9 where Jehu's murder of Joram and Ahaziah made it necessary to mention Jehoram and Ahaziah of Judah (2 Kings 8:16-29), who would not normally have been dealt with until after the death of Joram of Israel.

Problems

However, apparent problems arise on closer inspection. For instance, in Judah, the total from Rehoboam to Ahaziah's death is 95 years, whereas the identical period in Israel, from Jeroboam to Joram's death, is 98 years.

In the period from Jehu's coup to the fall of Samaria the combined total for Judah's kings is 165 years and that for Israel is 144 years.

Queen Athaliah, the usurper, reigned for six years (2 Kings 11:3),

but she was not included in the normal chronological scheme.

We have another headache in the seemingly conflicting dates for the accession of Joram of Israel (2 Kings 1:17 and 3:1). It is reasonably certain that Solomon's death occurred in 932 BC, 346 years before Jerusalem fell in 586 BC. But the lowest estimate of the biblical figures supplied for this period is about 372 years.

Clues

Four factors, however, go a long way towards resolving these problems completely.

■ Two different methods of reckoning the reigns of the kings were used: the 'non-accession-year' method and the 'accession-year' method.

In the non-accession-year (or ante-dating) system the death of a king meant that a year was counted twice, since the portion of the year falling to the deceased king was counted as a full year to him, whilst the remainder of the year was counted as a full year to his successor. So, to attain an accurate chronology, one year must be deducted for each king who reigned.

The accession-year (or post-dating) system did not count any portion of a year in the total years of a king's reign. The portion of the year occurring before a king's first full calendar-year was regarded as his accession year. In the early period of the divided monarchy Israel used the first method and Judah the second. The

discrepancy in totals between the two kingdoms corresponds to the greater number of Israelite kings in this period.

■ Allowance must be made for the fact that the calendar year in Judah, certainly in the earlier period, began in the month of Tishri (September/October), whilst in Israel it began in Nisan (March/April).

■ The practice of co-regencies meant that some reigns 'overlap'. The precedent for this is found in the case of David and Solomon, which thwarted Adonijah's attempted coup (1 Kings 1). Another example concerns Jotham, who acted as co-regent when Uzziah, his father, was smitten with leprosy (2 Chronicles 26:21). Other co-regencies generally accepted were between Asa and Jehoshaphat, Jehoshaphat and Jehoram, Amaziah and Azariah/Uzziah, Ahaz and Hezekiah, and Hezekiah and Manasseh. In certain cases the younger man (for example, Hezekiah) outshone his father (Ahaz) and events were dated by reference to the co-regent rather than to the reigning king (2 Kings 18:9-10).

An awareness of this custom allows a reduction of the overall total of the reigns and also helps us to interpret the biblical figures. For example, Manasseh reigned from 687 to 642 BC. 2 Kings 21:1 notes a reign of 55 years, which leads us to assume a co-regency from 697 to 687, made the more plausible by Hezekiah's severe illness.

▶▶

▶▶ ■ In the northern kingdom, Israel, during the last turbulent decades after the death of Jeroboam II, it is probable that rival kings were 'ruling' over different parts of the kingdom simultaneously. The combined reign of the six kings of this period is 41 years 7 months, whereas historically the period was about 24 years.

External checks

By a careful application of these factors, the chronologies of Judah and Israel can be integrated. But the process of relating the resultant chronology to the events of the surrounding world, to obtain an absolute rather than a relative chronology, has been advanced by archaeological discoveries. The more significant finds are as follows:

■ *The Assyrian Limmu or Eponym lists.* In Assyria an official, holding annual office, gave his name to that particular year. Remarkably complete lists of these officials have survived, covering the period 892- 648 BC, including significant events during their period of office. Since biblical and Assyrian histories converge at various points a precise date can be obtained.

■ *The Babylonian Chronicle.* These tablets deal with Babylonian history during the period from Hezekiah to the fall of Jerusalem and are of special interest to biblical scholars for the years when Judah was subject to Babylon, i.e. after 605 BC. As a result, our knowledge of the inter-relationships between the two kingdoms has been greatly increased. But it is not clear whether the Hebrew civil year uniformly follows the Babylonian pattern, which makes for an uncertainty of one year in dates during the reign of Zedekiah, Judah's last king.

■ Numerous contemporary inscriptions relate to particular events, such as:
• the battle of Qarqar in 853 BC, fought between Assyria and a coalition of small states including Israel;
• Jehu's payment of tribute to Shalmaneser III in 841 BC;
• or the fall of Samaria to the Assyrians in 723 BC.
Such records supply reliable pegs on which to hang the biblical details.

By applying the principles underlying the biblical chronologies and correlating them with the fixed chronology made possible by contacts with contemporary world-powers, we can establish an absolute biblical chronology which is accurate to within a year for the greater part of the monarchy. The reign of Saul remains an exception, with the 40 years given in Acts 13:21 being probably a round figure. Since '2' is the only figure remaining in the Hebrew text of 1 Samuel 13:1, most scholars accept that a tens-unit has dropped out. Twenty-two appears to be the most acceptable alternative since it fits in with other chronological data, such as the period of the Judges.

will not see (33). So Jeroboam brings ruin and destruction on his dynasty.

▶ **Josiah (2)** The king who initiated the most thoroughgoing reform in Judah. See 2 Kings 23.

▶ **Dried up/shrivelled (4)** Paralysed.

▶ **A lion (24)** Lions roamed Palestine, particularly the Jordan Valley, until the Middle Ages. Here the strange sight of the lion standing by its prey, but leaving both the body and the ass untouched, marks the event as having special significance. It is a 'sign' to Israel.

14:1-20 The blind seer

Even a blind prophet, if he is true, can see through pretence (5-6). Jeroboam's wife gets no chance to ask her question. Ahijah predicted Jeroboam's rise (11:29ff.). Now, because he has not been loyal to God, as David was, Jeroboam's whole dynasty 'will be swept away like dung' (see 15:29).

▶ **Properly buried (13)** Meaning that all the rest will die violently.

▶ **Scatter them beyond the Euphrates (15)** Israel was taken into exile by Assyria after the fall of Samaria (2 Kings 17).

▶ **Tirzah (17)** Capital of Israel in Baasha's day (15:33).

▶ **Book of the Chronicles (19,** some versions**)** Not the same as Chronicles in the Bible.

▶ **Verses 19, 29** The 'History of the Kings of Israel', which (like the 'History of the Kings of Judah') no longer exists, is mentioned 18 times in Kings. The writer is not interested in political or social history: loyalty or otherwise to God and true religion is the only measure of a king's success or failure.

14:21-31 Rehoboam of Judah 930-913

See 2 Chronicles 11:5 – 12:15.
Jeroboam's rule in Israel, covers the reigns of three kings – Rehoboam, Abijam and Asa – in the southern kingdom of Judah. Here too pagan religion flourishes under Rehoboam (son of one of Solomon's foreign wives, 21). The weakened state loses the Temple treasures to the invading Egyptian pharaoh, and north and south are constantly at war.

▶ **Shishak (25)** This is Sheshonq, Libyan founder of the Egyptian 22nd dynasty. He left a record of his campaign carved on a temple in Karnak, Egypt.

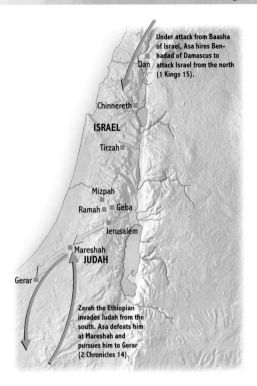

Under attack from Baasha of Israel, Asa hires Ben-hadad of Damascus to attack Israel from the north (1 Kings 15).

Zerah the Ethiopian invades Judah from the south. Asa defeats him at Mareshah and pursues him to Gerar (2 Chronicles 14).

1 Kings 15 – 16:28
Kings of Israel and Judah

The dates for the kings of Judah in this section include a number of periods of co-regency between one king and his predecessor. Almost all the dates given can be only approximate. See 'Unravelling the chronology of the kings'.

15:1-24 Abijam and Asa of Judah

See 2 Chronicles 13 – 16.
The writer of Kings defines a good king as one who promotes the worship of God; a bad king as one who strays into idolatrous practices. On this definition, Abijam's three-year reign (about 913-911) is a bad one (see 2 Chronicles 13). Asa, by contrast, is a good king. He rules for 41 years, about 911-870. The war with Israel continues until he succeeds in persuading Syria to change sides. It costs him all the silver and gold from his palace and the Temple, but diverts Baasha's attention and buys Asa time to improve his own defences.

▶ **The case of Uriah the Hittite (5)** See 2 Samuel 11.

▶ **Maacah (10, 13)** Asa's grandmother.

▶ **Ramah (17)** Only a few miles north of Jerusalem.

A short way down a track from the top of Mt Carmel lies a natural amphitheatre, littered with stones. There is a brook lower down. The details all fit the location of Elijah's contest with the prophets of Baal.

15:25 – 16:28 Kings of Israel

All Israel's kings were automatically bad by the writer's definition (see above), though some were worse than others. After ruling for two years (910-909), Nadab (15:25-32) is murdered by Baasha.

15:33 – 16:7: Baasha introduces a new dynasty and rules Israel for 24 years, about 909-886.

16:8-14: his successor, Elah, rules for two years (886-885) before his assassination by Zimri.

16:15-20: Zimri introduces a shortlived new dynasty (885) and commits suicide when under siege by Omri.

Elijah's journeys

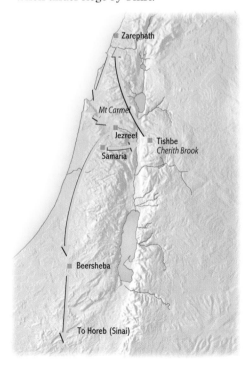

Zarephath

Mt Carmel

Jezreel

Samaria

Tishbe
Cherith Brook

Beersheba

To Horeb (Sinai)

▶ **16:21-28** Although only briefly mentioned here, Omri was one of Israel's most powerful kings politically. He introduces a new dynasty and rules for 12 years, about 885-874, fortifying Samaria as his new capital. For 150 years from this time, Assyria refers to Israel as 'the land of Omri'.

▶ **According to the word of the Lord (15:29)** See 14:6-16.

▶ **Jehu (16:1)** A prophet, not the later king.

1 Kings 16:29 – 2 Kings 1
King Ahab and the prophet Elijah

16:29-34 Ahab of Israel 874-853

In the writer's view, religious life in Israel reaches an all-time low in Ahab's 22-year reign. The king's marriage to Jezebel of Tyre, effecting an alliance between Israel and its northern neighbour Phoenicia, brings political strength and trade benefits. But Jezebel is strongly attached to her own religion, and she persuades Ahab to 'sin against the Lord' by imposing the worship of the Phoenician god Melqart (the 'Baal' of these chapters) on his people. The scene is set for the appearance of Elijah, and a classic conflict of 'church versus state'.

▶ **Verse 34** See Joshua 6:26.

17 Elijah forecasts drought

At a critical time, as if from nowhere, God's prophet makes his sudden and dramatic appearance. Elijah will be known as the greatest of all the prophets (see Matthew 17:3 and 10-13).

Baal was worshipped as a weather-god who could give or withhold the produce of the land. So, just as he had shown his power over the 'gods' of Egypt through the plagues, God now proves to king and people that he alone has power over the sun and rain without which nothing will grow.

God provides for Elijah's needs first from nature and then through a most unlikely person in the unlikeliest of places. The widow is a foreigner with no one to support her, and Zarephath is in the heart of Baal's own country! By providing for Elijah this way, God also shows his care for the poorest of the poor. (See Jesus' words in Luke 4:25-26).

Verses 17-24: this is the first account in the Bible of a revival from death. It is a heart-stopping story for the reader, too – happily closing with a remarkable expression of faith from one who knew nothing of God before Elijah came to her door.

▶ **Verse 1** Elijah's name means 'my God is Yah(weh)'. Gilead is in the north-east, across the Jordan. 'No dew or rain': the reason for the drought is sin (see Deuteronomy 11:17). Rain can normally be expected between late October and early January and again from April to early May.

▶ **Verse 21** Elijah may have used the 'kiss of life'; but the revival came in answer to his prayer, not just through a particular method of resuscitation.

18 Elijah's challenge: God or Baal?

Jezebel is fanatical for her religion. For three years she has done all in her power to eliminate the worship of God in Israel (4).

Now Elijah returns – one against 450 – with a challenge. Let's put this to the test and see who is the real God.

Baal is impotent – no more able to produce fire than to send the needed rain. It's God who is 'the living Lord'. The fire burns the saturated offering. The people shout 'The Lord alone is God.' The prophets of Baal are slaughtered. And the drought ends. But for all this, there will be no deep and lasting religious reform.

▶ **Verse 19** Mt Carmel, near modern Haifa, is at the seaward end of a range of hills rising to 530m/1600ft.

▶ **Verse 46** Elijah ran 17 miles to the summer palace at Jezreel.

Elijah's contest challenged the prophets of Baal (*above*) on their own ground. Baal as weather-god should have had no problem sending fire! Here he is depicted holding axe and thunderbolt.

According to the Bible story, God sent ravens to feed Elijah beside the Cherith brook, until it dried up.

The widow at Zarephath, who looked after Elijah in the great drought, would have used an oven like this to bake her bread.

19 Elijah runs for his life

Elation passes. Spiritual and physical strain leave Elijah in the grip of depression, fear, disappointment. Jezebel still holds the whip hand. Elijah escapes south to the desert and Sinai (Mt Horeb), drawing fresh strength from the food and drink provided by a practical angel. In the place where God made himself known to Moses, he speaks to Elijah, not in any spectacular way but out of the stillness. Self-pity is dealt with, a

Wars with Syria

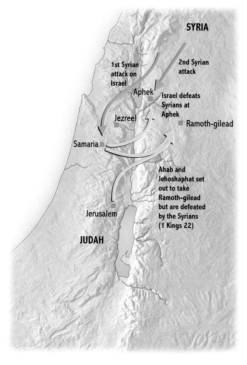

sense of proportion restored, and the path ahead mapped out.

Elijah had felt himself intolerably alone, his work finished. He is given a companion and successor, Elisha. God's work goes on.

(Chapter 21 follows this in the Greek translation of the Old Testament.)

▶ **Anoint Hazael... and Jehu... and Elisha (15-16)** Elisha is 'anointed', called to become a prophet, by Elijah's symbolic action in throwing his cloak around him. But the anointing of Hazael and Jehu is left to Elisha (2 Kings 8 – 9).

▶ **Verse 18** The number is probably symbolic: 7 (for perfection) x 1000. See Paul's reference to this episode: Romans 11:2-5

20 Israel and Syria at war

Benhadad of Syria and the allied kings of 32 city-states attack Samaria. The diplomatic exchange (2-9) is difficult to follow. But Benhadad has to eat his words in face of Israel's double victory. Ahab spares his life, but in doing so stores up trouble for Israel. He has made the same mistake as Saul: in a 'holy war' everything is made over to God in sacrifice. This war was meant to demonstrate that hills and plains alike are under God's dominion (28).

(Israel and Syria fought as allies against Shalmaneser III of Assyria at Qarqar in 853, but later fell out: see 22:1-2.)

▶ **All the people/the rest (15)** The Israelite army.

▶ **100,000... 27,000 (29-30)** The figures seem exaggeratedly high. See note on Exodus 12:37.

▶ **My father... your father (34)** Meaning ancestor, not actual father.

21 Robbery and murder – King Ahab indicted

Seizure or compulsory purchase of land was illegal in Israel. A man's heritage had to be handed on to the next generation. But other people's rights do not bother Jezebel. While her husband sulks like a spoilt child, she quietly arranges for Naboth's liquidation. She has only to contrive a blasphemy charge – backed of course by the statutory number of witnesses – and the 'criminal's' lands are forfeit. Elijah, the old prophet of doom, is the only fly in the ointment. But Elijah speaks true (see

22:37; 2 Kings 9:30-37) and for once the king takes notice, winning a stay of judgment for his lifetime.

22:1-40 Prophet warns of king's death

See also 2 Chronicles 18.

Jehoshaphat's son Joram has married Ahab's daughter Athaliah. Israel and Judah are, temporarily, allies against Syria. It is Jehoshaphat's request which brings Micaiah to the king with his fateful prophecy (one lone true voice against 400). The warning is ignored. Ahab cannot cheat death by being disguised and he dies in battle at Ramoth-gilead, east of the Jordan, as God had said. (For true and false prophets, see on 2 Chronicles 18.)

▶ **He has decreed (23)** The will of God, here as throughout the Old Testament, is seen as the immediate cause of events.

▶ **Verse 28** 'Listen, peoples, all together' has been mistakenly brought in here from Micah 1:2, from a marginal note by a scribe who thought Micaiah the same as Micah. There are very few scribal 'corrections' of this kind in the Hebrew text; all are obvious to scholars.

22:41-50 Jehoshaphat of Judah 873-848

See 2 Chronicles 17 – 20.

Jehoshaphat is a 'good' king. He reigns 25 years.

▶ **Verse 48** See chapters 9 and 10. The strong north winds may have blown the fleet on to the rocks.

22:51 – 2 Kings 1

Ahaziah of Israel 853-852

Ahaziah reigns two years, during which time Moab seizes independence. Ahaziah consults the Philistine god after a fall from the (flat) roof of his palace and Elijah pronounces God's judgment on his idolatry. It takes three military posses to bring Elijah to the king. But nothing can alter the sentence.

▶ **Baalzebub (1:3)** 'Lord of the flies': a derogatory pun on the god's real name, Baalzebul.

▶ **1:8** John the Baptist dressed similarly (Mark

This small vineyard close to the owner's house is like Naboth's small property, coveted by King Ahab and wrested from him by Queen Jezebel.

1:6). The prophet's clothing was rough and basic. He had no need of 'power dressing' to impress his audience. The message was sufficient.

2 Kings 2 – 8:15 Stories of Elisha

2 Elijah conveyed to heaven

Elijah seems to want to face this last experience alone. But Elisha stays with him right through the journey. The final scene – the whirlwind which catches up the prophet, and Elisha's vision of a fiery chariot and horses – is played out east of the Jordan, close to the place where Moses died. It is a remarkable end to a remarkable life. Elijah's reappearance at the transfiguration of Jesus (Matthew 17) underlines the

An ivory carving of the period suggests Queen Jezebel's style.

The remains of King Ahab's palace on the top of the fortified hill of Samaria.

unique position of this man amongst all the prophets of God. Elisha, left alone, takes up his task straight away.

▶ **Prophets (3)** Groups possessing ecstatic gifts; not always people of high spiritual calibre.

▶ **Jericho... Jordan (4, 6)** The river is 5km/ 3 miles east of the city.

▶ **A double share (9)** That is, the portion which fell to the heir, the eldest son, who inherited twice as much as anyone else. So Elisha asks, not for twice Elijah's spiritual power, but for the share which would mark him out as the prophet's successor.

▶ **Verse 11** In the Old Testament, fire often points to God's presence, as at Sinai.

▶ **Chariots of Israel (12)** Israel's defender; Elijah was of more value to the nation than its armed forces.

▶ **Some boys (23)** 'Boy' in Hebrew can be any age. These were young men – local louts, yelling abuse at the prophet and his God, telling him to 'Go up' like Elijah.

▶ **Verses 19-24** These miracles are evidence for the readers that God has indeed empowered Elisha.

3 Joram of Israel 852-841

Joram reigned 12 years. A punitive expedition against Moab by the allied forces of Israel, Judah and Edom, is made hazardous by drought. Elisha, his faculties stimulated by music (a common prophetic custom), promises an end to the drought, and victory.

▶ **A prophet (11)** Just as other nations consulted the will of their gods through diviners, so Israel sought God's will before battle, in earlier times through the priests and now through prophets.

▶ **Who poured water (11)** I.e. the assistant who served Elijah.

▶ **Verse 19** Deuteronomy 20:19 forbade the cutting down of fruit trees.

▶ **Slingers (25)** were skilled in hurling stones from hand-slings which they whirled and then let fly. David killed Goliath this way.

▶ **Verse 27** The sacrifice of the king's son so heartened the Moabites, or so appalled the Israelites, that the advance was halted.

4 Elisha performs wonders

Elisha's miracles, like those of Jesus, show God's care for ordinary people and their needs. The first two resemble those of Elijah

The Syrian general, Naaman, compared the River Jordan (here winding through Galilee) unfavourably with the rivers of his own country. But he washed in the river, as Elisha had instructed, and his skin disease was healed.

(1 Kings 17), perhaps to underline God's choice of Elisha as the true successor of the great prophet. The account is not necessarily in time order.

Verses 1-7: the widow whose children were to become slaves to discharge her debts; 8-37: the childless woman of Shunem who gave Elisha generous hospitality (her story is continued in chapter 8); 38-41 and 42-44: the feeding of the hungry.

▶ **My head (19)** The child had sunstroke.

▶ **Sabbath/new moon (23)** These were special times of religious observance when it would be natural to visit a holy man. The woman did not tell her husband the child was dead.

▶ **Wild gourds (39)** In the famine one man gathered colocynths, a powerful laxative, bitter and poisonous in large quantities.

▶ **Bread from the first-ripe grain (42)** This was the offering normally made to the priests at the beginning of the harvest.

5 Syrian general cured

This story, which Jesus refers to in Luke 4:27, like many others in both Old and New Testaments shows that God's concern is not limited to Israel. Syria was often at war with Israel, and Naaman was the commander of the enemy army.

A young Israelite slave-girl, captured in

a border raid, tells her Syrian master of Elisha's power. A visit is arranged through diplomatic channels. The prophet's instructions are not what Naaman expected. But his staff persuade him to try, and he is healed. Deeply impressed by the cure and Elisha's refusal of payment, the army chief of Syria becomes a follower of the God of Israel. Gehazi's greed might have ruined everything, and could not go unpunished.

▶ **Verse 1** A number of skin diseases come under the Old Testament term translated as 'leprosy'. Today the word applies only to Hansen's disease, hence Jerusalem Bible's 'virulent skin-disease/Good News Bible's 'dreaded skin disease'.

▶ **Talents, shekels (5)** There were no coins as yet; these were weights.

▶ **Verse 17** He took soil from the land of Israel's God because at the time it was believed that a god could be worshipped only on his own land (see David's words in 1 Samuel 26:19).

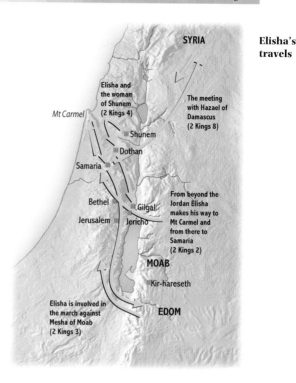

Elisha's travels

6:1-23 Army of God protects Elisha
Verses 1-7: the floating axe-head. The thick woods of the Jordan Valley provide a ready source of timber for the new community building needed by the prophets. Elisha's miracle was simply a kindly act.

Verses 8-23: his advice to the king (Joram) shows Elisha to be a true prophet of God. His confidence is in God's protection – a very real thing for those who have eyes to see (17). Far from being doomed (15), Elisha has them in the palm of his hand as he leads them home. The king, too, must show mercy. And so the raids, instead of continuing, come to an end.

▶ **Dothan (13)** Ten miles north of Samaria.

6:24 – 7:20 Israel's capital under siege
The peace secured by Elisha (23) does not last for ever. Benhadad of Syria returns to lay siege to Samaria, and the people are reduced to starvation and cannibalism. (A similar fate will befall Jerusalem: Lamentations 4:10.) The king blames Elisha for telling him to hold out and promising deliverance (33). The lepers, who depend on gifts of food, are worse off

than most. Their desperate hunger makes them the first to discover the truth of Elisha's prediction. The Syrian army fled at the approach, as they thought, of a relief force.

▶ **6:25** The ass/donkey was an 'unclean' animal, forbidden food; 'dove's dung' may be a nickname for some kind of vegetable. In the famine, both fetched astronomical prices.

▶ **6:30** Sackcloth was worn for grief and mourning.

▶ **7:2,19** 'Windows in the sky/heaven' or rain. There is no warrant for Good News Bible's 'grain'.

8:1-15 Petition to the king; Elisha's prediction
Verses 1-6: the second part of the story told in 4:8-37. This belongs to the time before Gehazi's leprosy, 5:25-27.

Verses 7-15: Elisha fulfils God's commission to Elijah (1 Kings 19:15). Hazael, like Macbeth, resorts to murder to turn prediction into fact and seize the throne.

▶ **Verse 10** The deception is presumably intended to give the king a false sense of security and enable Hazael to take the throne on his death. But he is not prepared to wait.

The Black Obelisk

This text on the 'Black Obelisk' which records the triumph of an Assyrian king, Shalmaneser III, mentions the biblical Jehu, King of Israel. The second panel on this face shows the king or his representative making obeisance to his Assyrian overlord.

❝ *The tribute of Jehu, son of Omri. Silver, gold, a golden bowl, a golden beaker, golden goblets, golden pitchers, lead, a royal staff, a javelin.* ❞

This part of the inscription reads: Yaua (Jehu) son of Humri (Omri).

The Black Obelisk is the only monument so far discovered which shows Israelites (*below*) bringing tribute to an Assyrian king.

The defences
of Samaria,
overlooking the
surrounding
country –
occupied in
Elisha's time
by besieging
Syrian troops.

2 Kings 8:16 – 17:41
Kings of Israel and Judah to the fall of Samaria

The writer returns to the history of the kings which has been interrupted by the stories of Elisha.

8:16-24 Jehoram of Judah 853-841
See also 2 Chronicles 21.
Jehoram was a 'bad' king, influenced by his wife Athaliah, daughter of Ahab and Jezebel (see chapter 11). He reigned eight years plus a co-regency, during which time successful revolts by Edom (to the south-east) and Libnah (on the Philistine border, south-west) crippled Judah.

8:25-29 Ahaziah of Judah 841
See also 2 Chronicles 22.
Ahaziah was another king who turned from God and went his own way. He reigned only one year.

9 Jehu of Israel: king by a coup 841-814
Elisha carries out the last of Elijah's commissions (1 Kings 19:16) while the armies of Israel and Judah are defending Ramoth-gilead against Syria. With the king conveniently recovering from his

wounds at Jezreel, 65km/40 miles away, the time is ripe for Jehu's coup. Jehu loses no time in killing King Joram of Israel, Ahaziah of Judah who is with him, and finally Queen Jezebel, so fulfilling the prophecy of Elijah (1 Kings 21:23).

▶ **This mad fellow (11)** The man's ecstatic state enables the army officers to recognize him as a prophet.

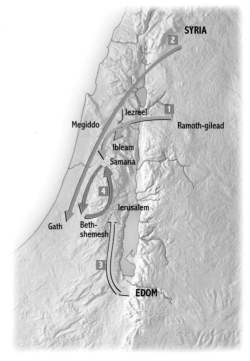

Jehu's coup; the Syrian invasion; Judah's wars with Edom and Israel

1 Jehu kills Joram, pursues Ahaziah, moves on to Samaria

2 Hazael invades Israel and Judah

3 Amaziah of Judah defeats the Edomites

4 Jehoash of Israel defeats Amaziah of Judah

▶ **The property of Naboth (21)** The vineyard seized by Ahab, 1 Kings 21.

▶ **Verse 26** See 1 Kings 21:19.

▶ **She painted her eyes (30)** Women's make-up, even in those days, was sophisticated: black kohl to outline the eyes; blue eyeshadow from lapis lazuli; crushed cochineal to serve as lipstick; and scarlet henna to paint finger- and toe-nails. There were also powders, and an array of perfumes and ointments.

▶ **You Zimri (31)** King Elah's assassin, 1 Kings 16:8-10.

▶ **The word of the Lord... by... Elijah (36)** 1 Kings 21:23.

10 Jehu's purge

Jehu's reign opens with a blood-bath in which all Ahab's family (1-11, 15-17), many of the royal house of Judah (12-14), and the prophets, priests and worshippers of Baal (18-27) lose their lives. Objects connected with Baal-worship are destroyed. But the shrines created at Bethel and Dan by Jeroboam, Israel's first king, are left and God's law neglected.

Jehu reigns 28 years, starting a new dynasty. During his reign, territory east of Jordan is lost to Syria.

11 Athaliah of Judah 841-835

See also 2 Chronicles 22:10 – 23:15. Queen Athaliah, Ahaziah's mother and the daughter of Ahab and Jezebel, reigned six years. These are some of the darkest days in the nation's history. The royal line of David is all but wiped out; only the baby Joash survives. The priest Jehoiada (husband of princess Jehosheba, who rescued Joash) leads the well-planned and virtually bloodless coup which puts Joash on the throne. The constitutional monarchy is restored, and loyalty to God reaffirmed in the swearing of a new covenant-pact.

▶ **Verse 12** Are these 'rules for kingship' (testimony) those set down by the prophet Samuel at the time of the nation's first kings (1 Samuel 10:25)?

12 Temple repaired: Joash of Judah 835-796

See also 2 Chronicles 24.
In the writer's estimation (less so in the Chronicler's), Joash is one of Judah's best

kings, ruling for 40 years. Under Jehoiada's guidance Joash rules well. But for some years money intended for Temple repairs gets no further than the priests. A new method of collection is devised and the work put in hand. Funds come from tax (2 Chronicles 24:6; Exodus 30:11-16) and freewill offerings.

Joash's later years see a decline in political (17ff.), moral and religious spheres (2 Chronicles 24:17ff.). Syria makes inroads into Judah and threatens Jerusalem. The king dies at the hands of his servants (see also 2 Chronicles 24:25-26 for more detail).

13:1-9 Jehoahaz of Israel 814-798

Jehoahaz reigns 17 years during which time Israel falls under Syrian domination.

▶ **Deliverer/'saviour' (5)** Various suggestions have been made: Adad-nirari of Assyria, who took tribute from Damascus and from Jehoash of Israel; Jeroboam II; Elisha.

▶ **Verse 7** Contrast Ahab's 2,000 chariots.

13 Jehoash of Israel 798-782

Jehoash reigns 16 years. There is war with Judah. Elisha's last prediction of victory over Syria is realized. The prophet dies, but even in death his body retains God-given power (21).

▶ **Chariots of Israel (14)** See on 2:12.

14:1-22 Amaziah of Judah 796-767

See also 2 Chronicles 25.
Amaziah is a 'good' king who reigns 29 years. Victory over Edom goes to his head. The disastrous challenge to Jehoash brings the forces of Israel right into Jerusalem, looting the Temple and other treasures. The people make Azariah co-regent. A further conspiracy against Amaziah ends in his death at Lachish.

▶ **In the book of the law of Moses (6)** Deuteronomy 24:16.

▶ **Valley of Salt (7)** The area south of the Dead Sea.

▶ **A thistle on Lebanon (9)** Jehoash replies in sneering parable to Amaziah's foolhardy challenge to battle.

▶ **Elath/Ezion-geber (22)** At the head of the Gulf of Aqaba, naval base of Solomon's Red Sea

fleet. The port fell into the hands of the
Edomites but was recovered by Amaziah's
victory.

14:23-29 Jeroboam II of Israel 793-753

Jeroboam II rules for 41 years, including a
time as co-regent. He is politically strong,
dominating the land from north of
Lebanon (Hamath = modern Hama in
Syria) to the Dead Sea (Sea of Arabah). He
defeats a weakened Syria. Jeroboam's reign
is Israel's Indian summer. After his death
the nation falls apart. The prophets Amos
(2:6ff.) and Hosea reveal the corruption
within Israel: extremes of wealth and
poverty; the grinding down of the poor and
the weak.

▶ **Jonah (25)** This is the only Old Testament
mention of the prophet outside the book which
has his name.

▶ **How he... are they not written (28)** The
meaning of the text is not clear.

15:1-7 Azariah (Uzziah) of Judah 791-740

See also 2 Chronicles 26.
Azariah, a 'good' king, reigns 52 years,
including a time as co-regent. Azariah is a
strong king, defeating the Philistines and
Arabs and reducing Ammon to a vassal
state. But pride brings him to an
unpleasant end (5; 2 Chronicles 26:16ff.).
The prophet Isaiah received God's call 'in
the year that King Uzziah died' (Isaiah 6).

15:8-31 Israel 753-732

Verses 8-12: Zechariah son of Jeroboam
rules six months (753-752) and is
assassinated by Shallum.

　　Verses 13-16: Shallum rules only one
month before his assassination by
Menahem.

　　Verses 17-22: Menahem introduces
another new dynasty, rules 10 years (752-
742) and becomes vassal to the powerful
Tiglath-pileser III (Pul) of Assyria.

　　Verses 23-26: Pekahiah son of
Menahem rules two years and is overthrown by an army coup led by Pekah,
740.

　　Verses 27-31: Pekah introduces a new
dynasty and rules 20 years, dating his

King Menahem
of Israel's
tribute was
reckoned by
scribes, as on
this Assyrian
relief of the
conquests of
Tiglath-pileser
III, from
Nimrud.

Tiglath-pileser
III, the Assyrian
king who
invaded Israel,
is pictured on
the palace walls
of Nimrud.

reign from Menahem's accession, 752-
732. His anti-Assyrian policy leads to mass
deportation of the people by Tiglath-pileser.
He is assassinated by Hoshea.

15:32-38 Jotham of Judah 750-732

Jotham is a godly king. During his 16-year
reign (and co-regency) he encounters
opposition from Syria and Israel.

16 Ahaz of Judah 735-716

See also 2 Chronicles 28; Isaiah 7.
Ahaz was one of Judah's worst kings.
During his 16-year reign and co-regency
Judah was under attack from all quarters:
Syria and Israel to the north; Edom and
Philistia to the south. The Temple was
stripped of silver and gold to pay the heavy
tribute demanded by Assyria in return for
help. Some of Isaiah's prophecies date from
this time.

▶ **Verse 5** See Isaiah 7:1.

▶ **Verse 7** In turning to Assyria for help, Ahaz ignored Isaiah's advice (Isaiah 7).

17 Hoshea, last king of Israel 732-723

Hoshea reigns nine years as Assyria's vassal. An attempt to win Egyptian support proves fatal. Samaria falls after a terrible three-year siege, and the whole remaining population is deported. Israel's fate is seen as the direct consequence of long-standing idolatry, of pursuing heathen practices, disobeying God's law, and ignoring the prophets (7-18).

Over the course of some years, Assyria repopulated the land with other conquered peoples, each with its own religion. But troubles are attributed to their failure to placate the local god, and an Israelite priest is sent back as a missionary. From this strange hotchpotch of religions a purer form of worship emerged amongst their descendants (41), the Samaritans (who nonetheless, right through to New Testament times, were *persona non grata* to the Jews – see John 4).

▶ **Verse 6** The people were deported to north and east Mesopotamia (Halah, Gozan, Media): i.e. north-east Syria/Turkey and Iran.

Remarkably, this 'Chalcedony seal' from the 8th century BC, with its gold holder, has the name of King Hoshea.

2 Kings 18 – 25
Kings of Judah to the fall of Jerusalem

18 Hezekiah 729-687
The Assyrian invasion

See also 2 Chronicles 29 – 32.

Isaiah 36 recounts the Assyrian invasion and Micah 1:10-16 probably also refers to it.

Hezekiah is one of Judah's finest kings. He rules for 29 years plus a co-regency.

Having dealt with Israel, in Hezekiah's reign the Assyrians turn their attention to rebel Judah. Lachish, in the lowlands 50km/30 miles south-west of Jerusalem, is besieged, and messengers are sent to Hezekiah (701 BC). The three Assyrians (the king's 'supreme commander, his chief officer and his field commander') are masters of psychological warfare. They refuse private talks with Hezekiah's cabinet, and insist on a public harangue. And they play on the people's fears by speaking Hebrew – not the diplomatic language, Aramaic – so that everyone understands. But their boast that God cannot save Judah from Assyria seals their fate.

▶ **The bronze snake (4)** See Numbers 21:4-9. This goes to show how easily an object which is innocent in itself can be misused once it has served its purpose.

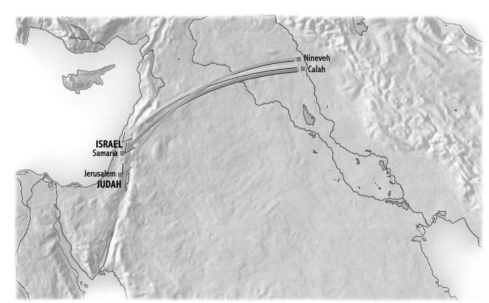

The Assyrian invasions

1 Tiglath-pileser III invades Israel and deports the people in the reign of Pekah (2 Kings 15)

2 Shalmaneser V captures Samaria and takes Israelites into exile on the Habor river and in the cities of the Medes (2 Kings 17 – 18)

3 Sennacherib attacks the fortified cities of Judah and besieges Jerusalem (2 Kings 18 – 19)

Nineveh
Calah

ISRAEL
Samaria

Jerusalem
JUDAH

19 The king and the prophet

See also Isaiah 36 – 39; 2 Chronicles 32:9-23.

Crisis brings out the best in Hezekiah. God answers his prayer and vindicates his trust. Isaiah's prophecy is fulfilled. Jerusalem is saved.

▶ **Isaiah (2)** One of the great prophets of Judah. According to Isaiah 1:1 he prophesied during the reigns of Azariah (Uzziah), Jotham, Ahaz and Hezekiah. His home was in Jerusalem. See further under the book of Isaiah.

▶ **Libnah (8)** Sixteen km/10 miles north of Lachish.

▶ **Tirhakah (9)** Pharaoh Taharqa, of Sudanese

A low-relief sculpture of Assyrian archers and slingers.

descent; in charge of the army, but not yet on the throne.

▶ **Gozan (12)** In north-east Syria; Eden: the

Sennacherib's Prism

King Sennacherib of Assyria left his own views about his attack on Hezekiah, written on clay prisms like this one, buried in the foundations of his palaces. They were meant for future kings to read, so they never reported any defeats or anything bad about the king. This example, called the 'Taylor Prism' stands 375mm/15ins high.

❝*As for Hezekiah of Judah who had not submitted to my yoke, I surrounded and captured 46 of his strong towns, the forts, and uncountable smaller places in their neighbourhoods, by means of heaping up siege ramps, bringing up battering-rams, by foot soldiers fighting, by undermining, breaching and sapping. I brought out of them 200,150 people, young and old, male and female, horses, mules, donkeys, camels, oxen and sheep beyond number and counted them as spoil. He himself I shut up in Jerusalem, his royal city, like a bird in a cage. I encircled him with watch posts and made it impossible for him to leave his city by the gate. His towns which I had captured I detached from*

his kingdom and gave to Mitinti, king of Ashdod, Padi, king of Ekron, and Sil-Bel, King of Gaza, and so reduced his land. In addition to their previous tribute payments, I imposed upon them a further payment as a due to my lordship. That Hezekiah – the fear of my lordly splendour overwhelmed him and the elite and his picked troops whom he had brought into Jerusalem, his royal city, as reinforcements, deserted. To Nineveh, my lordly city, he had brought after me 30 talents of gold, 800 talents of silver, precious stones, antimony, large blocks of carnelian, ivory beds, ivory chairs, elephant hide, ivory, ebony, whatever was very valuable, his daughters, his royal women, singers, male and female. He sent his messenger to pay tribute and homage. ❞

The siege of Lachish

In 701 BC, in the time of King Hezekiah of Judah, the city of Lachish, about 48km/30 miles south-west of Jerusalem, was attacked and captured by the Assyrians. King Sennacherib recorded his victory on his palace walls at Nineveh.

An aerial view of the 'tell' (mound of the ruined city) of Lachish. Extensive archaeological discoveries include a mass grave and unmistakable signs of burning on the walls.

left: The Assyrians attack the city.

below left: Israelite captives are led away by the victorious Assyrians.

Slingstones used by the Assyrian slingers in the attack.

Aramaean city-state of Bit-Adini on the Euphrates.

▶ **Winged creatures/cherubim (15)** See Exodus 25:22. They covered the Ark of the Covenant with their wings, in the inner sanctuary of God's Tent/Temple.

▶ **My hook (28)** God will lead them meekly captive as a person leads a bull or a horse. The Assyrians drove rings through the noses of captive kings.

▶ **The angel of the Lord went (35)** It is not clear what happened, possibly an outbreak of bubonic plague. See 2 Chronicles 32:21; Isaiah 37:36.

20 The king's illness; embassy from Babylon

Verses 1-11: to the people of the Old Testament hope of life after death was vague. The prospect of death reduces Hezekiah to tears (see also his poem, recorded in Isaiah 38:9-20). And God responds to the king's distress. This is one of a number of Old Testament stories in which God 'changes his mind', taking a more lenient course of action in response to people's pleas.

Verses 12-19: Babylon at this time was a small state south of Assyria, looking for allies. Isaiah predicts its future power, and the fate of Judah.

▶ **A poultice of figs (7)** Then the routine treatment for ulcers and boils.

▶ **Verse 11** 'Made the shadow go back ten steps on the stairway set up by King Ahaz' – a staircase used as a form of sundial.

21:1-18 Manasseh 696-642

Manasseh is to Judah what King Ahab was to Israel. He reigns 55 years, part of the time as co-regent, and brings Judah to the point of no return; a degradation worse than that of the Canaanite nations the Israelites had destroyed. The prophets declare God's inevitable judgment. Jerusalem will share the fate of Samaria. See also 2 Chronicles 33, which records a complete change of heart before the end of Manasseh's life (33:10-17).

21:19-26 Amon 642-640

See also 2 Chronicles 33:21-25.
Amon is another 'bad' king. After ruling two years he is assassinated by his own house servants.

22 Josiah the good 640-609

See also 2 Chronicles 34 – 35.
Josiah reigns 31 years. The writer portrays him as the best of Judah's kings, loyal to God and his laws, and carrying out thorough-going religious reform. A book of the law (probably a copy of Deuteronomy) is found in the course of repairing the Temple. (How had it come to be lost, within the Temple itself?) Reading it reveals that the nation has broken covenant with God, incurring the statutory penalties for such disloyalty. But the faithfulness of the king is taken into account.

▶ **Huldah (14)** Other women prophets named in the Old Testament are Miriam (Exodus 15:20-21); Deborah (Judges 4:1-10); Noadiah (Nehemiah 6:10-14).

▶ **Verse 20** Although Josiah actually died in battle (23:29-30) Jerusalem and the land were still safe.

23:1-30 Josiah's reforms

Josiah loses no time in acting on God's message through the prophet Huldah. Public reading of God's law is followed by renewal of the covenant-pact with God (1-3). Then comes a purge of public places, ridding the land of objects associated with pagan worship (4-14). The clean-up extends beyond Judah to former Israelite territory (15-20). The neglected Feast of Passover is celebrated once more (21-23; see 2 Chronicles 35), and private malpractices are dealt with (24-25).

God's judgment is delayed but not reversed: the nation's heart is not changed by the king's reforms. Josiah dies in futile conflict with Pharaoh Necho, who was marching to join forces with Assyria after the fall of Nineveh, the Assyrian capital, to the Babylonians (the rising power).

▶ **Verse 12** These were pagan altars. Manasseh worshipped the stars (21:3).

▶ **Verse 13** See 1 Kings 11:7.

▶ **Verses 16-18** For the prophet from Judah

Many small pottery figures found in Judah illustrate the superstitions which King Josiah tried to end by his reforms.

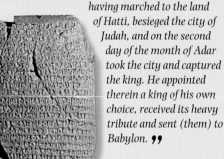

❝ *In the seventh year, in the month of Kislev,
the Babylonian king mustered his troops, and
having marched to the land
of Hatti, besieged the city of
Judah, and on the second
day of the month of Adar
took the city and captured
the king. He appointed
therein a king of his own
choice, received its heavy
tribute and sent (them) to
Babylon.* ❞

and the prophet from Bethel see 1 Kings 13.
(Samaria stands for the northern kingdom.)

23:31-34 Jehoahaz (Joahaz) 609
See also 2 Chronicles 36:1-4.
Josiah's son Jehoahaz, a 'bad' king, was on
the throne for only three months. Then he
was deported to Egypt by Necho. See
Jeremiah 22:10-11 for the prophet's

message about Jehoahaz.
▶ **Jeremiah (31)** Not the prophet.
▶ **Verse 34** The change of name indicated his
subjection to the Egyptian king.

23:35 – 24:7 Jehoiakim 609-597
See also 2 Chronicles 36:5-8.
Josiah's son Eliakim, renamed Jehoiakim as
a sign of his subjection, is put on the throne
by Pharaoh Necho. He rules for 11 years.
At first subject to Egypt, Jehoiakim becomes
Babylon's subject after Egypt is defeated at
Carchemish in 605. Judah remains a vassal
of Nebuchadnezzar for three years, then
defects to Egypt again. This brings more
attacks from the Babylonians, and repeated
warnings from the prophet Jeremiah. See
Jeremiah 22:13-19.

24:8-17 Jehoiachin 597
See also 2 Chronicles 36:9-10.
Jehoiakim's son, Jehoiachin, is removed
from the throne after three months by
Nebuchadnezzar. He is taken to Babylon in
597 with the treasures of Jerusalem and all
the leading men of Judah. The prophet
Jeremiah pronounced God's judgment on
Jehoiachin (Jeremiah 22:24-27).

24:18 – 25:30 Jerusalem falls;
Zedekiah 597-587
See also 2 Chronicles 36:11-21; Jeremiah
37 – 39.
The new puppet king also rebels. Jerusalem
suffers a terrible 18-month siege. Zedekiah
attempts to escape south but is caught and
taken to Babylon. The city falls to the
Babylonian army, is looted and utterly
destroyed. All but the poorest people, left
under governor Gedaliah, are taken into
exile. But Gedaliah is murdered and the
people escape to Egypt to avoid the
inevitable wrath of Babylon, taking the
prophet Jeremiah with them (Jeremiah 43).
25:27-30 conveys a glimmer of hope.
Under a new king in Babylon 35 years
later, Jehoiachin, the deposed king of

Just before King Nebuchadnezzar sacked Jerusalem in
587 BC, a junior Judean officer was sending reports,
written on broken bits of pottery, to his commander in
Lachish. One, perhaps the last, says they are watching
for the beacon signal from the city. Eighteen of these
notes were discovered in the gatehouse.

The lost Ark
Alan Millard

The Ark of the Covenant was a wooden box plated with gold, made to contain the two tablets of the law that Moses brought from Mt Sinai. It was kept in the innermost shrine of the Tabernacle and Temple. So the terms of the covenant – the law – were preserved in the sacred place, like treaty terms made between human rulers.

The lid of the Ark, also gold-plated, was known as the 'atonement cover' or 'mercy seat'. On the Day of Atonement, blood from the sacrifice was sprinkled on it to symbolize Israel's repentance for sins committed in the past year. In that way, the punishments due to the nation for breaking God's law were transferred to the animal.

The Ark was also seen as God's footstool: the place where he met those who served him. It was carried in front of the people when they were on the move together, as a sign of God's presence.

After the days of Jeremiah (see Jeremiah 3:16) the Ark disappears from history. Most likely, Babylonian soldiers destroyed it when they looted the Temple in 586 BC. There was no Ark in the later Temples in Jerusalem.

But this is the stuff of which legends are made!

Jewish tradition says Jeremiah hid it in a cave on Mt Nebo, or King Josiah hid it in a cave beneath Jerusalem.

Ethiopian legend claims that the son of King Solomon and the Queen of Sheba took it to Ethiopia, where it is supposedly hidden in a church in Aksum.

Ethiopian Christians carry boxes containing tablets bearing the Ten Commandments in procession. But this and other Jewish elements in their customs are less ancient.

Judah, is released from prison and kindly treated.

▶ **25:1** The date is January 588 BC.
▶ **25:2** 587 BC.
▶ **25:4** One of those who escaped brought news

of the city's fall to Ezekiel, already in exile in Babylon (Ezekiel 33:21).

▶ **25:9-10** The Temple was eventually rebuilt in 520-515 BC, after the return of the Jewish exiles. It was Nehemiah who restored the city walls.

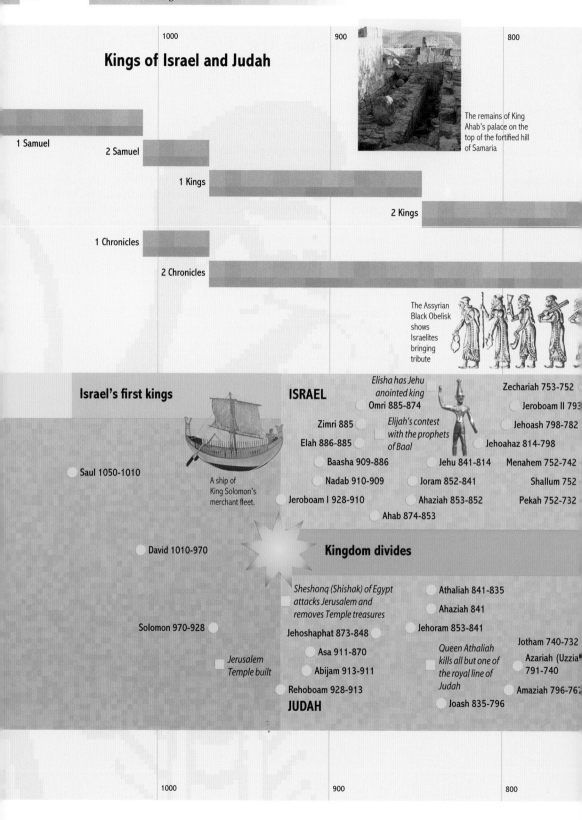

1000   900   800

Kings of Israel and Judah

The remains of King Ahab's palace on the top of the fortified hill of Samaria

1 Samuel

2 Samuel

1 Kings

2 Kings

1 Chronicles

2 Chronicles

The Assyrian Black Obelisk shows Israelites bringing tribute

Israel's first kings

A ship of King Solomon's merchant fleet.

ISRAEL

Elisha has Jehu anointed king

Omri 885-874

Zimri 885

Elijah's contest with the prophets of Baal

Elah 886-885

Baasha 909-886   Jehu 841-814

Nadab 910-909   Joram 852-841

Jeroboam I 928-910   Ahaziah 853-852

Ahab 874-853

Zechariah 753-752

Jeroboam II 793

Jehoash 798-782

Jehoahaz 814-798

Menahem 752-742

Shallum 752

Pekah 752-732

Saul 1050-1010

David 1010-970

Kingdom divides

Sheshonq (Shishak) of Egypt attacks Jerusalem and removes Temple treasures

Athaliah 841-835

Ahaziah 841

Jehoram 853-841

Solomon 970-928

Jehoshaphat 873-848

Jerusalem Temple built

Asa 911-870

Abijam 913-911

Rehoboam 928-913

JUDAH

Jehoram 853-841

Queen Athaliah kills all but one of the royal line of Judah

Joash 835-796

Jotham 740-732

Azariah (Uzzia) 791-740

Amaziah 796-767

1000   900   800

700   600   500

NB The period for
each Bible book
indicates its
historical setting,
not the date of
writing.
Overlapping dates
indicate periods of
co-regency

For the overall context see:
100 The Old Testament
      story

For further details see:
418 The prophets in their
      setting

Carved figure
of an Assyrian
slinger

722/1 *Samaria falls*
to Assyria – end of
kingdom of Israel

hea 732-723

742-740

This 8th-century
'Chalcedony seal'
has the name of
King Hoshea

The Babylonian
god Marduk,
depicted as a
dragon

Judah in exile   ## The return

Manasseh   *Discovery of the book*   *538 Fall of Babylon to the*
696-642   *of the law – Josiah's*   *Medes and Persians: Cyrus*
ezekiah 729-687   *religious reform*   Zedekiah 597-587   *allows Jews to return home*
: 735-716   *587 Nebuchadnezzar II destroys*
                          Jehoiachin 597   *Jerusalem and Temple – most*
                          Jehoiakim 609-597   *Judeans taken into exile*
Sennacherib attacks
Jerusalem   Jehoahaz 609
                                                      597 Nebuchadnezzar II takes Jerusalem –
          Josiah 640-609   *King Jehoiachin and people taken into exile*

      Amon 642-640

                          605 Daniel and others taken hostage

700   600   500

1 & 2 Chronicles

Summary

A selective history which concentrates on the royal line of Judah.

1 Chronicles 1 – 9
Family lines: Adam to after the exile
•
1 Chronicles 10
Death of Saul

1 Chronicles 11 – 29
King David's reign
•
2 Chronicles 1 – 9
Solomon's reign

2 Chronicles 10 – 36
The kingdom of Judah

On the face of it, Chronicles seems to repeat in duller and more moralistic fashion what has already been recorded in Samuel and Kings – the story of the nation from the Judges to the exile. So why this retelling? What is the Chronicler setting out to do? What lies behind his (or their, if this is not the work of a single individual) choice of material – it is highly selective? Since he never actually tells us, we must work out the answers from his writings.

Although clearly concerned with the past, the Chronicler cares less about what happened than about the *meaning* of events. He is an *interpreter* of history.

For most of Chronicles (1 Chronicles 10 – 2 Chronicles 36) the writer draws on Samuel and Kings. He expects his readers to know this history which he abbreviates, expands and modifies in keeping with his overall purpose. He ranges widely across other Old Testament books, particularly Genesis, Exodus, Numbers, Joshua, Ruth and some of the Psalms. He names as his sources various court records mentioned in Samuel and Kings.

He shares with the writers of Samuel and Kings the conviction that the key to the nation's peace and prosperity lies in obedience to God. To disobey is to court disaster. But he also has themes of his own, particularly:
■ true worship (focussed on the Temple)
■ and true kingship (the family-line of David).

The two come together in his account of David and Solomon, where he concentrates far more on the Temple than on other aspects of their reigns.

At the heart of his account are God's promise to David of a lasting dynasty (1 Chronicles 17:3-14) and God's message to Solomon, following his prayer at the dedication of the Temple (2 Chronicles 7:11-22). Because of this he concentrates on the kings of David's line, ignoring the northern kingdom altogether. His introduction (chapters 1 – 9) focusses on the southern tribes, Judah and Benjamin, and the priestly tribe of Levi, which was specially dedicated to God's service.

The Chronicler chose his themes to get a particular message across to his original readers. (He may have been writing in about 400 BC; and his books form part of the longer series, Chronicles-Ezra-Nehemiah.) These were the people who had returned from exile to rebuild Jerusalem under Ezra and Nehemiah. The new community had no king: the priests were their leaders.
■ They needed to be linked with the past.
■ They needed reassurance that God was still with them, working out his purposes.
■ They needed to know how best to re-establish worship.
■ They needed to be reminded that their future wellbeing depended on their faithfulness to God. They had experienced God's judgment in the destruction of Jerusalem and the Temple and in their own long years of exile. *It must never happen again.*

Today's readers have some problems with Chronicles. One is the Chronicler's tendency to 'modernize' – describing events in terms the people of his own day would understand. As in other Old Testament books (see notes on Exodus 12:37, and elsewhere) figures quoted often seem much too high. Chronicles frequently gives a higher figure than the comparable one in Samuel or Kings. The reason for this is not known. Maybe the intention is to stress the greatness of a victory God has given them, for example, not to provide actual statistics. Names, too, are often spelt differently in Chronicles from the earlier books, and some are no doubt copying errors. But these problems are partly of our own making. The ancient world was not as concerned as we are about exact statistics and standard spellings. We forget that the English language owes the latter to dictionaries which are relatively recent arrivals. In Elizabethan times the name Shakespeare, for example, could be spelt in many different ways and no one worried about it.

1 Chronicles 1 – 9
From Adam to the exile and after

The lists in these chapters provide only a skeleton family tree. They are not intended to be complete. In line with his purpose the Chronicler gives most attention to the family of David, and the tribes of Judah, Benjamin and Levi (see introduction above). The family lines are important for the Chronicler and those for whom the book was first written because they connect the people with all that has gone before in the purposes of God. They also prepare the way for the particular history, beginning at chapter 10, which will focus on David's line of kings and on the Temple as the centre of the nation's worship.

1:1 – 2:2 Adam to Israel (Jacob) and his 12 sons

1:1-27: Adam to Abram; Noah's descendants through Japheth, Ham and Shem. The list is drawn from Genesis, though the spelling of many names is slightly different here. (This is not reflected in some modern versions.)

1:28-54: Abraham, Isaac, Israel (Jacob); descendants of Ishmael and Esau. Attention narrows down to the father of the nation. 2:1-2: the 12 sons of Israel.

2:3 – 3:24 Judah: the royal line

2:3-55: the descendants of Judah, David's ancestors.

3:1-16: David's dynasty to the exile.
3:17-24: the royal line from the exile on.

4:1-23: more clans of Judah.

▶ **Judah (2:3)** Here the Chronicler's special interests begin to show through, with far more space given to Judah, the royal line (and in chapter 6 to Levi, the priestly line), than to the rest.

▶ **Tamar (2:4)** See Genesis 38:12-30.

▶ **Achar (2:7)** Achan. See Joshua 7.

▶ **Kelubai (2:9)** Caleb. Not necessarily Joshua's contemporary, who was not an Israelite although he was adopted into the tribe of Judah.

▶ **Boaz (2:11)** See Ruth 2 – 4.

▶ **Father of Kiriath-jearim (2:50)** I.e. founder of the town.

▶ **2:13** 1 Samuel 16 and 17 say eight sons.

▶ **2:16** Zeruiah's three sons are prominent in David's story: see 2 Samuel 2 – 3 and elsewhere.

▶ **Bathshua (3:5)** Bathsheba.

▶ **Elishama (3:6)** Elishua.

▶ **Johanan (3:15)** Not a king of Judah.

▶ **Zerubbabel (3:19)** A leader in the return from exile. See Ezra.

4:24 – 5:26 Simeon and the tribes east of the Jordan

4:24-43: Simeon.

Chapter 5: the two and a half tribes that settled east of the River Jordan – Reuben (5:1-10); Gad (5:11-22); the half-tribe of Manasseh (5:23-24).

▶ **Hezekiah (4:41)** Ruled 729-687 BC; see 2 Kings 18 – 20.

▶ **Reuben (5:1)** See Genesis 35:22; 49:3-4.

▶ **Tilgath-pilneser (5:5)** Tiglath-pileser.

▶ **5:17** Jotham, 750-732 BC: see 2 Kings 15. Jeroboam II, 793-753 BC: see 2 Kings 14.

▶ **5:26** Pul and Tiglath-pileser are one and the same, as modern versions make plain.

6 The priestly tribe of Levi

The line of the high priests (1-15); the families of Gershom, Kohath and Merari (16-30); families of the singers (31-48); descendants of Aaron (49-53); list of Levitical cities (54-81).

▶ **Levi (1)** Notice the space given to the priestly tribe, in which the Chronicler has a special interest (see on 2:3).

▶ **Verse 27** 'Samuel his son' should be inserted after Elkanah. The reference is to the prophet Samuel.

▶ **Verse 57** See Joshua 20:1-9 for cities of refuge.

7 The west Jordan tribes

Issachar (1-5); Benjamin (6-12). (This does not tie in with chapter 8, and it has been suggested that verses 6-11 refer to Zebulun, otherwise omitted altogether, and that verse 12 is the end of a lost list of Dan.) Naphtali (13); the half tribe of Manasseh (14-19); Ephraim (20-29); Asher 30-40.

8 Benjamin and King Saul

The families of Benjamin (1-28); the family line of Saul, Israel's first king (a Benjamite; 29-40).

When the ten northern tribes broke away to form the kingdom of Israel, Benjamin became part of the southern kingdom, joining Judah.

▶ **Gibeon (29)** An important Benjamite city, 8km/5 miles northwest of Jerusalem.

▶ **Verses 29-38** The list is repeated in 9:35-40, linking with the account of Saul's death which begins chapter 10.

▶ **Verses 33-34** Eshbaal = Ishbosheth; Meribbaal = Mephibosheth. See note on Jerubbesheth, 2 Samuel 11:21.

> ❝ *Sing praise to the Lord;*
> *tell the wonderful*
> *things he has done.*
> *Be glad that we belong*
> *to him;*
> *let all who worship him*
> *rejoice!...*
> *Give thanks to the Lord,*
> *because he is good;*
> *his love is eternal.* ❞
>
> 1 Chronicles 16:9-10, 34

The harp was a favourite instrument in David's day.

9:1-34 Exiles who returned from Babylon

This section, relating to the 6th century BC, interrupts the narrative of Saul and David (11th and 10th centuries), just beginning. The Chronicler wants to emphasize continuity: this is the exiles' own history; they belong to and have a part in the story. He focusses on the resettlement of Jerusalem (3), listing the people by tribe and family (3-9); the priests (10-13); the Levites (14-16); gatekeepers (17-27); those in charge of utensils and stores (28-32) and musicians (33).

▶ **Verse 3** Although the Chronicler will not tell the story of the northern kingdom, his concern is with the whole nation as the people of God (the 12 tribes, not just two): so here, Benjamin and Judah (the southern kingdom ruled by David's family line) and Ephraim and Manasseh (the two most powerful of the ten breakaway northern tribes, representing the rest). They are one people again.

▶ **Verses 10-27** These lists are paralleled in Nehemiah 11.

▶ **Bread (32)** Twelve loaves of bread, one for each tribe, presented to God and placed on a special table in the Temple.

9:35-44 Saul's family line

This list, repeated from chapter 8, serves to introduce the particular story beginning in the next chapter.

10 King Saul's death in battle

See on 1 Samuel 31 and 2 Samuel 1. The story of Saul's rise and fall is told in 1 Samuel 9ff.

For the Chronicler, the history of the monarchy begins with David. Verses 13-14 are sufficient comment on Israel's first king.

▶ **Verse 11** The people of Jabesh owed a debt to Saul: see 1 Samuel 11.

▶ **Verse 14** 'So the Lord killed/destroyed him' – for modern readers this is one of the most shocking instances of the way the Old Testament writers attribute direct action to God as first cause. If something happened, it was almighty God who made it happen.

1 Chronicles 11 – 29 King David's reign

The story of David's reign occupies the rest of 1 Chronicles. It is a selective history compared with 2 Samuel, missing out David's adultery with Bathsheba, the rape of Tamar and the family dissension which culminated in Absalom's rebellion. But if the Chronicler omits, he also adds to what we know, particularly the detailed plans and preparations for building the Temple (chapters 22 – 29).

11 – 12 David made king

See on 2 Samuel 5:1-10.
The story begins at the point where David

becomes king of the whole nation (11:1-3), and captures Jerusalem – David's city – making it his capital (11:4-9).

12:10-47: David's special guard – see on 2 Samuel 23:8-39.

12:1-22: David's supporters at Ziklag, the city the Philistines allowed him as base. This chapter is not paralleled elsewhere. The Chronicler is stressing the whole nation's support for David, so he tells how Saul's own kinsmen went over to him, and describes the warriors from Gad as so eager to join him that they crossed the River Jordan when it was in spate.

12:23-40: the troops who made David king at Hebron.

▸ **11:16** Bethlehem was David's home town. It is about 8km/5 miles south of Jerusalem.

▸ **11:29** Sibbechai = Mebunnai in 2 Samuel 23. The scribe has confused two Hebrew letters.

▸ **12:21** See 1 Samuel 30.

This is the area of modern Jerusalem where David's city once stood.

13 Moving the Ark: an aweful warning
See on 2 Samuel 6.

In line with his purpose of outlining the religious history of the nation, the Chronicler assigns this event first place in the record of David's reign. In actual point of time it came somewhat later.

▸ **Perez Uzzah (11)** means 'Uzzah's punishment' (10). Compare 1 Samuel 6:19. This is intended to show, not an angry God but the awesome holiness of everything connected with him. No unauthorized person may so much as touch the sacred Ark.

14 Foreign affairs
See 2 Samuel 5.

David was well able to handle the nations around. His family life was his weak point, as the other records make plain (2 Samuel 13ff.; 1 Kings 1:6).

▸ **Hiram (1)** See on 2 Samuel 5:11.

▸ **David's children (4-7)** The list in Samuel does not mention Elpelet or Nogah. Beeliada = Eliada.

15 – 16:6 The Ark installed in Jerusalem
See also 2 Samuel 6 (15:1-24, on the role of the priests and Levites, has no parallel). After leaving it three months at Obed Edom's house (13:13-14), David brings the Ark to Jerusalem and installs it in the tent he has had made for God. The original Tent of God (the Tabernacle) and altar remain at Gibeon. The Chronicler details the role of the Levites in the ceremony. David and the Levites wear the special clothes required (15:27). Proper worship is characterized by both order and joy. From earliest times music has held a special place in worship (note 16:7).

16:7-43 In praise of God
Extracts from various psalms are brought together in verses 8-36. These may be typical of what Asaph's choir sang before the Ark, rather than the actual words. At Jerusalem and at Gibeon provision is made for daily sacrifices and praise to God in words and music.

17 David's plan – God's promise
See on 2 Samuel 7.

It seems wrong to David that he should have a palace to live in while the Ark of God is still housed in a tent. And his attitude is right (contrast Haggai 1:4). God refuses his request, but expresses his love and approval of David in the promise of a dynasty which will never die out, and in allowing Solomon to build the Temple. David does not let disappointment shadow his glad acceptance of God's answer.

From God's promise to David sprang the hope of a Messiah (the once and future king: Isaiah 9). When Jerusalem was taken and the people went into exile in Babylon (587 BC) all seemed lost: despite the promise, David's line of kings ended. The Chronicler wants to revive that hope and trust in God. For the New Testament writers, the promise was fulfilled in Jesus, who came from the family of David and will reign for ever (Matthew 1 and 2).

18 – 20 David's victories: the expanding kingdom

See on 2 Samuel 8 (the Philistines), 10 (Ammonites and Syrians) and 12:26-31 (Rabbah, the Ammonite capital – modern Amman). These accounts are not in time order. The borders are pushed back: first to the west, then north and east. See map of David's wars (2 Samuel 8).

The Bathsheba and Uriah episode (recounted in 2 Samuel 11 and 12) fits between 20:1 and 20:2. The Chronicler regularly leaves out details of private life, in line with his purpose of focussing on true kingship and true worship, so this may not be a 'whitewash' or cover-up – especially since the story was already known from the earlier records.

▶ **18:4** The problem of over-high figures is not unique to the Old Testament. Other contemporary documents give similarly large numbers of soldiers and chariots. Statistics given by the opposing sides in a war rarely tally – even today! See introduction.

▶ **David's sons (18:17)** The writer of Samuel calls them 'priests', but by the Chronicler's time the word priest had acquired a technical meaning.

▶ **19:18** 2 Samuel 10:18 has 700 chariots, a more likely figure. But the word chariot here can mean simply 'mounted men'. The foot-soldiers here are the 'horsemen' of Samuel, since at this time in the ancient Near East the cavalry dismounted to fight.

▶ **20:5** See on 2 Samuel 21:19.

21 – 22:1 Census and plague; a site for the Temple

See on 2 Samuel 24.

For the Chronicler the census (assessing Israel's military strength suggests lack of trust in God) and plague are significant simply as the lead-in to David's decision (22:1) to build the Temple on the site of Ornan's threshing-floor, a fact not even mentioned in Samuel.

▶ **Satan (21:1)** 2 Samuel has 'God'. It is God who sets the limits to Satan's power (see Job 1 – 2). His existence in God's world, and the

The site David bought for the Temple was a threshing-floor – a flat, open space suitable for a building.

reason why God allows him power to act, remain a mystery.

▶ **The whole nation guilty (21:3)** National solidarity is a fact. When the king as leader sins the people suffer. The same is true of leaders and nations today.

▶ **21:5** These numbers differ from 2 Samuel 24:9. The Chronicler may have taken his figures from a different source.

▶ **21:18** The threshing-floor was a flat open space where the sheaves could be spread out. Oxen pulling studded sleds loosened the grain, which was then winnowed by tossing it into the wind. Ornan=Araunah in Samuel. Difficulty may have arisen because it was a foreign name.

▶ **Hid (21:20)** Perhaps in the cave beneath the rocky floor, which now lies under the Dome of the Rock mosque, erected on the Temple site.

▶ **21:25** 2 Samuel records the price paid for the threshing-floor, this verse apparently the price paid for the whole site.

22:2 – 23:1 Preparing for the Temple

This section has no parallel in Samuel. It follows naturally from the mention of the

Temple in verse 1. It probably belongs to the time of Solomon's co-regency with his father (23:1; 1 Kings 1), which may have lasted some years. David never stopped longing to build God a house fit for him. He accepted the set-back of God's refusal and turned all his energy and enthusiasm to the things he could do: selecting the site; amassing materials; deciding the plan.

▶ **Foreigners/aliens (22:2)** The Canaanites who remained in the land were pressed into a permanent slave labour force.

▶ **You have shed much blood (22:8)** This does not imply that Solomon was morally better than David, or that David's wars were not justified (God is often stated to have been with him in his campaigns). These very wars bought Solomon's reign of peace in a strong kingdom, and with it the freedom for king and nation to concentrate at last on the great task of building God's Temple.

▶ **22:9** The name Solomon comes from the Hebrew word for peace: 'shalom'.

▶ **22:14** Taken literally, this would make David far richer than Solomon. The meaning is clear: David had laid up colossal supplies; a fortune in gold; fantastic wealth of silver; a vast mass of bronze and iron.

▶ **23:1** The Chronicler makes no mention of the struggles over the succession recorded in 1 Kings 1. The focus right through these chapters is the Temple and the worship of God.

23:2-32 The Levites and their duties

The next five chapters record David's organization of the nation's religious (23 – 26) and civil (27) administration.

From the earliest days of desert-wandering, the job of the Levites had been the care and transport of the Tabernacle. They had also served the priests – in later times at the many shrines scattered throughout the land. Now the Ark was to have a permanent home, and worship was to be centralized in the Temple at Jerusalem. So David allocates new duties to the Levites: the care-taking and maintenance of the Temple; appointments as magistrates, janitors, musicians and choristers; and general assistance of the priests.

23:6-24 (with 24:20-31) provides a check-list of those who belong to the tribe of Levi and are therefore qualified to enter God's service.

▶ **Verses 3, 27** Thirty was the age at which a Levite began his work. David changed this to 20, once the Temple was completed.

24 The priests and their duties

Twenty-four groups of priests – all tracing their family lines back to Moses' brother Aaron, the first high priest – were to be in charge of the Temple sacrifices, each serving for two weeks a year. The order was decided by lot.

Verses 20-31: a further list of Levites (see above).

▶ **Nadab, Abihu (1)** See Leviticus 10.

▶ **Verse 4** The fact that Eli's family was descended from Ithamar partly accounts for the reduced numbers. Because of the sins of Eli's sons, many of their descendants met a violent death (see 1 Samuel 2:30ff.).

« Yours, O Lord, is the greatness and the power and the glory and the majesty and the splendour, for everything in heaven and earth is yours. Yours, O Lord, is the kingdom. »

David's last prayer
1 Chronicles 29:11

Music was an important part of Temple worship. This relief from 8th-century Carchemish shows a group of musicians playing various instruments.

25 Temple musicians

Music, both instrumental and vocal, was important in Jewish worship, as it was in social life generally. The Temple musicians were 'leaders in inspired prophecy', proclaiming God's message (25:1, 3). Asaph, Heman and Jeduthun were amongst the famous: they are named in the Psalms. But status does not come into the Temple service. Teacher and pupil alike share an equal place (8). David, himself a skilled musician (1 Samuel 16:15ff.; 2 Samuel 23:1), must have taken special delight in this part of the arrangements, which he supervised personally (2, 6).

26:1-19 Temple guards

A number of Levites were to act as door-keepers, taking turns on guard outside the Temple and storehouse. Presumably they were there to keep order. They also received gifts (2 Chronicles 31:14). All service in God's Temple was a high honour

– including that of these 'gate-keepers': see Psalm 84:10.

▶ **Verse 18** The meaning of 'parbar' is not known; it is variously translated 'court', 'colonnade', 'pavilion'.

26:20-32 Other Temple officers

Treasurers, clerks and magistrates are appointed to look after the Temple finances and legal affairs and to keep the records. The Temple treasuries – gifts and taxes from the people, and the spoils of war – were vast.

▶ **Verse 28** Samuel, Saul, Abner and Joab pre-date the Temple, so presumably these gifts were for the earlier Tent.

27 David's army and civil service

27:2-15: all 12 army commanders seem to have come from David's special guard of 'mighty men' (see chapter 11).

27:16-34: the officers in charge of the tribes (16-22), those in charge of the king's property – storehouses, produce and livestock – (25-31) and his personal advisers (32-34).

▶ **Verse 23** For the census see chapter 21. Those under 20 were not eligible for military service and so were never counted. The promise was made to Abraham (Genesis 15:5, at Ur; 22:17, after the testing over Isaac) and again to Isaac (Genesis 26:4).

▶ **Verse 32** Jonathan and Jehiel were tutors to the king's sons.

▶ **Verse 33** Ahithophel and Hushai both appear in the story of Absalom's rebellion, 2 Samuel 15:31ff. 'King's friend' is an official title.

28 – 29 David makes way for Solomon

Chapter 28: the story interrupted by the lists at 23:2 is now picked up again. A formal public assembly marks Solomon's official coronation, after the hasty affair of 1 Kings 1 (see 29:22). David presents his son to the people (1-8) and gives him a solemn charge (9, 10) before committing the plans for the Temple to his care (11-19). The design is God-given, closely following the pattern given to Moses for the construction of the Tabernacle. At the same time, David hands over the lists of Temple duties (21; see chapters 23 – 26).

Chapter 29: in addition to all he has put

by over the years, David makes a last lavish personal gift for the Temple building fund (1-5). His example and appeal (5) calls forth a willing, joyful response from the people, and the gifts pour in (6-9). Deeply moved, David thanks God from his heart that such giving is possible from people

An Egyptian worshipper.
Israel's Temple was the centre of the nation's worship, drawing people from all over the country to the great pilgrim festivals.

who apart from God's goodness have nothing. His prayer is one of the greatest in the whole of the Old Testament. It shows, as perhaps no other passage does, just why this man could be described as 'a man after God's own heart'.

▶ **29:4** See on 22:14.

▶ **Darics (29:7)** A Persian gold coin; anachronistic for David's day, but a clue to the date at which the Chronicler wrote.

▶ **All the sons of King David (29:24)** Earlier, Adonijah had attempted to wrest the throne from Solomon (1 Kings 1); later, Solomon put him to death. But for the present there was concord.

▶ **Records (29:29)** These may be what we have in 1 and 2 Samuel; otherwise they are lost to us.

2 Chronicles 1 – 9
King Solomon's reign

1 Solomon rules with the wisdom of God

The time is the 10th century BC. Solomon is now in firm charge of his father David's kingdom. God gives him the wisdom he asks for, plus power, wealth and fame. See on 1 Kings 3 and 10.

▶ **Shephelah/foothills (15)** The low hills between Judea and the Philistine coastal plain.

▶ **Verse 16** See 'Solomon's trade'.

2 Getting ready to build

See on 1 Kings 5.
Verses 4-6 add to the Kings account.

▶ **Verse 3** Huram is a variant of Hiram. See also on 2 Samuel 5.

▶ **Verse 13** Huramabi: short form Huram/Hiram.

3 Temple building begins

See on 1 Kings 6 – 7.

▶ **Mt Moriah (1)** It was on a mountain in the land of Moriah that Abraham was told to offer up Isaac (Genesis 22:2).

▶ **Parvaim (6)** Not known; possibly in Arabia.

▶ **The veil/curtain (14)** The sanctuary in which the Ark was kept was divided off from the main part of the building by this curtain, as it had been in the earlier Tent (Exodus 26:31). 1 Kings 6:31, 32 has wooden doors.

4 – 5:1 Fitting out the Temple

See on 1 Kings 7.

▶ **3,000 baths (4:5)** I.e. about 60,000 litres/14,500 gallons on the usual reckoning of 22 litres/4 gallons, 6³/₄ pints to one bath. 1 Kings 7:26 gives 2,000 baths.

▶ **4:6** See Exodus 30:17-21.

5:2 – 6:11 The ceremony begins

See on 1 Kings 8.

The Chronicler adds verse 6. The Ark is installed with joyful music and singing and great thanksgiving. The glory of God's presence fills the Temple (2-14). Solomon speaks to the people (6:3-11).

The Levitical singers (5:12) See 1 Chronicles 25.

▶ **6:2** In the desert days, when they themselves lived in tents, the people made a tent for God (the Tabernacle). Now that they are settled in houses, the Temple is built as a house for God. It was not a cathedral in which they met for worship. Assemblies took place in the open, in front of the Temple, where the altar and great basin stood.

6:12-42 Solomon's prayer

See on 1 Kings 8.

The ground for this prayer, and all prayer, is the fact that God and his promises are utterly dependable. The requests are based

The southern wall of the Temple area in Jerusalem, with the site of David's city in the foreground. There is a steep drop to the Kidron Valley on the right.

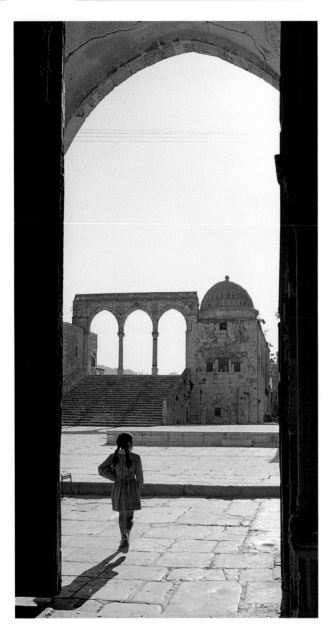

days of festivity run on into the week-long
Feast of Tabernacles, with a final day of
solemn meeting before they all disperse
(this clarifies 1 Kings 8:65-66).

Verses 11-22: in a second appearing,
God agrees to all Solomon's requests. But in
return he expects loyal obedience. The
Chronicler's readers, looking back to the
fall of Jerusalem and the years of exile that
followed, would see in these warning verses
the reason for those tragic events.

8 Solomon's building and trade

See on 1 Kings 9:10ff.
This account differs from Kings in verses 2,
11, and 12-15.
▶ **Verse 2** The cities of 1 Kings 9:10-14, redeemed
from Hiram by Solomon.
▶ **Verse 10** The 250 officers plus 3,600
overseers (2:18) add up to the same total as
the 550 plus 3,300 of 1 Kings 9:23; 5:16.
▶ **Verse 11** Compare 1 Kings 11:1-13. The
Chronicler is silent on Solomon's many foreign
wives and their influence, apart from what may
be implied here.
▶ **Law of Moses (13)** For the set feasts see
Leviticus 23; the sacrifices, Leviticus 1 – 7.
▶ **In front (12)** Because only the priests might
enter the Temple.
▶ **Verse 14** David's instructions are given in
1 Chronicles 23 – 26.

9:1-12 The Queen of Sheba

See on 1 Kings 10.
The Chronicler includes the visit as an
illustration of Solomon's widespread fame
and reputation.
▶ **Algum (10)** A foreign word, the 'almug' of
1 Kings 10:11; Good News Bible, 'juniper'.

9:13-31 Solomon's wealth and glory

See on 1 Kings 10:14-29.
The extent of Solomon's kingdom (26)
fulfils God's promise to Abraham (Genesis
15:18).
▶ **Verse 21** 'Ships plying to Tarshish'
(Tartessus) in Spain is highly unlikely. Probably
'ocean-going ships' as in Kings.
▶ **Verse 29** All of these sources are now lost to
us. Two of Ahijah's prophecies are recorded in
1 Kings 11 and 14. See on 1 Chronicles 29:29.

on other vital facts about God: his love for
his people; his absolute moral standards;
his readiness to hear and forgive those who
genuinely turn away from wrongdoing.
▶ **Verses 41-42** A free quotation of Psalm
132:8-10 which the Chronicler has added.

7 The consecration festival

See on 1 Kings 8 – 9.
Flame burns up the sacrifices in token of
God's presence and approval. The seven

2 Chronicles 10 – 36
The kings of Judah

The dates and length of reign of each king are given in the parallel sections of 1 and 2 Kings. Many of them include a period of co-regency with a predecessor, so there is often some overlap. See 'Unravelling the chronology of the kings', and 'Kings of Israel and Judah' chart.

The Chronicler does not recognize the kings of Israel. Only David's descendants are the nation's true kings. From the time of the split he therefore largely ignores the northern kingdom, and frequently refers to Judah as 'Israel'. Even so, the ten tribes are still considered part of the Israelite nation, and contain elements which continue loyal to God and to the rightful king.

10 Rehoboam: the kingdom divides
See also 1 Kings 12.
Rehoboam inherits from Solomon a wealthy kingdom beginning to show signs of weakness. By the time of his death only a fraction of that land and income are left to be handed down to his successor.

▸ **In Egypt (2)** See 1 Kings 11:26ff.
▸ **Verse 15** 'The will of the Lord... this is why': one of many places in the Old Testament where an event is attributed directly to God without reference to human freedom of choice. See on 1 Chronicles 10:14, etc. 'The word spoken by Ahijah': see 1 Kings 11:30-39.
▸ **Verse 18** Hadoram = Adoram (Adoniram) of Kings.

11 Rehoboam fortifies Judah
A timely word from Shemaiah averts civil war (1-4). Instead, Rehoboam concentrates on fortifying his tiny kingdom against attack from her larger and stronger neighbours, particularly Israel and Egypt. Refugee priests flock to Judah from Israel following Jeroboam's measures to break the religious ties with Jerusalem (see 1 Kings 12:26-33).
▸ **Shemaiah (2)** See 12:5, 7, 15.
▸ **Satyrs (15,** Revised Standard Version) The goat-like desert-demons of the old nature worship.
▸ **Abijah (20)** The Abijam of Kings.
▸ **Daughter of Absalom (20)** The Old

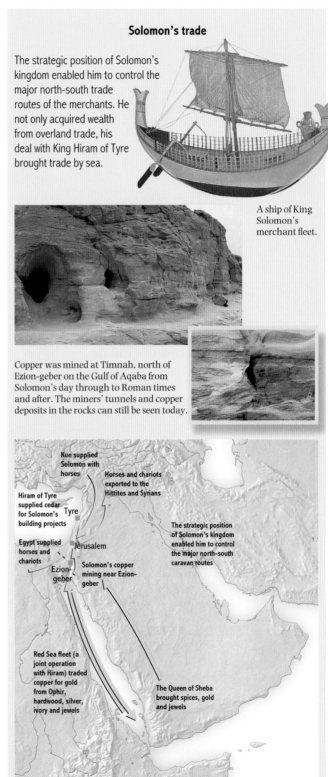

Solomon's trade

The strategic position of Solomon's kingdom enabled him to control the major north-south trade routes of the merchants. He not only acquired wealth from overland trade, his deal with King Hiram of Tyre brought trade by sea.

A ship of King Solomon's merchant fleet.

Copper was mined at Timnah, north of Ezion-geber on the Gulf of Aqaba from Solomon's day through to Roman times and after. The miners' tunnels and copper deposits in the rocks can still be seen today.

Kue supplied Solomon with horses

Horses and chariots exported to the Hittites and Syrians

Hiram of Tyre supplied cedar for Solomon's building projects

Tyre

Egypt supplied horses and chariots

Jerusalem

Ezion-geber

Solomon's copper mining near Ezion-geber

The strategic position of Solomon's kingdom enabled him to control the major north-south caravan routes

Red Sea fleet (a joint operation with Hiram) traded copper for gold from Ophir, hardwood, silver, ivory and jewels

The Queen of Sheba brought spices, gold and jewels

Testament often uses 'son of', 'daughter of' in the wider sense of 'descendant'. Maacah was Absalom's granddaughter (see 13:2).

12 Egypt invades Judah
See also 1 Kings 14.
Invasion, here and later, is seen as a direct consequence of disloyalty to God. National repentance (not mentioned in the Kings account) limits its effects, but Judah remains under Egyptian domination for some years.
▶ **All Israel (1)** The Chronicler means the true Israel, i.e. Judah.
▶ **Shishak (2)** Sheshonq I, Libyan founder of the 22nd dynasty of Egypt.

13 King Abijah: war with Israel
See also 1 Kings 15:1-8, which is more critical of the king. The fuller account here enlarges on what constitutes 'proper' worship, and on the reason for Judah's victory. Abijah's large family is meant to be seen as a sign of God's blessing.
▶ **Micaiah (2)** Maacah (11:20; 1 Kings 15:2).
▶ **Covenant of salt (5)** Salt had a ceremonial use in the ratification of treaties. It stood for faith, loyalty and long-lastingness (particularly in 'pacts' made with God).
▶ **500,000 (17)** Best taken as meaning simply 'a large number'.
▶ **Verse 20** See on 10:15 above.

❝*The Lord keeps close watch over the whole world, to give strength to those whose hearts are loyal to him.*❞

Prophet Hanani encourages King Asa
2 Chronicles 16:9

14 King Asa: peace and victory
See also 1 Kings 15:9-24.
The writer of Kings approves of Asa; the Chronicler sees good (chapters 14, 15) and bad (chapter 16) in his reign. Peace (verse 6) is the gift of God to an obedient king and people. The great victory, too, is God's doing.
▶ **Zerah (9)** Ethiopia/Cush is modern Sudan. Zerah was probably an Egyptian or Arabian chieftain (the earlier identification with Pharaoh Osorkon has now been abandoned).
▶ **A million (9)** Best taken to mean simply 'an enormous number'.

15 King Asa's reforms
Azariah (1) is mentioned only here in the Old Testament. His prophecy is the spur which sets Asa's reforms in motion.
▶ **Idols (8)** But see 14:3; 15:17. Asa probably destroyed the shrines where foreign gods were worshipped and left the others.
▶ **Ephraim, Manasseh and Simeon (9)** Loyal men from the two northern tribes migrated to Judah. But Simeon's territory had always been in the south, and the tribe had been assimilated long ago by Judah.
▶ **Maacah (16)** Asa's grandmother. See on 11:20.

16 The king's trust fails
Asa's faith weakens under test in his later years. Under threat from Israel he calls in foreign aid from Syria. And in sickness he turns, not to God, but to 'doctors'. These may in fact be mediums or medicine-men, since 'this is the only time in the Bible that consulting physicians is considered a sin'. Nonetheless, in death, his people honour him.
▶ **Ramah (1)** This city belonging to Ephraim, one of the northern tribes, is only 8km/5 miles north of Jerusalem itself.
▶ **Geba, Mizpah (6)** Two cities on the kingdom of Judah's northern border, close enough to Ramah for the building materials to be transported across.
▶ **Fire (14)** Not a cremation, but the burning of spices (see Jeremiah 34:5).

17 Jehoshaphat: a strong king
See also 1 Kings 15:24; 22:1-50.
The Chronicler gives Jehoshaphat, a

reforming king like Asa, much more space.

Jehoshaphat builds up a strong army and defences. He arranges for the people to be taught the law (7). And he is much respected by the surrounding nations. The worship of foreign gods clearly continues in the kingdom, since Jehoshaphat destroys their shrines (6), as his father had done. See also 20:32.

▶ **Book of the Law (9)** Part or all of the 'five books' – the Pentateuch.

▶ **Arabs (11)** Former nomads settling in Edom and Moab.

▶ **Verses 14ff.** As they stand, the figures for the muster are over-high. It is possible that the term 'thousand' is a group term rather than a number. See notes on Exodus 12:37, etc.

18 A near-fatal alliance

See on 1 Kings 22, which tells the same story.

▶ **The marriage alliance (1)** Jehoshaphat's son Jehoram married Athaliah, Ahab's daughter. Far from reuniting the kingdom, this link brought near-disaster to Judah in later years (22:10).

▶ **True and false prophets (4ff.)** It was never easy to distinguish between the two. Here Jehoshaphat senses from the shallow optimism of their message that these prophets are merely telling Ahab what he wants to hear. The false and the true can only be distinguished by their life and message, not by methods or manner (see Deuteronomy 18:17-22). No true prophet made a prediction which failed to happen; practised or encouraged immorality; or led people away from God and his law.

▶ **Like sheep... (16)** I.e. leaderless.

19 Jehoshaphat's law reforms

After Ramoth-gilead, Jehoshaphat concentrates on home affairs. He appoints civil judges, sets up local law-courts and a mixed court of appeal in Jerusalem. Compare Deuteronomy 16:18-20; 17:8-13.

▶ **Jehu (2)** Probably grandson of the Jehu in 1 Kings 16:1. It was not unknown for names to alternate like this within families.

▶ **Law of the Lord (8)** Cases covered by the law of Moses; the other lawsuits ('disputed cases', Revised Standard Version) are civil matters.

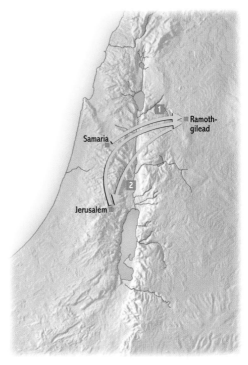

Battle at Ramoth-gilead

1 The allied forces of Israel and Judah attack the Syrians at Ramoth-gilead. Ahab dies

2 Jehoshaphat returns to Jerusalem

▶ **Verse 10** Fellow citizens or countrymen, not kinsmen as in New English/Revised English Bible.

20 Attack from the east

There is no account of this war in Kings. Judah's trust in God is amply vindicated. The invaders quarrel among themselves and leave the spoil to Judah. Only the alliance with Israel (35) mars the good record of Jehoshaphat's reign.

▶ **Meunites (1)** From a district of Edom near Mt Seir.

▶ **The Sea (2)** The Dead Sea.

▶ **Verse 17** Again and again the Chronicler stresses that victory comes through trust in God.

▶ **Tekoa (20)** Amos, the shepherd-prophet came from this town, 16km/10 miles south of Jerusalem.

▶ **Verse 33** This agrees with 1 Kings 22:43; but contradicts 17:6. (See 15:17.) The high places (often but not always on hills) were simply platforms on which cult objects stood. As the places themselves were regarded as holy, nothing short of the desecration carried out by Josiah could stop people using them.

▶ **Tarshish (36**, some versions) See on 9:21.

21 King Jehoram

See also 2 Kings 8:16-24.

The evil influence of Jehoram's wife (Athaliah was the daughter of Ahab and Jezebel) proved stronger than his father's good example. Jehoram lost control over Edom and Libnah (on the Philistine border), and led the nation into idolatry. 'Nobody was sorry when he died' (20): a terrible epitaph.

▶ **Elijah's letter (12)** It would appear from 2 Kings 3:11 (in Jehoshaphat's reign) that Elijah was no longer alive, though we cannot be certain. Possibly, foreseeing how things would go, the prophet left a written message which was delivered by a successor.

▶ **Jehoahaz (17,** some versions) An alternative way of writing Ahaziah (22:1). Both are a compound of 'Ahaz', meaning 'he has hold', or 'possession' and the name of God (written Jeho- or Jo- as a prefix; -iahu or -iah as a suffix). The whole name thus means 'God has possession'. Most of Judah's kings have names compounded in this way.

▶ **Not in the royal tombs (20)** Presumably because he displeased God. Other kings not buried in the royal tombs were Ahaziah, Joash, Azariah (Uzziah), Ahaz. Violent death or skin disease ('leprosy') also debarred them.

22:1-9 King Ahaziah

See also 2 Kings 8:25-29.

Ahaziah learnt nothing from his father's horrible end. Friendship with Israel led directly to his death in Jehu's purge.

▶ **Verse 2** Forty-two (some versions) should be 22, as 2 Kings 8:26.

▶ **Verse 9** This seems to be at variance with 2 Kings 9 and 10, where Ahaziah dies at Megiddo, and before his nephews' deaths. 'Samaria' may be used here of the kingdom rather than the city itself.

22:10 – 23:21 Queen Athaliah: blood-bath and revolt

See also 2 Kings 11.

Ahaziah's infant son Joash is the rightful heir. But so many of the royal family have been wiped out (21:17; 22:8) that the queen mother is able to make her bid for the throne unchallenged. After six years the usurper is overthrown. The Chronicler stresses the role of priests and Levites in restoring the rightful monarch to the throne.

▶ **23:11** 'The laws governing kingship'/ 'testimony' may have been those written down by Samuel (1 Samuel 10:25).

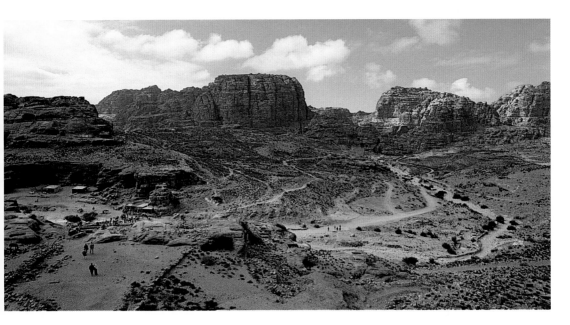

24 King Joash repairs the Temple
See also 2 Kings 11:21 – 12:21.
Under Jehoiada's influence, Joash begins well. The people are recalled to covenant-loyalty and the damaged Temple (7) is repaired. After the priest's death, however, the king comes under less healthy influences, till he sinks to the murder of Jehoiada's son for his outspoken criticism. In consequence his own life ends in ignominious defeat and assassination.

▶ **The tax (6)** See Exodus 30:12ff.

▶ **Verse 21** See Jesus' reference to Zechariah's death, Matthew 23:35.

25 King Amaziah
See also 2 Kings 14.
Amaziah's cruel victory over Edom (5-16, expanding on Kings) leads to his downfall. He brings home the foreign gods. And in his bumptious pride he throws down the gauntlet to powerful Israel (17ff.). Defeat turns the people against him. It seems that Uzziah, the 'Azariah' of 2 Kings, was made co-regent. After 29 years on the throne, a conspiracy ends Amaziah's life. The Chronicler sees the king's defeat and his death as punishment for worshipping the gods of Edom.

▶ **Verse 4** Deuteronomy 24:16.

▶ **100,000 (6)** Best taken as a round figure for a large number.

▶ **Israel... Ephraim (7)** The Chronicler makes it clear that he means the northern kingdom.

26 King Uzziah (Azariah)
See also 2 Kings 15:1-7.
The Chronicler describes the good (26:1-15) and the bad (26:16-23) in Uzziah's reign (as he has already done with Asa and Joash).

A strong king, Uzziah (aided by his religious adviser Zechariah, 5) begins well, seeking God and extending his sovereignty as far south as the Red Sea. He loves the land and protects the cattle from desert raiders (10). He sees that his army is well-equipped and armed with the latest in guided missiles (14-15). But as with many a good person before and since, power and success are his undoing. In his pride he takes on the role of priest. (Verses 16-20 add to the Kings account.) God strikes him with leprosy, a visible token of that unseen defilement of sin which makes him unfit for God's presence.

▶ **Verse 23** Isaiah received his call from God (Isaiah 6) in the year that King Uzziah died.

27 King Jotham
See also 2 Kings 15:32-38.
Jotham proves a 'good' king, faithful to God (2). He maintains and increases his father's power, adding Ammon to his

King Amaziah of Judah slaughtered the Edomites, throwing 10,000 men to their deaths from their cliff-top citadel at Sela (later Petra).

tributary-states. But the religion of the people remains mixed.

28 King Ahaz

See also 2 Kings 16; Isaiah 7.
The terrible apostasy of Ahaz brings Judah near to destruction. God even uses the idolatrous northern kingdom to punish his people – and to show them up by almost unheard-of clemency to the prisoners-of-war. There was still some good in Israel. Crisis brings some people to deeper faith, but not Ahaz (22ff.).

▶ **Valley of Hinnom (3)** Just south of Jerusalem, Hinnom (Gehenna) developed a sinister reputation; later it was where the city's rubbish was burned.

▶ **King of Syria (5)** Rezin, see 2 Kings 16.

▶ **Tilgath-pilneser (20)** Tiglath-pileser. This is not an invasion, but the imposition of crushing tribute.

▶ **Altars (24)** To pagan gods.

29 King Hezekiah

See also 2 Kings 18 – 20.
Hezekiah's first concern is to restore the Temple to its proper use. (His father Ahaz had robbed and closed it: 28:24.) The detailed account of the cleansing and rededication of the desecrated Temple is characteristic of the Chronicler. When the building has been made ready, king, priests and people are themselves made clean from sin by the offering of sacrifices.

▶ **Verse 25** See 1 Chronicles 25. Gad and Nathan were both prophets of David's day.

▶ **The song to the Lord (27)** Many of the psalms were written for use in the Temple on various occasions.

30 Celebrating the Passover

(For the origin and meaning of Passover see Exodus 11 – 13.) Samaria fell to Assyria in the reign of Ahaz (when Hezekiah was co-regent) – see 2 Kings 17. Most of the northern Israelites were taken captive and their land was re-settled. Hezekiah appeals to the few remaining Israelites to join with Judah for the feast (9). Despite the poor response, there had been no Passover to equal this since Solomon's day. And such was the general rejoicing that they extended the feast an extra week.

▶ **Verse 3** The normal date was the 14th of the first month, but Numbers 9 also allows the later date.

▶ **Verse 15** Many priests and Levites were slow to return to the reformed worship (29:34).

▶ **Verse 19** The Chronicler, who set great store by proper forms of worship, makes it clear that it is the attitude of heart that matters most.

31 Hezekiah's religious reforms

This whole chapter is an addition to the Kings account. The reforms even extend into the old northern kingdom (1).

The laws governing worship and the support of the priests are reintroduced (2ff.). The sheer volume of produce raised by the gifts for the priests and tithes for the Levites takes everyone by surprise (10). Special care is taken to see that it is properly distributed.

▶ **Verse 7** People began to give in May/June at the grain harvest and continued to the end of the fruit and vine harvests in September/October.

32 Assyrians invade Judah

See also 2 Kings 18 – 19; Isaiah 36 – 37.
Having wiped out the northern kingdom, the Assyrians make inroads into Judah, whose people have been showing signs of independence. But in his campaign of 701 BC Sennacherib fails to take Jerusalem. The reason, says the Chronicler, is that in the crisis Judah's king put his trust wholly in God. The theme is familiar.

The Assyrian attack on Lachish is pictured on Sennacherib's palace walls at Nineveh.

▶ **Verse 12** The Assyrian emissary misunderstood Hezekiah's reforms.

▶ **Verse 18** They used Hebrew. The people would not have understood Aramaic, the diplomatic language.

▶ **Verse 31** See 2 Kings 20:12ff. 'Left to himself' Hezekiah exhibits his treasures with foolish pride.

33:1-20 Manasseh's evil reign

See also 2 Kings 21:1-18.
For almost all of his long reign Manasseh was one of Judah's least God-fearing kings. He desecrated the Temple and practised human sacrifice (6-7). But the Chronicler

Hezekiah's conduit

To secure his water-supply from the invaders, Hezekiah channelled the water from the Spring of Gihon to the Pool of Siloam. The tunnel is over 620m/1700ft long, and winds to follow the lie of the rock.

In 1880 a boy who had been bathing in the Pool of Siloam found an inscription which tells its own story:

❝ ... And this is the story of the piercing through. While (the stone-cutters were swinging their) axes, each towards his fellow, and while there were yet three cubits to be pierced through, (there was heard) the voice of a man calling to his fellows, for there was a crevice(?) on the right... And on the day of the piercing through, the stone-cutters struck through, each to meet his fellow, axe against axe. Then ran the water from the Spring to the Pool for 1200 cubits, and 100 cubits was the height of the rock above the heads of the stone-cutters. ❞

Water was channelled from this spring – the Spring of Gihon – beneath the city walls by means of Hezekiah's tunnel to the Pool of Siloam, securing a water supply for Jerusalem in time of siege.

Hezekiah's conduit: the tunnel through which the water flows from the spring to the pool.

A detail from the inscription recording the stone-cutters' successful completion of the tunnel. It shows what Hebrew writing looked like at the time of the prophet Isaiah.

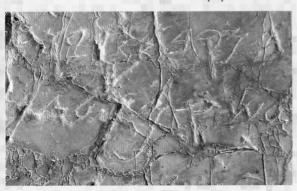

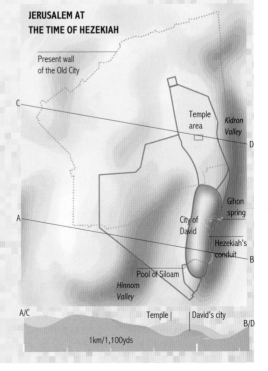

JERUSALEM AT THE TIME OF HEZEKIAH

Present wall of the Old City

C

Temple area

Kidron Valley

D

City of David

Gihon spring

A

Hezekiah's conduit

B

Pool of Siloam

Hinnom Valley

A/C   Temple | | David's city   B/D

1km/1,100yds

relates a change of heart not mentioned in Kings. Possibly Manasseh was caught up in the revolt of Ashurbanipal's brother, vassal-king of Babylon, and was called to account there after Ashurbanipal was victorious. God answered the king's desperate prayer, and his release and return changed him, but not the people.

▶ **Verse 6** Hinnom = Gehenna; see on 28:3 above.

▶ **Hooks (11)** Kings conquered by the Assyrians had hooks or rings driven through their noses.

▶ **Verse 18** There is a 'Prayer of Manasseh' among the Deuterocanonical writings.

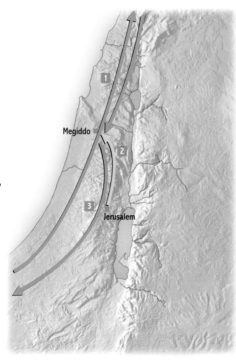

This small 6th-century BC clay tablet (part of the Babylonian Chronicle) records the defeat of the Egyptians at the Battle of Carchemish in 605. King Josiah of Judah lost his life by trying to intercept the pharaoh on his march north.

33:21-25 Amon
See also 2 Kings 21:19-26.
Amon reigned two years, 642-640. He followed Manasseh's evil example and was murdered by his servants.

34 Josiah: a reforming king
See also 2 Kings 22 – 23.
Josiah desecrates and demolishes places and objects of pagan worship, and repairs the Temple. During his reign the book of the law (probably Deuteronomy, perhaps in an earlier form) is discovered, and a measure of true repentance follows. But, despite the king's lead, the people's response is too little and too late to avert judgment.

There are some differences between the accounts in Kings and Chronicles, mainly in the order of events, but neither writer is primarily concerned with chronology. The real significance of the events lies in what they teach.

▶ **Verses 3, 7** Assyrian power was declining. So Josiah became gradually freer to take the politically dangerous step of extending his religious reforms into the former northern kingdom of Israel.

▶ **Verse 4** These were the altars built by Josiah's grandfather, King Manasseh.

▶ **Huldah (22)** See on 2 Kings 22:14.

35 Josiah's Passover; his tragic death
See 2 Kings 23:21-30.
Passover had been neglected under the Kings, though Hezekiah revived it (chapter 30). Now the celebration forms the climax to Josiah's reforms. The nation remember their deliverance from slavery in Egypt – within a few short years of a second slavery, to Babylon.

▶ **Verse 20** Necho was marching north in 609 to help Assyria fight off Babylon. On his way home he deposed and deported Josiah's successor, Jehoahaz. But in 605 he was defeated by Nebuchadnezzar of Babylon at Carchemish.

▶ **Jeremiah's lament (25)** This is not the Bible book of Lamentations; the lament has not been preserved.

36:1-4 Jehoahaz (Joahaz)
See also 2 Kings 23:31-34.
See on 35:20 above.

36:5-8 Jehoiakim
See also 2 Kings 23:35 – 24:7.
Jehoiakim began as a puppet of Egypt, and ended as a captive in Babylon.

36:9-10 Jehoiachin
See also 2 Kings 24:8-17.

Josiah's last battle

1 Pharoah Necho marches to Carchemish to aid the Assyrians in their battle against the Babylonians.

2 Josiah intercepts the Egyptian army at Megiddo – and dies in battle.

3 On his return Necho deposes Jehoahaz and takes him to Egypt.

Megiddo

Jerusalem

After only three months Jehoiachin was deposed and taken captive to Babylon. (He was 18 when he became king, not eight; and Zedekiah was his uncle.)

36:11-21 Zedekiah; Jerusalem destroyed

See also 2 Kings 24:18 – 25:30; Jeremiah 37:1; Ezekiel 17:3.

God gave Zedekiah and the nation many warnings through Jeremiah and the other prophets, but they were all ignored. The destruction of the city and Temple are seen as God's punishment – a judgment that spelt death or exile for the whole nation. The exile lasted about 70 years, until the Persians took over the Babylonian Empire.

▶ **Sabbath (21)** The Chronicler implies that these sabbaths were not kept under the kings. See Leviticus 25:1-7; 26:34-35.

36:22, 23 New hope

When the book of Ezra was detached from Chronicles, these verses were retained at the end of Chronicles and repeated at the beginning of Ezra. Chronicles could not end at verse 21. God had not utterly abandoned his people. Jeremiah had spoken scalding words of God's judgment and condemnation. But he had also spoken of God's continuing love for his exiled people, and of their eventual return (Jeremiah 24:4-7).

Ashurbanipal, king of Assyria, is represented in this relief from Babylon in a ritual act of slave-labour, serving the gods.

Ezra

Summary

The Jews return from exile, rebuild the Temple in Jerusalem and re-establish God's law.

Chapters 1 – 2
The first exiles return

•

Chapters 3 – 6
Rebuilding the Temple

•

Chapters 7 – 10
Ezra's return

Ezra and Nehemiah (one book in the Hebrew Bible, called Ezra) cover roughly 100 years, from 538 to 433 BC. Here the history of the Jewish nation related in the Old Testament ends. Ezra follows on from Chronicles (2 Chronicles 36:22-23 and Ezra 1:1-3 are identical), which closed with Nebuchadnezzar's destruction of Jerusalem in 587 BC and the people being taken into exile in Babylon.

Ezra and Nehemiah describe the three-stage return: the main party, who returned with Zerubbabel in 538/7; the exiles who returned with Ezra 80 years later, in 458 (this is the traditional date, which has strong archaeological support); and Nehemiah's party in 445. Because it is difficult to put the events of the two books in time order, some question whether Ezra and Nehemiah returned to Jerusalem in the reign of the same king (Artaxerxes 1, 464-423), prefering to place Ezra with the later Artaxerxes II (403-357).

On the wider plane, the Jewish events belong to the time following the overthrow of the Babylonian Empire by Cyrus, king of Persia, in 539, when a reversal of previous government policy not only allowed exiled peoples to return home but encouraged them in the practice of their own religions. The Jews could be themselves again, though firmly subject to Persia. They could rebuild their Temple at Jerusalem (work began in 538 and resumed in 520, when the prophets Haggai and Zechariah first spoke) and re-establish their own worship. This is the focus of the book of Ezra.

Ezra and Nehemiah span the reigns of five Persian kings, and a sixth, Darius II (423-404), is mentioned in Nehemiah 12:22.

It is not clear who wrote the books, or when they were written. The earliest date would be around 400 BC. The compiler may have been the Chronicler or one of his circle. Whoever he was, it seems he drew on the personal memoirs of Ezra and Nehemiah in editing the books named after them.

Nearly 50,000 Jews returned from exile – only a handful compared with the nation they had once been. Yet the survival of this 'remnant' was evidence of God's continuing love for his faithful people:

'What we see in Ezra-Nehemiah, is an Israel cut down almost to the roots, but drawing new vitality from its neglected source of nourishment in the Mosaic law and already showing signs, by its new concern for purity, of growing into the Judaism which we meet, both for better and for worse, in the New Testament' (Derek Kidner).

facing page: The decree of King Cyrus of Persia allowed the exiles to return to their home-land and to their 'holy city' of Jerusalem.

Return of the exiles under Zerubbabel and Ezra

1 – 2
The exiled Jews return

1 King Cyrus of Persia orders displaced people home

The policy of the Babylonian kings was to deport the peoples they conquered. But now (539 BC) Babylon has fallen to Persia

MEDIA
Ecbatana

BABYLONIA   Susa (Shushan)
Jerusalem   ELAM

PERSIA

The Jews under Persian rule

Persian kings				
Cyrus 559-530	Cambyses 530-522	Darius I 522-486	Xerxes I (Ahasuerus) 486-465	Artaxerxes I 464-423
The return from exile Ezra 1	Not mentioned	The Temple rebuilt Ezra 4:5, 24; 5	The king who made Esther his queen and Mordecai his grand vizier Ezra 4:6	The king who sponsored the return of Ezra and of Nehemiah. Jerusalem rewalled. Reforms. Ezra 4:7-23; 7:1ff.; Nehemiah 2:1

Prophets				
End of Daniel's life 1:21; 10:1		Haggai and Zechariah		Malachi

(as the prophets predicted). And one of
Cyrus' first actions is to repatriate the
exiled peoples, and allow them to reinstate
their national gods. Among those who
benefit from the change of policy are the
Jews. (See Isaiah's remarkable prophecy,
Isaiah 44:26-28; 45:1-13.)

▶ **Verse 1** See on 2 Chronicles 36:22-23. Cyrus'
action is God's doing: even foreign kings act at
the bidding of the 'King of kings'.

▶ **Verse 6** God saw to it that the exiles, like the
Israelites at the exodus (Exodus 12:35-36)
did not leave empty-handed.

2 List of returned exiles
See also Nehemiah 7. This chapter lists the
leaders, the clans of Israel, of priests and
Levites, of Temple workmen and Solomon's
servants. It lists the towns people returned
to, the places where their families had once
lived. Records like this are an important
proof of ancestry, a matter of vital
importance for the priests (61-62).

▶ **Verse 2** Nehemiah 7 lists 12 leaders,
representing the 12 tribes (i.e. the whole
nation). Zerubbabel is the grandson of exiled
King Jehoiachin (2 Kings 24:15); Joshua/Jeshua,
the son of Jehozadak, the leading priest, also

deported from Jerusalem by King Nebuchadnezzar (1 Chronicle 6:15). This is the Joshua of
Haggai 1:1 and Zechariah 3.

▶ **Nehemiah (2)** Not the same individual as the
later governor.

▶ **Barzillai (61)** 2 Samuel 17:27; 19:31ff.

▶ **Verse 63** The priest would use the sacred lots
(the Urim and Thummin) to ask God if these
priests were acceptable.

▶ **Verse 64** The figures given do not add up to
this total. There may have been mistakes in
copying or interpreting the numbers.

3 – 6
Rebuilding the Temple

3 The foundation is laid
The first thing to be rebuilt is the altar, so
that worship and sacrifice may begin
again, on the pattern laid down by Moses
(Leviticus 1 – 7). The phrase is almost a
refrain in Ezra: 'according to the
instructions written in the Law of Moses';
'according to the instructions handed
down...' Everything must be properly done:
this is not something new, but the old
authentic tradition restored. Lebanon

With the return
from exile the
happy sound of
children at play
in the streets of
Jerusalem could
be heard once
more.

again provides choice cedarwood for the building of this Temple as it did for King Solomon's (see 2 Chronicles 2). But the work makes little progress beyond the foundations.

▶ **Verse 1** This is the start of the religious new year, September/October, marked by key festivals including the Day of Atonement.

▶ **Verses 10-11** See 1 Chronicles 25. There are two choirs (or choir and soloist) singing alternately.

▶ **Verse 12** The older men wept for the glories of the Temple that had been destroyed.

4 Opposition brings work to a standstill

Verses 1-5: the settlers offer help. They too now offer sacrifices to the God of this land. But the Jews will have none of it, and so the settlers stir things up, managing to stop the work for 15 long years, until Darius is king (24).

Verses 6-23 interrupt the chronological sequence to carry the account of the opposition through to the time of Ezra and Nehemiah, nearly 100 years later. Here the bone of contention is the rebuilding of the city walls (12).

▶ **Judah and Benjamin (1)** It was mainly exiles from the southern kingdom who returned. Their 'adversaries' are the mixed people King Esarhaddon of Assyria had settled in the land, later known as Samaritans. They worshipped God, but alongside other 'deities' (2 Kings 17:24-41).

▶ **Verse 7** Aramaic was the international diplomatic language of the Persian Empire. Ezra 4:8 – 6:18 and 7:12-26 are written in Aramaic, not Hebrew like the rest.

▶ **Osnappar (10, some versions)** An Aramaic version of Ashurbanipal. 'Beyond the River'/'Trans (or West) Euphrates': this is the title of the fifth 'satrapy' or province, which included all Palestine and Syria.

▶ **Eat the salt (14, some versions)** I.e. they were maintained by the king; his paid officials.

▶ **Verse 23** This is the situation recounted in Nehemiah 1:3.

5 – 6 Rebuilding completed

Urged on by the prophets Haggai and Zechariah, the people again start building. This time an attempt to get the new king,

Darius, to stop it has the opposite effect. Darius checks the court records, and discovers the scroll on which King Cyrus' decree is written. The Jews have official authorization for their Temple, even to the dimensions and materials used.

In four years the Temple is finished and the people are able to celebrate Passover. For a nation that has recently come through a second exodus, delivered by God from their bondage in Babylon, this must have had very special meaning. In contrast to 4:3, 6:21 records that the sacrifices were enjoyed not only by the returned Jewish exiles, but also 'by all those who had given up the pagan ways of the other people who were living in the land and who had come to worship the Lord God of Israel'. Here is the 'remnant' of Israel, true to their

Excavations at the south-east corner of the Temple have revealed stonework which may go right back to the time of Zerubbabel who led the first group of returning exiles back home.

The scribe
Alan Millard

Most people in the biblical world had no need to learn to read or write, although many were aware of writing, as tax-collectors made their demands or the king listed his soldiers. To draw up a legal deed, or to write a letter, people went to a scribe who sat in the street or at the town gate, and paid him to create the document.

Probably more people could read than could write: even so, it was the scribe who usually did the reading – and interpreting if need be.

That was Ezra's position: one which had grown in importance in his day. Fewer people spoke the Hebrew language than before the exile, so they did not easily understand the law. By New Testament times the scribes had become specialists in that task.

Hebrew and Aramaic were usually written with pen and ink on papyrus or leather sheets or rolls. Notes and accounts might also be kept on wooden boards covered with wax. All these writing materials decay in the damp soil of most places in the biblical world.

A scribe outside a Middle-Eastern bank today fulfils much the same role as the scribes of ancient times. From Ezra's time on, Jewish scribes had a more specialized role.

Only in very dry places in Egypt, for instance, and in caves by the Dead Sea, have samples survived.

Pieces of broken pottery served as scrap paper and dozens of these have come to light from ancient Israel and Judah. They are mostly short notes and lists which either had no lasting value, or were discarded after their information had been entered into larger ledgers.

identity, bringing others into covenant relationship with God: separate but not exclusive.

▶ **6:11** A common form of execution in Persia; in effect, crucifixion.
▶ **6:19** Passover is celebrated in March/April.
▶ **King of Assyria (22)** I.e. king of what was once Assyrian territory.

7 – 10
Ezra

The rest of the book focusses on Ezra, a priest who can trace his line right back to Aaron, the first high priest (7:1-5). Ezra is a scholar of God's law. He will teach it to the new community of God's people, so that they will not repeat past mistakes.

7 More exiles return with Ezra
The story of Esther, the queen who saved the Jewish people from massacre fits into

the interval of nearly 60 years which separates 7:1 from 6:22.

Artaxerxes, the king now ruling Persia, is favourably disposed towards the Jews, and Ezra is given official sanction to teach the law and appoint magistrates in his homeland, to offer sacrifices and beautify the Temple. (Ezra's own memoirs would seem to be quoted from verse 27, where the text changes from the Aramaic of the Persian king's letter to Hebrew.)

▶ **Verse 1** On the traditional view, Artaxerxes I. But some think Artaxerxes II. See introduction.

▶ **Seventh year (7)** Or possibly 37th year.

▶ **Verse 9** The 1500-km/900-mile journey took four months.

8 Ezra's company

Ezra's party of over 1700 includes priests, people and, somewhat reluctantly, Levites. With them they take as gifts 22 tonnes/ 48,500lb of silver and 3,400kg/7,500lb of gold. Ezra is faced with a long and dangerous journey at a time of great unrest. And, having boasted his confidence in God, he can hardly now apply to the king for an escort! His prayer is heartfelt, and his faith rewarded by God's own safe-conduct.

▶ **Satraps (36)** Governors, usually only one to each 'satrapy' or province, with several subordinates.

9 – 10 The question of mixed marriages

Since their return, priests and Levites, rulers and people alike have intermarried with the heathen peoples around, a thing forbidden by God (Deuteronomy 7:1-5), not out of racial prejudice but because it led to idolatry. (God's concern – and the concern of those true to him – for non-Jews has already been seen in 6:21 and is a particular feature of the books of Ruth and Jonah.) This very practice had been a major factor in the nation's downfall under the kings. Yet even the horrors of defeat and exile have not taught the people their lesson. Ezra's bitter distress at the disclosure is therefore not surprising.

His close identification with the offenders and the deep grief of his prayer pricks the nation's conscience. They call on him to act. So, by their own choice, the whole assembly gathers to hear his judgment. We see them shivering in the December rains and can almost hear the interchange that follows (10:10-15).

The blame for all the unhappiness of broken marriages rests not on Ezra, but on those listed in 10:18-44 – the men who contracted those marriages in defiance of God's law. Some of them (as Malachi 2:10-16 makes clear) had even broken former marriages to Jewish wives to do so. See also under Nehemiah 13.

The Hebrew Bible continues straight on from Ezra 10:44, without a break, to the opening words of Nehemiah: the conclusion of the story. Ezra will reappear, in a more positive role, as the people assemble again in Nehemiah chapter 8 to hear God's law.

▶ **10:18** This list unlike that of chapter 2 begins with the names of the guilty priests, those who should have given a moral lead.

▶ **10:44** The text of the second part of the sentence is damaged. 1 Esdras 9:36 supplies the (likely) divorce and sending away of wives and children, painful though it is.

Nehemiah

Summary

The story of Governor Nehemiah, who made Jerusalem a city again.

Chapters 1 – 2
Nehemiah's return from Persia

•

Chapters 3 – 7
Rebuilding the walls of Jerusalem

•

Chapters 8 – 10
God's law and covenant

•

Chapters 11 – 13
Dedicating the city walls

The story of the exiles' return, begun in Ezra, continues in Nehemiah. It is 445 BC when King Artaxerxes I gives Nehemiah leave to return to Jerusalem, and the action comes thick and fast over the months that follow. Nehemiah tells his own first-person story in chapters 1 – 7, and from 12:27 to the end. Unlike the quiet, recessive Ezra, Nehemiah is vividly alive from the outset – a practical man, an organizer and leader, a man of courage and determination with deep spiritual resources to draw on.

1 – 2
Nehemiah returns to Jerusalem

1 Bad news from home; Nehemiah's prayer

In December 446, Nehemiah's brother Hanani (see 7:2) brings sad news of the colony in Jerusalem (see Ezra 4:23). Nehemiah holds the trusted position of king's cup-bearer at the Persian court, at that time resident in the winter capital of Susa. It is his job to taste the king's wine, in case it is poisoned. Although far from his homeland, he is so concerned for his people that for four months he continues to grieve and pray over the situation. Then characteristically, when the opportunity comes, he has a practical plan to put to the king.

▶ **Remember the word (8)** E.g. Deuteronomy 30:1-5.
▶ **Verse 10** Refers to the exodus – God's rescue of Israel from Egypt.
▶ **This man (11)** The Persian king.

2 Nehemiah's mission; the king consents

The sorry state of Jerusalem is a direct consequence of Artaxerxes' decree that building should cease (Ezra 4:7-23). Nehemiah therefore takes his life in his hands in championing a city which has been represented to the king as a hot-bed of rebellion. Even by letting his grief show in the king's presence he places himself in grave danger. But Nehemiah's concern for his people outweighs self-interest. God answers his prayer, and Artaxerxes grants his request. Unlike Ezra (Ezra 8:22), he sets out on his journey (longer than Ezra's by some 260km/200 miles: a total of around 1760km/1100 miles) with a military escort.

On arrival in Jerusalem Nehemiah mentions his plans to no one until he has made a secret personal inspection of the city.

▶ **Verse 6** Nehemiah returned after 12 years as governor (5:14), but the term agreed on here was probably shorter.
▶ **Sanballat, Tobiah (10, 19)** See also 4:1-9; 6:1-18; 13:4-9. These two were important men. 'A document of 407 BC (38 years after the events of this chapter) refers to Sanballat as "governor of Samaria", and the Jewish name Tobiah is borne by a powerful family in Ammon for centuries to come' (Kidner). 'Geshem' (Gashmu, 6:6): tribal chief of Kedar in north Arabia.

3 – 6
Jerusalem's walls rebuilt

Under Nehemiah's pro-active and inspirational leadership it takes just 52 days, despite all opposition, to build about 2.4km/1.5 miles of wall. The east wall was new (and 2.75m/9ft thick), the rest was rebuilt along the line of the previous walls, though much of the old stone was useless

'In those days I was the emperor's wine steward' (1:11).
Nehemiah served at the Persian court in the important position of king's cupbearer. Here a cupbearer attends King Ashurnasirpal II of Assyria at a banquet.

Nehemiah faced a huge task in rebuilding the walls which would make Jerusalem a fortified city once more.

(see on 4:2 below) and no doubt a good deal had been pillaged for other building work in the 150 years since the Babylonian destruction.

3 Organizing the work

This chapter describes the work from a starting-point on the north side and going anti-clockwise. Most of the places mentioned cannot now be identified. But the Sheep Gate (1) was on the north wall, eastern end; the Fish Gate (3) at the north-west corner; the Tower of the Ovens (11) at

the north-west corner of David's city. See map.

People of all sorts join together in the work of rebuilding. The list mentions priests and perfumers, goldsmiths and merchants, rulers – and women too. Some undertook a double section. Nehemiah, astute as always, sets the people to work on sections near their own homes, for which they naturally have a special concern. The leaders named are citizens of long standing; neither Ezra nor the men of his party are mentioned.

Nehemiah's enemies

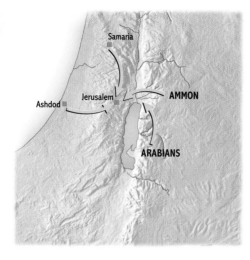

> ▶ **Verse 2** The walls had been burned, and fire made the local limestone disintegrate.
> ▶ **Verses 4-5** Old Testament prayers like this one fall short of Christ's standards. The motive behind them, however, is not personal vengeance but concern for God's honour which is at stake when his people are under attack.

5 Scandal of Jewish slaves

While Nehemiah has been buying back Hebrew slaves and loaning money and food to the poor (even providing his own support as governor), rich Jews have been exacting interest from their fellow countrymen, contrary to the law (Exodus 22:25) and selling them as slaves to foreigners. Nehemiah takes firm action to set this right.

Verses 14-19 take us 12 years on, as Nehemiah records, to his credit, his own style as governor. He acts as he does out of respect for God and his laws (15).

> ▶ **King's/royal tax (4)** The Persians imposed heavy land and other taxes on subject peoples.

6 Plots foiled, the work is completed

The opposition realize that their only chance of stopping the work is to get rid of Nehemiah. Their first move is to try to persuade him to leave Jerusalem for talks (2). When that fails they try blackmail (5-7) and intimidation (10). Nehemiah's replies (3, 8, 11) are superb. He will allow nothing to deflect him from his God-given task. And in under two months (by August/September, the work having been done in the summer heat) the walls are finished – such a fantastic achievement that even Israel's enemies are forced to acknowledge God's hand in it.

> ▶ **Ono (2)** Some 40km/24 miles north-west of Jerusalem.
> ▶ **Verse 10** Only priests were allowed into the Temple itself. This was an invitation, playing on fear, to break the law.
> ▶ **Verses 17-19** Chapter 5 revealed one 'threat from within'. These verses reveal a disloyalty on the part of leading Jews which jeopardized the whole effort.

7 The exiles who returned

The work completed, orders given and

> **❝ What you are doing is wrong!... Let's give up all our claims to repayment. Cancel all the debts... And give them back their fields, vineyards, olive groves, and houses at once! ❞**
>
> Nehemiah's social reforms 5:9-11

4 Nehemiah beats the opposition

The people have a will to work, and a dynamic leader. Nonetheless they have to face first ridicule, then terrorism from powerful opponents. Nehemiah's reply is prayer and faith, plus practical action: 'we prayed... and set a guard' (9); 'Remember the Lord... and fight' (14). His unshakeable confidence comes from the certainty that 'our God will fight for us' (20).

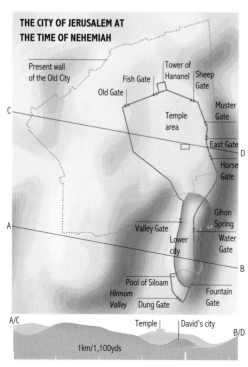

THE CITY OF JERUSALEM AT THE TIME OF NEHEMIAH

Present wall of the Old City

Tower of Hananel

Fish Gate
Old Gate
Sheep Gate
Temple area
Muster Gate
East Gate
Horse Gate
Gihon Spring
Valley Gate
Lower city
Water Gate
Pool of Siloam
Hinnom Valley
Dung Gate
Fountain Gate

Temple | David's city

1km/1,100yds

duties assigned (1-3), Nehemiah decides to create a register of all the families present, discovering as he does so an earlier listing.

Verses 6-73a (almost identical to the list in Ezra 2, see notes) refer to the first, and main, party of Jews to return home in 538 following Cyrus' decree.

8 – 10
God's law: the covenant renewed

The action in these chapters takes place only a few days after the work on the walls is finished. It is the 'seventh month', the beginning of the religious new year with its important festivals.

Ezra, the priest and law-scholar of chapters 7 – 10 of the book of Ezra, reappears to take the lead in religious affairs. These chapters, written in the third person, break into the memoirs of Nehemiah which are taken up again from 12:27.

8 Ezra reads the law
The people ask Ezra to bring out the book of the law (1). Ezra reads and the Levites explain to a patient and attentive audience. (Maybe they also translated for some who spoke Aramaic and knew no Hebrew: verse 8). When they learn the full measure of God's standards the people are overwhelmed with grief at the extent of their failures (just as King Josiah had been, long before; 2 Kings 22).

In the course of study, they rediscover the original instructions for the Feast of Tabernacles. And for the first time since Joshua (the leader who followed Moses) they make leafy shelters to live in, as a reminder of their ancestors' desert-wandering after the exodus from Egypt.

9:1-37 The people repent
Here, reversing the usual order, feasting is followed by fasting, joy by sorrow. The nation's repentance is genuine. Wrongs are righted and the people turn to God in

A gateway of the old city of Jerusalem today.

Excavation has revealed part of Jerusalem's walls going back to Nehemiah's time.

confession and worship. The people's prayer (the words 'and Ezra said', 6a in some versions, are borrowed from the Greek text) – the prelude to renewal of the covenant – begins with God's work of creation and recalls his loving and faithful dealings with a rebellious nation from the time of Abraham to their own day, when they come to him as slaves in their own land because of their sin.

▶ **Verse 1** The sackcloth and ashes are signs of grief – mourning for sin (see Jonah 3:6).

> 66 *You, Lord, you alone are Lord; you made the heavens and the stars of the sky. You made land and sea and everything in them; you gave life to all...* 99
>
> The start of the people's prayer 9:6

9:38 – 10:39 Signing the covenant

The review of their history in the great confession produces a longing to sign up once again to the covenant-agreement with God, so often broken. Nehemiah the governor, priests, Levites and leaders sign on behalf of the nation. The covenant is ratified in customary style with a curse (on those who break it) and an oath (of loyalty to God). The people pledge specifically to keep the law's requirements on marriage, the sabbath, and taxes, tithes and offerings to

support the Temple services, priests and Levites. 'We will obey all that the Lord our God commands... We will not neglect the house of our God.'

11 – 13
Nehemiah's work continues

11 – 12:26 Records of the people

11:3-19 is probably a list of those already living in Jerusalem (it is substantially the same as 1 Chronicles 9:2-17). The number was increased by a 10 per cent levy on the villages around.

11:25-36 lists occupied villages.

12:1-26 lists first the priests and Levites who returned with Zerubbabel, then descendants of high priest Joshua, then heads of families of priests, and records of the families of priests and Levites, ending with Temple duties.

'It is not bureaucratic pedantry that has preserved these names. The point is that these people and their chronicler are conscious of their roots and of their structure as God's company. This is no rabble of refugees, settling down anywhere' (Kidner).

▶ **11:23** See 1 Chronicles 25.
▶ **12:9** There were two choirs who sang or chanted in reply to one another.

12:27-47 Dedicating the city walls

At this point we return to Nehemiah's own first-person memoirs. Two processions, each led by a choir, make their way in opposite directions along the broad top of the wall, meeting in the Temple area for the concluding thanksgiving and sacrifices. It is an occasion of tumultuous joy and noisy celebration.

13 Abuses and reforms

12:44 – 13:3 are by way of editor's notes. At verse 4 we are back with Nehemiah.

In 433, after 12 years as governor, Nehemiah goes back to the court of King Artaxerxes. He is there some time. On his return he finds abuses that threaten the law of God (15-22), the nation's identity (23-27) and the priesthood (28-29). The people have already gone back on many of the promises so recently made to God (chapter 10).

The high priest, of all people, has given Nehemiah's old enemy, Tobiah (probably an Ammonite, despite his Jewish name), quarters in rooms attached to the Temple. The income for the Levites has not been forthcoming. Sabbath laws are being flagrantly broken. And yet again (see on Ezra 9 – 10, about 30 years before this) the Israelites have contracted marriages with foreign women. Nehemiah utters scalding words and roars into action to clean up these situations.

The achievements of Ezra and Nehemiah in the crucial years following the return of their decimated nation from exile are notable. Without the teaching of the law, without the invincible faith and fearless action of these two leaders, it is doubtful if a distinctive Jewish religion and community – with all that means for the wider world – could have survived. To this end their strong line on mixed marriage was essential. The objection to foreign women was not on the grounds of race, but because of their debased religions. (The Old Testament makes no objection to inter-racial marriage if both partners worship the God of Israel: the marriage of Moabite Ruth to Boaz is just one of many examples of 'foreigners' brought right in to the heart of God's family.) History had taught them that the admixture of paganism, with its easy standards and its appeal to the lowest in human nature, could quickly bring the Jewish faith to the brink of extinction.

▶ **Verse 24** Nehemiah is concerned for the new generation. What will happen to the nation's identity – barely recovered – if this goes on?

Jerusalem has been a walled city from earliest times. Walls built in Crusader times still surround the old city.

Nehemiah's rebuilding of the city walls meant peace and security for the people of Jerusalem.

Esther

Summary

The story of a Jewish girl who becomes queen of Persia and, with the help of her cousin Mordecai, foils a plot to eliminate the Jewish nation.

This Persian guard decorated the walls of the winter palace at Susa when King Ahasuerus divorced his queen, and Esther was brought to court.

Esther tells the story of a plot to exterminate the entire Jewish nation in the days of the Persian king, Ahasuerus (Xerxes I), and how it was thwarted. It also explains the origin of the Jewish Feast of Purim.

Estimates of the book vary – largely on account of the seeming improbability of the events. For the Jews, Esther is a book of instruction (law) and of history (narrative). Some Christians regard it as pure fiction. Others see it as a historical novel or short story based on genuine history. Others again think that the knowledge we have of Persian affairs in the 5th century BC – the writings of the Greek historian Herodotus, Persian inscriptions and tablets from Persepolis – give good grounds for treating Esther essentially as history.

Certainly many background details – court customs, the use of couriers, the forbidding of mourning, execution by hanging – accurately convey the Persian world at that time. Quite recently the word *puru* has been found inscribed on a dice, confirming what the writer says about the origin of Purim.

Who is the writer? We do not know. But his nationalism and accurate knowledge of Persian ways make it likely that he was a Jew who lived in Persia before the empire fell to Greece.

Although the book does not mention God by name, a belief in his power to overrule in human affairs, no matter where, and his unfailing care for his people, underlies everything.

Greek additions to Esther

The Greek Septuagint text adds whole paragraphs to the book, including references to God (and sometimes leaves out material in the Hebrew text). Jerome's 4th-century Latin Vulgate text made these passages part of the Deuterocanonical books. (They can be read there in Roman Catholic editions of the Bible, and in the Protestant Apocrypha). There are six major additions, amounting to 107 verses. The Jerusalem Bible reintegrates them, using italics to distinguish them from the rest of the text.

1 Ahasuerus dethrones his queen

The Persian emperor Ahasuerus (Greek, Xerxes) reigned from 486-465 BC over an empire stretching from the Indus to northern Sudan. He was the son of Darius I, who left him vast wealth and a new luxurious palace complex at Susa. Excavation has revealed the throne room, harem and a 'paradise' (garden). Ahasuerus is mentioned in Ezra 4:6.

His winter capital (unbearably hot in summer) was Susa, a city in Elam, about 260km/200 miles east of Babylon. The Greek historian Herodotus describes him as a cruel, capricious, sensual man – which fits well with his character in this book.

In 483 he gives a huge feast, the climax to a six-month display of his wealth and power. But his queen (we are not told why) refuses to play along with his wish to make her part of the exhibition. And on the advice of his astrologers the king deposes her.

▶ **Queen Vashti (9)** Herodotus says Amestris was Ahasuerus' queen. It is possible that Vashti ('best' or 'beloved') is her Persian name. Or there may have been other queens we know nothing of.

▶ **He sent letters (22)** Darius had set up an

Portrait of Esther

Frances Fuller

Esther was a beautiful Jewish girl who had been raised by her cousin Mordecai, after her parents died. Her Jewish name was Hadassah. They lived in Susa, the capital city of Persia during the time of King Xerxes (Ahasuerus), among the exiles taken from Jerusalem by Nebuchadnezzar.

King Xerxes chose Esther from among the most beautiful virgins in the land to be his queen, replacing Queen Vashti who had refused to come to him when summoned. But Esther was a queen without power or privilege. She could not even approach the king, without risking death, unless she had been called to him, and she shared the king's attentions with hundreds of other women.

Mordecai seems to have been a minor official in the palace. This enabled him to stay near the gates, check on Esther and send messages to her, though he did not have ability to communicate directly with the king. When Xerxes appointed a wicked man named Haman to the highest position among his nobles, and the others began to bow down to him, Mordecai refused to honour him in this way, even after being told that it was required by the king. Haman was enraged and when he learned that Mordecai was a Jew, he plotted to right the wrong by killing all of the Jews. He even persuaded Xerxes to turn this plot into a royal edict. Later he lost patience and built a gallows on which to hang Mordecai.

Esther, who had kept her alien identity from the king, was now the only hope of the Jews, and she asked them to fast three days, promising to approach the king at the end of this time. 'And if I perish, I perish.' When the potentially dangerous moment came, the king held out his sceptre to receive her, and in several meetings Esther acted with cunning and courage, asking the king for what she wanted, while continuing to show respect. Her behaviour is an amazing example of the use of feminine charm and even weakness to enlist support and authority for a cause. As a result, the Jews were saved, Haman was hanged on the gallows he built for Mordecai, his estate was given to Esther, and Mordecai was elevated

At his banquet the Persian king used lavish vessels like this beaten gold bowl, one of the Treasures of the Oxus.

to a position second only to the king. The Jews held a great celebration, which was made an annual event by the decree of Esther and Mordecai.

Though the story of Esther reads like a fairy tale, it has strong claims to historical accuracy, and the Jews trace the Feast of Purim (see 'The great festivals') to these events.

---

excellent fast-courier postal service which operated throughout the empire.

2 Esther becomes queen

The years of the disastrous Greek war – the battles of Thermopylae and Salamis – intervene between chapters 1 and 2. Four years pass before the king is able to get round to choosing a new queen. Among the beautiful girls rounded up to be taken to the capital for 12 months' beauty treatment, sampled by the king, and then for the most part forgotten, is a young Jewish girl, Esther, Mordecai's cousin. When her turn comes, she delights the king and he makes her his queen.

Esther's Jewish identity is kept secret (10): this is important for the plot as the story unfolds. So too is Mordecai's discovery of a plan to assassinate the king, which is written into the court records (23; see 6:1-2).

▶ **Verses 5-6** Mordecai would have been nearly 120 if he personally had been taken captive in

Esther took her life in her hands when she approached the Persian king unbidden. Here King Darius of Persia is seated on his throne; from the palace at Persepolis.

597. It probably means that his family was among the captives.

▶ **Hadassah/Esther (7)** Some make much of the fact that the names 'Esther' and 'Mordecai' are similar to those of the Babylonian gods 'Ishtar' and 'Marduk'. But this is not surprising if both were names given to them in captivity, as this verse says Esther's was. Hadassah means 'myrtle'. An official named Marduka appears on a text of this period, but there is no means of knowing if this is Mordecai.

▶ **Tebeth (16)** December/January 479.

> *Having once captured our imagination, a story can 'take off' and, like a seedling transplanted into receptive soil, begin a life of its own in the reader's mind.*
>
> Joyce Baldwin

3 Prime Minister Haman's plot to destroy the Jews

We are not told why Mordecai refuses to bow to Haman. He must have considered that Haman's demand went beyond court courtesy and required a degree of worship that cut across his own faith. In his unreasoning fury Haman determines on 'ethnic cleansing' to rid Persia of the entire Jewish race. Haman lived in a fate-ridden society where the court diary for the year's events was worked out by casting lots. So he must choose a 'lucky day'. Fortunately for the Jews it was 11 months off. The king's assent is easily won by accusing the Jews of rebellion and promising a huge rake-off: 340,000kg of silver . Haman plans to raise the money by plundering Jewish goods and confiscating their lands.

> *Who knows but that you have come to royal position for such a time as this?*
>
> Mordecai persuades Esther 4:14

4 Esther hears the news

The entire fate of the Jews now depends on Esther. She alone has access to the king. But she has not been summoned to him for a month. The only way open to her is the dangerous step of going to him unbidden. Anxiously she agrees to take the risk. The Jewish community must support her in fasting (and presumably the prayer that goes with it).

▶ **Verses 14-16** Mordecai makes no mention of God, but his faith makes him certain that help will come, even if Esther refuses. If she does, though, she will forfeit her own life. He piles on the pressure.

5 An invitation to dinner

The king permits an audience. But Esther proceeds cannily. She invites the king and his favourite to dinner. In the mellow after-dinner atmosphere she gives a second invitation. Haman – suspecting nothing, knowing nothing of Esther's relationship to Mordecai – is greatly flattered. He goes home and builds a gallows topping the city wall, on which he intends to hang his enemy.

6 The king rewards Mordecai

This is the turning-point of the story. The king cannot sleep, and reads the court diary, which reminds him of his debt to Mordecai.

'What should be done for the man I want to honour?' he asks Haman. And Haman, misunderstanding, finds he has heaped on his enemy the honours he had thought would be his own. Embarrassed and humiliated, he finds no comfort at home. His superstitious wife and friends see in this the beginning of his downfall. 'Mordecai is a Jew,' the writer has Haman's wife say, 'You cannot overcome him.'

7 Haman's villainy unmasked

After dinner on the second evening, Esther makes her request. Haman is dumbfounded. And his action in throwing himself at Esther's feet as she reclines on her couch only succeeds in adding attempted rape to the charges against him. In the supreme irony of things, he ends his life on the gallows he himself had made.

A Persian gold armlet decorated with griffins (from the Oxus Treasure) conveys the wealth and luxury of life at the Persian court, into which Esther was introduced.

66 The dramatic reversal of a disastrous fate that had seemed set to wipe out the whole Jewish race so impressed the writer that he applied himself with all his artistic powers to conveying the events in writing, and his account so fascinated Jewish readers that the book became a best seller… It continues to be the number one favourite with Jewish communities, and is read in the family every year at Purim. 99

Joyce Baldwin

▶ **My people (4)** Almost casually, Esther reveals her secret.

▶ **They covered Haman's face (8)** I.e. in token of the death sentence.

8 Mordecai promoted; a new edict

There still remains the problem of Haman's edict. Since it was issued in the king's name and under his seal it cannot be revoked (8). But in answer to Esther's further plea the king authorizes a second decree permitting the Jews to fight back.

▶ **Verse 2** Once the king had given his ring to Haman. Now he gives it to Mordecai, making him the second most powerful man in the land.

▶ **Verse 9** May/June.

▶ **Verse 11** The Jews were allowed to treat their enemies exactly as they were to have been treated themselves (see 3:13).

9 Jewish vengeance; Purim

When the appointed day arrives, the Jews rid themselves of their enemies, including Haman's ten sons; but there is no looting. There can be no excuse for Esther's vindictive request (unless it simply accounts for the feast being celebrated on different days in Susa and the country). She shows herself to be a child of her age. The bodies of Haman's sons are hanged (or impaled) to make their fate public knowledge.

Some have taken the casualty figures as conscious exaggeration to amuse the readers. They are certainly very high, though had Haman's plan succeeded, perhaps ten times as many Jews would have been slaughtered.

In commemoration of the nation's deliverance, the 14th and 15th Adar became annual feast days, preceded by a fast on the 13th. To this day the Jews celebrate Purim, reading the book of Esther aloud, and remembering many more recent miracles of deliverance.

10 Postscript

The final historical notes, attesting the good use Mordecai made of his power, seem to have been added later.

Poetry & Wisdom

JOB TO SONG OF SOLOMON

Derek Kidner

Poetry

The word 'poetry' may suggest to us a highly specialized branch of literary art, produced by the few for the few. But this would be a misleading term for any part of the Old Testament. A closer modern equivalent would be the measured oratory of, for instance, a Winston Churchill –

> *We shall fight on the beaches,*
> *We shall fight on the landing-grounds,*
> *We shall fight in the fields and in the streets*

– in which reiteration (or other devices) and rhythm join to make a passage doubly memorable and impressive.

Reiteration was a favourite Canaanite technique, and is also a mark of some of the earliest biblical poetry:

> *Spoil of dyed stuffs for Sisera,*
> *Spoil of dyed stuffs embroidered,*
> *Two pieces of dyed work embroidered for my neck as spoil.*
> Judges 5:30

The **rhythm**, though tighter than this in the original, is a flexible matter of stresses, or beats, not of fixed numbers of syllables. Most often there will be three stresses to a line, matched by another three in the following line which pairs with it to form a couplet. But this pattern may be varied by an occasional longer or shorter couplet, or by a triplet, in the same passage; or again the predominating rhythm may be of couplets in which a three-beat line is answered by another of two beats:

> *Hów are the mighty fállen*
> *in the mídst of the báttle!*

This last rhythm, with its touch of fading or drooping, is often used for **taunts** or **laments** (as in the book of Lamentations), and this has suggested the name *Qinah* (lament) for it, although its use is not confined to such themes.

What is almost the hallmark of biblical poetry, in contrast to our own, is **parallelism**: the echoing of the thought of one line of verse in a second line which is its partner:

> *Has he said, and will he not do it?*
> *Or has he spoken, and will he not fulfil it?*
> Numbers 23:19

There are many varieties of this, from virtual repetition to amplification (filling it out) or antithesis (putting in the opposite). It has a dignity and spaciousness which allow time for the thought to make its effect on the hearer, and often also the opportunity to present more than one facet of a matter:

> For my thoughts are not your thoughts,
> neither are your ways my ways,
> says the Lord.
> Isaiah 55:8

Bishop Lowth, whose lectures on Hebrew poetry in 1741 first introduced the name 'parallelism' for this poetic style, pointed out that this structure, based as it is on meaning, survives translation into the prose of any language with remarkably little loss, unlike the poetry that relies on complex metre or a special vocabulary.

There are, of course, such points of style in Old Testament verse, and occasionally such devices as assonance, rhyme, refrains, word-plays and acrostics; but they are secondary. The essence of this poetry is that it has great matters to convey forcibly to people of all kinds. It is therefore unselfconscious, and remarkably free from artificialities of language.

For this reason, poetry is not segregated into a few poetical books, but breaks out in various contexts at moments of special importance. The examples quoted above are drawn from books we might call

> **"** *The essence of this poetry is that it has great matters to convey forcibly to people of all kinds.* **"**

histories (but the Jews called them the 'Former Prophets' and 'the Law') and from prophecy. In fact nearly all prophetic utterances are in this form, and are rightly set out as lines of poetry in recent translations of the Bible.

Three books of the Old Testament, however, were given a more elaborate system of accents than the rest by the Jewish grammarians, to mark them out as distinctively poetic. These were **Job, Psalms** and **Proverbs**. To our ears, a better candidate than Proverbs would have been the Song of Solomon; its pure lyric poetry a third example of Hebrew poetry to stand beside the rich eloquence of Job and the singable verse of the Psalms.

On **Job**, more will be said under the heading of Wisdom, below; but purely as poetry it has been hailed as one of the masterpieces of world literature, for the wealth and energy of its language and the power of its thought.

In the **Psalms**, poetry is put to work, to be 'the way to heaven's door' in worship or in teaching, furnishing inspired words for public festivals and royal occasions, and for individuals who might come to confess their sins, or plead for healing, or rejoice over some deliverance or revelation.

The Hebrew text of some psalms names melodies, notation and musical instruments to be used, reminding us that the psalms are poems meant to be sung. The harp was a popular accompaniment in Old Testament times.

In Proverbs a wise elder teaches the young a wisdom that is grounded in reverence for God.

the books which we group under this name (in the Old Testament, **Proverbs, Job, Ecclesiastes**), for proverbs and pointed sayings are part of every culture, and Israel's was no exception. In the narratives we have, for instance, Jotham's fable of the trees, Samson's riddle, and various proverbs; while in the Psalms and prophetic oracles the teaching syle of the Wise makes itself clearly heard from time to time (e.g. Psalm 1; Isaiah 28:23ff.; Jeremiah 17:5ff.; Hosea 14:9). We are confirmed in identifying this as a distinct ingredient in Scripture by the fact that Israel itself heard it as a third voice alongside Law and Prophecy. There was even a proverb to this effect: 'The law shall not perish from the priest, nor counsel from the wise, nor the word from the prophet' (Jeremiah 18:18).

The **Song of Solomon**, by contrast, scarcely gives the name of God a mention, but responds rapturously to his creation and to its crowning glory, the gift of love between man and woman. Its presence in the Bible is the most graceful of tokens that God's world is not properly divisible into secular and sacred, and that holiness cannot be indifferent to beauty.

Solomon Of all reputations for wisdom, Solomon's is pre-eminent; and it rests not only on his own brilliance but on his patronage of learning and the arts. The Queen of Sheba was but one of a stream of visitors who poured into Israel to hear him and put him to the test. The names and places of 1 Kings 4:30-33 give a glimpse of an intellectual world that briefly found its capital in Jerusalem; and this openness to foreign enquirers finds some reflection in the authorship of Proverbs 30 and 31:1-9, which are apparently the work of non-Israelite converts.

Wisdom

Wisdom, in the Old Testament, is the voice of reflection and experience, rather than of bare command or preaching. We are persuaded, even teased, into seeing the connection between God's order in the world and his orders to people, and the absurdity of going against the grain of his creation.

> *Wisdom in the Old Testament is the voice of reflection and experience.*

> *A scholar's wisdom comes of ample leisure ... to be wise he must be relieved of other tasks.*
>
> Ecclesiasticus 38:24

Variety of forms Wisdom takes many forms. A vivid comparison, perhaps expanded into a parable or an allegory, is a favourite device; the Hebrew word for it, *mashal*, does duty for any of these, and equally for a proverb or a taunt. A riddle or an enigmatic saying is another means of pricking a person into thought. At a deeper level there will be searching reflection on the way God governs the world, and on the ends for which we live.

Like poetry, Wisdom is not confined to

The wisdom of the East Israel's Wisdom literature, then, never professed to have developed in an intellectual vacuum. Just how rich was the surrounding culture is becoming clear as the wisdom of Egypt and Mesopotamia comes increasingly to light. Some of their fables, popular sayings and precepts have been preserved, and they are largely concerned with the common stuff of life that occupies the biblical proverbs: teachability, sobriety, wise speech, kindness, trust in divine help, magnanimity, friendship. There is a certain amount of mere worldly wisdom here, but much, too, that is sound and high-principled, although the biblical material moves at a consistently higher level of informed faith. Another class of literature from these countries wrestles with the problems of suffering and the meaning of existence, arguing the points at considerable length in skilfully constructed poetic monologues and dialogues.

The fact that questions of this depth were being debated in writing, not only in the time of Solomon but for 1,000 years before him, and that the Israel of his day was anything but a cultural backwater, should dispose of the idea (still current in some circles) that Israel's stock of wisdom consisted at this time of short popular sayings, which supposedly developed by degrees into longer and more religious units, and only in the latest period into the connected discourses of Proverbs 1 – 9, or the probings of Job and Ecclesiastes. The dating of these calls for better criteria than a scheme of religous evolution.

A distinctive treatment But while it is illuminating to see how high a level of discussion existed from these early times, the Old Testament treatment of these themes remains distinctive.

In the book of **Job**, God is recognizably the faithful, righteous Lord whose ways, while they are past finding out, are to be trusted to the end. Job does not have to conclude, like one of the Babylonian sufferers, that what is evil on earth may be counted good in heaven; nor is there any question of placating God with gifts; still less of throwing in one's hand and renouncing him.

And in **Ecclesiastes** the apparent pessimism of the book has only a surface resemblance to the deep-dyed cynicism of the Babylonian *Dialogue between Master and Servant*, where nothing has meaning or value, and only caprice remains. Ecclesiastes does indeed reduce everything

True wisdom is a journey through life directed by God. 'Trust in the Lord with all your heart' is the teacher's advice to his pupil as he sets out on this path.

the world offers to a mere breath, but this is done precisely because we were made for something bigger than time and space: the fear of God, whose assessment of every deed and 'every secret thing' as good or evil invests the whole of life with meaning (Ecclesiastes 12:13-14).

That expression, the fear of God, to which Ecclesiastes moves as its conclusion, is the starting-point of **Proverbs** (1:7) and the pivot of all the Wisdom literature (see Job 28:28; Psalm 111:10; Proverbs 9:10). Secular philosophy tends to measure everything by human beings, and comes to doubt whether wisdom is to be found at all. But the Old Testament with this motto turns the world the right way up, with God at its head, his wisdom the creative and ordering principle that runs through every part; and people, disciplined and taught by that wisdom, finding life and fulfilment in his perfect will.

Job

Summary

The story of Job revolves around the issue of suffering and how we are to understand it. It is a conversation piece between the sufferer, Job – a good man – and his well-meaning but small-minded friends, until at last God speaks...

The book of Job stands alone amongst the books of the Old Testament. It forms a part of the 'Wisdom' material (with Proverbs and Ecclesiastes; see 'Poetry and Wisdom'), but in form and theme it is unique. No one knows who wrote it, or just when it was written, but the story is set in the days of the patriarchs. Job is a wealthy and influential sheikh – wealthy in terms of flocks and herds rather than cash. Part of the year he is a man of the city; for the rest, on the move with his cattle. He belongs either to the days before the priesthood and organized religion or to a region where these things were not needed. He reminds us very much of Abraham: a man of the East.

A prose prologue introduces the great debate between Job and his friends which the author records in magnificent poetry. The subject is as old as the hills and as modern as the space-age. If God is just and good, why does he let innocent people suffer? (Why the casual victims of war and terrorism? Why the child dying of cancer?) As a man Job is really good: about the best anyone could ever hope to be. Yet calamity overwhelms him. Loss of possessions and family is followed by grim, prolonged physical suffering that shakes his faith to the depths.

As they tussle with the problem, both Job and his friends are hampered by ignorance of the larger issue, the challenge of Satan related in the prologue. They have no assurance of a future life. For them death is the end. So justice must be seen to be done in this life. According to the orthodox theology of the day – the position championed by the three friends – prosperity was God's reward for good living, calamity his judgment on the sin of the individual. Generally speaking this held good. But the friends reduced a general truth to a rigid, invariable rule. If Job suffers, then he must be a wicked man. But

Job knows this is untrue. So the argument goes back and forth, neither side shifting position, until they reach complete impasse, at which point God himself intervenes. He does not answer Job's questions. But, seeing God, Job is satisfied. If his friends' theology had been too narrow, his own concept of God had been too small.

The book leaves much unsettled. It is only in the New Testament that we approach an answer to the problem. As we look at Christ on the cross we see the suffering of the only really innocent person. And we see a God who cares so much for us he is prepared to shoulder the whole burden of human sin and suffering. Yet the book of Job is not out-dated. Even today, suffering men and women find that this book speaks to their need as no other book in the Bible.

See also 'Understanding Job' and 'Wisdom in Proverbs and Job'.

1 – 2
Prologue

1:1-5: the main character, Job, a truly good man, is introduced in the 'Once upon a time' style which tells us this is a story.

1:6-12: off-stage, so to speak (to let the reader know something none of the characters in the story are aware of), in the court of heaven, Satan accuses Job of serving God for what he can get out of it. God allows Satan to test this out – a measure of his confidence in Job – but Job himself is to be spared.

1:13-22: in the space of a single day Job loses everything – possessions, servants, family – but his confidence in God remains

left:
One by one Job's servants bring him devastating news. The donkeys are stolen; lightning has struck and killed the sheep; Chaldean raiders have taken the camels, killing all but the servant who escaped to tell what happened.

Calamities
beset Job like a
whirling dust-
storm. This is the
time of testing.

unshaken (compare verse 21 with Paul's words in Philippians 4:11-12).

2:1-6: Satan has lost the first round. Now he says Job is only really concerned for his own skin. So God allows a further test, stopping short only at Job's life.

2:7-13: Job's body breaks out in running sores. The great man becomes an outcast. His wife fails him. The three friends who remain loyal sit in silence, appalled at what has happened. But still Job holds fast to God.

▶ **Uz (1:1)** A town somewhere to the east of Palestine – linked with Edom in Lamentations 4:21.

▶ **1:2** Job's large family and substantial estate indicate that Job has God's favour. Seven and three are ideal numbers.

▶ **Sons of God/heavenly beings (1:6)** Angels of God's court in heaven. Satan is among them, under God's authority.

▶ **Satan (1:6)** The 'adversary' of mankind.

▶ **Sabeans (1:15)** Nomads of south-west Arabia.

▶ **'Chaldeans' (1:17)** Nomads from south Mesopotamia, Abraham's homeland.

▶ **Rubbish heap/ashes (2:8)** Ashes are linked with suffering, mourning and humble repentance. The rubbish heap would be littered with bits of broken pottery.

▶ **Job's friends (2:11)** Wise men from towns in Arab and Edomite territory, a region renowned for its sages.

❝ Blessed is the man whom God corrects; so do not despise the discipline of the Almighty. For he wounds, but he also binds up; he injures, but his hands also heal. ❞

The words of Job's friend 5:17-18

3 – 14
First round in the debate

3 Job curses the day he was born
The seven-day silence is broken by Job in a shout of protest against his misery. He wishes he had never been born and longs to find peace and release in death. Why? Why? Why?

▶ **Verse 8** Job refers to magicians who can make a day 'unlucky'. Leviathan may be the monster supposed to have been imprisoned by God at creation. In chapter 41 Leviathan is the crocodile.

▶ **Verse 24** Sighs and groans are his daily diet.

4 – 5 Eliphaz reasons with Job
The three friends now begin the to-and-fro argument which makes up most of the book. Eliphaz has first turn. Job has often helped others in trouble, he says, now he should be prepared to swallow his own medicine. God destroys the guilty, not the innocent (4:7). No one is blameless before him (4:17). Trouble is an inevitable part of life (5:7). The best course is to turn to God (5:8), accept his reproof (5:17), and wait to be restored to favour.

There is much in what Eliphaz says, but his diagnosis happens to be wrong in Job's case.

▶ **5:4** Cases were tried and contracts made at the town gate; it was the hub of public life.

6 – 7 Job replies

It is nauseating advice (6:6-7) to tell a man at the end of his tether to be patient (6:11-12). Job wants only to cease to be. His friends have failed to show sympathy when he needed it most (6:14ff.). He has done nothing to deserve suffering (6:30). Life is a succession of pain-filled days and sleepless nights (7:3-6).

7:11-21: Job turns to God and pours out his heart to him – his fear, his longing for death. Why won't God leave him alone? If sin is the trouble, why won't he forgive?

▶ **6:18-19** The caravans of traders crossing the desert come looking for water, and not finding it move on to die of thirst.

▶ **7:5** Job's sores breed maggots.

8 Bildad takes up the argument

Eliphaz had begun gently. Bildad takes a firmer line as Job's words grow wilder. God is just. He rewards the good and punishes the wicked. Bildad's words are salt to an open wound (4).

9 – 10 Job's reply: how could God do this?

Job believes, as Bildad does, in the justice of God. But his own case will not square with his belief. God has condemned an innocent man. How can anyone call him to account? Good, bad – it is all one (9:22). Disaster strikes both. Why (10:2)? The Creator has turned Destroyer (10:8). Will he allow no respite before life is over (10:20-22)?

9:5-13 forms a hymn to God. Its images come from ancient creation stories.

▶ **Rahab (9:13)** The legendary monster of chaos.

▶ **9:16-19** In his bitterness Job sees God as an unjust judge. Like many people before and since, Job's basic problem was to get a hearing at all (19), and even if he got as far as the court he could not be sure of a fair hearing and impartial administration of the law.

▶ **10:21** See 'Old Testament views of the afterlife'.

11 Zophar joins in

Zophar's words are harshest of all. He has no patience with Job's irreverent talk. Does Job think himself innocent? God is letting him down lightly (6). Job must put away his sin (13-14); then God will restore him.

Everything is black and white to Zophar. He doesn't doubt that his position is right.

The story of Job is set in patriarchal times, his wealth measured in sheep and cattle.

Understanding Job
Katharine Dell

Job represents suffering humanity, struggling to understand in the face of calamity and despair. Despite his traditional reputation for patience, Job in fact represents those who are not prepared to take suffering lying down but feel the need to protest, argue and debate. The main dialogue of Job portrays this protesting figure, which many have ignored by only reading the prose sections of the book.

When good people suffer
The book of Job consists of a simple tale of a man who did all that he thought God required of him. He was generous to the poor and the underdog, he was a respected member of his community and he even sacrificed to God on behalf of his children just in case they had inadvertently sinned. He was a good man who did not deserve the destruction of his property, the death of his children and the infliction of a leprous disease that made him lose all standing and dignity.

Those around him, the friends who came ostensibly to comfort him, told him that he must have sinned to deserve this punishment from God but Job throughout maintained that this suffering was truly undeserved. He did not however give up on God but strove to understand his relationship with God despite the suffering and the hardship and the grief that he had to endure.

Tough questions
The book raises profound questions. One is what motivates people to be religious? Job is

The story of Job speaks to all who are bowed down by suffering.

accused by Satan, in a heavenly discussion that is going on without Job's knowledge, of just pursuing a religious life because of what he can get out of it. It was believed in those days that good behaviour led to all kinds of benefits – long life, children, and material rewards. But Job proves that his faith is not so superficial as this in the way that he holds on to it through thick and thin and in fact matures in his understanding.

Another question raised in the book of Job is how to understand suffering and still maintain a relationship with God. There are

some who say that we are not truly human until we have suffered. Of course, this is not true, but there are dimensions to our self-understanding and to our realization of what a relationship with God is about, that only emerge when we come face to face with ourselves, often in a situation of suffering or grief.

Job discovers new depths to his faith as a result of his questioning. He stages a protest against God and is not afraid to speak out. He finds

God to have turned cruel, to be ignoring him and yet at the same time to be pursuing him and making him feel hedged in. He longs to fly away from his suffering like a bird, to be free of the chains that bind him, and yet he also longs for the stability of a meaningful relationship with God, for the security and stability that gave him.

Why me?

In the long dialogue section of the book Job is a man in anguish and confused. He is preoccupied with death – in one sense he longs for death as an escape, but then he realizes that if he dies he will not be able to continue to argue his case with God. Who will hear him then when he is in the darkness of Sheol? He longs for God to respond to him so that he can receive an answer to his question, 'Why me?'

God responds

The climax to the book is when God does in fact make a response to Job, although it is not the response he expects. Instead of comforting words or a rational explanation God merely tells of the wonders of the universe that he has created and of the animals that roam the earth. The message here is that there are many things in life that we do not understand and that God is working on a different plane from human beings, one that we can only glimpse and never fully comprehend. This does not mean that he is inaccessible, but rather that we should not try to limit him by our imperfect understanding.

It is not an irrefutable principle that the good will prosper and that the wicked will be punished. God's justice cannot be reduced to such a simplistic theory. Unfathomable things do happen and sometimes for no apparent purpose. Job ultimately has to accept this, which he does on his knees, saying that he has spoken of things that he has not fully understood.

After this we read in a crucial verse, 42:7, that God was angry with the three worthless comforters of Job for they had not spoken right of him as Job had. This suggests that to attempt to understand, to reach the limits of our knowledge and comprehension and still hold on to faith is better than the friends' line, which was to keep reiterating that if Job was suffering then he must have sinned. They were locked into their narrow dogma, which maybe made life comfortable and easy to cope with. But the message here is that real life is not like that. It is full of uncertainty, of meaningless suffering and of riddles and contradictions. Faith in God is sometimes hard, but it is just that – faith.

Happily ever after?

At the end of the book we have Job restored to good fortune, in true folk-tale style. But there is a certain unease with this ending. We have just learned that Job was not in it for material reward and there he is with twice the number of camels that he had before. Maybe the author just allowed himself a touch of irony by ending the tale in this way.

Job is restored, but in his encounter with God he has reached a new level of faith that will mean that he can never really go back to what he was before. He is given a new set of children – yet will they ever really replace the original ones? He is given long life and sees his children's children grow up, a real sign of blessing in Hebrew thought.

Holding on to faith

Job then has much to offer those suffering today. The message here is not to give up on God because bad things happen in the world. Rather, in holding on to faith, we will perhaps reach a deeper level of understanding or maybe just a sense of God's presence alongside. But the most profound response to suffering is found in the Christian message that, in Christ, God suffered at the deepest level and so is able to be with us in our suffering and guide us when we are lost and perplexed, yet desperately wanting to hold on to our faith in God, as Job was.

> ❝ *Man that is born of woman is of few days and full of trouble.* ❞
>
> 14:1

Yet he hits the mark when he asks 'Can you fathom the mystery of God?' (7), for it is in these terms that God will 'answer' Job (chapters 38 – 42) and Job will be satisfied.

▶ **Verse 8** See 'Old Testament views of the afterlife'.

12 – 14 Job responds

Job is stung to sarcasm. His friends are not the only ones who can work things out. God is all-wise, all-powerful. If he turns the norms of wisdom and justice upside-down, what can anyone do about it (12:7-25)? Job's experience gives the lie to the arguments of his friends (13:1-4). He will put his case to God direct, and God will acquit him (13:18). What are the charges against him (13:23)? Life is short and there is no waking a person from the sleep of death (14:1-12). Job cries to God to hide him away in the land of the dead until his anger is past, and then to restore him (14:13-17). But despair floods back – what hope is there (14:19)?

▶ **12:1** See 'Wisdom in Proverbs and Job'.
▶ **14:13** See 'Old Testament views of the afterlife'.

> Transition from wealth to poverty can be swift for people dependent on occasional rains for pasture and the health of their flocks.

15 – 21
Second round in the debate

15 Eliphaz speaks again

The debate grows more heated. Job has needled his friends, and they make no

allowances for the stress he is under. It never crosses their minds he may really be innocent. They go on doggedly defending their position and trying to bludgeon Job into submission.

Job is a self-opinionated old windbag (2)! All he has said – his wild accusations against God; his attempts to justify himself – merely serve to prove his guilt (6). Job is wrong in saying that the wicked get off scot-free. Their fate is a terrible one (17-35).

16 – 17 Job repeats his complaint

It is cold comfort his friends have to give. How easy for them to talk, when it is Job who bears the pain. (Like many since, their silent sympathy, 2:13, helped more than their well-meaning words.) God has worn him out with suffering and the cruelty of others. The pictures Job paints (16:9, 12-14) convey his intense, unbearable agony – a tortured body and a mind tormented at the thought that God could do all this to him. Even now he cannot believe God is unjust: there must be one who will plead his cause in heaven (19; see 1 John 2:1). If his case rests till he is dead, what hope is there (17:13-16)?

▶ **17:3** Job speaks to God.
▶ **17:13-16** See 'Old Testament views of the afterlife'.

18 Bildad returns to the fray

Bildad bitterly resents Job's angry rejection

of their advice. The argument is getting personal (3). He replies by painting a terrible picture of the fate of the wicked (5-21), meant to put Job in his place. But Job is innocent, and Bildad's tirade irrelevant.

19 Job's hope that God will defend him

Job's friends have become his tormentors, levelling false accusations and offering no answer to his desperate questions. He is shut in on himself (8), despairing (10), utterly alone (13-16). He has become an object of loathing to those he loves most (17). Even pity is denied him (21-22).

Yet in his darkest moments, faith and hope still well up inside him. He is certain of vindication. One day God himself will take up his case and clear him – and he will be there to see it (25-27). Then those who have maligned him will find themselves answerable to God.

▶ **Book (23**, some versions) A scroll: the book form as such did not come until New Testament times.

▶ **Verses 23-27** This is a difficult passage and the lines which follow 25a are particularly unclear. It is important not to read back into this a full-fledged belief in resurrection, which came much later. (See 'Old Testament views of the afterlife'.) But Job's Redeemer/vindicator is clearly God, whom he hopes to meet after death (why else would he need to leave a written testimony?). See too his words in 14:13.

20 Zophar echoes Bildad's thoughts

Zophar, like Bildad, is upset by Job, and he takes up Bildad's theme: the fate of the wicked. Their prosperity is short-lived, their punishment certain. But this is not the point. They are not hearing Job because his case does not fit their general rule.

We hear no more from Zophar after this: either he has nothing further to add, or a section of the third round of speeches has been lost. It is possible that 27:13-23, which sounds so strange coming from Job, belongs in fact to Zophar.

21 Job tells it as it is

Zophar's theology is all very well, but it flies in the face of experience. The condition of Job, the good man, is pitiful (5). Yet more often than not, evil people flourish, live happily and die peacefully (7-18). The friends will argue that God's vengeance falls on their children (19). But what kind of justice is that? Their so-called comfort is nothing but a pack of empty lies.

Job challenges an inadequate orthodoxy and too narrow a view of the world. This 7th-century BC Babylonian plan of the world shows it surrounded by ocean, with Babylon on the Euphrates, mountains to the north of Assyria and swamps to the south.

22 – 31
Third round in the debate

22 Eliphaz will not give in

Eliphaz would rather invent sins for Job (5-9) than allow that his own view might be inadequate. He sticks to the same stubborn line of argument. Job is in the wrong! Job had thought to hide his sins from God (14). Let him make peace with God, put away his sin, and all will be well again.

▶ **Ophir (24)** So famous for the export of gold (see 2 Chronicles 8:18) that 'Ophir' and 'fine gold' became synonymous. The location is unknown.

66 *Where shall wisdom be found? And where is the place of understanding? Man does not know the way to it, and it is not found in the land of the living. The deep says, 'It is not in me,' and the sea says, 'It is not with me.' It cannot be gotten for gold, and silver cannot be weighed as its price... God understands the way to it... And he said to man, 'Behold, the fear of the Lord, that is wisdom; and to depart from evil is understanding.' 99*

28:12ff.

23 – 24 Job wrestles with his problem

Job's thoughts go round and round, always coming back to the same sticking-points. If only he could find God and put his case to him. But God is not to be found, and his ways are inexplicable.

Chapter 24: look what goes on in the world; life is neither fair nor just. God delays judgment, and those who trample the helpless underfoot seem to get away with it. (It may be that Zophar, not Job, is speaking in verses 18-25.)

▶ **Remove landmarks/boundary stones (24:2)** I.e. seize lands. The landmark was a stone sometimes inscribed with the landowner's title-deeds and boundaries.

▶ **Take in pledge (24:3, 9)** Take as security for credit, or seize in payment of debt.

25 Bildad rests his case

If the speech is complete as it stands (see on chapter 26), Job's friends have exhausted their argument. They have nothing more to say. Bildad merely reiterates the obvious truth that no one is 100 per cent perfect in God's sight. This does not help Job. What point is there in godly living if God's punishment falls equally on good and bad?

26 – 27 Job swears his innocence

26:1-4 may be Job interrupting Bildad, who then continues to speak of God's power, to the end of the chapter (in another hymn, like that of Job 9, with images drawn from ancient creation stories). In the created universe we catch a glimpse of God's dynamic power. But who can think to comprehend that power in all its fullness?

Chapter 27: his friends want him to deny his integrity, but Job will not perjure himself. Verses 13-23 sound strange coming from Job. This has previously been the argument his friends have put forward. Either Job's thinking has changed, or this passage really belongs to one of the others (perhaps Zophar).

▶ **Abaddon (26:6; 28:22, some versions)** Another word for 'Sheol', the shadowy land of the dead.

▶ **Rahab (26:12)** See 9:13.

28 In praise of wisdom

Is Job or the author speaking in this chapter? The text does not say. But the heart of Job's problem is how to understand the inscrutable ways of God. No miner can uncover a vein of wisdom; all the wealth in the world will not buy it. Only God knows where to find it. And people become wise through reverence for God and by rejecting evil. See 'Wisdom in Proverbs and Job'.

▶ **Ophir (28:16)** See on 22:24.

29 – 31 Job states his case

Job puts his case together in this final statement.

Chapter 29: 'If only... ' Job looks back longingly to the golden days of God's favour – past enjoyment of home, of success in business, of universal respect. He speaks movingly of his good deeds done in fulfilment of God's laws (12-17). He had expected long life and a good death (18) – the signs of God's favour.

Chapter 30: 'But now': he returns to the bitter present, which has made him the butt of all, an outcast, incessantly gnawed by pain. All this God has done to him, yet will never tell him why (19-20).

Chapter 31: all this has befallen a man who has avoided immorality, even in his thinking (1); who has played fair with his employees (13); been generous in relieving need (16); never become obsessed with money (24) or turned idolater (26-27); turned no one from his door (32); harboured no secret sins (33); never kept quiet for fear of what others might think or how they might react (34). Job is prepared to swear to all this before God (35). (How many of us could honestly do the same?) Yet how has God repaid him?

▶ **29:6** A picture of superabundance.

▶ **30:29** He conjures up lone creatures of the desert, whose very cries are mournful.

▶ **30:31** Lyre and flute or pipe, which once played joyful music now cry sorrow.

▶ **31:26** Sun and moon worship was widespread in the ancient Near East, but God's law forbade it.

▶ **My land cried out (31:38)** Because Job has taken it from its rightful owners.

32 – 37
Elihu's tirade

Elihu has not been mentioned, or spoken, before. He has been a silent bystander, holding back out of deference to his elders. But he can bear it no longer. His pent-up thoughts burst out in a long, unstoppable tirade.

Chapter 32: Elihu is the original angry young man. His elders are lost for words, but he is simply bursting with indignation at Job's attitude, dying to have his say.

Chapter 33: Job has declared himself the innocent victim of God (9-11); but God will not answer his charge (13). Elihu says God speaks to us through warning dreams (15) and through suffering (19) – in order to save, not destroy us (30).

Chapter 34: Job has said God is in the wrong (5-6), and there is nothing to be gained by making him our delight (9). But God is the judge of all people: supreme, just, impartial (10-30). Job has added to his other sins resentment and rebellion against God (36-37).

Chapter 35: Elihu (wrongly; see 2 Samuel 11:27; 12:13) sees good and bad conduct as a matter between people (8): God remains high above, untouched by either. People cry out to him in their need (9). But they are concerned for their own skins, not for him (10-12). This is why he does not answer (13).

Chapter 36: God is almighty, all-wise (5). He is a Teacher who uses suffering to open our ears to listen and learn where we

have gone wrong (8-10). Job should not be longing for death (20), but learning his lesson (22).

Chapter 37: God is great. He commands the thunder and lightning, rain and snow. He spreads out the clouds and the shining skies. We are as nothing beside God's awesome splendour, his unassailable holiness. We are right to fear him (24). He pays no attention to people (like Job!) who grow too big for their boots.

38 – 42:6
God's answer satisfies Job

God breaks in just when Elihu has finished his list of excellent reasons why Job cannot expect an answer! God is almighty, far and away above humanity. But he is also near. He hears, and he cares. Job had imagined himself putting his case to God, asking his questions. But imagination is not reality. It is God, not Job, who asks the questions now. And through the succession of searching questions Job finds his opinion of himself shrinking, his concept of God expanding. His mental image of God had been altogether too small. The God who confronts him is God on a different scale altogether.

Chapters 38 and 39: where was Job when God made the world, light and darkness, wind and rain, the constellations in their courses? What does Job know about the creatures of the wild – the lion, the goat, the wild ass and ox, the ostrich, the horse, the eagle? Did he make them? Can he feed them, tame them – as God can?

Chapters 40 and 41: is Job God's equal,

'Miners dig iron out of the ground and melt copper out of the stones,' says the writer in Job 28. But Wisdom, more precious than silver, gold or gems is to be found, not by mining, but in God. King Solomon's copper mines are still to be seen in the mountains north of Eilat.

In the end, Job's fortunes are restored. The sun shines for him again: the dark days are past. And his integrity is vindicated.

been dabbling in things beyond his understanding, totally out of his depth. Before, he had gone by hearsay; now he has seen God for himself, as he longed to do. There is now no question of putting his case; seeing God is enough. His questions remain unanswered, but he is satisfied. It is unthinkable that this God could ever let him down or act inconsistently. He can trust, where he does not understand. Now he can accept what comes. Self-righteousness melts away. Job regrets the bitter things he has said. As he looks at God and worships, he sees himself and his problem in perspective.

42:7-17
Epilogue

Verses 1-6 are the high point in the story. This final passage in prose merely rounds things off. Job has been vindicated, and this must be visibly demonstrated. (There is no promise of a fairy-tale ending to every case of suffering.)

God has taken Job to task for his reaction to suffering, but his integrity is beyond question. Job's good name is as clear as his conscience. It is the three friends who have been wrong. Job's was an honest search for truth. They would not allow for truth being bigger than their understanding of it – and so they were guilty of misrepresenting God. They must obtain Job's forgiveness before God will forgive them.

Significantly, it is at the point when Job has accepted his suffering and forgiven his friends, that God reverses his fortunes. Friends, prosperity, family are all restored to him, with a long life in which to enjoy them.

that he calls him to book, and questions his justice? (Job's wild words had brought him dangerously near the sin of Adam and Eve.) Look at just two of my creatures, says God – Behemoth (the hippopotamus) and Leviathan (the crocodile). Look at their strength (40:16; 41:27), their sheer untameability (40:24; 41:1-2). People are utterly powerless to control them. What folly then to claim equality with God who made them!

42:1-6 contains Job's reaction, the climax of the book. Job now realizes he had

Psalms

Summary

The Psalms are the timeless hymns of ancient Israel, collected into five books:

1. *Psalms 1-41*

2. *Psalms 42-72*

3. *Psalms 73-89*

4. *Psalms 90-106*

5. *Psalms 107-150*

Within the books the psalms are grouped by theme or purpose or under a collector's name.

In the Jewish Bible, Psalms belongs to the Writings, a miscellaneous collection which includes the Wisdom books.

The psalms express the whole range of human feeling and experience, from dark depression to exuberant joy. They are rooted in particular circumstances, yet they are timeless, and so among the best-loved, most-read, parts of the Bible. In our modern age we are stirred by the same emotions, puzzled over the same fundamental problems of life, cry out in need, or worship, to the same God, as the psalmists of old. We find it easy to identify with them. And we find their sheer, dogged faith, the depth of their love for God, both a tonic and a rebuke.

Composition

Psalms (the Old Testament hymnal) is a collection of five books: 1-41, 42-72, 73-89, 90-106, 107-150. At the end of each section (e.g. 41:13) the break is marked by a formal ascription of praise to God (a 'doxology'). Psalm 150 forms a doxology to the whole collection.

It is probably fair to say that, in general, Book 1 has mainly personal psalms, Books 2 and 3 mainly national (linked to the Temple choirs) and Books 4 and 5 psalms for public worship. Within the books the psalms are often grouped, according to common themes, a common purpose, or a common author/collector.

The Hebrew titles

Most of the psalms are prefaced by a title or heading (omitted or included only as notes in some modern versions) which is later than the psalm itself but preserves very ancient Jewish tradition. Some name the author or collector, and relate to specific events in history. Seventy-three psalms bear David's name (see 'David and the Psalms'): some, no doubt, dedicated to him as king; some collected by him; and a good

many, surely, his own composition. 1 Samuel 16:17-23 and 1 Chronicles 25:1-8 are not the only indications that the king was a gifted poet and musician. Many other titles concern the musicians, instruments, musical settings, or indicate the type of psalm (*Maskil*, *Miktam*), although the meaning of many of the terms used can now only be guessed at.

Classifying the psalms

There have been many attempts to classify the psalms, and they can be grouped in a number of ways, for example by theme. There are psalms which plead with God and psalms which praise him; appeals for forgiveness, or the destruction of enemies; prayers for the king, or for the nation; 'wisdom' psalms (see 'Poetry and Wisdom' introduction); psalms which probe life's problem-areas; and psalms (such as 119) which celebrate the greatness of God's teaching (*torah*: imperfectly translated 'law'). Many psalms are a blend of several of these common themes.

Perhaps one of the most helpful ways of grouping the psalms is by the main literary types:

- Hymns, in praise of God's character and deeds (e.g. Psalms 8, 19, 29).
- Community laments, arising out of some national disaster (44, 74).
- Royal psalms, originating in some special occasion in the life of the reigning king (2, 18, 20, 45).

There was music to enhance the language of the psalms. This clay figure of a lute player dates right back to the 16th century BC, before the Israelites left Egypt.

facing page:
A tree that grows beside water (Psalm 1), and does not dry up, is a vivid picture – in a country as dry as Israel – of those who find joy in God's law. These are the waters of the River Jordan, close to its sources.

■ Individual laments (3, 7, 13, 25, 51).
■ Individual thanksgivings (30, 32, 34).

Their history and use

All of the psalms are part of the religious life and worship of Israel, public and private, and have a specific historical background (see 'The Psalms in their setting'). Some relate to the time of the first Temple (from David to Solomon, about 950 BC to its destruction in 587). These focus on the ideals of kingship and justice, the covenant with Israel's God, and the land. Others relate to the exile (587-520), when there was no king or Temple and the nation was dispersed. They look forward to restoration under God. And a third group belongs to the time after the return (520-?167), when the Temple was rebuilt and worship restored but the people were without a king and under foreign rule. There was considerable development in religious understanding over this long 600-year period, and Psalms reflects this.

Overriding themes

Like any hymnbook, the great focus of Psalms is on God and the relationship with his people: God's glorious power and might; his steadfast love and readiness to help; the trust his people can confidently place in him; his justice; his impartial and inevitable judgment of all that is 'wicked'. The king also plays a large part in Psalms, quite often prefiguring for both Jews and Christians the hoped-for Messiah, the Christ.

David and the psalms

Nearly half the book of Psalms, 73 of them, including almost all of Book 1, have the note 'belonging to/by David' in the Hebrew titles. They are as follows: 3-9, 11-32, 34-41, 51-65, 68-70, 86, 101, 103, 108-110, 122, 124, 131, 133, 138-145.

Fourteen of these are linked with events in David's life: 3, 7, 18, 30, 34, 51, 52, 54, 56, 57, 59, 60, 63, 142.

Dating

It is very difficult to date individual psalms, or to discover just how and when they were collected and compiled, though the process began with David, if not before, and continued into the days after the exile. Manuscripts found at Qumran have shown that the whole collection as we have it must have been finalized some time before the Maccabean period (2nd century BC).

The psalms as poems

The words of C. S. Lewis underline one further important point: 'The psalms are poems, and poems intended to be sung: not doctrinal treatises, nor even sermons... They must be read as poems if they are to be understood... Otherwise we shall miss what is in them and think we see what is not.'

So, before turning to the psalms themselves, it is important to read the section in the introduction, 'Poetry and Wisdom', where the conventions of Hebrew poetry are explained. 'A poet looks at Psalms' helps us see them in terms of performance.

Psalms 1-41
Book 1

Most of the Psalms in this book have 'belonging to/by David' in the Hebrew title.

1 The way to happiness

The psalm the compilers have chosen to introduce the whole hymnal is a 'wisdom' psalm. It points the way to God's blessing (true happiness lies in pleasing God). There is another path, but those who choose it are doomed.

Verses 1-3 picture the happy people (the good) who resolutely turn their backs on evil and set their hearts and minds on doing what God wants. 4-6, in terrible contrast, picture the present life and future fate of the wicked. The two go their separate ways, and all are on one path or the other: there is no third way.

▶ **Note** Other 'wisdom' psalms are: 49, 73, 112, 127, 128, 133.
▶ **Verse 3** Compare this with Jeremiah 17:7-8.

The people of Israel looked to God as all-powerful against the forces of evil. This relief carving from Assyria, showing the head of a demon, illustrates the fears of other contemporary peoples.

2 Rebel world – sovereign God

This psalm is thought to be for a coronation (or its anniversary): see also Psalm 72. Verses 1-3: the world-rulers, the 'kings of the earth', enter into a futile conspiracy. 4-6 contrast the power of God and the king he has enthroned, as close to him as a son. In Jewish thought these words point to the coming Messiah. The New Testament applies these verses and especially verse 7 to Jesus (see also 'Christ in the psalms'). 7-9: God delegates authority. 10-12: the psalm ends on a note of solemn warning.
▶ **Zion (6)** God's Temple was built on Mt Zion in Jerusalem.

3 A cry to God in time of danger

The Hebrew title says this psalm is by David, at the time of his son Absalom's rebellion: 2 Samuel 15. This is the first of 14 psalms linked to events in David's life: see 'David and the psalms'.

Verses 1-2 outline the situation. 3-6: in God, the God who answers, is security and freedom from fear. 7-8: the psalmist calls on God to save him.
▶ **Sacred hill/holy mountain (4)** Zion, the Temple mount.

4 Inner peace: an evening prayer

Hebrew title, 'by David'. Trust in God sets mind and body at rest.

Verse 1: past answers to prayer give grounds for present confidence. 2-5: a reprimand is followed by command. 6-8 describe the joy and peace which nothing can shake.

5 Prayer at first light

Hebrew title, 'by David'. Beset by men who lie and flatter while they plot his downfall (6, 8-10), the psalmist appeals to the God who loathes every semblance of evil (1-5), the Defence and the Rewarder of the good (11-12). This is the God he will worship and serve (7).
▶ **Verse 3** may allude to the daily sacrifice.

6 A cry of anguish

Hebrew title, 'by David'. Sick at heart (disturbed in mind, ill in body), the psalmist

---

Psalms for special times and needs

Evening: 4, 141
Protection from enemies; safety: 3, 5, 44, 54, 58, 64, 71, 91, 121, 124, 140
Help in trouble, distress, illness: 6, 12, 13, 22, 28, 35, 38, 39, 41, 57, 69, 70, 77, 86, 88, 102, 120, 130, 142, 143
Justice: 7, 10, 17, 26, 73, 82
Guidance: 25, 27
Longing for God: 42, 43, 63, 84
When God is silent: 13, 35, 86, 88, 102, 130, 143

Answered prayer: 30, 34, 73, 116, 126
Evil in the world: 12, 14, 37, 82, 115
Comfort and assurance: 23, 27, 46, 121
Family life: 127, 128
Before worship: 24, 84, 95, 122, 133, 134
In praise of God: 8, 19, 24, 27, 29, 33, 47, 65-68, 75, 81, 92, 95-100, 103-107, 111-113, 115, 117, 127, 134, 135, 145-150
Thanksgiving: 9, 30, 34, 40, 48, 116, 118, 126, 136, 138, 144

Sin, confession and forgiveness: 32, 38, 51, 103, 139
Trust in God: 11, 16, 23, 27, 31, 46, 56, 62, 125, 131, 139

The Psalms in their setting

John Eaton

Two perspectives have been especially fruitful in modern study of the Psalms:

- enquiry into their original use
- and consideration of how the compilers of the final collection saw them.

A festival setting

The original use of the psalms appears to have been rooted especially in the pilgrimage festivals. And of the three annual pilgrimages (Passover/Unleavened Bread in March/April, Weeks or Pentecost in May/June, Ingathering or Tabernacles in September/October), the one in the autumn was especially productive of psalmody.

This outstanding holy season in some way combined the antecedents of the well-known New Year, Day of Atonement, and Tabernacles of the later Jewish calendar. In its pre-eminence, it could be referred to simply as 'the festival' or 'the festival of the Lord' (Leviticus 23:29; Judges 21:19; 1 Kings 8:2, 65).

After six months of drought and burning sun, this September/October observance was truly a time of 'new year'. The beginning of the rainy season was expected, when ploughing and sowing could begin. But the rains sometimes failed and starvation loomed. It was indeed a time to gather for prayer and praise of the Lord of all life (compare Zechariah 14:16-17).

Some psalms reflect the experience of the actual pilgrimage (84, 122). It was a journey of fellowship and of longing for renewal in the Lord's presence.

'God is my rock in whom I take refuge' (Psalm 18:2).

Early in the festival the need for purification and atonement was addressed, and some psalms may come from ceremonies that expressed human frailty and God's plentiful redemption (130, 51). The sanctuary itself was purged and its role as God's dwelling was renewed (87, 93, 132). Processions with the Ark towards the eastern wilderness and back into the Temple expressed the Lord's power to subdue chaos (24, 29, 46, 48, 68). It was like the victory over chaos at the first creation (74:12-17), and also like the beginning of the Lord's bond with his people (50:5). Proclamation was made that he now truly reigned, having asserted his supremacy, his divine glory (47, 93, 95-99). With the great renewal came also a vision of perfection, the ultimate kingdom of God.

His new presence was acclaimed with joyful shouts, music and dance, but this was soon followed by his address to his people through a prophetic voice. Here the desired message of peace (85:8-11) might sometimes give way to stern or ironic warnings (50, 81, 95; Isaiah 6). Colourful ceremonies joined with prayers for rain and healthy growth – pouring of water over the altar in the court, carrying of green branches, torch dances, sprinkling of the fields. Several psalms reflect the hope for such blessings (65, 126-128, 133).

From 1000 to 587 BC the kings of David's line convened and presided over the festival. It was the appropriate time for their first full installation and for subsequent renewals. It was understood that the only true king was God, whose kingship was served and mediated through his chosen servant David and his dynasty. This ideal was expressed in dramatic ceremonies (traceable in 2, 18, 21, 72, 89, 110, 118). Humility, righteousness, care for the poor, faith – with such qualities, the psalms and ceremonies declared, the Lord's royal Servant would be victorious and all the world saved.

Individuals in distress

Throughout the rest of the year there were many occasions for psalms at the Temple. In addition to daily morning and evening offerings and other set holy days, there were occasions of crisis for

▶▶

the king, the nation (44, 79, 80, 83) and individuals.

Some 20 psalms have been thought to belong to trials at the sanctuary, a sacred ordeal when ordinary evidence was insufficient (1 Kings 8:31-32). These psalms protest innocence, plead for justice, and denounce slanderers and other adversaries (3, 4, 5, 7, 17, 26, etc.). Confident endings have been thought to reflect a verdict in the suppliant's favour.

Others see these and many other psalms as prayers of fugitives requesting asylum or safe-conduct: hence the prayers for refuge and shelter under God's protection. However, there is no evidence that psalms were sung in these legal situations or adapted from inscriptions left at the Temple by such suppliants.

A more enduring theory for a great many psalms of individual supplication is that David or a descendant was praying (sometimes at a field altar) when threatened by martial enemies, rebels, sickness and so on. Sometimes it may be that the king is preparing to sleep at the sanctuary in hope of a dream-vision and word of assurance (17, 63 etc.). These psalms often have royal features and involve the people; a royal interpretation would come close to the tradition that David himself composed them.

Piety in later times

A rather different setting has been suggested for some psalms thought to be of later date (1, 19, 34, 37, 49, 111, 112, etc.) which have an air of the study circle. Teaching and discussion might be concluded with a psalm giving thanks or gathering up teaching. So the way of wisdom was taught, and the happiness

which came with devotion to the Lord's word or law. Perhaps it was in such circles that the seed of belief in resurrection developed (49, 73).

Arrangement

Original settings apart, what did the psalms mean to the compilers of the book? Their convictions have recently been studied in the light of their work of arrangement. It appears that they especially related the psalms to the Messianic kingdom, to the daily task of prayer and meditation, and to the all-encompassing work of praise.

Thus they placed Psalm 2 at the head of the largest group associated with David (3-41) to indicate that the royal figure was now taken up into the hope of the perfect king to come, the Messiah. The Psalms had always had a link with prophecy (1 Chronicles 25:1-3), but now this aspect was brought forward, as it was to be also in the New Testament.

The placing of Psalm 1 before the whole collection may also have deep significance. Here it commends the 'sheer happiness' of the person who rejects evil

influences and steeps heart and soul in the Lord's teaching, his word and will, a constant communion which (it is implied) the following collection of psalms can nourish.

And then all was wonderfully concluded by the placing of Psalm 150, which keeps the visionary joy of the great festival alive in all generations, all the more for us since the kingdom has shone through in the work of Christ. Before the revelation of God, all in heaven and earth rejoice in praise. The dancers and psalmist-musicians at the centre represent the pulsating joy of every living thing, not humanity alone, embraced in the Creator's will to make all well. So the compilers signal to us that this in the end is what their collection of psalms is all about.

pleads with God for his life (1-7), and is assured of God's answer (8-10).

▶ **Note** This is the first of seven 'repenting' (penitential) psalms: 6, 32, 38, 51, 102, 130, 143.

▶ **Sheol** (5, some versions) The shadowy world of the dead. Although the psalmists thought in terms of some kind of continued existence beyond the grave it was largely negative. Death cut people off from all they could experience of God during their lives. Their tongues were still; they could no longer sing God's praises. See 'Old Testament views of the afterlife'.

7 Refuge in God

According to the Hebrew title, David sang this song because of Cush the Benjamite (this may have been the Ethiopian who told David of the death of Absalom). The psalmist casts himself on God, knowing his cause is just (1-5). He calls on God to clear his name, to support the right and break the wicked (6-11). He describes the terrible fate awaiting those who refuse to repent (12-16) and closes on a note of thanksgiving.

8 The crowning glory

Hebrew title, 'by David'. Verses 2-4: as he contemplates the great expanse of the universe the psalmist is overwhelmed by a sense of the littleness of humanity. He marvels that God not only bothers about 'mere mortals', but has set them over all other creatures (5-8). The psalm ends, as it began, with a refrain of praise to God (1, 9). See further, 'God and the universe'.

▶ **Verses 4-6** See also Hebrews 2:6-9 and Genesis 1:28.

9 In praise of God the just

Hebrew title, 'by David'. This is one of a number of 'acrostic' psalms, in which the first letter of each verse follows the order of the 22-letter Hebrew alphabet. Only the first eleven letters (with one omission) are used here, and the acrostic seems to continue (imperfectly) in Psalm 10.

Verses 3-8 give the reason for the outburst of praise. God has executed justice and upheld the right. He is an unassailable fortress (9-10). Praise him (11)! Trouble is by no means over (13), but past experience

gives ground for fresh hope (15-20). 'Thy kingdom come'!

10 A prayer for the oppressed

Verses 1-11: times are bad. Evil people defy God and disregard his laws and get away with it. The poor are their helpless victims. 12-18: the psalmist calls on God to act, confident that he will break oppression and defend those who have no one but God to turn to.

▶ **Verse 1** There are times when every believer shares the psalmist's feeling that God is far away. See also 13:1; 22:1; 42:9; 43:2; 74:1.

11 A declaration of faith

Hebrew title, 'by David'. No matter what the danger, the ones who trust in God have no need to panic (1-3). They know God is still sovereign: the champion of justice, the Judge of evil (4-7).

▶ **Fire and brimstone** (6) As in the overthrow of Sodom and Gomorrah (Genesis 19:24).

12 A prayer for God's help

Hebrew title, 'by David'. Surrounded by those whose word cannot be trusted (1-4), the psalmist puts his faith in the utterly dependable promises of God.

13 From despair to hope

Hebrew title, 'by David'. In his misery it seems to the psalmist that God has forgotten him. How much longer must he bear it? Will only death bring an end to it (1-4)? No! All his past experience assures him he will again have cause to thank God for his goodness (5-6).

14 A wicked world

Hebrew title, 'by David'. Society is corrupt: the bias to sin universal (1-3). In wilful blindness humans pit themselves against a God who not only exists but punishes and avenges every aggressive act against his people (4-7).

▶ **Verses 1-3** Paul uses these verses to support his case that no human being is sinless when measured by God's standards (Romans 3).

▶ **Jacob... Israel** (7) The psalmist calls the nation by the two names of its founder. The wily Jacob was given the new name 'Israel' after his

A Bedouin squats in the market-place at Beersheba, demonstrating the present-day version of the ancient pipes.

> Verse 10 The psalmist is probably thinking of premature or sudden death. Paul, applying the words to Christ, sees their deeper significance (Acts 13:35-37).

17 A plea for justice
Hebrew title, 'A prayer by David'. David, like Job, is certain of his own integrity and this is the basis of his plea.
> Apple (8) The pupil; the part of the eye a person instinctively protects.
> Verse 14 This sounds vengeful (though Revised English Bible translates differently). The thought may be: 'heaping on them the very things they love. They are "men... of the world": give them their fill of it!' (F.D. Kidner). See also 'Self-justification, cursing and vengeance in Psalms'.

18 David's victory song
The Hebrew title says this is David's song when God saved him from Saul and all his other enemies. It is a revised version of the song recorded in 2 Samuel 22. The outburst of love and praise (1-3), and the cataclysmic terms in which David describes God's rescue (7-19), give some idea of his previous desperation. He owes his life, his triumphs, his throne, everything to God (28-50).
> Sheol (5) See on Psalm 6:5.
> Verse 8 God appears, 'breathing fire' in his anger at human sin. 'Burning coals': see Isaiah 6:4.
> Verses 10-12 Compare Ezekiel 1:4ff. The living or winged creatures are cherubim, the attendants who signify God's unapproachable holiness.
> Verses 20-24 See 'Self-justification, cursing and vengeance in Psalms'.
> Verse 49 Paul relates this to Christ, in Romans 15:9.

momentous encounter with God at Peniel (Genesis 32:28).

15 What God requires
Hebrew title, 'by David'. This psalm prepares the questioner (maybe a pilgrim come for one of the great festivals) for worship at the Temple.
What does God require of the one who seeks his company? He expects right conduct, right speaking (2-3a), right relationships with others (3b-4), and a right use of wealth (5). See also Psalm 24.
> Hurt (4) I.e. he keeps his word whatever the cost.
> Verse 5 One of the Jewish laws, see Leviticus 25:36-37. It was not a total ban on lending at interest, but applied to fellow Israelites.

16 The path to life
Hebrew title, 'by David'. The psalmist places all his trust in God, and in God finds everything he needs. Those who set their hearts on God and put their lives in his hands (1-6) find joy and security for the present and need not fear the future (7-11).
> Verse 6 The boundary lines of the plot of land a person inherited.

❝ You, Lord, are all I have, and you give me all I need; my future is in your hands. ❞

16:5

19 Creation displays God's glory; the law expresses God's will
Hebrew title, 'by David'. God's universe describes his glory in speech without words (1-4). The psalmist's thought leaps straight from the sun, with its all-pervading, searching rays, to the law of God – pure and clean, bringing joy and wisdom, instruction and enlightenment to our hearts (4b-11); and to his own need of

A poet looks at Psalms

Steve Turner

As a performance poet I feel an affinity with the psalmists. They weren't writing to impress other psalmists or to win the Psalmist of the Year Award. Nor were they writing for silent introspective reading. They were composing for the human voice and to be heard at public events.

When the psalms were first performed there would have been music to enhance the language, and probably physical movement too. After all, David, the best-known psalmist, was not only a writer and a spiritual thinker but a musician and a dancer. His work consequently had a sense of body, mind and spirit. He didn't write for the intellect alone and I'm sure that he had no ambitions to be merely 'appreciated'. He imagined the loud clash of cymbals, not the slow tread of feet down the aisles of a library.

I see a connection between this psalmic culture and the renaissance of public poetry in the English-speaking world in the second half of the 20th century, a time when poets became interested in the pre-literary roots of their craft, a time when the lyre inspired the lyric and the dancing foot gave its name to the basic unit of poetic rhythm.

Significantly, the most public English language poets of this period, Allen Ginsberg and Dylan Thomas, were heavily influenced by both the language and the tone of the psalms. 'The great rhythms had rolled over me from the Welsh pulpits,' Thomas wrote. 'I read, for myself, from Job to Ecclesiastes.'

The images from the Psalms – 'the valley of the shadow of death',

'the apple of the eye' – and the ringing phrases – 'the days of our years are three score years and ten', 'righteousness and peace have kissed each other', 'fearfully and wonderfully made' – have become so embedded in our cultural consciousness that we are apt to

> **66** *The psalmists were composing for the human voice and to be heard at a public event.* **99**

forget their biblical origins. Those people who manage to escape the direct effect of the Psalms pick up the resonances from Shakespeare, Dante, T. S. Eliot to writers of modern pop hits.

As tribal bards, the psalmists selected instantly recognizable images from the contemporary landscape. As universal poets they drew comparisons between what was seen and what was unseen; between still waters and inner peace, between the spreading wings of a bird and God's loving care, between the grass in the field and the brevity of life. As visionaries they could hear the waters clapping and see the heavens rejoicing.

Yet the Psalms aren't all jolly affirmation. There's a brutal honesty that we miss if we only pick out those recommended for comfort. The Psalms attain a level of emotional nakedness and self-knowledge which artists constantly strive for but which religious folk often avoid for fear of letting the side down. An argument with God doesn't appear to be good publicity for faith.

The psalmists don't wallow in misery, but they are frank about the days when it seems as though God has left the phone off the hook. Psalm 9 – 'I will praise thee, O Lord'– is followed by Psalm 10 – 'Why standest thou afar off, O Lord?'– and a reading through all 150 psalms has the effect of being taken on a spiritual roller-coaster ride.

The psalms continue to nurture and inspire me because they are a realistic record of a lifetime's walk with God with all the attendant joys, fears, doubts and certainties. They have the power to engage and enlighten precisely because of this ring of authenticity.

Together they form a model body of artistic expression which encourages me to value the variations in my own spiritual temperature. They also encourage me to make a record of those variations and then to share them in public.

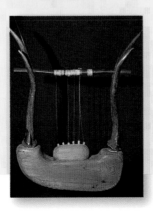

'By the rivers of Babylon we sat down and wept
    as we remembered Zion.
On the willows there we hung up our harps'
(Psalm 137:1-2).

protection and cleansing from sin (12-14). See also 'God in the universe', and Psalm 119 in praise of the law which reveals God's will.

20 'Victory to the king!'

Hebrew title, 'by David'. Battle will soon be engaged. The people (or the choir in the Temple) invoke God's blessing (verses 1-5). A single voice (the king, perhaps prefiguring the Messiah) responds in confident trust (6-8). And the people offer an urgent prayer.

▶ **Verse 1** 'You' = the king. Zion is the Temple hill.

21 Royal thanksgiving

Hebrew title, 'by David'. The occasion may be a victory, or an anniversary. The king counts his blessings (1-7), rejoicing in God's goodness. His confidence for the future (8-12) rests in God's constant love (7). With God's help, all his enemies will be put down. The last verse is the counterpart to 20:9. This time the people (or choir) cheer God to the echo.

22 Suffering and saving

Hebrew title, 'by David'. Kidner calls this 'The psalm of the cross', because Jesus used the opening words to cry his anguish on the cross (compare verse 1 with Matthew 27:46; Mark 15:34). The experience goes far beyond David's own, describing not an illness but what would appear to be 'an execution'. The terms in which the sufferer's agony of mind and body are described became an extraordinarily precise description of Jesus' last hours (see 'Christ in the psalms'). That feeling of desertion by God becomes a terrible reality for Jesus, enduring the crushing, suffocating weight of human sin which tears him apart, seeming to sever (if that were possible) the essential unity of Father and Son.

In the psalm, despair at God's silence (1-2) and the psalmist's own situation (6-8, 12-18) alternates with hope – hope that springs out of every recollection of God's past dealings with him (3-5, 9-11). The final prayer (19-21) brings new inward assurance, expressed in open praise (22-31).

66 *The Lord is my shepherd,*
    I shall not want;
    he makes me lie down in
      green pastures.
He leads me beside still waters;
    he restores my soul.
He leads me in paths of
      righteousness for his
      name's sake.
Even though I walk through
      the valley of the shadow
      of death,
I fear no evil;
    for thou art with me;
    thy rod and thy staff,
      they comfort me. **99**

Psalm 23

If, at the deepest level, the early verses of Psalm 22 speak of Christ's suffering, surely the closing verses speak of the worldwide deliverance he made possible.

▶ **Bulls from Bashan (12)** Bashan, north of Gilead on the east of the Jordan, was famous cattle country.

▶ **Verse 8** See Matthew 27:43.

▶ **Verse 18** See John 19:24.

23 'The Lord is my Shepherd'

Hebrew title, 'by David'. This best-known, best-loved of all psalms pictures God, the Good Shepherd (see also John 10). He provides all that his people need. He leads them through life. He secures them from all harm (1-4). Verse 5 introduces a second picture: God, the perfect host, feasting his people with good things. And it goes further: because 'in the Old Testament world, to eat and drink at someone's table created a bond of loyalty' the picture is not simply of a guest but of a friend.

▶ **Verse 1** The shepherd image is often used of God. See Psalms 28:9; 77:20; 78:52; Isaiah 40:11; Ezekiel 34:11-16. Jesus took this image for himself: see John 10.

▶ **His name's sake (3)** I.e. because this is his nature. God's love and care are wholly in keeping with his character.

▶ **Verse 4** 'Deepest darkness' has generally been taken to mean death: hence 'valley of the shadow of death'.

24 Worship

Hebrew title, 'by David'. This psalm is a processional hymn, possibly written for that great occasion in David's life when the Ark was first carried into Jerusalem (2 Samuel 6:12-15).

The whole world and everything in it is God's. Who then is worthy to stand in his presence (1-3)? The answer (4, and see Psalm 15) would lead to despair if God were not 'the God of Jacob' (6) – that mixed-up, twisted character God chose to become the founder of Israel. Verses 7-10: the Ark is at the gates: open the doors for God himself to enter and own!

25 A prayer in trouble

Hebrew title, 'by David'. This is an acrostic – alphabet – psalm (see on Psalm 9). The psalmist is harassed by the incessant attack of his enemies, and disquieted in his own conscience (1-3, 16-21). Deeply aware of his need, he turns to God for help and guidance, asking to experience again his love and forgiveness (4-15).

26 Prayer of someone good

Hebrew title, 'by David'. The psalmist is not claiming perfection (see 'Self-justification, cursing and vengeance in Psalms') but a consistent life of trust and obedience to God. He calls on God to acquit him of false charges. Compare this self-portrait with the first part of Psalm 1.

▶ **Wash my hands (6)** Compare Matthew 27:24.

27 Trust and commitment to God

Those (like the psalmist) whose priorities are right (4, 8) have nothing to fear (1-3, 5-6). They know where to turn in trouble (7-12) and their hope is well founded (13-14). The Hebrew title says this lovely psalm, springing out of a deep heart-hunger for God, is 'by David'.

28 Prayer – and its answer

Hebrew title, 'by David'. Danger leads to a cry for help, and a plea for the punishment of those evil people who are the source of the trouble (1-5). Prayer turns to praise at the assurance that God has heard and answered (6-9).

29 Glory to God!

Hebrew title, 'by David'. In the torrent of rain, the ear-splitting thunderclaps, the blaze of lightning, the roaring wind that sets the great forests in motion, the psalmist not only sees God's matchless power but hears God's voice. For God made and orders them all (3-10). Let the hosts of heaven sing his glory (1-2) – and may God bless his people on earth (11).

The style of this psalm, with its rythmic repetition, is close to that of ancient Canaanite as well as early Hebrew poetry.

▶ **Verse 5** Lebanon's cedars were the strongest and finest of all.

▶ **Sirion/Hermon (6)** This 3,000m/9,000ft mountain is in the far north, on the Israel/Lebanon border.

> *" Fling wide the gates... that the King of glory may come in! Who is the King of glory? The Lord of hosts, he is the King of glory! "*
>
> 24:9-10

> *" The Lord is my light and my salvation; whom should I fear? "*

> *" Though my father and my mother forsake me, the Lord will take me into his care. "*
>
> 27:1, 10

facing page:
Some psalms are
meditations in
the Temple.
Others reflect on
life: its light and
its darkness.

▶ **Kadesh (8)** A place in the desert south of Beersheba.

30 Thanksgiving for life restored

The events in 1 Chronicles 21 may possibly provide the background to this psalm. The Hebrew title says it is by David, written (in advance) for the dedication of the Temple. The dark days and tearful nights when life was in danger are past (2-3, 6-10): joy has returned with the daylight (5). Easy times bred self-reliance (6). But this experience has put life into perspective (5a) and shown the psalmist his own helplessness (7-10). Now that the danger is behind him – a humbler and wiser man – he gladly and openly acknowledges his debt of gratitude to God (11-12).

31 Trial and trust

Hebrew title, 'by David'. Verses 1-8: the psalmist turns to God for refuge (1-5); trust deepens as he recalls God's past dealings with him (6-8). 9-13: his mind returns to the painful present. 14-24: from his own trouble he turns to God again, with such renewed trust in God's goodness and love that he is able to give encouragement to others (23-24).
▶ **Verse 5** With his dying breath Jesus echoed these words (Luke 23:46).

32 Confession and the joy of God's forgiveness

Hebrew title, 'by David'. This is the second of the seven 'repenting' psalms: see note on Psalm 6. Guilt suppressed becomes an intolerable burden (3-4). Confession and forgiveness bring a joyous lightness of heart (1-2, 5): the relief of it! Out of his own experience the psalmist encourages others to pray to God with confidence. (In verses 8-9 God himself speaks.)
▶ **Verse 4** The psalmist feels the 'heavy hand' of God weighing him down. There is a self-inflicted 'judgment' for those who stubbornly refuse to do what they know is right (see too 1 Corinthians 11:30).

33 Everybody sing God's praise!

Tune up the instruments. Sing for joy and burst into song. Look, hear, what God has done! Sing God's praises for who he is

(4-5). Worship the Creator and stand in awe of him (6-9). Praise his sovereign rule in human affairs – his unfailing care for all who honour him (10-19). Sing a song of trust in him (21-22).
▶ **A new song (3)** To surpass the best of the old. Every fresh experience of God calls forth new praise. John, in his vision, heard a new song in heaven (Revelation 5:9-10; 14:3).

34 God's care for his people

An alphabet poem (see on Psalm 9). The Hebrew title says the psalm is by David and links it to the incident in 1 Samuel 21:10 – 22:1, although the king's name there is Achish.

A man with such a story to tell of God's faithfulness cannot help sharing it. He owes it to God and his fellow believers (1-10). In the psalmist's experience, the person who honours God finds life (11-14). His misfortunes may be many, but God brings him through them all (19-22).
▶ **Verse 7** An angelic host protected Elisha (see 2 Kings 6:16-17). See also 'Angels in the Bible'.

35 A prayer to God to uphold the right

Hebrew title, 'by David'. (For the ethical problems raised by the psalm see 'Self-justification, cursing and vengeance in Psalms'.) Confident that right is on his side (he states his case in 7, 11-16, 19-25), the psalmist calls on God to pay back his enemies in their own coin (1-6, 17, 26) and clear his good name. Then he will praise God and tell others of his righteousness (9-10, 18, 28).
▶ **Verses 5-6** The angel here is a punishing angel, as in Exodus 12:23 and elsewhere. See 'Angels in the Bible'.

36 God's unfailing love

Hebrew title, 'by David, the Lord's servant'. Verses 1-4 picture human wickedness: the person totally committed to his own evil ways. 5-10 contrast the character of God – loving, faithful, good; the source of life and light and all the good that we enjoy. 11-12 are a personal prayer, with the answer (12) concluding the psalm.

37 Good and evil

Hebrew title, 'by David'. An 'acrostic' poem in 22 sections, one for each letter of the Hebrew alphabet (see on Psalm 9). It is a collection of the proverbial sayings that the wisdom writers loved (see 'Poetry and Wisdom', introduction) and according to which, no matter how things look, the good will prosper, the wicked be punished.

Wherever you look, people are flagrantly disobeying God's law, and getting away with it. Don't be tempted to envy them, says the psalmist. Things are not what they seem (1-2, 7b-9). The wicked are in a far from enviable position. Their time will soon be up, but blessing and security await God's people (the message drummed home by the proverbial sayings of 10-40, which paint the contrast between the wicked and the good). Go on doing good; be patient; trust God to act (3-7a).

▶ **Verse 19** This is the traditional view, but not all psalms go along with it. See 73:4-14.

38 A sufferer's prayer

Hebrew title, 'by David'. This is the third of seven 'repenting' psalms: see note on Psalm 6. Sin has resulted in physical sickness (3, 5, 7), as well as mental anguish (2, 4, 6, 8). Friends and family stand aloof (11), and the opposition have the chance they have been waiting for (12, 16). The psalmist admits his sin, with bitter regret, and cries to God for help (21-22).

39 Our 'little life'

Hebrew title, 'by David'. The psalmist struggles to contain his thoughts, for fear of dishonouring God, but they burst out (1-3). He feels death at his shoulder; life as insubstantial as a puff of wind (5-6). And he cries out to God to reassure (4) and forgive him (8), and to remove his troubles (10-13).

▶ **Verse 13** The psalmist sees his suffering as punishment (the view expressed by Job's friends and refuted by God in Job's case). If there is no happiness in this life, nothing can be hoped for beyond death, when he will simply cease to be. See 'Old Testament views of the afterlife'.

40 Heartfelt praise and prayer

Hebrew title, 'by David'. The psalmist has openly declared God's marvellous dealings with him (9-10). He looks back to the moment of rescue with deep thankfulness (1-3), and spells out for others the things he has learned about God (4-8). But his troubles are not yet over (12-17). He is still conscious of his need. And he appeals afresh to God for help. (Verses 13-17 are repeated in Psalm 70.)

The New Testament sees a deeper significance in this psalm, especially verses 7-8: see Hebrews 10:5-7.

▶ **Verse 6** Obedience to God's law is more important than sacrifices, as the prophets often point out: see 1 Samuel 15:22; Amos 5:21-24.

▶ **Scroll (7,** some versions) Probably the book of the Law.

41 Ill and alone

Hebrew title, 'by David'. Verses 1-3 state a general truth. Happy are those who help the needy; in time of need, God will help them. 4-12 outline the psalmist's own case: his illness, his isolation, his reliance on God. Verse 13 is a formal stanza of praise to God, with the people's 'Amen!' added to mark the end of the first book of psalms.

▶ **Verse 9** This betrayal will bring Judas to mind for Christians (see John 13:18 and Luke 22:21). Sharing food binds people together in loyal friendship. See on Psalm 23.

Psalms 42-72
Book 2

According to the Hebrew titles (see introduction) the psalms in this book come from a number of different sources. Psalms 42-49 are headed 'Sons of Korah' (the Temple musicians). Psalm 50 is ascribed to Asaph, who belongs to another Temple group, with more psalms in Book 3. Psalms 51-65 and 68-70 have David's name attached, and Psalm 72 has Solomon's.

42 and 43 Longing for God

These two psalms share the same theme and the same refrain (42:5, 11; 43:5), and probably began as a single poem.

The psalmist is in exile in the north (42:6), surrounded by godless people who mock his faith (42:3, 10; 43:1-2). Deeply dispirited, he contrasts past joys (when he led the pilgrim throng to the sanctuary, 42:4) with the unhappy present. All his happiness rests in God, and he is filled with longing for God's presence, to come again to the Temple (42:2; 43:3-4). And, black as things are, at the very thought of God, faith and hope break through (42:5, 11; 43:5).

▶ **Verse 6** The River Jordan rises near the foot of Mt Hermon on Israel's northern border. 'Mount Mizar' remains unidentified.

44 National lament

This psalm is prompted by a disastrous defeat. Israel is bewildered. After all the stories of God's amazing actions in their early history (1-3), and their complete reliance on him (4-8, 17-18), now this! God had deserted them (9-12). They are disgraced (13-16), and cannot understand why (17-22). Verses 23-26 are a real cry from the heart for God's help.

The switch to 'me' and 'my' in 4, 6, 15 may indicate a single voice (that of the king or high priest) leading the public prayer.

▶ **Verse 19** The images conjure up danger and death (compare Psalm 23:4).

▶ **Verse 22** Paul quotes these words, describing the experience of Christians (Romans 8:36).

▶ **Verse 23** God seems to be asleep, like those false gods Elijah mocked for their failure to respond to prayer (1 Kings 18:27). Nowhere else in the Bible is God accused of sleeping.

45 Song for a royal wedding

The actual occasion may have been the wedding of King Ahab of Israel to Jezebel, princess of Tyre (12, and see on 8 below). If so, the king's reign soon changed for the worse (1 Kings 16:29-33).

Verses 1-9: the poet's eloquent praise of the king's majesty and godly rule. 10-15: a word to the bride in all her finery. Verses 16 and 17 are addressed to the king.

▶ **Verses 6-7** The language here seems to point beyond the present king to the kingdom of God, prefiguring the Messiah.

▶ **Palace ivory (8)** A further possible link with Ahab. Archaeologists have discovered beautiful

carved ivories in his palace at Samaria.
▶ **Ophir/finest gold (9)** See 1 Kings 9:28.
▶ **Tyre (12)** Important sea-port and city-state; modern Sour in Lebanon.

46 'A mighty fortress is our God'
This psalm – the one on which Luther based a famous hymn – may have been written following King Sennacherib of Assyria's attack on Jerusalem (2 Chronicles 32), some natural disaster, or in anticipation of the events heralding Messiah's coming. Verses 4-5 have a parallel in Revelation 22:1-5, where the ideal is perfectly realized. The psalmist glories in God's presence with his people (1, 4-5, 7, 11), and his real and unassailable protection.

47 Shout and sing!
A psalm acclaiming God as Israel's King and Lord of the world. Let everyone rejoice and sing his praises.

48 Zion, glorious city of God
An outburst of relief and joy at the city's reprieve from invasion (perhaps King Sennacherib of Assyria's: see 2 Chronicles 32).
▶ **North Zaphon (2)** The psalmist may have used this phrase because the north was the traditional seat of the gods.
▶ **Ships of Tarshish (7)** See on 1 Kings 10:22.

49 Meditation on life and death
This psalm is a typical piece of 'wisdom' on life's inequalities. See note on Psalm 1 for other wisdom psalms. At the end of the line death waits for the materialist – the

'As a deer longs for a stream of cool water, so I long for you, O God. I thirst for you, the living God' (Psalm 42:1).

wealthiest cannot buy themselves off. The 'moral' is similar to that of Jesus' parable of the rich man (Luke 12:16-21).

Generally speaking the psalmists have no clear concept of life after death, and verse 15 is therefore often taken as a reference to premature death. But this undermines the reasoning, which requires an ironing out of this life's inequalities beyond the grave. See 'Old Testament views of the afterlife'.

50 God calls us to account
In verses 1-4 the summons comes. 7-15: God speaks in warning to his loyal people. It is not enough to go through the ritual motions. Sacrifices are not required to satisfy God's hunger. It is the thankful heart, not the token thank-offering, that counts. 16-20: there are serious charges against those who can recite God's commandments, yet disobey them; who keep company with crooks and are prepared to ruin one of their own family. 21-23: they reckon God of no account because there has been no instant response. But they are wrong. If they ignore his words, nothing can save them.

God says,

❝ *I have no need of a bull from your stall or of goats from your pens, for every animal of the forest is mine, and the cattle on a thousand hills. I know every bird in the mountains, and the creatures of the field are mine.* **❞**

50:9-11

51 Plea for forgiveness
The Hebrew title says this psalm was written by David when the prophet Nathan confronted him over his adultery with Bathsheba and the murder of her husband Uriah (2 Samuel 12). Verses 18-19, which seem to belong to the time after Jerusalem fell to the Babylonians, may have been added later.

The psalm itself is deeply moving. It lets us see right into the soul of a man who has loved God yet fallen into grievous sin. He has been made to see himself through God's eyes, and he is heartbroken. He makes no excuse, simply accepts God's judgment and admits his guilt. All he can do now – knowing God's love and mercy – is ask forgiveness and the chance of a fresh start.

▶ **Verse 5** The meaning is not that conception or childbirth are sinful in themselves, but that sin is ingrained from the very first moment of existence.

▶ **Hyssop (7)** The herb used in the purification ritual described in Numbers 19.

▶ **Bloodguilt (14)** This certainly fits David's case. He arranged for Uriah's death in order to cover up his own sin (2 Samuel 11).

52 The doom of the wicked
The Hebrew title says this is a psalm by David at the time of Doeg's betrayal (1 Samuel 22). But the reference to the Temple in verse 8 would seem to make it later. Verses 1-4 describe the evil oppressor; verse 5 God's certain reprisal. 8 and 9 are a personal expression of trust and thanksgiving.

53 'There is no God!'
Hebrew title, 'by David'. See on Psalm 14, of which this is a revised version.

54 A cry for help
According to the Hebrew title, this is David's appeal to God after the Ziphites betrayed his position to Saul (1 Samuel 23:19ff.). The plea (1-3) is followed by trust (4-5). The promise of a thank-offering (6-7) shows the psalmist's confidence that God will answer his prayer.

55 Betrayed by a friend
Hebrew title, 'by David'. The content fits in well with the time of Absalom's rebellion (2 Samuel 15 – 17), when Ahithophel, David's most trusted adviser, defaulted.

Above and beyond all his other fears and troubles (1-4, 9-11), the treachery of a trusted friend – one who also loves God – has come like a knife to the heart (12-14, 20-21). The psalmist is torn by conflicting emotions: fear and longing to opt out of the whole situation (4-8); and the desire to see his enemies worsted (9, 15). But trust eventually wins (16-18, 22) – for friends may be faithless, but not God.

▶ **Verse 17** These are the regular times for prayer: see Daniel 6:10.

▶ **Verse 22** See 1 Peter 5:7.

56 'In God I put my trust'
Hebrew title, 'by David, after the Philistines captured him in Gath'. But neither 1 Samuel 21 nor 27 records this. The psalmist has plenty to worry him and shake his nerve (1-2, 5-6). But he knows the

In the morning, and as the sun goes down, the psalmists sing God's praise.

answer to fear (3-4, 10-11). And he can safely and thankfully (12-13) leave God to deal with his enemies (7-9).

57 Prayer from among ferocious enemies

Hebrew title, 'by David', from the time when he was in hiding from Saul (1 Samuel 22:1; 24). Circumstances may be black (4, 6), but those who fill their minds with God can sing his praise, come what may (1-3, 5, 7-11). Paul and Silas also knew the truth of this (Acts 16:19-25).

58 'There is a God who judges'

Hebrew title, 'by David'. The psalmist calls down God's terrible judgment on corrupt and evil people in power. See 'Self-justification, cursing and vengeance in Psalms'.

▶ **Gods (1**, some versions) A sarcastic reference to the rulers and judges.

▶ **Cobra (4)** 'Deaf' because it does not respond to the snake-charmer.

▶ **Verse 8a** In popular belief, slugs and snails left slimy trails because they melted as they moved.

59 Prayer for protection and punishment

The Hebrew title, 'by David', links the psalm to the incident in 1 Samuel 19:11-17 (where Saul sets watch on David to kill him), echoed in the refrain 'Each evening they come back...' (6, 14). The psalmist addresses his very personal prayer (1-4, 9-10, 16-17) to the Lord of all the nations (5, 8, 13). All his confidence flows from the certainty that God loves him (10, 17).

▶ **Jacob (13)** I.e. the nation of Israel.

60 The nation in defeat

The Hebrew title, 'by David', associates the psalm with the campaign recorded in 2 Samuel 8, when the faith of verse 12 and God's word in verse 8 were realized in eventual victory

▶ **Verses 6-8** God proclaims the land and people of Israel as his own: Shechem, in the heart of the country, between Mts Ebal and Gerizim; Succoth, a city east of the Jordan; Gilead, Israelite land east of the Jordan; Manasseh, Ephraim, Judah, the 'big three' of the 12 tribes. He declares his power over Israel's traditional enemies: the Moabites, east of the Dead Sea; Edomites, to the south-east; and Philistines, on the Mediterranean coast.

61 Prayer of a burdened king

Hebrew title, 'by David'. Far from home (2; maybe on campaign or fleeing from Absalom) and precarious on his throne (6-7), the king craves the safety and security only God can give (1-4).

▶ **Verse 3** The 'tower of strength' image comes from the city-wall defences.

62 A psalm of patient trust

Hebrew title, 'by David'. Humbly,

Psalm 58 is a cry for God's judgment on the wicked. When the psalmists call down punishment on their enemies, it is no more than was meted out to them by invading Assyrians and Babylonians. In this 7th-century BC carved relief from Syria, an Assyrian soldier carries the decapitated head of his enemy.

trustingly, the psalmist commits his cause to God. Human beings are bent on destruction (3-4), but what are they (9-10)? Power belongs to God, who wields it with love and justice (11-12).

'The land has produced its harvest. God, our God, has blessed us' (Psalm 67:6). A number of psalms were written to celebrate the Harvest Festival.

63 The thirsting heart
Hebrew title, 'by David when he was in the Judean desert' (as an outlaw hunted by King Saul). Having tasted the full joy and satisfaction of God's presence (2-8), who can bear to lose it (1)?

▶ **Verses 9-10** For dead bodies to be left unburied as prey to wild animals (10) is a deep disgrace. These verses are in sharp contrast to the rest of the psalm. See 'Self-justification, cursing and vengeance in Psalms'.

64 'Protect me, God'
Hebrew title, 'by David'. In verses 1-6 the psalmist pictures his trouble. In 7-9 he expresses his certainty that God will punish all who plot and scheme and slander. The punishment will fit the offence exactly (compare verse 7 with verses 3-4).

> **❝ In the shadow of your wings I sing for joy. ❞**
>
> 63:7

65 Hymn of thanksgiving
Hebrew title, 'by David'. This psalm may have been used at the harvest festival. All praise to God who hears and forgives faults (1-3), who blesses, satisfies and saves (4-5). Praise to God the Creator and Controller of the natural world (6-8). Praise to God who gives the harvest and makes the whole earth ring with joy (9-13).

66 Praise and worship
When prayer is answered and troubles are past (19, 14), the heart overflows with praise. Praise to God who has always come to his people's rescue, from the earliest days (verse 6 looks back to the escape from Egypt – the exodus) until now (8-12). Thanksgiving, and an offering of thanks (13-15), for God's love and care for every individual (16-20).

67 Thanksgiving for harvest
'The land has produced its harvest; God, our God, has blessed us' – and the watching world acknowledges not only God's provision for his people but his justice and leading, with gladness and joyful song.

68 Israel's song of triumph
Hebrew title, 'by David'. This psalm seems to be a battle-march cum processional hymn, maybe sung as the Ark was carried into Jerusalem (2 Samuel 6), or at the ceremony commemorating that event (see the allusions in verses 1, 7, 17-18, 24-25). The psalm paints a series of vivid pictures of God's victorious power.

Verses 1-6, a tribute to God; 7-10, God leads the nation through the desert; 11-14, the conquest of the land; 15-18, God chooses Mt Zion in Jerusalem to be his home; 19-23, salvation to Israel – death to the enemy; 24-27, the procession; 28-31, may God make a show of his strength to subdue the nations; 32-35, let everyone sing the power and majesty of Israel's God!

▶ **Sinai (8)** Where God gave the law and made covenant with Israel.

▶ **Verses 14-15, 22** 'Bashan' is the Golan Heights area, north-east of Lake Galilee. In the wide sense the region stretched as far as Mt Hermon, which may be the mountain referred to here. 'Zalmon' is probably another of the mountains in this region.

69 Prayer in suffering

Hebrew title, 'by David'. This psalm is often quoted in the New Testament (John 2:17; 15:25; Romans 15:3). Like Psalm 22 it is a cry for help from one in desperate straits and close to death. The psalmist's picture in verses 2, 14-15 could be taken for an actual description of the prophet Jeremiah's case (Jeremiah 38:6). Verses 34-36 seem to belong specifically to a time following the wholesale destruction of Judean cities, but before the fall of Jerusalem to the Babylonians.

The psalmist's trouble is through no fault of his own. His suffering is borne for God's sake (1-12). He prays that God, in his love, will rescue him (13-18) before he is totally overwhelmed. (The images could not be more powerful: he is up to his neck in the treacherous bog, out of his depth in the angry sea. Time is running out as he calls for help.) The guilt of his tormentors is clear (19-21): may they be punished for all they have done (22-28). May God set him free to praise; let the whole earth ring with praise at the restoration of God's people (29-36).

▶ **Verse 21** This is echoed in the Gospels, describing Jesus' crucifixion; see Matthew 27:34, etc.

▶ **Verse 28** The image of a book in which the names of all God's people are written occurs first in Exodus 32:32-33, is picked up here, in Psalm 87:6, Daniel 12:1, and carried into the New Testament (Philippians 4:3). Revelation uses it several times, culminating in the great judgment scene (20:12).

70 An urgent call for help

Hebrew title, 'by David'. These verses also appear at the end of Psalm 40 (13-17).

71 A prayer in old age

At the end of a long and troubled life (9, 20) there is still no let-up (4, 10-11). But trouble has schooled the psalmist in trust (6-7). Nothing can make him despair. As long as God is with him (9, 12, 18), the future is full of hope (14-16, 19-24).

72 Prayer for the king

Hebrew title, 'by/of Solomon' (Greek, 'for Solomon'). This last psalm in Book 2 (celebrating a coronation or its anniversary, like Psalm 2) is certainly a fitting one for Solomon's reign: Israel's golden age of peace, prosperity and power. But it also looks beyond it to the perfect ideal: an endless reign (5) over the entire world (8, 11); a rule of God-like justice and righteousness (7, 12-14); a time of unequalled fruitfulness (16).

▶ **The River (8)** Euphrates.

▶ **Tarshish, Sheba (10)** Meaning 'the remotest outposts of empire'. Sheba may be a region in Arabia. Tarshish is probably Tartessus in Spain.

▶ **Like Lebanon (16)** For a small country Lebanon produces an amazing abundance and variety of fruit and vegetables.

▶ **Verse 20** This editor's note belongs to an earlier collection of David's psalms.

Psalms 73-89
Book 3

According to the Hebrew titles (see introduction) 11 of the 17 psalms in this book (73-83) carry the name of Asaph (with Psalm 50). Psalms 84, 85, 87, 88 are attributed to the Sons of Korah (see on Book 2). Psalm 88 is also ascribed to Heman the Ezrahite. Psalm 86 carries David's name; 89 that of Ethan the Ezrahite. Heman led the first Temple choir, Asaph the second and Ethan the third (1 Chronicles 6:31-47).

73 This unjust world

This is one of the 'wisdom' psalms: see note on Psalm 1. The issue is God's justice: how is it that those who flout God's laws prosper, and trouble falls on those who least deserve it (3b-14)? It is enough to make the good turn cynical, envious and bitter (3, 21), tempting them to say things better left unsaid (15). Only as believers turn to God do they learn to see beyond appearances (16, 17). In reality, God's people have everything that matters (1, 23-26, 28). The wicked – for all their wealth – are destined for destruction (17-20, 27).

> *❝ My mind and my body may grow weak, but God is my strength; he is all I ever need. ❞*
>
> 73:26

74 A lament for God

The reason for this psalm is a sense of abandon. God has deserted his people (1-2). The Temple (whose existence told the people God was present with them) has been destroyed. The psalmist replays the appalling scene: the sounds of smashing axes, the ringing, triumphant shouts, the all-consuming fire (3-8). How long will the anti-God enemy remain master (9-11)? The psalmist thinks of the power of his God (12-17). He pleads with God to keep his promise to Israel (19-20) and sweep the blasphemous enemy away (18, 22-23).

▶ **Verses 13-15** The language comes from the ancient creation stories, as God brings order out of chaos. These verses can also be taken as referring to the deliverance from Egypt, pictured first as a dragon, then as Leviathan, the crocodile of the Nile.

75 God is Judge

Israel rejoices in God's sovereign justice. He alone has power to judge all people.
▶ **Verses 2-5** God is speaking.
▶ **Verses 4- 5** The Hebrew uses pictures to indicate arrogant power: 'lift up the horn', 'insolent neck'.
▶ **Cup (8)** This is used in the Bible as an image of God's wrath.

76 A song of deliverance

The victory may be David's or the psalm may refer to the (much later) Assyrians. It would be appropriate for a number of different occasions and may have been used at a festival time. Israel marvels at the terrible glory of the God who overthrows all the might of the enemy.
▶ **Salem, Zion (2)** Jerusalem.

77 The past and the present

Has God stopped loving us? He seems no longer to care for his people (5-9), and there is no comfort in present troubles (2-4). Wistfully, longingly, the psalmist reflects on better times, calling to mind God's past great deeds on behalf of his people (11-20).
▶ **Verses 2-6** The trouble which sets the psalmist thinking may be a personal, or a national, crisis.
▶ **Verses 16-20** The last verse clearly refers to the exodus from Egypt, but some of the

language recalls the creation. For the image of God as shepherd, see on 23:1.

78 Lessons from Israel's history

This psalm, taking lessons from the time of the exodus and the desert wanderings through to King David, was probably used at festival times. For a long time Ephraim (9) was the most powerful of the 12 tribes. Joshua was an Ephraimite, and the tribe had great prestige under the judges (Judges 8:2; 12). But with David's accession Judah took the lead. The psalmist thinks over the reasons for Ephraim's rejection, and finds them in Israel's history.

God gave Israel the law to remind them of him (5-8). But Ephraim disobeyed (9-11). They forgot what had happened in Egypt and the desert – the miracles (13-16, 23-29, 44-53), the rebellions and the punishments (17-22, 30-43). They forgot the pattern that repeated itself after the conquest of the land (54-66). And God chose Judah instead – a city of Judah (Jerusalem) as capital and a man of Judah (David) to be king (67-72).

▶ **Verse 9** This seems to be a reference to the defeat of Saul and Israel on Mt Gilboa (1 Samuel 31:1).
▶ **Zoan (12)** An ancient capital of Egypt.
▶ **Verses 13-16** See Exodus 14 and 17.
▶ **Verses 24-31** See Exodus 16; Numbers 11.
▶ **Verses 44-51** See Exodus 7 – 12.
▶ **Ham (51)** One of Noah's three sons, ancestor of the Egyptian people.
▶ **Shepherd (52)** See on Psalm 23:1.
▶ **Shiloh (60)** For a long time the principal sanctuary in Israel – presumably destroyed when the Ark was captured by the Philistines (1 Samuel 4).

79 Alas for Jerusalem

A lament for the destruction and bloodshed of the fall of Jerusalem (1-4; the city fell to Babylon in 587 BC: see 2 Kings 25:8ff.). The people call on God to forgive and help them (5, 8-10a, 11), and to destroy the pagan enemy (6-7, 10b, 12).
▶ **Verse 2** To leave bodies unburied was shameful.

80 'Come and save your people'

This is the people's desperate cry to God.

God and the universe

David Wilkinson

Although Christians disagree about the mechanism of creation, the Bible's view of the relationship between God and the universe is clear in principle.

One Creator

God is the sole Creator of the universe. Whatever the mechanism or timescale used, the Bible is emphatic that everything in the universe owes its existence to the sovereign will of God (see e.g. Genesis 1:1; John 1:3; Colossians 1:16).

Therefore, the Bible challenges 'scientism', that is the belief that science gives the only explanation of the origin of the universe. Science may describe how God did it, but it does not give an answer to why the universe exists.

It challenges any form of the worship of nature, whether in animism or in some strands of New Age, by emphasizing the distinction between God and creation.

It also challenges us in our concern for the environment. The world is not there to be used as we wish, but is the creation of God over which we have been given stewardship.

Order

God is the source of the order in the universe. God is the one who holds the universe in existence and his faithfulness underlies the faithfulness of what we call the laws of science (Colossians 1:17). This in fact provided a basis for modern science and today affirms science as a legitimate Christian activity. Science discloses the order of the universe or, as Kepler said, it is thinking God's thoughts after him.

Relationship

God puts relationship at the heart of the universe. In contrast to the Babylonian creation stories, where human beings are created simply as slaves to the gods, the Bible views the apex of the created order as the opportunity of men and women to be in relationship with the Creator God. They alone are created in the image of God, are given an intimacy of relationship and the responsibility of stewardship (Genesis 1:26-28; 2:4-25; Psalm 8:3-8).

The world is not to be worshipped as a divine organism or abused as an impersonal machine, it is to be used for good under responsibility granted by the Maker who wants to be in intimate relationship with human beings.

Worship

The God of the universe is meant to be worshipped. The Bible never discusses God's relationship with the universe in purely academic terms. As Psalm 8 and Psalm 19 make plain, when we consider God's universe we are inspired to worship – to marvel at the extravagance, care and beauty of the Creator.

Saving the universe

God achieves his saving work within the universe. The same God who is greater than the universe, who creates and sustains the universe every moment of its existence, also acts within it. Salvation is achieved by the eternal God acting at particular points in the space-time history of the universe, supremely in the life, death and resurrection of Jesus (Colossians 1:15-20).

Transforming the universe

God's purposes are not limited to this universe. Although the Bible insists that creation is good (Genesis 1:31), it also recognizes that because of humanity's fall the universe is not as it should be. This represents a central theme which finds fulfilment in the picture of God bringing about the new heaven and new earth of Revelation 21:1. The second coming of Christ means a transformation of the universe itself.

The time may be after the exile of the northern kingdom of Israel (2 Kings 17) but before the fall of Jerusalem (2 Kings 25). (The psalmist mentions Ephraim and Manasseh, two northern tribes, and the southern tribe of Benjamin which is sometimes linked with them, but not Judah.)

Israel is pictured as a great vine planted by God (8-16), stretching out to the mountains and cedars of Lebanon in the north (10), west to the Mediterranean and east to the River Euphrates (11).

▸ **Shepherd (1)** See on Psalm 23:1.

▸ **Walls (12)** I.e. the walls enclosing and protecting the vineyard.

81 God's message at harvest

This is a festival song. Verses 1-5: the people are summoned to celebrate the harvest festival (Tabernacles/Shelters). God reminds his people of all he has done for them (6-7) and all he longs to give (10, 14-16). Yet in obstinate disobedience they refuse him and choose trouble (8-9, 11-13).

▸ **Verse 3** The ram's-horn trumpet announced the start of the festival.

▸ **Unknown voice (5)** A puzzling statement, unless it refers back to the time before Moses' day (see Exodus 6:3).

▸ **Verse 6** A description of Israel's slave-labour in Egypt.

▸ **Meribah (7)** See Exodus 17:1-7.

82 The justice of God

This psalm can be taken as it stands: God takes the gods of the nations to task for their injustice and oppression (the Old Testament does not deny the existence of other supernatural beings, only their power: verse 6). This scene recalls Job 1:6. Or the psalm can be understood as referring to corruption and injustice in the law-courts: God calling the judges to account. In this case 'the gods' (1) is taken to mean those who exercise God's right of judgment over others. Verse 6a is quoted by Jesus: see John 10:34.

83 Under enemy attack

The nation is in grave danger from an alliance of all the old enemies (6-7), plus powerful Assyria (8). The people call on God's aid, remembering past deliverances (9-11): 'Do to them what you did...' Their victory will show that there is only one God and *all* the nations are subject to his sovereign rule (18).

▸ **Descendants of Lot (8)** Lot fathered Moab and Ammon (see Genesis 19:36-38).

▸ **Verses 9-12** See Judges 4 and 5. Oreb and Zeeb, Zebah and Zalmunna, were Midianite princes put to death by Gideon (Judges 7 and 8).

84 A pilgrim's song

The pilgrim comes to Jerusalem for one of the great annual festivals. His heart sings for joy at the prospect of worshipping God in his Temple. The happiest people in the world – it seems to him – are those who can be there always (4, 10).

▸ **Baca (6)** Possibly an actual valley the pilgrim passes on his way to Jerusalem. But 'the thirsty valley' gives the sense.

85 A prayer for the nation

The people praise God for his past forgiveness (1-3) and pray for his 'saving presence' now (4-7). All that the psalmist knows and has experienced of God's love and faithfulness fills him with optimism (8-13). What God has yet to give will far exceed his past goodness. All is well with the world in the lovely picture painted by verses 10 and 11.

86 Prayer in trouble

Hebrew title, 'by David'. Because the psalmist knows God – and all his love and goodness (5, 7, 13, 15) and power (8-10) – he can be confident in putting his case (1-4, 6-7, 14). Troubled though he is, he can trust God to help.

▸ **Poor (1)** A 'bankrupt', not financially, but before God.

87 City of God

This festival psalm looks forward to the glorious future God has planned for his holy city. Zion (Jerusalem's Temple hill) is to be the focus and capital of the nations. All are included as citizens (4-5), even old enemies like the Philistines and nations which have held Israel in bondage (Egypt and Babylonia). The Old Testament sees this triumph largely in material and

" How lovely is thy dwelling place, O Lord of hosts! My soul longs, yea, faints for the courts of the Lord; my heart and flesh sing for joy to the living God. Even the sparrow finds a home, and the swallow a nest for herself, where she may lay her young, at thy altars, O Lord of hosts, my king and my God. "

84:1-3

geographical terms, the New in spiritual (Revelation 21:1 – 22:5).

▸ **Rahab (4)** Here a poetic synonym for Egypt.

88 A cry of despair
This prayer (Hebrew title, 'by Heman the Ezrahite; see on Book 3 above and 1 Chronicles 6:33-38) is the darkest of all the psalms. Here is a man who feels life ebbing away (3-9a), and he has no hope beyond death (10-12). There is no one to turn to but God, who is crushing him with trouble (7-8, 13-18). He is in the grip of the blackest depression. Yet faith lives on – what else could account for his persistent cry to God?

▸ **Sheol, the Pit, Abaddon (3, 4, 11,** some versions) All refer to the shadow-land of the dead. See 'Old Testament views of the afterlife'.

89 A hymn and prayer
Hebrew title, 'by Ethan the Ezrahite': see on Book 3 above and 1 Kings 4:31. The psalmist sings the story of God's faithful love to Israel; his covenant and promise to David of an everlasting dynasty of kings (1-37). He rejoices in the power and justice of the Creator-God (5-14). But at verse 38 the tone changes dramatically. God is accused of breaking faith with his king (38-45). Where now are the promises of old? Where are the proofs of former love? How long... (46-51)?

Verse 52 is not related to what has gone before. It is the 'doxology' added to mark the end of this third book of psalms (see introduction).

▸ **Rahab (10)** A reference to God's taming of chaos at the creation, represented by this monster of the deep.

▸ **Tabor and Hermon (12)** Tabor, the rounded hump of mountain near Nazareth from which Deborah and Barak swept down to victory (Judges 4 – 5); Hermon, the 3,000m/9,000ft peak on the border with Lebanon.

▸ **Verse 19** This may refer to Nathan's message to David (2 Samuel 7:8-16).

Psalms 90-106
Book 4

Few of the psalms in this book have Hebrew titles making specific connections.

But like most of those in Books 2 and 3 they are in the main meant for public worship. All but three (90, 101, 103) are anonymous.

90 A short life and a hard one
The Hebrew title links this psalm with Moses, though few scholars accept him as author. It has an almost funereal tone and a sombre mood which the book of Ecclesiastes shares.

Compared with the eternal nature of God (1-4) we mortals are as transient as a blade of grass (5-6). Our span of life is short, yet even this must be worked out under God's judgment (7-10). The psalmist appeals to God's pity as he begs for the return of joy and gladness (13-17).

▸ **Verse 12** The truly wise are those who revere God and his teaching (see Proverbs 1:7).

91 Trust God and rest secure
In this psalm the voice of confident trust (1-13) and the voice of God (14-16) speak encouragement and reassurance. Nothing can touch those God protects – neither people nor beasts, by day or by night; not war, nor disease. (This is not to say life will be all roses, or verse 15 would have no meaning.)

▸ **Verses 11-12** Satan quotes these verses to tempt Jesus (Luke 4:9-12). But Christ had no need to test the truth of God's word, neither had he come into the world to take the soft option.

▸ **Verse 16** Long life was seen at the time as God's reward given to the good.

92 'A song for the sabbath'
This joyous thanksgiving in music and song for all that God has done (5-9) was used for public worship in the Temple. It goes on to celebrate God's goodness to each individual, and to all his people (10-15).

93 'The Lord reigns'
The Lord is King over all the earth – land and sea – eternal, almighty; his laws changeless and the Temple holy for ever with his presence.

94 God's justice
The psalmist calls on God as Judge to punish the wicked. How fully do these

> *It is good to give thanks to the Lord, to sing praises to thy name, O Most High; to declare thy steadfast love in the morning, and thy faithfulness by night, to the music of the lute and the harp, to the melody of the lyre.*
>
> 92:1-3

> *Whenever I am anxious and worried, you comfort me and make me glad.*
>
> 94:19

Self-justification, cursing and vengeance in Psalms

Christians reading the psalms are bound to come across two special problem areas:

■ the self-justification of the psalmists
■ and their tendency to call down and spell out the most terrible vengeance.

We cannot simply discard the offending passages. They appear alongside passages no one would question. The psalmists did not, of course, know Christ's teaching that we should love and forgive even our enemies. But they did possess the law, which instructed them not to bear grudges or take revenge (Leviticus 19:17-18). Even in the case of enemies, they were to return stray beasts and come to the rescue when a donkey fell under its load (Exodus 23:4-5). The law did not license retaliation, it set limits to it (an eye for an eye, *and no more*).

Self-justification

Two comments may help.

■ The psalmist is claiming comparative, not absolute righteousness (i.e. in comparison with other people, not measured by God's standards). Someone who is good may sin and still be a good person. There is all the difference in the world between those who endeavour to do right and those who deliberately set aside the accepted laws of God and society. King David is a good example: he was well aware of his shortcomings before God (see Psalms 51 and 19:12-13). Deep repentance features alongside self-justification in the psalms.

■ The psalmist is very often picturing himself as 'the indignant plaintiff' putting his case before God the Judge. And although we may dislike his self-righteous tone, from this point of view he is unquestionably 'in the right'.

Cursing and vengeance

Here a few points are worth bearing in mind.

■ The first concerns God's holiness. In emphasizing God's love we tend today to be unduly sentimental about rank evil. But the psalmists knew God as One 'whose eyes are too pure to look upon evil', who cannot countenance wrongdoing. And this is what motivates their call for vengeance on the wicked. God's own character – his good name – demands it.

■ The psalmists are realistic in recognizing that right cannot triumph without the actual overthrow of evil and punishment of wrong. We pray 'Thy kingdom come', but often shut our eyes to what this really means. The psalmists spell out what retribution means. We might ask ourselves if we are really superior to them in our revulsion, or if perhaps we are less in love with good, less opposed to evil than they were. Have we faced real persecution for our faith? Do we value life more than right?

If the psalmists *are* guilty of actually gloating over the fate of the wicked, if personal vindictiveness creeps in under the cloak of concern for God's good name, then they are clearly in the wrong. It is an awful warning: we can ourselves so easily be guilty of the same thing.

But in the psalms wrong thinking (if wrong thinking there is) never carries over into wrong action. There is no question of the psalmists taking the law into their own hands; no Inquisition. Vengeance is always seen as God's province, and his alone.

criminals deserve God's judgment for their oppression of God's people and deliberate flouting of his laws (1-6). How stupid they are to think they can hoodwink God (7-11). But, though the thought of vengeance is never far away (20-23), the psalmist's spirits lift as he thinks of God (12-19).

Psalms 95-100 are a group of psalms written in exultant praise of the God who reigns over all his creation.

95 Sing for joy
Let us praise and worship God our Maker (1-7a). Let us listen to him, for he expects us to obey (7b-11).
▶ **Verse 8** See Exodus 17:1-7.

96 'Sing a new song'
The song his people sing is a song of God's salvation, of his greatness and his glory – a song of universal joy when he comes to rule with justice.

97 'The Lord is King!'
The images are of awesome power, and shining, searching light. The spirit sings with gladness for all that God has done – for God, supreme, triumphant; the Saviour and delight of all who hate evil.

98 The Lord victorious
A song to God the Victor. He comes to rule the world with justice. Let the sea and its creatures, earth, rivers, hills – everyone and everything – go wild with joy.
▶ **Verse 6** Trumpets and horns are sounded for God's enthronement.

99 The Lord enthroned
God the King, the Holy One, is on his throne; God who forgives and disciplines his people, from the least to the greatest. Praise and worship him.

100 Give thanks and worship
'The Lord is God' – he made us – 'the Lord is good'. Let all the world sing and be glad. Psalm 100 is one of the best-known and most often sung of all the psalms.
▶ **Verse 3** See Deuteronomy 6:4. This is the faith of Israel.
▶ **His gates, his courts (4)** I.e. the Temple.

101 The king's manifesto
Hebrew title, 'by David'. The king pledges himself before God to root out evil from private and public life and to reward integrity.
▶ **House (2)** Household and court.
▶ **Verse 8** Most probably a reference to his daily administration of justice in Jerusalem.

102 On the rack
The psalmist is a young man (23), wearied by suffering. He pours out all his feelings to God. Verses 1-11 describe his suffering: ill in body, sick at heart, taunted by enemies, cast off by God. His life is slipping away (11), but God is not subject to time (24, 27). Verses 12-22 may be a hymn the psalmist has included within his prayer. God is Sovereign for ever (12). Surely he will pity his city and free his people (13-22). Verses 23-28 revert to the personal. Surely God will answer the psalmist's prayer .

103 The love and mercy of God
Hebrew title, 'by David'. A psalm of humble, heartfelt gratitude to God for all his goodness, but above all for his mercy and his unchanging, unchangeable love. What he has done for one (1-5), he does for all (6-18): so let everyone, everywhere praise him.
▶ **My soul (1, 22)** This is used to mean 'whole being', as 1b makes clear.

Psalm 104 celebrates the Creator, who set the oceans and mountains in place and created the habitats for all his creatures. The 'rock-badger that hides in the cliffs' (Psalm 104:18) is the shy rock hyrax.

❝ O come, let us worship and bow down, let us kneel before the Lord, our Maker! For he is our God, and we are the people of his pasture, and the sheep of his hand. ❞

95:6-7

104 Praise God the Creator

This wonderfully pictorial psalm to God the Creator and Sustainer of all has parallels in texts from Egypt and Mesopotamia. The psalmist conjures up the marvels, the grandeur, the detail of the earth and its creatures, sky and sea, sun and moon – the perfection and completeness of God's work in creation (1-24). All is summed up in verse 24. The whole of God's creation depends on his unfailing provision (27-30), for life itself. To contemplate his creation is to catch sight of God's glory and sing his praise (31-35).

▶ **Badgers/conies (18)** Probably the Syrian rock hyrax, a shy little animal about the size of a rabbit, which lives among the rocks.

▶ **Leviathan (26)** A name for the crocodile and also (as here) the monster of the sea.

105 'The Lord is our God'

This psalm focusses on God and his people. The call to praise (1-11) is followed by a history of how God chose Israel and gave them the land (12-45): the patriarchs (12-15); Joseph's story (16-22; Genesis 37 – 46); the deliverance from Egypt (23-38; Exodus 1 – 12); God's provision in the desert (39-42; Exodus 16 – 17) and the possession of Canaan (43-45). This is the covenant God (8) who protects and saves. 'Praise the Lord!'

106 God's rebel people

The psalm begins with praise of God's goodness and love (1-5). But from verse 6 it becomes a confession of the nation's sin, from Egypt to the psalmist's own day. Time and again God rescues his people and almost at once they break faith with him. Now they are in exile (47) as the psalmist cries out to God: 'Save us, O Lord.'

Verse 48 is the 'doxology' added to mark the end of the fourth book of Psalms.

▶ **Verse 7** The first instance of rebellion, see Exodus 14:10ff.

▶ **Craving (14)** For the good food of Egypt. God gave them meat but punished them with a plague (Numbers 11).

▶ **Verses 16-18** See Numbers 16.

▶ **A calf at Horeb (19)** Horeb = Mt Sinai. While Moses was on the mountain receiving God's instructions, the people made a golden bull-calf

> *Some sailed over the ocean in ships, earning their living on the seas.*
> *They saw what the Lord can do, his wonderful acts on the seas.*
>
> 107:23-24

idol to worship after Egyptian custom (Exodus 32).

▶ **Land of Ham (22)** Egypt; see Psalm 78.

▶ **Baal of Peor (28)** The people turned to idol worship and laid themselves open to God's judgment (Numbers 25).

▶ **Meribah (32)** See Numbers 20:2-13.

▶ **Did not destroy but intermarried (34-35)** Judges 1 and 2 summarize this part of Israel's history. From that time on (40-46) the story became a repetitive pattern of rebellion against God, followed by enemy occupation, followed by repentance, followed by freedom, followed by further rejection of God.

Psalms 107-150
Book 5

This final book contains several groups of psalms. The Hebrew titles designate 108-110 and 138-145 as 'according to/by David'. Psalms 113-118, 120-134 (with four more psalms of David) and 146-150 form further groups, as introduced in the text below.

107 Thanks to the God who saves

In this festival psalm, a single theme (we are beset by troubles of our own choosing or making, but God rescues us from them all) is spelt out in four word-pictures: the traveller, 4-9; the captive, 10-16; the sick man, 17-22; the sailor, 23-32.

Circumstances differ for each individual, but all share the same experience: as they cry out to God in their need, he hears and answers. All have equal cause to praise him. Verses 33-43 describe God's unchanging love in dealing with his people. 'The wise' will call to mind God's 'loving deeds' and ponder them.

108 A hymn to God

Hebrew title, 'by David'. The psalm is made up of extracts from Psalm 57:7-11 and Psalm 60:5-12.

▶ **Verses 7-13** See Psalm 60.

109 A cry for vengeance; a call for help

Hebrew title, 'by David'. People the psalmist has loved and treated well have returned evil for good. They have no excuse for the attack which has reduced him to a shadow (1-4, 22-25). In verses 6-19 his bitterness finds expression in a terrible curse, excused in the psalmist's mind as fitting punishment: 'he loved to curse – may he be cursed! He hated to give blessing – may no one bless him' (17). It is tit-for-tat, 'an eye for an eye', as the law allowed. See 'Self-justification, cursing and vengeance in Psalms'. For those who follow the way of Jesus, the longing for revenge must give way to love, even for enemies (Matthew 5:43-48).

110 'King and priest for ever'
Hebrew title, 'by David'. This royal psalm (for a coronation?) speaks in such prophetic terms (1-4) of the ideal, that it is seen as pointing to God's coming King: the Christ. Verse 1 is quoted more often than any other Old Testament saying by the New Testament writers, who identify this King – the Messiah – with Jesus. See, e.g., Matthew 22:44; Luke 20:42-43; Hebrews 10:12-13. See 'Christ in the psalms'.
▶ **Melchizedek (4)** The mysterious priest-king to whom Abraham gave a tenth of his possessions (see Genesis 14:17-20). Hebrews 5 – 7 applies this concept to Christ.

111 In praise of God
This psalm is identical in form with Psalm 112. Both consist of 22 phrases each beginning with a successive letter of the Hebrew alphabet.

The psalmist rejoices in God's greatness; his faithfulness and justice; his integrity and trustworthiness; his provision and his redemption. Central to the psalm is God's covenant, the promises by which he binds himself to his people and which he will never forget (5, 9). Respect for God is the true starting-point of all human wisdom (10).

112 To be happy, 'Trust and obey'
A 'wisdom' psalm (for others see note on Psalm 1). For the alphabet form, see on Psalm 111 above.

Happy are those who obey God and care for others. Their reward is sure. They can withstand life's knocks, secure and unafraid.

▶ **Verses 2-3** The psalmist describes the reward in material terms because in his day there was no clear concept of the afterlife. What he says is generally (but not invariably) true. God's people have their full share of trouble, but are given resources to meet it (7-8).

Psalms 113-118 are a group of psalms linked traditionally with the Jewish feasts of Harvest (Tabernacles/Shelters) and Passover. In Jewish homes Psalms 113 and 114 are sung before the Passover meal; Psalms 115–118 after it (see Matthew 26:30).

The Lord 'fills the hungry with good things,' rejoices the psalmist (Psalm 107:9).

113 Our incomparable God
God is above and beyond his creation, yet he is infinitely aware of human misery. His love reaches to 'the dust', to lift up the poor and needy. Feeling the heartache of the childless wife, God brings her joy – respect instead of disgrace.
▶ **Ash heap/dunghill (7)** The rubbish dump, the place for outcasts (see Job 2:8). Good News Bible, 'misery'.
▶ **Verse 9** Childlessness was viewed as a sign of God's disfavour – a punishment (1 Samuel 1:6; Luke 1:25).

114 Passover hymn
This is the festival which marks the escape

from Egypt at the exodus. The people remember how God freed them when they were slaves and made them his own people. Verse 3: he sent back the sea (Exodus 14) and the Jordan river (Joshua 3) to let them cross. He provided water in the desert (8; Exodus 17; Numbers 20).

> **"**Give thanks to the Lord, for he is good: his love is eternal.**"**
>
> 118:1

115 The one, true, living God
This psalm gives an indication of the way many psalms must have been sung – with a single voice leading and the congregation joining in the response (9-11, etc.). A powerful contrast is drawn between God – almighty, loving, faithful – and the lifeless, impotent idols of 'the nations' (1-8). From the response of trust (9-11) and confidence in God's blessing (12-15) the psalm comes full circle back to God and his people (16-18).

Psalm 119, like these modern Jews with their Torah scroll, celebrates the life-giving law of God. 'How sweet is the taste of your instructions – sweeter than honey!'

▶ **House of Aaron (12)** 'Priests of God'.

▶ **Verse 17** Praise is for the living; death stills all tongues.

116 'God saved my life'
Saved from death in answer to prayer, the psalmist comes to make his thank-offering in the Temple. The memory of that terrible time when the grave 'closed in' on him, with fear and danger all around, is vividly present as he pours out his heart in gratitude to God.

▶ **Cup of salvation (13)** A vivid compression: this is the cup of wine he will drink as part of the thank-offering he has promised to make. God gave him back his life; now he offers thanks.

117 Call to praise
The psalmist calls all nations to praise the Lord. In his love and constant care for Israel he shows his purpose for every nation (see Romans 15:11).

118 A victory hymn
The hymn was sung in procession by king, priests and people. As they approach the Temple, the king recalls the victory won with God's help (1-18). Verses 19-27: the procession, carrying branches, moves from the gateway to the altar.

▶ **Verse 22** The despised nation of Israel has become the great power. By Jesus' day Israel, in turn, had forfeited their privileged position (Matthew 21:42-43).

119 In praise of God's word
This is the longest psalm of all – and the most formal and elaborate in concept. There are 22 eight-verse sections. Each section begins with a successive letter of the Hebrew alphabet, and each verse within the section begins with the same letter.

Within this stylized pattern the psalmist makes a series of individual, though not isolated or disconnected, statements about the 'law' (God's teaching and instruction for life) and the individual – interspersed with frequent prayers. He uses ten different words to describe it: God's law, his testimonies (instruction), precepts, statutes, commandments, ordinances (decrees), word, ways (paths), promises and judgments (rulings). And one or other of these descriptions occurs in all but a very few verses. He seems to have taken the same delight in the discipline set by this complex poetic form, as he did in the study of the law itself. True freedom is found through constraint, in both cases.

In the psalm we see how eagerly and persistently he applies himself to the task of understanding the law. He learns it by heart. He longs for more. Nothing is allowed to deflect him from it. The will of God expressed in his teaching governs the psalmist's life-style and his conduct, gives him hope and peace, leads him into life and liberation. His confidence in it is unbounded. To see it broken genuinely distresses him. His glad obedience, love and regard for God's will (the heart of what will later be called God's 'kingdom') provide a constant challenge for every believer.

The psalm's focus on the truly happy life as one deep-rooted in reverence for God

connects it with other 'wisdom' psalms: see note on Psalm 1.

Psalms 120-134, each of which has the Hebrew title 'A song of ascents', are a collection of songs thought to have been sung by pilgrims on their way up the hill to the Temple in Jerusalem for a religious festival. In many of them the thought and imagery focusses on the holy city.

120 The whiplash of wagging tongues
Many psalms, like this one, are full of references to the sins of the tongue – lies, scandal, slander, hypocrisy. The follower of God may suffer as much from what people say as from what they do.

▶ **Verse 5** A poetic way of saying he is living among savages!

121 God, our Guardian
Those who trust God know where to turn

> **❝ *Your word is a lamp to my feet, a light on my path.* ❞**
> 119:105

Pilgrims sang as they went up to Jerusalem to celebrate the great festivals at God's Temple. Psalms 120-134 are some of these 'songs of ascents'.

Christ in the psalms

The primary meaning of the psalms is always to be sought first of all in their immediate, historical context. But this does not exhaust their significance.

No one can read Psalms without becoming aware that certain psalms and individual verses have a deeper, future significance beyond the simple meaning of the words. The Messiah is not mentioned by name, but his figure is foreshadowed, as later generations of Jews came to realize. And the New Testament writers are quick to apply these verses to Jesus as the prophesied Messiah.

■ Some psalms, particularly the 'royal psalms' (of which 2, 72, 110 are the most striking) picture an ideal divine king/priest/judge never fully realized in any actual king of Israel. Only the Messiah combines these roles in the endless, universal reign of peace and justice envisaged by the psalmists.

■ Other psalms depict human suffering in terms which seem far-fetched in relation to ordinary experience, but which proved an extraordinarily accurate description of the actual sufferings of Christ. Under God's inspiration, the psalmists chose words and pictures which were to take on a significance they can hardly have dreamed of. Psalm 22, the psalm Jesus quoted as he hung on the cross (verse 1; Matthew 27:46), is the most amazing example. Compare verse 16 with John 20:25; verse 18 with Mark 15:24. (See also Psalm 69:21 and Matthew 27:34, 48.)

■ There are also many other verses in the psalms which New Testament writers apply to Jesus as the Christ:
Psalm 2:7, 'You are my son': Acts 13:33
Psalm 8:6, 'everything under his feet': Hebrews 2:6-10
Psalm 16:10, 'not give me up to Sheol...': Acts 2:27; 13:35
Psalm 22:8, 'let him deliver him': Matthew 27:43
Psalm 40:7-8, 'I delight to do your will': Hebrews 10:7
Psalm 41:9, 'my close friend... has lifted his heel against me': John 13:18
Psalm 45:6, 'your throne endures for ever': Hebrews 1:8

Psalm 69:9, 'zeal for your house has consumed me': John 2:17
Psalm 110:4, 'a priest for ever after the order of Melchizedek': Hebrews 7:17
Psalm 118:22, 'the stone which the builders rejected...': Matthew 21:42
Psalm 118:26, 'blessed is he who comes in the name of the Lord': Matthew 21:9.

---

in trouble. With God to guard them they can come to no harm.
▶ **Hills/mountains (1)** They may signify danger, or the reference may be to the Temple hill (Mt Zion) and God's presence.
▶ **Moon (6)** Its rays were thought harmful.

122 Jerusalem, city of God
Hebrew title, 'by David'. The pilgrim prays for the peace of the city, the centre of worship and seat of government for the whole nation.

▶ **Verse 8** refers to his fellow-countrymen living in the city.

123 Plea for mercy
The appeal is to God, who cares for those the rich treat with contempt. Verse 1 is a single voice; then the group speaks.

124 God, the Rescuer
'If God had not been on our side...' The consequences are unthinkable. For without God's help the nation could not

have survived the onslaught of their enemies. The credit is God's alone. (How true this was in Israel's history, over and over again.)

125 Secure in God

Those who trust in God enjoy unshakeable security, solid as the Temple hill itself. The wicked will not always have the upper hand. Let them be warned!

126 Laughter and tears

This psalm is often associated with the return from exile and the hardships that followed. Verses 1-3 express the people's exuberant joy at God's blessing; verses 4-6 the need to experience this yet again (or a prayer for the restoration of the nation as a whole).

▶ **Verse 4** For most of the year the river-beds in the southern desert (Negev) are dry, but when the rain comes the water rushes down them in torrents.

127 Without God, nothing

Hebrew title, 'by Solomon'. This is a 'wisdom' psalm (see note on Psalm 1). Human effort is of no avail if God is not in it. The connection between verses 2 and 3 would seem to be that God's normal provision comes through the gift of sons, the key to the family's future financial security.

▶ **Verse 5** Disputes and business deals were settled at the city gate. Here the grown-up sons support their father in maintaining the family's interests.

128 'Happy, those who obey God'

This 'wisdom' psalm (see note on Psalm 1) sees obedience to God as the route to (material) blessing. The psalmist's picture describes everything the person of his own day asked of life. See also on Psalm 112:2-3. The New Testament changes the concept from material to spiritual reward.

▶ **Verse 3** The vine and the olive are symbols of peace and plenty – the fullness of God's blessing.

129 The enemies of Israel

In verse 1 a single voice (the cantor) invites the company to elaborate on Israel's ill-treatment by their enemies (2-4). Verses 5-8 are a call for God's judgment (see 'Self-justification, cursing and vengeance in Psalms').

▶ **Verse 3** The taskmasters' whips scored cuts and weals on their backs.

▶ **Verse 6** Grass and other seeds dropped or blown onto the flat clay roofs of houses would briefly root and begin to grow, but quickly be burned up in the heat of the sun.

▶ **Verse 8** The passer-by would normally call out a blessing by way of greeting (compare the English 'goodbye' = 'God be with you').

130 'Hear my cry, O Lord'

This is a 'repenting' psalm (see note on Psalm 6). Praying, hoping, waiting for God's help, the psalmist's attitude is one of eager trust. He implores Israel to trust as he does, for the Lord will save his people from the mess their sins have brought them to.

131 A psalm of simple trust

Hebrew title, 'by David'. The psalmist has put aside all arrogance and conceit. He is content to rest quietly in the Lord, like a child in its mother's arms. (This is one of the Bible's loveliest mother-images of God.)

132 God's promise to David

This 'royal' psalm reflects the bringing of the Ark to the city (see 2 Samuel 6:12-15) and Temple. The Ark contained the record of God's ancient covenant with his people, renewed in his promise of a lasting dynasty to David (11-12; see 2 Samuel 7:11-16). Zion (the Temple hill) is God's chosen home, his appointed centre for worship, in the city of Jerusalem, seat of kings. Verse 17 points to the future: there is a great king yet to come.

▶ **Ephrathah (6)** Bethlehem, David's birthplace.

▶ **Jaar/Jearim (6)** An abbreviation for Kiriath-jearim, where the Ark was kept for 20 years following its return by the Philistines.

133 The family-unity of God's people

Hebrew title, 'by David'. This is a 'wisdom' psalm (see note on Psalm 1). The theme is the family harmony of God's people, precious as holy oil or dewfall on bare hills.

▶ **Verse 2** The picture comes from the high

priests' consecration: the anointing with oil
(Exodus 29:7).
▶ **Verse 3** The dew is a symbol of blessing. Mt
Hermon's extra-heavy dew is seen as falling on
the parched hills further south, bringing fertility.

134 An evening prayer

The 'Song of ascents' group of psalms closes
with this little night-time prayer as the
pilgrims depart. Verses 1 and 2 would seem
to be their words to the priests and Levites,
who respond with the blessing in verse 3.

135 A hymn to God

This psalm echoes many earlier ones. God
is to be praised for choosing Israel (1-4), for
his greatness (5-7, 15-18) and his mighty
works (8-14). Let priests and people sing
his praise (19-21).
▶ **Sihon... Og (11)** See Numbers 21.

136 The 'Great Praise' (Hallel)

Hallel is the Hebrew word for praise (as in
Hallelujah: 'Praise the Lord!'), and this
psalm was sung at Passover. The
description of God's great works in creation
(4-9) and history (10-24) alternate with
the people's refrain to God's unchanging,
timeless love.
▶ **Verse 5** The idea of wisdom as God's partner
in creation is taken up in Proverbs 3:19-20;
8:22-31.
▶ **Verse 13** See Exodus 14.
▶ **Verses 19-20** See Numbers 21.

> ❝ *By the rivers
> of Babylon we sat
> down and wept
> as we remembered
> Zion.
> On the willows
> there we hung up
> our harps.* ❞
>
> 137:1-2

137 Lament of the exiles

'Sing us one of your songs,' the captors
demand. But how can the exiles sing to God
in the foreign land of Babylon? The old
joyful melodies bring a lump to the throat.
Memories of the terrible destruction of their
city and Temple overwhelm them. The
pain of it comes out in a cry for vengeance:
tit-for-tat, 'an eye for an eye'.
▶ **Edomites (7)** Descendants of Esau and
therefore closely related to Israel, but centuries-
old hostility divided the two. The Edomites
gloated at the news of Jerusalem's ruin
(Obadiah 8-14).
▶ **Verse 9** See 'Self-justification, cursing and
vengeance in Psalms'. The Israelites had no
doubt witnessed just such atrocities committed
in Jerusalem by the Babylonian army (8).

138 A song of thanks

Hebrew title, 'by David'. God has answered
prayer. Once again he has shown his
faithful love. He is great and high above,
yet he cares for the lowly (6). The psalmist
has a continuing story to tell of God's
loving and protective care for individuals.

139 The God who is there

Hebrew title, 'by David'. The psalm is
concerned with God's all-knowingness and
'everywhere-presentness', not in an
abstract, but in a highly personal way.
If God knows everything, he knows me
through and through, even my thoughts.
He has known me from before the day I was
born (1-6, 13-16). If God is present
everywhere, no matter where I go he is
there. He is always with me (7-12, 18b).
I will align myself with him in the fight
against evil. Let him search out and deal
with all that is wrong in me (23-24).
▶ **Verses 19-22** This angry outburst takes us
by surprise. But if the psalmist is in the right, his
logic demands that the wrong be punished.

140 'Save me, Lord!'

Hebrew title, 'by David'. The psalmist is in
real trouble from the plotting of violent
people, and from their venomous tongues.
He prays that God will guard him (1-8) and
punish them (9-11), in the confident
knowledge that God is for the right and
implacably opposed to evil (12-13).
▶ **Verses 9-11** See 'Self-justification, cursing
and vengeance in Psalms'.

141 'Help me now'

Hebrew title, by David'. This evening
prayer acknowledges the pull of evil as a
force to be reckoned with. The psalmist
asks God to keep him from the very things
he condemns in others, in thought and
word and action.

142 Prayer to God our refuge

The Hebrew title links this psalm with the
time when David was on the run and in
hiding from Saul in a cave (1 Samuel
23:19ff.). He cries to the One who knows
all about him: the Lord, his refuge.

143 Prayer for God's help

Hebrew title, 'by David'. This is the last of the seven 'repenting' psalms (see note on Psalm 6). The psalmist has reached the end of the line: no more reserve or resources (3-4). But in a desperate situation one refuge remains: God himself (5-12). 'O Lord... teach me... deliver me... lead me... bring me out of trouble'.

144 Song for the God of victory

Hebrew title, 'by David'. The king thanks God for victories won (2, 10). What are we 'mere mortals' that the great God should spare us so much as a passing thought (1-4)? Yet time and again God comes to the rescue (5-11). The song closes with a prayer for peace and prosperity for the future generation (12-15; this may originally have been a separate psalm).

Psalms 145-150 are a group of psalms in praise of God, probably intended for public worship. They are used by Jews today in daily prayer. Psalms 146–150 all begin and end with 'Praise the Lord!': in Hebrew, *Hallelujah*.

145 Praise the Lord!

Hebrew title, 'by David'. This is an alphabet psalm (see on Psalm 9). One letter, missing from the Hebrew text, has been taken into the English versions from the Greek as 13b.

The 'I' declares the personal nature of this psalm, pouring out praise to God for his greatness and power (1-7, 10-13a), and for his character: loving, forgiving, good and faithful, just and kind. God provides for and satisfies the needs of every living creature (8-9, 13b-21). So – 'let all flesh bless his holy name for ever and ever'.

146 Praise God, the helper

The focus of this personal psalm is on God as the hope and help of his people, utterly dependable, caring for all in need. Over and over again the Bible shows God as one who feeds the hungry, cares for the oppressed, sets free the prisoners, protects the alien and helps the defenceless. Compare verses 7-9 with Isaiah 61 and Luke 4:16-19.

147 'Praise God, his people'

The Greek version splits this psalm into two, ending the first at verse 11. Here is God the Almighty: the universe (4), the seasons (8), the nations (14), the elements (16-18), are his to command. His power sets him utterly above and beyond humankind. Yet his heart goes out to individuals; all who are hurt and unhappy (2-3). He takes pleasure in those who love

The psalmists drew many images from the natural world of God's creation to express, not just beauty, but suffering too.

and respect him (11). And he gives his people his word to live by (19). Praise the Lord!

148 Praise God, all creation!

This psalm calls on everything there is to praise its Creator: the angels in heaven; sun, moon and stars; the earth and its creatures; the elements; the wild and the tame; kings and all people everywhere. And who should praise him like his own (14)?

▶ **Waters above the skies (4)** I.e. the rain.
▶ **Horn (14)** Meaning God has given them strength and power.

149 Praise God, in triumph!

This is a public psalm, for the assembled people. They rejoice in military triumph, with drums and dancing, at the victory God has given. Their enemies are vanquished,

subject, and punished (7-9).

▶ **A new song (1)** See Psalm 33:3.
▶ **Double-edged swords (6)** In the New Testament the double-edged sword is a metaphor for the word of God (Hebrews 4:12; Revelation 1:16).
▶ **Vengeance (6b-9)** Victory for the downtrodden necessarily entails defeat for the forces of oppression. See also 'Self-justification., cursing and vengeance in Psalms'.

150 Praise God – with full orchestra!

This choral symphony of praise is the grand climax and finale to the whole collection of psalms. Every instrument in the Temple orchestra (3-5), everything with life and breath in the whole creation, is called to join in a mighty crashing paean of praise to God.

Proverbs

Summary

A textbook of wise sayings to school the young in the right way to live. True wisdom is based upon reverence for God.

Chapters 1 – 9
All about wisdom

Chapters 10 – 31:9
Collections of proverbs and sayings

Chapters 31:10-31
Poem on the good wife

Proverbs is a book of wise sayings: not simply an anthology, but an oriental textbook, schooling young people in wise and right living by the repetition of wise thoughts. It is wisdom distilled into short, sharp phrases, dramatic contrasts, and unforgettable scenes from life. It sets out what is right and what is wrong (not just a slick formula for success), because 'wisdom' in Proverbs is based on reverence for God and obedience to his laws.

The 'fear of the Lord' is the essence of all true human wisdom. This is the starting-point. Proverbs applies the principles of God's teaching to the whole of life, to relationships, home, work, justice, decisions, attitudes, reactions – everything we do and say, and even think. God has taught what is best for us. Experience proves it.

The book divides into eight main sections: a general introduction on wisdom (chapters 1 – 9); six collections of sayings (10:1 – 31:9); and an 'alphabet' (acrostic) poem on the good wife (31:10-31).

It is now fairly generally agreed that in content the proverbs belong to the days of Israel's first kings, although editing continued for some centuries. King Hezekiah of Judah, who organized some of the editorial work (25:1), reigned 250 years after Solomon. The book as we have it was finalized, at the latest, by the time of Joshua (or Jesus) ben Sira(ch) who composed Ecclesiasticus (a wisdom book included amongst the deuterocanonical writings) in about 180 BC.

The precise part Solomon played in all this is not known. His name appears in the title, and he is the author/compiler of the two longest collections (10:1 – 22:16 and chapters 25 – 29). Solomon was a man of outstanding wisdom (see 1 Kings 3; 4:29-34) and his court became an international centre for the exchange of learning. 1 Kings 4:32-34 tells us that

Solomon 'spoke three thousand proverbs – and his songs were a thousand and five. He spoke of plants... he spoke also of animals, and of birds, and of reptiles, and of fish. People of all nations came to hear the wisdom of Solomon, sent by all the kings of the earth, who had heard of his wisdom.'

Through marriage with pharaoh's daughter, Solomon had close links with Egypt, and perhaps knew the *Wisdom of Amenemope* which is so closely paralleled in Proverbs 22:17 – 23:14, as well as other collections of wise sayings. He and his wise men culled the wisdom of the East, but they incorporated nothing that was not in line with God's standards. See 'Poetry and Wisdom.'

From chapter 10 on, Proverbs is best digested a few sayings at a time. It may also be a help to study the proverbs under themes. This way we can weigh one saying against another, and get an idea of the general teaching on a particular topic. It is important to bear in mind that proverbs are by nature *generalizations*. They state what is *generally, not invariably*, true. The writers do not deny that there are exceptions. But exceptions are not within the scope of proverbial sayings. For instance, Proverbs states that those who live by God's standards will prosper in the world. This is generally the truth. But it is not an unqualified 'promise'. Job, and above all the life of Jesus, show the other side of the coin.

Proverbs is paralleled in contemporary cultures by other collections of wise sayings. This papyrus from Thebes, dating from about 1000 BC, contains part of the Egyptian *Wisdom of Amenemope*.

1 – 9
True wisdom

1:1-6 To the reader

> **The fear of the Lord is the beginning of wisdom, the foundation of knowledge.**
>
> 1:7

Proverbs opens with a statement of its purpose (2-6) and basis (7). It is aimed especially at the young and uninstructed – but no one is too old or too wise to learn. Proverbs and sayings encapsulate wisdom (not cleverness), and wisdom is the path to life.

▶ **Verse 1** Best taken as the title to the whole book, not just the first section. Solomon's own proverbs begin at 10:1.

1:7-19 Advice to the young

The teacher addresses his pupils as a wise father would his son. The young man has a vital choice to make: between the right course and the wrong one; between wisdom and folly; between going God's way through life and going his own. The teacher describes the two alternatives, and shows where each leads. In verses 10-19 he tries to arm his pupil against temptation. The theme of every lesson is the same: 'Get wisdom.' Repetition is still a good teaching method!

▶ **Fear of the Lord (7)** This is an important recurring phrase in Proverbs. It describes a wholesome awe and respect ('reverence') for God which expresses itself in obedience, reliance on God and deliberate avoidance of evil (3:7).

▶ **Verse 12** The pit of death, 'Sheol' – the place of the dead.

'Go to the ant, you sluggard. Consider her ways and be wise.' Many lessons are drawn from nature in Proverbs.

1:20-33 Wisdom calls out

> **Trust in the Lord with all your heart, and do not rely on your own insight. In all your ways acknowledge him, and he will make straight your paths.**
>
> 3:5-6

See 'Wisdom in Proverbs and Job.' Everywhere wisdom is crying aloud (20-21). She calls to everyone. Listen! What she says of those who refuse to learn is the simple truth (22-32). There is no greater folly than choosing not to 'fear the Lord' (29).

▶ **Wisdom (20)** The teacher pictures wisdom as a great lady. She competes for attention with another woman – Folly – who is no lady at all (see chapter 9).

2 'If you listen...'

Wisdom is to be found through knowing God. It is hard-won, but worth every effort (1-10). It is a safeguard against wrongdoing and bad company, both male (11-15) and female (16-19). It sets our feet on the right path (20).

3 – 4 The teacher's advice

Take wise teaching to heart; stay humble; trust God (3:1-12). Wisdom offers the things that money can't buy: peace, happiness, security (3:13-26). Wisdom was at work in creation and continues to be worked out in the dos and don'ts of everyday life and relationships (3:27-35).

The teacher passes on his own father's instruction (4:1ff.). Wisdom is the thing to go for: it leads to life. Steer clear of wrongdoing and of bad company.

▶ **3:19,20** See also 8:22-31.

5 Be faithful

Be wise when it comes to women. Don't fall for a cheap line, especially from a married woman. She is quite literally a *femme fatale*. Find pleasure in your own wife: love her and be happy. (This subject is taken up again in 7:6-27.)

6 – 7:5 Beware...

This section gives some timely warnings. Beware of accepting unlimited liability for anyone (6:1-5). Beware of idleness (6:6-11). Beware the fate of a 'bad lot' (6:12-19). Keep God's commands. They will save you from the schemes of seductive women.

▶ **Six things... seven (16)** See 30:15.

▶ **Flirting eyes (25)** Some things, it seems, don't change! And long before Solomon's time women wore eye make-up to improve on nature.

▶ **Verse 27** New Jerusalem Bible translates 'can a man carry fire inside his shirt... '

7:6-27 The temptress

The teacher describes a young man falling for a married woman's shameless seduction. To judge by the number of warnings in Proverbs this was common enough. Even Solomon, for all his wisdom, was as weak as any at this point – and in the end his foreign wives led him to worship other gods (1 Kings 11:1-13).

▶ **7:17** The same spices are mentioned in Psalm 45:8 (a love song) and Song of Solomon 4:14 (the bridegroom describing his bride).

Wisdom in Proverbs and Job
Katharine Dell

In the book of **Proverbs** we encounter wisdom in two ways.

■ First, through the many proverbs and instructions of the book, we learn that it is a quality that we should strive to acquire. The experience of many generations has been passed down in the pages of Proverbs and distilled into pithy sayings that represent truth about human nature and relationships.

■ Second, we find Wisdom personified as a woman. We find her in the streets calling out to youths to follow her paths of goodness and righteousness and we also find her described as an essential part of God's creative and ordering role from the beginning, created by God and yet alongside him at creation, participating in the event.

So wisdom is not just something that we can learn, it is on offer to us by God through the figure of Wisdom, who is the embodiment of right and truth and good living and part of the essential order of the created universe.

The youth is offered two paths, the one to folly and destruction represented by the prostitute or loose woman who entices and seduces unsuspecting young men into her perfumed bed, an image that contains overtones of ancient pagan fertility rites. The other is to wisdom and life and is represented by the figure of Wisdom who stands for truth and knowledge and understanding.

In Proverbs 8, Wisdom is pictured as a woman, calling people to follow her. She is God's creation, instructing human beings in his ways – unlike that other woman, Folly.

To know this wisdom is to know something of the nature of the Godhead, to know folly is only to run after false deities.

In **Job** we find a hymn to wisdom, praising the hiddenness of true wisdom – it is hidden deeper than the deepest mine and higher than the highest mountain. Ultimate wisdom is unattainable and known only to God, as shown in his speeches in the book. Yet to strive to acquire it is better than doing nothing at all, and the hymn ends with the plea to fear God, for he is the beginning and end of all wisdom.

Job himself strives for understanding in the midst of his suffering and ultimately realizes that whilst he may not ever understand the reasons for his suffering he was right to question and has a more profound relationship with God as result.

Wisdom personified

The female symbolism in the portrayal of personified wisdom in Proverbs is striking. Some have suggested that what we have here is vestiges of a goddess-myth, a consort for Yahweh, an image which fell from popularity at the rise of monotheism. Others have suggested that this is simply a way of affirming a feminine aspect to the divinity.

God's qualities, although described in predominantly male terms in the Bible, also include a feminine creative and ordering role. Wisdom is this ordering and creating force and yet her call to human beings is also an ethical one. To get wisdom is to be part of the order and design of the universe, to reach an understanding that pervades the depths of meaning that only God can truly fathom and also to know the kind of behaviour that God requires of us all. It is interesting to note that the language of wisdom is taken up in the New Testament in the understanding of Jesus as the divine 'Word', in the beginning with God and yet also sent on earth to dwell among us and to offer truth to all who have ears to hear.

8 In praise of Wisdom

See 'Wisdom in Proverbs and Job.' In marked contrast to the sly woman of chapter 7, slipping out at dusk to catch her man, Wisdom makes an open appeal to all as they go about their daily business (as in 1:20-21). Mere prose will not serve to describe her. It calls for poetry to sing her praise. Wisdom here is more than a simple personification: she embodies an aspect of God's own nature. The value of her instruction is beyond any earthly fortune (6-21). 'The Lord created me first of all,' she says, 'I was made... before the world began.' The lyrical description in verses 22-31 is poetic, not literal/historical.

9 Wisdom and Folly

All the teacher's previous lessons are crystallized in this vivid picture of Wisdom (1-6) and Folly (13-18). Each invites us – empty-headed, wayward – to a feast. Wisdom sets life before us. On Folly's menu there is only death.

> *Being cheerful keeps you healthy. It is slow death to be gloomy all the time. Corrupt judges accept secret bribes, and then justice is not done.*
>
> 17:22-23

The sayings in Proverbs are to do with the ordinary affairs of daily living and human relationships. Hard work, whether at the plough or spinning wool, is always commended.

10 – 22:16 Solomon's proverbs

The young man has been faced with the choice and urged to choose wisdom. Now the instruction begins; practical instruction that ranges over every aspect of life.

In this first collection, the sayings get their punch from contrast. The second line, or half, of each saying is the antithesis of the first. Each proverb is complete in itself, though some are linked by words or themes into series. They reveal sound psychology and accurate observation of life. They demonstrate the outworking of wisdom and folly in the practical business of living.

For the teaching in 10:1 – 31:9, see 'Important themes in Proverbs 10 – 31'.

▶ **15:11** Even the realms of the dead (Sheol and Abaddon) are open to God.

▶ **17:8** The man is confident his bribe will work, but the practice is wrong (see verse 23).

▶ **18:18** In Old Testament times it was common practice to discover God's will by casting lots.

▶ **20:10** Leviticus 19:35 condemns the giving of short weight, and the prophets also denounce all such cheating in business.

22:17 – 24:34 Thirty wise sayings

It seems likely that in this section Proverbs makes creative use of material from abroad (see 'Poetry and Wisdom'), in addition to material from Israel's own 'wise men'. The Egyptian *Teaching of Amenemope* is in 30 sections like these (Good News Bible numbers them) and the first ten are very alike.

The sayings in this section are more connected than in the previous one. They begin with 'things to avoid' (22:22-29). Then come the hazards of social climbing (23:1-8); father and son – discipline and advice (23:12-28); a portrait of a drunkard (23:29-35); teaching on wisdom and folly (24:1-14), and right living (24:15-22).

After the 30 sayings comes a 'postscript' of additional sayings (24:23-34) focussing on justice and hard work, with a sketch of the lazy person in verses 30-34.

▶ **Thirty sayings (22:20)** The Hebrew has

several possible meanings, but it seems to imply a book of sayings which consists of (roughly) 30 paragraphs or chapters.

▶ **Ancient landmark (22:28)** 'Old boundary stone.'
▶ **Narrow well (23:27)** I.e. one it would be difficult to get out of; 'deadly trap'.

25 – 29
More of Solomon's proverbs

Under King Hezekiah (25:1) Israel returned to the old neglected patterns of worship. He repaired the Temple and resumed the sacrifices, restoring the Temple music along the lines laid down by David (2 Chronicles 29). What is more likely than that he should then have turned his attention to the classic wisdom of Solomon? At any rate, it was his people who published this collection of Solomon's proverbs.

There is more grouping here than in 10:1 – 22:16, and the proverbs rely more

Important themes in Proverbs 10 – 31

Wisdom and folly – the wise man and the fool

This is the main strand of the whole book, the subject of the first nine chapters. The sayings point the contrast between wisdom – living by God's standards, keeping to what is right, and folly – people wilfully going their own way. Wisdom leads to life and all that is good – folly is a mere half-life that ends in death. The verses listed below detail the wise course of action in many different circumstances. They outline the character of 'the wise', in contrast to the life and character of the 'fool' who shuts his mind to God and reason.

10:8, 13-14, 23; 12:1, 15-16, 23; 13:14-16, 20; 14:1, 3, 7-8, 15-18, 24, 33; 15:5, 7, 14, 20-21; 16:16, 21-23; 17:10, 12, 16, 24, 28; 18:2, 6-7, 15; 19:25, 29; 21:22; 22:3; 23:9; 24:3-7, 13-14; 26:1, 3-12; 27:12, 22; 28:26; 29:8-9, 11.

The righteous and the wicked

How people respond to life's alternatives determines which of these two groups they join. The wise, on Proverbs' definition of wisdom, will be righteous. The gullible fool is always teetering on the edge of wrongdoing. It is more than likely he will end up among the wicked. The proverbs below describe the righteous life – the life of integrity – and the blessing it brings to the individual and the community. God loves and protects the righteous. The wicked are subject to God's wrath. If they flourish, it is only for a short time. They are heading straight for death and destruction.

10:3, 6-7, 11, 20-21, 24-25, 27-32; 11:3-11, 17-21, 23, 28, 30-31; 12:2-3, 5-7, 10, 12-13, 21, 26, 28; 13:5-6, 9, 21-22, 25; 14:9, 11, 14,

> **"** Just as God created the natural world by words ('And God said, "Let there be…"') so we create the social world by words. A kind word heals. A cruel one injures – and psychological wounds cut deeper than physical ones. Judaism rejects the idea that 'words will never harm me'. The Book of Proverbs says, 'Death and life are in the power of the tongue.' **"**
>
> Jonathan Sacks

19, 32; 15:6, 8-9, 26, 28-29; 16:8, 12-13; 17:13, 15; 18:5; 20:7; 21:3, 7-8, 10, 12, 18, 26-27; 24:15-16; 25:26; 28:1, 12, 28; 29:2, 6-7, 16, 27.

Words and the tongue

Proverbs places tremendous stress on the power of words and speech, for good and for ill. What we say, and how we react to what others say – advice, or rebuke, or gossip, or tempting suggestions – betrays what we are (see Matthew 12:34-37). The tongue is an incalculable force: it takes a wise person to master it (see also James 3). The proverbs below are full of sound advice and timely warning.

In Old Testament times the city gate was the place where business affairs and trade were conducted. These stallholders at the Damascus Gate in Jerusalem follow in an ancient tradition.

▶▶

> **6 6** *Singing to a person who is depressed is like taking off his clothes on a cold day...*
> *If your enemies are hungry, feed them; if they are thirsty give them a drink.* **9 9**
>
> 25:20-21

on comparison than contrast for effect ('*like* apples of gold... *is* a word spoken in season'). The proverbs draw their pictures from nature and everyday life.

▶ **25:6-7** Jesus uses the same theme in Luke 14:7-10, but he broadens it to cover a whole attitude to life.

▶ **26:4-5** These two verses are probably meant to be complementary, not contradictory. It is usually pointless to argue with a fool, but there are times when false reason must be shown up for what it is.

▶ **26:8** What could be more nonsensical than fixing a stone to a sling or catapult so that it can't come out?

30
Sayings of Agur

Both Agur and Lemuel (31:1) are non-Israelites. 'Massa' was an Arab tribe descended from Abraham's son Ishmael. The East was famous for its wisdom, right

▶▶ 10:18-21, 31-32; 11:9, 11-14; 12:6, 14, 17-19, 22; 13:2-3; 14:5, 25; 15:1-2, 4, 23; 16:1, 23-24, 27-28; 17:4, 7, 27; 18:4, 6, 13, 20-21; 19:5, 9; 20:19; 21:6, 23; 22:10; 25:11, 15, 23, 27; 26:22-28; 27:2; 28:23; 29:20.

The family

Fads and fashions change but the basic structure of family life, its joys and sorrows, remains constant. There are still unfaithful husbands, and wives who bicker and nag their husbands. There are still children from good homes who go off the rails. Proverbs' wise advice on the things that make for a happy and stable home-life, and the things that undermine it, is as sound today as ever.

■ **Parents and children**
   10:1; 13:1, 24; 17:21, 25; 19:13, 18, 27; 20:11; 22:6, 15; 23:13-16, 19-28; 28:7, 24; 29:15, 17; 30:11, 17.

■ **Wives**
   12:4; 18:22; 19:13-14; 21:9, 19; 25:24; 31:10-31. (The main advice to **husbands** comes in the earlier section, e.g. chapter 5.)

Laziness and hard work

Proverbs contains a good many sketches of the lazy, too idle to begin a job, too slack to see it through, yawning their way through life until it is too late, and poverty and hunger claim them. There is

SOME SECONDARY THEMES

■ **Rich and poor – poverty and wealth**
   10:15; 11:4, 24-25; 13:7-8, 11; 14:20-21, 31; 18:11, 23; 19:4, 7, 17; 21:13, 17; 22:1, 2, 7, 16, 22-23; 23:4-5; 28:3, 6, 11, 20, 22; 30:8-9.

■ **The world of business and affairs; plans and decisions**
   11:1, 15, 26; 15:22; 16:3, 9-11, 33; 17:8, 18, 23; 18:16; 19:21; 20:10, 14, 16, 18, 23; 21:14; 22:26-27; 27:23-27; 28:8.

■ **The proud and the humble**
   11:2; 12:9; 15:25; 16:18-19; 18:12; 21:4, 24; 22:4; 29:23.

■ **Friends**
   17:9, 17; 18:24; 19:4, 6; 27:6, 10.

■ **Neighbours**
   25:8-10, 17-18; 26:18-19; 27:10, 14; 29:5.

■ **Masters and servants**
   11:29; 14:35; 17:2; 29:19-21; 30:10, 22-23.

■ **Kings and rulers**
   16:13-15; 19:12; 20:2; 23:1-3; 24:21; 25:1-7; 28:15-16; 29:12, 14; 31:4-5.

■ **Hopes and fears; joys and sorrows**
   12:25; 13:12; 14:10, 13; 15:13, 30; 17:22; 18:14; 25:20; 27:9.

■ **Anger**
   14:17, 29; 15:18; 16:14, 32; 19:11-12, 19; 20:2; 22:24-25; 29:22.

■ **The 'fear of the Lord'**
   Although the phrase does not occur all that often, this is no secondary theme; as the basis of all wisdom, it is absolutely fundamental to the whole book: 10:27; 14:26-27; 15:16, 33; 16:6; 19:23; 22:4; 23:17; 24:21. See also in the earlier section, e.g. 1:7; 3:7.

nothing to commend slackness, but 'in all toil there is profit'.
   10:4, 5, 26; 12:11, 24, 27; 13:4; 14:23; 15:19; 18:9; 19:15, 24; 20:4, 13; 21:25; 22:13; 24:30-34; 26:13-16; 28:19.

Proverbs commends honesty in business: fair weights and measures.

down to Christ's own day (see Matthew 2:1). Agur is a man whose close observation of life and nature have taught him humility.

▶ **Three... four (15)** A device indicating that the list is not exhaustive. See also 18, 21, 29 and 6:16.

▶ **Verse 19** He finds four sources of wonder: how the eagle can soar; how the snake can move without legs; how the ship can ride the waves; and the mysterious attraction which draws a man to a woman.

31:1-9
Advice to King Lemuel

See under chapter 30 above. Lemuel outlines his mother's teaching. We seem to catch a tone of mild reproach in verse 2.

▶ **Son of my vows (2)** 'The answer to my prayers,' Good News Bible.

31:10-31
The good wife

Proverbs paints a remarkable picture of the power of woman, for good and for ill. It closes with this lovely acrostic poem (each of the 22 verses begins with a new letter of the Hebrew alphabet – *aleph*, verse 10, to *tau*, verse 31) about the best of wives. She is seen from the man's perspective and reflects a time when the woman's identity was defined largely by her place/role in the family.

The good wife is responsible, capable, hardworking and completely trusted. Who can find such a one? Her worth (to her husband) is beyond price (verse 10). Not only do her husband, family and household depend on her provision and foresight for their physical needs; they owe her their well-being at a much deeper level (11, 12, 26). Her influence extends beyond this immediate circle to society at large (20).

And she finds ample scope for all her gifts in the wider spheres of buying and selling and business transactions (16, 18, 24). Where does her secret lie? In that same 'fear of the Lord' in which all true wisdom has its roots.

Is this portrait simply an epilogue extolling the virtues of the ideal wife, or is there more to it? Placed as it is, at the end of Proverbs, it is surely more likely to have been intended as a summary of what the whole book is about: depicting the person – man or woman – who is truly wise. Just as Wisdom has been represented as a woman, so here it seems fair to see the wife as a representative figure too. In her noble character, she stands for the kind of person we are all meant to copy.

Weaving material to make clothes for her household and to trade at the market was one of the duties at which the 'capable wife' of Proverbs 31 excelled.

Ecclesiastes

Summary

The Philosopher takes a hard look at life: without God it is totally meaningless,

Chapters 1 – 2
Is there a purpose to life?

Chapters 3 – 11
Life, wisdom, folly

Chapter 12
'Remember your creator'

> ❝ *Life in this world does not fundamentally change, and we do not need a date for Ecclesiastes in order to receive its message. It is part of the genius of the Preacher's thought that it stands on its own feet at any time and in any place.* ❞
>
> Michael Eaton

Ecclesiastes is a piece of 'wisdom literature' (see 'Poetry and Wisdom'), a popular form of writing in Near-Eastern countries in Old Testament times. It is not a familiar form today, and can seem disjointed to us, with its apparently disconnected thoughts and sayings and observations on life. But the theme of Ecclesiastes is singularly 'modern': it is shared by any number of 20th-century novels and plays.

The book simply observes life around and draws the logical conclusions. This is life 'under the sun', life as we see it. The author imposes no preconceptions. Life as we live it, without God, is futile, meaningless, purposeless, empty. It is a bleak picture. Nature and history go round in circles: there is nothing new. Add up the profit and loss of human life and you are better off dead. Life is unfair; work is pointless; pleasure fails to satisfy; good living and wise thinking are rendered futile by death.

'Be realistic', says the book. 'If life without God is the whole story, see it for what it is. Don't pretend. Don't bury your head in the sand. This is the truth about life.'

But this is not – like so many modern writings – just cynicism and despair. God never intended us to leave him out of the picture. God can inject joy into every aspect of living: from food and work to home and marriage (2:24-26; 3:13; 5:18-20; 9:7-10). He intended us to find ultimate satisfaction not in life but in him. The wise person dies like the fool, it is true, but wisdom is still good and right (2:13). And God will judge the just and the wicked (3:17). Enjoy life, not as an Epicurean ('eat, drink, for tomorrow we die'), but as one faithful to God, because you depend on him for life and for enjoyment (3:13; 5:19). An empty, futile existence is not inevitable: remember God while you are still young (12:1); respect him and keep his commandments (12:13).

'Ecclesiastes' is the Greek translation of 'Qoheleth' (1:1, 2, 12; 7:27; 12:8, 9, 10 – the 'Teacher', 'Preacher', 'Speaker', 'Philosopher'), a word which seems to indicate the author's official title rather than his name. We are meant to identify this figure with Solomon, who was 'son of David, king in Jerusalem' (1:1, 12) and the embodiment of wisdom. Although it is doubtful that Solomon was in fact the author, who better qualified to pronounce on life, having tasted it to the full – power, fame, riches, women, all that anyone could wish for – and tested out what life was like both under God and without him? The author-editor is best seen as 'an admirer of

'What profit can we show for all our toil under the sun? A generation goes, a generation comes...' This is the voice of the world-weary Teacher, as he takes up his pen.

Solomon, writing up the lessons of Solomon's life in the tradition of wisdom for which Solomon was famous' (Michael Eaton).

1 – 3
All is futile – without God

1 – 2:23 Life is pointless…
The author states his theme: the emptiness and futility of life. People come and go. The cycles of nature and history are constantly repeating themselves. There is nothing new. Even the search for wisdom – our highest goal – is futile, for 'the more one knows, the more one has to suffer'.

What are we to do with our days (2:3)? If we live for pleasure – all that wealth and status can afford – life is still empty (10-11). Wisdom is far better than folly, but in the end death makes fools of us all. The things we work for must be left behind for others to enjoy. This is the futility of life 'under the sun'.

▶ **Verses 1, 12** See introduction.

▶ **Under the sun (3, 9, 14,** most versions) A recurring phrase in Ecclesiastes. It indicates 'the world, seen simply from a human standpoint'.

2:24 – 3:22 …pointless, without God
Here the tone begins to change. The new factor is the mention of God. There is no joy or satisfaction in life, it is true – apart from God (2:24-26).

And now we have a new perspective: 'under heaven' (3:1). And we see that there is a proper time for everything in life (3:1-8). God has made it so. We understand time, but we cannot comprehend the whole of God's work (11). So we learn to stand in awe of God. There *is* injustice and corruption in life (16ff.), but God has set a time for just judgment, although we must all die.

4:1 – 11:8
Life 'under the sun'

Chapter 4
There is so much oppression in life that we would be better dead; better still never to

have been born (1-3). We wear ourselves out with work, trying to outdo one another, never stopping to ask what it's all for (4-8).

From this point in the book the thoughts and observations are more frequently interspersed with advice and teaching, in the proverbial manner adopted by the 'wise'. Wisdom may look foolish in the world's eyes (1:17, 18; 2:14-17) but 'Qoheleth' clearly still believes in it and intends us to live by it (see 12:9-11).

▶ **A three-strand cord (12)** Three are even better than two. A rope made of three strands is hard to break.

'What do people gain from the efforts they make?' asks the Teacher. This relief carving from Assyria pictures a fisherman at work.

Chapter 5
Sound advice is given about promises made to God (1-7) and attitudes to money (10-12). Another of life's evils (13-17) is the business crash. The way to live is to enjoy work, and to enjoy prosperity if it comes, for these are God's gifts. Enjoyment is the antidote to gloom about the passing of the years (20).

▶ **Verses 8-9** The meaning is not clear. Revised English Bible translates verse 9, 'The best thing for a country is a king whose own lands are well tilled.'

Chapter 6
What value is long life, without the chance to enjoy all we have worked for (1-6)? Better be still-born or miscarried (3). The person ruled by appetite and desire will never be satisfied (7-9).

Chapter 7
It is wise to take account of death as well as life (2). A serious outlook on life is best (1-6). Know how to enjoy good times and learn from bad ones (14).

'Qoheleth' observes another of life's anomalies (15): there are good people who die young, and wicked people who grow old in their wickedness.

Everything is brought to the test of wisdom (23), but life will not add up. God is not to blame: there is nothing wrong with how God made us. Our troubles are all of our own making (29).

> **❝** *For everything there is a season, and a time for every matter under heaven:*
> *a time to be born, and a time to die;…*
> *a time to kill, and a time to heal;*
> *a time to break down, and a time to build up;*
> *a time to weep, and a time to laugh.* **❞**
>
> 3:1-4

▶ **Verses 16-17** sound like the cynical tones of worldly wisdom. God would never say we were overdoing real goodness, or advise a little wickedness!

▶ **Verse 18** The advice is to avoid extremes.

▶ **Verse 28** He has found only one man in a thousand worth the name, and not one woman!

Chapter 8

Faith cannot resolve the problem of evil: good people getting what the bad deserve; wicked people admired and having a cushy time. The people of God can only assert what they know is true, though all the evidence is against it (12). Enjoyment is the best thing in life, says 'Qoheleth' (15). Yet he applies his own energy to wisdom, even though God has concealed from us the answer to life's mysteries (16-17).

> **❝** *Of making many books there is no end, and much study is a weariness of the flesh.* **❞**
>
> 12:12

9:1-10 Death awaits all

One fate – death – comes to all people, good and bad alike (with this one difference, that the good are in God's hands, 1). There is no knowing how long anyone has (11-12). So work hard and enjoy life while it lasts, for death cuts us off from all the world has to offer (7-10).

9:11 – 11:8 Wisdom and folly

Wisdom may not pay, yet it is still worth more than power (9:13-18).

A collection of proverbs on wisdom and folly, wise sayings and practical advice, follows from 10:1 – 11:8.

'Remember your Creator while you are still young,' is the Philosopher-Teacher's wise advice.

11:9 – 12:8
'Remember your creator'

Practical advice leads straight in to the author's conclusions. If life is long, rejoice in it. Rejoice in the light before the dark night of death begins. Let the young rejoice in their youth, always mindful of God who calls us all to account. Don't wait till old age. Don't wait till life has become futile and empty and there is nothing ahead but death. Fear God – hold him in awe – and obey him.

> **❝** *Cast your bread upon the waters, for you will find it after many days.* **❞**
>
> 11:1

Verse 8 brings the Philosopher full circle. He ends as he began (1:2): all is useless, utterly futile.

▶ **12:2-6** Verse 2 depicts life drawing to an end, the darkness of death closing in. Verses 3-5 are a series of pictures of old age, when strength fails, teeth are few, sight grows dim. Moffatt translates verse 5: 'When old age fears a height, and even a walk has its terrors, when his hair is almond white, and he drags his limbs along, as the spirit flags and fades'. The 'silver chain...' (6): metaphors of death.

12:9-14
The end of the matter

The use of the third person seems to indicate that this postscript has been added by someone other than the author, unless he is adopting this convention by way of conclusion.

The Philosopher has spoken the truth about life, shown it for what it is without God. His constructive advice is scattered through the book. Now he pinpoints the one thing on which our life turns: our attitude to God. There is a judgment, when good and evil will be sorted out. We must live in the light of it. The 'fear of the Lord' (as Proverbs makes so plain) is where true wisdom – and real life – begins.

Song of Solomon

Summary

A series of love-poems, unique in the Bible in its celebration of human sexuality and the passionate love of a man and woman.

This 'song of songs' is a series of lyric poems on the theme of love between man and woman. The setting is pastoral: the poems are full of images from the countryside. The time, appropriately, is spring. They are full of the passion and delight of human love.

The poems defy complete analysis and, partly for this reason, have been subject to all kinds of interpretation.

- Jews and Christians down the ages have used them as allegories or 'types' – of God's love for Israel; of Christ's love for his bride the church. The poems themselves give no evidence of having originally been written for that purpose.
- Some see the poems as a drama with two or three characters (bride and royal bridegroom or Solomon, the girl, and her shepherd lover). There is, however, no evidence apart from the Song that this kind of literature existed in Israel.
- Others regard the poems as a series of songs sung during the week-long wedding-feast, as in Syria today, with the bride and groom crowned king and queen.

The natural approach is simply to take the Song as it stands. It explores the feelings, hopes, fears, passion of a man and woman. It can be seen as a filling out of that first-ever love-poem, the words of Adam to Eve, in Genesis 2:23. It is a celebration of male and female sexuality, of the erotic delight each lover takes in the body of the other. There is nothing illicit or lustful about it. 'The theme of sexual enjoyment and consummation runs through the whole book, and the theme of commitment is central to that whole relationship' (G. Lloyd Carr). It is therefore wholly in line with the general biblical view, from Genesis on, although it stands alone amongst the Bible books in concentrating on this theme.

Love poetry

The Song is clearly love poetry. It is a genre known the world over, and the ancient Near East had its own particular conventions which we find in the Song.

- Characteristically, the lovers use the intimate *tu/du* form of address retained in French and German but largely lost in modern English (the old 'thou').
- There are the familiar 'seek-and-find' and 'hazards-to-overcome' motifs.
- Physical beauty is celebrated with elaborate imagery, often from nature.
- The senses – sight, sound, smell, touch – are given full play.

Unlike other ancient Near Eastern love poetry, however, there is no connection here, not even verbal, with cult or religion: the Song uses none of the words of Israel's religion and worship. Nor does jealousy or infidelity feature in these poems, as it does in so many others.

Structure

The book can be 'divided up' in a number of ways. Most modern translations provide headings to show who is speaking. G. Lloyd Carr offers the following analysis:

1:2 – 2:7	Anticipation
2:8 – 3:5	Found, and lost – and found
3:6 – 5:1	Consummation
5:2 – 8:4	Lost – and found
8:5-14	Affirmation

The outline-guide which follows takes the book simply chapter by chapter.

Chapter 1

The bride, a country girl, speaks first, partly to her lover, partly to the women of Jerusalem (probably the court or harem), who serve as a kind of chorus in the Song (1-6). The bride and bridegroom then converse (7-17).

▶ Solomon's Song of Songs (1) The title may

Like an apple tree among the trees of the forest, so is my beloved among young men. To sit in his shadow is my delight, and his fruit is sweet to my taste.

2:3

imply that Solomon wrote it, or that it was written for, or about, him. He was as renowned in love (1 Kings 11:1-3) as he was in wisdom. But he can hardly be taken as the ideal of single-minded devotion! Nor does the country-shepherd image suit him, unless the language is pure literary-pastoral convention. Hence the appeal of the three-character interpretation of the Song, in which Solomon attempts to win the heart of the girl, who remains true to her shepherd lover. See also 8:11-12.

▶ **Kedar (5)** The Kedarites wandered the Sinai desert. Their tents were made of black goat hair.

▶ **Pharaoh's chariots (9)** Solomon ran a thriving import-export trade in the horses and chariots for which Egypt was famous (1 Kings 10:26-29).

▶ **Verses 12-13** 'Nard': spikenard, a perfumed ointment. Those women who could afford such luxuries wore sachets of fragrant myrrh, suspended from the neck, beneath their dresses.

▶ **Verse 14** A red cosmetic dye was made from henna. 'Engedi': a beautiful freshwater 'oasis' close to the barren shores of the Dead Sea.

Chapter 2

Compliment is exchanged for compliment (2 and 3ff.). The bride's thoughts dwell on her lover with passionate longing (3-6), thrilling at his voice (or the memory of his words; 8, 9). The bridegroom calls to her in the idyllic beauty of springtime (10ff.). It is all in a country setting. Only the aside of verse 7 contains any hint of the court.

▶ **Sharon (1)** The fertile coastal plain of northern Israel.

▶ **Verse 7** See also 3:5; 8:4. The significance of this refrain seems to be that love must be allowed to grow naturally, in its own time. It is not to be forced or given an artificial stimulus.

▶ **The foxes (15)** Jackals. If they damage the blossom there will be no fruit.

Chapter 3

The search-and-find motif is introduced in a dream sequence as the bride describes the distress of separation, and the joy of reunion (1-4). Verses 6-11 describe the grand procession of King Solomon.

▶ **Wood from Lebanon (9)** The famous cedar, imported for building the Temple and palaces.

> **❝** *You have stolen my heart, my sister,*
> *you have stolen it, my bride,*
> *with just one of your eyes, one jewel of your necklace.*
> *How beautiful are your breasts, my sister and bride!*
> *Your love is more fragrant than wine,*
> *your perfumes sweeter than any spices.* **❞**
>
> 4:9-10

Chapter 4

The bridegroom glories in the beauty of his bride. The imagery is oriental. Her eyes are shy and soft as doves; her hair shining silky-black like the coats of a flock of goats caught in the sun as they ripple over the hillside (1). Her teeth are white and even; her cheeks full and rosy; her neck like a tower hung with trophies; her breasts like deer (2-5). It is the nature of sexual love the world over to consider every detail of the body with delight. In the bridegroom's eyes the beauty of the woman he loves is flawless. She has stolen his heart, fired his senses, and he longs to take her for his own (9-12).

▶ **Senir, Hermon (8)** The 3,000m/9,000ft mountain on the Israel-Lebanon border.

▶ **Sister (9)** A term of endearment, not a literal statement.

▶ **Garden (12)** This image is taken up and repeated through the Song (4:15; 5:1; 6:2, 11; 8:13). It is used as a euphemism for the female sexual organs. Here the secret/locked garden indicates virginity.

▶ **Verse 16** The bride invites the bridegroom to enjoy his 'garden' – herself.

Chapter 5

The bride dreams again (2-8). This time the bridegroom comes and, although all is prepared (5), she is too slow in letting him in. Once again the enjoyment of love is frustrated. Eager anticipation turns to a deep sense of loss (6). In reply to the women (9) she describes her lover, begging them – if they find him – to tell him she is faint with love for him. He is, from head to foot, as 'totally desirable' to her as she to him (10-16).

▶ **Myrrh... (5)** She is perfumed as a bride on her wedding night.

▶ **Verse 7** Did they mistake her for a prostitute, so to mistreat her?

Chapter 6

The women question (1); the bride replies (2-3) – and the bridegroom again describes the beauty of his one and only love. There is no queen or royal concubine to match her.

▶ **Tirzah (4)** A beautiful city, the early capital of the northern kingdom of Israel.

❝ *Winter is past! The rains are over and gone; the flowers appear in the countryside; the season of birdsong is come, the turtle-dove's cooing is heard in our land.* **❞**

2:11-12

top:
The Song of Solomon is full of lovely images drawn from nature – as in this scene from Galilee.

above:
'Your cheeks, behind your veil, are halves of pomegranates.' The lover details the beauty of his sweetheart.

top:
The 'promised bride' in the Song pictures her lover as a gazelle, 'leaping on the mountains, bounding over the hills'.

above:
The Song of Solomon, appropriately for a series of love poems, is set in the springtime; the time when the cooing of doves is heard everywhere.

A happy bride, dressed in the traditional finery of the Yemenite Jews.

▶ **Verse 12** Revised English Bible translates, 'I did not recognize myself: she made me a prince chosen from myriads of my people.'

▶ **Shulam (13)** If 'Shulam' is a place, its location is not known. There are no grounds for linking the girl here with Abishag the Shunammite (1 Kings 1:3-4), as some have done.

Chapter 7

Again the bridegroom marvels at the beauty of his bride, ever more intimate in his description (1-7). He cannot tear his eyes away. Every detail is perfection. His mind and senses leap to the moment of possession (8-9).

The bride loves him utterly, without reserve (10-13), longing to give herself to him – in all the glory of the springtime (12).

▶ **Carmel (5)** The mountain of Elijah's contest with the prophets of Baal, which today makes an impressive backcloth to the port of Haifa.

▶ **Mandrakes (13)** A plant considered from very early days to have aphrodisiac powers.

Chapter 8

The bride longs to take the initiative and display her affection openly. In her mind her lover's arms are already about her in tender and passionate consummation of their love (verse 3; as 2:6).

At verse 5 the scene changes. The two are together at last. Love has found its fulfilment. *Nothing* can destroy true love. (Many people see 8:7 as the real ending of the Song.)

'The final invitation is to a continued celebration of the love and communion which the happy couple shares.' The inclusion of the Song of Solomon in the Bible means that 'the joys of physical union and mutual enjoyment are stamped with God's approval' (G. Lloyd Carr).

▶ **Seal (6)** A ring or cylinder seal engraved/imprinted with the owner's name was often hung from a cord around the neck. The point is ownership/possession. The girl wants her lover openly to own that she is his.

▶ **Verses 8-9** The girl's brothers, who are responsible for her, speak of their sister at the point of growing up. How will they preserve her honour? In verse 10 she speaks for herself as a woman ready for marriage.

▶ **Verses 11-12** The 'vineyard' is probably a poetic allusion to Solomon's harem and all its attendants. Let him keep it! The bride's love and person is her own to give: it is not for sale. These verses weigh against those who identify Solomon himself as the lover.

> **❝ Love is as strong as death, passion cruel as the grave; it blazes up like a blazing fire, fiercer than any flame. Many waters cannot quench love, no flood can sweep it away. ❞**
>
> 8:6-7

The Prophets

ISAIAH TO MALACHI

Mike Butterworth / Alec Motyer

Throughout the Bible God communicates with the people he has created. That communication always has a purpose and calls for action. Sometimes God speaks directly to a particular person with a promise or a warning. Sometimes the hearer is told to take a message to another person or other people. It is clear that God can speak directly to any person, but he often uses his own delivery service.

God's messengers

God's messengers are described in various ways (e.g. 'man of God', 1 Kings 13:1; 'seer', 1 Samuel 9:9, 11, 18-19; 2 Samuel 24:11) and the terminology certainly varied in different periods of history. But the most common word in the Bible to describe a messenger of God is 'prophet/

prophetess'. The word can describe the plain fact – someone really has a message from God – or what appears to be so – someone purports to give a message from God.

In early times the word 'prophet' probably referred mostly to people who exhibited rather wild behaviour, which was attributed to the Spirit of God (see, especially, Numbers 11:26-30; 1 Samuel 10:9-11; 19:20-24). As time went on, the people of Israel came to understand that outward displays of inexplicable behaviour

The prophets declared God's message to people throughout the land.

were of minimal importance. What mattered was whether a prophet had (or had not), in Jeremiah's words, 'stood in the council of the Lord' (23:18-22). The ideal prophet was one who spoke with God 'face to face', as Moses did (Numbers 12:6-8; compare Deuteronomy 18:15-22).

A true prophet

From the Old Testament stories about prophets and leaders, the hallmarks of a true prophet were:

> *" The message is what makes a prophet a prophet. "*

A call from God. We have accounts of how some of the great prophets were called:

Moses (Exodus 3:1– 4:17)
Samuel (1 Samuel 3)
Isaiah (Isaiah 6)
Amos (Amos 7:10-15)
Hosea (Hosea 1:2ff – not a typical case!)
Jeremiah (1:4-10)
Ezekiel (1 – 3).

This must have been of decisive importance for them, though we cannot say that all prophets received such a definite call. Some seem to have belonged to prophetic schools, as with the band/company of prophets, in 1 Samuel 10:10 and 19:20, or the sons of the prophets mentioned in connection with Elijah and Elisha (e.g. 2 Kings 2).

Some other important leaders also received direct calls from God:

- Abraham in Genesis 12:1-3 (a call that was later confirmed and expanded in13:14ff.; 15:1-7; 17:1ff., etc.)
- Joshua (see especially Joshua 1)
- Gideon (Judges 6:11ff.)
- Samson (via his parents in Judges 13).

A message from God. It is not clear whether the early prophets majored on this aspect: no message is mentioned in the cases of Moses, the 70 elders who prophesied (Numbers 11), or the band that met Saul. For the rest, however, it is clear that the message is what makes a prophet a prophet. The means of receiving it may vary (voice, vision, dream) and the method of passing it on may vary (proclamation at the sanctuary or Temple, speaking face to face with an individual, or acting out the message, as in Isaiah 20 and Jeremiah 19

True prophets trod a lonely path. Their task was daunting, and their message often unpopular.

and 27). The important factor is that the message is from God.

Prayer. Prophets are expected not only to speak to people on behalf of God, but to speak to God on behalf of the people. See especially Exodus 32:11-14, 30-32, where Moses offers to be punished instead of the Israelites who have made a golden calf (compare Genesis 20:7, where Abraham has the prayer ministry of a prophet, and Jeremiah 15:1).

False prophets

Not all those who claimed to be prophets were truly God's messengers. How were God's people to tell the difference?

In Deuteronomy 13 the false prophet is one who calls people away after 'other gods' and speaks 'rebellion against the Lord your God, who brought you out of the land of Egypt... to make you leave the way in which the Lord your God commanded you to walk'. When this prophet's words are tested against what is already recognized as the truth of or about God, they fail.

A second test is the test of time: if a prophet speaks for God, what he says

comes true. The false prophet's message fails this test too.

Prophets in the history of Israel

Israel was founded on God's promise to Abraham. They enjoyed a special (covenant) relationship with him, and that entailed weighty responsibilities. Israel was expected to be faithful to the Lord God only and to fashion their lives according to the instructions – the law – that God himself had given.

Right from the beginning they proved to be rather poor at keeping their side of the covenant and incapable of hearing what God had to say. God therefore sent a series of prophets to remind them of what he had done for them and of their proper response; to warn them of the consequences of disobeying God, the almighty and only true God, and to exhort them to return to him.

Prophets also had a more positive role:

- to encourage the people in times of suffering (deserved or undeserved)
- to offer them forgiveness when they had sinned
- and to renew the covenant promises made with their ancestors.

Most significantly, the prophets point forward to the time when God will intervene decisively in the life of the nation by sending his own special representative.

The Old Testament refers to this person as 'king', 'son of David' (2 Samuel 7:12ff.; Isaiah 9:7; 11:1ff.; Zechariah 9:9; compare Micah 5:2), 'servant of the Lord' (Isaiah 42:1-4; 49:1-6; 50:4-11; 52:13 – 53:12), 'righteous Branch' (Jeremiah 23:5-6; Zechariah 3:8; 6:12) , 'son of man' (Daniel 7:13f.: an ordinary title in itself, simply meaning human being, but very significant in the way it is used here, and in the Gospels), and so on.

The New Testament calls this person the 'Messiah', the 'Christ', the 'anointed one', and Christians from the time of Jesus until now have been enriched by their study of the pictures that the prophets present to us.

The message of the prophets

Some of the most important themes of the prophets of Israel may be summarized as follows:

The most important prophets

9th century BC	**Elijah and Elisha**	No book left; narratives in 1 and 2 Kings. Elijah prevented Israel from completely forsaking God: 1 Kings 18.
8th century	**Jonah**	The prophet belongs to this time, but many scholars think the book was written much later.
	Amos	Sent with a message of judgment from Judah to the northern kingdom of Israel.
	Hosea	Northern kingdom. God's love is emphasized in the midst of judgment.
	Isaiah	Chapters 1 – 39 refer mostly to about 750 onwards.
		Chapters 40 – 55 refer to the time of exile and return (from about 538 on).
		Chapters 56 – 66 are difficult to place in a particular period.
		All sections contain long-term prophecies about the Messiah.
	Micah	Both judgment and salvation. Predicts the birth of a ruler from of old, in Bethlehem.
7th century	**Nahum**	Rejoices over the destruction of Nineveh in 612 BC.
	Habakkuk	Struggles with the problem of evil – and how God deals with it!
	Zephaniah	Judgment with a closing promise.
7th to 6th centuries	**Jeremiah**	Began in Josiah's reign. When his calls to repentance failed, he warned the people they must submit to Babylon. Finally he gave salvation prophecies: God would make a new covenant.
Soon after 587 BC	**Obadiah**	Prophecy against Edom for their treatment of Judah when Jerusalem fell.
6th century (exile)	**Ezekiel**	Called in Babylon itself. Judgment prophecies at first. Salvation only after the fall of Jerusalem in 587 BC.
6th century (post-exile)	**Haggai**	Haggai and Zechariah encouraged the people to rebuild the Temple after the exile (520 BC onwards).
6th (to 5th?) century	**Zechariah**	Chapters 1 – 8 deal with the same time as Haggai. Chapters 9 – 14 belong to a later time. Both parts look forward to a time when all nations may participate in God's salvation.
5th to 4th century(?)	**Malachi**	Calls the people of Judah to full commitment. Looks forward to the future appearance of 'Elijah'.
Uncertain date	**Joel**	Links a plague of locusts with the 'Day of the Lord'.

God is the Ruler of all history. The prophets took this so seriously that they were prepared to risk depicting the mighty empires of their day as 'tools' in the hand of God (Isaiah 10:5-15).

This constitutes a problem for Habakkuk: how could the holy God use unholy, corrupt instruments? The answer the Bible offers is to re-affirm God's sovereign control of the world, a control so intricately exercised that people who do not own him act responsibly according to the dictates and pressures of their own natures. But God the just and holy Ruler nonetheless presides, governs and guides over all (see 2 Kings 19:25, 28; Ezekiel 38:3-4, 10-11, 16; 39:2-3).

The need to get right with God. For both the community and the individual, to get right with God is what matters most (see Isaiah 30:15). God is always at work to bring his people back to himself (Amos 4:6-11). The prophet summons men and women to personal readiness to meet with God (Amos 4:12).

Religion and right action. There is no place for religion without right living, both on the personal level and in terms of social justice (Jeremiah 7:1-15). To be right with God, men and women must live in obedience to God's standards and commands, and this produces a sound society. If people are alienated from God, their relationships with one another will go awry (compare Amos 2:7-8 with 9-12).

Judgment and hope. According to the prophets' analysis of the current situation, God's judgment is inevitable. Yet hope shafts through the darkest clouds (Isaiah 6:13; 28:5; 29:5; 31:5; Amos 9:11ff.).

This blend of darkness and light, judgment and hope springs directly from the character of God himself: God, the just and holy judge – God, the ever-loving, ever-merciful.

The messianic kingdom. God has a bright future state in store for his people. It is seen as the setting up of the perfect covenant relationship (Isaiah 54:10; Jeremiah 31:31-34; Ezekiel 37:26-27). And it is centred upon that great coming Person already described above.

opposite: Like watchmen who guarded olive-groves and vineyards, the prophets were 'look-outs', seeing what went on around them and speaking God's message to that situation.

The prophets in their setting

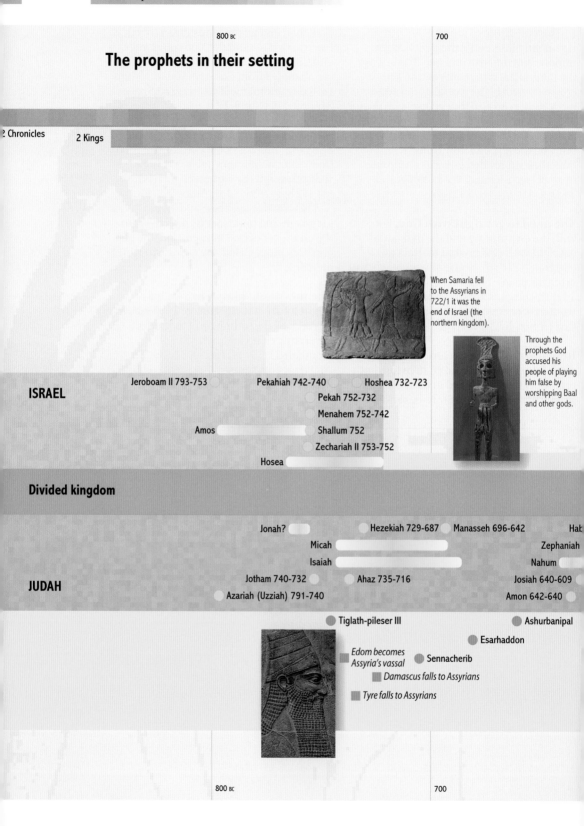

800 BC   700

2 Chronicles   2 Kings

When Samaria fell to the Assyrians in 722/1 it was the end of Israel (the northern kingdom).

Through the prophets God accused his people of playing him false by worshipping Baal and other gods.

ISRAEL

Jeroboam II 793-753   Pekahiah 742-740   Hoshea 732-723
Pekah 752-732
Menahem 752-742
Amos   Shallum 752
Zechariah II 753-752
Hosea

Divided kingdom

Jonah?   Hezekiah 729-687   Manasseh 696-642   Hab
Micah   Zephaniah
Isaiah   Nahum
Jotham 740-732   Ahaz 735-716   Josiah 640-609
JUDAH   Azariah (Uzziah) 791-740   Amon 642-640

Tiglath-pileser III   Ashurbanipal
Esarhaddon
Edom becomes Assyria's vassal   Sennacherib
Damascus falls to Assyrians
Tyre falls to Assyrians

800 BC   700

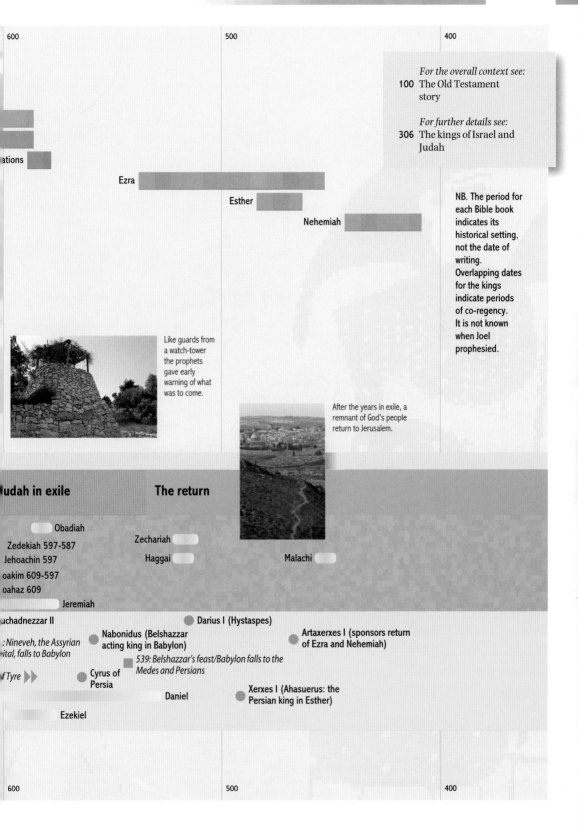

600 500 400

For the overall context see:
100 The Old Testament story

For further details see:
306 The kings of Israel and Judah

ations

Ezra

Esther

Nehemiah

NB. The period for each Bible book indicates its historical setting, not the date of writing. Overlapping dates for the kings indicate periods of co-regency. It is not known when Joel prophesied.

Like guards from a watch-tower the prophets gave early warning of what was to come.

After the years in exile, a remnant of God's people return to Jerusalem.

Judah in exile   **The return**

Obadiah

Zedekiah 597-587

Jehoachin 597   Zechariah

oakim 609-597   Haggai   Malachi

oahaz 609

Jeremiah

uchadnezzar II   Darius I (Hystaspes)

: Nineveh, the Assyrian   Nabonidus (Belshazzar   Artaxerxes I (sponsors return
ital, falls to Babylon   acting king in Babylon)   of Ezra and Nehemiah)

                          539: Belshazzar's feast/Babylon falls to the
                          Medes and Persians

Tyre ▶▶   Cyrus of
             Persia

             Daniel   Xerxes I (Ahasuerus: the
                             Persian king in Esther)

Ezekiel

600 500 400

Isaiah

Summary

Prophecies of God 'the Holy One', Lord of history, and the salvation of his people.

Chapters 1 – 39
Warnings and promises to Judah and the nations

•

Chapters 40 – 55
Comfort and encouragement for the exiles

•

Chapters 56 – 66
After the exile; future glory

Best-known passages

Isaiah's call *(6)*
'A child is born' *(9)*
Kingdom of peace *(11)*
The desert highway *(35)*
'Comfort my people' *(40)*
The suffering servant *(53)*
New earth, new heavens *(65:17-25)*

The Prophets

Isaiah stands at the head of 'The Prophets', the third great section of the Old Testament. Sixteen prophets are named, and we have 17 books of their visions and prophecies (the odd one out being Lamentations: known in the Greek versions as the 'Lamentations of Jeremiah'). The four 'major' prophets are Isaiah, Jeremiah, Ezekiel and Daniel; the twelve 'minor' prophets, Hosea, Joel, Amos, Obadiah, Jonah, Micah, Nahum, Habakkuk, Zephaniah, Haggai, Zechariah, Malachi. See 'The Prophets' and 'Prophets and prophecy'.

The books of the prophets belong to the time of the nation's decline, the exile and the return to their homeland. They span, altogether, a period of 250-300 years. See table in 'The Prophets' and chart, 'The prophets in their setting'.

God sent these prophets on a daunting and sometimes dangerous mission. They were for the most part despatched at the eleventh hour, to try to halt the people's headlong rush to destruction; to warn them of judgment; to call them back to God in repentance – and, after the great disaster of the fall of Jerusalem, to comfort the survivors with the assurance of God's continuing love and purpose for them. The prophets went out in the burning conviction that they had a message from God. Some braved death to make it known.

Isaiah

The prophet who gives this book its name lived in Jerusalem in the 8th century BC. He was married – his wife is described as 'the prophetess' and may have shared his calling. Two sons are mentioned by name in the book.

In chapter 6 Isaiah describes his call from God in the year of King Uzziah's death (about 740 BC). He prophesied for over 40 years through the reigns of Jotham (a godly man like his father), Ahaz (one of Judah's worst kings) and Hezekiah (died 687/6 BC). He may have lived on into the dark days of the evil King Manasseh.

The reigns of these kings are recorded in Kings and Chronicles: Uzziah in 2 Kings 15:1-7; 2 Chronicles 26; Jotham in 2 Kings 15:32-38 and 2 Chronicles 27; Ahaz in 2 Kings 16 and 2 Chronicles 28; Hezekiah in 2 Kings 18 – 20 and 2 Chronicles 29 – 32.

Isaiah knew from the outset that his words would fall on deaf ears, but he did have one great triumph. When Sennacherib's Assyrian army was hammering at the gates of Jerusalem in Hezekiah's reign (701 BC) the king took Isaiah's advice and the city was saved (chapters 36 – 37).

It is likely that Isaiah gathered a group of disciples or fellow-prophets around him who treasured and preserved his words.

The initial vision of God in all his glory in the Temple (chapter 6) coloured Isaiah's whole mission. He had seen God as the 'Holy One of Israel' and he never forgot it. He had seen human sin for the appalling thing it is, and he never forgot that either. And he had been forgiven and taken into God's service. Throughout his life, he preached God's righteousness, warned of the judgment on sin, and comforted his people with the knowledge of God's love, his longing to forgive, and all the glories in store for those who remained faithful to him.

opposite: In a parched land, a spring in the desert is a powerful symbol of hope and new life.

The book

The place of Isaiah at the head of the prophetic books is well deserved. There is nothing to equal its tremendous vision of God and the glory in store for God's people until we reach the book of Revelation, at the end of the New Testament.

In Isaiah we have a collection of visions and prophecies relating to various times. It is not always easy to follow – partly because we are unfamiliar with the language and ways of prophets and visionaries; partly because we do not know the principles which determined the present arrangement of material. In places there is clearly a time-sequence. Other parts seem to be arranged according to subject.

Composition

We do not know how the book was eventually put together. No doubt Isaiah himself wrote down at least some of his prophecies (see 30:8, and the use of the first person in chapters 6 and 8).

The book clearly falls into three sections: chapters 1 – 39, 40 – 55, 56 – 66. The style and language change from chapter 40 on, although the same themes appear right through the book.

Traditionally, Isaiah has been seen as the work of one author, the 8th-century prophet to whom God predicted the events of later history reflected in chapters 40 – 55, which address the people in exile in Babylon shortly before the time of their return (538 BC). The New Testament writers, quoting from various parts of the book, assume this.

Others see the book as a compilation of prophecies – Isaiah's own and those of his successors – given over a long period of time.

The important thing for scholars (and readers) today is the shape and structure of the whole of Isaiah, explored in 'Understanding Isaiah'.

1 – 5
Judah and Jerusalem

1 'You are doomed!'

Although Jerusalem was not finally destroyed until 587 BC, the nation had, a century before, virtually reached the point of no return. God's people have rejected him, breaking the sacred covenant that bound them to him. And God is sickened by their moral degradation, social injustice (16, 23) and religious hypocrisy (11-15). The language is extreme. Once-faithful Jerusalem is 'behaving like a whore', utterly betraying God's trust (21). God's people are his 'enemies'. Yet still God offers forgiveness (18). Swift and terrible judgment will fall on all who continue to defy him: he will cleanse his people from their sin.

▶ **The vision (1)** Isaiah describes what God enables him to see in his mind's eye: 'messages which God revealed'. The book includes

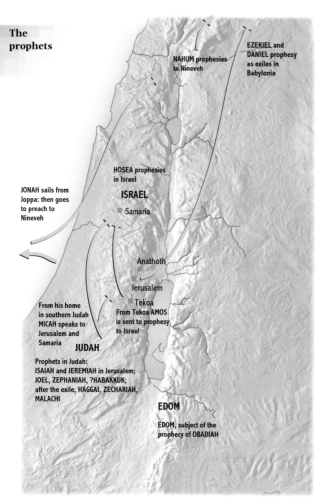

The prophets

NAHUM prophesies to Nineveh

EZEKIEL and DANIEL prophesy as exiles in Babylonia

HOSEA prophesies in Israel

ISRAEL

Samaria

JONAH sails from Joppa: then goes to preach to Nineveh

Anathoth

Jerusalem

Tekoa

From his home in southern Judah MICAH speaks to Jerusalem and Samaria

From Tekoa AMOS is sent to prophesy to Israel

JUDAH

Prophets in Judah:
ISAIAH and JEREMIAH in Jerusalem; JOEL, ZEPHANIAH, ?HABAKKUK; after the exile, HAGGAI, ZECHARIAH, MALACHI

EDOM

EDOM, subject of the prophecy of OBADIAH

prophecies about foreign nations as well as 'Judah and Jerusalem'. Isaiah's father, 'Amoz', is not to be confused with the prophet Amos.

▶ **Earth and sky/heaven and earth (2)** This is the language of an ancient Near Eastern overlord confronting subject kings who have broken covenant.

▶ **Holy One/Holy God of Israel (4)** This is Isaiah's special title for God, springing directly

out of the vision which accompanied his call to be God's prophet (chapter 6). It is used only twice in other parts of the Bible.

▶ **Verses 7-9** The Assyrians have overrun Judah, destroying 46 fortified cities. The northern kingdom of Israel has already fallen. Only Jerusalem (the 'daughter of Zion') remains. The destruction of Sodom and Gomorrah, two utterly corrupt cities at the southern end of the

'Though your sins are like scarlet, they shall be white as snow; though they are red as crimson, they shall be like wool' (1:18). Wool, dipped in scarlet dye, is hung up to dry, at Hebron.

Understanding Isaiah
Hugh G.M. Williamson

Many readers find the book of Isaiah difficult to grasp. It contains many well-known passages, but its overall shape is complicated.

One book: three parts

One way of finding some order is by noticing the setting of the three main sections. Chapters 1 – 39 mostly deal with Judah and Jerusalem under the monarchy. Chapters 40 – 55 suit the period of the exile in Babylon. And chapters 56 – 66 return us to Jerusalem, but at the time of the restoration after the exile. Many scholars believe that this reflects the work of different authors.

Whether or not that is true, the difference of setting and hence of atmosphere is clear.

- In the first part, we have the impression that Isaiah would have liked to bring good news to his audience but could not because they rejected his message. So he wrote it down to serve later on. In this way, people would realize that the judgment which took place really was from God. This would give them faith to believe that he could also bring them the salvation which he had prom- ised. See especially 8:16-18 and 30:8-14. This last passage shows (verse 8) that Isaiah came to realize that this would be long after his lifetime.
- The second part of the book announces that this time of sal- vation has finally arrived. It is as though the book which Isaiah had 'sealed up' can now be opened and the more positive message proclaimed. Many of

> *Understanding the shape of the book is not just an intellectual game; it is literally a matter of life and death.*

the themes of the first part of the book are taken up again, but whereas before they spoke of punishment, now they speak of restoration.

For just two examples, compare 5:26 with 49:22 and 6:9-10 with 43:8.

However, the promise follows the judgment, it does not replace it. So both parts of the book need to be put together to get the whole message. This may help explain why passages which sound like the second part of the book come at the close of sections of the first (e.g. chapters 12 and 35). They illustrate on a smaller scale the outlook of the wider book as a whole.

- In the last part of the book, however, we find that the audience begins to be divided into two groups, the righteous and the wicked. As readers, we are being challenged, as it were, to see whether we belong in the first section of the book, under judgment, or in the second, as recipients of the promise.

Introducing the themes

The first chapter serves to introduce these themes to its readers. From its general shape we can discern a pattern which is meant to help us find our bearings in the extensive material which follows.

It too is in three sections.

- First (verses 2-9) we learn of God's case against his people, and that their sin is going to bring judgment in the form of military defeat; in fact, it is already happening! And 'we' (verse 9) are left as those who have only just escaped. This corresponds to the first section of the book as a whole.
- Verses 10-20 then show that it is not enough to respond just with more religious rituals. God wants a whole change of lifestyle, to one of purity of living and concern for justice. 'If you are willing and obedient' (verse 19) there can be complete forgiveness for the past.
- Finally, just like the third part of the book as a whole, verses 21- 31 show that the readers are divided into two categories, and that God is making a distinction between them. The 'rebels and sinners will be destroyed' (verse 28), but there are also those in Zion who will be redeemed (verse 27).

As we approach the book through this introduction, therefore, we are urged to read it in a responsive manner – to heed the warnings and threats and to grasp hold of the promises. Under- standing the shape of the book is not just an intellectual game; it is literally a matter of life and death.

Dead Sea, is described in Genesis 19. There could be no worse fate.

▶ **The survivors (9)** The theme of the faithful few, the 'remnant' of God's people, is a key one in Isaiah. See 4:2, 3; 6:13; 10:20-22; 11:10-16; 28:5; 37:4, 30-32.

▶ **New moon (13)** The first day of each new month was a holy day.

▶ **Scarlet, red as crimson (18)** Both are colour-fast; only God could 'wash' these out.

▶ **Oaks (29)** The sacred groves where Canaanite rites took place; symbols of the nation's idolatry.

2 – 4 'The time is coming'

In these chapters Isaiah looks forward to a coming time of peace when Jerusalem will become the city of God for people of all nations (2:1-5; Micah 4:1-3 is almost the same). Before that, God will execute fierce judgment on all sin and wrongdoing (2:6 – 4:1). Human pride is marked for destruction (2:11-18). Isaiah (like Jesus) sees pride as the root of so much wrong. Evil has no place in the renewed city; only the few who are faithful to God will survive to enjoy it (4:2-6). This theme of a coming day and a kingdom at peace is developed in chapters 11 – 12.

▶ **2:6** The practice of magic (forbidden in Leviticus 19:31) and foreign alliances both led to idolatry.

▶ **2:10** Also Revelation 6:15; 2 Thessalonians 1:9.

▶ **2:13-16** Symbols of pride. Solomon used the famous Lebanese cedarwood for his Temple. The ships of Tarshish were great ocean-going vessels, the pride of the fleet.

▶ **The vineyard (3:14)** Symbol of the nation, see chapter 5.

▶ **Baldness (3:24)** Heads were shaved as a sign of mourning or degradation.

▶ **4:1** So many men have been killed in battle that the women offer to provide their own keep (unheard of in those days), if only the man will marry them.

▶ **The branch/plant (4:2)** New growth shooting from the old roots (see 11:1); the community is to be reborn.

▶ **4:5** Cloud and fire – the symbols of God's presence when they journeyed through the desert (Exodus 13:21).

5 Song of the vineyard

This song (verses 1-7), like Jesus' vineyard story (Matthew 21:33-41) is a parable. The Jewish nation is the vineyard of God. He has done everything necessary to ensure a heavy yield. But the vintage is bitter. 'Woe betide' (8ff.) those whose wrongdoing causes God to abandon the vineyard (not for ever, though: see chapter 27).

In the land of Judah the vast estates built up at the expense of the poor (8) will become waste land. Ten acres of vines will yield only 22 litres; the harvest will be only a tenth of the seed sown (10). Again the prophet denounces pride, luxury, drunkenness, injustice. God will give the signal for the enemy invasion (26ff.) which will overwhelm them.

▶ **Sheol (14,** some versions) The shadowy world of the dead.

▶ **Verse 26** Isaiah does not name the 'distant nation'. Assyria was the immediate threat; Babylon the later one.

6 'I saw the Lord!' – Isaiah's call to serve

The overwhelming experience of God's holiness described in this chapter shaped Isaiah's whole life as a prophet. He constantly spoke of the God he served as 'the Holy One of Israel'. The knowledge that he had seen God with his own eyes, experienced his forgiveness and been sent out in God's service would sustain him all his life. And he would need this: for God sent him to a nation deaf and blind to his entreaties (9-10); a nation that would be destroyed and taken captive (11-12). Yet there was hope: the germ of a new nation would survive (13).

▶ **Feet (2)** The whole body is meant.

▶ **Verse 5** Isaiah, face to face with God, is overcome with a sense of his own unworthiness. (In the Old Testament it was considered death to see God.) His experience is shared by Moses and Jeremiah in the Old Testament (Exodus 3; Jeremiah 1); Peter and Paul in the New (Luke 5:1-11; 1 Corinthians 15:8-10).

▶ **Verses 9-10** The Hebrew idiom expresses

> ❝ *In the year that King Uzziah died, I saw the Lord seated on a throne, high and exalted, and the train of his robe filled the Temple. Above him were seraphs, each with six wings: with two wings they covered their faces, with two they covered their feet, and with two they were flying. And they were calling to one another: 'Holy, holy, holy is the Lord Almighty; the whole earth is full of his glory.* ❞
>
> 6:1-3

result as if it were purpose. God did not intend to stop people repenting. He sent Isaiah out with the express purpose of saving people from judgment, and the prophet's message is clear. But the people shut their ears and refused to act.

▶ **Verse 13** This seems to mean a new beginning.

7 – 12
Present and future

7 – 8 'Immanuel': judgment and promise

The date is about 735 BC. Uzziah's grandson, Ahaz, is on the throne. Ahaz defied God (2 Kings 16), and in consequence his kingdom came under attack from all quarters. When he refused to join the Israel/Syria alliance against Assyria, they attacked Judah. It is at this point that Isaiah goes to him with God's message (3-9).

Isaiah offers Ahaz a sign that God will keep his promise to save Judah and its line of kings. Ahaz, with false piety, will not ask for one. So Isaiah promises him another sign, a child called 'God with us'. In the immediate future 'God with us' means judgment (7:15-25; 8:5-8; compare 8:1-4), though in the long term it will mean blessing (8:9, 10). For the king is set on the disastrous course of asking Assyria's help. And when the rebels are dealt with, Assyria will sweep on into Judah, till Jerusalem itself is surrounded (see chapters 36 – 37).

▶ **House of David (7:2)** The royal household.
▶ **Syria and Ephraim (7:2 and 5ff.)** Syria (strictly speaking at this date, Aram) was ruled from Damascus. As predicted, the kingdom was crushed by Assyria in 732. 'Ephraim' is the northern kingdom of Israel, which also fell to Assyria, 734-722 BC.
▶ **Shear-jashub (7:3)** The name means 'a remnant shall return'. The names of both Isaiah's sons stood as a constant reminder of his teaching – see chapter 8 and on 10:20.
▶ **Fuller's Field (7:3)** The fuller/clothmaker needed to be near water for his job of cleaning and whitening cloth.
▶ **7:14-16 'Immanuel' in Hebrew means 'God is with us'.** The sign seems to have both present and future significance. 1. In the few years it takes for a child conceived now to reach an age

when he can choose for himself, Israel and Damascus will cease to be a threat.
2. There will one day be born a child who will truly be 'Immanuel', 'God with us' (see Matthew 1:23). The word translated 'virgin' in some versions (and in the Greek text) is more like English 'maiden' than the technical term, 'virgin'.

▶ **Curds/milk and honey (7:15, 22)** These symbols of natural plenty, here stand for a waste land where cattle and bees afford the only remaining food supply.
▶ **The prophetess (8:3)** Isaiah's wife.
▶ **Maher-shalal-hashbaz, 'quick loot, fast plunder' (8:3)** The name carries the same (initial) message as 'God with us' – one of judgment at the hands of Assyria. Compare 8:3, 4 with 7:14-16.
▶ **Shiloah (8:6)** Probably an aqueduct outside Jerusalem. Hezekiah's Siloam tunnel (see feature) had not yet been constructed.
▶ **The River (8:7)** Euphrates.

9:1-7 A king will come

This prophecy moves right away from the dark days of the present to a vision of a bright and glorious future. A king will come from David's line to rule in peace and justice – for ever. Zebulun and Naphtali in Galilee, the first of the tribes to be crushed by Assyria, will be the first to see the light, to taste the joy, to be set free by the coming prince of peace.

Matthew 4:12-16 specifically links this prophecy with the coming of Jesus, whose home-town was Nazareth, in Galilee, and who began his public ministry at Cana in Galilee.

▶ **The way of the sea (1)** The main highway between Egypt and Syria passed through Galilee.
▶ **Day of Midian's defeat (4)** Gideon's great victory against the Midianites, Judges 7.
▶ **Mighty God (6)** No less than God himself: see 10:21 where the same word is used.
▶ **An everlasting kingdom (7)** See the angel Gabriel's words to Mary, Luke 1:32-33.

9:8 – 10:4 Punishment for Israel

We are brought back abruptly to the present. The people of the breakaway northern kingdom of Israel stand condemned for their arrogance and

Prophets and prophecy
Mary Evans

Painting the portrait of a typical Old Testament prophet would be very difficult indeed. Who would one choose as typical?

All sorts

Would it be a trained professional prophet who began as an apprentice and worked his way up to be the leader of a prophetic group – like Elisha (1 Kings 19:21; 2 Kings 4:38)? Or would you choose an independent prophet with no real training, like Amos (Amos 7:14)?

It could be a prophet who worked within court circles, acting as a key adviser to the government, like Isaiah (2 Kings 19;1-6; 20:1-21), or one who was often seen as a direct enemy of the state – like Jeremiah (Jeremiah 20:2; 32:3; 36:26).

Some prophets used music to help them in their work (Exodus 15:20-21; 1 Samuel 10:5; 2 Kings 3:15). Some used very strange pictures or dramatic presentations, whereas others seemed to find straightforward everyday speech was enough to help them get their message across.

Some were lifelong prophets, others apparently worked as a prophet for a fairly short period of time.

They all told of the same God and described the same responsibilities that are given to those who want to maintain a relationship with God, but they are very different people who present their message in very different ways.

There is no such thing as the typical prophet.

Women as well as men

Although all of the Old Testament prophets who have books written by them or named after them are men, this does not mean that women were not, or could not be, prophets.

It is possible, though perhaps unlikely, that when Isaiah describes his wife as 'the prophetess' (Isaiah 8:3) he is using the title in an honorary sense. But when Miriam (Exodus 15:20), Deborah (Judges 4:4), Huldah (2 Kings 22:14), or the rather more unpleasant Noadiah (Nehemiah 6:14) are called prophets there is no doubt that this reflects an active ministry.

There were not very many women prophets, but there seems to have been no prejudice against those there were simply because of their sex.

The good king Josiah sent several national government leaders to get the advice of the prophetess Huldah about one of the most significant events in his reign, the finding of the 'book of the law' (2 Kings 22:8-20). Her words were taken just as seriously as if they had come from Isaiah or Micah, who were both active prophets at the same time.

There were false prophets (see 'The Prophets'), both male and female, who were condemned for their false prophecy, but there is no hint that their gender was ever an issue.

Looking to the future

When prophets spoke of future events it is very clear that there was often a hidden question mark hanging over what they were saying. It is as if they were presenting alternative doors of possibility for the future. In many cases, whether that particular door will be passed through depends on whether or not the hearer or reader responds to the message the prophet has given.

Take Jonah, for example. (Whether we take the story as parable or history, does not alter the point.) The prophet is called to bring a clear message of judgment and destruction to the people of Nineveh. However, when the people actually responded to the message and repented, God chose to close that particular door for the present. Jonah was annoyed at this because he wanted the Ninevites to die, but he was not surprised. He knew that this was the way in which God worked (Jonah 4:2).

These alternative pictures of the future explain why it is possible for prophets to speak, without contradiction, both of the total destruction of God's people and of the hope of great renewal and prosperity. These are two alternative doors.

The Old Testament prophet's primary role was not to give people a glimpse of a blue-print of future events. They did 'foretell', as Deuteronomy 18:21-22 makes clear. But their main concern was to encourage people to live now in the way that God wanted, a way that reflected the fact of their relationship to him.

Let the hearer beware

Prophets were responsible to speak out clearly the things that God had given them to say. However, the

▶▶ listeners had responsibilities too. They were, of course, responsible to hear and heed the things said to them; to turn their faith into action; to live out the justice and holiness and love of their God. They were also responsible for critiquing what was said, for assessing whether or not the prophet really was speaking from God, responsible for being honest with themselves and with God and in particular for not trying to bribe the prophet to give nice warm messages that only ever contained the things they wanted to hear (Micah 2:11; Isaiah 30:10-11; Jeremiah 5:31).

New Testament prophets

In the New Testament too, prophecy played a very important role in the life of the people of God. There were those, like Agabus (Acts 21:10) or Philip's daughters (Acts 21:9), who were known for having specific prophetic gifts. However, very few people are actually identified as prophets; rather the gift of prophecy is presented as belonging to the whole church. Particular individuals might be used by God to bring specific messages from God to his people, but the emphasis is on the message and the response of the church rather than the one who brought it.

In the New Testament church, all believers were now viewed as having a priestly role, able to enter into the presence of God without need of any priestly mediator other than Christ himself (Hebrews 10:19-22; 1 Timothy 2:5). There are strong indications that all were also viewed as having a prophetic role, able to hear for themselves what God was saying and bring their understanding of that to the church for it to be weighed and worked out (1 Corinthians 14:29, 31).

And today?

For today's church and today's Christian the challenge of prophecy remains. We are still called upon to speak out about the justice and holiness and love of the great God whom we serve, and we are still called upon to live out that justice and holiness and love.

We may not all be among those who are recognized as prophets, regularly able to encapsulate the essence of the things that God wants his people to hear, in a way that is immediately recognized as valid by all those who belong to God and genuinely seek his word. But if all believers are in direct relationship with God, there is the potential for all believers to hear what God is saying.

If this is true, it is vitally important that we are all good listeners: able to listen to what God is saying so that we can share it with others; and able to listen to what others are saying to us so that we can judge whether God is speaking to us through them.

---

rebellion, injustice and oppression. They have already had a taste of judgment, but learnt nothing from it. Therefore God will not spare them. The prophecy is written in four stanzas, each ending with the same refrain (12, 17, 21, 10:4; it was used before, in 5:25).

The Assyrians took many Israelites captive in 734, but Samaria held out until 722/1. Israel had turned a deaf ear to the warnings of Amos and the appeals of Hosea (Isaiah's contemporary), the two prophets God had specially sent them.

10:5-34 'I sent Assyria'

God makes use of a proud and cruel nation to punish his people. But the emperor's arrogant boast (13, 14) does not go unchallenged (15) and Assyria's excessive ferocity is not excused: it will be punished (12, 24ff.). Even at the height of judgment God never loses sight of his purpose to save. A remnant – pathetically few – of his people will survive to trust and serve him (20ff.).

▶ **Verse 9** A list of cities and city-states conquered by Assyria — all Syrian except for Samaria.

► **Not one/not a (14)** A vivid way of expressing the total absence of any resistance.

► **The remnant (20)** This is one of the key themes in Isaiah. It goes back to the day God called him into service (6:13), and runs as a thread of hope through the darkest messages of judgment. See on 1:9 for references. This same faithful remnant, those who have survived, is to realize all the glorious promises for the future.

► **Verse 26** See Judges 7 and Exodus 14.

► **Verses 28ff.** Gibeah, just north of Jerusalem, was Saul's capital; Anathoth, a few miles east, the home of Jeremiah. Isaiah pictures an attack on Jerusalem from the north, the usual route of invading armies from countries to the north or east. Sennacherib actually approached from Lachish, to the south-west.

11 – 12 When all will be well

The theme of earlier passages (2:2-4; 4:2-6; 9:1-7) is developed more fully here. The coming king will be from David's family ('Jesse', 11:1, was David's father). He will possess the Spirit of God himself: just, righteous, faithful, like God. Nations will rally to him (11:10). His kingdom will be free of enmity and evil. The natural world reflects this total transformation (11:6ff.). There will be a great gathering in of all God's scattered people (11:12), and the song of God's salvation will be on everyone's lips (chapter 12). Isaiah pictures it all in physical terms. But what he sees is a radical change. This is a new earth, centred on God and obedient to his will (11:9; 12:6; see also 65:17ff. and Revelation 21).

13 – 23
The nations stand condemned

These chapters bring together a collection of prophecies against foreign nations given at various times. God's concern is not limited to his own people. The whole world is his.

The prophecies conjure up powerful pictures and use vivid imagery to describe the terrors to come. They have the form and language of poetry. For example, 14:4 makes it clear that what follows is a taunt-song. In addition to the headings – 'an oracle (or message) about...' – the prophecies are interspersed with brief explanatory prose notes (e.g. 13:1; 14:1-4; 16:13, 14; 17:7-9; 19:16 – 20:6). Some versions make this clear.

13 – 14:23 Babylon

See also chapters 46 – 47. In Isaiah's day Babylon was struggling for independence from Assyria. This prophecy concerns Babylon, 100 years later, at the height of its power – and looks forward to the day when Babylon in turn will be brought down.

In 539 Babylon fell to the Medes and Persians led by Cyrus. Xerxes destroyed the city in 478, and it was finally abandoned in the 4th century BC. In the New Testament, Babylon becomes a symbol. It is the city of rebel humanity, implacably opposed to God (Revelation 17; it also serves as a code-word for Rome).

► **Holy war (13:3)** On this concept, see 'Holy war'.

► **13:10** This is conventional language for the cataclysmic 'day of the Lord'. See e.g. Ezekiel 32:7; Joel 2:10 and New Testament passages, Matthew 24:29; Revelation 6:12-13.

► **Ophir (13:12)** See 1 Kings 9:28.

► **13:21-22** A list of repulsive creatures.

► **King of Babylon (14:4)** The taunt-song is addressed, not to a particular king, but to the dynasty, representing the whole kingdom.

► **Morning/Day star (14:12)** Venus; in Canaanite belief, a god who made a bid to be 'top god'.

► **14:13** The very same thoughts brought God's judgment on Babel, Babylon's predecessor (Genesis 11:1-9).

14:24-27 Assyria

Assyria's fate is also sealed (see on 10:5-34). Ultimately Babylon will break the power of Assyria. But before that there will be a signal defeat in God's own land (25; see chapters 36 – 37).

14:28-32 Philistia

The date is probably 716 BC (28). Assyria is in trouble, and the Philistines (old enemies of Israel, occupying the coastal plain) try to persuade Judah to join them in rebellion. But the Assyrians are far from finished (29, 31). Worse is to come – and the Philistines are doomed. God's poor and suffering people, however, find safety in him.

15 – 16 Moab

The Moabites were descendants of Abraham's nephew, Lot. They occupied the plateau land east of the Dead Sea. It was from Moab that Ruth came. At times the Moabites were on good terms with the Israelites, but they had no share in Israel's faith. Isaiah is stirred to sympathy at the spectacle of Moab's suffering (15:5), now only three short years away (16:14). Moab sends to Jerusalem for help, and God urges his people to take the fugitives in (16:1-5).

Isaiah's prophecies against the nations

The cities of Moab fell to Assyria in successive campaigns. They were to fall again to Nebuchadnezzar of Babylon.

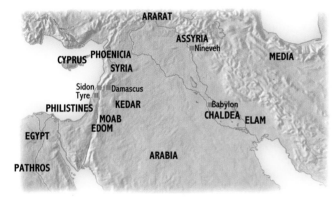

▶ **15:1-9** These are all towns in Moab. 'Nebo' is the mountain from which Moses viewed the promised land; 'Zoar' a town at the southern end of the Dead Sea, spared in the overthrow of Sodom. The 'valley of willows/poplars' is probably the boundary between Moab and Edom to the south.
▶ **Baldness (15:2)** See on 3:24.
▶ **Sela (16:1)** 'The rock' – Edom's fortress in Jordan; now part of the site of Petra. The fleeing Moabites have taken refuge here.
▶ **Arnon (16:2)** A deep gorge which formed the boundary between Moab, to the south, and Ammon, to the north.
▶ **16:3-4a** Moab's plea to Judah. 4b, 5 are an aside.
▶ **Vineyards of Sibmah (16:8ff.)** A region famous for its wine – here a symbol of national prosperity.

▶ **16:14** A person bound by contract works no more than the time contracted for; so, 'three years, and barely that'.

17 Damascus

This is a prophecy from Isaiah's early days – see on chapter 7. In response to King Ahaz's appeal for help against the Syria-Israel alliance, the Assyrians launched a series of raids in which Damascus was plundered and King Rezin met his death. This prophecy also attacks Israel for siding with Syria against their own kin – the nation of Judah.
▶ **Asherah symbols (8)** Canaanite cult-images and altars.
▶ **Hivites, Amorites (9)** Tribes destroyed by the Israelites in the conquest of Canaan.

18 Ethiopia/Cush

This is modern Sudan. In Isaiah's day Egypt was ruled by a Sudanese dynasty. The Assyrian threat brings envoys from afar. But God will deal with the invader on the very eve of victory (5-6 – see 37:36ff.). And the far-off nation will send gifts in grateful homage to God (7; see 2 Chronicles 32:23).

19 Egypt

This prophecy foretells the disintegration of Egypt: internal strife, followed by conquest, a ruined economy and breakdown of leadership (1-15).

Egypt was defeated by Assyria when Sennacherib's army besieged Jerusalem (701 BC). Further defeats culminated in the sack of Thebes in 663 BC, when the Assyrians pillaged centuries of temple treasures.

But God uses the sword for surgery, not anarchy. Verses 16-24 reveal his ultimate purpose: the revelation of himself to the Egyptian people. Amazingly (23-25), Egypt and Assyria (those most opposed to God's purposes) will be united with Israel in the worship of God, bringing blessing to the whole world. 'That day' (i.e. the day of God's judgment – both temporal and final – a frequent phrase throughout Isaiah) is the day of God's final intervention in judgment and salvation on a worldwide scale. The New Testament sees 'that day' as the day of Christ's return.

The comparison of God's people to a vine or vineyard is a recurring theme in the prophets.

After Jerusalem fell in 587 there were numerous influential colonies of Jews in Egypt and in Assyria. A copy of the Jewish Temple was even constructed at Leontopolis in Egypt about 170 BC. But all that was only a pale shadow of what is envisaged in Isaiah.

▶ **Verses 5-10** Egypt's whole economy depended on the yearly flooding of the Nile to water and fertilize the land beyond its banks. Too much or too little (as here) spelt disaster.

▶ **Verse 16** Poetry turns to prose for the rest of the chapter, and chapter 20.

▶ **Zoan (11)... Memphis (13)** Respectively the current and ancient capitals of Egypt. Zoan (Tanis) was in the delta region; Memphis just south of it on the Nile.

▶ **City of the sun (18)** Heliopolis = On; centre of Egyptian sun-worship.

20 Egypt and Sudan

'The year' (1) is 711 BC, when the Assyrians crushed the Philistine rebellion at Ashdod. The support expected from Egypt had not materialized. Three years earlier, God had instructed Isaiah to mime the role of a slave, stripping off his sackcloth and sandals to go about naked and barefoot (2). It was a startling demonstration (like Ezekiel's dramatic

actions) of the coming captivity of Egypt, designed to warn his people to place no reliance on help from that quarter. In 701 BC (see on chapter 19 above) Egypt was defeated by Assyria.

21 Three oracles

The 'wilderness' or 'desert by the sea' (1) is Babylonia (9). See on chapters 13 – 14. The downfall of Babylon will be good news to the captives from Israel (10). Even so, Isaiah is appalled by what he foresees. Being a 'seer' is a painful and costly business (3-4).

There is temporary respite for Edom (Dumah, 11-12) – but judgment was to follow (see 34:5).

Not even the remote tribes of Arabia (13-17) will escape the long arm of Assyria. This prophecy became reality when Sargon attacked Arabia in 715 BC.

▶ **Verse 16** 'Kedar', a powerful Bedouin tribe; 'servant/contract', see on 16:14.

22 'The Valley of Vision'

Jerusalem was Isaiah's home. It was here that he had his visions. The city is surrounded by valleys and mountains. The 'Valley of Vision' which stands for the city is probably the Hinnom Valley. Despite the

> 66 *A grim vision is shown to me: the traitor betrayed, the spoiler despoiled. Advance, Elam; up, Media, to the siege! Throw off all weariness! At this vision my limbs writhe in anguish, I am gripped by pangs like a woman in labour. I am distraught past hearing, disquieted past seeing, my mind reels.* 99
>
> 21:2-4

Phoenician warships from Tyre and Sidon safeguarded trade and fought off powerful enemies, the foremost being Egypt.

Sennacherib approached. As Assyria declined, Tyre regained its power, only to lose it again to the Babylonians.

▶ **Tarshish (6)** Probably 'Tartessus' in Spain.

▶ **Chaldeans/Babylonians (13)** Chaldea was part of south Babylonia, but when Chaldean kings came to power in Babylon the term was used of the Babylonian kingdom as a whole.

▶ **Seventy years (15)** Probably a round figure, meaning a lifetime.

reprieve in Hezekiah's day (chapters 36 – 37), Isaiah foresees the future destruction of Jerusalem. (Nebuchadnezzar II of Babylon eventually took the city after a terrible siege in 587 BC. The walls were broken down and the Temple destroyed.)

The people's reaction in the face of disaster is a mixture of frenzied activity and sheer escapism (8-13). They check their weapons and store water against a siege, but they do not 'look to the Maker of the city'.

Verses 15ff. relate to Isaiah's own day. Shebna, a high official in Hezekiah's court (36:3), is to be demoted, and Eliakim promoted. But he will find himself unable to cope with his hangers-on, and his authority will be short-lived.

▶ **Elam... Kir (6)** Outposts of the Assyrian Empire which no doubt supplied conscripts to the army.

▶ **House/palace of the forest (8)** The city's arsenal; see 1 Kings 7:2; 10:17.

▶ **Verses 9, 11** Water supply was vital in the event of siege. See 2 Chronicles 32 (and feature) for the Siloam tunnel, Hezekiah's solution to the problem.

23 Tyre

For centuries Tyre and Sidon (two Phoenician cities on the coast of modern Lebanon) dominated the sea-trade in the eastern Mediterranean. Tyre's colonies, of which Cyprus was the nearest, were widespread. And the city's merchantmen ventured as far afield as the Indian Ocean and the English Channel. A major tradeline was Egyptian grain (3).

Tyre was a city corrupted by its own wealth and success, and Isaiah warns of the approaching end. He spoke truly. In 722/1 the city fell to Sargon of Assyria. In 701 the ruler of Tyre fled to Cyprus as

24 – 27
Judgment and salvation

From the particular – God's judgment on specific nations – we move to the universal: the time when God will judge the whole world and everyone in it. Life will not go on for ever just as it is. One day God will step in and end the world as we know it. There will be a shaking of the foundations, and the world, weighed down by sin, will collapse (24:20). Isaiah was in no doubt about this. Neither was Jesus (see Matthew 24).

But God's purpose is not just to condemn. One chapter (24) on judgment is followed by three (25 – 27) on rescue and saving, when God removes 'the cloud of sorrow that has been hanging over all the nations' (25:7). Death itself will be destroyed, and grief will be no more (compare 25:8 with Revelation 21:4). The nations will sit down at God's great celebration banquet (a reference to this feast led to Jesus' parable story: Luke 14:15-24).

A song of joy in God, who makes the weak and helpless his concern (25:1-5), leads into a description of the joys awaiting God's people on the far side of judgment (25:6-12). Chapter 26 breaks into song again. Its theme is trust. In life there is waiting (8ff.), suffering and failure (16-18). But God holds fast his own, even through death (19). The song of the vineyard in 27:2ff. contrasts with chapter 5. The day will come when God's purpose for his people will be fulfilled. The present punishment is intended as a corrective. The exile will end. In the final harvest all God's people will be brought home.

▶ **That day (24:21**, etc.) See on chapter 19 above.

▶ **Moab (25:10)** The current enemy of God's people stands for all such enemies.

▶ **26:19** This graphic picture of resurrection (which some take to refer to the nation) marks a new stage in Old Testament belief. The 'dew' expresses God's power to revive the dead, who lie in the earth.

▶ **Leviathan (27:1)** The dragon/serpent figure from pagan mythology. God's judgment extends to the superhuman realm (see 24:21, where the 'powers above' may be the sun, moon and stars worshipped by other nations). The same figure is used in Revelation 12:9 to depict Satan.

▶ **Asherah (27:9)** See on 17:8 above.

▶ **27:10-11** Refers to the oppressors, whose suffering will be far greater than that of God's people.

28–31
More warnings to God's rebellious people

28 Woe to Samaria and Judah's leaders

Attention is turned once again to the sins of Isaiah's own day. Verses 1-6 are addressed to Israel. (The tribal name 'Ephraim' represents all 10 tribes of the northern kingdom.) They belong to the time before the fall of Samaria, the capital, in 722/1 BC. The pleasure-loving, luxury-loving city is ripe for the plucking – and Assyria's hand is outstretched to take it. Yet a core, 'remnant' (see on 10:20 above) will remain.

The leaders come under special attack (7ff.). Religious leaders and rulers alike have not led but misled the people. At verse 14 the prophet turns on Judah and the rulers in Jerusalem. They have made a treaty with Egypt, which the prophet mockingly refers to as a treaty with death (15) and think themselves safe. They will discover how wrong they are (18). Real security rests with God.

Verses 23-29 bring in a little Wisdom teaching. The farmer knows what to do because God teaches him. God's people would do well to learn that lesson.

▶ **Verses 9-13** J.B. Phillips translates 10, 13: 'The-law-is-the-law-is-the-law, The-rule-is-the-rule-is-the-rule.' Isaiah's hearers are

deliberately making nonsense of God's message; 9-10 may be their sneering reply to the prophet. To those who treat God's words as gibberish, Isaiah says that God will deliver his next message in Assyrian!

▶ **Death (15)** The word is the same as the Canaanite god of the dead, worshipped in Egypt under different names.

▶ **Stone/cornerstone (16)** See also 1 Peter 2:4ff. Here the meaning of the stone has to do with trusting God. Faith can wait patiently,

Carved figures of a horseman, archer and slinger were found at Tell Halaf, north-east Syria, called Gozan in the Bible. This was where King Sargon of Assyria settled Israelite captives after his victory in 722/1 BC.

confident of safety in God. There is no need for hasty, panic action.

▶ **Verse 21** Refers to David's victories; see 1 Chronicles 14:8-17.

29 Woe to Jerusalem

'Ariel' (the word has several meanings, the most likely here being 'altar of God') stands for Mt Zion/Jerusalem (8). The city will be besieged (3) and then reprieved (5ff. and see 37:36). God's word to his people has become a closed book, because they pay him only lip-service (11-16). But the day is coming (17ff.) when those who are deaf and blind to his message will hear and see, when God's people will once again fear and obey him.

▶ **Verse 14** Paul quotes the Greek version of Isaiah's words in 1 Corinthians 1:19.

▶ **Verse 17** A picture of things suddenly reversed: the forests become fields and fields forests. The same thought continues in the verses that follow.

▶ **Humble, needy (19)** People loyal to God, not simply the victims of social injustice (see Matthew 5:3, 5).

30 – 31 Woe to the rebels who rely on Egypt

Judah is in league with Egypt (see on 28:15) and they think themselves secure against Assyria, despite all Isaiah's earlier warnings. But when it comes to the crunch Egypt will sit tight (30:7) while the Assyrians invade Judah (chapters 36 – 37). It is God – the One they would not trust (30:9-12) – who will save them in the end (30:27-33; 31:5-9; 37:36). Like a lion standing over its prey, like a bird protecting its nest, God will unfailingly defend his people (31:4, 5). He pleads with them yet again to turn to him (31:6).

▶ **Zoan (30:4)** See 19:11.

▶ **30:6** The gifts are carried through the Negev desert to Egypt.

▶ **Rahab (30:7)** A poetic synonym for Egypt.

▶ **30:33** The oppressor will be utterly destroyed. 'Topheth' ('a burning place') is in the Valley ('Ge-' in Hebrew) of Hinnom, just outside Jerusalem, where in Israel's darkest days children were sacrificed to the pagan god Molech. The valley later supplied the name for hell, 'Gehenna'.

> *Let the wilderness and the parched land be glad, let the desert rejoice and burst into flower... Brace the arms that are limp, steady the knees that give way; say to the anxious, 'Be strong, fear not! Your God comes to save you.'*
>
> 35:1-4

32 – 35
Peace, justice and rescue

32 The future king; peace by a hard road

'Some day...' Briefly the prophet returns to the theme of a future king, of a time when justice will reign. Verses 6-8 echo the thoughts of the Wisdom writers. Verses 9-14 speak directly to the women of Isaiah's day. They are living a life of careless ease, but those days are numbered. Let them mourn their loss. Verse 15 looks forward again to a time of lasting peace, justice and righteousness brought about by the working of God's Holy Spirit in his people. And creation itself feels the effect. When they did wrong, the land suffered (12-13; compare Genesis 3:17-18). Now, when everyone does what is right, the land too revives (see Romans 8:20-21).

▶ **Verse 9** The cossetted women of Jerusalem typify the society of Isaiah's day.

▶ **Strip off (11b)** I.e. go in mourning.

▶ **Verse 19** The meaning is not clear; 'forest' and 'city' may refer to enemies.

33 When God intervenes

This is a chapter with many changes of speaker and mood. The destroyer/enemies of verse 1 are not named. Verses 2-4 are a prayer; 5-6 a hymn; 7-9 a lament which can apply to many times beside Isaiah's own. Only those who live by their faith in God remain unshaken in circumstances like these (2-6; 15-16). Again we glimpse the future king as a glorious vision unfolds in verses 17-24. God never deserts his own; the city defended by him is unassailable. Where God is king, all is safe, all are cared and provided for, sins are forgiven, sickness unknown.

34 Judgment on the nations

God will one day avenge the wrong done to his people (8; see also chapter 24). Edom – the enemy *par excellence* – is singled out as an example. The destruction is total and terrible: the whole land turned to a desert waste.

▶ **34:4** These images of the end-time recur through Scripture: see Matthew 24:29; Revelation 6:13-14 in the New Testament.

▶ **Bozrah (6)** At various times Edom's capital city.

▶ **Verse 16** We have no light on what this book is. The book of the Lord elsewhere is a record of those saved (Daniel 12:1; Malachi 3:16); it is 'the book of life' (Revelation 20:12ff.)

35 Salvation for God's people

Stern prophecy gives way to lyric poetry – in striking contrast to the horror of chapter 34. Destruction gives way to re-creation. God is coming to bring his people home by a safe highway. At the sight of him everything is changed. The dry and lifeless desert, bursting for joy, becomes a paradise of flowing streams, great trees, a carpet of flowers... There is healing and wholeness (3-6), gladness and song, as God's people enter Zion.

36 – 39
The Assyrian crisis

These three chapters are a straightforward historical account, after all the prophecies of chapters 1 – 35. See on 2 Kings 18 – 20, an almost identical account apart from Isaiah's omission (between verses 1 and 2) of Hezekiah's initial cave-in to Sennacherib (2 Kings 18:14-16), and Hezekiah's poem (38:9-20). See also 2 Chronicles 32.

Hezekiah's illness and the embassy from Babylon probably preceded the siege (about 705-702 BC). The events may have been reversed here to provide a lead-in to the following chapters, which focus on Babylon as the world power it later became.

'Peace in my time' was Hezekiah's reaction to the terrible prediction of conquest and captivity (39:5-8). Isaiah could draw no comfort from the thought.

40 – 55
Hope for the exiles; the Servant of the Lord

Up to this point the book of Isaiah has been largely taken up with the threat from Assyria. Chapter 39 provides a transition to the next major era: the time of Babylonian domination.

In 587 Judah was devastated for a second time (the first was in 598). The Temple was destroyed. The false confidence that God would protect Jerusalem, no matter what, was shattered. Thousands were taken into exile (Jeremiah 52:28-30).

Isaiah 40 – 55 addresses these dispirited exiles. Although God has punished them – as he had so often warned, and as they deserved – he still loves them. They can trust him. He (unlike all other 'gods') has the power to help them and fulfil his promises. (Babylon actually fell to Cyrus the Persian in 538 BC: see 44:28 – 45:1.)

These chapters are so full of hope and comfort that they are known as 'The Book of the Consolation of Israel'. They also look

The army of King Sennacherib of Assyria surrounded Jerusalem in Isaiah's time. Pictures of his terrifying campaigns line the walls of his palace. This one shows the beheading of captives.

far beyond the circumstances of Israel in the 6th century BC. Where the previous chapters spoke of a future king, these speak of a coming 'Servant' who will carry out God's purposes at great cost. The New Testament, with Christians ever since, sees particularly in the fourth 'Servant Song' (52:13 – 53:12) a remarkable portrayal of Jesus.

This whole section (40 – 55) speaks so powerfully of God's salvation that Christians see in it something much bigger than the rescue of Israel at a particular time in history. Here is God's firm purpose to deliver humankind from the 'bondage' of sin; his promise of a new life for all who will come to him.

The Assyrians
Alan Millard

The Assyrians occupied the northern part of what is now Iraq, along the Tigris river, for most of the Old Testament period. The hills and plains of this fertile land contrast with the desert to the west and craggy mountains to the north and east. For this reason the Assyrians had constantly to defend their country against invasion.

History

The Assyrians were mainly a Semitic people (the racial group to which the Arabs and the Jews also belong) and their language was closely related to Babylonian. They also used the same cuneiform writing system (see 'The Baby-lonians'). Assyrian king lists tell us that the Assyrians were in their land by about 2300 BC.

From 1350 BC Assyria became a leading state in the Near East. After a time of weakness (about 1050 to 925 BC), when Aramaean tribes from Syria pressed hard, a line of vigorous kings established the powerful Assyrian Empire.

Life and art

With the empire came wealth. The reports in the Bible and elsewhere and the battle scenes which decorated Assyrian palace walls give the impression of a cruel warrior people. But their purpose was to glorify the gods of Assyria who gave the victories to their kings and to display Assyria's power. There was more to Assyrian life than war.

At Nineveh, Ashur and Calah, their most important cities, the kings built great palaces and temples. Walls were lined with

stone slabs carved in low relief. These show the king out hunting, dealing with his subjects, and worshipping the gods, as well as depicting his victories.

Palace furniture was beautifully decorated with ivory panels, carved or engraved. The king, with the queen at his side, lay on a golden couch and drank from golden goblets.

Libraries

Thousands of clay tablets were stored in the palace libraries. Many deal with diplomacy and administration, and record details of the kings' reigns. There are legal documents and letters to the kings and also dictionaries and word lists.

The libraries collected Babylonian books, including legends of early history, such as *The Epic of Gilgamesh* which tells of the flood (see 'Flood stories') and myths about the gods and the creation of the world and human society.

Religion

Ashur, the national god of Assyria, was regarded as king of the gods. He and the other gods (moon, sun, weather; goddess of love and war,,,) were believed to control everything.

Each city had a main temple where the patron god was worshipped. On the god's special day and at major festivals people lined the streets to see the god's statues carried in procession.

The spirit world was taken very seriously. People wore charms to ward off evil spirits and demons who were thought to bring trouble

King Ashur-nasirpal II of Assyria.

Hunting, particularly lions, was a favourite pursuit of the Assyrian kings.

Bronze strips which decorated a temple door show the Assyrian king on campaign, with a chariot crossing a bridge of boats.

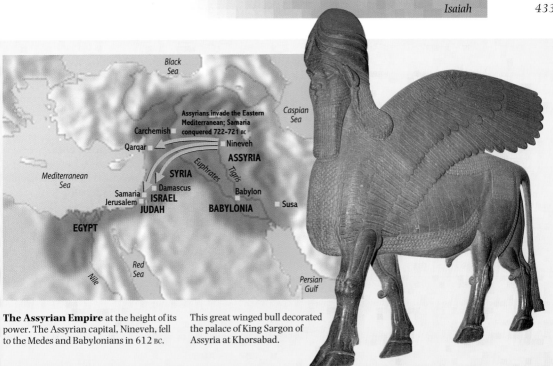

The Assyrian Empire at the height of its power. The Assyrian capital, Nineveh, fell to the Medes and Babylonians in 612 BC.

This great winged bull decorated the palace of King Sargon of Assyria at Khorsabad.

and illness. They consulted omens and astrologers about the future, believing marks on the livers of sacrificed sheep and movements of the stars were divine writing announcing good or bad luck.

It was very hard to know what the gods wanted: they were unpredictable.

Offerings were made to ensure the dead rested in the dusty underworld and did not haunt their descendants, but there was no real hope of life after death.

Assyria and Israel

The Assyrians came into contact with Israel as they extended their power to the south-west in the 9th century BC. Shalmaneser names Ahab of Israel among kings whose troops he defeated in 853 BC and Jehu as paying tribute in 841.

About 796, Joash of Samaria brought tribute to Adad-nirari V. Fifty years later, Tiglath-pileser III renewed Assyrian pressure on Israel, extracting payment from Menahem (2 Kings 15:19-20).

When Damascus and Samaria threatened Ahaz of Judah he made himself subject to Tiglath-pileser in return for his help. As a result the Assyrians took Damascus in 732 BC and appointed Hoshea king of Israel in place of Pekah, taking over many towns in the north (2 Kings 16).

Hoshea rebelled (2 Kings 17:4), so Tiglath-pileser's son, Shalmaneser V, attacked and captured Samaria after three years (722/1).

The next Assyrian king, Sargon II (Isaiah 20:1) records deporting '27,290 of its inhabitants together with their chariots... and the gods in whom they trusted'.

Assyria and Judah

Hezekiah, son of Ahaz, rejected his father's policy of submission to Assyria and so Assyrian forces marched to subdue him.

Although Sennacherib overran Judah (701 BC), he was unable to take Jerusalem or capture Hezekiah, a fact on which Assyrian

records and the biblical narratives agree. Hezekiah retained his throne but paid tribute, as did his son Manasseh.

When Assyrian control slackened in the west, after 635 BC, Josiah may have extended the frontiers of Judah again.

40 A message of comfort

There *is* comfort for God's people in their distress: he is coming as he promised (1-11; see chapter 35). Mortals are frail as grass beside him (6-8): yet he is tender and gentle as a shepherd with his lambs (11).

Israel's God is the Creator: incomparable, eternal (12-26). Yet he never stops caring for his people (27-31).

▶ **Double (2)** Either 'in full', or possibly 'a double portion in place of the punishment for her sins'.

▶ **Verses 3-5** These verses sum up the mission of John the Baptist, see Luke 3:1-6. Verse 3 is quoted (from the Greek text) in Matthew 3:3.

'A voice cries out, "Prepare in the wilderness a road for the Lord!"' Chapter 40 of Isaiah speaks hope to God's people.

▶ **Verses 6-8** See James 1:10-11; 1 Peter 1:24-25 (quoting from the Greek text).
▶ **Verse 11** See also Ezekiel 34. Jesus took up this picture, describing himself as the good shepherd; see John 10:11 and his parable of the lost sheep, Luke 15:4-7.

41 'Fear not... I will help you'

God's tone is that of the stern lawyer as he brings the nations to court (1). But with his own people he is infinitely loving and tender (8ff.). He is at hand to help. They have nothing to fear.

▶ **From the east (2)... from the north (25)** 44:28 names the new conqueror, Cyrus the Persian (from Israel the route was north, then east).
▶ **Verse 4** God as the Lord of history is a constant theme in Isaiah 40 – 66.
▶ **My servant (9)** The nation as God's servant is a recurring theme in Isaiah. See e.g. 43:10.
▶ **Verses 21-24** God calls the gods of the nations – who are no gods – to account. They can neither predict things to come nor make sense of the past. Only God, the one true God, can do that.

42 A light for the nations

A new theme begins to unfold, alongside the forecast of Babylon's downfall: God's plan to open the eyes of the whole world and bring them salvation. This was, from the very beginning, the intended role of Israel (Genesis 22:18).

Chapter 42 begins abruptly with the unexplained, 'Here is my servant'. It is left to the reader to work out exactly who this is. The servant is 'Israel', and at the same time someone else (49:3-5). As the picture develops through the four 'Servant Songs' – 42:1-4 (7); 49:1-6; 50:4-11; 52:13 – 53:12 – it becomes clear that no ordinary person or people fits the description.

The New Testament writers are in no doubt that the servant Isaiah foresees, the one who will save all humanity by suffering on their behalf, is Jesus Christ (Matthew 12:15-21). They have Christ's own authority for saying so (Mark 10:45; Luke 4:16-21; 22:37). See also Acts 8:32-35; 1 Peter 2:21-24.

God presents his servant (1-4), then commissions him (5-9). A new song follows the announcement of 'new things' to come (10-13). It is a song of praise and a battle song. Then God continues his address with a fresh promise of help (14-17) and a plea that this time his people listen (18-20). The exiles need to learn from their experience (21-25).

43 God's unfailing love and care

In all his people's sufferings God is beside them (2). He will set them free again, simply because he loves them (4ff.). In verse 8 the scene is again the courtroom (as in chapter 41): both Israel and the nations are on trial. By their constant disobedience, God's people have forfeited all right to his care (22-24) – yet he forgives (25).
▶ **Verse 1** The nation came into being when God brought them out of Egypt and made a covenant with them at Sinai.
▶ **Verses 16-17** The crossing of the Red Sea at the exodus from Egypt.

44 – 45 No God but God; the forecast of Israel's return

These chapters continue the themes that run through the whole section: Israel as God's servant, the object of his love (44:1-5); God as Lord of history, the only one able to draw back the veil on the future (44:6ff.); ridicule of the lifeless no-gods that humans worship (9-20); God's promise that he will set his people free.

In 44:26 – 45:8 we are taken a stage further. The general promise that God will rescue his people becomes specific. In the reign of Cyrus, Jerusalem and its Temple will be rebuilt (see on Ezra 1:1-4ff.). Verses 9-13: God speaks to his questioners. We return to the courtroom at verse 20.
▶ **Cyrus (44:28)** Did God reveal the king's actual name, far in advance? There is no doubt he could, though Old Testament predictions are rarely so specific (see Joshua 6:26 and 1 Kings 16:34 for one example). He has already set out his unique claim to be the Lord of history, the only one who can truly foretell the future or know the meaning of the past.
▶ **45:22-25** God's love reaches beyond Israel to the world. The New Testament applies verse 23 directly to Christ; see Philippians 2:10-11.

God promises his people rivers and springs of water, even in the desert (Isaiah 41), a symbol of life, blessing and prosperity. This boy is enjoying the water from the ancient springs at Jericho.

46 – 47 Proud Babylon will fall

See also chapters 13 – 14 above on Babylon. The indictment of pagan gods reaches its climax in the passive submission of the Babylonian gods Bel and Nebo. These dumb idols burden the backs of their worshippers. The real God is one who carries his people's burdens, who has power not only to speak but to act. Chapter 47 (like 14:4-21) is a taunt-song to the metre of a funeral procession. Babylon will be shown as little mercy as the Babylonians have shown others.
▶ **47:1** 'Virgin daughter', the city of Babylon; 'Chaldeans', see on 23:13.

48 God's patient love for faithless Israel

From Babylon, we turn back to Israel. This chapter is the climax to what has gone before in 40 – 47. It marks a break in the section as a whole: chapters 49 – 55 are 'part two'. There are harsh words for God's people. Stubborn, deaf to God, treacherous and rebellious (4, 8) they have fully deserved all they have suffered. Verses 1-11 largely concern the past, 12-22 the future. All that God foretold in their past history has come true (3-6). Now he is telling them

'This is the end for Babylon's gods,' cries the prophet in chapter 46. This fearsome terracotta demon comes from Babylon.

> 66 *Can a mother forget the baby at her breast and have no compassion on the child she has borne? Though she may forget, I will not forget you! See, I have engraved you on the palms of my hands.* 99
>
> 49:15-16

something new (6, 14). God always purposed peace for his people (18), but there could be 'no peace for the wicked'. Now the moment of liberation has come: he says 'Go out from Babylon, go free!'

> ▶ **Verse 16** Most versions include the Hebrew sentence which follows the quotation. This may be an addition, a biographical note, or it may introduce the Servant of the Lord, as God's spokesman in 17ff.

49 – 50 'I will never forget you'

Part two of the larger section (40 – 55) opens with the second 'Servant Song' (49:1-6). God's servant is Israel (3), yet also one who will bring Israel back (5). Comfort, compassion and restoration are the keynotes of 49:8 – 50:3.

In the third Servant Song (50:4-9), for the first time we glimpse his suffering and rejection (6ff; see chapter 53). But nothing can deflect him from his purpose.

> ▶ **50:1** God did not divorce his unfaithful 'wife', Israel; he brought her lovingly home (see Hosea 3:1; Hosea was declaring his message to Israel at the same time as Isaiah proclaimed God's word in Judah).
> ▶ **50:10-11** This 'tailpiece' to the Song concerns the people's response.

51 – 52:12 An end to suffering

God always keeps his promises. As he kept his word to childless Abraham and Sarah, so he will save his people and with them all the nations (51:1-8). It is the Almighty God, the Creator, who makes this promise (12-16). We hear the prophet's voice break in at 9-11. The terrible time of suffering is past (17-23). It is time to shake off grief and lethargy. There is good news. God is about to escort his people home (52:1-12).

> ▶ **Rahab (51:9)** See on 30:7.
> ▶ **52:3-6** God will lead a second exodus, from Babylon , like the escape from Egypt long before.
> ▶ **52:11** When Jerusalem was captured, the

Babylonians robbed the Temple of all its treasures. The people will take them back. See Ezra chapter 1.

52:13 – 53:12 God's suffering Servant

This fourth Servant Song is the best-known of all. The scene shifts from the joyous home-coming to the lonely figure who paid the price of it. How different this is from the people's understanding of the future king: no acclaim, only rejection – a figure despised and ignored. Could God's hand be in this (53:1)? Yes, 'It was my will that he should suffer'. He 'will bear the punishment of many and for his sake I will forgive them' (10-11).

The New Testament echoes Isaiah, seeing in Jesus the ultimate fulfilment of these words. He it was who willingly gave his life that all might be forgiven, taking 'the place of many sinners' to reconcile God and his people, 'undoing' the effects of that original downfall. Compare 53:5-9 with Matthew 27:11-13, 26-31, 41-43, 57-60. Compare 53:4-6, 10-12 with Romans 5:6-9, 18-19; 1 Peter 2:21-24; Philippians 2:5-11.

54 – 55 'Come to me'

God pledges himself in tender, unswerving, enduring love to his people. Though 'mountains and hills may crumble' God's love for them will never end (54:10). In peace and security the foundations of a new and dazzling city are laid (54:11ff.; and compare Revelation 21:18ff.). 'Come to me,' God invites. 'I make no charge.' And his responsive people, in turn, call the nations to come (55:1-7).

The vision in these later chapters of Isaiah (as earlier, at 2:2-4; 4:2-6; 9:2-7; 11 – 12; 25; 35) goes far beyond the events of the actual return from exile. The restoration of Israel which took place then merges into a vision of the final glorious day when sin and sorrow will be no more, and the whole Israel of God (see Romans 9 – 11; Galatians 3) will be for ever at home with the Lord (Revelation 21).

56 – 66
Shame and glory

In these chapters we return to a restored Jerusalem, and life back home, after the exile. Scenes of sin and failure mingle with scenes of future glory.

56:1-8 For all the nations
There is nothing exclusive about the love of God. There is a place among his people for all who will follow and obey him (1-8), even the most despised. God's own Temple is meant to be a 'house of prayer' for all the nations.

56:9 – 59:21 Israel accused
From the ideal (58:1-8) we come down to a far different reality. Spiritual and secular leaders alike have gone soft and failed in their jobs (56:9-12). The people have been guilty of many sins – the charges are quite specific. They have run after the Canaanite gods, sacrificing at the hill-top shrines and joining in sexual rites and child-sacrifice (57:4-13; see 2 Chronicles 33:1-9). This makes a mockery of their religious observance (including rigorous fasting): they neither love God nor their fellow human beings (58).

Chapter 59 crystallizes the issue. The prophet points the people to the heart of the matter – the problem is their sin which cuts them off from God (59:1-2). His indictment of a society rotten to the core, riddled with lies, dishonesty, injustice, malice and violence (1-8) leads to confession (9-15a) and God's answer to the problem (15b-21).

Two ways are opening up in these chapters: a safe path that leads to blessing for those who respond to God (the righteous); a dangerous road leading to destruction for those who choose not to (the wicked). What God, in his amazing love, wants for his people is made plain in 57:14-19; 58:6-14; 59:20-21.

▶ **Beds (57:2,** some versions) i.e. their graves.

▶ **57:5-8** The pagan rites involved prostitution. Idolatrous Israel, unfaithful to God, is pictured as a prostitute.

▶ **Molech (57:9)** See on 30:33.

▶ **Public square (59:14)** The 'lawcourt' of the day, where cases were heard and justice was dispensed.

▶ **59:21** Compare this with the new covenant described in Jeremiah 31:31-34.

60 – 62 The glorious city
In the unbridgeable gap between the shame of Israel and her glory stands the figure of God the Avenger and Redeemer (59:16-20). Now judgment gives way to promise realized.

Chapter 60 pictures the incredible transformation of Jerusalem: filled with glory, light, joy, excitement. The return to God's favour is seen in very 'earthly' terms: fabulous wealth, power, influence. Even so, this is a very different earth from the one we know (17-22); and the New Testament will translate Isaiah's concept into spiritual and universal terms (see on chapters 54 – 55 above).

The unnamed voice in 61:1ff. is that of the Servant. The passage is sometimes seen as a fifth Servant Song. (In Luke 4:16-21 Jesus announces his mission by reading these words.) In 61:5-9 God's people become the nation of priests he always intended them to be (Exodus 19:6; and see 1 Peter 2:9), breaking into a song of praise (10-11).

The day is coming (chapter 62) when God will be able to rejoice and delight in his people: a day to long for, pray for (6), prepare for (10).

▶ **60:6-7** 'Ephah', a Midianite tribe; 'Kedar' and 'Nebaioth', Arabian tribes. Their wealth lay in their camels, sheep and goats.

▶ **Double portion (61:7)** Here Isaiah has in mind the share of the firstborn son.

63:1-6 The Avenger
See also 59:16ff. Edom (which means red) with its capital, Bozrah, represents all the enemies of God's people. This is an appalling picture; but until the enemy is defeated, God's people cannot be set free (see Revelation 19:11-16).

63:7 – 64:12 The prophet prays
The prophet's prayer is very like a psalm. Recalling all God's past goodness and faithfulness, his acts of power in the days of Moses (63:7-14), leads to an impassioned

appeal (63:15ff.). Where is God's concern, his power now? Why does he not tear the heavens apart to come and rescue his people in their crying need? Is God unmoved? Will he do nothing?

▶ **63:9** Some translations render the Hebrew, 'the angel of his presence saved them', some 'not an angel but the Lord himself'. Either way, it is God making himself known, present, caring for his people. In Exodus 'the angel of the Lord' is often virtually synonymous with 'the Lord'.

65 – 66 God's answer: a new creation

God responds to the prophet. He has always been ready to help, but his people never sought him. He *will* answer the prayer for his people in a way which exceeds their wildest dreams. But the answer will be two-edged: for those who align themselves against him, total destruction, the sweeping away of every vestige of evil; for his faithful ones, life, joy, peace beyond imagining, in a heaven and earth made new.

So these final prophecies highlight two contrasting destinies, in a sharp play of light and darkness. God cannot overlook evil. Those who go their own sinful way (65:1-7, 11-14), who refuse to listen to God (66:3-4), will be judged. But God has a place reserved in his new world for those of humble faith (65:8; 66:2). The nation will be reborn (66:9), their suffering a thing of the past. These are the faithful ones (the 'remnant' of God's people). God is bringing the nations to judgment (66:18-19). Some he will spare, sending them to distant lands, to tell out his greatness to those who do not know him and to bring back those of his people still scattered abroad.

The final bright picture of Jerusalem, visited by pilgrims of all nations coming to worship God (66:23) has its dark shadow side in the fate of those who refuse God's mercy (24).

▶ **65:8** The bunch is poor, but it contains some good grapes which are not to be wasted.

▶ **Fortune, Destiny (65:11)** Pagan gods of fate, Gad and Meni, to whom sacrificial offerings were made.

▶ **65:25** See 11:6-9.

▶ **66:19** Isaiah pictures people streaming in from distant lands – from Spain (Tarshish) in the far west, from Africa (Put, Lud) to the south, from the far north, Anatolia (Tubal), and across from Greece (Javan).

Jeremiah

Summary

A reluctant prophet's anguished warnings of God's judgment in the years leading up to the fall of Jerusalem in 587 BC.

Prologue: chapter 1
Jeremiah's call

•

Part 1: 2–45
Jeremiah's life and prophetic messages to his own people during the reigns of Judah's last five kings

•

Part 2: 46–51
Jeremiah's prophecies against other nations

•

Postscript: 52
The fall of Jerusalem and its Temple to Babylon: exile for the people

Jeremiah appears on the scene about 100 years after Isaiah. He was born into a priestly family at Anathoth (Anata), a few miles north of Jerusalem, about 650 BC, and was called to be God's prophet in 627. 2 Kings 22 – 25 and 2 Chronicles 34 – 36 provide the historical background to Jeremiah's prophecies.

The power of Assyria was already crumbling when he began to declare God's message to Judah. For 40 years – through the reigns of Judah's last five kings – Jeremiah warned of coming disaster and appealed in vain to the nation to turn back to God. With the death of godly King Josiah in 609, religious and political affairs worsened. Judah was caught in the crossfire between two contending world powers: Babylon to the north, and a resurgent Egypt to the south.

Babylon emerged supreme, to become the instrument of God's judgment on his own people. In 598/7 Babylon defeated Judah and King Nebuchadnezzar put Zedekiah on the throne in Jerusalem. Despite Jeremiah's advice, Zedekiah rebelled against Babylon and precipitated the most serious defeat Judah had ever known. In 587 Nebuchadnezzar's army broke into Jerusalem, destroying the city and its Temple, and took the people captive into exile.

Jeremiah was offered a comfortable life at court, but chose instead to remain in Judah. When Gedaliah (the governor appointed by Nebuchadnezzar) was murdered, the people fled to Egypt, taking Jeremiah with them. As far as we know he ended his days there, still declaring God's words to those who refused to listen.

Jeremiah was not the only prophet of his day. Among his contemporaries were Habakkuk and Zephaniah – and Ezekiel among the exiles in Babylon. (Daniel is set in the Babylonian court from about 605 BC on.) But Jeremiah stands out, a lonely figure: isolated by a message from God which made him increasingly unpopular; branded a traitor for advocating submission to Babylon. He was imprisoned and often in danger of his life. Yet this sensitive, unselfconfident man never compromised his message from God. He could not help but declare the terrible fate he saw in store for his nation, and he grieved over their stubborn refusal to take notice. The times were dark; his message sombre; yet to write him off as a born pessimist is quite wrong. There is a strong streak of hope running through Jeremiah's prophecies. After the judgment, after the exile, God will restore the joy and prosperity of his people in their homeland.

Judah's last kings

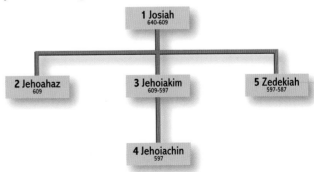

1 Josiah
640-609

2 Jehoahaz
609

3 Jehoiakim
609-597

5 Zedekiah
597-587

4 Jehoiachin
597

The book

The book of Jeremiah, like those of the other prophets, is probably best viewed as an anthology of his sayings which grew from the scroll dictated to Baruch (chapter 36) with bits added to it at various times. It is a glorious mixture of literary forms: prose and poetry, taunt and lament, acted parable, biography and history. The material is not arranged in historical order, which makes some of it difficult to set against the right background. The key events of Jeremiah's lifetime are listed in the table, and dates are indicated in the text wherever possible.

The message

Jeremiah's message can be summarized roughly as follows:

■ At first he calls for genuine repentance: if God's people turn to him, they may escape judgment.

■ From the time of the burning of the scroll (chapter 36; King Jehoiakim's fourth year) he tells them judgment is inevitable. The Babylonians will conquer them. The best course is to submit.

■ After the fall of Jerusalem in 587 Jeremiah encourages his stricken people: God's purposes still hold (31:31-34); he *will* restore them.

The prophecies are much concerned with the fact that the old Sinai covenant binding God and nation has broken down. Soon there will be a new covenant.

Unusually among the prophets, Jeremiah often reveals his personal feelings, especially the 'confessions' of his struggles with God: see 11:18 – 12:4; 15:10-21; 18:19-23; 20:7-18. See also 'Portrait of Jeremiah'.

One of Jeremiah's first two visions was of a cooking pot about to tip over. Destruction was 'boiling over' onto God's people from Babylon, the great power of the north.

1 – 45
Jeremiah's life and messages to God's people

Part one of the book contains all Jeremiah's prophecies to his own people. There are subsections within this. Chapters 2 – 25 record prophecies against Judah and Jerusalem during the reigns of four kings: Josiah, Jehoiakim, Jehoiachin and Zedekiah. Chapters 26 – 45 are linked with events in Jeremiah's life. Within this section, chapters 37 – 45 focus on stories of the prophet during and after the reign of Zedekiah, before and after the fall of Jerusalem to the Babylonian army.

1 The reluctant prophet

The date is 627 BC. Jeremiah is a young man, probably in his early twenties, and as reluctant to become God's spokesman as Moses before him (Exodus 3:10 – 4:17). But about one thing he had no doubt. His message was a word from God himself. 'The word of the Lord came to me' runs as a refrain right through the book, from first to last. In this lies his certainty, and his compulsion.

Straightway Jeremiah is given *vision* (11ff.). God shows and explains to the prophet what he is going to do: what Jeremiah must tell the people. They will not want to hear. They will be against Jeremiah from the outset. But God will protect him. The pattern of Jeremiah's whole life is set out in this initial encounter with God.

▶ **Verses 1-3** See introduction.

▶ **Verse 10** The prophet's ministry is negative and positive, destructive and constructive, about judgment and promise. He will speak to his own people, and to the nations.

▶ **Almond... watching (11-12)** The two words sound alike in the Hebrew: 'shaqed/shoqed'.

▶ **Verse 13** The forces of Babylon are like a cauldron about to pour its scalding contents on Judah. In this period of Jewish history trouble always came from the north: first the powerful armies of Assyria; then, in Jeremiah's day, the Babylonians.

2 – 3:10 The case against God's people

Chapters 2 – 24 are all prophecies against Judah and Jerusalem. Jeremiah begins (2:1-3) with a tender portrayal of 'first love': the time when the nation was faithful to God, when God led them towards their new land, protecting them from harm.

But in Canaan Israel betrayed God (4-8). And now God states his case against them (9ff.). The heathen nations are at least loyal to their idols (10-11). Not so the

Portrait of Jeremiah
David Barton

Jeremiah lived when the political map of the ancient world was being redrawn. Assyria was weakening, Babylon rising, and Egypt was eager to assert its authority. The tiny kingdom of Judah, caught in the middle of these great powers, would always have been under threat. But it was doubly threatened by a belief in its own invincibility. A century earlier Jerusalem had miraculously survived destruction. In consequence people came to have a dogmatic belief that the city would never fall, and that King David's dynasty would not end.

It was against this turbulent background and the stubborn refusal of his own people to face the tough political realities of a changing world that Jeremiah's life and ministry was shaped.

Images from childhood
Jeremiah was born in Anathoth, a village to the north-east of Jerusalem, where his father was a hereditary village priest. Jeremiah was a younger son in what was clearly a happy family. All his life Jeremiah was able to recall the images and experiences of his childhood.

He loved the natural world. He watched the migration of the birds (8:7). He knew the nesting habits of the partridge (17:11). But with his prophetic sight these things became something more: the almond tree putting forth its blossom, the farmer clearing his ground, were, for him, revelations of the mystery of God.

The reluctant prophet
Into this life Jeremiah's call comes. He was from the beginning a reluctant prophet, and he never ceased to discuss the trials of his office with God (1:6; 17:16; 20:7-9). From these and other passages we glimpse the sheer burden of the task he has to bear. He does not seem to be made of the stern stuff prophets are supposed to be made of.

Shaped by suffering
We sense how hard it must have been for him to be forbidden marriage, with its promise of a loved wife and children (16:1-9). Sensitive, with an exceptional capacity for affection, he was given a mission 'to pluck up and to break down, to destroy and to overthrow' (1:10) among the people he loved.

This was a path of pain, from which, though he might grumble, Jeremiah never flinched. His prophecies are moving and, at times, shocking. He longs to end his mission, but the power of God will not leave him: 'If I say I will no longer mention him... there is in my heart as it were a burning fire' (20:9).

The text, sometimes biography, sometimes autobiography, allows us to sense the way in which the suffering that comes from his calling deeply shapes the character of the man. His insights grow out of the personal experiences of a life lived against the grain of society but in total loyalty to God.

Loneliness
It is probable that early on in his ministry Jeremiah was associated with the reforms of Josiah. This involved closing down Judah's high places to centre the religious life of the nation on Jerusalem, a move that would bring conflict with his family. There is an underlying hurt in the prophecies of chapter 1 which probably stems from this. From now on loneliness is a

Jeremiah was born at Anathoth, in the barren hills just north of Jerusalem.

▶▶

characteristic of Jeremiah's life.

Jehoiakim, Josiah's son, was not sympathetic to his father's policy, and in reaction Jeremiah, with another prophet Uriah, came forward to defend the purity of the Temple worship (chapter 7). Jehoiakim saw this as open defiance and ordered their arrest. Uriah fled to Egypt, but was eventually brought back and put to death, while Jeremiah seems to have been protected by the powerful family of Shaphan (chapter 26), who are scribes, and who continue to be his support in the coming years.

Judah under attack

Increasingly now the tiny kingdom of Judah is threatened from the north-east. Jeremiah was convinced that, through Nebuchadnezzar, God would punish Judah for their faithlessness (27:5-11). He advised surrender without delay (38:17).

It was a terrible period: the king, the authorities and other prophets took a contrary view. The people hated Jeremiah. He was banned from the Temple. But, unable to abandon his task, he dictated his prophecies to Baruch, and they were then taken in to the king. The vivid description in Jeremiah 36 of the king contemptuously cutting off and burning the prophecies as they were read, underlines Jeremiah's isolation.

The warring parties of the court saw their opportunity. This was dangerous defeatism. So they took measures to remove him and Jeremiah was arrested and thrown into a well. It would have been difficult to kill a prophet in cold blood, so he was left to starve and to die (chapter 38). Only the intervention of a brave palace servant saves him.

Trust and hope

Yet Jeremiah was not defeatist. Although, during this long period, he prophesied against the false security of the king's advisers, he staked his personal faith on God's future restoration of Israel by buying a field and carefully preserving the deeds (chapter 32).

He might be called, mockingly, old 'Terror on every side', from his repeated warning (20:4; also 6:25; 20:10; 46:5). But he still points to the promise of God the other side of destruction. 'For I know the plans I have for you, says the Lord, plans for welfare and not for evil, to give you a future and a hope' (29:11).

That hope was powerfully expressed to the exiled Jews in Babylon in the vision of the two baskets of figs (24:5-7). And at the most tragic moment of his life, when, in Babylon's final attack, all the leaders were taken off into exile, he writes astonishing words of hope: 'God declares: I shall bring you back to the place from which I exiled you' (29:14).

The prophet who knew what it was to be shunned and ill-treated had never lost his own personal sense that God was always with him. Now, at his people's darkest time, he can speak with conviction of the God who will never forget them.

A new beginning

It is these prophecies that give us Jeremiah's final and lasting insight. Preaching for so long (his ministry lasted some 40 years) to an obdurate people, Jeremiah became convinced that there had to be a new beginning. The old covenant, conditional on people's obedience to the law, had failed. Jeremiah foresees that it will be replaced by a new covenant, within which God will take the initiative, touching each human heart directly, revealing himself as a God of compassion and overwhelming love. It is a vision of the era of the spirit, of which Paul speaks in Romans – 'the law of the spirit of life'.

But, before Paul wrote that, Jesus himself had turned to Jeremiah for words and images to sum up his own ministry. Often Jeremiah's life resembles that of the bleak passion of Jesus in its powerlessness and utter dependence on God. So it is not surprising that, on the night before his crucifixion, Jesus should bring Jeremiah's prophecy to fulfilment: 'This... is the new covenant sealed by my blood' (Luke 22:20).

people of the living God. Their offence is set before them in a series of vivid pictures. They prefer their own polluted water to God's fresh spring (13). They would sooner turn to Egypt and Assyria for help than to God (18). The vine of Israel has gone wild (21). Like a wife turned common prostitute, the nation has run after foreign gods (20, 23-25, 33; 3:1-10).

3:6-10: 'Israel' here refers to the northern kingdom whose people had been carried into exile a century before, in 722/1 BC (verse 8). King Josiah's religious reforms (beginning in 621 BC), far-reaching though they were, did not change the heart of the nation. The people, God says, did not come back to him in sincerity. It was just pretence.

▶ **Baal (2:8)** The Canaanite god.
▶ **Cyprus/Kittim... Kedar (2:10)** From west to east (Kedar is in Arabia): the whole pagan world.
▶ **2:13** Compare Jesus' words: John 4:13-14; 7:37.
▶ **Memphis... Tahpanhes (2:16)** Cities of Egypt: Memphis near Cairo; Tahpanhes a frontier town in the eastern Nile delta, on the route to Palestine.
▶ **Strangers (2:25,** some versions) Pagan gods.
▶ **3:1** Such a thing was unlawful; see Deuteronomy 24:1-4.

3:11 – 4:4 'Return, O Israel'
Even now God will save his people if they really repent. He will bring them back from exile a united nation (3:18) whose worship is a living reality, not a mere ritual (3:16; 4:4; and compare 31:31-34).
▶ **The Ark/Covenant Box (3:16)** In which the law was kept in the inner sanctuary of the Temple. It is no longer needed when God's law is written on every heart.
▶ **Shameful gods (24)** A euphemism for 'Baal'.
▶ **4:4** All Jewish boy babies were circumcised when they were eight days old, as a sign that they had entered into covenant relationship with God: Genesis 17:1-14. (There was no female circumcision, but Israel's women were God's covenant people too.) No external mark, however, can turn a person into God's child without an accompanying 'circumcision' of heart, mind and will.

4:5-31 Approaching disaster
Destruction and devastation are about to fall on Judah. Jeremiah is given a preview of the nation's collapse before the Babylonian army which fills him with unspeakable horror (19-31).
▶ **Verse 5** The trumpet sounded the alarm for war.
▶ **Verse 11** The scorching desert wind is a symbol of destruction.
▶ **Dan (15)** The northernmost town in the land; first in the path of the invader.

Major events of Jeremiah's lifetime

627 Jeremiah called to be God's prophet. Death of Ashurbanipal, last great king of Assyria.
621 Discovery of the book of the law. King Josiah's great reformation begins.
612 Nineveh, capital of Assyria, falls to Babylon.
609 The Egyptian army marches north to bolster collapsing Assyria. Josiah intercepts it at Megiddo and is killed. On his return from Assyria, Pharaoh Necho deposes the new king, Jehoahaz, placing Jehoiakim on the throne.

605 Egyptian forces routed at Carchemish by Nebuchadnezzar of Babylon.
604 Nebuchadnezzar subdues Syria, Judah and Philistine cities.
598 Alliance with Egypt brings the Babylonian forces down on Judah again.
597 King Jehoiakim dies, Jerusalem falls to Babylon after a two-month siege. The new king, Jehoiachin, is deported with others to Babylon. His uncle, Zedekiah, is put on the throne.

588 Under pressure from the pro-Egypt party, Zedekiah breaks faith with Babylon. Jerusalem under siege for 18 months.
587 The Babylonian army breaks into Jerusalem. The people are deported; the city plundered and burned; the Temple destroyed. Three months later, governor Gedaliah is murdered. Jeremiah is taken to Egypt.

God accuses his people of unfaithfulness on 'every high hill' (3:6). The pagan Canaanite shrines were typically sited on heights and hill-tops. This round 'high place' was built in the city of Megiddo about 2500 BC.

opposite: Among the Canaanite practices Israel was told to avoid was the erection of memorial pillars like these uncovered at Byblos in Lebanon (ancient Phoenicia).

▶ **Verses 19-21** Jeremiah's grief – or possibly that of the land, or Jerusalem.

▶ **Verse 23** God is unmaking the earth; see Genesis 1:2.

▶ **Verse 30** A picture of Jerusalem (the 'daughter of Zion'), unrepentant still; still seeking foreign aid.

5 National corruption

God searches in vain for a vestige of truth and justice among his people. The nation is steeped in idolatry; happy with a rotten society; untroubled by conscience. God and his prophets alike are disregarded. It is false prophecy the people want to hear. God has no option but to punish.

▶ **Verse 1** recalls Abraham's prayer for Sodom (Genesis 18:22-32). God would have spared the city for 10 innocent people. Here, even one would save Jerusalem.

▶ **Verse 28** Justice and care for the helpless have always been God's special concern, enshrined in the law and upheld by the prophets.

6 Declaration of war

All God's warnings have fallen on deaf ears. His call to walk 'the good way' (16) has met with flat refusal. So God has rejected his people (30) and turned them over to the invading armies. Even Jerusalem will be besieged.

▶ **Benjamin (1)** This was Jeremiah's own tribe, occupying land just north of Jerusalem. Tekoa, Beth-haccherem are two hills south of the city.

▶ **Shepherds (3)** A picture of the enemy encampments.

▶ **Noon (4)** It was not usual to attack in the heat of the day.

▶ **Sheba (20)** In Arabia; famous for the incense it exported.

7 – 8:3 In the Temple

The people had a superstitious faith in the Temple. They thought God would always protect Jerusalem as he had done in 701 (see 2 Kings 18 – 19; Isaiah 36 – 37) because his Temple was there. They were wrong. God sends Jeremiah to stand at the Temple gate and tell them that God knows the difference between religious ritual and real religion (7:10). He sees all that goes on (9). Jerusalem is no more sacrosanct than Shiloh, the sanctuary the Philistines destroyed (see 1 Samuel 4). Even now, if only they will stop what they are doing, change their ways, God will let them go on living in the land he gave them (7). Security and well-being rest on obedience to God (23).

▶ **7:6** See on 5:28.

▶ **7:11** Jesus quoted these words of the Temple in his day (Matthew 21:13).

▶ **Ephraim (7:15)** The leading tribe of the breakaway northern kingdom.

▶ **Queen of heaven (7:18)** The fertility goddess Ashtoreth/Astarte/Ishtar, whose worship involved sexual rites and prostitution.

▶ **7:22** Jeremiah is not denying that the system of sacrifices was instituted at God's command (see Leviticus 1 – 7). But the people were substituting sacrifice for obedience. Jeremiah is urging them to get their priorities right. As Samuel said long before, 'To obey is better than sacrifice' (1 Samuel 15:22).

▶ **7:29** They must cut off their hair – either in mourning, or as a sign that they are no longer pledged to God.

▶ **Topheth (7:31)** See Isaiah 30:33.

8:4-17 Condemned by God

The people refuse to repent. They are aided and abetted by religious smooth-talkers: the scribes (professional interpreters of God's law), the 'wise' to whom they turned for advice (see 2 Samuel 14:2ff.; 20:16ff.), the prophets and the priests. All alike are motivated by self-interest.

8:18 – 9:26 Grief on grief

It is not always clear here whether the speaker is Jeremiah, God or the people

Jeremiah contrasts the true, living God with lifeless idols, like Baal, the Canaanite fertility god to whom God's people offered sacrifices (11:17).

66 *The harvest is past, the summer has ended, and we are not saved...*
Oh, that my head were a spring of water and my eyes a fountain of tears!
I would weep day and night for the slain of my people. 99

8:20; 9:1

(Bible versions offer different options). Jeremiah shares God's own deep grief at his people's sin and its tragic consequences. Society is sick (9:3-6, 8): sick as a direct result of the nation abandoning God and his laws and going their own way (12-14). So inevitable has judgment become (15-16) that the professional mourners can already be called in (17).

▶ **Balm/medicine (8:22)** Gilead was famous for its healing ointment from very early times (Genesis 37:25).

▶ **Wormwood (9:15)** A bitter-tasting plant (as some versions translate), and so a symbol for sorrow.

▶ **9:25-26** Despite the outward mark of his covenant (see 4:4), God's people have made themselves like the pagan nations around. And like them they will be punished. See chapters 46 – 51.

10 The living God – and wooden idols

Idols made by human hands, no matter how elaborate they may be, are lifeless, powerless, motionless, speechless. Not so the God of Israel. It was he, not they, who created earth and sky (11ff.). (This was one of Isaiah's great themes: Isaiah 40:18-20; 44:9-20.) Now this same God is poised to destroy them (17ff.). Jeremiah can hear the enemy coming (22), as he prays.

▶ **Tarshish... Uphaz (9)** Tarshish, Tartessus in far-away Spain; Uphaz may be Ophir, famous for its gold.

▶ **Gather up your belongings (17)** Get ready to flee.

▶ **Shepherds (21)** Leaders.

▶ **Verses 23-25** Jeremiah's prayer on his people's behalf.

11:1-17 The broken covenant

The terms of God's covenant-agreement with his people, made at Sinai after the exodus (see Deuteronomy 5ff.), are still in force. By persistent disobedience to God's law, and by idol-worship, Judah has broken that agreement and come under the curse (see Deuteronomy 11:26-28; 27). Jeremiah must go and tell the people (another unpopular message). Nor does God want him to pray on their behalf (14; it sounds as if God has had many such pleas from the prophet!).

This chapter seems to belong to the period of reaction following Josiah's reforms (2 Kings 23).

11:18 – 12:17 Plot to kill Jeremiah

Jeremiah's message aroused such intense anger that the people of Anathoth, his home town, were prepared to kill him if he didn't stop (11:18-23). It is God, keeping his promise to protect the prophet, who alerts Jeremiah to the danger. The discovery leads Jeremiah to question God about the way evil people get on in the world (12:1-4). He is neither the first, nor the last, to puzzle over this (see Psalm 73; Habakkuk 1:12-13). In answer, God tells him there is worse to come (5-6)! Nonetheless, he *will* punish (7-13), and afterwards restore (14-17).

▶ **Jungle by the Jordan (12:5)** The Jordan runs below sea-level from Lake Galilee to the Dead Sea; and in Old Testament times the river was bordered by dense, steamy thickets which were the haunt of wild animals.

▶ **House, inheritance (7), vineyard (10)** Metaphors for the nation.

13 A dramatic parable

God makes use of many teaching methods to get his message across. The prophets sometimes act out their message (this is a feature of Ezekiel's ministry; it recurs in Jeremiah 18, 19, 32). The garment Jeremiah conceals so that it will be spoiled is variously translated loin-cloth, belt and shorts. Actions often speak louder than words, and stick in the mind. Here Jeremiah announces that Judah and Jerusalem will be thoroughly ruined, like his garment. He was full of grief at announcing God's vengeance (17), though he had earlier cried out for it (11:20): 'If you will not listen... I will cry bitterly.'

▶ **Perath/Euphrates (4-7)** This may be Parah, 6km/4 miles north-east of Anathoth. Or it may refer, as elsewhere, to the Euphrates, some 550km/350 miles from Jerusalem, and represent the captivity and exile of the nation.

▶ **King and queen mother (18)** Almost certainly Jehoiachin and Nehushta (see 2 Kings 24:8-16).

14:1 – 15:9 Drought!

There is severe and prolonged drought (14:1-6). The people once again appeal to God (7-9). But God will not listen (10-12). Neither will he hear Jeremiah's pleas that they have been duped by the lies of false prophets (13ff). Yet Jeremiah goes on praying for them (19-22) until God's terrible answer in 15:1.

▶ **Sword, famine, pestilence (14:12)** 'War, starvation, disease', all regarded, from earliest times, as punishments from God. The three together imply full-scale judgment (see also 16:4; 24:10; Ezekiel 14:21; Revelation 6:8; 18:8).

▶ **Your glorious throne (14:21)** The Temple.

▶ **Moses and Samuel (15:1)** Both interceded successfully for the nation (Exodus 32; 1 Samuel 12:19-25).

▶ **15:4** Under Manasseh the nation reached an all-time low: see 2 Kings 21; 2 Chronicles 33.

15:10-21 Jeremiah's distress

In deep suffering Jeremiah comes to God, praying *against* those who have paid back his faithful service and his care for them with hatred, making his life a misery. There is justice in his plea (though the teaching of Jesus goes beyond that: Matthew 5:43-48; Luke 23:34). It is for God's sake that Jeremiah is in trouble. It is God's cause, and in rejecting him they reject God.

God answers the prophet's self-pity with the strong reassurance he needs (19ff).

16 No time to marry

God's instruction to Jeremiah is plain: 'do not marry'. By remaining single, in a society where this was almost unheard of, Jeremiah becomes a living symbol of God's message. Very soon there will be the most terrible famine and slaughter in Jerusalem. This is no time, no place, to raise a family. As God removes his peace and his love from them (5) the people will at last know him as the Almighty (21). Yet God still has a future for them (14-15), and the prophet declares his confidence in God (19-20).

▶ **Verses 6-7** Customs connected with mourning, some of them pagan (see Leviticus 19:27-28).

17 Hope for the hopeless

This chapter contains a mixture of different material: a prophecy of judgment (1-4, in

Jeremiah was based in Jerusalem, where all his warnings fell on deaf ears. This view looks south from the walls of the Old City of Jerusalem into the Kidron Valley.

Someone who trusts in God is like a tree with its roots close to water, safe from drought. Jeremiah 17:7-8 echoes the words of Psalm 1.

prose); a Wisdom psalm (5-8, like Psalm 1); a personal poetic prophecy-cum-lament; and an early prose prophecy which offers hope of escaping judgment (19-27).

▶ **Verse 1** An iron stylus was used to incise inscriptions on rock or stone. The nation's sin is as permanently engraved, right at the 'heart' of things.

▶ **Asherah (2)** See on Isaiah 17:8.

▶ **Verses 14-18** This is Jeremiah's prayer. For verse 18, see on 15:10-21.

18 The potter and the clay

This is another dramatized parable (see on chapter 13). Like the human potter, God has the unquestionable right to remould the spoilt nation. We can never simply assume that things will always be the way they are (7-10).

Again, Jeremiah's unpopular message leads to threats against his life. In verses 19-23 he is so touched on the raw by those who spurn his God-given message that he comes out with a really vengeful prayer (very different from his reaction in 13:17): 'Do not forgive...' See on 15:10-21. 'Self-justification, cursing and vengeance in the Psalms' also looks at this issue.

▶ **Verse 1ff.** The same image is used in Isaiah (29:15, 16; 45:9; 64:8) and taken up by Paul in Romans 9:20-21.

▶ **Sirion (14,** some versions) Mt Hermon, usually capped with snow all year round.

▶ **East wind (17)** 'Trouble', see 4:11.

19:1 – 20:6 Jeremiah in trouble

Jeremiah breaks his pottery jar in another acted parable. Having got people's attention, he explains: God will break the city and people as surely and as irreparably as that jug.

Jeremiah goes straight from the Hinnom Valley to the Temple; and there his message lands him in trouble. With hands and feet made fast in the wooden stocks he pours out his heart to God.

▶ **Hinnom (19:2), Topheth (19:6,** etc.) See on Isaiah 30:33.

20:7-18 'A curse on the day I was born!'

Jeremiah was not a thick-skinned man; it hurt to be hated and ridiculed. Yet he *had* to make God's word known (9) – so his role as prophet put him under tremendous pressure.

His lament is an encouragement to all who feel as he does. Voicing his complaint to God brings him through to confident praise (13). Then he plunges into despair (14-18).

21 Zedekiah looks for a miracle

The year is 587, when Jerusalem was under siege in Judah's final struggle with Babylon. King Zedekiah turns to the prophet, hoping for a word of comfort, another miraculous reprieve (as in 701 against the Assyrians: 2 Kings 19). But none is forthcoming: God says defeat is certain. The only hope lies in surrender.

The story of Jerusalem's fall is told in 2 Kings 25 and 2 Chronicles 36. See too Jeremiah 39; 52.

▶ **Verse 8** God gives them the same choice, between the way that leads to life and the way that leads to death, as recorded in Deuteronomy (30:15-20).

22 King Jehoiakim warned

This prophecy is earlier than chapter 21. Jehoiakim reigned from 609 to 597 – the year Jerusalem first surrendered to Babylon; see 2 Kings 23:34 – 24:6 and 2 Chronicles 36:5-8.

The doom-laden diatribe in verses 13ff. contrasts Jehoiakim – who sees his kingship in terms of cedarwood palaces – with his godly father, Josiah. No one will mourn his passing or honour his death (the 'honours of a donkey', 19, is the ultimate insult).

Verses 24ff. concern Jehoiakim's 18-year-old son Jehoiachin (Coniah, 24) who reigned only three months (598) before he and his mother were indeed taken into exile with many other captives.

▶ **The dead (king) (10)** Probably King Josiah, killed at Megiddo. Good News Bible names Josiah and his son Jehoahaz (Shallum, 11, brother of Jehoiakim), who ruled only three months before being taken prisoner to Egypt by Pharaoh Necho on his return from Assyria in 609. Jehoahaz died in Egypt.

▶ **Lebanon, Bashan, Abarim/Moab (20)** Mountain ranges to the north, north-east and east of Judah.

▶ **Verse 30** The promised line of kings from David stops here. Jehoiachin's grandson Zerubbabel led the exiles home and became their governor, but not their king.

❝ *Like clay in the hand of the potter, so are you in my hand, O house of Israel.* **❞**

18:6

23 A stinging rebuke – and future hope

The government (1-8) and religious leaders (9ff.) alike receive a stinging rebuke. Misrule, and the lies pronounced in God's name, will not go unpunished.

Then comes a wonderful promise. One day God will set on the throne a king of his own choice (5-8). The deliverance from exile will put the old exodus from Egypt into the shade.

Verses 9-40 address the prophets. Those in the northern kingdom (Samaria) had served Baal. That was bad enough. But in Judah the prophets 'are all as bad as the people of Sodom and Gomorrah' (Genesis 18:20ff.)! With such a message, it is not surprising that Jeremiah encountered bitter hatred from the priests and prophets – as Jesus did (26:11; compare Matthew 21:45-46; 26:66).

▶ **Branch (5)** 'Descendant'; see Isaiah 4:2; 11:1. It is also a title for the Messiah in Zechariah 3:8; 6:12.

▶ **Adulterers/unfaithful (10)** Those who played God false by turning to pagan gods whose worship involved sexual rites and prostitution.

▶ **Burden (33)** Message.

24 Picture language

The date of Jeremiah's vision of the two baskets of figs in front of God's Temple is some time after 597 (verse 1; 'Jeconiah' is Jehoiachin). The exiles are the cream of God's people. (Ezekiel was among these first captives: Ezekiel 1:1-3. Daniel and his friends, according to Daniel 1:1-7, were in Babylon earlier still.) And God is shaping a future for them. For those who remain in Judah there is no future but destruction. Yet through Jeremiah God still perseveres with his 'bad figs'.

▶ **Heart (7)** The concept is all-inclusive: mind, will and emotions.

25 Coming invasion

The year is 605 (1), when Nebuchadnezzar of Babylon routed the Egyptians at Carchemish. For 23 years Jeremiah has been repeating God's message, and still the people remain unmoved. Now he tells them that the city will fall and they will serve the Babylonians for 70 years in exile. The judgment of God will also fall on the pagan nations who so richly deserve it, and on Babylon itself (12-38).

▶ **Verse 13** For Jeremiah's prophecies against the pagan nations, see chapters 46 – 51.

26 Jeremiah on trial

The date is 609, when King Jehoiakim's reign began, or soon after. The situation has links with chapter 7. It was one of those times when it is dangerous to declare the plain truth of God (15), and Jeremiah's straight speaking in the Temple almost cost him his life. The pronouncement that continued disobedience would lead to the destruction of the Temple so enraged the priests and prophets that they wanted him dead (11). But the name of God still counted for something among the rulers and people (16). Uriah (20ff.; known only from this passage) was less fortunate. The support of a court official, Ahikam saved the day for Jeremiah (24).

▶ **Shiloh (6)** See chapter 7.

▶ **Verse 16** The law said that a false prophet should be put to death (Deuteronomy 18:20). But Jeremiah is recognized as a true prophet of God.

▶ **Verse 18** See Micah 3:12. The prophet's words are remembered a century later (Micah was Isaiah's contemporary).

27 – 28 Rebel, or submit?

It is 597. The Babylonians have taken the first captives from Jerusalem and placed King Zedekiah on the throne. But the Babylonian king has troubles at home, and in the small nations to the west, including Judah, revolt is in the air.

Jeremiah walks the streets of the city wearing a wooden yoke in token of submission to Babylon. Only by servitude can Judah (27:12-15) and the nations (27:3-11) escape destruction. It was not a popular message, and provoked a head-on clash with the false prophets. Hananiah, claiming to have God's message, flatly contradicts Jeremiah, breaks the yoke (28:1-4, 10),

> **66** *'The days are coming,' declares the Lord, 'when I will make a new covenant with the house of Israel and with the house of Judah... I will put my law in their minds and write it on their hearts.'* **99**
>
> 31:31, 33

Two baskets of figs provided an object lesson for the prophet (chapter 24).

and tells the people what they want to hear. But time proves the truth of Jeremiah's words (28:15-17; and compare 27:19-22 with 52:17-23). Any prophet who falsely claims to speak for God is under sentence of death (Deuteronomy 18:20).

29 Letter to the exiles

The exiles to whom Jeremiah writes are the captives deported with King Jehoiachin, among them Ezekiel (see on Jeremiah 22). The false prophets predicted a swift return. Jeremiah advises the exiles to settle down and live a normal life: the exile will last 70 years. Then they *will* return. But even from Babylon his enemies try to stir up trouble for him (24ff.).

30 – 31 God's new covenant

At the nation's darkest hour, comes a message of hope. When it looks like total extinction, God promises his people (the whole nation, northern and southern kingdoms) a future. They will be saved (30:10ff.) and restored (18ff.). The exiles will return rejoicing to their homeland (31:7ff.). And a new covenant will replace the old one made at Sinai, which they have broken. This time God will remake them from within, giving them the power to do his will (31:31-34; and compare Romans 8:1-4; 2 Corinthians 5:17).

The words of Jeremiah here, like those of Isaiah, have a short-term and long-term future significance. He is talking of the actual return from exile, yet there is more to be fulfilled. The writers of the New Testament (which means 'new covenant') see in Jesus Christ the full realization of Jeremiah's prophecy (see Hebrews 8ff.). It is the Holy Spirit's work, through Christ, to 'write God's laws' on 'the hearts' of all believers.

▶ **Ephraim (31:9)** The most powerful northern tribe stands for all.

▶ **Shepherd (31:10)** For other references to this image of God see Genesis 49:24; Psalm 23; Isaiah 40:11; Ezekiel 34:11-31. The same image is applied to Jesus: John 10:7-16; Hebrews 13:20; 1 Peter 2:25; 5:4; Revelation 7:17.

▶ **Ramah, Rachel (31:15)** Rachel, mother of Joseph and Benjamin, died at Ramah near

Bethlehem. Jeremiah pictures her weeping for her exiled sons. Matthew 2:18 sees this as a picture of the grief caused by Herod's slaughter of the young children.

32 Jeremiah buys land

It is 588/7: Jerusalem is under siege, and Jeremiah's home town, Anathoth, in enemy hands. Cousin Hanamel is some optimist, coming to the imprisoned prophet (2-3) to try to sell land at a time like this! Amazingly, Jeremiah buys – and his purchase shouts the message: 'God has a future for Judah.' Everyone in the city must have heard about it. Jeremiah acts under orders from God; only afterwards does he admit his puzzlement (25). In answer God outlines his immediate, and his ultimate purpose for the nation.

Baruch, Jeremiah's secretary, makes his first appearance in verse 12. He comes to the fore in chapters 36 and 45. (Amongst the Deuterocanonical books is a 'Book of Baruch'.)

▶ **Verse 8** Land was a family heritage; it never came up for sale on the open market. See Leviticus 25:25.

▶ **Verse 35** See on Isaiah 30:33.

33 God's unbreakable promise

Jeremiah is still being held prisoner by King Zedekiah, as in the previous chapter. The theme is once again future restoration. Where God has torn down, he will rebuild (4, 6ff.). Joy and prosperity will return (10-11), and an ideal king will rule (14-16). This will happen as surely as night follows day according to God's ordering (20-21).

▶ **Verse 21** See 2 Samuel 7 and Numbers 25.

▶ **Two families (24)** Israel and Judah ('two kingdoms', New International Version), or, from verse 26, the family of Jacob (the nation) and the family of David (the kings).

34 Owners cheat on slaves

The date is still 588/7. After receiving God's message (1-7), King Zedekiah issues an order to free all Jewish slaves, perhaps hoping this will win God's favour. The law said Jewish slaves should be freed after six years (see Deuteronomy 15:12ff.), but the practice had lapsed. Now the owners free their slaves but go back on their undertaking to make this permanent. The slaves are forced into slavery again – and God condemns the owners as law-breakers.

▶ **Verses 4-5** See 39:7. There is no record of Zedekiah's death.

▶ **Verses 18-19** The ceremony invoked a similar fate on whoever broke the covenant. See Genesis 15.

▶ **Withdrawn/stopped its attack (21)** There was a temporary let-up while Nebuchadnezzar dealt with Pharaoh's army (37:5).

35 Nomad clan shames God's people

Chapters 35 and 36 take us back 10 years to the earlier siege of Jerusalem in the reign of King Jehoiakim (609-598). The Rechabites, pledged to abstain from wine and to a nomadic lifestyle, were descendants of Jehonadab, who took God's part against the Baal-worshippers in 2 Kings 10:15-23. (They are mentioned only here, in 2 Kings 10 and 1 Chronicles 2:55.) Fear of the invading army brings them to the city (11), where their obedience to a pledge made 200 years before puts the people of God to shame.

The Dung Gate of old Jerusalem: here people go about their business much as they did in Jeremiah's time.

36 King burns prophet's writings

This is one of the most vivid and dramatic chapters in the whole Bible. The year is 605/4. Jeremiah is banned from the Temple (5; no doubt to prevent him repeating what he said earlier, chapter 26). But the word of God cannot be stifled. The message is written; the prophet bides his time; and then within a single day it is read aloud three times – to the people fasting in the Temple, to the palace officials, and to the king himself. Jehoiakim (see also on chapter 22) may burn the scroll, but not even he has power to destroy the message, or prevent its fulfilment. Patiently, Jeremiah and secretary Baruch write the words again.

▶ **Scroll (2)** A long roll of papyrus or leather was used for written records in the days before books. Scrolls could be as much as 10m/33ft long and contain a large amount of material set out in columns.

▶ **Verse 30** Within three months of Jehoiakim's death his son was deported to Babylon.

37 – 38 Jeremiah locked up

Zedekiah is king, the year 588, and Jerusalem is temporarily reprieved from the besieging Babylonians (37:5). Jeremiah's counsel to surrender to an enemy from whom there will be no escape (37:8-10; 38:2) lands him in his deepest trouble yet. Setting out to inspect his property at Anathoth (32:6ff.) he is arrested as a deserter, beaten and shut up in a cellar. An appeal to the king, who is anxious to know God's word (37:3, 17; 38:14) but lacks faith and courage to act on it, wins him a move to the palace courtyard, but he remains in close custody on a daily ration of bread as long as supplies last (37:21). The next move is to the muddy bottom of the courtyard well, where he would have died but for Ebedmelech's appeal to the king (38:8ff.).

39 – 40:6 Jerusalem taken

See also chapter 52; 2 Kings 25; 2 Chronicles 36.

Jeremiah's terrible vision (38:22-23) becomes a reality (39:6-8). God's warnings finally give way to judgment (39:1-10). But even in the midst of judgment, God does not lose sight of individuals. Ebedmelech's life is saved (39:15-18). And the Babylonian king takes thought for the prophet (39:11-12). So Jeremiah is the only one to have any say in his own future (40:1-5). Offered a place of honour at the Babylonian court, he chooses instead to throw in his lot with the have-nots, left behind in the land of Judah.

▶ **Riblah (39:5)** Nebuchadnezzar's base was a town to the south of Hama in Syria.

▶ **Gedaliah (39:14)** Son of the man who earlier saved Jeremiah's life (26:24). The family may have supported Jeremiah's apparently pro-Babylonian stance, and so won favour with Nebuchadnezzar and his officers.

▶ **Mizpah (40:6)** A town a few miles north of Jerusalem; a place of national assembly from Samuel's time.

40:7 – 41:18 Governor's murder

Chapters 40 – 44 focus on those left behind when the rest are taken into exile. Gedaliah makes a good start as governor. With Jerusalem in ruins he makes his headquarters at Mizpah, 8km/5 miles to the north-west. Those who had fled before the army, escaping to neighbouring countries, return and they gather in a good harvest, after the hungry days of occupation. But after three months Gedaliah, ignoring warnings, is assassinated by the king of Ammon's hit-man. Fearing reprisals from Babylon, the people make ready to escape to Egypt.

▶ **41:5** They approach from the centre of the old northern kingdom of Israel whose capital was Samaria. Shiloh and Shechem were centres of worship.

▶ **Asa/Baasha (41:9)** See 1 Kings 15:16ff.

▶ **Pool of Gibeon (41:12)** A site of ancient treachery: see 2 Samuel 2:12ff. Gibeon is 8km/5 miles north-west of Jerusalem. The 'pool' for collecting water is 11.3m/37ft across and 10.6m/35ft deep.

42 – 43:7 Escape to Egypt

For all the people's declared willingness to obey God's word (42:5), when the message

Beneath Jerusalem, even today, are ancient cisterns designed to conserve every precious drop of water. The muddy cistern into which Jeremiah was thrown would have had a round shaft carved through the rock. This one is below the Eccle Homo Convent in Jerusalem.

comes telling them to stay put, they disobey. Egypt seems safer. They take Jeremiah and Baruch with them. And, as God said (42:15-18), in due course the long arm of Nebuchadnezzar, king of Babylon, reaches down into Egypt (568 BC). According to the Jewish historian Josephus, there were Jews among the captives he took back with him.

▶ **43:3** Jeremiah's secretary Baruch (32:12; chapters 36 and 45) had obviously already warned them against going to Egypt.

▶ **Tahpanhes (43:7)** See on 2:16.

43:8 – 44:30 Appeal from Egypt

Taken to Egypt against his will, Jeremiah enacts his last recorded parable (43:8ff.). The message is the same as 42:15ff. Despite all that has happened in consequence of playing God false, the people still refuse to listen. They will go back to worshipping the 'Queen of heaven' (44:17-19; see on 7:18), and all will be well again!

We hear no more of Jeremiah after this. Tradition has it he was stoned to death in Egypt.

▶ **The pavement (43:9)** Archaeologists have uncovered a large area of brick paving on the site.

▶ **Heliopolis (43:13)** See on Isaiah 19:18.

▶ **Hophra (44:30)** This pharaoh (589-570 BC) helped Jerusalem against Babylon in 588, then withdrew. In 569 a revolt deposed him. He died trying to regain the throne in 566.

45 Baruch

This short chapter connects with chapter 26, the writing of the scroll in 605. Baruch shared something of Jeremiah's distress. God promises he will escape the coming slaughter in the 'tearing down' and 'pulling up' of what God has built and planted (as he promised Ebedmelech, 39:15-18). That must suffice. This promise comes true in 43:5-6.

46 – 51
Prophecies against the nations

For Jeremiah, and Isaiah before him, God has charge of the whole world and all that goes on in it. God deals with evil wherever it occurs. These chapters, terrible though

The nations that inflict punishment on God's people will themselves be brought to ruin, says the prophet.

they are, contain some of the most magnificent poetry in the book. They expand on the latter part of chapter 25. Isaiah 13 – 23 and Ezekiel 25 – 32 contain similar prophecies against the nations.

46:1-26 Egypt

Verses 1-12 describe the defeat of Pharaoh Necho by King Nebuchadnezzar of Babylon at Carchemish in 605. Verses 13-26 forecast Nebuchadnezzar's invasion of Egypt (which took place in 568). See also Isaiah 19 – 20; Ezekiel 29 –32.

▶ **Verse 9** These are the mercenaries: from Sudan (Ethiopia) and Libya (Put). Lud/Lydia may refer to a place in north Africa, rather than Lydia in west-central Turkey.

▶ **Balm/medicine (11)** See on 8:22.

▶ **Verse 14** There were Jewish settlements in these cities in southern Egypt.

▶ **Apis (15)** The Egyptian sacred bull. God has overthrown the gods of Egypt.

46:27-28 'Don't be afraid'

These verses reassure God's people of rescue and return home. God will be fair in the punishment he metes out for their sins.

47 Philistia

See also Isaiah 14:28-32. The Philistines occupied the southern coastlands of Canaan from the 12th century on, often warring with the Israelites (see 'Canaanites and Philistines'). Pharaoh Necho controlled Gaza at the time of his march north in 609, but the city often changed hands. Calamity will come on Philistia from the Babylonians in the north. Nebuchadnezzar must have overrun the Philistine cities when he quelled Judah in 587. Other prophecies: Ezekiel 25:15ff.; Amos 1:6-8; Zephaniah 2:4-7; Zechariah 9:5-7.

▶ **Gaza, Ashkelon (1, 5)** Philistine cities.
▶ **Caphtor (4)** Crete, the island from which the Philistines originally came.
▶ **Anakim (5,** some versions**)** People of giant height who had some connection with the Philistines (Joshua 11:22). But this may not be the right word here.

48 Moab

See Isaiah 15 – 16. The Moabites occupied the high plateau-land east of the Dead Sea. Moab, and neighbouring Ammon and Edom, seem to have joined forces with

Jeremiah is taken to Egypt

Mizpah
Gibeon
Jerusalem
Bethlehem

EGYPT   Migdol

Tahpanhes   After the murder of Gedaliah at Mizpah, the people flee to Egypt, taking Jeremiah with them.

Heliopolis

Memphis

PATHROS

Judah in rebelling against Nebuchadnezzar (27:1-3). Presumably he dealt with them when he dealt with Judah. Other prophecies: Ezekiel 25:8-11; Amos 2:1-3; Zephaniah 2:8-11.

▶ **Nebo (1)** The city, not the mountain.
▶ **Chemosh (7, 13)** Chief Moabite god. Bethel was the sanctuary set up in the northern kingdom of Israel to rival Jerusalem.
▶ **Arnon (20)** The river boundary between Moab and Ammon, to the north.
▶ **Dibon (22)** This city, east of the Dead Sea and a short distance north of the River Arnon was taken by Israel early on, then changed hands more than once. In Jeremiah's time it belonged to Moab.
▶ **Horn (25)** An image of power, strength, might.
▶ **Kir-heres (31)** Original capital of Moab, 20km/11 miles east of the Dead Sea; present-day Kerak in Jordan.
▶ **Verse 37** A picture of mourning.

49:1-6 Ammon

See on Moab above; also Ezekiel 25:1-7. Ammon was an old enemy of Israel. David disposed of Uriah during a siege of the capital city, Rabbah/Rabbath-ammon (modern Amman, capital of Jordan). Ammon is condemned for seizing Israelite land, but will later be restored.

▶ **Verse 1** Milcom/Molech: the Ammonite god. See Joshua 13:24-28 for Gad's territory. It was at different times ruled by Moab, Ammon (in Jeremiah's time) and the Assyrians.

49:7-22 Edom

Other prophecies: Isaiah 21:11-12; Obadiah (who seems to have borrowed some passages from Jeremiah). Edom's judgment will be total: see Isaiah 34.

▶ **Verse 18** See Genesis 19.
▶ **Jungle by the Jordan (19)** See on 12:5.

49:23-27 Damascus

See also Isaiah 17:1-3; Amos 1:3-5; Zechariah 9:1. The Assyrians took the city in 732 BC, in Isaiah's time. It suffered further in the centuries that followed.

▶ **Hamath, Arpad (23)** Hama, in Syria; and a town just north of Aleppo.
▶ **Ben-hadad (27)** The name or title of a number of Syrian kings.

49:28-33 Kedar

The tribe of Kedar, descendants of Abraham's son Ishmael, lived as nomads in the Arabian desert. Nebuchadnezzar routed these tribes in 599.

▶ **Hazor/Hazer (30)** Probably nomad settlements; not the city in northern Galilee.

49:34-39 Elam

Jeremiah spoke in 597. Within a year Elam was attacked by Nebuchadnezzar. The country lay east of Babylon, across the Tigris River. The capital, Susa, is mentioned in Nehemiah 1:1; Esther 1:2; Daniel 8:2. It was the winter capital of the Persian Empire.

50 – 51 Babylon

See on Isaiah 13 – 14 and 46 – 47. The ruins of Babylon, capital of empire in Jeremiah's day, King Nebuchadnezzar's great pride and joy, lie in the desert 90km/55 miles south of modern Baghdad. Jeremiah's impressive prophecy was sent with the delegation that went to Babylon in

In prophesying invasion and ruin, Jeremiah was accused of undermining the people's morale. But he was not being pessimistic for the sake of it. Only by facing up to reality could they avoid the catastrophe of destruction and exile.

the fourth year of Zedekiah's reign, six years before the fall of Jerusalem. It was given a public reading, then sunk in the Euphrates, as Babylon itself would sink

Oppression and exile have been the fate of the ordinary people of the Middle East repeatedly down the centuries. Jeremiah saw only too clearly the suffering and tragedy that defeat and exile would bring in his own time.

The Babylonians
Alan Millard

Over 6,000 years ago, the ancient kingdom of Babylonia occupied the southern part of modern Iraq – the land through which the Tigris and Euphrates rivers flow to the Persian Gulf. The land is flat, and cities grew up there soon after people had learned how to use the river water for irrigation.

Early civilization
Babylonia, with Egypt, was one of the early centres of civilization in the Middle East. A thousand years before Abraham, Sumerians were living in Babylonia. The highly organized cities were ruled by kings and priests and often fought for control of water.

Temples were set on brick platforms which developed into towers of several stages, each smaller than the one below, rising 50m/162ft or more above the ground (the ziggurat).

Worshippers presented carefully carved stone statues and vases, hoping the gods would remember them. Craftsmen worked metals (all imported) with great skill to create outstanding pieces of jewellery in gold and silver, tools and weapons in copper and bronze.

Writing
Large populations need organizing, which is probably why the Sumerians invented writing, shortly before 3000 BC. At first, simple pictures stood for common objects, then their names were used for their sounds (as pictures of a car and a cat could be read 'carpet'). The conventional system used about 600 signs for words or syllables. Speed of writing resulted in the

pictures losing recognizable forms. The pressure of the reed stylus on soft clay, the normal writing material, produced the wedge-shaped strokes of the cuneiform script. The Babylonians adopted the script for their Semitic language.

Babylon's power
The city of Babylon enjoyed power briefly under Hammurabi (about 1792-1750 BC). His kingdom,

The Babylonian Empire at the height of its power. King Nabopolassar captured the Assyrian capital of Nineveh in 612 BC. Persian and Median armies took Babylon in 539 BC.

which covered the rest of Babylonia and Assyria, did not last long after his death.

Babylon dominated the Near East for another short period, of lasting fame. After the fall of Assyria in 612 BC, Babylon took

above King Nebuchadnezzar II realized his dream in building 'Great Babylon'. This brick is stamped with the king's name.

centre King Nabonidus of Babylon stands before the symbols of the moon-god Sin, the sun-god Shamash and the goddess of love and war, Ishtar.

right This tablet of the Babylonian Chronicle, written in cuneiform, tells of the fall of Nineveh, capital city of Assyria, to the conquering Babylonians.

control of the whole area from the Persian Gulf to the border with Egypt. In 605 BC, Nebuchadnezzar (605-562 BC) defeated the Egyptian Pharaoh Necho at Carchemish and he and his successors maintained their rule with a few campaigns to suppress rebels and secure their frontiers.

A stone stele shows King Merodach-baladan, at the left, and a courtier, with symbols of the gods above, about 712 BC.

The last king, Nabonidus (555-539 BC) lived in northern Arabia for ten years, probably for religious reasons, leaving the kingdom in the hands of his son Belshazzar.

Babylon and Judah

Judah became subject to Babylon after Carchemish, but a few years later King Jehoiakim rebelled. Nebuchadnezzar's army marched to Judah and besieged Jerusalem. The new king, Jehoiachin, was taken prisoner to Babylon with many leading citizens.

Cuneiform tablets record rations issued to him and his family there. The siege with its date (15/16 March 597 BC) is entered in the Babylonian Chronicle: 'The king of Babylon... marched to the westland, besieged the city of Judah, capturing it on the second day of Adar. He captured its king, appointed a ruler of his own choice...'

Ten years later Nebuchadnezzar returned because Zedekiah, the king he had appointed, revolted. This time the Babylonians destroyed Jerusalem and its Temple and took most of the people to Babylonia (587/6 BC).

Nebuchadnezzar's Babylon

The exiles from Judah were brought to the great city of Babylon which Nebuchadnezzar had rebuilt. The inner city was protected by a wide moat and double walls of brick (3.7m/12ft and 6.5m/21ft thick), with room for a military road at parapet level between them. Of the eight great gateways, the Ishtar Gate, built to honour the Babylonian god Marduk, is best known today.

The gateway is decorated with alternate rows of bulls (symbol of the weather god Adad) and dragons (symbol of Marduk) made of glazed brick. The Procession Street (along which statues of the gods were carried at the New Year festival) led from the gate to the city centre and the great temples. Its walls were of blue enamelled brick with a relief of lions (symbol of Ishtar) in red, yellow and white. Babylon contained dozens of temples. Most important was the ziggurat of Marduk (biblical Merodach), the patron god of the city, with his temple beside it.

Nebuchadnezzar built a complex of palaces at the north, beside the Ishtar Gate. It was here that Daniel came, to join the king's court.

Babylon's fall

For all its glory, the Babylonian Empire lasted less than a century. The army of Cyrus the Persian captured Babylon in 539 BC.

Archaeologists have reconstructed the Ishtar Gate which stood at the entrance to the processional way which led to the great temples of the gods in Babylon. Figures of dragons and bulls on the Gate are made of glazed brick.

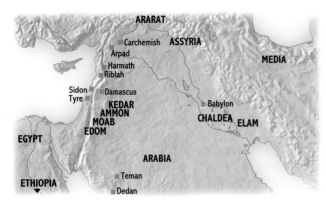

before its conqueror (51:59-64). The Medes (51:11) would pour in on Babylon from the north like the sea. God's people are warned in advance to be out of harm's way when it happens.

Cyrus, at the head of an army of Medes and Persians, took Babylon in 539. In 482 BC the city was destroyed by Xerxes I.

Babylon was God's instrument to punish his people (as the Assyrians had been earlier), but the sinful pride of the city calls out for judgment, and God declares that the looters will themselves be looted (50:10), the Babylonian hammer will be hammered (50:23). Evil cannot be ignored: judgment *will* come.

▶ **Bel, Merodach/Marduk (50:2)** The Babylonian gods.

▶ **50:21** There is a play on the names Merathaim and Pekod, two Babylonian tribes.

▶ **Vengeance for his Temple (50:28; 51:11)** These notes were written after the destruction in 587.

▶ **51:27** Ararat in eastern Turkey; Minni in north-west Iran; Ashkenaz, the Scythians, in the same area. All were subject to the Medes.

▶ **Her sea (51:36)** Babylon's prosperity and security depended on its elaborate system of canals and lakes.

▶ **Seraiah (51:59)** Brother of Jeremiah's secretary, Baruch (32:12).

▶ **The words of Jeremiah end here (64)** Chapter 52 is an addition.

52
Historical 'postscript'

This chapter fills out the account of the fall of Jerusalem, the destruction of the Temple, and the deportation of the people given in Jeremiah 39. It is almost identical to the story in 2 Kings 25 (see comment there).

▶ **Verses 28-30** The captives were deported in 597, 587 and 581. 2 Kings says 10,000 were taken; 2 Chronicles 36 says it was all the survivors.

▶ **Verse 31** With the accession of Nebuchadnezzar's son (562-560), things improved for Jehoiachin, a token of new hope for the nation.

Lamentations

Summary

A collection of five laments which grieve for the destruction of Jerusalem by the Babylonian army in 587 BC.

We do not know who wrote the five poems collected in this short book. The laments are anonymous in the Hebrew text. The oldest Greek translation of the Old Testament (the 'Septuagint' or 'LXX', which dates from the 2nd and 3rd centuries BC) names Jeremiah. But these laments differ in style and content from Jeremiah's prophecies. They are most likely the work of a single author, a contemporary of the prophet and an eye-witness to the destruction of Jerusalem by Nebuchadnezzar's Babylonian army in 587 BC.

To the people of Judah, the fall of the city meant more than the loss of their beautiful and almost unassailable capital. Jerusalem was in a very special sense God's city. His Temple was there. This was where he chose to live with his people. And when Jerusalem was burned, the Temple destroyed, the people deported, they knew that God had given them up to the enemy. Otherwise it could not have happened.

So these laments express the poet's grief, not simply over the suffering and humiliation of his people, but over something deeper and far worse: God's rejection of his own people, because over and over again, despite repeated appeals and warnings, God's covenant people had broken faith with him.

The first four poems are in the dirge rhythm used for funeral songs and are written as alphabet poems (acrostics). In 1, 2 and 4, each of the 22 verses begins with a new letter of the Hebrew alphabet. In 3, each letter has three verses. The fifth poem (chapter 5) has 22 verses, but is otherwise quite different from the rest.

The poems are still read aloud in Jewish synagogues in mid-July to mark the anniversary of the destruction of the Temple in 587, and in memory of the final destruction in AD 70.

Chapter 1 Lament for Jerusalem

In verses 1-11 we hear the voice of the poet; in 12-22 the city itself is grieving. Jerusalem is alone, deserted, mourning; the people gone; the Temple defiled and destroyed. God has judged and punished the city for the enormity of its sin. Now, at last, Jerusalem cries out to him.

Chapter 2 God has done this!

In this second lament (1-12) the poet revisits the dreadful scene. All the ruin and desolation, the starving children, the slaughter *are God's doing*. That is the worst of it, as the poet stresses again and again. He speaks to the city (13-19), then cries to God on the city's behalf (20-22): let God look, and pity.

Chapter 3 Hope against hope

In the third lament the agony of the nation is focussed in the experience of a single individual. In the darkness, crushed and battered to the point where all hope dies (18), his faith still rekindles at the thought of God whose character is steadfast love and mercy (19-33). When he is all but lost, there comes the knowledge that God is near (55ff.). But he cannot forgive the bitter provocation of his enemies (59-66).

Chapter 4 'Zion has paid for her sin'

This lament contrasts the city's former glory, and the horrors of siege: the cries of starving children; wizened faces; shrivelled bodies; never to be forgotten (1-11). Who is to blame? It is the sins of the people, the prophets and the priests that have brought the city low (12-16). And Edom – Judah's old arch-enemy – gloats, not knowing that its own punishment is yet to come (21-22).

Chapter 5 'Bring us back to you, Lord'

In the prayer to God which rounds off this little collection of laments, the poet vividly

An old woman, veiled in black, in the Old City of Jerusalem – a figure of mourning that fits Lamentations, the collection of laments for the destruction of the city by the Babylonians.

describes 'what has happened to us': the loss of freedom, loss of land, loss of respect; rape and cruelty; forced labour; near-starvation. He sees this as a consequence not only of the people's own sin but that of previous generations. And he prays to God for restoration, if it is not, after all, too late.

Ezekiel

Summary

Ezekiel's prophecies in Babylonia, before and after the fall of Jerusalem.

Chapters 1 – 3
Ezekiel's vision and calling

•

Chapters 4 – 24
God's judgment on Judah

•

Chapters 25 – 32
God's judgment on the nations

•

Chapters 33 – 37
The fall of Jerusalem: God's promises

•

Chapters 38 – 39
Prophecy against Gog

•

Chapters 40 – 48
God's plan for a new Jerusalem – the vision of the Temple

Best-known passages

Vision of God *(1)*
The watchman *(33)*
Valley of dry bones *(37)*
A new Temple *(40ff.)*

In 597 BC King Jehoiachin surrendered Jerusalem to the Babylonian army, and was taken into exile. With him went 10,000 of Judah's statesmen, soldiers, craftsmen (2 Kings 24:14). Among them was Ezekiel, Jeremiah's younger contemporary, then in his mid-twenties.

The man

Ezekiel was in training to be a priest, looking forward to serving God in the Temple, like his father before him. Instead he found himself an exile in Babylonia, far from Jerusalem.

It seemed like the end of all his hopes. But when he was 30 (the age at which he would probably have taken up his duties as a priest: Numbers 4:3, and see 1:1), God called him into service as a prophet. The call was accompanied by a vision which coloured his entire ministry (just as Isaiah's had done long before). He saw God in all his awesome majesty, above and beyond our human world, all-seeing, all-knowing. It was a vision of fire and glory. And against this dazzling brilliance Ezekiel saw his people's sin in all its blackness.

He saw the inevitability of judgment and for six years this was his message. Only after the city and Temple of Jerusalem were destroyed in 587 did he really begin to stress God's intention to 'resurrect' (chapter 37) and restore the nation, and to look forward to the time when the ideal would be realized: to the new Temple in which God's people would offer him perfect worship (chapters 40ff.).

As he declared God's message to the exiles, a great weight of responsibility rested on Ezekiel. He saw himself as a 'look-out', who must warn of danger or be held accountable. One of his most characteristic themes is that of individual responsibility before God.

Ezekiel was an extraordinary man, a visionary, imaginative, by training someone who appreciated and understood ritual and symbol. He was passionate, dedicated, utterly obedient to God. The most hardened onlooker could not fail to be impressed as Ezekiel acted out his sobering messages.

The book

Ezekiel is written entirely in the first person, apart from the note in 1:2-3, and is in keeping with the man.

The structure is balanced and clear, with the fall of Jerusalem as the pivotal point. Unlike those of the other major prophets, Ezekiel's prophecies are meticulously ordered and dated (1:1, 2; 8:1; 20:1; 24:1; 26:1; 29:1; 30:20; 31:1; 32:1, 17; 33:21; 40:1).

The message is consistent throughout. So too is the style and language. Characteristic themes and repeated phrases run right through. Ezekiel's message, with its acted parables, is very close to that of Jeremiah, whom he may have heard as a young man in Jerusalem. But although he writes for the most part in rather solid prose, Ezekiel is more flamboyantly visual than the other prophets. With him, prophecy merges into 'apocalyptic': see on Revelation, the Bible book closest in spirit to Ezekiel, which borrows many of his images.

For many Christians, Ezekiel is a closed book, apart from a few familiar passages: the extraordinary vision of God in chapter 1; the watchman (33); the valley of dry bones (37); the vision of the Temple (40ff.). Many of the prophecies seem laboured and over-complicated. He uses language meant to shock, and irony is one of his verbal tools. Yet we desperately need to catch something of Ezekiel's vision of Almighty God. We need to see sin as God sees it. We need to be reminded of our own accountability. We need to know that God is God.

Reading the Old Testament also helps in understanding the New. We need to be acquainted with Ezekiel in order to understand Revelation.

1 – 3
Ezekiel's vision and calling

Ezekiel is a book of visions and symbolic actions – beginning with this great vision of God.

1 'I saw a vision of God'

As Ezekiel gazes out over the Babylonian plains, he sees what looks like an approaching storm: thunder, lightning, black clouds. Then he makes out the figures of four cherubim (see 10:15), angelic creatures, standing wing-tip to wing-tip, forming a hollow square. At the centre, fire glows; and above, under the blue vault of the heavens, is the Lord of glory in human form, seated on a throne, encircled by a dazzling rainbow. Beside each four-faced cherub is a terrifying, whirling wheel, moving like a castor and full of eyes. The Almighty, the God of Israel is present in all his power in far-flung Babylonia! Who can look on this and live?

▶ **Thirtieth year (1)** Most probably Ezekiel's own age. If, as seems likely, this was the age at which a priest took up his duties, it would have been a year of special significance for the prophet. But to become eligible at last for his life's work as a priest, when in exile, hundreds of miles away from Jerusalem and its Temple, must have been a bitter experience.

▶ **Chebar (1)** Usually identified as the great canal which ran from the Euphrates north of Babylon, close to the city of Nippur.

▶ **Verses 2-3** A note added to explain Ezekiel's opening sentence. The date was 593 BC (see introduction).

▶ **Living creatures (5)** Cherubim (10:15), the figures which spread their wings over the mercy-seat above the Ark of the Covenant (Exodus 25:18ff.). As the son of a priest, Ezekiel may have been familiar with the figures of cherubim which decorated Solomon's Temple. Similar winged, sphinx-like creatures frequently appear in Babylonian art.

▶ **Verse 26** In Isaiah 6:1 the prophet says bluntly 'I saw the Lord', but Ezekiel makes it clear that we cannot see or experience God as he really is. So he uses phrases like: 'as it were the appearance of', 'the likeness of the glory of'. Compare Exodus 24:9-11 and 33:18-23; also Daniel 7; Revelation 4.

2 – 3 Ezekiel's God-given task

The purpose of God's coming is to make Ezekiel his messenger to the exiles, the watchman sent to warn the remnant of God's rebel people (2:1-7; 3:16-21). And the words of God, though hard, are satisfying (2:8 – 3:3). From this point on it will be Ezekiel's life-mission to let God's people know that he is the Lord. They will learn it first through the terrors of judgment (7:4). Afterwards they will see his power to restore and renew (36:8-11).

▶ **Son of man/mortal man (2:1)** Ezekiel is addressed in this way throughout the book. It simply means 'human being'. Jesus most often used 'Son of man' to describe himself, with an intended allusion also to Daniel 7:13, 14.

▶ **Lord God/Sovereign Lord (2:4)** Ezekiel constantly uses the double title, 'Adonai Yahweh', emphasizing God's almighty power and the personal covenant relationship with his people. See 'The names of God'.

▶ **Briers and thorns… scorpions (2:6)** A vivid picture of the hostile reception.

▶ **2:10** Normally a scroll had writing on only one side; perhaps the implication is that there was no room left for Ezekiel to add anything of his own.

▶ **3:7** The calls of Isaiah (6:9-12) and Jeremiah (1:17-19) were equally daunting.

▶ **Watchman (3:17)** This concept is expanded in chapter 33.

▶ **3:25-27** The meaning seems to be that Ezekiel would be dumb except on the occasions when God had a message for him to give. Was he forbidden to speak or did he actually lose the power of speech? Either way, the utterances he did make had added force. Not until news reached him of the fall of Jerusalem (24:27) did he speak normally again.

God's judgment on Judah

4 – 5 Ezekiel acts out the siege of Jerusalem

The 'props' for the drama are ready to hand: a large sun-dried brick on which Ezekiel draws an outline of the city; and the metal plate on which they bake their flat loaves of bread. We are in the realm of symbol, as so often in this book.

The people watch, and get the message. With growing horror they see him weigh out his meagre measure of mixed grain and eke out his water ration. They see the prophet wasting away, as the population of Jerusalem will do under siege.

Next (chapter 5) they watch him shave his head, sharing Jerusalem's disgrace. They see him burn the hair and toss it away, till only a tiny handful – representing the exiles themselves – remains. It is an awesome lesson.

▶ **4:5-6** The instructions given in 4:9 – 5:4 make it likely that Ezekiel lay on one side for a part of every day, rather than continually. The Greek version has 190 days; from the fall of Samaria in 722/1 BC to the return of the exiles in 538 is 184 years. From the fall of Jerusalem in 587 to 538 is 49 years. 40 may represent a generation, rather than being an exact figure.

▶ **4:9,12** Under siege no one is fussy about the ingredients they use to make bread. Nothing here contradicts the food laws.

▶ **Twenty shekels (4:10)** About 230gm/8oz.

▶ **Sixth part of a hin (4:11)** Just over half a litre; about a pint.

▶ **Unclean (4:13ff.)** Ezekiel could accept the limited diet imposed on him but the use of human dung for fuel revolted him. Even in exile he had kept himself ritually clean, observing the food laws (see on Leviticus 11 and 'Strictly kosher'), as Daniel and his friends also did at the Babylonian court (Daniel 1). This would make everything he ate 'unclean'. God understands the prophet's feelings and lets him use cow dung (still a normal fuel in the East) instead.

6 – 7 This is the end

The acted message is reinforced by the spoken word. The people's flagrant idolatry is about to bring destruction upon them – judgment from which there is no escape. Then they will know that the Lord is God indeed. Terrible, total calamity is befalling the land.

▶ **Riblah (6:14**, probable reading, though Hebrew has Diblah) From south to north. Riblah, on the River Orontes, is near Israel's northern boundary.

▶ **Disgusting conduct/abominations (7:3, 4, 8, 9)** The reference is to worship of other gods and the ritual prostitution and other practices that went along with this.

▶ **The seller grieve (7:12)** Because he has been forced to sell the land which was his heritage.

▶ **7:18** Shaven heads were a sign of disgrace as well as of mourning.

8 – 11 A second vision: God deserts the Temple

In September 592 God comes to Ezekiel a second time (compare 8:2 with 1:27). He is

The winged creatures of Ezekiel's vision may have resembled familar images from contemporary art and sculpture – like this ivory sphinx. More winged creatures appear on an ivory panel made to decorate a piece of furniture (below).

transported in vision to Jerusalem, and set down beside the Temple (8:1-4). What he sees may be actual practices, or the description may be symbolic. Either way the meaning is plain. There has been a total departure from the true religion of Israel. An image of the Canaanite goddess Asherah/Astarte (the 'image of jealousy', 3) has been set up in God's Temple. The nation's leaders are secretly practising animal worship (8:7-13). The women (8:14) are mourning the Sumerian god Tammuz, who was supposed to die with the old year and rise again with the spring. Men turn their backs on God to worship the sun (8:16).

Contrary to popular belief (8:12), God both sees and judges (9:9-10). Only those who grieve for the loss of the true faith will be spared (9:4-6).

Chapter 10: following the terrible slaughter which makes Ezekiel cry aloud for his people (9:8), he sees again the vision of the cherubim, the glory, the whirling wheels, that he describes in chapter 1. What greater contrast imaginable than this sight of God in all his glory – and the loathsome scenes of idolatry in his Temple (chapter 8). This is why God's presence will be withdrawn, leaving the Temple an empty shell and Jerusalem without its heart and soul.

But first Ezekiel sees two men he recognizes, rulers who are advocating resistance to Babylon, despite the insistence of God's prophets that this would prove fatal (11:1-4). Ezekiel pronounces God's judgment, and as he speaks, to his alarm, Pelatiah falls dead (11:5-13) in confirmation of God's word. But God is not making a 'full end' (13). The future lies with the exiles. And on this note, and with this message (25), the vision ends.

▶ **Jaazaniah (8:11)** His father was King Josiah's secretary of state; his brother Ahikam, Jeremiah's friend. Not the same man as in 11:1.
▶ **The branch... (8:17)** Possibly a reference to some pagan practice.
▶ **9:2** Linen was worn by the priests. It indicates purity.
▶ **A mark (9:4)** Jeremiah, Baruch and the foreigner, Ebed-melech, were among those 'marked' to be spared (Jeremiah 40:4; 45;

> **❝** I will give them a new heart and a new mind. I will take away their stubborn heart of stone and give them an obedient heart. Then they will keep my laws and faithfully obey all my commands. They will be my people, and I will be their God. **❞**
>
> 11:19-20

39:15ff.). In Revelation those true to God are marked (7:3; 9:4; 14:1), and so are those who sell out to the forces of evil (13:16). The 'mark' here is the last letter of the Hebrew alphabet, taw, written as a cross in the oldest script.
▶ **9:9** Idolatry has been the chief sin so far. Here it is clear that the most basic laws have been broken.
▶ **11:3** A difficult verse, most likely meaning that this was not the moment for peace-time building. The cauldron protects the meat from the flames.
▶ **A new spirit (11:19)** See Ezekiel 36:26 and compare Jeremiah 31:33-34.

12 Ezekiel acts the refugee
Although most people refuse to listen, the prophet continues to make God's word known (1-3). As he puts together the bare necessities, ready for flight, and as he breaks through the mud-brick wall at night, Ezekiel is playing the part, not just of any escapee, but of King Zedekiah ('the prince', 10). Compare 12-13 with Jeremiah 52:7-11.

Ezekiel's prophecy proved accurate to the last detail. Zedekiah could not see because his eyes were put out. It was as God said it would be, and within a very short space of time (21-28).

13 False prophets
The work of Jeremiah and Ezekiel was constantly undermined by false prophets, who told people what they wanted to hear, and claimed God's authority for their message of false hope. They were like plaster, concealing the crumbling structure of the nation, but unable to stop it falling (10-16). There were also prophetesses, practising magic and holding helpless individuals in thrall (17ff.).

Unlike the false prophets, when God says something will happen, he means it – and he has the power to carry it out. There is often a conditional aspect to prophecy, even so: the response of the people (in repenting, for example) may bring about a change in the way God carries out his plans (see chapter 18 and 29:17-20; also Amos 7:1-3, 4-6).
▶ **Verse 18** The magic may have to do with amulets, or represent some kind of 'binding'

power. The hunt is for 'lives' – the whole person – not 'souls'. Disembodied spirits had no place in Jewish thinking.

14 God will punish the unfaithful

God claims a unique place in the hearts of his people. Those who deny him his rightful place, worshipping other 'gods' alongside, are destined for destruction. The majority regard the few godly people among them as an insurance against disaster. But at this point in time not even Noah or Job could save anyone but themselves.

▶ **Verse 14** It is interesting that the exemplary ancient heroes, Noah and Job, are non-Israelites. Danel is not the Daniel we know of – Ezekiel's contemporary in exile. That name is in any case spelt differently. There is a 'Dan'el', an upright character, in an ancient Canaanite epic. The reference may be to him or to some other ancient hero standing for the same godly ideal.

▶ **Verse 21** These judgments represent the worst fears of ancient peoples (see Jeremiah 14:12).

15 Parable of the vine

The vine was a popular symbol for Israel. There is by this time no question of it bearing fruit, and as wood the vine is useless, fit only for burning. Israel is already partially destroyed (4): there is nothing for it now but total destruction (6-8).

▶ **Verse 6** The fire the residents of Jerusalem have escaped is the earlier deportation in 597 BC, which took Ezekiel himself into exile.

16 Like a wife who sleeps around

The issue is faithfulness. Jerusalem (the nation) has been unfaithful to God. So the sexual image in this parable is a natural one, especially in view of the sexual rites and prostitution linked with worship of pagan gods.

God took Israel up when she was nothing – an abandoned baby that no one has cared for – and lavished his love on her, making her into a great and glorious nation. She owed him everything. But prosperity turned her head and, like a wife turned prostitute, she played fast and loose with foreign nations. She 'courted' them and worshipped their gods, with all the

hideous practices that involved (20-29). God was forgotten; the covenant (like the marriage-vow) broken. God must punish (35-43), but will also restore his people (53, 60), making a new covenant with them that will last for ever (60, 62; see also Jeremiah 31:31).

▶ **Amorite... Hittite (3)** The reference is to moral, not literal, parentage. Israel had become as decadent as the nations they destroyed at the conquest of Canaan.

▶ **Verse 4** These were the midwife's duties.

▶ **Verse 8** With the symbolic gesture of covering he claimed her in marriage. See Ruth 3:9. God sealed the contract with the Sinai covenant.

▶ **Verse 38** Adultery was punishable by death.

▶ **Verse 46** 'Samaria': capital of the northern kingdom; destroyed in 722/1. 'Sodom': the Dead Sea city wiped out for its gross immorality (Genesis 19).

17 Parable of the eagles and the vine

The parable in 1-8 is explained point by point in 11-15. The first eagle is Nebuchadnezzar of Babylon, who took King Jehoiachin captive (3, 4; see introduction). The seed he plants (5, 13) is Zedekiah. But Zedekiah soon turned to Egypt (the second eagle) for help (7, 15), bringing the Babylonians back to destroy Jerusalem.

In 587, within three or four years, the prediction of 17-21 came true (see Jeremiah 52). But God will take a 'cutting' from the line of Israel's kings (the cedar) which will take root (22-24).

▶ **Verse 8** It seems best to take this as stressing the fact that Zedekiah was well off under Nebuchadnezzar (as in 5).

▶ **Verse 15** One of the 'Lachish letters' (about 590 BC) excavated from the ruins of the city says that 'Coniah, the son of Elnathan, commander of the army, has gone down on his way to Egypt'. Was he one of the king's agents, seeking help from Pharaoh Psammetichus II?

18 Called to account

Contrary to popular belief (2), God is not so unjust as to punish one generation for the sins of another (20). He holds everyone answerable for their own sins. It gives God no pleasure to sign the death warrant for

Ezekiel shared the life of a refugee settlement, acting out his prophecies to a people in exile.

It is the one who sins who will die. A son is not to suffer for his father's sins, nor a father because of the sins of his son.

18:20

anyone (23). His concern, always, is that people should turn away from evil and live (30-32). And he makes his standards plain (5-9; 14-17).

▶ **Soul (4)** 'Life' – see on 13:18 above.
▶ **Verses 5-9, 10-13** Both examples mix ritual and social laws. All are part of God's covenant-law set out in Exodus, Leviticus and Deuteronomy.
▶ **Verse 20** Ezekiel is redressing the balance, not denying the basic principle that in life children do suffer the consequences of their parents' wrong-doing (Exodus 20:5).

19 Lament for Israel's rulers

The poem is written in the familiar dirge-rhythm. The lioness is Judah; the kings her cubs. The first (3) is Jehoahaz, carried off to Egypt by Pharaoh Necho in 609. The second (5) is Jehoiachin (see introduction). Now, thanks to Zedekiah's rebellion, both the nation and its line of kings will be destroyed (10-14).

20:1-44 A history of the nation's rebellion

July/August 591. Ezekiel turns from allegory to historical fact. From the time in Egypt and the wilderness right down to his own day,

Israel's history has been a weary repetition of idolatry and rebellion against God. All along, God held back from making an end of the nation. But now he will cut off the rebels (38). His own, he will restore (40-44).

▶ **I gave them... (25-26)** These difficult verses seem best understood in the light of Romans 1:24, etc. God 'gave them up' to the evil things they wanted.
▶ **Bamah (29)** High place. There is a play on words in this verse.
▶ **Verse 37** Jerusalem Bible translates: 'I mean to make you pass under my crook and I will bring a few of you back.'

20:45 – 21:32 Fire and sword

God's judgment will sweep across the land from south to north like a forest fire (20:45-48). The sword of God is drawn against Israel. It is in the hands of the king of Babylon (21:19), who will destroy the capital cities of both Ammon and Judah (21:20). (Five years after Jerusalem fell, Nebuchadnezzar attacked Ammon.)

▶ **Negev (20:46, some versions)** Today this region is arid desert, but Palestine as a whole was more wooded in Old Testament times.
▶ **Rabbah (21:20)** Amman, present capital of Jordan.

▶ **Until he comes... (21:27)** See Genesis 49:10. There is one coming to whom the kingship rightly belongs.

22 Charges against Jerusalem

God's people are guilty – guilty of bloodshed, oppression, extortion, bribery, and sexual sin; they have made a mockery of their religion (6-12). When God tests them by fire, no trace of genuine metal will be found (17-22). Every section of society shares the guilt: rulers, priests, prophets and common people alike (23-31).
▶ **Unclean and clean (26)** See Leviticus 11.
▶ **Verse 28** See 13:8-16.

23 Parable of the two sisters

Oholah is Samaria, capital of the northern kingdom of Israel. Oholibah is Jerusalem. Both sisters have behaved like common whores. Their appetite for their lovers (the pagan gods) is insatiable; their behaviour utterly disgusting. They have run, in turn, after Egypt and Assyria. Now Judah, outdoing her sister, is running after Babylon. Jerusalem will share Samaria's fate – shame and destruction at the hands of her latest lover. Her punishment is fully deserved (45).
▶ **Verse 10** The Assyrians destroyed Samaria in 722/1 BC.
▶ **Verse 23** Pekod, Shoa and Koa were probably tribes on the eastern borders of the Babylonian Empire. The Babylonians and Chaldeans were not separate peoples.

24 Jerusalem besieged; Ezekiel's wife dies

The date is the same as in 2 Kings 25:1; Jeremiah 52:4 – usually thought to be 15 January 588 BC. Jerusalem is like a rusty cooking-pot, set on the fire to burn. The behaviour of the people has polluted the city. The very same day that the siege is laid, Ezekiel's much-loved wife is suddenly taken from him. But God forbids him the customary forms of mourning. Ezekiel's personal loss is part of a grief beyond expression. People will eat their hearts out for the fate of Jerusalem, though they go about dry-eyed, like the prophet. And when news of the city's fall reaches them, Ezekiel will at last be able to speak freely (27; see

3:26-27); the judgment will be over.
▶ **Verse 17** The mourning customs of the day: noisy lamentation; bared head sprinkled with dust and ashes; bared feet; veiled face; and the funeral meal provided for the mourners.

25 – 32
God's judgment on the nations

Although the prophets concentrated mainly on Israel/Judah, all of them were very conscious that God was Lord of the whole world. There is no nation beyond the reach of his judgment: and what he condemns and punishes in his own people, he condemns and punishes in other nations too. This collection of prophecies effectively marks the break in Ezekiel's ministry before, and his ministry after, the fall of Jerusalem in 587 BC.

25 Ammon, Moab, Edom, Philistia

For other prophecies, see on Jeremiah 47 – 49. These four nations were Israel's closest neighbours, and her oldest enemies.

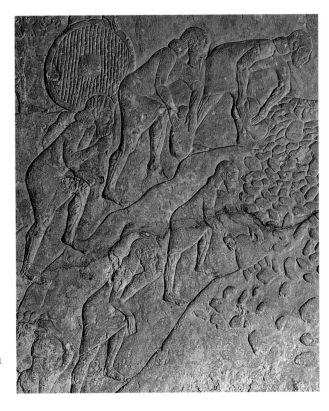

Captive people are a useful labour force. Slaves under guard dump earth in this Assyrian relief-carving.

Rich silk brocade, still woven on hand-looms in the city of Damascus, evokes the wealth and luxury of ancient Tyre denounced by the prophet Ezekiel.

All took a vengeful delight in Israel's downfall, for which God will punish them. Shortly after this, Ammon, Moab and Edom were overrun by Nabataean tribesmen. The Philistines disappeared from history a century before the birth of Jesus

26 – 28:19 Tyre

See on Isaiah 23. The date of Ezekiel's prophecy is probably the end of the 11th year – February 586 – assuming that Ezekiel learnt of the fall of Jerusalem that year, rather than the following one (see 33:21). The forecast of chapter 26 proved all too true. Tyre did not laugh long over Jerusalem's fate. Within a few months Nebuchadnezzar's army was at her own gates, and for 13 years she was under siege.

Tyre was a tempting prey. The city lay at the foot of the Lebanese mountains and possessed the finest natural harbour in the eastern Mediterranean. It was in fact a double harbour, as the main city was built on an offshore island (26:5). As a centre of

trade and commerce Tyre was fabulously wealthy, and her own glassware and purple dye were world famous. Ezekiel fittingly pictures the city as a great trading vessel (chapter 27) laden with the choicest of cargoes, and commanding human skills and resources from far and wide. News of her wreck will put the world into mourning. Chapter 28:1-19 is a lament for the king of Tyre, whose pride has proved his downfall.

▶ **Senir (27:5)** Mt Hermon.
▶ **Gebal (27:9)** Byblos, now Jubail, in Lebanon.
▶ **Daniel (28:3)** See 14:14.
▶ **28:12ff.** Much of the imagery is drawn from Genesis 2 – 3.

28:20-26 Sidon

Another famous Old Testament sea-port, Sidon is in Lebanon, 20 miles north of Tyre. Today both Tyre (Sour) and Sidon are small fishing-ports. The charge against Sidon is, again, contempt for God's people (24). Sidon, like Tyre, fell to Nebuchadnezzar. Verses 25-26 are a message of hope for Israel.

29 – 32 Egypt

A collection of seven prophecies, all (except the one beginning at 30:1) carefully dated.

- 29:1-16, January 587. By his insufferable pride in placing himself among the gods, Pharaoh has exposed his whole land to God's anger. But he will learn who is God!

- 29:17-21, New Year's day, 571 (the latest prophecy in the book). The long and costly siege of Tyre ended about 574. Ezekiel declares that Egypt will be Babylon's next prey.

- 30:1-19, undated. Ezekiel depicts the judgment Nebuchadnezzar will execute on Egypt and her allies. God will put an end to Egypt's wealth (10-12) and her 'gods' (13ff.).

- 30:20-26, April 587. Pharaoh Hophra's army had made a half-hearted attempt to relieve besieged Jerusalem, but had been defeated. His power will be yet further broken.

- 31:1-18, June 587. Egypt is likened to a great cedar tree (2-9). Because of its overbearing pride the tree will be felled

Ezekiel's prophecies against the nations

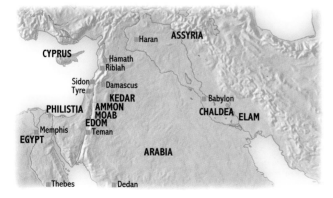

CYPRUS

Haran   **ASSYRIA**

Hamath
Riblai

Sidon   Damascus
Tyre   **KEDAR**
PHILISTIA **AMMON**   Babylon
MOAB   **CHALDEA** **ELAM**
EDOM
Memphis   Teman
EGYPT

ARABIA

Thebes   Dedan

Those who shepherded God's flock (the leaders of the people) had abused their power. God promised a 'good shepherd', who would care for them.

(10-14). Egypt will be removed to the place of the dead (15ff.).

■ 32:1-16, March 585 (after the news of Jerusalem's fall had reached the exiles). A lament for Pharaoh.

■ 32:17-32, (? March) 585. Egypt will join the other fallen nations: Assyria, Elam, Meshech, Tubal, Edom, Sidon. They are consigned to a great burial-chamber full of graves.

▶ **Pharaoh/king of Egypt (29:2)** The particular pharaoh is Hophra. All the pharaohs were worshipped as gods. So also was the Nile crocodile (verse 3).

▶ **Migdol to Aswan (29:10)** I.e. from north to south – the whole land. Migdol was a city on the Nile delta.

▶ **Pathros (29:14)** Upper (i.e. southern) Egypt.

▶ **30:5** Egypt's allies.

▶ **Assyria (31:3,** many versions) Good News Bible, 'You are like a cedar in Lebanon', and Jerusalem Bible make better sense.

▶ **32:22-30** 'Assyria', the great power in Isaiah's day, overthrown by Babylon. 'Elam', a nation east of Babylon. 'Meshech and Tubal', little-known nations on Assyria's northern frontier. 'Princes of the north', presumably city-states north of Palestine.

33 – 37
The fall of Jerusalem: God's promises

33:1-20 The watchman
These verses reiterate the teaching of two earlier passages, 3:17-21; 18:5-29.

33:21-33 News of Jerusalem's fall
The news did not take Ezekiel by surprise. God had already given him back his speech, as promised (24:27), by the time the messenger arrived. Some texts have 'eleventh year' for 'twelfth' in verse 21, in which case the news takes the more likely time of six months to reach them. Those left behind in Judah, far from repenting, were busy annexing other people's property. And in Babylonia the exiles who seemed to lap up Ezekiel's words came simply for entertainment. They neither believed them nor acted on them: a depressing state of affairs after all that had happened!

34 Leaders and people denounced
Both 'shepherds' (1-10) and 'sheep' (17-22) come in for condemnation. They have greedily, cruelly, selfishly exploited those committed to their care. But God will be a true shepherd, bringing his scattered flock back to good pasture in their homeland

Ezekiel's vision was a detailed reconstruction of the Jerusalem Temple area. Yet it was remarkably different. For out of it flowed a widening, deepening stream that became a life-giving river.

N

(11-16; and see Luke 15:4-7). He will appoint a good shepherd – a new David – to care for them (23-24; and see John 10:11), and the flock will dwell secure.

35 Prophecy against Edom

Edom is marked out for destruction, because of her callous reaction to Israel's downfall. She not only gloated, but planned to make capital out of it by seizing the land (10; the two nations are Israel and Judah). See 25:12-14 above. Other prophecies against Edom: Isaiah 34:5-15; Jeremiah 49:7-22; Obadiah.

36 Return to the homeland

God tells the desolate land it will soon be inhabited. His people are coming home. Israel's defeat has made people despise the God of Israel as powerless. Their return will vindicate his honour. The nations will know, and God's people will know, that he is the Lord. Those who returned from exile were truly and permanently cured of idolatry (25). But the total transformation of a 'new heart' is realized only 'in Christ' (2 Corinthians 5:17). Ezekiel was thinking of something far more complex than a heart transplant: the heart, in Jewish thought, stood for the whole personality, the essential person.

37 Vision in the valley of dry bones

After ten years in exile, and with Jerusalem destroyed, the people have given up hope. Not all Ezekiel's promises of restoration can raise a spark in his hearers. The nation is dead. But God can take even skeletons and make them into a living army. Ezekiel plays his part by making God's word known, but it is the Spirit of God who gives life. Israel will be remade and live again. The two warring kingdoms will become one nation under one king – a new David. And here (21-28) the promise to the exiles merges into the full blessing of the future golden age. The return is only a foretaste of all God has in store for his people.

▶ **Into one (17)** 'Hold the two sticks end to end in your hand so that they look like one stick,' Good News Bible.

▶ **David (24)** The ideal, messianic king, who will rule for ever in peace and righteousness.

38 – 39
Prophecy against Gog

Magog, Meshech, Tubal (2) and Gomer (6) were all sons of Japheth (Noah's son). They gave their names to Indo-European peoples living in the Black Sea/Caucasus region, on the northern fringe of the then-known world. Ezekiel pictures an invasion of these barbaric hordes from the north, led by the unidentified Gog, who may personify the cosmic forces of evil. Allied with armies from far and near (Persia, Sudan and North Africa, 5) he will wage war on the Lord's people. And God will demonstrate his power in the sight of all by taking on all the forces of evil singlehanded, and destroying them once and for all. 'Gog' is responsible for the plan, but the Lord's hand is always in control.

Chapter 39 repeats and enlarges on 38. So vast is Gog's army that the weapons provide Israel with seven years' fuel supply. And the carnage is so great it takes seven months to clean up the land. (For the Jews, the number seven symbolized perfection and completeness.) The judgment of God is a terrible thing, and Ezekiel conjures it up in horrifying pictures. The fact that these chapters immediately precede Ezekiel's vision of the new Temple in which God dwells among his people, gives added point to John's choice of Gog and Magog to represent all who oppose God in the last great battle instigated by Satan at the end of time (Revelation 20:8).

40 – 48
A new Jerusalem: the vision of the Temple

These chapters were written some years after the rest (except for 29:17-21), in 573 BC. Although, for the most part, they make rather dull reading, they are in a very real sense the climax to the whole book. Ezekiel began with a vision of God in the plains of Babylon. It ends with a vision of God returning in glory to a new Temple – God in the midst of his people once again, never to depart.

For all the detail, Ezekiel's description is

The Dead Sea is so salt that nothing can live in it. Yet in Ezekiel's vision, the water that flowed from the Temple, down the Jordan Valley to the Dead Sea, made its salt water fresh, and brought life to its shores.

no mere blueprint for the second Temple. It was not the old Jerusalem, but a structure like a city that he saw (40:2). It is true that the new Temple follows much the same layout as Solomon's Temple, and is all set out for the sacrifices (40:38ff.). But when God returns in all his glory it is to live for ever in a Temple and among a priesthood and people cleansed from evil (chapter 43). Everything is perfect. This is the ideal. Yet it is not as far-reaching as the vision in Revelation. It is still envisaged in earthly terms: there is still a Temple and sacrifices; the people of God are synonymous with Israel (44:6ff.); the laws continue, so does

death, so does the need for a sin-offering (44:15-27).

Again there is the subtle blending and telescoping of near and distant future which is characteristic of the prophets. The laws, the offerings, the feasts of Exodus and Leviticus are reinstated (chapters 45 and 46). Yet suddenly, in chapter 47, we are given something gloriously new. Out of God's Temple flows a great life-giving river bordered by trees whose fruit is for food and whose leaves are for healing (see Revelation 22:1-2). The new tribal boundaries with which the book concludes (47:13ff.) are stylized, rather than geographically feasible. And at the very end the city is named. It is not now Jerusalem, but 'The Lord is there' (compare Revelation 21:22ff.).

▶ **Long cubit (40:5)** About 21in/520mm; so the measuring-rod was nearly 3 metres.

▶ **Sons of Zadok (40:46)** Zadok, who replaced Abiathar (1 Kings 2:26-27, 35), was the first high priest to officiate in the Temple.

▶ **43:3** See chapter 10 and chapter 1.

▶ **47:9-10** The salt water of the Dead Sea is made fresh. The 'Great Sea' is the Mediterranean.

Daniel

The book of Daniel falls into two parts. The first six chapters relate to historical events in Babylon, spanning the years of the nation's exile: 605 (1:1) to 537 BC (10:1). They tell stories of Daniel and his three friends, Shadrach, Meshach and Abed-nego. The remaining chapters, written in the first person, record four visions of future events given to Daniel in his old age.

Two languages are used: the central core (2:4 – 7:28) is in Aramaic, the rest in Hebrew. No one knows the reason for this.

When was Daniel written?

Although according to the text the book of Daniel belongs to the 6th century BC, most scholars do not believe the book was written then. They opt for a 2nd-century BC writer, drawing on well-known stories and adding the visions to bring things up-to-date. His purpose in writing was to give God's people new heart at a time when the nation was under great threat.

The issues underlying this are complex. They relate mainly to questions of history (people and events not known from any other source: see text), and the use of two languages.

It is possible to argue the early date for Part 1 and a later date (and author) for Part 2.

The crunch point is whether the kind of detail in chapter 11 (which seems to relate so clearly to the time of Antiochus IV in the 2nd century) is to be regarded as prophecy, made 400 years in advance. God does not normally work this way in life or, generally, in the rest of Scripture (though God being God we can hardly deny the possibility!).

What kind of book?

Daniel has a historical setting and is concerned with history, but is not a history in the same way as, for example, the books of Kings. Nor is it quite like the other prophets, who speak to the people in the name of God.

It is one of the earliest examples (the only one in the Old Testament), of the genre known as 'apocalyptic' writing, setting out a world-view of history within the great purposes of God. See on the New Testament book of Revelation.

Message

The main thrust of the book is clear: God, the God of Israel, is sovereign ruler of the world, at all times and in all places. For his people this means one thing: total loyalty to him. No matter how powerful the opposing forces, God will in due time (his own time) defeat them all.

The man

From the text we learn that Daniel was a Judean exile at the court of Babylon, taken there as a boy a few years earlier than Ezekiel and the first main batch of exiles. He belonged to a noble (possibly royal) family and was exceptionally able and intelligent. Daniel's role in the stories which make up the first part of the book is as much that of statesman as prophet.

Summary

Stories of Daniel, an exile in Babylon, and his visions of the future.

Part 1: chapters 1 – 6
Daniel and friends at the Babylonian court

•

Part 2: 7 – 12
Daniel's visions

Best-known passages

Nebuchadnezzar's dream (2)

The fiery furnace (3)

Belshazzar's feast (5)

Daniel in the lions' den (6)

Daniel's prayer (9)

MEDIA

Babylon
**BABYLONIA
(CHALDAEA)**

Jerusalem

PERSIA

1 – 6
At the Babylonian court

1 Daniel and friends win favour
Daniel arrives in Babylon in 605 (see below). Good looks and natural ability ensure a place for him and his friends among those selected for special training. But the Babylonians do not observe Jewish rules on clean and unclean food (Leviticus 11), nor do they drain away the blood when they slaughter animals (Leviticus 17:10ff.). Young as they are, Daniel and his friends are determined not to compromise their religion. So their only course is to restrict themselves to a vegetarian diet – and they thrive on it. What is more, they graduate from the king's school with honours!

▶ **The third year... (1)** That is 605 BC. After defeating Egypt at Carchemish, Nebuchadnezzar attacked Jerusalem. Daniel and others were taken hostage for the good behaviour of King Jehoiakim, who had been placed on the throne by the Egyptian pharaoh. Daniel uses the Babylonian reckoning for Jehoiakim's reign, beginning the year following the accession year. So 'the third year' here is the same as the fourth year (Jeremiah 25:1; 46:2) in Palestinian reckoning. The historical books do not mention this attack/siege, only those of 597 and 587 BC.

▶ **Shinar (2, some versions)** The old name for Babylonia.

▶ **Verse 4** The literature of Babylon was one 'in which magic, sorcery, charms and astrology played a prominent part' (J. Baldwin). Daniel and co. would need the determined hold on their own faith already shown, if they were not to be caught up in things their law forbade (Deuteronomy 18:10-12).

▶ **Verse 7** The endings of the Hebrew names (-el, -iah) link them with the name of Israel's God. At least one of the new names (Belteshazzar) is linked to that of a Babylonian god (see 4:8).

▶ **First year of King Cyrus (21)** The year of the decree repatriating the exiles (Ezra 1:1-4).

▶ **Until Cyrus... (21)** That is 539 BC.

2 King Nebuchadnezzar's dream
Daniel had only just graduated when he was faced with this test. The interpretation of dreams was a well-established role of the Babylonian magicians and the rest (verse 2). But anyone can come up with an interpretation, and who is to tell which is right – so Nebuchadnezzar devises his own test. Daniel believes that God can reveal the dream as well as its meaning, and has the faith to pray for this.

The image represents four world empires, beginning in the present and stretching into the future. The two most widely held interpretations are:
■ Babylonian, Medo-Persian, Greek and Roman;
■ Babylonian, Persian, Median and Greek.

The first is a better fit with the historical situation and with the fact that Christ (the kingdom of God) comes in the Roman period. The second view has the merit that the bulk of Daniel 7 – 12 refers to the Greek period.

▶ **Chaldeans (2)** In its general sense the term simply means 'Babylonian'; later it was used in a restricted sense of a class of wise men. Daniel uses the word in both ways. New International Version translates, 'astrologers'; Good News Bible, 'wizards'. The Chaldeans were the experts in the 'art' of magic. Their writings include 'omens, magic incantations, prayers and hymns, myths and legends, scientific formulae for skills such as glass-making, mathematics and astrology' (J. Baldwin).

▶ **Verse 4** The text changes from Hebrew to Aramaic here, continuing to 7:28.

3 The ordeal of the fiery furnace
The years pass and Nebuchadnezzar, forgetting he once acknowledged Daniel's God as supreme, sets up his gold-covered image 27m /90ft high, demanding that all his people worship it. But Daniel's companions will not compromise. There is only one God, and God's law forbids them to worship any other (Exodus 20:3). They know God *can* deliver them from a terrible death; they do not know if he *will* (17). But come what may, they will not deny him (18). In the event, the flames kill those who fling them in, and burn through their own bonds; but they come out with not so much as a smell of burning about them. And a god-like figure walks through the fire with them. Again the king is compelled to worship.

Marduk may be the Babylonian god which King Nebuchadnezzar honoured with a golden statue 27m/90ft high, according to Daniel 3.

▶ **Satrap (2)** One of a number of Old Persian words which occur in Daniel.

▶ **Lyre, trigon/zither, harp (5)** These are all Greek words. The instruments themselves are Mesopotamian, but Greek cultural influences had spread across this part of the world before Nebuchadnezzar's time. Greek colonies were widespread, and Greek mercenaries served in many armies.

▶ **Furnace (6)** A kiln (probably for baking bricks) with an open top and an open door at the side through which the king could see the men.

▶ **Verse 23** Here the Greek version adds two songs included in the Deuterocanonical books: 'The prayer of Azariah' and 'The Song of the three children (young men)'. See 'Deuterocanonical books'.

4 The king's madness

Nebuchadnezzar himself authenticates this extraordinary story (1-18, 34-37). Perhaps sensing that this dream is against himself, he does not turn to Daniel straight away (6-8). It is clear from Daniel's dismay that he does not wish the king ill. But the king's pride in his achievements (and archaeology shows they really *were* something to boast of) overrides Daniel's wise advice.

On Nebuchadnezzar's illness, consultant psychiatrist Dr M.G. Barker sees in Nebuchadnezzar's case the characteristics 'of a depressive illness with relatively acute onset (and) delusional beliefs of a morbid nature'. In the days before modern treatments, he says, 'most such illnesses had a spontaneous remission within a period of one, two and, occasionally, more years'. The form of the delusion (a person assuming an animal identity) is unusual today, though Dr Barker has himself encountered two cases.

There is some evidence of a tradition that the king became ill in his later years, although contemporary official records, not surprisingly, are silent about this.

▶ **Verses 3 and 34-35** The echoes from Psalms and Isaiah may reflect Daniel's influence on the king.

▶ **Seven times (16)** The length of time here as elsewhere in Daniel is unspecified. It was a definite, limited period of time fixed by God. ('Seven years', Good News Bible, is also possible.)

When the musicians played, everyone was supposed to bow down to the statue King Nebuchadnezzar erected. This group of musicians comes from Assyria.

5 The writing on the wall

Strictly speaking, Nabonidus (556-539 BC) was the last king of Babylon. But he retired to Arabia early in his reign, leaving his son Belshazzar acting king in Babylon (hence the fact that Daniel could be made only 'third ruler', 16).

The date is 539, 23 years after Nebuchadnezzar's death. The great feast at the palace is going with a swing, when a mysterious hand begins to write on the wall. Three words are written. They are weights, or units of money: 'a mina, a mina, a shekel and a half-shekel'. Daniel, now an old man, is summoned to interpret; and he goes to the root meanings of the words: 'number', 'weigh', 'divide'. The

The writing on the wall at Belshazzar's feast had to do with weights and numbers: the king was weighed on the scales and found wanting. This is the mina weight of the inscription.

Gold cups and bowls plundered from the Temple were drunk from at King Belshazzar's feast. The Oxus Treasure included gold drinking vessels from ancient Persia.

king's days were indeed numbered. That very night Cyrus the Persian took the impregnable city of Babylon, so the ancient historians tell us, by diverting the course of the River Euphrates and entering along the dry river-bed, while the Babylonians were at a feast of their gods.

▶ **Father (2)** I.e. ancestor, predecessor. The word often has this sense in the Old Testament.

▶ **The queen (10)** As Belshazzar's wives were there already, this may have been the queen mother, Nebuchadnezzar's widow.

▶ **Darius the Mede (31)** No other historical record so far found mentions anyone of this name, or places any ruler between Nabonidus/Belshazzar and Cyrus. Darius has been variously identified, but none of the suggestions is completely satisfactory. This does not mean we can write Darius off as a fictional character. Since Cyrus was so well known the author could hardly have hoped to get away with such an invention. Perhaps this is another name for Cyrus, who had mixed ancestry. In that case verse 31 would be translated 'Cyrus the Persian, even Darius the Mede'.

6 Thrown to the lions

All his life Daniel has been a man of God. He is now in his eighties, and his enemies still cannot fault him. They can only attack him through his religion (4-5). Daniel could have stopped praying for a month, or he could have prayed in secret. But he is no more ready to compromise now than he was as a boy. So his enemies have him. The king's hands are tied by his own decree, but God's hand is not. Daniel was as safe from harm in the lion-pit as his friends had been in the furnace.

▶ **Verses 8, 15** See Esther 1:19; 8:8.

▶ **The den/pit (16)** Most probably an enclosure with an open top around which was a spectator's gallery. There was also a small entrance at the side, which Darius sealed up (17).

7 – 12
Daniel's visions

7 The four beasts

Like chapter 2, Daniel's first vision is a pictorial representation of history. Again

In his first vision, Daniel saw winged beasts that stood for different empires. Such creatures were often represented in sculpture and ivory carvings at the time. This bearded sphinx is carved on the walls of the council hall at Persepolis, palace of the kings of Persia.

there are four successive empires, and then the kingdom of God is established. The winged lion is Babylon; and verse 4 has Nebuchadnezzar particularly in mind. Verse 6 depicts the Greek Empire of Alexander the Great, on his death divided among his four generals. Seleucus founded a dynasty in Syria. Ptolemy founded a dynasty in Egypt. The other two kingdoms were Greece and Asia Minor. The 'ten horns' (7, 24) equate with the toes of the image in chapter 2, though the precise identification has been much debated.

Verses 9-12 picture God's judgment of the world empires. In 13-14 God gives total dominion to 'one like a son of man'. This was Jesus' favourite title for himself. The kingdom inaugurated at Christ's first coming will be finally realized when he returns (see Matthew 26:64).

Opposing God's people in different guises throughout history is the 'little horn' (8, 20-21), until God finally removes its power. It is from this chapter that Revelation 13 draws its imagery.

▶ **Verse 1** 544 BC, the year Belshazzar became co-regent with his father – that is, before the events of chapter 5.
▶ **Verse 9** Compare Revelation 1:14; 20:4.
▶ **The books (10)** Recording everyone's deeds. See e.g. Malachi 3:16; Revelation 20:12.
▶ **A time, two times, and half a time (25)** Often taken to mean 3.5 years; but see 4:16. Evil is given its head, but for a strictly limited time.

8 The ram and the he-goat

At this point the text reverts from Aramaic to Hebrew. The second vision focusses on the second and third empires. The two-horned ram which symbolizes Medo-Persia will be superseded by the swift-footed goat – Alexander's Greek Empire. Alexander himself is the 'great horn'. The 'four horns' are the kingdoms into which his empire was divided (see chapter 7). The little horn, in this chapter, refers to Antiochus IV, who ruled Syria 175-164 BC. Verses 9-14 vividly depict the atrocities of his reign (see chapter 11), which resulted in the Jewish Maccabean revolt. 1 Maccabees 1 – 6 (in the Deuterocanonical books) recounts this period of Jewish history.

▶ **Susa (2)** East of Babylon; one of the four capitals of Persia.
▶ **Prince (11, 25)** God himself. In attempting to wipe out the Jewish religion Antiochus was directly challenging the God of Israel.
▶ **Verse 13** In 167 BC Antiochus desecrated the Temple by installing a pagan altar for sacrifices.
▶ **Verse 14** I.e. 2,300 days (see Genesis 1). Antiochus first meddled in Jewish affairs in 171; he died in 164.
▶ **Gabriel (16)** This is the first time God's messenger-angel is named in the Bible. It was Gabriel who appeared to Zechariah, father of John the Baptist, and again to Mary before the birth of Jesus.
▶ **The end (17)** This usually refers to the winding-up of history, and God's final judgment. But verse 26 relates the vision to the distant future, and 19 to the period when the suffering will be over. The Bible writers often seem to step clear of time, and view contemporary and future events as one aspect of the total, final events of 'the end'.

9 Daniel's prayer

The date is 538. Babylon has virtually ruled Judah since the Battle of Carchemish in 605. The 70 years' captivity spoken of by Jeremiah is almost up. Daniel pleads with God for the return of his people to their homeland. He is completely one with his people, sharing the blame for sin (5ff.), and his request rests solely on God's mercy (18). He saw the answer to his prayer that same year, but Israel's troubles were not over. God now shows Daniel something of what lies ahead.

Verses 24-27 are very difficult, and numerous interpretations have been suggested. God has ordained a period of 70 x 7 ('seventy weeks of years') in which the salvation of his people will be completed (24). For the Jews, the number seven itself symbolized completeness, perfection. It may therefore be best to take the numbers

Kings in Daniel's time used cylinder seals to authorize their documents. This is the seal used by Darius 1 of Persia, who reigned at the time of Ezra and the rebuilding of the Jerusalem Temple.

symbolically, though the period of time between the decree to rebuild and restore Jerusalem and the beginning of Jesus' ministry (25) comes very close to the 7 + 62 weeks = 483 days, standing for the same number of years. This is the total reached if we take the figures literally (though there is more than one possible starting-point, and even the end-date is not absolutely fixed). Verse 26 seems to point to the death and rejection of Christ and the destruction of the Temple which followed in AD 70 – with a wider reference at the end. But the subject of verse 27 is not at all clear. 'He' is taken by some to be the Messiah, by others to be the destroying prince of the previous verse.

Old Testament views of the afterlife

Philip Johnston

The Old and New Testaments say different things about death and the afterlife. In the New Testament, Christ's resurrection is the basis of our faith now and of our hope for life after death, as Paul explains in 1 Corinthians 15. But in the Old Testament there is very little reference to meaningful life after death, and many texts imply that this life is all that counts (e.g. Psalm 39:13).

This should not surprise us. After his transfiguration, Jesus told the disciples of his coming resurrection, but they did not understand what this meant (Mark 9:10). Later Paul wrote that Jesus 'brought life and immortality to light' (2 Timothy 1:10). In other words, before Christ (i.e. BC) people knew little about eternal life.

The Old Testament's focus on this life explains some of its other important differences from the New Testament. For instance, the absence of reward or punishment after death explains why the righteous want themselves to be rewarded and the wicked to be punished in the present life. It is the only way they think God's justice can be seen.

The underworld and the dead

Most peoples in the ancient Near East believed that at death everyone went down to the underworld. This was a dark dreary place under the earth, ruled by various gods. People who went there had a shadowy, sleepy existence, and there was no escape. The Hebrews called the underworld *Sheol*. Isaiah gives a brief poetic description of it (Isaiah 14:9-11): when the mighty king of Babylon descends there, its inhabitants will need to be roused to meet him, and he will become as weak and powerless as they are. Job sees it as a place of rest (Job 3:11-19).

However, Israel's view of the underworld and the dead differed from that of its neighbours in important ways:

■ Unlike several ancient Mesopotamian poems which have detailed descriptions, the Old Testament shows little interest in the underworld. It mentions dying and death about 1,000 times, but the underworld only about 100 times. And there is very little description. Death was inevitable, but the Israelites were not generally concerned with the afterlife. Israel's God was a God of the living, and his people had to respond to him in this life.

■ Perhaps many Israelites, like their neighbours, thought that everyone went to the underworld. One text (Ecclesiastes 9:10) suggests this. However, in most of the relevant texts it is the wicked who should go to Sheol (e.g. Psalm 9:17), not the righteous (e.g. Psalm 30:3). Good people only talked of going there if they felt God was punishing them (e.g. Genesis 37:35; Job 14:13), or that he was judging all humanity (Psalm 49:7; 89:48). So Sheol is usually seen as an undesirable destiny. At the same time, there is no mention of punishment in Sheol (unlike hell in the New Testament).

■ Consulting the dead was strictly forbidden (Deuteronomy 18:10-11). The account of Saul and the witch of Endor (1 Samuel 28) shows that it was possible, but Saul is roundly condemned by the spirit of the dead Samuel. So too were the Israelites by Isaiah, centuries later (Isaiah 8:19). God's people were to look to him for guidance and support, not to the dead or

10 – 11:1 Daniel and the angel

After a long fast, Daniel receives an awe-inspiring vision of a glorious figure: very like John's vision of Christ in Revelation 1:12-16. He is given insight into the continual battle raging in the spiritual realm between those protecting God's people and those bent on their destruction (see Ephesians 6:12). Michael is the special

Daniel's later visions concern crushing powers and empires. This foot of a giant statue was found at Caesarea.

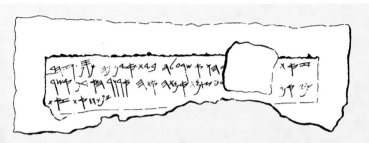

This Hebrew inscription was engraved on the lintel of a tomb chamber in Silwan, Jerusalem. It belonged to a royal steward who may have been the Shebnah criticized by Isaiah (22:15-19), and whose full name could have been Shebnaiah. Intended to warn off grave robbers, it reads: *The tomb of [...]iah, royal steward. There is no silver or gold here, only his bones and the bones of his mistress with him. Cursed be the person who opens it.*

to the supposed underworld gods.

- The Israelites did not venerate dead ancestors. Some neighbouring peoples did this at regular festivals, but there is no mention of it in the Old Testament. Family tombs in Israel were cut in soft rock, with ledges where bodies were left to decompose. When the tomb was needed again, the bones of the previous corpse were simply put into a pit in the centre and the ledge re-used. Bones held no special significance. The single mention of 'food for the dead' (Deuteronomy 26:14) refers to an offering at burial or to a funeral meal (compare Jeremiah 16:5), since placing food regularly in tombs would certainly have been condemned.

Life beyond death

Two Old Testament men avoided death and were taken directly to be with God: Enoch (Genesis 5:24) and Elijah (2 Kings 2:1). But no Israelite ever prayed to be taken to heaven like them, so they were

obviously seen as exceptions. However, a few psalmists clearly believed they would avoid Sheol and continue in fellowship with God (Psalm 16:10-11; 49:15; 73:24). These writers glimpse by faith an alternative destiny to the underworld.

Job's triumphant declaration (Job 19:26-27) seems to present a ringing confidence in life beyond death. This may well be the case, even if it goes against what Job says both before and after this (e.g. 17:13-16; 21:23-26). But unfortunately the Hebrew text is difficult to interpret here, as the footnotes in most translations indicate, so we cannot be certain.

Resurrection

The idea of resurrection is rare in the Old Testament, and it comes at times of extreme crisis. The idea is first used by Hosea as a metaphor to describe the restoration of the nation after its punishment and exile (Hosea 6:1-3), and then more fully by Ezekiel (37:1-14). The resurrection of humans first occurs in an apocalyptic passage in Isaiah

(26:19), but only for God's persecuted people, not their enemies (compare verse 14). A more general resurrection is mentioned only in Daniel. It leads to everlasting life for the righteous and everlasting shame for others (Daniel 12:2).

These passages represent a growing belief in a positive afterlife, which various Jewish books written between the Testaments developed further. However, there remained a great variety of views, as is illustrated in the disagreement between Sadducees and Pharisees (Acts 23:8). It was only the resurrection of Jesus which 'brought life and immortality to light' (2 Timothy 1:10).

The Persians
Alan Millard

The Persians were a nomadic people who moved into Iran from Central Asia about 1000 BC. They settled east of the Persian Gulf in an area still called Farsistan. The first Persian king known in history is Cyrus I, who ruled about 640 BC.

Cyrus the Great
The Persians make a dramatic entrance into the Bible story at the time when Cyrus' grandson, Cyrus II (the Great), marched into Babylon.

In 550 BC Cyrus had taken control of Ecbatana, capital of the Median king, Astyages, his father-in-law. The Medes ruled much of Persia and what is now Turkey. Cyrus took over their realm, conquered King Croesus of Lydia in western Turkey, then moved east into north-west India. By 540 BC he was ready to challenge the power of the great Babylonian Empire.

The fall of Babylon
Cuneiform inscriptions mention the fall of Babylon without a battle in 539 BC. Later tradition tells how

The Persian Empire at the height of its power. The Persian and Median army conquered Babylon in 539 BC. Alexander the Great and his Greek army began the conquest of the Persian Empire in 333 BC.

Cyrus' army marched into the city along the course of the River Euphrates, which had been diverted.

King Darius I (the Great) slays a mythical beast.

These figures line the wall of the council hall of the palace at Persepolis.

Policy of peace

Cyrus was a beneficent ruler. In Babylonia he repaired temples and returned to their own shrines images of the gods which had been brought to Babylon. The Assyrians and Babylonians had deported many conquered peoples. Now Cyrus allowed the Jews to return from Babylon to Judah. They took with them the treasures looted from the Temple in Jerusalem, and they had permission to rebuild it.

The Persian Empire

The books of Ezra, Nehemiah, Esther, Haggai, Zechariah, Malachi and parts of Daniel belong to the time of the Persian Empire under Cyrus, Darius, Xerxes (Ahasuerus) and Artaxerxes. They reflect the power and wealth of the Persian kings.

With the Near East under his control, Darius (522-486 BC) took Macedonia in northern Greece in 513. After a setback at Marathon, his son Xerxes (486-465) pushed as far as Athens before losing the sea battle at Salamis. Despite revolts in Egypt and attacks by Greek states, the Persians held their empire for 200 years. Then in 333 BC, Alexander crossed the Hellespont and within a few years Greece had become the new power.

Enlightened government

Wise government and administration made it possible for Persia to control far-off nations, Cyrus the Great divided the empire into provinces, each with its own ruler or 'satrap'. These were Persian or Median nobles, but nationals under them retained some power. People were encouraged to keep their own customs and religions, and this helped to keep the peace.

Darius I (see Ezra 6) further improved the system of government. He also introduced coinage and a legal system. His new postal network was a vital aid to communication.

A further unifying factor was the use of Aramaic as the diplomatic language of the empire from Egypt's southern frontier at Aswan to the River Indus. Aramaic was already known, even in far-off Judah, from Assyrian times. 'Speak Aramaic to us,' King Hezekiah's officials said to the Assyrian messengers, 'we understand it.' The official letters preserved in the book of Ezra are written in this Imperial Aramaic.

Art and culture

The empire created great wealth

This ornate silver flagon, from the Oxus Treasure, is a fine example of Persian craftsmanship.

and craftsmen were brought to the capital cities from every region. Darius I built a magnificent palace at Persepolis and there were others at Pasargadae, Susa and Ecbatana. Gold plate and jewellery display the wealth and luxury of the Persian court, reflected in the book of Esther.

The Cyrus Cylinder was found about 100 years ago. It records how Cyrus II of Persia took the city of Babylon by surprise, without a battle, and how he returned the gods taken from various Babylonian cities to their homes, together with their servants. This was the policy which returned the Jews to their homeland after the long years of exile.

A Babylonian boundary stone, carved with the emblems of many different gods (the origin of the signs of the zodiac).

guardian angel of the Jewish people (12:1). The 'princes' in this chapter are patron angels of the various nations.

11:2-45 Struggle for power

This chapter presents a detailed account of the struggle that took place in the Persian and Greek periods. Those who believe that the book was written *after* these events naturally do not consider this chapter to be real prophecy. The intention would still be to declare that God has full knowledge and control of all history.

There are to be three more Persian kings (2; Cambyses, Gaumata and Darius I), followed by a fourth (Xerxes). Xerxes invaded Greece but was defeated at Salamis in 480 BC. The power then passed to Greece (3-4; see chapter 7). Verse 5 refers to Egypt (the 'king of the south') and to Ptolemy's one-time general, Seleucus, who became 'king of the north' – the powerful kingdom of Syria and the east. Fifty years later (6) the daughter of Ptolemy II married Antiochus II of Syria. But she was divorced and murdered, and her brother avenged her by attacking Syria (7). Verses 9-13 reflect the struggles between the two powers at the end of the 3rd century BC. The Jews then joined forces with Antiochus III of Syria to defeat Egypt (14-15). They gained their freedom from Egypt (16), and Antiochus made a marriage alliance with Ptolemy V (17). Antiochus invaded Asia Minor and

Greece but was defeated by the Romans at Magnesia in 190 BC (18-19).

The 'exactor of tribute' (20) was his son Seleucus IV, who was shortly succeeded by his brother Antiochus IV, the persecutor of the Jews. Verses 21-24 aptly portray his character and policies. Through the treachery of Ptolemy's own men, Antiochus briefly gained control of Egypt in 173. On his return he attacked Jerusalem and slaughtered 80,000 Jews (25-28). The next time he attacked Egypt he was thwarted by the Roman fleet (29-30). He turned on Jerusalem again and desecrated the Temple (31). He was aided and abetted by some Jews, but others refused to compromise their faith, though they died for it (32-33). Judas Maccabaeus instigated a successful revolt, so helping the faithful (34).

Verses 36-45 do not describe actual events at the end of Antiochus' life. They may refer to the end of Syrian domination, at the hands of Rome, the new king from the north. Or they may anticipate events at the end of time (see 8:17), which the sufferings of God's people under Antiochus foreshadow. This then leads in to chapter 12.

12 Deliverance

Daniel is the first Old Testament book to speak explicitly of the resurrection of individual people (verse 2). When that day comes, and all the terrible troubles are past, those who have shown themselves wise by their faithful obedience to God will rise to shine like stars for ever. All evil will be done away. But as for times, those are in God's hand. Not even Daniel understands this (6-8) – so a cautious approach to these matters may still be the wisest course!

Hosea

Summary

The relationship between God and Israel is vividly portrayed in the prophet's own marriage – unfaithfulness, breakdown and healing.

Chapters 1 – 3
Hosea's experience
•
Chapters 4 – 14
God's messages to his people: judgment and restoration

This is the first and longest of the 'Minor' (shorter) prophets, called 'The Book of the Twelve' in the Hebrew Bible. Chronologically, Amos is a few years earlier.

The man and his times

Hosea was one of Isaiah's contemporaries, a prophet of God in the 8th century BC. He was a northerner and his message was for Israel, the northern kingdom, although he occasionally refers to Judah.

Hosea became a prophet at the end of the reign of the nation's last powerful king, Jeroboam II. He prophesied for the next 40 years, until just before Samaria fell to Assyria in 722/1 BC. During that time the country went rapidly downhill. Rejection of God and the wholesale adoption of pagan religious practices brought about a moral and political landslide. 2 Kings 14:23 – 17:41 gives the history of the period. The fact that after Jeroboam's death Israel had six kings in just over 20 years, four of them assassinating their predecessors, gives some idea of the nation's instability.

The message

Hosea's great themes are love – God's covenant-relationship with his people – judgment and hope.

What Israel's unfaithfulness meant to God – how he continued to love his covenant people and long for their return to him – the prophet learnt through bitter personal experience, as the wife he loved betrayed and deserted him. His message comes straight from the heart. That is what makes his book so moving, so universal and so special.

1 – 2:1 Hosea's wife and children

God instructs Hosea to marry Gomer, a woman God knows will prove unfaithful. This seems to be the meaning of verse 2, which reads, literally, 'Marry a woman (wife) of harlotry (whoredom).' 'Harlotry'

in Hosea has a double meaning, describing both illicit sexual relations and religious acts of unfaithfulness.

Three children are born, and each is given a name which speaks God's message to Israel: 'Jezreel' (standing for bloodshed and punishment), 'Unloved' and 'Not my people'. Through the prophet, God is giving his people a last opportunity to repent before judgment breaks on the land (2 Kings 17:13-14). Yet even though they refuse, his loving purpose is not thwarted (1:10 – 2:1). Those punished will be blessed. 'Not my people' will become God's own again. 'Unloved' will once more be loved.

▶ **Jezreel (14)** The site of many bloody battles; here the reference is to the slaughter recounted in 2 Kings 10.

2:2-13 Unfaithful wife – faithless nation

Hosea's voice, pleading with his unfaithful wife, becomes one with the voice of God addressing Israel. The people are worshipping Baal, the Canaanite fertility god, thinking he is the one who gives good crops and plentiful harvests; when all the time it is God. They will be punished.

2:14-23 God, the lover

In the infinitely tender language of love, God speaks of a better future, a new covenant protecting his people from all danger (both from wild beasts and from military aggression), a people betrothed and faithful to him.

▶ **Achor/Trouble Valley (15)** Near Jericho; the place where Achan sinned and was punished (Joshua 7).

▶ **My Baal (16)** A substitute word must be used because 'baal', which was the everyday word for 'lord/master/husband' was also the name of the Canaanite god.

▶ **Jezreel (22)** The word means 'God sows'.

3 Hosea's wife on probation

Gomer, now seemingly the slave of another man, is bought back and put on probation. Again, Hosea's action and his continuing love provide an object lesson. For a while, Israel too will be deprived of the things they counted on – their king and their religious emblems – but in time they will turn back to God.

▶ **Raisin cakes (1)** Dried grapes were offered to the fertility gods in the hope of a good harvest.

▶ **Verse 4** Sacrifice and ephod (part of the priest's regalia) belonged to the proper worship of God; pillar and teraphim (household gods) were part of the pagan admixture.

4 God's case against Israel

From now on there is no further mention of Hosea's family. But the experience is there, and it colours the rest of the book. Real faith in God finds expression in loving obedience, delight in his laws. The pros-

titution of Israel's religion led to literal prostitution (10-14). Pagan religion with its temple prostitutes brought in its wake sexual degradation (13-14) and the breakdown of law and order in society (the basic Ten Commandments are being broken, verse 2). The priests, who failed to make God's laws known and feathered their own nests into the bargain (4-9), and the men of Israel (14) are responsible for what has happened. God holds them accountable.

▶ **Verse 15** 'Bethaven' = 'House of evil', a derisory name for Bethel ('House of God'), one of the religious centres in the northern kingdom. Gilgal, near Jericho, was also an important place of worship.

▶ **Ephraim (17)** The leading tribe stands for the nation of Israel.

5 Judgment

A generation has grown up to whom God is a stranger (7). The alarm is sounded on Judah's borders, for Judah shares the sin to which Israel has become addicted (8-12). Not even the great king of Assyria (13; Tiglath-pileser III – see 2 Kings 16:5ff.) can

A nation reaps what it sows. God will restore prosperity to the land if his people will return to him.
Threshing out the harvest in the hills of Judea.

save them from God's judgment.

These verses probably refer to the Israel/Syria war against Judah (2 Kings 15:27-30; 16:5-9).

Verse 15 expresses God's longing. Will suffering achieve what prosperity has not, serving, as C.S. Lewis puts it, as God's 'megaphone to rouse a deaf world'?

▶ **Mizpah, Tabor, Shittim/Acacia City (1-2)** Places where there were shrines for Baal worship.

6:1-6 A short-lived change of heart

Suffering turns the people to God again. But there is no deep or long-term change. Their 'love' evaporates like dew in the hot sun. It is lasting love and real knowledge of him that God looks for.

Verses 4-6 express God's loving perplexity about his people. Jesus picks up the important statement that God wants his people's love, not placatory sacrifices, in Matthew 9:13 and 12:7.

6:7 – 7:16 Catalogue of evil

Priests have turned butcher. At the heart of the nation's religion, at Shechem, there is

intrigue and murder (6:7-10). At court it is the same. Kings fall at the hands of hot-heads and conspirators (7:6-7; see intro-duction). Israel turns to foreign peoples (8-9), foreign powers (11), foreign gods (16): but never to the Lord. Hosea's language is vividly pictorial (8, 11, 12).

▶ **Oven (7:4)** They baked their flat loaves on saucer-shaped 'hot-plates' placed upside down over the embers. The loaf (8) must be turned over to cook both sides.

8 God forsaken

Israel will be caught up in the whirlwind of God's judgment. They have made gods, made up laws, set up kings to suit them-selves: as if God and his laws did not exist. But neither idols nor allies will avail when the God they have forgotten strikes.

▶ **Bull-calf (5)** Israel's first king set up two images at shrines in his own land to rival Jerusalem as religious centres (1 Kings 12:28). The calf had a long association with pagan cults in Egypt and in Canaan.

9 A terrible destiny for Israel

It was probably at the height of the festival to mark the grape-harvest that Hosea spoke out (1-5). The people may call him a fool, but he knows he is God's watchman, and he will not hold his tongue (7-8). Israel will become a slave-nation to Assyria, as they once were to Egypt (3, 6). Sin has become habitual, ingrained, to the point where God finally withdraws his love (12, 15). Having wandered from God they will become wanderers among the nations (17). David Hubbard makes the sad point that 'from the time of Hosea's threat until the present the vast majority of Israel's sons and daughters have listed *Diaspora* (Dispersion) as their address'.

▶ **Memphis (6)** The pyramid tombs of Egypt's kings had stood there since the 26th century BC.

▶ **Gibeah (9)** For the evil deed referred to, see Judges 19.

▶ **Baal-peor (10)** See Numbers 25.

▶ **Gilgal (15)** A centre of Baal worship, but also the place where Saul was acclaimed king (1 Samuel 11:14-15). It is probably this that Hosea has in mind. The people's eagerness to have a king had in it the seeds of danger. Some

Understanding Hosea
Grace I. Emmerson

Hosea is a book about love, God's love and human love. It is also about human responsibility, about the choices for or against God that Israel had to make, and that we too have to make. Wrong choices have consequences for our lives.

A lesson from life
It was never easy to be one of God's prophets, but for Hosea it was especially difficult. He was not only to preach about God's persistent love in the face of rejection. He was to live out that love, illustrating his message by his life. It was a costly ministry.

God's first instruction to Hosea was a strange one. The wife he was to marry was immoral. A surprising start for a prophet! These words have been written with hindsight and describe, not what Gomer was at the time of her marriage, but what she became, a picture of Israel's unfaithfulness to God.

Yet despite wrong choices which brought not freedom but slavery, this was not the end of Gomer's story or of Hosea's marriage. God gave him a second instruction to keep on loving with a love that never gives up, just like God's love (chapter 3).

We are given no glimpse of Hosea's emotions, of the hurt he felt when Gomer left him or the courage he needed to renew the relationship. We don't know whether his marriage had a happy ending. For this is not the love story of Hosea and Gomer. It is God's love story; not simply past history but God's word for us today.

God told Hosea to take a wife he knew would be unfaithful. The prophet's heartbreak mirrored God's own feelings about his unfaithful people.

Uncomfortable reading
Hosea is not an easy book to read and is often uncomfortable, even frightening. God is pictured several times as a wild animal, destructive and dangerous. It sounds offensive,

> **❝** *Love cannot help becoming hope.* **❞**
>
> Kazoh Kitamori

but it is an important aspect of Hosea's message. Sin is serious, its consequences devastating. God's love is not superficial and sentimental but costly and transforming. It cost Jesus the cross.

Hosea's contemporaries, however, had forgotten the first commandment: 'no other god beside me'. They wanted to 'hedge their bets' so that if the Lord failed them they had another god to rely on. And so they turned to Baal, a Canaanite fertility god, and found Baal's worship less demanding than God's.

What of Gomer?
Recently, feminist studies of Hosea have brought fresh, sometimes disturbing insights into the story of Hosea and Gomer (chapters 1 – 3) and the patriarchal culture from which it comes. Not only is the nation's idolatry symbolized by a woman's unfaithfulness but the story is told entirely from the husband's viewpoint. The woman is passive throughout, given neither choice nor voice. Both accusation and restoration are the husband's doing. Love and discipline are imposed on her.

Equality for all
But this is where the symbol is inadequate. God's love is freely offered. The choice is ours. Here is the greatness of the Bible. It reflects an ancient patriarchal culture but transcends it with equality for all, proclaiming to every new generation that God, though grieved by our rejection, yet endlessly forgives, offering through Jesus a way back into his love.

of the later kings would usurp God's place as the true Leader of his people.

10 Disgrace and destruction

Outwardly, affluent Israel made a great show of religion (1), but inwardly the people moved further and further away from God. The calf-image at Bethel had become the nation's only 'king' (3-5), a king marked for destruction (6-8). Now they are reaping what they have long sown (13). Yet they could still sow an altogether different crop (12).

▶ **Shalman (14)** Probably a reference to the recent invasion of Gilead by Salamanu of Moab.

11 Loved as God's children

This chapter lets us see right into the infinitely loving parent-heart of God. All down the long years of history, from Egypt on, and despite all he has done for them, Israel has rejected God's love (1-4). The nation deserves no mercy (5-7). Yet God still shrinks from destroying them (8-9). He is torn between love and justice, neither of which can be denied. This is the pain he took to himself in the cross of Christ.

▶ **Admah and Zeboiim (8)** Two cities to the south of the Dead Sea, presumably destroyed with Sodom and Gomorrah (Genesis 19).

12 Lessons from history

This is not an easy chapter to follow. Israel needs to be reminded of scheming Jacob (3-6, 12) and how he learnt to lean on God, and to forget their proud independence and reliance on foreign powers. The people deride the prophets of their own day. They need the reminder that it was through a prophet (Moses, 13) that God brought the nation into being.

▶ **Verses 3-4, 12** Incidents recounted in Genesis 25:21-26; 32:22-32; and 29.

13 The east wind of God's judgment

Israel may turn to Baal and other idols, but there is in fact no God but God. People may forget him, or discount him, but he exists: and he has power to carry out all that he has warned of.

▶ **East wind (15)** The scorching wind from the desert which dries and shrivels everything in its path.

14 'Return, O Israel'

After the fierce tones of chapter 13, this last chapter is full of love and pleading. The way is open. There is no need to pass through the fire of judgment. The only requirement is loyalty to God (2-3): this is the way to find love and forgiveness, and to embark on a new, transformed life (4-7). This is the truly wise course (9).

Hosea sets it out so clearly. Yet his contemporaries ignored it all. The Assyrians swept down and destroyed their splendid capital, Samaria. They took the remaining Israelites into exile and repeopled their land with foreigners. When God gives warning of judgment, he is not playing with words.

'I will be to the people of Israel like rain in a dry land. They will blossom like flowers' (14:5). God promises his people new life when they return to him.

Joel

Summary

A locust plague in Judah warns of the Day of the Lord. But God is ready to forgive and bless his people if only they will turn to him.

> **❝** *What the locust has left, the swarmer devours; what the swarmer has left, the hopper devours; and what the hopper has left, the grub devours.* **❞**
>
> 1:4

We know virtually nothing about this prophet, except his father's name (1:1), and the prophecy contains few clues to the date when it was written. We may guess at dates – and guesses range from the 8th century BC to the 4th century BC and later – but the book itself is timeless.

Joel is obviously familiar with themes which also occur in Isaiah, Amos and Ezekiel – particularly the 'Day of the Lord', when God will finally judge the world and his own people. What prompts the prophet's message is a dire emergency, a plague of all-consuming locusts. As the insect swarms hide the sun and eat up the food supply, the prophet sees in them the darkness and suffering which will characterize that Day. He calls the nation to repent, for God still loves his people and longs to rescue and restore them.

1 Locusts lay waste the land

Even in the past 100 years Jerusalem has been stripped of all vegetation by a plague of locusts like the one Joel describes so vividly. The swarm of several million insects is carried into Palestine by the desert wind from Arabia.

The locust grows rapidly from larva to winged adult (4), and at every stage its appetite is insatiable. It is worse than an invading army: when it moves on there is no green or growing thing left (6-12). There is nothing to offer to God (9, 13), or so little that the people are using all they have to ward off starvation. For Joel, the locust swarm is a sign, a warning of the terror of the Day of the Lord, God's approaching judgment day (15). He calls for a national day of prayer (14).

In his mercy, God restores fertility to the land. 'I am going to give you corn and wine and olive-oil' (2:19). The olive press will have work to do.

2:1-11
Warning of God's judgment on his people

The locust army becomes a picture of the invading army of God on the day of his judgment: the sky black with insects (2); the 'scorched earth' in their wake (3); their inexorable, totally irresistible, onward march (4-9). This is what God's judgment will be like. Who can bear it (11)?

2:12-17 A call to repent

The good news is that no one *need* endure God's judgment. He is still calling people to repent (12). Joel calls the whole nation to turn to God and plead for mercy (13-17).

2:18-32

Moved with pity and compassion, God promises to restore in profusion all that the locusts have taken. He will rid the land of the locust army he has sent against them (25).

More than this, God promises a great outpouring of his Spirit, not just on priests and prophets, but on ordinary people, regardless of gender, age, or class (28-32). In Acts 2:16-21, Peter, addressing a crowd of Jews gathered in Jerusalem from 'every nation under heaven', announces that this prophecy of Joel is being fulfilled.

▶ **Northerner (20)** Locust hordes generally invade Palestine from the south or east. The military threat, however, was from the north. So northerner here may indicate a hostile enemy, rather than saying where the locusts came from.

3:1-21 God calls the nations to account

The nations will be punished for all they have inflicted on God's people (3:2-8). Multitudes will be gathered for God's judgment. There he will decide their destiny (14).

Then God will make his home in a city and among a people at last made holy; and

the whole land will share in this abundant blessing (16-18).

▶ **Tyre, Sidon, Philistia (4)** See Ezekiel 25 – 28. Artaxerxes III sold the Sidonians as slaves in 345 BC, and in 332 Alexander the Great sold the people of Tyre and the Philistine city of Gaza into slavery.

▶ **Sabaeans (8)** Famous Arabian traders.
▶ **Verse 10** Joel reverses Isaiah's famous words (Isaiah 2:4).
▶ **Verse 12** Some versions have 'Jehoshaphat' which means 'the Lord judges' – hence the alternative translations, 'Valley of Judgment', 'valley of Decision'.

Joel sees a swarm of locusts as an object lesson about the great and terrible day of God's judgment.

God's blessing is expressed in a green and fruitful land which his people can enjoy.

Amos

Amos was a layman: a shepherd and dresser of fig-trees. His home was in Tekoa (1:1), about 20km/12 miles south of Jerusalem, on the edge of the Judean desert. But God sent him as his prophet to the northern kingdom of Israel (7:14-15). His base was the religious centre of Bethel, where King Jeroboam I had set up a calf-image when the nation had first split into two rival kingdoms.

Amos lived in the reign of Jeroboam II (793-753 BC), Israel's Indian summer of prosperity and influence. Beneath its affluence, however, the nation was rotten. Amos was sent to denounce the social and religious corruption, and warn of God's impending judgment. But the people turned a deaf ear, as they did to his contemporary, Hosea. And the king's chaplain told him to get back to Judah (7:10ff.)!

Thirty years after Jeroboam's death, in 722/1, the Assyrians attacked from the north to destroy Samaria and take the people into exile. Israel ceased to exist. But the prophet's voice still sounds down the years, crying out for justice on behalf of the poor and helpless of every age and nation, and warning that God will judge those in power who continue to oppress them. God cares.

The prophet Amos was a shepherd when he received God's call.

1 – 2 God's judgment on the nations – and Israel

Amos condemns the nations round about Israel, one by one – Syria, Philistia, Tyre, Edom, Ammon, Moab. The Syrians are guilty of wanton cruelty (running studded threshing-sledges over the bodies of their captives, 1:3); the Philistines of selling their own people. Tyre and Edom have transgressed the laws of kinship. Ammon's atrocities have been committed simply to gain more land. By desecrating a corpse Moab has violated one of the most universal of all ancient unwritten laws. God will punish each and every one. No doubt the listening Israelites were happy to hear their enemies condemned.

But Amos does not stop there. Judah too is condemned (2:4-5). Now the prophet is getting uncomfortably close to home.

Even so, nothing can have prepared his hearers for the shocking punch-line, the refrain that this time is for them: 'For crime after crime of *Israel* I shall grant them no reprieve' (2:6). This was the main purpose of Amos's preaching: to warn the Israelites that they too were under the judgment of God.

Hosea makes it plain that Israel's basic sin was in turning away from God to worship idols. But Amos emphasizes the moral and social decline which resulted. They have grown hard and callous in their dealings with others; young and old make use of temple prostitutes; and they have

Summary

The shepherd-prophet Amos delivers God's warnings of judgment to the northern kingdom of Israel.

Chapters 1 – 2
God's judgment on neighbouring nations – and on Israel
•
Chapters 3 – 6
Warnings of punishment; appeals for repentance
•
Chapters 7 – 9:6
Visions of judgment
•
Chapter 9:7-15
A remnant of Israel restored

Justice and the poor
Evelyn Miranda-Feliciano

Justice and the poor is a main motif in Scripture. It runs through the warp and woof of the salvation story from the day Abel was slain by his brother, Cain, to the wiping away of tears in the book of Revelation.

A matter of heart and will
The biblical idea of justice is not a theoretical construct which simply stretches the intellect. Rather, it exercises the heart and the will. It is summarized by Jesus' saying that to love God with all our heart, with all our soul and with all our mind; and to love our neighbour as ourselves sums up all the law and the prophets (Matthew 22:37-40). These two statements concretized the expression of God's justice and righteousness in the Old Testament.

Seen in this light, justice therefore has a dynamic relational quality; in fact, a quality of a loving determined act between God and humans, and between one human and another. An act which fulfills the demands of a relationship, whether with God or fellow humans, is called righteous. Any act within the covenant relationship that maintains, preserves or restores the foundation of a communal life is just.

Living life together
Justice brings together humanity and community, two important elements very much eroded in our times. For instance, world leaders and strong nations are happy enough to make a global economic village of the world, but are they willing to make it a community of compassionate caring and just sharing of resources?

In the Old Testament, the law of Moses, exemplified in the Ten Commandments, and all the other laws were forged within a covenantal pact of obedience and faithfulness – between God and his people, and among themselves. Everything was open and nothing was forced. All the laws were meant to create a sound basis for living life together.

God's bias to the poor
So biblical justice does not wear a blindfold, impartially holding the balance like the symbol of justice we have today. Rather, it has an open, magnificent, holy face; the face of God kindly turned towards the poor, the helpless and the downtrodden. In a fallen world of chronic injustice, then and now, God firmly stands as Protector and Vindicator of the dispossessed (Psalm 10:14-18). This is God's social bias, his partiality.

It is not that the poor are necessarily sanctified by the scarcity in their lives, or are more virtuous because of their suffering than the rich. 'There is no distinction', Paul says in the New Testament, 'since all have sinned and fall short of the glory of God' (Romans 3:23).

It is that on God's social scale, in the midst of all the evil and distortion of human sinfulness, those on the underside of life are on the 'wronged' side; they are the 'sinned-against' ones. And being the ultimate measure of what justice is, God takes up their causes. For he loves righteousness and justice (Psalm 33:5); he is near to the broken-hearted, and he saves the crushed in spirit (Psalm 34:18).

Rulers and judges
As the Lord of Righteousness (Jeremiah 23:6), God expects, first and foremost, rulers and judges

▶▶ (i.e. the leadership of the land) to be just and right (2 Samuel 8:15; 1 Chronicles 18:14; 1 Kings 10:9; Deuteronomy 1:16; Exodus 23:7-8; Psalm 82:3-4).

The duty of the king is not to debauch himself but to be constantly vigilant to speak on behalf of those who are unable to articulate their suffering. He is to judge righteously and maintain the rights of the poor and needy (Proverbs 31:4-5, 8-9).

On the other hand, judges are not to take bribes, not to be intimidated by the powerful, but rather to uphold the right of the afflicted and the destitute, and to succour the weak and needy.

The role of the prophets

To remind the leaders of this is the role of the prophets, who thunder against idolatry and injustice – on personal, national and international levels. They often dramatized in their own persons the consequences of a people enamoured only by their own whims and appetites.

In the economy of Scripture, faithfulness to the One God and people's wellbeing go together (as idolatry goes with injustice). This is something we need to reflect on in today's world of secularism and pluralism and enormous scientific advancement, where injustice seemingly abounds, getting more sophisticated by the day. Is this because of a stubborn refusal to recognize an absolute God of justice in our midst?

Our own world

Today, the world's poor have vastly increased in number, and they come in many guises.

The recent ethnic wars which have wiped out whole peoples is a grim repeat of Cain slaying Abel.

The unwanted refugees who have become stateless are worse off than the exiles of olden times.

Women and children all over the world still bear the brunt of numerous oppressions brought about by their gender and helplessness.

The old, the sick and the infirm take a back seat in life.

The teeming workers from poor countries scour the face of the earth. Severely culturally and socially dislocated, they often work under onerous conditions.

Famine in many parts of the world leaves millions, if not yet dead, mere spectres of themselves. And at the same time there are nations who worry about obesity among their citizens, spending billions on weight-reducing technologies.

Today also, a great part of humankind suffers oppression not only at the hands of neighbours but also from the unseen hands of powerful elites in their own countries and in the wider world.

By creating laws, structures and systems biased towards the interest of the few, people today have devised a way of distancing themselves from directly oppressive acts against not only individuals or communities but also whole nations and peoples.

Some economic/political laws, structures and systems which operate today keep weaker nations in constant dependency and underdevelopment. That the poor will always be with us remains a fact – proof of a universal unregenerate conscience under God's judgment.

Who will help?

The prophet Isaiah surveyed the moral and social landscape of his day and found it utterly barren. He lamented:

*'There was no justice,
    and when the Lord saw it he was
        displeased.
He saw that there was no help
    forthcoming
    and was outraged that no one
        intervened.'*
Isaiah 59:15-16

To intervene was the great challenge for Isaiah and all faithful prophets before and after him.

Today, with injustice globalized and structured, and the poor further marginalized and reduced to statistics, the challenge to 'stand in the gap' remains as strong as ever.

gagged God's spokesmen. None will escape God's punishment.

▶ **1:3, 6, etc.** The formula 'For three... for four' (some versions) indicates an indefinite number: so, 'again and again', 'for crime after crime'.

▶ **Hazael, Ben-hadad (1:4)** Kings of Syria. Hazael seized the throne in Elisha's time and founded a dynasty.

▶ **Kir (1:5)** The place the Syrians originally came from.

▶ **Gaza, Ashdod, Ashkelon, Ekron (1:6-8)** Four of the five Philistine cities.

▶ **His brother (1:11)** Edom and Israel were descendants of two brothers, Esau and Jacob.

▶ **Rabbah (1:14)** The Ammonite capital; modern Amman, capital of Jordan.

▶ **2:8** The law humanely ordered that garments taken in pledge were to be returned by nightfall (Exodus 22:26-27).

▶ **Amorite (2:9)** Used inclusively, meaning the original inhabitants of Canaan.

▶ **Nazirites (2:11)** Men consecrated to God by a special vow which involved renouncing wine.

▶ **Cart/wagon (2:13)** More likely the threshing-sledge (as Jerusalem Bible).

3 Punishment

Israel, the people who have known God's special love and care, the people he brought out of Egypt (1-2) have broken their covenant-agreement with God. In consequence they must suffer punishment. It is simple cause and effect (like the other instances given in verses 3-6). God has spoken; he will act. Of beautiful Samaria, with its great stone houses and exquisite ivory panels, only a trace will be left; just enough to show that the city once existed. And God will demolish the trappings of debased religion at Bethel (verse 14).

4 God's warnings ignored

The luxury-loving women of Samaria who have 'fattened' themselves (like the well-fed cows of fertile Bashan), at the expense of the poor, will be led away with hooks. (The Assyrians actually did this to their captives.) At the same time as they were crushing the helpless (those for whom God had special care, protected under God's law), the people still kept up the religious façade (4-5). But 'insurance policy' religion is a mockery of the real thing (see James

God will judge the luxury-loving people of Samaria, who furnish their homes with fine ivory carvings – and trample on the poor. That is the prophet's message.

1:26-27). By famine and drought, blight and disease God had warned them where they were heading – all to no avail.

5:1-17 'Seek me and live'

The funeral song for Israel (1-3) is quickly followed by an appeal. God calls on his people to save their lives by seeking him. And this means, not yet more sacrifices at the nation's corrupt sanctuaries (5), but reformed living – a return to God's standards of justice and right conduct in public as well as private life.

▶ **The gate (10)** 'Court'; the city gate was the place for business transactions and the administration of justice.

▶ **Joseph (15)** Ephraim and Manasseh (descended from Joseph's two sons) were leading tribes in the northern kingdom.

5:18-27 Bad news, not good!

The Day of the Lord is coming. The people of Amos's day used this expression to describe a time when God would act for them against their enemies. They looked forward to it. Shockingly, Amos says that on that day God will act *against them* because of their wickedness. The Day of the Lord will not be what they expect: it will be like a leap from the frying-pan into the fire (5:19). Shock on shock, God declares that he does not appreciate or accept their worship. What he wants is justice, to see them do what is right.

> **❝** *Woe to you who long for the day of the Lord! Why do you long for the day of the Lord? That day will be darkness, not light... I hate, I despise your religious feasts; I cannot stand your assemblies... Away with the noise of your songs! I will not listen to the music of your harps. But let justice roll on like a river, righteousness like a never-failing stream!* **❞**
>
> 5:18, 21-24

Israel will be 'sieved', said Amos, as this woman sieves grain at Sychar.

The Old Testament prophets often speak of the Day of the Lord: see Isaiah 13:6; Ezekiel 30:2-3; Joel 1:15ff.; Zephaniah 1:7ff.

▶ **Sakkuth, Kaiwan (26)** Assyrian gods associated with the planet Saturn.

6 Ruin and exile
Affluence and comfortable living (then as now) insulate people from the real issues, and breed false security. Self-sufficiency and pride have been the downfall of human beings from first to last (e.g. Genesis 11:1-9; Ezekiel 28). Now the pride of Israel, which God hates (8), will be brought low. Ruin and exile await God's people.

▶ **Calneh, Hamath (2)** Two towns in Syria; Hamath is modern Hama.

▶ **Lo-debar, Karnaim (13)** Towns east of the Jordan, which Israel took from the Syrians.

▶ **Arabah (14)** The dry valley running south from the Dead Sea to the Gulf of Aqaba.

7:1-9; 8:1-3; 9:1-6 What the prophet sees
Five visions of doom are described in these passages. After each of the first two, the locusts and the fire, Amos begs God to forgive his people, and God relents. But the second two (the plumb-line, 7:7-9, and the

basket of fruit, 8:1-3) allow no such opportunity. Judgment is necessary and certain. The last vision (9:1-6) gives a terrifying picture of total destruction.

▶ **The Lord repented/relented (3, 6)** I.e. he mercifully changed his mind.

7:10-17 Confrontation
God's prophet and 'official religion' meet head-on in the confrontation between Amos and Amaziah (10-17). The prophet has God's authority for his message and will not be silenced. Amaziah will die in exile. The invading army will abuse his wife, kill his children and seize his land.

▶ **Verses 14-15** Amaziah insinuates that prophecy is just a job. Amos replies that he has a different job and only prophesies because God has told him to.

▶ **Sycamore (14)** A kind of fig-tree; not the tree we call sycamore.

8:4-14 Israel ripe for ruin
People like to think their 'little' sins too small for God to notice. But he sees everything: greed and sharp practice; short weight and sub-standard goods. And the poor, who always come off worst, are his special concern.

▶ **Verse 5** The traders are cheating by overcharging, using false measures and tampering with the scales.

▶ **Ashimah (14,** some versions) A Syrian goddess worshipped in Israel. Dan, in the far north, was the town where Jeroboam I erected a calf-image to divert the people from worship in Jerusalem.

9:7-15 A faithful remnant restored
For the nation as a whole, judgment will be inescapable. God will deal with them like any foreign nation (7a). But for the faithful few the future holds unimagined blessing (11-15).

▶ **Caphtor (7)** Crete, where the Philistines originally came from.

Obadiah

Summary

A prophecy against Edom.

Nothing but his name (which means 'servant of God') is known of this prophet. His prophecy concerns the downfall of Edom (for other prophecies against Edom, see Isaiah 34:5-15; Jeremiah 49:7-22; Ezekiel 25:12-14; 35:1-15; Amos 1:11-12).

Edom occupied the mountainous region south-east of the Dead Sea. The capital, Sela (now Petra), was perched high on a plateau above a sheer rock cliff approached by a narrow gorge. It was virtually impregnable. From mountain strongholds like this the Edomites launched their raids on Palestine. As Esau's descendants they were in fact kin to Israel, but there was never any love lost between the two. The final outrage – and the occasion of Obadiah's prophecy – was their invasion of Judah while Jerusalem was being sacked by the Babylonians in 587 BC.

Obadiah denounces Edom's pride (3). The Edomites thought their strongholds invincible, but they would be utterly destroyed (8-10).

In the 5th century BC Arabs took Edom, and in the 3rd century the region was overrun by the Nabataeans (who built the rock-city of Petra in present-day Jordan). Some Edomites settled in southern Judah. Herod the Great, ruler of the Jews at the time of Jesus' birth, was one of their descendants. After AD 70 the Edomites entirely disappear from history.

In contrast to dispossessed Edom, Israel will return to possess a greatly extended land including former Edomite territory (17-21).

▶ **Teman (9)** An important town in Edom, home of Job's friend Eliphaz; Mt Esau is Mt Seir.

▶ **Verse 19** 'Negeb'/'Negev', the southern desert; 'Shephelah', the hill-country behind the western coastal plain; 'Ephraim and Samaria', the northern kingdom of Israel; 'Gilead', east of the Jordan.

▶ **Verse 20** 'Zarephath' 1 Kings 17:9; Luke 4:26), between Tyre and Sidon in Phoenicia (now Sarafand in Lebanon); 'Sepharad' may be Sardis in present-day Turkey.

Obadiah denounces Edom. Visible beyond the old high place of sacrifice is 'Aaron's tomb' on one cliff-top, and the stronghold of 'Sela' (Umm al Biyara, which means 'cisterns') – Edom's capital – on the other.

Jonah

Summary

The story of the prophet Jonah's mission to Nineveh, capital city of enemy Assyria, with a call to repent or face God's punishment.

Jonah is a little masterpiece: a rattling good tale with a dramatic plot that is full of surprises. No wonder children love it. But the author did not write it as a story for children. Jonah carries a vital message. And whether we take the book as in the style of a Jewish folk-tale, as 'fiction with a message', or as 'history with a moral', there is no doubt about the main themes. The book is about justice and mercy. Jonah has to learn that Israel's special relationship with God does not make him their exclusive possession. God's care and concern – his purpose to save – extends to the whole world, even the Assyrian enemy that in 722/1 destroyed Israel. The story must have conveyed a strong message to those of the Jewish establishment who shared Jonah's view.

Jesus focussed attention on two further points: the parallel with the three days between his own death and resurrection; and the ready repentance of the Ninevites in contrast to his hearers (Matthew 12:41; Luke 11:32).

The Old Testament provides no detail about the author of Jonah or the date of writing. The only other mention of a prophet of this name is in 2 Kings 14:25. That would set this story in the mid-8th century BC. Nineveh, capital of powerful Assyria and subject of this book, was destroyed by the Babylonians in 612 BC. Nothing completely rules out the early date implied by the setting, but most scholars place it during or after the exile on grounds of language and certain historical problems (see on 1:17; 3:3 below).

Jonah was so set on evading God and the mission he had been given that all his natural fears of a long sea voyage were swept aside. To the Jews the sea was fearful, the great unknown, the habitat of mythical sea monsters and chaos.

1 Jonah rejects God's mission

Called by God to go to Nineveh and denounce the wickedness of the people, Jonah takes ship in the opposite direction: 4:2 tells us why. It is not that he's afraid (verse 12 shows plenty of courage!), but he knows God too well. If the Ninevites repent and change their ways, God will forgive them. And Jonah wants this cruel threatening enemy nation destroyed. So he disobeys. By trying to save his life, the heathen sailors display more humanity than the man of God (13).

▶ **Verse 3** 'A ship bound for Tarshish': maybe Tartessus in Spain. Jonah is heading west, away from Nineveh, as far as he can get.

▶ **A great fish (17)** Although sperm whales and large sharks capable of swallowing a person are not unknown in the eastern Mediterranean, this incident is clearly intended to be seen as a miracle. It is one of the many things God 'appoints' or 'ordains' in the story (see 1:4; 4:6-8). Argument over this must not blind us to the whole point.

2 Jonah's prayer

This moving psalm records Jonah's cry from the belly of the fish. He vividly describes his near death by drowning, the fate from which God has saved him. Uncomfortable though he now is, he has come to his senses, remembering his 'true loyalty' (8). And God responds by returning him to the world of light and air (10). He will have the chance to begin again.

▶ **Verse 2** 'Sheol' is the world of the dead.

3 Nineveh responds

Now, when God's call comes again, Jonah leaps to obey. He is on his way to Nineveh –

at once! And his message produces a remarkable effect. The whole city, from the greatest to the least, repents. And God spares them.

▶ **Three days' journey (3)** If this is not storyteller's exaggeration for the sake of effect, it may apply to the district of Nineveh as distinct from the city whose inner wall was enlarged from three to more than 12 km/7 miles round by King Sennacherib.

▶ **God repented (10)** See on Amos 7:3.

4 A hard lesson for Jonah

Jonah wanted God to confine his love and mercy to Israel. Let the heathen get their deserts. Far from being delighted that his message provoked such a fantastic response, he was furious. And it wasn't simply that he didn't want to look a fool. There was no spark of compassion for the people of Nineveh in Jonah's heart. And so God used a plant (the shady castor-oil plant) to teach him an important lesson (6ff.). There is a subtle play on words here: 'pity' can also mean 'be sorry to lose' something. Jonah is sorry to lose the plant as God is sorry to lose Nineveh. But God's feelings, unlike Jonah's, stem from a deep compassion (11).

Rather than obey God's instructions, Jonah took ship in the opposite direction. The model is of a Greek merchant ship, 6th century BC.

Micah

Summary

Prophecies of God's judgment on Samaria and Jerusalem for injustice and crimes against the people: God will punish and afterwards restore.

Micah was one of the 8th-century BC prophets, contemporary with Amos and Hosea (in the northern kingdom of Israel) and Isaiah (in Jerusalem). He was a countryman, from a town in south-west Judah, on the Philistine border.

His message is for Samaria and Jerusalem, capital cities of the two kingdoms. From a comparison with Amos it is clear that Judah had become infected with the same sins that beset Israel. So Micah, too, denounces rulers, priests and prophets; deplores the money-grubbing exploitation of the helpless; dishonesty in business; sham religion.

God's judgment will fall on Samaria and Jerusalem; only after that will there be restoration. But Micah also sees a glorious future, when Jerusalem will become the religious centre of the world, and Bethlehem give birth to a greater David who will rule over all God's people.

1 The two cities

In the prophet's lament, God is pictured coming down from heaven, treading upon the mountains, to destroy Samaria for her persistent idolatry. The gangrene has spread into Judah, and God's judgment is at the gates of Jerusalem. Micah pictures the approach of the invading army. Stronghold after stronghold falls. The order is not that of the Assyrian army's march, however: the towns (those known) encircle Micah's own home town of Moresheth-gath (10ff.). (The place-names frequently conceal a play on words: Moresheth-gath is like the Hebrew for fiancée; Mareshah like the word for conqueror.) The parents in Judah will mourn for their exiled children.

In 722/1 BC the Assyrians destroyed Samaria. In 701 they besieged Jerusalem, and the city escaped by a miracle (see 2 Kings 18:9 – 19:37). Micah most probably lived through both these traumatic events.

> 66 *Woe betide those who lie in bed planning wicked deeds, and rise at daybreak to do them, knowing that they have the power to do evil! They covet fields and take them by force; if they want a house they seize it; they lay hands on both householder and house, on a man and all he possesses. Therefore these are the words of the Lord: I am planning disaster for this nation.* 99
>
> 2:1-3

▶ **Verse 1** Jotham (750-732) and Hezekiah (729-687) were good (God-fearing) kings; Ahaz (735-716) was one of the worst, introducing terrible heathen practices, including child-sacrifice. (Overlapping dates indicate periods of co-regency.)

▶ **Gath (10)** A Philistine, and therefore enemy, city.

▶ **Verse 13** Lachish led the nation into idolatry.

2 – 3 Exploitation and misrule

Those with power and influence are all on the make, and not fussy about the means they use. So property is seized and families made destitute; and the preacher is told this is none of his business. (2:12-13 moves abruptly to the future, picturing God at the head of the remnant of his people.) Far from promoting justice, the nation's leaders 'hate good and love evil'. They fleece the people (3:1-3 are not meant literally!). Rulers, priests and prophets, there is nothing to choose between them – all have their price (3:11). They will bring Jerusalem to ruin (3:12).

4 Future greatness

The doom of chapter 3 is followed by fresh hope. Verses 1-8 speak of a new Jerusalem, from which God's word goes out to all people, and to which the nations flock, in an era of peace and plenty.

God will bring home a remnant of his people. Salvation – rescue and restoration – will come: but only on the other side of suffering, after the trauma of the Assyrian invasion and the exile in Babylon (verse 10 shows that the 'now' of verse 9 takes in the whole sweep). Then God will judge, not his people alone, but all the nations massed against them (11-13).

▶ **Verses 1-3** Almost identical with Isaiah 2:2-4. One may borrow from the other, or both use an existing prophecy.

▶ **Babylon (10)** The enemy in Micah's day was

Assyria, but like Isaiah he looks ahead to the power which would destroy Jerusalem a century later.

5 The King from Bethlehem

'Now' (verse 1), in the midst of the Assyrian siege, Micah speaks of a deliverer – the ultimate deliverer – who will come, like David of old, from Bethlehem (see Matthew 2:1-6). Historical perspectives blur, as so often in the prophets, and current events melt into those of the near and far distant future. In the messianic peace, even the Assyrian will be overcome. But Judah too will be purified 'in that day' (10ff.). All that they have relied on in place of God will be destroyed: armies, defences, witchcraft and false gods.

▶ **Ephrathah (2)** The district around Bethlehem.

▶ **Seven... eight (5)** Idiomatic, for 'an indefinite number', perhaps meaning that no matter how many leaders are needed they will be forthcoming.

▶ **Nimrod (6)** Assyria (see Genesis 10:8-12).

6 Pleasing God

God sets out his case, lays his charges, against his people. Don't they know what pleases him? It is so plain, so simple (verse 8). There can be no substitute for love and loyalty and fair dealing. Though they may try to buy him off with extravagant offerings and impressive gifts, God sees his people's dishonesty, the false scales that he hates because they cheat the helpless. And he will punish sharp practice, violence and deceit.

▶ **Verse 5** See Numbers 22 – 24.

▶ **Shittim to Gilgal (5)** I.e. at the crossing of the Jordan (Joshua 3 – 4).

▶ **My firstborn... (7)** The sacrifice of the firstborn crept into Israel with other pagan practices in the dark days of the nation's last kings.

▶ **Verse 11** See Amos 8:5.

▶ **Omri... Ahab (16)** Two kings of Israel notorious for introducing Baal-worship.

7 Darkness and light

The prophet opens his heart to us in this final chapter. He mourns for what is happening among his own people as society breaks down (1-6). Faithfulness, honesty, trust: all are gone. The rot which began at government level has permeated the whole nation. And now all human relationships are crumbling. Friendship and family count for nothing.

The human scene is black, but hope remains because Micah knows his God. With God there is yet light. He may still be relied on. His promise will not fail. He will build again. He will deliver again. In his compassionate love he will forgive again.

So Micah will watch (7) and wait for the time when God will once again shepherd his people (14ff.), doing miracles for them as of old, showing compassion: faithful to the age-old promises he made to the founding fathers of his people (20).

▶ **Watchmen (4)** The prophets were posted as watchmen to warn of coming judgment (see Ezekiel 3:17-21).

> **" What does the Lord require of you? To act justly and to love mercy and to walk humbly with your God. "**
> 6:8

Nahum

Summary

God's judgment against the city of Nineveh and the whole Assyrian Empire.

The subject of Nahum, like that of the book of Jonah, is Nineveh, the great capital city of Assyria. But whereas Jonah records the city's reprieve, Nahum predicts its destruction. The date is somewhere between the fall of Thebes to the Assyrians in 663 BC (already in the past in 3:8-10), and the fall of Nineveh to the Babylonians and Medes in 612 BC. Nahum seems to have been a Judean, but apart from this we know nothing about him, except that he was capable of writing some of the most graphic poetry in the whole of the Old Testament.

1 'I will end Assyria's power'

Nahum starts, not with Nineveh, but with God: his power, his anger, his goodness. God says that the days of Assyria, whose armies destroyed Israel and threatened

Jerusalem itself less than a century before, are now numbered.

Verses 2-8 are an alphabet psalm (incomplete), either the prophet's own composition or perhaps an existing poem he turned to his purpose. Every phrase speaks God's power, over earth, seas, rivers, mountains. Bashan's rich pasture and forest turn brown at his presence as if stricken by drought. The hills melt. God is his people's powerful protector (7): his coming spells death to their enemies (8-10).

▶ **An overwhelming flood (8)** Impregnable Nineveh eventually fell when floodwaters breached her walls, making way for the attacking army.

▶ **One/a man (11)** Perhaps Sennacherib, the Assyrian king who took Lachish and then laid

Nahum writes of the fall of Nineveh, capital city of Assyria. The Assyrians were the great power of his day, whose armies inflicted great suffering on subject peoples. They had destroyed the kingdom of Israel in 722/1 BC.

siege to Jerusalem in 701 BC (see Isaiah 36 – 37).

2 Assault on Nineveh

The prophet's description uses every resource of sound and vision: we can see and hear, almost smell, the onslaught. Once, God had used the armies of Assyria to punish his people. Now the forces attacking Nineveh are his instruments. Blood and thunder; plunder and desolation; the den of the Assyrian lion is no more. Nahum's scenes are vivid to the eye and to the imagination – even to the wailing slave-girls.

▶ **Mantelet (5**, some versions) A siege-engine armed with battering-ram.

▶ **Verse 6** See 1:8.

3 Doom city

Nahum pictures the city as a prostitute, enticing the nations into submission. Now she will receive a prostitute's punishment (5-6). She will share the terrible fate she inflicted on the Egyptian city of Thebes (No-Amon). (At Thebes, city of Amun, state-god of Egypt, the treasures of centuries had been accumulated. The Assyrians took the city with fire and slaughter and plundered all its wealth.) Though the nation is as

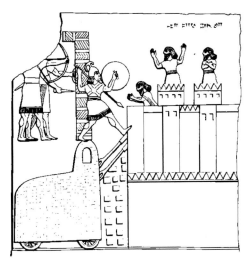

The armies of Assyria with their siege-engines and battering-rams, stormed cities and slaughtered God's people.

great as a swarm of locusts they will vanish like a swarm that has flown. The final verses are addressed to the emperor. All is now lost for ever.

For all its might, Nineveh fell quickly into ruin after the Babylonians took it, leaving no trace but a mound which is known today as Tell Kuyunjik, 'the mound of many sheep'.

▶ **Ethiopia/Cush (9)** Present-day Sudan, which supplied a dynasty of Egyptian kings. 'Put' may be Libya or possibly Somalia.

Habakkuk

Summary

Why does God let the wicked flourish? Is there no justice? Habakkuk asks the great, universal questions – and God replies.

66 *The righteous will live by being faithful.* 99

2:4

The prophet Habakkuk is battling with much the same problem as Job and the writer of Psalm 73: the fact that while the good, the innocent, suffer, the wicked flourish. So Habakkuk, believing that God is just and good, asks his questions. Why, God, why?

The book belongs to the latter part of the 7th century BC, when Jeremiah was prophesying in Jerusalem. Some would place it before, some just after, the fall of the Assyrian Empire (Nineveh, the Assyrian capital, fell to the Babylonians in 612 BC) and the defeat of Egypt by King Nebuchadnezzar of Babylon at Carchemish in 605. Babylon is on the march, but so far Judah has escaped. In 597 BC, not long after this, Jerusalem fell into enemy hands, and in 587 the Babylonians destroyed the city.

'I will climb my watchtower and wait to see what the Lord will tell me to say,' says Habakkuk.

1 'O God, why?'

'O God, why are you deaf to my prayer? Why don't you *do something* about the breakdown of law and order, about the *wickedness* in the land?' the prophet cries (1-4).

God's answer (5-11) seems only to aggravate the problem: 'My punishment will be an invasion of savage Babylonian (Chaldean) soldiers!'

So Habakkuk replies (12-17), 'How can you, the all-good, the just God, use such a vicious instrument of judgment – you who cannot bear the sight of evil? Will you let Babylon fish the sea of humanity for ever?'

2 God cares: right will prevail

The prophet takes his stance high on the watchtower, on the look-out, waiting with bated breath for God's response (1). And the assurance comes: God has not changed his nature; he has not joined sides with the wicked. When the final scores are added up, only those who trust God and remain true to him will live (4). God will punish all humanity's arrogant pride. Woe betide those who greedily grab what belongs to others; who for selfish ends justify the cruellest means; who climb to power on the backs of others; who destroy and dehumanize; who give their worship to idols shaped by human hands. The lives of all such people are forfeit, whatever their nationality.

▶ **Verse 17** The armies stripped the forests for which Lebanon was famous.

3 Let God be God! – the prophet's prayer

Habakkuk's prayer comes with a great sigh of relief. God, his strength and joy, is God after all!

The prayer is a psalm, to be sung with accompanying instruments. This has led some to believe that Habakkuk was a Levite, attached to the Temple.

The focus is on God himself; God approaching from the mountains of the southern desert (Teman is in Edom; Paran part of Sinai); God wrapped about with thunder and lightning in the storm of his wrath; God setting the world trembling with a glance.

Habakkuk sees the inevitability, the fury of judgment. Yet, though it means the loss of every good thing in life, God is still to be trusted. The prophet will wait for the day when God deals with the invader (16). He will rejoice in God, though life is stripped of all that gives natural joy and satisfaction.

> **"** *The fig tree has no buds, the vines bear no harvest, the olive crop fails, the orchards yield no food, the fold is bereft of its flock, and there are no cattle in the stalls. Even so I shall exult in the Lord and rejoice in the God who saves me.* **"**
>
> 3:17-18

Zephaniah

Summary

Prophecies of
God's day of universal
judgment, and his
judgment on Judah.
God's promise to restore
the faithful few.

Zephaniah prophesied in the reign of King Josiah of Judah (640-609 BC), about the time Jeremiah's ministry began. From his stern words to the nation, it seems he spoke before Josiah launched his great programme of reform in 621, following the discovery of the law-book in the Temple. The two previous kings, Manasseh and Amon had brought the religion and morality of Judah to an all-time low. Zephaniah himself may have been of royal blood, tracing his ancestry back to Hezekiah (1:1), who was king in Isaiah's day, 70 years or so before.

1 The day of God's judgment – on Judah, too

In popular thinking the 'day of the Lord' would bring untold blessing to all God's people, and destruction to their enemies. Amos, years before this, had warned that on that day all evil would be punished, making it a black day for many in Israel. Zephaniah spells out the same message, in detail, to Judah. The day is close at hand when all who are guilty of idolatry (4-6), violence, fraud (9), all who sit by in idle indifference (12), will be set apart for destruction (this is the meaning of verse 7). And their cry will be heard in every quarter of the city of Jerusalem (10-11).

▶ **Baal (4)** The Canaanite god of fertility whose worship involved sexual licence and prostitution.
▶ **Milcom (5)** Molech: the national god of the Ammonites.
▶ **Wine left on its dregs (12)** A picture drawn from wine-making; one of the secrets in making wine is not to let it settle.

2 Judah's neighbours doomed

The only hope for God's people is to seek him, and begin living by his standards (3).

If they do not, they will share the fate of the nations around: Philistia (4-7) to the west; Moab and Ammon (8-11) to the east; Ethiopia (12) to the south; Assyria (13-15) to the north.

▶ **Gaza, Ashkelon, Ashdod, Ekron (4)** The four remaining Philistine city-states.
▶ **Kerethites (5)** The Philistines, who originally came from Crete.
▶ **Sodom, Gomorrah (9)** Cities at the southern end of the Dead Sea, destroyed by God for their wickedness (Genesis 19).
▶ **Ethiopians/Cushites (12)** Sudanese; at this time the ruling dynasty in Egypt.
▶ **Nineveh (13)** Capital of Assyria; see Nahum, particularly chapter 3.

3 God will save the faithful few

The 'tyrant city, filthy and foul' is none other than Jerusalem (1-7)! Beginning with rebellion against God, and the corruption of religion, the rot spreads into every sector of society. In the end, God has no alternative but to wipe the city out.

But that is not the end of the story. Zephaniah has already spoken of 'survivors' and 'a remnant' (2:7, 9). Now he enlarges on God's purpose for the humble, faithful few who will remain when all human pride and self-sufficiency is done away with and the nation is purged and purified (11-13).

There is cause for great rejoicing. God is in the midst of his people, protecting and keeping them safe, pouring out his love on them. Israel will no longer do wrong (13). With exultant song they will be brought home and restored to favour. All the nations of the world will share in this as they come to worship God (9).

Haggai

Summary

The prophet speaks
to the returned exiles in
Judah and Jerusalem: get
your priorities right –
complete the rebuilding
of God's Temple if you
want to enjoy his
blessing.

The last three books of the Old Testament – Haggai, Zechariah and Malachi – take us on past the exile to the time when the Jews were repatriated: the time of Ezra and Nehemiah.

Haggai's little book is one of the gems of the Old Testament. It has permanent relevance, because its basic concern is with priorities.

Haggai delivered his 'word from the Lord' in 520 BC, Zechariah in 520-518. When the first party of exiles returned to their homeland under the leadership of Zerubbabel (grandson of King Jehoiachin) in 538, they made an enthusiastic start on rebuilding the Temple which had been destroyed by the Babylonians in 587. But opposition and apathy very soon brought the work to a standstill (Ezra 4:4-5). Sixteen years after the decree of the Persian Emperor Cyrus which allowed the people to return, Haggai and Zechariah began to stir things up (Ezra 5:1-2). Thanks to them, by 516 the Temple was completed.

Why was it so important to rebuild the Temple? Because God's honour was at stake. As Joyce Baldwin explains: 'The nations had to know beyond any doubt that the God of Israel had not gone out of existence when the Israelites were removed from their land.' The Temple and the covenant were bound up together (see Ezekiel 37:26), and 'while the Temple lay in ruins there was no outward sign of the Lord's presence with the restored community'. The Temple, set on Mt Zion, stood for God's continuing purposes.

Four times Haggai comes to the people with a message from God (1:2-15; 2:1-9; 2:10-19; 2:20-23). The messages are precisely dated (see notes below) and were all given within a 15-week period.

1:2-15: life is hard, with food and clothing in short supply, and prices soaring. Why? Because the people have their priorities wrong. They are all wrapped up in their own selfish concerns. God is neglected. And so the very things they work for evade them. For all the good

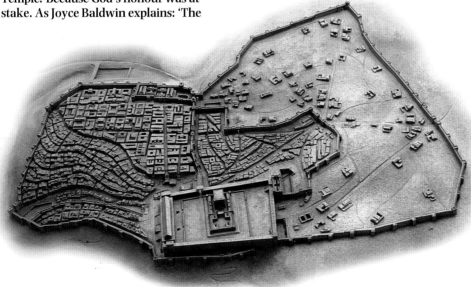

Haggai and Zechariah stirred up the former exiles to complete the rebuilding of Jerusalem's Temple. It was Nehemiah who organized the rebuilding of the city walls.

things of life are God's to give or withhold. Haggai's words strike home to the nation's conscience. Within three weeks, work on the Temple is resumed.

2:1-9: Solomon's fabulous Temple had been demolished 70 years before. Few of those now building would have seen it – but all had heard of it. And its glory had lost nothing in the telling. The new Temple seems a feeble thing in comparison. But let the builders take heart. The present building is just a foretaste of the splendour and glory of the end-time, the era of peace and prosperity to which the prophets all looked forward.

2:10-19: work on the Temple has been resumed, but this in itself will not make the workmen 'holy' (dedicated to God and fit for his service). It is rottenness, not soundness that is contagious (Haggai makes his point from the ritual law). Their previous neglect of God brought all kinds of unpleasant consequences. But from the day they begin to put first things first, God will bless every aspect of life.

2:20-23: a word for Zerubbabel. It is to Zerubbabel the heir to David's throne, rather than to Zerubbabel the individual, that these messianic promises are made. He stands in the line from David to Christ. (Compare the way 'David' is used in Jeremiah 30:9, and see notes on Zechariah 4.)

▶ **1:1** 29 August 520 BC. Darius the Great ruled the Persian Empire from 522-486 BC. Judah was a province of the Empire.

▶ **1:15** 21 September 520 BC: just over three weeks after Haggai's appeal.

▶ **2:1** 17 October 520 BC.

▶ **2:10 and 20** 18 December 520 BC.

▶ **2:23** Zerubbabel is not given the title 'king', but it seems as if the curse on King Jehoiachin recorded in Jeremiah 22:24-30 is being lifted.

Zechariah

Summary

Prophetic messages and visions of judgment and restoration.

Part 1: chapters 1 – 8
Zechariah's visions at the time the Temple was rebuilt, 520-518 BC

•

Part 2: chapters 9 – 14
Judgment on Israel's neighbours
The future king
God's people delivered and restored
The Day of the Lord – judgment and salvation of all nations

It seems that Zechariah came from a family of priests (1:1, 7). With Haggai he was closely involved in the rebuilding of the Temple following the return from exile (see on Haggai, and Ezra 5 – 6 for the historical background). Like Daniel and Ezekiel he was a visionary. His book at one and the same time distils the wisdom of many of the earlier prophets, and brings the events of the far future into clear focus.

There is a sharp contrast between chapters 1 – 8 and 9 – 14, and most scholars believe that the second part is the work of a later author writing in the same tradition as Zechariah himself. This is based on difference of content and language, the apocalyptic style without the visions of part one, and the fact that the prophet's name is not mentioned.

Both parts, however, share the same basic concerns: judgment and salvation for Judah and the nations; the rebuilding of the Temple as a sign of God's presence; and the nation's leaders in relation to God. In both parts of Zechariah there are passages about leaders which point to the coming Messiah. The figures differ: in part one, priest, governor (= king-substitute), Branch (chapters 3 – 4, 6); and in part two, humble king and afflicted shepherd (chapters 9, 11 – 13).

The New Testament Gospels quote Zechariah (part two) more than any other prophet in their narratives of Jesus' last days, reflecting on Jesus as the Messiah. Zechariah, with Ezekiel, also has a major influence on the book of Revelation.

1 – 8
Part 1

1:1-6 Introduction
The date is October/November 520 BC (verse 1). Zechariah began to speak for God at the same time as the prophet Haggai.

This first message falls between the speech recorded in Haggai 2:1-9 (given on 17 October) and Haggai's last recorded message (2:10ff., dated 18 December).

Zechariah was probably a young man at the time (his grandfather, Iddo, returned with the exiles less than 20 years before: Nehemiah 12:4).

Verses 2-6 relate past history, warning the present generation not to behave as their forebears had done.

1:7-17 Vision 1: The four riders
Eight visions are recorded in chapters 1 – 6. Each contributes to a picture meant to be seen as a whole.

Zechariah's first vision, dated 15 February 519 (1:7), is of four horsemen patrolling the world on God's behalf, like the mounted patrols which 'policed' the Persian Empire. (The significance of the colours, if any, is now lost.) God used other nations to execute judgment on his people. But they went too far, stirring God's compassion for his people. Now those nations will be judged and God will comfort and restore his own. This message is reinforced in the chapters that follow.

▶ **Verse 10** Darius, the Persian king, so transformed the roads that his envoys could do in a week journeys that before had taken merchant travellers 90 days.

1:18-21 Vision 2: The four horns
The second vision is a vivid picture of the destruction of the hostile powers which had ground the nation down: the powerful 'horns'. ('Four' indicates completeness – the 'four corners' of the earth.) Their power will

> *If Haggai was the builder, responsible for the solid structure of the new Temple, Zechariah was more like the artist, adding colourful windows with their symbolism, gaiety and light. To make sure that their symbolism is rightly understood an interpreting angel acts as guide.* ""
>
> Joyce Baldwin

be smashed by four workmen: smiths, who presumably hammer them on the anvil.

2:1-5 Vision 3: The measuring-line

Now a man is seen with a measuring-line, come to measure up the city for rebuilding. The walls had been broken down and set on fire in 587. They were not rebuilt until Nehemiah's day (445, 75 years after this prophecy). God will be a protecting wall around Jerusalem, 'and a glorious presence within it'.

2:6-13 Exiles called home

The rest of this chapter – not now a vision – is poetry (as in Jerusalem Bible).

Zechariah addresses first the exiles, then the Jews in Jerusalem. God is calling the exiles home from Babylon. His message to Jerusalem will make them want to 'sing for joy'. For God is coming home too! He will return to his own people, to live once again in his own place. The nations will become God's people (11).

▶ **The land of the north (6)** Babylonia; in point of fact, east, but that way desert lay between, so the invading armies of Assyria and Babylonia all entered Palestine from the north.

3 Vision 4: The high priest rerobed

Joshua, the high priest, stands before God representing the people, as Satan levels his charges against them. Joshua's filthy clothes are sin-stained. But God's set purpose is to restore and renew his people. He issues clean clothes to fit them for his presence, and a 'solemn charge' (6ff.). As a token of good things to come God speaks of his servant, the Branch from the family of David (the coming Messiah; verse 8 and Isaiah 11) who will usher in a day of universal peace and prosperity (the meaning of the vine and fig-trees symbol in verse10).

▶ **Verse 9** Because of the abrupt change of image here from Branch to stone, Jerusalem Bible (taking the 'seven' of 4:10b to refer to the stone rather than the lamps) and Revised English Bible rearrange the text (the latter drastically).

▶ **Stone (10)** The seven facets (Hebrew 'seven eyes') may make it all-seeing, all-knowing. It may be a building-stone, or a jewel engraved with some symbolic meaning. The same Hebrew word, *'ayin*, is used for eye and spring. So 'seven springs' is a possible alternative translation.

4 Vision 5: Lamps and olive-trees

The vision in this chapter is interrupted by a word from God to Zerubbabel (8-10), telling him that as he started the rebuilding of the Temple, he will complete it. Verse 6 unlocks the meaning of both word and vision: everything that is achieved is by the spirit of God.

The lampstand stands for the Temple and faithful Jewish worshippers. Like a city set on a hill (the picture used in Matthew 5:14), their light shines out for God and 'cannot be hid'.

The olive-trees are two men chosen (anointed) by God to serve him (14). The roles of priest and prince (king) go together here. Jointly they supply what God's people need to shine with God's light in the world. (The New Testament sees Jesus as the fulfilment of this priest-king ideal.)

▶ **Verses 6ff.** Zerubbabel was the heir to David's throne (Haggai 2:20-23), but he is not called king. To have done so at that time would have created (unnecessary) problems with the Persian emperor.

5:1-4 Vision 6: A giant flying scroll

The enormous scroll (9 metres/10 yards long) comes from God and represents his law. It is inscribed with a curse on all who have disobeyed it and broken the covenant-agreement with him (see Deuteronomy 27:14-26). The seventh and the third commandments, specifically mentioned in verse 3, stand for the whole law. God's word carries with it the power of punishment: evil is dealt with.

5:5-11 Vision 7: A basketful of wickedness

Zechariah now sees an outsize basket (like those for measuring grain) in which all this wickedness is contained. God's angel ensures that no evil can escape. All of it is carried off on strong wings, far away to the east: to Babylon, the land of the exile. The cleansing is complete.

▶ **Verse 8** 'Wickedness', an all-inclusive word, is feminine in Hebrew: hence the figure of a woman.

▶ **Verse 9** The 'wind' in the women's wings (most versions) could equally be read as 'Spirit' (the same word in Hebrew), emphasizing that the cleansing is God's work.

6:1-8 Vision 8: Four horse-drawn chariots

Zechariah's last vision recalls the first (1:7-17), though that was of riders, not charioteers, and there are puzzling differences of detail. God's patrols compass all 'four corners' of the earth. The nations have been judged. Now God's spirit is at rest (verse 8) – in contrast to 1:15 – and there will be peace.

▶ **Verse 6** The lines of attack were north, south and west: east lay the desert.

6:9-15 The crowning

Verse 9 (in the same manner as 4:8; 7:4; 8:1, 18) marks the end of the vision and introduces a word from God (an oracle). Surprisingly the crown is given to Joshua, the priest. It may be that the crown was placed first on the head of Joshua, then on the head of Zerubbabel (verse 13) – or that two crowns were made. Both men seem to be present (as in chapter 4's vision of the lampstand and the olive-trees). The king – 'the Branch' (a messianic title) – and high priest work in harmony together (13). The

A rider in the desert: in his first vision Zechariah saw four horsemen sent by God to patrol the earth.

New Testament sees the two roles become one in the person of Jesus.

▶ **Crown (11)** The Hebrew is 'crowns'. 'Eastern crowns were circlets, which could be worn singly or fitted together to make a composite crown' (Joyce Baldwin). Compare Revelation 19:12.

7:1 – 8:23 Fasts become feasts

The date is 7 December 518. Chapters 7 and 8 round off the first part of the book.

Some men come to the Temple to ask about keeping fasts (7:2-3). Zechariah does not give a straightforward answer. It is the *purpose* of fasting that really matters. He challenges their motives: they have not obeyed the commands God gave through the earlier prophets (7:5-7). He reminds them of the covenant they have broken. Because they refused to listen to God, God did not answer their prayers, and they suffered exile (7:8-14).

Then comes a heartwarming message from God (chapter 8), a total transformation, a great swing from sorrow to joy. Out of his deep love, God renews his central purpose, to bless and to save his people: to be their God (see on 2:6-13; 13:7-9). Things will be different for the survivors of the destruction and exile. They themselves will be different. They must pay heed to the words of the prophets: something their ancestors failed to do. They must love truth and justice and peace, as God does. And if they do – their sad commemorative fasts will become feasts!

The time is coming (8:20-23) when the nations themselves will turn to God. They will come to Jerusalem saying, 'We want to share in your destiny, because we have heard that God is with you.'

▶ **7:2** It is not clear who sent the men: Bethel (the town that was the centre of worship for the northern kingdom of Israel), Darius (verse 1), or Bethel-Sharezer.

▶ **7:3, 5** The fast in the fifth month (July/August) marked the fall of Jerusalem to the Babylonians in 587 BC, when the Temple was destroyed. The fast in the seventh month (September/October) commemorated the death of Gedaliah, governor of Judah after the fall of the city (2 Kings 25:25).

▶ **Verse 19** The two additional fasts were probably to mark the beginning of Nebuchadnezzar's siege of Jerusalem (the tenth month) and the breaching of the walls 18 months later (the fourth month).

9 – 14
Part 2

9 – 11 Israel and the nations

For the changes which set chapters 9 – 14 apart from chapters 1 – 8, see introduction.

Chapter 9 pictures God's conquest (1-8) and the joyous arrival of the Messiah to claim the land (9-10). He comes riding a donkey (not a war-horse) to inaugurate a rule of peace (compare Matthew 21:5). All Israel's old enemies fall before him (1-8). There will be no more oppression. The Philistines (5-7) will be absorbed into Israel, as the Jebusites (from whom David captured the city of Jerusalem) had been long before. The Jewish captives will be released, and Israel's military power will equal even that of rising Greece. God is his people's protection and salvation.

Chapter 10: it is God, not pagan gods, who makes the fields green and the earth a fertile place (verse 1). Without a leader, God's people wander like lost sheep, an easy prey to fortune tellers and those who interpret dreams (verse 2). God is full of pity for the straying flock. He will come to their rescue as a shepherd does (the image is already there, in 9:16). Every one will be brought home. Verse 3 returns to the victory theme: God at the head of his hosts, working miracles for his people (11).

Chapter 11: the poem of verses 1-3 is an ironic lament for the fallen forests of Lebanon and Bashan. Verse 4 returns to the shepherd and flock images: the nation's leaders and its people. The prophet is sent to shepherd God's flock – but the people prefer exploitation to the genuine care of a good shepherd. So God sends his prophet as the worthless leader they seem to want (15,16). The covenant with God is broken and the nation divided.

▶ **9:1-7** Many relate these verses to the advance of Alexander the Great after his Greek army defeated the Persians in 333 BC.

▶ **9:7** The Philistines eat food forbidden and abhorrent to God's people (see Leviticus 11).

▶ **10:2** In the absence of any real spiritual lead, the people are dabbling in magic. The old household gods (teraphim) were used in divination.

▶ **11:1-3** This is the 'clearance' in preparation for the returning Israelites. In Old Testament times the thickets fringing the Jordan were the haunt of lions.

▶ **11:8** Who are these three shepherds? So many different suggestions have been offered by scholars that it seems best to say we do not know!

▶ **Thirty shekels/pieces of silver (11:12)** The prophet sarcastically calls it a 'lordly price' – this was the price of a slave (Exodus 21:32; and see Matthew 26:15; 27:3-5). In both Zechariah and Matthew, 30 shekels of silver is the value put on the good shepherd.

12:1 – 13:6 Jerusalem besieged – and delivered

The nations attack Jerusalem but they are defeated. God gives victory to the fighting forces of Judah and protects his people (12:1-9).

12:10 – 13:1: the triumph of victory turns to deep mourning for a man they have killed (verse 10). The overwhelming sense of compassion which leads to this mourning comes from God himself. The Hebrew of 12:10 says (literally), 'They shall look on *me* whom they have pierced...', suggesting that it is God's own representative the people kill. They are filled with remorse for what they have done and God cleanses them from their sin (13:1). (John's Gospel quotes from this passage, applying Zechariah's words to the death of Christ: see John 19:34-37.)

13:2-6: this cleansing includes the removal of all false prophets. If any persist in prophesying, their own parents will turn against them and finish them off.

▶ **12:11** Rimmon is both a place name and the name of a god in the Old Testament. The reference may be to the ritual weeping for the god at the dying of the year (compare Ezekiel 8:14).

▶ **13:6** The wounds are ritual gashes (compare 1 Kings 18:28, of the prophets of Baal).

13:7-9 'Strike the shepherd!'

This short and surprising poem again picks up the shepherd image and the theme of leadership which is so often in the prophet's mind. God summons the sword to strike shepherd/leader (unidentified) and scatter the sheep/people. They are tested and purified until just the faithful few remain. With this remnant, the special relationship between God and his people will be renewed (verse 9, compare 8:8; see also Jeremiah 31:31-34; Mark 14:27; Hebrews 8:8-11).

14:1-21 The last battle

Chapter 14 pictures the final war of the nations against Jerusalem, and its outcome: the day of God's judgment. God himself will appear with his angels (5), ushering in perpetual day. The whole earth will become God's kingdom and all will worship him (9).

Those who set themselves against God (the city defended by his people) will meet a horrendous fate. All those who survive will join God's people in worship. Everything, down to the humblest pot in the kitchen, will be made over to God, cleansed and dedicated to his service (20-21).

The New Testament book of Revelation, chapters 21 and 22, echoes many of the details in this great finale to the book of Zechariah.

▶ **Verse 8** The idea of life-giving water flowing from Jerusalem echoes Ezekiel 47.

> 66 *Rejoice, rejoice, people of Zion! Shout for joy, you people of Jerusalem! Look, your king is coming to you! He comes, triumphant and victorious, but humble and riding on a donkey – on a colt, the foal of a donkey. The Lord says, I will remove the war chariots from Israel and take the horses from Jerusalem; the bows used in battle will be destroyed. Your king will make peace among the nations; he will rule from sea to sea.* 99
>
> 9:9-10

Malachi

Summary

Malachi brings God's message to a downcast people who have grown careless of him. God's love is constant. His Day is coming. Set things right and make ready.

The name Malachi means 'My messenger'. It may have been the prophet's actual name or a pen-name. From the book itself we can deduce the historical setting. It would seem to be around 460-430 BC – either just before Nehemiah became governor of Jerusalem, or during his absence later on. That is about 80 years after Haggai and Zechariah spurred the people on to rebuild the Temple.

It is a difficult waiting time, and disillusion has set in. Times are hard, the people are poor, ground down by foreign powers. The prosperity promised by Haggai if they get their priorities right has not materialized, and Zechariah's glorious predictions of the future messianic king and the day of God's judgment and restoration have not come to pass. It is hard to hold on to hope as the waiting drags on. The people are beginning to doubt the words of the prophets, to feel God has forgotten them and let them down.

This shows in an increasingly casual attitude to worship and the standards God set them.

God's messages for his people through Malachi begin with a reassurance of his constant and continuing love for them. The rebukes that follow call them back to the covenant-agreement which binds his people to him in a very special relationship. The Day of the Lord *is* coming! It is vital God's people live in the light of that certainty.

1:1-5 'I have always loved you'

Malachi's starting-point is God's love (verse 2a). His people, struggling with economic hardship and persistent sniping from the opposition (see e.g. Nehemiah 1:3; 4), cannot see much evidence of it (2b). In answer they are told to look at their brother-nation Edom – overrun like themselves by Babylon, but not restored (see Obadiah).

▶ **Love... hate (2-3)** The Hebrew idiom is over-strong in English. It means, not literal love/hate, but the special choice of one and not the other.

1:6 – 2:9 The priests' failure

Israel enjoys a unique Father-child relationship with God. God is in a special sense their Lord. But not even the priests have honoured him. The rule for the sacrifices is 'the very best for God' (Leviticus 22; Deuteronomy 15, 17), not poor sick beasts the owner is glad to get rid of. Offerings like this belittle the greatness of God and all that his people owe to him. It would be better to close the Temple and stop the sacrifices altogether (1:10) than show such contempt.

God instructed the descendants of Levi – those set apart especially to serve him – to teach his people the truth about him, to tell them what is right, and by their own lives to set an example (2:6). But instead of

Like a flower among thorns, the prophets' predictions of a glorious future stand out from the warnings of judgment and disaster.

> **"** *For you who fear my name the sun of righteous-ness shall rise, with healing in its wings.* **"**
>
> 4:2

turning people away from wrong, they lead them into it. The priests have broken their covenant-promise to God.

▶ **1:11** God is receiving more acceptable worship from people of other nations – a statement intended to shock Malachi's Jewish hearers.

2:10-16 Broken promises

By marrying women who worship other gods, the men of Israel are breaking their promise to shun pagan practices. (See also Ezra 9 – 10 and Nehemiah 13, which deal with the same situation). The issue is not a

racial one. Foreign women who loved God could be taken into the heart of the nation, as is clear from the story of Ruth. Marriage makes husband and wife 'one body and spirit' (15) and God wants the children to be taught at home what it means to be his (15).

Indifference towards God is soon reflected in callousness towards one another. The older men are cruelly discarding their ageing wives for these attractive young foreigners. God cares about these things. He hates to see the promise to be faithful broken: divorce is cruel. These older women are cast aside with no means of support and no one to protect them.

2:17 – 3:18 The justice and mercy of God

God's people can always look around and see godless men and women flourishing. It seems unfair (2:17; 3:13-15). But in the final winding-up of things justice and right will prevail (3:1-5). The Lord is coming, first to purify, and then to judge. First a herald-messenger will come to prepare the way (3:1a; and see on 4:5). Then a messenger will come who is the Lord himself (3:1b).

God does not change (6). Nor, sadly, do his people (7). They have been fickle from first to last. God gives them all they have, yet they rob him even of his legal dues. Anything given to God is only a small return on all that people owe him. To hold back from giving, through self-interest, is to deprive themselves of all the good things God would otherwise give them.

Verses 16-18 come as a welcome relief. There are still some who encourage one another in the love of the Lord; and he knows and honours them.

▶ **Tithes (3:10)** The law required that a tenth of all crops and farm animals should be given as a kind of income tax to provide for the upkeep of the Temple and the support of the priests and Levites engaged in God's service.

▶ **Book (3:16)** There are a number of references to this record: Exodus 32:32; Psalm 69:28; Isaiah 30:8; Daniel 12:1; Revelation 3:5; 13:8.

4 The Day of the Lord

The day is surely coming, as so many prophets have foretold, when God will even things out once and for all. For some (the wicked) the fierce brilliance of that day will burn like fire. But those who honour God will rejoice in its healing rays.

Verses 4-5 serve as postscript, not just to Malachi but to the Old Testament as a whole. They look back to the laws given at Sinai (Horeb), which must always be kept in mind. They look forward to a new age of joyful freedom, when evil will be totally destroyed and all ills healed.

With Malachi the voice of Old Testament prophecy falls silent.

▶ **Sun (2)** Malachi draws his picture (but not his theology) from the winged disk which represented the sun-god in Persian and Egyptian art.

▶ **Elijah (5)** According to 2 Kings 2, Elijah, the great reforming prophet of that time, did not die but was taken up to heaven. The New Testament Gospels see John the Baptist as the 'Elijah' prophesied by Malachi – the last prophet sent by God to herald the coming Messiah (Matthew 17:10-13). But he was not literally Elijah come again, as John's questioners probably expected (John 1:19-26).

Deuterocanonical books

Mark Elliott with Stephen Travis

The 'Deuterocanonicals' or 'Apocrypha' are a group of Jewish writings which were never part of the Jewish canon of Scripture, but have been accepted as authoritative in some parts of the Christian church. In some editions of the English Bible they are included as a supplement, usually placed between the Old and New Testaments. Roman Catholic Bible versions integrate them with the other Bible books (see below). They were written between about 300 BC and AD 70, and include stories, historical books, Wisdom literature, liturgical material, a letter and an apocalypse.

Many Jews of this period believed that prophecy lasted only from Moses to Ezra (see Josephus, *Against Apion* 1.40-41; 2 Esdras 14). So several of these books were attributed to heroes from the period before Ezra, such as Solomon, Jeremiah and Baruch. Most were originally written in Hebrew. Highly valued by many Jews, they were included in the Greek translation of the Hebrew Scriptures, known as the Septuagint. Hence they became familiar to 1st-century Greek-speaking Christians, who read the Scriptures in their Septuagint form.

The destruction of Jerusalem and its Temple by the Romans in AD 70 threatened the identity and survival of Judaism. At the same time the Christian church was experiencing significant growth. The Jewish community responded to these challenges by 'closing' the canon of Scripture. They affirmed the 24 books of the Law, the Prophets and the Writings (which Christians call the Old Testament), but rejected the additional books found in the Septuagint.

Christians meanwhile, among whom Gentiles now predominated, naturally used the Scriptures in the form most accessible to them: the Greek Septuagint was their Bible. So the deuterocanonical books were widely known in the churches during the early centuries of the Christian era.

However, in the 4th century Jerome was appointed to make a definitive translation of the Bible into Latin. This became known as the Vulgate, and has had official status in the Roman Catholic Church to this day. Becoming convinced that only the Hebrew text was authoritative, he excluded those books found only in the Greek version. These books he called 'apocrypha' (the Greek means 'hidden'), though his reason for choosing this word is obscure.

Surprisingly, perhaps, Jerome's view did not prevail. The Western Catholic Church soon added the Apocrypha in Latin to the Vulgate, and acknowledged this fuller collection of books as canonical Scripture.

Jerome's view came into its own in the 16th century, when the Protestant Reformers excluded the Apocrypha from the canon of Scripture. They were suspicious of apocalyptic thought (as found in 2 Esdras), and of 2 Maccabees because 12:43-45 had been used to justify the Roman Catholic doctrine of purgatory. And they rejected the teaching on salvation by good deeds which some had attempted to prove from Tobit and other books.

Nevertheless, Martin Luther included the apocryphal books in his German translation of the Bible, placing them in a separate section after the Old Testament.

In reaction to this reduction of the Apocrypha's status, the Roman Catholic Church declared at the Council of Trent (1546) that these books are part of the Christian canon of Scripture. Soon afterwards they were given the name 'Deuterocanonicals' (Greek *deuteros* means 'second'). According to the Roman Catholic Church, the term indicates that they belong to a second layer of the canon, but does not imply that they are of less worth than the other Old Testament books.

The Deuterocanonical books

Books which are in the Septuagint and form part of the Eastern Orthodox and Roman Catholic canons:

- Tobit
- Judith
- Additions to the Book of Esther
- Wisdom of Solomon
- Ecclesiasticus, or the Wisdom of Jesus son of (ben) Sira(ch)
- Baruch
- The Letter of Jeremiah
- Additions to the Book of Daniel
  The Prayer of Azariah and the Song of the Three Jews
  Susanna
  Bel and the Dragon
- 1 Maccabees
- 2 Maccabees

Other books in the Septuagint which are not included in the Roman Catholic canon, but are accepted by Eastern Orthodox churches:

- 1 Esdras (placed in an appendix to the Latin Vulgate)
- Prayer of Manasseh (placed in an appendix to the Latin Vulgate)
- Psalm 151
- 3 Maccabees
- 4 Maccabees

A book in the Slavonic (Old Russian) Bible and in the Latin Vulgate appendix:

- 2 Esdras (sometimes known as 4 Ezra)

The Eastern Orthodox churches have always regarded the Deuterocanonicals as part of Scripture, though they attribute a somewhat lesser status to them than to the Old Testament proper.

Most Protestants have continued to exclude these documents from their canon of authoritative Scripture. But in recent years many have come to value them for their literary merit, spiritual wisdom, and the insight they give into developments in the Jewish community in the critical period between 200 BC and the time of Jesus.

It is appropriate for us to let these books speak for themselves, asking to what extent they reinforce the teaching of the Hebrew Scriptures and the New Testament, and to what extent they introduce new ideas which seem to be in conflict with those Scriptures. They come from a period when Jews were often under extreme pressure to compromise their faith and commitment to

❝** God of my father, God of the heritage of Israel, Master of heaven and earth, Creator of the waters, King of your whole creation, hear my prayer. **❞

Judith prays that she may kill Holofernes: 9:12

God. And because of this they offer much insight into God's justice and providence, his promise of eternal life to those who remain faithful to him, and the ultimate triumph of his purpose for the world.

The books of the Apocrypha should be distinguished from other surviving Jewish literature of the same period such as *1 Enoch, Jubilees, 2 Baruch*, which are often known as 'Pseudepigrapha' (meaning 'books written under a false name'). Though popular among specific groups of Jews and Christians in ancient times, they have never been assigned canonical status by Jews or by mainstream Christian churches.

The contents of the books

Tobit is a romantic tale, composed around 180 BC. Its writer was concerned to preserve Israel's religion from the poisonous fashions of Greek culture, and to teach that God helps those who observe his laws.

Blind for four years after sparrows' droppings landed on his eyes while he slept, Tobit suffers in Nineveh. So does his relative Sarah, far off to the east in Ecbatana, from a demon that has successively killed her seven husbands on their wedding nights.

On the way to reclaim a debt, Tobit's son Tobias and the angel Raphael (incognito as a distant cousin) stop to stay with Sarah's family. God has already provided remedies for them in the form of a fish which attacks but is killed by them. Its liver and heart, when smoked, drive off demons.

Thus Tobias wins Sarah as his wife. And the fish's gall bladder cures Tobit's blindness.

Judith, written during the 2nd century BC, attained prominence in Jewish tradition in the early Middle Ages, when the reading of it was incorporated into the festival of Hanukkah. It is the fictitious story of a woman who uses feminine wiles to achieve the assassination of an Assyrian general, and so delivers her nation. Its historical references are confused and inaccurate.

For example, Nebuchadnezzar is taken to be king of Assyria rather than Babylon. He represents human strength which sets itself up to defy God and sends his forces against Judah. Judith, a godly widow, turns up when the garrison defending the approach to Jerusalem has sworn to surrender after five days if God does not intervene.

In going over to the enemy camp, she swears loyalty to the king as lord of the earth, and to his general Holofernes, who lusts after her. Against him, Judith symbolizes weak Israel. But she has trust in God, courage and feminine ingenuity as her weapons – and the wisdom to apply a sword to Holofernes' neck while he is drunk and drowsy.

The story ends with Judith's song of praise: 'For the Lord is a God who crushes wars.... The Lord Almighty has foiled them by the hand of a woman.'

The Additions to the Book of Esther are six passages found in the Greek, but not the Hebrew text of the Old Testament book of Esther. They appear to be added to give a religious tone to the book, famous as it is for not mentioning God. They may have been added in stages during the 2nd and 1st centuries BC.

The six passages are:
- Mordecai's dream
- King Artaxerxes' letter ordering the Jews to be exterminated
- prayers by Mordecai and Esther
- Esther's successful audience before Artaxerxes
- the king's further letter in praise of the Jews
- and the interpretation of Mordecai's dream.

The Wisdom of Solomon is a poem designed to stir up love for wisdom. Though attributed to the king famous for his wisdom, it must have been written sometime between 100 BC and AD 50. It begins with an appeal to seek wisdom and righteousness (1:1 – 6:11). It continues with what purports to be Solomon's personal testimony to the value of wisdom, which is here depicted as a feminine person, God's agent in his relations with the world (6:12 – 10:21). The final part (11:1 – 19:22) reflects on God's

❝... the potter, sitting at his work,
turning the wheel with his feet;
constantly on the alert over his work,
each flick of the finger premeditated; ...
pummels the clay with his arm,
and with his feet he kneads it;
he concentrates on applying the glaze right
and stays up late to clean the kiln. ❞
Ecclesiasticus 38:29ff.

❝ Treat the doctor with the honour that is his due,
in consideration of his services;
for he too has been created by the Lord.
Healing itself comes from the Most High...

The Lord has brought forth medicinal herbs from the ground,
and no one sensible will despise them. ❞
Ecclesiasticus 38:1ff.

❝ See the rainbow and praise its Maker,
so superbly beautiful in its splendour.
Across the sky it forms a glorious arc
drawn by the hands of the Most High. ❞

Ecclesiasticus 42:15 – 43:23

involvement with humanity and his protection of his chosen people.

Passages with particular theological significance include the reflection on the immortality of those who are faithful to God (chapter 3), the explanation of how God rules the world justly (11:15 – 12:27), and the appeal to Jewish readers to reject false religions (chapters 13 – 19). The book expresses Jewish wisdom traditions in language which is at home in the Greek world of thought.

Ecclesiasticus, The Wisdom of Jesus son of (ben) Sira(ch), is another wisdom book, written in Hebrew by Sira around 175 BC and translated into Greek by his grandson Jesus about 130 BC. More traditional than the Wisdom of Solomon, it is often reminiscent of the Book of Proverbs.

Its purpose was to convince Jews, and perhaps well-disposed Gentiles, that true wisdom is to be found primarily in Jerusalem and not in Athens.

The book requires honour of parents and respect for the past, while the final section (chapters 44 – 51) is devoted to the praise of Israel's heroes. Its name 'Ecclesiasticus' is derived from the fact that it attained great popularity in the early church (Greek *ekklesia*).

Baruch dates from the 2nd or 1st century BC and combines various elements. The central section (3:9-4:4) is an example of wisdom literature, being a poem rejoicing in God's gift of wisdom to Israel. It is preceded by a long confession of Israel's sins as the cause of the Babylonian exile. 4:5– 5:9 is a poem about God's restoration of Israel after exile.

Though presented as coming from the early 6th century BC, when the exile began, the message of the book spoke to Jews scattered across the world at a later period, for whom exile had in effect become a permanent experience.

The Letter of Jeremiah, written possibly as early as 300 BC, urges those living under foreign influences not to fear or worship idols. It is partly dependent on the thought of Jeremiah 10:1-16. The document is often counted as chapter 6 of Baruch.

The Additions to the Book of Daniel consists of three passages added in the Greek version of Daniel during the 2nd century BC.

The Prayer of Azariah and the Song of the Three Jews is inserted between Daniel 3:23 and 3:24. Azariah was the original name of Abednego who, with Shadrach and Meshach was thrown into the fiery furnace (see Daniel 1:7; 3:23).

Azariah's prayer acknowledges the sins of the Jews which have led to exile, and prays for God's mercy and intervention (verses 3-22). The brief central section tells how God protected his servants from the force of the fire (verses 23-28). The song of the three men celebrates God's greatness and his intervention in times of distress and danger (verses 29-68).

Susanna is the story of a beautiful young woman who, after she resisted their advances, was falsely accused by two Jewish elders of committing adultery with a young man in her garden. Daniel cross-examined them and exposed the inconsistencies in their testimonies. In the Septuagint the story appears at the beginning of the Book of Daniel, to show how Daniel's wisdom led to his high reputation in Babylon (verse 64). It has provided inspiration for artists throughout the centuries.

Bel and the Dragon contains two stories. The first relates Daniel's mockery of the idol Bel, exposing Bel's priests as the ones whose secret nightly feasts were the reason why food placed before his statue was devoured. The second tells how Daniel destroyed a dragon which the Babylonians worshipped as a god. When he fed it with cakes made from pitch, fat and hair it exploded. For this Daniel was thrown into the lions' den. Instead of being eaten by the lions there he was fed with stew miraculously supplied by the prophet Habakkuk, who was whisked all the way from Judea to Babylon by an angel. So Daniel was delivered, and those who had tried to destroy him were thrown to the lions instead.

1 Maccabees gives an account of the struggle of Jewish patriots to overthrow the oppression of the Syrian ruler Antiochus IV.

It tells how Antiochus tried to suppress Jewish religious practice and the Temple rituals, and how the resistance led by Judas Maccabaeus and his four brothers between 167 and 142 BC liberated the Jews from foreign rule.

The author, writing about 100 BC, was

working from written sources and paid careful attention to dates and historical detail. His concern was to show how faithful Jews fought in order to keep faith with God's law (see 2:19-22; 14:29).

The story reaches its climax in 142 BC when 'the yoke of the Gentiles was removed from Israel, and the people began to write in their documents and contracts, "In the first year of Simon the great high priest and commander and leader of the Jews"' (13:41-42). This marked the beginning of a period of Jewish independence from foreign interference, during which Simon (one of Judas' brothers) and his descendants combined the office of ruler and high priest.

2 Maccabees is an alternative account of the same period. Written at about the same time as 1 Maccabees, it summarizes the lost five-volume history by Jason of Cyrene. It is more concerned with theology than historical detail.

It stresses, for example, belief in the resurrection of the body, the ability of martyrdom to cleanse the nation's sins and remove God's anger against it, and the power of miracles to reveal the nature and purpose of God.

1 Esdras, written between 150 and 100 BC, is an alternative version of the narrative in 2 Chronicles 35:1– 36:23, Ezra, and Nehemiah 7:38 – 8:12. (Esdras is the Greek form of Ezra.)

Unique to this book is the story in 3:1 – 5:6. It tells of a banquet given by the Persian king Darius, at which three of his bodyguards debate what is the strongest thing in the world. One says 'wine', another 'the king'. The third, who is the Jew Zerubbabel, says 'women' but then changes his answer to 'truth'. At this the people present shout, 'Great is truth, and strongest of all' (4:41), and Darius grants Zerubbabel permission to rebuild the city and Temple of Jerusalem.

The Prayer of Manasseh expresses what the penitent king Manasseh might have prayed when he was being carried off to Babylon for a short period of exile (see

2 Chronicles 33:11-13). The prayer speaks of God's power and mercy and states, like Jesus in Mark 2:17, that repentance is not for the righteous but for sinners. It probably dates from the 1st century BC.

Psalm 151, which dates perhaps from the 3rd century BC, is a psalm attributed to David in which he describes God's choice of him to be king and his killing of Goliath.

3 Maccabees is not concerned with the same period of history as 1 and 2 Maccabees, but with events in the late 3rd century BC. It tells how Jews living in Egypt were delivered by God's providential protection from oppression by the ruler Ptolemy IV Philopator. There are similarities to the story of Esther in the Old Testament.

Written in the 1st century BC or 1st century AD, it is a historical novel designed to encourage Jews in Alexandria threatened with persecution. Like the Jews in the story, they are to pray (1:16 – 2:20; 6:1-17; 7:20), to hold fast to God's law and destroy apostates (2:33; 7:10-15) and to trust in God's providence (4:20).

4 Maccabees is a philosophical discussion in the Greek style, to demonstrate that 'devout reason is sovereign over the emotions' (1:1). But the author is Jewish, convinced that reason chooses wisdom, and wisdom is nothing other than education in the law (1:15-17). In chapters

The Maccabees won the Jews a brief period of independence from occupying forces. It was a movement to restore not only freedom of worship but personal devotion to God's law – the Torah being studied here.

❝ *Judas Maccabaeus, strong and brave from his youth, let him be your general and conduct war against the gentiles... Pay back the gentiles to the full, and hold fast to the ordinance of the Law.* ❞

Judas' father charges his sons: 1 Maccabees 2:68-69

Rulers of Palestine 'between the Testaments'

333-166	GREEK/HELLENISTIC RULE	166-63	JEWISH INDEPENDENCE	63-4	ROMAN RULE
333-323	Alexander the Great	166	Maccabees lead revolt against Antiochus	63	Pompey adds Judah to province of Syria
300	The Ptolemies, kings of Egypt	166-160	Judas Maccabaeus	63-40	Hyrcanus II
200	Syrian Seleucid dynasty rules	165	Temple rededicated	48	Pompey overthrown by Julius Caesar
175-166	Antiochus IV Epiphanes, the Syrian king who defiled the Temple in 168	160-143	Jonathan (Judas' brother)	44	Julius Caesar assassinated
		142-134	Simon (Judas' brother)	40-37	Antigonus: Jewish ruler under Romans
		134-104	John Hyrcanus	37-4	Herod the Great
		104-103	Aristobulus	27	Octavian/Augustus Caesar rules the Roman Empire
		103-76	Alexander Jannaeus		
		76-67	Alexandra Salome		
		67-63	Aristobulus II		

> 66 *Maccabaeus and his companions, under the Lord's guidance, restored the Temple and the city, and pulled down the altars erected by the foreigners in the market place... They purified the sanctuary... This day... fell on the twenty-fifth of Chislev... They decreed by public edict... that the whole Jewish nation should celebrate those same days every year.* 99

King Antiochus IV had desecrated the Temple. 2 Maccabees 10 recounts its restoration.

5-12 he supports his argument particularly from the stories of Eleazar and the seven brothers which he has learnt from 2 Maccabees 6 – 7.

He writes eloquently of the power of the martyrs' suffering to atone for the sins of the people as a whole, and promises them eternal blessedness. In contrast with 2 Maccabees, his Greek framework of thought leads him to express this in terms of 'deathless souls' (18:23) rather than bodily resurrection.

The book probably dates from the 1st century AD.

2 Esdras is a Jewish work from about AD 100, to which Christians later added chapters 1 – 2 and 15 – 16. The central part is apocalyptic in character (see on Revelation), reporting revelations given to Ezra in seven visions by the angel Uriel. It reflects on the meaning of the Temple's destruction and how to trust in God when there are no easy answers. Though ostensibly referring to the destruction by Nebuchadnezzar in 587 BC, its actual audience is Jews troubled by the disaster of AD 70.

The Greeks

From the time of Israel's later kings, the world of the Old Testament was dominated by a succession of great powers and empires: the Assyrians to whom northern Israel fell; the Babylonians who destroyed Jerusalem and took the people into exile; the Persians, who returned the Jews to their homeland.

But between the last stories of the Old Testament and the birth of Jesus, the dominant power was Greece, and the influence of Greece was more widespread and far longer lasting than any that had gone before. Many of the Deutero-canonical books, including the histories of the Maccabees who won Jewish independence for a while, belong to this time: the Hellenistic age (from *hellas*, the old name for Greece).

The Greek Empire in about 275 BC, nearly 50 years after the death of Alexander.

The Parthenon at Athens was one of the glories of the ancient world.

Figures of Scythian archers and a bronze helmet found at Corinth are from the time of the Greek and Persian wars.

philosopher, Aristotle, had been his tutor, and he was possessed, not simply with the urge to conquer, but to spread Greek ideas and Greek culture wherever he went.

He was only 32 when he died (in 323 BC). His generals divided up the empire, continuing the spread of the Greek language and civilization he had begun. Ptolemy won Egypt. Seleucus and his line ruled the East from Antioch in Syria. Palestine was involved in a tug of war between the two powers.

Greek culture spreads

Although Greek civilization was at its greatest before Alexander, it was during the Hellenistic age after his death that Greek influence was most widely felt in Bible lands.

Greek became the main language of common speech and communication for trade, education and writing. Greek

and Egypt (founding the city of Alexandria), winning victory after victory until he reached the banks of the Indus – weeping, it was said, that there were no more worlds to conquer.

Alexander was more than a legendary general. The famous Greek

The 'golden' or classical age of Greece began about 480 BC. The city-state of Athens was then a model of democracy, with all the citizens playing their part in its affairs. But bitter, local wars divided the country and the Greeks had to fight hard to keep the Persians at bay.

Alexander the great

In 338 Philip of Macedon won control over the whole of Greece. On his assassination, he was succeeded by his 20-year-old son Alexander, who defeated the Persians in 334, then won Syria

Alexander stamped his impression not only on Greek coinage, but across the whole of the ancient world, east to the borders of India.

A Hellenistic house dating from the 2nd century BC has been excavated at Araq al Amir in Jordan. It is said to have been built by Hyrcanus, who belonged to the influential Jewish Tobiad family. It is an interesting example of how Greek architecture and building styles were adopted across the Bible lands. The largest of the stone blocks measures 7x3m/23x10ft!

The marble bust of a woman displays Greek fashion; 1st century BC.

architecture changed the appearance of many towns. Greek-style gymnasia, theatres and stadia were built everywhere.

At Alexandria in Egypt the Old Testament was translated into Greek (the 'Septuagint') for the large colony of Greek-speaking Jews who lived in the city.

The New Testament as we now have it was written in Greek, rather than the Aramaic of Palestine (the earlier diplomatic language of the Persian Empire) or the Latin of the Roman Empire (although first drafts of parts of the Gospels may have been written in Aramaic or Hebrew).

From 167 BC the Romans began to take over former Greek cities and kingdoms. But the Greek language and Greek influence remained.

Greek slaves were taken into Roman households, some as doctors, teachers or accountants. The Romans adopted many of the Greek ways of thinking. Romans learned to speak Greek. The old Roman gods were equated with the Greek system, and the Greek gods were given Roman names: Zeus became Jupiter; Poseidon became Neptune; Ares became Mars; Artemis became Diana.

Greek influence in Palestine

The customs and ideas of the Greeks formed an important part of the life and culture of Palestine in New Testament times.

Just across the Lake, south-east of Galilee, there was a federation of ten free Greek towns, 'Decapolis', on the Greek pattern. Jesus went to teach there. The towns included Scythopolis (modern Beth-shean), where archaelogists have been uncovering the remains of the classical city with its theatre, gymnasium and temples. Recently archaeologists have also been working at Sepphoris, an important Hellenistic city only a few miles from Nazareth (see 'Jesus and the cities').

See also 'Roman rule, Greek culture', 'The city of Athens', 'The city of Corinth', 'The city of Ephesus'.

THE NEW TESTAMENT

3

THE GOSPELS AND ACTS

Matthew to Acts

THE LETTERS

Romans to Revelation

Nazareth, home-town of Jesus.

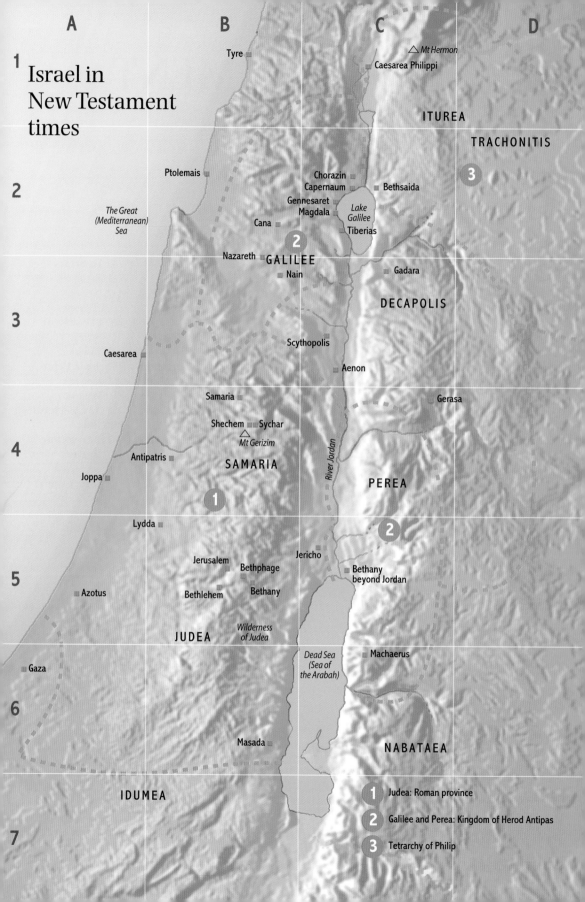

Israel in New Testament times

A   B   C   D

Tyre

△ Mt Hermon
Caesarea Philippi

ITUREA

TRACHONITIS

③

Ptolemais

The Great
(Mediterranean)
Sea

Chorazin
Capernaum   Bethsaida
Gennesaret
Magdala   Lake
Galilee
Cana   Tiberias

②

Nazareth   **GALILEE**
Nain   Gadara

DECAPOLIS

Caesarea

Scythopolis

Aenon

Samaria   Gerasa
Shechem   Sychar
△ Mt Gerizim

Antipatris   **SAMARIA**   River Jordan   **PEREA**

Joppa

①

Lydda

②

Jerusalem   Jericho
Bethphage   Bethany
beyond Jordan
Bethlehem   Bethany

Azotus

JUDEA   Wilderness
of Judea

Gaza

Dead Sea
(Sea of
the Arabah)   Machaerus

NABATAEA

Masada

IDUMEA

① Judea: Roman province

② Galilee and Perea: Kingdom of Herod Antipas

③ Tetrarchy of Philip

1 2 3 4 5 6 7

What is the New Testament?

The New Testament, like the Old, is a collection of books: 27 books and letters written over a period of about 50 years, in different styles, by a number of authors.

The Old Testament story covers a period of about 2,000 years, the New Testament story about 100 – the 1st century 'AD', the time of the Roman Empire.

The Old Testament tells the stories of many people, but essentially is the story of the nation of Israel. The New Testament focusses on one special person belonging to that same nation: Jesus Christ.

The word 'testament' means 'covenant' or agreement. The Old Testament, the Hebrew Bible, is about the covenant between God and the people of Israel (the Jews). They were to be his special people through whom the whole world would be blessed. In response to God's love and care, and to fulfil his purposes, they were to keep God's laws and be faithful to him.

But time and again they failed. And so their prophets began to talk about a new covenant, one that people would keep because it would be 'written on their hearts': not something external, but a new life within.

That new covenant, Christians believe, was what Jesus made possible through his life and death and resurrection. Through Jesus, God offers the gift of new life, a sharing in God's own life, now and for ever. This 'special offer' is not for one nation only, but for all the people of the world, anyone willing to receive it. This new beginning for a sinful world will be completed when Christ returns and 'all things are made new'. That is why the Christian message is called 'good news' (a 'gospel').

The first four books of the New Testament are all called 'Gospels'. They are four complementary accounts of the life of Jesus, each by a different writer with a particular purpose, or 'angle', related to those he was writing for (see 'The Gospels and Jesus Christ' and 'Studying the Gospels').

The Acts of the Apostles, which follows the Gospels of Matthew, Mark, Luke and John is the second part of Luke's story, telling how Jesus' first followers spread the Good News of what he had done – out from Jerusalem and the province of Judea to the wider world of the Greek East and the Roman Empire.

A key figure in this expansion is the apostle Paul. He was not one of Jesus' original 12 disciples. In fact he was fiercely opposed to what they were saying about Jesus and his resurrection – until a dramatic encounter with the risen Jesus completely changed his mindset and his life.

After Acts come the letters. Thirteen of these have Paul's name attached to them. The rest are by other close followers of Jesus. Most are written to the new groups of Christians in different places, answering questions, explaining more about what Jesus did, and showing them how to live out their new faith in practical ways.

The last book in the New Testament is Revelation. It belongs to a special kind of writing called 'apocalyptic' (see 'Jewish religion in New Testament times' and 'Understanding Revelation') and looks forward to the final triumph of God as an encouragement to believers when times are especially hard.

> **The Gospels tell the story of Jesus not just to give us interesting facts about a historical person. They tell it so that we may discover good news about how Jesus can make a life-changing impact on us!**
>
> Stephen Travis

Jewish religion in New Testament times

Dick France

Jesus was a Jew. The Christian church began its life in Palestine, and its first members were Jews. To understand the New Testament we need to have some knowledge of the Jewish religion as it was in and around the time of Jesus.

The last of the Old Testament prophets lived 400 years or more before John the Baptist came on the scene. Since that time the Jewish religion had not stood still. The classical religion of Old Testament Israel had evolved into Judaism.

By the 1st century AD Jews were to be found all over the Roman world and beyond (see 'The Jewish Dispersion'). Here we focus on the Jews of Palestine.

Some important institutions in Judaism

The Temple Solomon's great Temple had been destroyed by the Babylonians in 587 BC. After the exile the Jews who returned to Jerusalem built a less impressive structure, which lasted for 500 years. Then Herod the Great decided to replace it with a magnificent new temple, which became one of the seven wonders of the ancient world. (See 'Herod's Temple'.) It was begun in 19 BC, and was still not complete in the time of Jesus (John 2:20). It was finished eventually in AD 64 – six years before it was destroyed by the Romans!

It was this imposing complex of buildings which excited the admiration of Jesus' disciples (Mark 13:1). Here the age-old ritual of sacrifice and worship continued, with its elaborate establishment of priests and Temple servants, though all under the watchful eye of the Roman garrison in the fortress of Antonia, which overlooked its courts (Acts 21:31ff.). The Temple buildings proper were separated off from the vast outer courtyard, the 'Court of the Gentiles', by a barrier which bore notices forbidding any Gentile to enter on pain of death (see Acts 21:28-29; Ephesians 2:14).

When the Gospels describe Jesus as teaching and carrying out his work 'in the Temple' it was usually in this wide public area, where teachers set up their stands in the shaded porticos and people would gather to listen and ask questions. Here too, at festival times, was the thriving market in sacrificial animals and sacred money for the Temple offerings, which so angered Jesus.

The Temple was not merely a place of worship. It was a symbol of Jewish identity and national pride. One of the chief reasons why Jesus and his followers became unpopular was that they were perceived as anti-Temple (Matthew 26:61; 27:40; Acts 6:13-14).

The synagogue There was only one Temple, but each community had its synagogue. Here there was no sacrifice. It was the local centre for worship and study of the law. On the sabbath the community would meet, men and women separated, to listen to the reading and exposition of set passages from the Law and the Prophets (Luke 4:16ff.) and to join in liturgical prayers. During the week the synagogue was the local school, the community centre, and the focus of local government. Its elders were the civil authorities of the community, the magistrates and guardians of public morals.

Law and traditions Israel had had a law since the days of Moses. But after the exile and the destruction of the Temple, Ezra (in the 5th century BC) led a movement of intensive study of the law, and the Jews became increasingly 'the people of the book'.

This detailed study gave rise to a body of traditions, still developing in the time of Jesus, which aimed to spell out more fully how the law should be followed. **Scribes,** professional students and guardians of the law and traditions, worked out exact regulations for all occasions. There were, for example, 39 types of action prohibited on the sabbath, and one of those ('taking anything from one place to another') lent itself to further elaboration sufficient to cover almost any activity. Travel was limited to a 'sabbath day's journey', about two thirds of a mile (Acts 1:12).

> ❝ *The rules about the Sabbath are as mountains hanging by a hair, for Scripture is scanty, and the rules many.* ❞
>
> Mishnah, Hagigah 1.8

Scribal teaching was meant to help people keep the law, but sadly Jesus' comments on the scribes show that sometimes concern with details overshadowed the more fundamental concerns of the law (Mark 7:1-13; Matthew 23:23).

The marks of a Jew The survival of the Jews in the face of hostility and persecution led them to prize those aspects of the law which marked them out as the people of God. Three 'identity markers' became especially important: circumcision, the keeping of the sabbath, and the food laws (based on Leviticus 11 and on the command not to eat blood) which made it impossible for Jews to share normal meals with non-Jews. One of the biggest problems faced by the early Christians was how Jewish and non-Jewish believers could be integrated into one community (read Acts 10:1 – 11:18; Acts 15:1-29).

Parties and movements in 1st-century Judaism

The Pharisees Readers of the Gospels tend to think of the Pharisees as self-righteous hypocrites, but this is not the way most Jews at the time saw them. They were the religious purists, enthusiastically committed to preserving and obeying the law and keen to encourage others to do so. Judged by this standard, they were model Jews (Philippians 3:5-6), and they were widely respected. Most scribes belonged to the Pharisaic party, and from them came the rich development of legal traditions already mentioned.

Their concern for meticulous legal observance (particularly over matters of ritual purity in food) limited their social contact with less scrupulous Jews, and could lead to a sense of superiority over the 'people of the land' (John 7:49). This separation, and their tendency to place a higher value on precise ritual observance than on such broad principles as love and mercy, led them into conflict with Jesus. He did not dispute their orthodoxy, but accused them of getting the service of God out of perspective, so that their well-meant attempts to define the requirements of law actually made things more difficult for ordinary people.

The number of Pharisees was probably not very great, but their influence was strong. It was the Pharisees who worked out the lines along which Judaism developed after the destruction of Jerusalem in AD 70. They ensured a continued emphasis on individual piety and strict ethical standards, as well as ritual observance.

The Sadducees The Sadducees were the other main party at the time of Jesus, though their influence was already declining. They were drawn from the rich, landowning families. The chief priests were mainly Sadducees, and it was from among their ranks that the High Priest was chosen. They controlled the organization of the Temple, and were still the dominant party in the Sanhedrin (the Jewish supreme Council), where they and the Pharisees frequently took opposite positions (Acts 23:6-10).

Their religious stance was conservative, accepting no revelation beyond the Five Books of Moses (Genesis to Deuteronomy). So they rejected more recent beliefs favoured by the Pharisees – such as immortality, resurrection, angels and demons (Mark 12:18; Acts 23:8). As an aristocratic minority they did not enjoy as much popular support as the Pharisees.

The Essenes This previously rather shadowy group has come dramatically to light since 1947, with the discovery of the Dead Sea Scrolls. These ancient scrolls are

In the time between Old and New Testaments, Jewish religion developed into Judaism. Orthodox Jews in the Old City of Jerusalem today.

from the library of the Qumran Community, a 'monastic' sect of Essenes who lived in deliberate isolation in the barren desert near the Dead Sea. The sect was founded by the otherwise unknown 'Teacher of Righteousness' about 165 BC, and survived until AD 68 when it was destroyed in the Jewish Revolt (against the Romans). They saw themselves as the true people of God, and other Jews, including the Temple establishment in Jerusalem, as his enemies. Out there in the desert they waited for the coming of the Messiahs (the priestly Messiah of Aaron and the royal Messiah of Israel), and the great final battle between the Sons of Light and the Sons of Darkness, when God would vindicate their faithful witness and restore the true sanctuary.

Meanwhile, they were occupied in the diligent study of the Scriptures, bound by a strict monastic discipline, keeping the law more rigorously even than the Pharisees,

> **66** They shall separate from the habitation of ungodly men and shall go into the wilderness to prepare the way of the Lord. **99**
>
> Qumran Community Rule 8.13

loving one another and hating those outside. They produced elaborate biblical commentaries, applying every phrase of the Old Testament passages to their own situation and expectations.

Not all Essene groups shared the separatist lifestyle of Qumran, but the documents from Qumran give vivid evidence of an ascetic, apocalyptic type of Judaism which was very much alive as a real alternative to the better-known Pharisees and Sadducees.

The Zealots While Pharisees and Sadducees tried to make the best of Roman rule, and the men of Qumran dreamed of God's mighty intervention in the future, many Jews were not prepared to wait. A serious revolt led by Judas of Galilee when the Roman poll-tax was introduced in AD 6 (Acts 5:37) was the inspiration for later groups of freedom fighters, often lumped together under the title 'Zealots'. The Barabbas who was a prisoner at the time of Jesus' trial probably led one such group. The Romans suppressed several earlier uprisings, but the great Jewish Revolt provoked by the Zealots in AD 66 led to the fall of Jerusalem in AD 70. At their best, Zealots were religiously motivated patriots, believing that the people of God should not be subject to a foreign empire.

Apocalyptic Many 'apocalypses' (revelations) were written in Palestine from the 2nd century BC onwards to offer a message of hope to a people near despair. They recount extra-ordinary visions allegedly received by great men of the past (Enoch, Elijah, Ezra, etc.), usually in cryptic imagery, with symbolic numbers and carefully calculated dates. They are marked by a strong dualism: good and evil, God and Satan, light and darkness are involved in cosmic conflict. The present world-order is controlled by the forces of evil, but the final battle is about to be fought. Then God will crush all opposition, evil will be destroyed, and his people will reign in glory. Revelation, in the New Testament, is a Christian apocalypse.

Messianic hopes The extravagant visions of the apocalypses expressed only one among a number of hopes cherished by Jews at that time. Several messianic figures from the Old Testament had gripped the popular imagination: the prophet like Moses (Deuteronomy 18:15-19), the returning Elijah (Malachi 4:5-6), but above all the Son of David, a warrior king whose mission it would be to bring victory, peace and glory to Israel. Some thought of spiritual renewal, most of victory over the Romans.

The word Messiah (Greek 'Christ') inevitably triggered hopes of political independence, so Jesus was cautious about letting others call him 'Christ'. He came to a people 'looking for the consolation of Israel' (Luke 2:25); but none expected it to come by way of a cross.

Proselytes While Jews were often misunderstood and ridiculed, a considerable number of Gentiles were attracted to the Jewish religion and took the serious step of becoming 'proselytes'. This involved circumcision and baptism, and the keeping of the whole law, including the sabbath and food laws. It was in effect a change of nationality.

Many more, attracted to the monotheistic faith and strict morality of Judaism in contrast with the decadent polytheism of Rome, identified themselves with the faith and ideals of Israel but stopped short of the proselyte's full commitment. These fellow-travellers, often rich and influential officials, sometimes appear in the New Testament as 'those who fear God' or 'the devout' (Acts 13:26, 43, 50; 17:4).

The Samaritans These were the descendants of the surviving Israelites of the northern kingdom who intermarried with the newly imported alien population after the fall of Samaria in 722/1 BC. They never reintegrated with Judah, and by the time of Nehemiah the rift was irreparable. The building of the Samaritan temple on Mt Gerizim, over-looking Shechem (John 4:20), set the seal on Jewish repudiation of the Samaritans. It was the Jewish king Hyrcanus who destroyed the Samaritan temple in 128 BC.

Yet the Samaritans worshipped the same God. Their authority was the Five Books of Moses (but not the rest of the Old Testament), hardly altered from the Jewish version. Like many of the Jews they hoped for the coming of a prophet like Moses. Jewish hatred and disdain for Samaritans sprang more from historical and racial considerations than from any fundamental difference of religion.

Herod's Temple

The first Temple, built by King Solomon, was destroyed by the Babylonian army in 587 BC. On their return from exile, the Jews rebuilt it as best they could, though it had little of its former glory.

When Herod became king under the Romans he embarked on a great building programme, the most ambitious project being a grand new Temple. Herod was an Idumean, and this seemed a good way to curry favour with his Jewish subjects.

Work began in 19 BC , with most done by 9 BC, but it was not actually finished until AD 64. Parts of its massive structure are still visible on the western ('Wailing Wall') and eastern sides. Recent excavations have uncovered a flight of steps leading to the southern gates, and carved stone blocks from the parapets and porches.

Descriptions by the Jewish historian Josephus, and notes in rabbinic writings, supply us with information about this splendid building.

A great courtyard (the Court of the Gentiles) was surrounded by a portico where schools were held and business was transacted (John 10:23; Luke 19:47; John 2:14-16). A barrier divided this outer courtyard from the inner ones, which only Jews could enter: prominent notices forbade others to go further, on pain of death.

Beyond the barrier were three further courts,

- the Women's Court where 13 money-boxes shaped like upside down trumpets were placed to collect donations (this is the scene of the 'widow's mite' story, Mark 12:41-44)
- the Court of the men of Israel
- and finally the Priests' Court in which the altar and the Temple proper stood.

This was larger than Solomon's, but built to the same design and richly decorated. The outside was

> **66** *He who has not seen the temple of Herod has never seen a beautiful building.* **99**
>
> Talmud, Baba Bathra 4a

gilded, and inside the walls glowed with gold

The inner sanctuary was empty. The Ark which held the terms of God's covenant with his people was no longer in existence (see 'The lost Ark'). The Roman general Titus reduced the Temple to piles of ash and rubble in AD 70, following the Jewish Revolt. For Christians it is significant that the Temple disappeared at the time a new covenant was established, opening the way to God for people of every nation (see Hebrews 8 – 10; Ephesians 2:11-22).

This is the market where people purchased their sacrificial offerings. They then went through the central Hulda Gates, crossing the Court of the Gentiles, to the inner courts.

This photograph of A.W. Garrard's model gives a general view of the Temple enclosure from the north-east. The Temple Court and the Temple sanctuary are in the centre. The Royal Portico (so named because of its size) is in the background.

The Priests' Court. The place where the animals were slaughtered is in the foreground, with the altar for burnt offering in the centre and the 'laver' filled with water in the background. On the left is the Hall of the Priests. The steps on the right lead up to the Temple sanctuary.

A view looking into the Temple from the Women's Court through the Nicanor Gate (named after the Alexandrian Jew who gave it), reached by a flight of 15 'steps of ascent'.

These are the underground baths (*mikvaot*) used by the priests. Before going on duty each morning the priests took a ritual bath for purification, and again during the day if they became 'unclean' because of their duties. The passageway and immersion rooms are preserved beneath the present-day Temple mount.

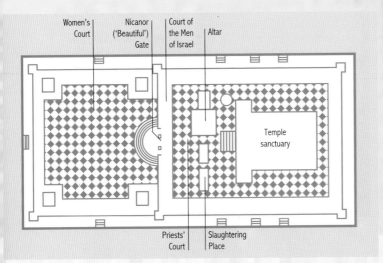

The high priest reads from a scroll in the outer room of the Temple. Only once a year could he enter the inner sanctuary. He wears his special clothes. The breastplate with 12 stones represents the 12 tribes of Israel. His head coverings, linen breeches, coat and girdle are in the four colours of the sanctuary – white, blue, purple and scarlet – interwoven with threads of gold.

Jews under Roman rule: the province of Judea

David Gill

The world of the New Testament is the world of the Roman Empire. The Jewish people, who had won a brief period of freedom under the Maccabees (from 166 BC to 63 BC), were very soon subject again, this time to the Romans.

Following the conquests of the Roman general, Pompey (who sacked Jerusalem), Rome formed the province of Syria in 58 BC, with control over the whole region. But Judea remained on the edge of the Roman world.

Rome endorsed the appointment of Herod, first as governor (47 BC), then as king of Judea (40 BC, though it took three years to establish his position). In his turn, Herod supported Octavian (later the Emperor Augustus) at the battle of Actium in 31 BC, and was rewarded with further cities to add to his kingdom.

On Herod's death in 4 BC Rome was forced to send legions into Judea from the province of Syria, in part to secure the portion of the royal treasury at Jerusalem bequeathed to Augustus.

In AD 6, Archelaus, Herod's heir, was exiled to Gaul and large parts of Herod's former kingdom then became part of the new province of Judea, controlled by a Roman official of the equestrian rank based at the harbour city of Caesarea.

The Roman 'prefects'

The first of these 'prefects' – a lower rank than the governors of most other provinces but the same as Egypt – appointed by Augustus to govern Judea was Coponius. The prefect was allowed to appoint the Jewish high priests. This meant that the ruling Jewish families of the province were willing to co-operate with him.

The prefect had few troops of his own. In times of unrest, he had to turn to the frontier province of Syria for help.

Pontius Pilatus (see 'Pilate'), who sentenced Jesus to death, was the fifth prefect of Judea. Appointed by the Emperor Tiberius in AD 26, he offended the Jews through a number of acts which included introducing images of the emperor into the city of Jerusalem by night. He caused a riot by using one of the sacred treasuries to pay for an aqueduct for the city. Large quantities of running water were needed for ritual washing but there may also have been an attempt to introduce Roman culture in the form of bath-houses.

The tensions between Roman authority and the Jews is reflected in the Gospel accounts of Pilatus offering to release Jesus at Passover time. Pilatus was finally removed from office in 36 following an incident in Samaria.

In 39/40, the Emperor Gaius (Caligula) tried to have a statue of himself placed in the Temple at Jerusalem, and the province went through a period of such instability that military intervention from Syria was necessary to restore order.

King Herod Agrippa

When Claudius became emperor in 41, Judea was given as a kingdom to Agrippa I, the grandson of Herod the Great. He had been brought up in Rome and supported Claudius

far left: Head of the Roman Emperor Augustus, from Pergamum. It was Augustus who ordered the census at the time of Jesus' birth.

left: Head of Emperor Tiberius, who appointed Pontius Pilate Governor of Judea.

when Gaius was assassinated. This is the Herod who features in the Acts of the Apostles. Agrippa's reign was shortlived. He died at Caesarea in AD 44 (Acts 12:23).

The Roman 'procurators'

At this point the kingdom reverted to being a Roman province, this time governed by equestrian officers with the rank of 'procurator'. The right to control the roles of the Jewish high priest was reasserted.

Interestingly, the second procurator, Tiberius Iulius Alexander, came from a Jewish family from Alexandria in Egypt. The Jewish historian Josephus noted that he 'abstained from all interference with the customs of the country and kept the nation at peace'.

One of Emperor Claudius's appointments was the imperial freedman (i.e. former slave of the imperial household) Felix in 52. He was responsible for the imprisonment of Paul at Caesarea (Acts 23:23-24). Felix married into the Herodian royal family. His wife Drusilla was the daughter of Agrippa I. He was himself the brother of the imperial freedman Antonius Pallas.

Felix's governorship saw a rise in the number of political assassinations by the *sicarii* ('daggermen'). One of their more important victims was Jonathan the high priest, who had been part of a delegation sent to Rome.

In 54 Felix had to deal with a revolt by an Egyptian prophet who had planned to storm Jerusalem, and it was this individual for whom Paul was mistaken when arrested in the city (Acts 21:38).

Felix was himself recalled by the emperor, probably around AD 60, because of tensions between the

The Pontius Pilatus inscription from Caesarea

The Roman governor of Judea, Pontius Pilatus, is known from the four Gospel accounts as well as from the Jewish writers Josephus and Philo. One of the records of his time in Judea was the stone inscription found re-used in the theatre at Caesarea. This inscription records the establishment of a temple dedicated to the 'divine emperor' Tiberius. The Latin inscription correctly identifies Pilatus as *praefectus*:

'Pontius Pilatus Prefect of Judea has dedicated to the people of Caesarea a temple in honour of Tiberius.'

Jewish and Gentile populations in the province. It was probably owing to these sensitivities that his replacement, Porcius Festus, decided to leave Paul in prison.

The Jewish Revolt

In 66 the great Jewish Revolt against Rome broke out. This led to the destruction of Jerusalem by (the later emperor) Titus in AD 70. The province was then reorganized under the Emperor Vespasian and a permanent garrison of the 10th Legion was stationed there.

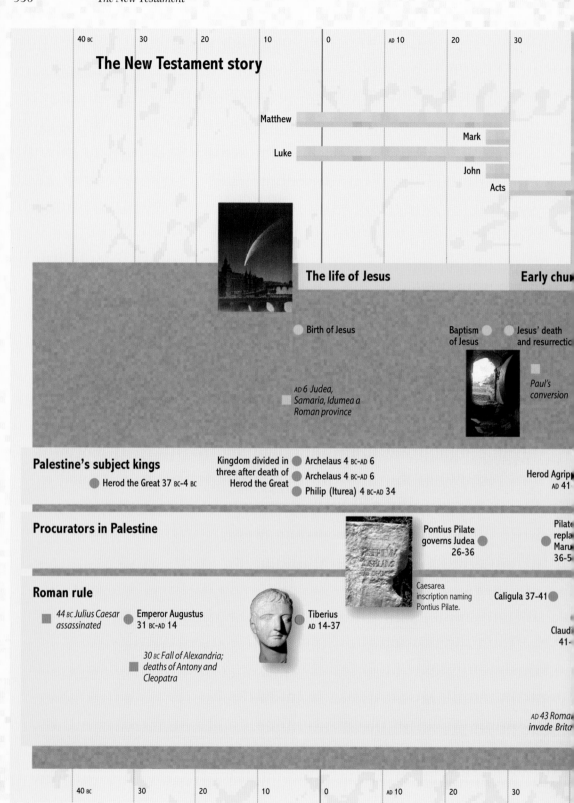

The New Testament story

40 BC   30   20   10   0   AD 10   20   30

Matthew

Mark

Luke

John

Acts

The life of Jesus

Early chu▶

Birth of Jesus

Baptism of Jesus

Jesus' death and resurrectio▶

AD 6 Judea, Samaria, Idumea a Roman province

Paul's conversion

Palestine's subject kings

Herod the Great 37 BC-4 BC

Kingdom divided in three after death of Herod the Great

Archelaus 4 BC-AD 6

Archelaus 4 BC-AD 6

Philip (Iturea) 4 BC-AD 34

Herod Agrip▶ AD 41

Procurators in Palestine

Pontius Pilate governs Judea 26-36

Pilate replac▶ Maru▶ 36-5▶

Caesarea inscription naming Pontius Pilate.

Roman rule

44 BC Julius Caesar assassinated

Emperor Augustus 31 BC-AD 14

Tiberius AD 14-37

Caligula 37-41

30 BC Fall of Alexandria; deaths of Antony and Cleopatra

Claud▶ 41-▶

AD 43 Roma▶ invade Brita▶

40 BC   30   20   10   0   AD 10   20   30

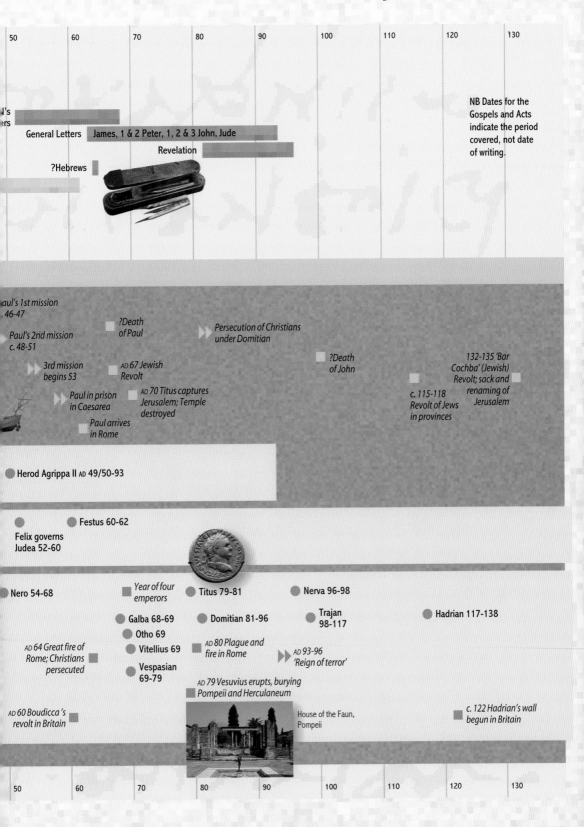

50   60   70   80   90   100   110   120   130

ul's
rs

General Letters   James, 1 & 2 Peter, 1, 2 & 3 John, Jude

Revelation

?Hebrews

NB Dates for the Gospels and Acts indicate the period covered, not date of writing.

aul's 1st mission 46-47

Paul's 2nd mission c. 48-51

?Death of Paul

Persecution of Christians under Domitian

3rd mission begins 53

AD 67 Jewish Revolt

?Death of John

132-135 'Bar Cochba' (Jewish) Revolt; sack and renaming of Jerusalem

Paul in prison in Caesarea

AD 70 Titus captures Jerusalem; Temple destroyed

c. 115-118 Revolt of Jews in provinces

Paul arrives in Rome

Herod Agrippa II AD 49/50-93

Festus 60-62

Felix governs Judea 52-60

Nero 54-68

Year of four emperors

Titus 79-81

Nerva 96-98

Galba 68-69

Domitian 81-96

Trajan 98-117

Hadrian 117-138

Otho 69

Vitellius 69

AD 80 Plague and fire in Rome

AD 93-96 'Reign of terror'

AD 64 Great fire of Rome; Christians persecuted

Vespasian 69-79

AD 79 Vesuvius erupts, burying Pompeii and Herculaneum

House of the Faun, Pompeii

c. 122 Hadrian's wall begun in Britain

AD 60 Boudicca's revolt in Britain

50   60   70   80   90   100   110   120   130

The Gospels and Jesus Christ

I. Howard Marshall

Virtually all we know about the earthly life of Jesus is to be found in the four Gospels contained in the New Testament.

Outside sources

The life of a travelling preacher in an obscure corner of the Roman Empire was not likely to find its way into the writings of Roman historians, who had (as they thought) more important things to occupy their attention. Tacitus refers very briefly to Jesus, and then only by way of explanation of the name of the 'Christians' who were put to death by Emperor Nero.

Even Jewish historians offer us little more. The standard history of the Jews was written by Josephus towards the end of the 1st century, and he does refer to Jesus at one point in his narrative as a miracle-worker who was the Messiah; he was put to death by Pilate but later reappeared to his disciples. The passage may have been tampered with in the course of transmission by later Christian scribes (for would Josephus have called Jesus the Messiah?), but is probably genuine in essentials.

Other Jewish traditions about Jesus have been preserved in the writings of the rabbis. They tell us that he practised magic, beguiled the people, and said that he had not come to destroy the law or add to it. He was hanged on the eve of Passover for heresy and misleading the people, and had five disciples who healed the sick. This gives some idea of how Jesus would have been regarded by people who shared the outlook of the Sanhedrin, the Jewish Council that condemned him to death.

A more promising source of information lies in various 'gospels' which were not included in the New Testament. Such works have long been known, but in recent years interest has been rekindled by the discovery of the *Gospel of Thomas* at Nag-Hammadi in Egypt. This work contains a set of sayings ascribed to Jesus. They have obviously been worked over by radical Christians, but it is possible that here and there in this and other similar documents fragments of genuine tradition about Jesus may be preserved. However, the fact that

The Dead Sea Scrolls, the library of a Jewish sect living just before and during the time of Jesus, discovered hidden in these caves in 1947, shed light on the thought-world of ancient Palestine. Although some writers have tried to find references to Jesus in them and use them to create bizarre portraits of him, in fact the Scrolls contain no mention whatever of Jesus and his followers. What is recorded of the members of the sect and their enemies has no connection with the story of Jesus, although it helps us better understand the world in which he lived and the religious ideas that were current in it.

John the Baptist, a lone figure coming from the Judean wilderness, heralded the coming Messiah.

the early church excluded them all from the approved list of Scripture is some indication that the hunt is not likely to be very successful.

This means that for all practical purposes our knowledge of Jesus comes from the New Testament alone. Even here the field quickly narrows down. The letters of Paul and the other apostolic writers make very little reference to the events in the life of Jesus – although they attached great importance to his ministry as a historical fact, and were strongly influenced by what he had taught.

A story remembered and retold

It is, then, to the Gospels that we must turn for the written record of the life and teaching of Jesus. The Gospels were not composed until at least 30 years after the death of Jesus. During this period the material for them was preserved and handed down both by word of mouth and by written records that no longer survive.

The tradition would have been passed on carefully. In Jewish schools the children were taught to remember oral material accurately, and later Jewish rabbis were equally careful in handing down unwritten teaching. It would be natural for Jewish Christians to remember and preserve accurately what Jesus taught. The Gospel material was originally taught in Aramaic, the language spoken by Jesus, and in a poetic form which was easy to memorize.

People remember what they want to remember. This does not mean that Jesus'

hearers conveniently forgot what they found disturbing and unpalatable. On the contrary, there is much in the Gospels that must have been challenging and difficult, and yet it has been faithfully preserved.

The story of Jesus was remembered and retold because it was relevant to the life of the church. For example, the first Christians had to argue with those Jews who were opposed to them, so it was essential to remember how Jesus had debated with them. Faced with decisions on ethical issues such as marriage and divorce, they needed his teaching as their authority on such matters. So it is good, when we read a passage in the Gospels, to ask what significance it had for the early church. The story of Jesus was not preserved out of an academic interest in history for its own sake, but because of its practical relevance for the first Christians. It was not 'pure' but 'applied' history.

People also tend to remember and pass on stories and teaching in a certain pattern. Stories of healing miracles, for example, describe in turn the condition of the sufferer, the way in which the cure was effected, and the results it produced. Many stories about Jesus describe a situation in which he was placed, or a question which was put to him, and culminate in the essential point: an authoritative saying of Jesus on the topic at issue.

'Studying the Gospels' shows how the Gospel writers were authors rather than simply editors of the information that they received. The clearest example is John's Gospel, for the author has to some extent interpreted the story of Jesus to show its significance for his readers. He has offered a kind of commentary on the ministry of Jesus in which it is hard to distinguish between the original 'text' and its 'interpretation'.

The important point, however, is that there really is a 'text' which he is explaining for us; he is not commenting on something that never existed. Behind the Gospel stands the figure of John the apostle, just as apostolic testimony is the basis of the other Gospels. It is also being increasingly recognized by scholars that it is one and the same Jesus who is described in all four

Gospels. Whereas the critics of a former era argued that the Gospel of John had little or no basis in history, it is now seen that all four Gospels build on historical tradition, each preserving different aspects of it.

The purpose of the Gospel writers

John's Gospel raises the question of the relation of the Gospels to history. Did what is described in the Gospels really happen? We have already indicated that the Gospels rest on reliable tradition, handed down with care in the church. At the same time we must bear in mind that the Gospels are concerned to present the Christian significance of Jesus. Their basic purpose is to preach the gospel in order to convert the unbeliever and to build up believers in their faith.

> **" The greatness of this person could not have been captured in one picture. So we have four portraits, each bringing out its own distinctive facets of the character of Jesus. "**

This means that they are not simply historical reports, as for example the biography of some famous soldier might be. The writers were not trying to give a detailed historical account of Jesus' life with everything in proper chronological order. We have only to compare the order of events in Mark 4 – 5 with Matthew 13; 8; 9 to see this fact plainly.

Or again, the Gospels record very little of some aspects of Jesus' life: scarcely anything is mentioned before he reached the age of 30; and even the account of his ministry is incomplete. There is by no means enough incident to fill the whole of his active public life. We should not blame the Gospel writers for not doing something they never intended.

But this does not mean they were unconcerned about history. The Gospels are not invention. In the preface to his Gospel (Luke 1:1-4), Luke lays particular stress on the fact that he was making use of authentic eye-witness testimony. History certainly mattered for him, and there is no reason to suppose that the other writers thought differently.

What, then, were they trying to do? They were preaching the gospel, the good news. They were presenting Jesus as the Christ, the Son of God (Mark 1:1). They wrote in order that their readers might believe in him and so have eternal life (John 20:31). They therefore portrayed Jesus as his followers saw him. To them he was no ordinary man, not even a unique prophet. He was the Lord whom God had raised from the dead and who was now alive and active in heaven. They knew no other Jesus than this. They might have thought differently about him before the resurrection (see Luke 24:19-24), and even the resurrection did not compel everybody who heard about it to believe. But they had come to believe in Jesus as a result of the total impact which he had made upon them, and so they could not present him in any other way.

So the history in the Gospels is history as seen by Christians. A non-Christian would see it differently – claiming, for instance, that the resurrection could not have happened. It might be interesting to have an account of Jesus written from that point of view, but none has come down to us. What we have are the Gospels, written by Christian believers, written to persuade people to believe, but none the less historical for that.

Four portraits of Jesus

Each of the Gospel writers presents Jesus to us in his own characteristic way. The greatness of this person could not have been captured in one picture. So we have four portraits – four camera angles on the same scene – each bringing out its own distinctive facets of the character of Jesus.

Matthew concentrates on the relationship of Jesus to the Jewish faith. He shows how Jesus came to fulfil the Old Testament, but at the same time to judge the Jews for their unfaithfulness to their religion. No other Gospel denounces so forcibly the hypocritical outlook of the Pharisees. The Jews are called to see Jesus as the promised Messiah, the Son of David; and judgment is pronounced upon them for the failure of so many to respond to him. Matthew portrays Jesus very much as a teacher. He has given us systematic accounts of Jesus' teaching for the church's inner life and evangelistic mission.

Mark emphasizes action rather than teaching. He stresses how Jesus taught his disciples that the 'Son of man' must suffer and be rejected, and that they must be prepared to tread the same path. Those who tried to understand Jesus other than as a crucified Saviour would misunderstand him. The Jews expected a Messiah who would be a political leader and a figure of glory. They found it hard to recognize Jesus as the Messiah because he chose the path of humble service and suffering. Only

at his second coming would he appear as the King in his glory.

Luke stresses the blessings of salvation brought by Jesus. His Gospel emphasizes the signs of the coming of the Messiah, prophesied in the Old Testament and seen in Jesus' healing of the sick and preaching of the gospel to the poor and needy. Luke especially brings out the grace of God revealed in Jesus and bestowed upon those who seemed least worthy of it – sinful women and rapacious tax-collectors. For this is precisely what grace means, that men and women can do nothing to deserve it.

The life of Jesus

Jesus was the son of the virgin Mary, born at Bethlehem shortly before the death of Herod the Great in 4 BC.
(Picture: Manger Square, Bethlehem.)

He spent his early life in Nazareth where he worked as a village carpenter.

When John the Baptist began to preach beside the River Jordan (about AD 27), Jesus came and was baptized by him.

He immediately received the gift of God's Spirit, commissioning him for his work.

In the strength of the Spirit, in the Judean wilderness, he withstood Satan's inducements to divert him from his calling.

He then commenced a ministry of preaching and healing, mainly in Galilee.

This was preceded by a period in Judea (John 1 – 3) and included visits to Jerusalem.

It concluded with a journey to Jerusalem which culminated in his arrest and death at Passover time about AD 30.
(Picture: the great doors of the Church of the Holy Sepulchre, Jerusalem.)

Finally **John** reveals Jesus as the One sent by God the Father into the world to be its Saviour. As the Son, he has his Father's authority, living in close communion with him. John goes deepest into the things God has revealed and brings out the eternal significance of the 'God-become-man'.

What Jesus taught

Jesus' message centred on the good news of the rule (or kingdom) of God. In the Old Testament the prophets looked forward to a future era when God would act in power and set up his rule over Israel. This hope was associated with the coming of a king ('anointed' for this role, and hence called 'Messiah', Greek 'Christ') who would belong to the kingly line of David. In the time of Jesus, the people had come to expect a warrior-king to deliver them from their Roman overlords. See 'Jesus and the kingdom'.

Jesus taught that this hoped-for era had already dawned and he looked forward to the future consummation of God's rule, with himself as King. But the significant thing was that God's powerful intervention in history had already begun. It was to be seen, not as many people may have expected, in military victories but in Jesus' mighty works of healing and his preaching of salvation. God was already acting in the ministry of Jesus.

This good news demanded a response. Jesus called people to repent of their sin; he offered forgiveness to the penitent; and he summoned people to become his disciples. To accept the good news of the rule of God meant accepting Jesus as Master. Out of the many who responded, Jesus appointed 12 men to be the leaders of the new people of God who were to replace the old Israel which rejected the message of God, and to be associated with his missionary work. See 'The twelve disciples of Jesus'.

Jesus taught his disciples a new way of life. It is summed up in the Sermon on the Mount (Matthew 5 – 7). Jesus took over the Old Testament commandments to love God and one's neighbour and filled them with new life and vigour.

Mad, bad, or 'Son of God'?

Jesus taught with such self-confident authority that people asked who he thought he was. Some people dismissed him as mad. Others were prepared to see him as Messiah, but when he showed no inclination to lead them to war against Rome they turned away from him. This was probably why Jesus did not claim the title of Messiah openly. He preferred to speak of himself cryptically as the 'Son of man', a phrase which could simply be a kind of self-reference but which he on occasion filled powerfully with meaning on the basis of its use in Daniel 7:13. For Jesus it meant a figure who would one day be invested with power and glory by God (Mark 14:62), but who was, for the time being, humble and unknown (Matthew 8:20) and destined for suffering and death (Mark 8:31).

After his disciples had begun to realize who he was, he tried to teach them that he must die, although they were slow to take it in. Jesus saw himself fulfilling the role of the Servant of the Lord who suffers humiliation and death (Isaiah 52:13 – 53:12). He laid down his life as a ransom to save people from death (Mark 10:45; John 10:11). Only to his closest disciples did he reveal that he was the Son of God in a unique, intimate manner. And

On the first Easter Day, Jesus' disciples found his tomb empty. Later that day they met their risen Lord. This rock-cut 1st-century tomb lies beneath a convent in Nazareth.

he shared with them his privilege of addressing God in prayer by the name of *Abba*, 'Father' (Matthew 6:9; 11:25-27; Mark 14:36).

Throughout his public life Jesus was involved in conflict with the religious authorities, mainly because of his scorching criticisms of their man-made traditions which diverted people from the real purposes of God's law. He attacked the hypocrisy which substituted tradition for the law of Moses. His messianic claims spurred the Jewish leaders on to arrest him. They feared he might be the centre of a popular uprising against Rome which would lead to grim reprisals and the loss of their own positions (John 11:47-53). So when Jesus came to Jerusalem and flung down the gauntlet by his attitude to the Temple, they took steps to arrest him with the connivance of one of his followers.

God's new covenant

Meanwhile Jesus held a last meal with his disciples. He filled a familiar table ritual with new content by using the bread and wine as symbols: his body was about to be broken in death on their behalf, and his blood about to be shed sacrificially to ratify God's new covenant with people and to bring in his kingdom. After the meal, he went out to pray and to meet his enemies.

He was put through a trial which appears to have broken the appropriate legal rules. When the witnesses failed to produce sufficient evidence to condemn him, he was forced to make what his judges regarded as the blasphemous statement (to Christians it was the simple truth) that he was the Messiah.

He was condemned to death.

The Jews handed him over to the Roman governor as a political rebel against Rome, and although the governor was privately convinced of his innocence he allowed him to be put to death by the Roman punishment of crucifixion.

From the third day after his death, however, many of his disciples claimed that his tomb was empty and that he had himself appeared to them. God had raised him from the dead. The appearances took place over a period of 40 days, and in the course of them he gave his final command to his disciples to be his witnesses throughout the world, and ascended from their presence as a symbol of his return to be with God and as a promise of his second coming to them at the end of the world.

That is the gospel story in brief. There is no other Jesus. The attempts of sceptical scholars to peel off the Christian interpretation and leave behind an ordinary, human person as the real 'historical' Jesus have proved fruitless.

It leaves with us the picture of a person about whom people must make up their minds. Throughout the Gospels Jesus appears as more than a man. His message, his deeds, and his person force the reader to decision.

Studying the Gospels

Richard A. Burridge

People have studied the Gospels in different ways, almost from the moment they were written.

The first Gospel commentaries were written in the 2nd century, explaining and applying the Gospels to the lives of early Christians.

The church fathers discussed the merits of various approaches – the literal, spiritual or allegorical understandings.

Having made the Bible available to people in their own language, the 16th-century Reformers realized that for it to be authoritative and useful in the church, all possible tools, methods, and approaches must be used to understand it.

During the 19th century, the great strides made in literary-critical study of ancient texts began to be applied also to the Gospels.

The explosion of Gospel studies this century means that probably no other documents in the world have been subjected to so much research and scholarship, with a wide range of methods now available.

What are the Gospels?

Before we can understand any communication, we need to know what it is. A radio receiver cannot decode television pictures! And the same is true for writings. We do not listen to a fairy story in the same way as to a news broadcast, or interpret legends as if they were history.

Unfortunately, some people do read the Gospels like legends, while others treat them like a modern history book. Both approaches will result in misunderstanding. We must interpret them in the same way as those who first wrote, produced, read or heard them.

Although the Gospels look like 'stories about Jesus', biblical scholars early in the 20th century said they were not biographies of Jesus. After all, they tell us nothing about Jesus' human character or appearance, nor about the rest of his life apart from his brief ministry – concentrating on his last days, death and resurrection.

However, although *modern* biography reckons to cover the whole of a person's life and analyze their upbringing and personality, ancient 'lives' (even the word 'biography' goes back no further than the 9th century) were much shorter. Graeco-Roman writers described their understanding of a person through his deeds and words, detailing his death as the final revelation of his character.

The Gospel accounts of what Jesus 'did and taught' (Acts 1:1), their focus on him as subject, and their extended 'Passion' narratives of his last days on earth, are very similar in form and content to ancient 'lives'. We must therefore study them concentrating on the person of Jesus, and use all possible literary tools to see how each Gospel writer composes his particular portrait.

What does the text actually say?

After we know what the text is, we need to discover what it says, putting aside modern ideas of printing and publishing.

The Gospels are between just over 11,000 (Mark) and 19,000 words (Luke), about the amount that fitted on one single scroll, about 30ft long.

Even the most careful scribes are liable to make errors when copying them by hand in lamplight! However, we have over 5,000 manuscripts containing all or part of the New Testament, many more than for most other ancient texts. Through careful comparison of these in the light of scribal methods, scholars specializing in such textual studies ('**textual criticism**') can establish what the original texts said.

There are, of course, minor variations here and there, and

> **❝** *In the first part of my work, Theophilus, I gave an account of all that Jesus did and taught from the beginning.* **❞**
>
> Acts 1:1

translations record these in the margins or footnotes, as 'some ancient authorities read...'. Nonetheless, the text of the New Testament is better established than the rest of the classics.

Most of us read the Gospels in our own language, so it is sensible to have two or three good translations to study, compare and contrast. We must understand what the text is actually saying, and not what we want it to say!

How were the Gospels composed?

We regard copying another person's work as plagiarism, or

even theft. This is another modern concept. For the ancients, following a predecessor's account was not only a compliment, but accepted his authority. Thus Luke says that his sources include eye witnesses, preachers and other writers (Luke 1:1-4).

A quick look shows that the first three Gospels are closely related: around 90 per cent of Mark's 661 verses appear in Matthew, with about 50 per cent also in Luke. As they can be studied side by side, these three are called the 'Synoptic' Gospels, from the Greek *syn-opt-*, to see together. On the other hand, less than 10 per cent of the Synoptics' material appears in John. How are we to explain these facts?

Matthew and Luke are probably using the shorter account of Mark as their 'authority', writing with his scroll open before them, combining it with other material. Of course, Mark could be a later abbreviation, but why would he leave out all the others' material?

Matthew and Luke share about 200 additional verses in common, mostly Jesus' teaching which they place in different contexts. This suggests that they had a collection of Jesus' sayings, since lost, which we call 'Q', from the German *Quelle*, 'source'.

In addition, Matthew and Luke each have their own special material.

This analysis of the texts, called **'source criticism'**, reveals helpfully how each evangelist writes his account of Jesus. Although the fourth Gospel contains some material in common with the others (derived perhaps from oral tradition), it was composed independently of the other three.

What types of stories do they contain?

The Gospels are composed of separate stories of a few hundred words connected together into narratives.

Mark begins his Gospel with several events of Jesus' ministry in chapter 1, followed by a collection of stories of conflict with the religious authorities in chapters 2

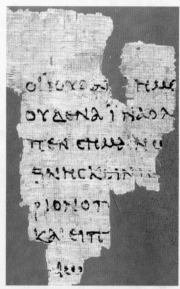

The earliest surviving fragment of a Gospel text – part of John 6 – dates from about AD 125/130; from the John Rylands Library.

and 3, and a set of parables in 4.

Such **'form criticism'** analyzes the different types of material in the Gospels and shows how they contain miracle stories, healings, parables, sayings, or 'pronounce- ment stories' leading up to a 'punch line' from Jesus (see how Mark 2:28 concludes 2:23-28). This helps us understand how individual stories were preserved and used within the early church.

John tells us that the Gospel writers had too much material, so they made a selection (John

20:30-31); Luke writes an 'orderly' account (Luke 1:1-4). Form criticism reveals that this 'order' is more logical than chronological, as the writers collect together their material about what Jesus said and did.

Were the Gospel writers editors or authors?

After form-critical study of small sections during the middle of the 20th century, scholars turned to how each Gospel writer ('evangelist') develops the story.

If Matthew and Luke follow Mark, the way they handle his material reveals their different interests. Similarly, newspapers today report events with a different 'spin' or angle, reflecting the interests of their editors. News- paper editorial work is called *redaktion* in German, and so this study of the evangelists as editors is called **'redaction criticism'**. This kind of comparative study reveals how Matthew is interested in the relationship of the church to Judaism, while Luke is writing for a more Gentile readership.

Once the evangelists were seen as editors and theologians, they could be studied as authors, describing their understanding of Jesus in a particular way. As Luke put it, recognizing that others had already written about Jesus, 'it seemed a good idea to me too' (Luke 1:3)! So often we study small chunks of about 10 or 20 verses of the Gospels; redaction study sets each section in the context of the writer's whole picture.

Different kinds of literary criticism

Increasingly today a wide range of literary-critical methods are being used to help our understanding of the Gospels.

So **'composition criticism'** considers how each evangelist arranges his material – for instance, Matthew's five great blocks of Jesus' teaching (chapters 5 – 7, 10, 13, 18, 23-25) or Luke's geographical arrangement of Galilee (4 – 9:50), the journey south (9:51 – 19:27), and Jerusalem (19:28 – 24:53).

'Narrative criticism' studies how the whole story works, with its plot, characters, tension, irony, motifs and patterns.

Structuralist approaches analyze the structure of episodes to see how they actually work, as well as the deeper structure of the whole book.

'Rhetorical criticism' considers the use by the evangelists of techniques in ancient oratory to persuade their readers of the truth about Jesus.

Approaches like these, together, show how this most exciting area of literary study of the Gospels reveals the richness of each evangelist's account.

Who were the Gospels written for?

All books are written for a particular audience or readership. Since not everyone could read in those times, ancient books were made known through public readings, at a dinner party or other gathering.

The Gospels would have been read aloud, in worship or other groups, more than they were read privately by individuals.

'Sociological analyses' describe the social or educational level of each Gospel's intended audience, and reconstruct the kind of church Matthew was writing for, or the 'Johannine community' suggested by the argument with 'the Jews' and the synagogue in the fourth

Gospel. This *can* become circular – reconstructing the community in the light of the text and interpreting the text in the light of the reconstructed community!

Recently, attention has moved away from the communities to the kind of reader or listener implied within each Gospel, with **'reader-response criticism'** looking at how each Gospel achieves its particular effect on people.

Dare we 'criticize' the Gospels?

Some people are worried by all these different 'criticisms' being applied to the Gospels.

Christians believe the Bible to be inspired by the Holy Spirit, as the Word of God. Are these approaches not about the words of human beings? Yes, they are. But God has communicated his Word through inspiring human beings to write and compose, to read and pass on these stories – and he can also inspire the humble biblical scholar trying to understand them!

The Gospels are not interpreted as magic books floating down from heaven, nor should we expect them to conform to modern notions of reporting and writing. Criticism need not be negative; rather, the use of these critical tools helps us understand more fully the depths and the riches of these books, how God inspired the first Christians to tell the story of Jesus in their day as we seek to do the same today.

Matthew

Summary

Matthew's life of Jesus focusses on his teaching.

Key passages and best-known stories

'Immanuel' *(1)*
Visit of the Magi *(2)*
The Sermon on the Mount *(5–7)*
The golden rule *(7:12)*
Parables of the kingdom *(13)*
Peter declares his faith *(16:13-20)*
Jesus transfigured *(17)*
Jesus and the children *(19:13-15)*
The rich young man *(19:16-22)*
Tribute to Caesar *(22:15-22)*
The greatest commandment *(22:34-40)*
Future events and the judgment *(24–25)*
Jesus' last week: suffering, death and resurrection *(26–28)*

Each of the four Gospels has its own special emphasis (see 'The Gospels and Jesus Christ', four portraits of Jesus). Although Matthew comes first, it is the one that many readers today find most difficult. But for the first Christians it was most important to show that the new faith was rooted in Judaism, and this is what Matthew, with all its quotations from the Jewish Bible, does. The Gospel is a 'bridge', connecting Jesus with what has gone before.

The author, a Jewish Christian writing for a church mainly composed of Jewish Christians, concentrates his skills on presenting Jesus as the long-awaited Messiah – the Christ predicted in the Old Testament (see 'Jewish religion in New Testament times'). He carefully records what Jesus said about his kingdom, a radically different concept from the idea of Messiah current in his day, when most Jews expected a political leader who would free them from Roman domination.

Matthew concentrates on Jesus' teaching, carefully structuring his material to alternate narrative and teaching, which he arranges in five main sections:

- chapters 5 – 7 (the famous 'Sermon on the Mount'): discipleship
- 10: mission
- 13: Jesus' parables
- 18: his disciples' relationships
- 24 – 25: the future

But Matthew does not confine the 'good news' to his own people, the Jews. Most have and will reject it (something so painful to the writer that he often sounds anti-Jewish). So the Gospel which begins by looking back to the Old Testament closes with Jesus' great commission to make disciples of all nations.

The writer

The Gospel does not name its author, but from earliest times it has been attributed to Matthew, the apostle and one-time tax

facing page:
Man, boy and donkeys, in an arched street in the Old City of Jerusalem.

Stories and events found only in Matthew

Parables	Miracles	Incidents
The tares/weeds	The two blind men	Joseph's dream
Hidden treasure	The dumb man who was possessed	The visit of the wise men
The pearl	The coin in the fish's mouth	The escape to Egypt
The net		Herod's massacre
The hard-hearted servant		Pilate's wife's dream
The workers in the vineyard		The death of Judas (also in Acts)
The two sons	Some of Jesus' **teaching** is found only in	The saints resurrected in Jerusalem
The marriage of the king's son	Matthew, including his wonderful invitation	The bribing of the guard
The ten 'bridesmaids'	to 'Come to me'.	The great commission
The talents		

collector for the Romans. Little is known of him. And beyond the fact that the Gospel belongs to the period between AD 50 and AD 100 no one knows for certain when or where it was written. Much of Matthew's material is almost identical with Mark's – and Mark was informed by the apostle Peter. Most scholars today believe that Matthew drew on Mark (not vice-versa) and date the Gospel some time after AD 80.

Main themes
- The Old Testament points forward to Jesus, in whom all God's purposes are fulfilled.
- Jesus is the Messiah, 'son of God' and 'son of man', God's promised King.
- Jesus both fulfils and transforms the law God gave to Israel through Moses.
- The people of God, now, are those who respond to the message of Jesus.

1 – 2
Jesus, the Messiah, is born

1:1-17 Dynasty of the true King
See also Luke 3:23-38. The two lists are in reverse order and give a different set of names from David onwards (only Zerubbabel and Shealtiel appear in both).

The lights of Bethlehem shine out across the terraced 'fields' which surround the hill-top town.

The point, for Matthew, is to show Jesus as the true King, descended from the royal line of David, as God had promised. He may be listing the heirs to the throne, while

'Genealogies are important'

❝ Our notions of the core of the gospel may not be the same for other cultures.

There are cultures where these genealogies are important. It's certainly important in my culture, where we want to know exactly where you have come from. Who are your ancestors?... I think the Chinese know this, the Filipinos know this, the Africans know this. The genealogies are important. ❞

Melba Maggay

Luke lists Joseph's particular line.

Matthew's list is stylized and abbreviated to fit his pattern: 14 names from Abraham to David; 14 from David to Jechoniah; 14 from Jechoniah to Jesus. Fourteen is 2 x 7, and the number 7 signified perfection. 'Six sevens' (3 x 14) are past and the 'seventh seven' is about to begin. Matthew's list has two turning-points: David (the start of the monarchy) and the exile (its end). His purpose is to establish a base for what will follow: his great theme that in Jesus scripture is fulfilled.

It is possible that 14 is the numerical value of the name David, since the letters/consonants of the Hebrew alphabet served also as numbers: d (4) + v (6) + d (4) = 14.

▶ **Son/descendant of David (1)** King David was promised an unfailing succession. But Judah ceased to be a monarchy at the time of the exile. And the promise came to be applied to the Messiah.

▶ **Verses 3-6** It was unusual to include women in a list like this, yet four are mentioned here. None of these would have been included if God had been concerned only with respectable Jewish people. Tamar had children by her father-in-law, Judah, who had wronged her (Genesis 38); Rahab was a Jericho prostitute who helped the Jewish spies (Joshua 2); Ruth, a Moabite woman who made her mother-in-law's God her own (Ruth 1-4); and Solomon's mother (Uriah's wife) was Bathsheba, with whom David committed adultery (2 Samuel 11).

▶ **Verse 11** 'Father', like 'son' (verse 1), can be used in a wider sense. Josiah was Jechoniah's grandfather.

1:18-25 'God is with us'

Luke's fuller account of the birth of Jesus focusses on Mary; Matthew's on Joseph. Joseph is a descendant of David (verse 20) and it is his naming/adoption of Jesus (who was not his son) that makes Jesus officially a 'son of David' as the Scriptures require. In verse 23 Matthew gives us the first of five Old Testament quotations used in chapters 1 and 2 to show that Jesus fulfils all that the prophets foretold (see also 2:6, 15, 18, 23).

Here Isaiah's words take on a new dimension: in Jesus (Hebrew 'Joshua', a name that means 'God saves') God is actually here in our world with us (the meaning of the name 'Immanuel') . See also 'God with us' and 'The virgin birth'.

▶ **Verse 18** In Jewish society this pledge was legally binding and could be broken only by divorce.

▶ **Verse 25** The implication is that after the birth Mary and Joseph lived a normal married life (see

'God with us' – the incarnation

Dick France

One of the more puzzling things about the New Testament is the way its writers suggest, and occasionally say openly, that Jesus, a young carpenter from an obscure village who was executed in his early 30s, was also God. Not just 'a god', but God, the one true God of the Old Testament, present in human form.

They do not often say this in so many words. John's Gospel begins by telling us that 'the Word' (a title for Jesus, as becomes clear in the Gospel) 'was God', and that this Word 'became flesh and lived among us' (John 1:1, 14). At the end of the same Gospel the apostle Thomas, who notoriously refused at first to believe that Jesus had risen from the dead, hails him as 'My Lord and my God' (John 20:28).

In a few other places in the New Testament Jesus appears to be called 'God' (e.g. Acts 20:28; Romans 9:5; 2 Thessalonians 1:12; Titus 2:13; Hebrews 1:8; 2 Peter 1:1; 1 John 5:20), though it is intriguing that in all these cases either there is some question about the right reading of the text or the Greek words can be understood in a

different way. This sort of language apparently did not yet come easily to the writers.

But these apparently direct statements that Jesus is God are only the tip of a huge theological iceberg. After all, the people who wrote the New Testament books were Jews, brought up from childhood to believe that there is only one God and that to speak of any human being in divine terms was

> **❝** You must make your choice. Either this man was, and is, the Son of God: or else a madman or something worse. You can shut him up for a fool, you can spit at him and kill him as a demon; or you can fall at his feet and call him Lord and God. But let us not come with any patronising nonsense about his being a great human teacher. He has not left that open to us. He did not intend to. **❞**
>
> C.S. Lewis, *Mere Christianity*

blasphemy. No wonder phrases like 'Jesus is God' did not trip easily off their tongues. But in many other more subtle ways that belief comes to light all over the New Testament books.

Jesus often referred to himself as the Son of God, and to God as in a unique sense his Father (e.g. Matthew 11:25-27; 24:36) and the Gospel writers tell us that God himself described Jesus in this way (Mark 1:11; 9:7). His followers took up the theme: for instance, Jesus is called the Son of God 22 times in the five short chapters of 1 John, and John says he wrote his Gospel so that his readers might believe that Jesus is the Son of God (John 20:31).

Such language from a Jew is not just politeness: no one else was ever described in this way, and no one else had dared to address God simply as '*Abba*' (Father) as Jesus did (Mark 14:36). Sayings such as 'I and the Father are one' (John 10:30), 'whoever has seen me has seen the Father' (John 14:9), and 'I am in the Father and the Father in me' (John 14:10-11) take us far beyond the ordinary worshipper's sense of belonging to God. This is a

Wise men from the East brought Jesus gifts of frankincense and myrrh. Both are contained in this incense burner from the Temple of the Winged Lions at Petra.

also 13:55-56). The birth took place some time between 6 and 4 BC, when King Herod the Great died.

2 Homage – and a threat

Men from the East (Persia, Babylonia or Arabia) come to pay homage to the infant King. They are astrologers. Studying the stars and their meanings is what makes them 'wise'. And they have no doubt that the new star

means the birth of the promised King in Judah. (It is tradition that identifies the Magi as three kings and attaches specific meaning to their presents – gold for a king; incense for God; myrrh for a mortal man.)

Their news is not welcome at the palace. Herod the Great, king of the Jews from 37-4 BC, was murderously jealous of all rivals. 'Herod was suspicious of anyone whom he thought could try to

---

unique family relationship; Father and Son share the same divine nature.

In Luke 1:35 the title 'Son of God' is linked with Jesus' virgin birth. Although the title does not depend on Jesus' being born of a virgin (after all, John, who stresses the title most, never mentions the virgin birth), the two ideas fit comfortably together (see 'The virgin birth').

Sometimes Jesus claimed to do things that only God can do, such as forgiving sins (Mark 2:5-12), judging (Matthew 7:21-23; 25:31-46), or giving life (John 5:25-29). Paul and John took this even further in the extraordinary claim that it was through Jesus that the world was created – and that means that he must be older than the universe! (John 1:1-4; 1 Corinthians 8:6; Colossians 1:15-17.) The New Testament writers associated Jesus so closely with God that they saw no problem in applying to him Old Testament texts which were in fact about God (e.g. Romans 10:9-13; Hebrews 1:8-12).

Already within the New Testament there is evidence that Christians had begun to worship Jesus and pray to him (Acts 7:59; 9:10-17; 1 Corinthians 1:2; Revelation 5:8-14, etc.). Paul, writing to the Greek-speaking Christians in Corinth, preserves the

prayer 'Our Lord, come' in the Aramaic form *Maranatha*, which shows that this was already by the mid-50s a familiar formula from the early Aramaic-speaking churches (1 Corinthians 16:22). Remember that these were Jewish people, praying to a man whom they had seen executed only a few years earlier, and you realize how amazing it is.

There are a few places in the New Testament where the language used to express Jesus' divine nature and authority is so exalted that they are thought to be echoes of hymns or creeds which were already in use in the church's worship. Chief among these are Philippians 2:6-11; Colossians 1:15-20; Hebrews 1:2-3, and of course John 1:1-18. To read these passages carefully is to gain a thrilling impression of how Jesus' followers had come to understand who he was within not much more than a generation after his life, death and resurrection. They speak of him not just as a man whose life began at Bethlehem in the days of Herod, but as one who has been from the beginning, who shared the Father's glory before the world began (John 17:5, 24), and whose life on earth was only a temporary 'interruption' of his heavenly glory.

This is what later came to be formulated as the 'doctrine of the incarnation' (which means literally

the 'enfleshing', taking up the language of John 1:14). It is not presented to us in the New Testament as a systematic doctrine. Rather we share the exhilarating experience of Jesus' first Jewish followers as they tried to make sense of the man they knew, and gradually came to realize who he really was.

But in their different ways they have left for us a rich source for theological discovery, and in their writings are all the raw materials for the fully developed Christian doctrine of the Son of God who 'for us and for our salvation came down from heaven, and was incarnate of the Virgin Mary, and was made man'.

Perhaps Matthew expressed the truth most appropriately when he reminded his readers that the name Immanuel, the name of the virgin's son, means simply 'God with us' (Matthew 1:23).

The star of Bethlehem
Colin Humphreys

The comet of 1858 (Donati's comet) seen 'standing over' Paris. The star of Bethlehem may have looked like this.

What was the star of Bethlehem? Did it really exist? There are three key characteristics of the star that we can deduce from Matthew's Gospel:

- It was a star which had newly appeared. Matthew 2:7 states, 'Then Herod summoned the Magi secretly and ascertained from them the exact time when the star had appeared.'
- It travelled slowly through the sky against the star background. The Magi first 'saw his star in the east', then they came to Jerusalem where Herod sent them to Bethlehem, then 'they went on their way and the star they had seen in the east went ahead of them.'

Since Bethlehem is almost due south of Jerusalem, the star must have moved slowly through the sky from the east to the south in the time taken for the Magi to travel from their country (Arabia, or Mesopotamia or Persia) to Jerusalem, probably one or two months.

- The star 'stood over' Bethlehem. Matthew 2:9 records that the star 'went ahead of them and stood over the place where the child was'. Popular tradition has the star pointing out the very stable in which Christ was born, but according to Matthew, viewed from Jerusalem the star stood over the place where the child was born, i.e. Bethlehem.

There is one and only one astronomical object that satisfies the above criteria: a comet with a long tail. A comet newly appears in the sky and it travels slowly through the sky against the star background, at typically 1-2 degrees per day. The picture shows how a comet can appear to stand over a place, with the long tail pointing the head of the comet to a particular place. Thus a comet uniquely fits the description in Matthew of the star.

The Chinese kept a close watch on comets and other interesting stars. According to ancient Chinese records there was a spectacular comet with a long tail which appeared in 5 BC and was visible for over 70 days. This is the only long-tailed comet recorded by the Chinese in the period 20 BC - AD 10, hence the comet of 5 BC may be uniquely identified as the star of Bethlehem. In addition, the Chinese records tell us the position in the sky where this comet first appeared and from this we know that the Magi would first have seen this comet in the east, just as described in Matthew.

---

take the throne away from him. One-time friends, servants, countless enemies, priests, nobles and all who crossed him in some way were killed' (A.R. Millard). The massacre at Bethlehem is quite in character with other cruelties on record. But God is able to protect his own and, warned by the angel, the little family escapes to Egypt.

Jesus, as Messiah, had to be born in Bethlehem (in verse 6 Matthew part-quotes, part-interprets the prophet Micah's words). Verse 15 (quoting Hosea 11:1) makes the link with Israel as God's son, rescued from Egypt at the exodus. Verse 23 is not a scripture quotation as such, though there are many pointers to Messiah's lowly origin. It explains the name by which he was known: 'Jesus of Nazareth'.

▶ **Verse 18** Jeremiah (31:15) is pointing to the grief of the Babylonian exile. Rachel, the mother-figure of Israel, was Jacob's much-loved wife. She died in childbirth at Ramah on the way to Bethlehem.

▶ **Archelaus (22)** inherited a third of Herod's kingdom, ruling Judea, Samaria and Idumea from 4 BC - AD 6. His repressive measures led the Romans to depose him and take control of Judea themselves. See 'The Herod family'.

3 – 4
Jesus' mission begins

3 John the Baptist
See also Mark 1:2-11; Luke 3:2-22. Luke 1 tells the story of John's birth.

There is an interval of some 30 years between chapters 2 and 3 of Matthew's Gospel. Now the compelling voice of the adult John, calling on God's people to make ready for the Messiah, draws crowds out into the desert-wilderness of Judea to listen. Peter's brother, Andrew, was one who responded and was baptized by John (John 1:35-40).

The 'washing' of baptism symbolized a radical cleaning up of a person's life – wiping the slate clean of all previous wrong – a return to God. John's baptism, unlike the customary ritual washings was once-only. Jesus had no need of this, as verses 14-15 and the rest of the New Testament

make plain. He had no need to be baptized in order to be forgiven because he 'had no sin'. Yet it is right, 'for now', because Jesus must do 'all that God requires' to save the world. So he steps into the River Jordan, accepting his destiny, to receive God's commission and blessing.

Matthew has already shown that Jesus is the Messiah, David's 'son'. In verse 17 (Psalm 2:7; Isaiah 42:1) Jesus is affirmed as God's own Son. Now his feet are set on the path of 'the Servant whose mission is to bear the sins of the people' (R.T. France).

▶ **Kingdom of heaven (2)** See 'Jesus and the kingdom'.

▶ **Verse 4** See note under Mark 1:1-8.

▶ **Pharisees and Sadducees (7)** See 'Jewish religion in New Testament times'.

4:1-11 The testing of Jesus
See also Mark 1:12-13; Luke 4:1-13. In the severe testing – the 'temptations' – that follows his 40-day fast, Jesus faces up to the things which will go on testing his intent to do God's work in God's way all through his ministry. He now has power – power to feed the hungry, heal the sick, raise the dead. How will he use it? To satisfy his own (legitimate) needs? To test God out? To

It was through inhospitable country like this Mary and Joseph fled with the infant Jesus, escaping to Egypt to be safe from the murderous King Herod.

command a following? When it comes to it, will he use his power to save himself or, trusting God, tread the path to the cross in order to save others? Jesus answers Satan's test questions with words from scripture, quoting Deuteronomy 8:3; 6:16; 6:13 – key passages from Israel's 40 years in the desert, when God tested his people's obedience to him (Deuteronomy 8:2).

▸ **Verse 1** God intended to test Jesus but the agent is 'the devil' (from the Greek word for 'tempter'), who uses all his powers to try to turn people away from God.

▸ **Took him (8)** Either literally or in a vision.

4:12-25 In Galilee

John is put in prison. Jesus, when he hears the news, travels north in what may be a tactical withdrawal. Matthew sees in this the fulfilment of another Old Testament prophecy (14-16).

Jesus has left his home-town of Nazareth. Now, for the whole of his ministry in Galilee, his base will be the lakeside town of Capernaum. Here he calls his first disciples (see 'The twelve disciples of Jesus') and begins his public ministry: travelling all over to teach, 'proclaim the good news of the kingdom' and heal the sick.

▸ **Decapolis/Ten Towns (25)** Ten free Greek cities south-east of Galilee.

Satan, testing Jesus, suggested he throw himself from 'the pinnacle of the Temple', trusting the angels to save him, as Scripture promised.

5 – 7
Following Jesus: The Sermon on the Mount

See also Luke 6:20-49. The 'sermon' is the first and longest of the five sections in which Matthew gathers together the teaching of Jesus. Sitting on the hillside with his followers all around him Jesus tells them how his disciples are meant to live. This is no simple set of rules. Their whole attitude and outlook is to be transformed: from the inside out. Their goal is a goodness like God's, which knows no bounds (5:48).

5:1-16 True happiness

Jesus turns ordinary human ideas about happiness upside down. Contrary to general opinion, it is not the rich, the ruthless, the powerful who are really 'well off'. The genuinely fortunate are those who recognize their dependence on God (the 'poor in spirit', verse 3), trusting in God and not their own resources. The hallmarks of God's people are suffering (4), 'meekness' (5), a longing to be right with God and to

66 *Blessed are the poor in spirit, for theirs is the kingdom of heaven. Blessed are those who mourn, for they shall be comforted. Blessed are the meek, for they shall inherit the earth...* 99

Jesus' 'Beatitudes': 5:3ff.

'You are like light for the whole world,' Jesus said to his disciples. 'A city built on a hill cannot be hidden.' Tsefat, in northern Galilee, is just such a city.

'see right prevail' (6), readiness to forgive (7), having their hearts set on God (8), peacemaking (9).

Their reward will be to receive what they long for. And their lives are effective in the world: they put the seasoning into life, they stop the rot (13), they light up the way (14). By what they do and say and how they react, they reflect something of what God himself is like – so that others see and give God the credit (16).

5:17-48 A new standard
It may have seemed to some, from Jesus' attitude to the sabbath and other laws, that he wanted to remove the law completely. Far from it. Rather, he will *fulfil* the law God gave through Moses. It is all too easy to take the law in a superficial, legalistic way, to be content with keeping the letter. It is the spirit, the principle behind the law, that reveals God's will.

In verses 21-48 Jesus introduces six examples with the words: 'You have heard... but I say to you...' He shows how the principles expressed in the law are meant to be applied. In every case – murder (21-26; Exodus 20:13), adultery (27-30; Exodus 20:14), divorce (31-32; Deuteronomy 24:1-4), oaths (33-37; Numbers 30:2; see also Matthew 23:16-22), retaliation (38-42; Exodus 21:24), loving others (43-48; Leviticus

'Look how the wild flowers grow,' Jesus said to his disciples, as they sat around him on the open hillside to be taught a lesson in trust.

19:18; see also Luke 10:29-37) – the standard is raised. Jesus shows how sin begins in the mind and will. That is where it must be rooted out. Law-courts deal only with wrong*doing*: in God's eyes the thoughts and motives behind the action are culpable too.

▸ **The law and the prophets (17)** I.e. all the Old Testament precepts. There are three divisions in the Jewish Bible: the Law (Genesis to Deuteronomy); the Prophets (Former: Joshua, Judges, Samuel, Kings; and Latter: all the prophets except Daniel); and the Writings (the rest of the 'Old Testament').

▸ **Verse 22** Even a trivial insult indicates an attitude of disdain/hatred that is culpable.

▸ **Verse 23** An offering to God means nothing if a grudge or grievance is not first put right.

▸ **Verses 31-32** In Moses' day a wife could be dismissed at whim. His law gave her some security. Jesus goes back to the fundamental meaning and purpose of marriage. The bond made when the two become 'one flesh' is indissoluble. Divorce is unthinkable, except where one of the partners has broken the bond already. See 19:3-9.

6:1-18 Giving, praying, fasting
Motives, thoughts, intentions, what goes on deep inside, are what matter when it comes to religious practice, too. God gives no prizes for an outward show of piety. So Jesus tells his followers to give and pray and fast (the three 'most prominent practical requirements for personal piety in mainstream Judaism') without drawing attention to themselves. God will reward them. Prayer is to be simple, trusting: as children come to a loving Father, eager to please, conscious of failings. It is expressed in the model prayer Jesus gives his disciples (9-13), which we know as 'The Lord's Prayer' (see also on Luke 11:2-4).

6:19-34 First things first
People can choose what to set their hearts on. They can go all out for money and material things, or for God and spiritual things. But not for both. Everyone must decide their own priorities. Those who put God first can rest assured he knows all their needs and will not fail to supply them. They can be free from anxiety.

The twelve disciples of Jesus

Andrew McGowan

Out of all his followers, Jesus chose 12 men to be his disciples (Mark 3:13-19), giving them the title 'apostles' (Luke 6:13). They were to spend three years with him, hearing his teaching and learning about the kingdom of God.

Peter, the recognized leader of the disciples, was originally called Simon son of Jonas. He and his brother Andrew came from Bethsaida, and later lived in Capernaum. They worked together as fishermen in partnership with the sons of Zebedee. See Matthew 16:17; John 1:44; Mark 1:16-17; Luke 5:10.

Jesus gave him the nickname 'Peter' (meaning 'Rock') and from then on he was known as Simon Peter, though for a long time he was anything but solid and reliable. He was fiery, impetuous, and constantly swinging from one position to another. For example:

- In Matthew 16:13-26 Peter declares that Jesus is the Christ, the Son of the living God. But only a short time later he is rebuking Jesus for suggesting that he must be crucified!
- On another occasion he saw Jesus walking on the water and started to walk out towards him (Matthew 14:28) but then his faith failed and he began to doubt and to sink.
- At the Last Supper he says that he will be loyal even if all the others desert Jesus (Mark 14:29ff.), but then three times denies he even knows Jesus (Mark 14:66ff.).
- When they came to arrest Jesus he lashed out with a sword

The inner circle

Peter, James and John formed the inner circle of disciples who were present with Jesus on such significant occasions as the raising of Jairus' daughter to life, Jesus' transfiguration and his prayers before the arrest in Gethsemane.

See Mark 5:37; 9:2; 14:33.

(John 18:10) but then ran away (Matthew 26:56).

Nevertheless, by the power and grace of God, Peter was transformed into a leader, a writer (he wrote two New Testament letters) and a preacher of tremendous courage and authority. His sermon on the Day of Pentecost led to the conversion of 3,000.

After the resurrection Jesus asked Peter three times to reaffirm his faith, paralleling the three denials (John 21:15ff.).

Jesus said that Peter was the Rock on which he would build the church. He shares this with the other disciples (Matthew 16:18) since it is the apostles and their teaching which lay the foundation of the church (Ephesians 2:20).

Andrew, Peter's brother, had previously been a disciple of John the Baptist. We know little else about Andrew, although he seems to have been a practical man. His great contribution was to bring Peter to Jesus. The Bible records that he was with the other apostles after the ascension.

See John 1:35-40; John 6:8-9; 12:21-22; Acts 1:13.

James and his brother John, the sons of Zebedee, were both disciples. They seem to have had stormy natures, which is probably why Jesus called them 'Boanerges' or 'Men of Thunder'. James and John were the ones who wanted to call down fire from heaven to destroy a Samaritan village which didn't welcome Jesus! They also proudly sought high position in Jesus' kingdom.

Yet James was the first of the Twelve to be martyred for the faith. Here was a man whose commitment and passion, which could easily have been used for terrorism, were used in the service of God's kingdom.

See Mark 3:17; Luke 9:54; Mark 10:37; Acts 12:2.

John, brother of James, was not only a disciple but also a major contributor to the New Testament. John's name appears in the titles of five books – a Gospel, three letters, and the Revelation – though scholars debate whether all are by the same John.

While he was dying on the cross Jesus committed his mother into John's care and keeping (John 19:25-27). From various other references in the New Testament it would seem that John may have been a cousin of Jesus on his mother's side, so perhaps this was a natural decision for him to make.

Philip, like Peter and Andrew, was from Bethsaida. His call to follow Jesus came the day after that of Simon and Andrew.

Philip was a very down-to-earth

▶▶ sort of person. He quickly calculated exactly what it would cost to feed 5,000 people! It was Philip who asked Jesus to show them 'the Father'. Clearly he didn't always understand what Jesus was doing, but he persevered. He was also responsible for leading Nathanael to Christ.

See John 1:43-46; 6:5-7; 14:8.

Nathanael (also called Barthol-omew) was from Cana in Galilee. When Philip told him about Jesus, he doubted whether 'any good thing' could come out of Nazareth. 'Come and see,' Philip said. And when he did come Jesus amazed him by describing exactly what he had been doing just before.

Nathanael was convinced!

He was a man of sound charac-ter. In fact, Jesus described him as 'An Israelite in whom there is no guile'. He was one of those to whom

The doubter

Thomas is well known as 'doubting' Thomas. Although devoted to his Master and even prepared to risk death, he did not understand Jesus' comments about his impending death and could not believe in Jesus' resurrection until he actually saw him.

Thomas's name comes from the Aramaic word meaning 'twin'. In his Gospel, John uses the Greek version 'Didymus' three times.

Thomas has gone down in history with something of a bad character reference but Jesus did not reject him. Instead he called him to believe, using the occasion to speak of those who, in the future, would believe without having seen Jesus in person.

See John 11:16; 14:5; 20:24-29; 21:2.

The forgotten men

There are three disciples of whom we know practically nothing.

James, son of Alphaeus was probably the 'James the Younger', son of Mary, mentioned in Mark 15:40.

Thaddaeus is mentioned in Matthew 10:3 and Mark 3:18 as

Thaddaeus, but is also called Judas the son of James in Luke 6:16; Acts 1:13.

Simon the Zealot may have been one of the Zealots who sought the liberation of Israel from Roman rule, or his name may simply be a description of his 'zealous' personality.

the risen Christ appeared by Lake Galilee

See John 1:43-51; 21:2.

Matthew (also called Levi) was a tax collector. He was actually collecting taxes when he received his call from Jesus. He was one of the 'sinners' with whom Jesus associated, much to the fury of the Pharisees. Jesus said that these 'sinners' were the very people who most needed and most appreciated his teaching. On one occasion in Matthew's house, Jesus went so far as to say that only those who recognized themselves to be sinners would receive any benefit from his ministry. Most Jews would have rejected Matthew as a quisling and traitor because he worked for the Romans, gathering taxes. But in Jesus he found a Saviour.

See Matthew 9:9ff.; 10:3; Mark 2:13-17.

Jesus drew all these very different characters to himself and made them his disciples. What a Saviour, to be able to transform the world by means of men like these.

The traitor

Judas Iscariot is known to everyone as the disciple who betrayed Jesus for 30 pieces of silver. He was the treasurer for the disciples and was stealing from the 'poor bag' which he held for them. No wonder that he objected to the action of Mary in anointing Jesus with expensive ointment which he said should have been sold.

Jesus made it clear at the Last Supper that he knew who would betray him, but Judas went ahead and made a deal with the chief priests. And so the soldiers came to arrest Jesus, led by Judas who identified and betrayed him with the kiss of greeting from a friend.

Afterwards Judas was filled with remorse and his tragic death is recorded.

See Matthew 26:14-16, 25; Mark 14:10-11, 43-45; John 12:3-6; 13:27-30; Matthew 27:3-10 – compare Acts 1:18-19.

▶ **Verses 22-23** The eyes were thought of as windows, letting light into the body. There is a word-play here on single = generous and evil eye = stingy.

7 Dos and don'ts

Do *not* be harshly critical (1-5); *do* be discriminating (6). Never give up praying (7-11).

Verse 12, 'the golden rule', puts the whole sermon in a nutshell: 'Do as you would be done by.' This is the essence of both Law and Prophets. So:

- Make sure you are on the right road to eternal life (13-14).
- Beware of being misled – tell true from false 'by their fruits' (15-20).
- Words are not enough; many are self-deceived (21-23).
- The safe course is to act on Christ's teaching: a house built on rock can stand the storm (24-27).

The 'sermon' over, Matthew notes the *authority* that sets Jesus apart from all other teachers and impresses his hearers.

8 – 9:34
Healing and teaching

8 – 9:8 Healings

Jesus responds to human need. Teaching, preaching and healing go together: his authority is expressed in what he says and what he does.

8:1-4: the leper. To the Jew lepers were unclean, untouchable. Jesus could have healed the man with a look, or a word – instead he reaches out and touches him. (For the leprosy regulations, see Leviticus 13 – 14; the term 'leprosy' in the Bible covers a number of skin diseases.)

8:5-13: the centurion's boy. Jesus' mission is to Israel, but nowhere among his own people has he found faith to equal that of the Roman officer who recognized authority when he saw it. (See also 15:21-28.)

8:14-17: at Capernaum Jesus uses his healing power to cure sickness and demonstrates his authority over evil spiritual powers which were seen to be at the root of many ills. Matthew applies Isaiah's words

quite literally to Jesus' healing ministry.

8:18-21: Jesus' response to two would-be followers provides a lesson on commitment.

8:23-34: tellingly, Matthew has the story of Jesus' control of the wild and violent storm immediately followed by the calming of two wild and violent men. In their accounts, Mark and Luke focus on just one of the men, 'Legion' or 'Mob' (Mark 5:1-17; Luke 8:26-37). They may draw on a different tradition. Or perhaps Matthew has in mind the two witnesses required for a valid testimony under Jewish law. Jesus restores both men to sanity. But the residents of Gadara – one of the Ten (Greek) Towns 10km/6 miles south-east of the Lake – were so scared that they sent Jesus away.

9:1-8: the man with paralysis. Jesus uses the physical healing as proof of the spiritual cure: the man's forgiveness.

▶ **Son of man (8:20)** A phrase Jesus often uses to describe himself. It emphasizes his humanity

Jesus' first disciples were fishermen, called while mending their nets. These fishing-boats are in the harbour of Acco, on Israel's Mediterranean coast.

**Jesus in
Galilee and
the north**

Mt Hermon
Zarephath/Sarepta
Tyre
Caesarea Philippi
Chorazin
Capernaum   Bethsaida
Gennesaret
Cana
Magdala
Tiberias   Lake
Nazareth   Galilee
Nain   Gadara
GALILEE

(Psalm 8:4), yet points beyond it (Daniel 7:13-14).

▶ **8:21-22** The disciple wants to wait till after his father's funeral before joining Jesus. This need not mean that his father is already dead. 'I must first bury my father' is a colloquial way of saying, 'I will follow you sometime – when my father is dead and I am free to go.' Jesus' response overrides one of the most basic requirements of Jewish society, using shock-tactics to make the point that following him is an absolute priority.

▶ **8:23-27** See also Mark 4:36-41, with some differences of detail.

▶ **His own/home town (9:1)** Capernaum – see 4:13.

9:9-17 Matthew's call; questions about fasting

In Mark (2:13-17) and Luke (5:27-32) the tax collector is called Levi, and the feast is held at his house. 'Matthew' may have been Levi's first name, as 'Peter' was Simon's. Jesus' presence in such company scandalizes the religious Pharisees. John's followers are also puzzled. Why does Jesus feast whereas John fasted? Luke (5:36-37) gives Jesus' answer most clearly. His radically new teaching cannot be squeezed into the mould of the old legalism. It must find new forms of expression, or the old will be destroyed and the new spoilt.

▶ **Tax collectors (9-10)** The tax is likely to have been customs duty. Collectors 'were heartily disliked both as collaborators and

*66 As Jesus
saw the crowds,
his heart was
filled with pity
for them,
because they
were worried
and helpless,
like sheep
without a
shepherd. So
he said to his
disciples,
'The harvest is
large, but there
are few workers
to gather it in.
Pray to the
owner of the
harvest that he
will send out
workers to
gather in his
harvest.' 99*

9:36-37

extortioners. As a class they were regarded as dishonest... Matthew must therefore have been the richest of the apostles' (Leon Morris). When he walked out of his job there was no going back.

9:18-34 More healings

Verses 18-26: Jairus' daughter; the woman with a haemorrhage (see on Mark 5:21-43; Luke 8:40-56).

Verses 27-31: two blind men. The reason for secrecy (30) is not explained. Presumably Jesus is anxious to avoid his miracles giving people the wrong ideas about his mission.

Verses 32-34: the dumb man who was possessed.

▶ **Verse 23** Musicians were often hired to play dirges at a house where someone had died.

9:35 – 10:42
Jesus' charge to the Twelve

This is Matthew's second teaching section. See also Mark 6:7-13; Luke 9:1-6, and other parallel passages.

Jesus' pity for the people, God's 'harvest' (9:36-37), leads straight into the account of his selection of the 'Twelve' (see 'The twelve disciples of Jesus'). The choice and training of this inner ring of disciples was a vital part of Jesus' mission. The word 'apostle' means 'messenger', and the task of spreading the word about Jesus would rest with them after his death.

Now, having called them, he sends them out for the first time, with his own authority to heal. He gives them their instructions (some only temporary – see Luke 22:35-36) and warns them of the kind of reception they are likely to get, both now and in the future. They are to expect hardship, to trust in God's care and to fear no one.

▶ **10:1** The Twelve represent God's new community, as the 12 tribes did the old.

▶ **The tax collector (10:3)** It seems Matthew could never forget he was once a social outcast.

▶ **10:23** echoes Daniel 7:13. The subject is authority/sovereignty, not Jesus' 'second coming'. The reference here may be to his triumphant return from death at the resurrection.

▶ **Beelzebul (10:25)** Even Jesus' enemies do not deny that he casts out demons. But they do their best to discredit him. The Jews seem to have taken the name of a heathen (Canaanite) god, which in their own language sounded like 'lord of dung', and applied it to a demon chief, perhaps Satan.

▶ **The housetop (10:27)** The flat roof of the house was a favourite place for gossip and discussion.

▶ **10:28** Only God, not Satan, has this power.

▶ **10:34-35** The division is a 'result' of Jesus' teaching. The Bible often expresses consequences as if they were deliberate intention.

▶ **10:39** 'Whoever finds': i.e. those who deny their faith to save their skins.

11 – 12
The claims of Jesus

This is one of Matthew's narrative sections: it also contains a good deal of teaching.

11:1-19 'Are you the one?'
John, held prisoner by Antipas (the younger son of Herod the Great; ruler of Galilee and Perea), is puzzled by the reports of Jesus. He expected the Messiah to come in judgment. Jesus' reply reminds John of the other aspect of Messiah's work (predicted in Isaiah 35:5-6; 61:1), which he is fulfilling. Jesus thinks no less of John for his doubts. He is the greatest of the prophets, the latter-day Elijah predicted by Malachi (4:5). But John, though he heralds Christ's new kingdom, belongs to the old order, and at this point remains outside it. So the humblest person within the kingdom is more privileged than John.

▶ **Verse 12** Jesus may be referring to Zealot militants, from whom he disassociated himself, or to the fact that the kingdom opens its gates to those who are desperate (see Luke 16:16).

▶ **Verses 16-17** Like sulky children, Jesus' contemporaries refuse to 'play weddings' with him, or to 'play funerals' with John. They will listen neither to good news, nor to warnings.

▶ **Verse 19** This is God's Wisdom. The sentence means that 'the proof of the pudding is in the eating'.

11:20-30 'Come to me'
Most of Jesus' miracles took place in the small area at the northern end of Lake Galilee, around Capernaum, Chorazin and Bethsaida. They created much excitement. But as evidence of the coming kingdom, they were meant to change people's lives, to lead to repentance. This did not happen, so God's judgment on their stubborn disbelief was inevitable. If the people of Tyre and Sidon (the prosperous, godless seaports denounced by the prophets: see e.g. Isaiah 23) – even Sodom (a byword for evil: Genesis 19) – had seen what they had seen, they would have been in sackcloth and ashes to show grief for their sins and their intention to change.

It was the ordinary folk who received Jesus – and he was glad. To all who are worn down by burdens, he offers relief. Those who enter his service will find him no crushing task-master.

▶ **Son (of God) (27)** Jesus claims a unique relationship to God. The parent-child picture says that his relationship to God is *something like* that. 'Sons of/children of' is a common Hebrew idiom. It conveys the idea of shared nature or characteristics. 'So when the New Testament says that Jesus is "the Son of God" it is stating that Jesus shared the characteristics and nature of God himself. He was claiming to be really and truly divine' (John Drane).

12:1-14 Trouble over the sabbath
See on Mark 2:23 – 3:6. Verse 14 gives us the first hint of what is to come: the antagonism runs so deep that Jesus' life is threatened.

12:15-37 Devil's emissary?
The Pharisees see Jesus as the devil's agent (24), despite the transparent goodness of his work (22-23). If they were right, Satan would be set on a suicide course (25-29) – as are all who, like the Pharisees, call good evil. They are stubbornly denying the work of God's Spirit, and that makes it impossible for God to forgive them (31-32).

12:38-50 'Show us a miracle'
The lawyers and Pharisees want to *see* Jesus do a miracle – a 'sign' that will bear out his claims. But he will not perform for

> 66 *Come to me, all you who labour and are overburdened, and I will give you rest. Shoulder my yoke and learn from me, for I am gentle and humble in heart...My yoke is easy and my burden light.* 99
>
> 11:28-30

> 66 *Our Lord did not invent the codex of canon law. He did not dictate the Summa of Thomas Aquinas. He sat upon a hillside, perched himself in a rocking boat just off the beach. He spoke in the synagogues and in the houses of the people. The images he used were the simplest images of rural life.* 99
>
> Morris West

their benefit. One sign only will be given – Jesus' resurrection from the dead: the incontrovertible proof that his message is true; that he is who he claims to be.

Verses 43-45: the story is a warning to those who have repented and made the 'about-turn' in their lives as a result of what they have seen and heard. Unless they take the further step of whole-hearted commitment, they are in grave danger.

Verses 46-50: Jesus' apparent lack of filial respect would have shocked his hearers, as he no doubt intended. He is making the point that the bond between those who respond to God is stronger even than family ties.

▶ **Verses 39-40** See Jonah 1:17; 2:10. By Jewish reckoning any part of the 24 hours which make up day and night could count as the whole. So, in Jesus' case, Friday afternoon to Sunday morning is spoken of as three days and nights.

▶ **Verse 42** The Queen of Sheba (1 Kings 10:1-10).

▶ **Verse 49** seems to indicate younger children of Mary and Joseph (see on 1:25), though the Hebrew and Aramaic word also includes cousins and close relatives (see also 13:55-56). Joseph is generally thought to have died by this time.

13:1-52
Jesus' kingdom stories

The parables about God's kingdom form Matthew's third teaching section. By using story, Jesus can teach at a number of different levels. There are layers of meaning beyond the obvious point, for those who are prepared to think. The parables sorted out those who came simply to see miracles and be entertained, from serious followers who really wanted to understand Jesus' teaching. He told his stories to the crowds but kept the explanation for his disciples. There was so much misunderstanding about the nature of the kingdom that Jesus makes one point at a time in these stories.

The first story, the seed and the soils (1-9, explained in 18-23), pictures the varied response his message will bring. All the others are picture-stories introduced by

66 You are the Christ, the Son of the living God. 99

Peter's declaration: 16:16

the words: 'The Kingdom of heaven is like...'

Verses 24-30: the wheat and the weeds (explained in 36-43). This story is concerned with the mixture of good and bad in this life, to be sorted out at the judgment.

Verses 31-33: the mustard-seed, and the yeast. From small beginnings, quietly and unnoticed, the kingdom will make great growth.

Verses 44-45: the treasure, and the pearl. So valuable is the kingdom, it is worth all we have to make sure of it.

Verses 47-50: the fisherman's net. This describes the sorting out of good and bad at the end of time.

See further, 'Jesus and the kingdom'.

13:53 – 14:12
Nazareth rejects Jesus; John beheaded

See on Mark 6:1-6 and 14-29.

14:13 – 17:27
Teaching and miracles in Galilee and the north

14:13-36 Food for 5,000; Jesus walks on the water
See on Mark 6:30-56. See also Luke 9:10b-17; John 6:1-21. The supernatural power of Jesus is brought out in both stories.

15:1-20 The Pharisees and the question of 'tradition'
See also Mark 7:1-23. From the first, Jesus' teaching on religion (6:1-18) brought him into conflict with the Pharisees. For them 'tradition' (the oral teaching of the rabbis which supplemented and interpreted scripture) was binding. But Jesus never hesitated to denounce tradition wherever it watered down or undermined scriptural principles. The ruling on vows is a case in point. People were allowed exemption from their duty to maintain their parents if they dedicated the money to God. That way they could still enjoy the proceeds. It is not simply 'clean hands' (what is done, 2) but a

Jesus and the kingdom
David Field

John the Baptist was surrounded by excited crowds when he shouted in the desert, 'The kingdom of heaven is near.' The sense of anticipation grew when, a little later, Jesus echoed John's words as he began his ministry in Galilee. 'The time has come,' he exclaimed. 'The kingdom of God is near.'

God's kingdom (or the kingdom of heaven – the meaning is the same) was obviously central to Jesus' mission and message. It was vitally important to him. When he taught his disciples how to pray, he told them to ask God, 'May your kingdom come.' When he sent his disciples out on their first preaching expeditions, it was the kingdom of God which was to be at the heart of the good news they were told to spread (see Matthew 10:7).

An electrifying picture
But what did Jesus mean by this 'kingdom' language? He used the phrase often himself (it comes over 100 times in Matthew, Mark and Luke), but the Old Testament does not mention it at all, and it occurs only rarely in the New Testament outside the Gospels. It was special, and special to *him*.

Today it would be hard to get the same 'tingle factor' if a preacher stood up in the pulpit to announce the nearness of God's kingdom. Very few modern people know what it is to live under a monarchy, and even citizens of the United Kingdom regard their queen in a way which is totally different from the electrifying picture John the Baptist's hearers would have seen in their minds' eyes when they were told, 'The King is coming.'

What would they have expected? With the Old Testament monarchy in mind, their image of a king would have had three major features:

■ **A person of power.** Unlike most modern monarchs, an Old Testament king had unlimited authority and no accountability. The lives of his subjects were in his hands. (See the story about Ahab and Naboth in 1 Kings 21.)

■ **A person of status** A king was a revered figure. His affluent lifestyle matched his exalted rank. Wherever he went, he received the royal red-carpet treatment. (Compare David's deference to Saul in 1 Samuel 24 and 26.)

■ **A national figurehead** The nation's aspirations found a focus in the king, as head of state. Victory over his enemies raised the people's profile. Defeat for him spelled national disgrace and disaster. (See the sad story of Jehoiakim and Nebuchadnezzar in 2 Kings 24.)

With this vivid picture of human royalty in their minds, it was not hard for Old Testament believers to think of God as the world's great King. 'How awesome is the Lord Most High, the great King over all the earth!', sang the psalmist.

And if he was King of the world the Lord was also, in a very special way, the ruler of the nation – 'Jacob's King', who would display his glory one day in such a devastating way that Israel's enemies would be left confused and defeated.

Through his Messiah, a king descended from David's royal line, Israel's God would overturn all opposition and establish his rule of justice and peace (see Isaiah 41:21 and 40:10).

A living reality
Into this seething cauldron of popular expectation Jesus launched his dramatic announcement, 'The kingdom of God is near.' No wonder everyone stopped and took notice! Was the great moment of God's royal intervention, forecast so urgently by the Old Testament prophets, about to arrive?

It was. In fact, with Jesus' arrival on the world scene, *it had already come*. As Gabriel told Mary just before she became pregnant, 'The Lord God will give him the throne of his father David. His kingdom will never end.' God's kingdom is 'my kingdom', Jesus told his followers later, and Paul does not feel at all awkward in writing about 'the kingdom of Christ and of God' (Ephesians 5:5).

In Jesus the kingdom of God had become a living reality. 'If I drive out demons by the finger of God,' he commented, 'then the kingdom of God has come to you.'

Shocks and surprises
Nevertheless, Jesus' expectant audience was in for a shock. He certainly was the promised King, but he turned their ideas about God's rule upside down.

■ They were expecting **a display of power**, but Jesus taught them that the focal point of God's kingdom was the gentle, merciful empowerment of the weak and disabled members of society. He crushed the powers of evil in a stunning series of miracles, but the whole purpose of these 'signs' was to bring divine healing and release to ordinary people who had been crippled by physical, psychological, social or spiritual disorders.

The kingdom of heaven belongs to the poor, the distressed and the suffering, he taught his disciples, not to the rich, the powerful and the self-sufficient (see Matthew 5:3, 10).

- They were expecting **a parade of status**, but God's King was not born with a silver spoon in his mouth. He began his human life in the squalor of a stable. 'I did not come to be served, but to serve,' he explained to his followers later. He was a self-emptying monarch, comments Paul (see Philippians 2:5-8). He turned his back on conventional royal respectability by spending time with those whom the rest of society regarded as inferior – lepers, foreigners and (of course) women. And he left life carrying a cross, the mark of ignominy, not waving a royal banner.

- They were expecting **a national figurehead**, someone to throw the Roman occupation force out of the land and establish exclusive Jewish supremacy. Jesus refused to fill that political role. There was to be no passport control which favoured Jews at the entry point to God's kingdom.

'People will come from east and west and north and south,' he taught, 'and will take their places at the feast in the kingdom of God.' Instead of fighting to keep foreigners out, Jesus gave his followers their mission marching orders to bring outsiders in (compare Matthew 28:18-20).

A dynamic idea

In Jesus' hands the kingdom of God becomes a dynamic idea – 'rule' rather than 'realm'. It describes God's active reign in the world.

The qualification for entering it is not the right kind of birth certificate but a radically changed lifestyle, characterized by repentance and faith. There are

> **“** *Great is, O King,*
> *our happiness*
> *in thy kingdom,*
> *thou, our king.* **”**
>
> A Zulu prayer from South Africa

patterns of behaviour which are totally incompatible with a genuine submission to God's rule.

Conversely, all who submit their wills to his, find that his royal power is immediately available to help them conquer bad habits and live lives which really please him (see 1 Corinthians 6:9-10).

Now, but not yet

There is also a 'now, but not yet' dimension to Jesus' teaching about the kingdom of God. Although God's rule is powerfully present in his own words and actions, his stories-with-a-purpose (the parables) paint word pictures of slow growth as the kingdom is gradually established, like yeast in dough or a small seed's slow transformation into an impressive tree (see Matthew 13:31-33).

The final outcome, however, is inevitable. When Jesus comes again to wind up the history of the world as we know it, the kingdom of God will be displayed in total triumph. Like it or not, all creation will submit to his **power**. His royal status will be blazoned from one end of the universe to the other. And he will emerge as his church's great **figurehead** as it demonstrates 'the fullness of him who fills everything in every way' (see Philippians 2:9-11; Matthew 24:30; Ephesians 1:22-23).

Here, at Caesarea Philippi, are the springs of the River Jordan. Earlier the town was named Paneas from its shrine to the Greek god Pan. This was the dramatic background when Jesus asked his disciples the pivotal question, 'Who do you say I am?' And Peter replied, 'You are the Messiah, the Son of the living God.'

'clean heart' (motive and intent, 18) that matters.

15:21-39 A foreign woman's faith; cures, and a second feeding miracle

Tyre and Sidon (21) lay outside Jewish territory. The Canaanite woman is quick to seize her opportunity. The case of the centurion's servant (8:5-13) makes it clear that race is not a barrier: God's kingdom is inclusive (8:11). So the harsh response would seem to be a test of faith. Quick as a flash, the woman quips back. And Jesus will not refuse a request made with such tenacious faith.

Verses 29-39: the differences of detail

Jesus was scathing about religious leaders who 'led little ones astray'. They were fit only to have a millstone tied around their necks and be cast in the sea! These millstones are in the Agricultural Museum at Jerusalem.

between this passage and 14:13-21, and the fact that Mark also records both miracles, make it unlikely that this is a second account of the same event, despite the basic similarity. The context (21ff. and 31) suggests that on this occasion non-Jews (Gentiles) were fed.

▶ **The dogs (26)** An abusive term for Gentiles.
▶ **Magadan (39)** The location is not known.

16:1-12 Jesus' warns...

See also Mark 8:11-21. The Pharisees had demanded a sign once before (12:38ff.). Now the Sadducees, the ultra-conservatives, join them in putting Jesus to the test. But his answer is still the same.

▶ **Yeast/leaven (6)** An evil force, working unseen. The disciples must not be like those Pharisees and Sadducees whose hostility prevents them from recognizing the work of God.

16:13-28 'You are the Christ'

Simon speaks for all the apostles in asserting his belief that Jesus is the Messiah. And Jesus

sees in him the man of rock (Peter) he will become after the shattering experience of denial and forgiveness (26:69-75). It is Peter, the natural spokesman, who will be responsible more than any other for the formation of the church at Pentecost (Acts 2 – 5).

Verses 21-28: Jesus begins to prepare his disciples for the suffering that lies ahead. But the recent promise has gone to Peter's head. The rock becomes an obstacle. God's spokesman turns devil's advocate.

▶ **Verse 19** The authority given to Peter is given equally to the others (see 18:18). The idea of the keys echoes Isaiah 22:22. God is not bound by whatever Peter may say. But anything done by the disciple in accordance with Christ's will is to have permanent validity.
▶ **Verse 28** See on 10:23.

17 The transfiguration

See on Mark 9:2-13.

▶ **Verses 24-27** As Son of God, the one on whose behalf the tax is levied, Jesus is exempt.

Jesus and money

David Instone Brewer

About half of Jesus' parables involve money in some way. This reflects the importance of money and business for Jesus' hearers. Palestine, and especially Lower Galilee, was an important trade route and was also an important production site for many goods and foodstuffs.

Exports and imports

Palestine exported vegetables, grain, olive oil, rushes for rope-making, bitumen and asphalt from the Dead Sea, and balsam. Palestine was almost the only source of balsam, which was used for medicines and spices. The revenue was so important that Herod built large fortifications to protect the balsam

route. Another large export was salted fish, which was also an important part of Palestinian diet.

Imports included beer from Babylon and Egypt, cheese from Bythinia, mackerel from Spain,

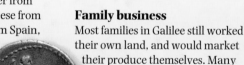

wines and asses from Lydia, purple from Tyre, jewelry, parchment and papyrus from Egypt.

Family business

Most families in Galilee still worked their own land, and would market their produce themselves. Many families specialized in particular businesses.

Fishing, for example, was big business, so that even a small firm like the family of John and

The Roman silver *denarius* was a day's pay for labourers in Jesus' time. In his story of the 'Good Samaritan', the innkeeper was given two *denarii* to look after the injured man.

Roman relief showing a money changer at his table.

But as a human being, identified with us, he pays it.

18
Life in God's community

This is Matthew's fourth teaching section, on relationships in the new community. God's kingdom operates by totally different standards from the world's. Status-seeking is out (1-4). So is the policy of 'the weakest to the wall'. On the contrary, the spiritually weak are the special responsibility of the strong (5-14). In the new community wrongdoing matters; every effort must be made to set the defaulter right (15-20). Unlimited forgiveness is expected of those who enjoy the limitless forgiveness of God (21-35).

▶ **Verses 8-9** See on Mark 9:44-45.

▶ **Verses 24, 28** The point is the immeasurable extent of our 'debt' to God, compared to anything we may have to forgive our fellow human beings.

19 – 20
From Galilee to Jerusalem

John's Gospel mentions several visits to Jerusalem, Matthew just this one, leading to the climax of Jesus' last week. The country east of the Jordan is Perea (see 'Israel in New Testament times' map).

19:1-12 Marriage and divorce
See also 5:31-32; Mark 10:2-12; Luke 16:18. The rabbis disagreed about divorce. Some allowed it for anything that displeased the husband; others only for unfaithfulness. Jesus goes back to God's purpose for man and woman at the very beginning. That is how God meant it to be. Moses, dealing with a situation that fell far short of the ideal, placed a restriction on divorce. Jesus says that adultery is the only legitimate reason. See on 5:31-32.

The standard seems too high to Jesus' followers (10) and he recognizes this (11): it *is* too hard without God's help. Even so,

---

James could use hired labourers (Mark 1:20).

Sometimes a village produced a single product which they supplied to a wide area. The pottery villages of Kefer Hanania and Shikhin supplied all of Galilee.

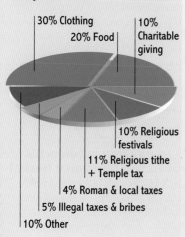

Expenses for a working-class family in New Testament Palestine

- 30% Clothing
- 20% Food
- 10% Charitable giving
- 10% Religious festivals
- 11% Religious tithe + Temple tax
- 4% Roman & local taxes
- 5% Illegal taxes & bribes
- 10% Other

Currency
Money changers were an important part of commerce because of the wide variety of coins. Large cities each produced their own coinage, all with slightly different values.

In Palestine the coins of Tyre were the standard currency. The Temple refused payment in any other coins, probably because Tyrian coinage had higher percentages of precious metal than other currency.

Taxes
Everyone needed coinage to buy goods which they did not produce themselves and to pay taxes. The taxes included the imperial Roman tax, taxes for local administration and the Temple tax. On top of this were the religious tithes for the poor, for the synagogue, and the

'second' tithe which had to be spent in Jerusalem during festivals.

One of the most common coins was the silver denarius, which was the day-wage for an agricultural worker, and which bore the head of Tiberius Caesar (see Matthew 22:19-21).

Jesus tried to warn about the insidious effect of money in his teachings, but he did not reject the use of coinage. He paid his Temple tax (Matthew 17:24-27) and encouraged the payment of secular taxes (Matthew 22:19-22), and the only named role we know about among his group of followers is 'treasurer' (John 12:6).

celibacy is not the answer for most people (it was very unusual for Jews). Jesus is one of those who forgo marriage to carry out a special commission from God.

19:13 – 20:16 In God's kingdom
19:13-30: see also Mark 10:12-31; Luke 18:18-30.

The ancient streets of the Old City of Jerusalem speak of their long history. Here Jesus spent his last days.

Verse 12 reintroduces the subject of God's kingdom, whose values turn the world upside down. Unlike his disciples, Jesus regards children as important, making a point about status in the kingdom as he gives them his blessing.

Jesus' first answer to the rich young man's question about good deeds and eternal life (16) is the one any Jewish teacher would have given. And the man – a ruler in the synagogue – could claim he had kept the commandments. But Jesus pinpoints the root of this man's trouble. His commandment-keeping is not whole-hearted. His possessions mean too much to him. Because of them he is failing to love God and his neighbour without reserve. So Jesus tells him to sell up and follow him. It is better to possess nothing than to love things more than God.

The disciples were surprised (25) because they thought riches were a reward for goodness, an index of someone's spiritual state – so they go on to ask about rewards (27ff.)

20:1-16: this story, illustrating Jesus' words in 19:30, comes only in Matthew. He is not talking about pay structures, or saying that all will be equal in heaven. The point is that many who expect to be made much of will be in for a rude shock in God's kingdom. God will honour some very unexpected people. Eternal life is for all who will receive it: 'good' and 'bad', young and old. The remarkable thing is the land-owner's (God's) generosity – not his unfairness.

▸ **19:24** There have been various 'explanations' of the 'needle's eye'. But it seems that Jesus is deliberately suggesting the impossible.

▸ **19:28** The apostles have a special place in the new kingdom. Only Matthew records these words.

▸ **19:29** Those who follow Christ will be repaid many times over, here and now – but 'with persecutions' (see Mark).

▸ **20:2** The denarius (a Roman silver coin) was the normal day's wage for a labourer.

▸ **20:3-6** The times are 9 a.m. (the third hour), 12 noon, 3 p.m. and 5 p.m. – an hour before sunset, which was when the men were paid for the day's work.

20:17-34 Jesus again predicts his death; status; two blind men healed
See also Mark 10:32-52; Luke 18:31-43. Jesus' patience is amazing. Over and over again he explains that the kingdom is for the humble. There is to be no lording it.

Yet, even when he speaks of his death as they near Jerusalem, the disciples are taken up with their own status. The place at the top is reserved for the disciple who – like the master – is prepared to live for others and if need be to die for them.

Verses 29-34: Mark and Luke mention only one blind man – perhaps because Peter, who probably supplied the information, knew Bartimaeus personally (see Mark).

▶ **Sons of Zebedee (20)** James and John.

▶ **The cup (22)** I.e. the cup of suffering. James

was the first of the loyal apostles to meet a violent death (Acts 12:2).

21 – 25
Jesus in Jerusalem

It was spring, and people from far and near were crowding into Jerusalem for Passover, the great feast commemorating the nation's liberation from Egypt. Not all could find lodgings in the city itself. Jesus

Jesus and the Old Testament
Dick France

Jesus' Bible was the Old Testament. He quoted it frequently (at least 40 direct quotations are found in the Gospels) and more often referred indirectly to its stories and teaching (some 70 clear allusions in the Gospels). His quotations often came with the simple but decisive introduction 'It is written'. Sometimes he spoke more directly about its importance:

■ 'Do not think that I have come to abolish the Law or the Prophets; I have not come to abolish them but to fulfil them. I tell you the truth, until heaven and earth disappear, not the smallest letter, not the least stroke of a pen, will by any means disappear from the Law until everything is accomplished' (Matthew 5:17-18).

■ 'Everything must be fulfilled that is written about me in the Law of Moses, the Prophets and the Psalms' (Luke 24:44).

■ 'The Scripture cannot be broken' (John 10:35).

Some of his harshest words were reserved for those who tried to evade the plain commands of God in the Old Testament by means of

human traditions, however venerable (Mark 7:1-13).

The authority of the Old Testament
In public controversy Jesus regularly used a quotation from the Old Testament to settle the argument (see, for instance, Matthew 12:3-4, 5-7; 21:13, 16; 22:31-32, 43-44). It was an effective method, since other Jews also accepted the

> 66 *Without the Old Testament you will never understand the New.* 99

authority of the Old Testament, but this was no mere public stance to meet people on their own grounds. Even in private the Old Testament was the basis of his life. When tempted in the wilderness, it was to the Old Testament that he turned for guidance (Matthew 4:4, 7, 10), and even in his final agony on the cross it was words from the Old Testament that he uttered (Mark 15:34; Luke 23:46, quoting Psalms 22:1; 31:5).

In teaching his disciples, Jesus was always using Old Testament language, sometimes by direct quotation, but often simply weaving familiar Old Testament words into his sayings. For instance, his mysterious prediction of future events in Matthew 24:29-31 draws on no fewer than seven Old Testament passages in just three verses (Isaiah 13:10; 34:4; Daniel 7:13; Zechariah 12:12; Isaiah 27:13; Deuteronomy 30:4; Zechariah 2:6).

Some of Jesus' most central ethical teaching comes directly from the Law of Moses (see Matthew 19:18-19, drawing on the Ten Commandments, and Matthew 22:37-40 drawing on Deuteronomy 6:5 and Leviticus 19:18). His Sermon on the Mount contains a striking sequence of examples where he examines Old Testament texts and themes, and explains how they should be applied to practical Christian living (Matthew 5:21-48).

His complaint about other Jewish teachers was that they did not explore the full implications of these divine commands; their

▶▶

and his friends stayed at nearby Bethany, where Martha, Mary and Lazarus had their home. Each day they walked the two miles into Jerusalem, over the shoulder of the Mount of Olives and down through the thick groves of trees.

21:1-11 Messiah triumphant

See on Luke 19:28-44. See also Mark 11: 1-10. Characteristically, Matthew quotes the prophecy from Zechariah 9:9.

21:12-17 Temple purge

See also on John 2:13-25. Having entered the city in triumph as the Messiah, Jesus shows his authority in the Temple, the nation's central shrine. His dramatic overturning of the money-changers' tables is a major demonstration against the commerce and big business that had taken over God's 'house of prayer'.

The blind and lame (excluded from the Temple it would seem from 2 Samuel 5:8) are welcomed and healed by Jesus. And

superficial and wooden interpretations missed the point, and prevented them from discovering the revealed will of God.

The fulfilment of the Old Testament

Jesus came to 'fulfil' the Old Testament (Matthew 5:17). In his teaching we soon discover that this did not mean merely reinforcing its teaching. Indeed sometimes he offered quite daring new insights, as, for example, his pronouncement that 'What goes into your mouth does not make you unclean, but what comes out of your mouth, that is what makes you unclean' (Matthew 15:11; contrast the food laws in Leviticus 11). It was more by his own life, and supremely his death, that he brought its fulfilment.

So he often talked about his own role in the light of Old Testament models. As Jesus walked with two disciples after his resurrection, Luke tells us that 'beginning with Moses and all the prophets, he explained to them what was said concerning himself in all the Scriptures' (Luke 24:27). But this was merely the climax of the way he had been teaching them all through his ministry.

Sometimes he referred to Old Testament people or events as 'foreshadowings' of his own life

(e.g. Matthew 12:40-42); sometimes he quoted explicit predictions of one who was to come (e.g. Luke 4:17-21; 22:37). Again and again he insisted that he *must* suffer and die, because this was what had been written about him (e.g. Mark 8:31; 9:12-13; Luke 18:31; Mark 14:21, 27; Matthew 26:54; Luke 24:44-47).

He had come to 'fulfil', and there was a divine compulsion about what was written. It *must* be fulfilled.

The Old Testament was for Jesus not just a book of interesting historical records, but the authoritative word of God. He believed its statements, endorsed its teaching, obeyed its commands, and set himself to fulfil the pattern of redemption which it had laid down.

His uncompromising acceptance of the Old Testament as the Word of God set the pattern for his followers, including the writers of the New Testament books, who delighted to trace the connections between Jesus and the Old Testament, and fully shared his conviction of its authority. The Old Testament has rightly been described as 'the sub-structure of New Testament theology'. Without the Old Testament you will never understand the New – indeed you will never make sense of Jesus.

children recognize what the religious officials are blind to, as they chant the earlier tributes of the crowds.

▶ **Verse 12** The annual Temple tax had to be paid in the special Temple coinage – hence the need for money changers.

21:18-22 The fig-tree
See also Mark 11:12-14, 20-24. Jesus' action is generally taken as symbolic. The fig which bears no fruit is good for nothing but destruction. From the context, it seems we are meant to see the tree as a symbol of the Temple which, for all its ritual, is spiritually barren. Jesus uses the incident as an object lesson on the power of faith. God is able to do the impossible.

21:23-46 Jesus' authority questioned
The question asked by the chief priests and elders is natural, in the light of what has happened (12-17). Jesus makes no direct answer, but it is clear that he and John derive their authority from the same source. In the three parables that follow, his critics find themselves under fire.

Verses 28-32: the two sons. The first represents the social outcasts, who have made a genuine response to John and to Jesus; the second the religious leaders, with their mock obedience.

Verses 33-41: the vineyard (the nation of Israel whose owner is God: Isaiah 5:1-7). The men to whom God has entrusted spiritual leadership have abused the prophets and are about to kill his Son.

Verses 42-43: see Psalm 118:22-23. Jesus transfers the picture from Israel to himself – cast aside, crucified by his own people, but reinstated by God.

22:1-14 The invitation
Jesus' parable of the guests invited to the wedding feast illustrates what he has just said (21:43). The day will come when God no longer invites those who repeatedly refuse him. The invitation will go to others. Verses 11-13 are a warning to the newcomers. Those who come must come on God's terms.

▶ **Wedding garment (12)** Not special wedding clothes but clean clothes for a special occasion.

'Whited sepulchres' was Jesus' harsh phrase for hypocritical religious leaders: whitewashed outside, but rotten within.

22:15-46 Test questions
See on Mark 12:13-44.

23 'You hypocrites!'
Jesus launches into a scathing attack on Israel's legalistic, but much-respected religious leaders. The man who cared so deeply and had such patience with ordinary people – even the wicked, the weak-willed and the stupid – could not stomach the religious sham, the self-righteous pride, the hair-splitting pedantry he saw in these Pharisees and scribes. Do as they say, he tells the crowd and his followers, but not as they do.

Jesus makes seven specific charges (13-26), each introduced with the same words: 'Woe to you...' (a regretful 'alas', not a pronouncement of doom).

▶ **Moses' seat/chair (2)** Meaning they are the authorized interpreters of the law God gave through Moses.

▶ **Verse 10** 'Teacher' gives the sense. The same Greek word is used today of a 'professor'.

▶ **Verse 15** 'Twice as fit for hell' gives the sense. New converts are often more fervent than those brought up in the faith.

▶ **Mint, dill, cummin (23)** Common garden herbs.

▶ **Verse 27** Tombs were specially white-washed for Passover to prevent people inadvertently touching them and becoming ceremonially defiled.

Jewish Christians heeded Jesus' warning (24:16) to flee when the Romans invaded their country, some escaping to Pella, *below* (where ruins of an early church can still be seen), some to Petra, *left*, whose 'Nazarene quarter' is in the foreground of the picture.

Two coins: one bears the head of the conquering Emperor Titus, the other bears the inscription 'Jud[ea] Cap[ta]', marking the fall of Judea in AD 70.

On the Titus Arch in Rome is this stone carving of the seven-branched candlestick and other Temple plunder being carried away by the victorious Romans.

▶ **Verse 35** This is Zechariah, son of Jehoiada (there is no record of the prophet Zechariah being murdered). Genesis 4:8; 2 Chronicles 24:20-21.

▶ **Verses 38-39** Jesus may be predicting the destruction of the city. Verse 39 refers to his return in glory and judgment.

24 – 25
Fall of Jerusalem; Jesus' return

This is Matthew's fifth and last teaching section. The subject is the future: the end-time and Jesus' own return. A key theme here, as in chapter 23, is judgment.

The disciples' admiration for the great Temple buildings (see 'Herod's Temple') lead to Jesus' astonishing prediction of its utter destruction. Further questions follow. When will the Temple be destroyed? What indications will there be that the age is coming to an end? The disciples make a close connection between the two events. Jesus can tell them about 'these things', but as to the timing of 'that day' – the great day of judgment – God alone knows (24:36). The important thing is to be ready.

The disciples must not be misled – there will be many wars and natural disasters, persecutions and false Messiahs (24:4-13, 23-27). These are not signs of the end. There will be time for world-wide preaching of the gospel (14). And when the end does come, it will be totally unexpected (36-44). But there will be clear warning signs of the destruction of Jerusalem (15-22, 32-35). (The city and Temple were in fact destroyed by the Romans in AD 70.)

The rest of Jesus' teaching in this section (24:45 – 25:46) comes in the form of parables: he uses stories to drive home the points of the previous chapter.

24:45-51: the good and bad servants. Because his return will be unexpected, Jesus' followers must always be ready.

25:1-13: the wise and foolish girls. This story makes the same point, stressing that one day time will run out. Preparedness is an individual thing. It cannot be borrowed from someone else.

25:14-30: the 'talents'. A talent was a large sum of money, not a coin. Each man is entrusted with a capital sum in line with his business ability, and he is expected to trade with it. How people use what is given them in this life will determine their future destiny.

25:31-46: the sheep and the goats. At the judgment God takes account of how each one has treated others in this life. In the parable, the 'goats' are punished for failing to do what they should have done.

▶ **24:15** Daniel 11:31. An alternative rendering, in line with Luke's paraphrase is 'so when you see the abominable sign spoken of by the prophet Daniel (let the reader understand)'. This could be a reference to the emperor's image on the ensign carried by the Roman soldiers.

▶ **24:21** Over 1,000,000 people lost their lives in the fall of Jerusalem, and Herod's magnificent cream stone and gold Temple was razed to the ground.

▶ **24:28** is a proverb. Gathering vultures are tell-tale signs of a corpse. The coming of the Son of man will be equally obvious.

▶ **24:29-31** Symbolic language. In the light of verse 36, 'immediately' cannot be taken literally. Jesus appears to telescope the two 'comings in judgment'.

▶ **24:34** A reference to the destruction of the Temple within the lifetime of his hearers. It took place about 40 years after Jesus' prediction.

26 – 27
Jesus' last days

Matthew's account closely follows Mark's story of Jesus' last days.

26:1-5 Conspiracy
It is two days before Passover Day, when the lambs were killed in re-enactment of that day, long ago in Egypt, when their blood kept death from the Israelites' door (Exodus 12:21-30). The symbolism is deeply significant for Matthew. The chief priests and elders of the Sanhedrin Council (not now the scribes and Pharisees of previous chapters) make the death-plot official.

26:6-13 A woman anoints Jesus

See on Mark 14:3-9.

26:14-29 Betrayal – and the Last Supper

See also Mark 14:12-25; Luke 22:7-38; John 13 – 14.

At this crucial moment, Judas, perhaps disillusioned about the kind of Messiah Jesus has turned out to be, or for some other motive, unexplained, changes sides (verses 14-16).

On the first evening of the festival, Jesus and his close friends meet as a family to eat the Passover meal together – and the old Passover is transformed into the Lord's Supper as the Lamb of God (John 1:29) prepares to lay down his life for the world. This is as the scriptures said it would be, but that does not remove the guilt from Judas (24).

To the familiar words of the blessing (26): 'Blessed art Thou, O Lord our God, King of the Universe, who bringest forth bread from the earth,' Jesus adds his own startling words, 'this is my body'. He is going to be killed. And by his death a new covenant will be made, in place of the old covenant between God and Israel made at the exodus. His blood is 'poured out for many for the forgiveness of sins'. By eating and drinking, his disciples share in the benefits of his sacrifice.

▶ **Keeping Passover (18)** John's Gospel makes it plain that the Last Supper took place the evening before the regular Passover meal, and that Jesus died at the time the Passover lambs were killed. Knowing what would happen to him, Jesus most probably arranged for his Passover meal to be held in secret the previous evening.

Passover and the Last Supper

Michele Guinness

Of all the Jewish festivals, Passover is the most important (see 'The great festivals'). Eight days with no bread, cake, nothing with a raising agent in it, only *matzah* – flat, crisp slices of fairly tasteless unleavened bread, all in memory of the great escape from Egypt, so swift there was no time for the daily home-made bread to rise.

But at Passover there are compensations. The first night, *Seder* ('Service') night, is a wonderful extended-family celebration of the freedom God gives his people. It's a little like Christmas, except that the Seder has a long, age-old liturgy, accompanied by a number of important symbolic rituals.

This was almost certainly the setting for the Last Supper.

Jesus used the rituals as a kind of audio-visual aid, so that in years to come, as they celebrated the Passover, his disciples would understand the full significance of the occasion.

The service, which lasts about four hours, and revolves around a slap-up meal, is contained in a book called the *Haggadah* ('the telling'), recounting the story of how the Jews were delivered from slavery in Egypt, and set out for the promised land. As a child I had my own special edition – with graphic illustrations of the ten plagues, and the drowning of the Egyptians in the Red Sea.

The table, today, is resplendent with the best silver and crockery, glowing in the light of two trad-itional candles. In the father's place three squares of *matzah* are hidden inside a satin holder. In the centre

is the Seder dish, containing bitter herbs, and two items added after the time of Christ: a burnt egg to symbolize the Great Temple which was destroyed, and the shankbone of a lamb, the only reminder of the lambs whose blood was used to daub the doorposts of the children of Israel at the time of the final plague in Egypt, so that the Angel of Death would pass them by.

Every major festival is celebrated with red wine, the symbol of rejoicing, and on Seder night it is compulsory to drink four cups.

After the traditional blessing the first cup is drunk and the youngest child asks four questions, basically, 'Why is this night different from all other nights?' The rest of the service, by way of reply, tells the exodus story. 'We were slaves in Egypt, and God heard our cry and

26:30-56 Jesus arrested

See also Mark 14:26-52; Luke 22:39-53 (it is Luke who depicts most vividly the agony of Christ's prayer in the garden).

On the way to their special place, the olive-orchard of Gethsemane on the Mount of Olives, Jesus prepares his followers – Peter most of all – for their own failure (30-35).

The prospect of his suffering fills Jesus with horror. It was more than the fear of a terrible death, though no reasons are given here. Peter, writing later, says that Jesus 'was bearing our sins in his own body on the cross' (1 Peter 2:24).

The moment passes. Jesus accepts the path of suffering as his Father's will. And as the mob comes out to arrest him he is once more in command. He expresses only love for the traitor. When one of his followers (identified as Peter in John 18:10) draws his sword and cuts off the ear of the high priest's servant, Jesus arrests the violence (and heals the injured man: Luke 22:51). He had come to fulfil the prophecies of scripture, says Matthew. And at this point all his followers desert him, as he had known they would (31).

26:57-68 Trial at the high priest's house

See on Mark 14:53-65.

26:69-75 Peter disowns Jesus

See on Luke 22:54-65.

27:1-26 The traitor's suicide; Jesus questioned by the Roman Governor

Only Matthew records Judas' remorse. He flings back the money, but a clear conscience is not so easily bought. (Acts 1:16-20 has a different version of the

came down and rescued us.' No mention is ever made of Moses.

An hour or so later, after singing Psalms 113 and 114, known as the small *Hallel* ('praise'), and a second cup of wine, when I was desperate with hunger, came that dreaded moment.

Bitter herbs, usually eye-smarting pieces of horseradish root, dipped in *charoseth* (a sweet mixture made out of nuts, apples and wine), are distributed around the table, and swallowed with a certain amount of groaning. They represent our ancestors' pain, made bearable only by the sweetness of the hope of the promised land. Everyone present, says the *Haggadah*, should feel as if they had actually been a slave in Egypt. A special guest is given this delicacy first. Jesus offered it to Judas.

The men wash their hands (this was probably the moment when Jesus washed the disciples' feet), and at last it's dinner time (roast lamb at the time of Christ, but not today). The middle of the three *matzahs* (or *afikomen*) has always been the special symbol of the Passover lamb. Earlier, the father has broken it in half, and while the children are distracted by the food, hides it. Immediately after the meal they search until they find it, then sell it back to the father, who breaks it and gives a piece to every guest. No more food must pass their lips that night.

It would be impossible not to make the connection here with Jesus' institution of the Communion, especially as it is followed by the third cup, known as the 'Cup of Blessing'. 'The cup of blessing which we bless, is it not a sharing in the blood of Christ?' asks the apostle Paul (1 Corinthians 10:16).

The service continues with lots of joyous singing, including the great Hallel (Psalm 136), and ends with the fourth cup, which is accompanied by a prayer to God to 'send your wrath on the nations that despise you'.

Jesus joined in the singing, then went out into the Garden of Gethsemane (Matthew 26:30). 'Let this particular cup pass from me,' he prayed, before he yielded to the ordeal ahead. In other words, 'I am the Passover lamb broken for you, the blood shed for you. God's wrath will be poured on me, so that you are truly free.'

Jesus was dead and buried, his followers utterly miserable. They were not to know that this was simply a waiting time, that he would rise again. The figures here, gazing across the graves to the distant Temple area, catch the mood.

story.) For the trial before Pilate, see on Luke (23:1-25).

27:27-56 Mockery and crucifixion
See on Mark 15:16-41.

27:57-66 Jesus' burial; a guard is set
See on Mark 15:42-47. Matthew is the only one to mention the guard; see also 28:11ff.

28
The empty tomb: Jesus alive!

See on Luke 24 and 'Jesus' resurrection'.

Verses 1-10: sorrow turns to awe and joy as the women hear the angel's message and see the risen Jesus for themselves. The first to know, they hurry to share the amazing news.

Verses 11-15: the guards are bribed to lie, to say the tomb is empty because Jesus' followers stole the body while they slept. The penalty for falling asleep on duty was death, but perhaps Pilate too could be squared with a bribe.

Verses 16-20: the eleven remaining apostles return to Galilee. There Jesus, now possessing 'all authority', gives them his last command – to make disciples of *all* nations.

All through his Gospel Matthew has referred back to the Jewish scriptures, showing how Jesus fulfilled them. But there is nothing exclusive about the good news. And the final words of the Gospel are universal: God's kingdom is open, the invitation is extended, to people of every nation.

▶ **Verse 19** 'Father, Son and Holy Spirit': this phrase became a standard expression in the formal liturgy of the early church.

> ❝ *Go... make disciples of all nations... And I will be with you always, to the end of time.* ❞
>
> 28:19-20

Mark

Summary

Mark's life of Jesus is the shortest and most action-packed.

Key passages and best-known stories

John the Baptist's proclamation *(1)*

The Twelve *(3:13-19)*

Parable of the sower *(4)*

Jairus' daughter *(5)*

Death of John the Baptist *(6:17-29)*

Jesus transfigured; the boy with fits *(9)*

Jesus predicts his death and resurrection *(8:31; 9:31; 10:33-34)*

Blind Bartimaeus *(10:46-52)*

The widow's mite *(12:41-44)*

The last week – betrayal, arrest, trials; Jesus' death and resurrection *(11 – 16)*

This is the shortest of the Gospels and probably the first to be written. The date may be about AD 65-70, though if Acts is dated at 63 (see introduction to Acts), Mark must be earlier, since Acts follows Luke, and Luke draws on Mark. There is a strong early tradition that John Mark wrote the Gospel in Rome, setting down Jesus' story as he had heard it directly from the apostle Peter.

Papias, writing not later than AD 140 says:

'Mark, who was the interpreter of Peter, wrote down accurately all that he remembered, whether of sayings or doings of Christ, but not in order. For he was neither a hearer nor companion of the Lord.'

A little later, Irenaeus says that Mark was written 'when Peter and Paul were preaching the gospel in Rome and founding the church there'. After their deaths, 'Mark, Peter's disciple, has himself delivered to us in writing the substance of Peter's preaching.'

This would certainly account for the Gospel's extraordinary vividness. And the writer obviously had non-Jewish readers in mind, because he often explains Jewish customs.

This Gospel concentrates on telling the story, moving swiftly through from Jesus' baptism to the critical events of the cross and resurrection. Within this framework, the material tends to be grouped by subject. Mark's Gospel bustles with life and action. It goes into more detail than Matthew's in the accounts of what Jesus did, but deals with Jesus' teaching more briefly.

Only four paragraphs in Mark's 16 chapters are unique to his Gospel. All the rest is covered in Matthew or Luke, or appears in both. Yet because each writer adapts his material to his own particular purpose we have more than a simple duplication of accounts. None is dispensable. And to lose Mark would mean the loss of far more than the few paragraphs we do not find elsewhere. Mark shows us Jesus in action, convincing us by the things he does that his claim to be the Son of God is true.

Who was Mark?

The name 'John Mark' occurs often in Acts and the New Testament Letters ('John' is the Jewish name, 'Mark' the Latin). His mother had a house in Jerusalem where Jesus' followers met in the days of the early church (Acts 12:12). And he was cousin to Paul's companion, Barnabas. Mark blotted his copybook with Paul by going home half-way through the first missionary tour. But Barnabas gave him a second chance, and he later won the love and respect of Paul and of Peter. He was a real comfort to Paul in prison (Colossians 4). And Peter, whose companion he became, loved him as his own son (1 Peter 5:13).

1:1-13
Good news!

Mark's opening sentence – 'The beginning of the good news of Jesus Christ, *the Son of God*' – packs a real punch. The startling truth is out: the purpose of the Gospel and its message are on the table from the outset.

1:2-8 John the Baptist
See also Matthew 3:1-12; Luke 3:2-22.

The word 'gospel'

The word 'gospel' translates Greek *evangelion* = good news (hence 'evangelist').

It was the Anglo-Saxons who coined the term 'Godspell', a word that may mean 'good news' or 'news about God' for the new faith when it reached them.

For everyone who welcomes the gospel story, it is both.

Mark passes over Jesus' birth and John's early history. For him the good news begins with the adult John, the prophetic voice Isaiah had predicted, crying out from the desert, urging the nation to make ready for God's coming. The rest of Mark's account will show that Jesus, the one whose coming John announced, is the Messiah, the Son of God.

▶ **Verses 2-3** Mark combines three Old Testament references: Exodus 23:20; Malachi 3:1; Isaiah 40:3.

▶ **Verse 8** Water is a symbol. It can clean only the outside. God's Holy Spirit can cleanse a person from within.

▶ **The prophet from the desert** John has only the simplest of food and rough clothing. His camel-hair tunic and leather belt may have been worn in conscious imitation of Elijah (see 2 Kings 1:8 and the prophecy in Malachi 4:5). He was certainly recognized instantly as a prophet. Not only did he look the part, he possessed the prophet's conviction that he came with a message from God. People flocked from far and

The River Jordan, where John baptized, winds from Lake Galilee, well below sea level, down through the semi-tropical rift valley to the Dead Sea.

After his baptism Jesus spent 40 days in the Judean Desert, fasting. But he would not yield to the temptation to misuse his God-given power, by changing the stones into bread to satisfy his gnawing hunger.

wide to hear him, probably gathering beside the Jordan near Jericho, close to the place where Joshua had led the Israelites into their promised land so many centuries before.

1:9-13 Jesus' baptism and testing

Mark gives only a brief summary. See on Matthew 3 – 4; Luke 3:21; 4:1-13.

1:14 – 8:26
Jesus in Galilee

Galilee, though subject to Rome, was under the jurisdiction of a 'native' ruler: Herod Antipas, one of Herod the Great's four sons. The region lay to the west of Lake Galilee. In Christ's day it was prosperous and densely populated, criss-crossed by Roman military roads and ancient trade routes – north, south, east and west. The fresh-water lake – 21km/13 miles long, 11km/7 miles wide, sunk in the deep trough of the Jordan rift valley over 180m/600ft below

sea-level – is the focal point in Jesus' travels. It divided Herod's territory from that of his half-brother Philip, to the east.

Most of the apostles came from the towns around the lake-shore, which enjoyed a sub-tropical climate. Capernaum was Jesus' base. Tiberias, 16km/10 miles away, was a spa town famous for its hot baths. Many of the sick people Jesus healed would have come to the area for the mineral waters at Tiberias. On the hill behind the town was Herod's splendid summer palace.

The lake is ringed around with hills – brown and barren on the east; in those days green, fertile, wooded on the west. Over the tops, and funnelling down through them, races the wind that can whip the lake into a sudden fury of storm. North, the snow-capped summit of Mt Hermon (which some identify as the mountain where the disciples of Jesus saw him transfigured in glory) dominates the skyline.

In Jesus' day, palms, olives, figs and vines grew on the hillsides around the lake. And the little towns and villages on its western shore were thriving centres of industry: fish pickled for export; boat-building; dye-works; potteries. John the Baptist lived an ascetic life in the desert. By contrast, Jesus chose to be in the thick of things, in Galilee, one of the busiest, most cosmopolitan regions of Palestine.

At Capernaum the local Roman centurion had contributed to the building of the synagogue. The ruins of the Capernaum synagogue (pictured here, and probably built two or three centuries later) show a combination of Roman style and traditional Jewish symbols: grapes, the star of David, and a carving of the lost Ark of the Covenant which once stood in the Temple sanctuary.

1:14-20 'Come with me!'

King Herod's arrest silences John's voice and is the signal for Jesus' return to the north to begin his own public proclamation of God's good news. Now is the time, God's kingdom is close at hand, repent and believe. (See 'Jesus and the kingdom'.)

By Lake Galilee Jesus calls four fishermen. He will teach them to catch, not fish, but people (John 1:35-42 fills in the background).

1:21-45 A teacher who can heal

From now on Capernaum is Jesus' headquarters.

Any Jewish man could be called on to explain the readings from the Scriptures in a synagogue service. What impressed those who heard Jesus was his authority: unlike other teachers he did not quote or rely on the authority of others.

The first recognition of Jesus as 'the Holy One of God' comes from a man possessed, and Jesus immediately tries to keep his identity secret. He exercises his power for good over the forces of evil, first by muzzling the voice (25), then by healing the man. In verse 34, again, when he heals the sick he forbids the demons to speak. And the man with the skin-disease (not strictly a leper, see note below) is warned not to tell of his cure (43-44). In fact he disobeys and the publicity restricts Jesus' movement (45). But is this the only reason why Jesus tells people (at least nine times in this Gospel) not to reveal his true identity? Why make a secret of the fact that he is the Messiah?

The reason seems to lie in the wrong ideas about Messiah and his mission that were current at the time. The people were expecting a political leader to free them from the Romans. Jesus needed time to explain the kind of 'kingdom' he had come to inaugurate: it was something even his close followers would find hard to grasp.

▶ **Evil/unclean spirit (23)** 'Unclean' because the man did not keep the strict rules which would make him fit to join in public worship. In Jesus' day, the Jews believed that many illnesses (mental illness especially) were caused by evil spirits. (God and the world he has made is good, therefore suffering must be rooted in evil.) So it

is often hard for us to know whether mental illness or actual 'possession' is being described. Either way, Jesus' authority is clear – and astonishing. See also note on Luke 4:33.

▶ **Verse 32** The sabbath, with its rules restricting movement, begins at sunset on Friday and ends at sunset on Saturday. So this was when people were able to bring the sick to Jesus.

▶ **Verse 44** See Leviticus 14:1-32. In the Bible, the term 'leprosy' covers a variety of skin diseases.

2:1-12 A paralyzed man walks!

Here it is the initiative, and faith, of his friends that leads to the man's healing. Jesus' action demonstrates his power in both physical and spiritual realms. When he says the word, the man is healed. When he says the word, the man is forgiven. In both cases something really happens.

▶ **Verse 4** The house would have an outside staircase leading to a flat roof, giving extra living-space. The roof would be made of tiles or lath and plaster – not difficult to break through.

▶ **Son of Man (10)** This is Jesus' preferred title for himself, perhaps because the title 'Messiah' was so misunderstood. In the Old Testament 'Son of man' generally means simply 'human being', but in Daniel 7:13-14 'someone like a Son of man' ('human being' in most recent translations) is given power by God. Jesus says that the Son of man has authority and power on earth to forgive sins (2:10). He is 'Lord of the sabbath' (2:28). He says that the Son of man must suffer, die and rise again (8:31; 9:9, 12, 31; 10:33, 45; 14:21, 41). And he says that the Son of man will reign in glory (8:38; 13:26; 14:62).

▶ **Verse 11** Ordinary people slept on the floor on a mat or bedding which could be rolled up in the daytime.

2:13-22 Unsuitable friends; the time to fast

Levi (Matthew) is an outsider, an unsuitable friend for any respectable Jewish teacher. His dinner guests are equally beyond the pale. See on Matthew 9:9-17; Luke 5:27-39.

▶ **Scribes, Pharisees (16)** See under 'Jewish religion in New Testament times'.

Fishing in Lake Galilee

Lake Galilee is the world's lowest fresh-water lake, with a surface some 207m/680ft below sea level and a maximum depth of 45m/150ft. It measures roughly 20 x 11km/13 x 7 miles.

Much of Jesus' ministry was based around the lake, and at least seven of the 12 disciples were Galilee fishermen. Peter, Andrew and Philip lived at the lakeside town of Bethsaida, a name that means 'a place of nets', or 'fishery'.

In New Testament times the lake was a rich fishing ground, the principal catch most probably being the *tilapia*, 'St Peter's fish'. The suitability of this fish in warm-water fish-farming today, for instance in Africa, gives a new slant to the 'feeding of the 5,000', in which bread and two small fish were used to feed the hungry.

The cast net – a circle weighted at the edges, with a cord attached to the centre to draw it in – seems to have been the one generally used. The long drag net (seine), which catches all sorts and sizes of fish is mentioned only in Matthew 13:47, where the kingdom of heaven is likened to it.

In 1985, the level of the lake fell so low that the hull of an old boat was revealed. Its style, and objects found within it, together with Carbon 14 testing of the wood, showed that it was 2,000 years old, dating from close to the time of Jesus – scuppered perhaps when the Romans overran the area in AD 67. The hull was raised and preserved and the 'Jesus boat' can be seen today at Ginosar, north of Tiberias.

2:23 – 3:6 Breaking the rules?

See also Matthew 12:1-14; Luke 6:1-11. Jewish interpretation of the commandment to keep the sabbath as a work-free holy day (Exodus 20:8-11; 34:21), had hedged it about with so many petty rules and restrictions that its primary purpose was lost. The day of rest was intended for people's physical and spiritual good, not to deny them food and help. It is a day for doing good – and not only in an emergency. Mark reports two clashes over the issue, in the cornfield, when Jesus' disciples are hungry (23-28) and in the synagogue, a case of human need (3:1-6). Jesus' apparent defiance triggers a terrible reaction: a death-plot against him.

▶ **2:25-26** See 1 Samuel 21:1-6. The loaves David took were those the priests placed each week on the altar.

▶ **Herodians (3:6)** Supporters of Herod Antipas; see 'The Herod family'. They collaborated with the Romans, and were therefore normally abhorrent to scrupulous Pharisees.

Jesus' parable of the soils (or the sower) is illustrated in this scene from Galilee, with good soil, rocky ground, thorns and growing grain.

3:7-19 The Twelve

Crowds flock to Jesus from the south (Judea, Jerusalem, Idumea); from the east across the Jordan; and from Tyre and Sidon, the coastal towns in the north-west.

Jesus chose an inner circle of 12 (see 'The twelve disciples of Jesus') who became founder-members of the new kingdom – the counterparts of Jacob's 12 sons, who gave their names to the tribes of Israel. Three – Peter, James and John – were specially close to him. Four, all from Galilee, were partners in a fishing business (Peter and his brother Andrew; James and his brother John). One (Matthew/Levi, who may have been the brother of James, son of Alphaeus) was a tax collector, serving the Romans. Simon, at the other extreme, belonged to a nationalist guerilla group (the Zealots) working to overthrow the occupation. We know little of the others. Judas Iscariot, marked out as the one who betrayed Jesus, may be the only non-Galilean ('Iscariot' may mean 'from Kerioth', in Judea).

The full list also appears in Matthew 10:2-4 and Luke 6:12-16. The 'Thaddaeus' of Matthew and Mark seems to be the same as 'Judas, son of James' (Luke 6:16; Acts 1:13). Bartholomew is often identified with the Nathanael of John 1. The group was certainly a very mixed bunch of men; not one was from the religious establishment.

▶ **Verse 12** See on 1:21-45.

3:20-35 Jesus in league with the devil?

See on Matthew 12:15-37 and 49.

4:1-34 Parable-stories about God's kingdom

See on Matthew 13:1-52. The parables here are drawn from farming, and are about growth.

Verses 1-8, 13-20: the seed and the soils.

Verses 9-12: listening and understanding.

Verses 21-25: the lamp. Good news is for sharing. (See also Matthew 5:15; Luke 11:33.)

Verses 26-29: the growing seed (recorded only in Mark). The farmer sows his seed, as Jesus and his followers sow the seed of God's kingdom. But it is God who determines the coming of his kingdom.

Verses 30-32: the mustard seed.

▶ **Verse 12** In Jewish idiom, result is often expressed as if it were intention. This verse refers to the 'consequence', not the 'purpose' of Christ's teaching. It is clear from verses 22-23 that the reason for wrapping up the meaning is to encourage listeners to search it out for themselves.

4:35-41 Jesus calms a great storm

See Matthew 8:23-27; Luke 8:22-25. Sudden storms sometimes whip Lake Galilee into fury. This story shows Jesus' power over nature as he calms the furious elements. His quiet confidence contrasts sharply with the disciples' fear, first of the power of the storm, then of the greater power of Jesus. 'Who *is* this man?'

5:1-20 Madman in the graveyard

See also Matthew 8:28-34; Luke 8:26-39. Crossing the lake brings Jesus into non-Jewish (Gentile) territory. The man sheltering among the burial-caves is a pitiful sight – a fragmented personality at the mercy of a hundred conflicting impulses; totally incapable of a normal life. But Jesus has authority over wild elements *and* wild people: the picture in verse 15 is of total transformation. The exorcism is followed by mischief and disturbance, as the herd of pigs runs headlong into the lake

– a sight which must have convinced the man that his tormentors had really gone for good.

▶ **Verse 1** Some MSS have Gadara, some Gergesa, some Gerasa. The general area is south-east of the lake. At only one point on the eastern bank is there a steep slope (13).

▶ **Decapolis (20)** 'Ten Towns'; ten free Greek cities.

5:21-43 Jairus' daughter; and the woman who touched Jesus' cloak

See also Matthew 9:18-26; Luke 8:40-56. The two stories run in parallel; both are about females, about faith, and about people beyond the help of doctors.

The woman tries not to advertise her presence, because the bleeding makes her polluted and untouchable to her fellow Jews. As a woman she is in any case regarded as a 'second-class citizen' (but not by Jesus). Jesus' cloak has no magic properties. He knows the difference between the casual contact of the crowd and someone reaching out in need. The woman's faith not only leads to her physical healing: it 'saves' her.

The incident must have encouraged Jairus. The fact that this synagogue official, a big man in the local community, came to Jesus shows that not all religious leaders were against him. Because of his trust in Jesus his little girl is brought back to life. Jesus has power over life and death.

Jesus astonished his disciples by calming one of Lake Galilee's fierce and sudden storms.

below: Here, on the east side of Lake Galilee, the demented herd of pigs rushed into the lake and drowned, following Jesus' healing of 'Legion'.

below left: At Gadara, one of the Ten (Greek) Towns there was no ban on pork as there was for the Jews.

Jesus in Galilee and the north

Map labels: Mt Hermon; Zarephath/Sarepta; Tyre; Caesarea Philippi; Chorazin; Capernaum; Bethsaida; Gennesaret; Cana; Magdala; Lake Galilee; Nazareth; Tiberias; Nain; Gadara; **GALILEE**

In the story of Jesus' miracle, five loaves and two small fish, probably pickled rather than fresh like these, became enough to feed 5,000. These fish from Lake Galilee are known as 'St Peter's fish', as their large mouths, in which they carry their eggs, could hold a coin (see Matthew 17:27).

▶ **Verse 39** This was not just a coma – the child really was dead. Everyone knew it (40). Jesus' words describe death as God sees it – a sleep from which we wake to a new day.

6:1-13 Jesus rejected in Nazareth; the Twelve sent out

Verses 1-6: in Jesus' home town it is not a case of 'local boy makes good' but 'who does this jumped-up carpenter think he is?' It was not in line with Jesus' purpose to make a display of his powers in order to

convince sceptics (see Matthew 4:6-7).
Verses 7-13: see on Matthew 9:35 – 10:42.

▶ **Verse 3** See on Matthew 12:49. James later became the leader of the church in Jerusalem (Acts 15:13). Judas wrote the Letter of Jude.

6:14-29 King Herod has John beheaded

The context of this story is the question of who Jesus is (14-16). Guilt and superstition make Herod Antipas think Jesus is John come to life again. Herod had divorced his own wife to marry Herodias, wife of his half-brother Philip. John had denounced this as incest (Leviticus 18:16; 20:21), and been imprisoned for his pains. But Herodias wanted to still the preacher's tongue permanently and did not miss the opportunity when it came.

6:30-44 Food for 5,000

See also Matthew 14:13-21; Luke 9:10b-17; John 6:5-14. The Twelve report back, and Jesus sees their need for rest and a time away from the incessant demands of the crowds. His plan is foiled – yet instead of being annoyed or irritable with the pursuers, his heart goes out to them (34). Jesus meets their hunger for teaching *and* for food.

▶ **Verse 37** Needless to say they did not have this kind of money: the denarius 'silver coin' was a working man's wage for the day – this would be over six months' wages.

6:45-56 Jesus walks across the lake

It was some time between 3 a.m. and 6 a.m. Again it is the disciples' need that calls out Jesus' love. And again he demonstrates his supreme power over creation: he is Lord of wind and water.

▶ **Fringe/edge (56)** The blue-tasselled border of his (rabbi's) cloak.

7:1-23 The 'tradition of the elders'

See on Matthew 15:1-20. Mark adds an explanatory note for non-Jewish readers (3-4). The washing rituals had to do with religious 'cleanness', not simply hygiene or table manners. But it is possible for the observance of 'tradition' to empty God's plain command of all meaning (13). Jesus

points out that humanity's real problem is not dirty hands but the deep-down pollution of mind, heart and will, which no amount of washing can clean. The concept is so radical (the idea of clean and unclean foods is so much part of Jewish thinking) that even the disciples need further explanation.

7:24-37 Across the border

Verses 24-30: see on Matthew 15:21-28. Jesus is in Gentile territory: Mark's account moves from the idea of clean and unclean foods (19) to that of 'clean' (Jews) and 'unclean' people (non-Jews). God's kingdom is *inclusive*.

Verses 31-37: the man's speech defect was the result of his deafness, as is often the case. Saliva was popularly thought to have healing power: Jesus treats the man in the way his contemporaries expect.

8:1-21 Food for 4,000; the demand for a sign

Verses 1-9: see on Matthew 15:29-39. Dalmanutha is not known.

Verses 11-21: see on Matthew 16:1-12. The disciples' lack of spiritual discernment disappoints Jesus. They are so taken up with the bread-supply, they cannot see that he is warning them against the ever-present dangers of religious hypocrisy (see Luke 12:1) and materialism (the prime concern of the pro-Herod faction).

8:22-26 Sight for the blind

This story 'matches' that of the deaf man (7:32-37): so with the coming of God's kingdom the blind see and the deaf hear, as Isaiah had predicted (Isaiah 35:5). But still Jesus guards against publicity – see on 1:21-45.

The story can also be taken as a 'frame' to the section that follows, and which closes with the healing of another blind man (10:46ff.).

8:27 – 10:52
Jesus' identity and mission: towards Jerusalem

8:27 – 9:1 'Who do people say I am?'

See on Matthew 16:13-28. Here and

elsewhere Mark records in full incidents which show Peter's failings, but plays down the credit side. This is understandable if the information came from Peter himself. This episode is a pivotal point in the story. The focus shifts, as for the first time Jesus tells his followers that he will suffer death, and afterwards rise again (see too 9:31; 10:33-34).

▶ **Caesarea Philippi (8:27)** 40km/25 miles north of Lake Galilee.

▶ **9:1** The reference may be to those who witnessed his transfiguration, or more likely to the witnesses of his death and resurrection.

9:2-13 Jesus transfigured

See also Matthew 17:1-13; Luke 9:28-36. The apostles are sure now that Jesus is the Messiah. This special glimpse of his glory, given to the inner ring of three, must have been tremendously reassuring through all that lay ahead. Moses (Israel's great law-giver) and Elijah (the first great prophet) converse with Jesus, and the subject is his coming death (Luke 9:31). From now on Jesus will talk more and more of his suffering and death: this is the Messiah's glory. But even his closest friends do not find it palatable.

▶ **Verse 2** The mountain may have been 2,700m/9,000ft Mt Hermon, 19km/12 miles north-east of Caesarea Philippi (8:27). Mt Tabor, another possibility, would have meant a journey south. Peter wants to prolong the present moment. Perhaps Moses and Elijah will

According to the contemporary Jewish historian Josephus, John the Baptist's prison was Herod's fortress at Machaerus in the far south, east of the Dead Sea.

❝ Anyone who wants to be a follower of mine must renounce self: he must take up his cross and follow me. Whoever wants to save his life will lose it, but whoever loses his life for my sake and the gospel's will save it. ❞

8:34-35

stay if they make shelters for them, like the Tent (Tabernacle) where God was present in the old days, before the Temple was built. The glory of all he saw that day imprinted itself indelibly on Peter's memory (2 Peter 1:16-18).

▶ **Verse 9** Jesus again pledges his followers to secrecy.

▶ **Verse 13** 'Elijah', i.e. John the Baptist (see Matthew 17:13). Malachi (4:5) had predicted a reappearance of Elijah to announce the day of God's coming.

9:14-29 The boy who had fits

See also Matthew 17:14-19; Luke 9:37-42. The symptoms described here, attributed to an evil spirit by Jesus' contemporaries, sound like a case of epilepsy (which modern medicine can treat but not cure). The disciples fail because of their lack of faith (see Matthew 17:19-20). Yet Jesus does not turn the child away because his father's faith is limited. In line with the beliefs of the time, Jesus commands the spirit to leave the boy, and he is healed. The key to success is prayer (29; some manuscripts add 'and fasting').

9:30-50 Lessons for disciples

See on Matthew 18. Jesus again forewarns the disciples of his coming death and resurrection (30-32). Then Mark brings together a number of Jesus' sayings loosely linked by theme (reward, belonging) or key word ('salt', 'fire').

No one who is preoccupied with selfish ambition can become a 'great' Christian (33-37). It has to be other people first, self last. It is better deliberately to limit personal self-fulfilment, even to go handicapped through life (44-45), than miss God's kingdom altogether.

▶ **Verses 43-48** Jesus draws his terrible picture of hell from Jerusalem's permanently smouldering refuse-tip in the Valley of Hinnom (Gehenna), and the dead bodies gradually eaten away by worms.

▶ **Verse 49** 'Salted with fire' – i.e. purified in the 'refinery' of suffering.

10 On the way to Jerusalem

Jesus leaves Galilee and travels south. He spends some time in Perea, on the east side of the River Jordan (1) before making his way to Jerusalem via Jericho (32, 46).

The New Testament Letters may throw light on the arrangement of this chapter. Paul, for example, similarly brings together advice for husbands and wives, children, masters and slaves, leaders (see e.g. Ephesians 5:22 – 6:9).

Verses 1-12: divorce. See on Matthew 19:1-15.

Verses 13-16: Jesus blesses the children. See also Matthew 19:13-15; Luke 18:15-17. Jesus has already used a child to point a lesson (9:36-37). Here he does so again. To enter God's kingdom we must all become, not childish, but childlike – receiving him with humble, loving trust (15). Children (along with women) had no standing in Jewish society at this time, but Jesus welcomes and values them.

Verses 17-31: the danger of wealth. See on Matthew 19:16-30; Luke 18:18-30. This incident does not imply that all Christ's followers must become penniless. He is speaking to one man, not to all, and in this case the man's possessions kept him from becoming a disciple. Anything that takes first place in our lives – the place meant for God (Mark 12:29-30) – must go. Jesus takes one steady look at the man (21) and sees to the heart of his problem. 'Go, sell,' he says, and, 'Come, follow me.'

Verses 32-45: Jesus' coming death and resurrection. Jesus repeats his prediction for the third time (see 8:31; 9:31). See on Matthew 20:17-34.

Verses 46-52: blind Bartimaeus cured. This story can be seen as closing the 'frame' around this section, with the healing of another blind man at the beginning (8:22ff.), and symbolic of the disciples' blindness/enlightenment. See also Matthew 20:29-34 (where there are two men); Luke 18:35-43. The story is wonderfully vivid. Only Mark tells us the name of the beggar who was so determined to ask Jesus for his sight that he threw aside his cloak and leaped to answer Jesus' call. As he afterwards joined the company of Jesus' followers, Peter presumably came to know him.

▶ **Verse 12** See 'Jesus and women' on Jewish rules regarding divorce.

▶ **First, last (31)** In importance.

Jesus and the cities
David Instone Brewer

Lower Galilee, where Jesus spent most of his years of ministry, was relatively densely populated. There is archaeological evidence of several large cities in the area – Ptolemais, Tiberias, Scythopolis and Sepphoris – but there is only one incidental reference to any of these in the Gospels (John 6:23).

Important cities in Galilee

Sepphoris is especially important because it was only about an hour's walk from Nazareth, where Jesus grew up. It was a cosmopolitan city of about 30,000 people. It had two markets, a fine central street lined with a colonnade of pillars, a central archives office, a royal bank with a mint for making its own coins, and a sophisticated water system which delivered fresh water by aqueduct and removed soiled water through drainage channels.

Tiberias (pictured here), which was about the same size as Sepphoris, was being built as the new capital of the region while Jesus was growing up.

It is almost certain that Jesus was familiar with these cities, even though they are not mentioned.

Jesus would have regularly passed through Tiberias on any journey between Capernaum and southern Galilee or Judea. He would have had to come off the main road and climb a steep escarpment to avoid it.

The absence of any mention of these cities in the Gospels probably indicates that Jesus deliberately avoided preaching in them. This was perhaps for the same reason that he neglected Jerusalem till the

end of his ministry, to be out of the public eye and avoid trouble with the authorities before time. While he was in the villages he was unimportant to the rulers, though they undoubtedly received reports of him.

Images from urban life

Jesus' teaching shows that he was well aware of urban life and what it involved. Although his teaching drew largely on agricultural images, he also used images which fit better into urban settings.

He spoke about the administration of a large estate (Luke 16:1-8), the actions of absentee landlords (Mark 12:1-12), investment banks (Matthew 25:27/Luke 19:23), court and prison (Matthew 5:25-26/Luke 12:57-59).

He met with people who undoubtedly lived in cities, like the wealthier tax collectors, and a

The city of Tiberias on the shores of Lake Galilee may have been regarded as 'unclean' by the Jews of Jesus' time, since it was said to have been built on a graveyard.

centurion (Matthew 8:5).

Jesus did visit some of the larger towns which had market-places (Mark 6:56) and although we have no record that he personally visited the cities, he sent his disciples to evangelize them (Matthew 10:11, 14/Luke 10:1, 10 – where the Greek word *polis* should be translated 'city').

11 – 13
Jesus in Jerusalem

11:1-11 The Messiah enters his city
See introduction to Matthew 21; and see on Luke 19:28-44.

11:12-26 The fig-tree; Jesus purges the Temple
See on Matthew 21:18-22 and 12-17.

11:27– 12:12 Jesus in the Temple – on whose authority?
See on Matthew 21:23-46. Jesus, the carpenter from the north, with no formal training in the Jewish law, strolls among the shaded colonnades of the Temple, teaching his followers in the manner of the best-qualified rabbi. No wonder the religious 'professionals' question his authority. His reply, and the condemnatory parable that follows, silences them. They withdraw to take stock and renew their attack.

12:13-44 Test questions
See also Matthew 22:15-46; Luke 20:19 – 21:4. Luke 20:19-20 gives the background to these questions.

Verses 13-17: this question is a test of Jesus' political stance. Will he align himself with the Zealots in refusing to pay the poll-tax? The answer clearly repudiates their ideology: you can give to Caesar *and* to God.

Verses 18-27: the Sadducees try to ridicule the idea of resurrection with an absurd case of Levirate marriage (see on Ruth, chapter 3). But the laugh is on them, because there *is* a resurrection – to a life where there is no sexual union or procreation because there is no death.

Verses 28-34: the third question is a genuine one. With 613 commandments to choose from, Jesus replies in the words of Israel's creed (the *Shema*; Deuteronomy 6:4-5) and Leviticus 19:18. If the Pharisees hoped for an unorthodox reply (Matthew 22:34-35) they were disappointed. The astonishing wisdom of Jesus silences his opponents – but *he* has not finished with *them* (35-40).

The scribes (lawyers) took the prophecy that Messiah would be a son of David literally, as a matter of physical descent. To the delight of the listening crowd, Jesus shows that David's own messianic psalm makes their position untenable (35-37).

In strong contrast to the self-advertisement of the men of religion (38-40) comes the little incident in verses 41-44. What counts with God is not the size of the cheque, but the amount of love and self-sacrifice it represents.

▶ **Verse 15** The tax had to be paid in Roman coinage. The denarius was stamped with the head of the Emperor Tiberius.

▶ **Son of David (35)** Matthew 1 and Luke 3 show that Jesus was in fact a descendant of David, but much more than that. He is the Son of God – David's son and David's Lord.

▶ **Verses 41-42** In the Women's Court were 13 trumpet-shaped collection boxes. A 'poor widow' is the poorest of the poor.

13 Coming events, for Jerusalem and the world
See on Matthew 24. See also Luke 21 and 17:22ff. Some of the language Jesus uses and the things he describes echo Old Testament prophecies of the end-time and the symbolic language of 'apocalyptic' writing, familiar to his hearers (see on Revelation): for example, verses 7-8 (battles, earthquakes, famines) and 24-25 (eclipse of sun and moon...).

14 – 16
Jesus' death and resurrection

14:1-11 Plot and betrayal
See also Matthew 26:6-13; John 12:1-8. Jesus' public ministry is at an end. As the Passover festival approaches (see Matthew 26) events move swiftly to a climax. Against a dark backcloth of hatred and treachery shines the story of one woman's love for the Lord (3-9).

It was common courtesy to pour a little perfume on arriving guests. Perfume was also used to anoint a body for burial. And the word 'Messiah' means the 'one anointed' for God's service. Perhaps intuitively sensing the tragedy ahead, Mary (see John 12:3) pours out the whole flask of precious perfumed oil in a lavish, extravagant gesture of affection. (A working man earned one denarius/'silver coin' a day. This luxury import was worth nearly a year's wages.) John (12:1-8) places the event some days earlier and tells us the unpleasant truth about Judas' embezzlement of the funds.

14:12-25 The Last Supper
See on Matthew 26:14-29.

14:26-52 Arrest in Gethsemane
See on Matthew 26:30-56. There seems little point in the mention of the young man (51-52) unless this is Mark himself.

14:53 – 15:15 Trials and denial
See on Luke 22:54-71.

Jesus and women
David Instone Brewer

Jewish women lived very restricted lives in 1st-century Palestine.

In the cities they rarely left the house, and wore a heavy veil when they went to synagogue or to buy and sell goods. In the countryside they worked outside and collected water, but never on their own.

No man would speak to a woman he did not know. It was a mark of piety not to speak to any women.

Girls were not sent to school, and they did not attend the teaching portion of a synagogue service, which took place in the *androne* or 'men's room'.

Women could not teach and they did not even say the blessing at family meals.

Women belonged to their fathers before they were married, then to their husbands, and they were looked after by their sons if they were widowed.

They were not allowed to be witnesses in a trial, and any religious vow they made could be annulled by their husband.

Their husband could marry a second wife or keep a concubine or divorce them for any reason. Women could get a divorce only by convincing a panel of judges that they were neglected, in which case their husband would be fined until he gave them a divorce.

As a result of all this, the birth of a girl was often greeted with sorrow, and a daily prayer contained the line, 'Blessed be God who did not make me a woman.'

Jesus breaks the mould
The attitude of Jesus towards women stands in complete contrast to all this.

He is the only rabbi who has women among his disciples. Although all of his close disciples were men, there are several named women among the wider circle.

Mary and Martha are portrayed as close friends, and he spent time teaching them. Some women even travelled with him, and supported him (Luke 8:1-3).

Jesus taught that men should marry only one wife, and that marriage should be lifelong.

He taught that repentant prostitutes were closer to God than many of the religious leaders (Matthew 21:31), and he allowed a prostitute to anoint him and kiss his feet in public (Luke 7:36-50).

Women were the first to see Jesus alive again after his crucifixion, and their testimony is given credence in the Gospels.

The trials

The Jewish court which tried Jesus was the Sanhedrin, the supreme court at Jerusalem. Its 71 councillors came from influential families – elders, lawyers, Pharisees and Sadducees. The high priest for the year presided.

The Sanhedrin had wide powers in civil and religious matters in Judea, but under Roman rule was not empowered to carry out the death sentence. So Jesus had also to appear before the Roman governor on a charge which would merit the death sentence under Roman law. Blasphemy was sufficient for the Jews. To be sure that Pilate would ratify the sentence, the safest charge was treason.

The Jewish trial was far from regular. It was held at night. There were no defence witnesses. The witnesses for the prosecution could not agree. And the death sentence, which should not have been pronounced till the day following the trial (the Jewish day ran from sunset to sunset), was immediate.

15:16-41 The cross

Jesus is now utterly alone, isolated from the soldiers, the jeering crowd of onlookers and the little group of women who loved him enough to endure one last watch.

The Gospel writers play down the physical horror of the hours on the cross when Jesus plumbed the depths of suffering. But why did he die? The Gospel writers and the whole New Testament see Jesus' death as the climax of his mission, the final

General Gordon, at the end of the 19th century, suggested that this strikingly skull-like rocky outcrop, outside the walls of the Old City of Jerusalem, could be Golgotha ('Skull Hill') where Jesus was crucified.

Roman soldiers in the New Testament
Harold Rowdon

Roman soldiers had many duties besides active service in military conquest. They policed the streets when there was danger of rioting – so there was always a force stationed in Jerusalem. This was heavily reinforced during the Jewish festivals, when huge crowds of excitable people filled the city to overflowing. Soldiers also stood guard on prisoners, acting as escort to those who were being moved.

They were always present at the execution of criminals, both to prevent a last-minute rescue and to carry out the actual execution.

Centurions were officers in charge of a nominal group of 100 men. Usually they had risen from the ranks and were chosen for their courage and reliability.

Several centurions are mentioned in the Gospels and Acts, two by name. All appear in a favourable light on account of their regard for the Jews, their fairmindedness and the positive response of some of them to Christ.

- Jesus healed the servant of a centurion stationed at Capernaum (Matthew 8:5-13; Luke 7:1-10). The local Jewish leaders regarded him as a friend of the Jews – as well they might, since he had built a synagogue for them.
- The centurion in charge of the soldiers who crucified Jesus was so impressed by what he saw and heard that he concluded Jesus was both innocent and divine (Matthew 27:54; Mark 15:39, 44ff.; Luke 23:47).
- In Acts 10 we read of Cornelius, the God-fearing centurion who

A Roman soldier, from the Damascus Museum.

was converted through the preaching of Peter.

- Several unnamed centurions were involved in the arrest and imprisonment of Paul (Acts 21:31ff.; 22:25; 23:17, 23; 24:23).
- Julius was the centurion in charge of Paul and other prisoners sent to Rome (Acts 27:1). He treated Paul kindly (27:3), though he paid more attention to the captain and the owner of the ship than he did to Paul's advice (27:9-11).

Six 'centuries' of men formed a **cohort**, which was commanded by a **tribune** (Acts 21:31). Claudius Lysias was the tribune in charge of the force keeping order in the outer courts of the Temple when the Jews rioted and Paul was arrested (Acts 21:26ff.; 23:17ff.). Cohorts were often named. The Italian Cohort (Acts 10:1) was probably recruited in Italy. The Augustan Cohort was named in honour of Augustus, first emperor of Rome.

Ten cohorts formed a **legion** which was commanded by a **legate**. On paper, at least, its strength was 6,000 men.

Pilate

Harold Rowdon

Evidence for the life of Pontius Pilate (Pilatus) is scanty, but enough survives from non-biblical sources to confirm the accuracy of the biblical account.

A stone slab discovered in 1961 in a theatre at Caesarea refers to Pilate as 'prefect' of Judea. The Roman historian, Tacitus, describes him as 'procurator'; but this title was probably used only after AD 41. The Bible accurately describes him as 'governor'. Two Jewish writers, Philo and Josephus, relate several incidents from his stormy governorship which confirm the biblical picture of him as a mixture of heavyhandedness and weakness.

A middle-class Roman with military and administrative experience, Pontius Pilate was appointed in AD 26, with very wide powers, especially in military and financial matters. For example, he appointed the high priest and controlled the Temple funds. Unlike most other governors, Pilate issued local coins bearing pagan symbols, some of which have survived.

Philo describes Pilate as a harsh, spiteful and brutal man. According to Josephus, in one of his historical works, Pilate antagonized the Jews almost as soon as he was appointed. He allowed the Roman troops to bring their regimental standards into Jerusalem. These contained representations of the emperor, and the Jews were furious because they felt that the holy city had been desecrated by these idolatrous symbols. Pilate bowed to the storm and ordered the removal of the standards.

On another occasion, according to Philo, the Jews took violent objection to some golden shields which Pilate had dedicated in his Jerusalem residence. This time, Pilate at first refused to remove

A coin issued by Pontius Pilate.

them, but the threat of an appeal to Emperor Tiberius induced him to order their removal to his headquarters at Caesarea.

Josephus records an incident arising from Pilate's plan to use money from the Temple treasury to finance the building of an aqueduct to bring water into Jerusalem from a spring 25 miles away. Mass protests were met by force, and many Jews died. This may be the incident referred to in Luke 13:1. (See also 'Jews under Roman rule: the province of Judea'.)

Each of the Gospels records the trial of Jesus before Pilate (Matthew 27:1-26; Mark 15:1-15; Luke 23:1-25; John 18:28 – 19:16). Mark records the basic story. Luke

adds the sending of Jesus to Herod (23:6-12) and Pilate's triple assertion that Jesus was innocent (23:4, 14, 22). Matthew relates the dream and message of Pilate's wife (27:19), his disclaimer of responsibility for Jesus' death (27:24f.), and his setting a guard at the tomb (27:62-66). John, who had been present at the trial, adds even fuller details.

Pilate's final blunder was to seize a number of Samaritans who had assembled on Mt Gerizim as a result of a rumour that sacred vessels from the Tabernacle were hidden there. Some of the ringleaders were executed. In response to a Samaritan protest, Vitellius, governor of Syria and Pilate's superior, ordered the ham-fisted prefect to answer to the emperor for his handling of the affair. But the reigning emperor, Tiberius, died before Pilate reached Rome, and we do not know the outcome of the affair. Eusebius, the 4th-century Christian historian, recorded a report that Pilate committed suicide.

Several unreliable traditions regarding Pilate's body are in existence. A number of *Acts of Pilate*, alleged records of Pilate's rule, appeared during the early Christian centuries. They are forgeries, intended to discredit Christianity. The Ethiopian Church lists Pontius Pilate as a saint!

The body of Jesus was bound in linen cloths and laid in a rock-cut tomb. The picture on the right is of the Garden Tomb in Jerusalem.

The Church of the Holy Sepulchre marks the traditional site of Jesus' crucifixion and burial. Inside the church an ancient shrine covers the rock-cut tomb.

fulfilment of God's purpose. His suffering was 'for us and for our salvation'. By his death he paid the full penalty for 'the sins of the world', once and for all. In Jesus' own words, recorded in the Gospel accounts of the Last Supper, his body was broken and his blood was shed to make a 'new covenant' between human beings and God. By his death he reconciled us to God, making possible the free gift of eternal life.

▶ **Verse 21** Cyrene in North Africa had a strong Jewish colony. Alexander and Rufus evidently became Christians. This may be the same Rufus as the one mentioned in Romans 16:13.

▶ **A son of God (39)** Greek-speakers used this phrase of someone heroic: 'a truly great man'.

▶ **Salome (40)** Zebedee's wife; mother of James and John (Matthew 27:56).

15:42-47 Burial

Death by crucifixion was long drawn out. It often took two days or more. But by 'three in the afternoon' (33) Jesus is dead. Joseph, a member of the Sanhedrin Council and a disciple of Jesus (Matthew 27:57) saves him from the final indignity of a mass grave.

▶ **Preparation Day (42)** I.e. the day before the sabbath, which began at 6 p.m.

16 The resurrection

See on Luke 24. For some unknown reason – most probably damage to very early copies of the Gospel – the best surviving manuscripts of Mark end abruptly at 16:8. Verses 9-20 represent early attempts to round the Gospel off more satisfactorily.

Luke

Summary

Luke tells his story of Jesus for non-Jewish readers.

Key passages and best-known stories

Birth stories of John and Jesus *(1 – 2)*
Magnificat *(1:46-56)*
Nunc Dimittis *(2:29-32)*
The boy Jesus in the Temple *(2:41-50)*
Jesus' testing *(4:1-13)*
Sermon in the synagogue *(4:16-22)*
The Good Samaritan *(10:25-37)*
Martha and Mary *(10:38-42)*
The lost sheep *(15:4-6)*
The 'Prodigal' son *(15:11-32)*
Zacchaeus *(19:1-10)*
Jesus' last week *(22 – 24)*
On the Emmaus Road *(24:13-35)*
Jesus' ascension *(24:50-53)*

Luke, of all the Gospels, gives us the fullest life-story of Jesus. It is also the only one to have a sequel. The Gospel is part one of a two-part history of Christian beginnings: Luke/Acts. Both parts are dedicated to the same man, the Roman Theophilus, and both are written for the same reason, to show God working out his purpose in the life and work of Jesus and his followers.

The Gospel is carefully compiled from reliable, first-hand sources. Luke is not simply a biographer. His overriding concern is to get at the truth of what happened in Palestine in the critical years of Jesus' lifetime. His Gospel shows Jesus as the Saviour of all: his coming, a world event. In Luke we have the clearest picture of Jesus the human being. And his selection of stories reflects his own warm interest in people, especially the sick and helpless, the poor, women, children, the social outcasts. It has been suggested that whereas Matthew's keynote is royalty and Mark's power, the keynote of Luke is love. The Gospel is also full of joy, as the love of God transforms human lives.

The writer
The Gospel does not mention the author's name, but all the evidence points to Luke the much-loved doctor, Paul's friend and companion on his missionary journeys (Colossians 4:14; see introduction to Acts). The precise way diseases are described in the Gospel fits well with this. Unlike Matthew, Mark and John, Luke was almost certainly not a Jew. He may have come from Antioch in Syria or Philippi in Greece.

From the Gospel itself it is clear the writer is a cultured, educated man with a wide vocabulary and a 'tidy' mind: he enjoys compiling, ordering and selecting material. He is an artist with words, combining formal journalist-reporting with a sensitive, sympathetic approach to personal stories. And although he writes for non-Jews, he is at home with both Greek and Jewish backgrounds.

Luke writes from a historical basis, naming kings, emperors and officials, and archaeology has generally proved him an accurate historian, though some points (the census in 2:2, for instance) are still debated.

Sources
Luke worked with Mark and knew him well (Colossians 4:10, 14; Philemon 24), and the Gospel of Mark is clearly one of his main sources. He uses 65 per cent of the same material, reproducing some of it almost word for word. In addition he draws on eye-witness accounts and spoken reports of actual events. He also uses material found in Matthew but not in Mark. Many believe this points to a written record, now lost, but used by both. It is labelled 'Q' (from German *quelle*, 'source', 'spring').

Date of writing
There is no conclusive evidence to tell us when Luke was written and various dates have been put forward. It must have been written (at least in its first edition) before Acts, since that is a sequel, and Acts does not mention any event after AD 62. So there are good arguments for a date in the early 60s. Others, however, argue strongly – from the date of Mark's Gospel (probably late 60s) and apparent references to the fall of Jerusalem to the Romans in AD 70

The virgin birth

John Simpson

Both Matthew (1:18-25) and Luke (1:30-35) state that Jesus Christ was conceived by an action of God's Holy Spirit without the intervention of a human father, and thus born of a virgin, Mary. We call this event the virgin birth – or, more accurately, the virginal conception – of Jesus.

In both Matthew and Luke the emphasis lies on the power and activity of the Holy Spirit in the birth of Jesus. It is this, not the absence of a human father, nor even the co-operation of the virgin mother, which is the important point. From his mother, Jesus was born as a man, but by the creative act of the Spirit his is a new humanity, the starting-point of a new race.

It is arguable that this would have been possible apart from a virgin birth, but the biblical evidence points to this miracle as the means which God employed in order to bring his Son into the world. We are not told anything about the physiology of the incarnation, but simply that it was through the activity of the Spirit that Mary became pregnant.

That is indeed all that can be said, since we are concerned here with the entry of the infinite God into his creation, and this is something that cannot be described, any more than the act of creation itself can be described.

Nor can the virgin birth be rejected simply because it is a miracle. The supreme miracle is the incarnation itself, and, if we can accept that miracle, there should be no difficulty about accepting the means by which God chose to effect it.

The virgin birth is seldom mentioned elsewhere in the New Testament. That is a warning to us not to get it out of proportion. The fact is stated, but Scripture nowhere makes the deity of Christ, nor his incarnation, nor his sinlessness stand or fall by the method of his birth.

The prophecy of Isaiah 7:14 that a 'young woman' should conceive and bear a son called 'Immanuel' ('God with us') was seen to have a deeper meaning after the birth of

(21:20) – for placing the Gospel some time between AD 75 and 85. A revision of Luke, after Acts was written, and perhaps with fuller access to Mark's material, is possible. But there is no conclusive evidence on dating.

1:1-4
Preface: Luke explains

As the number of Jesus' followers grew, and Christian groups sprang up in many places after Jesus' death, it soon became apparent that the stories and teaching of Jesus which were circulating by word of mouth must be written down.

Mark was one of the 'many people' Luke says had already written about 'the things that have happened among us' (1). Mark's Gospel was in existence before Luke set out 'to investigate the whole course of these events in detail'. This may have been when Paul was in prison in Caesarea: Luke was then in Palestine, with time and oppor-

tunity to check on the facts. At any event, he decides to write 'an orderly narrative' for Theophilus, most probably Luke's patron and a high-ranking Roman official who would meet the publishing costs. Theophilus (whose name means 'dear to/friend of God' in Greek) has some interest in Christianity, and Luke wants him to know the truth.

1:5 – 2:52
John and Jesus: birth stories

Neither Mark nor John is interested in the stories of Jesus' birth, and Matthew focusses on Jesus as the Messiah, from the royal line of David. Luke alone tells of John the Baptist's birth, and his fuller account of Jesus' birth adds much to what we know. He must surely have interviewed Mary, Jesus' mother, to have obtained such privileged information. The language and ideas of these chapters reflect his Jewish sources.

Jesus (see Matthew 1:22-23).

In Mark 6:3 the people of Nazareth call Jesus 'son of Mary', a phrase that may well have been an insult based on the rumour that Joseph was not his father. John 8:41 contains a similar slander.

Some have found further references to the virgin birth in Galatians 4:4 where Paul says that God 'sent forth his Son, born of woman', and again when he spoke of Jesus as the 'second Adam', the first of the new race (1 Corinthians 15:45-47).

See also '"God with us" – the incarnation'.

A geneticist comments

66 Genetics has always seemed to be a barrier to belief in the virgin birth of Jesus Christ. Even if one of Mary's eggs had developed without fertilization (a process called parthenogenesis which happens regularly in some aphids and bees), the resulting child would have been female like her mother. Somehow Jesus must have got a Y-chromosome or he would not have been a male.

However, we now know that there are genetic mechanisms by which this could in theory occur. These do not 'explain away' the virgin birth or make it less of a miracle, but they do help us to understand ways in which God might have worked.

We have to recognize that if Christ was going to be fully divine, he must somehow be different. If God is going to bring his Son into the world, he could, as it were, have snapped his fingers and produced a full-blown infant. But Christ was fully human as well as fully God. So, we are told, he had a normal mother but a divine father.

I have no problems whatever with the virgin birth. To me, this is a theological neccessity. 99

R.J. Berry

1:5-25 The priest and the angel

A new age is dawning, heralded by wonders. Luke shows that God is intimately involved in the events which lead up to the birth of Christ.

In the Old Testament, barren years frequently preface the arrival of those with a special part to play in God's purposes: Isaac, Jacob, Samuel, Samson. So it is with Zechariah and Elizabeth, both of them good (godly) people from priestly families, who have long suffered the pain and stigma of childlessness, despite their prayers.

Zechariah is in Jerusalem for his annual two-week spell of duty as a priest. This year, comes the honour of a lifetime: he is chosen to offer the incense, alone in the Temple. And at that moment God's angel brings word that the deep inner longing of this couple will be answered. God *will* give them a son, and in so doing fulfil his larger purposes for the nation, and for the world. John is destined to be the bridge between the 'old' and the 'new'. He will be the new Elijah, heralding the long-promised, long-

Zechariah, serving the Temple, was chosen to go inside to burn the incense. Here he received the angel's message that he would have a son (John the Baptist) with the special role of announcing God's kingdom.

awaited Messiah. But this is too big a stretch for Zechariah's imagination, and in consequence he emerges speechless.

▶ **Verse 15** Compare Samson's dedication to God (Judges 13:4-5); and the Nazirite rules (Numbers 6).

▶ **Gabriel (19)** 'The mighty one of God' who explained Daniel's vision and prophecy (Daniel 8:16; 9:21).

1:26-38 Mary's message from God

Six months after Zechariah's encounter with the angel, God sends Gabriel to announce the birth of 'the Son of the Most High (God)'– this time to the young

66 *My soul tells out the greatness of the Lord, my spirit has rejoiced in God my Saviour* 99

The beginning of Mary's 'Magnificat': 1:46-47

Bethlehem, set on a ridge in the hill-country south of Jerusalem, is still surrounded by fields where 'shepherds watch their flocks'.

These stone mangers standing against a wall are a reminder of Jesus' birth, and the manger that served as his cradle.

woman chosen to be his mother. Mary's response is in marked contrast to Zechariah's. Her quiet acceptance of a situation bound to cause scandal, and possibly the cancellation of her marriage contract, shows something of the kind of woman God has chosen. See also 'Mary, the mother of Jesus' and 'The virgin birth'.

1:39-56 Mary and Elizabeth: sharing the news

Having heard that Elizabeth, too, is pregnant, Mary sets straight out on the four- or five-day journey south from Nazareth to 'a town in the Judean hills'. The meeting of these two kinswomen is one of special joy and significance. Their

thoughts and feelings are crystallized in Elizabeth's benediction and Mary's hymn of praise. Perhaps the words of her 'Magnificat' had taken shape in her mind during the journey. It is full of Old Testament echoes, words which Mary must have known and loved from childhood, especially Hannah's song after Samuel's birth (see 1 Samuel 2:1-10).

What happened when Mary got home is recorded in Matthew 1:18-25.

1:57-80 'His name is John'

The fact that the child was not to be given a family name, and Zechariah's sudden recovery of speech as the Holy Spirit fills him, giving his pent-up thoughts voice in

2:1-20 The birth of Jesus

Bethlehem, 9km/6 miles south of Jerusalem and 110km/70 miles south of
Nazareth, was the home of Ruth and Boaz
and later the birthplace of King David. But
for Jesus there was no special guest-room in
the town. His cradle was the manger which
served the beasts of some householder who
took pity on the shelterless couple in their
obvious need.

So God's deliverer, 'the Messiah, the
Lord' is born. And the message, 'glory to
God... and peace on earth', is borne by
choirs of angels to simple shepherds
minding their flocks on the hillside.

▶ **Verse 2** See 'The census'.

▶ **Manger (7)** In poor households the animals
were often 'stabled' in a lower part of the
general living-area.

2:21-40 Recognition in the Temple: Simeon and Anna

See Leviticus 12 for the Jewish background
to the custom described here. Forty days
after Jesus' birth his parents present him to
the priest in the Temple. They are not
wealthy enough to sacrifice a lamb, so they
offer two doves or pigeons. It is all routine
procedure – until Simeon sees the child.
This faithful Jew not only recognizes the
Messiah God promised he would see before
he died: he sees in him the fulfilment of
God's saving purpose for the whole world.
Anna, like Simeon, realizes the hope of a
long lifetime in this brief encounter.

The joy of this child's coming is the
keynote of the chapter. Simeon's word to
Mary (35) comes in sharp contrast to the
general tone.

▶ **Verse 39** Matthew 2 fills in more of what took
place before the family settled in Nazareth.

2:41-52 Star pupil amazes Temple teachers

This one story is all we know of Jesus'
boyhood. It must have stood head and
shoulders above all Mary's other memories,
as perhaps the first indication of all that
would follow.

At 12, a Jewish boy underwent
preparation for adult status in the religious
community (today's *bar mitzvah*). This visit
to Jerusalem is therefore a special one for

Mary and Joseph
offered a sacrifice
of two doves or
pigeons when
they took the
baby Jesus to the
Temple to be
dedicated to God
because he was a
first-born son.

prophetic song (the 'Benedictus'), make a
deep impression on the people around.
Great things are now expected of John.

▶ **In the desert/wilderness (80)** Here both
John and Jesus were 'honed' for their ministry.
The desert had long been associated with
prophetic inspiration. In John's time, the Essene
community (whose writings, known as the 'Dead
Sea Scrolls', were discovered in 1947), had its
base in the Judean desert close to the northern
end of the Dead Sea. Some suggest John was
brought up by this or some similar desert sect,
leaving it as an adult to go public with his special
message from God.

The census
Colin Humphreys

Luke 2:1-5 states that a census was taken by the Roman Emperor Caesar Augustus around the time of the birth of Jesus, and that Joseph travelled with Mary from Nazareth to his home town of Bethlehem in order to register.

This census is one of the most difficult problems in the New Testament to resolve and much has been written about it.

There are three well-documented major censuses conducted by Augustus: in 28 BC, 8 BC and AD 14. But these were apparently for Roman citizens only, and Joseph was not a Roman citizen. In addition, there are various records of provincial censuses under Augustus for non-citizens for purposes of taxation. For example, in AD 6, ten years after the death of Herod the Great, Josephus refers to a census in Judea administered by Quirinius, the governor of Syria, and Luke also refers to this census in Acts 5:37.

However, there is no record of a census for taxation purposes in Judea around the time of the birth of Christ, hence the problem in interpreting Luke 2:1-5. But if the census was not for taxation purposes but was instead a census of allegiance to Caesar Augustus, the problem is solved. Some translations of Luke 2:1-5 refer to a census for taxation, but taxation is not mentioned in the Greek manuscripts of Luke's Gospel.

The 5th-century historian Orosius states: 'Augustus ordered that a census be taken of each province everywhere and all men be enrolled. So, at that time, Christ

was born and was entered on the Roman census list.'

The Jewish historian Josephus appears to refer to the same event: 'When all the people of the Jews gave assurance of their goodwill to Caesar, and to the king's government, these very men [the Pharisees] did not swear, being about six thousand.'

From the context of these words in Josephus this census of allegiance to Caesar Augustus

An inscription with the name of 'divine' Augustus Caesar, the Roman emperor who gave the decree for the census that took Mary and Joseph to Bethlehem.

A coin of the Emperor Augustus.

place *before* the one when Quirinius was governor of Syria'. As we have said, this latter census occurred in AD 6 and Luke was well aware of it (Acts 5:37).

Thus the earlier census referred to by Luke in Luke 2:1-5 provides a clue to the date of the birth of Jesus, The census of allegiance which occurred about a year before the death of Herod is consistent with Christ being born in 5 BC.

occurred about a year before the death of Herod the Great, which fits very well the census referred to in Luke 2:15.

There is one further problem with this census. Luke 2:2 is usually translated 'this census was first made when Quirinius was governor of Syria', but Quirinius did not become governor of Syria until AD 6. However, the Greek sentence construction of Luke 2:2 is unusual and an alternative translation is 'this census took

Jesus. Visitors flocked into the city for Passover, travelling in large parties for safety. (See 'The great festivals'; also 'Passover and the Last Supper'.)

Jesus' parents have no reason to suspect he is missing till the evening halt. Next day they retrace their steps, and on the following morning find him in the Temple. For Jesus, on a rare visit from distant Nazareth, the opportunity to engage with the best teachers is not to be missed. He forgets all about his parents. 'My Father' has priority. This is the first indication that Jesus realized his special relationship with God. The next 18 years are passed over in total silence.

▶ **Verse 49** Jews would normally say 'our Father' or 'Father in heaven'.

3:1 – 4:13
John the Baptist and Jesus

3:1-20 John's message
See also on Matthew 3; Mark 1:2-8. Luke's historical detail makes it possible to date John's ministry (and the beginning of Jesus' ministry a few months later) around AD 27-29.

Verses 10-14, which explain what it means to 'produce fruit in keeping with repentance' (8), occur only in Luke. Genuine repentance will show itself in daily life – in kindness, generosity, honesty. The soldiers are told, 'No bullying; no black-mail; make do with your pay!'

▶ **Annas and Caiaphas (2)** Annas was high priest AD 6-15; Caiaphas, his son-in law, AD 18-36, with Annas still so influential that their names can be bracketed.

▶ **Verses 19-20** See on Mark 6:14-29.

3:21-22 Jesus' baptism
See on Matthew 3. Only Luke says that it was as Jesus was praying that a dove-like form was seen and God's voice heard.

▶ **Heaven opened (21)** Meaning that what followed is a revelation from God.

▶ **Verse 22** A dove became the symbol of the Holy Spirit for Christians. For Jews it stood for Israel.

3:23-38 Jesus' family line
See on Matthew 1:1-17. Luke places his genealogy as a preface to Jesus' ministry. He had reached the age at which a priest, with a proven line of descent, could take up office. Unlike Matthew, Luke takes the line right back to Adam, 'son of God'. The two lists are almost the same from Abraham to David: then they diverge. As a 'son of Adam' Jesus is real man; as 'son of David' he is Messiah. His unique status as 'Son of God' has already been made clear in the birth stories (1:32, 35).

4:1-13 Tried and tested
See on Matthew 4; Mark 1:9-13. Matthew and Luke begin with the same temptation but differ on the order of the other two. Luke does not bother with the place from which the 'kingdoms of the world' are viewed: the glory and authority offered are more important.

The real target of Satan's attack is Jesus' relationship to his Father: 'if you are the Son of God...' These attempts to undermine his confidence and sow doubts are not so different from the serpent's approach in Genesis 3 – 'Did God say...?' But this time the agent of evil does not succeed. Jesus has the final word, and is left in peace – for a time (13).

4:14 – 9:50
Jesus at work in Galilee

4:14-30 'Is this the carpenter's son?'
Luke chooses to start with Jesus' keynote 'sermon' at the synagogue back home in Nazareth, although this was not the first event in his ministry. Astonishment at Jesus' teaching quickly changes to

A rabbi stands with a group of Jewish children at the Western, or 'Wailing' Wall, still standing from the Temple King Herod built, and to which Jesus went as a boy, to learn from the teachers.

❝ *The Spirit of the Lord is upon me, because he has anointed me to bring good news to the poor. He has sent me to proclaim release to the captives and recovery of sight to the blind, to let the oppressed go free, to proclaim the year of the Lord's favour.* ❞

Jesus uses Isaiah's words to announce in his home synagogue at Nazareth that 'today this scripture has been fulfilled': 4:18-19, 21

hostility. And at the implication that because of their disbelief the gospel will be offered to non-Jews, the people are all set to lynch him. See also Matthew 13:53-58; Mark 6:1-6.

▸ **The synagogue (16-17)** Any Jewish man might be invited to take part in the service of prayers, readings and sermon. The leader stood to pray and read from the scrolls, sat down to teach (20).

▸ **Verses 26-27** See 1 Kings 17:8-16; 2 Kings 5:1-14.

4:31-44 Sabbath at Capernaum

See on Mark 1:21-45. Luke picks up Mark's narrative at this point, but by placing the two synagogue/sabbath stories next to one another brings out the sharp contrast in people's response to Jesus. He also adds personal touches. The 'high fever' of verse 38 is a medical term, and he tells us that Jesus laid his hands on those he cured (40).

▸ **Demon (33)** 'In the ancient world it was widely held that many troubles are caused by

Mary, the mother of Jesus
Frances Fuller

Mary, a peasant girl in an oppressed country, was probably only a teenager when she became the mother of Jesus, but her words reveal her as a knowledgeable girl, acquainted with the ways of God and the history of her people. And she was a model of wisdom and poise.

It is all in her story. Being troubled, she pondered. Told the impossible, she asked a practical question. Offered a miracle from God, she believed. Handed the humiliation of an illicit pregnancy, she saw God as holy, herself as a servant, and she accepted his will.

In spite of what the neighbours might think, she saw instantly how she had been honoured. Not offered a chance to refuse, she decided to do the required thing with joy. Overwhelmed, she hurried to share her news with another who would understand. Congratulated, she praised God, seeing herself as just part of the stream of history in which God does great things.

Being chosen by God for great honour cost Mary a lot of stress and heartache. Joseph, whom the Bible calls a just man, resolved to divorce her. It took another visit by the angel to prevent that. Then

she had to travel just at the wrong time and delivered the baby in a strange place, not very clean or comfortable.

Unexpected visitors kept arriving, telling about amazing signs.

When she and Joseph took the baby to the Temple to present him to God, a devout man, who took the infant in his arms and said he had been living for this moment, told Mary that a sword would pierce her soul.

Then there were threats to kill the baby, so instead of going home the young family had to flee across the desert to Egypt and hide until Herod was dead. Many other babies died when the soldiers were looking for Jesus, and Mary heard this.

The child was extraordinary – brilliant, inquisitive, with a searching awareness of his own identity. Mary must have felt at times unsure what to do with him, but she knew he was still a child and maintained her authority over him, teaching him to obey.

Like other mothers, she undoubtedly told him the stories of his birth and his childhood. Watching him grow, she kept on pondering, putting it all together.

When he became a man, she let him live his own life, appearing in his story rarely, only enough for us to know that she believed in his destiny and was concerned for his welfare.

She raised a son who resembled her in profound ways. He obeyed God unflinchingly. He could accept both humiliation and honour. As Mary had endured shame for the joy of being his mother, he endured the cross for the joy that would follow.

The predicted sword did pierce her heart, but Mary stood by him, witnessing the injustice and agony of his death and hearing him ask a beloved disciple to take care of her.

As faithful child of God, as exemplary woman, as mother, Mary is unsurpassed.

Mary's story is told in Matthew 1:16-25; Luke 1:27-56; 2; John 2:1-5; 19:25-27; Mark 3:21.

KEY PASSAGES

The angel's message Luke 1:28-38
Mary's song (the 'Magnificat')
Luke 1:46-56

Women's perspectives in the Gospels

Richard Bauckham

In the social world of the New Testament period it was mostly men who had official authority in the public sphere, whereas women often had real power and influence, alongside men, in the domestic sphere of the household. The latter was far from unimportant, but literature of the period written from the male perspective, as most is, can easily give a misleading impression by focussing on those aspects of life in which men were dominant.

A striking feature of the Gospels is the extent to which they take readers into the spheres of life in which women were active. This reflects the important place of women in the life and ministry of Jesus and in the early church which told the Gospel stories.

Elizabeth and Mary, in Luke

The first two chapters of Luke's Gospel are notable for the way the story is told from the perspective of the two women, Elizabeth and Mary.

This is one of the differences between Luke and Matthew, who tells his story of the birth and infancy of Jesus from the perspective of the male characters. This is appropriate to a narrative which moves in the public, political sphere, where male authority rules.

Luke, on the other hand, sets most of his story in the domestic sphere of the household, where women could have decisive influence on events.

Mary is the key human agent in these chapters of Luke. By accept-ing her God-given role as the mother of Jesus, she becomes an agent of God's deliverance of his people, with decisive effect on human history (1:46-56). Had the story been told from a male perspective, her significance might well have been confined to the household but, from the female perspective that Luke's narrative adopts, Mary's role in God's purposes transcends the purely domestic sphere.

Events seen through women's eyes

The stories about Jesus' ministry which all four Gospels recount are seldom told from Jesus' own perspective. Instead they invite the reader to adopt the many different perspectives of the people who hear, encounter and follow Jesus. Among these are many women, who follow Jesus as disciples, welcome Jesus into their homes, or come to him for healing.

Jesus interacts with women most often within the household or the synagogue, less often in the public places which were a predominantly (though not ex-clusively) male world.

One reason the Gospels so often feature the perspectives of female characters is that Jesus' ministry was not confined to the public world of male dominance. He is often to be seen in the spheres in which women could most easily exercise independence and initiative, such as the home of his friends Martha and Mary.

A teaching role for women

One Gospel scene which shows a woman in an unusual role in that society is when Mary, sitting at Jesus' feet like the disciple of a rabbi, learns her master's teaching in order to become a teacher herself (Luke 10:38-42).

The fact that this scene is set in her home foreshadows the way in which, in the earliest churches, women took an active part in leadership and teaching, unusual for the culture.

This was possible partly because the early Christians met and worshipped in homes. So the inevitable constraints of the non-Christian public world outside were avoided and the domestic setting of early church gatherings opened up fresh possibilities for women.

evil spirits. The Bible says little about demon possession before or after the incarnation, but much during Jesus' ministry... : this phenomenon is part of the conflict between Jesus, who came to destroy the works of the devil, and evil' (Leon Morris).

▶ **Judea (44)** The term is used here of Palestine generally, not the south in particular. Jesus went there later.

5:1-11 Record catch for Peter and partners

Matthew (4:18-22) and Mark (1:16-20) simply record Jesus' call to the fishermen to follow him. Luke's story shows that this was based on more than casual contact. In the first of the three miracles recorded in 5:1-26, Jesus moves in on Peter's area of expertise. The huge catch, made against all the norms, brings Peter to his knees (8). God is at work, and Peter is no saint.

▶ **Gennesaret (1)** Another name for Galilee.

5:12-16 Jesus' touch heals a 'leper'

This miracle, and the one that follows, shows Jesus' compassion. The man was an advanced case, 'full of leprosy'. Yet Jesus is prepared to touch the untouchable. See on Matthew 8:1-4.

5:17-26 A paralyzed man walks!

See on Mark 2:1-12. Jesus reads the thoughts of his questioners (21-22). And Luke notes that the man and all who saw what happened recognized the miracle as God's doing (25-26).

▶ **Scribes and Pharisees (17)** See 'Jewish religion in New Testament times'.

5:27-39 Levi throws a party for Jesus

See on Matthew 9:9-17. For other parties where Jesus was guest: see Luke 7:36; 11:37; 19:7.

6:1-11 Clash over sabbath rules

See on Mark 2:23-3:6.

6:12-16 Jesus chooses the Twelve

See on Mark 3:7-19, and 'The twelve disciples of Jesus'. Only Luke tells us of Jesus' night of prayer before announcing his choice. He tells us more about Jesus as a man of prayer than any other Gospel writer. See, for example, 9:18, 28; 10:21; 11:1; 18:1. Jesus takes time away from the crowds in lonely places.

6:17-49 Teaching for disciples

Luke's 'Sermon on the Plain', parallels Matthew's collection of teaching in the 'Sermon on the Mount' (chapters 5 – 7), but is shorter. Jesus must have taught the same truths on many different occasions.

Having chosen the Twelve, Jesus comes some distance down the mountainside to a level area. Here he sits down to teach, and gathered around him are the apostles, his followers and a great crowd of people who have come to hear him and be healed. After all are healed (19), he speaks directly to his followers. They know what it is to be literally poor and hungry and sad and hated 'on account of the Son of Man' (20-22). Their hardships will be turned to blessing, Jesus says, 'for surely your reward is great in heaven'.

By contrast (24-26), alas for those who have it all now. (These 'woes' appear only in Luke.)

Verses 27-36: the law of love is to 'do to others as you would have them do to you', including those who do us down. See on Matthew 5:17-48.

Verses 37-49: see on Matthew 7.

7:1-10 Officer's slave healed

See on Matthew 8:5-13 and 'Roman soldiers in the New Testament'. Luke's

The New Testament miracles

I. Howard Marshall

The Gospels contain various reports of happenings, such as instantaneous healings of sick or disabled people or displays of control over natural phenomena, which cannot be accounted for by normal explanations. On about 35 different occasions Jesus performed various kinds of deeds that seemed miraculous to those who saw them. In addition there are several passages where we are told in quite general terms that Jesus performed miracles.

Jesus' miracles

The majority of these stories about Jesus tell how he healed the sick of various diseases including fever, leprosy (a skin disease, but probably not the modern disease of that name), dropsy, paralysis, blindness, deafness, and dumbness, doing so without any apparent medical aids. In general these cures were effected by his simple word (Mark 1:27; 2:11), sometimes by touch (Mark 5:41), and not by the use of magical gestures or devices.

In other cases he cast demons out of people who were suffering from physical or mental disorders. Three times we hear that he raised people from the dead.

The remaining stories show his power over inanimate things – to feed a large crowd of people with very little food, to walk on the surface of a lake and to still a storm, to curse a fig-tree so that it withered away, to change water into wine, and to catch enormous quantities of fish.

These stories testify to the tremendous impression which the work of Jesus made on those who

saw it. Even if the stories contained some legendary elements, we should still want to know what it was about Jesus that made people tell such stories about him. They were not intended to make people marvel at him personally, but were meant to bring glory to God (Luke 7:16). They testified to

The Gospels are full of accounts of Jesus' healings – how the crippled, the deaf, the blind, and people with all kinds of illnesses were made well.

God's love for suffering humanity (Mark 1:41; 8:2).

In a significant passage Jesus sent a message to John the Baptist, who was in prison, to assure him that he was the coming deliverer whom John had heralded. He used words to describe the mighty works which showed that they fulfilled the Old Testament promises of the coming time of salvation when God would heal people's bodies as well

as their souls (Luke 7:22; Isaiah 29:18-19; 35:5-6; 61:1).

The mighty works were thus indications that God's power was at work through Jesus, and signs that the kingly rule of God had begun to make its presence felt in the world that was under the sway of Satan. Casting out demons was the indication that their master was facing a superior power and that the reign of God was already present (Luke 11:20).

The intended effect of the mighty works, therefore, was to lead people to faith in the saving power of God at work in Jesus (Mark 9:23f.). They were not compelling signs of God's power: the Pharisees felt able to attribute them to the power of Satan (Mark 3:22). But to those with the eyes to see, they constituted the sign that God was at work in Jesus, fulfilling his promises, and were meant to awaken and confirm faith in him.

Miracles in the early church

All this applies to the miracles of Jesus himself. It also applies to the miracles in the early church. The early Christians displayed powers similar to those of Jesus. We hear of sick people being cured, the dead being raised, the miraculous release of prisoners and even the power to inflict physical judgment. These were signs that the same power of God which was at work in Jesus was still at work in his disciples, confirming their message of salvation, and also warning of the reality of God's judgment.

▶▶ **Modern objections
to miracles**

The accounts of Jesus' mighty works are an integral and central part of the story. We cannot dismiss them and end up with a non-miraculous Jesus. Why, then, do people try to eliminate them from the picture of Jesus?

▪ In the first place, it is argued that science rules out the possibility of miracles. In fact, this argument is nothing more than the statement of a presupposition: that in a purely material universe nothing can happen that cannot be accounted for in terms of natural causes.

But that is simply an assumption about the nature of the universe which cannot be proved to be true. Certainly single, unrepeated events can generally not be verified scientifically, but neither can they be ruled out as impossible. At most it could be argued that normally miracles do not occur; but it is illegitimate to claim that therefore miracles can never occur. After all, the characteristic of miracles is precisely that they are abnormal! We ought at least to have open minds on the point.

▪ Second, it is argued that we have no reliable historical evidence for miracles. We must have good testimony that the alleged miracle happened, and that it cannot be explained in a non-miraculous manner. Since we are dealing with something as unusual as a miracle, the evidence needs to be extremely strong, since (it is argued) it is more likely that the witnesses got it wrong than that a miracle actually happened.

If, however, only one of the miracles of Jesus could be claimed as historical, this would be enough both to demonstrate that miracles are possible and to make further ones probable.

Such an event is the resurrection.

The evidence that reliable witnesses claimed to have seen Jesus alive after his death (1 Corinthians 15:3-8) is incontrovertible. For many people the only explanation that makes sense of the evidence is that he was miraculously raised from the dead. People who want to disagree must produce some convincing alternative explan-

> **❝ People who don't like
> to talk about miracles often
> find no trouble at all in talking
> about the paranormal. ❞**
>
> Keith Ward

ation. (See 'Jesus' resurrection').

If the resurrection did take place, then it makes the fact of other miracles highly likely. For, first, it establishes the possibility of the miraculous taking place at all. It means that God can and does act in the natural order in an unusual manner. Then the resurrection is God's 'Yes' to the life of Jesus – including Jesus' own claim to work miracles (Luke 7:21f.; 11:19). It would be highly unlikely that God acted miraculously only once in the resurrection and never at other times in the life of Jesus.

This evidence is confirmed by the reliable historical tradition that Jesus did work miracles, which is found in the Gospels. To be sure, we cannot test and affirm on purely historical grounds the truth of every single miracle story. There may be occasions where a miraculous event has another 'complementary' explanation in terms of natural causes. In some cases, what seemed miraculous to 1st-century people may be explicable today in natural terms (e.g. in the psychological healing of a psychosomatic disease). In other cases there may not be enough evidence to confirm or disprove the Gospel story.

▪ A third point often raised against the historicity of the New Testament miracles is that similar stories are told of other great men of the period. Hence it is likely that Christians, who shared the superstitions of their day, would invent similar stories about Jesus.

One could reply that if it was necessary for Jesus to be a miracle-worker in order to be seen by the people of that time to be 'the greatest' in 1st-century terms, then God could certainly condescend to their level of understanding and do mighty wonders through him. More important is the fact that the stories of Jesus display some telling differences from those told about other men.

The significance of Jesus' miracles lies not so much in the miraculous power which he displayed in them, as in the testimony they bear to the saving and healing power that is part and parcel of the reign of God.

greater detail emphasizes the humbleness of the man. And Jesus marvels at his faith.

7:11-17 Back from the dead!

Only Luke, with his concern for the underprivileged, records the raising of this widow's son (her only means of support). He brings the story in at this point in relation to the report back to John (22). Jesus, ever-compassionate, is Lord of life and death.

▶ **Nain (11)** A village south-east of Nazareth. See map.

▶ **Verse 13** Luke is the only Gospel writer to refer to Jesus as 'the Lord', a term probably not much used during his lifetime.

7:18-35 Messengers from John

See on Matthew 11:1-19.

▶ **Verse 35** 'God's wisdom, however, is shown to be true by all who accept it.' People turned to God in response to the preaching of both John and Jesus.

7:36-50 At dinner with a Pharisee

This is a different incident from the one recorded in the other Gospels. Simon shows Jesus no special courtesy. But a common prostitute, to whom he has opened up the possibility of forgiveness, pours out her gratitude in lavish love, not caring what anyone thinks. Jesus reads Simon's thoughts (39) and takes them up in his story. The woman's love does not earn forgiveness (47), it follows it.

▶ **Verse 37** Meals like this were not private: people could come and watch. But it took courage for this woman to go to a house where she knew she was not welcome. Jewish women often wore small flasks of perfume, like a necklace. The long neck of the flask was broken to release the contents. It was easy for the woman to reach Jesus' feet, as guests reclined on couches: heads towards the table, feet away from it.

8:1-21 Secrets of God's kingdom

Verses 1-3: only Luke tells us the part the women played in Jesus' mission. Susanna is not mentioned again. Mary Magdalene stood watching at the crucifixion, and she and Joanna were at the tomb and saw the Lord on the resurrection morning. Their love, and that of many other women who followed him from Galilee, never wavered.

Luke takes up Mark's material from verse 4 to 9:50, but misses out Mark 6:45 – 8:26.

Verses 4-15: see on Matthew 13:1-52. See also Mark 4:1-20.

▶ **Verse 2** Mary's trouble is more likely to have been mental illness than the sexual immorality often assumed. She is not the woman of 7:36ff.

▶ **Verse 5** In Palestine, sowing came before ploughing.

▶ **Verse 10** See on Mark 4:12.

▶ **Verse 19** See on Matthew 12:49.

8:22-39 Stormy crossing; a man possessed

See on Mark 4:35-41; 5:1-20.

▶ **Verse 32** Pork was forbidden food for Jews. But the country east of the lake was largely non-Jewish.

8:40-56 Jairus' daughter; woman with a haemorrhage

See on Mark 5:21-43, the fuller account. Verse 56: Luke, as so often, notes the effect of the miracle on those around.

9:1-17 The Twelve sent out; Herod is puzzled; 5,000 fed

Verses 1-6: see on Matthew 9:35 – 10:42. This time (though not always: 22:36) they are to go as they are, travelling light.

Verses 7-9: Luke seems to have a special source of information about Herod, perhaps through Joanna (8:3).

Verses 10-17: see also Matthew 14:13-21; Mark 6:30-44; John 6:1-14. The feeding is a miracle and a 'sign' which indicates Jesus' true identity. It may also anticipate the Messiah's banquet-feast with his people.

Model of a rich man's house at the time of Jesus.

▶ **Verse 1** The apostles were not together all the time. It would have been easy for those with homes and families around Capernaum to have seen something of them.

▶ **Blessed (16)** I.e 'said the blessing'.

9:18-27 'Who do you say I am?'; Jesus speaks about his suffering

See the fuller version in Matthew

16:13-28, and Mark 8:27 – 9:1. Luke abridges at this point.

9:28-36 Jesus transfigured
See on Mark 9:2-13.

9:37-50 A boy with fits; 'Who is the greatest?'
Verses 37-43: see on Mark 9:14-29.
Verses 46-48: see on Matthew 18 and Mark 9:30-50.

9:51 – 19:27
Galilee to Jerusalem

Much of what is recorded in these chapters is unique to Luke. Jesus' sight is set on Jerusalem and what lies before him there. The framework of the journey is clear, but not the route. The 'interval' between the Galilee days and Jesus' last week is used by Luke to bring together much of Jesus' teaching on the general theme of discipleship.

9:51-56 Samaritans refuse Jesus hospitality
The direct route from Galilee to Jerusalem passed through Samaritan territory. Jerusalem was the centre of worship for the Jews but not for the Samaritans. They had their own temple on Mt Gerizim, close to Shechem. So this village was not going to help Jesus on his way to the rival shrine. See Samaritans in 'Jewish religion in New Testament times' and on 10:29ff.

▶ **Verse 54** No wonder Jesus nicknamed these two brothers 'sons of thunder'!

9:57-62 No turning back
See on Matthew 8:18-22.

Martha and Mary
Frances Fuller

The Gospels record three incidents involving Martha and her sister Mary; twice their brother Lazarus is present.

A question of priorities
The first time, Martha had invited Jesus to their home. She was likely the eldest in a family of young adults who had lost their parents. The occasion was probably the Feast of Dedication, which lasted eight days and involved traditional foods and ceremonies and lamps in the windows. So Martha had a lot to do.

While Martha was rushing around feeling overworked, Mary was 'sitting at Jesus' feet', an expression which refers not to posture but to purpose. She was studying with a rabbi.

Women were not supposed to study with rabbis, but that was not what bothered Martha. She thought that Mary should help with the chores. If Jesus were not talking in his fascinating way, she probably would, so Martha needed Jesus on her side.

Jesus could have told Mary, 'Run along then; maybe we can talk after dinner.' But, instead, he said that Mary had chosen the one necessary thing. He chided Martha gently for worrying about details.

A brother's death
In the second event, Lazarus had been dead four days. A grief-stricken Martha met Jesus in the road where they had a discussion about death and resurrection and about Jesus' identity. The same woman who, just the last time they met, had been obsessed about being a good hostess, now pronounced the same stunning discovery for which the apostle Peter was praised (Matthew 16:16):'You are the Christ, the son of God.'

Mary appeared later, and fell on her face at Jesus' feet to say,'Lord, if you had been here...'

Then the two of them, with a crowd of friends, watched Lazarus walk out of the tomb.

Mary's extravagant gesture
In the third story, at a dinner in honour of Jesus, Mary bent over his feet, pouring expensive perfume on him and wiping it with her hair. Judas criticized the waste, and again Jesus defended Mary.

(In Luke 7:36-50 there is a similar but different story, and the woman involved is not

Mary poured precious perfume on Jesus, from an alabaster flask like this Hellenistic one from Egypt. The inscription labels it as containing cinnamon.

▶ **Verse 60** 'The duty of burial took precedence over the study of the Law, the Temple service, the killing of the Passover lamb... But the demands of the kingdom were more urgent still' (Leon Morris).

10:1-24 Jesus commissions 70

Compare this with Jesus' instructions to the Twelve (Matthew 10:5-15). See also Matthew 11:20-27. The number 70 (or 72) may perhaps symbolize the nations of the world (from the list in Genesis 10). They are sent out in pairs. Entrusted with God's good news, they are entitled to support from the people they go to. But they are not to look for luxury (the 'going from house to house', 7, is with a view to a better living). Time is too precious to waste on endless social formalities (4). There is work to be done, a message to be made known. And God himself will judge those who reject it. The 70 are overjoyed at their new power. But greater cause for joy is the certainty of eternal life (20).

▶ **Verses 13-17** 'Alas for... ', rather than 'Woe to... ' We have not previously heard that the Galilean towns of Chorazin and Bethsaida have rejected Jesus. Capernaum was Jesus' base. Tyre and Sidon: heathen cities denounced by the Old Testament prophets. 'Hades': the place of the dead — a metaphorical phrase: 'brought down to the depths' .

▶ **I saw Satan fall (18)** Their ability to exorcize evil spirits is a sign that Satan's power is broken. The preaching of the new age means defeat at last for the power of evil. Jesus rejoices in this fulfilment of his ministry.

▶ **Verses 21-24** echo the tone of John's Gospel.

10:25-37 'Who is my neighbour?'

Only Luke tells the famous story of the 'good Samaritan'. Jesus gives a textbook

Mary. It takes place in the home of a Pharisee named Simon in the Galilee area. Mary anointed Jesus in Bethany, in the home of a leper with the same popular name. The messages of the two stories are totally different.)

Martha was there, being herself, serving the table, though this was not even her house! The one difference was that Martha did not complain.

Mary and Martha both loved Jesus. But Mary was Mary and Martha was Martha. Because of Mary, Christian women feel free to put study and devotional time on the top of their list and know it's OK to love Jesus with passion and express it extravagantly.

Martha followed traditional patterns, worked hard and took her theology lesson at the moment it became relevant, while standing in the road. And the Holy Spirit revealed to her the profoundest of truths.

The oldest daughter

In the modern Middle East there is an 'oldest daughter syndrome' in many families. It happens often, whether or not by plan, that the eldest daughter, taught by her mother how to cook and clean and serve others, becomes trapped in these duties. She will help to raise the younger children, often at the sacrifice of part of her education. Unless someone asks for her early, she is likely not to marry, because she is always at home and invisible to the community.

Usually, she masters the feminine crafts, doing the most perfect embroidery in the village or making the most delicious sweets. When guests come she will jump up to make coffee and to do the scrubbing up after meals. The harder she works, the more the family depends on her.

As the parents age, she is expected to stay at home and care for them, while younger siblings are free. And if the parents should die relatively young, her situation becomes static, because not only does she now have no one to arrange marriage for her, but she is responsible for the house and younger members of the family.

Even after the others marry, she will have no independence. Since it is not proper for a woman to live alone, she must live in the home of a brother, where she may be little more than a servant.

This eldest daughter may accept her role and perform it cheerfully, or she may feel used and be openly jealous of her younger sisters or even her brothers. More commonly she will be driven by responsibility to perform her duty, though she harbours anger underneath.

What elements of this scenario fit the story of Mary and Martha? How did Jesus speak to their situation?

The three stories about Martha and Mary are told in Luke 10:38-42; John 11; and John 12:1-8 (Matthew 26:6-13; Mark 14:3-9).

The desert road drops steeply down from Jerusalem to Jericho. Among these barren hills it is easy to imagine the robbers of Jesus' 'Good Samaritan' story.

An ancient inn stands beside the old road from Jerusalem to Jericho.

The Samaritan in Jesus' story (Luke 10) brought the injured Jew to an inn, like the one modelled *right*, to be cared for.

answer to the lawyer's question about eternal life. Chagrined, and attempting to save face, he asks another. Instead of answering directly, Jesus replies with a parable.

There was a long history of hatred between Jew and Samaritan (see 'Jewish religion in New Testament times'), though the Samaritans, like the Jews, held the law sacred. The Jews regarded them as scum – untouchables. Yet Jesus has this 'enemy' carrying out the law, whereas the injured man's fellow Jews – even the religious leaders – fail. A real 'neighbour' is one who does the loving thing whenever and wherever occasion arises, regardless of the deepest enmity or antagonism.

10:38-42 Martha and Mary
Only Luke tells this story. The two sisters and their brother Lazarus lived at Bethany, near Jerusalem. Martha gets into a state, slaving to prepare an elaborate meal. She would have done better to keep the menu simple and leave time to listen to Jesus, as Mary did. See 'Martha and Mary'.

11:1-13 'Teach us to pray'
Matthew (6:9-13) gives the longer form of the Lord's Prayer. Jesus is supplying both a prayer to be prayed ('when you pray, say...' 2,) and a 'model' (Matthew 6:9, 'in this way') on which to base other prayers.

Jesus' followers come to God, not as subjects to 'the Master of the Universe' but as children to the best of fathers: simply, sharing his concerns and confidently telling him of their own needs. They must not be discouraged if time goes by and they see no answer. Persistence, in the end, wins over even the most reluctant friend – and there is no reluctance to answer on God's part. See also Matthew 7:7-11.

▶ **Hallowed be your name (2)** This expresses reverence for all that God is: 'name' means whole character.

▶ **Daily bread (3)** 'Daily' most probably means 'for tomorrow', and 'bread' 'our essential needs'.

▸ **Verse 4** 'Forgive us… for (not because or insofar as) we forgive.' Since we human beings do forgive others, we can be confident of God's mercy.

▸ **Verse 7** In a poor family everyone slept on a raised section of the one all-purpose room. Hospitality, at whatever time, was regarded as a sacred duty.

▸ **Verses 11-12** Fish and serpents look alike, so do eggs and curled-up scorpions.

11:14-36 Opponents draw Jesus' fire

Verses 14-23: see on Matthew 12:15-37.
Verses 24-26: see on Matthew 12:43-45.
Verses 29-32: see on Matthew 12:38-42.
Verses 34-36: see on Matthew 6:22-23.

Only Luke, typically, records the woman's voice from the crowd. Jesus does not reject her words but makes a more important point (27-28).

▸ **Demon (14)** See on 4:33.

▸ **Beelzebul (18)** See on Matthew 10:25.

▸ **Verse 24** People thought of desolate places as the haunt of evil spirits.

▸ **Verse 26** 'No one can live for long in a moral vacuum. The kingdom of God… means such a victory over evil that evil is replaced with good and with God' (Leon Morris).

11:37-54 Jesus rebukes the Pharisees

Verses 37-41: see on Matthew 15:1-20.
Verses 42-52: see on Matthew 23. In verses 53 and 54 the level of hostility grows.

▸ **Verse 38** The hand-washing was a religious ritual, not a matter of hygiene. The teacher is expected to keep the rules.

12 – 13:9 Warning and reassurance

A warning to the disciples about the danger of saying one thing and doing another (12:1) leads into general teaching about the coming judgment, and how it should affect life here and now. It is essential to be prepared, to get priorities right. Much of this section is paralleled in Matthew.

12:1-12: see Matthew 10:26ff. Jesus' intention is not to frighten but to reassure (6-7). But there is a right 'fear' of God that holds people steady against other fears (4-5, 8-9).

12:13-21: only Luke records the story of the rich but foolish man bent on amassing money and all that it can buy, instead of being 'rich towards God'.

12:22-34: see on Matthew 6:19-34.

12:35-48: see on Matthew 24:45-51.

13:1-9: Roman troops had slaughtered some Galilean pilgrims in the Temple at Passover. People assumed that the victims of the two disasters must have been specially wicked, but that was not true. The whole nation is ripe for judgment and will meet an equally horrible fate if present opportunities for a change of heart are let slip.

▸ **Thousands (12:1)** Not a head-count: a very great crowd.

▸ **12:10** This 'blasphemy' is a whole mind-set: the kind that can attribute Jesus' good works to the devil (11:15).

▸ **12:35** 'Be ready for action'; for freedom of movement at work the long tunic was drawn up through a belt.

▸ **12:49-50** The good news of the gospel will run through the earth like fire. But first Jesus must plumb the depths of suffering.

13:10-17 Woman with a bent back

Only Luke records the story of a woman who would be diagnosed by doctors today as suffering from a particularly crippling form of arthritis. Jesus' compassionate straightening of her fused spine adds to all his other clashes with the Pharisees over healing on the sabbath. See also Mark 3:1-6.

▸ **A spirit (11), Satan (16)** See on 4:33. Satan bears ultimate responsibility for bringing suffering into the world along with sin.

13:18-21 Pictures of God's kingdom

See on Matthew 13, and 'Jesus and the kingdom'.

13:22-35 'Will only a few be saved?'

Jesus does not answer the question directly. Don't ask 'how many'. Just make sure you seek entrance to God's kingdom. Many will try, yet fail (22-29). And there will be surprises (30). Time is limited.

Verses 31-35: Jesus is not bothered by Herod's threats. He knows what lies ahead, and grieves at the fate of the city that will destroy him.

> **❝** *Life does not consist in the abundance of possessions… Do not worry about your life, what you will eat, or about your body, what you will wear. For life is more than food and the body more than clothing.* **❞**
>
> 12:15, 22-23

Jesus' story of the shepherd searching for his lost sheep evokes a timeless image.

A shepherd leads the flock through barren country in the hills of Judea, seeking fresh pasture.

commends a genuinely humble spirit, not false modesty.

Verses 12-14: real generosity does not look for return.

Verses 15-24: Jesus' story of the 'great banquet' is triggered by one of the dinner guests (15). In order to 'eat bread in God's kingdom' (to be saved) it is necessary only to say yes when the invitation comes. But those who rate other things more important will exclude themselves, with no second chance.

▶ **Dropsy (2)** In this condition fluid collects in parts of the body, causing swelling and pain.

▶ **Verse 3** Nothing in Moses' law forbade healing on the sabbath. But Jewish rabbinic rules allowed it only in life-or-death cases.

▶ **Verse 5** The first case may be either 'child' or 'ass'.

14:25-35 Following Jesus will cost

Great crowds are following Jesus, unaware of what it will mean to be his true followers. Loyalty to Jesus must outweigh all other, quite proper, claims. (He is not saying 'hate your family!' but 'love me more', 26.) No one can follow him unless they are prepared for all that this means. They need to reckon up. Can they afford to follow (28-30)? (The price is no less than everything they have, 33.) On the other hand, can they afford to refuse (31-32)?

▶ **Verse 34** Pure salt cannot lose its taste, but the impure 'salt' used in 1st-century Palestine could. Then it was no use on the land, nor would it degrade.

15 A lost sheep; a lost coin; a lost son

In marked contrast to the serious tone of chapter 14 come these three stories about God's joy in finding the lost. Like the shepherd, like the woman, like the father of the 'prodigal son', God never stops caring. He goes out of his way to welcome them back, and every one who is 'found' and returns is a cause for celebration (5, 7, 9, 10, 23, 32).

The Pharisees and scribes who find fault with Jesus for welcoming 'bad' people (1-2) are like the elder son in the story. Unlike God, they show neither love nor pity for those who fail to meet their standards.

14:1-24 One day at dinner

Verses 1-6: on his way to dinner, confronted by human need, Jesus heals a man swollen with 'dropsy', even though it is the sabbath (see also 13:10-17; Mark 3:1-6). His questions, 'Is it lawful?' (3) and 'Wouldn't you...?' (5) leave his critics speechless.

Verses 7-11: guests were carefully seated according to rank and status (as at a formal banquet today), but everyone wants a seat at the top table. Jesus

▶ **Verse 8** Each of the silver coins was a day's wage for a labourer, a real loss for a poor woman.

16 The case of the shrewd manager

Verses 1-13: the story Jesus tells his disciples commends the manager's astuteness, not his dishonesty. He knows how to make money work for him. The debtors are put in his debt by taking up his offer of large discounts. So his future is secured.

Verses 16-17: compare Matthew 11:12-13. The emphasis here is different.

Verse 18: see on Matthew 19:1-12.

The story of the rich man and Lazarus (the only 'named' character in Jesus' stories; 19-31) is special to Luke. Jesus may have taken a popular folk tale, using it in his own way. The scenes are vividly pictured: a rich man with everything, a poor man with nothing. Yet Lazarus goes to bliss, his head resting against the great 'father Abraham' at the heavenly feast (as John's would rest against Jesus at the Last Supper). Justice has been done and there is no changing it (the great chasm). In response to the rich man's plea, Abraham tells him that if the words of scripture do not persuade his brothers to repent, neither will a man coming back from the dead.

Those words are bound to make Luke's readers think of Jesus' own resurrection.

▶ **Verse 9** Friends bought by money cannot get us to heaven. But the way we use our money now may affect our eternal destiny. It is a test of how we could handle wealth of a different kind. Is God, or money, our master?

▶ **Force (16)** 'All who will, press their way into it' (Knox).

17:1-10 Forgiving; faith; duty

To place a hindrance in the way of any believer is a terrible thing (1-2). Sin must be opposed, but with a readiness to forgive and go on forgiving (3-4). The apostles think they need more faith to do that, but it is not a question of 'more' (5-6). Nor must they look for special favours when they have done what they should (7-10).

17:11-19 Ten 'lepers' healed

The men are sent to the priests in order to be declared fit to return to normal society. By going, they demonstrate their faith in Jesus' word. All are cured, but only one, a despised Samaritan, takes the trouble to say thank you.

▶ **Verse 12** 'Leprosy' can refer to several diseases.

▶ **Samaritan (16)** See on 9:51-56 and 'Jewish religion in New Testament times'.

17:20-37 Teaching about Jesus' return

See on Matthew 24. No amount of calculation can fix the time (20-21) or place (37) of Christ's return in judgment. It will be plain for all to see – no secret (23-24). And the world will be caught unprepared, as it was by the flood (26ff.).

▶ **Verse 21** The kingdom is already present in the person and work of Jesus. 'Among', not 'within', is the correct translation.

18:1-14 Two stories about prayer

These parables-from-life appear only in Luke.

Verses 1-8: God is not like the unjust judge. If this woman can persist with her plea, winning justice against such odds, how much more confident of a hearing and of justice can God's 'chosen ones' be. They need to pray and not lose heart, even if the answer is delayed.

Verses 9-14: the Pharisee 'prays' simply to congratulate himself on being better than others, and to rehearse his good deeds. It is the tax collector – the one who finds nothing in himself to be proud of – whom God hears.

18:15-17 Jesus and the children

See also Matthew 19:13-15; and on Mark 10:13-16. To the disciples, the children were a nuisance. But Jesus loved them. Verse 17 makes the same point as the story of the Pharisee and the tax collector. God's kingdom is wide open to all who come in humble trust.

18:18-28 The question of eternal life

See on Matthew 19:16-30. See also Mark 10:17-31 and 'Jesus and money'.

18:31-34 Jesus again predicts his death

See also Matthew 20:17-19; Mark 10:32-34. This is the seventh time Luke has recorded Jesus predicting his suffering: in general terms in 5:35; 12:50; 13:32-33; 17:25; with specific detail in 9:22, 43-45 and here, where he speaks of being handed over to the Gentiles, and of his resurrection.

18:35 – 19:10 Sight for a blind man; a change of heart for Zacchaeus

Jesus nears Jericho, on his journey to Jerusalem.

18:35-43: see on Mark 10:46-52.

19:1-10: Zacchaeus is chief collector for the area, unlike Matthew, who was simply a local collector. But both were social outcasts because of their job. Zacchaeus has made himself a fat living by adding a rake-off to the Roman taxes he was responsible for collecting – fleecing his own people for personal advantage. But, like tax collector Matthew and unlike the 'rich ruler'(18-25), Zacchaeus does not allow his wealth to become an obstacle. The encounter with Jesus makes a new man of him.

> 66 *The Son of Man has come to seek out and save the lost.* 99
>
> 19:10

▶ **Your faith has saved you/made you well (18:42)** His faith did not effect the cure: it was the channel by which he received it.

▶ **Son of Abraham (19:9)** Not simply a Jew, but one whose faith shows him to be a true descendant.

19:11-27 A loan to invest

This story is similar to the parable of the talents in Matthew, though here each is loaned the same modest sum. Verse 11 gives the reason for the story. Jesus, like the 'nobleman', is about to leave his people for a time. In his absence they must faithfully carry out the work given them to do. It is a case of 'use it or lose it'. For the nobleman returns, with authority, to call his servants to account and to execute summary judgment on his enemies.

> 66 *Blessed is he who is coming as King in the name of the Lord! Peace in heaven and glory in the highest heavens!* 99
>
> Jesus enters Jerusalem in triumph: 19:38

▶ **Verse 12** Herod the Great got his kingdom by going to Rome. His son, Archelaus, also went to Rome to be given his title to the kingdom of Judea (followed by a delegation of Jews opposed to his rule). The allusions would not be lost on Jesus' hearers.

▶ **Pound/gold coin (13)** The Greek mina: about three months' wages for a labourer. The men are servants entitled to carry out business transactions, not slaves.

19:28 – 21:38 Jesus in Jerusalem

19:28-48 In triumph, to the Temple

See also Matthew 21:1-17; Mark 11:1-19. Jesus rides into the city on an ass (Zechariah 9:9), not a war-horse. He comes on a peace mission. Sadly, Jerusalem will have none of it, missing God's moment and embarking on a course which eventually led to total destruction at the hands of the Romans in AD 70. The lament in verses 41-44 comes only in Luke.

The purging of the Temple (45-46), Mark says, was the next day. Jesus returned each day, holding people spellbound with his teaching, to the frustration of those who wanted him silenced for ever.

▶ **Bethphage and Bethany (29)** Villages east of the Mount of Olives, two miles from Jerusalem.

▶ **Verse 38** Luke paraphrases for his non-Jewish readers.

▶ **Verse 45** See Matthew 21:12-17. Luke, like Matthew, compresses the events; compare Mark 11:11 and 15ff.

20:1-18 'By what authority...?'; vineyard parable

See on Matthew 21:23-46. See also Mark 11:27 – 12:12.

20:19 – 21:4 Jesus' enemies set traps

See on Mark 12:13-44. See also Matthew 22:15-46.

21:5-38 Signs of destruction and the end time

See on Matthew 24. See also Mark 13.

Verses 8-11: signs of the end.

Verses 12-19: persecution of Jesus' followers.

Verses 20-24: the fall of Jerusalem: phase one of the end.

Verses 25-28: cosmic upheaval and Jesus' return: phase two of the end.

Verses 29-33: the certainty of these events. 'All' (32) must refer to the warning signs, including the fall of Jerusalem. All the indications are that Christ's coming is near: yet God still delays, giving time for the good news to be made known throughout the world. The fig-tree is the first to come into leaf in Palestine.

Verses 34-36: the need to be ready.

▶ **Verse 37** may mean Jesus lodged there, rather than camped out.

22 – 24
Jesus' last hours: the cross and resurrection

22:1-38 Judas turns traitor; the Last Supper
See on Matthew 26:14-29. See also Mark 14:12-25; John 13 – 14.

▶ **Verse 10** It was usually the woman's job to carry water, so this man would have been conspicuous.

22:39-53 On the Mount of Olives; the arrest
See on Matthew 26:30-56. See also Mark 14:26-52. Jesus' real trial takes place among the olives, as he consents to sacrifice his life. Arrest follows swiftly.

▶ **Verses 43-44** are omitted in some texts, on the view that they were added by an early scribe. The evidence points strongly that way. The word agony/anguish, describing Jesus' horror at facing a God-forsaken death (Mark 15:34) occurs only here in the New Testament.

22:54-65 Peter denies Christ; soldiers mock him
Peter is brave enough to keep within sight of Jesus as he is led away. But with nothing to do but wait, courage oozes away and fear takes control. Three times Peter says what he swore he would never say (22:33; Mark 14:29-31). Even his leading disciple denies Jesus. But one look from him is enough to break the big fisherman's heart.

22:66 – 23:12 The trials
See also on Mark 14:53 – 15:15. Blasphemy was a capital charge under Jewish law. The trial by the Sanhedrin Council makes it clear they condemned Jesus to death for his claim to be Son of God.

This model of Jerusalem at the time of Jesus looks towards the Temple area. The houses of the Upper City are on the left. The Roman garrison (the Fort of Antonia) is at the far end of the Temple complex.

The Fort of Antonia, where the Roman garrison was stationed at the time of Jesus' trial, was conveniently close to the Temple in case of trouble.

Jesus was taken to the Fort of Antonia to be tried. There on the 'Pavement' he was mocked and ridiculed. Paving-stones from the 2nd century AD discovered below the Ecce Homo Convent are scratched with the games the Roman soldiers played.

But the accusation is rephrased for the Roman governor. Pilate is not interested in offences against Jewish religious law, so the charges are 'perverting our nation' (sedition), forbidding payment of tax (totally false: 20:20-25) and the treasonable claim to be 'King of the Jews' – the charge on which Pilate's condemnation will rest (see verse 38).

Herod is in Jerusalem for the Passover. If Pilate is attempting to shift responsibility by sending his prisoner to Herod, it does not work. It is strange to find the exchange over Jesus bringing these two old enemies together.

▶ **23:3** The answer is non-committal. What Jesus would mean by the title, and what Pilate would understand, are two very different things. See the fuller record in John 18:33-38.

23:13-31 Sentenced to death

Although acquitted by both Herod and Pilate, Jesus is condemned to death – because Pilate dare not risk another unfavourable report reaching the emperor (John 19:12). So a convicted murderer is

freed, and an innocent man scourged and crucified.

23:32-49 On the cross

See on Mark 15:16-41. Only Luke tells us that one of the mocking robbers repented and was forgiven.

A cross could be the traditional shape or T, X, Y or I-shaped. It had a projection to take the main weight of the body. Prisoners were fastened, hand and foot, by ropes or nails, sometimes with legs twisted and bent to contort the body. Dying this way was a prolonged torture: an object lesson to all who passed by. But the Gospel writers all focus on the meaning of Jesus' death rather than horrific descriptions.

▶ **About the sixth hour/noon (44)** This was the fixed point of the day. Without clocks and watches, times can only be approximate. John says Jesus was sentenced by Pilate at the sixth hour, but may mean simply 'late morning'; Luke that Jesus was on the cross about midday. Mark's 'third hour' seems to place the crucifixion earlier, but again may be taken less precisely as 'getting on in the morning'. The differences are not hugely important.

▶ **Verse 45** The curtain divided the sanctuary from the body of the Temple. Just once a year the high priest passed through to intercede for the people (Hebrews 9:7). Now no intermediary is needed – all may have access to God (Hebrews 10:19-22).

23:50-56 A hurried burial

See on Mark 15:42-47.

24 Jesus alive from the dead!

In the stillness of Sunday morning, as day breaks, so does the extraordinary news. The tomb is empty. Jesus, so recently dead and buried, is alive again!

The details given in the four accounts of what took place on that momentous morning are difficult to harmonize. With any major event, it is hard to piece together information from a number of independent witnesses. But all are clear about the fact – see 'Jesus' resurrection'.

Only Luke records the story of the two otherwise unknown disciples going to Emmaus (13-35), so vividly told that it seems to come first-hand. What happens when Jesus catches up with them – the dramatic mood-swing, and their new understanding: 32, 45 – encapsulates what happened to all Jesus' followers.

When Jesus died, they not only lost a much-loved friend and teacher, but the focus of all their hopes. They were alone and terribly afraid. Jesus had several times spoken not only of his coming death but also of his resurrection (see on 18:31-34), but they did not expect a sequel to the story. Peter, the natural leader, was crushed beyond bearing by the knowledge that he had denied Christ.

Yet within 12 hours everything has changed. The tomb is empty – and Jesus himself has been seen on at least five different occasions, not only by the apostles

The Herod family tomb in Jerusalem, like that of Jesus, was rock-cut and sealed with a heavy circular stone. The bigger picture is taken from the inside, the smaller from outside.

Two friends were making their sad way from Jerusalem to Emmaus, thinking Jesus dead, when a stranger who was Jesus himself caught up with them.

but by other followers too. They recognize him as the real Jesus, not a ghost. They see the crucifixion scars (39-40). He eats with them (43). He appears to Peter (34; 1 Corinthians 15:5), and the apostle is a new man. Despondency, mourning, fear are replaced by indescribable joy (41).

Everything written about Jesus in the scriptures has been fulfilled (44). Now those who have witnessed these things must go out and tell the world that because of Jesus' suffering they can be forgiven (47). Jesus' return to heaven closes Luke's chapter on his life on earth.

▶ **Verses 50-52** Luke compresses events. As he makes clear in his sequel – Acts – the ascension took place 40 days later.

Jesus' resurrection
David Wheaton

In Old Testament teaching the idea of resurrection does not feature prominently (see 'Old Testament views of the afterlife').

Although the idea of rising again was not linked to expectations of the Messiah, Peter in his sermon on the Day of Pentecost (Acts 2:25-28) sees Jesus' resurrection as the fulfilment of Psalm 16:8-11.

Jesus' teaching
Jesus taught about the resurrection in his parables (Matthew 13:36-43; 25:31-46, etc.) and maintained it against the teaching of the Sadducees (Mark 12:18-27). He spoke of a resurrection to judgment, when believers will be raised to experience eternal life in its full and final reality, and unbelievers will rise to condemnation (John 5:19-29; 6:39, 40, 44-59; 11:25-26).

In preparing his followers for his death, Jesus had promised them that he would rise again on the third day (Mark 8:31; 9:31 and 10:34 – Hebrew reckoning is inclusive, and so 'after three days' here = Matthew's 'on the third day', 16:21, etc.).

All four Gospel writers give prominence to the resurrection of Jesus in their narratives (Matthew 28; Mark 16; Luke 24 and John 20 – 21). Paul highlights it as a fundamental fact in the earliest Christian tradition (1 Corinthians 15:1-8).

The evidence
The evidence for Jesus' resurrection demonstrates how, in spite of his promises, the disciples were not

The early morning sun slants across a stone used to seal a 1st-century tomb. 'He is not here. He is risen', said the angels.

expecting Jesus to rise from the dead. The Bible records give a graphic description of their progress from despair to confidence, and so for us there are the following strands of evidence:

■ **The empty tomb** On the first Easter morning the women came to embalm Jesus, expecting to find the tomb sealed and his body inside. Instead, the tomb was open and empty (Mark 16:1-7, etc.).

■ **The missing body** Not only was the body not there, but Matthew, Mark and Luke tell of angels proclaiming that Jesus had risen, while John relates

how the position of the grave-clothes, left as if the body of Jesus had evaporated through them, was enough to convince him (20:6-8). Had Jesus' enemies stolen the body, they could have produced it to disprove the early preaching of the resurrection; had his friends stolen it, they could never have preached with such conviction or displayed such endurance in suffering.

■ **The risen Jesus** All accounts emphasize that the disciples were not expecting to see Jesus alive again. He had to give them proof that it was really Jesus who appeared to them (John 20:15-16, 20, 27; Luke 24:30-31, 37- 39).

■ **The transformed disciples** If we compare John 20:19 with Acts 2:14 we can see how fear was changed to boldness as the disciples became convinced of the fact that Jesus was alive again.

The effects of Jesus' resurrection
■ **For Jesus**
– It vindicated his claims to be the Son of God (Romans 1:4).
– It began the process by which he returned to the glory of heaven (Luke 24:50-51; Ephesians 1:19-21) and released the gift of his Spirit to his followers (John 16:7; Acts 1:8; 2:4).
– It demonstrated the power of God the Father at work in him (Ephesians 1:19-22).

■ **For Jesus' followers** (including Christians in the 21st century!):
– It offers hope for the future, of

▶▶ sharing the glories of heaven (1 Peter 1:3-5; John 14:2-3).
– It gives firm assurance for faith in Christ here and now (1 Corinthians 15:12-20).
– It tells us that Christ has 'pioneered' the way to his Father's presence for all who place their trust in him (1 Corinthians 15:22-23; Hebrews 2:10-15). So he is called 'the firstfruits of those who have fallen asleep'(picture language showing that others will follow where he has led).
– It encourages Christian believers here and now to enter into the benefits of Christ's resurrection (Ephesians 2:6) by developing new attitudes of mind (Colossians 3:1-3), a new experience of victory over sin (Romans 6:5-14) and power for living (Ephesians 1:18-20; Philippians 3:10).

What happened after

All four Gospel writers relate various appearances made by Jesus in the period following his resurrection. In Acts (1:3) Luke tells us that these appearances were spread over a period of 40 days, after which Jesus returned to heaven by ascending from the earth.

His disappearance in this way assured them of its finality (he had vanished into thin air following previous appearances). To have moved in any other direction would have left them with a confusing message, still wanting to search for him on the earth.

The Bible writers portray Jesus as returning to the place of privilege and power, 'seated at the right hand' of the Father (Ephesians 1:20-21; Colossians 3:1; Hebrews 1:3) and waiting for the Father's timing for him to return to earth in

The first Easter Day

Drawing together the evidence of the four Gospel writers, we can suggest a sequence of events as follows:

■ A group of women go to the tomb early on the first day of the week to embalm the body of Jesus (Matthew 28:1; Mark 16:1-2; Luke 24:1, 10; John 20:1a).

■ They discover that the stone has been rolled back (Matthew 28:2-4; Mark 16:3-4; Luke 24:2; John 20:1b).

■ The body of Jesus is no longer in the tomb; instead they see an angel who explains the situation and gives them a message (Matthew 28:5-7; Mark 16:5-7: Luke 24:3-7).

■ The women run back to Jerusalem to tell the other disciples, and are greeted in the main with disbelief (Matthew 28:8; Luke 24:8-11, 22-23; John 20:2).

■ Peter and the 'other disciple whom Jesus loved' go to the tomb and find it empty; they then return home (John 20:3-10; see Luke 24:12, 24).

■ Mary Magdalene follows them back to the tomb, and remains there after they have left. Jesus then makes his first appearance, to her (John 20:11-18; Matthew 28:9; Matthew names Mary Magdalene and 'the other Mary').

■ On that same day he appears to Peter (Luke 24:34; 1 Corinthians 15:5), to the two going to Emmaus (Luke 24:13-32; see Mark 16:12-13), and then to the rest of the disciples, except Thomas, back in Jerusalem (John 20:19-23; Luke 24:36-43; Mark 16:14).

Other appearances are recorded in the four Gospels, Acts 1 and 1 Corinthians 15. What emerges from all the accounts is a remarkable consistency on two points – that Jesus could now reveal himself and disappear at will, and that he showed himself only to his followers.

glory (Mark 13:26-27, 32), to raise the dead (1 Thessalonians 4:13-18) and give them their resurrection bodies (1 Corinthians 15:35-44).

Until then he is our great high priest, having taken our humanity into heaven. He lives to share the concerns of his people (Acts 7:55-56; Hebrews 2:17-18; 4:14-16) and to make intercession for us (Hebrews 7:24-25; 9:24). The fact that he is pictured as being seated at the right hand of God is evidence that his work is completed and that it has been accepted (Hebrews 1:3-14; 10:11-14).

John

Summary

John's story of Jesus is a Gospel of light and love.

Key passages and best-known stories

The Word (1)
Wedding at Cana (2)
Nicodemus (3)
Woman at the well (4)
5,000 fed: 'I am the bread of life' (6)
'I am the light of the world' (8:12-59)
Cure of a man born blind (9)
'I am the good shepherd' (10:1-21)
'I am the resurrection and the life': raising of Lazarus (11)
Mary anoints Jesus (12:1-7)
Jesus' last meal with his disciples (13–17)
'I am the way, the truth, the life' (14)
The true vine (15)
Jesus' prayer (17)
Trial, death and resurrection (18–21)
Jesus and Mary Magdalene (20:11-18)
Thomas the doubter (20:24-29)
Jesus and Peter (21:15-19)

John's Gospel, like the other three, tells the story of Jesus, covering much of the same ground, yet it is strikingly different from Matthew, Mark and Luke. An early church leader, Clement of Alexandria, labelled John as the 'spiritual' Gospel.

■ John supplements the other accounts: he concentrates on the meaning of what took place.

■ John works to a different plan and pattern from the others. His Gospel is much less episodic.

■ He selects from Jesus' many miracles certain 'signs' which show most clearly who he was.

■ He records mainly what Jesus said – especially about himself – in a style very different from Matthew, the other Gospel which concentrates on Jesus' sayings. He includes no parable-stories, but gives us Jesus' great 'I am...' claims.

■ Whereas the other three focus mainly on Galilee, most of the events recorded in John take place in and around Jerusalem at the various festivals. It is possible that Jesus adopted a different teaching style for the nation's capital city and theological centre.

■ John's Gospel speaks of 'the Jews', almost as if Jesus' disciples were not Jews themselves. This is probably for his non-Jewish readers – quite natural, if he was writing the Gospel in Ephesus (see below). His use of the term, without distinction, for Judeans in general and the Jewish religious authorities who opposed Jesus has often been misinterpreted as anti-Semitic. But John is a Jew himself, and he points out that 'many (Jews) believed', particularly as events move towards their climax (see e.g. 11:45; 12:11, 42). And the unbelief of others is something he struggles to account for (12:37-43; compare Paul, agonizing over the same issue in Romans 9 – 11).

The great keynote of John's Gospel is love: 'God so loved the world that he gave his only Son, so that everyone who believes in him... may have eternal life' (3:16). John portrays Jesus as an unquenchable light, shining in the darkness: one who offers the gift of life.

The writer and his readers

The author refers to himself simply as 'the disciple whom Jesus loved' (21:20, 24). He is one of the Twelve, and one of those closest to Jesus and to Peter. The Gospel makes no mention of the apostle John and describes the Baptist simply as 'John'. These clues all point to John, son of Zebedee, brother of James and business partner of Peter and Andrew. If John was not the actual writer (and he may, like Paul, have used a secretary), the connection with him is clearly very close. The early church held that the aged apostle wrote or dictated the Gospel in Ephesus in present-day Turkey.

This is interesting, because the Gospel is clearly written by a Jew from Palestine who combines concepts also found in the Dead Sea Scrolls with 'pre-Gnostic' language and ideas from the Greek and Roman world (see 'Understanding Colossians'). The Jewish 'kingdom of God' translates into 'eternal life' in John. In his prologue he uses the word *logos* (translated 'Word') which has special meaning for both Jews and those in the Hellenistic world. Other examples are his light and darkness themes and the glory revealed through the life of Christ on earth.

The Gospel seems to assume that the readers already know the facts about Jesus' life, and is generally regarded as being written for Christians, Jews and non-Jews. The words 'so that you may believe' in 20:31 which appear to refer to non-believers, may mean 'continue to believe'/ 'be confirmed in your faith'.

The apostle John

John may have been Jesus' cousin (his mother, Salome, being Mary's sister: Matthew 27:56; Mark 15:40; John 19:25). The family fishing business at Capernaum must have been a flourishing one, as the household had hired servants. If the 'other disciple' of 18:15-16 is John it may have been through the business that John was acquainted with the high priest (John 18:15-16). He may also be the unnamed disciple of John the Baptist referred to in John 1:35, 40.

John was certainly one of those who knew Jesus best. John and James (nicknamed by Jesus 'sons of thunder'), with Peter, formed the privileged inner ring of Jesus' band of 12.

When was the Gospel written?

Most scholars think this was the last Gospel to be written, towards the end of the 1st century, though some would place it before AD 70, when the Jewish Revolt against Rome resulted in destruction for Jerusalem.

1:1-18
Prologue

Matthew and Luke begin their story at the time of Jesus' birth, Mark at the start of his ministry. John's introduction goes right back to the very beginning. The story of Jesus does not begin with a human birth: this Gospel concerns 'the Word', one who shares God's own nature (1), who was God's executive in creation (3). When God spoke (see Genesis 1), his Word brought life itself into existence.

In his Gospel, John makes great use of the image of light breaking into the world.

Now comes the stupendous truth: this same Word became a human being in the person of Jesus Christ (14). 'He lived among us,' John says. 'We *saw* his glory.' His life shone out against the darkness of a world which largely failed to recognize him (10) – even his own people (11). But those who did receive him are blessed with God's loving forgiveness (grace, 16). They are accepted and welcomed into God's family, his adopted children (13).

God sent his messenger to prepare his people for Christ's coming (6-7), but the role of his only Son is to make God known (18).

▶ **Word (1)** Greek *logos*. John chooses a word that for both Jew and Gentile 'is the starting-point of all things' (William Temple). It combines the Jewish thought of God's self-expression with the Greek idea of 'Reason' behind everything.

▶ **John (6)** John the Baptist (see Luke 1, Matthew 3, Mark 1), herald of the coming Christ.

▶ **Verse 14** John may be thinking especially of the time when he and Peter and James saw Jesus in his glory, transfigured (Matthew 17:1-8).

1:19 – 2:12
John and Jesus: opening scenes

1:19-34 'There is the Lamb of God!'
John the Baptist's dramatic preaching attracts much attention. But he directs it away from himself. He is not Messiah. Nor will he admit to being the predicted second Elijah (Malachi 4:5; in contrast, Jesus leaves us in no doubt that this prediction was realized in John – Matthew 17:10-13). Nor is he the prophet like Moses, spoken of in Deuteronomy 18:15. As soon as God has shown him his 'Chosen One' (32-34), John directs people to Jesus.

▶ **The Jews (19)** As often elsewhere in the Gospel, John does not distinguish between the general term and 'the Jewish religious authorities' (his meaning here). See introduction.

▶ **Pharisees (24)** See 'Jewish religion in New Testament times'.

▶ **Bethany (28)** This is not the Bethany close to Jerusalem mentioned elsewhere. Its exact location is not known.

▶ **The Lamb of God (29)** A phrase from the Old

Testament sacrifices (Leviticus 4:32-35; see also Isaiah 53:4-12). Sin separates the guilty person from a holy God. But in Old Testament times an animal could be offered as an 'atonement'. Further sin meant repeated sacrifices. Jesus is God's 'Lamb', giving up his life once-and-for-all to 'take away the sins of the world'. Significantly, Jesus dies at the time the lambs are killed for Passover.

1:35-51 Jesus' first followers
See 'The twelve disciples of Jesus' and on Mark 3:7-19. At John's words, two of his followers leave him for Jesus – Andrew, the fisherman (see also 6:8-9; 12:22) and an unnamed follower, possibly the apostle John. The news is too good not to share; so Andrew brings Peter, and Philip (see also 6:5; 12:21; 14:8) brings Nathanael.

▶ **Verses 32-34** John is the first of four witnesses in this chapter who identify Jesus as Son of God/God's Chosen One (41, 45, 49).

▶ **Tenth hour (39)** 'Four in the afternoon' (some versions) is arrived at by counting from 6 a.m. (sunrise). 6 a.m. to 6 p.m. and 6 p.m. to 6 a.m. was the customary Jewish way of reckoning time. But it has been argued that John's Gospel may reckon time in the Roman way, from midnight to 12 noon and 12 noon to midnight.

▶ **Verse 42** 'Cephas' (the Aramaic name) and 'Peter' (from the Greek) both mean 'the rock-man'.

▶ **Verse 48** Nathanael was following the Jewish custom of meditating on the scriptures under his fig-tree. It seems likely, from Jesus' words in verse 51, that he was thinking about Jacob's dream of a stairway between heaven and earth (Genesis 28:12). Jesus applies the picture to

> 66 *In the beginning was the Word: the Word was with God and the Word was God. He was with God in the beginning... The Word became flesh, he lived among us, and we saw his glory... No one has ever seen God; it is the only Son, who is close to the Father's heart, who has made him known.* 99
>
> 1:1-2, 14, 18

Nathanael was meditating under a fig-tree – a place of deep shade out of the fierce heat of the sun – when Philip came to tell him about Jesus.

himself. In 21:2 Nathanael appears to be one of the Twelve, but he is not named in the lists, unless Bartholomew was another name for him.

▶ **Son of man (51)** Jesus' favourite description of himself. The title echoes Daniel's vision of the future king (Daniel 7:13-14).

2:1-12 Jesus at a wedding

Jesus' first miracle has a homely setting. The wedding festivities normally lasted a week, and when the wine ran out the bridegroom (who provided it) must have been highly embarrassed.

This is the first of seven 'signs' selected by John. All have a purpose – they actively support the claims Jesus made, and are intended to lead to/confirm faith. No lesson is drawn from this story, but the water is generally taken as a symbol of the old religious system which Jesus transforms.

▶ **Cana (1)** Nathanael's home town (21:2) about 6km/4 miles north of Nazareth.

▶ **Verse 4** No one, not even his mother, has the right to put pressure on Jesus. But his reply is not as harsh as some translations make it sound. 'Your concern and mine are not the same' is probably the meaning. 'My time' is significant in John, pointing to the fulfilment of Jesus' mission.

▶ **Verse 6** The water pots were there for the ritual washing of hands and utensils.

> **❝** *For God so loved the world that he gave his only Son, so that everyone who believes in him may not perish but may have eternal life.* **❞**
>
> 3:16

2:13 – 3:36
Jesus in Jerusalem for Passover

2:13-25 Traders ejected from the Temple

See on Matthew 21:12-17. John places this incident at the beginning of Jesus' ministry, the other Gospels at the end. He may be overruling strict chronology for more important considerations. Jesus, the Messiah, visits 'his' Temple and asserts his unique authority – to be instantly questioned by the authorities about his right to do so.

▶ **Passover (13)** See Matthew 26:14-29.

▶ **Verses 20-21** John assumes his readers know about Jesus' death and resurrection. The Temple was in a special sense the place of God's presence – the closest people could come to God himself. With the coming of Jesus that changed: he could describe himself as the Temple of God. Those who had seen Jesus had seen the Father (14:9). See 'Herod's Temple', for the Temple in Jesus' day.

3:1-21 Interview with Nicodemus

Nicodemus, a member of the Jewish (Sanhedrin) Council chooses to come to the teacher unobserved, at night. Later he comes out openly on the side of Christ (7:50-51; 19:39). Jesus' harsh words about

At the wedding at Cana, in Galilee, Jesus performed his first miracle – changing water into wine, when supplies ran out.

some Pharisees clearly did not apply to all.

Verse 3 is John's only use of 'kingdom of God', the phrase so frequently used in the other three Gospels. 'Eternal life' (16) he uses constantly. To enter God's kingdom means a radical new beginning. The new age Jesus brings in is not bound by the old cycle of physical birth and death. Eternal life involves something which can only be described as rebirth, being 'born of the Spirit'.

Verses 16-21 may be Jesus' words or John's comment. They contain the heart of the Gospel message. Jesus comes to save – all the world can benefit, but only if they believe. The consequence of Jesus' coming, for those who refuse him, is judgment.

▶ **Wind/Spirit (8)** In Greek as in Hebrew the same word has both meanings. So there is a play on words here.
▶ **Serpent/snake (14)** See Numbers 21:4-9. The 'lifting up' of Jesus is at his crucifixion.

3:22-36 John says 'I am not the Messiah'

For a while Jesus' ministry overlaps with John the Baptist's, and Jesus draws the bigger crowds. John's reaction is exemplary. No trace of bitterness or jealousy sours his gladness at Jesus' God-given success. He is happy to let Jesus (rightly) take the limelight, and to fade into the background himself (30).

Verses 31-36 may be the Baptist's words or John's comment.
▶ **Verse 22** See 4:1-2.
▶ **Verse 24** See Mark 6:17-29. The writer here as elsewhere assumes that his readers know the basic facts (though Mark 1:14 and Matthew 4:12 say John was in prison before Jesus began his public ministry).

4:1-42
Jesus and a Samaritan woman

Jesus chooses the short route from Jerusalem to Galilee which takes him through Samaria – normally avoided by Jews, since over 700 years of religious and racial prejudice separated the Jew from the Samaritan (see on Samaritans in 'Jewish religion in New Testament times'). Add to

---

Jesus' seven 'I am...' statements: the seven 'signs'

1. **The bread of life** (6:35)
   Sign: 5,000 fed (6:5-14)
2. **The light of the world** (8:12)
   Sign: cure of the man born blind (9:1-41)
3. **The gate for the sheep** (10:7)
4. **The good shepherd** (10:14)
5. **The resurrection and the life** (11:25)
   Sign: Lazarus raised from the dead (11:1-44)
6. **The way, truth and life** (14:6)
7. **The true vine** (15:1)

The rest of the signs:
– Water into wine at the wedding in Cana (2:1-11)
– Cure of the official's son (4:46-54)
– Cure of the sick man at the Pool of Bethesda (5:1-9)
– Jesus walks on Lake Galilee (6:16-21)

See 3:2; 6:14; 7:31; 20:30-31 for why John recorded these signs. 2:13-22 points to the ultimate sign: Jesus' own resurrection.

Women at a well in the hills of Judea. A Samaritan woman, coming to a well near her home, had a life-changing encounter with Jesus.

The Pool of Bethesda – where Jesus healed a sick man – with its five shady 'porches', has been discovered deep below the level of present-day Jerusalem.

this the Jewish prayer, 'Blessed art thou, O Lord... who hast not made me a woman', and the Samaritan woman's surprise (9) when Jesus talks to her is understandable.

Tired and thirsty though he is, Jesus never ignores human need. As the conversation develops it becomes clear that the woman's need is not physical (as she thinks) but spiritual (7-15), that she has a moral problem which she side-steps with a theological question (16-24). She sees Messiah as the answer to everything – and he stands before her (25-26).

As a result of this seemingly insignificant encounter, many others believe – some through the woman's testimony, more through Jesus' own words.

▶ **Sychar (5)** Probably Askar, within walking distance of Jacob's well.

▶ **Verse 13** See Jesus' promise: 7:37-38.

▶ **Verse 20** For the Samaritan, Mt Gerizim was the centre of worship; for the Jew, Jerusalem. Jesus says that the place is unimportant. What matters is that worship should be from the heart and with true faith.

4:43-54
Galilee: Jesus heals an official's son

This is the second of the signs recorded by John (see on 2:1-12 above). Jesus never performed miracles simply to impress. They were intended, as here (verse 53), to lead to and strengthen faith. John's purpose in recording them is precisely the same.

5
Jerusalem again

5:1-18 Trouble on the sabbath
The healing of a chronically sick man at the Pool of Bethesda (Bethzatha) is John's third sign (see 2:1-12; 4:43-54).

Jesus clashed with the religious authorities a number of times over healing on the sabbath (Mark 3:1-6; Luke 13:10-17; 14:1-6; John 9). It was not the general principle of the sabbath as a special day that he disagreed with (he regularly attended the synagogue) but the petty restrictions imposed by the religious authorities, which often worked against God's purpose in giving people a weekly day for rest and worship. Here he is attacked on two counts – sabbath-breaking and blasphemy – because he puts his own work on the same level as God's (17). God's activity in the world did not finish with the creation.

▶ **38 years (5)** gives us some measure of the man's despair. He had been there so long and tried so many times to be first into the water, that he had virtually given up hope.

▶ **The Jews (10)** Clearly here and in 18, religious authorities opposed to Jesus.

5:19-47 In the name of God
Those who opposed Jesus were right: he was making himself 'equal to God' (18) – though not independent of him (19). 'I can do nothing on my own... (I do) the will of him who sent me' (30). But his claims for himself are mind-blowing. As 'Son of God'
■ he knows God's plan (20)
■ he has God's authorization for all he says and does (19, 30)
■ he has power to give eternal life (21, 24, 40)

he has the right and authority to judge all people, living and dead (25-29).

A man who makes these claims must be 'mad, bad, or (truly) God'. What support can he give them?
- the word God spoke at his baptism (37)
- the testimony of John the Baptist (33-35)
- the evidence of his own miracles (36)
- the words of Old Testament scripture (39).

▶ **Moses (45)** See Deuteronomy 18:18. Jesus is the Prophet God told Moses he would raise up.

6
Galilee

6:1-21 Food for 5,000; Jesus walks on the lake

See on Mark 6:30-56. See also Matthew 14:13-36; Luke 9:10b-17. These are John's fourth and fifth signs (see 2:1-11;

The Herod family
E.M. Blaiklock

When the Romans organized the East in 63 BC, Pompey appointed a priest named Hyrcanus to rule Galilee, Samaria, Judea and Perea. Hyrcanus had an astute vizier, an Idumean named Antipater, who knew how to use his power shrewdly for his family's advantage. He secured his two sons, Phasael and Herod, in key governorships and, when Antipater was murdered in 43 BC, the two young men succeeded jointly to the viziership in Hyrcanus' court.

Herod the Great

Phasael was soon a victim of a Parthian raid which followed the assassination of Julius Caesar, who had intended pacifying their frontier. Herod escaped to Rome, and so impressed Octavian (the future Augustus) that he received a mandate to recover Palestine, which he did between 39 and 36 BC. He successfully carried on a pro-Roman administration for 34 years, marked by the building of the Roman port and base at Caesarea and a temple to Augustus at Samaria.

Simultaneously, he conciliated the Jews, who hated him for his Edomite blood, by building the great Temple at Jerusalem (see 'Herod's Temple'). He was a superb diplomatist. He divided the opposition by suppressing the old aristocracy – yet married Mariamne, one of their number, and set up a nobility of officials. He stimulated loyalty to his house by founding a pro-Herod Jewish party, the 'Herodians'; established a bureaucracy modelled on that of the Ptolemies in Egypt; and secured his power by a mercenary army and a system of strongholds. The price he paid for his dangerous living was tension within his own family, murder, and ultimately paranoia.

This was the Herod who was king when Jesus was born. Herod's jealousy of this 'rival king' and ruthless slaughter of the children at Bethlehem is in keeping with what we know of his character.

Herod's will divided the kingdom which he had ruled so long, so dexterously, and so ruthlessly.
- **Archelaus**, son of the Samaritan woman Malthace, took over

Judea and Idumea, by far the choicest share.
- **Herod Antipas**, son of the same mother, received Galilee and Perea.
- And **Philip**, son of a Jewess named Cleopatra, took Iturea, Trachonitis, and the associated territories in the north-east.

Archelaus

Archelaus, who inherited his father's vices without his ability, bloodily quelled disorders which broke out in Jerusalem. The result was a wider uprising, which required the strong intervention of Varus, Governor of Syria.

Archelaus' stupid rule continued until AD 6, when Jewish protest secured his banishment. Judea was placed under the control of a procurator (a governor responsible to the Roman authorities).

Herod Antipas

Herod Antipater (Antipas), on the other hand, equalled his father's long reign. The Herodian flair for diplomacy bolstered the puppet rule while Tiberius was emperor. But Antipas misread the mad Caligula.

4:46-54; 5:1-9).

That day when Jesus fed the crowd of people stands out clearly in John's mind, and he tells us details missing from the other three accounts. He remembers which disciples replied to Jesus' question; he recalls the lad who gave up his lunch. And in the account of how Jesus came to them that evening, walking across the Lake, he remembers how far they had rowed from shore when they saw him.

▶ **Passover (4)** This is the second Passover

> **66** *What God wants you to do is to believe in the one he sent.* **99**
>
> 6:29

mentioned in John (see 2:13). A year later, at the next Passover, Jesus died (11:56; 12:1).

6:22-59 'I am the bread of life'

In the synagogue at Capernaum (59) Jesus takes the bread as his starting-point for a deeper lesson.

The crowd is all in favour of a Messiah who can provide free meals for the asking (26, 34). No one can live without food. But Jesus comes to provide 'bread' that will satisfy more than physical hunger. He is

---

▶▶ He sought a royal title, was deposed and exiled, an ordeal loyally shared by the notorious Herodias.

It was Antipas who imprisoned and executed John the Baptist. He also had a brief meeting with Jesus, when Pilate referred the prisoner to Herod during the trial.

Herod Agrippa I

Herod Agrippa I, the grandson of the first Herod, was brought up at Rome, managed Caligula better, and so succeeded to Philip's tetrarchy when Philip, the best of the three brothers, died. When Antipas was exiled, Galilee and Perea were added, and in AD 41, Agrippa received from the Emperor Claudius the whole of his grandfather's domains.

This is the Herod who appears in Acts 12. He died of a grave intestinal disorder in AD 44 at the age of 34, and Palestine came wholly under Roman rule.

Herod Agrippa II

Agrippa left a teenage son who was set up by Claudius as king of Chalcis in AD 48. In AD 53, the domains of Philip the tetrarch and Lysanius were added by Claudius to this realm, together with an area on the western side of Galilee, including the new town of Tiberias.

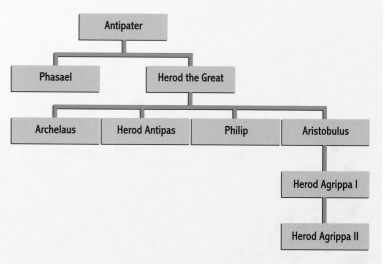

The appointment carried the title of king, so in AD 53 Agrippa became Agrippa II, last of the Herodian line.

He appears in the New Testament only in the brilliantly told story of Acts 25, where, as the procurator Felix' guest, he heard the defence of Paul.

the bread God gives, the one who comes to give life to the world (33). Those who believe in him will never hunger (35).

Paradoxically, it is by laying down his own life that Jesus is able to give others a life 'for ever' (51). To receive this life it is necessary to accept his sacrifice (52-58). At the Last Supper Jesus gave visible expression to this same truth (Matthew 26:26-28).
▶ **Manna (31)** See Exodus 16 and Deuteronomy 8:3.

6:60-71 Reaction
Those who put a crudely literal interpretation on Jesus' words were disgusted. The

The hills across Lake Galilee glow with the reflection of the setting sun. This was the time of day when Jesus was called on to provide food for a hungry crowd of people.

law forbade the drinking of blood. Meat had to be specially butchered to meet the law's requirements. Yet the reason for that rule would have helped them to understand Jesus. Leviticus 17:11 says, 'it is the blood that makes atonement, by reason of the life'. So Jesus is saying, 'I am atoning for your sin; avail yourselves of my sacrifice.'

Many of his followers turn away: they do not want this sort of Messiah. But the Twelve remain, in growing faith. Peter speaks for them all: 'Lord... you have the message of eternal life... we have come to know that you are the Holy One of God' (68). Yet one will betray him (70-71).

'I am the bread of life,' Jesus said. Bread is not an optional extra. It is a basic staple food on which life depends. A boy in Bethlehem ('house of bread') carries home the day's bread supply for his family.

7 – 10:21
To Jerusalem for the Feast of Shelters

7:1-13 Danger
Last time Jesus visited Jerusalem there was trouble, ending in a plot against his life (chapter 5). In Judea his life is still in danger. But his 'time' (the time of his death) has not yet come, so he avoids publicity.
▶ **The Jews (1, 13)** See introduction.
▶ **Shelters/Tabernacles (2)** September/October: the eight-day Jewish harvest festival, commemorating the nation's desert wanderings. See 'The great festivals'.
▶ **Brothers (3, 5)** See Matthew 13:55-56.
▶ **Not going (8)** Some manuscripts add 'yet'.

7:14-52 A mixed response
As opposition mounts, individuals take sides. Jesus' teaching (40) and his miracles (31) convince some. Others raise difficulties (27, 41-42). But no one who genuinely wants to do God's will is left in doubt (17).

Jerusalem in New Testament times

Peter Walker

Within the Jewish world of Jesus' day no city could compare with Jerusalem. Jewish people from Galilee and all the countries of the Jewish Dispersion made regular pilgrimages to the 'holy city', going up for the three major festivals and paying an annual Temple tax. For 100 years (163 – 63BC) they had sovereignty over Jerusalem, but in the New Testament period their city was under Roman rule.

By this time the city had expanded from the tiny 'Zion' of King David (now the Lower City) to include the wealthy district of the Upper City to the west and (more recently) the northern suburbs. Yet the Temple enclosure still made up a fifth of the city. Overlooking the Temple there was the Antonia fortress, where the Roman soldiers were garrisoned —

THE CITY OF JERUSALEM

- Present wall of the Old City
- Fort Antonia
- Pool of Bethesda
- ?Golgotha
- Temple mount
- Kidron Valley
- Gennath Gate
- The Temple
- Herod's palace
- **UPPER CITY**
- Tyropean Valley
- Pinnacle of the Temple
- **LOWER CITY**
- Aqueduct
- Pool of Siloam
- Hinnom Valley

ready to quell any unrest (see Acts 21:31ff. and 'Herod's Temple').

There was a bridge across the Tyropoean Valley so that the Temple could be entered directly by

those coming from the Upper City (an area which included Caiaphas' house, the home of John Mark and Herod's palace).To the north of the Temple was the pool of Bethesda with its five porticos (John 5:2), to the south the Temple steps – the regular means of access to the Temple (Luke 2:22ff.). Further to the south was the ancient pool of Siloam (John 9:7).

Unlike the present Turkish walls of the Old City (the grey dotted line on map), the northern wall (the 'Second Wall', built by Herod the Great) was almost certainly indented. Although Jesus' crucifixion clearly took place outside the wall of his day it is not impossible that the traditional location *within* the present city is correct. A few years later this site was brought within

The main sites of importance in New Testament times are:

1 Herod's Temple
2 *Kidron Valley*
3 *Mount of Olives*
4 Garden of Gethsemane
5 Fort of Antonia
6 Pool of Bethesda
7 Pool of Siloam
8 *Hinnom Valley*
9 Herod's palace
10 Golgotha ('Place of a skull', the traditional site of the crucifixion)
11 [Gordon's Calvary]
12 City of David
13 [Western (Wailing) Wall]

the 'Third Wall' built by Herod Agrippa I (AD 41 – 44).

Jesus clearly made several visits to Jerusalem (Luke 2:22-51; 10:38-42; 13:34; cf. John 2:13; 7:14), but his final visit was the climax of his ministry. He hinted to his disciples at what it would involve: 'for it is impossible for a prophet to be killed away from Jerusalem' (Luke 13:33; compare Mark 8:31).

But some had other ideas. Would Jesus usher in the 'kingdom of God' (Luke 19:11)? If he was truly the Messiah, would he build a new, cleansed Temple, or expel the Roman authorities?

Jesus would fulfill some of these hopes in unexpected ways, but he also had his own agenda: to challenge Israel's leaders, to assert God's reign and his own authority over the Temple, to pronounce solemn words of judgment, to reveal his own identity, and also to accomplish for God's people a profound rescue (or new 'exodus': Luke 9:31).

This clash of agendas is seen most clearly when Jesus enters the city (Luke 19:37-46). Inspired by the panoramic view from the Mount of Olives (*below*), the crowds welcomed Jesus as Zion's King (even though, strictly, God himself was its true King: Isaiah 52:7). Yet

Jesus then burst into tears because of what he knew would soon happen to Jerusalem and its Temple: 'they will not leave within you one stone upon another; because you did not recognize the time of your visitation from God' (Luke 19:44).

Jerusalem was missing its moment of destiny: the Son of God entering the City of God. No wonder his arrival in the Temple caused a stir!

After this, Jesus taught the crowds in the Temple daily (Luke 20:1ff.), but it was on the Mount of Olives that he gave his disciples more details about Jerusalem's destruction (Mark 13). And it was here – in Gethsemane, an olive-grove at the foot of the Mount – that he prayed before his arrest.

The next day, after his trial before Pilate in Herod's palace, he was led out through the Gennath Gate to be crucified.

These dramatic events, culminating with Jesus' resurrection outside the city walls, affected the way that Jerusalem was viewed by the New Testament writers – the 'holy city' had become, instead, the place of the Messiah's crucifixion.

They were still loyal to the city (e.g. 1 Corinthians 16:1-9; Acts

21:17) but Paul concluded that the earthly city, unlike the 'Jerusalem above', was 'in slavery with her children' (Galatians 4:25-26; cf. Revelation 11:9; 21:2). Hebrews 13:12-14 sums up this new way of thinking: 'Jesus also suffered outside the city gate; let us then go to him outside the camp and bear the abuse he endured. For here we have no lasting city, but we are looking for the city that is to come.'

When the city and its Temple were destroyed in AD 70 this confirmed for Christians their new perspective on Jerusalem, signalling that God's purposes had entered a decisive new stage with the coming of Jesus to the city.

Present-day Jerusalem, the view of the city from the Mount of Olives, looking across the Kidron Valley to the ancient Temple area.

empty-handed, to the anger of the Pharisee authorities. The rabble may know nothing of the law (49) but Nicodemus does – yet they will not hear him (50-52).

▸ **Verse 15** Jesus did not have a rabbi's training to interpret the law.

▸ **One work (23)** The earlier healing of the sick man at the Pool of Bethesda: 5:9.

▸ **Dispersion (35, some versions)** The Jewish communities in Greek (Gentile) cities abroad.

▸ **Verse 42** They cannot have heard the story of Jesus' birth. The Old Testament reference is Micah 5:2.

One of the great annual festivals was Tabernacles/Shelters. This was one of the occasions when Jesus went up to Jerusalem (John 7). The priests enter the Temple through the Water Gate, carrying a golden flagon of water. A trumpeter follows, heading a lively procession of people carrying branches and bowls of fruit.

Jesus' words on the last day of the feast (37-38) draw their imagery from the ceremony appointed for each of the previous days of the festival, when water from the Pool of Siloam was offered to God. They echo Isaiah 55:1: 'Oh, come to the water all you who are thirsty', calling the people back to God. Jesus is a bubbling spring, reviving and transforming thirsty human hearts. 'He was speaking of the Spirit,' John explains (39).

Again the response is mixed, and the guards sent to arrest him come back

When Jesus gave sight to a man born blind, he spread mud on the man's eyes and told him to wash in the Pool of Siloam (pictured here).

7:53 – 8:11 Caught in the act
Although this story is probably genuine, it is unlikely that it originally belonged here (some manuscripts place it at the end of John's Gospel, others insert it after Luke 21:38). The lawyers are trying to trap Jesus. They intend to push him either into contradicting the Mosaic law, or into falling foul of the Roman authorities, who did not allow Jews to carry out a death sentence. But Jesus did neither – nor did he condemn, or condone, the woman's conduct. He gave her a second chance.

8:12-59 'I am the light of the world'
Jesus again uses one of the ceremonies of the feast to explain his own mission. At dusk they lit four great golden candelabra to symbolize the pillar of fire by which God guided his people through the desert by night (Exodus 13:21). Jesus says he will give the light which is life itself to all who follow him (12).

There is no validity in claims like these, made without back-up, say the Pharisees (13). Jesus calls God to witness (18), but they are mystified by his talk of 'the Father'.

He goes on to strengthen his claims (12-30). Unlike everyone else, he knows where he comes from and where he is going. And he knows what lies ahead.

Many Jews believe him (30). But his promise that the truth will make his disciples free upsets those who reckon they 'have never been slaves'. Physical descent from Abraham is not enough, Jesus says (39ff). All are slaves to sin and need the Son to give them the freedom of God's household (34-36). Those who have spiritual life will respond to God's message (47).

Jesus can be no Jew himself, to say such things: he must be a crazed Samaritan (48, 52)! Does he claim to be greater than Abraham? Yes. What is more, he takes to himself the name of God: 'I am' (58), the eternal one.

9 A blind man sees; the sighted close their eyes

This sixth sign underwrites Jesus' claim to be the light of the world. It also says something about the problem of human suffering.

- The Bible makes a clear connection between suffering and the sin which has been endemic since the original downfall of the human race. But this does not mean that particular people suffer because of their own (or their parents') sin (3).
- God can bring good out of suffering.

Here the man's blindness leads to an encounter with Jesus. His eyes are opened and he sees (7). His mind is opened and he believes (35-37).

By contrast, the sighted allow prejudice and pride to blind them to the truth (40-41). Confronted by a miracle, all they can see is a broken sabbath rule (16). Their minds are closed. They will not listen to the man's own simple logic (30-34).

▶ **Verse 6** Jesus uses the methods of popular medicine (saliva was thought to have healing properties). But the important thing is the man's faith, demonstrated by his ready obedience (7).

▶ **Sent (7)** Because the water was channelled from another source.

10:1-21 'I am the good shepherd'

This passage follows straight on from chapter 9. The shepherd was a familiar figure in Palestine. He spent much of his life with his flock. His own sheep knew and responded to his voice. He led (not drove) them to fresh grazing, and guarded them from wild animals by lying across the entrance to the sheepfold at night (so Jesus can say, 'I am the gate', 9). In the Old Testament, God is often called the shepherd

of Israel. And his chosen leaders are also the nation's 'shepherds'.

Now Jesus chooses to describe himself as the good shepherd. The phrase sums up so much: the close, personal relationship between himself and each of his followers; the absolute security they have in him; his leadership and guidance; his constant company; his unfailing care; his life, 'laid down for the sheep'.

Again, his claims divide his hearers (19-21). He has power to lay down his life and to take it up again. Everything rests on his special relationship with the Father (15, 17, 18).

▶ **Other sheep (16)** Jesus' concern goes out beyond the Jewish nation to the waiting world. Jew and non-Jew, slave and free, man and woman, all are one flock (see Galatians 3:28).

'I am the good shepherd,' Jesus said. He spoke of himself as both the shepherd and the 'gate' of the sheep, caring for his people and keeping them safe. Having gathered the sheep into the fold, walled and topped with thorns, the shepherd lay across the entrance to sleep.

Places mentioned in John's Gospel

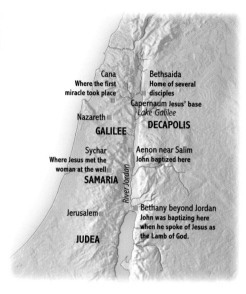

Cana
Where the first
miracle took place

Bethsaida
Home of several
disciples

Capernaum Jesus' base
Lake Galilee

Nazareth

GALILEE

DECAPOLIS

Sychar
Where Jesus met the
woman at the well

Aenon near Salim
John baptized here

SAMARIA

River Jordan

Jerusalem

JUDEA

Bethany beyond Jordan
John was baptizing here
when he spoke of Jesus as
the Lamb of God.

10:22-42
Jerusalem: Feast of Dedication

The eight-day feast of Hanukkah – the festival of lights – takes place in December. It commemorates a great Jewish victory under the Maccabees and the rededication of the desecrated Temple.

The people remain in suspense over Jesus' identity because they will not believe (24-26). Again he rests his authority on God, 'the Father' with whom he is one (29). They are ready to stone this man who tries to make himself God (33). But all that he does bears witness to the truth of his claim, 'The Father is in me and I am in the Father' (38).

11
'I am the resurrection and the life'

The raising of Lazarus is the seventh and last great sign in John's Gospel. Jesus claims he can give people new, eternal, spiritual life: here is the proof. Ahead lies Jesus' own death and resurrection.

Jesus knows that Lazarus will die – but death will not have the last word. It is for the 'glory' of God (4) and so that the disciples will believe (15). So he does not

hurry. The disciples take Jesus to mean that the illness is not terminal (12), and try to dissuade him from a dangerous journey (8).

Neither the disciples nor the two sisters could understand Jesus' behaviour, but the outcome for them all was a strengthening of trust in him (15, 26-27, 40, 42). Jesus himself *is* resurrection-and-life. Martha already knows him to be Messiah and Son of God. Mary knows he could have saved Lazarus from death. Neither could have imagined what they were about to witness. Behind the tears of Jesus (33) lies more than natural sorrow for his friends: he is 'deeply moved' (33, 38) with anger at the tyranny of death, 'the last enemy'.

The raising of Lazarus is decisive – for faith and life on the one hand (45); for hatred and death on the other (53). Only a little while now to Passover, when Jesus' own 'hour' will come. He is already a wanted man (57).

▶ **Thomas (16)** See also 20:24-29.
▶ **Verse 50** The high priest's words took on a significance he never dreamed of.

12
Final days of public teaching in Jerusalem

12:1-8 Mary's precious perfume
See on Mark 14:1-11.

12:9-11 Plot to kill Lazarus
Many Jews believe in Jesus because of the man brought back from the dead (see also 11:45-48; 12:18-19). So the chief priests plot to kill Lazarus too.

12:12-19 Jesus rides in triumph into Jerusalem
See on Luke 19:28-48 and introduction to Matthew 21. See also Mark 11:1-11. John's account is the briefest, and the only one to connect the welcoming crowds with the news of Lazarus' resurrection (17-18). To the Pharisees opposed to Jesus it seems as if 'the whole world is following him'.
▶ **Branches of palm (13)** The symbol of victory.

12:20-36 Death and glory

Some Greek (= Gentile/non-Jewish) converts seek Jesus out – and all at once he is face to face with his destiny. He knows 'the hour has come'. His discourse (23-36) is full of paradox: life multiplied through death; the glory that comes by way of the cross; light and darkness (echoing 1:4-11).

With a final appeal to 'believe in the light', Jesus withdraws. His last days will be spent with his disciples (13 – 17): there is much to tell them, and little time left.

▶ **Love, hate (25)** The meaning is 'love more'/'love less'. The other Gospels talk about 'trying to save' and 'losing'.

▶ **Verse 27** This prayer is very like the one the other Gospels record, in Gethsemane.

▶ **Ruler of this world (31)** Satan, the 'prince' of evil; see also 14:30; 16:11.

12:37-50 The unconvinced

At the end of Jesus' public ministry and despite all his miracles, most of his own people, the Jews, remained unconvinced. Many of the religious authorities *did* believe, but were too afraid of the Pharisee hard-liners to say so openly. So it happened as the prophet Isaiah said it would.

'I have not come to judge the world but to save the world,' Jesus says (47). Nonetheless, to reject him is to reject God, to spurn life and light and invite judgment (44-50).

▶ **God has... (40)** 'We have to remember the Hebrew idiom, which often states what God foresees is going to happen as though it was inevitable' (Tasker). In the Greek text of Isaiah 6:10 it is the people themselves who stop up their ears.

▶ **Saw his glory (41)** Since the Father and Son are one, Isaiah, in his vision of God in the Temple (6:1), saw Christ.

13 – 17:26
Jesus' last words to the Twelve

13:1-20 The Master's example

Jesus is at supper with the Twelve for the last time (see on Matthew 26:14-29). They have been arguing over who is greatest (Luke 22:24). Jesus' reply is to strip and wash their dusty feet. The Master willingly makes himself their slave (Luke 22:27). Here is the role-model for his followers.

▶ **I am (19)** See also 8:24, 28. This is God's own name: Exodus 3:14.

13:21-30 Judas, the traitor

We know from Luke 22:3-6 that Judas has already volunteered to help the priests make a secret arrest. Now the moment has come. The rest of the disciples have no idea of what is afoot. But Jesus knows. 'It was (literally) night.' But in this Gospel light and darkness take on deeper meaning (1:4-9). These were Jesus' darkest hours,

Jesus taught in the porches of the Temple area in Jerusalem.

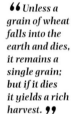

66 *Unless a grain of wheat falls into the earth and dies, it remains a single grain; but if it dies it yields a rich harvest.* **99**

Jesus speaks of his death: 12:24

Jesus withdrew from stressful days in the city of Jerusalem to the nearby village of Bethany, to enjoy the hospitality of his friends.

though nothing could extinguish the light of his life (1:5). Judas, by contrast, stepped from the light into a darkness from which there would be no return (3:19-20; Matthew 27:3-5).

▶ **The disciple Jesus loved (23)** Generally taken to mean John (see introduction). It seems an unnatural way for John to refer to himself, but no more natural if this is someone else referring to him.

13:31-38 'Love one another'

Jesus sees his approaching death (and what it will achieve) as God's glory revealed. He spoke similarly of the death-and-raising of Lazarus (11:4). He has set the supreme example of love. His 'new commandment' to his followers is to love one another with a love like his.

Peter, puzzled by Jesus' talk of going where he cannot follow, claims more than

The peace of God
Robert Willoughby

Peace is one of the main things which human beings long for. So it is hardly surprising that the risen Jesus makes peace central to what he says to the disciples when he meets them behind locked doors.

'Peace be with you! As the Father has sent me, I am sending you' (John 20:21).

Jesus probably used the Hebrew word *shalom* which can be taken simply as a greeting. But it is equally likely he is pointing out that, in his death and resurrection, he has obtained peace for his followers.

Jesus knew that his disciples were agitated and worried about their own future and he has kept on reassuring them that things will work out for the best (John 14:1, 27; 16:33).

The idea of peace, *shalom*, has a rich Old Testament background. It can simply mean the absence of war, but more often it implies a sense of wholeness and general well-being. Sometimes it even implies prosperity or safety. This is usually tied up with society's or the individual's relationship with God.

It is God who brings peace, both politically and spiritually. It is for this God-given peace that the priests were instructed to pray in

the words of Aaron's blessing:

'The Lord bless you and keep you; the Lord make his face to shine upon you and be gracious to you; the Lord turn his face toward you and give you peace' (Numbers 6:24-26).

In Jeremiah 28 we read about false prophets who were so aware of the people's longing for peace that they promised it even when the people had forfeited any right to it by their disobedience. Jeremiah makes it clear that real peace cannot be experienced by people who are in rebellion against God.

Only God can truly bring peace and we are conscious of this when Jesus stands amongst his disciples after the resurrection. This is what the company of angels had promised when they witnessed the birth of Jesus:

'Glory to God in the highest, and on earth peace to those on whom his favour rests' (Luke 2:14).

Paul understood this and links the gift of peace to the cross of Christ where humanity is put right with God. The sin which cuts a person off from God can be forgiven and that person can become a friend of God. According to Paul, such peace leads to joy even as we suffer because perseverance,

character and hope are the result.

For individual believers peace is a 'fruit' of God's Spirit in their lives as they rely upon God and live for him. They are described as particularly blessed when they take up the role of peacemaker. Clearly the peace which they have experienced in their relationship with God is good news for others, too.

Just as the cross could bring about peace between Jews and Gentiles – the greatest racial barrier in the ancient world – so the good news of what Jesus has done can bring peace and overcome all barriers today.

Christ's followers have a responsibility to deliver that message. This is why Jesus adds, 'As the Father has sent me, I am sending you.'

KEY PASSAGES ON PEACE

John 20:19-23; Romans 5:1-11; Ephesians 2:14-18; Philippians 4:6-7; Numbers 6:22-27; Jeremiah 28

Love
Robert Willoughby

'A new command I give you: Love one another. As I have loved you, so you must love one another. By this everyone will know that you are my disciples, if you love one another.'

For most people, these words from John's Gospel (13:34-35) would sum up the Christian message. They occur early on in Jesus' farewell message to his disciples, before he is arrested and sent to his death. They follow on from Jesus' own great example of humble, practical love, when he took the servant's role and washed his disciples' feet.

These chapters (John 13 – 16) present a group of disciples who are anxious at the prospect of losing Jesus and concerned about how they will cope in his absence. So it is significant that Jesus stresses the basis of their Christian commitment, to love each other.

Throughout John's Gospel Jesus points to the closeness of the loving relationship which he himself has with his Father in heaven. God himself *is* love and is the source and measure of all love.

It is because God loves the world that he sends Jesus to be the Saviour of the world. And it is because of Jesus' obedience to the will of God his Father that the Father loves him and does everything that Jesus asks. They are completely one in what Jesus says and does.

This is the kind of discipleship which Jesus wants from his followers. It is rather like the Old Testament concept of covenant, where the loving God makes and keeps an agreement with others,

binding himself to those who love him in a way akin to marriage.

Christ's followers are also expected to show love towards those who might naturally be their enemies.

Luke records Jesus' parable of the Good Samaritan, told in answer to a lawyer who, knowing God commanded him to love his 'neighbour', asked the question,

> **❝** *Love is patient, love is kind. It does not envy, it does not boast, it is not proud. It is not rude, it is not self-seeking, it is not easily angered, it keeps no record of wrongs. Love does not delight in evil but rejoices with the truth. It always protects, always trusts, always hopes, always perseveres. Love never fails.* **❞**
>
> 1 Corinthians 13:4-8

'Who *is* my neighbour?'

Samaritans and Jews normally hated each other but Jesus approved of the actions of the Samaritan in the story, who helped a Jewish man ambushed, robbed and left for dead.

Paul writes that the requirements of the Old Testament Law are completely fulfilled by those who act in love. On several occasions he links love with hope and faith as the essential characteristics of the Christian – love being the greatest of the three. He also describes love as a 'fruit of God's

Spirit' – a natural product in all who have the new life God gives in Christ.

However, like us, the early Christian churches were far from perfect. The Christians in Corinth thought of themselves as being especially 'spiritual'. But they were quarrelsome and took sides with a number of different leaders and splinter groups. Their actions showed that they had not understood the basic Christian attitude of love towards others.

At the heart of his first letter to the Corinthians, Paul describes in detail what true Christian love is really like. He points out that no matter what great knowledge or gifts a Christian possesses, the true measure of spiritual worth lies in self-giving love.

KEY PASSAGES ON LOVE

John 13 – 17; 1 John 4:7-21;
Matthew 5:43-48; Luke 10:25-37;
1 Corinthians 13; Galatians 5:22-23;
Exodus 34:6-7

he can deliver. Jesus knows he will deny, rather than die (38; 18:15-18).

▶ **As I told the Jews (33)** See 7:34; 8:21.

14 'I am the way, the truth, the life'

The disciples are worried and upset by the talk of betrayal and the thought of Jesus leaving them. So Jesus speaks reassurance, but leaves Thomas even more mystified (5). Jesus is the way to God, the truth, and the one who makes the eternal life of God available to all who will receive it (6). Philip wants to see God, not realizing that he has already seen him, in Jesus (8, 9).

Soon Jesus will return to the Father (12, 28), and it is something to be glad about (28). He is making the approach-road for men and women to come to God (6). He is going to get a permanent home ready for his disciples, and in due course he will come for them (2-3). His return to God will bring new power in action, new

certainty in prayer (12, 14). Best of all, his followers will have a Helper: the Holy Spirit will come to be with them always and everywhere (not limited by a physical body as Jesus had been). He will teach and counsel and bring to mind all that Jesus has said (16-17, 26). And Jesus' own unshakeable peace will be theirs (27).

For their part, the disciples must continue to love and trust him (1). And the way to show their love is to do all that he says (15, 21, 23).

15 – 16 'I am the true vine'; more about the promised Helper

Supper is over. Jesus and his disciples are leaving for Gethsemane (14:31; 18:1). The conversation continues. There is not much time left.

15:1-17: in the Old Testament, Israel is pictured as the vine, brought out of Egypt by God and planted in the new land – but so often failing to yield the fruit God expects. Jesus is the *real* vine, fulfilling God's purpose where Israel had failed and bringing into being a new Israel (the 'branches' are those who believe in him).

Every branch of a vine grows directly from the main 'stock'. When they are cut back, branches which have borne fruit are pruned to within an inch or two of the stock. They remain/'abide' in the stock for most of the year as it grows around them. Then the branches grow out rapidly to bear fruit again. Branches which have not borne fruit at all are cut right back, and are fit only for burning.

15:18 –16:4a: Jesus' followers no longer belong to the world as they once did. He has made them part of himself and they will inevitably attract hatred, just as Christ himself did. But Help is at hand (15:26). Even so, there will be those who think they are serving God in seeking to kill the followers of Jesus. (Paul confesses he was one such: Acts 22:3-4.)

16:4b-15: Jesus returns to what he has already said to them (13:33; 14:16, 25): his going means the coming of the Spirit in his place, to prove to people how wrong they are about sin and judgment (8-11) and to lead his followers into a deeper understanding of the truth (13-15).

A vine with the main 'stock', branches growing from it, bunches of grapes on the fruitful branches, and the unfruitful branches cut off to be burnt. 'I am the vine,' Jesus said. 'You are the branches.'

16:16-33: there will be grief and sadness (at Christ's death), but only for a little while. The disciples will see him again (at the resurrection) and know lasting joy. There is a testing time ahead, but the battle between Jesus and the world is won (31-33)!

▸ **Bear fruit (15:4, 16)** Galatians 5:22 gives examples: love, joy, peace, patience, kindness, goodness, faithfulness, humility and self-control.

▸ **16:25, 29** Jesus has been using 'figures of speech', 'veiled language': he has taught often by picture and (in the other Gospels) by parable. Soon he will speak plainly. 'Now', it seems to the disciples, he is beginning to do so.

17 Jesus' prays for himself and for his followers

Jesus' work is complete (4), all but the final 'hour'. He has passed God's message on. He has made God known. Now there remains only death and the glory he set aside to become a human being.

But his followers (the disciples and those who believe through their teaching, 20) will be left bereft in a hostile world. So he prays that God will protect them (15); that their lives may be shaped by the truth of God's word (19); that they may display such unity among themselves that the world will be shaken out of its disbelief (21); and that they may, in the end, be with him in his glory (24).

▸ **Verse 12** The reference is to Judas.

▸ **Verse 24** Compare John 1:14.

18 – 21
Trial, death – and resurrection

18:1-12 Betrayal and arrest

See on Matthew 26:30-56. See also Mark 14:26-52; Luke 22:39-53. John omits Jesus' prayer in the garden. But he tells us the name of the slave, and that the swordsman was Peter.

▸ **Verse 1** See map, 'Jerusalem in New Testament times'.

18:13 – 19:16 Jesus stands trial

See on Mark 14:53 – 15:15, which covers the sequence of events; Luke 22:54 –

23:31. See also Matthew 26:57 – 27:26. John, perhaps in the interests of non-Jewish readers (see introduction), gives more space to the Roman trial than to the Jewish one.

The detail John fills in shows a close knowledge of what happened – the cold night; the charcoal fire (18:18); the blow to the prisoner (18:22); Jewish religious scruples over entering the Roman's house at such a time (18:28); the exchanges between Jesus and Pilate, and Pilate and the Jews; the terrible national apostasy as God's people declare they have no king but Caesar.

▸ **Annas and Caiaphas (18:13-14)** Unlike the other Gospels John does not mention the Jewish Sanhedrin Council. Jesus answers to the powerful former high priest, Annas (18:12-13, 19-24), father-in-law of the then high priest Caiaphas. The others have the actual trial before Caiaphas, which is much more likely.

▸ **That year (18:13)** The high priest held office for more than a year. John means 'this particular year'.

▸ **A cock crowed (18:27)** As Jesus had predicted: 13:38.

▸ **19:14** Preparation Day/the day before Passover: the lambs were killed that day, to be eaten at the Passover meal after sunset (the 'next day' by Jewish reckoning). There is a deep significance in Jesus dying on the day the lambs were killed. In this event, he held his Passover meal a day early (with no lamb).

On the question of time, see on Luke 23:44 and on John 1:39.

19:17-37 Jesus crucified

See on Mark 15:16-41; Luke 23:32-49. See also Matthew 27:27-56. Again John's account shows a vivid, eye-witness recollection of events – the details of the inscription (20-22); the seamless tunic (23-24); the moment when Jesus entrusted his mother to John's care (26-27); the incontrovertible evidence of Jesus' death (34).

▸ **Verse 31** Jewish law said that the bodies of criminals must not be left hanging after sunset (Deuteronomy 21:23).

▸ **Verse 34** John is implying more than that Jesus was without question dead. As a Jew, he could not help seeing special significance in the flow of

> *Love of God is the root, love of our neighbour the fruit, of the Tree of Life. Neither can exist without the other; but the one is cause and the other effect, and the order of the Two Great Commandments must not be inverted.*
>
> William Temple

> *Eternal life is this: to know you, the only true God, and Jesus Christ whom you have sent.*
>
> 17:3

blood (for sacrifice) and water (for cleansing). Jesus' death brings forgiveness and new life.

19:38-42 Burial

See on Mark 15:42-47. See also Matthew 27:57-66; Luke 23:50-56. The death of Jesus brings two secret disciples out into the open. Only John mentions the part played by Nicodemus (see 3:1-15).

20 Jesus alive again!

See on Luke 24. See also Matthew 28; Mark

16. This Gospel gives a personal account of what happened – what John heard and saw for himself, and what he learned from Mary Magdalene. Thomas the realist's momentous declaration of faith – 'My Lord and my God!' – is the climax of the whole Gospel. John's purpose in writing is to bring his readers to just such an assured and clear-cut belief in Jesus (31): that they may find 'life' by trusting him. He cannot tell everything about Jesus (30; 21:25), but what is told is enough.

Across the Kidron ravine from the city of Jerusalem is the Garden of Gethsemane, the twisted forms of the ancient olive-trees recalling Jesus' agony on the eve of his death.

Mary Magdalene
Frances Fuller

Mary Magdalene was singularly well prepared to witness to the facts about Jesus' ministry, his death and his resurrection.

She was a woman changed by Jesus, having had seven demons driven out of her life. We can't know exactly what these were, but at that time a mental disorder or an extremely painful and disruptive illness was often blamed on a demon.

After her healing she travelled with Jesus and his disciples, along with other women who believed in him and supported his ministry. Whenever any of these women are named, she appears in the short list, often being mentioned first. This probably indicates leadership in the group. She would have witnessed his miracles, heard his sermons and profited from his teaching.

Mary had some material resources and used them for Jesus, because the group of women not only cared for his needs and those of his disciples in practical ways, but also financed their journeys.

She is the only one of the women who is mentioned by every Gospel

writer in the record of who was present when Jesus was crucified. Though many followers ran away before that fearful event, several faithful women, including Mary Magdalene, were there. John pictures her standing with the mother of Jesus.

She was present when Joseph of Arimathea laid Jesus in the tomb, hastily on Friday before sunset. She then went home to prepare spices and perfumes for anointing his body, and on Sunday morning she was the first at the tomb. She found it empty and went to tell the disciples.

After two of the disciples came and saw and ran back home, she lingered in the garden weeping, apparently because she had been robbed of the opportunity to honour him by taking care of his body. Jesus then appeared to her and sent her to proclaim the news that she had seen the risen Lord (she was the first!) and that he would ascend to his Father. When she told the disciples, they did not believe her. Later he rebuked them for this.

And then she disappears from

the record, not being mentioned in Acts or in any of the Letters. Does this mean that she had no role in spreading the gospel? Or did she go on quietly telling others what she had seen and heard? Did they believe her? Was she among those scattered in the persecution of the church in Jerusalem? Where did she go? What would she like to say to modern Christian women?

Mary Magdalene's story is told in John 19:25; 20:1-18; Luke 8:1-3; 23:49, 55-56; 24:1-11; Mark 15:40-41, 47; 16:1-11; Matthew 27:55-56, 61; 28:1-10

After Jesus' resurrection the disciples returned to Galilee. Early one morning, after they had spent a whole night fishing but made no catch, Jesus called to them from the water's edge. He had lessons still to teach them.

▶ **Verse 7** John sees the grave-clothes and head-cloth lying undisturbed, still in place. But now an empty space separates the head-cloth from the rest. No one could steal a body and leave the grave-clothes like that. Jesus' body can only have passed through them. So John took note, and believed.

21 Jesus in Galilee with his followers

Only John tells us how Jesus came to the seven of them as they were fishing, just as in the old days. John was there. He remembers how many fish they caught, and their surprise and relief at finding the net intact. He remembers how Jesus gave Peter the chance to cancel out his three-fold denial with the three-times-repeated question, 'Do you love me?'; how he restored Peter to his old place as leader, and gave him the task of caring for his people. He remembers Peter's question about his own destiny – and sets the record straight.

The Gospel closes with an affirmation of the truth of what is written. It was 'that other disciple, whom Jesus loved' (20) who 'spoke of these things and wrote them down'. The community testifies to the truth of what he said (24).

▶ **Verse 18** A prediction of Peter's execution. Tradition says he was crucified in Rome when Nero was emperor.

Acts

Summary

The Good News of Jesus spreads from Jerusalem to Rome, from the Jewish to the Gentile world.

Chapters 1 – 5
The church in Jerusalem
Jesus' ascension
Pentecost

•

Chapters 6 – 9
The gospel spreads
Stephen, the first martyr
Saul's conversion

•

Chapters 10 – 12
Peter and Cornelius:
God accepts all nations!
Escape from prison

•

Chapters 13 – 15
Paul's first mission
Jerusalem conference

•

Chapters 16 – 18
Paul at Philippi, Athens, Corinth

•

Chapters 19 – 20
Paul at Ephesus

•

Chapters 21 – 28
Paul, the prisoner
Arrest in Jerusalem
Caesarea: Paul's defence
Voyage to Rome

The book of Acts covers a period of some 30 years, from the birth of the church on the Day of Pentecost to Paul's imprisonment at Rome. It describes the spread of Christianity around the northern Mediterranean – through present-day Syria, Turkey and Greece, to the heart of the Roman Empire. The 'acts' related are mainly those of the apostles Peter and Paul, though the book might well be called 'the acts of the Spirit of God'. It is under the direction of the Holy Spirit that the new-born church bursts through the national frontiers of Israel to become an international, worldwide movement. (See 'The Holy Spirit in Acts'.)

Acts is the only book of its kind in the New Testament. Like the Old Testament histories, it is more than a simple history book. Acts is 'salvation history'. God's purpose to save the world, revealed gradually in the Old Testament and fulfilled in Jesus, continues in the mission of the church.

The present order of the New Testament books hides the fact that Acts is a sequel to Luke's Gospel – book two of a two-part work addressed to an individual. Luke writes for Theophilus, a sophisticated, educated Roman who already knows something about Christianity (see on Luke 1:1-4).

Who wrote it?
All the evidence, from earliest times, points to Paul's 'dear friend Luke, the doctor'. Luke is the only non-Jewish (Gentile) writer in the New Testament. He may have come from Antioch, or Philippi. Although we have few facts about his life, his writings prove him to be a skilful writer and a generally reliable historian. We know, from the way he changes from 'they' to 'we' in Acts (16:10;

Time-chart
There are not enough fixed points to be exact, but the dates below are accurate within a year or two either way.

AD 30	The founding of the church in Jerusalem (Acts 1 – 2)	48	Apostles confer at Jerusalem (Acts 15)	58-60	Paul in prison at Caesarea (Acts 24 – 26)
32/35	Paul's conversion (Acts 9)	48-51	Paul's second mission (Acts 15:36 – 18:22)	60-61	Paul appeals to Caesar and sails for Rome (Acts 27)
34/37	Paul's first visit to Jerusalem (Acts 9:26ff.)	50	Paul reaches Corinth (Acts 18)	61-63	Paul under house arrest in Rome (Acts 28:30)
45 or 46	Famine relief sent to Jerusalem from Antioch (Acts 11:27ff.)	53	Paul's third mission begins (Acts 18:23)		
45 or 46	James executed (Acts 12:2)	54-57	Paul at Ephesus (Acts 19)		
46 or 47	Paul's first mission (Acts 13 – 14)	57-58	Paul in Greece (Acts 20)		
		58 (June)	Paul reaches Jerusalem (Acts 21)		

It was on the Mount of Olives that the risen Jesus took leave of his disciples, and was 'taken up to heaven'.

66 *When the Holy Spirit comes upon you, you will be filled with power, and you will be witnesses for me in Jerusalem, in all Judea and Samaria, and to the ends of the earth.* 99

Jesus' last words to his followers: 1:8

20:5; 27:1), that he witnessed many of the events he describes with such dramatic detail.

He was with Paul at Philippi. He made the fateful journey with him to Jerusalem, stuck by him during a two-year detention at Caesarea, and shared the voyage and shipwreck on the way to Rome. Luke had plenty of opportunity to obtain his other information first-hand – from Paul and Barnabas and others in the church at Antioch; from James, the Lord's brother, among others at Jerusalem; and from Philip and his daughters at Caesarea. And we know from Luke 1:1-4 just how concerned he was to get at the facts.

Why did he write?

In the preface to his Gospel Luke tells us that having gone carefully over the whole story, he decided to write an ordered account for Theophilus, 'so that your Excellency may learn how well founded the teaching is that you have received'. His earlier work dealt with all that Jesus 'began to do and teach', from the beginning to the day he 'was taken up to heaven'. In Acts he tells how the salvation Jesus claimed to bring works out in reality, for Gentiles as well as Jews. Opposition cannot stifle it. In every place new groups spring up and

continue to meet together.

As Luke describes all this, he takes pains to show that, although the new teaching often led to disturbances, the Roman authorities themselves cleared Christians of the charges brought against them.

See also '"Good news!" – from the first Christians'.

When was Acts written?

Paul has been in prison in Rome for two years at the end of Acts. The book ends on an optimistic note, though without prospect of Paul's release. There is no hint of his death (probably AD 64-65), of Emperor Nero's persecutions, or the Jewish Revolt (AD 66-70). The most likely date would therefore seem to be about AD 63, though a later date is possible.

1 – 8:1a
The church is born: Jerusalem

1:1-14 Luke's preface; Jesus' 'ascension'

The first part of Luke's work (his Gospel) is an account of all that Jesus did and taught during his life on earth. Acts continues the story after his return to God (the 'ascension' described in verses 9-11), when his work continues through the apostles, empowered by the Holy Spirit at Pentecost (chapter 2). It shows how the promise in verse 8 was fulfilled:

- in Jerusalem (2:1 – 8:1a)
- Judea and Samaria (8:1b – 11:18)
- and way beyond (11:19 to the end).

▶ **Verse 6** The question stems from verse 3. It seems the apostles still see God's kingdom in nationalistic terms, expecting Israel in the end to become an independent state.

▶ **A cloud (9)** The sign of God's glory (compare also Exodus 40:34 and Luke 9:34-35) and the means of conveying Jesus from them.

▶ **Verse 10** The white clothing indicates angels.

▶ **Sabbath day's journey (12)** Jewish law limited travel on the sabbath to 2,000 cubits – about 1km/two-thirds of a mile.

▶ **Mary... and his brothers (14)** This is the last time Jesus' mother is mentioned in the New Testament, and the first time his brothers are associated with the disciples. We know that James, at least, had seen the risen Jesus (1 Corinthians 15:7).

1:15-26 The twelfth apostle

As far as we know, this is the last time the apostles use the time-honoured method of casting lots. It is not just a 'lucky dip'– the decision is made after much prayer. The 12 apostles parallel the 12 tribes of Israel, so the number must be made up. The twelfth man must have been with Christ through-out his earthly ministry, and have seen him after the resurrection.

▶ **Verses 18-19** Matthew 27:3-8 says Judas hanged himself. Maybe two different stories were circulating.

2:1-13 'These men are drunk!'

With the coming of the Holy Spirit at Pentecost the waiting is over. Tongues of flame that all can see denote an inner change which is quickly evident. The apostles and disciples become the new church, full of life and power, utterly different from their former fearful selves. And the change is permanent.

▶ **Pentecost (1)** The old Jewish festival of Firstfruits, which took place at the beginning of the wheat harvest. It was 50 days after the Passover, the time of Jesus' crucifixion.

▶ **Verses 2 and 3** Both Hebrew and Greek use the same word for 'wind' and 'Spirit'. The wind and the tongues of flame are signs of the presence and power of God.

▶ **Each heard in his own language (6)** The audience of Jews and converts were from widely scattered countries (see map below). Now, to their astonishment, each hears his own mother tongue being spoken by these Galileans. The curse of Babel (Genesis 11:1-9) is dramatically reversed.

2:14-47 Peter's moving speech

The impassioned address delivered by a transformed Peter evokes an immediate response. They have killed Jesus by allowing him to be crucified. God has raised him to life (23-24). But they can be forgiven (38-39). God is calling them to himself. (Peter delivers a similar message in chapters 3 and 10; Paul in chapter 13.)

The baptism of 3,000 people is followed by a new, joyous sense of community. This finds practical expression in a readiness to share money and possessions. It is sustained by a new pattern of life (46).

▶ **The third hour (15)** 9 a.m., and on that day there was fasting till mid-morning.

▶ **Breaking of bread (46)** Luke's term for Paul's 'Lord's Supper'. It took place in the context of a shared meal.

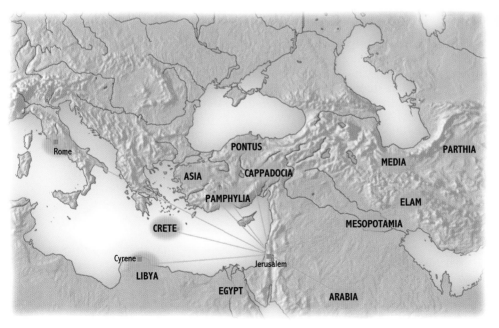

Peter's audience on the Day of Pentecost

Following the gift of God's Spirit at Pentecost, Peter and the others met daily in the Temple courts. These shady colonnades where people gathered to listen to the teachers are re-created in this Temple model.

3 A cripple walks!

Healing and teaching, both made possible by the power of the Spirit of God, go together here, as they did in the ministry of Jesus. The man was sitting at the Temple gate because his disability barred him from entry (2 Samuel 5:8). As soon as he can walk, he goes in. Something begins to happen when the passersby really *look* at the beggar and he looks up at them (4-5). Peter's message here is much the same as in chapter 2, calling his fellow-Israelites to repentance and faith.

▶ **The ninth hour (1)** 3 p.m. Prayer times were early morning, afternoon (as here) and sunset. The first two coincided with the morning and evening sacrifices.

▶ **Solomon's Porch (11)** The colonnade that ran along the east side of the Court of the Gentiles.

4:1-31 Peter and John questioned

It is the teaching, centring on the risen Christ, which annoys the Sadducees – naturally enough, since they denied the possibility of resurrection. (Paul later divides the Pharisees and Sadducees over the very same question: 23:6.) The resurrection was at the heart of the Christian message from the beginning. Despite the arrest of Peter and John, numbers continue to grow (4-5). The Council may warn, but the apostles cannot stop speaking (18-21). Released, they pray for boldness, and their prayer is answered (24-31).

▶ **Annas... Caiaphas (6)** Annas was senior ex-high priest, his son-in-law, Caiaphas, ruling high priest (AD 18-36).

▶ **He is the stone (11)** A quotation from Psalm 118:22.

▶ **Verse 13** 'Ordinary men of no education'; 'untrained laymen'.

▶ **Miracles (30)** This prayer too was answered: see 5:12ff.

4:32 – 5:11 Ananias and Sapphira

The pooling of property was voluntary, but some were prompted less by real generosity than by a desire to impress. In lying to the church, Ananias and Sapphira were practising deceit against God himself. The terrible consequences serve as an example to the whole community.

▶ **Barnabas (4:36)** Later chapters show how aptly he was named. A leader in the church at Antioch, he and Paul were sent out together as missionaries. Paul benefited from Barnabas' encouragement – so too did Barnabas' young cousin, John Mark.

▶ **5:9** 'Similar occurrences can be attested from primitive societies where a curse of this kind can have a cataclysmic effect in causing death by shock' (Howard Marshall).

5:12-42 Apostles arrested and questioned

It was like the days of Jesus in Galilee all over again, so many were being healed by the apostles. No wonder the Jewish authorities grew jealous of their enormous influence. Their swift deliverance from prison and the angel's command further convince the apostles of their mission. Threats, imprisonment, even the lash, are of no avail against the power of God.

▶ **Peter's shadow (15)** Shadows were thought to have magical powers.

▶ **Verse 28** The apostles openly held the Council responsible for Jesus' death, and they fear reprisals.

▶ **Hanging him on a tree (30)** The upright of the cross was a fixture, and might well be a sawn-off tree trunk. See also Deuteronomy 21:22-23.

▶ **Gamaliel (34)** A well-respected leader of the Pharisees (Paul's teacher).

▶ **Verses 36-37** The Jewish historian Josephus tells Theudas' story by name, but dates it a generation later than Judas! Judas, for the resistance, headed a protest in AD 6 against paying tax to Rome.

6:1-7 Administrators appointed

Complaints come from the Greek-speaking, non-Palestinian Jews of unfairness in the daily share-out. The apostles' answer is to let them choose seven of their own number – men of spiritual calibre – to oversee these practical matters. At least two left a permanent mark on the young church: Stephen, a powerful preacher, the first martyr (chapter 7), and Philip the evangelist (8:4-40).

6:8 – 8:1a Stephen martyred

Stephen is (falsely) charged with blasphemy (6:11) and brought before the Jewish Council, just as Jesus was. He seems to have been among the first to foresee the inevitable break with Jewish worship which the new teaching entailed. He wants to 'alter the traditions Moses handed down' say his accusers (6:14).

Stephen's lengthy defence (7:2-53) takes the form of a review of the nation's history. The court knows the facts, but the interpretation is revolutionary. And the sting lies in the tail (51-53). Israel of old rejected the prophets from Joseph and Moses onwards. The present generation has rejected the Messiah himself. Verses 44-50 are Stephen's answer to the charges about the destruction of the Temple. A permanent building to 'house' God was never more than second-best.

▶ **Freedmen (6:9)** Roman prisoners and their descendants, later given their freedom.
▶ **Forty (7:23, 30, 42)** A round figure for a generation but also a number with special significance, marking 'each new development in the history of God's mighty acts' (R.A.H. Gunner).
▶ **7:42** God allows people to suffer the consequences of their wrongdoing.
▶ **Handed down by angels (7:53)** According to Jewish tradition, accepted by the first Christians (Galatians 3:19; Hebrews 2:2).
▶ **The witnesses... Saul (7:58)** The prosecuting witnesses, by law, had to cast the first stones – though in other respects this was little more than a lynching. The 'young man' Saul was probably in his 30s. He appears here for the first time, sharing the responsibility for Stephen's death. ('Consenting' may mean that as a member of the Jewish Council he cast his vote against Stephen.)

The scene burnt into Saul's mind (22:20), and must have played a part in preparing him for his dramatic conversion to the new faith (chapter 9). From chapter 13 on, as the apostle Paul (the Roman version of his name) he takes the leading role in Acts.

8:1b – 9
Persecution spreads the Good News about Jesus

8:1b-25 Simon the sorcerer
The persecution that follows Stephen's death leads to the first broadening of the church's outreach. The attack seems to have concentrated on Stephen's fellow-Hellenists (Greek-speaking Jews), leaving the apostles free to remain in Jerusalem.

Wherever the scattered believers went they took the message with them – in Philip's case with such marked success that two of the apostles come down to see what is happening. It is Philip's *power* which draws Simon, and he covets the power to convey the gift of the Spirit, needing Peter's stern words to set him right (21ff.).

▶ **Verse 5** Though hated by the Jews (see on Luke 10:25-37), the Samaritans, too, believed

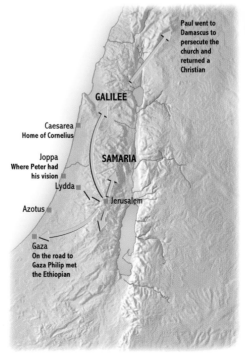

Paul went to Damascus to persecute the church and returned a Christian

The gospel begins to spread

GALILEE

Caesarea
Home of Cornelius

Joppa
Where Peter had
his vision

SAMARIA

Lydda

Jerusalem

Azotus

Gaza
On the road to
Gaza Philip met
the Ethiopian

in a coming Messiah (John 4:25). See Samaritans in 'Jewish religion in New Testament times'. They were ready to hear, as Jesus had said (John 4:35-42), and responded eagerly.

▶ **Verse 10** Simon sees himself as the sole agent of the supreme God, which explains his offer in verse 18.

▶ **That they might receive the Holy Spirit (15-17)** Every believer has the Spirit of God – see Romans 8:9; 1 Corinthians 12:13. But there is special significance in the visible sign of the coming of the Spirit – given when the apostles officially recognize these members of the despised enemy nation as equal citizens in God's kingdom.

8:26-40 Queen's treasurer converted

At the height of Philip's flourishing Samaritan campaign God calls him away to meet the need of an individual. Eunuchs were barred from the Temple, but God knows this foreigner is ready to receive the Good News about Jesus.

▶ **An Ethiopian (27)** The man, a Jewish convert, was treasurer of the old kingdom of Cush, in northern Sudan.

" As (Saul) was... approaching Damascus, suddenly a light from heaven flashed around him. He fell to the ground and heard a voice saying to him, 'Saul, Saul, why do you persecute me?' "

9:3-4

Saul was on his way to Damascus, determined to stamp out the whole Christian movement, when Christ challenged him, in a vision.

▶ **Candace (27)** The title of the queen mother who ruled the country on behalf of her son. The king himself, deified as the child of the sun-god, was considered too holy for such secular functions.

▶ **Scripture (32)** Isaiah 53:7-8. The quotation is from the Greek (Septuagint) text which differs slightly from the Hebrew (Masoretic) text on which our Old Testament is based.

▶ **Caesarea (40)** Philip seems to have settled at this sea-port and brought up a family. See 21:8-9. Azotus: the old Philistine city of Ashdod.

9:1-31 Saul meets Jesus

Saul's confrontation with Jesus, on the road to the old Syrian capital, Damascus, marks a turning-point in the history of the early church. The story is told three times in Acts: once, here, by Luke, and twice by Saul/Paul himself – 22:5-16; 26:12-18. Never has any conversion brought a more radical change. The blinding light leaves Saul sightless for three days, with nothing to do but think. By the time Ananias reaches him, Saul the persecutor has become 'Brother Saul' – a man who will suffer much for the cause he tried to stamp out. His immense energy is given at once to preaching Jesus as Son of God (20): and opposition begins.

When Paul escapes to Jerusalem, no one will believe him – until Barnabas comes to the rescue (27; see 4:36-37)

▶ **The Way (2)** The church was known by this name before the people of Antioch invented the new name 'Christian' (11:26).

▶ **Persecute me (4)** Those who persecute his followers persecute Jesus himself.

▶ **Tarsus (11)** A university city with a population of half a million; meeting-place of East and West, Greek and Oriental.

9:32-43 Peter raises the dead

Now there is peace at last (31), Peter is free to visit the Christian groups. A healing at Lydda leads to a call from the port of Joppa (20km/12 miles to the north-west), where Tabitha, a much-loved Christian woman, has died. Peter brings her back to life, and settles for a time at Joppa. His host is a tanner, an 'unclean' occupation for the Jews because it involves handling dead animals. Is Peter already to some extent

liberated from his Jewish religious taboos and ready for the next big challenge?

10 – 11
Good News for Gentiles too

10 Cornelius sends for Peter
Up to this point the gospel has been preached only to Jews, converts to Judaism (proselytes) and Samaritans (who observed the law of Moses). Now God steps in to make it plain that the message is for everyone (34-35). God prepares the Roman officer, Cornelius, and he prepares Peter. Three times the vision and message come – apparently instructing Peter to break the Jewish food laws (see Leviticus 11). But when the men from Cornelius arrive, he is quick to realize the far deeper,

Blinded by the light that met him on his journey, Saul was led to a house on Straight Street, Damascus. Today, the street is a main artery of the old covered market.

human implications of his dream (28). A second Pentecost – the coming of the Holy Spirit on the Gentiles – follows his teaching. No one can now deny baptism to those who have received such an obvious mark of God's favour.

▶ **Cornelius, a centurion (1)** One of those who formed the backbone of the Roman army. The centurions stationed in Palestine appear in a very favourable light in the New Testament. (See 'Roman soldiers in the New Testament'.) Cornelius was an adherent to Jewish faith and

worship, but not a circumcised convert.

▶ **Peter's trance (9-16)** It was midday when Peter fell into his waking dream, and Cornelius' men were already nearing Joppa. Peter's hunger, and perhaps the leather awning overhead, shape the images of a vision which God uses to convey his message.

11:1-18 Peter reports back

The recounting of the events at Caesarea (5-15) underlines their significance. The criticism Peter faces from a particularly

A historian looks at the New Testament
E.M. Blaiklock

The New Testament tells a story that was to change the course of all subsequent history. The four Gospels, describing the active years of Jesus, are set in various levels of society in Rome's most turbulent province, highlighting the imperial administration and clearly indicating the situation which led, in AD 66, to Rome's most awful provincial war.

The Acts of the Apostles picks up the theme. It is a narrative written by an educated Greek, a major historian in his own right, and shows the triumphant spread of the movement which was to change the world.

That movement was shaped by one who can justly be called the first European – the educated rabbi Paul, who was thoroughly at home with Greek literature and philosophic thought (as the Areopagus address demonstrates), and who was also a Roman citizen, supremely conscious, as his plan of evangelism demonstrates, of the worth, the power, and the significance of the Empire and the Roman Peace.

Test Luke on detail, as

archaeology has demonstrated he can be tested, and he emerges as a man of meticulous accuracy. Read him at length, and see Ephesus and Corinth come to life. Pick single words – 'proconsuls', for example, the *plural*, in the Ephesus riot story – and see a small fact of history accounted for...

Paul's letters, in the full stream of ancient correspondence, are just as historically illuminating. Corinth, vicious, cosmopolitan, pseudo-philosophical, polyglot, disordered, argumentative, controversy-ridden, comes to life in the letter to its turbulent church, into which the restless spirit and urban vice of the place had infiltrated.

Or turn to the poetry of Revelation – the last New Testament book – a riot of symbolism, which this age above all should richly appreciate. Here is Rome as seen nowhere else – through the eyes of a bitter provincial foe. Rome, tyrranous, drunk with blood, madly persecuting... and doomed.

Anyone who knows the New Testament in its context, and

against its background, has an open window into the mind, the society, the problems, the spirit of the 1st century. Its brewing storms – the last Jewish Revolt, for example – are visible. Its fumbling administration in the East which set the stage for disaster, is clear to view. Its experimentation with puppet kings, its repressive legislation, its patches of anachronistic city rule, its frontier life (as for example at Lystra), its philosophic divisions, its collaborating groups, the obvious symptoms of coming catastrophe – the New Testament reveals them all.

As a collection of historical documents, the New Testament is unique.

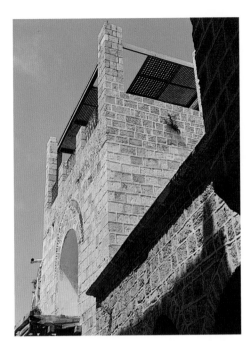

narrow faction of Jewish Christians in Jerusalem will dog every stage of Paul's missionary work. The admission of Gentiles to full membership of the church, without circumcision, is the most controversial question of the apostles' generation. But Luke makes it clear that the apostles and leaders fully approved Peter's action, the hand of God was so evident in it all (17-18).

11:19-30 Antioch: the first Gentile church

At about the same time as the events in Caesarea, things are moving in the north, at Antioch, third largest city in the world (after Rome and Alexandria), busy commercial centre and capital of the Roman province of Syria.

The warm response of the Greeks to the Christian message leads the Jerusalem church to despatch Barnabas (see on 4:36) to Antioch. He in turn tracks Saul down at his home city of Tarsus. And the stage is set for the next great advance, described from chapter 13 onwards.

▶ **Greeks/Hellenists/Gentiles (20)** The general Greek-speaking population of Antioch.

▶ **Lord (20, 21, 23)** A more suitable title for Jesus in the Roman world than the Jewish 'Messiah'. As the Romans declared 'Caesar is

Lord' so the Christians declared 'Jesus is Lord'.

▶ **A severe famine... in the days of Claudius (28)** Claudius was emperor AD 41-54. The famine hit Palestine about AD 46.

12
King Herod persecutes the church

12:1-19 James executed; Peter jailed

While Paul and Barnabas are in Jerusalem, handing over Antioch's donation for the famine relief, King Herod (posing as a champion of the law) instigates a new wave of persecution. James, one of the three apostles closest to Jesus, dies. But Peter is rescued (as he was before: 5:19), even as the Christians gather to pray. A maximum security prison presents no problems to God! And there is more for Peter to do. The story is graphically told, with suspense closely followed by humour, as Rhoda leaves Peter standing at the door (14).

▶ **King Herod (1)** Herod Agrippa I, grandson of Herod the Great (Luke 1:5). The kingdom was given him by his friend, the Emperor Caligula, and extended by Claudius. See 'The Herod family'.

▶ **Unleavened Bread (3)** The seven-day feast

A thriving church was quickly established at the city of Antioch, in Syria. Two of its best men – Saul and Barnabas – were sent out as missionaries. Antioch remains a major city today.

Lattice-work shades the roof of a house in Joppa. In Peter's waking dream, the canvas canopy overhead was full of clean and unclean animals. God's gift of new life in Christ was meant for Gentiles as well as Jews.

A famine during the reign of Emperor Claudius (shown on this coin) prompted the Christians at Antioch to send a generous gift to the stricken Christians in Judea.

immediately following Passover, and regarded as part of that festival (4).

▶ **Four squads of soldiers (4)** One squad of four soldiers for each watch of the night, two with Peter, two at the door.

▶ **James (17)** The brother of Jesus (Mark 6:3; Acts 15:13; 21:18).

12:20-25 King Herod dies

The Jewish historian, Josephus, also describes the king's sudden death in AD 44. Luke sees it as a direct consequence of Herod's self-aggrandisement and disrespect for God.

▶ **Eaten by worms (23)** The description points to an intestinal illness, perhaps peritonitis. Poor hygiene might well admit roundworms. But the phrase may be symbolic. It seems to have been routinely used of the death of a tyrant.

13–14
Paul's first pioneer mission

From this point on in Acts, Saul/Paul is the central figure.

The church at Antioch, directed by the Holy Spirit, selects its best men for pioneer work.

Barnabas and Saul, with young John Mark to help them, go first to **Cyprus** (13:4-12: Barnabas' native island; see also 11:19-20), where they confound magician Elymas and make a notable convert, the proconsul Sergius Paulus. Saul adopts the Roman version of his own name: Paul. From now on it is 'Paul and company', as he takes the lead.

They have barely begun their mainland

New missionaries, Saul and Barnabas, first preached the Good News at Salamis in Cyprus. After a meeting with the Roman proconsul on the island, Saul adopted the Roman form of his name – Paul.

Paul's first mission

Paul and Barnabas sailed from Cyprus to Attalia (Antalya) on the south coast of modern Turkey (*main picture*), making for the nearby city of Perge (Perga). Here archaeologists have uncovered the remains of the great city square (*agora*) with its central fountain and mosaics (*right*). Shops opened off the shaded colonnades on all sides.

In a remote, mountainous area of what is now Turkey, Pisidian Antioch is a remarkable example of a Graeco-Roman colony. Typically, Paul headed for the main centres in his evangelistic mission.

Rocks, distant mountains and sky make up the landscape near the 'pagan' city of Lystra, where Paul healed a cripple and he and Barnabas were fêted as the Greek gods Hermes and Zeus. Timothy, who later accompanied Paul on his journeys, came from Lystra.

journey when, at **Perga** (13:13), John Mark returns home. (Paul sees this almost as desertion: 15:37ff.)

Paul's first reported sermon, at **Antioch in Pisidia** (13:14-52), is given to a mixed audience of Jews, Gentile converts and sympathisers. A brief resumé of Jewish history (like Stephen's speech: 7:2-53) is given to show that Jesus is God's promised Saviour. Opposition from the Jews sends Paul and Barnabas to the Gentiles (13:46).

Driven out of Antioch, they go to **Iconium** (14:1-6), where the pattern is repeated.

Following an attempted stoning, they escape to **Lystra** (14:6-20), where the healing of a cripple leads the people to acclaim Barnabas as Zeus (chief god of the Greeks) and Paul as Hermes (the messenger-god), despite their protests.

Further trouble from the Jews of Antioch takes them on to **Derbe** (14:20-21), the furthest point of this first mission, where the response is good. Returning by the same route they encourage the new believers, appointing leaders for each church.

15:1-35
Jerusalem conference

Ten years or more have passed since the apostles approved the admission of Cornelius' Gentile household to the church (chapters 10–11), and opposition has hardened. When reports of Paul's successes among the Gentiles reach the salvation-by-faith-*and*-circumcision party, they see the red light and openly oppose his teaching.

On such a vital matter, an authoritative decision by the apostles and elders is essential to avoid a complete split. Peter's reminder of the earlier events, and the account given by Paul and Barnabas of God's work among the Gentiles, carry the day.

The final summing-up and verdict given by James, the Lord's brother and leader of the Jerusalem church, finds general acceptance. The Gentiles are asked simply to accommodate the Jewish Christians by respecting Jewish food-laws, so that Jews and Gentiles can share the same table and the church meet together as one.

This chapter is a turning-point in Acts. The centre now shifts away from Jerusalem and the apostles, with the emphasis on the mission to the Gentiles, and the new churches.

15:36 – 18:28
Paul's second mission: from Asia to Europe

15:36 – 16:5 Separation
A 'sharp argument' about John Mark results in two missionary campaigns instead of one. Barnabas, the 'encourager', no doubt helped his young nephew to make the grade and eventually win Paul's approval (2 Timothy 4:11).

Barnabas and Mark return to Cyprus. Paul takes Silas and revisits the mainland cities of the first campaign. At Lystra and Derbe, Timothy is added to the company.
▶ Silas (Silvanus) (15:40) Representative of the Jerusalem church (15:22). Like Paul, he was a Roman citizen. He travelled with the apostle as far as Beroea (17:14) and rejoined him at Corinth. Silas was associated with Paul in the writing (from Corinth) of 1 and 2 Thessalonians; also with Peter in the writing of his first letter.
▶ Timothy (16:3) The decision to circumcize Timothy was taken in order to regularize his position as a Jew, not in order to secure his

Drawn by the vision of a Macedonian man calling for help, Paul sailed from Troas on the west coast of Turkey to Neapolis (Kavalla) in northern Greece, pictured here. So the gospel first came to Europe.

'Good News!' – from the first Christians

Michael Green

> **66** *Nothing could keep them quiet. They had found the key to life, and they would not be silent.* **99**

The Christian gospel burst on the world like a thunderclap. Its preachers had a message so exciting and so urgent that they took every opportunity to pass it on, whatever the cost to themselves in hardship and suffering.

- ■ It was not a religion.
- ■ It was not a morality.
- ■ It was a story – a story about the most wonderful person the world had ever seen, Jesus of Nazareth.

The great story

The story began long before the birth of Jesus, with the great Creator-God who made mankind to know and enjoy him: but mankind turned the other way. So God chose a man, Abraham, and his family which became the people of Israel. They were intended to show a rebel world what the true God was like, and what he offered to mankind and expected from them. But it was a story in search of an ending. The people chosen to bring God's healing to the world were themselves in need of rescue and restoration.

The first Christians were united in their belief that the great story of God's dealings with mankind had reached its climax in the life, death and resurrection of Jesus of Nazareth. They were convinced that he was the Messiah, whom the Jewish leaders had misunderstood and delivered up to the Roman occupying power for execution.

What is more, they were convinced that this Jesus was not only the long-awaited Jewish Messiah but the Lord God himself who had come as a man to rescue not only the Jews but all humankind

from the terrible results of our rebellion.

His death dealt with the guilt we have all incurred.

His risen life supplied the power for change, companionship throughout this mortal life, and the pledge of life with God after the grave.

A new age

The early Christians saw themselves as living in the first days of the new age which dawned when Jesus rose from the tomb on Easter morning. Because of that, they saw every-thing in a new light.

They devoted all their energies to understanding Jesus better (by studying the Old Testament of which he was the fufilment) and making him real to people who had never met him. The core of their proclamation was the Risen One whom many of them had known personally and had followed for several years while he had been a carpenter and a rabbi.

The essential message

Careful analysis of Acts, the Gospels and the Letters has shown that these first Christians had a broadly uniform pattern for their proclamation. It ran something like this:

'The ancient prophecies have been fulfilled, and the new age has dawned with the coming of Jesus the Messiah.

'He was born of David's family,

and died on the cross in accordance with the prophecies of scripture, in order to deliver us from this present evil age.

'He was buried and rose again the third day, as scripture had foretold. He is now exalted to God's right hand as Christ (Messiah) and Lord of the living and the dead.

'He has given his Holy Spirit to his followers as an assurance of his Lordship, and as the foretaste of his return to be the Judge and Saviour of mankind at the Last Day.'

This pattern of announcement was developed very early. You can see it in the sermons in Acts, Romans 1:3-4; 1 Corinthians 15:3- 4 and 1 Timothy 3:16. The Gospels themselves represent a good deal of the evangelistic content of the early sermons: the material was preached before it was written down. Philippians 2:4-11 is very early, probably coming from the Aramaic-speaking church, and yet is as doctrinally developed as anything in the New Testament. The main thrust of their message was uniform from the start.

Telling people about Jesus

Naturally there was nothing rigid and inflexible about their proclam-ation. They began where people were:

- ■ a cynical Roman official
- ■ a poor beggar
- ■ a small group of Jews meeting by a riverside.

But, as examination of the addresses in Acts makes plain, they went on to tell people all about a *person*, Jesus.

They offered a *gift*, indeed two

▶▶

▶▶ gifts impossible to procure elsewhere: forgiveness from the past and the gift of the Holy Spirit.

They went on to call for a *response*: repentance and faith, baptism into the community of Christians, and reception of the Holy Spirit.

Different audiences

When preaching mainly to **Jews**, the first Christians drew deeply from their common heritage, the Old Testament, and they proclaimed Jesus as the fulfilment of its hopes and promises. Jesus offered deliverance from the guilt of breaking God's laws. So justification, forgiveness, cleansing are stressed.

When addressing **pagans**, they emphasized deliverance from the demonic powers, of which people in the ancient world were so acutely aware.

So to the Jews Jesus was shown as Christ, the Messianic Deliverer, the climax of the Old Testament revelation.

To the pagans he was presented as the conqueror of the forces of evil who had brought life and immortality to light.

When preaching to **Gentiles** who were totally ignorant of the Old Testament, the early missionaries started further back, by establishing the existence of one true God and deriding the prevalent idolatry.

Acts gives two examples of their approach, one to unsophisticated people (14:15-17) and the other to the cultured (17:22-31). In both cases they point to one true God, the Creator and Sustainer of all life, and this natural revelation prepared for the specifically Christian message to follow.

This way of proceeding had been used by Jews in the previous century or so, when seeking to commend the ethical monotheism of Israel to an immoral and idolatrous but wistful pagan world. It formed a useful introduction to the gospel, and remained the staple approach for centuries.

A versatile approach

There was tremendous versatility in the way they went about making Christ known. The Acts of the Apostles shows them preaching in the streets, in synagogue and Temple, when arrested, in debate, when visiting, in the context of works of mercy, and especially in homes.

Home meetings were the great way in which the gospel spread so fast in the three centuries when Christians were not allowed to own any churches. The passion, the self-sacrifice and the imaginative initiative of these early evangelists are most striking.

Moreover, Acts makes plain the depth at which this early preaching was carried on. Words are used which indicate that the Christians acted like heralds, teachers, and debaters. They discussed the gospel, argued it, gave testimony to its efficacy, and showed how it fitted in with the Old Testament scriptures.

Women chattered the good news at the laundry, philosophers argued it on the street corners, prisoners told their fellows. People of every culture and background demonstrated its power by their transformed lives (see 1 Corinthians 6:9-11) and their willing acceptance of hardship and death (e.g. Acts 20:22-24).

These were the qualities which commended the new message, while the power of God's Spirit in their social and personal lives backed up their claims.

Nothing could keep them quiet. They had found the key to life, and they would not be silent.

Making connections

When engaged in interpreting the person of their Master they used the language and thought-forms familiar to their hearers.

If the early Jewish 'kingdom of God' language sounded politically suspect in Gentile circles, they spoke of 'eternal life' instead, which meant much the same but was readily comprehensible to pagans.

There are many examples of this gift they developed for translating words and concepts without compromising their original force. None is more memorable than the first 14 verses of John's Gospel, where the Christian message of the incarnation is clothed in language very close to Stoicism, so as to cut ice in a Greek setting.

Colossians 1:15-20 shows Paul using the language of his unbelieving opponents but filling their terms with his Christian concepts.

The address at Athens (Acts 17:16-31) is a brilliant example of putting the orthodox Christian message in essentially Athenian dress, complete with classical allusions instead of Old Testament texts.

Throughout this process of 'translation' their aim remained constant. It was to make crystal clear the unique saving work of the divine, crucified and risen Jesus. He was both the Lord they served and the message they so tirelessly proclaimed.

salvation. Paul had a special affection for his loyal, though timid, companion and successor. He came to regard him almost as his own son.

Paul's second mission

16:6-40 Earthquake shakes Philippi

At Troas, close to ancient Troy, Luke joins the party for the first time, and Paul receives his call to cross to Europe. It is tempting to think that Luke (whose home town may have been Philippi) was the man in Paul's dream.

In each place he visited, Paul normally went first to the synagogue (for which a minimum of ten men was required). At Philippi there was simply a group of women, meeting for prayer (14). So the church at Philippi, whose loving, faithful support and unfailing concern would bring Paul such joy (Philippians 1:3ff.; 4:10ff.; 2 Corinthians 8) begins with the response of Lydia, a local businesswoman.

When Paul frees a slave-girl whose psychic powers earn her owners easy money (16-19), trouble quickly follows. Philippi was a Roman colony (see Philippians introduction) and the owners clamour for their rights as Roman citizens (20-22). Paul the Jew has the same rights (37-39), but no one knows that.

The arrest of Paul and Silas is followed by the dramatic conversion of their jailer (23-36), after an earthquake opens the prison doors and parts the prisoners' chains.

Offered release next day, Paul will not accept until he has an official apology for the illegal beating of a Roman citizen. When he does move on, Luke remains behind (20:f.).

▶ **Thyatira (14)** A church was later formed in Lydia's home town (see Revelation 2:18ff.).

17:1-15 City in uproar!

Paul and Silas travel the great Roman highway, the Egnatian Way, from Philippi to **Thessalonica**. The response to Paul in this sea-port, the capital city of Macedonia, was no mere flash in the pan (see 1 Thessalonians 1:2-10; 2 Thessalonians 1:3-4). The Jews were 'jealous' because here as elsewhere Paul won over the 'devout Greeks', those already attracted to

Judaism – the very people they themselves hoped to win as converts.

In **Beroea** (10-15), 100km/60 miles to the west, the Jewish group is notable for their open-minded study of the scriptures. Jews, Greek women and men respond. But troublemakers from Thessalonica ensure that Paul moves on again, escorted by believers to Athens ahead of Timothy and Silas.

Philippi, a Roman colony in Macedonia, stood on the great east-west Egnatian Way, sections of which can still be seen.

17:16-34 Paul and the philosophers of Athens

Paul was a strategist. He campaigned in the great cities of the Roman world. He selected centres on trade-routes, sea-ports, places where there was much coming and going. From these centres the message would run like fire far and wide. He started with Roman Asia (present-day Turkey), moved on to Greece, then set his sights on Rome, and Spain beyond.

So he comes to Athens, a city with 1,000 years of history, glorying in past greatness; Athens, the originator of democracy, home of Aeschylus, Sophocles, Euripides, Thucydides, Socrates, Plato; the greatest university of the world, centre of philosophy, literature, science and art. See 'The city of Athens'.

In the synagogues Paul argues his case from the Jewish scriptures. Addressing the Greek philosophers in Athens he takes his cue from a local inscription (23) and quotes from their own writers (28). The message, that they must repent and believe in Jesus, whom God has raised from the dead (18, 30-31) does not change, but a different audience calls for a different presentation. Athens proves hard ground for the gospel (18, 32).

▶ **The Epicureans (18)** Materialists whose philosophy often amounted to little more than the pursuit of pleasure.

▶ **The Stoics (18)** Rationalists, propounding a philosophy of self-sufficiency and dogged endurance.

▶ **Foreign gods (18)** So inseparably did Paul speak of Jesus and the resurrection ('anastasis') that the Athenians took these to be the names of two new-fangled deities. Several philosophical schools believed in the immortality of the soul, but the Greeks regarded the idea of 'bodily' resurrection as completely ludicrous (32).

▶ **The Areopagus (19)** An ancient court of great prestige, possibly responsible for licensing public lecturers.

▶ **In him we live and move... (28)** Paul quotes the Cretan poet Epimenides. According to legend, it was he who advised the Athenians to erect 'anonymous' altars.

18:1-17 Paul in Corinth

See 1 Corinthians introduction and 'The city of Corinth' for background. Paul probably arrived in Corinth in AD 50, when Gallio was proconsul. He was joined there by Timothy and Silas (5; 17:15).

Most of the Jews oppose the new teaching, though the president of the synagogue is convinced (8) and Paul continues teaching for 18 months. When angry Jews take him to court, proconsul Gallio is swift to judge that Paul has committed no crime, and hustles them away (12-17). His decision is an important one for the Christian faith.

▶ **Aquila and Priscilla (2)** Tent-makers or leather-workers. They became staunch friends of Paul. Travel took them to Corinth, Ephesus and back to Rome. Everywhere, this hospitable pair were a great support to the young churches.

▶ **Claudius' edict (2)** Issued about AD 49-50 against the Jews for 'constantly rioting at the instigation of Chrestus' (possibly referring to disputes between Christian and non-Christian Jews in Rome).

18:18-23 Back to Antioch

A lot of travelling is packed into this short passage. Paul goes by sea from Corinth via

---

The Nazareth Decree

This remarkable inscription most probably dates from the 1st century AD. It was sent to a French collector from Nazareth in 1878. Was it the rumour that Jesus of Nazareth had risen from the dead that made the decree necessary?

66 *ORDINANCE OF CAESAR. It is my pleasure that graves and tombs remain undisturbed in perpetuity for those who have made them for the cult of their ancestors, or children, or members of their house. If, however, any man lay information that another has either demolished them, or has in any other way extracted the buried, or has maliciously transferred them to other places in order to wrong them, or has displaced the sealing or other stones, against such a one I order that a trial be instituted, as in respect of the gods, so in regard to the cult of mortals. For it shall be much more obligatory to honour the buried. Let it be absolutely forbidden for anyone to disturb them. In the case of contravention I desire that the offender be sentenced to capital punishment on charge of violation of sepulture.* 99

The city of Athens
David Gill

In the 5th century BC Athens had been one of the leading cities of ancient Greece, and had controlled a substantial empire. During the time of the leading politician Pericles, the city undertook a major building programme which included the construction of the Parthenon, the Erechtheion and the Propylaia which still dominate the skyline of the modern city.

The city of Athens was sacked

The rich cultural life of Greek cities is represented by this carving of a Muse, playing a *cithara*.

by the Roman general Sulla in 86 BC, and from that time was a relatively minor provincial city; Corinth, not Athens, would become the administrative capital of the Roman province of Achaia.

Subsequent benefactions to Athens by notable Romans (including Julius Caesar, who donated a new market), may have been a gesture of appeasement to a city which had suffered at Roman hands.

Nevertheless, Athens' great past meant that it continued to attract

The city square at Athens, with the Parthenon on the acropolis in the background. The headless statue is of the Emperor Hadrian. His breastplate shows Athena standing on the she-wolf which is suckling Romulus and Remus, Rome's founders.

The colonnaded *stoa* (the gift of King Attalos of Pergamum) has been rebuilt along one side of the great city square (*agora*) which was the heart of ancient Athens. Here Paul debated with the Areopagus Council.

The Greek heroes Ajax and Achilles concentrate on a board game in this Athenian black-figured vase-painting.

benefactors to finance its public buildings. The Emperor Augustus constructed a temple – now dismantled – to himself and the goddess Roma on the Athenian acropolis next to the Parthenon.

The *agora*, the main city square, was the location for the political buildings of the city of Athens. Augustus added to the market first started by his adopted father, Julius Caesar. The agora was surrounded on each side by long colonnaded buildings or stoas, some of which had been gifted to the city by benefactors.

When Paul came to Athens he was 'revolted at the sight of a city given over to idolatry'. His response was to engage in debate with all-comers, preaching 'Jesus and Resurrection' to the bemusement of some, who thought these were two more gods!

Eventually he made a formal speech to the Areopagus Council, casting his whole address in a form which took full account of their history, literature and religious beliefs (see '"Good News!" – from the first Christians').

The city of Athens, dedicated to the Greek goddess Athena, is still dominated by the remains of the ancient Parthenon with its temple complex. A colosssal bronze statue of the goddess was dedicated on the acropolis in the 5th century BC. The tip of her spear could be seen out at sea. Athens in Paul's day was as famous for its university as for its temples.

The Holy Spirit in Acts
G.W. Grogan

The Holy Spirit figures so largely in Acts that the title might well be expanded to read: 'The acts of the risen Christ by the Holy Spirit through the apostles'.

God in Person

The Spirit is not some abstract power, but a person: he does what only a person can be said to do. He speaks (1:16; 8:29; 10:19, etc.), enables others to speak (2:4; 4:8, 31, etc.), bears witness (5:32), sends out Christian workers (13:4), forbids certain courses of action (16:6-7) and appoints people to serve in the church (20:28). He is linked with us (15:28) and at the same time one with and equal to God (5:3, 9).

The agent of Christ

Acts 1:1 may imply that Jesus' work after the ascension continued through the Holy Spirit. The Spirit is the gift of the ascended Christ to his disciples (2:33; compare John 7:39) and is called 'the Spirit of Jesus' (16:7; compare Romans 8:9). He is also called 'the promise of the Father' (1:4; compare Luke 24:49).

The creator of the church

The church as we know it today was initiated at Pentecost. Wind and fire (2:2-3) are Old Testament symbols of deity (see Exodus 19:18; 1 Kings 19:11-12). 'Tongues' (the ability to speak different languages (Acts 2:4-13) may be the way God chose to indicate the church's ultimate universality, its presence among people of every language. (There are various ways of understanding the relationship between the 'tongues' of Acts and those in evidence at Corinth: 1 Corinthians 12 – 14.) The Spirit creates a fellowship of love and unity (Acts 2:43-46) and he is promised to those who respond to the gospel (2:38; see also 5:32).

The Spirit unites

Luke is vitally interested in the progress of the gospel and the consequent expansion of the church through the Spirit's activity.

The church on which the Spirit came at Pentecost was composed of *Jews and proselytes* (Gentiles committed to Judaism and therefore regarded as if they were Jews; 2:11). Soon other groups were to be brought in.

Jews hated Samaritans, who were of mixed race and deviant religion, but in Acts 8:14-17 the Spirit comes on *Samaritan believers*. This happens only after the (Jewish) apostles lay their hands on them, indicating love and fellowship on their part as well as the fact that 'salvation is from the Jews' (John 4:22). (In his Gospel, too, Luke shows a positive attitude to Samaritans: Luke 9:51-56; 10:33; 17:15-16.)

In Acts the barrier between Jews and Gentiles is broken down (10:44-48; compare also 11:1-18) when the Pentecost phenomena occur a second time as Peter preaches to *Gentiles*. (Luke's Gospel records Jesus' Nazareth sermon in which he showed God's concern for Gentiles – Luke 4:24-27 – and his commendation of a Roman centurion – Luke 7:1-10).

It was through John the Baptist that the promise of the Spirit was first given (Luke 3:16; compare Acts 1:5; 11:16), so Luke records in Acts 19:1-7 how a group of *John's disciples* also received the Spirit.

These passages reveal how the Spirit binds together these divergent groups, preventing division in the infant church. The uniting power of Christ is shown to be a reality. Speaking with tongues (recorded by Luke on two of these occasions: 10:44-46; 19:6) witnesses to the equal standing of these groups with the Jews and proselytes converted at Pentecost. Peter makes this plain when he refers to the conversion of the Gentiles (11:15-18).

The power behind the church's witness

The Holy Spirit was given to the church to enable men and women to witness for Christ (1:8; compare 4:33). Filled with the Spirit they speak with power (2:4, 14ff.; 4:8, 31; 6:10). But 'filled with the Spirit' also describes certain Christians whose quality of character specially fits them for various forms of service (6:3, 5; 11:22-24). So the Holy Spirit in his fullness gives people power to reveal Christ both by lip and life.

On some occasions Christians are told to preach the gospel to particular people (Acts 8:29; 10:19ff.), but Luke does not say how these instructions came. But the account in Acts 13:1-3 makes it clear that the church was directed by the Spirit to send Barnabas and Saul to evangelize the Gentiles, most probably through a word from a prophet present in the Antioch church.

▶▶

Agabus' gift of predictive prophecy is also mentioned (11:27-28; 21:10-11; compare 21:4). The second of these was fulfilled, not so much literally as in its essential content, for Paul was imprisoned by Gentiles. Four prophesying daughters of Philip are mentioned in Acts 21:8-9, and the disciples of John at Ephesus prophesied as well as speaking in tongues (19:6).

Prophecy was not concerned only with prediction but also with the encouraging and strengthening of the church (15:32; compare 1 Corinthians 14:3). All this prophetic activity illustrates the fulfilment of the promise made by the prophet Joel: 'In the last days... I shall pour out my Spirit on all people' (Acts 2:17-21).

There are references to healing and other miracles performed by the apostles (e.g. 3:6-7; 5:12-16; 19:11-12) without specific reference to the Holy Spirit, although doubtless they were due to his activity.

The life of the church

The Spirit of God was concerned with the inner life of the church in every place, strengthening, encouraging and enabling the church to grow (9:31).

It was the Spirit who appointed elders of the church as its guardians (20:28).

The church in council sought guidance on a matter of great importance and believed this was given through the Holy Spirit (15:28). On this occasion there is no reference to prophetic activity but rather to discussion, consideration of the clear activity of God and study of the Old Testament scriptures.

Acts is unique in its revelation of the person and role of the Holy Spirit. It records a fulfilment which is also a new beginning. The prophecies of the Old Testament (e.g. in Joel 2:28-32) and the promises of the Lord Jesus (e.g. in John 14:16) about the Holy Spirit find their fulfilment at Pentecost. The age of the Spirit, preached by Jesus and so evident in the New Testament Letters, has now begun.

Ephesus (where Aquila and Priscilla were going) to Jerusalem and Antioch. He then returns to Ephesus by road through Phrygia and Galatia (central Turkey) for a further missionary campaign.

▶ **Verse 18** Cenchreae was the port for sailing east from Corinth. 'Jews made vows to God either in thankfulness for past blessings (such as Paul's safe-keeping in Corinth) or as part of a petition for future blesssings (such as safe-keeping on Paul's impending journey)' (Howard Marshall). Under a Nazirite vow, hair was cut only when the vow came to an end and a sacrifice was offered.

18:24-28 Eloquent Apollos

Thanks to Aquila and Priscilla's instruction (26), the eloquent Apollos became a man of great influence in the Corinthian church (27-28; 1 Corinthians 1:12; 3:4ff.).

▶ **Alexandria (24)** This city on the Mediterranean coast of Egypt was a centre of learning and home of the Jewish philosopher, Philo.

▶ **John's baptism (25 and 19:3)** It would seem there were disciples of John who became believers in Jesus without being baptized into the new faith (or fully informed about it).

19 – 21:6
Paul's third mission

19 Silversmiths riot at Ephesus

See 'The city of Ephesus'.

19:1-7: see note on 18:25 above.

If Paul could win the people of Ephesus (the provincial capital) to the Christian faith the news would spread through the whole province of Asia. Verse 10 indicates that this is just what happened. It is likely that all seven churches mentioned in Revelation 1:11, as well as those at Colossae and Hierapolis, were founded during this period.

Teaching and healing go together, and the news of a remarkable exorcism (13-17) spreads like wildfire through the city.

So effective is Paul's ministry in communicating the message that 'gods made with hands are not gods at all' (26) that it

Paul's preaching at Ephesus, that there are no gods but God, led to a riot. His companions were dragged to the largest assembly place in the city – a theatre seating 24,000 people.

Just a litter of stones and a single re-erected pillar remain of the great temple at Ephesus dedicated to the Greek goddess Artemis (Roman, Diana). In Paul's day, silversmiths did a roaring trade, selling shrines of the goddess to worshippers and tourists.

cuts the takings of the silversmiths making images of the city's famous goddess, Artemis. They stir the whole place to uproar, dragging Paul's companions to the great theatre, and chanting slogans. After two hours of this, the town clerk manages to calm them down. Like Gallio at Corinth he declares the Christians innocent (37).

▶ **Hall of Tyrannus (9)** A lecture-hall which, according to some manuscripts, Paul used

MACEDONIA
Philippi
Troas
Assos
Mitylene
ASIA
GALATIA
Ephesus
Samos
PHRYGIA
Miletus
ACHAIA
Cos
Patara
Antioch
Rhodes
Tyre
Ptolemais
Caesarea
Jerusalem

The Asiarchs (31, some versions) Important officials responsible for maintaining order at religious functions.

▶ **The town clerk (35)** The leading civic official, answerable to the Romans for such an illegal assembly.

20:1-16 Paul sets out for Jerusalem

2 Corinthians fills in some of the details on Paul's return to Greece, so briefly covered in 20:1-6.

The apostle is preoccupied with the collection for the poverty-stricken Christians in Jerusalem (the men listed in verse 4 are delegates from the Gentile churches). His mission to the Gentiles has been much criticized by the Jews. This is his great gesture – a practical expression of the unity of Jew and Gentile in the church of Christ. It is supremely important to him – hence his determination to get to Jerusalem.

Before he left Ephesus, Paul wrote 1 Corinthians. From Macedonia (1) he wrote 2 Corinthians. From Corinth he wrote the letter to the Romans. It is likely he also visited present-day Albania and Yugoslavia ('Illyricum', Romans 15:19) at this time.

Paul's third mission

during siesta-time, from 11 a.m. to 4 p.m.

▶ **Magic... books (19)** Such was the city's name for magical papyrus scrolls of spells that these were known in the Roman world as 'Ephesian letters'.

▶ **Artemis (Diana) (24)** The cult adopted the name of the Greek goddess, but continued to worship the mother-goddess fertility figure of the region's ancient religion. The temple was one of the seven wonders of the world, four times the size of the Parthenon. The 'sacred stone' (35) was a meteorite, supposed to resemble the goddess, and kept in the temple.

▶ **The theatre (29)** An ideal place for the crowd to gather, since it could hold 24,000 people.

Travelling from Ephesus to Jerusalem, at the end of his third mission, Paul took ship on a coaster, calling in at various places around the south-west of Turkey.

On the way back from Greece, Luke joins Paul at Philippi, where they begin their voyage to Jerusalem, picking up the party waiting for them at Troas.

Troas (7-12) provides an interesting glimpse of early Christian worship – they meet on a Sunday evening in a private house for the Lord's Supper followed by a meal together (11). The sermon is very long: Paul has so much to say to them. The effort to listen for so long, late at night in the fuggy warmth of the lamps, proves too much for the weary Eutychus.

Verses 13-16 detail the island-hopping voyage to Miletus, 48km/30 miles south of Ephesus.

▶ **Verses 9-12** It is not entirely clear whether the miracle is one of resurrection or of preservation. But Luke states that Eutychus was dead (9) before Paul went down, and alive after Paul attended to him (10).

20:17 – 21:14 Painful partings

Paul's address to the elders from Ephesus (20:18-35) is the only one in Acts which was given to Christians – and the only recorded address by Paul which Luke actually heard him give.

The apostle foresees so clearly the troubles the church will face, from inside and out. 'Be on your guard,' he warns (28-30 ; Revelation 2:2 shows what notice the elders took). Paul's speech is deeply personal (18-27, 31-35). He is fully aware of the dangers ahead and does not expect to see these friends again. His words move them to tears as they put their arms around him in farewell.

Further voyaging takes Paul and company to Tyre, and another parting (21:1-6), then down the coast to Ptolemais (60km/40 miles south), and Caesarea (a similar distance south again), where Philip is still living (8:40). Nothing can shake Paul's determination to go to Jerusalem, not even a prophecy of his fate (21:10-14).

▶ **Trials/hard times (20:19)** There was serious trouble in Asia, quite apart from the riot at Ephesus (see 2 Corinthians 1:8-11).

▶ **Philip... one of the seven (21:8)** See Acts 6:5; 8:4-40.

▶ **Agabus (21:10)** Acted prophecy of this kind is familiar from the Old Testament (e.g. Ezekiel).

21:15 – 22:29
Paul arrested in Jerusalem

On his arrival Paul receives a warm welcome from his fellow-Christians, including the church leaders (21:17-20a). But garbled tales are circulating, that Paul teaches Jews to abandon circumcision and the law. If he openly identifies with a group of men under a strict vow (21:23; compare Numbers 6:13-21) all will see that he respects and observes the law. (This issue looms so large that Luke makes no mention of the relief fund on which Paul set such store.) But before the week-long term of the vow is over, a group of conservative Jews from the province of Asia (Turkey) create such a ferment that soldiers from the fort step in to prevent a lynching (21:27-35). Permitted to speak in his defence, Paul recounts his own story (22:1-21). But the mention of his mission to the Gentiles (21) creates a fresh furore. Taken inside to be questioned under torture (24), Paul is strapped down, and about to be flogged, when he declares his Roman citizenship –

Determined to visit Jerusalem, Paul sailed from the south coast of Turkey to Tyre, in Syria.

❝ *I do not place any value on my own life, provided that I complete the mission the Lord Jesus gave me – to bear witness to the good news of God's grace.* **❞**

Paul's farewell to the elders of Ephesus: 20:24

Feeling ran so high when it was thought Paul had taken a non-Jew into the Temple that he was mobbed. Remarkably this Greek inscription from Herod's Temple was found by archaeologists. It forbids non-Jews to enter the inner courts of the Temple, on pain of death.

to general consternation (see on 16:6-40).

▶ **Brought Greeks into the Temple (21:28)**
Anyone might go into the outer court, but
notices in Greek and Latin forbade Gentiles, on
pain of death, to enter the inner courts.

▶ **The barracks/fortress (21:34)** The cohort
was stationed in the Fort of Antonia. Two flights
of steps led down from the fort to the outer
court of the Temple.

▶ **The Egyptian (21:38)** Leader of the
'dagger-men' who specialized in assassinating
Romans and pro-Roman Jews. They murdered
Ananias the high priest in AD 66.

▶ **Is it lawful... ? (22:25)** A Roman citizen had
the right to a fair trial, and even if guilty was
spared the scourge. This horrible whip of
several thongs armed with pieces of lead or
bone was a far more deadly instrument than the
'rods' used at Philippi (16:22 – not all versions
make this clear).

Paul spent two
years in custody
in Caesarea, the
port where the
Roman governor
of Judea was
based. Herod the
Great had rebuilt
the city in
honour of
Augustus, the
first Roman
emperor. Roman
pillars now litter
the shore outside
the harbour from
which Paul took
ship to Rome. See
further, 'Bringing
the past to life'.

22:30 – 26:32
Paul, a prisoner

22:30 – 23:11 Jewish Council hears Paul's case

Jesus stood silent before his accusers, but
Paul is vocal. He does not hesitate to play
one party against another in the Council,
by stating that he is on trial for his belief in
the resurrection of the dead. (See 'Jewish
religion in New Testament times' on
Pharisees and Sadducees.) Again the
Roman troops remove him to the safety of
the fort.

At this low point, Paul is given a word of
encouragement: he will be Christ's witness
in Rome (23:11).

23:12-22 Assassins' plot uncovered

Forty men vow to kill Paul when he is
taken to the Council for further questioning. But Paul's nephew alerts the tribune in
time for a counter-plan.

23:23-35 Transfer to Caesarea

The Romans administered the province of
Judea from the port of Caesarea. The size of
the escort provided for Paul and his friends
on the journey – heavy-armed infantry,
cavalry, light-armed troops – is an indication of the unrest in the province. Paul's
emergency transfer turned into a weary

two-year imprisonment (probably AD 58-60), punctuated by three hearings of his case, without resolution.

▶ **Felix (23:24)** The violent but ineffective governor of Judea, AD 52-59. He was eventually recalled to Rome for mishandling riots in Caesarea. His residence was the palace built by Herod the Great (35).

24 Governor Felix hears Paul's case

Five days after the transfer, Paul's case comes before the Roman governor, Felix.

Tertullus opens ingratiatingly for the Jewish prosecution (2-8). Paul, confident of Roman justice, gives a succinct summary of events. His only 'crime' concerns his belief in resurrection. Felix adjourns the case, giving Paul limited freedom (22-23).

He later returns with Drusilla, a Jewess, daughter of Herod (Acts 12:1), his third wife and the likely source of his information about 'the (Christian) Way'. Paul's talk of 'justice and self-control and future judgment' is too near the bone for this pair, especially as Felix was hoping for a fat bribe from his prisoner (26).

25 'I appeal to Caesar!'

Two years pass, and Felix is succeeded by Porcius Festus. (He was not governor for long, dying in AD 62.) His attempt to curry favour with the Jews compels Paul to appeal to Caesar. He has offended against neither Jewish nor Roman law (8). But he has more hope of justice from the Emperor Nero than from the Sanhedrin!

When King Agrippa comes to pay his respects to the new governor, Paul's case is put to him (13-21). This is Agrippa II, son of the Herod of Acts 12:1, great-grandson of Herod the Great. Bernice, his sister and acting wife, crowned an inglorious career by becoming mistress to the emperors Vespasian and Titus.

Festus is satisfied Paul has committed no crime, so what charge can he write in his letter to the emperor about the prisoner he is sending to Rome (25-27)?

26 King Agrippa hears Paul's case

Once again Paul is called to speak in his own defence. As he told his story to the Jews in Jerusalem (chapter 22), now he tells it to the king. The central issue is resurrection – 'Why does it seem incredible to you that God should raise the dead?' (8) – specifically Christ 'as the first to rise from the dead' (23).

At this point he is interrupted. 'You are out of your mind,' shouts Festus. Agrippa laughs it off – he cannot afford to lose face with Festus or to offend the Jews by denying the prophets.

The governor and the king agree that 'this man could have been set free if he had not appealed to Caesar' (32).

> 66 *You have appealed to Caesar, to Caesar you shall go.* 99
>
> 25:12

Paul's voyage to Rome

▶ **Paul's conversion (12-23)** The story here differs in emphasis from the account in chapter 22. The 'goads' are the pressures compelling Paul to a complete change of direction in life. Verses 16-18 summarize the Lord's words on the Damascus road, what Ananias said, and the message which came to Paul in the Temple (22:17ff.).

27 – 28
Rome at last

27 Storm and shipwreck
The voyage to Rome is made in three ships: a coaster from Caesarea to Myra, on the south coast of Turkey (Asia); a cargo vessel (carrying grain on the regular run from Alexandria in Egypt to Rome) from Myra to Malta; and another from Malta to Puteoli in the Bay of Naples. Luke gives a superb account of the eventful passage.

They start late in the season (sailing ceased for winter in mid-November) and by the time they reach Crete 'the Fast' (27:9;

The vessel in which Paul was shipwrecked was a cargo ship like this one, carrying grain from Alexandria to Rome.

Atonement, September/October) is over. As they seek a safe winter harbour, the favourable south wind changes to a dreaded 'north-easter'. For two weeks they run before the storm, with no means of knowing where they are (27:20: they fixed their position by sighting sun and stars).

Paul, the prisoner, commands extra-ordinary authority (21-25, 30-32, 33-36, 42-43), giving hope and courage to all '276 souls' aboard. God has promised them safety: Paul *will* appear before Caesar (23-24). When the ship runs aground, all make it safely to shore on an island they discover to be Malta.

▶ **Secure the boat (16)** The dinghy had been towed behind – now they bring it on board.

▶ **Syrtis (17)** Quicksands and whirlpool off the North African coast.

28 From Malta to Rome
Paul makes an impact on the people of the island, surviving a snakebite, and healing the father of the island chief. So winter passes and the third phase of the voyage

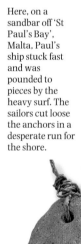

Here, on a sandbar off 'St Paul's Bay', Malta, Paul's ship stuck fast and was pounded to pieces by the heavy surf. The sailors cut loose the anchors in a desperate run for the shore.

Paul was the first to bring the gospel to Malta. Deep beneath the streets of Mdina, the ancient capital, are catacombs where it is believed that persecuted early Christians met and held their 'love-feasts' – the shared meal which was part of the Communion service.

takes them safely to Puteoli, where a Christian welcome awaits.

So Paul reaches Rome at last, though hardly in the way he imagined. He is allowed his own lodgings, with a single guard. And for two years he bears witness to Jesus at the heart of the Empire, as God had promised.

What happened after this is not known. Most probably he was released, went to Spain as planned, and then back East before further imprisonment and execution in about AD 64-65.

▶ **The twin gods (28:11)** Castor and Pollux, the sailors' patrons.

At last Paul arrived in Rome, marched into the city along the Appian Way, as a prisoner. But there were Christians already there, who came out to meet him.

Roman rule, Greek culture
David Gill

In the Gospels, Acts and Letters we find Greek-speaking Jews, and frequent mention of 'the Greeks'. Sometimes this simply means 'non-Jews': but those who spoke Greek and belonged to Greek city-states were also reckoned to be the only 'civilized people' – the rest being 'barbarians'. Within walking distance of Jesus' home area of Galilee there were ten of these Greek cities. In Turkey today there are splendid ruins of similar ones.

In warships like this the Romans won supremacy by sea.

The coming of Rome

In the two centuries before the birth of Christ, the Greek Empire fell to the Romans. In 133 BC the bequest of King Attalos of Pergamum effectively created the province of Asia, essentially the western coast of modern Turkey. Further provinces in the region included the creation of Cilicia in south-eastern Turkey around 80 BC and the acquisition of the kingdom of Galatia in central Anatolia in 25 BC.

Civil war between Octavian (later the Roman Emperor Augustus) and Mark Antony led finally to the battle of Actium (31 BC), the fall of Alexandria in Egypt (30 BC), and the suicide of both Antony and the Ptolemaic ruler, Cleopatra. This left Rome in charge of Egypt and other Ptolemaic possessions in the eastern Mediterranean. Octavian awarded King Herod several former Egyptian cities in Judea in 30 BC.

Augustus subsequently reorganized the provincial structure of the Empire, making provinces accountable either directly to the emperor or to the senate at Rome.

Several Roman provincial governors, within Judea and outside it, feature in the New Testament: for example, Sergius Paulus of Cyprus (Acts 13:7) and Gallio of Achaia (southern Greece; Acts 18:12). It is perhaps significant that, having met Sergius Paulus on Cyprus, Paul adopts that form of his name (he was 'Saul' until then), and makes his way to Pisidian Antioch (Acts 13), where the governor had family estates.

Despite the imposition of Roman rule in the eastern Mediterranean, it was, remarkably, the Greek ('Hellenistic') culture that continued and became a key element in the spread of the gospel. Roman roads and the Roman Peace enabled Paul and his companions to travel in safety: but it was the Greek *koine* – common language – that made communication possible. Hellenistic settlements (at Ephesus, for example) became centres for the spread of the gospel among non-Jews.

Even as part of the Roman Empire the communities established by the Greeks continued to write public inscriptions in Greek. Cities often adopted Greek institutions for administration – so they had standard forms of magistrates, councils, and assemblies. Likewise

An impressive example of a rich man's house built in Hellenistic style has been found at Araq al Amir in Jordan.

the city was often focussed on a particular religious cult (that of Artemis/Diana at Ephesus, for example).

Greek cities and Roman colonies

Within this framework of Greek cities with Greek institutions, and using Greek as their main language, Rome started to establish a series of colonies in which to settle veterans from the campaigns. One of Julius Caesar's eastern colonies, founded just before his assassination, was at Corinth (the city Paul visits in Acts 18, later writing two letters to the Christians there – see 'The city of Corinth').

In the province of Galatia, established in 25 BC, colonists from the 5th and 7th legions were settled on land acquired from the temple estates of Mên Askaenos near Pisidian Antioch, a city visited on Paul's first missionary tour (Acts 13).

Jerash (in present-day Jordan) was one of the 'Ten Towns' – Greek cities – close to Jesus' home area of Galilee. Archaeologists have uncovered a huge area of the city, including the theatre, wide main streets (*right*) and the spectacular columned temple of Artemis (*above*).

All these cities had Roman administrative structures and used Latin, but only as the public language – Greek remained the language of the people. They naturally became the focus for Roman culture within a province. Certainly at Corinth it is clear that members of the local élite from other cities and regions in the province were attracted to the colony to acquire the benefits of Romanization.

Roman citizenship was rare, at least in the 1st century AD, amongst the Greeks in the east, though it became fashionable to adopt Latin names (such as Rufus, Mark 15:21; Romans 16:13). This explains the centurion's surprise at Jerusalem when Paul declares he is a Roman citizen (Acts 22:28).

Citizenship gave Paul the right to appeal to the emperor ('Caesar') when his imprisonment in Judea seemed to be a permanent arrangement (Acts 25:11).

Brushes with the authorities
The Roman colonies not only had a Roman constitution, they also had a Roman legal framework. Thus when Paul was arrested at Philippi – a Roman colony – the city magistrates (*duoviri* in Latin), acted illegally (Acts 16:20). Instead of being given privileged treatment as a citizen, Paul was imprisoned and beaten.

At Corinth, the case against Paul was (correctly) brought before the governor (Acts 18:12-17). Corinth is also the setting for legal hearings which are discussed by Paul (1 Corinthians 6:1-11).

The New Testament reveals a different legal approach in Greek cities which, although coming under the jurisdiction of the Roman provincial governor, also retained some of their own constitution.

The tension between the two authorities within a province is well illustrated by the account in Acts 19 of a riot which occurs at Ephesus in response to Paul's teaching. The rioters gathered, chanting, in the theatre, and it was the task of the secretary of the city, the *grammateus*, to calm them and remind those present that the

▶▶ provincial governor would deal with any grievances.

Brushes with civic authorities are also noted elsewhere, especially in Acts.

For example, at Thessalonica, the civic magistrates, correctly identified by Luke as 'politarchs' (Acts 17:8), were faced with hearing a possible charge of treason against Paul and Silas: 'They are all defying Caesar's decrees, saying that there is another king, one called Jesus' (Acts 17:7). Interestingly no formal charges were made and Paul and Silas were expelled from the city before the governor of Macedonia could be called to intervene.

At Athens, Paul was brought before the traditional civic court of the Areopagus (Acts 17). Again, the safest solution, both for Paul and the civic authorities, was for him to leave the city.

The Games

One of the characteristics of cities in the Greek east was the establishment of games which modelled themselves on the great pan-

In days long before the benefits of modern medicine it is not surprising that healing cults had such a following. The god Asclepius and his daughter Hygeia (health and healing) are represented on this marble carving from the 5th century BC.

The ancient city of Ephesus, where Paul caused a riot by the impact of his teaching, is one of Turkey's major tourist attractions today. This is one of its main streets.

Hellenic festivals of Olympia and Delphi.

Events like these were thought to help develop good citizens. They were primarily athletic, including, for example, a foot-race or wrestling, as well as equestrian events in some places. The cultural side might include musical and oratorical skills. Games of this kind were held at periodic intervals, often every four years, like the Olympic Games.

The Syrian King Antiochus IV had tried to introduce such games at Jerusalem, along with a gymnasium where the young men of the city were trained. This caused riots from the Jews, who saw the spread of Greek culture as a threat to Jewish identity.

The temple of Asclepius at Pergamum includes water conduits and a tunnel which were part of a medical centre. They may have been used to give patients shock treatment.

The sacred games, where the winner was awarded a crown as a prize, were the most prestigious. However, in some cities cash prizes were awarded. These games, known as *themides*, often seem to have been instituted by a wealthy benefactor who left money to provide for the prizes. They might then be named after him, like the Balbilleia festival established at Ephesus by Tiberius Claudius Balbillus.

Sometimes games were established in conjunction with the imperial cult (see 'Emperor worship and Revelation'). Pergamum in the province of Asia had a festival of this kind, linked to the cult of Roma – the personification of the city of Rome – and Augustus.

Emperors took an interest in the games, notably Nero who travelled around Greece participating in the major events – some of which had to be moved forward to allow him to take part – and culminating in a speech in the stadium at the pan-Hellenic sanctuary of Isthmia where he declared Greece to be free.

The widespread interest in games may explain Paul's frequent allusions in his letters to 'running the race' (1 Corinthians 9:24, 26; Galatians 2:2; 5:7; Philippians 2:16) and 'gaining the prize' (1 Corinthians 9:24, 27; Philippians 3:14).

Religious cults

Each city of the Roman Empire had a wide range of cults. The core cults for a Greek city might be based around the Greek Olympian gods, such as Zeus, Ares, Artemis, and Aphrodite. In Roman colonies, the cults of gods such as Jupiter, Mars, Diana and Venus were common. The gods were visualized in human form.

Some of the most important statues of antiquity were designed

A Roman theatre still stands in the city
centre of Amman, in Jordan.
This comic actor wearing a mask is
Roman, from the 2nd century BC.

to portray the gods. One of the
seven wonders of the ancient world
was the colossal gold and ivory cult
statue of Olympian Zeus which was
placed in the god's temple at
Olympia. The importance of such
worship in the landscape of the
ancient city is reflected in the
account of Paul's arrival at Athens,
a city perceived as being 'full of
idols' (Acts 17:16).

Although these cults may share
a common name, for example
Aphrodite or Artemis, they were far
from uniform and sometimes
totally different from one another.
For example, at the city of Paphos
on Cyprus, Aphrodite was
worshipped in the form of a conical
rock or *baetyl*. At Ephesus, Artemis,
a goddess normally associated with
hunting, was perceived as a figure
with what appear to be multiple
breasts. Paul's preaching had a
dramatic effect on the income of the
silversmiths of the city, who were
clearly making offerings which
could be dedicated to the goddess
(Acts 19). In Acts the city-clerk of
Ephesus comments that the image
of Artemis had fallen from heaven,

a possible allusion to the worship of
sacred rocks (Acts 19:35).

One of the unifying cults of the
eastern Roman Empire was the
worship of the Roman emperor. In
the Greek, Hellenistic, period, rulers
had encouraged their subjects to
worship them as gods, and this
practice was continued under
Rome.

In 29 BC, after the battle of
Actium and the suicide of Mark
Antony, Augustus allowed the
cities of Asia and Bithynia to
establish temples where his deified
adopted father Julius Caesar could
be worshipped alongside Roma.
Moreover he allowed himself to be
worshipped by Greeks – but not
Romans – at Pergamum and
Nicomedia. At Ancyra in the
province of Galatia there was a
temple dedicated to Augustus and
Roma. It is on the walls of this
building that the text of the
achievements of Augustus –
originally placed on bronze plaques
outside the imperial Mausoleum at
Rome – can still be read.

Inscriptions from the Roman
colony of Narbo (Narbonne) in
southern France, dated to AD 11
and AD 12 or 13, outline how each
sector of the community would be
drawn into making provision for

the worship of the emperor. For
example, three Roman equestrians
and three freedmen would be
expected to 'sacrifice one animal
each' as well as provide incense
and wine for each member of the
colony at their own expense.

Other cults were linked to
healing, through the worship of
the god Asclepius whose cult
could even be found at Rome.
One of the most important
centres was at Epidauros in
Greece. The complex remained
popular in the Roman period,
attracting people who would come
and sleep in the confines of the
sanctuary. A rival sanctuary at
Pergamum expanded in the 2nd
century AD through wealthy
Roman benefactors.

The spirituality of the cults and
mystery religions appealed
particularly in the area of Roman
Asia (modern Turkey) to which
Paul addressed several of his letters.
In Ephesians and Colossians he
uses the language of these religions
to show the far greater power of
Jesus. See 'Understanding
Colossians'.

See also 'The Greeks' and '"Good
News!" – from the first Christians'
(for the way Paul approaches his
different audiences).

The Letters

Donald Guthrie / Stephen Motyer

The Letters make up about a third of the New Testament. Sometimes readers find them difficult to understand, and return with a sense of relief to the Gospels. But the Letters contain much teaching of vital importance from the apostles and their associates, and the difficulties begin to fade when we are able to see the Letters in their contemporary setting, and understand the story-line behind them. Then, like the light suddenly shining behind a photographic slide, they spring to life, and we are able to see their message both for then, and for now.

The world of the Letters

The letters were all written as Christianity expanded out from Palestine into the wider world, which was dominated by the Roman Empire. What was it like, living under Roman power at this time?

A world of prosperity The Romans had brought peace and wealth. Pirates had been banished from the Mediterranean, and huge fleets of merchant ships ferried grain and luxury goods to Italy. The tentacles of Roman trade and power reached far and wide – as far as West Africa and northern India. Rome itself was a very wealthy city, and other cities to which letters were sent – Ephesus, Philippi and Corinth, for example – had grown rich through this trade.

Many roads had been built, travel was easily possible, the Greek language was spoken right around the eastern Mediterranean, and the Roman army was stationed in all the main cities, to safeguard Rome's interests.

There was, however, a dark side to all this. In some places, especially in Palestine, the burden of taxes was very high. As always, the rich grew richer at the expense of the poor. With prophetic passion, James' letter denounces the exploitation of the poor by the rich, and the merchants who plan their wealth without concern for God. Paul devoted several years of his ministry to collecting money from the comparatively rich churches in Greece and Asia Minor, to take to the poor in Jerusalem.

At the bottom of society were the millions of slaves who owned no property and belonged completely to their masters. The empire was built on their labour.

Many, like Onesimus (the slave who is the subject of Paul's Letter to Philemon), ran away to hide in the big cities. Slaves were supposed to adopt the religion of their master, but the Good News of Jesus Christ, who makes us all children and heirs of God, brought a sense of freedom to many. Paul encouraged Christian slaves not to rebel against their masters, but to serve them even better, for Jesus' sake.

A world of fear All the first readers of the letters had seen Roman soldiers – like the one on whom Paul bases his picture in the Letter to the Ephesians, where he encourages Christians to put on the 'whole armour of God'. The omnipresent Roman army reminded everyone of the basis of Roman power: fear and subjection. There were constant rumours of the wars on the edges of the Empire, and stories of Roman brutality towards rebellious subjects.

But there were other causes of fear. Life was short, and painful. Food shortages rarely affected Italy, because in times of famine the limited grain would be shipped there, leaving the local population with nothing. Medicine was crude, and very unsuccessful.

Above all, for many people, life was dominated by fear of unseen powers, much more threatening than the Roman army. Astrology was widely practised, and linked with magic, in which many people put their trust. They believed that the right spells or incantations would give them power and safety – make the rain come,

ward off disease, give them wealth, keep the demons at bay, defeat their enemies. Even Jews, living in the cities of Asia Minor, had been caught up by this way of thinking, and used the name of 'the Lord' as a magic talisman. Virtually everyone knew that the powers of evil were a horrible, daily threat. Hostile magic could kill. Sorcery was often connected with the many temples to Greek and Roman deities.

For the first believers, stepping into Christian faith was truly coming 'out of darkness into (God's) marvellous light', as Peter puts it. Now they were safe, delivered by a Saviour who had 'triumphed over the principalities and powers', and from whose love nothing could separate them. But they still faced great challenges, living in this dark, pagan society.

In order to earn a living, they were expected to join in the celebrations and rituals of their 'trade guild', offering sacrifices to the gods or goddesses associated with their trade. Could they still do this, as Christians? Some said that, since Jesus had defeated all evil powers, they could join in, knowing that the idol had no real power any more. But others felt that they should not participate in pagan worship, even if that meant poverty because they could not rise to leadership in the trade guild.

Paul agreed that 'for us there is only one

Paul travelled by sea to the Roman province of Asia (modern Turkey), where he founded many churches. When he left, he kept in touch by letter. Some of those letters now form part of the New Testament.

God, the Father, from whom are all things and for whom we exist, and only one Lord, Jesus Christ, through whom are all things and through whom we exist'. But he drew the line at Christians joining festivals in pagan temples. 'I do not want you to be partners with demons!' he said. Instead, Christians must learn to live by the power of God – filled with the *Holy* Spirit – amongst these dark powers, shining like lights in the world and living lives of love, joy and real peace in the midst of the fear and uncertainty of their society.

A world of confusion Fear and confusion often go together. The confusion of the world of the Letters was very real, producing a spiritual yearning, a longing for solid truth in a changing and unsure world. The confusion was produced partly because people could move around so freely, and so discovered how many different philosophies and religions were on offer, all promising answers to doubt. The sheer variety was bewildering.

Take a walk down a street in Ephesus in the 1st century, for instance, and we are struck by the number of small shrines to different deities, tended by devotees who feel that the god or goddess has shown them favour. We may bump into a procession – perhaps in honour of the goddess 'Roma'. The imperial cult which worshipped 'Rome' was very popular at this time, because of the general peace and prosperity. (See 'Emperor worship and Revelation'.)

We pass large temples, dedicated to various gods, and become aware of the cult prostitutes, both men and women, who work in several of them, offering union with the power of the deity through sexual encounters. We realize, though, that the huge temple of Artemis in the centre of Ephesus is served by hundreds of virgin priestesses, promoting sexual abstinence and the superiority of women – and offering power through magic arts.

As we walk along, we see some of the *malakoi*, homosexual young men with coiffured hair – all dressed to kill – some of them with their older lovers. We remember the teaching of the great philosopher Plato, who believed that homosexual love was the most exalted form of human love. We know that young children are regularly drawn into these activities, and into sexual service in the temples.

Nearby is the cult-centre of one of the many 'mystery-religions', offering experience of divine power through special knowledge revealed only to cult members. We know that many of them use drugs or dancing to produce ecstasy.

We pass the synagogue, and notice that many ordinary Ephesians are going in. They are attracted by the antiquity of Judaism. Moses, the law-giver, lived hundreds of years ago, long before even the poet Homer! For many, Judaism has become a solid rock in a confusing world, although few go so far as to be circumcised and commit themselves wholly. Many try to combine the worship of several gods.

Now we arrive in the market-place at the centre of the city, and see the travelling philosophers and their schools of students. We pause to listen, first to the **Cynics**, who teach a simple, down-to-earth morality – how to live a good life. They cannot be bothered with the intellectual Stoics, teaching nearby. The **Stoics** tell us that God is present in everything, and that we must learn to live in harmony with God by practising 'indifference', so that we are not affected by extremes of emotion, whether joy or sorrow. They disagree totally with the **Epicureans**, who are also here: they do not believe in the existence of gods or the supernatural, and teach that pleasure is the supreme goal of life.

Where can we find truth in all this confusion?

Down a side-street we find the Hall of Tyrannus, where a strange Jew called Paul is teaching yet another religion, centred on Jesus who promises victory over death and all the powers of evil to any who will simply believe in him and confess him to be 'Lord'. Sounds interesting...

It is not difficult to draw parallels between the world of the Letters and our world today, in all its cultures! The message of the Letters has as much relevance now as it did then.

The readers of the Letters

The readers of the Letters all belonged to the world we have just described. Our own time is so distant that it is sometimes hard to realize how fresh, and totally revolutionary, Christianity then was. The Christian message was completely different from anything else on offer on Main Street, Ephesus.

But because the members of the first churches were often drawn from very diverse backgrounds, it was difficult for them to settle down in one, new fellowship. In particular, relations between Jews and Gentiles were often strained. This was partly because there was much puzzlement over the status and relevance of the Jewish law. Jewish Christians could see no reason to give up observing their food laws and festivals, but strict obedience to these laws made it impossible to have deep fellowship with Gentile Christians. Conversely, Gentile Christians could see no reason to start obeying such laws, especially if they had already worshipped in a synagogue without doing so. Paul devotes much space to this issue in Romans and Galatians.

We see the powerful influence of the surrounding culture in other ways too.
- Pagan sexual practices were creeping into the church in Corinth, and probably also worship-styles drawn from the mystery religions.
- The fear of evil powers was still very real for the Christians in Ephesus, and in Colossae.
- Hebrews was written to a group of Jewish Christians alienated from their fellowship, who felt that they wanted a bit more of the old, and less of the new.

They were real people, like the readers of the Letters today. So each letter had a specific purpose, addressing the particular needs of the readers, which varied greatly from letter to letter.

The variety of the Letters

The variety of the Letters is enormous, as a quick survey reveals. The obvious way to group them is by author, as the New Testament does.

There are 13 letters under Paul's name, one anonymous letter (Hebrews), one by James, two under Peter's name, three under John's and one by Jude.

Paul's letters fall naturally into four groups:
- 1 and 2 Thessalonians are probably the earliest, and are particularly concerned with Christ's return.
- Romans, Galatians and 1 and 2 Corinthians share a common emphasis on the gospel which Paul preached.
- The 'prison letters', in all of which Paul mentions that he is a prisoner, consist of Ephesians, Colossians, Philippians and Philemon. Some of his most profound teaching is included in these letters.
- The 'pastoral letters', 1 and 2 Timothy and Titus, are concerned with practical matters of church leadership and organization.

The other letters are often grouped under the title of 'General Letters'. They are addressed to a more general, less precisely defined, readership than Paul's letters, although Hebrews and 2 and 3 John were in fact written to specific churches or individuals.

The story of the Letters

The story of the different letters is not always easy to discover. Because they were written in response to people's needs and questions, they supply much basic Christian teaching, but not in an organized way. They are vigorous and dynamic, vivid snapshots from the lives of the first churches.

Acts is our only other source of information about the early church. But Acts too does not claim to present a complete record of events. So there are gaps in our knowledge, and details about which we cannot be certain. However the main lines of the picture can be drawn clearly.

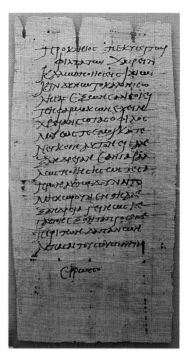

Paul's letters played a key role in his relations with the churches. Recorded for posterity, they were to prove the basis of Christian teaching and practice down the centuries to this day. This papyrus letter from the 1st century AD begins: 'Prokleios to his good friend Pekysis, greetings...'

The first letters 1 and 2 Thessalonians were written during Paul's time at Corinth described in Acts 18. An inscription at Delphi helps to fix this date at about AD 50-51.

By this time Paul had been a Christian for about 15 years, and had already devoted some years to teaching and church-planting. So these first letters were written by someone whose Christian thinking and ministry had already matured.

Even so, they have a wonderful freshness as we hear Paul recalling his ministry in Thessalonica, encouraging the believers to love and holiness, and explaining his revolutionary teaching on the second coming of Christ.

The 'gospel' letters The next group may be placed later, during the period covered by Acts 19 and 20 (although Galatians may have been written earlier from Antioch, Acts 14:26-28).

Paul had sailed from Corinth to Ephesus. After some time there he heard reports of difficulties in the church back at Corinth. He also received a letter from the church itself.

1 Corinthians was his reply. It is essentially a practical letter, in which he tries to heal the divisions in the church, and responds to some of the problems facing new Christians in a pagan city notorious for its immorality.

Paul's various contacts with the church at Corinth are not easy to unravel. It seems that he visited Corinth after writing his first letter, and may have written another letter which has been lost. At any rate, it is clear that he was not happy about the Corinthians' response to him. So he sent Titus to Corinth, and eventually received better news of the situation.

So then he wrote 2 Corinthians to express his relief and anxiety to preserve good relations, and to warn and encourage the church further.

Soon afterwards Paul visited Corinth again himself. While there (Acts 20:3) he wrote his famous letter to the Romans, the longest of his letters, and the nearest to a full summary of the Christian message. In it, he explains 'the gospel of God, of which I am not ashamed', and shows its implications for mission and for Christian living.

It is not certain why he wrote this powerful letter to the Romans. He had never been to Rome, but at this time he was hoping to travel there soon. So he may have wanted to introduce the church to the basics of his teaching, perhaps so that they would support his projected missionary journey to Spain. It also looks as though he wanted to bring about reconciliation between the Jewish and Gentile groups in the church there.

But it was not to work out as Paul had hoped. Soon afterwards, he travelled to Jerusalem, where he was arrested. After two years in prison in Caesarea, without trial, he claimed his right as a Roman citizen to be tried before the emperor. Eventually he arrived in Rome – in chains.

The prison letters Paul was allowed considerable freedom during his two-year imprisonment in Rome. He was under house arrest, but no restrictions were put on his visitors or his correspondence. So tradition favours Rome as the place from which Paul wrote the 'prison' letters.

Ephesians and Colossians are close in content, just as Ephesus and Colossae are quite close geographically. In spite of its title, Ephesians may have been a circular letter, sent to several small churches in Ephesus and the surrounding area, giving general teaching about Christ, the world and the church, in order to help the believers resist the pressure of pagan society around them and live faithful lives.

Colossians has a similar thrust, but in it Paul tackles some particular false teaching which was threatening the churches in Colossae and nearby Laodicea.

The little letter to Philemon belongs to this period. Paul writes tactfully, pleading on behalf of Onesimus, a runaway slave. By a huge divinely-engineered coincidence, Onesimus had run away from Paul's old friend Philemon, only to meet Paul hundreds of miles away in Rome. He became a Christian, and now returns to his old master bearing this lovely letter, no longer a mere slave but a brother in Christ.

Philippians deals with a different situation. Paul wanted to thank the Christians at Philippi for the concern they had shown in sending him gifts. His main reason for writing was to encourage them to remain united and joyful in the face of opposition and threats of various kinds. But he also wanted to pave the way for Timothy to visit them.

The remarkable feature of these 'prison letters' is the depth of Christian understanding Paul shows in them, particularly in Ephesians. Perhaps this resulted from long hours of reflection and prayer, while physical freedom was denied him.

The Pastoral Letters If Paul wrote these letters in his old age, as seems likely, he must have been released from his captivity in Rome, and had a further period of missionary travel not recorded in Acts.

1 and 2 Timothy and Titus show his deep care and concern for his churches and their organization, and his desire to leave them in good hands. 2 Timothy was written just before his death, encouraging Timothy to remain true to the gospel.

Hebrews The Letter to the Hebrews may also have been connected with the church in Rome. It is addressed not to a whole church, but to a group of Christian Jews who, it seems, were separating themselves from the main church and looking for security and peace again in Judaism. The unknown author – possibly Apollos – is deeply concerned about this, for he knows that Jesus the Messiah is not just a nice addition to Judaism, but the focus of all God's plans for the world. So he writes passionately, painting a vivid picture of Jesus' greatness, and encouraging them to remain faithful even if persecution comes their way.

Letters from other apostles 1 Peter is addressed to scattered Christians in five provincial districts of Asia Minor, at a time when persecution was looming. Peter wanted to encourage them with the example of Jesus, and with the thought of his victory on the cross by which salvation has been won. 2 Peter was presumably sent to the same circle of readers, but this time Peter warns against a particular false teaching which encouraged immorality.

1, 2 and 3 John may be the last New Testament writings. They date possibly from the 90s AD. According to tradition, John lived in Ephesus, so the background to the letters is probably church life in Asia Minor. Here 'docetism' was spreading – the view that 'the Christ' was a heavenly being incapable of suffering, so that he could not really have become flesh and died on the cross.

These letters oppose this teaching vigorously, and emphasize love and unity in the truth.

The Letter of James, on the other hand, is quite possibly the earliest part of the New Testament, written in the late 40s AD from Jerusalem, where James was the leader of the church. He wrote to Jewish Christians everywhere, at a time when many of them still belonged to synagogues, to encourage them to be distinctive disciples of Jesus.

Finally the brief letter of Jude is closely linked to 2 Peter, since much of the material about the false teaching occurs in both, often in similar language. Jude describes himself as James' brother, and it is reasonable to suppose that both were brothers of Jesus.

By their sheer variety, the Letters encourage us to see that it is always possible to live a faithful Christian life, whatever our circumstances, however difficult or strange or different from others'. The God and Father of our Lord Jesus Christ is with us, by his Spirit.

The New Testament Letters

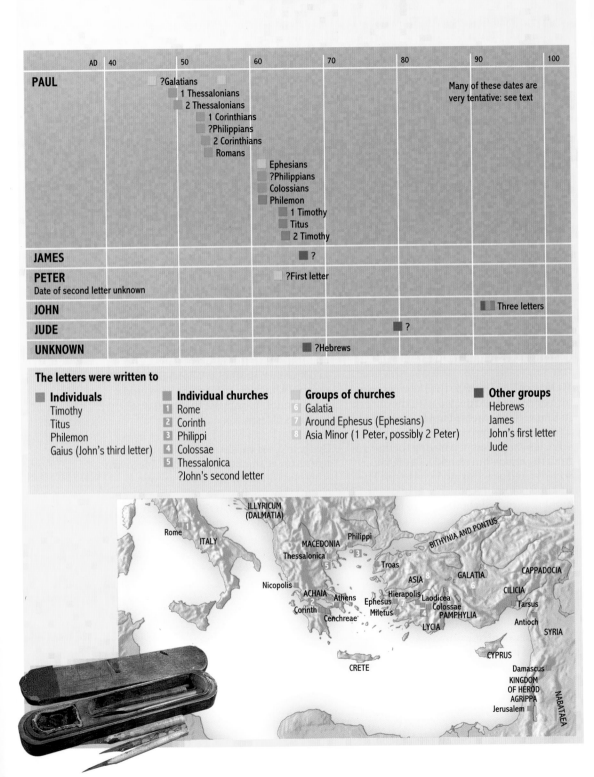

	AD 40	50	60	70	80	90	100
PAUL		?Galatians				Many of these dates are very tentative: see text	
		1 Thessalonians					
		2 Thessalonians					
		1 Corinthians					
		?Philippians					
		2 Corinthians					
		Romans					
			Ephesians				
			?Philippians				
			Colossians				
			Philemon				
			1 Timothy				
			Titus				
			2 Timothy				
JAMES			?				
PETER Date of second letter unknown			?First letter				
JOHN						Three letters	
JUDE				?			
UNKNOWN			?Hebrews				

The letters were written to

■ Individuals
Timothy
Titus
Philemon
Gaius (John's third letter)

■ Individual churches
1 Rome
2 Corinth
3 Philippi
4 Colossae
5 Thessalonica
?John's second letter

■ Groups of churches
6 Galatia
7 Around Ephesus (Ephesians)
8 Asia Minor (1 Peter, possibly 2 Peter)

■ Other groups
Hebrews
James
John's first letter
Jude

Romans

Summary

Paul writes to the Jewish and Gentile Christians in Rome, whom he hopes soon to visit, on the great themes of law, faith and salvation.

Chapters 1 – 11
Paul's gospel
Introducing the theme
(1:1-17)
The universal need
of salvation *(1:18 – 3:20)*
God's provision for all
(3:21 – 4:25)
New life in Christ *(5 – 8)*
The Jews in God's plan
(9 – 11)
•
Chapters 12 – 15:13
The Christian life
•
Chapters 15:14 – 16:27
Personal news and
greetings

Paul, the traveller and Roman citizen, had still not been to Rome when this letter was written (about AD 57). He had made three prolonged and extensive journeys, pioneering the Christian message throughout the eastern provinces of the empire and establishing churches. Now, probably in Corinth, about to take his relief fund to Jerusalem (see Acts 20), Paul's thoughts turn to pioneering the gospel in the west. He will travel to Spain and on the way fulfil the ambition of years by visiting the Christians at Rome.

Paul was not to know that three weary years would elapse between the letter and the visit, or that when he eventually entered Rome it would be as a prisoner (Acts 28).

The city and the church
See 'The city of Rome'. Rome in Paul's day was the capital of an empire which stretched from Britain to Arabia. Wealthy and cosmopolitan, it was the diplomatic and trade centre of the then-known world. All roads led to Rome. The Roman Peace made travel safer, though never quite free from danger (see 2 Corinthians 11:26); Roman roads made it relatively swift and easy. Visitors from Rome heard Peter's first sermon in Jerusalem on the Day of Pentecost.

So it is not surprising that there was a large and flourishing Christian community there by the time Paul wrote. Most were not Jews, and one reason for this letter may be that Paul wanted to encourage respect for their fellow Jewish Christians (see chapters 9 – 11 especially).

Some time earlier there had been trouble with the authorities. And although all was now quiet, the Christians were still suspect. Their Founder had, after all, faced a charge of treasonable activity against the emperor. And despite their efforts to live as loyal citizens of Rome, only a few years after this letter (in AD 64) Emperor Nero was able to make a scapegoat of the Christians, laying the blame on them when the city went up in flames. Tradition says that both Paul and Peter died in the ferocious persecution that followed.

The letter
Romans takes pride of place among the New Testament Letters, although it was not the first to be written. 1 and 2 Thessalonians, 1 and 2 Corinthians and Galatians are earlier, and some of the themes of those letters are taken up again in Romans. What impelled Paul to write at this particular point we do not know. Perhaps he already sensed he was risking his life by going to Jerusalem, and felt he might never speak to the Roman Christians in person. So he sets out vital elements of the Christian message important for them in their current situation and to help them understand more about his teaching.

The great theme of Romans is faith in the death and resurrection of Christ as the only ground of acceptance by God – a God who treats all people alike, Jew and Gentile.

Paul pulls no punches in describing the state the world is in (1:18-32). Everyone stands condemned by God's standards. Even the Jew, who has the unique privilege of knowing God's law, cannot keep it (2 – 3:20). But God offers us free pardon and new life. What we cannot do for ourselves, Jesus has done for us (chapter 5). We are free to make a fresh start – this time with all the power of God at our disposal (chapters 6 – 8).

Why, then, when the Gentiles respond eagerly to God's way of salvation, do most Jews reject it? This is something peculiarly painful to Paul, as a Jew himself. It seems they are so caught up with obedience to the law that they are unable to see that God has done something new in Christ. The old way of relating to God is still assumed to be *the* way, and binding on them. But in the end they too will 'come in' (chapters 9 – 11).

God's forgiveness and love spur us on to

> **" I am not ashamed of the gospel: it is the power of God for salvation to everyone who has faith. "**
>
> 1:16

Paul is harsh about the gross immorality and decadence of the Roman world. But he was not exaggerating. We can see this from some contemporary writing and from Pompeii, where the town and its people, in the midst of normal life, were buried in lava when Mt Vesuvius erupted soon after Paul wrote his letter to the Romans.

live up to our new calling – to reshape our whole way of thinking and manner of life. God's 'good news' is not an end in itself. It is meant to transform human relationships, making it possible for Jews and Gentiles to treat one another as equals in the church, and to permeate every aspect of daily living (chapters 12 – 15).

The impact and influence of Romans is immeasurable. It has fired the imagination of great men – Augustine, Luther, Bunyan, Wesley – and through them shaped the history of the church. But God has also touched the lives of countless individuals through this letter – ordinary men and women who have read and believed and acted on the apostle's teaching.

1:1-15
Opening lines

The apostle's whole life-mission is captured in his first few sentences. Paul, Christ's slave and emissary, commissioned to carry God's good news to the nations, writes to his fellow Christians in Rome. His 'grace' and 'peace' blend the traditional Greek and Jewish greetings into something uniquely Christian. What is the 'good news'? It is about the Son of God, raised from the dead – 'Jesus Christ our Lord' (2-4). (This is the gospel message: its effect is summarized in verses 16-17.)

Verses 7-15 are full of warm, human feeling. Paul greatly appreciates this group of Christians he has never met. He longs to see them and share with them all that the gospel means.

▶ **Verse 7** 'Saints' (older versions) are not a special, super-grade elite, but all who belong to Christ: God's people.

▶ **Verse 14** 'Greek and non-Greek/barbarian': those who were not Greek were considered uncivilized.

1:16 – 11:36
Paul's gospel

1:16-17 God's power to save
Paul glories in the good news from God which he has been called to make known to everyone. He will go into much more detail about it in the course of his letter. Here, he summarizes its effect:

■ it is God's power to save all who believe
■ it reveals God's 'righteousness'.

This is not simply an abstract moral perfection: it is the fact that he is true to his promises (his 'covenant faithfulness'). So 'when Paul announces that Jesus Christ is... Lord of the world, he is... unveiling before the world the great news that the one God of all the world has been true to his word, has dealt decisively with the evil that has invaded his creation, and is now restoring justice, peace and truth' (Tom Wright).

1:18 – 3:20 A world in need
Paul begins his thesis with a penetrating analysis of the human condition. Everyone

– Gentile (18-32) and Jew (2:1ff.) alike – is under God's judgment.

Humanity in general (1:18-32) refuses to acknowledge God. They have no excuse, for God can plainly be seen and known in his creation. So God lets them do as they want, and they sink deeper and deeper into the morass of their own perverse and perverted behaviour. Wrong thinking (irrationality) and wrongdoing go hand in hand. If reason is rejected (25), conscience will not be heard either (32).

Paul turns to **the Jews (2 – 3:20**, although they are not named until verse 17). They are quick to judge others, but ignore God's call to repent of their own wrongdoing. So they too stand condemned. God has no favourites. He judges all by the same standard (11). Those who do not have God's law and those who do will be judged, not by what they know but by what they do (13).

2:17-29: the Jews will be saved neither by the law (12-24) nor by circumcision (the outward sign of belonging to God; 25-29). They pride themselves in God and the law. They know what God wants them to do – but do they actually keep the law? If not, they 'might as well never have been circumcised'! The real Jew is one who obeys God from the heart.

3:1-20: Paul imagines the questions the hecklers will fling at him and meets their points one by one.

■ Have the Jews any advantage over others? Yes, the fact that God has entrusted them with his revelation (3:1-2).

■ What if some have failed in their trust? Will God go back on his promises? No. God still keeps his word (3:3-4), but promises will not save them.

■ Wrongdoing seems to serve a good end, since it highlights God's goodness. So why not 'do evil that good may come' of it? Because God is a just Judge – and the end does not justify the means (3:5-8).

■ Are the Jews any better off than other people? No. Everyone is in the grip of sin. The law makes people know they have sinned; it makes the Jews accountable – it is powerless to put anyone right with God (3:9-20).

▶ **Abandoned/given over (1:26, 28)** God does not force obedience. The Bible uses strong language. Those who will not hear will have their own way, and bear the consequences. But God never abandons people against their will.

▶ **2:6, 13** This seems to contradict what Paul has already said in 1:17. But the point he is making in these chapters is that no one actually does all that God requires. There is a new way of being put right with God.

▶ **Circumcision (2:25)** See Genesis 17.

▶ **2:29** There is a play on words here. 'Jew' is derived from 'Judah', which means praise.

▶ **Justified (3:20)** Also translated 'put right with God', 'found upright in the tribunal of God'. See 4:25.

3:21 – 5:21 God's provision

A free gift (3:21-31). Since God is just, and Jews and Gentiles alike are 'under the power of sin', how are things to be put right? The law cannot do it, so some new way must be found. The good news is that God himself, through the death of his own Son, Jesus Christ, has provided the means of our forgiveness (see also chapter 5). God has dealt with sin and shown himself true to his promises. The essence of the good news Paul was commissioned to preach, and the heart of the Christian message still, is that all who believe this are 'justified'– not by their own faith (that is only the channel by which pardon is received), but in the merciful kindness of God (his 'grace') through the death and resurrection of Jesus.

The faith of Abraham (chapter 4). Paul picks up on his statement in 3:21-22 that this same faith-principle is inherent in the Old Testament scriptures. If he can prove his point in the case of Abraham – father of the Jewish nation, and the prime example of an upright person – surely the Jewish objectors will be convinced. And he can. God accepted Abraham not because of his good life, but because of his faith (4:3; Genesis 15:6) – because against all the odds Abraham stuck to his conviction that God would do what he promised (Romans 4:21). The covenant-agreement, of which circumcision was the outward sign, came later (Genesis 17). So God's people are not those of Abraham's race who lay claim to

The city of Rome
David Gill

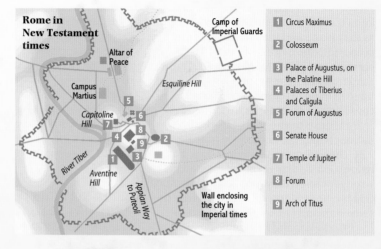

Rome in New Testament times

Altar of Peace

Campus Martius

Capitoline Hill

River Tiber

Aventine Hill

Appian Way to Puteoli

Esquiline Hill

Camp of Imperial Guards

Wall enclosing the city in Imperial times

1 Circus Maximus

2 Colosseum

3 Palace of Augustus, on the Palatine Hill

4 Palaces of Tiberius and Caligula

5 Forum of Augustus

6 Senate House

7 Temple of Jupiter

8 Forum

9 Arch of Titus

Rome is located on the River Tiber, and takes advantage of the 'seven hills' on which it is built.

Some of the earliest structures in Rome have been discovered on the Palatine Hill. Before the time of the emperors, the city was a relatively modest affair. It was Augustus (the first emperor) who apparently claimed to have transformed it into a city of marble. Certainly from reading Augustus' achievements, it is clear that he transformed Rome into a capital fit for domination of the Roman world.

The city itself was huge. Hints at its size can be gained from the size of the hand-outs given during Augustus' reign, which included gifts to 320,000 members of the urban plebs in 5 BC. If slaves, women and children are taken into account, the population of the city is likely to have been well over a million.

The administrative heart of Rome was the forum. It was here that the Senate met in the Curia. The forum was dominated by a massive temple dedicated to Julius Caesar, who had been turned into a god.

In fact there were two other fora in the 1st century AD (until Trajan added a further complex).

The first was a forum initiated by Julius Caesar and completed by Augustus. This included a temple of Venus Genetrix, the deity from whom Caesar believed his family had descended.

Next door was the Augustan forum dominated by a massive temple of Mars the Avenger, vowed before the battle of Philippi, fought between Augustus and Mark

The mad Caligula (Gaius), who succeeded Emperor Tiberius in AD 37 was murdered in AD 41. After him came Claudius.

AD 69 was the year of four emperors. Finally the troops declared for Vespasian. It was his son Titus who destroyed Jerusalem in AD 70. Vespasian ruled until AD 79, dying two months before Vesuvius erupted, burying Pompeii.

Antony on one side, and Brutus and Cassius, the assassins of Caesar, on the other.

To give some idea of the scale of religious buildings in Rome, Augustus claimed that in a single year, 28 BC, he restored 82 temples! An elaborately decorated Altar of Peace celebrated one of the gifts that the emperor bestowed on Rome and the empire.

The emperor's palace was located on the Palatine Hill above

the Roman forum. This was the site of Augustus' house, which was gradually expanded into a major complex under Domitian.

Augustus allowed part of his property to be used for the construction of an important temple of Apollo; contemporary writers made the point that the emperor had become a neighbour of the gods.

Other emperors had equally grand plans. The imperial

biographer Suetonius recorded that Gaius (Caligula) reputedly turned the temple of Castor and Pollux in the Roman forum into an entrance to his palace which lay up the slope behind. Nero constructed a huge complex in the area near the later Colosseum. Known as the Golden House, it contained numerous dining-rooms, a colossal statue of Nero, baths, and parks.

This was the city to which Paul came at last, as a prisoner. He had earlier written a long letter to the Christian group in the capital, many of whom were known to him.

Here he would spend two years in custody, having appealed to Caesar to judge his case. His movement was limited, but that did not stop him writing and making plans. Nor did it prevent people coming to him to learn more about Jesus and the new life he offers.

It is likely that Paul eventually died at Rome, where tradition has it that the apostle Peter was crucified.

The armies of Rome not only won the empire, they kept order in every part of it.

The forum of ancient Rome. In the centre is the temple of Castor and Pollux; on the left, the temple of Vesta; in the background, Emperor Titus' victory arch and Colosseum. On the right is the Palatine Hill.

the covenant promises as their birthright but those of any race who share Abraham's faith.

Christ and Adam (chapter 5). The death and resurrection of Jesus has given us a new standing before God. We have life. We have peace. We have hope. We have the presence of the Holy Spirit. There is point and meaning now to the rough and tumble of life (1-5).

But how can one man's death result in pardon for millions of others? The key lies in the solidarity of the human race. Sin, disobedience, began with one man (Adam) and spread to all his descendants. We all share the 'disease' and its inevitable consequence, the reign of sin and death which cuts us off from God. On the same principle, Jesus' 'righteous act', his obedience, has made acquittal and life available to all. The effect of God's gift far outweighs the effect of 'one man's sin'.

> **Justified (4:2)** Paul is using law-court language. There was no public prosecutor in a Jewish law-court – simply an accuser and a defendant. 'Having heard the case, the judge finds in favour of one party, and thereby "justifies" him: if he finds for the defendant, this action has the force of "acquittal". The person justified is described as "just", "righteous", not as a description of moral character but as a statement of his status before the court' (Tom Wright).

> **Grace (5:2)** One of Paul's favourite words. It means the (wholly undeserved) favour of God.

> **5:20** We all have an innate tendency to feel that laws were made to be broken. The fact that something is forbidden actually makes us want to do it more (see 7:8).

66 *The wage paid by sin is death; the gift freely given by God is eternal life in Christ Jesus our Lord.* **99**

6:23

66 *Christianity is the faith of ever-new beginnings.* **99**

Desmond Tutu

6 – 8 A new life!

Set free from sin (chapter 6). Since God has provided a way for sins to be forgiven, 'shall we persist in sin, so that there may be all the more grace?' What an absurd idea! Christians are 'joined' to Christ, sharing his death and resurrection. Baptism – going down into the water – signifies that the old life is dead and buried. We come up out of the water to begin a new life. We were dead to God before; now we are alive to him. Sin's stranglehold is broken. We must live in the light of that new freedom (10-11). We have a new master now: we serve God (17-18). And the wages paid by these two 'bosses' do not bear comparison (23).

Set free from the tyrant, law (7 – 8:4). Paul has already made it plain that the law cannot save: we cannot work our passage to heaven by keeping rules. The law is also limited to a person's lifetime (1-3). The new life God gives releases us from the law (4-6). Not that there is anything wrong with God's law in itself. It is wholly good. But by its very existence it creates an awareness of sin. Paul takes a personal example (7-24). He describes his own situation as a Jew, knowing the law and finding himself condemned by it, to the point of despair. This is how it was before he found deliverance from the grip of sin. He knew what was good and right, yet he found himself unable to do it. Sin held him prisoner. Who could effect his escape? 'Who but God?... through Jesus Christ our Lord' (25).

Set free from death (8:5-39). God has done what the law could not do (3). We are no longer controlled by our human nature:

Many stone carvings that illustrate Roman life have survived to the present day. Here Roman farmers pay for a lease of land.

we can live according to the Spirit. The Spirit of God is alive and actively at work in everyone who belongs to Christ (9). Even our bodies, which still die, will be raised to life by God's Spirit (11). It is his presence that convinces us we really are God's children (16). He is our foretaste (first instalment, 23) of glory to come – a living spring of hope within us. And he turns our inarticulate longings into prayer (26-27).

It is God's intention that every one of us should be like Christ (29). Like him in character now; like him in glory eventually. God is recreating us 'in his own image' (Genesis 1:27). And every little circumstance of life is worked into this great overall purpose (28). Nothing can shake it. No one can ever make God write us off – we have Christ in heaven to plead our cause. And no power in heaven or earth can cut us off from his love (38). So whatever life may bring, we can win through.

▶ **Sinful body (6:6**, some versions) Not the human body, but the 'sinful self'.

▶ **6:11** This is not a matter of playing games, pretending to be what we are not – but of being what we are. 'Dead to sin': in the sense that the score for the old life has been settled, not that we no longer feel its pull.

▶ **Flesh (7:5**, etc., some versions) Other versions translate as 'human nature', 'natural inclinations'. Here Paul is talking about the 'old person' that has passed away. But he often uses it in distinction from the 'spirit'. He is not subscribing to the Greek idea that the body (the physical) is sinful in itself. However, it remains, for the Christian, the vehicle through which sin can gain access. 6:13 tells Christians how to avoid this.

▶ **Body/state of death (7:24)** Human nature, subject to the laws of sin and death.

▶ **Likeness of sinful man (8:3)** Paul chooses his words with care. Jesus was a real person, but in one respect he was not identical to other people. He did not share the sinfulness that ordinarily goes with human nature.

▶ **8:10** 'Your bodies are going to die.'

▶ **8:11** Christians are promised a resurrection like Christ's.

▶ **Abba, Father (8:15)** The ordinary word a Hebrew-speaking child still uses for his 'daddy'.

▶ **Creation (8:19ff.)** Because we are part of nature, our sin brought pain and death not only

on ourselves but on the whole created world. So, in the day we are transformed, the creation will share our transformation. There will be 'a new heaven and a new earth' (Revelation 21:1).

▶ **Predestined/already chosen (8:29)** See 'God's sovereign choice'.

9 – 11 About Israel

As Paul dwells on God's glorious provision for all who are 'in Christ', he is filled with distress for Israel, God's own specially chosen and privileged people. How could they refuse to believe in their own, promised Messiah? The Gentiles responded eagerly to the gospel – but not the Jews. And Paul would have sold his own soul to have had it otherwise.

How can he account for this strange anomaly? God has not broken his word (9:6). All along he exercised his sovereign right of choice (9:6-13). And we can hardly call him to task for it. The Maker has an indisputable right to do as he pleases with what he makes (9:14-21). It is only by virtue of his patience and mercy that even a remnant of stubborn, rebellious Israel survived his judgment (9:22-29). People of other nations, knowing their failure, welcomed God's gift and achieved 'a righteousness based on faith'. The Jews, pursuing righteousness on the basis of deeds, refused God's better way (9:30-33).

Paul himself once shared this misplaced zeal. Now he longs for the Jews to believe as he does that 'Christ is the end of the law' (10:1-4). All who acknowledge Jesus as Lord and believe that God raised him from the dead will find salvation (10:5-13; and

The great city square (the forum) with its public buildings was the hub of ancient Rome, to whose Christians Paul wrote his letter. Even its ruins speak of the power and magnificence of empire.

❝I am convinced that neither death nor life..., nor things present, nor things to come... nor anything else in all creation. will be able to separate us from the love of God in Christ Jesus our Lord. ❞

8:38-39

Paul, writing about Jews and Gentiles (Romans 11), took an image from the practice of grafting new branches onto olive-trees.

see Philippians 2:11). The messenger's task is to make sure that everyone hears the good news. And Israel has heard, and understood – yet still refused to believe (10:14-21).

Has God rejected his people, then (11:1)? No. Paul himself is a Jew, one of the few who are true to God, as in the days of the prophet Elijah. The nation's blindness is partial and temporary. It has given the Gentiles their opportunity (11). They owe the Jews a great debt and should never disparage them. In due course their own faith will lead to a great turning to God among the Jews (25-26). God's ways are beyond understanding, but his purpose is 'to show mercy to all mankind' (32).

▶ **9:12-13** The quotations are from Genesis 25:23 and Malachi 1:2-3. Both refer to nations – Israel, descended from Jacob; Edom,

descended from Esau – rather than individuals. See Obadiah.

▶ **9:18, 22** See 'God's sovereign choice'.

▶ **Like Sodom... like Gomorrah (9:29)** I.e. utterly obliterated. See Genesis 19:24ff.

▶ **10:6-10** In the style of a Jewish teacher of his day, Paul gives a running commentary on Moses' words in Deuteronomy 30:11-14.

▶ **11:7** See 'God's sovereign choice'.

▶ **All Israel (11:26)** Israel as a whole.

▶ **Mercy to all (11:32)** Without distinction, rather than without exception.

12 – 15:13
The Christian life

Out of sheer love, and at great cost, God has saved his people's lives. Ought they not to be offered back, so that God can transform

Paul

Stephen Motyer

The apostle Paul was the first, and possibly the greatest, Christian theologian and missionary.

- He was the first fully to explain the death and resurrection of Christ as the focus of God's plan of salvation.
- It was he who first understood the new nature of God's people, now made up of Jews and Gentiles bound together in one 'body'.
- It was he who first saw how God's new action in Christ fits together with his special relationship with his 'old' people, Israel.
- And it was he who first spread the gospel effectively around the Gentile world, telling people simply of Jesus the Saviour, and not requiring them also to become Jews.

What a man!

Great hardship

He was criticized, hated and physically abused by Jews and Gentiles alike. His missionary travels involved terrible hardship, which he describes in detail in 2 Corinthians 11.

At times he felt great fear, but pressed on, sustained by revelations from God, by the love and support of his converts, by an overwhelming sense of call and of the love of Christ urging him on – and by a deep experience of the power of God working through him.

He thought of himself as continuing the ministry of Jesus by

The city of Antioch in Syria was the home-base from which Paul went out on missionary service. Antioch remains a major city today, and the ancient Byzantine church speaks of its long Christian history.

issuing God's appeal to the world to repent and 'be reconciled' to him through Christ.

As an apostle he even thought that his daily example of joy in suffering, and strength in weakness, was a public demonstration of the truth of the gospel, and the reality of Jesus' resurrection power.

He felt as though he had a debt to discharge by preaching and living the Good News before all people.

So it was not possible to be neutral about Paul. People either hated him, because he disturbed their comfortable certainties, or loved him, because his message had proved life to them, too.

He saw his life as a race run at full stretch for Christ and others, as a battle waged with spiritual weapons against the powers of evil, even as a sacrifice offered up to Christ, like the animal sacrifices of the Old Testament.

Passionate love

His love for his converts was passionate. In his letters he pictures himself variously as their father, mother, nurse, servant, and brother. He held himself up as an example for them to follow, and lived every moment knowing that he must one day appear before Christ to give account for his ministry.

What made him do all this?

Paul's early life

- He was born probably around AD 5, in Tarsus in Cilicia (the south coast of modern Turkey), where his father was a leading citizen and also a very strict Jew.
- Paul inherited Roman citizenship from his father, a rare privilege for someone born outside Rome.
- At a young age Paul was sent for his education to Jerusalem, where he had relatives.
- He grew up passionately committed to 'the traditions of the fathers', as he puts it, a Pharisee of intense devotion, and violently opposed to the suggestion that a cursed criminal could be the Messiah. In his passion for the Jewish law he began a violent campaign

Paul spent two years in prison at Caesarea before taking ship from its harbour to have his case heard by the emperor in Rome.

against those who believed such blasphemy.

The turning-point

Then came the conversion experience described three times in Acts (9:3-19; 22:3-21; 26:9-18), when he discovered that his zeal for the law had led him to persecute the Messiah – and that God had nonetheless accepted him, forgiven him, and called him to be a prophet and apostle on behalf of Jesus.

His conversion was also his call.

But he knew that he could not simply add belief in Jesus as Messiah to his previous Jewish beliefs. So he had to rethink his whole theology, wrestling again with the scriptures in the light of this amazing discovery of a Messiah who had died and risen again, and of his call to preach him to the Gentiles.

How could he tie it all together? He could not simply reject God's law, but clearly God had now done something wonderfully new – though promised by the prophets.

It is likely that the first few years after his conversion were spent in intense prayer and thought in the Roman province of Arabia.

Then he started work!

The travelling preacher

Barnabas called him from Tarsus to help the ministry in Antioch, where for the first time Jewish Christians abandoned the food laws which kept them separate from Gentiles, and formed a single community with Gentile believers. Paul knew that this was right, and the church there became his home, and the base for the three missionary journeys that followed.

These began probably in AD 47, and over the next 15 years Paul travelled all over the eastern Mediterranean with various companions, preaching the gospel first in the synagogues, and then among the Gentile communities.

He paused in Corinth (to stay over 18 months) and in Ephesus (over two years), because these were great trading centres, from which the Good News would easily spread. After 10 years of hard work his boast was that 'from Jerusalem in a circle right round to Illyricum (Bosnia) I have fully preached the Gospel of Christ!'

He longed to reach Rome,

but first had to endure two years' imprisonment without trial in Caesarea. Eventually he exercised his right as a Roman citizen to appeal for trial before the emperor in Rome, and so was transported there as a prisoner.

After waiting for two years for his trial, he may have been freed for a further period of travel and ministry before his final arrest and execution, possibly by the Emperor Nero in Rome in AD 65.

Thirteen of Paul's letters are included in the New Testament. All date from the period of his travels and imprisonments, probably starting with Galatians (about AD 49) and ending with 2 Timothy (about AD 65). His letters are one of the great foundation-stones of the church of Jesus Christ. But he points away from himself. 'We proclaim not ourselves,' he wrote, 'but Jesus Christ as Lord! – and ourselves as your servants for Jesus' sake!'

Through his writings, he serves us still.

KEY PASSAGES FOR PAUL'S LIFE AND WORK

Acts 9:1-30; 11:19-26; 13 – 28; 1 Thessalonians 1:1 – 2:12; Galatians 1:11 – 2:16; 2 Corinthians 2:14 – 6:13; Romans 1:1-17, 15:14-24.

'Don't let the world mould you to its pattern,' Paul urges his Christian readers. This mould and the image produced from it gives us the picture.

and renew them? This will mean a complete re-orientation, changing outlook and attitude as well as behaviour (12:1-2).

12 Family relations

The transformation begins as individuals take their place in the new 'family' of Christ. Our own stock must go down: our opinion of others, up. The gifts God gives are to be used for the good of the whole Christian community. Love is the hallmark. We are to serve God without flagging. Old attitudes must change – not only towards fellow Christians but towards the outside world. Instead of giving tit-for-tat when we are wronged, we treat the enemy as our best friend, and leave God to do the judging.

13 The powers that be

Because the authorities are given their power by God, for the public good, Christians are required to 'submit' to them. Taxes are to be paid, and laws observed. The Christian has a duty to meet all 'Caesar's' lawful demands. But submitting does not mean that every command must be obeyed. There are times when these demands directly conflict with the

commands of God. Then it is right to say 'No', and suffer the consequences (Acts 5:29).

No debt must be incurred, other than the permanent obligation to love – and not wrong – others. Paul is conscious of living in a time of crisis (11). 'Salvation is nearer' than when they first believed. So his call to live as God requires has a note of urgency about it.

14 Freedom and responsibility

There are some matters of conscience over which Christians disagree. (Paul instances the eating of meat, 2-3 – see on

> ❝ Romans 13... is the opposite of a totalitarian charter... Caesar and his henchmen actually work for the one God of Israel, and are accountable to him. This does not legitimise their particular style, laws or mode of operation; it locates them on the cosmic map, in which the creator God desires peace and justice, not anarchy. At the same time Paul is urging Roman Christians not to repeat the mistakes made in the late 40s, when Jews (including Jewish Christians) were expelled from Rome following riots. ❞
>
> *Tom Wright*

> **"** *Accept one another as Christ accepted us, to the glory of God.* **"**
>
> 15:7

1 Corinthians 8 – and observance of Jewish feast days, 5). It is not helpful to argue over 'doubtful points'. Those who are strong in the faith may feel free to do things that would give others a bad conscience. That is no reason to despise them. Neither side should pass judgment on the other. All of us, Paul says, are answerable, not to one another, but to Christ. It is better to limit our own freedom than exercise it at a fellow Christian's expense.

▶ **14:2, 14** There was the problem that meat sold in the market had been sacrificed to pagan gods; also, the Jews had strict laws about 'clean' and 'unclean' animals and the method of slaughter. If Jewish Christians insisted on the letter of the law, and Gentile Christians stuck out for freedom, the two sections would never share a meal together.

15:1-13 Make Jesus your model

There is nothing Christian about pleasing ourselves. Good relations between Christians are far more important than 'my rights'. With Christ as our role-model, we must do all we can to promote real oneness, no matter what background we come from.

15:14 – 16:27 In closing...

15:14-33 Personally speaking

In closing, Paul speaks personally. For more than 20 years he has been an apostle to the non-Jewish world. He has seen churches established all over Cyprus, Syria, Turkey and Greece (to use their modern names). Now he has completed this work and discharged his responsibilities. Once

God's sovereign choice

In Romans 9 and 11 we have perhaps the most forthright treatment of God's sovereign right to choose his people in the whole Bible.

Paul's starting-point is that no one has any claim on God's mercy. He shows how God in his love has chosen certain individuals down the ages to play a special role in his purpose for the world (9:6-13). And he emphasizes the wideness of God's mercy (11:28-32). God the Creator has the right to choose, and we have no right at all to question his choice or doubt his justice.

If God selects some for forgiveness, does he select others for judgment? Paul is much more cautious about this ('What if...?' 9:22). He contents himself with asserting God's right to do so but at the same time stresses God's patience (9:22). He talks about God hardening people's hearts

(9:18; and see 1:28), but in every instance these are people who have exercised the freedom God has given us *not* to listen to him – our right deliberately to go against him if we so decide.

Paul declares the sad truth: 'Not all the Israelites accepted the glad news' (10:16). God never hardens the hearts of those who *want* to know him and do his will:

'*Everyone* who calls on the name of the Lord will be saved' (10:12).

Human beings are not helpless pawns in the hands of a capricious god. The Bible teaches God's sovereign right to choose those he will save. It also teaches human responsibility.

It may be beyond our limited understanding how God's 'election' and human freedom can operate simultaneously (just as it is hard to understand how scientists can describe light in terms of waves *and*

particles – two ideas which seem mutually contradictory). God is not subject to the things which limit our understanding. So we can only take God's word, holding on to both his sovereignty and our freedom to choose – not trying to find a compromise between them.

the business of delivering the money given by the Gentile churches to Jerusalem (a visit about which he has real misgivings) is over, he can look west to Spain, calling at Rome on the way.

▶ **Illyricum (19)** Former Yugoslavia.

▶ **Macedonia and Achaia (26)** Northern and southern Greece.

16 Greetings to friends

It is in one way surprising to find such a long list of friends in a church which Paul had never visited. (For this reason some believe this chapter originally belonged to a copy of Romans which was sent to Ephesus.) Yet all roads led to Rome, and many Christians from the eastern provinces must have passed through the capital at one time or another. It is obvious that despite his busy life Paul did not lose interest in people or lose touch with them.

As he signs off he feels compelled to warn the Roman Christians against a set of troublemakers (17ff.). He knows their disruptive influence on the churches all too well.

But then, as always at the close of his letters, his thoughts return to the wisdom and glory of the eternal God he has been called to serve.

▶ **Phoebe (1)** It was probably Phoebe – travelling from Cenchreae, the port of Corinth – who carried Paul's letter to Rome.

▶ **Priscilla and Aquila (3)** A couple whose home was in Rome, but who travelled extensively in the course of their leather-working business. They did sterling Christian work at Corinth and Ephesus (Acts 18:2-3, 18-28).

▶ **Rufus (13)** May be the son of Simon of Cyrene (Mark 15:21).

▶ **Verse 21** Timothy is well known in the Letters. He was like a son to the aging Paul. Jason may be Paul's host from Thessalonica (Acts 17:5-9). Sosipater may be Sopater from Beroea (Acts 20:4).

▶ **Tertius (22)** The Christian who acted as Paul's secretary in writing this letter.

▶ **Erastus (23)** This may be the same public official whose name has been found inscribed on a marble paving-block at Corinth, dating from this time.

In Romans 16 Paul names many friends, both men and women, at Rome. This head of a Roman woman reminds us of those real people.

1 Corinthians

Summary

Paul writes in response to a number of reports and questions from the church at Corinth.

Chapters 1 – 4
Divisions in the church:
Paul's message

•

Chapters 5 – 10
Issues of sexual morality and Christian behaviour
Food offered to idols:
rights and duties

•

Chapters 11 – 14
Order and disorder in the church: proper dress, the Lord's Supper, spiritual gifts

•

Chapter 15
About resurrection

Chapter 16
Closing messages and greetings

Best-known passage

On love *(13)*

Paul wrote this letter from Ephesus (15:32; 16:8), in about AD 54. Acts 18 recounts Paul's 18-month stay at Corinth on his second missionary journey – and describes the founding of the church.

The city

See 'The city of Corinth'. The old Greek city of Corinth was destroyed and rebuilt by the Romans. It stood in a strategic position to control trade across the narrow neck of land between the Aegean and Adriatic Seas. A thriving centre of commerce and a cosmopolitan city where Greeks, Latins, Syrians, Asiatics, Egyptians and Jews rubbed shoulders, it was an obvious target for Paul. Establish a church here, and the Christian message would quickly spread far and wide.

Yet in other ways it is hard to imagine a less likely place for the new faith to take root. The town was dominated by the temple of Aphrodite (goddess of love), built on the heights of the acropolis. Thousands of temple prostitutes, a large floating population, and the general racial hotch-potch, all contributed to the city's unsavoury reputation. Corinth was a by-word for excess and sexual licence. There was even a word for it: to 'Corinthianize'.

The church

The Christian church, like the city, was racially and socially mixed. There were a few Jews, but more Gentiles. Few if any Christians belonged to the patrician 'nobility' (1:26). The Christian community ranged from slaves at one end of the spectrum to 'upwardly mobile' office holders (like city-treasurer Erastus, Romans 16:23) at the other. Many were converts from a permissive pagan back-ground. They had little to boast of – yet they prided themselves in their intellectual prowess. They bandied about such slogans as 'Liberty' and 'Knowledge'. Those Paul is primarily concerned to correct in his letter are a number of relatively high-status Gentile men who, though they have become Christians, want their social lives to continue unchanged. This is the group causing most of the problems in the church.

The letter

Two factors lie behind the writing of 1 Corinthians.

First, Paul had received reports of the church which made him very uneasy (1:11; 5:1).

Second, a delegation arrived from Corinth, and (or with) a letter seeking his advice on various questions (7:1; 16:17).

In the letter, Paul takes up five of the matters reported to him:
- divisions in the church;
- a case of incest;
- court-cases between members;
- the abuse of Christian 'freedom';
- the general chaos reigning in church services, even in the Lord's Supper.

He also answers questions the Corinthians have written about:
- questions about marriage and single life (see 'Sexual issues in the church at Corinth');
- problems over food consecrated to idols and social functions held in the temples;
- whether or not women should cover their heads to pray, and their place in public meetings (Paul also insists that men should pray and prophesy bare-

headed, although Greek and Roman men and women customarily covered their heads during an act of worship or sacrifice);
- the matter of spiritual gifts;
- the fact and the meaning of resurrection.

Paul's reply to these questions gives us a fascinating glimpse of what actually went on in one of the early churches, and it is none too savoury!

1:1-9 Greeting and prayer

Paul's opening and thanksgiving (1:4-9) are characteristic. He believes in encouragement. Of all his letters to churches, only Galatians lacks this note of praise.

▶ **Sosthenes (1)** Possibly the synagogue leader mentioned in Acts 18:17. He may be acting as Paul's secretary.

▶ **Verse 8** The 'Day' refers to Christ's return and the final judgment.

1:10 – 4:21 Rival cliques

In a day before church buildings, when Christians met in houses or halls, and a large group might well have to split up, it is easy to see how divisions could arise. Paul mentions three factions centred on rival 'leaders': Paul (their founder), Apollos and Cephas (Peter). A fourth division, in their pride, claimed exclusive rights to the label 'Christian'.

Apollos (1:12) was a Jewish Christian from Alexandria (Egypt). When he arrived in Ephesus, Aquila and Priscilla took him aside for fuller instruction (Acts 18:24ff.). He travelled to the province of Achaia (of which Corinth was capital), where he proved a powerful and eloquent teacher.

The mention of Peter (Cephas, 1:12) does not necessarily mean he visited Corinth. As leader of the 12 apostles it would be natural for him to have a following, particularly among Jewish Christians.

It seems from these chapters that the groups were making invidious comparisons between Paul and the more eloquent Apollos. Paul, although a trained scholar, had had his troubles at Corinth (Acts 18:9-10; 1 Corinthians 2:3). A clear statement of God's message, not style without substance, was his main concern.

66 The message about the cross is foolishness to those who are perishing, but to us who are being saved it is the power of God... For God's foolishness is wiser than human wisdom and God's weakness is stronger than human strength. 99

1:18, 25

The road leading down from Corinth to its port. Behind the ruins of the ancient city lies its fortified acropolis.

The city of Corinth
David Gill

The ancient city of Corinth stood at one of the key cross-roads of the Mediterranean. It dominated the important Isthmus of Corinth which joins the Greek mainland to the Peloponnese.

This narrow neck of land separates the eastern Mediterranean from the Adriatic Sea (and thus Italy and the western Mediterranean). A direct route across it avoids a potentially dangerous voyage around the southern Peloponnese and Cape Malea. A special paved road was built in about 600 BC to help move cargoes from one side to the other. (Much later, when the Roman Emperor Nero visited Greece in AD 67 he initiated a grand scheme to cut a canal through the Isthmus, but the project was not completed.)

The Greek city of Corinth was destroyed by the Romans in 146 BC. It lay desolate for the next

century, and the neighbouring city of Sikyon took over responsibility for the Isthmian Games. These were one of the four main pan-Hellenic Games – the other centres being Olympia, Delphi and Nemea – in which Greeks could compete.

In 44 BC the city was refounded

The great temple at Corinth was dedicated to the sun-god, Apollo (see picture on p. 705). This head of Apollo is Roman, from Perge, 2nd century AD.

as a Roman colony by Julius Caesar. It was given a Roman feel through the use of Roman rather than Greek architecture for its buildings and public spaces.

Most of the public inscriptions for the first century or more of the colony's life were in Latin rather than Greek, reflecting the cultural identity of the city. These texts indicate the way that, as in other Roman cities, wealthy individuals expressed their generosity by donating buildings and other facilities for the benefit of the colony.

A well-known example was the provision of a square next to the theatre in the middle years of the 1st century AD, given by Erastus, *aedile* (a Roman magistrate) of the city (see inscription). A man of the same name described as 'steward of

The Isthmian Games held at Corinth were famous throughout Greece. This figure of a young athlete is Roman, late 1st century BC – 1st century AD. The wreaths and inscriptions record the athletes' triumphs in several of the important Games of the Greek world.

The city of Corinth as it is today. The acrocorinth rises behind the ruins.

In his account of Paul's time in Corinth, recorded in Acts 18, Luke mentions an important judgment made by Governor Gallio. An inscription from Delphi records Gallio's time as governor of the province of Achaia.

the city' appears in Paul's Letter to the Romans (16:23), written from Corinth.

Corinth remained a major city throughout the Roman period, with its two harbour complexes of Cenchreae on the eastern Saronic Gulf, and Lechaeum on the Corinthian Gulf. It was the administrative centre for the Roman province of Achaia, which covered the Peloponnese and most of the southern mainland of Greece.

As a result it became fashionable for the social élites of other cities in the province to fulfil magistracies in Corinth. For example, we find members of the Euryclid family from Sparta taking a leading role and becoming benefactors of the city.

As the centre of a Roman province with good communications to the eastern Mediterranean and to Italy itself, Corinth became a natural focus for Paul's ministry.

Paul's first visit to Corinth lasted some 18 months. It can be dated fairly precisely because during his stay he was brought before Gallio, the governor of Achaia. Gallio's time as governor is recorded in an inscription from Delphi which can be dated to AD 51 or 52.

Paul wrote two letters to the church at Corinth, and his Letter to the Romans seems to have been written from there, as it includes greetings from members of the Corinthian church.

Excavations by the American School of Classical Studies have revealed evidence for a range of religious cults within the city. Further details about the cults have been provided by inscriptions as well as descriptions by authors writing in the Roman period.

The geographer Strabo, writing during the reign of the Emperor Augustus, commented that the temple of Aphrodite on Acrocorinth (the mountain dominating the city) was only a small building

An inscription originally set in bronze letters into the pavement at Corinth names the city magistrate, Erastus, as the donor (honouring his election promises!). Paul mentions a city official with this name.

in his day. The major complex of the Hellenistic period disappeared with the sack of the city by the Romans.

Aphrodite was a particularly important deity for Julius Caesar and his adopted son the Emperor Augustus, as they claimed to trace their ancestry back to Venus, the Roman equivalent of Aphrodite.

This portrait from Corinth of the Roman Emperor Augustus wearing a toga, reminds us of the Roman background to this cosmopolitan city.

But the Corinthians were infected with something of the spirit of nearby Athens. They fancied themselves as thinkers and took pride in their supposed intellectual superiority. In fact, as Paul points out (3:1-4), their argumentative, judgmental attitude shows they are still bound by the world's way of thinking. They stand in need of teaching. They have to be reminded that human cleverness is a far cry from God's wisdom (1:18 – 2:16). It is not proud and clever people who appreciate the wisdom of God's plan of salvation through Christ's death on the cross, but those who are spiritually wise. This kind of wisdom, and with it true values and real judgment, is God's gift through his Holy Spirit. A person must become a fool in the world's eyes in order to be really wise (3:18).

So Paul and Apollos are not rivals but partners, sharing the work of building God's church (3:5-9). Once the basic foundation of faith in Christ is laid, every Christian is responsible for what they do with the new life they have been given. See to it that you build to last, Paul says (3:10-17).

There should be no place for pride among Christians and no looking down on others. The greatest Christians regard themselves as no more than God's slaves. That is the example to follow (chapter 4).

▸ **Chloe's people (1:11)** Presumably members of Chloe's household.

▸ **Stephanas (1:16)** A founder-member of the church at Corinth, and one of the delegation sent by the church to Paul at Ephesus (16:15ff.).

▸ **1:17** Evangelism – telling the Good News – not baptism, was Paul's main work.

▸ **Jews and Greeks (1:22)** National character-istics show through. The Jews want evidence (miracles). The Greeks are into speculative philosophy. Nor do the two share the same concept of salvation. For the Greeks, to be saved means rescue, healing or being set free from slavery.

▸ **1:26** See introduction.

▸ **Mystery/secret truth (2:1,** some versions) Other manuscripts have 'testimony'.

▸ **You are God's temple (3:16)** Here Paul means the whole church; later (6:19) he refers to the individual.

▸ **Guardians/tutors (4:15)** Slaves who looked

after their master's children and took them to school.

▸ **Timothy (4:17)** Paul's younger colleague in the work (16:10-11; Acts 16:1-4).

5 Incest in the church

In the name of their boasted 'liberty' the church is condoning incest (both Roman and Jewish law forbade marriage between a man and his stepmother). It is a case which would shock even the pagans in that notorious city. These Christians have brought their old values with them into the church, and never given them up. So the whole church is endangered (as Paul had warned in a previous letter, though they had mistaken his meaning, 9-13).

▸ **Hand over to Satan (5)** The phrase is used only here and in 1 Timothy 1:20. Short-term discipline is to be exercised for the long-term good of both the church and the individual concerned. The man is to be expelled from the church: 'delivered over into that region where Satan holds sway' (Leon Morris). It is hard to see how this would result in the 'flesh' (perhaps 'sinful lusts') or 'body' being destroyed.

▸ **Leaven (6-8)** Yeast – often (though not always) used as a picture of the corrupting power of evil. Bread for the Passover was made without leaven, as a reminder of the Israelites' hasty departure from Egypt. Christ has become our Passover sacrifice, says Paul; it is time we got rid of the old yeast of evil in our lives.

6:1-11 Lawsuits between Christians

Christians should not take one another to court, as some of the Corinthians have done. Jews did not take cases before Gentile courts – not because the courts were corrupt (although that was often the case, and bribery was rife), but because it would be an admission of Jewish inability to operate their own laws. Surely the Christ-ian community – these 'wise' Corinthians – should be capable of settling internal disputes. Better to be wronged than drag one another to court.

▸ **Judge the world (2), judge angels (3)** Paul is speaking of the final judgment. This is a development from Christ's teaching in Matthew 19:28. The 'angels of the cosmos' are mentioned as the highest order in the created universe.

6:12-20 Freedom, or licence?

The Corinthians claim they are free to do anything (see also 10:23). 'No doubt,' says Paul, 'but I for one will not let anything make free with me' (6:12). Sexual needs, they argue, are like hunger: they must be satisfied. The body is not important anyway. But this is wrong thinking, a carry-over of old (Greek) ideas. For the Christian the body cannot be separated off from the whole personality. (Paul deliberately avoids the Greek body/soul language and the concepts that go with it.) You cannot sin with the body and keep the 'real' person untarnished: every individual is a unity. Christians have been joined to Christ's body: they must honour God in the way they use their own bodies.

7 Answers to questions on marriage

In their letter to Paul, the Corinthians have raised six questions about single and married life.

- Are married couples to continue normal sexual relations after conversion? Yes (7:1-7).
- Should single people marry? Paul prefers the single life – but only for those with the gift of self-control (8-9).
- Is divorce between Christians permissible? No (10-11).
- What about the unconverted husband or wife? Christians are to stick to their pagan partners, unless the partner wants separation (12-16).
- The fifth question is not so clear. Most likely it is: 'Should engaged couples marry?' This must be a matter for personal decision, but in the very troubled times Paul sees ahead, single people will find it easier to work out their Christian priorities (25-38).
- May widows remarry? Yes, but Paul qualifies this (39-40).

▶ **Verses 10, 12** Paul is careful to distinguish between commands given by Jesus (or a tradition which he began) and his own teaching.
▶ **Verse 29** Paul doesn't mean the men to desert their wives, or be irresponsible. He is talking about priorities, and how everyday concerns can dominate life.

8 The question of food offered to idols

It was hard in Corinth to make a clean break with paganism. Trade groups and clubs held their social functions at the temples. Most of the meat sold in the shops had first been offered in sacrifice.

Some Christians maintain that since other gods do not really exist ('idols are nothing') they are free to eat meat and attend club dinners. But others are worried. Freedom is right, says Paul. But no one should exercise personal freedom at the expense of another person's conscience. Love is more important than knowledge.

The issue is not so much the food as where it is eaten. It is never right – not even on social occasions – to eat at the table of demons in a pagan temple. (This was only an isssue for the social élite: the poor were not normally invited to temple feasts.)

9 Rights and responsibilities

Paul takes examples from his own life, to drive home the lesson that Christians should curtail their own freedom if there is any risk it will damage others or lead them astray.

If anyone has rights, surely it is the apostle. Yet he has gladly given up his right to take a wife with him on his trips and his right to expect the church to provide his keep. There are more important things than rights. For the gospel's sake this 'free man' willingly subjects himself to

This diagram of the Asclepion at Corinth helps to explain the question raised by the Christians about 'food offered to idols'. The dining-rooms used for social functions by trade groups are directly beneath the temple's holiest place.

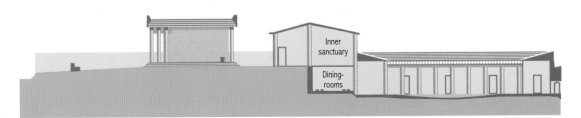

Inner sanctuary

Dining-rooms

Writing from Ephesus, where this sculpture of a winged Victory bearing a wreath and a palm was found, Paul compares the Christians to athletes: they compete for a fading wreath, Christians for one that never fades.

restrictions laid on him by others in order to win people for Christ.

▶ **In a race... (24-27)** The Isthmian Games (second only to the Olympics) were held every three years at Corinth. Each competitor underwent 10 months' stiff training, hoping to be crowned with the victor's pine wreath. Paul was afraid, not of losing his salvation, but of failing to measure up to his calling. Hence the need to keep striving for the goal, and not throw salvation away (like the Israelites in the wilderness: chapter 10).

10:1-13 A warning from history

It is easy to be over-confident, especially when life is smooth (10:12-13). The fate of many of the people of Israel during the wilderness wanderings stands as a solemn warning. (Hebrews 3:7ff. draws similar lessons from the same events.)

▶ **Verse 7** Exodus 32:6.
▶ **Verse 8** Numbers 25:1-9.
▶ **Verse 9** Numbers 21:5-6.
▶ **Verse 10** Numbers 16:41-49.

10:14 – 11:1 Paul's appeal and summary

Christians must choose between the Lord and idols (empty in themselves but, behind them, real demonic powers). There can be no compromise. It is playing with fire to have any part in pagan sacrifices. As far as meat is concerned, the rule is unselfish

concern for the good of others.

▶ **The cup of blessing/thanksgiving (10:16)** The name given to the third cup in the Passover feast, over which a prayer of thanksgiving was said. This may well have been the cup with which Jesus instituted his memorial Supper – hence the thought here.

11:2-16 Disorder in the church: the question of proper dress

Some of the women in the church at Corinth have flouted custom by praying bareheaded. What is the proper (head)dress for men and women when they pray and prophesy in the church? Since Jewish customs differed from those of the Greeks and Romans, Paul needs to give a ruling.

The men, he says, should pray bareheaded (contrary to Greek and Roman custom), but women should cover their heads. A covered head is the symbol of authority given to women by God. This is a difficult passage and the meaning is not wholly clear. In the end Paul falls back on what is customary in the churches (16).

The issue is one of order and disorder, of God's glory and human glory. In contemporary usage, 'head' did not convey control, authority or leadership, though it *was* used to mean 'source', which seems to be the meaning here.

'Paul was writing to the most licentious city in the ancient world, and... in such a place modesty had to be observed and more than observed;... it is quite unfair to wrest a local ruling from the circumstances in which it was given, and to make it a universal principle' (William Barclay).

▶ **Dishonours his head (4-5)** I.e. 'disgraces Christ'.
▶ **Have her hair cut off (6)** The punishment for a prostitute at that time.
▶ **The image and glory of God (7)** Genesis 1:26-27 includes both sexes in God's 'image', but does not mention 'glory'.
▶ **Verse 10** In Jewish teaching the angels represent order. A woman who does not cover her long hair when she prays aloud in church or speaks God's message contravenes the 'proper order' in worship. She is displaying her own (human) glory, when the focus should be on God's glory. Some versions have 'husband' in this verse, but Paul is talking about men and

In 1 Corinthians 11 Paul answers questions about proper dress for worship, particularly covering the head, where traditions were contradictory. This figure, probably of an early emperor, with his toga pulled up over his head was found at Corinth.

women, not husbands and wives in this whole passage.

11:17-34 Disorder in the church: greed at the Lord's Supper

In the early days the Lord's Supper took place in the course of a communal meal. It was 'bring-and-share', with everyone bringing what food they could. But in Corinth the loving, sharing principle has broken down. Some begin to eat before others have arrived. And some get drunk while others go hungry. It is a disgrace – a serious offence. Paul has to remind them of the circumstances in which the first Lord's Supper took place.

▶ **This is my body (24-25)** The earliest record of Jesus' words.

▶ **In an unworthy manner (27-30)** No Christian is ever 'worthy' to come into God's

---

Sexual issues in the church at Corinth

Vera Sinton

Some members of the Corinthian church were Jewish, brought up with clear rules against incest, adultery and same-sex intercourse. It had been agreed, however, that Christians need not keep the whole Jewish law. Jesus had brought freedom and change into the lives of his followers. The question was, how much freedom in matters like sex?

In Corinth there seem to have been 'abstainers', who thought Christians were already 'raised from the dead' to a new life free from sex. They were choosing not to sleep with their husbands or wives. Some were separating or divorcing (7:5-11). There were also 'indulgers' who thought Christians were free to have sex with prostitutes, to satisfy a physical need similar to hunger (6:13-15). Paul uses five great Christian themes to indicate the boundaries of Christian freedom.

■ **Creation** God designed sexual intercourse to help a man and a woman form a bond in marriage which is like one organism, 'one flesh' (6:16). It is a relationship of equality. Each rules over the body of the other (7:4) in the sense of having freedom, not control. If they agree to be apart for a while, they should come together again soon.

■ **Redemption** Though created for good, sexuality contains the potential to hurt and damage. Sexual sins, along with things like greed and drunkenness, are the past history of many believers (6:9-11). (Paul includes same-sex intercourse as harmful.) Christians have been saved from sin at great cost. The Holy Spirit lives in them. To have sex, where the body is saying 'I love you and give myself to you', while the heart is withholding commitment, is not just sin against the other person. It is sin against self (6:18), because it damages the integrity of body and mind. It devalues what is precious to God.

■ **Resurrection** The resurrection is another sign that body cannot be separated from heart and mind. The risen Jesus had a body and God will raise his people to life after death in a new kind of body (6:14; 15:12-50).

■ **Community** Meanwhile, Christians belong to a community. Each person is connected to Christ and to other Christians like the parts of a body (6:15; 12:12-27). If members join their bodies sexually in a wrong relationship, it affects the well-being of this wider body. There was a bad instance of this in the Corinthian church. They should have been grieved, not proud of it (5:1-6).

■ **God's calling and gifts** So sexual union outside marriage is not for Christians. Sexuality is treasured, but that does not mean that all the potential of each person must be fulfilled. Circumstances – being a slave, for example (7:21) – will often impose painful limits. Yet within those limits all Christians are free to understand their lives as a calling from God to be lived to his glory.

A single life can also be accepted as a gift from God and lived to the full within the Christian community. Paul sees no spiritual value in abstaining from sex, but he robustly advocates a single life (7:32-35), where it brings freedom for serving the Lord.

presence, but that is not the point here. Judgment has overtaken the Corinthians not for insufficient self-examination, but for stuffing themselves at the meal as if it had no connection with the Lord's death. What is more, they have eaten without thought for their fellow-Christians (this is what Paul means by 'discern the body', 29).

12 – 14 Disorder in the church: abuse of spiritual gifts

In contemporary religions, trances or strange, ecstatic speech showed a person's spiritual status. It was therefore not surprising that the Christian church at Corinth, to whom God gave a variety of gifts by his Holy Spirit (12:4-11), should have been especially taken up with the more spectacular ones, among which was the ability to speak in unknown 'tongues'.

Paul does not underestimate these gifts. He would have them all speak in tongues, he says (14:5); and he himself excels in this gift (14:18). But it does not top the list on his scale of values. Those seeking experiences for themselves need to be reminded that the life of the church is more important. There are other gifts Christians should seek even more strenuously.

Christian unity does not imply uniformity (12:12-29). The gifts come from a single Source, and are given for the good of the whole church. Every individual has an indispensable part to play in the life of the one body. This should prevent a universal scramble for the same gifts. The important thing is not which gifts are most impressive, but which best serve to build up the church. This means that prophecy – a message from God which everyone can understand – is of more value than tongues.

Yet there are things more important still (12:31). Three qualities of life – faith, hope, love – will outlive all the gifts. And these are for everyone. Without them no one is anything. And Christian love outshines all. This is the best way of all; this is what Christians should really set their hearts on. Paul bursts into a great hymn on the theme (chapter 13), one of the most glorious passages in the whole Bible. And as he paints his picture of what love is, he consciously or unconsciously draws us a portrait of a person – Jesus himself. He is the living embodiment of this outgoing, long-suffering, self-giving, self-effacing love. Without it – without him – there would be no church.

See also 'Spiritual gifts'.

14:26-40, Paul's instructions for how things should be done, provides a fascinating glimpse into an early-church service. Again Paul stresses the need for order. He forbids the women to disturb the service by talking (34-35). (From verse 35 it seems that some were calling out questions and comments.) Their new liberty is not to be abused. 'Paul is not discussing whether and how qualified women may minister, but how women should learn' (Leon Morris). He is certainly not denying them a vocal part in worship (from 11:5 it is clear that women prayed and prophesied – and Paul makes no adverse comment on this).

▶ **Faith (12:9)** A special gift. Not the faith in Jesus which every Christian has.

▶ **Prophecy (12:10)** The gift of speaking God's message. 'Tongues': inspired speech to express the praise of God or other deeply-felt emotion; the person uttering it does not know its meaning, hence the need for interpretation.

▶ **14:34** There is no Old Testament law about

66 If I speak in the tongues of mortals and of angels, but do not have love, I am a noisy gong or a clanging cymbal. And if I have prophetic powers, and understand all mysteries and all knowledge, and if I have all faith, so as to remove mountains, but do not have love, I am nothing... 99

The beginning of Paul's famous passage on love: 1 Corinthians 13

'Now we see in a glass, darkly' (13:12): in Paul's day, like this bronze one from Egypt) were made of polished metal and gave a poor reflection.

Spiritual gifts

Michael Green

After centuries of neglect, 'spiritual gifts' are very much to the fore today, and what Paul writes in 1 Corinthians 12 – 14 is central to the discussion.

'Charismatics' major on these gifts, and 'anti-charismatics' often argue that they ceased with the last apostle. This is untrue. They flourished in the 2nd and 3rd centuries. However, spiritual gifts are not the essence of the Christian life. Had it not been for their misuse at Corinth we should have heard little about them in the letters of the New Testament, though of course they are very evident in Acts.

Paul, who wrote in 1 Corinthians 12 – 14 about the *gifts* of the Spirit also wrote Galatians 5:22-24, on the *fruit* of the Spirit. The Holy Spirit is given us to make us effective for Christ. His gifts are for service, his fruit for character. We need both.

What are these spiritual gifts? Paul mentions here:

- The gift of wise words.
- The gift of 'knowledge', which means insight into a situation without having been told. It may come in words or mental pictures.
- 'Faith' – that means trusting God, even 'in the dark' and against all the probabilities.
- 'Gifts of healing' – and healing includes physical, spiritual, psychological and relational damage.

The Holy Spirit continues to heal today, but why this is not more widespread than it is remains a mystery, despite much discussion.

- 'Miracles' (literally 'acts of power') – probably the ministry of deliverance from evil spiritual forces.
- 'Prophecy'. Highly valued in the early church, this was the gift of speaking directly from God into a situation. It might be predictive (see Acts 11:28) or encouraging (1 Corinthians 14:3). Prophecy differs from scripture, though both come from God. Prophecy is for the particular situation, whereas scripture has universal validity.

> **❝** *We are made for complementarity. I have gifts that you do not.* Voilà! *So we need each other to become fully human.* **❞**
>
> Desmond Tutu

- 'Tongues' – the ability to praise God and pray in words inspired by the Spirit, though their meaning is unknown to the user.
- 'Interpretation of tongues'– the ability to know what those words indicate.

In the early days of the Charismatic Movement there was excessive preoccupation with tongues. It appears at the bottom of Paul's list because, although it is a blessing to the user, it is no good to anyone else (unless interpreted), and spiritual gifts are not designed for personal gratification but for building up the Christian community (1 Corinthians 12:7). That is why, in chapter 14, Paul so values 'prophecy' – it helps other people.

Other important passages to study on this subject are Romans 12:3-8; 2 Corinthians 12:12; Hebrews 2:4; 1 Peter 4:10-11, and the whole of Acts.

From these it is clear that there is no fixed number of spiritual gifts, that the Holy Spirit distributes them as he sees fit, that they are intended to challenge unbelievers, to encourage edification and interdependence in the church. Love (1 Corinthians 13) is the supreme gift.

Interestingly, the use of this word 'gift' is almost confined to Paul in the New Testament. He uses it of the vocation to marriage or celibacy (1 Corinthians 7:4-7), and of our eternal life (Romans 6:23). Clearly the word is not restricted to so-called 'charismatic' gifts, so it is unhelpful to divide Christians into 'charismatic' and 'non-charismatic'. No one can even *be* a Christian without receiving the gracious gift, the *charisma*, of the Holy Spirit!

Paul speaks of fighting wild beasts at Ephesus (literally or metaphorically) among his various trials. This mosaic comes from Paphos, Cyprus.

this. Paul may mean Genesis 3:16 (or Genesis 2:21-22).

15 About resurrection

> **If Christ has not been raised from death, then we have nothing to preach and you have nothing to believe.**
>
> 15:14

Most of the Jews believed in the resurrection of the body (the same body that had died). To the Greeks it was the soul that was immortal. The very idea of resurrection seemed ridiculous to them (see Acts 17:32).

Paul begins with his gospel message (1-4) and the evidence for Christ's resurrection (5-8). This is of the first importance. On it the Christian faith stands or falls. What is more, it is a well-attested fact. Most of those who saw the risen Lord are still alive (about 25 years after the event).

Christ's resurrection is the guarantee that his followers, too, will be raised from death (12-23). But what kind of body will they have (35)? The body which is raised will be better than the body which is buried. The old was physical, the new will be 'spiritual' (not an insubstantial spirit, but like Jesus himself) and immortal. It will as far outshine the old body as a full-grown plant outshines the shrivelled seed from which it grows (36-49). At the end, when Jesus comes to rule, death itself will be defeated (24-28). With Paul, we can sing a

facing page: The columns of the temple of Apollo (the sun-god) dominate the ruins of ancient Corinth.

victory song of praise and thanksgiving to God (51-57).

▶ **James (7)** Jesus' brother; leader of the Jerusalem church.

▶ **Baptized on behalf of (or for) the dead (29)** Possibly by proxy for those who died unbaptized. But the meaning may be that people became baptized in order to be reunited with Christian friends and relatives who had died.

▶ **Wild beasts at Ephesus (32)** One of the spectacles at the arena was to watch men fighting savage wild animals. But Paul is probably speaking metaphorically about what he went through there. Ephesus had a magnificent theatre (see 'The city of Ephesus') but no arena as such.

16 Personal and practical matters

16:1-4: Paul answers the last of their questions, giving directions for collecting money for the poor at Jerusalem (the Gentile churches were contributing).

5-12: he looks forward to an extended visit to Corinth. And he gives news and instructions about various individuals.

13-24: the letter closes with a final appeal, and greetings from the Asian churches (Ephesus was the provincial capital), especially from Aquila and Priscilla, the leatherworkers in whose house Paul lived during his stay in Corinth.

The warm and loving final greeting he writes himself (the rest having been dictated to a secretary: a common practice).

▶ **Macedonia (5)** Philippi and Thessalonica were both in this province.

▶ **Apollos (12)** He is probably reluctant to return because of the split (3:4).

2 Corinthians

Summary

Paul has been under attack from the church in Corinth. Longing for better relations, he writes to explain himself and his calling as an apostle.

•

Chapters 1 – 7
Paul and the church at Corinth

•

Chapters 8 – 9
About aid for the Christians in Jerusalem

•

Chapters 10 – 12:13
Paul the apostle: accusations and defence

•

Chapters 12:14 – 13:14
The coming visit and final greetings

An interval of not much more than a year separates Paul's two letters to Corinth. The second letter was probably written about AD 56, from a town in Macedonia (the Roman province in northern Greece whose capital was Philippi).

After the first letter was written, affairs seem to have come to a head, and Paul paid a swift unscheduled visit (his second; on his first visit to Corinth the church was founded) which proved unpleasant both for him and for the church (2:1). He promised to return (1:16). But instead, to avoid an even more painful visit (1:23), he returned to Asia (where he ran into grave danger, 1:8ff.) and wrote them a sharp letter which caused him a great deal of anguish (2:4). He could enjoy no peace of mind until he heard their reaction, so he left for Troas, on the coast, hoping for news. Although things were going well there, he could not bear to wait, and crossed the Aegean into Macedonia (2:12-13) where at last Titus reached him with the news that the letter had brought the Corinthians to their senses (7:6ff.). His relief knew no bounds.

Now, as he writes again, the worst is over. He looks forward to a third visit which he hopes will be a happier one. So the final part of the letter is specifically intended to clear the air (13:10). (He did pay his visit, and wrote his letter to the Romans during his stay at Corinth. So there was presumably a happy ending to the troubles.)

2 Corinthians is perhaps the most intensely personal of all Paul's letters. As we read, we feel the weight of his burden of care for all the churches (11:28): the depth of his love for them and his anguished concern for their spiritual progress. We see in personal terms the cost of his missionary programme: hardship, suffering, deprivation, humiliation, almost beyond human endurance. And we see unshakable faith shining through it all, transforming every circumstance.

The personal nature of the letter makes it difficult to analyze. Paul's thought flows on, with recurring themes, almost unbroken (apart from the break before chapter 8, when he turns to the matter of the relief fund for Jerusalem; and again before chapter 10, when he takes up the accusations made by his critics). In the main, Paul writes in defence of his ministry and his God-given authority as an apostle.

1:1-17 Greeting and thanksgiving

Paul's associate in this letter is Timothy. His readers are the Christians at Corinth and the surrounding province of Achaia which would include the groups at Athens and Cenchreae.

His prayer strikes a more personal note than usual. Instead of praise for the church, Paul thanks God for his special goodness during recent trials. His suffering has had two wholly good side-effects:

- the experience of God's comfort in it all;
- a new ability to help and comfort those in similar circumstances.

1:18 – 2:17 News and explanations

- **Facing death (1:8-14).** The reason for Paul's prayer is now explained. While in the province of Asia (whose capital city was Ephesus) Paul ran into trouble so serious it seemed likely to cost him his life. At first sight this looks like a reference to the uproar at Ephesus recounted in Acts 19:23-41. But there

Paul's life was not in danger. It is perhaps more likely he was either seriously ill, or in danger from mob-violence somewhere in Asia (modern Turkey).

■ **Paul accounts for his changes of plan (1:15 – 2:11).** In his first letter (1 Corinthians 16:5) Paul promised to come to Corinth via Macedonia (northern Greece). Later he decided to make two visits, on the way to and from Macedonia (1:16). In the event he has done neither, and the Corinthians have criticized him for shilly-shallying. But this is not the reason for the changes of plan. He took his decision because of the state of affairs in the church. Having had one head-on clash, he wanted to delay visiting them again until relations were happier. So he tried to sort things out by letter – a letter he feared would hurt them, and which was painful to write.

The trouble seems to have been personal antagonism to Paul on the part of one man (2:5-11; not the man guilty of incest, 1 Corinthians 5:1). Now that the church has dealt with him, Paul urges his forgiveness.

■ **Paul's recent travels (2:12-17).** After writing the letter, Paul could not rest. He went to Troas hoping to meet Titus on his way back from Corinth with news of the church's reaction. Not finding him there, he crossed the Aegean Sea to Macedonia. The reason for the thanks-giving of verses 14-17 becomes clear in chapter 7. In Macedonia he met Titus, and the news from Corinth was good.

▶ **Verse 14** Paul takes this picture from the triumphal procession accorded to a victorious Roman general. He headed a parade through the streets of Rome in which incense was burnt to the gods. The victor was followed by his captives and the spoils of war. Paul sees himself as Christ's slave (at the end of the procession, among the prisoners in chains who were to be executed), being led around the empire in his triumphal march. For the captives, the smell of incense had the scent of death about it, as the aroma of Christ does for Paul. In the end he will suffer a death like Christ's. Compare 4:10-12. (Another view, which underlies some translations, sees Paul led as a soldier in the procession.)

3 – 6:10 Paul's ministry

Past, present and future interweave in these chapters. As for the past, the old covenant has been replaced by a new life-giving one (3:6-18). The present is an anomaly: on the one hand the apostle is appointed ambassador of God himself, charged with his amazing message to humanity (3:4-6; 4:1ff.; 5:16 – 6:2); on the other, he is subjected to every kind of human weakness, persecution and suffering (4:7-12; 6:3-10). But the future, in all its glorious certainty, eclipses any suffering the present can hold (4:13 – 5:10). Weigh the cost of discipleship, incredible though it seems, against the 'eternal weight of glory' being made ready for Christ's faithful followers and you have the true balance of things.

▶ **Letters of recommendation/introduction (3:1)** In the early days, Christians moving to a new town often took with them such letters from the old church to the new. Paul has no need of such a letter – the very existence of the Corinthian church is sufficient testimony.

▶ **Stone tablets (3:3)** On which the law God gave to Moses was written (Exodus 24:12).

▶ **Moses' face (3:7ff.)** When Moses came down from Mt Sinai with the tablets of the law, his face dazzled the Israelites, so close had he been to God. In order to overcome their fear he veiled his face (Exodus 34:29ff.).

▶ **Reflecting the glory (3:18)** The 'glass' or 'mirror', being made of polished metal, gave only an imperfect reflection.

▶ **Clay pots (4:7)** Cheap pottery lamps (see verse 6), or, if Paul is picturing the Roman triumphal procession, earthenware pots

Listing some of the dangers he had undergone for the sake of the gospel, Paul mentions several shipwrecks. Many passenger-carrying Mediterranean vessels were (and still are) quite small. With no power but the wind, travelling by ship could be hazardous, particularly out of season.

❝ *The God who said, 'Out of darkness the light shall shine!' is the same God who made his light shine in our hearts, to bring us the knowledge of God's glory, shining in the face of Christ.* ❞

4:6

deliberately chosen as a foil to the magnificent treasures inside.

▶ **Tent (5:1)** Our physical body. Paul uses an ordinary Greek expression, which at the same time reminds us of the body's impermanence.

▶ **Found naked (5:3)** 'Without a body'; as a disembodied spirit.

6:11 – 7:1 The need for a clean break

Paul's feelings are deeply stirred (6:11-13). He longs for the Corinthians to match his own complete open-heartedness towards them.

The change of tone at 6:14 is abrupt – but there is no evidence that this section

The light of God's glory shines in the heart of all Christ's followers. 'But we have this treasure in jars of clay,' says Paul, lest it should seem to be our own.

Clay pots, including amphorae like these, were used to store and transport wine and all kinds of goods in Paul's day.

has been misplaced, as some argue. Paul's love for his churches always holds them to the highest standards. He has warned them before of the dangers of compromise with the pagan world (1 Corinthians 8:10). Now he stresses the utter incongruity of permanent relationships between Christians and heathen. The issue here is the same as in 1 Corinthians 8 – 10. Verse 16 is the key: Paul makes it clear that there is no common ground between God's Temple and a temple which honours false gods. Clearly, his earlier letter had not resolved some of these issues: the Corinthians still clung to their old ideas and social patterns.

7:2-16 Paul's joy at the good news from Corinth

He had reached this point in the story at 2:13. Now he takes it up again. At last Titus is able to set Paul's mind at rest. The Corinthians' reaction to his letter is all he could have hoped. The result has been entirely good. The apostle's relief and joy are overwhelming. His faith in them has been completely vindicated.

▶ **Not on account of/for the sake of (12)**
A Jewish idiom meaning 'not so much on account of'.

8 – 9 Money matters

Now that confidence is restored, it is possible to raise the matter of the relief fund for the poor in Jerusalem. Titus had helped the Corinthians make a start, following Paul's instructions in his earlier letter (1 Corinthians 16). Now he is to return and supervise the completion of the collection, accompanied by delegates from the Macedonian churches (8:18, 22) as a safeguard against any charge that Paul was embezzling the fund (8:20-21; 12:16-17).

The Jerusalem church seems to have been in financial trouble almost from the start, probably because the break with Judaism cut converts off from their families and often cost them their jobs. Paul was quick to encourage the Gentile churches in Galatia, Macedonia and Corinth to help their Jewish fellow Christians. By doing so they would learn the duty and blessing of systematic Christian giving, and at the

same time show their appreciation of what they owed the Jewish parent-church.

Practical instructions rub shoulders with spiritual principles in these chapters. Christian giving is a loving response to the self-giving of the Lord Jesus. Christians should need no urging to give cheerfully and generously. Those with more than they need will make up the incomes of those with too little, so that all have enough.

▶ **The churches of Macedonia (8:1)** included Philippi (see Philippians 4:15ff.), Thessalonica and Beroea. Harsh treatment from the Romans and a succession of civil wars had impoverished the province, and the persecuted Christians must have been worse off than most.

▶ **Inexpressible/priceless gift (9:15)** Paul seems to have coined a special adjective to describe the grace of God, as expressed in 8:9.

10 – 12:13 Paul answers his critics

Paul now turns his attention to the hostile minority at Corinth who have challenged his authority and criticized his behaviour. This sounds very like a continuation of the old rival cliques of 1 Corinthians 1 – 4. They show the same conceit, the same old mistaken standards of judgment. They have attacked Paul on a number of counts:

- He may be a brave letter-writer, but meet him face to face and he's a coward (10:1, 9-11).
- He is no speaker (10:10; 11:6).
- He is a second-rate apostle (11:5; 12:11) – his insistence on earning his own living underlines this (11:7ff.).

Paul answers every charge, showing the hollowness of their standards of judgment:

- When he comes, they will discover he is as ready to act as he is to write: but he would much rather use his authority to build up the church (10:1-11).
- Their boasting counts for nothing: it is God's commendation which is all-important (10:12-18). Paul engages in some mock boasting of his own, tongue-in-cheek, to shame his converts and opponents. He relates the vision and revelation God has given him, but (mockingly again) says he cannot

66 You know the generosity of our Lord Jesus Christ: he was rich, yet for your sake he became poor, so that through his poverty you might become rich. 99

8:9

tell them what he heard or saw
(11:16 – 12:10).

■ Apostleship does not consist in oratory
and lording it over the church (11:6,
13-15, 19-20). Paul is not lacking in
any of the qualities of true apostleship
(11:6; 12:12). As for earning his own
living, he was concerned that no one
should think him a sponger, and
anxious not to burden them (11:7ff.).

▶ **King Aretas (11:32)** Aretas IV ruled the
Nabataean kingdom (stretching from the
Euphrates to the Red Sea) from his capital,
Petra, 9 BC – AD 40. The Jews were behind the
governor's action – see Acts 9:22-25.

▶ **Visions and revelations (12:1)** We know of
three early visions from Acts: on the Damascus
road (9:4ff.); at the house of Judas (9:12); and
in the Temple at Jerusalem (22:17ff.).

▶ **A man in Christ (12:2-3)** I.e. a Christian.
Paul is speaking of himself. 'Fourteen years
ago': AD 41-42, six or seven years after Paul's
conversion, but before the great Gentile
missions. The 'third (or highest) heaven' is a
Jewish expression meaning to be actually in the
presence of God. Paul is describing the most
sublime experience imaginable.

▶ **A thorn in my flesh (12:7)** This may be
some physical illness (a painful eye disease, or
malaria) or a reference to the unremitting
opposition he encountered. Either way, it was a
constant source of pain and depression –
Satan's work – yet the means God used to keep
Paul humble and to demonstrate his power.

12:14 – 13:10 The coming visit

Paul looks forward to his third visit to
Corinth. And the reason for the tone of
these last chapters becomes clear. He is
afraid he will find the same bickering
splinter-groups, the same arrogance and
general disorder that made him write the
first letter. He is afraid his pride in them
will take a knock, in the face of typical
'Corinthian' sins: sexual promiscuity, bitter
quarrels and disorder (12:20-21). And so
he calls them to put things right before he
comes, so that when he does he may not
have to call them to order with harsh
discipline.

▶ **Two or three witnesses (13:1)** The
procedure laid down under Jewish law (see
Deuteronomy 19:15).

13:11-14 Conclusion

After last-minute instructions, and
farewell, Paul closes with the lovely words
of 'the grace'.

▶ **A holy/brotherly kiss (12)** A kiss on the
cheek had become the customary Christian
greeting, expressing a loving family relationship.

Galatians

Summary

An urgent letter in which Paul deals with serious problems. The basic issue concerns teachers who insist that Gentile Christians must be circumcised and keep the Jewish law.

•

Chapters 1 – 2
Introduction: Paul's authority as an apostle

•

Chapters 3 – 4
The gospel: law or faith?

•

Chapters 5 – 6
Responsible freedom: the caring community

Who were the Galatians?

Galatia was a huge Roman province extending almost from coast to coast through the mountain and plain of central Turkey. How much of it Paul evangelized we do not know. But Acts 13 and 14 record how he founded churches in the southern cities of Antioch, Iconium, Lystra (Timothy's home town) and Derbe on his first missionary journey. And we know of two follow-up visits made later on (Acts 16:6; 18:23). (The ethnic Galatians were three Celtic tribes, living in the north of the province.)

Why did Paul write to them?

Paul wrote to address some serious problems in the churches. Not long after his first visit, other Jewish-Christian teachers arrived in Galatia. Paul had taught that repentance and faith were all that was needed in order to receive God's forgiveness and live the new life God had given them. These teachers insisted that non-Jewish converts must also be circumcised and observe the Jewish law – virtually become Jews. (The same thing happened at Syrian Antioch, Acts 15:1.) When Paul heard this he was distraught (Galatians 4:20). He saw that it struck at the roots of the Christian message. Salvation – new life – is God's gift to all who believe. This teaching 'made obedience to the law just as essential to salvation as trust in the crucified Messiah' (R.A. Cole). Having begun on the basis of faith, to return to the law as the basis of Christian living undoes all. Christians are freed and free people, subject only to Christ's law (of love; chapter 6). This situation led to the most strongly worded of all Paul's letters.

When was the letter written?

The date is probably about AD 49. This is the year when the committee of enquiry met in Jerusalem to resolve this very issue (Acts 15). Paul may be referring to this Council (or to the consultations which no doubt preceded it) in 2:1-2, though he is not explicit. If that is not his meaning, the letter must have been written shortly before it took place. Several years later, in his letter to the Romans, Paul raises many of the same points. Less extreme circumstances then allowed a more dispassionate consideration of the issues. The letter to the Galatians stands out, nonetheless, as the great charter of Christian freedom.

1 'There is no other gospel'

Paul's urgency is clear from the start. The abrupt assertion of authority (1) and lack of any word of praise are most unlike him. He gets straight to the point (6-8): there is only one 'gospel of Christ'. May those who say otherwise be damned! He is not saying this to curry favour with people (his gospel may have been seen by the Judaizers as a soft option compared with keeping the law). The only approval he cares about is God's (10).

What Paul teaches is simply what Christ himself revealed to him (12). There was no greater devotee of the traditions of Jewish religion than Paul, before his experience of Jesus on the Damascus road (13-15; Acts 9).

His brief autobiography (13-24) underlines the fact that his authority comes from God. It does not need 'authorization' – though he was fully acquainted with the leaders of the Jerusalem church who presumably approved his God-given message (as they

66 *The gospel I preach is not of human origin. I did not receive it from any human being, nor did anyone teach it to me. It was Jesus Christ himself who revealed it to me.* 99

1:11-12

Galatia was a large province in what is now central Turkey. This picture was taken near Isparta, Turkey, on the road to Pisidian Antioch, which Paul and his companions visited on their first mission.

> *You began by God's Spirit; do you now want to finish by your own power?*
>
> 3:3

later also fully endorsed a law-free gospel for the Gentiles: Acts 15).

▶ **Verses 4-5** Paul stresses the fact that the initiative was God's.

▶ **My former life... (13)** See Acts 8:1; 9.

▶ **Verse 17** It is not easy to fit the events Paul says followed his conversion with the (very compressed) account in Acts 9. 'Arabia' may be the area around Damascus, or the wider Nabataean kingdom of Aretas (whose capital was Petra in present-day Jordan). The 'three years' may have been one full year and part of two others. Paul does not say why he went. Since the point is his God-given authority to spread the gospel it is likely he was doing just that. (It had got him into trouble with King Aretas earlier in Damascus: 2 Corinthians 11:32.)

▶ **Cephas (18,** some versions) Peter. This seems to be the visit of Acts 9:26ff.

▶ **Syria and Cilicia (21)** Antioch was in Syria, Tarsus (Paul's home town; Acts 9:30) in Cilicia – the south-east corner of the coast of modern Turkey.

The big issue in Paul's letter to the Galatians arose out of the wrong teaching of the 'Judaizers', pushing for all Christians to be circumcised and conform to the Jewish law. Paul (the converted Jew) sees this as exchanging Christian freedom for slavery.

2 Paul's mission approved

Paul's next visit to Jerusalem is either that of Acts 11:30 (over famine relief) or that of Acts 15 (raising the issues which led to the Council). He has a private meeting to discuss his 'gospel for the Gentiles'. Paul did not want to have his work invalidated, and he was afraid that his ministry might be hindered or even disapproved of by the Jerusalem leaders. But they fully endorse what God is so clearly doing through Paul (7-9).

But at Antioch Peter, for fear of the strict party men sent by James, went back on his former approval of a law-free gospel for the Gentiles. And others – even Barnabas, Paul's former partner in mission – followed his example. Because of the Jewish food laws they would not eat with Gentiles. Paul had this out with Peter, in public (11ff.).

Having once gained freedom through faith in Christ, how could they rebuild the system of law they had torn down (11-21)? The Christian life is to be lived just as it began – by faith (20).

▶ **Fourteen years (1)** Either from his conversion or from his time in Cilicia.

▶ **From James (12)** But James did not share their view: see Acts 15:13-21.

▶ **Ate with the Gentiles (12)** See on Romans 14:2, 14.

▶ **Verses 17-18** The real sin lies not in breaking Jewish food laws, but in turning back to the system of law.

▶ **Verses 19-20** See on Romans 6 – 7.

3 – 4 It is faith, from first to last

Anyone willing to exchange Christian freedom for the Jewish law, says Paul, is a fool. These Jewish Christians talk about making the Gentiles sons of Abraham through the rite of circumcision. But Gentile Christians are already Abraham's sons and heirs – because they share his faith (3:7, 29). God accepted Abraham centuries before the law was given through Moses. So how can the law win people free pardon (3:15-18)? The law was like a child-minder (verse 24: Greek *paidagogos* – the slave who escorts and protects a child, sometimes helping with the homework!) until the promise made to Abraham was fulfilled in the coming of Christ (3:19-24).

Now, by faith in him, we are all God's children – regardless of race or status or sex.

The Galatians had responded eagerly to Paul's preaching. What happened to make them change (4:8-20)? Paul's loving, anxious concern is palpable in this passage. Can they really want to throw their freedom away (4:8-9)? Those under the law are like the son Abraham had by his slave-woman, Hagar. But Christians are free-born – heirs, like Isaac, to all God's promises.

▶ **3:12** Leviticus 18:5.

▶ **3:13** Deuteronomy 21:23.

▶ **Angels (3:19)** The Greek text of Deuteronomy 33:1-2 has 'The Lord has come from Sinai... on his right hand were his angels with him.'

▶ **Elemental/ruling spirits (4:3, 9)** The forces that once controlled them; the false gods they once served.

▶ **Days... (4:10)** Jewish feast days.

▶ **I was ill (4:13)** See 2 Corinthians 12:7.

▶ **4:21** The story Paul uses here is from Genesis 16 and 21.

▶ **Mt Sinai (4:24)** Where the law was given to Moses.

5 – 6 'Christ has set us free!'

Freedom is precious – much too precious to throw away (5:1). The issue is not so much circumcision as what it stands for. Paul is so incensed by those who have unsettled his young converts that he could wish they would go all the way and emasculate themselves (5:12)! Christians are not to be subject to the law but led by God's Spirit (5:16). When the life-giving Spirit of God is in charge, human lives yield a rich harvest of love, joy, peace... (5:22) – qualities as unlike what 'natural' human nature produces as can be (5:16-21).

The Christian community cares and shares (6:1-6). Those who stumble are set right (gently). Burdens are shared. People harvest exactly what they sow in life (6:7-9): a harvest of death on the one hand and eternal life on the other. So 'we should do good to everyone, and especially to those who belong to our family in the faith'.

At this point (6:11) Paul takes the pen from his secretary to write the last lines himself. For him there is only one thing worth glorying in: the power of the cross of Christ to re-create and transform human lives. Like the brand burned onto a slave, the scars Paul bears from his work for Christ show to whom he belongs.

▶ **5:11** Some of Paul's opponents were saying he was in favour of circumcision.

▶ **6:17** 'The scars I have on my body show that I am the slave of Jesus.' See 2 Corinthians 4:7-12; 6:4-10; 11:23-29. The scars of his Christian service are living proof, if proof is still needed, that he is Christ's true apostle.

Paul was concerned that the Galatian Christians, released from their enslavement to the pagan gods, should not fall into a new bondage to a religious calendar – observing 'days and months and years'. A sundial inscribed with Greek symbols, from Ephesus.

> **66** *All of you are the children of God, through faith, in Christ Jesus... There can be neither Jew nor Greek, there can be neither slave nor freeman, there can be neither male nor female – for you are all one in Christ Jesus.* **99**
>
> 3:26-28

Ephesians

Summary

A circular letter from Paul to the churches around Ephesus.

Chapters 1 – 3
About Christ and the church

•

Chapters 4 – 6
Living out the new life in Christ

Best-known passages

Christian unity *(4)*
The 'armour of God' *(6)*

Paul's letter to the Ephesians differs considerably from his other letters. There are none of the usual personal greetings, although Paul had spent some years in Ephesus and had many friends there (see Acts 19). Nor does Ephesians deal with particular problems or news. Even the words 'at Ephesus' (1:1) are missing from some of the early manuscripts. It is more of a sermon than a letter (rather like Hebrews and 1 John), focussing on the character of Christ's church.

It seems likely that Ephesians began as a 'circular', written to a group of churches in what is now western Turkey – of which Ephesus itself was the most important. The 'seven churches' listed in Revelation 1:11 were in this general area; so too was the church at Colossae.

The fact that Paul wrote as a prisoner (probably under house arrest in Rome in the early 60s) links this letter with Philippians, Colossians and Philemon – the other 'letters from prison'. (Prison was not a form of punishment under the Romans: they simply held the worst criminals in custody awaiting sentence.) Of the three, Ephesians is closest in thought to Colossians. Because of its general nature the letter provides few clues to the situation in the churches. But it is clear that the Gentile Christians predominated, and that they tended to look down on their Jewish fellow Christians.

Paul had been specially commissioned to work among the Gentiles, but he held no brief for a divided church. Hence his stress in this letter on God's glorious plan to bring people of every nation and background together in Christ (1:10). As Christians, all are on equal terms. All are one, in Christ. That 'oneness' has to be demonstrated in personal relationships and Christian behaviour.

> **❝** Christians not only have faith in Christ; their life is in him. As the root in the soil, the branch in the vine, the fish in the sea, the bird in the air, so the place of the Christian's life is in Christ. **❞**
>
> Francis Foulkes

1 – 3
God's great plan

1:1-14 The eternal purpose of God

God has poured out his love on us, blessing on blessing. Paul catches his breath in wonder at the very thought of it: 'Let us give thanks... Let us praise God... Let us praise his glory' – verses 3-14 are one long sentence in Greek! (They are so hymn-like that the New Jerusalem Bible sets them out as verse.)

From the very beginning God determined to share his spiritual riches and glory with us – 'in Christ' (the key phrase of Ephesians). Christ stands at the very heart of God's plan. As we believe in him, his death sets us free: we can be forgiven. We can also share his new, risen life. We are made one with him, part of him. And in him we too are caught up in God's great world-plan as we live to his glory.

▶ **Saints** (1, some versions); **grace and peace** (2) See on Romans 1.

▶ **Heavenly places/realm/world** (3 and 1:20; 2:6; 3:10; 6:12) The spiritual realm of all the unseen forces of good and evil.

▶ **Chose/chosen** (4, 12) Everything, including God's choosing, comes to us in and through Christ. He was the one chosen by God to save the world, before ever it was made. We benefit in so far as we are 'in him' by faith.

▶ **Blood** (7) In the Old Testament, sin could not be set aside without a sacrifice. Christ's death meets this requirement, and breaks sin's stranglehold. So we are forgiven and set free. 'This is the priceless gift God gave to us, free of all charge, in his Son.'

▶ **Mystery** (9) 'Secret plan'; no human mind could have guessed God's intention. Paul usually uses this word to mean the 'open secret' of the gospel.

1:15-23 Paul prays

It warms Paul's heart to hear of the faith and love of these Christians. He prays that they may have greater understanding, a surer grasp of their glorious destiny, and increased awareness of the power at their disposal. The power God exercised in raising Christ from the dead and setting him in supreme control of the universe is at work in us, too!

▶ **Head, body (22-23)** The picture carries the concept of the same life flowing through both; of the church carrying out Christ's work in the world.

2:1-10 Past and present: from death to life

Because of our disobedience and sin, we were 'spiritually dead', cut off from God. But in and through Christ God has brought us to life again. He has made us part of his new creation. We are saved to live as God wants, here in this world – and to reign with Christ in the spiritual realm (6; see on 1:3).

▶ **Ruler of the spiritual powers (2)** Satan, whose rebellious spirit is actively at work in the world of human beings.

2:11-22 Breaking the barriers

In the ancient world Jews were separated from Gentiles by racial, religious, cultural and social barriers. (Non-Jews were, for example, forbidden on pain of death to enter the inner courts of the Temple in Jerusalem.) The Jews were God's chosen people, near to him; the Gentiles were sinful heathens, far off. If Christ could bring these two together, there is no human gulf too great for him to bridge. And he did. His death on the cross is the one means of peace with God for all people, without distinction, those who are near and those who are far off (14). And all who belong to him have a common bond which is deeper and stronger than any of their former differences – of race or colour or status or sex or background. Jew and Gentile are one in Christ, a new people.

▶ **The circumcised (11)** I.e. the Jews. See Genesis 17.

▶ **Verse 12** The Gentile Christians have no cause to give themselves airs. Up till now they have been outsiders. The Jews, as God's people, were the only ones for whom there was hope.

▶ **Saints/God's people (19** and 3:18) Here Paul uses the term to mean the Jewish Christians as distinct from the 'incomers', the Gentile Christians.

3:1-13 Paul's mission to the Gentiles

Before Christ came, God's promises were largely confined to the Jews. The Old Testament gives only glimpses of his purpose for the wider world. The gospel of Christ was itself largely a 'mystery', 'kept secret' until now (4-6) – and at the heart of this secret was God's intention to make the Gentiles, too, heirs to all his promises. When Paul was commissioned to bring them the message of salvation (8-9), a new phase in God's plan was begun.

As people of all nations are brought together in Christ they demonstrate God's power and wisdom, not only to the watching world (see John 17:21), but to the cosmic powers beyond and behind it (10). Through faith in Christ we can be confident of access to God (12). Since such

West met East at Ephesus, a prime example of Roman rule and Greek culture, where notices were displayed in Latin and Greek and the mystery religions flourished alongside temples dedicated to the Roman emperors.

66 By grace you have been saved through faith, and this is not your own doing; it is the gift of God. 99

2:8

The city of Ephesus
David Gill

The city of Ephesus was a major port at the mouth of the river Cayster in the Roman province of Asia (now western Turkey). The river today is silted up and the archaeological remains are some distance from the sea.

It had originally been a Greek city, and one of its main cult sites was the great temple of Artemis, one of the seven wonders of the ancient world, which lay outside the urban settlement. The fabled King Croesus was reported to have been a benefactor of the temple, which was destroyed by fire in 356 BC and subsequently rebuilt.

In the hellenistic period Ephesus had formed part of the Attalid kingdom which was bequeathed to Rome in 133 BC, and it later became the administrative centre of the province, eclipsing the old royal capital of Pergamum.

The city itself was built on the slopes of mounts Koressos and Pion. The site today is dominated by the massive theatre which looks out towards the ancient harbour and the sea. Originally a Hellenistic structure, it was enlarged during the reign of Claudius, and could hold some 24,000 people. It was to the theatre that an angry mob dragged two of Paul's companions, when the silversmiths created a riot over the loss of trade in images of Artemis (Roman Diana) caused by Paul's preaching.

Nearby was the commercial *agora* (or market-place, the equivalent of a Roman forum), and this too was developed in the Roman period, notably during the reign of Augustus.

To the north of the theatre lay

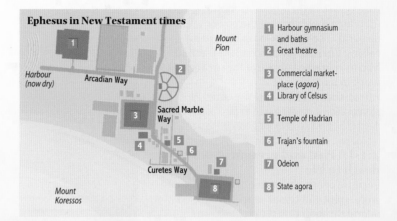

Ephesus in New Testament times

Mount Pion

Harbour (now dry)   Arcadian Way

Sacred Marble Way

Curetes Way

Mount Koressos

1 Harbour gymnasium and baths
2 Great theatre
3 Commercial market-place (*agora*)
4 Library of Celsus
5 Temple of Hadrian
6 Trajan's fountain
7 Odeion
8 State agora

The beautiful façade of the Library of Celsus has been carefully restored. It was one of many magnificent buildings in ancient Ephesus.

the stadium which seems to have been developed during the reign of Nero.

The political buildings for the city were in the upper State *agora*, and these included places for the council and smaller groups to meet. Between the two main political buildings was placed a double temple, almost certainly dedicated to the cult of Roma – the

personification of the city of Rome – and Julius Caesar. In the centre of the open space was located the temple for the Divine Augustus.

Paul spent two years in Ephesus, teaching first in the synagogue, then in the lecture hall of Tyrannus – and the Good News went out from there to the whole province. From prison he wrote a circular letter to Ephesus and the churches in the area. A further letter in Revelation 2, some years later, calls on the Ephesian Christians to return to the love for Christ they showed when they first heard the gospel.

1 Timothy was also written and sent to Ephesus, where Timothy was acting leader of the church.

A priestess of Artemis, the goddess to whom the great temple at Ephesus was dedicated.

top: The Arcadian Way leads from the harbour at Ephesus (long silted up) to the theatre.

Two of the key features of Ephesus are the main street known as Curetes Way (*above*) and the State (upper) *agora*, the main city square (*middle*). Behind the colonnade on the right were the public buildings and the orators' *odeion*.

Artemis (Greek) or Diana (Roman) was the goddess of hunting portrayed here. But the figures of the goddess at Ephesus took a very different form (see picture p. 663).

> 66 *There is one body and one Spirit, just as you were called to the one hope of your calling, one Lord, one faith, one baptism, one Lord and Father of all.* 99
>
> 4:4-5

benefits flow from the spread of the gospel, Paul's readers must not let his present suffering discourage them (13).

▶ **Verse 3** Paul is referring to what he has just told them, not to a previous letter.

3:14-21 Paul prays again

Paul has prayed that the church might have understanding (1:15-23). Now he prays more urgently than ever that they may have love; that they may be strong; that Christ may make his home in their hearts; that God may fill them completely.

4 – 6
Christians in action

4:1-16 Unity – in practice

Christian unity is a fact. Christians are bound together by a common faith, a common life, common loyalty, common purpose. They serve one Master. He is the head, they are the limbs of a single body (4-5; see also 1 Corinthians 12-13). But they are not all identical in temperament, personality or gifts (11ff.). The bond must constantly be cemented by a loving, forbearing attitude to one another, and by using the different gifts for the common good. We have to grow up together until we are all Christ wants us to be (14-16).

▶ **Verse 8** Following his ascension Christ gave gifts to all people (see verse 11).

4:17 – 5:20 'Live in the light!'

Salvation is God's free gift, but it carries with it the obligation to live and behave from that point on as God wants (4:1, 17). This means deliberately discarding the old,

This temple at Ephesus was dedicated to the Roman Emperor Hadrian.

selfish way of life, shedding former habits –
and letting the new life change our thinking
and remould our pattern of behaviour. Paul
does not stop at generalities: he is quite
specific in his 'dos' and 'don'ts'. The new life
calls for truth and honesty; no harboured
grudges, no spite and bitterness – instead
kindness and a new readiness to forgive.
In a word, we are to copy God's own
character, living lives of sacrificial love
(5:1-2) which will bear the searching light
of God. Once we belonged to the dark: now
we are 'children of light' (8).

5:21 – 6:9 Christian relationships: family and household

'Submit yourselves to one another,' Paul
says, speaking to all his readers, men and
women alike. There is no verb in verse 22
in the Greek: first the wife and then the
husband is used to illustrate Paul's
instruction in verse 21. So the Christian
wife gives her husband complete respect
and loyalty; the Christian husband cares
for his wife with unselfish, undemanding
love. Each depends on the other, and both
model themselves on Christ. Their relationship, in turn, reflects the relationship Christ
has with his church. In the family, children
owe their parents respect and obedience.
Parents must exercise discipline – not
behave like petty tyrants; Christian slaves
(and, presumably, employees) serve their
masters as willingly and well as they serve
Christ. Christian masters (and employers)
will not bludgeon or bully, knowing that
they must answer to a Master themselves.

▶ **5:32** The close physical bond between
husband and wife is an illustration of Christ's
spiritual union with his church: 'one flesh'/one
body.

6:10-24 'Put on the armour of God'

Paul does not pretend it will be easy to
maintain these standards. There is a need
for 'body-building' (10). The fight is on. We
are up against powerful forces in a spiritual
struggle. We need spiritual weapons – and
these God provides. Like the Roman soldier,
we have a belt and breastplate, shoes and
shield, helmet and sword. God fits us out
with all the armour we need for defence
and protection. With these we can make
our stand against all-comers.

Most important of all, is the unseen
weapon of prayer. The prayers of his
readers can help Paul keep up his courage
and speak up for God in that faraway
prison (19-20). So the letter closes on a
personal note. Tychicus, Paul's 'postman'
here, also carried the letters to the
Colossians and Philemon. Paul's closing
prayer for his brothers and sisters in Christ
matches and expands on his opening
greeting: may God grant peace, love and
faith to all – and his grace be with them.

A seat reser-
vation in the
theatre at
Miletus, a city to
the south of
Ephesus, reads
'For Jews and
God-fearers
only'. Paul's
message that in
Christ the
barriers of race
and status are
broken down
was a revol-
utionary idea.

'Put on God's
armour,' Paul
instructed the
Ephesian
Christians: in his
mind was the
figure of a
typical Roman
soldier.

Philippians

Summary

Paul, a prisoner awaiting sentence, writes to a group of Christian supporters in Philippi who have a special place in his heart. The keynote of his letter is joy.

Chapter 1:1-26
Greetings, prayer and personal news
•
Chapters 1:27 – 2:30
Jesus: model of humility
•
Chapter 3
A warning; run to win
•
Chapter 4
Instructions and thanks

Best-known passages
'Let this mind be in you'
(2:5-11)
'Whatsoever things are true...'
(4:8)

Philippi, like Corinth in Paul's day, was a Roman colony, on the Egnatian Way – the great northern east-west highway. The town was occupied by Italian settlers following Octavian's great battles, first against Brutus and Cassius, then against his former ally Antony. The colonists were proud of their special rights and privileges, and intensely loyal to Rome. In Philippi, as in the province of Macedonia as a whole, women enjoyed high status. They took active part in public and business life – a situation which is reflected in the church.

Who were the Philippians?

Philippi, in northern Greece, was the first church established by Paul in Europe. It was founded about AD 50 during his second missionary tour (see Acts 16:12-40). When Paul, Silas and Timothy left, Luke, the doctor, stayed on. Philippi was a medical centre, and may possibly have been Luke's home town. He no doubt did much to put the group on its feet and continue the evangelistic outreach.

The letter reveals a church taking its share of suffering (1:29), and in some danger of division (1:27; 2:2). There may have been some leaning to a doctrine of perfectionism (3:12-13). But this letter was written to encourage progress rather than to solve problems: hence the warning against some Jewish Christians who insisted that non-Jewish Christians must be circumcised and keep the Jewish law (see 3:2ff.). Paul loved this church and rejoiced over its progress (the words 'joy' and 'rejoice' are used 16 times in this short letter).

The letter

Paul was 'in chains' when he wrote this letter (1:12). If this refers to the time of his house arrest while waiting for his case to be heard by the emperor in Rome (Acts 28:16, 30-31), the date is in the early 60s. But the conditions he describes seem harsher than in Acts; judgment is imminent, and there is a real possibility of death. Timothy, but not Luke (to judge by 2:20-21), is with him. It may therefore be that the 'imprisonment' is an earlier one – Caesarea, or one not recorded in Acts (the Romans did not sentence people to prison, they simply held them in custody awaiting judgment). A good case has been made out for Ephesus, which would make the date of writing about AD 54. We cannot be certain either way.

Why did Paul write?

There are several reasons for writing. Paul wanted to explain why he was sending Epaphroditus back. He wanted to thank the Philippians for their gift (also to make sure they did not send another one, creating a cycle of gift and return-gift according to the conventions of the day). He had news for them. And what he had heard about them made him long to encourage and advise. Further news reached him while he was writing that made it imperative to add a word of warning (3:1b).

1:1-2 Opening greetings

The letter comes from Paul 'and Timothy' – the young man who was with Paul when the church was founded, and who would shortly be coming to Philippi again (2:19). The 'slaves of Christ Jesus' write to the

66 To me, living is Christ and dying is gain. 99

1:21

'saints': not an élite, but all God's people, as men and women set apart for his service. The 'overseers' (church leaders; 'bishop' is too specific) and helpers ('deacons') receive special mention.

1:3-11 Paul's prayer for the church

Paul's prayer is full of love, joy (a keynote of the whole letter) and thankfulness. He longs for them to enjoy progressively richer and deeper spiritual knowledge which will mould their lives to God's pattern.

▶ **The first day (5)** See Acts 16:12-40.

▶ **My imprisonment (7)** See introduction above.

1:12-26 Personal news

Paul speaks of the past (12), present (13-18) and future (19-26), weighing the alternatives of life and death. Living or dying, Christ is everything to Paul, and he is hard put to choose. Only the need of the Philippian Christians tips the balance in favour of life.

▶ **What has happened to me (12)** If Paul writes from Rome, this includes mob violence, injustice, plots, prison, shipwreck and long detention under constant guard.

▶ **The whole praetorian/palace guard (13)** The crack imperial force from which Paul's warders were drawn. Normally a guard would stay with someone under house arrest around the clock. The person concerned provided his own food and shelter.

▶ **Deliverance (19)** If the judgment goes against him, death will deliver him into Christ's presence; if it goes for him, his captors will release him to serve the church.

▶ **To live is Christ... (21)** Possessing more and more of him, becoming more and more like him, until on his death the process is completed in one glorious moment.

1:27 – 2:18 Plea for a united stand

There is more than a hint of division in the church (see for example 4:2). Paul urges them all to pocket their pride, and to live and work and think as one. Anything less is unworthy of the One whose life on earth is the supreme example of humility. It is because Jesus gave up all that was his by right – even his life – that God has given him the highest place of all (2:5-11 is

probably a quotation from an early hymn in praise of Christ – most modern versions recognize this by setting the text as verse). So his followers need to 'work out' their salvation, by living out the new life God has given them (12ff.).

▶ **The form of God (2:6, some versions)** The actual nature, not just the appearance (as also in verse 7).

▶ **Emptied himself (2:7)** 'Gave up all he had'; 'made himself nothing'. In becoming human Jesus retained his essential nature as God, but waived his status and willingly accepted limitations, for example, to his omnipotence, omniscience and omnipresence. He lived a life of humble obedience, limited to the resources God gives to human beings: the power of his Spirit; the guidance of his word; prayer...

▶ **Name (2:9)** The supreme name, 'Lord', is the Greek for 'Yahweh', the name of God.

▶ **Day of Christ (2:16)** The day of his return.

▶ **A libation/offering (2:17)** Paul's death adds only the finishing touch to the real offering, the faith and life of the church.

2:19-30 Paul commends his fellow workers

Verses 19-23: Timothy (see 1:1-2).

Verses 25-30: Epaphroditus. The

Littered stones and a few standing pillars remain at Philippi. In Paul's time it was an important town and Roman colony on the Egnatian Highway. Ruins of a Byzantine church, in the distance, show the lasting influence of Paul's mission.

'I press towards the goal to win the prize,' Paul wrote, describing his Christian life. All his effort was concentrated on this one thing, like the Roman charioteer.

Philippians had sent him to help Paul. In sending him home, Paul is anxious to make it clear he has not fallen down on his job. Far from it.

> ❝ *There is only one mark of a true Christian – a life lived for Jesus Christ in faith and love.* ❞
>
> Marcus Morris
> on 3:1-4

3 Warning and example

Paul is about to round off his letter (3:1a), when fresh and alarming news compels him to take up his pen again. He does not mind repeating former advice, as a safeguard (3:1b). They must beware of those 'dogs' (a term of abuse used by Jews about Gentiles) the Judaizers – that group of Jewish Christians who followed Paul everywhere, insisting that Gentile converts must be circumcised and keep the law (despite the official edict of Acts 15:19ff.). They are in fact altering the whole basis of salvation, making it 'by faith and…', instead of 'by faith only': hence Paul's anger.

> ❝ *Whatever is true, whatever is honourable, whatever is just, whatever is pure, whatever is pleasing, whatever is commendable, if there is any excellence and if there is anything worthy of praise, think about these things.* ❞
>
> 4:8

▶ **The true circumcision (3)** The true Israel, the true people of God.

▶ **Profit/assets… loss (7-8)** God does not operate a credit and debit account (though Paul does believe that God rewards those who do his will and serve him well on earth). This is a rabbinic concept which underlies Jesus' words in Matthew 16:26.

▶ **I press on… (12ff.)** Like the athlete or charioteer, who does not waste time looking back, but strains every nerve and concentrates every effort to cross the line or pass the post.

Paul counters the idea that perfection can be reached here and now. (He does, however, encourage Christians to 'grow up' and reach maturity.)

▶ **Their god is their stomach/belly (19,** some versions) I.e. appetite; whatever they want; revelling in things they should be ashamed of.

▶ **Our citizenship (20)** They are to regard themselves as a colony of heaven. The Philippians, being intensely proud of their status as a Roman colony, would be quick to grasp all that that meant.

4 Advice and encouragement

Verse 1: a general appeal.

Verses 2-3: two women, Euodia and Syntyche have quarrelled. Since Paul deals with this in a public letter, it seems to have been more than a private squabble. It suggests they were two of the church's leaders (Paul's 'co-workers', 3).

Verses 4-9: rejoice, rejoice! The advice comes from a man in chains, facing death; a man who has been stoned and beaten and hounded by the mob. Yet experiences which leave others sour and bitter leave Paul overflowing with joy! How does he do it? The key lies in verses 6-7: Paul knows how to off-load all his cares – and to fill his mind with good and positive things (8). (He has also learned the secret of contentment, whatever his circumstances, 12: nothing is beyond him, in Christ's strength, 13.)

Verses 10-20: the apostle's appreciation of the church's gifts. From the very first they have supported him (15), with a generosity that extends to all in need (2 Corinthians 8:1-5). At real cost they have given themselves and all they possess. No wonder Paul loves these Christians: a group of faithful, loyal, thoughtful, generous, outgoing men and women.

▶ **Caesar's/the emperor's household (22)** Christian members of the emperor's staff (the palace staff, if Paul is at Rome).

Colossians

Summary

Paul writes to a church he did not found, which is adopting a hotch-potch of beliefs and losing sight of all that Christ means.

Chapter 1:1-14
Opening greetings and praise for the church

•

Chapters 1:15 – 2:5
Christ and his work; the apostle's task

•

Chapters 2:6 – 4:6
New life in Christ

•

Chapter 4:7-18
News and closing messages

Colossae was a small town in the beautiful Lycus Valley, about 100 miles east of Ephesus, near Denizli in modern Turkey. Its near neighbours were the more prosperous Laodicea (Colossians 4:16; see Revelation 3:14ff.) and Hierapolis. There were Christian groups in all three towns.

The church
We have no record of how the church began. But it was probably during Paul's three years in Ephesus (Acts 19) that two prominent men from Colossae – Epaphras and Philemon – became Christians. And they were active in spreading the Christian message in their home area (Colossians 1:6-7; 4:12-13; Philemon 1-2, 5).

When and why did Paul write?
Although Paul had never visited the group at Colossae, he had heard all about it from Epaphras. There was much to be thankful for, but some of the news was worrying. So he wrote to them from prison.

Where this was, is still subject to debate: there is no conclusive proof. If Paul was in custody waiting for his case to be heard in Rome (Acts 28), the date would be about AD 61. (Later in the 60s, Colossae was levelled by an earthquake.) If he wrote from Ephesus it would be the early 50s (Ephesus is much closer to Colossae than Rome is, and much easier for Philemon's runaway slave, Onesimus, to reach.)

Paul had a ready-made opportunity to send the letter with Tychicus (if he was travelling from Rome he may well have carried the letter to the Ephesians at the same time: the two letters are markedly similar) and Onesimus, whom he was sending home (see Philemon).

A problem to address
The trouble at Colossae which Paul addresses is 'syncretism' – that tendency to introduce ideas from other philosophies and religions on a level with Christian truth, which we know very well today. It was (and is) understandable. There were Greeks and Jews in the Colossian church, as well as 'native' Phrygians. It was natural that they should cling to their own ideas and want to incorporate them into the new faith. It seemed harmless enough, and appears to have been a longstanding tendency, taken over into the church from Judaism. But Paul knew that it struck at the heart of his gospel message. By trying to retain circumcision, their food-laws and festivals (2:11, 16), not to mention angel-worship and mysticism (2:18), the Jewish Christians were changing the whole basis of Christian living, which depends on Christ just as it begins with him (2:19; see on Galatians). The idea of angel intermediaries

Colossae lay at one side of the Lycus Valley (in Roman Asia/modern Turkey), near Laodicea and Hierapolis, two other towns mentioned in the New Testament. With mountains, streams and a fertile landscape it was a likely breeding-ground for pantheism and the mystical and 'Gnostic' (secret knowledge) ideas Paul opposes in his letter.

(2:18) denied the supremacy of Christ. And the introduction of asceticism and high-flown philosophy threw people back on themselves and on human wisdom (2:18-23) – which had already failed them. Although Paul does not deal with these issues point by point these are the thoughts that lie behind his letter (see 'Understanding Colossians'). The Colossians need to take fresh hold on Christ, on his complete supremacy and utter sufficiency. This is Paul's theme.

> **" Christ is the image of the invisible God; his is the primacy over all creation. "**
>
> 1:15

1:1-14 Opening greetings and prayer

It is characteristic of Paul to begin with thanksgiving. He has his Christian priorities – and his psychology! – right. But his warm-hearted praise is genuine, not just sugar to coat the pill of the lecture to follow. His loving care (and his prayer list) extended beyond the churches he himself had brought into being, to groups of Christians he had never even met (2:1). It cheered him immensely to hear of their faith and love and hope. And he longed for God to give them fuller understanding and spiritual maturity.

▶ **Epaphras (7)** A native of Colossae and founder of the church. He worked tirelessly there and in nearby Hierapolis and Laodicea. He was with Paul when the letter was written (4:12-13).

1:15-23 Christ Jesus – supreme

The thought of God's rescue mission (13-14), lifts Paul into pure poetry as he attempts to capture in words the nature and work of Christ (as in Philippians 2:5-11, he may have drawn on an early hymn). Jesus is the living expression of God himself – active in creation, upholding all that exists. Christ is first – in existence, in power, in position. He has first place in God's new creation. He is the head of the church and the source of its life. Through the death of his Son God has made us his friends. This is Paul's gospel – good news indeed!

▶ **Firstborn (15,** some versions) Not first to be created, but the heir whose position is unique.

Understanding Colossians
Paula Gooder

Paul's major concern in his Letter to the Colossians is to encourage the Christian community at Colossae to worship Christ and to reflect this worship in their daily lives. Yet in chapter 2 Paul turns to specific concerns: the Colossian Christians should not allow themselves to be led astray from the proper worship of Christ by the false teaching which they have encountered.

A return to Jewish customs

This false teaching seems to have been affected by a certain type of Jewish mysticism. The false teachers were encouraging the Colossian Christians to return to specifically Jewish customs:

■ to practise circumcision (2:11)
■ to observe the Jewish regulations about food and drink
■ and to keep the laws about regular worship, not only at major festivals but also on the sabbath (2:16).

This teaching would have affected not only what the Colossian Christians believed but also how they lived their daily lives: what they ate and drank and how they worshipped week by week.

In the letter as a whole Paul tries to show the Colossians that the proper worship of Christ affects the whole of their lives and thus rules out such practices.

Mystical practices

Even more worrying for Paul was the type of worship which these false teachers practised (2:18). Early Jewish mystics believed that it was possible for humans to ascend from earth into heaven and, once there, to see God's throne and the angels in heaven. The false teachers at Colossae seem to share this belief. Unfortunately the language of 2:18 is unclear. It could mean that the Colossian Christians are being condemned by their opponents because they do not practise ascent into heaven, or the condemnation may be because they do not worship the angels which the mystics saw during such an ascent.

▶ **Thrones... (16)** Unseen beings and powers outside our visible world.

1:24 – 2:5 Paul's own task

The apostle's job is to make God's message known. The philosophers hint at secrets, at deep things known only to the initiated. This is God's open secret: 'Christ – in you!' A share in God's own glory for every Christian! This is a 'secret' worth knowing. It makes all Paul's struggle and effort 'to preach Christ to everyone' worthwhile.

▶ **1:24** 'Paul applies to himself the same pattern, of suffering on behalf of others, that was worked out on the cross' (Tom Wright). He is not adding to that work: Christ's saving work is complete. But in the overlapping of the ages, between Christ's resurrection and his return, God's new people will suffer as their Master did.

2:6 – 4:6 An appeal for Christian maturity

False argument was filtering into the Colossian church from various quarters (see 'Understanding Colossians' and

In Colossians 3 and Ephesians 5 – 6, Paul teaches about right relationships within the family and household. This mother and daughter are depicted on a funerary relief from Palmyra.

introduction). It was misleading and dangerous because it was based on human teaching and not on Christ (2:8).

Christ is the One who embodies 'all the fullness' of God and in him Christians find their own fulfilment (2:9-10). By his death the Jewish law (Judaism itself) has been superseded: the shadow has given way to reality. 'Then why behave as though you were still living the life of the world?' (2:20). There may be good sense in rules,

Either way, the problem for Paul, and hence the Colossians, is that the beliefs of these mystics have made them arrogant and they no longer worship Christ as the head of the church (2:19).

Secret knowledge

Another belief of these mystics was that they had special revelations from God about mysteries unknown by everyone else. They maintained that they had a special knowledge which was not available to all. This belief is sometimes called Gnosticism.

At various points in the letter (particularly 1:26-27 and 2:2) Paul makes a point of countering these beliefs. The mysteries of God are revealed to all in Christ. The Colossian Christians should not be made to feel inferior by anyone teaching any other message.

False teaching

The false teaching and wrong ideas Paul contests in this letter seem to be a type of Judaism which not only attempted to force the Colossian church back to particular Jewish practices like circumcision, but which also believed that they were the recipients of a special revelation not available to everyone, a revelation which they received while ascending into the heavenly realms. In this letter Paul seeks to draw the Colossian church back to the true worship of Christ, the image of the invisible God, the head of the church.

Borrowed language

Paul deliberately uses the 'Gnostic' terms of his readers: for example, 'mysteries', 'wisdom' and 'knowledge'. Words like these were often used to describe the special

revelation received from God by these mystics.

Yet in this letter, Paul makes them serve his Christian purposes: the mysteries of God are revealed to all in Christ. In using the language of those he is trying to convince, Paul clearly shows that all they hope for has indeed been revealed through Christ Jesus.

Paul urged his Christian readers to cast off the old life and live the new. That meant behaving differently. It also meant changing the mind-set and abandoning wrong ideas.

Superstition held many people in thrall: it is represented by this statue of the goddess of good luck.

There was also a false division in Greek thinking between body (material, evil) and soul (spiritual, good). The mosaic from a Byzantine church in Jerash (one of the old Hellenistic 'Ten Towns', now in Jordan) of a caged bird symbolizes the soul imprisoned in the body.

renewed in the likeness of Christ, taking on his character (3:10). The loving, forgiving Lord is the model for Christian behaviour (3:12ff.). His word (3:16) shapes our thinking. The new life is one of prayer (4:2-4) and thanksgiving to God (3:15-17). Home and household are transformed by outgoing, unselfish love in every relationship (3:18 – 4:1).

▶ **2:12** See Romans 6.

▶ **2:16** These things are no longer relevant.

▶ **Elemental/ruling spirits (2:20)** The old pagan superstitious idea that spirits control the world.

▶ **3:18 – 4:1** See on Ephesians 5 – 6, where Paul treats the same subject more fully.

4:7-18 Personal news

The reference to Tychicus and Onesimus links this letter with Ephesians (see 6:21-22) and Philemon. All three letters would seem to have been sent at the same time by the same messenger. (The letter from Laodicea, 16, may be Ephesians.) It is good to find Mark reinstated after the trouble he once caused between Paul and Barnabas (Acts 13:13; 15:36-40). Aristarchus, who though a Jew came from Greece, was another longstanding companion of Paul's and had been involved in the riot at Ephesus (Acts 19:29). Luke stayed with Paul to the end, but Demas defected (2 Timothy 4:10-11). Epaphras, the Colossian, has been mentioned already (1:7, and see introduction). Archippus may be Philemon's son (Philemon 2). Nympha, in Laodicea, is only one of those who opened their homes to the local Christian group long before there were church buildings. Aquila and Priscilla at Ephesus (1 Corinthians 16:19) and later at Rome (Romans 16:5), Philemon at Colossae and Gaius at Corinth (Romans 16:23) all did the same. The whole church is deeply in their debt.

but they cannot qualify or disqualify anyone who has found life in Christ.

Chapter 3: becoming a Christian means a definite break with the old self-centred, self-indulgent way of life. There is a new self, moving in a new direction, being

Angels in the Bible
Stephen Noll

Angels appear throughout the pages of the Bible from Genesis to Revelation, with some 300 allusions to them in the Old and New Testaments. Though neglected by scholars over the past 200 years, angels have made a comeback, not only in popular opinion but in biblical study, with its renewed interest in mythology and apocalyptic as background to the Old and New Testaments.

The word 'angel' (Hebrew *malak*; Greek *angelos*) describes the function of a messenger rather than the nature of an angel.

■ There are holy angels like the cherubim and seraphim, who serve before God's throne.

■ There are evil angels like Satan, who are utterly cast out.

■ And there are 'principalities and powers' who are corrupt but who continue to uphold the fallen world order.

The 'council of the holy ones/gods' in the Old Testament, is a notion akin to the Mesopotamian and Greek concepts of a 'pantheon', an assembly of gods presided over by the father god. Rather than denying the existence of other divine beings, the Bible uses the council to assert that the Lord is incomparably above them (Exodus 15:11; Psalm 89:6). Thus the Bible grants a certain reality behind the myths of polytheism but also represents those myths as a corruption of God's original rule over the nations (Psalm 82; Deuteronomy 32:8-9).

The Old Testament 'angel of the Lord' is an enigmatic figure, who sometimes speaks as a messenger and sometimes as God himself (Exodus 3:1-6). Often interpreted as prefiguring Christ, the angel of the Lord is probably an archangel, one of an inner circle of angels who convey God's word and guide his people in salvation history (Exodus 23:20-22).

The only two named archangels in the Bible are Michael and Gabriel (Raphael appears in the apocryphal book of Tobit). In the New Testament, angels appear at the beginning of Jesus' life and ministry and at the end, providing a 'framework of mystery' for his unique person and work.

Although the Holy Spirit comes as an internal witness to God's presence and power, angels continue to appear in the history and mission of the church (Acts 8:26-40).

The New Testament clearly teaches that angels watch over God's people (Luke 15:10). It is less clear whether each believer has a personal guardian angel (Matthew 18:10; Acts 12:15).

In the Letters, angels are mentioned primarily to highlight the Sonship of Jesus Christ. The risen Christ is exalted above the 'principalities and powers' of this present evil age, and no earthly or heavenly creature can separate us from his love (Ephesians 1:20-23; Romans 8:38-39).

The Letter to the Hebrews uses angels as foils to establish Christ's full deity and humanity (Hebrews 1 – 2).

When Jesus taught his disciples to pray, 'your will be done on earth as in heaven,' he clearly assumed the existence of a heavenly society of praise and obedience.

A recently published Dead Sea Scroll describes an elaborate 'angelic liturgy' in heaven, and Paul envisages angels all around when Christians gather to worship (1 Corinthians 11:10).

Angels are a feature of apocalyptic writing (see on Revelation). Daniel's vision of the coming of the Son of man is strongly reflected in New Testament teaching about the end-time (Daniel 7:9-13; 12:1-3). Angels announce and accompany Jesus Christ at his second coming, serving to execute the judgments of God (1 Thessalonians 4:16; Matthew 24:31). They also form a society of witness and praise to his completed work (Revelation 4 – 5).

1 & 2 Thessalonians

Summary

Paul writes to the faithful, suffering church at Thessalonica. He has been anxious for them, but now has received good news. He instructs them in the Christian life and sets them right about various issues related to Jesus' return and God's judgment.

Thessalonica was a free city, capital of the Roman province of Macedonia (northern Greece). It was a prosperous port on the Aegean Sea, across the bay from Mt Olympus. It also stood on the Egnatian Way, the land trade route from Dyrrachium on the Adriatic to present-day Istanbul. Thessaloniki is today a flourishing modern city, centre of government for northern Greece, and second only to Athens.

The church

The church was founded about AD 50 after Paul (with Silas and Timothy) left Philippi on the second missionary tour. See Acts 17:1-9. According to this account Paul did not stay in Thessalonica long: just three successive sabbaths preaching in the synagogue, followed by a short time based at Jason's house. Then the Jews stirred up trouble because Paul was winning converts from those interested in Judaism. Jason and the other Christians were hauled before the magistrates and bound over to keep the peace. For safety's sake the newly-formed church sent the missionaries away. But persecution continued, from Jews and others.

The letters

From Thessalonica, Paul and his party went to Beroea, then Paul continued alone to Athens. It seems Timothy joined him there (1 Thessalonians 3:1-2), but was almost immediately sent back to Thessalonica for news. Paul was acutely anxious to know what had become of the little group of Christians. He was in Corinth by the time Timothy returned with good news.

Paul's first letter to the Thessalonians was written at this point. It is full of relief and joy. Paul answers questions that had arisen, and repeats his teaching on matters where the church was weak. It was to be read to all the believers (5:27), some at least of whom would not have been able to read. It may have gone the rounds of several house churches.

The second letter followed a few months later, reinforcing the teaching and clearing up misunderstandings, particularly over Christ's return. These two letters are the earliest of Paul's surviving writings (with the possible exception of Galatians) and probably the oldest writing in the New Testament. They were written only 20 years after the crucifixion of Jesus.

1 THESSALONIANS

1:1 Opening greetings

Paul is the author of the letter. But he writes in association with Silvanus (= Silas, see Acts 15:40) and Timothy, his companions on the mission to Thessalonica, and now in Corinth. This co-authorship is reflected in the use of 'we', something which distinguishes 1 (and 2) Thessalonians from Paul's other letters.

Little remains of ancient Thessalonica today. As Thessaliki it is the second biggest city in Greece. In later Roman times the Egnatian Highway Paul travelled passed under the Arch of Galerius, pictured here. The street is still called by its old name.

1:2-10 Faith, love – and hope

The response of the people of Thessalonica to the gospel message, and all that has happened since, is something to thank God for. This little group of Christians has endured persecution. They were deprived of their teachers far too soon. Yet they have stood firm. More than that, within months they have become an example of unwavering faith to the rest of Greece (7), spreading the Good News far and wide by word and life.

▶ **True (9)** The God who is faithful and true to his covenant promises.

▶ **Verses 9-10** summarize Paul's gospel. He has taught them about the character of God; about Jesus, his Son, who died to rescue them from judgment; and about his resurrection. The promise of Christ's return is especially precious to all who suffer. These letters are shot through with it.

2:1-16 Paul relives his time in Thessalonica

It is clear that Paul's enemies have been engaged in a smear campaign. The apostle clears himself of their charges by reminding the Christians of what actually happened when he was with them. He did not come as an itinerant quack teacher, peddling dubious wares and out to deceive (3). Nor was he on the make, in any sense (5). He came to give, not get (8), willing to face more trouble while still smarting from his wounds at Philippi (2; see Acts 16:22ff.). Nor did he rely on them for his keep (9; though the Philippians helped support him – see Philippians 4:16). The conventions of the patronage system would have put him under obligation to them, and required him to do as they told him. Obviously Paul would want to avoid that, and – perhaps even more – the odium of the itinerant preacher who would say almost anything to earn a living.

▶ **Verses 15-16** Paul speaks like an Old Testament prophet. Nowhere does he speak so harshly of his own people.

2:17 – 3:13 'How we missed you!'

Paul is as close to his converts as parent to child. No matter how far away, they are deep in his heart and thoughts. The knowledge that they are in trouble fills him with unbearable anxiety. Paul's happiness – his life, even – depends on their continuance and progress in the faith. So he longs to see them and hear from them. He is even prepared to face Athens alone, rather than do without news. So Timothy's welcome report brings the apostle an influx of joy, a new lease of life. His one thought now is to see them again (11).

▶ **Satan hindered us (2:18)** It is in the enemy's interests to keep the missionary and his converts apart.

▶ **We told you beforehand... (3:4)** 1st-century Christians were taught from the outset to expect trouble and suffering.

4:1-12 Living for God

Verses 1-8: sexual life. Pagan standards of sexual behaviour fell far short of Jewish and Christian ones. The pull of the old ways was strong for the young converts. But they must exercise self-control. Christian must not wrong Christian in sexual affairs.

Verses 9-10: Christian love. Even where love already exists there is always room for more.

Verses 11-12: work. Patrician Greeks looked down on those who worked with their hands (though the artisans and manual labourers themselves took pride in their work). And there were idlers in the church quite happy to sponge on the generosity of fellow-Christians. Paul himself worked with his hands. He was prepared to step down the social ladder and identify with the labourers. And he encourages the Thessalonians to do the same. The prospect of Jesus' return was a great temptation to opt out of humdrum daily work (see also 2 Thessalonians 3:11-12).

▶ **Wrong his brother (6)** The same principle applies before and after marriage – sexual promiscuity deprives others of what is rightly theirs.

4:13 – 5:11 When Jesus returns

Two problems have arisen out of Paul's teaching on the subject:

■ Some had died in the months between Paul's departure and the writing of this letter. So, will Christians who die before

Christ comes lose out (13-18)? Far from it, says Paul. They will be raised first when Christ comes. And dead and living together will join in the Lord's triumph and enjoy his presence.

■ When will the Lord come (5:1-11)? No one knows. But he will come suddenly and unexpectedly – and we need to be ready.

▶ **Asleep (4:13)... fallen asleep (14)** This is a Jewish metaphor, used by Jesus and other Jews who believed in the resurrection of the dead. Paul is saying that death is no more permanent than sleep: we awake refreshed and renewed, through resurrection, to the new life. He is not affirming the concept of soul-sleep after death.

▶ **The breastplate (5:8)** Faith, love and the certainty of future salvation are the Christian's defences against all attack. Compare Ephesians 6:14ff.

5:12-22 Final instructions

Time, or space, is running out. But Paul manages to pack 17 practical and characteristic commands into these few verses.

5:23-28 Conclusion

Paul's prayer is comprehensive: for the whole person in every aspect ('spirit, soul, body'). Authority (the stern command to read the letter to the whole church) sits beside humility. The apostle, who never ceases to pray for his readers, knows how much he needs their prayers.

▶ **A holy/brotherly kiss (26)** See 2 Corinthians 13:12. This was standard family practice: the practices of the family became the practices of the church, which met as family and in homes.

2 THESSALONIANS

1:1-2 Opening greetings

1:3-12 Praise and encouragement

Verses 3-4: the Thessalonians seem to have protested against the extravagant praise of Paul's first letter (chapter 1). He replies that it is only right to thank God for their growing faith and love, and their firm stand in face of persecution.

Verses 5-12: God is a just God: he will do what is right. It is therefore certain

The Thessalonians raised questions about the resurrection and Christ's return, which Paul answers in both his letters. He had to instruct them to get on with their work, whatever it might be, not simply to down tools and wait for Christ's coming.

that those who make his people suffer, and reject his truth, will themselves suffer 'eternal destruction' (permanent separation from God, in contrast to the believer, who has 'eternal life', permanently in God's presence).

2:1-12 The Day will come

This passage is one of the most difficult in all Paul's letters. (Even Peter found Paul hard to understand – 2 Peter 3:16!) He alludes to teaching of which we have no surviving record, so that much which was clear to his first readers is now obscure. It is better, in some cases, to admit we do not know the meaning, than to speculate.

Some of the Thessalonian Christians thought the Day of the Lord had already begun. But Paul has never said (or written, 2) so. Before this happens, he explains, there will be a great, final rebellion against God, headed by an individual utterly opposed to him. (Compare Revelation 13 and 1 John 2:18-25). At present there are forces at work restraining evil – but in the end these will be swept away. Victory will come only through Christ, when he appears.

▶ **Man of lawlessness/Wicked One... (3)** Not Satan himself, but the leader of the anti-God forces, who sets himself up as God. ('Son of perdition' is Hebrew idiom, meaning 'the one who is doomed to destruction'.)

▶ **The one who holds it back/restraining hand (7)** Perhaps Paul personalizes the principle of law and government which holds evil in check; perhaps he means an angelic being. We really do not know.

▶ **Those who will perish (10)** Because they do not welcome the gospel. They turn their backs on the truth which offers salvation. In effect, like Milton's Satan in *Paradise Lost*, they say 'Evil be thou my Good' (12).

▶ **Verse 11** Paul sees God as the one in ultimate control. The Bible often attributes evil to God, for the same reason. Yet God wants everyone to accept his invitation 'to be saved'.

2:13 – 3:5 Thanksgiving and prayer

Paul turns, with tremendous contrast, to the Thessalonians. They were chosen and called by God – and they responded gladly to the truth. They will share in the glory of Jesus himself.

▶ **From the beginning (2:13)** From eternity (see Ephesians 1:4).

▶ **The traditions (2:15, some versions)** Not customs, but the truth about Jesus and his teaching, faithfully handed down by the apostles: the same truth that we have in written form in the New Testament.

▶ **Comfort (2:17, some versions)** In the old sense of strengthen.

3:6-15 'We were not lazy'

Paul stressed the need to work in his first letter (4:11). But excitement about Christ's coming seems to have made the situation worse, not better. So Paul speaks out in strong terms against those who idle their life away and sponge on others. They can find no warrant for this in the example he has set.

3:16-18 Conclusion

The present is tough, the future will be tougher (2:3-12). But no matter what times may be like, no matter what may be going on around, the Christian has an inexhaustible, unfailing source of peace.

At verse 17 Paul takes over from his secretary. His own signature authenticates this letter (see 2:2). He added his personal signature to each of his letters in the same way.

> **❝ May the Lord of peace himself give you peace at all times and in all ways. ❞**
>
> 3:16

1 & 2 Timothy

Summary

1 Timothy
A letter about leadership in the church. Paul warns of the dangers of false teaching, tells Timothy how to choose the right kind of leaders, and gives the younger man personal guidance for his own leadership role.

2 Timothy
Personal advice – encouragement, warnings, instructions – to Timothy to follow in Paul's footsteps as a true and faithful witness for Jesus.

Timothy was the child of a mixed marriage – his mother being Jewish, his father Greek. His home was at Lystra in the Roman province of Galatia (not far from Konya in present-day Turkey). Paul came to Lystra on his first missionary tour, and it must have been then that Timothy was converted. He made such strides as a Christian that when Paul called again he decided to take Timothy with him on his travels. The local church leaders formally commissioned the young man and gave them their blessing. And from then on he became Paul's constant, loyal, trusted and greatly loved companion.

Timothy was not naturally brave, and he was often unwell. He needed a good deal of encouragement. But Paul's confidence was not misplaced. In the letters to the different churches he speaks most warmly of this 'son in the faith'. Timothy not only travelled with Paul and was associated with him in many of his letters, he frequently acted as Paul's envoy to the churches. Very early on he was left behind in Beroea to consolidate and follow up Paul's work there and at Thessalonica. He was sent to Corinth when Paul heard of the troubles in the church there – no easy assignment. And at the time Paul wrote to him he was in Ephesus, supervising the local Christian groups and responsible for choosing and training church leaders.

The letters
1 and 2 Timothy and Titus belong to the end of Paul's life. Paul was free when he wrote 1 Timothy and Titus, and had recently been engaged in further evangelism in Greece and what is now Turkey. This does not tally with anything we know from Acts, and it may be assumed that Paul was released from the imprisonment described in Acts 28, resumed his preaching for some time, and was then re-arrested and taken to Rome for trial. In

2 Timothy he is in prison and expecting to be executed.

In these 'pastoral letters' – the general title for the three letters, because they concern the leaders' 'pastoring' of the church – we have a directive from Paul on the way Timothy and Titus should handle the various problems they encountered in the oversight of the churches in their charge. Paul sets out the qualities to look for in appointing church leaders. He gives advice on personal conduct. And in the face of much false and misleading teaching he urges them to concentrate on essentials and not be side-tracked. The best way to counter wrong ideas is to teach the truth.

The early church had no doubt that these letters were genuinely written by Paul to the two men named. Modern scholars have questioned this on the grounds that they differ in language and content from Paul's other letters, and that they counter 2nd-, rather than 1st-century heresies. Some suggest they are the work of a later writer who incorporated some genuine Pauline material. This raises fresh problems, however, and there may be a simpler explanation.

We know that Paul often used a secretary, for instance, and if he was given a good deal of freedom this would make arguments based on vocabulary very uncertain (even with computer analysis!). The vocabulary and style in these letters is often very like Luke's, and he may have written them for Paul. In 2 Timothy 4:11 Paul says 'only Luke is with me'. The problem over content is that Paul tells Timothy and Titus things they must surely have known already. The reason may be that the instructions were meant to be read to their churches. Even the point about heresies is by no means certain. There is nothing in the letters that we can categorically say Paul could not have written.

1 TIMOTHY

1 The trouble at Ephesus; Paul and Timothy

There had been a tremendous response to Paul's preaching in and around Ephesus (Acts 19; see also 'The city of Ephesus'). A great many Christian groups had sprung up almost overnight. And Paul was quick to realize how vulnerable they were to wrong teaching (Acts 20:29-30). Ten years later his fears had materialized. Apocryphal Jewish legends and family trees (4) were being made the basis of strange teaching. This was a wrong approach to the Old Testament law, and Timothy must stop it spreading. The Christian message should result in faith and love and a clear conscience – not idle speculation. It has always seemed more exciting to argue over abstruse topics than to live the Christian life.

Paul had been a Christian for over 30 years. He had been on the road with the gospel message for 20. Yet he never forgot that he had once gone all out to destroy this sect (13; Acts 8:1-3; 9). He never ceased to be amazed that God should have taken a man like him into his service. Paul's directive is a good one: 'hold to your faith; obey your Christian conscience'.

▶ **Sound (literally, 'healthy') doctrine/teaching (10)** This is a frequent emphasis in the Pastoral Letters. This 'healthy teaching' means not simply beliefs which conform to the gospel the apostles taught, but the living out of those beliefs in Christian behaviour, as this verse makes clear.

▶ **Words of prophecy (18)** The indication (given either to Paul, or at Timothy's commissioning) that God had chosen Timothy for this work.

▶ **Handed over to Satan (20)** We do not know exactly what this means – but see on 1 Corinthians 5:5.

2 Men and women in the church

Prayer is of prime importance. That means prayer for the authorities, if Christians are to lead the kind of peaceable lives which

> **❝** Here is a saying that you can rely on and nobody should doubt: that Christ Jesus came into the world to save sinners. **❞**
>
> 1:15

Timothy was a young man needing to exercise authority in a group which included people older than himself. Paul offers wise advice on his relationship with those in the church, both men and women.

These portraits of a man and a woman come from a tomb relief at Palmyra.

allow them to concentrate on making the
Good News known to everyone, as God
intends (4).

In the assembly, the men are to pray
without anger or argument. Christian
women are to be conduct-conscious, not
clothes-mad, and must not lord it over the
men. The Christian message upgraded the
status of women (see e.g. Galatians 3:28).
But God did not intend them to take over.
Men and women are equal in his sight, but
their roles are not identical. Paul is not
singling women out for special censure
here. He is evenhanded, correcting abuses
in worship, both by grumbling men and
usurping and untrained women. (Nothing
that Paul says here rules out women
exercising the gifts God has given them for
ministry.)

▶ **Verse 15** Paul would never have made
childbirth the means of a woman's salvation
(compare verse 5)! The thought may follow on
from verses 13-14 — i.e. though woman was
the first to sin, it was through woman that the
Saviour was born. Or it may be that she will be
kept safe through childbirth. Paul clearly expects
that Christian women will marry and have
children.

3 Church leaders

It was Paul's practice to appoint several
elders (*episkopos,* translated 'bishop' in
some versions, means, literally
'overseer') to take charge of each
church (Acts 14:23). 'Overseeing' what
went on was one of the functions of the
elder's role. These in turn were assisted by
'helpers' ('deacons', 8).

Paul's list of qualifications for these
leaders makes sound sense. They must be
men who can control themselves and their
families, who have proved to be stable
Christians, and who have the respect of
the outside world. Timothy was not a
naturally forceful character. To have
Paul's written authority was the next best
thing to having the apostle with him
(14ff.).

▶ **Mystery (9,** some versions) God's revealed
secret in Jesus Christ; the Christian faith is God-
given, not made by people.
▶ **Verse 11** 'Wives' or 'women' – the Greek
word can mean either, depending on the

context. Here it is not clear if Paul means
women helpers or deacon's wives.
▶ **Verse 16** Paul seems to be quoting a
Christian hymn.

4 False teachers – and true

The ultimate source of false teaching is
Satan, the Enemy, himself. It is promoted
by those who are dead to conscience. They
ban marriage and lay down rigid rules
about diet – things God has designed for
our good. They claim that their thinking is
super-Christian. In fact it is sub-Christian.

Timothy, as a true teacher, has to make
this clear. And this does not stop at words.
His whole life must bear out what he
teaches others. So he has to let the truth
mould his own life (6); he has to keep
spiritually fit (7-8). He has always to watch
himself, and watch his teaching. Those
who are older will not recognize his
authority because he is young. Christian
character commands authority at any age.

5 – 6:2 How to deal with people in the church

5:1-2: Paul's advice is sound. Treat other
people as if they were your own family
(1-2).

5:3-16: widows who have no means of
support deserve special consideration.
Their lot was unenviable. There was a
grain dole in Rome and some other places,
but no other state welfare in Paul's day.
The church was quick to realize and accept
its responsibility to help (Acts 6:1). It soon
had a sizeable problem, and not all of the
cases were equally deserving. Paul's rule is
that the church should reserve its help for
those who are really destitute. It should
take on to its books only older widows of
good Christian character, and committed
to Christian work. The younger ones
should remarry. And wherever possible
widows should be cared for by their own
relatives. In the city where the goddess
Diana was served by a host of prostitutes,
the reputation of those who serve Christ
must be beyond reproach.

5:17-22, 24-25: elders must be carefully
chosen, treated with respect, and paid for
their work. They are especially open to false
charges against them. Timothy must take

care to deal fairly in such cases.

Verse 23 is in parenthesis, a personal note. Timothy is clearly not strong. He needs to take care of himself.

6:1-2: as Christians, slaves are free people – but they are not to drag Christ's name in the mud by turning on their masters (see also on Ephesians 6:5ff.; Philemon).

▶ **5:9** The Greek means, literally, 'a one-man woman'.

▶ **5:22** 'Lay hands on': i.e. commission for Christian service.

▶ **5:23** Sound medical advice at the time; wine counteracted some of the harmful impurities in the water.

6:3-21 'Fight the good fight of faith'

The subject of false teaching comes up yet again. Verses 3-5 give us a none-too-happy picture of what Timothy had to contend with in the church: questions, arguments and endless disputes. The superior 'know-ledge' (*gnosis*, 20) claimed by these people soon grew into the full-scale heresy of 'Gnosticism', whose initiates felt free to discard some of the cardinal Christian truths, including the fact that Christ was truly human.

Some see religion as a road to riches (5). And Christians are rich – though not in money. Money is not wrong in itself, but the craving for money leads to all kinds of evil. 'Rich Christians' (17ff.) count their wealth in terms of generous sharing, and good done to others.

As someone 'dedicated to God', Timothy will steer clear of the pitfalls of money. Faith, love, perseverance and gentleness are his goals in the 'good fight of faith'. One day Jesus will return in glory: life is to be lived in the light of that fact.

▶ **The root/source (10)** More accurately, 'a root'.

▶ **Verses 15-16** This doxology has a strongly Jewish flavour: Paul may have recalled it from synagogue worship.

2 TIMOTHY

This is Paul's last and most moving letter. After a lifetime of service and suffering for Christ he is in prison again, and death is imminent. He is alone except for Luke, and longs to see Timothy again. Yet there is no hint of self-pity; no regrets. His last word is one of encouragement to all who follow after. He can face death without fear and without doubt. The race is over – ahead is his reward.

> **"** The love of money is the root of all evils. **"**
>
> 6:10

1 'I thank God'

Deep thankfulness fills Paul's heart as he thinks of Timothy. And he longs for this man of many fears, as well as real faith, to share his own confidence. He urges Timothy to hold to the truth he has taught him, and not be ashamed of the gospel or of Paul. The secret of Paul's confidence is *knowing* Christ (12; and see Philippians 3:10). God's grace is sufficient; he will give the needed strength to endure in the face of opposition and suffering.

▶ **Tears (4)** Shed when they parted.

▶ **That day (12)** The day of the Lord's return; the day of judgment.

▶ **All... in Asia (15)** False teaching took such a hold in Ephesus (see 1 Timothy 1) that Christians rejected the very man to whom they owed their faith. Here, however, Paul may mean those Christians from Asia who were in Rome, rather than the whole Christian community in the province of Asia. Phygelus and Hermogenes are not mentioned anywhere else in the New Testament.

▶ **Onesiphorus (16)** His household is mentioned in 4:19. Verse 18 may indicate that he has already died.

> **"** God did not give us a spirit of timidity, but a spirit of power, of love, and of self-discipline. **"**
>
> 1:7

2 Paul's charge to Timothy

No one knew better than Paul what it costs to be a Christian. 'From the soldier Timothy must learn endurance, from the athlete discipline and from the farmer perseverance' (3-7, Donald Guthrie). The theme of Paul's gospel is Jesus Christ, risen from the dead (8): it is for this he has suffered. He offers Timothy a lifeline to hold onto, in the lines of a hymn (11-13). He must stick to the true gospel, not be side-tracked into empty chatter, wild specul-ation or fruitless, divisive argument (16,

23). The true servant of Christ is kind, not quarrelsome, a good teacher, tolerant, and gentle with those who need discipline (24-25).

▸ **Verse 17** Philetus is mentioned only here; Hymenaeus in 1 Timothy 1:20.

▸ **The resurrection (18)** They denied the reality of resurrection by treating it as a spiritual experience.

3 Troubled times ahead

Paul describes in detail the character of the final age of turmoil (2-7). We can see something of it in our own time, indeed in every age. He warns that, as the time for Christ's return draws near, evil will intensify – even within the church (5-6). Those who are true to Christ will endure persecution (as Jesus himself predicted: John 15:20). For his part, Timothy must stand firm in the truths taught him from the scriptures. In them lies wisdom and the way to salvation in Christ. They are 'God-breathed' (inspired): the breath of life for all who seek to walk in God's ways.

▸ **Jannes and Jambres (8)** In Jewish tradition, the names of Pharaoh's magicians (Exodus 7).

▸ **Verse 11** See Acts 13 – 14. Timothy would vividly recall these events since they took place near his home. Paul was stoned and left for dead at Lystra, Timothy's home town.

4 A final charge – and news

Death is close for Paul (6). He can face it without fear: he has run the course and kept the faith. The Olympic victor's wreath, the sovereign's award for faithful service is in prospect, not just for him but for all who have loved the Lord and long for his return.

He has a last charge for Timothy: go on declaring God's message, 'press it home in season, out of season', come what may. The time will come when people prefer to follow their own whims, choosing fable and legend in preference to truth.

Personal news is left until last. Paul's fellow missionaries – Titus, Tychicus, Trophimus – are all away. One is ill, and one (Demas) has defected. At the first stage of his trial (16) Paul, like Jesus, stood alone. All his friends deserted him, and his enemies were not slow to make capital. Now winter is coming and he wants his books and papers, and his thick cloak. He has only Luke's presence, and the faithful Christians in Rome (21), to warm his heart – and the hope that Timothy and Mark will reach him in time.

▸ **Endure suffering (5)** Despite his fears, Timothy did just that (see Hebrews 13:23).

▸ **Verse 8** Best understood as 'the crown which is the reward of the righteous'.

▸ **Books and parchments (13)** Possibly copies of Old Testament books, Paul's own notebooks, or personal papers.

▸ **Alexander (14)** See 1 Timothy 1:20.

▸ **The lion's mouth (17)** This may just be a manner of speaking; or it may refer to the lions in the arena, to Nero, or to Satan.

What awaits Paul, and all Christ's faithful followers, is a 'crown of righteousness'. This carving from Ephesus shows a dove bearing a victor's 'crown'.

" *I have fought the good fight, I have finished the race, I have kept the faith. Now there is in store for me the crown of righteousness, which the Lord, the righteous Judge, will award to me on that day.* **"**

Paul, on his approaching death, to Timothy: 4:7-8

Titus

Summary

Instructions and encouragement to Paul's companion and fellow-missionary, Titus, who has been placed in charge of an unruly and difficult group of Christians on Crete.

See introduction to 1 and 2 Timothy.

Titus is not mentioned in Acts, but it is clear from the Letters that he was one of Paul's trusted inner circle. As a Greek he was made a test case on the visit to Jerusalem, to clarify the position of non-Jewish converts (Galatians 2:1-4). Later, when, despite Timothy's work, trouble flared up in Corinth, Paul chose Titus as the man for the job. He not only sorted things out, but established very good relations with the church – no small tribute to his tact and strength of character (2 Corinthians 2; 7; 8; 12). Some years later again, when Paul wrote this letter, Titus had been left to consolidate the apostle's work in Crete. He faced a situation very similar to Timothy's at Ephesus (see 1 Timothy). The last mention of Titus is in 2 Timothy 4:10, when he was away (presumably still furthering the Christian cause) in Dalmatia (former Yugoslavia).

Crete
Crete was probably one of the first places to hear the Christian gospel. There were Jews from Crete in the crowd that listened to Peter on the Day of Pentecost (Acts 2:11). But the message fell on rough ground. The Cretans were such habitual liars (1:12) that the Greeks coined a special verb for lying – 'to Cretize'. And it is plain from Paul's letter that even the Christians were an unruly, hot-headed, volatile bunch who needed firm handling.

1 Instructions for Titus' task on Crete
The unusually long and formal introduction to this letter matches the 'semi-official' nature of its contents. Is it the thought of the Cretans and their lies (12) that makes Paul dwell on the dependability of a God 'who does not lie' (2)? The promise of eternal life which he holds out is utterly reliable.

For the qualifications of church leaders (5-9) see on 1 Timothy 3. The requirement that any leader of the church must hold firm to 'the trustworthy message' leads straight into a description of those who flout this. They are rebellious talkers and deceivers, teaching what they should not teach. The situation is so bad it calls for a really strong line – a sharp rebuke to those who propound 'Jewish myths' (pointless speculations based on the Old Testament) and others who reject the truth (10, 14; and see 1 Timothy 1).

▶ **Verse 12** The proverb 'All Cretans are liars' was coined by a Cretan writer, the 6th-century BC philosopher Epimenides. This sort of stereotyping was very common in antiquity.

▶ **Verse 16** The acid test of faith is how we live.

2 – 3:11 Living the faith
The way Christians behave can discredit, or reinforce, the Christian message. Paul's instructions throw no flattering light on the Cretan temperament. They were a naturally belligerent, argumentative people, uncontrolled, resentful of authority and partial to the bottle! But the Christian life calls for discipline, obedience and respect for others. Paul has a word for older men and women (2:2-4) and younger ones (2:5-6). Titus himself must set the example

> ❝ *To the pure, all things are pure, but to those who are corrupted and do not believe, nothing is pure.* ❞
>
> 1:15

The setting of the Pastoral Letters

MACEDONIA
Thessalonica
Troas Pisidian **GALATIA**
Nicopolis   Antioch
Iconium
Ephesus
Corinth   Lystra
Miletus

CRETE

(2:7-8). Slaves must try to please, not answer back or steal from their masters (2:9-10). Those who have trusted in God and found salvation will be eager to do what is good (2:14; 3:8). Once, says Paul, we were all slaves to passion and pleasure. But that was before we discovered the loving kindness of God, who saved us and renews us by his Holy Spirit, giving us the 'hope of eternal life'.

▶ **Washing (3:5)** A picture of the cleansing, renewing work of the Holy Spirit which is symbolized in Christian baptism.

▶ **Genealogies/lists of ancestors (3:9)** See 1 Timothy 1.

3:12-15 Last instructions

When his 'relief' arrives, Titus is to join Paul at Nicopolis on the west coast of Greece. Tychicus is another member of Paul's inner circle of partners in the gospel (Ephesians 6:21, etc.). Zenas and Apollos (see Acts 18:24-28) may have been the ones who brought Paul's letter to Titus.

Philemon

Summary

Paul writes to his friend Philemon about the return of his runaway slave, Onesimus, now a Christian.

This is a personal (though not private: see verse 2) letter from Paul to Philemon, one of his converts and a good friend.

Philemon was a man of some standing. A group of local Christians regularly met in his home at Colossae. One of his slaves, Onesimus, had deprived his master of his service by running away to the big city (Rome, or perhaps Ephesus) where he could easily escape detection. There he somehow came into contact with the imprisoned apostle, and through him became a Christian.

Paul loved this young man like a son, but he was Philemon's legal property. It was hard for Paul, and hard for Onesimus – who was liable to terrible punishment for what he had done – but he must go back and make amends. Paul could not keep him without Philemon's willing consent.

So he wrote this 'covering note' for Onesimus. And Tychicus went with him for company and moral support, taking the latest news and a letter from Paul to the Colossian church (Colossians 4:7-9).

A very different Onesimus is returning from the one who ran away, and Paul appeals to Philemon to treat this slave as a brother in Christ – as if he were the apostle himself (16-17)!

Philemon is under considerable pressure to do as he asks: Paul points out in verse 8 that he could have dictated where his duty lay, but he prefers to make a request on the basis of love. His description of himself as an old man, a prisoner (9), tugs at the heartstrings. He is, in effect, asking Philemon to give Onesimus his freedom and send him back (13), in part for services Paul rendered to Philemon. Paul uses the conventions of the day: a gift given requires a gift in return. Hence his appeal (19): Philemon owes his Christian life to Paul. There is added pressure from the fact that this letter is to be read to the church in his house. But Paul is confident Philemon will comply and 'set his mind at rest'. Everything is couched in terms of praise and encouragement.

This letter provides the clearest evidence of how Paul would deal with slavery within the community of Christ. It is not acceptable – and he intends the Christian community to be an example of what the world should be like. Although Paul does not specifically address slavery as an institution, his requirement lays a depth charge beneath it.

▶ **Apphia (2)** Probably Philemon's wife. Archippus may be their son.

▶ **No use... (11)** Paul plays on Onesimus' name, which means 'useful'.

▶ **Verses 15-16** Slavery was an integral part of the social structure of the day. But Paul wants Onesimus to be accepted, not as a piece of property but as a brother. He is no longer to be treated as a slave. Although he does not say so outright, the force of verse 16 is that Paul wants him set free. The new Christian community should be different, both spiritually and socially, from society at large.

▶ **Verses 18-19** Paul's 'IOU' recalls the Samaritan's good neighbourliness in Jesus' story (Luke 10:35).

▶ **Epaphras, Mark... (23-24)** See Colossians 4.

The mosaic of a slave comes from Paphos, Cyprus, 3rd century AD.

This Roman slave-tag reads: 'Seize me if I should try to escape and send me back to my master.'

Hebrews

Summary

The old system of laws and sacrifices has been replaced with something new and altogether better in Christ. The writer encourages his Jewish Christian readers to 'grow up' in their faith – and warns against going back.

Chapters 1 – 4
Christ, the complete revelation of God:
greater than the angels;
greater than Moses;
our great high priest

•

Chapters 5 – 10
Jesus, our salvation:
priest and sacrifice;
mediator of a new and better covenant

•

Chapters 11 – 12
Faith and its heroes
Jesus, our example

•

Chapter 13
A life that pleases God
Closing prayer and messages

The origin of Hebrews is something of a mystery. The oldest manuscripts are anonymous, and there are none of the conventional greetings with which a lst-century letter usually began.

In 13:22 the writer refers to it as 'a word of exhortation', 'a message of encourage-ment', not a letter. (He may have adapted a sermon or address given on some special occasion.)

Even in the first few centuries AD no one knew for certain who the author was, though many people attributed it to Paul. Today this is considered very unlikely. Hebrews reflects neither Paul's style nor his thought. But having said that, we are no nearer to solving the puzzle. From the letter, we know that the author knew Timothy (13:23). He writes extremely polished Greek. And he is plainly an able teacher. He knows the Old Testament inside out. And the version he quotes is the Greek Septuagint – which means he is probably a Greek-speaking (Hellenistic) Jew, writing to fellow Greek-speaking Jews. He is a Christian who has thoroughly thought through the relation of his faith to Judaism.

To whom was it sent?
The title 'To the Hebrews' is very old, but may not be original. It is a fair inference from the letter – with its discussion of priests and sacrifice and its many Old Testament quotations – that it was written to a group of Jewish Christians of some intellectual ability. The group had been established a good many years (2:3; 13:7), and had a history of persecution. They should have been mature Christians by this time, capable of teaching others (5:11 – 6:2). Instead they are withdrawn and inward-looking. And they seem to have half a mind to turn back to Judaism. They need a forceful reminder that what they possess in Christ is far better.

When was it written?
If Jerusalem and the Temple had already fallen to the Romans, the author would have been almost bound to mention it when he referred to the priests and sacrifices. So it is fairly certain the letter was written before AD 70. If it was sent to Rome (see 13:24), it was most likely written in the 60s, perhaps just before Nero's persecution (if 12:4 is to be taken literally).

What is it about?
The big question that Hebrews addresses is: how can human beings approach God? Few questions are more important or more universal. It is this issue which gives an undeniably difficult letter its lasting significance. See 'Understanding Hebrews'.

The letter was written for a group of Christian Jews wavering between Christ-ianity and Judaism. It is in a sense the counterpart to Paul's Letter to the Romans, this time directed to a Jewish audience and explaining Christ's relationship to all that had gone before in the religious history of Israel. So the writer compares and contrasts the person and the achievements of Jesus with the Old Testament priesthood and sacrificial system. He is not only incomparably greater and better than these, he is the ultimate realization of all they stand for. He is the perfect priest, offering the perfect sacrifice. He has finally removed the barrier of sin and given people access to God in a way the sacrificial system could never do. That was the copy: he is the original pattern. That was the shadow: he is the reality men and women have always been searching for. To turn away from him – back to an inferior substitute, back to a proven failure – is to lose everything.

1 God's Son – greater than the angels

The letter begins with the most amazing statement on the nature of God's Son (compare Colossians 1:15-20). Jesus is not only God's complete, supreme and final revelation of himself. He is the actual embodiment of the character and glory of God: the imprint of his Person; God's express image. He is the 'heir of all things', the creator and sustainer of the universe, the one who has effected God's great purpose of salvation. Through him sin has been dealt with, forgiveness made possible. His work complete, he is seated now at God's side, in the position of supreme power.

The angels (whom some Jews came close to worshipping) themselves worship Christ (6). They are spiritual beings, but no more than God's servants (14). The Son is far and away above them – as the scriptures prove.

The writer's use of the Old Testament. The quotations in Hebrews are from the Greek Septuagint version, which differs in some respects from our own Old Testament. The writer is in any case more taken up with the meaning than with the precise words used. Comment and quotation are often merged, as was quite customary in his day. And if we look up the references, we find that the writer – like other New Testament writers – exercises a surprising freedom of interpretation. Some verses are filled with meaning far beyond their original context. See 'The Old Testament in the New Testament'.

The quotations in this chapter are: verse 5, from Psalm 2:7 and 2 Samuel 7:14; verse 6, from Psalm 97:7 or Deuteronomy 32:43; verse 7, from Psalm 104:4; verse 8, from Psalm 45:6-7; verse 10, from Psalm 102:25-27; verse 13, from Psalm 110:1.

▸ **At the right hand (3)** The place of highest honour. It speaks of Jesus' closeness to God.

2 The saviour

If the message of the angels – that is the law of Moses, Acts 7:38, 53 – proved true, how much more important is the Son's message of salvation (1-4).

For a little while Christ shared our human nature. Now he is crowned with glory because he willingly suffered death for our benefit, to free us from the power of death (5-9) and to cleanse us of sin (11). It is 'as if the whole created order was designed on the principle that glory could be secured through suffering' (Donald Guthrie). He is the 'pioneer', blazing the way to salvation for all who follow (10). What is more, because he was one of us – like us in every way – we can be sure he is able to help us (16-18).

▸ **Verses 6-8, 12-13** The texts quoted are Psalm 8:4-6; Psalm 22:22; Isaiah 8:17-18.
▸ **Made perfect (10)** The meaning is 'bring to completion'. The idea which underlies these verses is the (Platonic) notion that this world is the realm of the imperfect and that through death we enter heaven, the realm of the perfect.
▸ **Verse 17** This idea is more fully explained in chapter 5.

❝ *We see Jesus, who for a little while was made lower than the angels, now crowned with glory and honour because of his suffering and death.* ❞

2:9

'A gospel to my culture'

Some parts of the Bible which seem difficult or even irrelevant in one culture may be precisely right for another. The Letter to the Hebrews is a case in point.

Dr Melba Maggay, speaking of her own, Filipino, culture, says:

❝ For us God is high and lifted up – a dark Lord... inaccessible. A basic need in our culture is for a God who will go between us. We have a text in Scripture that speaks to this need, this longing for a mediator, for this go-between God: Hebrews. We have a high priest who is not unable to sympathize with human weakness, a high priest who has gone ahead of us into the heavens. We can with confidence draw near and not be turned away. This distant God can be reached through this go-between God, this Mediator, Jesus Christ. That is good news in my culture. That is a gospel to my culture. ❞

3:1-6 Jesus, God's Son, is greater than Moses, God's servant

Moses made Israel into a nation. He led them out of slavery in Egypt and through the desert. He gave them God's law and their forms of worship. No one was more revered by the Jews, and rightly so. But he could never be more than God's faithful servant. Jesus is God's Son.

3:6 – 4:13 Rest for the people of God

This whole passage is rooted in the Greek version of Psalm 95:7-11.

Those to whom this letter is addressed are in a very similar position to Israel at the time of the exodus. Both have seen God at work in an amazing way. But despite this the Israelites rebelled against God in the desert. 'They did not believe' – and so a whole generation forfeited their right to enter the promised land and enjoy the rest God would have given them (3:11). Be warned. What happened then can happen now, if those who hear God's message do not accept it (4:1-2).

The parallel is made more explicit. The 'rest' God spoke of was more than just a stable and secure life in the land he had promised. Through the psalmist (Psalm 95), hundreds of years after Joshua's day, God was still appealing to people to enter his rest. There is a spiritual counterpart to the promised land, and the passport to it is faith (4:3). God's resting-place has existed from the time of the creation (4:4; Genesis

The Old Testament in the New Testament

Dick France

The Old Testament was the Bible of Jesus (see 'Jesus and the Old Testament'), and the writers of the New Testament books continued to appeal to its authority. There are something like 250 direct quotations from the Old Testament in the New, and around 1,000 clear allusions.

The early Christians were so steeped in the Old Testament that its language came naturally to them.

To take two examples:

■ The Beatitudes (Matthew 5:3-10) do not actually quote from the Old Testament, but verses 3-4 are obviously modelled on Isaiah 61:1-3 and verse 5 on Psalm 37:11 – and practically every phrase can be roughly paralleled in the Old Testament.

■ The Book of Revelation contains no formal quotation, but it is modelled throughout on Old Testament passages, particularly from Daniel, Ezekiel and Zechariah.

Sometimes, no doubt, they used familiar scriptural language just because it was part of their normal vocabulary. Sometimes they quoted legal and ethical texts as continuing guides for the life of the people of God. But often when they quoted or echoed the Old Testament they had a more deliberate theological purpose. They believed, as Jesus himself had made clear, that he had come to fulfil what had gone before, and they delighted to trace the connections.

Fulfilment of scripture

Often the New Testament writers point out how the predictions of the Old Testament prophets have come true in the events of Jesus' life, death and resurrection, and continue to be fulfilled in the growth of his church.

Matthew includes in his Gospel a dozen quotations with introduc-

tions such as 'all this happened to fulfil what was spoken by the prophet' (Matthew 1:22-23; 2:5-6, 15, 17-18, 23, etc.).

The records of early Christian sermons in Acts are full of claims for the fulfilment of scripture (e.g. Acts 2:25-36; 3:22-26; 13:32-41).

Some passages seem to have been special favourites and are quoted repeatedly (e.g. Psalm 110:1; 118:22; Isaiah 53; Daniel 7:13-14). These were passages which Jesus himself had used to explain his mission, and his followers continued to draw on them in preaching and debate.

Prefigurings

But sometimes the New Testament writers appealed to passages which were not in themselves predictions of the future, but which they nonetheless believed to have been 'fulfilled' in the coming of Christ.

Jesus had made many such claims (e.g. Matthew 12:3-6,

2:2). It is still there. We enter into that eternal rest, God's peace, as we trust him and take him at his word.

The writer has been arguing from God's word: now he steps back to consider it (12-13): alive, active, penetrating, exposing everything to the One to whom all must give account.

▶ **3:8** See Exodus 17:1-7; Numbers 20:1-13.

4:14 – 5:10 Jesus, the great high priest

The writer moves on from Jesus as the Son of God, to Jesus, our great high priest, a title given him nowhere else in the New Testament.

Aaron (5:4) was appointed by God as the first high priest of Israel. He was the intermediary between a holy God and a sinful people, the go-between who represented each to the other. The Jewish religion – the system these Jewish Christians were tempted to return to – still had its high priest. But in Christ, the writer says, we have a high priest who fulfils all the statutory requirements, and far more, because he has no need to atone for his own sins. He is the perfect high priest appointed by God as mediator for all time.

▶ **Melchizedek (5:6, 10)** The king/priest of Salem to whom Abraham gave a tenth of the plunder recovered from the invading kings (Genesis 14:18-20). Chapter 7 develops the thought of these verses.

▶ **5:8** Not learning to obey, but learning the full

> **"** *The word of God is something alive and active: it cuts more incisively than any two-edged sword.* **"**
>
> 4:12

40-42; 13:13-14; Mark 7:6-7), but the fullest use of this method is found in Hebrews, where the writer goes through the most important people and institutions of Old Testament Israel, especially the ritual of worship in the Tabernacle, and shows how they find their fulfilment in Jesus, as the true high priest and the perfect, final sacrifice.

This principle is known as 'typology'. Persons, institutions and events of the Old Testament are understood as 'types' (models, prefigurements) of the decisive work of God which was to take place with the coming of Christ. The aim of typology is to show how Jesus fulfils not only the explicit predictions of the Old Testament, but its whole fabric, to establish his coming as the final, complete embodiment of God's saving work through the ages.

Sources and use of quotations

Quite often the words quoted in the New Testament are not the same as we find in our Old Testament text. Usually the differences are insignificant, but sometimes they are quite striking (e.g. Matthew 27:9-10 compared with Zechariah 11:12-13).

Often the difference is due to the fact that the New Testament writers are using a different text from the one now found in our Old Testament. Most New Testament quotations reflect the Greek Septuagint text, which quite often differs from the Hebrew. Sometimes they seem to be quoting other forms of the text, such as we can now find in the Aramaic *targums* (paraphrases).

But sometimes the explanation is that the New Testament writers were not reluctant to adapt the wording themselves, in order to bring out the interpretation and the application of the text as they saw it. The purpose was not to change the meaning, but to bring it out more clearly for their readers, sometimes by incorporating the interpretation into the wording of the quotation, just as a modern preacher will often paraphrase a biblical text in order to 'get the message across' and to help those who listen to see how it applies to their circumstances.

Once the first Christians had understood that Jesus was the fulfilment of the Old Testament, they came to read it not simply for its own sake but in the light of that fulfilment. So they were able to find pointers to Jesus in places where other Jews would not see them, and were willing to exercise a freedom in interpretation from which we might shrink in order to give full expression to their conviction that, as Jesus himself put it, Moses (and the other Old Testament writers) 'wrote about me' (John 5:46).

cost and meaning of obedience through suffering.

▶ **5:9** See on 2:10.

5:11 – 6:20 Grow up and move on

The writer is frustrated in what he wants to say because of his hearers' lack of understanding. They have got stuck at the ABC level in their faith (5:11 – 6:3). This lack of progress is bad enough in itself. But it is symptomatic of something much more serious. They are in danger of abandoning their faith altogether. So the writer gives his sternest warning (6:4-8). If, despite all their Christian knowledge and experience, they wilfully reject their faith, they will become Christ's enemies, effectively crucifying Jesus afresh (6). There will then be no hope for them, for they have refused the one available means of forgiveness. This is where their thinking is leading them, though they have not yet reached the point of no return.

Warning is quickly followed by encouragement (9-12). The writer cannot

The Letter to the Hebrews is written to Jewish Christians tempted to turn back to Judaism. This synagogue from the early centuries AD is at Baram in northern Israel.

believe they will go so far – or that God will allow it. God's promise is certain (13-18). Our hope of receiving God's blessing is therefore certain too. Jesus has gone into the 'heavenly Temple' before us: there on our behalf in the presence of God (19-20) – and we will share his glory.

▶ **6:2** 'Baptisms' – not the usual word for Christian baptism. The teaching may be on the difference between Christian baptism and Jewish ritual washings. 'Laying on of hands', at baptism and commissioning for special service, symbolized the empowering of the Holy Spirit.

▶ **6:18** The promise and the vow are taken as the two witnesses which the law of Moses required (Deuteronomy 17:6; Hebrews 10:28).

7 A new high priest

6:20 brings us neatly back to the point made in 5:10: chapter 7 carries it forward. Jesus has superseded the Levitical priesthood by becoming high priest for all time. This fact is anticipated in Psalm 110, where the Messiah is described as a priest of a different order. The shadowy figure of Melchizedek (Genesis 14:18-20) reflects something of the nature of Christ's priesthood – the dual role of king *and* priest; the timelessness of it; its superiority to the old order. Levi in a sense acknowledged this by paying Melchizedek tithes through his ancestor Abraham (9)!

If the priesthood of Aaron and his fellow Levites had been good enough, no change would have been needed (11-12). But in fact neither these men nor the old religious system could meet the needs of sinful humanity. A different and better kind of priesthood, one not resting on the correct line of physical descent, was needed.

Jesus, who came from the royal tribe of Judah, not the priestly tribe of Levi (14), is the one who has given us 'a better hope, through which we approach God' (19) and the guarantee of a better covenant (22). He offered himself as a once-and-for-all sacrifice (27), so he is able to save, for all time, those who approach God through him (25). The old order has been replaced with a better one.

8 The promise of better things

Jesus is different from all other high priests.

His priestly work in heaven is the reality of which theirs are mere copies and shadowy reflections. 'If there had been nothing wrong with the old covenant, there would have been no need for a new one' (7). But God's people were unable to keep their side of the agreement, as the prophet Jeremiah made plain in looking forward to the day when God would draw up a new one. The old agreement was external, based on obeying God's rules. It was bound to fail. The new rests on knowledge and understanding, a unity of heart and mind between God and his people (10-11).

▶ **Verse 5** The Alexandrian Jews, influenced by the thinking of the Greek philosopher, Plato, regarded the Tabernacle 'as only an imperfect copy of what already existed in heaven, which Moses himself saw' (Donald Guthrie).

▶ **Verses 8-12** quote Jeremiah 31:31-34, in the Greek version. This is the longest scripture quotation in the New Testament.

9 – 10:18 Shadow and reality; the perfect sacrifice

The writer's thoughts are again back in the time of the exodus, when God made his covenant with Israel through Moses, and gave them the pattern on which to construct his Tent, the Tabernacle. (The Temple was later modelled on it – but it is not the Temple he has in mind here.) Although God had chosen to live with his people, in a tent like their own, they had no right of access to him. The layout of the Tabernacle (see 'The significance of the Tabernacle') and the whole system of animal sacrifice emphasized God's separateness and the people's sin. The high priest, the only person allowed to enter the inner sanctuary, went in every year on the Day of Atonement (*Yom Kippur*, still the great Jewish day of fasting; 9:7). And the very repetition of the sacrifice made its ineffectiveness all too clear (9:25). It was also limited. For 'sin with a high hand' or deliberate, premeditated sin, there was no atonement, only punishment.

When Christ came, the whole system was reformed (9:10): a new order began. As perfect high priest he offered himself as the perfect sacrifice (9:14) – a single voluntary offering, effective for all time, setting people free from the wrongs they have done. And his death brought the terms of his will (the new covenant) into effect (9:16ff.). For he went into heaven itself, to stand on our behalf in the presence of God (9:24). Sin has been removed. When he returns it will be to save (9:28).

10:1-18: the writer continues to press home his point that the old repeated sacrifices could only *remind* people of their sins, not remove them. What the law could not do, Christ has done. His offering is effective for ever. No further sacrifice is needed. Sins and misdeeds are not only forgiven but forgotten (17-18).

▶ **9:22** The context is worship, not people forgiving one another.

10:19-39 'Come near to God'

Jesus has won for us open access to the presence of God. 'So let us come near to God', the writer urges (19-22). Hold firm to the hope that is ours in Christ. God can be trusted to keep his promise.

There is no sacrifice left that will save those who oppose God, despise God's Son and insult his Spirit. It is a fearsome thing to face judgment at the hands of the living God (26-31).

These are people who have suffered for their faith, who have gladly endured loss. Keep up your courage, the writer urges. Hold on. Patient endurance will be rewarded. 'Just a little while longer...' (35-39).

▶ **Through the curtain (20)** See Mark 15:38.

11:1 – 12:11 Have faith!

The substance of this whole passage follows directly from 10:39: 'We are not people who turn back... we have faith.' The faith that is needed is an ongoing confident reliance on God, come what may. To have faith is to be certain – not of the here and

> **" When Christ had offered for all time a single sacrifice for sins, he sat down at the right hand of God. "**
>
> 10:12

The sacrificial system of the old covenant with Israel (represented by this model of an offering at the Tabernacle) has now been replaced, says the writer of Hebrews, by God's perfect once-and-for-all self-sacrifice in Christ.

Understanding Hebrews
Joy Tetley

Hebrews is an intriguing and powerful work. We do not know who produced it, nor the precise location and identity of those who first received it. Yet its message takes us into the depths of God and points us to the fundamentals of Christian discipleship.

Its author is essentially a preacher, on fire for God and with pastoral concern for a community in crisis. Yet his passion is expressed through a work that is carefully structured and carefully argued. Both mind and heart are very much engaged.

God and God's mission of salvation are the author's primary focus. The language and imagery used have much to do with worship and our means of access to God. In all this, Jesus is crucial. For the writer of Hebrews, 'looking to Jesus' (12:2) means seeing into the life and character of God.

The opening of this sermon declares that God's Son is the 'radiance of God's glory and exact imprint of God's very being' (1:3). God's 'Son' took on 'flesh and blood' (2:14) in the one we know as Jesus, so expressing God's longing and commitment to meet us where we are and lead us into the glory of God's presence. That life-changing truth should be a spur to faith and hope, even when circumstances push us to the limits of endurance.

Hebrews highlights the significance of Jesus in a particular way. The writer presents Jesus as great high priest – an image unique to Hebrews in the New Testament. It is a picture which would have been especially meaningful to those from a Jewish background. It is also a perceptive vision which has much

to say at all times and in all places.

The priesthood of Jesus is a fleshing out of God's yearning that all should know him, all should have free and confident access into his presence, all should share his life. For God in Jesus, that meant sharing fully in human experience and going through incalculable suffering. It also meant bursting out of the boundaries of existing Jewish understandings of priesthood.

In Jewish tradition, the priests were responsible for an extensive ritual system which sought to enable safe access to and communication with a holy God. This system (laid out especially in Leviticus) was seen as God's way of dealing positively with human sin and uncleanness.

Sacrifices had a central role. One of prime and focal significance was made on the annual Day of Atonement (see Leviticus 16). On this Day, the high priest (and he alone) went into the 'holy of holies', the innermost sanctuary of the Tabernacle (and later Temple) where God was believed specially to dwell. On behalf of all the people he offered the blood of the animal sacrifice, praying that by that offering, with the repentance it betokened, God would set aside the people's sins. It was a sacrifice that had to be repeated year after year by a high priest who, despite all the rites of purification he went through, remained a sinful human being.

He was also, like all his fellow priests, from a particular dynastic tribe. Only those of the tribe of Levi and the house of Aaron could be priests (Leviticus 8). In effect, being a priest depended on being born into the right family.

What Hebrews is saying, however, is that God has made a new covenant, in which sacrifice and priesthood take on a revolutionary meaning. What the old system was feeling after is brought to fulfilment by God's initiative and God's doing. By the life, death and ongoing work of Jesus (the self-expression of God), God and humankind are brought together. The 'shadows' of the former things give way to the real thing. The only sacrifices that continue to be appropriate are the sacrifices of praise and generosity (Hebrews 13:15-16).

Here is a God who does not fit in with traditions and expectations (that is something of what is meant by the 'order of Melchizedek', Hebrews 7). Jesus did not come from the right tribe to be a priest (7:13-14). God does a new thing. And Jesus in no way stands between humankind and God. Nor does he simply act on our behalf. Rather, Jesus opens the way for everyone to draw near with confidence to the 'holy of holies'. Through Jesus, we are all invited into a heart-to-heart relationship with God.

In Jesus, God's heart is both expressed and broken. For Jesus is both priest and victim. In Jesus, God offers his life, for us and to us. There can be no other priesthood to match this. This is the 'end ' of priesthood. Of this priesthood, all can taste the fruits. In this priesthood, all are invited to share.

now, the tangible things – but about the realities we cannot see (1). To believe that God made the world, creating what we see from invisible resources is itself a matter of faith (3).

The Old Testament abounds in examples of people who won God's approval by trusting him to keep his promises, taking him at his word. The stories of how they lived and died 'in faith' stand on record, and the writer runs through the list of the most remarkable of these examples of faith. All of them looked forward to the time when God would fulfil his promises: none of them actually lived to see it (13). Their sights were set on a 'better country'. And God has a place prepared for them: he is proud to own them and be known as their God (16).

- Abel's offering showed his faith – and his jealous brother killed him (Genesis 4).
- Enoch's faith saved him from experiencing death (Genesis 5:21-24).
- Noah's faith meant acting on God's warning word – so saving his whole family (Genesis 6 – 8).
- Abraham's trusting obedience to God's call took him away from his settled life at home (Genesis 12:1-7) to become a lifelong alien and refugee. His faith made him willing to offer up his only son, trusting that God would bring him back to life (Genesis 22).
- Isaac, Jacob and Joseph in turn all demonstrated their belief in God's promise (Genesis 27; 48; 50:24-25).
- Faith overcomes fear (23).
- It determined Moses' choice to leave court and throw in his lot with a nation of slaves (Exodus 2; 12; 14).
- The city of Jericho was taken by faith, not superior force (Joshua 2 and 6).

And so on through the Judges – Gideon (Judges 6 – 7); Barak (Judges 4); Samson (Judges 15 – 16); Jephthah (Judges 11 – 12) – through King David and the prophets.

- Daniel's faith saved him from the lions (33; Daniel 6).
- Elijah and Elisha brought the dead back to life (35; 1 Kings 17; 2 Kings 4).

In answer to faith, God has given remarkable triumphs and victories. But not always. Faith is demonstrated – equally – through those who have endured imprisonment, torture and death.

- Jeremiah was beaten and imprisoned (36; Jeremiah 38).
- Isaiah, it is said, was sawn in half (37).
- Zechariah was stoned (37; 2 Chronicles 24).

And there were many more like these. Yet none of them received what God had promised – because he had a better plan, says the writer, one that included us too (39-40).

As for us (12:1), we are surrounded by these heroes of faith. They are looking on, crowding round the track to see us run. So, strip off everything that hinders, and run the Christian race to the finish. Consider Christ – the ultimate example of faith: its pioneer and perfector (there is no 'our' before 'faith' in the Greek of verse 2). He did not give up when he faced the cross. Fix your eyes on him. Think what he went through – and don't be discouraged (1-3).

Verses 5-12: accept suffering as correction from a loving Father, evidence that he cares and wants the best for us. This discipline is like an athlete's training. The pain is short-term: the reward, lasting. So brace the trembling limbs, and keep going!

▶ **12:5-6** The writer quotes Proverbs 3:11-12 and Job 5:17.

12:13-29 No turning back

This section is one of encouragement, and warning. Count your assets (22-24) and don't turn back.

You have come to God by a better way than the terrors of Sinai, the writer says (18-21; Exodus 19), and he sets out the glories of heaven for us to see (22-24, 28). Be thankful, be grateful, respond to God in worship. Live to please him (14). There is no escape for those who refuse him: they will find him 'a consuming fire' (15, 25, 29).

▶ **Esau (16-17)** See Genesis 25:29-34; 27:34-40.

▶ **Mount Sinai (18-19)** See Exodus 19:16-22; 20:18-21.

▶ **Verse 23** 'Firstborn': those specially dedicated to God. 'Names written in heaven':

> 66 *To have faith is to be sure of the things we hope for, to be certain of the things we cannot see.* 99
>
> 11:1

> 66 *Run with determination the race that lies before us... our eyes fixed on Jesus.* 99
>
> 12:1-2

How may we approach God? Not as Moses and God's people once met him in fire and cloud on Mt Sinai. We may now come by a better way, through Christ himself – a way that is open to all.

see also Daniel 12:1; Luke 10:20; Philippians 4:3; Revelation 3:5.

▶ **Blood of Abel (24)** See Genesis 4:10.

▶ **Verse 26** quotes Haggai 2:6, Greek version.

13:1-17 How to please God

❝Jesus Christ is the same yesterday, today, and for ever.❞

13:8

God is concerned with the whole of life – the use of the home; response to the need of others; marriage; use of money. Love (1) shows itself in practical living (2-5). Follow the good example of those who have gone before – for Christ does not change (7-8). Live, not by the rule-book, but by drawing on the inner strength which God provides (9).

Verses 10-15: the writer returns, briefly, to his earlier themes. Not the old order but the new. Not the old sacrifices, but Jesus.

Not a permanent home on earth, but a city yet to come.

Verses 16-19: a final appeal. Do good and help one another. Follow your leaders. And 'please pray for us': a personal touch, at last.

13:18-25 Closing prayer and personal messages

The writer closes with a deeply moving prayer and blessing (20-21). He has written to encourage, not censure. He hopes the readers will take this kindly, and that he will see them soon.

▶ **In/from Italy (24)** The letter may have been sent from Italy, or the writer may be with a group of Christians from Italy who add their greetings to a letter going home.

James

Summary

An appeal addressed particularly to Jewish Christians to live out the faith, especially within the Christian community.

James speaks of faith and actions, wisdom, riches and poverty, testing and trouble, pride and prejudice, patience and prayer, in a style which recalls the Old Testament book of Proverbs.

James is the first of a group of seven 'general' letters, so called because they are addressed to groups of Christians in different parts of the Greco-Roman world, not to one particular church.

James, although it begins as a letter (with its 'from' and 'to') is more of an address, giving practical guidance on Christian conduct, covering various topics: rich and poor, pride and humility, wisdom, patience, prayer, controlling the tongue – and most importantly, faith and actions. There should be no discrepancy between the two. *Real* faith shows in the way Christians behave. It affects how they think of themselves and how they regard and treat others. James reminds his readers of the need for genuinely Christian standards and values in every area of life.

We know little or nothing of how the letter came to be written, or who it was sent to. From 1:1 it would seem the readers are Jewish Christians, although some take the 'twelve tribes of the Dispersion' to mean the 'new Israel', Christians of all nations.

We cannot be sure who the author was. The most likely candidate is James, the brother of Jesus. He became a Christian when he saw the risen Jesus (1 Corinthians 15:7) and went on to become the leader of the Jerusalem church (Acts 12:17; 15:13ff.; 21:18). The letter has a Jewish-Christian flavour and many of its characteristics sit well with this James as author.

- It has a marked sense of community.
- It echoes the concept of wisdom found in later Jewish wisdom literature.
- There are several parallels and allusions to Jesus' teaching, particularly in the Sermon on the Mount.
- Some of the words and phrases in this letter resemble those in James' speech at the Jerusalem Council recorded in Acts 15.

- The author's air of authority may be a further indicator.

The letter was probably written around AD 60, although some argue for an earlier, some for a later, date.

1 Deeds, not words

This opening chapter mentions almost all the topics dealt with more fully later: testing (2, 12-15), endurance (3; 5:7-11), wisdom (5; 3:13-18), prayer (5-8; 4:2-3; 5:13-18), faith (6; 2:14-26), riches (9-11; 2:1-13; 5:1-6), the tongue (19, 26; 3:1-12; 4:11), Christianity in action (22-25; 2:14-26). The crisp, succinct style and some of the themes recall both the Old Testament book of Proverbs and Jesus' own way of speaking in the Sermon on the Mount (Matthew 5 – 7).

James' comments in this chapter provide us with a fair idea of what Christians should be like. They have a positive attitude to the difficulties of life, knowing their value. They do not blame God when things go wrong. They know where to turn for help and guidance. Their values are right. They have control of their tongues and their tempers. They set themselves to discover God's standards and to live them out. They put faith into practice – and it shows.

▶ **Dispersion (1)** See introduction and 'The Jewish Dispersion'.

▶ **Verse 5** Jesus also told his followers to ask God, who gives good things (Matthew 7:7-11).

▶ **Verse 12** Echoes the style of Jesus' Beatitudes (Matthew 5:3-12).

▶ **Verses 22-23** Compare Jesus' words in Matthew 7:21, 24-27.

▶ **Verse 27** Real religion shows itself in care for the needy and in an exemplary life.

❝ If any of you is lacking in wisdom, ask God, who gives to all generously and ungrudgingly, and it will be given you. ❞'

1:5

If faith does not show itself in what we do and the way we behave, says James, it is dead! Genuine faith means that Christians will care for others and show them respect regardless of appearances and social status.

The figure of a bejewelled woman comes from Cyprus.

2:1-13 Respect the poor

> **66** *Those who were poor according to the world... God chose to be rich in faith and to be the heirs to the kingdom.* **99**
>
> 2:5

It is a natural human tendency to defer to social superiors and despise those below us on the social scale. There is nothing Christian about this. The right thing is to treat everyone with equal respect – to love our neighbour as ourself, as God's commandment teaches us (8; Mark 12:28-31).

▶ **Law that gives/of freedom (12)** Christ's law is a law of mercy, freeing people from the penalty of sin – something the law of Moses could not do. Paul also speaks of the law of Christ in 1 Corinthians 9 and in Galatians.

▶ **Verse 13** Compare Matthew 6:14-15; 18:21-35.

2:14-26 Faith and actions

> **66** *Resist the devil, and he will run away from you. The nearer you go to God, the nearer God will come to you.* **99**
>
> 4:7-8

Faith that stops at words is not faith at all. Even demons *believe* in God, and fear him, but that won't save them from God's judgment. Real faith *works*. God accepted Abraham (Genesis 15:1-6; 22) and Rahab (Joshua 2) because their faith resulted in action: it was genuine. If what we believe does not affect the way we live, what we do, it is *dead*.

▶ **Verse 24** James may be reacting to a garbled understanding of Paul's teaching (that we are 'justified' by grace through faith) on the part of some Jewish Christians out there in Paul's territory. His teaching here has been (wrongly) used by some to defend a doctrine of salvation by works.

3:1-12 Taming the tongue

Those who want to be teachers in the church must first learn to control their tongues. To master this most uncontrollable and contradictory member of the body is to have perfect self-control. One spark can light a forest fire. A single word can be just as destructive – a deadly venom. The same tongue can bless and it can curse, do good and do untold harm. This inconsistency, James says, is against all the laws of nature (11-12).

▶ **Verse 6** is very difficult. It seems to mean that through the tongue 'all the evil characteristics of a fallen world... find expression'. It not only pollutes the whole personality, its evil influence continues through the whole course of life.

▶ **Verse 12** Similar to Jesus' imagery in Matthew 7:16-18.

3:13-18 True wisdom

'Pure wisdom' comes from God and shows itself in gentleness, peace, mercy. It is a very different thing from being worldly-wise. The worldly-wise are full of selfish ambition, eager to get on, asserting their own rights. James offers a sort of counter-order wisdom, in contrast to the conventional wisdom of the wellborn and educated in the Greco-Roman world.

4 Whose friend are you?

James turns from peace (3:18) to conflict (4:1-2). The root cause of quarrels and fighting is envy: setting our hearts on something we want and determining to get it, no matter what. We align ourselves with the world when we behave like that, James says. And the world's friend is God's enemy (4). Don't be proud – be humble. Resist evil and submit to God who lifts up the humble (6-10).

Don't criticize and judge others: judgment is God's business (11-12).

Don't assume you have total control of

your life: that is in God's hands too
(13-16).

5:1-6 A warning to the rich

There is a special danger in wealth (5:1-6;
2:6-7). It wraps people up in false security.
They are so well-insulated that they cease
to feel for those who are cold and hungry.
This life is so pleasant that they forget the
day of reckoning. But God sees and hears
all.

In the style of an Old Testament prophet,
James denounces those who pile up riches
yet pay out no wages. There are echoes of
Proverbs, too, in these phrases.

Compare Jesus' parable of the rich fool
(Luke 12:16-21).

▶ **Verse 2** Compare Matthew 6:19.

5:7-20 Patience and prayer

James continues the thought of the day of
God's coming. Christians need patience in
the waiting time, the patience of the
farmer, the patient endurance of suffering
that we see in the prophets and Job. All was
well for Job in the end, and so it will be for
us.

Are you in trouble? Pray, then. Are
you happy? Praise God. Are you ill? God
heals in response to trusting prayer.
Elijah is no different from us. Think of the
power of his prayer (1 Kings 17:1; 18:1),
and be encouraged.

James' final words, perhaps still in the
context of prayer, concern the backslider.
When one of the fellowship turns away
from God, another must go and bring them
back. That return means a soul saved and
sins forgiven.

> ❝ *The
> prayer of the
> righteous is
> powerful and
> effective.* ❞
>
> 5:16

1 & 2 Peter

Summary

1 Peter
Peter writes to encourage Christians facing suffering and hard times. He reminds them of all they have to be glad about in Christ and urges them to live lives which reflect God's own holiness.

2 Peter
This letter combats false teaching, which will incur God's judgment. Peter urges his readers to live blameless lives as they await the day of the Lord's return, which will surely come.

The author of these letters declares himself as 'Simon Peter, servant and apostle of Jesus Christ' (1 Peter 1:1; 2 Peter 1:1). He is 'a witness of the sufferings of Christ' (1 Peter 5:1).

Peter
Peter met Jesus first of all through his brother Andrew (John 1:40-42). The two brothers came from the fishing village of Bethsaida. But they were living at Capernaum, at the northern end of Lake Galilee, when Jesus called them to leave their fishing business and follow him.

Peter quickly became the leader and spokesman of the group of 12 disciples who were with Jesus throughout the years of his public ministry. He was one of the inner three who saw some of Jesus' greatest miracles and who were allowed to see him in his true glory (Mark 9; 2 Peter 1:16-18). But when Jesus stood trial, Peter, for all his fine words, denied all knowledge of him – a fact he never forgot. Knowing his remorse, the risen Jesus appeared to Peter before any of the other apostles. And he became a leader of the new-born church, as Jesus had predicted (Matthew 16:13-20) – the very first to declare the Good News about Jesus (Acts 2).

Tradition has it that Peter's final years of preaching and teaching (he was accompanied in his travels by his wife) took place in Rome. There he was crucified, head downwards, during Emperor Nero's terrible persecution which began in AD 64. The reference to 'Babylon' in 1 Peter 5:13 may well be a code-word for Rome (as in Revelation 16:19, etc.).

1 Peter
The first letter was sent to scattered groups of Christians in the five Roman provinces which covered the greater part of modern Turkey, north of the Taurus mountains. Peter most probably wrote from Rome, at the outbreak of Nero's persecutions (if 5:13 refers to the city). He had John Mark with him, and Paul's companion Silvanus (Silas) to help him write. Christians in other parts of the empire would soon be suffering as they were in Rome. Peter's message is one of comfort, hope and encouragement to stand firm.

2 Peter
The second letter mentions neither place of writing nor destination. Scholars have very great doubts whether the letter is really Peter's. It certainly differs in language and subject from 1 Peter. Some scholars point out anachronisms and believe the writer 'borrowed' from Jude (see below). Maybe the writer (perhaps a disciple of the apostle) gave the letter Peter's name because he was the most important source of the material included. There is no conclusive proof.

Longstanding tradition, and the care taken by the early church Councils to exclude documents they regarded as forgeries, weigh in favour of Peter as author. And despite the differences, the letters have a great deal in common. 2 Peter 1:12-18, speaking of Peter's approaching death and of Christ's transfiguration, match 1 Peter in grammar, style and vocabulary. Michael Green lists a number of other allusions to the life of Jesus and of Peter: the prophecy of Peter's death (John 21:21-23; 1:14); denial of Jesus (2:1); the last state worse than the first (Matthew 12:45; 2:20); the Day of the Lord coming like a thief in the

In his great mercy God has given us new birth into a living hope through the resurrection of Jesus Christ from the dead.
1:3

night (Matthew 24:43; 3:10).

The letter addresses the issue of false teaching, which is rife in the churches. Countering this, the author's main theme is true knowledge. He re-emphasizes the certainty of Christ's return in judgment and rescue, pointing out what this means in terms of Christian living.

2 Peter and Jude

Fifteen of the 25 verses in Jude also appear – some wholly, some partly – in 2 Peter, and the two letters have many ideas in common. This means that:

- they were written by the same author
- or that one draws on the other
- or that both draw on a common source.

Since it is widely believed that Peter draws on a catechism (or an address) used at baptism in his first letter, he may well have made use of existing material in his second letter too.

The Jewish Dispersion

Dick France

'Dispersion' (Greek, *diaspora*) is the term which was used to mean those Jews who lived outside Palestine. After the disastrous Jewish War of AD 66-73 and the Roman destruction of the Temple in AD 70 large numbers of Jews moved away from their traditional home, especially eastwards into Mesopotamia. But the process of 'dispersion' began long before that. At least since their exile in the 6th century BC Jews had settled around the Middle East and the eastern Mediterranean.

By New Testament times probably more Jews lived outside Palestine than in it. There were estimated to be a million Jews in Egypt alone. In Alexandria, Jews made up such a significant proportion of the population that they formed a distinct political unit, living in their own areas of the city and maintaining their own culture and lifestyle.

Their distinctiveness, here and elsewhere, often led to strained relations with the non-Jewish population. Greek and Roman writers often speak disparagingly of the Jews who lived among them but

whom they did not understand, and anti-Jewish riots were not uncommon.

By the New Testament period most of the main cities had a Jewish colony, with its own synagogue (or at least a place for prayer, Acts 16:13). These expatriate Jewish communities were a natural first contact for Paul, as a Jew, and other Christian missionaries as they moved around the Mediterranean world.

Jews of the Dispersion are sometimes referred to as 'Hellenistic Jews'. Hellenism – the wave of Greek culture and ideas which rolled over the Mediterranean world following the conquests of Alexander the Great – remained the dominant strand in the culture of the eastern part of the Roman Empire. The dispersed Jews, away from the more conservative atmosphere of Palestine, adapted more readily to the Greek way of life. They did not abandon their distinctive religion and culture and cease to be Jews, but they were more willing to learn from and enter into dialogue with Greek ideas.

Many of the later Jewish writings, particularly those from Alexandria (e.g. the Wisdom of Solomon in the Deuterocanonical books, and the voluminous writings of Philo) are deeply influenced by Greek philosophy, and use language which would have been quite unfamiliar to Palestinian Jews. Apollos, the learned Jew from Alexandria (Acts 18:24), no doubt belonged to this school, before his gradual conversion to Christianity.

1 PETER

1 Looking forward in hope

Even in times of suffering, there is so much to gladden the heart and to thank God for: his gift of new life; the resurrection of Jesus which gives us 'living hope'; a legacy we will one day possess, which is 'kept safe' for us by God himself (3-5). Trials have a purpose: they test faith out and prove it genuine. The dark days are short in comparison with the joy to come (6-9).

The prophets spoke of this gift of salvation, predicting Christ's suffering – and glory (10-12). These are the things 'you have now heard' from the messengers who brought God's Good News – things that the angels themselves longed to catch a glimpse of. With such a ransom price paid (18-21), the new life must be different from the old. It demands 'holy living' (13-17), purity, love from the heart (22).

▶ Dispersion (1:1, some versions) See on James 1:1, and 'The Jewish Dispersion'. Versions which take the word to mean the scattered church (Jews and Gentiles), translate, e.g., 'strangers in the world'.

▶ Pontus, etc.: see map in 'Letters', introduction.

▶ Verses 10ff. The Old Testament prophets had a message for their own generation – but they also looked to the future, when Christ would come. The author of Hebrews writes in much the same vein (11:39-40).

2 – 3 Living as God's people

■ Don't get stuck at the baby stage, Peter says to his readers. Grow up in faith! Remember who you are (2:1-10): God's own people, chosen to make known the wonderful things he has done; living stones being built into a spiritual Temple that rests on the foundation stone of Christ himself.

■ Live exemplary lives (2:11-17). Make sure there are no grounds for any accusations brought against you. (Christians in Peter's day had to live down unsavoury rumours that they practised incest, held sexual orgies – even that they were cannibals.) Obey the civil authorities (Peter writes this with Nero ruling the empire!).

On this subject, see also Mark 12:17; Romans 13:1-7.

Peter writes to scattered groups of Christians enduring persecution in the reign of the sadistic Emperor Nero, whose head is shown on this coin.

> **66** *Like newborn babies, crave pure spiritual milk, so that by it you may grow up in your salvation.* **99**
>
> 2:2

- Slaves, harshly treated, find their model in Christ, who endured undeserved suffering without threat or argument in his own defence (2:18-25). As God, 'the righteous Judge' brought blessing for all from the suffering of Jesus, so he will bless those who suffer because they want to do his will.
- Wives, too, are to submit to their husbands' authority (3:1-6), and win over unbelieving husbands by their conduct. (This does not mean they are less important or inferior. Wayne Grudem makes the point that 'Jesus was subject to his parents and to God the Father'.) They are to take as their examples, not fashion models but women of faith – women like the matriarch Sarah, who radiate inner beauty. They are not only to live good lives, but to be free of fear and worry (6). Christian husbands, for their part, will show consideration to their wives (7). In terms of God's gift of new life, husbands and wives are equals. A good relationship is vital, not only for their happiness but for spiritual health too, for prayer withers in an atmosphere of friction.
- Verses 8-17, concluding, address *all* believers. Be loving, be kind, be humble. Pay back good for evil. Do good: keep a clear conscience. There is no need to be anxious or afraid. It is better to suffer for doing good than for doing wrong. Christ suffered death, the blameless for the guilty, in order to bring us to God (18ff.). The risen Jesus, now at God's right hand, enables us to stand before him in good conscience, washed clean of sin.

▶ **Living stone (2:4)** A favourite New Testament metaphor for Christ (see Mark 12). The quotations are from Isaiah 28:16; Psalm 118:22; Isaiah 8:14-15.

▶ **Spiritual sacrifices (2:5)** See, e.g., Romans 12:1; Hebrews 13:15-16.

▶ **Spirits in prison... (3:19-22)** Wayne Grudem sets out the issues raised by these difficult verses under three questions:
– Who are the spirits in prison? Are they unbelievers who have died; Old Testament believers who have died; fallen angels?
– What did Christ preach? Was it a second chance for repentance; the completion of his

True feminine beauty, says Peter, writing of the duties of husbands and wives, comes from 'the inner self', not 'outward adornment'. The gold disc inlaid with garnets is from a necklace (2nd century AD).

redemptive work; final condemnation?
– When did he preach? Was it in the days of Noah; between his death and resurrection; after his resurrection?'

He argues the view that Christ was 'in spirit' preaching through Noah when the ark was built. Augustine, Aquinas and some modern scholars agree with this.

An alternative view, from parallels in Jude and 2 Peter, takes the 'spirits in prison' as fallen angels who are in *tartaros* (not hell) – a holding cell also referred to by Isaiah. The point of this proclamation is not redemption but to declare victory over the powers of darkness.

There are a number of other views.

The flood-water which destroyed the world saved Noah and his family by floating the ark, so Peter sees the water of baptism as a symbol of rescue from death. It was the ark, not the water, which really saved Noah — as it is the risen Christ, not baptism in itself, who saves those who trust him and are cleansed from sin.

'Be on the alert,' says Peter. 'Your enemy (Satan) is prowling around like a hungry lion looking for his next meal!'

4 – 5 When suffering comes

Peter anticipates a time of suffering and persecution for his readers. When it comes, they will need to be ready – level-headed, alert, prayerful and unfailingly loving to others (4:7-8). The life of the past is done with (4:3-4). Now each of Christ's followers is given grace for some special service (4:10). It should come as no surprise to Christians to suffer for Christ's sake (4:12). It is a cause for joy, not discouragement! Christ's suffering led to glory – a glory Christ's faithful followers will share.

As a leader himself – and a witness of the crucifixion – Peter appeals for a real 'shepherd spirit' in all church leaders (5:1-4; and see John 10 and 21:15ff.). The younger people (5:5) must respect their authority. Christians need to acquire a genuinely humble spirit. They also need stout hearts to face formidable and unrelenting opposition (8-9). But God never ceases to be concerned for his people. Suffering is only for a little time: God's strength and power are endless.

▶ **4:1** 'Whoever suffers... ' Peter is talking about those who suffer for doing right (3:17), not sufferers in general.

▶ **To the dead... (4:6)** I.e. Christians who are now dead. They suffered the judgment of death, like other people, but they will live.

> ❝ *Leave all your worries with God, because he cares for you.* ❞
>
> 5:7

▶ **Love covers... (4:8)** A proverb also quoted in James 5:20.

▶ **Judgment (4:17)** The thought may link with 4:6 – see above.

▶ **5:5ff.** These verses echo the thought in James 4:6ff. The 'roar' is intended to terrify, but Satan no longer has the power to destroy those who belong to Christ.

▶ **Silvanus (5:12)** Silas, companion to Paul on his second missionary journey (Acts 15:22, 32ff.), and his associate in writing to the Thess-alonians.

▶ **Babylon (5:13)** Probably a code-name for Rome (see Revelation 17).

▶ **Mark (5:13)** See introduction to Mark's Gospel.

2 PETER

1 Knowing God and the truth

God's purpose for his people is that they should come to share his own nature and character – nothing less (4). So to faith must be added other qualities (5-8). In this way knowledge of Christ is translated into action (8). Peter does not hesitate to refresh his readers' memory of truth already known, especially as he sees his own death approaching (12-15).

Peter uses vivid imagery in his writing, drawing many pictures (as Jesus did) from the countryside: shepherds and flocks, seedtime and harvest, waterless springs and storm-driven mists. These would be familiar to his readers from the surrounding landscapes in what is now Turkey.

The Christian message does not rest on myth and legend, but on the evidence of eye-witnesses (16). Peter could never forget what he saw and heard, that day on the mountain when Jesus stood before them in his glory, and gives his own account of its significance (16-18; Matthew 17:5, etc.). The testimony of the prophets has been confirmed as a word from God himself (19-21).

▶ **Verse 14** Peter, facing death, recalls the Lord's words: John 21:18-19.

▶ **Verse 19** The Scriptures light our path through life until the dawning day of Christ's return: Psalm 119:105; Revelation 22:16.

▶ **Verse 20** This may mean either 'it is not the interpretation that authenticates the prophet's message', or 'the true interpretation, like the message itself, is God-given'.

2 False teachers, and their fate

The argument of this chapter is closely paralleled in Jude 4-16. To be forewarned is to be forearmed – so the writer warns his readers against false teachers who have already disrupted other Christian groups. They are anti-authority (10). They respect no one. They teach self-gratification, and their dissolute lives deny the Lord and shame his church (13-15). They trade in false hope, promising freedom from restraint which is in reality another enslavement (19). Their punishment is certain and terrible (4-10): the rescue of God's people is equally sure. The writer takes Old Testament examples: the flood, and the rescue of Noah (Genesis 6 – 8); the destruction of Sodom and Gomorrah, and the rescue of Lot (Genesis 19).

▶ **Angels (4, 10-11)** See on Jude.

▶ **Balaam (15)** It seems this true prophet

turned traitor when the price was high enough (Numbers 31:16).

▶ **Verses 19-22** These false teachers were once orthodox Christians. Now their state is worse than before they knew anything of Christ.

3 God will keep his promise

Years have passed and still Christ's expected return has not happened. The created world runs on as it always has done. What then of God's promise? There are always people ready to scoff (3ff.). But God's word, spoken through the prophets and apostles, will prove dependable (2). His word commands such power, it brought our whole world into being (5; Genesis 1:3). If God 'delays' it is out of mercy, not weakness (8-9). There is no difference of opinion between Peter and 'our dear brother Paul': both speak of these matters in the same way (15-16). Of course, says Peter, we all find some of Paul's teaching a bit hard to understand!

The certainty that Jesus will come, that it could happen any day, is the strongest possible incentive to Christian living (11, 14). The writer's closing instruction is to be ready: 'Grow in the grace and knowledge of our Lord and Saviour Jesus Christ.'

▶ **Second letter (1)** The first may be 1 Peter, or some other letter now lost.

▶ **The fathers (4)** Either the Old Testament fathers, or the first Christians. Fell asleep: this is the way Jesus talked of death.

▶ **Verses 5-7** 'There is a neat parallelism in these three verses. By his word and by means of water God created the world (5); by his word and by means of water, he destroyed it (6); by his word and by means of time he will destroy it in future judgment (7)' (Michael Green).

66 Make every effort to add to your faith goodness; and to goodness, knowledge; and to knowledge, self-control; and to self-control, perseverance; and to perseverance, godliness; and to godliness brotherly kindness; and to brotherly kindness, love. 99

2 Peter 1:5-7

66 The Lord... is patient... not wanting anyone to perish, but everyone to come to repentance. 99

3:9

1, 2 & 3 John

Summary

1 John
An address written to warn the readers against false teaching, calling on them to hold to the truth – that God is both light and love, requiring his children to 'live in the light' and to love one another.

2 John
A brief letter on the same theme, addressed to a particular church.

3 John
A personal note to a friend about a church leader who has become a real problem in the church.

1 JOHN

How did this anonymous piece of writing (called a letter, yet not written in letter form) come to be named as John's? The primary reason must be its striking likeness to the fourth Gospel. The obvious conclusion is that they are by the same author: so if the Gospel is by John this is also his work. (See introduction to John's Gospel.) The noticeably authoritative tone of 1 John and the author's claim in the opening verses to be an eye-witness support this. Some modern scholars, however, see the author of 1 John as a different person, consciously imitating the content and style of John's Gospel.

Both the Gospel and 1 John belong to the close of the 1st century. The Christian faith was 50 or 60 years old by this time and had spread throughout the Roman Empire. John, by tradition living out his last years at Ephesus in modern Turkey – a strategic centre of the Christian church – was probably the only apostle still alive. There was pressure on many Christian groups to incorporate ideas from other philosophies as part of the faith (a pressure the church still feels today).

1 John was written to counter some early form of 'Gnosticism' being propounded by people who were once church members but had now withdrawn from the group. They liked to think of themselves as intellectuals – possessing a superior knowledge of God. Contrary to the traditional Jewish and Christian holistic view of the world, they drew a line between the spiritual (good) and the material (evil). In practice this often led to immorality, because nothing the body did could tarnish the purity of the spirit. It also led to a denial of Christ's human nature, which was either 'make-believe' or only temporary. They reasoned that Christ, being spirit, could not have died.

In this strong but tender appeal to his 'little children' in the faith, John makes it plain that these ideas cut out the heart of the Christian message. If Christ did not become truly human and die to win forgiveness for 'the sins of the world' (2:2) there is no Christian faith.

The message John declares is twofold:
- God is light: he calls all who follow him to walk in the light of his commands;
- and God is love: he requires his people to love one another.

1:1-4 The Word of life

John's theme is 'the Word of life'. At the beginning of his Gospel John spoke of the person who is God's Word of life: Jesus Christ, someone John actually *knew*. Here too he speaks of his own experience: this living embodiment of God's Word could be seen and touched. The Word is both a person and a message: the two are inseparable. John had seen God's message of eternal life in Christ, had heard it from him, and now he joyfully declares it with a confidence born of certainty.

1:5 – 2:2 God is light

What is this message? First, that 'God is light'. This is the light that generates life and dispels darkness. Anyone who claims 'fellowship' or communion with God yet lives 'in the dark' is telling a lie (1:5-7). But to say we never sin is equally false. If we live in the light we will recognize and confess our sins. God can be relied on to keep his promise of forgiveness and

> **"** *John's three letters have struck me as still extraordinarily relevant to the current scene in the world and the church.* **"**
>
> John Stott

> **"** *God is light; in him there is no darkness at all.* **"**
>
> 1 John 1:5

cleansing (8-10). What is more, we have Jesus – the one through whom we are forgiven – to plead our cause (2:1-2).

2:3-29 Living in the light

How can we be sure that we really know God? To know is to obey. So the first test is obedience. If we obey God's commands, if we live as Jesus did, we *can* be sure (3-6).

2:7-17: the second test is love. Living in God's light means keeping the old-and-new command to love one another (the 'new commandment' Jesus gave his disciples – John 13:34 – which John knows these Christians have already been taught).

At this point John digresses. First he speaks to the church. His 'children', 'fathers', 'young men', reflect three stages in spiritual growth or maturity (12-14). From the church he turns to the world (15-17), which Christians must not love. What does this mean? John characterizes the world as humanity at loggerheads with God, self-centred, proud, acquisitive: the whole evil system. To love the world is to accept its values and attitudes. But this world is destined to end (17), and John says that end is near (18).

The early Christians were taught that an arch-enemy of Christ – the embodiment of evil – would come on the scene when the Lord's return was imminent (18; the actual word 'antichrist' occurs only in John's letters, but 2 Thessalonians 2 makes the same point). John sees many antichrists already on the scene (false teachers, once within the church, who deny that the man Jesus was the Messiah and Son of God). These early manifestations of the Great Evil are a sign that the time is near.

John comforts his readers that they are different. They know the truth. They have God's Holy Spirit to teach them. If they stay with the message they have heard, they will stay with the Son and the Father – which means eternal life.

▶ **Remaining in him (6, 28)** See John 15.

▶ **Verses 12-14** As some modern translations make clear, these verses are written in the form of poetry, unlike the rest of the letter.

▶ **Anointing/pouring (27)** John refers to the discernment the Holy Spirit gives to Christians. See also 4:4-6. He is talking about false

teachers, not saying that Christians have no need of teaching.

3 Living as the children of God

The child of God shares God's own nature. It is against that nature – out of character – to live a life of sin, to go on breaking God's law deliberately and habitually (the tenses of the verbs in the Greek make a distinction between this and the particular 'one-off' sins referred to in 1:10). The difference between 'God's children and the devil's children' (10) is that 'the devil's children' do not do what is right, or love others.

The message 'heard from the very beginning' is that God's people must love one another. What does that mean? John tells us plainly: 'This is how we know what

Light and love are the themes of John's first letter.

love is: Christ gave his life for us!' (16). This love is not just talk. It expresses itself in sacrifice and self-giving. And it will touch our pockets (17)! If our conscience is clear on this score, we can approach God with confidence. He answers the prayers of those who obey him.

God commands us to believe that the Jesus of history is in fact the Son of God, the Christ – and to love one another as Jesus commanded. Those who do so 'live in him, and he in them'. We know it by his gift of the Spirit.

▶ **Verses 19-20** 'Often our conscience accuses us justly... But our conscience is by no means infallible; its condemnation may often be unjust. We can, therefore, appeal from our conscience to God, who... knows everything... Stronger than any chemical tranquillizer is trust in our all-knowing God' (Stott).

> 66 *God is love.* 99
>
> 4:8

4:1-6 Testing, testing...

John sets one basic test by which to judge any teacher – he must recognize that Jesus Christ came as a human being. He is not ignoring the equally essential recognition of Jesus as Son of God (3:23 and 4:15). But it was Jesus' humanity that the heretics of John's day denied. So they cannot possibly come with a message from God. Because we belong to God, John says, we can tell truth from error.

> 66 *It is not we who loved God, but God loved us and sent his Son to expiate our sins... If God loved us so much, we too should love one another.* 99
>
> 4:10-11

4:7-21 God is love

God is light (1:5) – and God is love (4:8). He showed his love for us in sending his Son to bring us forgiveness and new life (9-10). The proof that we really share his life – his nature – is the love we show towards others. John has touched on this already in chapter 2: here he looks at it from all angles. Love and obedience are bound up together (21). If we love and obey God, we need not dread the day of judgment (17-18).

> 66 *Whoever believes that Jesus is the Christ is a child of God.* 99
>
> 5:1

5 We can be sure

Faith is what brings us into God's family (1). To love God is to share God's nature and to love others. Love for God makes obedience natural, not burdensome (3). Faith is what 'overcomes the world' (4-5). God himself stands witness that Jesus is his

Son. 'To believe is life, to disbelieve is death' (12). John is writing to those who do believe, that they may know for certain that eternal life is theirs (13).

The false teachers loved to talk about 'knowledge'. John makes his own list of things 'we know' for a certainty (18-20).

■ We know that Christ himself keeps his followers from continuing in the old sinful way of life.

■ We know we belong to God in an alien world.

■ We know that through the Son of God we know God himself, and share his eternal life.

Having set out the certainties, John urges his readers in closing: 'Do not abandon the real for the illusory' (Blaiklock).

▶ **Verses 6-8** The King James/Authorized Version incorporates words that do not form part of the original letter, but are a late addition. These are omitted in all modern versions.

▶ **Three witnesses (8)** The Holy Spirit, the water of Christ's baptism and the blood of his death.

▶ **Verse 16** 'The way to deal with sin in the congregation is to pray. And God hears such prayer' (Stott). But there is a sin which leads to death. John does not say what this deadly sin is. It is unlikely he means a specific sin. He could mean apostasy – rejecting the faith once held – but that runs counter to his own teaching in this letter. Jesus referred to just one 'unforgivable' sin: to see the work of God's Holy Spirit as the work of Satan (Matthew 12:31-32). John may have had in mind those counterfeit Christians, the false teachers.

2 JOHN

Unlike 1 John, 2 and 3 John are 'real letters, each long enough to be accommodated on a standard size sheet of papyrus (25 x 20cm) and conforming to the letter-writing pattern of the time' (I.H. Marshall). There is little doubt that 1, 2 and 3 John are the work of one author, most likely the apostle John or a close disciple of his. The writer calls himself 'the Elder' in both 2 and 3 John, the one addressed to 'the dear lady and her children' (most probably a disguised address for a church), the other a private letter, like Paul's letter to Philemon.

2 John, like 1 John, warns against false teachers, encourages the readers to hold to the truth (to stay with Christ's teaching), and focusses on a favourite theme: Jesus' command that those who follow him should love one another (5; 1 John 2:7 and 3:11; John 15:12-17). To love others as Jesus loves us means keeping God's commands. For Christians, love and truth go hand in hand.

Christ's teaching is the test by which to judge visiting teachers. Those who 'go beyond' it cannot be from God (9-10). John is combatting the same sort of trouble here (7) as in his first letter. From the start of the Christian mission there had been travelling evangelists and teachers, usually responsible to one of the apostles, who were given hospitality by the local churches. The time has come to tighten up. Those whose teaching contradicts the fundamental truth about Jesus Christ should not be made welcome.

John looks forward to a visit. There is so much more to be said than he can put in writing (12). The 'children of your dear sister' are presumably members of John's own church.

3 JOHN

See on 2 John above. This is a personal letter from the Elder to his friend **Gaius**. The name was a common one at the time, and there is nothing to connect this Gaius with any of the others mentioned in the New Testament. If tradition is anything to go by, he may have been a leader of the church at Pergamum. More importantly, Gaius was a man who 'lived in (and lived out) the truth' (3). His life and conduct are in striking contrast to that of another local leader, **Diotrephes**. Gaius, a man of integrity, is doing all in his power to help his fellow Christians, especially the travelling evangelists and teachers who depended on Christian hospitality and support. (The situation here is clearly very different from that of the church in 2 John, where members are faced with false teachers they are warned against welcoming.) Diotrephes is damaging John's own character, suppressing his letter, spreading lies, hugging his own position as leader and hindering missionary outreach.

The third character in the letter, **Demetrius**, may have been John's messenger (there being no postal service). This man's life speaks for itself. He richly deserves the high regard in which John holds him.

A letter is a poor substitute for personal contact. John longs to come soon to see his friend and have a good, long talk (13-14).

This clay statuette of a woman with a writing-tablet and stylus was found at Salamis in Cyprus. It dates from the 4th century BC.

Jude

Summary

A powerful warning letter to arm the readers to resist the fatal persuasion of false teachers within the church.

The author of this letter is Jude, the younger brother of Jesus and James, now an old man (the date is uncertain, but may be around AD 80). He was already thinking of writing, when alarming news of false teaching (see below) made him pen this short, vigorous letter with all speed. The letter is obviously Jewish – full of Old Testament references and allusions, and drawing its illustrations from at least two Jewish apocryphal writings (see below). Jude is dealing with a situation very like that dealt with in 2 Peter. And in fact the bulk of Jude's letter is paralleled in 2 Peter 2 (see introduction to 1 and 2 Peter). The two are so similar that either one made use of the other, or both drew on an existing tract against false teaching.

Though he had wanted to write 'about the salvation we share', Jude writes, instead, urging the Christians to hold fast to the truth. For 'certain men' have infiltrated the group and are now creating division by their false teaching (1-4). These men are so arrogant as to deny Christ. And Christian freedom has been turned into license.

Jude reminds his readers of examples from Jewish history and tradition (5-7): those who fall away, or give themselves up to pride or lust will suffer God's judgment.

These men reject authority. But they are marked out for destruction – as Sodom and Gomorrah were for their sexual immorality and perversion (7; Genesis 19); as Cain was for murdering the brother whose life showed up his own (11; Genesis 4); as Balaam was for betraying his position as a prophet (11; Numbers 31:8, 16 – see 2 Peter 2:15); and as Korah was for his rebellion against God-given authority (11; Numbers 16). The examples are carefully chosen. These are the very things of which these teachers are guilty.

Jude's intention is to stiffen resistance to such teachers. The Christians are not defenceless, but they must make full use of their defences. They must build on 'the faith' – that definitive body of truth they have been taught. They must pray and use the power of the Holy Spirit. They must live in the light of Christ's coming again. There is no need to be afraid or despair, for God is indeed able to keep them from falling.

▶ **The angels (6)** The statement about the 'sons of God' in Genesis 6:1-2 led to a belief in an earlier war in heaven between good and evil angels whose pride and ambition led to their downfall. 'The Greek myth of the destruction of the Titans by Zeus, the Zoroastrian legend of the fall of Ahriman and his angels, and the rabbinic elaboration of Genesis 6:1 all show how widespread such a belief was in popular religion, as an attempt to rationalize the contradictions and the evil in the world' (Michael Green). It was an apt illustration for Jude's argument.

▶ **Verse 9** The story comes from the apocryphal *Assumption of Moses*. Michael was sent to bury Moses, but the devil challenged his right to the body, on the ground that Moses had murdered an Egyptian. Jude uses Michael's circumspect reply as a lesson to people to watch their words, and not to treat the devil lightly.

▶ **Love feasts (12)** The Lord's Supper/Holy Communion was celebrated in the context of a shared meal in the early church.

▶ **Verses 14-15** A quotation from the apocryphal *Book of Enoch*. Jude takes his illustrations from books he and his readers know and respect, as well as from the scriptures themselves.

> *To him who is able to keep you from falling and to present you before his glorious presence without fault and with great joy – to the only God our Saviour be glory, majesty, power and authority, through Jesus Christ our Lord.*

Jude's doxology: 24-25

Revelation

Summary

Letters to seven churches introduce a series of prophetic visions heralding judgment – the final destruction of death and evil – and the remaking of all creation for God and his people together.

Chapters 1 – 3
John's vision of Christ
Letters to seven churches
•
Chapters 4 – 16
Visions of what is to come:
The scroll with seven seals
The seven trumpets
Seven signs: God's people under attack
The seven last plagues
•
Chapters 17 – 20
God's final triumph:
The last battle
Millennium
Judgment
•
Chapters 21 – 22
God's new world
John's closing words

Best-known passage

A new heaven and a new earth *(21:1-8)*

The full title of this book is 'The Revelation (Greek *apokalysis*) to John'. It is the only 'apocalyptic' writing included in the New Testament. Jewish apocalypses were written in times of crisis. They encourage readers by looking at the 'big picture' of human history and focussing on the end of the world when God will reign supreme in peace and justice. Many of the things that modern readers find most difficult about the book of Revelation are features of this kind of writing – the use, for example, of:

- visions
- symbols
- Old Testament 'echoes' (a kind of 're-reading of the Scriptures and bringing them up to date')
- numbers which carry special meaning.

Even those who fully appreciate the richness of symbol still have to wrestle with the problem of what John meant his readers to understand from the images he chooses.

The writer and his situation

The author tells us his name is John. He does not call himself an apostle: he says he is a 'servant' of Jesus (1:1), and a prophet (22:19). He is enduring suffering as a prisoner on the island of Patmos because he has been spreading the word about Jesus.

From his close knowledge of the Old Testament and the fact that he writes 'Hebraic Greek' (quite unlike that of John's Gospel and the Letters of John), it is likely he is a Jewish Christian, probably from Palestine. It is generally thought that this John is a different person from the John of the Gospel and Letters, though the fact that Revelation is apocalyptic writing may account for the marked difference of style, and a secretary may have been involved in the writing of the Gospel and Letters.

John was not an uncommon name at the time but, apart from the apostle, the only other John in the New Testament is John Mark.

Tradition says that the apostle John left Palestine to make his home in Ephesus – capital city of the Roman province of Asia, in which the seven churches of Revelation 2 – 3 are located, and itself the recipient of one of the letters.

The book was written during a time of persecution. John's own exile on Patmos (1:9) probably entailed hard labour in the island's quarries. Some Christians had been killed (2:13) and others imprisoned for their faith. And there was worse to come (2:10), as worship of the Roman emperor became obligatory (see 'Emperor worship and Revelation'). The date of writing would seem to be some time during the reign of the persecuting Emperor Domitian (AD 81-96).

Theme and purpose

The whole focus of Revelation is on Jesus. John says his book is a record of the events that Jesus Christ revealed to him. His first vision (1:11-20) is of Christ. It is Christ – the Lion of Judah, the Lamb of sacrifice (chapter 5) – who breaks the seals on the scroll which marks the beginning of God's final judgment. The redeemed are those

> 66 *In this book the translator is carried into another dimension – he has but the slightest foot-hold in the Time-and-space world with which he is familiar. He is carried, not into some never-never land of fancy, but into the Ever-ever land of God's eternal Values and Judgments.* 99
>
> Modern Bible translator, J.B. Phillips

Was Revelation written by John the apostle or another John? We canot be certain. Ancient tradition has it that the apostle spent his last days at Ephesus, which the writer clearly knows well. His tomb is said to be here, in the Basilica of St John at Ephesus rebuilt by the Emperor Justinian in the 6th century AD.

who follow the Lamb (chapter 14). God's people, the citizens of the new Jerusalem – the bride of the Lamb – are those whose names are written in the Lamb's 'book of life' (21:27). And Revelation closes with the repeated promise of Jesus, 'I am coming soon.'

The first Christians lived in eager expectation of Christ's return. But 60 years after his death it still had not happened, persecution was increasing, and some were beginning to doubt. So Revelation's letters to the churches, and the book as a whole, were needed to encourage them to stand firm. God is in control, no matter how things may look. Christ, not the emperor, is Lord of history. He has the key of destiny itself. And he is coming again to execute justice. There is a glorious, wonderful future for every faithful believer – and especially for those who lay down their lives for Christ. This world and all that happens in it is in God's hands. His love and care for his people is unfailing.

John's message was conveyed in a form designed to inspire as well as instruct. The vivid symbols which puzzle us were clear to those who first heard his circular letter to the churches. They understood the veiled references, but there was nothing to arouse the suspicion of authorities eager to charge these Christians with sedition.

Christians still find themselves in similar situations, terrorized and victimized by anti-Christian regimes. Every age needs the timeless realities, the perspective, the assurance of 'The Revelation to John': to know that the final victory of Christ and his people over death and evil is certain.

Approaching Revelation

A few simple rules of interpretation may help in understanding this book.

- Revelation, as we have said, belongs to a special kind of writing: 'apocalyptic' (see 'Revelation and Jewish apocalyptic writing' and 'Understanding Revelation'). It is closer to poetry than prose in the way it is meant to be understood.
- Revelation is rooted in the Old Testament: this is where to look for clues to the meaning of the various symbols.
- This is a book of visions. It is the main thrust of each picture that is important. As with parables, we need to look first at the whole, to discover the main idea.
- Chronology is largely a modern Western preoccupation. John's visions are presented as a series of graphic images,

---

Numbers with special meaning

Revelation, in common with other apocalyptic writing, makes frequent use of numbers. Their importance lies not in their literal value but in the fact that some numbers have special significance. For example:
4 usually refers to the earth (7:1), or a place (4:6)
6 falls short of perfection (ultimately so in the number of the beast: **666**)
7 has the meaning of perfection or completeness
12, the number of the tribes, speaks of God's people
1,000 stands for 'a great number'.

If a number is squared or multiplied it is even more significant. So **144** (12 x 12),**000** is the whole host of God's people.

Some letters of the Greek alphabet also served as numbers. It is therefore possible for figures to be used in place of letters for some names. But 'numerology', which attempts to identify names on the basis of the numeric value of letters, is full of pitfalls. See for example the note on 13:17-18.

The seven churches of Revelation

A messenger from John in exile on the island of Patmos would have crossed to Ephesus and then taken a circular route. The seven churches (Revelation 2 and 3) are listed in the order he would have visited them.

1 Ephesus

Paul spent two years teaching at Ephesus, capital of the Roman province of Asia, on his third missionary tour. His letter to the 'Ephesians' is addressed primarily to the Christians there. The city has been extensively excavated, and the visitors who throng its streets today can see the magnificent Library of Celsus at the foot of the main street down the hill. See 'The city of Ephesus' and Acts 19.

2 Smyrna

This is modern Izmir, a main city and busy port on the west coast of Turkey. The most important remains from Roman times are those of the forum (the main city square), pictured here. It was at Smyrna in about AD 155 that the aged bishop Polycarp refused to renounce Christ, and was martyred.

3 Pergamum

The ruins of the ancient town lie on the acropolis, high above modern Bergama. 'Satan's seat' (mentioned in the letter) may refer to the great Altar of Zeus, pictured here, which overlooked the town. Pergamum was also a centre of emperor worship, and drew many for the medical treatments associated with the temple of Asclepius, god of healing. See 'Emperor worship and Revelation' and 'Roman rule, Greek culture'.

4 Thyatira

This commercial centre on the road east is now the small town of Akhisar. The letter refers to earthenware, which may have been a main industry. Another was purple dye. Lydia, who welcomed Paul at Philippi (Acts 16:14), came from Thyatira and traded in these dyed stuffs. She may have returned home to help form the church here. A very different woman was instrumental in leading church members away from their faith and into immorality; her evil influence earns her the code-name 'Jezebel', after her Old Testament counterpart.

5 Sardis

Sardis was the former capital of the ancient kingdom of Lydia. The wealth of Croesus, king of Sardis, was legendary ('as rich as Croesus'). The Greeks then colonized the area. Pillars of the great Greek temple still remain. The gymnasium has been reconstructed. And archaeologists were surprised to discover this early Jewish synagogue.

6 Philadelphia

Philadelphia, a small town, was set in this landscape – on the edge of a broad valley which made fertile farming country. Today the town of Alaçehir derives its prosperity from the same source. The promise in the letter to make the church 'a pillar in the temple of my God' may be a reference to the temple on the hill, up behind the town.

7 Laodicea

This was a prosperous city near Hierapolis and Colossae in the Lycus Valley. The letter is full of local colour. Fine wool and eye-salve were two of Laodicea's products. It was also a banking centre. 'Lukewarm' refers to the tepid water coming from Hierapolis – see picture on page 769.

- not a sequence or timetable of events.
- ■ Ask, 'What did this mean for the original readers?' before relating it to the present day.

1
An authentic vision

John's introduction (1-3) declares his book a 'prophetic message'. It is 'the revelation of Jesus Christ' (1). Jesus is John's source *and* his subject. He draws back the veil on future events for John to make them known. This is not speculation: these are certainties, things that will take place 'soon'.

John's Revelation takes the form of a letter 'to the seven churches in the province of Asia' (western Turkey; 4, 11). The focus, from the outset, is on Jesus Christ: his death which 'freed us from our sin', his resurrection, his kingly rule, his coming again in glory.

Verse 9 begins the account of John's visions, when God's Spirit came upon him on the Lord's Day – the visions he was to write down and send to the churches. The radiant figure 'like a man' (12-16), with its echoes of Daniel 7 and 10, is Christ himself, the Master of life and death and human destiny.

▶ **Soon (1)** We do not know God's timetable or concept of time. The word serves to remind us to be ready.

▶ **Reads (aloud) (3)** This was how the scriptures were made known in John's day.

▶ **Seven churches (4, 11)** John makes great use of the number seven (seven seals, seven trumpets, seven bowls, etc.), which usually in this book stands for completeness, perfection. Here the number is also literal. Of the seven churches named in chapters 2 and 3, only Ephesus is well known (Acts 19). Acts 16:14 mentions Thyatira as Lydia's home town. The church at Laodicea is mentioned in Colossians 4:15-16. The rest occur nowhere else in the New Testament.

▶ **Mourn, lament (7)** In repentance or remorse.

Emperor worship and Revelation
J. Nelson Kraybill

The notion of treating the Roman emperor as a god started among people in the East who were grateful to Rome for having united 'all the world' (Luke 2:1) under one government and one economic system. During the 'Roman Peace' (*Pax Romana*) after 31 BC, civil wars largely ceased, piracy disappeared from the seas, and trade flourished.

In 29 BC provincial élites from Asia Minor registered their gratitude by requesting permission from Octavian (the new world ruler, later known as Caesar Augustus) to worship him as a deity at the city of Pergamum. Octavian authorized a new cult honouring both Roma (goddess of Rome) and Augustus (the emperor). John of Patmos, writing Revelation, later referred to Pergamum as the place 'where Satan's throne is' (Revelation 2:13).

From this small beginning grew an empire-wide practice of honouring the emperor as a god. The Roman Senate declared Caesar Augustus divine after his death in AD 14, allowing his stepson and successor Tiberius (AD 14-37) to call himself 'son of a god'.

This and other titles, such as 'saviour of the world', given to 1st-century emperors were parallel to titles Christians gave to Jesus. First-century coins frequently declared the reigning emperor *DIVUS* ('divine'). Caligula (AD 37-41) wanted a statue of himself placed in the Jewish Temple at

Roman coins of the 1st century frequently bore titles or images of the emperor that some Christians and Jews considered idolatrous. Domitian (AD 81-96), emperor during the time many scholars think John wrote Revelation, appears on this coin standing in a temple. Three figures kneel before him with outstretched arms.

▶ **Alpha and Omega (8)** The first and last letters of the Greek alphabet – meaning the 'eternal' God.

▶ **Patmos (9)** A small Greek island off the west coast of Turkey (see 'Seven churches' map).

▶ **Lord's day (10)** Usually taken to mean Sunday.

▶ **Sword (16)** See Hebrews 4:12. Jesus' words are double-edged. They can cut a person free, or administer judgment.

▶ **Hades (18)** The place where the dead await resurrection and judgment.

▶ **Verse 20** The 'mystery' is the secret meaning which Christ makes plain and no human being could have guessed. Some see 'angels' as a reference to pastors (although elsewhere in Revelation angels are always heavenly beings), some to guardian angels. But the best interpretation, in the light of what follows, is 'the essential spirit' of each church.

2 – 3
God's messages to the seven churches

The letters are intended to meet the needs of real churches at Ephesus and in the surrounding area, but they also deal 'with topics which have relevance to God's people at all times and in all places' (Morris). They follow a set pattern. The greeting is followed by a particular description of Christ. His 'I know...' commends what is good about the church. In five out of the seven cases this is followed by a criticism, and a warning. Each letter closes with a plea – 'If you have ears, then listen...' – and a promise. In the first three letters the plea comes first, in the last four, the promise.

> ❝ The churches are no more than lampstands. The light is Christ, and they are to show him forth. ❞
>
> Leon Morris

2:1-7 Ephesus
See on Acts 19. The church at Ephesus was firmly established and spiritually discerning. It had endurance, but their love

---

Jerusalem, but died before it was finished. Domitian (AD 81-96) liked subjects to address him as *Dominus et Deus Noster* ('Our Lord and God').

John of Patmos may have had emperor worship as a concern in writing Revelation. Many scholars think the 'beast rising out of the sea' (Revelation 13:1-10) refers to the Roman Empire with its 'seven heads' (succession of seven emperors), each bearing 'blasphemous names' (titles of deification).

A second beast (Revelation 13:11-18) may represent the vast guild of priests of the imperial cult, many of whom served as political and business leaders in the East. This guild of priests 'makes the earth and its inhabitants worship the first beast' (Revelation 13:12).

The comment that no one 'can buy or sell who does not have the mark (of the beast)' (Revelation

The following inscription from a city in Asia Minor north of the area of the seven churches of Revelation, dated 3 BC, reflects the kind of gratitude among élites in the provinces that helped generate the imperial cult:

❝ In the third year from the twelfth consulship of the Emperor Caesar Augustus, son of a god... the following oath was taken by the inhabitants of Paphlagonia and the Roman businessmen dwelling among them: I swear by Jupiter, Earth, Sun, by all the gods and goddesses, and by Augustus himself, that I will be loyal to Caesar Augustus and to his children and descendants all my life in word, in deed, and in thought, regarding as friends whomever they so regard... that in defence of their interests I will spare neither body, soul, life, nor children... ❞

13:17), perhaps is a reference to the fact that participation in the imperial cult was almost obligatory for doing business with late 1st-century trade guilds and financial institutions. Christians who maintained exclusive loyalty to Jesus apparently found themselves impoverished and politically powerless (see Revelation 2:9; 3:8).

(whether for Christ, for one another, or for humanity) is not what it had been. They need to repent, for a church without love is no church.

▶ **Nicolaitans (6)** Unknown outside this book. Their abhorrent behaviour sprang from false teaching (15), which had infiltrated the church at Pergamum.

▶ **Tree of life (7)** The ban of Genesis 3:22-24 is lifted for all who are faithful to Christ. Eternal life is his to give.

2:8-11 Smyrna

The little church at Smyrna (now the port of Izmir, in Turkey) was poverty-stricken – but rich in all that mattered. Jesus' word to them is all encouragement. He has set a definite limit to their suffering – and he holds out to them the gift of life. They will not be condemned at the judgment.

▶ **Synagogue of Satan (9)** Those Jews who harass the church are not God's people. See John 8:39-44.

▶ **Second death (11)** Explained in 20:14-15.

2:12-17 Pergamum

At Pergamum the church had made a brave stand despite external pressure, but some members are addicted to false teaching. As a result, old pagan practices are creeping in. Their choice is to repent or have Christ 'fight against them'.

▶ **Satan's throne (13)** Pergamum was the principal centre of emperor-worship in the region (see 'Emperor worship and Revelation'). An immense altar to Zeus dominated the town from its acropolis. People also flocked to be healed at the Temple of Asclepius: Pergamum could be described as 'the Lourdes of the ancient world'. One or all of these may be referred to.

▶ **Balaam, Balak (14)** See Numbers 31:16; 25.

▶ **Food offered to idols (14)** See on 1 Corinthians 8. The issue here is the same: food eaten in the presence of idols ('venue rather than menu').

▶ **Verse 17** Manna (Exodus 16) – i.e. food which God supplies. The meaning of the white stone is unknown. The name stands for the whole character: so a new character, a secret between the individual and God.

2:18-29 Thyatira

Thyatira (now Akhisar, in Turkey) was a town with many skilled workers, and the trade guilds held meals associated with pagan worship ('food offered to idols': see note under Pergamum, above).

This was another very mixed church. In many ways it was healthy. But an influential woman in the fellowship is advocating easy compromise with the immoral, idolatrous pagan world. And many have fallen in with her way of thinking. There are 'Christians' who have plunged deep into evil – perhaps to demonstrate their moral superiority; perhaps because they make a false separation (common in Greek thinking) between soul and body. Those who remain faithful are promised Christ's power and his presence (the morning star – see 22:16).

Revelation and Jewish apocalyptic writing

The period from 200 BC to AD 100 was one of the hardest in all Jewish history. Instead of the golden age the prophets foresaw, the Jews suffered defeat, occupation and violent religious persecution. It is not surprising that a number of writings emerged from this period of tension with common characteristics and the same preoccupation – a distinctive body of literature known as 'apocalyptic'.

Pessimistic about their own age, the writers harked back to the vision and inspiration of the prophets. Their concern was the messianic kingdom – God's age, in contrast to the present evil age – and its cataclysmic coming. To authenticate their message, they assumed the pen-name of some great Old Testament figure. By taking the standpoint of someone in the distant past they were also able to 'predict' events up to their own time. Their theme was expressed in visions and revelations in the style of Daniel, making great use of symbolism and (often bizarre) imagery.

In form, style and subject-matter John's Revelation is clearly similar to this type of literature. His concern, like theirs, was with eternal realities, the end of the world, new heavens and a new earth. Like the apocalyptists, John is steeped in the Old Testament and draws on the rich, evocative imagery of the prophets. But there are vital differences.

■ John uses his own name, not the name of some illustrious person who will give his writing authenticity.

■ He does not 'retrace history in the guise of prophecy'. He calls his book prophecy, as confident as Isaiah, Jeremiah, Ezekiel or Daniel that what he wrote was directly revealed to him by God, stamped with his authority (1:1-3; 22:6, 18-20).

■ He does not write of a future Messiah, but of Jesus the Messiah's return.

▶ **Jezebel (20)** King Ahab's evil wife; see 1 Kings 21:25-26.

3:1-6 Sardis

For all its reputation, the church at Sardis was dying on its feet. It is not opposition this church has to overcome but apathy, indifference and self-satisfaction. Yet there are a few whose faith is untarnished.

▶ **Verse 2** 'Be watchful', rather than 'Wake up!' Twice in its history this city had been captured because of its lack of watchfulness.

▶ **White (4-5)** may represent purity, festivity or victory.

3:7-13 Philadelphia

Philadelphia is present-day Alaçehir in Turkey. This letter, like the letter to Smyrna, contains no word of blame. To judge by these letters, it is not the biggest, most impressive-looking churches, or those with most prestige, which are necessarily in best spiritual shape. Christ opens the door for effective work (8 and 1 Corinthians 16:9), not to those who are strong, but to those who are faithful.

▶ **Verse 9** See on 2:9.

3:14-22 Laodicea

The worst case of all seven is a church so self-satisfied as to be totally blind to its true condition. It is so far from what it should be that Jesus stands outside, knocking for admittance to the lives of individuals who call themselves Christians (20). This letter is full of local colour. Banking and the manufacture of black woollen clothing made Laodicea affluent (17-18). The town was proud of its medical school, and renowned for a special ointment for sore eyes (18). Laodicea's water supply was channelled from hot springs some distance away, reaching the town tepid (16). The church is like its water – lukewarm. There is nothing to commend it.

▶ **Beginning (14)** 'Origin' or 'source'.

4
John's vision of heaven

The scene and the perspective shift from earth to heaven. The picture of the struggling churches fades before this sublime vision of the throne – the 'control centre' of the universe – ringed by an emerald rainbow. The One who is seated there defies description. John can only say that he seems to be shot with diamond light, to glow red as a ruby.

Around him are the 'elders': possibly Israel's 12 patriarchs, plus the 12 apostles, but probably angelic beings who represent all God's faithful people. Everything speaks of God's power and glory, his utter faithfulness (3, and see Genesis 9:12-17), and purity (the white garments, the shining, transparent 'sea'). Lightning and thunder speak of his awesomeness. Four living creatures, all-seeing, represent the whole creation, ceaselessly singing in honour of the Almighty, the Holy One, 'who was, who is, who is to come'. The elders join them to worship the eternal Lord of life.

▶ **Seven spirits (5)** The Holy Spirit. See 1:4 for the meaning of seven.

▶ **Four living creatures (6)** Similar, but not identical, to Ezekiel's 'cherubim' (Ezekiel 1 and 10).

The city of Laodicea had no water supply of its own. Its water was channelled from nearby Hierapolis, with its hot springs – so Laodicea's water was lukewarm, an image the letter applies to its church.

5 – 8:1
Vision of the scroll with seven seals

5 The sealed scroll

At this point John begins to see the things which 'must happen' in the future (4:1). A scroll completely covered with writing, inside and out, and sealed with seven seals – the scroll that contains the world's destiny (revealed in a series of pictures from 6:1 to 8:1) – must be opened. John is full of anguish that no one is found worthy. Then one of the elders calls his attention to 'the Lion from Judah's tribe': the Lion who won his victory as the slain Lamb.

Chapter 4 pictured God the Creator. This chapter pictures God the Redeemer. The response to both is universal praise and worship (4:8-11; 5:8-14, and see

❝ Look, I am standing at the door, knocking. If one of you hears me calling and opens the door, I will come in. ❞

Jesus' appeal: 3:20

❝ Worthy is the Lamb who was slain, to receive power and wealth, wisdom and might, honour and glory and praise! ❞

5:12

Philippians 2:8-11). The elders and living creatures are joined by countless myriads of angels.

▶ **Seven horns, seven eyes (6)** I.e. all-powerful, all-seeing.

6 The breaking of the seals

The breaking of the seals sets in train a series of disasters. (Many see the seven seals, the seven trumpets and the rest as parallel descriptions of the same reality – not a sequence in time order.) On the heels of conquest (2) come slaughter, famine and disease (4-8) – the classic judgments of God so often predicted by the prophets (see Jeremiah 14:12; Ezekiel 14:21; the riders come from Zechariah 1:8). But no matter what the disaster, God is in control. His love and care for his people never fails (9-11). Verses 12-17 picture the cataclysmic events which usher in God's great day of reckoning. In apocalyptic language John depicts the disintegration of the fixed and stable world we know. See also Matthew 24:29; Joel 2; Zephaniah 1.

▶ **Verse 2** Not the same figure as in 19:11.
▶ **Verse 6** The price of basic essentials is so inflated that ordinary people must give their whole day's wage for bread.

7 Interlude: God's people sealed

The four winds (1) may be the same as the four horsemen of chapter 6 (see Zechariah 6:5). If so, John sees the forces of destruction held back while God sets his mark of ownership on everyone who belongs to him. Christians are not promised a trouble-free life on earth. But they will come through their struggles to the permanently trouble-free life of heaven (14-17).

▶ **After this (1, 9)** indicates a new vision, not later in time than the events of chapter 6.
▶ **144,000 (4)** A symbolic number: the total of all God's people (12 x 12 x 1000), identical with the 'great multitude' (9). See 'Numbers with special meaning'. We take Israel to mean, not the nation, but God's people – Old Testament believers and New Testament Christians alike.
▶ **Verses 5-8** Dan is omitted from this list. Unusually, both Joseph and his son Manasseh

are included (but not Joseph's other son, Ephraim).

8:1 The seventh seal

Solemn silence follows the breaking of the last seal. We are brought to the time of the end.

8:2 – 11:19
Vision of the seven trumpets

8:2-13 The first four trumpets

The first six judgments which follow the trumpet-blasts echo the plagues of Egypt recorded in Exodus 7 – 12.

The trumpets which signal God's judgments parallel the seven seals (see on chapter 6 above), but the judgments are intensified. The prayers of God's people play a significant part in all this (5:8; 8:3-4). The trumpets sound a note of warning. The judgments, though severe, are not total. They are intended to bring people to their senses (9:20-21). In symbolic picture-language John describes four calamities affecting the natural world – earth, sea, water and the heavens. The 'woes' of the lone eagle imply that there is worse to come. The remaining judgments directly affect humanity.

9 The fifth and sixth trumpets

Demonic forces (monstrous stinging locusts), servants of 'the Destroyer' (Apollyon/Abaddon, 11), are next unleashed. But God sets them a time-limit (five months is the approximate lifespan of the real locust). Though human beings are their target they have no power to touch those who belong to God (4).

The 'locusts' torture. The angels released after the sixth trumpet is blown, with their hosts, have power to kill – within limits. Yet even in the face of the most fearsome warnings people stubbornly refuse to change their ways (20-21). This is the world we live in: a world that resists God to the bitter end; a world that creates its own 'gods' and has no qualms about murder, theft or moral standards.

▶ **200 million (16)** There were so many, John had to be told the number. He could not count

Understanding Revelation

Richard Bauckham

The book of Revelation is the Bible's climactic and concluding prophecy. It completes the message of all the biblical prophets by disclosing the way in which the rule of God over his whole creation is finally to come about.

Readers generally find it the most obscure of the New Testament writings and, in order to avoid the gross misinterpretations to which it has so often been subject, it is essential to appreciate the kind of literature it is.

Revelation is both a circular letter and an apocalyptic prophecy. Both categories help us to read it correctly.

A circular letter

Revelation is a circular letter to the seven churches of the Roman province of Asia (1:4) at the end of the 1st century. The seven messages to these churches (chapters 2 – 3) are not themselves letters, but introductions (one specific to each church) to the rest of the book.

- Each is a prophetic analysis of the state of one of these churches.
- Each addresses one local variation of the broader context which the prophecies of the rest of the book address.

This means that, just as when we read one of Paul's letters we have to remember the 1st-century context to which it was initially addressed, so we cannot hope to understand Revelation if we ignore the situation of the first readers.

Although Revelation does portray the final completion of God's purposes for the world, it does this

in direct relation to the situation of its first readers. It calls them to share in God's victory over the anti-Christian forces of their time and place – the power and influence of Rome and pagan culture.

As we can tell from the seven messages, not all of these Christians were suffering persecution. Many of them were avoiding suffering by compromising with pagan society and Roman power. Revelation is written not only to encourage those who are already suffering, but also to stir the complacent to uncompromising witness to God and to enable them to face the persecution which will come if they are faithful to Jesus Christ in their context.

Apocalyptic prophecy

Revelation (or the Apocalypse) is also an apocalyptic prophecy. Its first readers were more familiar with this literary form than we are (its closest analogy in the Bible is Daniel 7 – 12).

The visions full of symbolic images are not intended to be obscure, but to evoke imaginative insight. The meaning of the symbolism is often conveyed through allusions to the Old Testament or through allusions to the world in which the first readers lived.

The prophet describes how he was taken up into heaven in order to see the world from God's heavenly perspective. He is also transported in vision into the final future, in order to see the present from the perspective of God's final purpose for the world.

The world described in the

visions is the one in which the first readers lived, but it is seen from a perspective quite different from that of the dominant ideology of their time. This perspective counters the Roman imperial ideology, exposing its idolatrous deceits and disclosing instead the truth of things. Despite appearances, it is not 'the beast' who is supreme but God, and it is not through violent power that ultimate victory is achieved, but through suffering witness to the truth.

By enabling the readers to grasp this imaginatively, the visions enable them to resist the lies of the beast and to follow Christ in his sacrificial faithfulness even to the point of death.

Revelation's continued relevance to later readers lies in its power to bring this heavenly perspective to bear on every situation in which God's rule appears to be subverted by the powers of the world. Its purpose is not to give mere information about the future, but to enable Christians to live in the way that God's final purpose for the world requires.

them. The powers at God's disposal are colossal.

10 – 11:14 Interlude: the little scroll and the two witnesses

There is a break between the sixth and seventh trumpets, as there was between the sixth and seventh seals. God delays his final judgment, but not for ever (6-7). Another mighty angel (as in 5:1), radiant and glorious, brings John an open scroll. It contains a message for the world – the angel stands on land and sea. God's word is bitter-sweet (9). The believer tastes its sweetness (see Jeremiah 15:16; Ezekiel 3:1-3), but John's stomach churns at the bitter message he must make known to those who refuse God.

11:1-14 closely reflects Jewish apocalyptic writing (a text from Qumran, for example, concerns the measurement of the new Jerusalem) and is particularly difficult. John draws his symbols from Ezekiel 40 – 41 (the measuring of the Temple) and Zechariah 4 (the olive trees). The measuring indicates God's protection and care for his people. The two olives represent the church, faithful to the death. (Old Testament law required that evidence must be attested by at least two witnesses:

> 66 *After that, appeared a great sign in heaven: a woman robed with the sun, beneath her feet the moon, and on her head a crown of twelve stars. She was about to bear a child...* 99
>
> 12:1-2

Deuteronomy 19:15.) Warring against them are the anti-God forces of the Satanic 'beast', with power to kill and dishonour, but not to destroy or prevent their triumph.

▶ **10:4** John is under orders about what he writes. Not all he sees is for public knowledge.

▶ **Forty-two months (11:2)** Equal to 1,260 days (3), and 'a time (one year), times (two years) and half a time (six months)' (12:14). This may be derived from the length of the Syrian King Antiochus Epiphanes' tyranny in Jerusalem, which began in 168 BC, or from Israel's 42 encampments in the desert. But the precise length of the trial is less important than the fact that God has set a definite limit to it.

▶ **Sodom and Egypt (11:8)** Bywords for evil and oppression. The final phrase suggests Jerusalem, but it is more likely that the 'great city', here as later in the book, stands for the city of rebel humanity.

11:14-19 The seventh trumpet

The seventh trumpet announces the end. Jesus reigns: the world is his kingdom. Praise God! The Ark of the Covenant, once hidden away in the most sacred and inaccessible part of the Temple, is now visible to all (19). The way into God's presence is thrown open amid awesome flashes of lightning, peals of thunder, and a shaking of the foundations.

12 – 14
Seven signs: God's people under attack

The main thrust of these visions is clear: not so the details. The signs are:

- a woman in labour (12:1-2)
- a fiery red dragon (12:3)
- a beast from the sea (13:1)
- a beast from the earth (13:11)
- the Lamb, with his people, standing on Mt Zion (14:1)
- three angels (14:6, 8-9)
- a heavenly reaper, harvesting the earth (14:14ff.).

It has been suggested that John may have taken some of the material in these chapters from current myths. If this is so, the application is all his own. He was writing for a persecuted church, and these

John's visions set forth God's judgment on evil in terrible images of destruction. Within his own lifetime destruction had fallen unannounced on the town of Pompeii, as the volcano Vesuvius poured lethal gases and lava upon its fine houses, overcoming the townspeople as they went about their daily business. Excavation has revealed much, including the elegant 'House of the Faun', belonging to the Cassia family – and the horrifying figure of a girl, vainly trying to avoid suffocation from the fumes by pulling her tunic over her face.

chapters are full of encouragement to take heart.

12 A woman and a red dragon

The star-crowned woman clothed with the sun (1; contrast the prostitute of 17:3ff.) stands for God's chosen people, from whom first the Messiah (5), and through him the church (17), was born. The dragon bent on destruction is Satan himself (9). Verses 7-12 are a reminder that the struggle Christians are caught up in is part of a much greater conflict (Ephesians 6:11-12).

The main message is clear. Although Satan is strong and powerful, and his attack fierce, his time is short. He has been overpowered by Christ: he can be overcome by Christ's followers. He is destined for destruction, the church for triumph. God's people are at all times and everywhere under his sovereign protection.

▶ **Michael (7)** Israel's special guardian angel.

13 Two beasts

The beast from the sea (an evil place in Jewish thinking) is a composite creature drawn from the four beasts which represent successive world empires in Daniel 7. With its crowns and horns (sovereignty and power) and its open defiance of God, it stands for the author- itarian anti-God state. It derives its power from the evil one (2, 4) and it is seemingly indestructible (3). It dupes the world, but not those whose names are written in the Lamb's 'book of life' (8).

The second beast – the pseudo-lamb which speaks with Satan's voice (11) – is state-sanctioned, state-dominated religion. 16:13 and 19:20 identify it as the 'false prophet'. It apes the real thing, and mis- directs people's worship. Refusal to worship costs some their lives (15), others their livelihood (17). For John, the two beasts were the Roman Empire and emperor- worship. But every age has its equivalents.

▶ **Verses 13:3, 14** There was a rumour (known as the Nero *redivivus* myth) that the Emperor Nero had not really died in AD 68, and would return at the head of great (Parthian) armies from the east.

▶ **Forty-two months (5)** See on 11:2.

▶ **The mark (17)** Indicating ownership, and

acceptance of the beast's authority. People bear either the 'mark' of the world or the 'seal' of God – and it shows (16; 7:3).

▶ **The number (17-18)** Many have tried to identify an individual, since the letters of the alphabet doubled as numbers in ancient times. 'Nero Caesar' is the modern favourite, 'but to get this result we must use the Greek form of the Latin name, transliterated into Hebrew characters, and with a variant spelling' (Morris). The key may, rather, lie in the symbolism of the numbers, 6 being 'a human number', the number of humanity. No matter how many times repeated, it always falls short of 7, God's number of completeness, perfection. No matter how powerful the 'beast', it is not God.

14 Joy of the redeemed; the final harvest

This chapter stands in dramatic contrast to chapters 12 – 13. The Lamb stands on Mt Zion – the new Jerusalem – with *all* those who bear his name, not just a spiritual élite (1; see on 7:4 and note below). John now sees seven angels, appearing one by one as the agents of God's judgment.

- The first (6) calls people to respond to God's message of Good News.
- The second (8) announces the fall of 'Great Babylon', the city which symbolizes humanity combined in opposition to God. (In John's time 'Babylon' could be a 'code-word' for Rome: see chapter 17.)
- The third angel (9) declares judgment on all who have sold out to the forces of evil.

A voice speaks reassurance to God's people. These are the happy ones. They are called to endure, but they will enjoy rest from their labour.

Now the harvest of God's judgment begins. Four more angels appear in turn, coming from God's sanctuary in heaven.

The first (crowned) sits on a cloud, sharp sickle in hand. At the command of the second (15), he begins to harvest the earth.

A third (17) appears with another sharp sickle. At the command of the fourth, he harvests the vineyard, casting the grapes into the winepress of God's wrath.

▶ **Verses 3-4** See on 7:4. Verse 4 cannot be meant literally. That would exclude women from

> **❝** The real victory is not to live in safety, to evade trouble, cautiously and prudently to preserve life; the real victory is to face the worst that evil can do, and if need be to be faithful unto death. **❞**
>
> William Barclay

> **❝** Most of John's fantastic images are drawn from the Old Testament, and the beast from the sea is a composite of the four beasts in Daniel 7. **❞**
>
> Marcus Maxwell

the all-inclusive 144,000, the number which signifies all God's people. And to see sexual intercourse as defiling in itself would run counter to the rest of Scripture. Nor is there any scriptural warrant for saying it is more godly to be celibate than married. The meaning must therefore be those who are faithful to God (in John's day, those who have refused to take part in pagan worship and are 'virgin' in that sense). This is in line with the prophets, who frequently use the same figurative language: idolatrous Israel is described as a 'prostitute' and 'adulteress'.

The 'firstfruits' are that part of the world harvest which belongs to God.

▶ **Babylon (8)** See chapter 17.

▶ **One like a son of man/human being (14)** Since he is under orders (15) this must be an angel, not Christ himself.

▶ **1,600 stadia (20)** The stadion was about 202 yards — so, literally, 300km/185 miles. But 1,600 stadia is clearly another symbolic number — 4 (which stands for the earth) x 4 x 10 x 10 — meaning the complete destruction of the wicked throughout the earth.

15 – 16
The seven last plagues

Now come seven more angels with seven plagues. In 5:8 John pictured golden bowls filled with the incense of prayer. The bowls in chapter 16 pour out plagues upon the earth, the expression of God's anger. These plagues, like the judgments in chapter 8, vividly recall those which fell on Egypt at

According to Revelation 16:6 the place where the kings of the world gather for the final battle against God is 'Armageddon'. The word means 'Hill of Megiddo'. The mound of the ancient city can be seen beyond the pass it guards through the Carmel hills. So many battles were fought here that John adopts this name for the battle to end all battles.

the time of the exodus. But first (15:2-4) we see the joy and security of God's people. They are not subjected to the final terrors, which are specifically directed against evil (16:2, 9, 11). Heaven (it would appear from Revelation) is full of joyous song. Praising God, at last, comes naturally.

▶ **Name... number (15:2)** See on 13:17-18.

▶ **Song of Moses (15:3)** The great rejoicing after the crossing of the Red Sea (Exodus 15). Both songs are songs of deliverance and freedom.

▶ **Tent (15:5)** A reference to Israel's wilderness time. The Tent symbolizes God's presence.

▶ **16:12** The Euphrates separated the civilized world from the barbarian hordes beyond.

▶ **Armageddon (16:16)** The hill (mound) of Megiddo, the famous fortress on the edge of the plain of Jezreel which guarded the pass through the Carmel hills. Megiddo was so often a battle site, the name came to stand for battle.

▶ **The great city... great Babylon (16:19)** See on chapter 17.

17 – 20
God's final triumph

17 –19:5 The fall of prostitute 'Babylon'

So often and so vigorously did the Old Testament prophets denounce the literal Babylon (see references below) that it became a byword for human pride and vainglory.

For John and his readers, Babylon, the luxury-loving prostitute (in contrast to the woman of chapter 12 and the bride of chapter 21), was Rome, city of the seven hills (see verse 9) – rich, splendid, pampered, decadent Rome; Rome, where Christians were thrown to the lions and burnt alive as public entertainment; Rome, the cess-pit of the empire.

But every age has its 'Babylon', the personification of all the greed and luxury and selfish pleasure-seeking which entice people away from God; the things that promise so much and give so little. And Babylon, the epitome of all that cheats, is doomed!

Chapter 18, describing Babylon's fall, echoes the spirit and language of all the great 'downfall' prophecies of the Old Testament (Isaiah 13 – 14; 24; Jeremiah 50 – 51; Ezekiel 26 – 28). It is one final, comprehensive pronouncement of doom on every power in every age that grows fat on evil and treats people as mere commodities to be bought and sold (13).

God's people are tempted to come to terms with the world. But they are called to take an uncompromising stand (4). They will be vindicated. Justice will be done. It is so certain, it can even be said to have happened already. Babylon *has* fallen!

19:1-5: a great shout of triumph and hymn of praise is heard from heaven. This is not sheer vindictiveness, or gloating over the fate of others. God's people stake their lives on his truth and justice. They rejoice to see God vindicated and militant, unrepentant evil overthrown.

▶ **The beast (17:3)** See 13:1. Babylon is supported by a satanic power. The beast in these verses is sometimes a kingdom, sometimes a ruler.

▶ **Was, now is not (17:8)** At times evil powers rampage through human history; at times they go underground – but they always return.

▶ **Seven kings (17:10)** These may be the Roman emperors. If so, the five past are Augustus to Nero; the sixth is either Galba or Vespasian; the seventh Titus. Alternatively, the seven may be empires. Perhaps it is best to give the number seven its symbolic meaning: so 'the whole historic Roman Empire'.

▶ **Ten kings (17:12)** Sometimes taken to mean Roman emperors, but John is describing a future coalition. See also 13:3, 14, on the Nero myth.

19:6-10 The wedding of the Lamb

In the Old Testament, Israel is portrayed as the (usually unfaithful) wife of the Lord, so the image of the bride is a natural one here. So too is the feast. People expected Messiah's coming to be celebrated with a great banquet. John brings the two together in his lovely image of the wedding-feast of the Lamb and his faithful followers, the bride – the fine linen of her wedding-dress made from 'the good deeds of God's people'. What happiness to be an invited guest at *this* wedding!

▶ **The feast/banquet (9)** See Matthew 8:11; 22:2-9; 25:10; Luke 13:29; 14:15-17.

19:11-21 A rider on a white horse

We expect to see the Lamb – the Bride-groom – at this point. Instead we are shown a Warrior. The name we know him by (and there are depths to his character we cannot fathom, 12) is the Word of God (13). His victory is certain. He is King of kings and Lord of lords: supreme. Carrion are summoned already to gorge at a feast far removed from the banquet of the Lamb. The beast and the false prophet (chapter 13; 16:13), Satan's two henchmen, and their allies are seized and destroyed – in a 'war' without weapons, armour, or battle, so great is the power of this horseman.

▶ **A name (12)** See on 2:17.

▶ **Blood (13)** That of the crucified Christ, or the blood of his enemies. John may have either, or both, in mind.

20 Millennium; Satan overthrown; the last judgment

The 'thousand years' (millennium) of this chapter is mentioned nowhere else in the Bible, and no other chapter in the Bible has given rise to such heated argument about its meaning. However, certain things are clear.

■ John sees Satan under God's firm control (1-3).

■ He sees the souls of the martyrs, not

Humanity has two faces. The message of Revelation is that a day will come when justice will prevail. God will totally eradicate all that is evil, and take those who love him to be with him for ever.

*** I saw a
great white
throne and the
one who sits on
it... And I saw
the dead, great
and small
alike, standing
before the
throne. Books
were opened,
and then
another book
was opened, the
book of the
living. The dead
were judged
according to
what they had
done, as recor-
ded in the
books. **

20:11-12

*** I saw a new
heaven and a
new earth...
And I saw the
Holy City, the
new Jerusalem,
coming down
out of heaven
from God. **

21:1-2

*** Now
God has his
dwelling with
mankind... he
will wipe every
tear from their
eyes. There
shall be an end
to death, and to
mourning and
crying and
pain. **

21:3-4

every Christian (and this is important for the persecuted early church), resurrected to reign with Christ for 'a thousand years' (4-6).

■ At the end of it, the forces of evil muster to attack God's people, but are utterly destroyed. Satan himself shares the fate of the beast and the false prophet in 'the lake of fire' (7-10).

■ There is a general resurrection, when everyone stands before God to be judged, each on their own record. The verdict is life or death. And for those who live there will be no more death (11-15).

With regard to detail, here as in the rest of the book, it pays to be cautious. And the basic rules of interpretation (see introduction) need to be applied. To ask 'where' the reign takes place, or try to work out a timetable of events, runs counter to the whole spirit of the thing. It is true that in early Judaism the messianic kingdom happened on earth. Some Jews thought in terms of a messianic reign for a particular period of time, others of an interim sabbath of 1,000 years. The earliest Christian interpreters assumed that this chapter refers to an earthly millennium.

But John records something new. The reign here is not a general one of all believers, but only of the martyrs. Nor does he actually say that this reign is on earth (elsewhere in Revelation, thrones, 4, are in heaven). And although there has been fierce argument about the relation of the millennium to Christ's return, John in fact makes no mention of the 'second coming' in this chapter.

▶ **Note** John's vision may be compared with Paul's teaching in 1 Corinthians 15:24-28.
▶ **1,000 years (2)** Other numbers in Revelation are symbolic figures. A thousand years is long enough to show God's complete authority over Satan, and to far outweigh the earthly sufferings of the martyrs.
▶ **Gog and Magog (8)** See on Ezekiel 38.
▶ **The city he loves (9)** The community of God's people, in contrast to the 'great city' of Babylon.

21 – 22:5
God's new world

Death and all that is evil have been destroyed. Will God renew, or replace, the present heaven and earth?

What John describes is *all new*. If it is pictured in earthly terms, what others can we understand?

The new life is one long unclouded wedding day for all God's people – the happiest, most joyful time imaginable. And there is nothing to spoil it: no sorrow; no pain; no parting with loved-ones; no darkness. For God is always present. He is near. There is no sin or temptation to spoil the perfect relationship; no guilt; no shame.

The bride of chapter 19 appears as a city: the new Jerusalem and its people. The finest cities of the world are nothing to the breathtaking splendour, the shining radiance, of *this* glowing, golden city, with its perfect dimensions, its jewelled foundations, its glittering diamond walls, its gates of pearl. Those gates stand always open. And the city has no Temple, for God himself is *present*. There is peace here, and freedom and security.

From God's throne and through the centre of the city flows the river of life, crystal-clear. Trees which bear fruit all year round, and healing leaves, line the river-banks. All speaks of wonderful, endless life. Night is gone. God's own 'light perpetual' shines on his worshipping people.

▶ **12,000 stadia (21:16)** 2,400 km/1,500 miles. But this is not intended to be taken literally. It is 12 x 1000 (see on 7:4 and 14:20). On earth God's people seem few and scattered. But they are part of a vast community – the eternal city of God.
▶ **21:19-20** The list of jewels echoes those which were set into the high priest's breastpiece, to represent Israel.
▶ **22:2** The fall resulted in barred access to the 'tree of life' (Genesis 3:22-24). Now the edict is reversed. Humanity, redeemed, will never again abuse its freedom.

22:6-21
In closing

This is all true, the angel says to John. 'He is coming soon. Make these things known.' Then the vision of the angel fades – and it is Jesus himself who speaks.

The final statements are somewhat disjointed, but lack nothing in vigour. John affirms the truth of what he has written. In the sternest terms of his day, he warns against tampering with it. His closing words are full of urgency. The things he has described will happen soon. Christ's coming is imminent. Then people's attitudes will be fixed. It will not be possible to change. In the end, those who are not saved will be lost; those who do not enter into eternal life and the presence of God will be shut out for ever.

So 'let all who are thirsty come'. Let them 'have the water of life', for which there is no charge.

“ All shall be Amen and Alleluia.
We shall rest and we shall see,
We shall see and we shall know,
We shall know and we shall love,
We shall love and we shall praise.
Behold our end which is no end. ”

St Augustine

RAPID FACTFINDER

The Rapid Factfinder is a directory both to the Bible and to the material contained in this book.

First it gives main Bible references. It can be used to find where in the Bible events took place, or to follow up some of the Bible's main teaching, or to look up people and places.

It also serves as an index to the Handbook. The entry for each place, name or subject includes relevant articles and pictures as well as significant text references.

A tablet dating from the 9th century BC records the boundaries of land restored by the King of Babylon (*left*) to a priest (*right*). Above are the emblems of various gods, called upon to protect them and the gift.

A

AARON Moses' brother and spokesman; first high priest of Israel: Exodus 4 – Numbers 33/pp.160ff.
• *Before Pharaoh*: Exodus 5ff.
• *Aaron's robes and consecration*: Exodus 28 – 29; Leviticus 8
• *the golden calf*: Exodus 32
• *atonement ritual*: Leviticus 16
• *Aaron and Miriam challenge Moses*: Numbers 12
• *Aaron's rod*: Numbers 17
• *death*: Numbers 33:38-39.
Picture p.202 (Aaron's tomb).

ABANA One of two rivers of Damascus mentioned by Naaman: 2 Kings 5:12.

ABEDNEGO One of Daniel's companions exiled to Babylon: Daniel 1 – 3/pp.473ff.

ABEL Second son of Adam and Eve; brother of Cain: Genesis 4/pp.120, 121.

ABEL-BETH-MAACAH Town in the north of Palestine, near Lake Huleh, to which Joab pursued Sheba: 2 Samuel 20; also 1 Kings 15:20/ *Map* p.104C1.

ABEL MEHOLAH Place to which Gideon pursued the Midianites; birthplace of Elisha: Judges 7:22; 1 Kings 19:16/ *Map* p.245.

ABIATHAR Son of Ahimelech priest of Nob who joined David; became joint high priest with Zadok; conspired to make Adonijah king and was expelled by Solomon: 1 Samuel 22:20ff.; 1 Kings 1 – 2/ pp.276-277.

ABIGAIL Nabal's wife; later married David: 1 Samuel 25/ p.263.

ABIHU Son of Aaron; destroyed with Nadab: Exodus 6:23; Leviticus 10/p.184.

ABIJAH Son of Jeroboam I: 1 Kings 14.

ABIJAM (ABIJAH) Son of Rehoboam; king of Judah 913-911 BC: 1 Kings 15; 2 Chronicles 13/p.289.

ABILENE Region around Damascus of which Lysanius was tetrarch: Luke 3:1.

ABIMELECH 1. King(s) of Gerar: Genesis 20; 26/pp.135, 140. **2.** Son of Gideon: Judges 8:31ff.

ABIRAM Conspired against Moses with Korah and Dathan: Numbers 16/p.197.

ABISHAG The girl from Shunem who attended David: 1 Kings 1 – 2/p.276.

ABISHAI Brother of Joab and one of David's 30 warriors: 1 Samuel 26:6ff./p.263.

ABNER Saul's army commander; killed by Joab and Abishai: 1 Samuel 14:50 – 2 Samuel 3/ pp.261-266.

ABRAHAM/ABRAM Father of the nation of Israel; man of outstanding faith: Genesis 11:26 – 25:10/pp.110-111, 127-139.
• *God's call*: Genesis 12
• *meeting with Melchizedek*: 14
• *God's covenant*: 17
• *'sacrifice' of Isaac*: 22
• *death*: 25:8.
See 'Abraham', pp.132-134. *Picture* p.266 (Abraham's tomb).

ABSALOM Son of David; led a rebellion against his father: 2 Samuel 13 – 18/pp.272-273.

ACCAD See Akkad.

ACHAIA Province of southern Greece governed from Corinth: Acts 18:12, etc./*Map* p.680.

ACHAN Stoned for taking spoil from Jericho: Joshua 7/p.230.

ACHISH King of Gath with

whom David took refuge:
1 Samuel 21; 27 – 29/
pp.262-264.

ACHOR Valley near Jericho
where Achan was stoned:
Joshua 7:24.

ACTS OF THE APOSTLES
pp.643ff.

ADAM 1. The first man;
created by God and given
charge of the Garden of Eden.
By his disobedience he
brought sin and death on the
whole human race: Genesis
1 – 4; see Romans 5:12ff.,
etc./pp.116, 120-122, 686ff.
2. Place where the River
Jordan was blocked, allowing
the Israelites to cross into
Canaan, the promised land:
Joshua 3:16/*Map* p.104C4.

ADMAH Near Sodom; one of
the 'cities of the plain':
Genesis 10:19; 14:2/
Map p.127.

ADONIJAH David's son who
attempted to seize the throne
destined for Solomon: 1 Kings
1 – 2/pp.276-277.

ADRAMYTTIUM Paul set sail for
Rome in a ship from this port
near Troy on the west coast of
modern Turkey: Acts 27:2/
Map p.667.

ADULLAM David, on the run
from Saul, hid in a cave near
this town in Judah: 1 Samuel
22:1; 2 Samuel 23:13/
Map p.264.

AENON NEAR SALIM Where
John baptized: John 3:23/
Map p.634.

AGABUS Prophet who
predicted famine and Paul's
imprisonment: Acts 11:27-
30; 21:7-14/pp.665.

AGRIPPA Herod Agrippa II,
who heard Paul's defence
at Caesarea: Acts 25:13 –
26:32/p.667. See 'The Herod
family', p.627.

AHAB King of Israel 874-
853 BC (husband of Jezebel)
who seized Naboth's vine-
yard; opponent of Elijah:
1 Kings 16:29 – 22:40/
pp.290-293 *Picture* p.293
(Ahab's palace).

AHASUERUS King of Persia
who made Esther his queen:
Esther/pp.341-343.

AHAVA River and place in
Babylonia where Ezra
camped: Ezra 8:15, 21, 31.

AHAZ Son of Jotham, king of
Judah; father of Hezekiah:
2 Kings 15:38ff.; 2 Chronicles 27:9ff./p.324.

AHAZIAH 1. Ahab's son; king
of Israel 853-852 BC : 1 Kings
2:40ff./ p.293.
2. Son of Joram, king of
Judah 841 BC: 2 Kings 8:24ff.;
2 Chronicles 22:1ff./pp.297,
322.

AHIJAH Prophesied to Jeroboam the revolt of the ten
tribes: 1 Kings 11:29ff.;
14/p.289.

AHIMAAZ Son of Zadok who
passed information to David
during Absalom's rebellion
and brought news of victory:
2 Samuel 17:17ff.; 18/p.273.

AHIMELECH Priest of Nob,
killed for assisting David:
1 Samuel 21 – 22/p.262.

AHITHOPHEL David's trusted
adviser who gave his support
to Absalom: 2 Samuel
15:12 – 17:23/pp.272-273.

AI Site of one of Joshua's first
battles in the promised land:
Joshua 7 and 8/p.230 *Map*
p.104B4. See 'Cities of the
conquest', p.229.

AIJALON An Amorite town; a
city of refuge; fortified by
Rehoboam: Joshua 19:42;
21:24; 1 Chronicles 6:69;
8:13, etc./*Map* p.104B5.

AKKAD, AKKADIANS The
northern neighbours of the
Sumerians in 3rd-millen-
nium BC Mesopotamia.
From the Akkadian Semitic
language Babylonian and
Assyrian developed. Akkad,
as a place, is mentioned only
in Genesis 10:10, as a major
city founded by Nimrod.

ALEXANDER 1. Son of Simon
of Cyrene: Mark 15:21.
2. Leader in Jerusalem: Acts
4:6.
3. A Jew present during the

riot at Ephesus: Acts 19:33.
4. A Christian who lapsed:
1 Timothy 1:20.
5. Opponent of Paul:
2 Timothy 4:14. (These may
not all be different people.)

ALEXANDRIA Egypt's major
port on the Mediterranean,
founded in 332 BC by Alexander the Great. It had a large
Jewish community; home of
Apollos: Acts 6:9; 18:24, etc.

ALEXANDRINUS, CODEX See
under Codex.

ALPHABET p.231.

ALTAR See Sacrifice, Tabernacle, Temple. *Pictures*
pp.176, 281 (incense), 181
(horned), 236 ('high place'),
445 (Byblos), 765 (Altar of
Zeus, Pergamum).

AMALEK, AMALEKITES The
grandson of Esau and his
descendants; nomadic people
of Sinai and the Negev. At the
time of the exodus they
attacked the Israelites who
put them under a permanent
vow of destruction. Samuel
commanded Saul to destroy
them. David fought them,
and later they declined:
Exodus 17; 1 Samuel 15; 30/
Map pp.814-815.

AMASA Commander of
Absalom's army; killed by
Joab; 2 Samuel 17:25;
20/pp.273-274.

AMAZIAH Son of Joash, king of
Judah 796-767 BC: 2 Kings
12:21 – 14:21; 2 Chronicles
24:27ff./pp.298, 323.

AMMON, AMMONITES The
Ammonites (regarded as
relatives of the Israelites since
they were the descendants of
Lot's younger son) early on
occupied the land between
the River Arnon and the
River Jabbok, though part of
this territory was later lost to
the Amorites. Modern
Amman stands on the site of
the chief Ammonite city,
Rabbath-Ammon (earlier
Rabbah). The Israelites did
not conquer Ammon after
the exodus, and there were

struggles between the two
peoples at the time of the
Judges. They were defeated
by David. The Ammonites
were incorporated, successively, into the Assyrian,
Babylonian and Persian
empires. But during their
period of independence
they formed a threat to the
Israelites, at least until
Maccabean times when
the capital was known as
Philadelphia: Genesis 19:38;
Deuteronomy 2:19; Judges
3:13; 10 – 11; 2 Samuel 12,
etc.; 1 Maccabees 5:6/
Map p.209.

AMNON Son of David; raped
Tamar and was killed by
Absalom: 2 Samuel 13/
p.272.

AMON Son of Manasseh, king
of Judah 642-640 BC: 2 Kings
21; 2 Chronicles 33/p.303.

AMORITES A Semitic-speaking
nomadic people, stemming
from the middle Euphrates
area, who spread to Mesopotamia and Syria-Palestine,
settling there in the late 3rd
and early 2nd millennium
BC. Their language, known
only from personal names, is
the earliest recorded example
of West Semitic. They were
prominent in the population
of Mari, whose documents
throw much light on patriarchal customs. When the
Israelites invaded Canaan,
they defeated the Amorite
kings (Sihon and Og) who
controlled most of the land
east of the Jordan. The tribes
of Gad, Reuben and half
Manasseh occupied the area,
and the subject Amorites who
remained were gradually
absorbed: Joshua 12:1-6;
Judges 1:36; 1 Samuel
7:14/*Map* pp.814-815.

AMOS Prophet from Tekoa
whose book records God's
message to Israel.

AMOS, BOOK OF pp.490ff.

AMPHIPOLIS Town on Paul's
route through northern

Greece: Acts 17:1/
Map p.657.

ANANIAS 1. Disciple who tried to deceive the church:
Acts 5/p.646.
2. Disciple at Damascus sent to Saul: Acts 9/p.648.
3. High priest who laid charges against Paul: Acts 23:2; 24:1.

ANATHOTH Jeremiah's birthplace, just north of Jerusalem: Jeremiah 1:1/
Map p.104B5 *Picture* p.441.

ANCIENT NEAR EAST See 'The Old Testament and the ancient Near East', pp.105-107; 'Covenants and Near Eastern treaties', pp.210-211; and time-chart pp.100-101.

ANDREW Peter's brother, also a fisherman; one of the 12 apostles (see 'The twelve disciples of Jesus', p.557): Matthew 4:18, etc.; John 1:40ff./p.623.

ANGELS See 'Angels in the Bible', p.727; also Gabriel, Michael.

ANIMALS, BIBLE Visual feature pp.38-39 and additional pictures listed there.

ANNA Prophetess in the Temple at the time the infant Jesus was presented: Luke 2:36-38/p.599.

ANNAS Jewish high priest; father-in-law of Caiaphas before whom Jesus stood trial: John 18:13ff./ p.639.

ANTIOCH 1. Important city on the River Orontes in Syria; major centre for the early church; base from which Paul and Barnabas set out on their missions: Acts 11; 13:1, etc./*Map* p.652 *Pictures* pp.651, 689.
2. Antioch in Pisidia; town visited by Paul on his first mission: Acts 13:14ff./*Map* p.652 *Picture* p.653.

ANTIOCHUS Name of Seleucid kings of Syria in the time between the Testaments: pp.482, 518-519, 520.

ANTIPATRIS Paul was brought here under escort from Jerusalem on his way to Caesarea: Acts 23:31/
Map p.526B4.

APHEK Here the Israelites lost the Ark of the Covenant to the Philistines: 1 Samuel 4:1; also 29:1/*Map* p.104B4.

APOCALYPTIC pp.51, 473, 527, 531, 763-764, 768, 771.

APOCRYPHA See 'Deutero-canonical books', pp.515-520.

APOLLOS Jew from Alexandria instructed by Priscilla and Aquila; powerful preacher influencing the church at Corinth: Acts 18:24ff.; 1 Corinthians 1 – 4/pp.662, 695f.

APPIAN WAY Roman north-south highway in Italy.
Picture p.669.

AQABA, GULF OF *Picture* p.322.

AQUILA AND PRISCILLA A Christian couple who instructed Apollos and served the church in various places: Acts 18; Romans 16:3, etc./pp.658, 693.

AR Chief town of Moab: Numbers 21:15/
Map p.104C6.

ARABAH Rift valley running from Lake Galilee to the Gulf of Aqaba; the Sea of Arabah is the Dead Sea: Deuteronomy 1:1; 3:17, etc.

ARABIA, ARABIANS Semitic-speaking nomadic and semi-nomadic inhabitants of the northern part of the Arabian peninsula, which adjoined the areas of settled civilization. During most of the 1st millennium BC, the Arabians appear mainly as raiders, but there was a continual drift of small numbers into the settled areas. From the 3rd century BC onwards the region south-east of Palestine was occupied by one group of Arabs, the Nabataeans, who built up a flourishing

civilization based on the incense trade (see Sabaeans) centring on Petra.
In New Testament times the Nabataean dominion extended to the area east of Damascus, where there seems to have been an agent of their King Aretas. Paul spent some time in Nabataean territory after his conversion: 2 Corinthians 11:32; Galatians 1:17/
Map pp.814-815.

ARAD Canaanite town in the Negev 'wilderness' defeated by Joshua: Numbers 21:1; Joshua 12:14/*Map* p.104B6.

ARAM, ARAMAEANS A Semitic-speaking people, closely related to the Israelites, who spread throughout Mesopotamia and Syria during the later part of the 2nd millennium BC, and are found in the early 1st millennium dominating such Syrian city-states as Damascus and Hamath (see also Cilicians). The Hebrew name 'Aram' is usually translated 'Syria' but the Greek name *Suria* occurs in the New Testament. Abraham and his family migrated from Ur to Harran in 'Aram-naharaim' on the way to Canaan, and some of them stayed on as 'Aramaeans'. Some centuries later Balaam was hired from Aram to curse Israel. David became the overlord of the Aramaean states, which began to break free later in Solomon's reign. There were clashes between the northern kingdom of Israel and Damascus/Syria. In 732 BC the Assyrians defeated Damascus and the Aramaeans were deported: Genesis 11:28-32; 24:28ff.; Numbers 22:5; Deuteronomy 26:5; 2 Samuel 8; 10; 2 Kings 14; 16/*Map* pp.814-815.

ARARAT/URARTU Mountains where Noah's ark came to rest after the great flood; Lake Van area of Turkey and

Armenia: Genesis 8:4/
Map p.124.

ARAUNAH/ORNAN The man whose threshing-floor David bought, site of the Temple: 2 Samuel 24:16ff; 1 Chronicles 21:15ff./pp.312-313.

ARCHAEOLOGY See 'Bringing the past to life', pp.30-35.
• *Old Testament*: 'Creation stories', pp.117-118; 'Flood stories', pp.123-124; 'Cities of the conquest', pp.228-229; 'Settled life', pp.242-243; 'King Solomon's fortified cities', p.283; 'The Black Obelisk', p.296; 'Sennacherib's Prism', p.301; 'The seige of Lachish', p.302; 'Hezekiah's conduit', p.325. See also Assyrians, Babylonians, Greeks, Persians.
• *New Testament*: the 'Jesus boat', p.581; 'Jesus and the cities', p.587; 'Pilate', p.593; 'Jerusalem in New Testament times', p.630; 'The city of Athens', pp.659-660; 'Roman rule, Greek culture', pp.670-673; 'The city of Rome', pp.684-685; 'The city of Corinth', pp.696-697; 'The city of Ephesus', pp.716-717.

ARCHELAUS Son of Herod the Great; ruler of Judea: Matthew 2:22/p.554. See 'The Herod family', pp.627-628.

ARCHIPPUS Colossians 4:17; Philemon 2/p.726.

AREOPAGUS Paul was brought before the council which formerly met on this hill (Mars hill) in Athens: Acts 17/p.658 *Picture* p.660.

ARETAS Ruler of Arabia: 2 Corinthians 11:32/p.710.

ARGOB Part of the kingdom of Og in Bashan, east of the Jordan: Deuteronomy 3; 1 Kings 4:13.

ARISTARCHUS Paul's companion and fellow worker: Acts 19:29ff.; Colossians 4:10; Philemon 24/p.726.

ARK, NOAH'S Genesis 6:14ff./ p.125.

ARK OF THE COVENANT
Exodus 25; 1 Samuel 4ff.;
2 Samuel 6; 1 Chronicles
15–16/pp.174, 178, 258,
268, 311. See 'The lost Ark',
p.305.
ARMAGEDDON Assembling-
place for the great final battle
(see also Megiddo):
Revelation 16:16.
ARMOUR *Armour of God*:
Ephesians 6/p.719.
Pictures pp.592, 719 (Roman
soldiers). See also War,
weapons.
ARNON River flowing into the
Dead Sea from the east; boun-
dary between the Amorites
and Moabites: Numbers
21:13, etc./*Map* p.209.
AROER Town on the north
bank of the River Arnon:
Deuteronomy 2:36, etc.;
2 Kings 10:31/*Map* p.104C6.
ARTAXERXES King of Persia:
Ezra 4:7ff.; Nehemiah 2:1/
p.334.
ARTEMIS Goddess of the
Ephesians (Roman Diana):
Acts 19/pp.663, 664 (with
pictures). See also 'The city of
Ephesus', pp.616-617.
ASA King of Judah 911-870
BC: 1 Kings 15:8ff.; 2 Chronicles 14:1ff./pp.289, 320.
ASAHEL David's nephew;
killed by Abner: 2 Samuel
2:18ff./pp.264-265.
ASAPH A Levite; leader of
David's choir; named in the
titles of some of the Psalms:
1 Chronicles 15:17ff.; 25:1ff/
p.314.
ASHDOD Philistine town
where the Ark of the Coven-
ant stood in the temple of
Dagon: 1 Samuel 5; also
2 Chronicles 26:6; Isaiah
20:1, etc./*Map* p.104A5.
ASHER 1. Jacob's eighth son;
one of the 12 tribes of Israel:
Genesis 30:13. Family tree
p.147.
2. Territory of the tribe of
Asher: Joshua 19:24-31/
Map p.235.
ASHKELON Philistine town:
Judges 14:19; 1 Samuel

6:17/*Map* p.104A5 *Picture*
p.246.
**ASHTAROTH/ASHTORETH/
ASTARTE** Mesopotamian
Ishtar; mother goddess linked
with fertility, love and war,
like the Canaanite god Baal.
Picture p.303.
**ASHTAROTH/ASHTEROTH-
KARNAIM** Town sacked by
Chedorlaomer; capital of Og
of Bashan: Genesis 14:5;
Deuteronomy 1:4, etc./
Map p.104D2.
ASHURBANIPAL King of
Assyria 668-627 BC.
Picture p.327.
ASIA Roman province of
which Ephesus was capital;
western part of modern
Turkey: Acts 19, etc./
Map p.680.
ASSOS Sea-port on the west
coast of modern Turkey: Acts
20:13/*Map* p.664.
ASSYRIA, ASSYRIANS
Neighbours of the Babylonians whose homeland was
north Mesopotamia. During
the 2nd millennium, Assyria
came under the rule of
Amorites, and from about
1350 to 1100 BC built up a
powerful state exercising
some control as far west as
the Mediterranean. In 883 BC
Ashurnasirpal II moved his
capital from Assur to Kalhu
(biblical Calah, modern
Nimrud). His successors,
including Shalmaneser III
(858-824), Adad-nirari III
(810-783), Tiglath-pileser III
(or Pul; 744-727), Shalmaneser V (726-722) all of whom
had contacts with Israel,
continued there until Sargon
II (721-705) founded a new
capital at Dur-Sharrukin,
modern Khorsabad. His son
Sennacherib (704-681)
moved the capital to Nineveh,
where it remained under
Esarhaddon (680-669),
Ashurbanipal (668-627;
probably the Osnappar of
Ezra 4:10), and other minor
kings until its destruction in

612 BC by the Chaldeans and
Medes. See 'The Assyrians',
pp.432-433.
• *Invasions of Israel and Judah*:
2 Kings 15–19; 2 Chronicles
32; Isaiah 9–10; 36–37/
pp.299-301, 324, 424, 431.
See also 'Sennacherib's
Prism', p.301; 'The Black
Obelisk', p.296; 'The seige of
Lachish', p.302; 'Hezekiah's
conduit', p.325.
Maps pp.126, 300, 433
(Assyrian Empire)
Pictures pp.263, 286, 296,
299, 301, 302, 314, 326,
334, 362, 375, 401, 429,
431, 432, 433, 467, 475,
482, 500-501.
ASTARTE See Ashtaroth.
ATAROTH Town east of
Jordan: Numbers 32:31/
Map p.104C5.
ATHALIAH Daughter of Jezebel
who married Jehoram of
Judah and seized the throne
after her son's death: 2 Kings
11; 2 Chronicles 22/pp.298,
322.
ATHENS Cultural centre of
Greek civilization and
university city, where Paul
preached: Acts 17/p.658
Map p.657 *Picture* p.521.
See 'The city of Athens',
pp.659-660 (with pictures).
ATONEMENT God and
humanity made 'at one' by
the 'covering' of people's sin
before God: Leviticus 4; 16;
Romans 3:25; 1 John 2:2;
4:10. See 'Sacrifice', pp.182-
183; 'Priesthood in the Old
Testament', p.186. See also
Reconciliation, Redemption.
ATONEMENT, DAY OF
Leviticus 16/pp.187-188.
See 'The great festivals',
p.191.
ATRAKHASIS EPIC pp.118,
123.
ATTALIA Sea-port of Paul's
first missionary journey, on
the south coast of modern
Turkey: Acts 14:25/
Map p.652.
AUGUSTUS First Roman
emperor, who ordered the

census which brought Mary
and Joseph to Bethlehem:
Luke 2:1.
Pictures pp.534, 600, 697
(and see Coins).
AZARIAH (Uzziah) Name of a
number of individuals,
notably the son of Amaziah,
King of Judah 791-740 BC:
2 Kings 14:21ff.; 2 Chron-
icles 26/pp.299, 323, 421.
AZEKAH Town to which
Joshua pursued the Amorites:
Joshua 10:10.

B

BAAL Canaanite god of
weather, war, fertility.
Elijah's contest: 1 Kings 18/
pp. 290-291.
Pictures pp.15, 238, 240,
291, 306.
BAASHA Seized the throne of
Israel from Jeroboam's son;
ruled 909-886 BC: 1 Kings
15:16ff./p.290.
BABEL Site of the great tower
identified with Babylon:
Genesis 11/pp.125-126
(with ziggurat picture).
BABYLON City on the River
Euphrates; became capital of
Babylonia in southern
Mesopotamia: 2 Kings
20:12ff.; Jeremiah 50,
etc./*Map* p.456 *Picture*
pp.457.
BABYLONIA, BABYLONIANS
Heirs of the Sumerians and
Akkadians in southern
Mesopotamia; capital city
Babylon. Best-known king of
the 1st Babylonian dynasty
(18th century BC, roughly
the time of Abraham) was
Hammurabi, author of a
famous code of laws (see
p.171). During the early part
of the 1st millennium BC the
Babylonians were subject to
the Assyrians. Then from
612 to 539 BC the Neo-
Babylonian or Chaldean
dynasty dominated Western
Asia. Rulers mentioned in the
Old Testament are:

Nebuchadnezzar (604-562), Amel-Marduk (biblical Evil-Merodach; 561-560), Nergal-shar-usar (biblical Nergal-Sharezer, Greek Neriglissar; 559-556). Babylon (and with it the Babylonian Empire) fell to Cyrus the Persian in 539 BC. See 'The Babylonians', pp.456-457.
• *Invasion of Judah*: 2 Kings 24 –25; 2 Chronicles 36; Jeremiah 39/pp.303-305, 326-327, 425, 452 *Map* p.456 (Babylonian Empire) *Pictures* pp.7, 213, 304, 307, 326, 327, 355, 436, 456, 457, 474, 482. See also under Exile.

BABYLONIAN CHRONICLE p.288. *Pictures* pp.326, 456.

BABYLONIAN GENESIS p.117.

BALAAM Prophet called on by Balak to curse the Israelites: Numbers 22:5 – 24:25/ pp.202-203.

BALAK Moabite king who hired Balaam to curse Israel: Numbers 22:2 – 24:25/ pp.202-203.

BARABBAS Robber released in preference to Jesus: Matthew 27:16ff., etc.

BARAK One of the Judges; with Deborah he defeated Sisera and the Canaanites: Judges 4:6ff./pp.221, 240-241.

BARNABAS A Levite from Cyprus; commissioned with Paul by the church at Antioch for missionary service: Acts 4:36; 9:27; 12:25ff./ pp.646, 652, 654.

BARTHOLOMEW (NATHANAEL) One of the 12 apostles (see 'The twelve disciples of Jesus', p.558): Matthew 10:3, etc.

BARTIMAEUS Blind man healed by Jesus: Mark 10:46ff./p.586.

BARUCH The prophet Jeremiah's secretary: Jeremiah 32:12ff./ pp.451-453.

BARZILLAI Loyal friend of David during Absalom's

rebellion: 2 Samuel 17:27ff.; 9:31ff./pp.274, 277.

BASHAN Region east of Lake Galilee; kingdom of Og; famous for its cattle: Numbers 21:33; 32:33, etc./*Map* p.104C2.

BATHSHEBA Wife of Uriah the Hittite; David committed adultery with her and later married her; mother of Solomon: 2 Samuel 11 – 12; 1 Kings 1 – 2/pp.270-271.

BEDOUIN *Pictures* pp.24-25, 117, 134, 138, 199, 348, 354-355, 486. See also Nomads, nomadic life.

BEERSHEBA Southernmost town of Israel, on the trade route to Egypt: Genesis 21:14, 31; 26:23ff., etc./ *Map* p.104A6 *Picture* p.147.

BELSHAZZAR King of Babylon overthrown by the Persians: Daniel 5/p.475.

BELTESHAZZAR Babylonian name given to Daniel: Daniel 1:7/p.474.

BENHADAD The name of several rulers of Damascus: 1 Kings 15:18ff.; 20:1ff.; 2 Kings 6:24ff.; 8:7ff.; 13:3ff./p.292.

BENAIAH One of David's officers responsible for proclaiming Solomon king: 1 Kings 1 – 2/ p.277.

BENJAMIN 1. Jacob's twelfth and youngest son; Rachel died giving birth to him; father of the tribe of Benjamin which sided with Judah at the division of the kingdom: Genesis 35:18; 42 – 49/ pp.146, 148-150.
2. Territory of the tribe of Benjamin: Joshua 18:11-28/ *Map* p.235.

BERNICE Sister of Herod Agrippa II; with him when he heard Paul's case at Caesarea: Acts 25:13ff./ p.667.

BEROEA Town in northern Greece where Paul preached: Acts 17:10/*Map* p.657.

BETH-HORON (UPPER AND LOWER) Near the scene of Joshua's victory: Joshua

10:10/*Map* p.104B4.

BETH-SHAN Town on whose walls the Philistines hung Saul's body: 1 Samuel 31:10/*Map* p.104C3 *Picture* p.266.

BETH-SHEMESH Place to which the Ark of the Covenant was returned by the Philistines: 1 Samuel 6; also 2 Kings 14:11/ *Map* p.104B5.

BETH-ZUR Town settled by Caleb's descendants; fortified by Rehoboam: 1 Chronicles 2:45; 2 Chronicles 11:7/ *Map* p.104B6.

BETHANY Home of Martha, Mary and Lazarus just outside Jerusalem: John 11:1; 12:1/*Map* p.526B5 *Picture* p.635.

BETHEL Place of Jacob's dream; sanctuary town which became an official shrine of the northern kingdom of Israel: Genesis 28; Judges 20:18, 26; 1 Samuel 7:16; 1 Kings 12:28ff.; Amos 7:10ff., etc./*Map* p.104B4.

BETHESDA/BETHZATHA Pool in Jerusalem where Jesus healed an invalid: John 5:2/ *Map* p.630 *Picture* p.626.

BETHLEHEM Town a few miles south of Jerusalem; here Ruth settled and both David and Jesus were born: Ruth; 1 Samuel 16; 2 Samuel 23:13ff.; Matthew 2; Luke 2/*Map* p.104B5 *Pictures* pp.24-25, 42, 47, 253, 269, 542, 550, 598.

BETHPHAGE Place near Bethany from which Jesus sent disciples to fetch the ass on which he would ride into Jerusalem: Mark 11:1/ *Map* p.526B5.

BETHSAIDA Town on the shore of Lake Galilee; home of Philip, Andrew and Peter: John 1:44; Mark 8:22; Matthew 11:21/ *Map* p.526C2.

BEZALEL The craftsman chosen to construct the Tabernacle and its

furnishings: Exodus 35:30ff.

BIBLE See 'The books of the Bible', pp.14-17; 'What is the Bible?', pp.18-20; 'Introducing the Old Testament', pp.98-99; 'What is the New Testament?', p.527.
• *Bible and Qur'an*: pp.86-88
• *cultural perspectives*: pp.80-82, 95
• *English versions*: pp.21, 77
• *formation of*: see 'Passing on the story', pp.62-73
• *Hebrew Bible*: article pp.68-69; 70, 98-99; 'Jesus and the Old Testament', pp.569-570
• *historians' perspectives*: see 'Our world – their world', p.95; 'A historian looks at the New Testament', p.650
• *scientists' perspectives*: see 'A scientist looks at the Bible', pp.92-94; 'A geneticist comments' (on the virgin birth), p.597; 'New Testament miracles', pp.605-606
• *translation*: pp.74-76
• *understanding and interpretation*: see 'Reading the Bible', pp.22-23; 'Understanding the Bible', pp.46-59
• *women's perspectives*: see 'The Bible through women's eyes', pp.89-91; 'Women of faith', p.143; '(Ruth) A story through women's eyes', p.254; 'Women's perspectives in the Gospels', p.603.
See also 'Jesus and the Old Testament', pp.569-570; 'The Old Testament in the New Testament', pp.742-743.

BIBLE BACKGROUND See 'The Bible in its setting', pp.26-43.

BIBLE READING pp.22-23.

BIBLE REFERENCES p.21.

BIBLICAL CRITICISM See 'The text and the message', pp.58-59; 'Studying the Gospels', pp.545-547.

BILDAD One of Job's three friends: Job 2:11, etc./ pp.351ff.

BILHAH Rachel's servant; mother of Dan and Naphtali:

Genesis 29:29; 30:3, etc.
Family tree p.147.
BIRDS Visual feature
'Animals and birds', pp.38-
39 with further information
and pictures listed there.
BITHYNIA Roman province
bordering the Black Sea: Acts
16:7/*Map* p.680.
BLACK OBELISK Visual
feature, p.296.
BLESSING AND CURSING
Leviticus 26; Deuteronomy
27 – 28/pp.189, 192, 211,
217. See under Covenant.
BOAZ Landowner of Bethlehem who became Ruth's
husband and ancestor of
David: Ruth 2 – 4/ pp.252-
253.
BOOK OF THE DEAD, EGYPTIAN
p.156.
BOOK OF THE LAW *Josiah's*
discovery: 2 Kings 22;
2 Chronicles 34/pp.303,
326.
BOUNDARY STONE *Pictures*
pp.213, 482.
BOZRAH Town in Edom
denounced by the prophets:
Isaiah 34:6, etc./p.431.
BURNING BUSH Exodus 3 – 4/
p.160.

C

CAESAR Emperor of Rome. In
the Gospels, Augustus (Luke
2:1) or Tiberius; in Acts,
Claudius; elsewhere, Nero:
Matthew 22:17ff.; John
19:12ff.; Acts 17:7; 25:8ff.;
Philippians 4:22. See 'The
New Testament story',
pp.536-537.
Pictures pp.534, 697
(Augustus), 534 (Tiberius),
684 (Caligula and
Vespasian), 754 (Nero), 766
(Domitian).
CAESAREA Roman town on
the coast of Palestine;
residence of the procurators;
home of Philip and of
Cornelius; place where Paul
was imprisoned: Acts 10; 11;
21; 23/*Map* p.526A3 *Pictures*

pp.32-33, 479, 666, 690.
CAESAREA PHILIPPI Town at
the foot of Mt Hermon and
source of the Jordan; near
here Peter made his great
confession of faith in Jesus as
God's Messiah: Matthew
16:13ff./*Map* p.526C1
Pictures pp.83, 565.
CAIAPHAS High priest before
whom Jesus stood trial:
Matthew 26:3; Luke 3:2;
John 18:13ff./ pp.590, 639.
CAIN Eldest son of Adam and
Eve, who killed his brother
Abel: Genesis 4/pp.120-122.
CALAH One of the chief cities
of Assyria, founded by
Nimrod: Genesis 10:11/
Map p.300.
CALEB Sent to spy out
Canaan; only he and Joshua
of the 12 spies advised
advance; in his old age he
claimed possession of Hebron
and drove out the Anakim:
Numbers 13 – 14; Joshua
14 – 15/pp.197, 235.
CALENDAR, Israel's Visual
feature pp.42-43.
CALL *Of Abraham*: Genesis
12ff./pp.127ff.
• *of Moses*: Exodus 3 – 4/
p.160
• *of Samuel*: 1 Samuel 3/
p.256
• *of Isaiah*: Isaiah 6/p.421
• *of Jeremiah*: Jeremiah
1/pp.440-441
• *of Ezekiel*: Ezekiel 1 – 3/
p.462
• *prophet's call*: pp.409-410.
See under Twelve apostles.
CANA Village in Galilee where
Jesus turned water into wine:
John 2:1ff./*Map* p.526B2
Picture p.624.
CANAAN Son of Ham, cursed
by his grandfather, Noah:
Genesis 9:18ff./p.122.
CANAAN, CANAANITES The
people settled in Palestine
and southern Syria, who had
a flourishing urban civilization in the 2nd millennium
BC. The land of Canaan was
Israel's 'promised land':
Genesis 11:31; Numbers

33:51ff., etc. The Canaanites'
corrupt religion, criticized in
the Old Testament, is
illustrated in texts from
Ugarit (modern Ras Shamra).
Hebrew is a dialect of the
Canaanite language (Isaiah
19:18) and the related Ugar-
itic language greatly helps
our understanding of it.
See 'Canaanites and
Philistines', p.231; 'The
promised land', pp.214-215;
'Cities of the conquest',
pp.228-229; 'Holy War',
p.234.
Map pp.814-815.
Pictures pp.152-153, 231,
236, 238, 240, 276, 291,
306, 444.
CANON OF SCRIPTURE See 'An
approved list – the "canon" of
Scripture', pp.70-73; 'The
Hebrew Bible', pp.68-69.
CAPERNAUM Town beside
Lake Galilee; Peter's home
and Jesus' base during his
ministry: Matthew 4:13;
Mark 1:21; Luke 7:1-10; 10;
15, etc./*Map* p.526C2 *Picture*
p.579.
CAPPADOCIA Roman province
in what is now eastern
Turkey: Acts 2:9; 1 Peter 1:1/
Map p.680.
CARCHEMISH City on the
Euphrates in northern Syria;
here Nebuchadnezzar of
Babylon defeated the
Egyptians: Jeremiah 46:2/
p.453 *Map* p.456 *Picture*
p.326.
CARIANS An Indo-European-
speaking people of south-west
Asia Minor. They were used
by the Israelites as mercenary
troops in the 9th century BC:
2 Kings 11:4, 19.
CARMEL Range of hills jutting
into the sea by the modern
port of Haifa; scene of Elijah's
contest with the prophets of
Baal: 1 Kings 18:19ff.; also
2 Kings 2:25; 4:25/*Map*
p.104B2 *Pictures* pp.290,
774.
CEDAR The wood used in
building King Solomon's

Temple. *Pictures* pp.279,
281.
CENCHREAE Harbour of
Corinth: Acts 18:18; Romans
16:1/*Map* p.657.
CENTURION See 'Roman
soldiers in the New Testament', p.592; Cornelius: Acts
10/pp.649-650.
CEPHAS See Peter.
CHALDEA, CHALDEANS As the
Aramaeans spread across
northern Mesopotamia so the
Chaldeans (related tribes-
people) occupied the southern marshes. Chaldea was
Abraham's family home (see
Ur): Genesis 11:28.
During the 9th and 8th
centuries BC the Chaldeans
often won control of Babylon
(e.g. Merodach-baladan,
2 Kings 20:12ff.). After a long
struggle with Assyria, the
Chaldean dynasty established
itself there in 626 BC.
Map pp.814-815.
CHEBAR River in Babylonia
beside which Ezekiel and the
exiles settled: Ezekiel 1:1, etc.
CHEDORLAOMER King of Elam
who headed a punitive raid
against Sodom and Gomor-
rah; pursued and killed by
Abraham: Genesis 14.
CHERITH Brook beside which
Elijah lived during the
famine: 1 Kings 17:3/
Map p.104C3.
CHILDLESSNESS See 'Women
of faith', p.143.
• *Sarah*: pp.131ff.
• *Rebecca*: p.140
• *Rachel*: p.141
• *Hannah*: pp.255-257
• *Elizabeth*: p.597.
CHINNERETH Another name
for Lake Galilee (possibly
because of its 'harp' shape),
and a lakeside town:
Deuteronomy 3:17/
Map p.104C2.
CHORAZIN Town in Galilee
which Jesus condemned for
its unbelief: Matthew
11:21/*Map* p.526C2.
CHRONICLER, THE pp.223-
224, 308.

CHRONICLES, BOOKS OF
pp.308ff.

CHRONOLOGY OF THE KINGS
Article pp.287-288.

CHURCH *The people of God*: John 1:12-13; 1 Corinthians 12:12-31; 2 Corinthians 6:16-18; Galatians 3:6-29; Ephesians 2:11-22; Colossians 1:15-20; 1 Peter 2:4-10
• *foundation*: Matthew 16:18-20; 28:16-20; John 10:7-18; Acts 1:6-8; 2
• *mission and purpose*: Matthew 28:19-20; John 17:18, 22ff.; Acts 1:8; 26:16-18; 2 Corinthians 5:18-21; Ephesians 3:7-13; 5:25-27; Philippians 1:5-11; 1 Peter 2:5, 9; Jude 24-25
• *unity*: John 17; 1 Corinthians 1:10ff.; 11:17ff.; Galatians 1:6-9; 3:23-29; Ephesians 4; 1 Peter 3:8ff.
• *leadership*: Acts 6:1-6; 13:1-3; 14:21-23; 20:17-35; 1 Corinthians 12:4-30; 1 Thessalonians 5:12-13; 1 Timothy; Titus; Hebrews 13:17
• *gatherings*: Acts 2:41-47; 11:19-26; 19:8-10; 20:7-12; 1 Corinthians 11:17-33; 14:26-39; Hebrews 10:23-25
• *discipline*: Matthew 18:15-20; Acts 4:33 – 5:11; 1 Corinthians 5; 2 Corinthians 2:5-11; Galatians 6:1-3; 1 Timothy 5:17-22
• *message*: see under Gospel.

CILICIA, CILICIANS Roman province (in what is now southern Turkey), with Tarsus as its capital, and the inhabitants of the area. In the Old Testament Cilicia (Kue) is mentioned as a source of horses for Solomon's trade with Syria (see 'Solomon's trade', p.319): 1 Kings 10:28-29; Acts 21:39/ *Map* p.680.

CIMMERIANS A steppe people who crossed the Caucasus in the 8th-7th centuries BC, coming up against the Assyrians in north-west

Persia, and overrunning the Phrygian and Lydian kingdoms in Asia Minor. Mentioned in Ezekiel 38:6 (Gomer) in association with other northern peoples (see under Phrygians).

CIRCUMCISION For the men of Israel, the sign of belonging to the people of God: Genesis 17; Joshua 5; Acts 15; Romans 2 – 4; Galatians 2/pp.131, 135, 163, 529, 654, 683, 711-713.

CISTERN For storing water. *Picture* p.452.

CIVILIZATIONS See 'Making connections – the Bible and world history', pp.26-27.

CLAUDIUS Emperor of Rome: Acts 11:28; 18:2/pp.651, 658 *Picture* p.651.

CLAUDIUS LYSIAS Military tribune in Jerusalem who took Paul into custody: Acts 21:31 – 23:30.

CLEAN AND UNCLEAN CREATURES *Jewish food laws*: Leviticus 11/p.184.
• *Peter's vision*: Acts 10:3/ pp.649-651.

CLEMENT Philippian Christian; Paul's fellow worker: Philippians 4:3.

CLEOPAS One of two people the risen Jesus met on the road to Emmaus on the first Easter Day: Luke 24:13ff.

CO-REGENCIES See 'Unravelling the chronology of the kings', pp.287-288.

CODEX See 'From scroll to book', p.71.
• *Sinaiticus* (with picture): p.71
• *Alexandrinus* (with picture): p.72.

COINS *Pictures* pp.522 (Alexander), 566 (denarius), 572 (Titus and Judea capta), 588 (Tiberius), 593 (Pilate), 600 (Augustus), 651 (Claudius), 684 (Caligula and Vespasian), 754 (Nero), 766 (Domitian).

COLOSSAE Town in what is now south-west Turkey; Paul wrote a letter to the church

there: Colossians 1:2/p.723 *Map* p.680 *Picture* p.723.

COLOSSIANS, LETTER TO THE pp.723ff.

COMPILERS, BIBLE See Editors, Canon of Scripture.

CONQUEST OF CANAAN Joshua 5ff./pp.227ff. See 'The promised land', pp.214-215; 'Cities of the conquest', pp.228-229; '"Holy War"', p.234.

CORINTH See visual feature 'The city of Corinth', pp.696-697. Leading city of southern Greece, where Paul founded a church: Acts 18/p.658 *Map* p.657 *Pictures* pp.695, 699, 700, 705.

CORINTHIANS, LETTERS TO THE pp.694ff., 706ff.

CORNELIUS Roman centurion to whose household Peter was sent to preach the gospel: Acts 10/pp.649-650.

COUNCIL AT JERUSALEM Acts 15/p.654.

COVENANT A 'treaty' or 'agreement' setting out God's promises, first to mankind, later to his people: pp.110-111, 125, 143. See also 'Covenants and Near Eastern Treaties', pp.210-211.
• *With Noah*: Genesis 6:18; 9:9-17/p.125
• *with Abraham*: Genesis 15; 17/pp.127, 130
• *with Israel*: Exodus 19ff.; Deuteronomy 4ff./pp.168-169, 179, 205, 236-237
• *with David*: 2 Samuel 7; Psalms 89; 132/p.268
• *the 'new covenant'*: Jeremiah 31:31-34; Matthew 26:26-28; 2 Corinthians 3; Galatians 4:21ff.; Hebrews 9:15ff./pp.450, 544, 574, 707, 712-713, 745, 746.

CREATION AND PROVIDENCE pp.108-110, 115-116. Genesis 1 – 2; Job 38 – 42:6; Psalms 8; 33:6-22; 104; Isaiah 40:21-26; Matthew 6:25-33; Acts 14:15-18; Romans 1:18-23; 8:18-23; 13:1-7; Colossians 1:15-20; Hebrews 1:1-3. See also 'God

and the universe', p.379. For the new creation, see Life; for the new heaven and earth, see Heaven.

CREATION, CARE FOR See 'People as God's caretakers', p.119.

CREATION STORIES Article and *pictures* pp.117-118.

CRESCENS Companion of Paul; sent to Galatia: 2 Timothy 4:10.

CRETE, CRETANS The island of Crete and its inhabitants, seat of the great Minoan civilization in the 3rd and 2nd millennia BC. In the Old Testament Crete is referred to as 'Caphtor': Genesis 10:14; Deuteronomy 2:23. The Philistines are said to have come from the area under Cretan control: Jeremiah 47:4; Amos 9:7. The Minoan civilization of Crete did not survive the Sea People upheavals of the late 2nd millennium BC (see 'Cities of the conquest', pp.228-229 and 'Canaanites and Philistines', p.232) and in the 1st millennium Crete was simply a part of the Greek cultural area.
• *Old Testament*: The Old Testament speaks of some Cretans, the 'Cherethites', who settled near the Philistines in southern Palestine. Some, like the Philistines, joined David's mercenary troops: 1 Samuel 30:14; 2 Samuel 8:18; 15:18; 20:7, and see 1 Kings 1:38, 44.
• *New Testament*: Jews from Crete heard Peter's sermon at Pentecost; Titus was later in charge of the church there: Acts 2:11; Titus 1:5/pp.645, 737 *Map* p.737.

CRISPUS Convert at Corinth baptized by Paul: Acts 18:8; 1 Corinthians 1:14.

CRITICISM See Biblical criticism.

CRUCIFIXION See under Jesus Christ.

CUNEIFORM The wedge-shaped script of ancient Mesopotamia (Sumerian, Babylonian, Assyrian). *Pictures* pp.117, 123, 132-133, 139, 237, etc.

CURSING See Blessing and cursing.

CUSH The Sudan: Genesis 10:6, etc./*Map* p.126.

CUSHAN-RISHATHAIM Oppressor of Israel at the time of the Judges: Judges 3:7ff./pp.239-240.

CYPRUS, CYPRIOTS The island of Cyprus and its inhabitants, referred to in the Old Testament by the ancient name 'Elishah': Genesis 10:4, Ezekiel 27:7. This appears in other documents as Alashia. The Cypriots are also sometimes referred to as Kittim: Genesis 10:4; Numbers 24:24.
• *Old Testament*: Cyprus does not appear often in the Bible in this period. The name Kittim is applied to the island in Isaiah 23:1, 12, but it is qualified by 'coastlands' in Jeremiah 2:10 and Ezekiel 27:6, which suggests an extension to the adjacent mainland areas. In Daniel 11:30 it is used in a figurative way of Rome.
• *New Testament*: In the New Testament the island of Cyprus figures frequently in Acts. The home of Barnabas, it was the first stage on Paul's first missionary journey: Acts 4:36; 13:4.
Map p.652 *Pictures* pp.652, 750.

CYRENE In Libya, north Africa; home of Simon who carried Jesus' cross: Matthew 27:32; also Acts 2:10; 11:20/*Map* p.645.

CYRUS King of Persia who overthrew the Babylonians and returned the Jews from exile: Ezra 1:1ff. – 6:14; Isaiah 44:28ff.; Daniel 1:21/pp.328-330, 435, 474. See 'The Persians', pp.480-481.

D

DAILY LIFE See Work.

DALMATIA Roman province on the east of the Adriatic, where Titus preached: 2 Timothy 4:10/*Map* p.680.

DAMASCUS Leading city of Syria; home of Naaman, visited by Elisha; denounced by the prophets; on his way to Damascus to persecute the church, Paul was converted: Genesis 15:2; 2 Kings 5; 8; Isaiah 17; Acts 9, etc. *Picture* p.649.

DAMASCUS ROAD Conversion of Paul: Acts 9; 22; 26/p.648.

DAN 1. One of Jacob's 12 sons and ancestor of the tribe of Dan: Genesis 30:5-6, etc. Family tree p.147.
2. Territory of the tribe of Dan; northernmost town of Israel in which Jeroboam set up a shrine: Joshua 19:40ff.; Judges 17 – 18; 1 Kings 12:25ff./pp.235, 249 *Maps* pp.104C1, 235 *Picture* p.286.

DANIEL Taken captive to Babylon as a young man and trained for service at court; interpreter of dreams and a visionary; one of the great Old Testament heroes: Daniel/pp.473ff.

DANIEL, BOOK OF pp.473ff.

DARIUS 1. Darius the Mede who succeeded to the kingdom of Babylon after Belshazzar's death; known only from the book of Daniel: Daniel 5:31/p.476.
2. Darius I, king of Persia, under whom the Jerusalem Temple was rebuilt: Ezra 4 – 6; Haggai 1:1; Zechariah 1:11/pp.329, 331; 'The Persians', pp.480-481 (with picture). *Picture* p.342.
3. Darius II: Nehemiah 12:22.

DATHAN Rebelled against Moses with Korah and Abiram: Numbers 16/p.197.

DAY OF THE LORD See under Future destiny.

DAVID The shepherd boy who became Israel's second king and founded the royal line from which the Messiah was eventually born; composer/collector of many of the Psalms: 1 Samuel 16 – 1 Kings 2; 1 Chronicles 11 – 29/pp.261ff., 310ff. See 'David', pp.269-271. Family tree p.267.
• *Anointed king*: 1 Samuel 16
• *David and Goliath*: 1 Samuel 17
• *David and Jonathan*: 1 Samuel 18 – 20
• *the outlaw*: 1 Samuel 19 – 31
• *David's lament*: 2 Samuel 1
• *capture of Jerusalem*: 2 Samuel 5
• *the Ark brought to Jerusalem*: 2 Samuel 6; 1 Chronicles 15
• *God's promise of a lasting dynasty*: 2 Samuel 7; 1 Chronicles 17
• *Bathsheba*: 2 Samuel 11f.
• *Absalom's rebellion*: 2 Samuel 15 – 18
• *arrangements for the Temple*: 1 Chronicles 22ff.
• *Solomon's accession; David's death*: 1 Kings 1 – 2:11; 1 Chronicles 29.

DEAD SEA Salt sea into which the River Jordan flows; in Ezekiel's vision of the Temple, fresh water flowing from the sanctuary brings the Dead Sea to life: Ezekiel 40 – 48/p.472 (with picture). *Maps* pp.104, 526 *Picture* p.136.

DEAD SEA SCROLLS Manuscripts of the Qumran Community: pp.32 (with pictures), 65, 529-530, 539 (with picture).

DEATH The physical and spiritual consequence of humanity's sin-alienation from God: Genesis 2:17; Romans 5:12ff.; 6:23; Ephesians 2:1-5.
• *Victory over death*: John 5:24; 8:51; 11:25; Romans 5:17ff.; 6; 8:6-11, 38-39; 1 Corinthians 15:26, 54-56; 1 John 3:14; Revelation 21:4
• *the 'second death'*: Revelation 2:11; 20:6, 14; 21:8.

DEATH OF THE FIRSTBORN Exodus 11 – 12/p.164.

DEBORAH Prophetess and judge in the time of the Judges; joined with Barak to overthrow Sisera: Judges 4 – 5/pp.221, 240-241.

DECAPOLIS/TEN TOWNS A group of free Greek cities, mainly south of Lake Galilee and east of the River Jordan: Matthew 4:25; Mark 5:20; 7:31/*Map* p.526C3.

DEDAN, DEDANITES Modern Al-'Ula, in north-west Arabia. By about the 7th century BC the Dedanites were prospering from their position on the trade route to South Arabia: see e.g. Isaiah 21:13; Jeremiah 25:23; Ezekiel 25:13; 38:13. In about the 5th century BC the Mineans established a trading colony at Dedan, and in about the 1st century BC it became part of the Nabataean dominion. *Map* pp.814-815.

DEDICATION/LIGHTS, FESTIVAL OF See 'The great festivals', p.191 (and picture p.43).

DELILAH Philistine woman who betrayed Samson: Judges 16/p.246. See 'Understanding Judges', p.248.

DEMAS Paul's fellow worker who in the end deserted him: Colossians 4:14; 2 Timothy 4:10/pp.726, 736.

DEMETRIUS 1. Silversmith at Ephesus: Acts 19:24.
2. Christian commended by John: 3 John 12/p.761.

DERBE Town in modern Turkey visited by Paul on his first and second missionary journeys: Acts 14; 16:1; 20:4/*Map* p.652.

DESERT WANDERING The Israelites' 40 years in the Sinai wilderness: Exodus 16ff.; Numbers/pp.166ff., 193ff. *Map* p.166.

DEUTEROCANONICAL BOOKS pp.16, 70; article pp.515-520.

DEUTERONOMY, BOOK OF p.205.

DIANA See Artemis.

DIASPORA See Dispersion.

DIBON Moabite town: Numbers 21:30; 32:34; Isaiah 15:2/Map p.104C6.

DINAH Jacob's daughter, whose rape by Shechem was cruelly avenged by Simeon and Levi: Genesis 34/p.146.

DIONYSIUS Member of the Areopagus council at Athens who became a Christian: Acts 17:34.

DIOTREPHES A self-seeking church leader denounced by John: 3 John 9-10/p.761.

DISCIPLES OF JESUS See Twelve apostles.

DISPERSION Jews living in settlements outside Palestine. See 'The Jewish Dispersion', p.753.

DIVISION OF THE KINGDOM The split after Solomon's reign into Israel (north) and Judah (south): 1 Kings 12; 2 Chronicles 10/pp.285 (and map), 319.

DIVISION OF THE LAND among the 12 tribes, after the conquest of Canaan: Joshua 13 – 21/pp.235 (and map).

DIVORCE See under Marriage and family relationships.

DOEG Edomite servant of Saul who told him that Ahimelech had helped David: 1 Samuel 21:7; 22:9ff./p.263.

DOR Canaanite town in northern Palestine: Joshua 11:1-2; 1 Kings 4:11/Map p.104B3.

DORCAS/TABITHA Woman noted for her good works, whom Peter raised from the dead: Acts 9:36ff.

DOTHAN Joseph's brothers sold him to the Midianites at Dothan; here Elisha was delivered from the surrounding Syrian army: Genesis 37:17; 2 Kings 6/Map p.104B3.

DREAMS AND INTERPRETATIONS *Jacob's dream*: Genesis 28/pp.140-141
• *Joseph's dreams*: Genesis 37/p.149
• *dreams of the butler and baker*: Genesis 40/p.148
• *Pharaoh's dream*: Genesis 41/p.148
• *Nebuchadnezzar's dream*: Daniel 2/p.474
• *Joseph's dream*: Matthew 1
• *dreams in Egypt*: p.156 (dream manual picture p.150).
See also Visions.

DRUSILLA Jewish wife of the Procurator Felix, who heard Paul's case: Acts 24:24/p.667.

E

EBAL Mountain near Shechem on which the tribes were to stand to pronounce the curse on those who broke the law: Deuteronomy 11:29; Joshua 8:30/Map p.104B4.

EBEDMELECH Ethiopian servant of Zedekiah who saved Jeremiah's life: Jeremiah 38; 39:16ff./p.452.

ECCLESIASTES, BOOK OF pp.400ff.

EDEN 'Garden' cradle of the human race, in Mesopotamia: Genesis 2:8.

EDITORS, BIBLE See 'Editors at work', pp.66-67 and p.547.

EDOM, EDOMITES Mountainous area south of the Dead Sea occupied by Esau's descendants: Genesis 32:3. The Edomites were the southern neighbours of the Moabites, whose territory lay mainly to the east of the Wadi Arabah. Like the Moabites, they refused passage to the Israelites at the time of the conquest: Numbers 20:14ff. Hostilities continued between the Edomites and the Israelites: 1 Samuel 14:47, etc.; Isaiah 34:5ff., etc. In the

6th century, after the fall of Jerusalem, many migrated to southern Judah, and were followed by others in later centuries, when their home territory became part of the Nabataean kingdom (see Arabians). Southern Judea came to be called Idumaea, and the inhabitants Idumaeans: 1 Maccabees 4:29; 5:65; Mark 3:8. The Herods who ruled Judea in New Testament times were Idumaeans. See 'The Herod family', p.627. Map pp.814-815 Pictures pp.203, 323, 495.

EDREI Town where Og was defeated: Numbers 21:33/Map p.104D3.

EGLON 1. King of Moab killed by Ehud: Judges 3/p.240. **2.** Town destroyed by Joshua: Joshua 10:34/Map p.233.

EGNATIAN WAY The great east-west highway in Roman times. Pictures pp.657, 728.

EGYPT, EGYPTIANS See 'Egypt', pp.154-158. The Egyptians' highly developed civilization matched that of Mesopotamia. When Abraham had contact with Egypt in the Middle Kingdom period (about 2100-1800 BC) its civilization was already over 1,000 years old. It was probably in about 1800-1600 BC that Joseph and his people settled there: Genesis 46 – Exodus 14/pp.155ff. The exodus took place under the New Kingdom (about 1600-1100 BC), probably in the time of Pharaoh Ramesses II. Israel is mentioned as one of the nations in Palestine on the victory stele of his successor Merneptah (about 1208 BC; picture p.31). By the 1st millennium BC, the great days of Egyptian civilization were over. A fresh attempt at Asiatic conquest was made in the 10th century by Sheshonq I

(biblical Shishak): 1 Kings 11:29-40; 14:25-26. And Solomon traded with Egypt in the same century (see Cilicians). He also married a pharaoh's daughter. But though Egyptian rulers intervened in Palestine and Syria after this, Egypt was now a 'broken reed': 2 Kings 18:21; 19:9 – see under Ethiopians; 23:29; 24:1-7; Isaiah 36:6; Jeremiah 37:5-19; 46:1-26; Ezekiel 17:11-21. The country became successively part of the Persian, Hellenistic and Roman Empires.
Pictures pp.31, 101, 106, 149, 150, 151, 152-158, 163-165, 194, 315, 393.

EHUD Israelite champion who assassinated Eglon of Moab: Judges 3/p.240.

EKRON One of the five Philistine towns, where the Ark of the Covenant was held; denounced by the prophets: 1 Samuel 5:10; Jeremiah 25:20, etc./Map p.104A5.

ELAH 1. The name of a number of individuals, notably the son of Baasha king of Israel 886-885 BC, assassinated by Zimri: 1 Kings 16/p.290. **2.** Valley where David slew Goliath: 1 Samuel 17:2/Map p.104B5.

ELAM, ELAMITES Country east of the Sumerians and Babylonians (Elam – modern Khuzistan in south-west Iran), whose capital, Susa, became important under the Elamites' successors, the Persians: Genesis 14:1; Nehemiah 1:1; Isaiah 21:2, etc.
Pilgrims from Elam were in Jerusalem for Pentecost: Acts 2:9/Map p.645.

ELATH (ELOTH)/EZION-GEBER Settlements at the northern end of the Gulf of Aqaba; here Solomon built his fleet: Deuteronomy 2:8; 1 Kings 9:26, etc./Map p.319.

ELEAZAR Aaron's son; consecrated priest and put in charge of the Levites: Exodus 6:23; Leviticus 10; Numbers; Joshua 14:1, etc.

ELECTION God's sovereign choice; his right to single people out for blessing (see pp.110, 692): Romans 9:18ff.
• *God's choice of individuals for a particular purpose or job*: Genesis 12:1-2; Exodus 3; 1 Samuel 3; Isaiah 6; 45; 49; Jeremiah 1
• *God's choice of a people*: Deuteronomy 7:6ff.; Romans 8:28-30; 1 Corinthians 1:27ff.; Ephesians 1:4-12; 1 Peter 1:2; 2:9.

ELI Priest and Judge at Shiloh who preceded Samuel: 1 Samuel 1 – 4/ pp.255-258.

ELIAKIM Name of several individuals, the most notable being the steward over Hezekiah's household who negotiated with Sennacherib's officers: 2 Kings 18:18ff.; Isaiah 36.

ELIASHIB High priest in the time of Nehemiah; took part in rebuilding the city walls; later compromised with Nehemiah's enemies: Nehemiah 3:13.

ELIEZER Name of several individuals, notably Abraham's chief servant and adopted heir: Genesis 15:2.

ELIHU Angry young man in the story of Job: Job 32:2ff./ p.357.

ELIJAH One of Israel's greatest prophets, contemporary with Ahab: 1 Kings 17 – 2 Kings 2/pp.290ff.
• *The drought*: 1 Kings 17
• *contest with the prophets of Baal*: 1 Kings 18
• *the 'still, small voice'*: 1 Kings 19
• *the chariot of fire*: 2 Kings 2
• *appearance at the transfiguration of Christ*: Mark 9:4ff.

ELIMELECH Husband of Naomi: Ruth 1:2.

ELIPHAZ One of Job's friends: Job 2:11, etc./pp.350ff.

ELISHA Elijah's successor as prophet of Israel: 1 Kings 19:16ff.; 2 Kings 2 – 9; 13/pp.293ff.
• *Elisha and the Shunammite woman*: 2 Kings 4
• *healing of Naaman*: 2 Kings 5.

ELIZABETH Wife of Zechariah and mother of John the Baptist: Luke 1/p.597.

ELKANAH Father of Samuel: 1 Samuel 1.

ELYMAS Magician who opposed Paul and Barnabas in Cyprus: Acts 13/p.652.

EMMAUS On the day of his resurrection Jesus appeared to two disciples on their way to this village: Luke 24:13.

EMPEROR WORSHIP See 'Emperor worship and Revelation', p.766; pp.673, 763.

EN-ROGEL Spring near Jerusalem; here Jonathan and Ahimaaz waited for news of Absalom; Adonijah was feasting here when Solomon was proclaimed king: 2 Samuel 17:17; 1 Kings 1:9.

END OF THE WORLD See Future destiny, Heaven, Jesus Christ, return.

ENDOR Place in northern Israel where Saul consulted the medium: 1 Samuel 28:7/*Map* p.104B3.

ENGEDI Freshwater spring in the arid hills west of the Dead Sea; David's hide-out when he was outlawed by King Saul: 1 Samuel 23:29, 24:1ff. *Map* p.104B6 *Pictures* pp.263, 270.

ENGLISH VERSIONS See under Bible.

ENOCH Descendant of Adam's son Seth who walked with God and was taken into his presence without dying: Genesis 5:18-24/ p.122.

EPAPHRAS Paul's friend and fellow worker: Colossians 1:7, etc./p.724.

EPAPHRODITUS Christian sent to Paul by the Philippian

church: Philippians 2:25ff./pp.721-722.

EPHESIANS, LETTER TO THE pp.714ff.

EPHESUS See visual feature 'The city of Ephesus', pp.716-717. Capital of the Roman province of Asia (western Turkey); important centre of the early church: Acts 18:19; 19; 20:17; Ephesians 1:1; Revelation 2:1-7/pp.662-664 *Map* p.657 *Pictures* pp.663, 672, 700, 713, 715, 718, 736, 764, 765.

EPHRAIM 1. Son of Joseph; ancestor of the tribe of Ephraim: Genesis 41:52; 48:13ff. etc./p.151. Family tree p.147.
2. Territory of the tribe of Ephraim: Joshua 16:4-10, etc./*Map* p.235.

EPHRATHAH Bethlehem.

EPHRON Hittite from whom Abraham bought the cave of Machpelah: Genesis 23.

EPIC OF GILGAMESH, THE pp.123-124 (with picture), 432.

EPICUREANS pp.658, 676.

EPONYM LISTS p.288.

ERASTUS 1. Paul's assistant; sent to Macedonia with Timothy: Acts 19:22; 2 Timothy 4:20.
2. City treasurer of Corinth: Romans 16:23/p.693. See 'The city of Corinth', p.696. *Picture* p.697.

ERECH Town in Babylonia: Genesis 10:10; Ezra 4:9.

ESARHADDON Succeeded Sennacherib as king of Assyria: 2 Kings 19:37.

ESAU Son of Isaac and Rebecca; twin brother of Jacob; bartered away his blessing and was cheated of his birthright: Genesis 25:25ff.; 27 – 28:9; 32 –33; 36/pp.140, 142, 144-146.

ESHCOL Valley from which the spies brought back grapes: Numbers 13:23.

ESHTAOL Town mentioned in the story of Samson: Judges 13:25; 16:31/*Map* p.104B5.

ESSENES Ascetic group to which the Qumran Community belonged: pp.529-530.

ESTHER Jewish exile who became the queen of the Persian king Ahasuerus; heroine of the book of Esther/pp.340, 343. See 'Portrait of Esther', p.341.

ESTHER, BOOK OF pp.340ff.

ETERNAL LIFE See under Life.

ETHIOPIA, ETHIOPIANS The Ethiopians were Egypt's southern neighbours. Their land was not modern Ethiopia, but the territory along the Nile from Aswan to Khartoum, the northern part of which corresponds to Nubia. This was known in ancient times as Cush. In the 1st millennium, Ethiopia, with its capital at Napata, at times equalled the power of Egypt, its former ruler. In the 9th century the Egyptians employed an Ethiopian general against Palestine: 2 Chronicles 14:9-15. In the 8th-7th centuries an Ethiopian dynasty took over Egypt and intervened in Palestine: 2 Kings 19:9. They continued to serve under the Saite pharaohs of the next dynasty: Jeremiah 46:9. Ethiopia was at the furthest limit of the Persian Empire and though its officials might travel in the Near East, it was too remote to be permanently ruled by the great powers: Esther 1:1; 8:9; Acts 8:27. *Map* pp.814-815.

EUNICE Mother of Timothy: 2 Timothy 1:5.

EUPHRATES Great river of Mesopotamia which flows from Turkey into the Persian Gulf, often called 'the River' in the Old Testament; one of the rivers of the garden of Eden: Genesis 2:14; 15:18, etc.

EUTYCHUS Young man who fell from a window during Paul's sermon at Troas and was restored to life: Acts 20:9ff.

EVE The first woman and first mother; prompted by the evil serpent in the creation story to disobey God: Genesis 3/pp.116-120.

EVIL-MERODACH Amel-marduk, king of Babylon, who released Jehoiachin from prison: 2 Kings 25:27; Jeremiah 52:31.

EXILE IN BABYLON When Jerusalem fell to the Babylonians in 587 BC, the population was deported. The Jews were exiles in Babylonia until King Cyrus allowed them to return in 538 BC. This period falls between the end of Kings/Chronicles and the beginning of Ezra: Ezekiel, Daniel; 'The Babylonians', pp.456-457.

EXODUS Israel's escape from slavery in Egypt, led by Moses: Exodus 13:17ff./p.165; also p.113.
•*Route of the exodus*, with *map*, p.166.

EZEKIEL Great Old Testament prophet and visionary whose prophecies to the Jewish exiles in Babylonia are recorded in the book of Ezekiel/pp.461ff.
• *Visions of God*: Ezekiel 1; 10
• *the watchman*: 3; 33
• *death of Ezekiel's wife*: 24
• *valley of dry bones*: 37
• *vision of the Temple*: 40ff.
• *the river of life*: 47.

EZEKIEL, BOOK OF pp.461ff.

EZION-GEBER See Elath.

EZRA Priest and scribe who returned to Jerusalem with a company of exiles; responsible for re-enforcing the Jewish law: Ezra 7 – 10; Nehemiah 8 – 9/pp.328ff., 337-339.

EZRA, BOOK OF pp.328ff.

F

FAIR HAVENS Harbour in Crete on Paul's voyage to Rome: Acts 27:8/*Map* p.667.

FAITH *Trust in God; belief in his promises*: Genesis 15:6; Psalm 37:3ff.; Proverbs 3:5-6; Jeremiah 17:7-8
• *a way of life*: Habakkuk 2:4; Hebrews 11; James 2
• *commitment to Jesus Christ, trusting him for salvation*: John 1:12; 8:24; Acts 16:30-31; Romans 1:16-17; 4; Galatians 3; Ephesians 2:8-9; 1 John 5:1-5
• *the means of access to God's power*: Matthew 17:20-21; Mark 9:23; James 5:13-18.

FALL The disobedience of mankind which leads to the spoiling of the world in the creation story: Genesis 3/pp.119-120; also pp.109-110.

FALSE TEACHERS Acts 20:28-31; 1 Timothy 4; Titus 1; 2 Peter 2; 1 John 4; 2 John; Revelation 2:2, 14-15, 20ff./pp.734, 737, 757, 760, 761.
• *In the Old Testament*: see under Prophets.

FAMILY See Marriage and family relationships.

FAMILY TREES pp.147 (Abraham and the 12 tribes), 267 (David), 628 (Herod).

FARMER, FARMING *Pictures* pp.42, 43, 253, 312-313, 376, 396, 484-485, 494, 686, 730, 778.

FASTING *Jesus' teaching*: Matthew 6; 9; Mark 2; Luke 5/pp.556, 560, 580.

FEASTS See Festivals.

FELIX Roman procurator who kept Paul in prison at Caesarea: Acts 23:24 – 24:27/p.667.

FESTIVALS, JEWISH Leviticus 23/p.189. See 'The great festivals', pp.190-191.

FESTUS Successor to Felix as procurator of Judea; heard Paul's case at Caesarea: Acts 25 – 26/ p.667.

FISH, FISHING Visual feature, 'Fishing in Lake Galilee', p.581. *Pictures* pp.10, 17, 20, 194 (Egypt), 401 (Assyria), 559, 584 (St Peter's fish), 629, 642, 654.

FLESH *Flesh and blood; mortals*: Genesis 6:3, 12; Psalm 78:39; Job 19:26; 34:15; Isaiah 40:5
• *the sinful self*: Romans 7:13-25; 8; Galatians 5:16-24.

FLOOD, FLOOD STORIES Genesis 7 – 8/pp.122, 125; article pp.123-124.

FOOD LAWS See under Clean and unclean creatures.

FORGIVENESS *God's loving mercy*: Exodus 34:6-7; Psalm 51; Isaiah 55:6-7; 1 John 1:5-10
• *Christ's death as the basis of God's forgiveness*: Matthew 26:26-28; John 1:29; Acts 5:31; 13:38; Ephesians 1:7; 1 John 2:2, 12
• *forgiving others*: Matthew 6:14-15; 18:21-35; Ephesians 4:32; Colossians 3:13.

FRANKINCENSE Gift of the wise men to the infant Jesus; aromatic resin used to make anointing oil, and burned with offerings to God: Matthew 2/p.552 (with picture) *Picture* p.16.

FREEDOM Isaiah 61:1; Luke 4:18; John 8:31-36; Romans 6:16-23; 8:2, 21; 2 Corinthians 3:17; Galatians 3:28; 5:1, 13; James 1:25; 2:12; 1 Peter 2:16.

FUTURE DESTINY The day is coming (Old Testament 'that day', 'the Day of the Lord') when God will judge everyone; when all his glorious promises to his people will be realized in a new heaven and earth : Isaiah 2 – 4; 65:17-25, etc.; Daniel 12:1-3; Joel; Amos 5; Zephaniah; Matthew 24 – 25; Acts 1:6-11; 1 Corinthians 3:10-15; 15:20-28, 35-58; Revelation, especially 19 – 22.

See also Heaven, Jesus Christ, return, Resurrection.

G

GABRIEL The angel sent to interpret Daniel's vision; to Zechariah to announce the birth of John the Baptist; to Mary to announce the birth of Jesus: Daniel 8:16; 9:21; Luke 1:19, 26/pp.477, 597. See 'Angels in the Bible', p.727.

GAD 1. Son of Jacob and Leah's maid, Zilpah; ancestor of one of the tribes of Israel: Genesis 30:11; 49:19. Family tree p.147.
2. Territory of the tribe of Gad: Joshua 13/*Map* p.235.

GADARA One of the 'Ten (Greek) Towns' in Palestine: see Decapolis. *Pictures* pp.84-85, 583.

GAIUS 1. A Macedonian involved in the riot at Ephesus: Acts 19:29.
2. Paul's companion on the journey to Jerusalem: Acts 20:4.
3. A Corinthian whom Paul baptized: 1 Corinthians 1:14.
4. The person to whom John wrote his third letter: 3 John 1/p.761. (These may or may not be four different people.)

GALATIA Roman province in what is now central Turkey, where Paul founded churches, to which he wrote: Acts 16:6; 18:23; Galatians 1:2/*Map* p.680 *Picture* p.712.

GALATIANS, LETTER TO THE pp.711ff.

GALILEE Region and lake in northern Israel; home area of Jesus and a number of the disciples; centre of much of Jesus' ministry: 1 Kings 9:11; 2 Kings 15:29; Isaiah 9:1; Luke 4:14; 5:1ff.; 8:22ff.; John 21, etc.; Acts 9:31/p.579/*Map* p.526B3 See 'The land of Israel', pp.36-37 (with picture) *Pictures* pp.10, 37, 39, 241, 358, 375, 405, 448, 542, 583, 587, 604, 624.

GALLIO Proconsul of Achaia (and brother of Seneca the

tutor of Nero) whose decision against the Jews who brought charges against Paul gave the church new freedom: Acts 18/pp.658, 697 *Picture* p.697.

GAMALIEL Influential rabbi and member of the Sanhedrin who advised cautious handling of the apostles: Acts 5:34ff.; 22:3/p.646.

GAMES *Greek, pan-Hellenic*: p.672; *pictures* pp.696; 660 (board game)
• *Roman: picture* p.722 (chariot race), 616 (soldiers' games).

GATH One of the five Philistine towns; home of Goliath; later refuge of David: Joshua 11; 22; 1 Samuel 5:8; 17:4; 21:10ff. etc./*Map* p.258.

GATH-HEPHER Place from which Jonah came: 2 Kings 14:25/*Map* p.104B2.

GAZA One of the Philistine towns; features in the story of Samson: Joshua 13:3; Judges 16; 1 Samuel 6:17, etc./ *Map* p.104A6.

GEBA Town which features in the exploit of Jonathan and his armour-bearer; northern limit of Judah: 1 Samuel 14; 2 Kings 23:8; Nehemiah 11:31/*Map* p.104B5.

GEBAL Phoenician town of Byblos in Lebanon; provided workmen for the Temple: Joshua 13:5; 1 Kings 5:18.

GEDALIAH Appointed governor of Judah by Nebuchadnezzar; assassinated after only a few months: 2 Kings 25; Jeremiah 39:14 – 41:18/ pp.304, 452.

GEHAZI Servant of Elisha; punished for seeking reward from Naaman: 2 Kings 4 – 5; 8:4ff./p.295.

GENEALOGIES See Family tree and note 'Genealogies are important', p.550.

GENESIS, BOOK OF pp.115ff.

GENNESARET Another name for Lake Galilee.

GERAR Town in southern Israel ruled by Abimelech in

Abraham's days: Genesis 10:19; 20:1ff. etc./ *Map* p.104A6.

GERASA Jerash, one of the 'Ten (Greek) Towns' in Palestine: see Decapolis. *Pictures* pp.47, 671.

GERIZIM Mountain opposite Mt Ebal near Shechem where blessing was pronounced on those who kept the law; place of Jotham's parable, and later of the Samaritan temple: Deuteronomy 27:12; Judges 9:7; John 4:20/*Map* p.104B4.

GERSHON, GERSHONITES Son of Levi; head of one of the three Levitical families: Exodus 6:16-17; Numbers 3:17ff./pp.193-194.

GESHEM An Arabian; one of Nehemiah's main opponents: Nehemiah 2:19; 6:1ff./ p.334.

GESHUR Region and town in southern Syria; Absalom took refuge here, in his mother's home: Joshua 12:5; 2 Samuel 3:3; 13:38, etc./*Map* p.268.

GETHSEMANE Garden across the Kidron Valley from Jerusalem where Jesus went on the night of his arrest: Matthew 26:36; John 18:1, etc./*Map* p.630 *Picture* p.640.

GEZER Joshua campaigned against this Canaanite town; Pharaoh gave it to Solomon, who fortified it: Joshua 10:33, etc.; 1 Kings 9:15-16/ p.284; 'King Solomon's fortified cities', p.283/ *Map* p.233 *Picture* p.276.

GEZER CALENDAR *Picture* p.43.

GIBEAH Town a few miles north of Jerusalem; home of Saul: Judges 19; 1 Samuel 10:5, 10, 26ff.; 13; 14; 23:19, etc./*Map* p.104B5.

GIBEON The inhabitants of this town tricked Joshua into an agreement, which Saul later broke; David and Ishbosheth's men fought here; sanctuary in Solomon's day, where the Tabernacle was kept: Joshua 9; 2 Samuel

2:12ff.; 20:8; 21; 1 Kings 3:4ff.; 1 Chronicles 21:29/ *Map* p.104B5.

GIDEON Delivered Israel from the Midianites in the time of the Judges: Judges 6 – 8/ pp.221, 244-245, with map and diagram.

GIHON 1. One of four rivers of the garden of Eden.
2. A spring outside Jerusalem where Solomon was anointed king and from which Hezekiah channelled water by a tunnel into the city: Genesis 2:13; 1 Kings 1:38; 2 Chronicles 32:30/visual feature 'Hezekiah's conduit', p.325.

GILBOA Ridge of hills where Saul gathered his army for the battle against the Philistines in which he and Jonathan died: 1 Samuel 28:4; 31, etc./*Map* p.104B3.

GILEAD Israelite land east of the Jordan; famous for its flocks and spices; region from which Jair, Jephthah and Elijah came: Genesis 37:25; Joshua 17:1; Judges 10:3; 11; 1 Kings 17:1; Song of Solomon 4:1/*Map* p.209.

GILGAL Place near Jericho where the Israelites marked their crossing of the River Jordan; site of an important shrine; on Samuel's circuit as Judge: Joshua 4:20; Judges 3:19; 1 Samuel 7:16; 10:8, etc.; 2 Samuel 19:15; Hosea 4:15, etc./*Map* p.104C5.

GIVING Exodus 35:5ff.; 2 Kings 12:4-16; Matthew 6:1-4; Luke 12:16-21; 21:1-4; 1 Corinthians 8 – 9; 16:1-2/p.599; see also under Tithes.

GNOSTICS, GNOSTICISM pp.71ff., 723, 725. See also Mystery religions.

GOD One God who has disclosed himself in three persons – Father, Son (Jesus Christ) and Holy Spirit: Deuteronomy 6:4; Genesis 1:1-2 and John 1:1-3; Judges 14:6, etc.; Isaiah 40:13;

45:18-22; 61:1; 63:10, etc.; Matthew 28:19; John 14:15-26; 2 Corinthians 13:14; Ephesians 2:18; 4:4-6; 2 Thessalonians 2:13-14; 1 Peter 1:1-2.
• *The 'otherness' of God: the eternal Spirit; the Creator*: Genesis 1 – 2; Deuteronomy 33:26-27; 1 Kings 8:27; Job 38ff.; Psalms 8; 100; 104; Isaiah 40:12-28; 55:9; John 4:23-24; Romans 1:19-20; Revelation 1:8
• *the power of God*: Genesis 17:1; Exodus 32:11; Numbers 24:4; Job 40 – 42:2; Isaiah 9:6; 45 – 46; Daniel 3:17; Matthew 26:53; John 19:10-11; Acts 12; Revelation 19:1-16
• *God's knowledge*: Genesis 4:10; Job 28:20-27; Psalm 139:1-6; Daniel 2:17-23; Matthew 6:7-8; John 2:23-25; 4:25-29; Ephesians 1:3-12
• *God's presence everywhere*: Genesis 28:10-17; Psalm 139:7-12; Jeremiah 23:23-24; Acts 17:26-28
• *God's holiness and righteousness*: Exodus 20; Leviticus 11:44-45; Joshua 24:19-28; Psalms 7; 25:8-10; 99; Isaiah 1:12ff.; 6:1-5; John 17:25-26; Romans 1:18 – 3:26; Ephesians 4:17-24; Hebrews 12:7-14; 1 Peter 1:13-16; 1 John 1:5-10
• *God's love and mercy*: Deuteronomy 7:6-13; Psalms, e.g., 23; 25; 36:5-12; 103; Isaiah 40:1-2, 27-31; 41:8-20; 43; Jeremiah 31:2-14; Hosea 6; 11; 14; John 3:16-17; 10:7-18; 13:1; 14:15-31; 15:9, 12ff.; Romans 8:35-38; Galatians 2:20; Ephesians 2:4-10; 1 John 3:1-3, 16; 4:7-21.

GOG Leader of invading northern peoples to be destroyed by God; Ezekiel 38 – 39/p.471. 'Gog and Magog': quoted as symbol of the anti-God forces in the final onslaught: Revelation 20:8/p.776.

GOLD AND JEWELLERY *Pictures* pp.139, 406 (Yemenite), 132, 133 (from Ur), 154, 165, 286 (Egyptian), 341, 343, 475 (Persian), 185, 284, 755.

GOLIATH Philistine champion killed by David: 1 Samuel 17/pp.261-262.

GOMER The prophet Hosea's unfaithful wife: pp.483-484 and see p.486.

GOMORRAH See 'Where were Sodom and Gomorrah?', p.136. Town at the southern end of the Dead Sea violently destroyed for its wickedness: Genesis 14; 19; Isaiah 1:9-10, etc.; Matthew 10:15, etc./*Map* p.127.

GOSHEN Nile delta region in Egypt, where Jacob and his family settled: Genesis 45:10; Exodus 8:22, etc./*Map* p.166.

GOSPEL The 'good news' brought by Jesus – see margin note p.577 and '"Good News!" – from the first Christians', p.655: Mark 1:14-15; Luke 8:1, etc.
• *The gospel message*: e.g. Matthew 4:17; John 1:11-13; 3:1-21, 31-36; Acts 2; 13; 17; Romans 1 – 8 (especially 1:16-17; 5:1; 6:23); 2 Corinthians 5:17ff.; Galatians 2:20; 4:4-7; Ephesians 1:3ff.; 1 John 1:1-4; 5:11-12.
See also Kingdom, Life, Salvation.

GOSPEL OF THOMAS p.539.

GOSPELS See Matthew, Mark, Luke, John/pp.549ff.; 'The Gospels and Jesus Christ', pp.538-544; 'Studying the Gospels', pp.545-547.

GOZAN Town in northern Mesopotamia annexed by the Assyrians, to which the Israelites were deported: 2 Kings 17:6; 19:12.

GRACE God's love poured out on undeserving humanity (the Old Testament uses a number of different terms):

Deuteronomy 7:6-9; Psalms 23:6; 25:6-10; 51:1; Jeremiah 31:2-3.
• *God's grace in salvation*: Ephesians 2:4-9; Romans 3:19-24; 6:14
• *the Christian's dependence on God's grace*: 2 Corinthians 12:9; Ephesians 4:7; 1 Timothy 1:2; 1 Peter 5:5, 10; 2 Peter 3:18.

GREAT SEA Name used throughout the Old Testament for the Mediterranean.

GREECE, GREEKS Known in the Near East by the name of their Asiatic territory, Ionia – the 'Javan' of the Old Testament: Isaiah 66:19; Ezekiel 27:13; Daniel 8:21; 10:20; 11:2; Zechariah 9:13. Alexander's conquests brought Israel under Greek control (with the rest of the eastern Mediterranean) and under the influence of Greek civilization, culture and thought; see 'The Greeks', pp.521-523 (with pictures): Daniel 11; John 12:20; Acts 6; 17; 18.
• *In Daniel*: pp.477, 482. *Map* p.521 (Greek Empire). The New Testament word for Greeks is *hellenes* (Romans 1:14, though this word was often used of Gentiles in general, e.g. John 7:35). See 'Roman rule, Greek culture', pp.670-673; 'The city of Athens', pp.659-660; 'The city of Corinth', pp.696-697; 'The city of Ephesus', pp.716-717, all with pictures. Ship picture p.497.

HABAKKUK Prophet whose book records his puzzlement over God's use of the Chaldeans to punish his people.

HABAKKUK, BOOK OF pp.502-503.

HABIRU p.237.

HABOR Tributary of the

Euphrates; Gozan stood on its banks: 2 Kings 17:6.

HADADEZER/HADAREZER King of Zobah, defeated by David: 2 Samuel 8; 10; 1 Kings 11:23; 1 Chronicles 18 – 19.

HADASSAH Esther's earlier name.

HAGAR Sarah's Egyptian servant; mother of Ishmael: Genesis 16; 21/p.137. See 'Hagar', p.131.

HAGGAI Prophet who stirred the people to rebuild the Temple after Jews returned from exile.

HAGGAI, BOOK OF pp.505-506.

HAM Noah's son; father of a number of nations: Genesis 5:32; 9:18ff.;10:6ff./pp.122, 125 *Map* p.126.

HAMAN Villain of the book of Esther, who plotted against the Jews: Esther/pp.342-343.

HAMATH Hama on the River Orontes in Syria; ideal northern limit of Israel; conquered by Assyria: Joshua 13:5; 2 Samuel 8:9; 1 Kings 8:65; 2 Kings 17:24; 18:34, etc./*Map* p.458.

HAMMURABI King of Babylon, compiler of a code of laws: pp.106, 171 (with picture).

HANAMEL Jeremiah's cousin who sold him the field at Anathoth during the Babylonian invasion: Jeremiah 32/p.451.

HANANI Nehemiah's brother, who told him of the trouble in Jerusalem: Nehemiah 1:2/p.334.

HANANIAH False prophet denounced by Jeremiah: Jeremiah 28/p.450.

HANNAH Mother of Samuel: Samuel 1 – 2/pp.255-256. See 'Hannah', p.257.

HAROD Spring where Gideon camped and chose the small force which defeated the Midianites: Judges 7:1/ *Map* p.245.

HARRAN Town in north Mesopotamia to which Abraham went on the first

stage of his journey to Canaan; where Jacob served Laban; later dominated by Assyria: Genesis 11:31; 12:4-5; 29:4, etc.; 2 Kings 19:12/*Map* p.127.

HARVEST *Pictures* pp.42, 190, 253, 312-313, 376, 484-485, 730.

HAZAEL Seized the throne of Syria after assassinating Benhadad, following Elisha's prediction: 1 Kings 19:15-17; 2 Kings 8ff./pp.292, 295.

HAZOR Important Canaanite city in the north of Israel; Joshua defeated Jabin of Hazor and destroyed the city; the army of a later Jabin of Hazor was defeated by Deborah and Barak; rebuilt and fortified by Solomon; fell to Assyria: Joshua 11; Judges 4; 1 Kings 9:15; 2 Kings 15:29/p.233; 'King Solomon's fortified cities', p.283 (with picture)/*Map* p.104C2 *Pictures* pp.231, 236.

HEALING Cult of Asclepius, p.673.

HEAVEN The 'home' of God; the perfect, unseen world (also sometimes simply a word for 'sky'): Deuteronomy 26:15; Nehemiah 9:6; Matthew 5:45; 6:9; Mark 13:32; 1 Peter 1:4.
• *The 'new heaven and earth'*: Isaiah 65:17ff.; 2 Peter 3:10-13; Revelation 21 – 22.

HEBREWS, LETTER TO THE pp.740ff.

HEBRON Early name Kiriath-arba, in the Judean hills; base of Abraham and the patriarchs, who were buried in the cave of Machpelah; conquered by Caleb; David's first capital; where Absalom staged his rebellion: Genesis 13:18; 23; 35:27; Joshua 14:6-15; 2 Samuel 2:1-4; 15:9-10, etc./*Map* p.104B6 *Pictures* pp.140, 266.

HELIOPOLIS (ON) Sacred city of the sun god in ancient Egypt: Genesis 41:45;

Jeremiah 43:13/*Map* p.152.
HELL *Sheol*, Old Testament place of the dead (= New Testament 'Hades'): Psalms 88:3-5; 139:8; Proverbs 9:18; Isaiah 5:14; 38:18; Amos 9:2. See 'Old Testament views of the afterlife', pp.478-479. New Testament *Gehenna*, the fate of those finally cut off from God: Matthew 5:22, 29-30; 10:28; 23:33; 25:41; 2 Peter 2:4; Revelation 1:18; 20:13-15.
HELLENISTS, HELLENISM See Greece, Greeks.
HEMAN Appointed by David as one of the leaders of the Temple music: 1 Chronicles 16:41-42; 25/p.314.
HERMON 3,000m/9,000ft mountain on the borders of Israel, Lebanon and Syria; also called Sirion; its snows form part of the source of the Jordan; probably the mountain where Jesus was transfigured: Joshua 12:1, etc.; Psalms 42:6: 133:3; Matthew 17:1, etc./ *Map* p.526C1.
HEROD 1. Herod the Great: Matthew 2; Luke 15.
2. Herod Antipas: Matthew 14; Mark 6; Luke 3; 9; 23; Acts 4:27; 13:1.
3. Herod Agrippa I: Acts 12. See 'The Herod family', pp.627-628. *Pictures* pp.585 (Herod's fortress, Machaerus),617 (Herod family tomb).
HERODIAS Wife of Herod Antipas who brought about the death of John the Baptist: Matthew 14; Mark 6; Luke 3:19/p.584.
HESHBON Moabite, Amorite and later Israelite town east of the Jordan: Numbers 21:25ff., etc./*Map* p.104C5.
HEZEKIAH One of Judah's most outstanding kings; contemporary of Isaiah; besieged in Jerusalem by the Assyrians: 2 Kings 18 – 20; 2 Chronicles 29 – 32; Isaiah

36 – 39/pp.300-303 (including 'Sennacherib's Prism'; 'The siege of Lachish') ; 324, 325, 431. See also 'The Assyrians', p.433.
HEZEKIAH'S CONDUIT Visual feature p.325.
HIERAPOLIS Town with hot medicinal springs in the Lycus Valley (western Turkey) near Laodicea and Colossae; Epaphras may have founded the church there: Colossians 4:12-13/ *Map* p.680 *Picture* p.769.
HIEROGLYPH Egyptian pictographic writing. *Picture* p.157.
HIGH PLACE Pagan worship site: *pictures* pp.236, 276, 444, 495.
HIGH PRIEST Exodus 28 – 29/ p.174. See 'Priesthood in the Old Testament', pp.185-186 (with picture).
• *High priesthood of Jesus*: Hebrews 4:14 – 10:25/ pp.743-745.
HILKIAH High priest at the time of Josiah; discovered the book of the law: 2 Kings 22 – 23; 2 Chronicles 34.
HINNOM Valley outside Jerusalem; in the time of the prophets the pagan god Molech was worshipped here, with child sacrifice; later a place where corpses and refuse were burned; it provided the name for hell – Gehenna: 2 Kings 23:10; Jeremiah 7:31-32, etc./ *Map* p.630.
HIRAM King of Tyre, in alliance with David and Solomon; supplied cedar and skilled labour for the Temple; joined with Solomon to operate a Red Sea trading fleet: 1 Kings 5; 9 – 10/ pp.278, 284, 318 and 'Solomon's trade', p.319.
HISTORIANS' PERSPECTIVES 'Our world – their world', p.95; 'A historian looks at the New Testament', p.650.
HISTORY, OF ISRAEL See 'Israel's History':

introduction, pp.220ff. and the Old Testament history books: Joshua – Esther/ pp.225ff.; also p.67.
HISTORY, WORLD See 'Making connections – the Bible and world history', pp.26-27.
HITTITES An Indo-European-speaking people who established a civilization in central Asia Minor and controlled much of northern Syria in the 14th and 13th centuries BC. Their empire was destroyed by northern invaders (see Philistines) about 1200 BC. After the destruction of the Hittite Empire in Asia Minor, some of the people migrated to north Syria where they dominated such city-states as Carchemish (see also Cilicia). These people, now known as Neo- or Syro-Hittites, were the biblical Hittites of the period of Israel's kings. Abraham purchased a burial-plot for Sarah from Hittites occupying the Hebron area, and Esau married two Hittite women: Genesis 23; 27/p.139.
Uriah the Hittite served as a mercenary in David's army – his wife, Bathsheba, was seduced by the king: 2 Samuel 11/pp.270-271. *Pictures* pp.139 (Hittite marriage contract), 210 (Hittite law-code).
HIVITES See under Hurrians.
HOLINESS God's moral perfection, separation from evil and distinctive character: Exodus 3:4-6; 15:11; 1 Chronicles 16:10; Isaiah 6:3-5; 10:20; Hosea 11:9; John 17:11; Revelation 4:8.
• *Expressed in Jesus*: Acts 4:27, 30; John 1:14-18; 14:6ff.
• *in God's people*: Exodus 19:6; Luke 1:74-75; 2 Corinthians 7:1; Ephesians 4:23-24; Colossians 3:12ff.; Hebrews 12:10-11; 1 Peter 1:15-16; 2:9.
HOLY SPIRIT One with God the Father and Jesus Christ,

actively at work in the world, particularly in and through God's people.
• *Nature and person*: Genesis 1:1-2; 2 Samuel 23:2-5; Psalm 139:7-12; Matthew 12:25-32; 28:19; John 14:15-17; 15:26-27; Acts 5:1-3; 20:28; Romans 8:9-11; 2 Corinthians 3:15-18; 13:14; Ephesians 4:29-31
• *work*: Exodus 31:3; Judges 3:10; 14:6, etc.; Psalm 51:10-12; Isaiah 11:1-3; 32:14-18; 42:1-4; 63:10-14; Ezekiel 36:26-27; John 3:5-8; 14:25-26; 16:7-15; Acts 1:6-8; 2; 11:16-18; Romans 5:1-5; 8:1-27; 1 Corinthians 2:1-13; 12:3-13; 2 Corinthians 1:20-22; Galatians 5:16-25; 2 Peter 1:20-21. See 'The Holy Spirit in Acts', pp.661-662.
'HOLY WAR' p.204; article p.234.
HOPE The confident expectation which comes through trust in God: Romans 4:18; 5:1-5; 8:24-25; 12:12; 15:4; 1 Corinthians 13:13; 15:19ff.; Colossians 1:5, 27; 1 Peter 1:3ff.; Hebrews 11:1ff.
HOPHNI AND PHINEHAS Eli's unprincipled sons: 1 Samuel 2; 4.
HOREB Another name for Mt Sinai.
HORMAH Here, because of their disobedience, the Israelites were defeated by the Canaanites: Numbers 14:45; also 21:3; Joshua 15:30, etc./*Map* p.104B6.
HOSEA Prophet whose book concerns God's love for his faithless people.
HOSEA, BOOK OF pp.483ff.
HOSHEA Last king of the northern kingdom of Israel, 732-723 BC; 2 Kings 17/p.300.
HOSHEA, SEAL *Picture* p.300.
HOUSE *Pictures* pp.34-35 (Herodian), 132 (Ur), 231

(Canaanite), 232 (Philistine), 242 (Israelite), 523, 607 (of the rich), 670 (Hellenistic).

HULDAH Prophetess consulted by Hilkiah after he discovered the book of the law: 2 Kings 22:14ff.; 2 Chronicles 34:22ff./p.303. See 'Prophets and prophecy', p.423.

HURRIANS A northern people who spread through the Near East during the 2nd millennium BC. Prominent in the population at Nuzi, where customs similar to those of the patriarchs are attested in 15th-century BC documents. Hurrians appear in the Bible as 'Horites' and probably 'Hivites' (the v represents Hebrew w, which could be confused with r in later forms of the script).
The Horites were driven out of Edom by Esau. Hivites occupied land close to Mt Hermon, in the north. Solomon conscripted them for his building projects.
• *Horites*: Deuteronomy 2:12; Joshua 9:6-7
• *Hivites*: Genesis 10:17; Deuteronomy 7:1; 1 Kings 9:20.

HUSHAI David's friend who persuaded Absalom not to take Ahithophel's advice: 2 Samuel 15:32 – 17:15/ p.272.

HYMENEUS Disciplined by Paul for unsettling people's faith with false teaching: 1 Timothy 1:20; 2 Timothy 2:17.

I

IBLEAM Town in the north of Israel where Jehu killed Ahaziah: Joshua 17:11-12; 2 Kings 9:27; 15:10/ Map p.104B3.

ICONIUM Modern Konya in Turkey; Paul preached here on his first mission: Acts 13:51; 14:19-21/ Map p.652.

IDEOLOGIES See 'Making connections – the Bible and world history', pp.26-27.

IDOLS, IDOLATRY The people of Israel, called to exclusive worship of the one true God, were constantly 'seduced' by the appeal of gods worshipped by the nations around them. The Old Testament records this centuries-long struggle to keep the faith: Exodus 20; 32; 2 Kings 17 – 18; Isaiah 40; 44; Jeremiah 10; Ezekiel 14; Daniel 3; Hosea 2; 4/pp.175, 290-291, 434-435, 446, 465, 474, 483.
• *Food offered to idols*: 1 Corinthians 8; 10/pp.694, 699.
Pictures of pagan gods: 97, 175 (Egyptian apis bull), 362 (Assyrian demon), 436 (Babylonian demon), 663, 718 (Artemis/Diana of Ephesus). See also Ashtaroth, Baal, Worship.

IDUMEA Edom, including part of Judah after the exile; the Herod family were Idumaeans/Map p.526A7.

ILLYRICUM Roman province in present-day Bosnia, where Paul preached: Romans 15:19/Map p.680.

INCARNATION God become one of us: Matthew 1 – 2; Luke 1 – 2; John 1:1-18; Romans 8:3; Philippians 2:6-11; Colossians 1:13-22; Hebrews 1 – 2; 4:14 – 5:10; 1 John 1 – 2:2. See '"God with us" – the incarnation', pp.551-552.

INN Picture p.610.

INSCRIPTIONS Gezer calendar, p.43; Babylonian creation account, p.117; 'Epic of Gilgamesh' flood account, p.123; Sumerian document from Ur, p.132; cuneiform multiplication table, p.133; marriage contract tablet, p.139; Hammurabi's law-code, p.171; Hittite law-code, p.210; Boundary stone, p.211; seal of Shema, p.285; Black Obelisk,

p.296; Hoshea seal, p.300; Sennacherib's Prism, p.301; Lachish letter, p.304; capture of Jerusalem, p.304; Hezekiah's tunnel, p.325; Babylonian Chronicle, Battle of Carchemish, p.326; Nebuchadnezzar's brick, p. 456; Babylonian Chronicle, fall of Nineveh, p.456; Seal of Darius I, p.477; Shebna's tomb, p.479; Cyrus Cylinder, p.481; of Pontius Pilate, p.535; of Augustus Caesar, p.600; Nazareth Decree, p.658; forbidding non-Jews to enter the Temple, p.665; of Gallio, p.697; of Erastus, p.697; theatre-seat at Miletus, p.719; on slave-tag, p.739.
See 'Bringing the past to life', p.31 (with pictures including the Rosetta Stone, Merneptah stele and Hoshea's servant's seal).

INTERPRETING THE BIBLE See 'Keys to understanding', pp.46ff.; 'Understanding the Bible', pp.50-51; 'Interpreting the Bible down the ages', pp.53ff; 'The text and the message', pp.58-59.

ISAAC Son of Abraham; father of Jacob and Esau: Genesis 21 – 35/pp.133 and 135ff.
• *'Sacrifice' of*: Genesis 22
• *wife for*: 24
• *blessing of Jacob*: 27.

ISAIAH Great Old Testament prophet: 2 Kings 19 – 20; Isaiah/pp.300-301, 409ff., 417ff.
•*Call*: Isaiah 6
• great prophecies: the branch, Isaiah 4; Immanuel, 7; the great light, a son is born, 9; a shoot from Jesse, wolf shall dwell with the lamb, 11 – 12; desert shall blossom, 35; comfort my people, 40; 'Servant Songs', 42; 49; 50; 52 – 53; 61; arise, shine, 60
• Assyrian invasion: 36 – 39.

ISAIAH, BOOK OF pp.417ff. Picture p.32 (Isaiah Dead Sea Scroll).

ISHBOSHETH Saul's son, made king by Abner: 2 Samuel

2 – 4/pp.264, 266.

ISHMAEL, ISHMAELITES Son of Abraham and Hagar, and his descendants: Genesis 16 – 17; 25/pp.131, 135, 137, 146.

ISHTAR See Ashtaroth; 'The Babylonians', p.457 (with Ishtar Gate picture).

ISLAM See 'Making connections – the Bible and world history', p.27; 'The Qur'an and the Bible', pp.86-88.

ISRAEL 1. Later name of Jacob, and the nation descended from him.
2. The land occupied by the 12 tribes: after the division, the northern kingdom, excluding Judah and Benjamin/Maps pp.104 (Old Testament), 526 (New Testament). See also 'The land of Israel', pp.36-37; 'The promised land', pp.214-215 (both with pictures).

ISSACHAR 1. Son of Jacob and father of one of the tribes of Israel: Genesis 30:18; 49:14ff. Family tree p.147.
2. Territory of the tribe of Issachar: Joshua 19:17-23/Map p.235.

ITHAMAR Son of Aaron; priest of Israel: Exodus 6:23; Numbers 3ff./p.194.

ITTAI Philistine from Gath who stood by David during Absalom's rebellion: 2 Samuel 15; 18.

ITUREA Philip's tetrarchy north-east of Lake Galilee: Luke 3:1/Map p.526C1.

IVORIES Pictures pp.31, 107, 279, 293, 463, 493.

J

JABBOK Tributary flowing into the River Jordan from the east, beside which Jacob wrestled with an angel; boundary of Ammon: Genesis 32:22ff.; Numbers 21:24/ Map p.104C4 Picture p.145.

JABESH-GILEAD Town east of the Jordan which features in

Judges 21 and the story of Saul: 1 Samuel 11; 31:11-13/*Map* p.104C4.

JABIN King of Hazor whose army was defeated by Deborah and Barak: Judges 4/p.241.

JACOB Son of Isaac who supplanted his elder brother Esau; father of the 12 tribes of Israel: Genesis 25 – 49/pp.140ff. and 'Jacob', pp.144-145.
• *The birthright*: Genesis 25
• *Isaac's blessing*: 27
• *dream at Bethel*: 28
• *Jacob and Laban*: 29 – 31
• *Jacob wrestles with God*: 32
• *God's promise*: 35
• *journey to Egypt*: 44
• *blessing of his sons*: 49.

JAEL Wife of Heber; killed Canaanite general Sisera with a tent peg: Judges 4/p.240.

JAIRUS Synagogue official whose daughter Jesus restored to life: Mark 5:1ff./p.583.

JAMES 1. Son of Zebedee, brother of John; one of the 12 apostles (see 'The twelve disciples of Jesus', p.557): Matthew 4:21f.; 10:2; 17:1ff.; Mark 10:35ff.; Acts 12:2/p.651.
2. Son of Alphaeus: another of the apostles (see 'The twelve disciples of Jesus', p.558), probably the same as 'James the younger': Matthew 10:3, etc./p.558.
3. Brother of Jesus who became leader of the Jerusalem church; author of the letter of James: Matthew 13:55; Acts 12:17; 15:13ff.; 21:18; 1 Corinthians 15:7; Galatians 1:19; 2:9; James/pp.654, 704, 749-751.

JAMES, LETTER OF pp.749ff.

JAPHETH One of Noah's three sons; ancestor of a number of nations: Genesis 5:32; 9:18ff.; 10:1ff./p.125 *Map* p.126.

JASON Paul's host who was held answerable for him at Thessalonica: Acts 17:5ff.

JAVAN Coastlands and islands occupied by the Ionians (Greeks).

JAZER Amorite town captured by the Israelites, famous for its vines: Numbers 21:32; 1 Chronicles 26:31; Isaiah 16:8-9.

JEBUS Early name for Jerusalem: Joshua 18:28, etc.

JEDUTHUN Appointed by David as one of the leaders of the Temple music: 1 Chronicles 16:41-42; 25/p.314.

JEHOAHAZ 1. Son of Jehu, king of Israel 814-798 BC: 2 Kings 13 – 14/p.298.
2. Son of Josiah, king of Judah 609 BC; deposed by Pharaoh Necho: 2 Kings 23:30ff.; 2 Chronicles 36/pp.304, 326.

JEHOASH King of Israel 798-782 BC: 2 Kings 13/p.298.

JEHOIACHIN Son of Jehoiakim, king of Judah 597 BC; taken to Babylon by Nebuchadnezzar, released from prison by his successor: 2 Kings 24; 25:27ff.; 2 Chronicles 36; Jeremiah 52:31ff./pp.304, 326, 449, 458.

JEHOIADA The name of a number of individuals, notably the chief priest responsible for the coup which dethroned Athaliah and placed Joash on the throne of Judah: 2 Kings 11 – 12; 2 Chronicles 23 – 24/pp.298, 323.

JEHOIAKIM Eliakim, son of Josiah, king of Judah 609-597 BC; placed on the throne by Pharaoh Necho; king who burnt Jeremiah's scroll of prophecies: 2 Kings 23:34ff.; 2 Chronicles 36; Jeremiah 22:18ff.; 26; 36/pp.304, 326, 448-449, 450, 452.

JEHONADAB/JONADAB 1. One of David's family, involved in the rape of Tamar: 2 Samuel 13.
2. Son of Rechab, who helped Jehu wipe out the worshippers of Baal: 2 Kings 10.

JEHORAM/JORAM 1. Son of Ahab, king of Israel 852-841 BC, killed by Jehu: 2 Kings 3; 8 – 9; 2 Chronicles 22/p.294.
2. Son of Jehoshaphat, king of Judah 853-841 BC: 2 Kings 8:16ff.; 2 Chronicles 21/pp.297, 322.

JEHOSHAPHAT Son of Asa, king of Judah 873-848 BC; allied by marriage to Ahab of Israel; fought with him against the Syrians at Ramoth-gilead: 1 Kings 22; 2 Kings 3; 2 Chronicles 17 – 21/pp.293, 320-321.

JEHOSHEBA/JEHOSHABEATH Princess of Judah and wife of Jehoiada who saved the life of Joash: 2 Kings 11:2-3; 2 Chronicles 22:11-12.

JEHU Anointed by God through Elisha to destroy Ahab's line and become king of Israel 841-814 BC: 2 Kings 9 – 10/pp.297-298 *Picture* p.296 (Black Obelisk).

JEHUDI Officer at Jehoiakim's court who read Jeremiah's scroll to the king: Jeremiah 36.

JEPHTHAH The Judge whose vow resulted in the death of his daughter: Judges 11 – 12/pp.221, 244-245.

JEREMIAH Great prophet of Judah at the time of its fall to Babylon: 2 Chronicles 35:25; 36:12, 21-22; Jeremiah/pp.327, 439ff.; 'Portrait of Jeremiah', pp.441-442.
• *Call*: Jeremiah 1
• *the potter*: 18 – 19
• *the yoke of Babylon*: 27 – 28
• *the new covenant*: 31
• *purchase of the field*: 32
• *reading of the scroll*: 36
• *in the cistern*: 38
• *taken to Egypt*: 43.

JEREMIAH, BOOK OF pp.439ff.

JERICHO An 'oasis' in the desert north of the Dead Sea, blessed with a perennial freshwater spring, the reason for a history of settlement stretching back to about 8000 BC!

Jericho, guarding the fords of the River Jordan, was the town to which Joshua sent the spies, and the site of Israel's first great victory in the promised land. It features in Judges and the Elijah-Elisha story. Here Jesus gave Bartimaeus his sight, and Zacchaeus was converted; in the parable of the Good Samaritan, the Jew was attacked on the Jerusalem-Jericho road: Joshua 2:61; 6; Judges 12:13; 2 Kings 2; Mark 10:46; Luke19:1ff.; 10:30/pp.227, 230; 'Cities of the conquest', p.229/*Map* p.104C5 *Pictures* pp.101, 224, 435.

JEROBOAM 1. Jeroboam I, first king of the northern kingdom of Israel 931-910 BC, who set up shrines to rival Jerusalem: 1 Kings 11:26 – 14:20/pp.285-286, 289.
2. Jeroboam II, one of Israel's most illustrious kings 793-753 BC; social evils and empty ritual of his reign attacked by the prophets: 2 Kings 14:23-29; Amos 7/pp.299, 490.

JERUBBAAL Another name for Gideon.

JERUSALEM Probably the 'Salem' of which Melchizedek was king. Taken from the Jebusites by David (see capture diagram p.267), Jerusalem became the capital and holy city of Israel, and of the southern kingdom of Judah after the kingdoms divided. Here Solomon built the Temple. Jerusalem was besieged by the Assyrians in Hezekiah's reign; besieged again and destroyed by the Babylonians in 587 BC. Zerubbabel rebuilt the Temple after the exile; Nehemiah rebuilt the walls. Both city and Temple were despoiled and desecrated by the Syrian King Antiochus Epiphanes. When the Romans took over the Greek

Empire, Jerusalem remained subject. King Herod rebuilt the Temple; here Jesus was presented as a baby, and came when he was 12; he visited Jerusalem during his ministry; his trial, crucifixion and resurrection all took place here. In Jerusalem the church came into being at Pentecost, and from here it spread far and wide; here too the council on the position of the Gentiles was held. Jerusalem fell to the Romans in AD 70, after the Jewish Revolt. See 'Jerusalem in New Testament times', pp.630-631.

See Genesis 14:18; 2 Samuel 5; 1 Kings 6; 2 Kings 18 – 19; 25; 2 Chronicles 32; Ezra 5; Nehemiah 3ff.; Isaiah 36 – 37; Luke 2; 19:28 – 24, etc.; John 5, etc.; Acts 2; 15/pp.130, 266-268, 278ff., 324, 330-331, 334ff., 599, 614ff., 626ff., 644ff., 654. *Maps* pp.104B5, 274 (City of David), 336 (at the time of Nehemiah), 630 (in New Testament times) *Pictures* pp.19, 34-35, 243, 274, 278, 311, 316-317, 318, 329, 330, 337, 338, 339, 387, 397, 400, 447, 451, 452, 542, 543, 548, 555, 568, 590, 626, 630, 631, 632, 635, 640, 644 *Models and reconstructions* pp.505, 532-533, 533, 597, 607, 615, 616, 632, 646.

JESSE David's father; grandson of Ruth and Boaz: 1 Samuel 16 – 17.

JESUS CHRIST, LIFE See 'The Gospels and Jesus Christ', pp.538ff. (with outline life and pictures); '"God with us" – the incarnation', pp.551-552; 'Jesus' resurrection', pp.619-620; 'Jesus and the Old Testament', pp.569-570; 'Jesus and the kingdom', pp.563-564; 'Jesus and money', pp.566-567; 'Jesus and the cities', p.587; 'Jesus and women', p.589.

• *Birth*: Matthew 1; Luke 12/pp.550-551, 596-599 ('Virgin birth' article)
• *family line*: Matthew 1; Luke 3/pp.550, 601
• *baptism*: Matthew 3; Mark 1; Luke 3/p.554
• *temptation*: Matthew 4; Mark 1; Luke 4/pp.554-555, 601
• *transfiguration*: Matthew 17; Mark 9; Luke 9/p.585

• *triumphant entry into Jerusalem*: Matthew 21; Mark 11; Luke 19/p.614
• *trial*: Matthew 26; Mark 14 – 15; Luke 22 – 23; John 18 – 19/ p.590
• *crucifixion*: Matthew 27; Mark 15; Luke 23; John 19/ pp.590, 594, 616, 639
• *resurrection*: Matthew 28; Mark 16; Luke 24; John 20/ pp.616-620, 641

• *ascension*: Luke 24; Acts 1/pp.618, 644.
JESUS CHRIST, GOD IN HUMAN FORM *Son of God – his own claims*: pp.543, 551-552: Matthew 26:59-64; 27:41-44; Mark 2:1-12; John 5:17-47; 6:25-51; 7:16-31; 8:54-59; 10:22-39; 14:8-11; 17:1-5, 20-24; 19:7; also God's word: Matthew 17:1-8; Mark 1:9-11

MIRACLES OF JESUS

	Matthew	Mark	Luke	John
Healing of physical and mental disorders				
Leper	8:2-3	1:40-42	5:12-13	
Centurion's servant	8:5-13		7:1-10	
Peter's mother-in-law	8:14-15	1:30-31	4:38-39	
Two Gadarenes	8:28-34	5:1-15	8:27-35	
Paralysed man	9:2-7	2:3-12	5:18-25	
Woman with a haemorrhage	9:20-22	5:25-29	8:43-48	
Two blind men	9:27-31			
Man dumb and possessed	9:32-33		11:14	
Man with a withered hand	12:10-13	3:1-5	6:6-10	
Man blind, dumb and possessed	12:22			
Canaanite woman's daughter	15:21-28	7:24-30		
Boy with epilepsy	17:14-18	9:17-29	9:38-43	
Bartimaeus and another blind man	20:29-34	10:46-52	18:35-43	
Deaf and dumb man		7:31-37		
Man possessed, in the synagogue		1:23-26	4:33-35	
Blind man at Bethsaida		8:22-26		
Woman bent double			13:11-13	
Man with dropsy			14:1-4	
Ten lepers			17:11-19	
Malchus' ear			22:50-51	
Official's son at Capernaum				4:46-54
Sick man, Pool of Bethesda				5:1-9
Man born blind				9
Command over the forces of nature				
Calming of the storm	8:23-27	4:37-41	8:22-25	
Walking on the water	14:25	6:48-51		6:19-21
5,000 people fed	14:15-21	6:35-44	9:12-17	6:5-13
4,000 people fed	15:32-38	8:1-9		
Coin in the fish's mouth	17:24-27			
Fig-tree withered	21:18-22	11:12-14, 20-26		
Catch of fish			5:1-11	
Water turned into wine				2:1-11
Another catch of fish				21:1-11
Bringing the dead back to life				
Jairus' daughter	9:18-19, :23-25	5:22-24, :38-42	8:41-42, :49-56	
Widow's son at Nain			7:11-15	
Lazarus				11:1-44

• *Son of God – the opinion of his disciples and others*: Matthew 16:13-20; 27:50-54; Mark 1:21-27; 5:1-13; Luke 1:31-35; John 1:29-34, 43-51; 6:66-69; 11:23-27; 20:28; Acts 2:22-36; 7:54-60; 9:17-22; 10:34-43; Romans 1:1-4; Ephesians 1:20-23; Philippians 2:5-11; Colossians 1:15-20; Hebrews 1; 1 John 1:1-4; 2:22-25; 4:9-16
• *Son of man – truly human, yet sinless*: Luke 4:1-13; 23:39-41; John 8:46; 2 Corinthians 5:21; Hebrews 4:15; 1 Peter 2:22-23; 3:18; Galatians 4:4; Matthew 4:2; 21:18; Mark 1:41; 10:21; Luke 7:13; John 4:6; 11:33, 35, 38; 13:1; 15:13; Acts 2:22-23; Hebrews 2:14-18; 4:15; 1 John 4:2

• *significance of his death*: Mark 8:31-33; Luke 24:13-27, 44-48; John 1:29; 3:14-15; 11:50-52; 12:24; Acts 2:22-42; 3:12-26; 10:34-43; Romans 5:6-21; 1 Corinthians 11:23-26; Philippians 2:5-11; Hebrews 10:5-14; 1 Peter 2:24 (see also Forgiveness, Redemption)
• *promise of his return*: Matthew 24; 26:64; John 14;

Acts 1:11; 3:19-21; Philippians 3:20; Colossians 3:4; 1 Thessalonians 1:10; 4:13 – 5:11; 2 Thessalonians 1:5 – 2:12; 2 Peter 3:8-13. See also 'Jesus in a plural society', pp.83-85, and Messiah.

JETHRO/REUEL Moses' father-in-law and wise adviser: Exodus 2:16ff.; 3:1; 4:18; 18/p.166.

JEWELLERY See Gold and jewellery.

JEWISH REVOLT against the Romans in AD 66: pp.531, 535. Visual feature p.572. *Pictures* p.35 (objects from Masada).

JEZEBEL Princess of Tyre and Sidon who married Ahab and introduced Baal worship in Israel; responsible for Naboth's death; thrown to her death on Jehu's orders: 1 Kings 16:31; 18:4, 13, 19; 19:1-2; 21; 2 Kings 9/ pp.290ff.

JEZREEL Town and valley in northern Israel where King Ahab had his palace and Naboth his vineyard: the wounded Joram came to Jezreel; Jezebel died here: 1 Samuel 29:1; 1 Kings 18:45-46; 21; 2 Kings 8:29; 9:30-37/*Map* p.104B3.

JOAB Nephew of David and commander of his army; responsible for Abner's death; reconciled David and Absalom; supported Adonijah against Solomon: 2 Samuel 2 – 3; 10; 11; 14; 18 – 20; 24; 2 Kings 1 – 2; also 1 Chronicles 11ff./ pp.266, 271ff.

JOANNA One of the women who provided for Jesus and the 12; present on the resurrection morning: Luke 8:3; 24:10/p.607.

JOASH Rescued from Athaliah's massacre to become king of Judah; repaired the Temple: 2 Kings 11 – 12; 2 Chronicles 24/ pp.298, 323.

PARABLES OF JESUS

	Matthew	Mark	Luke
Lamp under a bushel	5:14-15	4:21-22	8:16; 11:33
Houses on rock and on sand	7:24-27		6:47-49
New cloth on an old garment	9:16	2:21	5:36
New wine in old wineskins	9:17	2:22	5:37-38
Sower and soils	13:3-8	4:3-8	8:5-8
Mustard seed	13:31-32	4:30-32	13:18-19
Tares	13:24-30		
Leaven (yeast)	13:33		13:20-21
Hidden treasure	13:44		
Pearl of great value	13:45-46		
Drag-net	13:47-48		
Lost sheep	18:12-13		15:4-6
Two debtors (unforgiving servant)	18:23-34		
Workers in the vineyard	20:1-16		
Two sons	21:28-31		
Wicked tenants	21:33-41	12:1-9	20:9-16
Invitation to the wedding feast; man without a wedding garment	22:2-14		
Fig-tree as herald of summer	24:32-33	13:28-29	21:29-32
Ten 'bridesmaids'	25:1-13		
Talents (Matthew); Pounds (Luke)	25:14-30		19:12-27
Sheep and goats	25:31-36		
Seedtime to harvest		4:26-29	
Creditor and the debtors			7:41-43
Good Samaritan			10:30-37
Friend in need			11:5-8
Rich fool			12:16-21
Alert servants			12:35-40
Faithful steward			12:42-48
Fig-tree without figs			13:6-9
Places of honour at the wedding feast			14:7-14
Great banquet and the reluctant guests			14:16-24
Counting the cost			14:28-33
Lost coin			15:8-10
The prodigal son			15:11-32
Dishonest steward			16:1-8
Rich man and Lazarus			16:19-31
The master and his servant			17:7-10
The persistent widow and the unrighteous judge			18:2-5
The Pharisee and the tax collector			18:10-14

JOB Central figure of the book of Job which explores the problem of bad things happening to good people/ pp.349ff. See also 'Understanding Job', pp.352-353.

JOB, BOOK OF pp.349ff.

JOEL Prophet in the time of Uzziah/Azariah, known only from his book.

JOEL, BOOK OF pp.488-489.

JOHANAN Jewish leader who warned Gedaliah of the plot to kill him; sought but ignored Jeremiah's advice about going to Egypt: Jeremiah 40 – 43.

JOHN 1. The apostle John, son of Zebedee, brother of James (see 'The twelve disciples of Jesus', p.557); the fourth Gospel and three New Testament letters bear his name; The Revelation to John may also be his work: Matthew 4:21ff.; 10:2; 17:1ff.; Mark 5:37; 10:35ff.; Luke 9:49ff.; Acts 3 – 4/ pp.621, 622, 758.

2. John the Baptist, forerunner of the Messiah: Luke 1; 3; 7:18ff.; Matthew 3; 11; Mark 1; 6, etc.; John 1; 3:22ff./pp.554, 561, 578-579, 584, 596-599, 607, 623, 625.

3. John Mark, see Mark.

JOHN, GOSPEL OF pp.621ff. *Pictures* pp.74 (Coptic), 546 (early fragment).

JOHN, LETTERS OF pp.758ff.

JONAH Prophet whose book recounts his mission to Nineveh.

JONAH, BOOK OF pp.496-497.

JONATHAN Eldest son of Saul; sworn friend of David: 1 Samuel 13 – 14; 18 – 20; 23:16-18; 31:2/pp.260, 262, 264.

JOPPA Sea-port in Israel (modern Jaffa); where Jonah embarked; here Peter had his dream and Cornelius sent for him: 2 Chronicles 2:16; Jonah 1:3; Acts 9:36ff.; 10/ *Map* p.104A4.

JORAM See Jehoram.

JORDAN Israel's chief river, flowing from the foot of Mt Hermon, through Lake Galilee, to the Dead Sea; the Israelites crossed this river to enter the promised land; David fled back across it from Absalom; Naaman washed in the Jordan and was healed; John baptized the people, and Jesus, in the Jordan: Joshua 3; 2 Samuel 17:22ff.; 2 Kings 2:6-8, 13-14; 5; Mark 1:5, 9, etc./*Map* p.104C *Pictures* pp.37, 294, 344-345, 361, 542, 543, 578.

JOSEPH 1. Jacob's favourite son; one of the great Old Testament heroes: Genesis 30:24; 37 – 50/ pp.146ff. See 'Joseph', pp.149-150.

• *Joseph sold into Egypt*: Genesis 37

• *Potiphar's wife*: 39

• *in prison*: 40

• *Pharaoh's dream*: 41

• *Joseph and his brothers*: 42 – 45

• *death*: 50.

2. Husband of Mary the mother of Jesus: Matthew 1 – 2; Luke 1:27; 2/p.551.

3. Joseph of Arimathea, secret disciple of Jesus who provided his tomb: Matthew 27:57ff.; Mark 15:43; Luke 23:50ff.; John 19:38ff./ p.594.

JOSHUA Succeeded Moses as leader of Israel; led the Israelites into the promised land: mentioned from Exodus 17:9 on, but particularly the book of Joshua/pp.166, 203, 218, 225ff.

• *Victory against Amalek*: Exodus 17

• *the spy*: Numbers 13 – 14

• *appointment as Moses' successor*: Numbers 27

• *placed in charge*: Deuteronomy 31; 34:9ff.

• *crossing the Jordan*: Joshua 4

• *Jericho*: Joshua 6

• *division of the land*: Joshua 13ff.

• *Joshua's charge to Israel*: Joshua 23 – 24.

JOSHUA, BOOK OF pp.225ff.

JOSIAH King of Judah 640-609 BC who embarked on thoroughgoing religious reform; killed fighting Pharaoh Necho at Megiddo: 2 Kings 21:24 – 23:30; 2 Chronicles 33:25 – 35:27/ pp.303, 326.

JOTHAM Son of Azariah/ Uzziah, king of Judah 750-732 BC: 2 Kings 15; 2 Chronicles 26 – 27/pp.299, 323-324.

JOY A hallmark of the believer, in both Old and New Testaments – joy derived from a relationship with God: Psalms 16:11; 30:5; 43:4; 51:12; 126:56; Ecclesiastes 2:26; Isaiah 61:7; Jeremiah 15:16; Luke 15:7; John 15:11; 16:22; Romans 14:17; 15:13; Galatians 5:22; Philippians 1:4; 1 Thessalonians 2:20; 3:9; Hebrews 12:2; James 1:2; 1 Peter 1:8; Jude 24.

JUBILEE Leviticus 25/p.189.

JUDAH 1. One of Jacob's 12 sons; ancestor of the royal tribe of Israel: Genesis 29:35; 37 – 38; 43ff.; 49:8-9/ pp.141, 146-147, 152.

2. Territory of the tribe of Judah, of which the hill-country of Judah and the wilderness of Judea (bordering the west side of the Dead Sea) form part; later the name of the southern kingdom: Joshua 15; 1 Kings 12:21, 23/*Map* p.235. *Picture* – see under Judea.

JUDAISM See 'Jewish religion in New Testament times', pp.528ff.; 'Making connections – the Bible and world history', pp.26-27; 'The Hebrew Bible', pp.68-69.

Pictures pp.43, 191 (Purim), 47, 48, 64, 66, 69, 386, 519 (reading Torah, Torah scrolls), 65 (scribe), 190 (celebrating harvest and Passover), 191 (sabbath candles, Festival of lights),

212, 712 (binding on the law; phylactery), 579 (Capernaum synagogue), 744 (Baram synagogue), 765 (Sardis synagogue), 54, 62, 170, 172, 530.

JUDAS/JUDE Name of a number of individuals in the New Testament, among them:

1. Judas son of James, one of the 12 apostles: Luke 6:16, etc.

2. Judas Iscariot, who betrayed Jesus: Matthew 10:4; 26:14ff.; 27:3ff.; John 13; 18/ pp.574-575, 635-636.

On 1. and 2. see 'The twelve disciples of Jesus', p.558.

3. The brother of Jesus, who may have written the letter of Jude: Matthew 13:55.

JUDE, LETTER OF p.762.

JUDEA Greek and Roman name for Judah; sometimes includes, sometimes excludes, Galilee and Samaria: Luke 4:44; 3:1, etc./*Map* p.526B5 *Pictures* pp.36, 416, 434, 469, 484-485, 540, 542, 572, 625.

JUDGMENT See Future destiny.

JUDGES, BOOK OF pp.238ff.

JUSTICE God's concern for justice (especially for the poor and defenceless) is embedded in his law (e.g. Exodus 22:21-27) and is a theme that runs right through the Bible, especially the prophets: see e.g. Amos/p.490 and article 'Justice and the poor', pp.491-492.

JUSTIFICATION A legal term: a judge's acquittal. The New Testament declares that God can acquit people of breaking his law because the penalty has been paid in the death of Jesus (see also Forgiveness): Exodus 23:7; Job 13:18; 25:4; Psalms 51:1ff.; 103:6; 143:2; Isaiah 50:8-9; 53:11; Luke 18:14; Acts 13:39; Romans 2:13; 3:4, 19-30; 4:2ff.; 5:1-10; 8:30-34; 1 Corinthians 6:11; Galatians

2:15-21; 3:6-14; Titus 3:7; James 2:14-26.

K

KADESH-BARNEA An oasis in the desert south of Beersheba; in this general area most of Israel's years of desert wandering were spent: Numbers 13:26; 20:1, 14; 33:36, etc.; Joshua 14:7/*Map* p.166.

KEDESH Canaanite town in Galilee conquered by Joshua; home of Barak: Joshua 12:22; Judges 4:6; also 2 Kings 15:29, etc./ *Map* p.104C1.

KEILAH Town David saved from Philistine attack, and where he took refuge: 1 Samuel 23/*Map* p.264.

KETURAH Abraham's second wife, after Sarah's death: Genesis 25:1ff./p.139.

KIDRON VALLEY Between Jerusalem and the Mount of Olives; David crossed it, fleeing from Absalom; Jesus crossed it to Gethsemane: 2 Samuel 15:23; 1 Kings 15:13; 2 Kings 23:4/John 18:1/*Map* p.630 *Picture* p.447. See 'Jerusalem in New Testament times' (with picture).

KINGDOM God's rule: the new age (see p.413 and 'Jesus and the kingdom', pp.563-564): Psalms 103:19; 145:11-13; Daniel 2:44; 4:3; 7:13-14, 27; Matthew 3:2; 4:23; 5:3, 10, 19-20; 6:9-10, 33; 13:11, 19, 24-52; 16:19, 28; 18:1-4, 23ff.; 19:12, 14, 23ff.; 20:1ff.; 21ff.; 21:43; 22:2ff.; 23:13; 24:14; 25:1ff., 34; 26:29; many similar references in Mark and Luke; John 3:3, 5; 18:36; Acts 14:22; 28:31; Romans 14:17; 1 Corinthians 4:20; Galatians 5:19-21; Colossians 1:13.

KINGS, BOOKS OF pp.276ff.

KING'S HIGHWAY Road running from the Gulf of

Aqaba, east of the Dead Sea, to Syria; Edom refused Moses access to it: Numbers 20:17, etc./*Map* p.209 *Picture* p.203.

KINGS OF ISRAEL AND JUDAH *Chart* pp.306-307; 'Unravelling the chronology of the kings', pp.287-288.

KIR/KIR-HARESETH Fortified town in Moab: 2 Kings 3; Isaiah 15:1; 16:7/ *Map* p.104C7.

KIRIATH-ARBA Earlier name for Hebron.

KIRIATH-JEARIM Chief town of the Gibeonites; where the Ark of the Covenant was kept for 20 years before David took it to Jerusalem: Joshua 9; 1 Samuel 6:19 – 7:2/ *Map* p.104B5 *Picture* p.259.

KIRIATHAIM Place east of Jordan allotted to the tribe of Reuben; later in Moabite hands: Joshua 13:19; Jeremiah 48:1/*Map* p.104C6.

KISH Father of King Saul: 1 Samuel 9:1ff.

KISHON River referred to in the story of Barak's victory, and Elijah's slaughter of the prophets of Baal; flows into the sea north of Mt Carmel: Judges 5:21; 1 Kings 18:40/*Map* p.104B2.

KITTIM Name for Cyprus; later for east Mediterranean coastlands generally.

KOHATH, KOHATHITES Son of Levi and ancestor of Moses. Head of one of the three Levitical families – the Kohathites: Exodus 6:16ff.; Numbers 3/pp.193-194.

KORAH Levite who with Dathan and Abiram conspired against Moses and Aaron and was destroyed: Numbers 16/p.197.

KUE Region of what is now southern Turkey (Cilicia) from which Solomon imported horses: 1 Kings 10:28/*Map* p.319.

L

LABAN Rebecca's brother; uncle to Jacob who outplayed him at his own cunning game: Genesis 24:29; 28 – 30/pp.141-142.

LACHISH See visual feature 'The siege of Lachish', p.302. Important fortified town in the foothills south-west of Jerusalem; features in the story of the conquest; the place where Amaziah was assassinated; a target of Assyrian and Babylonian attack: Joshua 10; 2 Kings 14:19; 18:14, 17; Jeremiah 34:7/*Map* p.104A6 *Pictures* pp.30, 102, 304.

LAMECH 1. Descendant of Cain: Genesis 4/pp.121-122. **2.** Father of Noah: Genesis 5:28ff.

LAMENTATIONS, BOOK OF pp.459-460.

LAMP *Pictures* pp.11, 242, endpapers.

LAODICEA Town in the Lycus Valley of present-day western Turkey; Paul's letter to the Colossians was also to be taken to the church there; one of the seven churches addressed by John in Revelation: Colossians 2:1; 4:13-16; Revelation 1:11; 3:14-22/Note, map and picture p.765. *Picture* p.769.

LAST SUPPER/LORD'S SUPPER Matthew 26; Mark 14; Luke 22; John 13 – 14; 1 Corinthians 11:17-34/pp.574, 635-636, 638. See 'Passover and the Last Supper', pp.574-575.

LAW OF GOD/TORAH God's instructions for right living.
• *The 'five books' of the law* (Genesis – Deuteronomy), pp.109-113, 115ff.
• *giving of the law*: Exodus 20ff./ pp.168ff.
• *ritual and ceremonial law*: Exodus 25 – 30; 34 – 40; Leviticus 1 – 9; 11 – 17; 22 – 25; Deuteronomy 14; 16; 18; 26

• *moral and social law*: Exodus 20:1-17; 21 – 23; Leviticus 18 – 20; Deuteronomy 5:1-21; 10:12-21; 15; 19 – 25
• *delight in the law*: Psalms 1; 19; 37:31; 40:8; 119; Proverbs 29:18
• *its permanent value*: Matthew 5:17-20; 22:36-40; 23:23; Luke 10:25-28; Romans 3:31; 8:3-4
• *the impossibility of meeting God's standards by human effort; the law's limitations*: John 7:19; Acts 13:39; Romans 2:25-29; 3:19-21; 7:7-25; 8:3; Galatians 2:16; 3:21-24; Hebrews 7:18-19; James 2:8-12
• *Jesus and the law*: Matthew 5/p.556
• *law and traditions*, pp.528-529.
See also 'A way of life: the Ten Commandments', pp.170-172; 'Sacrifice', pp.182-183; 'The Hebrew Bible', pp.68-69. Torah *pictures*, pp.47, 48, 64, 69, 71, 519.

LAZARUS Brother of Martha and Mary; raised from the dead by Jesus: John 11 – 12:11/p.634.

LEAH Elder daughter of Laban; Jacob's wife and mother of six of his sons: Genesis 29:16 – 33:7/ pp.141-142. Family tree p.147.

LEBANON The modern country and its mountain range; famous for its cedars (used in building the Temple) and its fruit: 1 Kings 5:6; Psalm 72:16; Isaiah 2:13, etc./*Picture* of cedars p.279.

LEMUEL The king whose mother's teaching is set out in Proverbs 31:1-9/p.399.

LETTER *Picture* p.677.

LETTERS (EPISTLES), NEW TESTAMENT Romans – Jude/ pp.681ff. Introduction pp.674-680.

LEVI One of Jacob's 12 sons; ancestor of the tribe which gave Israel their priests and

ministers: Genesis 29:34;
34:25ff.; 49:5ff./pp.146,
152.

LEVITES AND PRIESTS
Leviticus 21 – 22; Numbers
1:47-54; 3 – 4; 1 Chronicles
23ff./pp.189, 193-194, 309,
313-314. See 'Priesthood in
the Old Testament', pp.185-
186.
• *Levitical cities*: Numbers 35;
Joshua 21/p.236.

LEVITICUS, BOOK OF pp.180ff.

LIBNAH Fortified lowland
town taken by Joshua;
revolted against Joram;
attacked by Sennacherib:
Joshua 10:29-30; 2 Kings
8:22; 19:8, etc./
Map p.104A5.

LIFE *Human life (creation)*:
Genesis 2/pp.115-116. See
Creation and providence
• *God, the source of life*: his life-
giving laws and wisdom:
Deuteronomy 30:15-20;
Psalms 36:9; 133:3; Proverbs
8:35; 14:27; Jeremiah 21:8
• *'eternal' life (new creation)*:
Matthew 7:14; 10:39;
16:25-26; 18:8-9; 19:16ff.,
29; Luke 12:15; John 1:4;
3:15-16, 36; 4:14; 5:24;
6:27, 35, 40, 47-51; 10:10,
28; 11:25; 14:6; 17:3;
20:31; Romans 6:4ff., 22-23;
8:6; 2 Corinthians 4:10-12;
5:17ff.; Galatians 6:8;
Ephesians 2:2ff.; 1 Timothy
6:12; 1 John 1:1-2; 3:14;
5:11-12; Revelation 22:1-2,
17.

LIGHTS, FESTIVAL OF See
Dedication.

LIMMU LISTS, ASSYRIAN
p.288.

LO-DEBAR Place east of
Jordan where Mephibosheth
lived: 2 Samuel 9:4/
Map p.104C3.

LOCUST PLAGUES Exodus
10/pp.163-164 (Egypt); Joel
1/p.488 (Israel)
Pictures pp.165, 489.

LOT Abraham's nephew who
chose to live in Sodom and
narrowly escaped destruc-
tion: Genesis 11:31 – 14:16;

19/pp.127, 130, 135.

LOVE Article p.637. 1 Corinthians 13; Galatians 5:22;
1 John 4:7 – 5:3.
• *The love of God; Christ's love*:
Deuteronomy 7:7-81;
Proverbs 3:12; Isaiah 63:7-9;
Jeremiah 31:3; Hosea 3:1;
14:4; John 3:16; 13:1; 15:9,
12-13; Romans 8:35-39;
Galatians 2:20; Ephesians
2:4; 3:17-19; Hebrews 12:6;
1 John 3:1
• *loving God*: Exodus 20:6;
Deuteronomy 6:5; 11:1, 13,
22; Psalms 31:23; 116:1;
119:47-48; John 14:15,
21-24; Romans 8:28;
1 Corinthians 8:3;
1 Peter 1; 8
• *loving others*: Leviticus
19:18, 34; Matthew
5:43-46; John 13:34-35;
14:15, 21-24; 15:9-14;
Galatians 5:13-14; Ephesians
4:2, 15-16; Philippians 2:2;
Hebrews 10:24; 1 John
4:7 – 5:3
• *love between man and woman*:
Genesis 29:20; 2 Samuel
13:15; Proverbs 5:18-19;
Song of Solomon; Ephesians
5:25ff.; Colossians 3:19.

LUD See under Lydians.

LUKE Author of the third
Gospel and Acts; a doctor;
companion of Paul in his
missionary journeys:
Colossians 4:14; 2 Timothy
4:11; Philemon 24/pp.595-
596, 643-644, 657, 736.

LUKE, GOSPEL OF pp.595ff.

LUZ Former name of Bethel.

LYCIA Region in what is now
south-west Turkey: Acts
27:5/*Map* p.680.

LYDDA Old Testament and
modern Lod, near Jaffa: Acts
9:32, 35/*Map* p.526B5.

LYDIA A business woman
from Thyatira converted at
Philippi: Acts 16:14-15/
p.657.

LYDIANS An Indo-European-
speaking people of western
Asia Minor who succeeded to
the territories of Phrygia,
confronted Media, and

succumbed to Persia in the
6th century BC. They are
probably the 'Lud' of Isaiah
66:19; Jeremiah 46:9; Ezekiel
27:10; 30:5, though the
associated names in the
second and fourth of these
passages might point to north
Africa.

LYSTRA Timothy's home
town; where Paul healed a
cripple and was acclaimed as
a god (not far from Konya in
modern Turkey): Acts 14:6ff.;
16/*Map* p.652.

M

MAACAH Region south-east of
Mt Hermon, mentioned in
David's campaigns: Joshua
12:5; 2 Samuel 10/
Map p.268.

**MACCABEES, MACCABEAN
REVOLT** Jewish uprising led by
Judas Maccabaeus against
the oppressive Syrian King
Antiochus Epiphanes:
pp.477, 482, 518-520.

MACEDONIA Roman province
of northern Greece, including
Philippi, Thessalonica and
Beroea: Acts 16:9ff.; 20:1ff.;
2 Corinthians 9, etc./
Map p.680.

MACHAERUS East of, and
overlooking, the Dead Sea;
one of King Herod's
fortresses; here it is said that
John the Baptist was
beheaded: *picture* p.585.

MAGIC AND WITCHCRAFT See
'Magic in the Old Testament',
p.265 (with pictures).
• *The Bible's teaching*:
Deuteronomy 18:9-14;
Jeremiah 27:8-11; Daniel 2;
Galatians 5:19-21;
Revelation 21:8; 22:15
• *magic in Egypt*: Genesis 41;
Exodus 7ff./pp.148, 163; also
154-155, 156
• *Babylonian magic*: Isaiah
47:8-15; Daniel 2
• *Saul and the witch of Endor*:
1 Samuel 28.

MAGOG See Gog.

MAHANAIM Place east of the
Jordan near the River Jabbok;
mentioned in the story of
Jacob's return; headquarters
of David during Absalom's
rebellion: Genesis 32:2;
2 Samuel 17:24, etc./
Map p.268.

MAKKEDAH Joshua captured
the town and killed five
Amorite kings in a nearby
cave: Joshua 10:16ff./
Map p.104B5.

MALACHI Name or pseudo-
nym of the 'minor prophet'
whose book bears his name.

MALACHI, BOOK OF pp.512ff.

MALCHUS Servant of the high
priest; Peter cut off his ear
when Jesus was arrested in
the garden of Gethsemane:
John 18:10.

MALTA Here Paul was
shipwrecked on the way to
Rome: Acts 27:39 – 28:10/
Map p.667 *Pictures* pp.668,
669.

MAMRE Place close to Hebron
where Abraham stayed:
Genesis 13:18; 18:1;
23:17, etc.

MANASSEH 1. Joseph's son;
ancestor of one of the tribes of
Israel: Genesis 41:51; 48/
pp.148, 151. Family tree
p.147.
2. Territory of the tribe of
Manasseh, Joshua 13:29-31;
17:7-13/*Map* p.235.
3. Son of Hezekiah, king of
Judah 696-642 BC: 2 Kings
21; 2 Chronicles 33/pp.303,
324, 326.

MANKIND Created by God –
mortal, yet with a moral and
spiritual nature – to worship,
obey and enjoy God's friendship: Genesis 1 – 2; 17:1ff.,
etc.; Deuteronomy 5:28-33;
8; 2 Samuel 19:12-13;
Psalms 8; 27; 66; 78:5-8;
Isaiah 40:6-8; 43; Ecclesiastes 12:1-7; Micah 9:6-8;
Luke 12:13-21; Romans
1:18-25; 8:18ff.; 1 Corinthians 15:45-50; 2 Corinthians
5:1-5; 6:16-18.
• *In rebellion against God*:

Genesis 3; Judges 2:11-23; Psalm 2:1-3; Daniel 9:3-19; Romans 1 – 3; 7:13-25; Hebrews 3:7-19; Revelation 17 – 18. See also Sin and evil. For humanity's re-creation in Christ and glorious destiny, see Future destiny, Life, Regeneration, Heaven, etc.

MANNA The food God provided for his people in the wilderness: Exodus 16; Numbers 11/pp.166, 196.

MANNEANS See Scythians.

MANOAH Father of Samson: Judges 13.

MAON Town near which David took refuge from Saul and where Nabal lived: 1 Samuel 23:24; 25:2/ *Map* p.104B6.

MARESHAH Town fortified by Rehoboam, near which Asa defeated Zerah of Ethiopia: 2 Chronicles 11:8; 14:9; 20:37; Micah 1:15/ *Map* p.104A6.

MARK Author of the second Gospel; companion of Paul and Barnabas, also of Peter: Acts 12:12, 25; 13:13; 15:36ff.; Colossians 4:10; 2 Timothy 4:11; Philemon 24; 1 Peter 5:13/pp.577ff., 652, 654, 726, 736.

MARK, GOSPEL OF pp.577ff.

MARKET *Pictures* pp.42, 47, 81, 147, 351, 397, 399.

MARRIAGE AND FAMILY RELATIONSHIPS Genesis 2:18-24; Proverbs (see p.398); Matthew 5:31ff.; 19; Mark 10; 1 Corinthians 7; Ephesians 5:21 – 6:4; Colossians 3:18-21; 1 Peter 3:1-7.

• *Divorce*: Deuteronomy 24:1-4; Ezra 9 – 10; Malachi 2:10-16; Matthew 5:31ff.; 19:3-9; Luke 16:18; 1 Corinthians 7:10-16

• *celibacy*: Matthew 19:10-12; 1 Corinthians 7:7-9

• *marriage and God's relationship with his people*: Jeremiah 3; Hosea 1 – 3; Ephesians 5. *Pictures* pp.139 (marriage contract), 406 (Yemenite bride).

MARTHA Sister of Mary and Lazarus in whose home Jesus stayed: Luke 10:38ff.; John 11; 12:2/pp.610, 634. See 'Martha and Mary', pp.608-609.

MARY Name of a number of women in the New Testament.
1. Mary the mother of Jesus and wife of Joseph: Matthew 1; 2:11; 13:55; Luke 1 – 2/ pp.596ff., 644. See 'Mary, the mother of Jesus', p.602; also 'The virgin birth', pp.596-597.
2. Mary the sister of Martha and Lazarus, who anointed Jesus: Luke 10:39ff.; John 11; 12:3ff./pp.589, 610, 634. See 'Martha and Mary', pp.608-609.
3. Mary Magdalene, who was healed by Jesus and was the first to see him after the resurrection: Matthew 27:55-56, 61; 28:1ff.; Mark 15:40ff.; Luke 8:2; John 20/p.641 (with article).
4. Mary the mother of John Mark: Acts 12:12.
5. Mary the mother of James, 'the other Mary', and Mary wife of Clopas – who are probably one and the same: Matthew 27:56, 61; 28:1; John 19:25.

MASADA Herod's fortress close to the Dead Sea; site of the last Jewish stand against the Romans, ending in mass suicide in AD 73. *Pictures* of everyday objects from Masada p.35.

MASTERS See under Slaves and servants.

MATTHEW Tax collector who became one of the 12 apostles (see 'The twelve disciples of Jesus', p.558) and author of the first Gospel: Matthew 9:9; 10:3, etc./pp.549-550, 560.

MATTHEW, GOSPEL OF pp.549ff.

MATTHIAS Chosen after Jesus' death to take the place of Judas Iscariot as the twelfth apostle: Acts 1:15ff.

MEDIA, MEDES An Indo-European-speaking people who controlled an empire in Persia and Asia Minor in the 7th and 6th centuries BC, from their capital Ecbatana, modern Hamadan, in northwest Persia (Iran). The Medes were subject to Assyria and allies of Babylonia. In 550 BC Cyrus of Persia incorporated Media into his growing empire. From then on, Medes held a prominent place in Persian life. On their presence at Pentecost, see Elamites. *Map* pp.814-815.

MEDIATOR A go-between, reconciling two conflicting parties. The New Testament describes Jesus as the mediator between God and mankind (see also under Reconciliation): Galatians 3:19-20; 1 Timothy 2:5; Hebrews 8:6; 9:15; 12:24.

MEGIDDO Joshua defeated the king of this Canaanite city which dominates the pass through the Carmel hills; its strategic position has made it the site of numerous battles, hence its symbolical use as Armageddon (*Har-Magedon*, hill of Megiddo), site of the final battle, in Revelation. Sisera was defeated near here; Solomon fortified the city; Ahaziah died here; so did Josiah, killed in the battle against Pharaoh Necho: Joshua 12:21; Judges 5:19; 1 Kings 9:15; 2 Kings 9:27; 23:29/p.283 *Map* p.104B3 *Pictures* pp.223 (model), 242, 444, 774.

MELCHIZEDEK Priest and king of Salem who met and blessed Abraham: Genesis 14:18ff.; see Hebrews 5 – 7/pp.130, 744.

MEMPHIS Ancient capital of Egypt: Jeremiah 2:16; 46:14, etc./*Map* p.154.

MENAHEM King of Israel 752-742 BC: 2 Kings 15/p.299.

MEPHIBOSHETH Son of Saul's son Jonathan; honoured by

David for Jonathan's sake: 2 Samuel 4:4; 9; 16:1ff.; 19:24ff./pp.268-269, 273-274.

MERAB Saul's daughter, promised to David: 1 Samuel 14:49; 18:17ff.

MERARI, MERARITES Son of Levi; founder of one of the three Levitical families: Exodus 6:16ff.; Numbers 3/pp.193-194.

MERCY Kindness; readiness to forgive (see also under Grace): Exodus 34:6-7; Nehemiah 9:7, 31; Psalms 23:6; 25:6; 40:11; 51:1; 103:4, 8; Daniel 9:9; Jonah 4:2; Micah 6:8; Matthew 5:7; Luke 18:13; Romans 9:15; 12:1; Ephesians 2:4.

MERODACH-BALADAN Marduk-apla-iddina II, king of Babylon who sent an embassy to Hezekiah: Isaiah 39.

MESHACH One of Daniel's three companions in exile at Babylon; thrown into the fiery furnace but unharmed: Daniel 1; 2:49; 3/pp.473ff.

MESOPOTAMIA Land between the Tigris and Euphrates rivers; the term is often extended to include Babylonia to the south; includes Harran and Paddan-aram where some of Abraham's family settled: Genesis 24:10; Deuteronomy 23:4, etc.; Acts 2:9/*Map* pp.814-815.

MESSIAH, MESSIANIC KINGDOM God's chosen deliverer – the Christ – and his rule of peace and justice: Deuteronomy 18:15ff.; Psalms 2; 45:6-7; 72; 110; Isaiah 9:2-7; 11; 42:1-9; 49:1-6; 52:13 – 53:12; 61:1-3; Jeremiah 23:5-6; 33:14-16; Ezekiel 34:22ff.; Daniel 7; Zechariah 9:9-10; Matthew 1:18, 22-23; 16:16, 20; 26:63; Mark 14:61-62; Luke 2:11, 26; John 4:25, 29; 7:26-27, 31, 41-42; 9:22; Acts 2:36; 3:20-21; 4:26-28; 18:28; 26:22-23/pp.411,

413, 531, 549-550. See 'Christ in the psalms', p.388; 'Jesus and the kingdom', pp.563-564.

METHUSELAH Longest lived of the patriarchs listed in Genesis 5/p.122.

MICAH/MICAIAH 1. Prophet in Isaiah's time whose prophecies we have in the book of Micah/pp.498-499.
2. The Ephraimite who installed a Levite as priest to his house: Judges 17 – 18/p.249.
3. The prophet summoned by Ahab: 1 Kings 22; 2 Chronicles 18/p.293.

MICAH, BOOK OF pp.498-499.

MICHAEL The guardian angel of Daniel 10; 12:1; also Jude 9; Revelation 12:7/pp.479, 762, 773. See also 'Angels in the Bible', p.727.

MICHAL Saul's daughter; wife of David, who helped him escape Saul, but disapproved of him dancing before the Ark of the Covenant: 1 Samuel 14:49; 18:20ff.; 19:11ff.; 25:44; 2 Samuel 3:13-16; 6:16ff./pp.262, 268.

MICHMASH Where Saul's army mustered against the Philistines: 1 Samuel 13:2; 14/Map p.104B5.

MIDIAN, MIDIANITES Region of north-west Arabia. The Midianites were the southern neighbours of the Edomites. Their territory extended at times into the Hijaz of Arabia. Moses stayed in Midian after escaping from Pharaoh. The Midianites were camel-riding semi-nomads. A threat to the Israelites in the time of Judges, they were routed by Gideon: Exodus 2:15; Judges 6, etc./Map pp.814-815.

MILETUS Sea-port where Paul spoke to the elders from Ephesus: Acts 20:15, 17; also 2 Timothy 4:20/Map p.664.

MILLENNIUM In John's vision, the '1,000 years' during which Satan is 'chained up', his seductive power bound:

Revelation 20/p.775.

MIRACLES See 'The New Testament miracles', pp.605-606; note on p.160. See also Jesus' miracles list, p.795.

MIRIAM Elder sister of Moses and Aaron; sang in triumph at the crossing of the Red Sea; later punished with leprosy for rebellion against Moses: Exodus 2:4ff.; 15:20-21; Numbers 12; 20:1/pp.163, 165-166, 196, 199.

MIRROR *Picture* p.702.

MISSIONARY JOURNEYS, PAUL'S Acts 13 – 14; 15 – 18; 18 – 20/ pp.652ff.

MITYLENE Paul's ship put in here, at the island of Lesbos, on his way to Jerusalem: Acts 20:14/Map p.664.

MIZPAH The name (meaning watch-tower) denotes a number of different places, primarily one near Jerusalem where the Israelites assembled in the time of Samuel and the Judges. Here Saul was presented as king; later fortified by Asa; residence of Gedaliah: Judges 20:1; 1 Samuel 7:5ff.; 10:17; 1 Kings 15:22; 2 Kings 25:23/Map p.104B5.

MOAB, MOABITES Country bounded on the north by Ammon, on the west by the Dead Sea, and on the south by Edom. The Moabites passed through much the same phases as the Ammonites (see above). They refused to allow the Israelites to pass through their territory at the time of the conquest. The home of Ruth, Moab was in constant conflict with Israel. Their own account of one episode in the 9th century is given on the Moabite Stone, which shows that they spoke a Semitic-Canaanite language closely akin to Hebrew. Moab was frequently denounced by the prophets: Ruth 1; 2 Samuel 8:2; 2 Kings 3; Isaiah 15, etc./ Map pp.814-815.

MODELS AND RECONSTRUCTIONS
• *Ziggurat*: p.126
• *Tabernacle*: pp.177, 745
• *high priest*: p.185
• *Solomon's Temple*: pp.280-281
• *Herod's Temple*: pp.532-533, 597, 616, 646
• *eastern inn*: p.610
• *rich man's house*, p.607
• *New Testament Jerusalem*: pp.615, 630
• *Fort of Antonia*, p.616. See also Ships.

MONEY See 'Jesus and money', pp.566-567 (with picture). See also Giving, Tithes. *Pictures* – see Coins.

MORDECAI Cousin to Esther, who prompted her to act and save the Jewish people from massacre: Esther 2:5 – 10:3/ pp.341-343.

MOREH Hill where the Midianites encamped against Gideon: Judges 7:1/ *Map* p.104B3 *Map* and diagram p.245.

MORESHETH/MORESHETH-GATH Home of the prophet Micah: Micah 1:1, 14.

MORIAH Mountains where Abraham was told to go to sacrifice Isaac. 'Mt Moriah' was the site of Solomon's Temple: Genesis 22:2; 2 Chronicles 3:1.

MOSAICS *Pictures* pp.704, 726, 739, 755.

MOSES Great leader and law-giver who led Israel out of Egypt to Sinai, and through the years of desert wandering: Exodus 2 – Deuteronomy 34/pp.156ff. See 'Moses', pp.206-208.
• *Birth, and upbringing by Pharaoh's daughter*: Exodus 2
• *the burning bush*: Exodus 3 – 4
• *the contest with Pharaoh*: Exodus 7 – 12
• *crossing of the Red Sea*: Exodus 14
• *water from the rock*: Exodus 17; Numbers 20
• *Sinai; the law*: Exodus 19ff.

• *the golden calf*: Exodus 32
• *the spies*: Numbers 13 – 14
• *appointment of a successor*: Numbers 27
• *instruction to the people when they possess the land*: Deuteronomy 6ff.
• *final charge to the nation*: Deuteronomy 31
• *Moses' blessing*: Deuteronomy 33
• *death*: Deuteronomy 34.

MOULD *Picture* p.691.

MOUNT OF OLIVES Hill over-looking Jerusalem; David fled this way from Absalom; from the Mount Jesus entered Jerusalem in triumph, and wept over the city; on its slopes was Gethsemane; the village of Bethany lay on the far side; the place of Christ's ascension: 2 Samuel 15:30; Zechariah 14:4; Luke 19:29, 37, 41; 22:39; Acts 1:12, etc./for location see model p.630 *Picture* p.644.

MUSIC, MUSICAL INSTRUMENTS
• *In the Temple*: 1 Chronicles 25/p.314
• *in Babylon*: Daniel 3/p.475. *Pictures* pp. 42, 195 (trumpet), 132, 261, 345, 367 (harps), 107, 134, 314, 366, 475, 659 (musicians), 166 (tambourine), 227 (shofar), 359 (lute).

MYRA Port on Paul's journey to Rome: Acts 27:5/ *Map* p.667.

MYRRH Gift of the wise men to the infant Jesus; aromatic gummy resin used, like frankincense, to make anointing oil; also in cosmetics: Matthew 2/p.552 (with picture).

MYSIA Region Paul passed through on his way to Troas: Acts 16:7-8/Map p.657.

MYSTERY RELIGIONS A group term for various Greek cults and others from Egypt, Persia and elsewhere in the East which share the same concept of personal commitment by initiation into what amounts to a secret society whose rites were never divulged to an outsider. A number of sects began to develop about the time the New Testament Letters were written which later (in the 2nd century) came under the general heading of 'Gnosticism' (Greek *gnosis*, 'knowledge'), from the belief that special knowledge was required in order to be redeemed. This was made known to initiates in sects like those of the mystery religions. Paul uses some of their language, for example in the Letter to the Colossians, turning it around to speak of God's 'open secret' – the gospel message. See pp.673, 676.

NAAMAN Syrian army commander healed of leprosy by Elisha: 2 Kings 5/pp.294-295.

NABAL Husband of Abigail; landowner who refused David's request for hospitality: 1 Samuel 25/p.263.

NABATAEANS See Arabians.

NABOTH Killed so that Ahab could seize the vineyard he coveted: 1 Kings 21/pp.292-293.

NADAB Aaron's son who, with Abihu, committed sacrilege and died: Leviticus 10/p.184.

NAHOR Abraham's brother who settled at Harran and became the ancestor of several Aramaean tribes: Genesis 11:27ff.; 22:20ff.; 24:10ff.

NAHUM Prophet whose prophecy against Nineveh is recorded in the book of Nahum/p.500.

NAHUM, BOOK OF pp.500-501.

NAIN Place in Galilee where Jesus restored the widow's son to life: Luke 7:11/

Map p.526B3 *Picture* p.604.

NAMES 'Personal names in Genesis 1 – 11', p.121; 'The names of God', p.162.

NAOMI Mother-in-law of Ruth; from Bethlehem: Ruth/pp.251-253. See 'A story through women's eyes', p.254.

NAPHTALI 1. One of Jacob's 12 sons; ancestor of one of the tribes of Israel: Genesis 30:8; 49:21. Family tree p.147.
2. Territory of the tribe of Naphtali in Galilee: Joshua 19:32-39/*Map* p.235.

NATHAN Prophet who delivered God's word to David and helped place Solomon on the throne: 2 Samuel 7; 12; 1 Kings 1; 1 Chronicles 17/pp.272, 276.

NATHANAEL One of the 12 apostles, (see 'The twelve disciples of Jesus', p.558), probably the same as Bartholomew; from Cana: John 1:45-51; 21:2/pp.623-624.

NAZARETH Town in Galilee where Joseph and Mary lived; Jesus' home; Luke 1:26ff.; 2:39, 51; 4:16ff., etc./ *Map* p.526B2 *Pictures* pp.524, 542, 544.

NAZARETH DECREE Inscription p.658.

NAZIRITE VOW Numbers 6/pp.195, 246 (Samson).

NEAPOLIS Port near Philippi in northern Greece (modern Kavalla): Acts 16:11/ *Map* p.657 *Picture* p.654.

NEBO Town and mountain in Moab from which Moses viewed the promised land and where he died: Deuteronomy 32:49-50; 34:1ff./ *Map* p.104C5 *Pictures* pp.208, 215.

NEBUCHADNEZZAR King of Babylon who captured Jerusalem in 587 BC and took the Judeans into exile; Daniel interpreted his dreams: 2 Kings 24 – 25; 2 Chronicles 36; Jeremiah 21:2 – 52:30;

Ezekiel 26:7ff.; 29:18ff.; 30:10; Daniel 1 – 4/pp.304, 449, 451-455, 468, 474-475. See 'The Babylonians', pp.456-457.

NEBUZARADAN Nebuchadnezzar's captain of the guard at Jerusalem: 2 Kings 25; Jeremiah 39; 52.

NECHO Pharaoh who killed Josiah in battle at Megiddo, deposed Jehoahaz and put Jehoiakim on the throne: 2 Kings 23; 2 Chronicles 35:20 – 36:4/pp.303-304, 326 *Map* p.326.

NEGEV Arid region in the far south of Israel merging with Sinai, on the route to Egypt; here the patriarchs led their flocks, and the Israelites wandered before entering Canaan: Genesis 20:1, etc.; Numbers 13:17; 21:1, etc./ *Map* p.166 *Pictures* pp.37, 99, 112, 174, 179, 197, 216, 357.

NEHEMIAH Cup-bearer to the Persian king; returned to Jerusalem and organized the rebuilding of the walls; his memoirs are recorded in the book of Nehemiah.

NEHEMIAH, BOOK OF pp.334ff.

NERGAL-SHAREZER Senior official with Nebuchadnezzar's army: Jeremiah 39.

NICODEMUS The Jewish leader who came secretly to Jesus: John 3; 7:50ff.; 19:39/ pp.624-625, 632, 641.

NILE Great river of Egypt on which its whole economy rested; occurs in Pharaoh's dream; here the Hebrew babies were drowned and Moses was hidden; polluted in the plagues; often mentioned by the prophets: Genesis 41:1ff.; Exodus 1:22; 2:3ff.; 7:14ff.; Isaiah 18:2, etc./ *Map* p.154.

NINEVEH City which became capital of Assyria in Sennacherib's reign; Jonah was sent to save it; Nahum prophesied against it; when it fell to the

Babylonians the power of Assyria crumbled: Genesis 10:11; 2 Kings 19:36; Jonah 1:2; 3; Nahum 1:1/ *Map* p.300 *Picture* p.456.

NOAH Godly man saved from the flood which destroyed the rest of mankind; father of Ham, Shem and Japheth: Genesis 6 – 9/pp.122, 125. See 'Flood stories', pp.123-124.

NOB Place where David came to Ahimelech, and took Goliath's sword; its priests were killed by Doeg: 1 Samuel 21; 22/*Map* p.264.

NOMADS, NOMADIC LIFE Visual feature pp.198-199. *Pictures* pp.24-25, 38, 100, 117, 128-129, 134, 216, 350, 351, 354-355.

NUMBERS, BOOK OF pp.193ff.

OBADIAH 1. Steward over Ahab's household who saved 100 prophets: 2 Kings 18.
2. The prophet whose message against Edom is recorded in the book of Obadiah/p.495.

OBADIAH, BOOK OF p.495.

OBED Son of Ruth and Boaz; grandfather of David: Ruth 4:13ff.

OBED-EDOM Philistine in whose house the Ark of the Covenant remained after Uzzah's death: 2 Samuel 6:10ff.; 1 Chronicles 13.

OG King of Bashan east of the Jordan conquered by the Israelites: Numbers 21:32ff.; Deuteronomy 3/pp.202, 209.

OMRI Powerful king of Israel 885-874 BC who made Samaria his capital: 1 Kings 16/p.290.

ON See Heliopolis.

ONESIMUS Runaway slave; subject of Paul's letter to Philemon/ pp.726, 739.

ONESIPHORUS Christian who helped Paul in prison:

2 Timothy 1:16ff.; 4:19.

OPHIR Country of unknown location famous for its gold: 1 Kings 9:28, etc.

ORAL TRADITION See Story.

ORNAN See Araunah.

ORPAH Daughter-in-law of Naomi: Ruth 1/p.251.

OTHNIEL One of the Judges: Judges 3:7-11/p.240.

P

PADDAN-ARAM Where Laban lived, in north Mesopotamia: Genesis 28:2, etc./ *Map* p.127.

PAGAN GODS See Idols.

PAMPHYLIA Region in what is now southwestern Turkey, including Perga: Acts 2:10; 13:13/*Map* p.680.

PAPHOS Town in the south-west of Cyprus visited by Paul on the first missionary journey: Acts 13:6ff./ *Map* p.652 *Picture* p.704.

PAPYRUS The 'paper' of ancient times, made from stems of the papyrus reed. See 'From scroll to book', p.71. *Pictures* pp.41, 73, 74, 546, 677.

PARAN Desert area near Kadesh-barnea which the Israelites passed through after the exodus: Numbers 10:12, etc./*Map* p.166.

PASHUR Priest who put Jeremiah in the stocks: Jeremiah 20.

PASSOVER Exodus 12/p.164. See 'The great festivals', p.190 (and picture p.42); 'Passover and the Last Supper', pp.574-575.
• *Hezekiah's Passover*: 2 Chronicles 30/p.324
• *Josiah's Passover*: 2 Chronicles 35/p.326.

PATMOS Island off the coast of Turkey where John had his visions: Revelation 1:9/*Map* p.765.

PATRIARCHS Founding fathers of the nation of Israel. See Abraham, Isaac, Jacob. See

also 'Women of faith', p.143.

PAUL (JEWISH NAME SAUL) See 'Paul', pp.689-690. Apostle to the Gentiles and author of 13 New Testament letters: Acts 7:58 – Philemon/pp.647, 648, 651, 652ff., 677ff.
• *Stephen's martyrdom*: Acts 7:58ff.
• *persecution of the church*: 8:3; 9:1ff.
• *conversion*: 9 (22; 26)
• *first mission*: 13 – 14
• *Jerusalem council*: 15
• *second mission*: 15:36 – 18:22
• *third mission*: 18:23 – 20:37
• *at Jerusalem; the arrest*: 21 – 23
• *Caesarea; defence before Felix and Agrippa*: 24 – 26
• *voyage to Rome*: 27 – 28. See also the more personal passages in the letters: e.g. 2 Corinthians 1 – 2; 7; 11 – 12; Galatians 1:11 – 2:21; Philippians 1:12ff.; 3; 1 Thessalonians 2 – 3:2; Timothy 4:6ff., etc.

'PAVEMENT' In the Fort of Antonia; the place where the soldiers mocked Jesus. *Picture* p.616.

PEACE See 'The peace of God', p.636. Numbers 6:26; Psalms 4:8; 85:8-10; 119:165; Proverbs 3:17; Isaiah 9:6-7; 57:19-21; Jeremiah 6:14; 16:5; Ezekiel 34:25; Matthew 10:34; Luke 1:79; 2:14; 7:50; 19:38, 42; John 14:27; Acts 10:36; Romans 1:7; 5:1; 8:6; 14:19; Galatians 5:22; Ephesians 2:14-17; 4:3; 6:15; Philippians 4:7; Colossians 3:15; 2 Thessalonians 3:16; James 3:17-18.

PEKAH Seized the throne of Israel from Pekahiah, 752-732 BC: 2 Kings 15:25 – 16:5/p.299.

PEKAHIAH King of Israel 741-740 BC assassinated by Pekah: 2 Kings 15:22-26/ p.299.

PELATIAH Leader at Jerusalem whose death Ezekiel saw in a vision: Ezekiel 11/p.464.

PENINNAH Elkanah's second wife, who taunted the childless Hannah: 1 Samuel 1/p.256.

PENTATEUCH See Law of God/ Torah.

PENTECOST, DAY OF When Jesus' followers received the gift of God's Holy Spirit to enable them to spread the message of Jesus: Acts 2/p.645.

PENUEL Beside the River Jabbok, where Jacob wrestled with the angel: Genesis 32:22ff./*Map* p.104C4 *Picture* p.145.

PERGA Paul's first mainland stopping-place on his first mission, in what is now Turkey: Acts 13:13; 14; 25/*Map* p.652 *Picture* p.653.

PERGAMUM Town of one of the seven churches to which John wrote: Revelation 11:1; 2:12-17/Note and *map* p.765 *Pictures* p.672, 765.

PERSIA, PERSIANS An Indo-European-speaking people who conquered the Babylonians in the 6th century BC and went on to control an empire stretching from India to the Aegean and Egypt. Their main capital cities were Pasargadae and Persepolis in the mountains of south-west Persia, and the ancient Elamite capital Susa (biblical Shushan) in the lowland plain. Their liberally administered empire lasted until it became part of the still more extensive empire of Alexander the Great in the 4th century BC. Cyrus king of Persia allowed the Jews to return from exile; Esther was queen of Persia: Ezra 1:1; Esther 1:3; Daniel 8:20; 10:1, etc./pp.328ff. See 'The Persians', pp.480-481 (with pictures). *Map* p.480 (Persian Empire) *Pictures* pp.340, 341, 342,

343, 475, 476, 477.

PETER Apostle and leader of the early church (see 'The twelve disciples of Jesus', p.557); two New Testament letters bear his name: the Gospels; Acts 1 – 15; Galatians 1 – 2; 1 and 2 Peter/pp.566, 582, 615, 642, 645-646, 648-651, 752ff.
• *Call*: Matthew 4:18ff., etc.
• *recognition of Jesus as Messiah*: Matthew 16:13ff., etc.
• *presence at the transfiguration*: Matthew 17, etc.
• *denial of Jesus*: Matthew 26:69ff., etc.
• *Jesus' charge*: John 21
• *sermon at Pentecost*: Acts 2
• *healing at the Temple*: Acts 3
• *before the authorities*: Acts 4
• *release from prison*: Acts 5,12
• *at Samaria*: Acts 8:14ff.
• *raising of Tabitha*: Acts 9:36ff.
• *vision;visit to Cornelius*: Acts 10
• *Jerusalem Council*: Acts 15.

PETER, LETTERS OF pp.752ff.

PHARAOH Title of the kings of Egypt. Notably the following:
1. Abraham's pharaoh: Genesis 12:10ff.
2. Joseph's pharaoh: Genesis 40ff./pp.148, 151. See 'Joseph', pp.149-150.
3. The pharaoh of the exodus: Exodus 5ff./pp.159ff. See 'Egypt', p.156.
4. The pharaoh who gave Solomon his daughter in marriage: 1 Kings 9:16, etc./ p.156.
5. The pharaoh who sheltered Hadad: 1 Kings 11.
6. Shishak, who aided Jeroboam and attacked Jerusalem: 1 Kings 11:40; 14:25ff.; 2 Chronicles 12/ pp.157, 289, 320.
7. So: 2 Kings 17:4.
8. Tirhakah: 2 Kings 19:9; Isaiah 37:9/p.301.
9. Necho (see Necho).
10. Hophra: Jeremiah 44:30; Ezekiel 29:2/p.469.

PHARISEES AND SCRIBES The religious purists within 1st-century Judaism: p.529.
• *Clashes with Jesus*: Matthew 15:1-20; 16:1-12; 23; Mark 7; Luke 11:37 – 12:3; 18:9-14/pp.562, 571.

PHILADELPHIA Town of one of the seven churches to which John wrote: Revelation 1:11; 3:7-13/Note, *map* and picture p.765 (local landscape).

PHILEMON Christian owner of the slave Onesimus to whom Paul wrote his letter/p.739.

PHILEMON, LETTER TO p.739.

PHILIP 1. One of the 12 apostles (see 'The twelve disciples of Jesus', pp.557-558): Matthew 10:3; John 1:43ff.; 6:5ff.; 12:21-22; 14:8/p.623.
2. Son of Herod the Great; husband of Herodias: Mark 6:17/p.584.
3. Another son of Herod; tetrarch of Iturea: Luke 3:1.
4. Official and evangelist of the early church: Acts 6; 8; 21:8-9/pp.647, 648, 665.

PHILIPPI Roman colony in northern Greece, on the great Egnatian Highway; first place in Europe where Paul established a church; here an earthquake set him free from prison; later he sent a letter to the church at Philippi: Acts 16; 20:6; Philippians/ pp.657, 720 *Map* p.657 *Pictures* pp.657, 721, 754.

PHILIPPIANS, LETTER TO THE pp.720ff.

PHILISTIA, PHILISTINES Part of a group known as the Sea Peoples, who migrated into the Near East from the Aegean area in the 14th-13th centuries BC. Repulsed from Egypt, they settled on the southern coast of Palestine where they threatened the recently settled Israelites until they were finally conquered by David. The Philistines who had dealings with the patriarchs (Genesis 21; 26), were probably earlier

Aegean peoples, distinct from those of the late Bronze Age. The Philistines continued to occupy the southern coast of Palestine, and a contingent formed part of David's bodyguard. They finally lost their independence to David, and were probably largely assimilated, though they retained some cultural distinctiveness: Genesis 10:14; 20 – 21; 26; Joshua 13:2-3; Judges 3; 10; 13 – 16; 1 Samuel 4; 2 Samuel 5:25; Nehemiah 13:24; 1 Maccabees 10:83-84; Mark 7:24ff.; Acts 11:19; 15:3/*Map* p.426 *Pictures* pp.175, 258. See 'Canaanites and Philistines', p.232 (with pictures).

PHINEHAS 1. A priest; grandson of Aaron: Exodus 6:25; Numbers 25; 31:6; Joshua 22:13ff.
2. Son of Eli; killed by the Philistines when the Ark of the Covenant was captured: 1 Samuel 2:12ff.; 4/pp.258.

PHOEBE Deaconess from Cenchreae: Romans 16:1-2/ p.693.

PHOENICIA, PHOENICIANS Semitic-speaking inhabitants of today's Lebanese coast, north of Palestine. The Phoenicians were active in east Mediterranean trade from the 11th century BC onwards, operating from such cities as Tyre, Sidon, and Byblos. The name is Greek, *Phoinike*, probably meaning '(land of the) purple dye' (from *phoinos*, 'red'). They referred to themselves as Canaanites, whose descendants they were, and appear in the Old Testament as the people of Tyre, or, less commonly, Sidonians: 1 Kings 5:6, 18; Ezekiel 27:9, etc. *Pictures* pp.282, 665 (Tyre harbour), 281, 428 (models of Phoenician ships).

PHOENIX Harbour in Crete: Acts 27:12/*Map* p.667.

PHRYGIA, PHRYGIANS An Indo-European-speaking people who occupied west central Asia Minor (Turkey) after the collapse of Hittite power, and established a kingdom there in the early 1st millennium BC. Phrygia was overrun by the Cimmerians in the 7th century BC, and subsequently became part of the Lydian kingdom. The Phrygians are probably to be identified with the Mushku of the Assyrian inscriptions and 'Meshech' of the Bible, who appear as a warlike northern people: Ezekiel 32:26; 38:2-3; 39:1. Pisidian Antioch and Iconium, towns visited on Paul's first missionary journey, are in this region: Acts 2:10; 13:14ff.; 16:6/ *Maps* pp.652, 814-815

PHYLACTERY Small box containing texts from God's law, worn on the forehead by Orthodox Jews. *Pictures* pp.212, 712.

PILATE See article p.593 and 'Jews under Roman rule: the province of Judea', p.534 (both with pictures). Roman procurator of Judea who, fearing he would lose his position, allowed the Jewish authorities to crucify Jesus: Matthew 27; Mark 15; Luke 3:1; 13:1; 23; John 18 – 19.

PISGAH One of the peaks of Mt Nebo/*Map* p.209.

PISIDIA Mountainous region of inland Turkey: Acts 13:14; 14:24/*Map* p.652.

PITHOM One of the Nile delta stone-cities built for Pharaoh by Israelite slaves: Exodus 1:11.

PLAGUES OF EGYPT Exodus 7 – 12/pp.163-164.

PLAINS OF MOAB Where the Israelites assembled before crossing the Jordan: Numbers 22:1; 35:1, etc./ *Map* p.104C5.

PLANTS See Trees and plants.

POETRY OF THE BIBLE Notably, the books of poetry – Job; Psalms, etc. But there is poetry in many other books, e.g. Exodus 15 (Miriam's song), Deuteronomy 32 (Moses' song), Judges 5 (Deborah's song) and the Prophets. See 'Poetry and Wisdom', pp.344ff; 'A poet looks at Psalms', p.367.

POMPEII *Pictures* pp.537, 772.

PONTUS Roman province bordering the Black Sea: Jews from here were in Jerusalem at Pentecost; Aquila's home area: Acts 2:9; 18:2; 1 Peter 1:1/*Map* p.680.

POTIPHAR Officer of Pharaoh in whose household Joseph served: Genesis 37:36; 39. See 'Joseph', p.149.

POTSHERD A fragment of pottery; often used in Bible times as writing material for short messages. *Picture* p.31.

POTTERY *Pictures* pp.30, 31, 32, 232, 242, 304, 708. See also Work.

PRAYER, PRAYERS *Jesus' teaching*: Matthew 6:5-15; 7:7-11; 26:41; Mark 12:38-40; 13:33; 14:38; Luke 11:1-13; 18:1-14/ pp.556, 610, 613. And see 'Prayers of the Bible', p.805.

PRIESTS See Levites and priests.

PRISCILLA See Aquila and Priscilla.

PROCURATOR Roman governor: pp.535 and 536-537. See also Pilate, Felix, Festus.

PROMISED LAND Article pp.214-215. See also 'The land of Israel', pp.36-37.

PROPHECIES AGAINST THE NATIONS Many prophets pronounced God's judgment on the nations of their day: see Isaiah 13 – 23; Jeremiah 46 – 51; Ezekiel 25 – 32; Amos 1 – 2:5; Obadiah (against Edom); Nahum (against Nineveh); Zephaniah 2/pp.425ff.,

PRAYERS OF THE BIBLE
in Bible book order

Abraham's prayer for Sodom Genesis 18:22-33

Abraham's servant prays for guidance Genesis 24:12-14

Isaac's blessing Genesis 27

Jacob's vow at Bethel Genesis 28

Jacob's desperate prayer at Penuel Genesis 32

Jacob blesses his sons Genesis 48 – 49

Moses asks to see God's glory Exodus 33

Moses blesses the people of Israel Deuteronomy 33

Moses' plea for Israel when they had worshipped the golden calf Exodus 32; Deuteronomy 9

Moses pleads with God to forgive his rebellious people Numbers 14

Aaron's blessing Numbers 6

Balaam, on God's instruction, blesses Israel Numbers 22 –24

Moses' song: God and his people Deuteronomy 32

Moses' song of thanksgiving for deliverance from Egypt Exodus 15

Joshua's prayer after defeat at Ai Joshua 7

Joshua prays for time to complete his victory Joshua 10

Deborah's song of thanksgiving for victory Judges 5

Gideon's prayer for signs Judges 6

Hannah's prayer for a son 1 Samuel 1

Hannah's thanksgiving 1 Samuel 2

Samuel's prayer for the nation 1 Samuel 7

David's prayer following God's promise of a lasting succession 2 Samuel 7; 1 Chronicles 17

David's song of thanksgiving for deliverance 2 Samuel 22; Psalm 18

Solomon's prayer for wisdom 1 Kings 3; 2 Chronicles 1

Solomon's prayer at the dedication of the Temple 1 Kings 8; 2 Chronicles 6

Elijah's prayer on Mt Carmel 1 Kings 18

Elijah and the 'still, small voice' 1 Kings 19

Hezekiah's prayer at the time of Sennacherib's siege 2 Kings 19; Isaiah 37

Thanksgiving as the Ark of the Covenant is brought to Jerusalem 1 Chronicles 16

David prays for Solomon 1 Chronicles 29

Ezra's confession of the nation's sin Ezra 9

Nehemiah's prayer for his people Nehemiah 1

Public confession led by Ezra Nehemiah 9

Job seeks the reason for his suffering Job 10

Job pleads his case Job 13 – 14

Job's confession Job 42

The Psalms include an enormous number of prayers. See 'Psalms for special times and needs', p. 362, which lists them under themes.

Prayers of Isaiah Isaiah 25; 33; 63 – 64

Hezekiah's prayer in his illness Isaiah 38

Jeremiah's prayers Jeremiah 11; 14; 20; 32

Laments for the fall of Jerusalem Lamentations 1 – 4

Prayer for restoration Lamentations 5

The king's dream: Daniel's prayer Daniel 2

Nebuchadnezzar praises God Daniel 4:34-37

Daniel's prayer at the end of the exile Daniel 9

Jonah's prayer Jonah 2

Habakkuk questions God Habakkuk 1

Habakkuk's prayer Habakkuk 3

Prayers of Jesus:
- *the Lord's Prayer* Matthew 6:9-13; Luke 11:2-4
- *praise that God reveals himself to simple people* Matthew 11:25-26; Luke 10:21
- *in the Garden of Gethsemane* Matthew 26:36-44; Mark 14:32-39; Luke 22:46
- *from the cross* Matthew 27:46; Mark 15:34; Luke 23:34, 46
- *At the raising of Lazarus* John 11:41-42
- *facing death* John 12:27-28
- *for his followers* John 17

Mary's thanksgiving (Magnificat) Luke 1:46-55

Zechariah's prayer (Benedictus) Luke 1:68-79

Simeon's prayer (Nunc Dimittis) Luke 2:29-35

Prayers of the Pharisee and the tax collector Luke 18:10-13

The church's prayer in the face of threats Acts 4:24-30

Stephen's prayer at his death Acts 7:59-60

Prayers of Paul:
- *for the Christians at Rome* Romans 1:8-10
- *for Israel* Romans 10:1
- *for the church at Corinth* 1 Corinthians 1:4-9; 2 Corinthians 13:7-9
- *thanksgiving for God's comfort in trouble* 2 Corinthians 1:3-4
- *thanksgiving for spiritual riches in Christ* Ephesians 1:3-14
- *for the Ephesian Christians* Ephesians 1:16-23; 3:14-19
- *for the Philippian Christians* Philippians 1:3-11
- *for the church at Colossae* Colossians 1:3-14
- *for the Thessalonian Christians* 1 Thessalonians 1:2-3; 2:13; 3:9-13; 5:23; 2 Thessalonians 1:3; 2:13, 16-17; 3:16
- *for Timothy* 2 Timothy 1:3-4
- *for Philemon* Philemon 4-6

Peter's thanksgiving 1 Peter 1:3-5

John's prayer for Gaius 3 John 2

Doxologies – praise to God – and benedictions:
Romans 16:25-27
Ephesians 3:20-21
Philippians 4:20
1 Thessalonians 3:11-13
Hebrews 13:20-21
1 Peter 5:10-11
2 Peter 3:18
Jude 24-25

453ff., 467ff., 490, 495, 500, 504.

PROPHETS, PROPHECY See 'The Prophets': introduction, pp.408ff. and p.222; chart 'The prophets in their setting', pp.414-415; 'Prophets and prophecy', pp.423-424.
• *Old Testament books*: Isaiah – Malachi/pp.417ff.
• *true and false prophets*, pp.321, 410, 449, 464
• *in the New Testament*: p.424 and see 'Spiritual gifts', p.703.

PROSELYTES Gentiles who adopted the Jewish religion: p.531.

PTOLEMAIS Greek name for Acco: Acts 21:7/ *Map* p.526B2.

PSALMS, BOOKS OF pp.359ff.

PUBLIUS Head man on the island of Malta whose father Paul healed: Acts 27:7ff.

PUL Name for Tiglath-pileser as king of Babylon.

PURIM Esther 9/p.343. See 'The great festivals', p.191. *Picture* p.43.

PUT An African country, probably part of Libya: Jeremiah 46:9; Ezekiel 27:10, etc.

PUTEOLI Italian port where Paul landed on his way to Rome: Acts 28:13/ *Map* p.667.

Q

QUAIL Note and picture p.196.

QUIRINIUS Governor of Syria when Jesus was born: Luke 2:2; see 'The census', p.600.

QUMRAN COMMUNITY *Pictures* pp.32, 539. See also Dead Sea Scrolls.

QUOTATIONS New Testament quotations from the Old Testament, see article pp.742-743; also p.741.

R

RAAMSES One of the Nile delta store-cities built for Pharaoh by Israelite slaves: Exodus 1:11/*Map* p.166.

RABBAH Capital city of Ammon (modern Amman): Deuteronomy 3:11; 2 Samuel 12:26; 17:27; Jeremiah 49:2, etc./*Map* p.104C4.

RABSARIS, RABSHAKEH, TARTAN Titles of Assyrian officials sent by Sennacherib to parley with Hezekiah and intimidate the people: 2 Kings 18 – 19; Isaiah 36 – 37.

RACHEL Laban's daughter; Jacob's favourite wife; mother of Joseph and Benjamin: Genesis 29 – 35/ pp.141-142, 146. See 'Women of faith', p.143; 'Jacob', pp.144-145.

RAHAB The Jericho prostitute who hid the two spies: Joshua 2; 6; Matthew 1:5/pp.225-226, 550.

RAMAH Town to the north of Jerusalem; place of Rachel's tomb; mentioned in connection with Deborah, the story of the Levite, fortifications of Baasha and Asa, and Jeremiah's release: Matthew 2:18; Judges 4:5; 19:13; 1 Kings 15:17, 22; Jeremiah 40:1.

RAMESSES II Probably the pharaoh of the exodus (see Pharaoh): p.156 *Picture* p.164.

RAMOTH-GILEAD City of refuge east of the Jordan which featured in wars with Syria; chief of one of Solomon's districts; here Ahab was killed in battle and Jehu anointed: Joshua 20:8; 1 Kings 4:13; 22; 2 Kings 8:28ff.; 9/ *Map* p.104D3.

REBECCA Wife of Isaac, brought to him by Abraham's servant; Jacob her favourite son: Genesis 24 – 28/pp.139-140.

RECONCILIATION *Between God and humanity*: Romans 5:6-11; 11:15; 2 Corinthians 5:18-20; Colossians 1:20-22
• *between fellow humans*: Matthew 5:23-24; John 17:11, 20-23; 1 Corinthians 7:11; 12:12ff.; Galatians 3:28; Ephesians 2:11-22.

RECONSTRUCTIONS See Models and reconstructions.

RED SEA 'Sea of reeds' crossed by the Israelites at the exodus: p.165.

REDEMPTION Payment of a price to buy deliverance and freedom: Leviticus 25:25-55; Exodus 13:13; 21:30; 30:12; Numbers 18:15-16.
• *God's redemption of his people*: Exodus 6:6; Deuteronomy 7:8; 21:8; 2 Samuel 4:9; Job 33:22-28; Psalms 103:4; 107:2; 130:8; Isaiah 50:2; 63:9; Hosea 13:14.
• *Christ as a ransom*: Matthew 20:28; Romans 3:24; 8:23; 1 Corinthians 1:30; Galatians 3:13; Ephesians 1:7; 4:30; Colossians 1:14; Hebrews 9:12, 15; 1 Peter 1:18-19; Revelation 5:9; 14:3, 4.

REGENERATION Being re-born, re-created, made alive to God: Psalm 51:10; Jeremiah 24:7; 31:33-34; Ezekiel 11:19; 36:26; Matthew 19:28; John 1:12-13; 3:3ff.; Romans 8:9ff.; 2 Corinthians 5:17; Ephesians 2:5; Titus 3:5; 1 Peter 1:23; 1 John 2:29; 3:9; 4:7; 5:1, 4, 18.

REHOBOAM Solomon's son whose oppressive rule split the kingdom in two: 1 Kings 11:43 –14:31; 2 Chronicles 9:31 – 12:16/pp.285, 289, 319.

RELIGION, JEWISH See Judaism.

REPENTANCE Turning from sin and self-centredness to God: 2 Kings 17:13; 23:25; 2 Chronicles 33:10ff.; Job 42:6; Psalms 51; 78:34; Isaiah 1:16-20; 55:6ff.; Jeremiah 3:12-14; Ezekiel 33:12ff.; Daniel 9:3-20; Hosea 14:1ff.; Joel 2:12-14; Matthew 3:2, 8; 11:20-21; Mark 1:4; Luke 5:32; 13:3, 5;

15:7, 10, 18-21; 24:47; Acts 2:38; 17:30; 20:21; 26:20; 2 Corinthians 7:10; Hebrews 12:17; 2 Peter 3:9; Revelation 2:5.

REPHAIM Valley where David fought the Philistines: 2 Samuel 5:18, etc.

RESURRECTION Being raised from death to a new life (a bodily resurrection like Christ's): Job 19:25-27; Psalm 49:14-15; Isaiah 26:19; Ezekiel 37; Daniel 12:2; Matthew 22:30-32; Luke 14:14; 20:34-38; John 5:29; 6:39-40, 44, 54; 11:25; Acts 2:22-36; 4:33; 17:18, 32; 23:6-8; 24:15; Romans 1:4; 4:24-25; 6:5ff.; 1 Corinthians 15; Philippians 3:10-11; Colossians 2:12; 3:1-4; 1 Thessalonians 4:13ff.; Hebrews 11:35; 1 Peter 1:3; 3:21; 1 John 3:2; Revelation 20:4-6, 11-15.
• *Accounts of Jesus' resurrection*: Matthew 28; Mark 16; Luke 24; John 20; 1 Corinthians 15:3-8. See 'Jesus' resurrection', pp.619-620; 'The New Testament miracles', p.605.

RETURN FROM EXILE See books of Ezra and Nehemiah, pp.328ff.

RETURN OF JESUS CHRIST See under Jesus Christ and Future destiny.

REUBEN 1. Eldest of Jacob's 12 sons (the one who tried to save Joseph); ancestor of one of the tribes of Israel: Genesis 29:32; 30:14; 35:22; 37:42; 49:3ff./p.146, 149, 152. Family tree p.147.
2. Territory of the tribe of Reuben: Joshua 13:15-23/ *Map* p.235.

REUEL Another name for Jethro.

REVELATION What God chooses to make known to people. Christians regard the whole Bible as the record of God's revelation, for example: Deuteronomy 29:29; 1 Samuel 3:7, 21; Isaiah

22:14; 40:5; Daniel 2:22, 28ff.; Amos 3:7; Luke 17:30; John 12:38; Romans 1:17-18; 2:5; 8:18; 16:25; 1 Corinthians 14:6, 26; 2 Corinthians 12:1, 7; Galatians 1:12; 3:23; Ephesians 1:9-10, 17; 3:3, 5; 1 Peter 1:5, 12-13; 5:1; Revelation 1:1.

• *Christ as the revelation of God*: e.g. John 1:1-18; 14:7; Colossians 1:15ff.; Hebrews 1:1-3; 2 Peter 1:16ff.; 1 John 1:1ff.; Revelation 1:12-16

• *God revealed in creation*: Job 38 – 40; Psalms 8; 19; 104; Romans 1

• *God's power and glory revealed*: Exodus 24:9-11; 33:18 – 34:9; 1 Kings 19:9ff.; Isaiah 6; Ezekiel 1:10; Daniel 7:9-14; Matthew 17:1-5 (Christ's transfiguration); Revelation 4.

REVELATION OF JOHN, THE pp.763ff.

REZIN/REZON 1. Rezin, king of Syria, who attacked Judah and was killed by Assyrian King Tiglath-pileser: 2 Kings 15:37 – 16:9; Isaiah 7:1ff. **2.** Rezon, king of Damascus, who harassed Israel in Solomon's time: 1 Kings 11:23ff./ p.285.

RHEGIUM Italian port where Paul's ship put in: Acts 28:13/*Map* p.667.

RHODA The girl who answered the door to Peter after the angel had released him from prison: Acts 12:12ff.

RIBLAH This town on the Orontes was the military base of Pharaoh Necho and later of Nebuchadnezzar; here Zedekiah was blinded and his sons killed: 2 Kings 23:33; 25:6-7.

RIGHTEOUSNESS The right action and justice which characterize God and which God requires of people: Genesis 15:6; 18:23ff.; Leviticus 19:15; Deuteronomy 4:8; Job 4:7; 36:7; Psalms 1:5-6; 11:7; 23:3;

34:19; 37:25; 97:6; 98:9; Proverbs 10:2; 11:4ff.; Isaiah 53:11; 64:6; Ezekiel 3:20-21; 33:12ff.; Habakkuk 1:4, 13; Matthew 5:6, 10, 20; 6:33; 9:13; 13:43; Luke 18:9; John 16:8-10; Romans 3:10-26; 4:3ff.; 5:17ff.; 6:13ff.; 10:3ff.; 2 Corinthians 5:21; 6:14; Ephesians 6:14; Philippians 1:11; Hebrews 12:11; James 5:16; 1 Peter 2:24; 2 Peter 3:13; 1 John 2:1; 3:7.

RIZPAH Saul's concubine whose sons David gave to the Gibeonites to put to death: 2 Samuel 3:7; 21/pp.266, 274.

ROMANS, LETTER TO THE pp.681ff.

ROME, ROMANS Capital of the Roman Empire, Jews from Rome were in Jerusalem on the day of Pentecost; later Claudius expelled them; Paul wrote to the Christians at Rome, planned to visit them, and eventually reached the city as a prisoner: Acts 2:10; 18:2; Romans 1:7, 15; Acts 28/p.681. See 'Roman rule, Greek culture', pp.670-673; 'Jews under Roman rule: the province of Judea', pp.534-535; 'The city of Rome', pp.684-685; also 'Roman soldiers in the New Testament', p.592; 'The census', p.600 – all with pictures. For religious cults, see pp.672-673.

Pictures pp.33, 663, 673, 717 (theatres), 35, 588 (glass), 525 (pens), 566 (money changer), 686 (farmers), 739 (slave tag), 47, 693, 718 – see also under Caesarea, Coins, Pompeii, Ships.

RULERS OF PALESTINE, NEW TESTAMENT See 'Jews under Roman rule: the province of Judea', pp.534-535.

RUTH Moabite woman whose love for her Israelite mother-in-law Naomi led her to Bethlehem, to become the wife of Boaz and great-

grandmother of King David: Ruth/pp.251-253. See 'A portrait of Ruth', p.252.

RUTH, BOOK OF pp.251ff. See 'A story through women's eyes', p.254.

S

SABBATH The seventh day (Friday sunset to Saturday sunset) set aside under the Jewish law for rest from work and for worship; based on the pattern set by God at the creation. Jesus frequently clashed with the religious purists of his day over their interpretation of the sabbath law. See Genesis 2:2-3; Exodus 16:22-30; 20:8-11; 31:12-17; Leviticus 25; Deuteronomy 5:12-15; Nehemiah 13:15-22; Isaiah 56; 58; Matthew 12; Mark 2:23 – 3:6; Luke 4:16ff.; 6; 13:10-17; 14:1-6; John 5/pp.339, 582, 626. See 'The great festivals', p.191.

SABBATH DAY'S JOURNEY A ruling that limited travel on the sabbath: p.644.

SACRIFICE See article pp.182-183.

• *Old Testament sacrifice and offerings*: Genesis 4:2-4; 8:20; 22:1-14; Exodus 12 (the Passover); 29 – 30; Leviticus 1 – 9; 16 (the Atonement); 17; 1 Samuel 15:22; Psalms 50:5; 51:15-19; 107:22; Proverbs 15:8; Isaiah 43:23-24; Jeremiah 6:20; Hosea 3:4; Amos 4:4-5; 5:21-24. See also Tabernacle.

• *In the New Testament*: Matthew 9:13; 26:28; Luke 2:24; John 1:29; 6:51ff.; Romans 12:1; 1 Corinthians 10:14ff.; Ephesians 5:2; Philippians 2:17; 4:18; Hebrews 5:1-3; 7:27; 9:11-28; 10; 13:15-16; 1 Peter 2:5. See 'Understanding Hebrews', p.746 and pp.740ff.

SADDUCEES The conservative party within 1st-century Judaism: pp.529, 646.

SALAMIS Town in Cyprus visited by Paul and Barnabas: Acts 13:5/*Map* p.652 *Picture* p.652.

SALEM See Jerusalem.

SALOME One of the women who accompanied Jesus and the disciples from Galilee; present at the crucifixion and on the resurrection morning: Mark 15:40-41; 16:1/p.594.

SALT SEA Old Testament name for the Dead Sea.

SALT, VALLEY OF Where David defeated the Edomites: 2 Samuel 8:13.

SALVATION God's rescue of mankind from sin and death to 'eternal' life, a new quality and dimension of existence. The theme of salvation – God as saviour – runs right through the Bible. It is the heart of the Christian message: Exodus 14:30; Numbers 10:9; Deuteronomy 33:29; Judges 2:16-18; 1 Samuel 15:23; 1 Chronicles 11:14; Job 22:29; Psalms 28:8-9; 34:6; 37:40; Isaiah 30:15; 43:11-13; 45:21-22; 59:1; Jeremiah 30:10-11; Hosea 13:4; Matthew 1:21; 10:22; 19:25; 27:42; Luke 2:11; 8:12; John 3:17; 10:9; Acts 2:21; 4:12; 16:30-31; Romans 5:9-10; 10:9-13; 1 Corinthians 3:15; Ephesians 2:8; 1 Timothy 1:15; 2:4; 4:10; Hebrews 7:25. Salvation is also described in a series of metaphors or pictures: God covers people's sin – see Atonement; God acquits – see Justification; God reconciles – see Reconciliation; God redeems – see Redemption; God gives new life – see Regeneration, Life. See also Gospel.

SAMARIA Built by King Omri as capital of the northern kingdom of Israel; Ahab added a temple and palace; besieged by Syria; denounced for its wealth and corruption by the prophets; besieged and captured by the Assyrians in 722/1 BC; after this Samaria becomes the name of the general area: 1 Kings 16:24, 32; 22:39; 2 Kings 6:24; Amos 3:9ff., etc.; 2 Kings 17; Nehemiah 4:2; John 4:4ff., etc./pp.290, 295, 300, 493, 625-626 *Map* p.104B4 *Pictures* pp.19, 31, 293, 297.

SAMARITANS Descendants of the mixed Israelite/Assyrian population after Samaria fell to Assyria in 722/1 BC; worshipped according to the 'Five Books' of Moses, offering sacrifices not at Jerusalem but on Mt Gerizim; opposed Nehemiah's rebuilding of Jerusalem's city walls; hated by Jews in New Testament times – making Jesus' conversation with the Samaritan woman at the well (John 4) and his 'Good Samaritan' parable (Luke 10) shocking to his fellow Jews: pp.223, 531, 610, 649. *Picture* p.183.

SAMSON Champion of Israel against the Philistines in the time of the Judges: Judges 13 – 16/ pp.222, 246-259.

SAMUEL Judge and prophet who anointed Saul and David as Israel's first two kings: 1 Samuel 1 – 4:1; 7 – 16; 19:18ff.; 25:1; 28/pp.255ff.
• *Birth*: 1 Samuel 1
• *he hears God's voice*: 3
• *Israel's request for a king*: 8
• *Samuel and Saul*: 9ff.
• *Samuel anoints David*: 16
• *death*: 25:1
• *Saul summons Samuel by witchcraft*: 28.

SAMUEL, BOOKS OF pp.255ff.

SANBALLAT Persistent opponent of Nehemiah: Nehemiah 2:10, 19; 4; 6/ p.334.

SANCTIFICATION Making holy, setting apart for God (see Holiness); having an increasingly Christ-like character: Exodus 31:12-15; Leviticus 22:9; Deuteronomy 5:12;

Joshua 3:5; 1 Chronicles 15:14; Ezekiel 37:24-28; John 10:36; 15:1-17; 17:17-19; Romans 12:1ff.; 15:16; 1 Corinthians 1:2, 30; 6:11; 7:14; Ephesians 4:24; Philippians 1:9-11, 27; Colossians 1:10; 1 Thessalonians 3:11-13; 4:3-4; 5:23; 2 Thessalonians 2:13; 1 Timothy 4:5; Hebrews 10:10, 14, 29; 2 Peter 1:3-11; 1 John 3:2-3.

SANHEDRIN Jewish ruling Council in New Testament times/pp.590, 646, 647.

SAPPHIRA With her husband Ananias, guilty of deceiving the church: Acts 5/p.646.

SARAH/SARAI Wife of Abraham; mother of Isaac, in old age.: Genesis 11:29 – 23:19/pp.127ff.; 'Sarah', p.138.
• *Sarah gives her servant to Abraham to provide a child*: Genesis 16
• *the promise of a son*: 18
• *birth of Isaac*: 21
• *death*: 23:1.

SARDIS Town of one of the seven churches to which John wrote: Revelation 1:11; 3:1-6/Note, *map* and picture p.765.

SATAN See under Sin and evil.

SAUL 1. First king of Israel: 1 Samuel 9:2 – 31:13/ pp.259ff.
• *Anointed king*: 1 Samuel 10
• *rejected for disobedience*: 15
• *jealousy of David*: 18ff.
• *David spares his life*: 24; 26
• *consulting the medium*: 28
• *death*: 31 (also 2 Samuel 1).
2. See Paul.

SCRIBES Article pp.64-65; 'The scribe', p.332. *Pictures* pp.65, 332 (present-day), 299 (Assyrian).
• *New Testament*: see Pharisees and scribes.

SCROLL See 'From scroll to book', p.71. *Pictures* pp.32, 47, 64, 66, 69, 71, 98 – see also under Dead Sea Scrolls.

SCYTHIANS A nomadic steppe people, a group of whom

followed the Cimmerians over the Caucasus from south Russia into north-west Persia in the 7th century BC, where they became neighbours and allies of the Manneans. This association is reflected in Jeremiah 51:27 where Urartians (Ararat), Manneans (Minni) and Scythians (Ashkenaz) are summoned against Babylon. For a time they rivalled the Medes, but eventually became part of their empire and that of the succeeding Achaemenids. The main body of Scythians remained in south Russia. *Picture* p.522 (archers).

SEA PEOPLES See 'Cities of the conquest', pp.228-229; 'Canaanites and Philistines', p.232. See also Philistines.

SEALS *Pictures* pp.31 (Old Hebrew), 285 (of Shema), 300 (of King Hoshea), 477 (of Darius the Great).

SEIR Mountain, land and people of old Edom; where Esau went to live: Genesis 36:19-20.

SELA 'The cliff': capital of Edom; probably on the same site as later Petra: Isaiah 16:1. *Picture* p.323.

SELEUCIA Port of Antioch from which Paul set out on his first mission: Acts 13:4/ *Map* p.652.

SENIR Another name for Mt Hermon, or a nearby peak.

SENNACHERIB King of Assyria whose army besieged in Jerusalem in King Hezekiah's reign: 2 Kings 18:13ff.; 2 Chronicles 32; Isaiah 36:1ff./pp.300, 324.

SENNACHERIB'S PRISM Visual feature p.301.

SEPHARVAIM People from this town conquered by the Assyrians were brought to Samaria: 2 Kings 17:24; 18:34.

SEPTUAGINT The Greek translation of the Hebrew scriptures: pp.74, 515-516, 523.

SERGIUS PAULUS Pro-consul of Cyprus who asked to hear Paul's message: Acts 13:7ff./ p.652.

SERMON ON THE MOUNT Matthew 5 – 7 (Luke 6)/ pp.555-559.

SERVANT SONGS Isaiah 42 – 61/pp.434-437.

SERVANTS See Slaves.

SETH Son of Adam and Eve born after Abel's death: Genesis 4:25ff./ p.122.

SEVEN-BRANCHED CANDLESTICK Kept constantly burning to give light in the Tabernacle and Temple. *Picture* p.177.

SEVEN CHURCHES OF ASIA Revelation 1 – 3 records God's messages to these churches, inland from Ephesus in present-day Turkey/pp.767-769 Notes, *map* and pictures p.765.

SHADRACH One of Daniel's three companions in exile at Babylon; thrown into the furnace but unscathed: Daniel 1; 2:49; 3/pp.473ff.

SHALLUM Usurping king of Israel 752 BC who reigned only a month: 2 Kings 15:10ff./p.299. Also another name for Jehoahaz of Judah.

SHALMANESER Successor to Tiglath-pileser of Assyria who captured Samaria and took the Israelites into exile: 2 Kings 17.

SHAMGAR One of Israel's Judges: Judges 3:31; 5:6/ pp.239-240.

SHAPHAN Official of Josiah who reported to him the discovery of the book of the law: 2 Kings 22; 2 Chronicles 34.

SHARON Coastal plain of Israel: Isaiah 35:2, etc./ *Map* p.37 *Picture* p.368.

SHEBA Arabian country whose queen visited King Solomon: 1 Kings 10; 2 Chronicles 9/pp.284, 318; 'Solomon's trade' *map* p.319.

SHEBNA(H) High official under Hezekiah who parleyed

with Sennacherib's Assyrian delegation: 2 Kings 18 – 19; Isaiah 36 – 37.

SHECHEM 1. Important ancient town near Mt Gerizim; features in the stories of Abraham and Jacob, Joshua's renewal of the covenant, and Gideon's son Abimelech; first capital of the northern kingdom of Israel: Genesis 12:6; 33:18; 34; 37:12ff.; Joshua 24; Judges 9; 1 Kings 12/*Map* p.104B4.
2. Prince who raped Jacob's daughter Dinah: Genesis 34/p.146.

SHEM One of Noah's three sons; ancestor of a number of nations: Genesis 6:10 – 10:31/p.125 and Nations *map* p.126.

SHEEPFOLD *Picture* p.633.

SHEPHERD *Pictures* pp.137, 144, 262, 269, 350, 368, 469, 490, 633.
• *Shepherd psalm*: Psalm 23/pp.368-369
• *God, the shepherd of Israel*: Psalms 80:1, 100:31; Isaiah 40:10-11
• *shepherd leaders*: Jeremiah 25:34ff.; Ezekiel 34; Zechariah 11
• *Jesus, the 'good shepherd'*: John 10/p.633.

SHESHBAZZAR Entrusted with treasure for rebuilding the Temple after the Babylonian destruction; Sheshbazzar laid the foundations: Ezra 1:8ff.; 5:14ff.

SHILOH Sanctuary-town where Eli was priest and Hannah made her vow; here the Ark of the Covenant was kept, and Samuel heard God's call; probably destroyed by the Philistines: 1 Samuel 1 – 4/*Map* p.104B4 *Picture* p.255.

SHIMEI Benjaminite who cursed David at the time of Absalom's rebellion: 2 Samuel 16; 19; 1 Kings 2/pp.273, 277.

SHINAR Another name for Babylonia.

SHIPS *Pictures* of models pp.232 (Philistine warship), 281 (Phoenician merchant), 306 (Solomon merchant), 428 (Phoenician warship), 497 (Greek merchant), 668 (Roman corn ship) 670 (Roman warship).

SHISHAK See Pharaoh.

SHITTIM Israelite camp from which the spies were sent to Jericho; probably where Balak, king of Moab, required the prophet Balaam to lay a curse on the invading Israelites, and where Joshua was appointed Moses' successor: Joshua 2:1; 3:1; Numbers 22ff.; 25ff./*Map* p.104C5.

SHUNEM Where the Philistines camped for the battle of Gilboa in which King Saul and his son Jonathan died ; town from which Abishag, comfort of King David's old age, came; where Elisha stayed and restored a child to life: 1 Samuel 28:4; 1 Kings 1:3; 2 Kings 4/*Map* p.104B3.

SHUR Desert region to which Sarah's servant Hagar fled and through which the Israelites passed: Genesis 16:7; Exodus 15:22/*Map* p.166.

SIDDIM Valley (probably now under the waters of the Dead Sea) where King Chedorlaomer's alliance fought the kings of the plain: Genesis 14:3/*Map* p.127.

SIDON Phoenician port and merchant city, linked with Tyre; condemned by the prophets; visited by Jesus: Genesis 49:13; 1 Kings 17:9; Isaiah 23, etc.; Matthew 15:21; Luke 6:17; Acts 27:3/*Map* p.233.

SIHON Amorite king east of Jordan conquered by the Israelites: Numbers 21/p.202 *Map* p.209.

SILAS/SILVANUS A leader of the Jerusalem church who went with Paul on his missionary journeys and acted as his secretary for

some of the letters to the churches: Acts 15:22 – 18:5; 2 Corinthians 1:19; 1 Thessalonians 1:1; 2 Thessalonians 1:1; 1 Peter 5:12/pp.654, 728, 756.

SILOAM Pool in Jerusalem to which Hezekiah channelled water through a rock tunnel from the Gihon spring: 2 Kings 20:20; see visual feature 'Hezekiah's conduit', p.325. Here Jesus sent the blind man for healing: John 9:7. *Picture* p.632.

SIMEON 1. One of Jacob's 12 sons; ancestor of one of the tribes of Israel; left as hostage with Joseph in Egypt: Genesis 29:33; 34:25ff.; 42:24ff.; 49:5ff./pp.146, 152. Family tree p.147.
2. The godly man present when Jesus was brought to the Temple, whose prayer is known as the Nunc Dimittis: Luke 2:22-35/p.599.
3. Territory of the tribe of Simeon: Joshua 19/*Map* p.235.

SIMON 1. Simon Peter: see Peter.
2. Simon the Zealot, one of the 12 apostles (see 'The twelve disciples of Jesus', p.558): Matthew 10:4, etc.; Acts 1:13.
3. One of Jesus' brothers: Matthew 13:55.
4. Simon the leper, in whose house at Bethany Jesus was anointed: Matthew 26:6; Mark 14:3.
5. A Pharisee: Luke 7:40ff.
6. Simon of Cyrene who carried the cross: Matthew 27:32, etc.
7. Simon Magus, who tried to buy the gift of the Spirit: Acts 8/pp.647-648.
8. Simon the tanner in whose house at Joppa Peter had his vision: Acts 9:43ff.

SIN AND EVIL Wrong-doing; disobedience; rebellion against God.
• *Its entry into the world*: Genesis 2 – 3; 2 Peter 2:4;

Jude 5-7; Revelation 12:7-12
• *Satan – the personification of evil – and his work*: Genesis 3:1-6; Job 1 – 2; Matthew 4:1-11; 12:22-28; 16:23; Luke 13:16; 22:3-6, 31; John 8:43-47; Acts 26:15-18; 2 Corinthians 2:10-11; 11:14; 12:7; 1 Thessalonians 2:18; Hebrews 2:14; 1 Peter 5:8; 1 John 3:8-10; Revelation 2:13; 12:7-17
• *the universality of sin*: Genesis 3:16-24; 4; Deuteronomy 9:6-24; Psalm 14; Isaiah 59:1ff.; Jeremiah 44; Ezekiel 36:22-32; Matthew 15:16-20; Romans 1:28-32; 5:12; 6:23; Galatians 5:19-21; Ephesians 2:1-3; James 1:12-15; 4:1-3, 17; 1 John 3:4
• *God's victory; sin's ultimate destruction*: Psalm 103; Romans 5:15-21; 1 Corinthians 15:54-57; 1 John 3:4-10; Revelation 20.

SINAI Mountain in the Sinai peninsula where Moses received the law and the people worshipped the golden calf; also the surrounding area of desert: Exodus 19ff./*Map* p.166 *Pictures* pp.167, 748 (Mt Sinai), 112, 173, 194, 216, 348 (Sinai desert), 168 (site of Israelite camp).

SINAITICUS, CODEX See under Codex.

SINUHE, STORY OF p.155.

SISERA Canaanite army commander killed by Jael: Judges 4 – 5/ p.241.

SLAVES AND SERVANTS
• *Masters and slaves in the Old Testament*: Exodus 21; Leviticus 25, Deuteronomy 15; Jeremiah 34
• *masters and servants in Proverbs*: p.398
• *Jesus, the servant* (see also the Servant Songs in Isaiah 42 – 61): Matthew 20:28; John 13:1-17
• *Christians as Christ's slaves*: Matthew 20:26-28; Romans

1:1, etc.; Philippians 2:3-8
• *masters and slaves in the New Testament*: Ephesians 6:5-9; Colossians 3:22 – 4:1; 1 Timothy 6:1-2; Philemon; 1 Peter 2:18ff.
Pictures pp.467, 739.
SMYRNA Modern Izmir in Turkey; town of one of the seven churches to which John wrote: Revelation 1:11; 2:8-11/Note, *map* and picture p.765.
SO See Pharaoh.
SOCIETY, PLURAL See 'Jesus in a plural society', pp.83-85.
SODOM Notorious town at the south of the Dead Sea where Lot settled; destroyed with Gomorrah: Genesis 14; 19/ *Map* p.127.
SOLOMON David's son; king of Israel in its golden age; gifted with great wisdom; builder of the Temple; composer/ collector of wise sayings: 2 Samuel 12:24; 1 Kings 1 – 11; 1 Chronicles 22:5 – 23:1; 28 – 2 Chronicles 9; Proverbs 1:1; 10:1; 25:1, etc./pp.277ff., 316ff., 393, 396-398, 403ff.
• *Birth*: 2 Samuel 12:24
• *made co-regent*: 1 Kings 1
• *prayer for wisdom*: 1 Kings 3; 2 Chronicles 1
• *building of the Temple*: 1 Kings 6 – 7; 2 Chronicles 3 – 4
• *dedication of the Temple*: 1 Kings 8; 2 Chronicles 5 – 7
• *visit of the Queen of Sheba*: 1 Kings 10; 2 Chronicles 9
• *death*: 1 Kings 11:43; 2 Chronicles 10:31.
'SOLOMON'S MINES' See 'Solomon's trade', p.319. *Picture* p.357.
SON OF MAN See Jesus Christ.
SONG OF SOLOMON, THE pp.403ff.
SOSTHENES Ruler of the synagogue at Corinth: Acts 18:17; perhaps the same man as named in 1 Corinthians 1:1/p.695.
SPIES *Twelve spies sent by Moses into Canaan*: Numbers

13 – 14/ pp.196-197
• *Rahab and the two spies*: Joshua 2/pp.225-226.
SPIRIT Mind, heart, will; spirit as distinct from, or opposed to 'flesh' (see above; see also Holy Spirit): 2 Kings 2:9; Job 32:18; Psalms 31:5; 34:18; 51:10; Isaiah 26:9; 31:3; Ezekiel 37:1-10 ('breath' and 'spirit' translate the same Hebrew word); Matthew 5:3; 26:41; John 3:6; 4:23-24; Romans 2:29; 8; 1 Corinthians 2:11ff.; Galatians 5:16-25; Ephesians 4:23.
SPIRITUAL GIFTS See article p.703: 1 Corinthians 12 – 14; also Romans 12:4-8; Ephesians 4:7-16/p.702.
SPIRITUALITY See Life, ('eternal' life/new creation), Prayer, Psalms, Regeneration, Worship.
STANDARD OF UR *Picture* p.130.
STAR OF BETHLEHEM Article p.553.
STATE Authority of the powers that be: Matthew 18:24-27; 22:17-21; John 19:11; Acts 4:19; 5:29; Romans 13; 1 Peter 2:13-17/ p.691.
STEPHANAS Corinthian Christian baptized by Paul: 1 Corinthians 1:16; 16:15ff./ p.698.
STEPHEN One of the seven men chosen to take care of practical matters in the church; first Christian martyr: Acts 6 – 7/ p.647.
STOICS p.676.
STORY, STORIES See 'Storykeepers – the oral tradition', pp.62-63; 'The Bible as story', p.52; pp.47-48, 115. See also 'Creation stories', pp.117-118; 'Flood stories', pp.123-124.
Pictures pp.60-61, 63 (storytellers).
SUCCOTH 1. First stopping-place on the Israelites' journey from Egypt to Canaan: Exodus 12:37/ *Map* p.166.

2. A town where Jacob stopped, and which refused help to Gideon: Genesis 33:17; Judges 8/ *Map* p.104C4.
SUFFERING Central theme of the Book of Job, pp.349ff. (see 'Understanding Job', pp.352-353): Genesis 3:15-19; Psalms 37, 38, 73, etc. – see 'Psalms for special times and needs', p.362; Isaiah 53; Jeremiah 31:7-9 and 'Portrait of Jeremiah', p.441; Habakkuk 1; Matthew 8:14-17; 10:24-39; 24:9ff.; Luke 22:41ff.; John 9; Romans 8:18-39; 1 Corinthians 15:26; 2 Corinthians 6:3-10; 12:7; Hebrews 2:18; 12:3-11; James 5:13ff.; 1 Peter 1:3-9; 4:12ff.; Revelation 21:4.
SUMER, SUMERIANS The southern part of Babylonia and its early inhabitants; creators of Babylonian civilization, which later absorbed and succeeded them. Sumer's great period was during the 3rd millennium BC. After about 2000 BC, their language was replaced in common use by Akkadian. It was, however, preserved as a scholarly language, and in Sumerian literary texts, down to Hellenistic times. The Sumerians are not mentioned in the Bible, but 'Shinar' in Genesis is probably the counterpart of Sumerian *kengir* = Akkadian *sumeru*, meaning the land of Sumer. In Genesis it seems to refer to the whole of Babylonia. *Map* pp.814-815 *Picture* p.132 (document).
SUSA Capital of Elam; where the Persian kings spent part of the year: Ezra 4:9; Nehemiah 1:1; Esther 1:2/ *Map* p.480.
SYCHAR Samaritan town close to or identical with Shechem; site of Jacob's well: John 4:5-6/*Map* p.526B4.

SYENE Modern Aswan in Egypt: Isaiah 49:12; Ezekiel 29:10.
SYNAGOGUE p.528.
Pictures pp.66 (Tsefat), 69 (modern synagogue), 579 (Capernaum), 744 (Baram), 765 (Sardis).
SYNCRETISM The mixing of ideas from different religions: p.723.
SYRACUSE Town in Sicily where Paul stayed briefly on his way to Rome for his case to be heard by Caesar: Acts 28:12/*Map* p.667.
SYRIA, SYRIANS In the Old Testament, the Aramaean (later Syrian) land whose capital was Damascus; at times the ally, often the enemy, of Israel; see Aram, Aramaeans. In the New Testament the Roman province of which Palestine was part/*Map* p.526C1.

T

TAANACH Canaanite town near which Barak fought Sisera: Joshua 12:21; Judges 5:19/*Map* p.104B3.
TABERNACLE Exodus 25 – 27; 35 – 40/pp.169, 174. See 'The significance of the Tabernacle', pp.176-178. *Pictures* pp.176-177, 745.
TABERNACLES/SHELTERS, FEAST OF See 'The great festivals, p.191. *Pictures* pp.43, 632.
TABITHA See Dorcas.
TABOR Distinctive mountain in the plain of Jezreel where Barak gathered his forces to fight Sisera: Judges 4/ *Map* p.104B3 *Picture* p.241.
TAHPANHES Nile Delta town in Egypt to which Jeremiah was taken: Jeremiah 43:7-8/ *Map* p.454.
TALE OF TWO BROTHERS p.148.
TAMAR 1. Daughter-in-law of Judah who bore him twin sons: Genesis 38/p.148.

2. David's daughter raped by Amnon: 2 Samuel 13/p.272.

TARSHISH Far-off destination of Jonah, and source of minerals; may be Tartessus in Spain; the phrase 'ship of Tarshish' describes the vessel rather than its destination: Jonah 1:3; Isaiah 23:6; Ezekiel 38:13, etc.

TARSUS Important town in what is now southern Turkey; birthplace of Paul: Acts 9:11, 30; 21:39/ *Map* p.652.

TARTAN See Rabsaris.

TEKOA Town in the Judean hills from which the wise woman came to David; home of Amos: 2 Samuel 14; Amos 1:1/*Map* p.418.

TEMAN Part of Edom; its inhabitants were famous for their wisdom; home area of Job's friend Eliphaz: Jeremiah 49:7; Job 2:11/*Map* p.458.

TEMPLE, JERUSALEM See 'Solomon's Temple and its successors', pp.279-284 and 'Herod's Temple', pp.532-533 (both with pictures).
• *Solomon's Temple*: 1 Kings 6; 2 Chronicles 3ff./pp.278-282, 316-318
• *repair by Joash*: 2 Kings 12; 2 Chronicles 24/pp.298, 323
• *rebuilding of the Temple*: Ezra 3 – 6; Haggai; Zechariah/ pp.330-332, 505ff.
• *Ezekiel's vision*: Ezekiel 40 – 48/ pp.470-472
• *Jesus purges the Temple*: Matthew 21; Mark 11; John 2/pp.570-571, 624
• *Jesus predicts its destruction*: Matthew 24; Mark 13; Luke 21.
Pictures pp.572 (Temple plunder, Arch of Titus), 256, 274, 316-317, 318, 331, 387, 555, 576, 635 (Temple area).

TEMPLE SITE 2 Samuel 24:16ff.; 1 Chronicles 21:15ff./pp.275, 312-313.

TEMPLES *Pictures* pp.156 (temple of Amun, Karnak), 663, 718 (temples of Artemis/Diana and Hadrian, Ephesus), 671 (temple of Artemis, Jerash), 705 (temple of Apollo, Corinth).

TEMPTATION Trial, testing: Genesis 3; 22:1; Exodus 17:7; Deuteronomy 6:16; Psalm 95:9; Matthew 6:13; 22:35; 26:41; Acts 5:9; 1 Corinthians 7:5; 10:9-13; Hebrews 2:18; 4:15; James 1:2-4, 13-15.
• *The temptation of Jesus*: Matthew 4:1-11; Mark 1:12-13; Luke 4:1-13/ pp.554-555.

TEN COMMANDMENTS Exodus 20; Deuteronomy 5/pp.168-169, 209-212. See 'A way of life: the Ten Commandments', pp.170-172.

TEN TOWNS See Decapolis.

TERAH Father of Abraham: Genesis 11:24ff./pp.126-127.

THADDAEUS See Judas, son of James.

THEBES Capital city of Egypt sacked by the Assyrians: Jeremiah 46:25; Nahum 3:8, *Map* p.154.

THEOPHILUS Roman to whom Luke addressed his Gospel and Acts: Luke 1:3; Acts 1:1/ pp.596, 644.

THESSALONIANS, LETTERS TO THE pp.728ff.

THESSALONICA Important city of northern Greece (modern Thessaloniki) evangelized by Paul; he wrote two letters to the church there: Acts 17; 1 and 2 Thessalonians/ pp.657, 728 *Map* p.657 *Picture* p.728.

THOMAS One of the 12 apostles (see 'The twelve disciples of Jesus', p.558) who was absent when the others first saw the risen Christ: Matthew 10:3, etc.; John 11:16; 14:5; 20:24ff./ pp.634, 638, 641.

THYATIRA Home town of Lydia who was converted at Philippi; one of John's letters to the seven churches was addressed to Thyatira: Acts 16:14; Revelation 1:11; 2:18-29/Note, *map* and picture p.765.

TIBERIAS Spa town on the west shore of Lake Galilee, built by Herod Antipas and named after the Emperor Tiberius: John 6:23/ *Map* p.526C2.

TIBERIUS Roman emperor: Luke 3:1 *Picture* p.534 (and see Coins).

TIGLATH-PILESER Powerful king of Assyria to whom Ahaz turned for help against Syria and Israel: 2 Kings 15:29; 16:7ff.; 2 Chronicles 28:16ff./pp.299 (with picture), 324, 433.

TIGRIS Second great river of Mesopotamia: Genesis 2:14.

TIME-CHARTS 'Making connections – the Bible and world history', pp.26-27; 'The Bible in its time', pp.28-29; 'The Old Testament story', pp.100-103; 'Kings of Israel and Judah', pp.306-307; 'The Jews under Persian rule', p.329; 'The most important prophets', p.411; 'The Prophets in their setting', pp.414-415; 'Major events of Jeremiah's lifetime', p.443; 'Rulers of Palestine "between the Testaments"', p.520; 'The New Testament story', pp.536-537; Acts, p.643; 'The New Testament Letters', p.680.

TIMNAH Home of Samson's Philistine wife: Judges 14/ *Map* p.104A5.

TIMNATH-SERAH Town where Joshua was buried: Joshua 24:30/*Map* p.104B4.

TIMOTHY Paul's young companion and fellow missionary, later with responsibility for the church at Ephesus; Paul sent him two letters on the subject of leadership in the churches: Acts 16:1ff.; 17:14; 18:5; 19:22; 20:4; 1 Corinthians 4:17; 16:10; 2 Corinthians 1:19; Philippians 2:19ff.; 1 Thessalonians 3:2ff.; 1 and 2 Timothy; Hebrews 13:23/ pp.654, 657, 720, 728, 732ff.

TIMOTHY, LETTERS TO pp.732ff.

TIRHAKAH See Pharaoh.

TIRZAH Former Canaanite town which became the early capital of the northern kingdom of Israel: Joshua 12:24; 1 Kings 14:17; 15:21, etc./ *Map* p.104B4.

TISHBE Home of Elijah, in Gilead: 1 Kings 17:1/ *Map* p.104C3.

TITHES The custom of each individual giving back to God, each year, one tenth of the year's livestock and produce; received by the Levites in Jerusalem: Genesis 14:17-20; Leviticus 27:30-33, Numbers 18; Deuteronomy 14; Malachi 3:8-12/pp.213, 514.

TITUS Paul's companion and fellow missionary; smoothed things over with the Corinthian church; sent to Crete, where Paul sent him a letter of advice: 2 Corinthians 2:13; 7:6ff.; 8; 12:18; Galatians 2; 2 Timothy 4:10; Titus/ pp.707, 709, 736, 737-738.

TITUS' ARCH *Picture* p.572.

TITUS, LETTER TO p.737.

TOB Aramaean region northeast of Israel mentioned in connection with Jephthah and David: Judges 11:3; 2 Samuel 10:6/*Map* p.268.

TOBIAH An opponent of Nehemiah: Nehemiah 2; 4; 6; 13/pp.334, 339.

TOMBS *Pictures* pp.479 (Tomb of Shebna inscription), 571 ('whited sepulchres'), 544, 594, 617, 619 (1st-century tombs).

TOPHETH Place of child-sacrifice in the Valley of Hinnom.

TORAH See Law of God/Torah.

TRACHONITIS Area north-east of Israel in Herod Philip's tetrarchy at the time of Jesus: Luke 3:1/*Map* p.526D2.

TRANSFIGURATION See under Jesus Christ.

TREATIES See Covenant.

TREES AND PLANTS, BIBLE See visual feature pp.40-41, and references listed there: additional pictures pp.279 (cedar), 512, 591 (thistles/ thorns).

TROAS Port near Troy in north-west Turkey, used several times by Paul; here he had his dream of the man from Macedonia, and restored Eutychus to life: Acts 16:8ff.; 20:5ff.; 2 Corinthians 2:12/*Map* p.657.

TROPHIMUS Ephesian Christian who went with Paul to Jerusalem: Acts 20:4; 21:29; 2 Timothy 4:20/p.736.

TRUTH, SEARCH FOR See 'A scientist looks at the Bible', pp.92-94.

TWELVE APOSTLES See 'The twelve disciples of Jesus', pp.557-558.

• *Call and mission*: Matthew 10; Mark 3; 6; Luke 6; 9; John 1:35ff./ pp.560-561, 582, 584, 604, 607, 623-624.

TYCHICUS Christian who went with Paul to Jerusalem; accompanied Onesimus to Colossae, taking Paul's letters: Acts 20:4; Ephesians 6:21; Colossians 4:7ff.; 2 Timothy 4:12; Titus 3:12/ pp.726, 736.

TYPOLOGY The Old Testament prefiguring of the New: p.743.

TYRE Phoenician sea-port and city-state on the coast of Lebanon; famous centre of trade; Hiram of Tyre supplied David and Solomon with timber and materials for the Temple; Jezebel was the daughter of a king of Tyre and Sidon; the prophets condemned Tyre's pride and luxury: 2 Samuel 5:11; 1 Kings 5; 9:10-14; 16:31; Isaiah 23, etc./*Map* p.104B1 *Pictures* pp.282, 665.

U

UR Famous city in south Babylonia; family home of Abraham: Genesis 11:28ff. etc./*Map* p.127 *Picture* p.130 (Standard of Ur). See also visual feature within 'Abraham', pp.132-133.

URARTIANS A people speaking a language related to Hurrian, who emerged as a military power in the area of Armenia in the 9th century BC; possibly descendants of Hurrians who had occupied that area; a military threat to the Assyrians with whom they were often at war. Their chief god was Haldi, after whom some authors have referred to them as Chaldians (not to be confused with Chaldeans). Noah's ark is said to have landed on the mountains of Ararat (Genesis 8:4), i.e. somewhere in what was later Urartu, not necessarily modern Mt Ararat, which only received this name at a later date.

URIAH/URIJAH 1. A Hittite warrior in David's army; husband of Bathsheba; sent to his death by David: 2 Samuel 11/pp.270-271. **2.** Priest in Jerusalem: 2 Kings 16. **3.** Prophet in Jeremiah's time put to death by Jehoiakim: Jeremiah 26:20ff./p.450. **UZ** Home country of Job, probably in the region of Edom: Job 1:1.

UZZAH Man who touched the Ark of the Covenant as it was being moved from Kiriath-jearim and died: 2 Samuel 6/p.268.

UZZIAH See Azariah.

V

VALLEY OF AIJALON Where the sun 'stood still' while Joshua fought: Joshua 10/*Map* p.104B5.

VALLEY OF DRY BONES Ezekiel 37/p.471.

VASHTI Queen whom Ahasuerus deposed: Esther 1/p.340.

VINE, VINEYARD *Naboth's vineyard*: 1 Kings 21/pp.292-293 *vineyard of Israel*: Isaiah 5/p.421

• *parables of Jesus*: Matthew 20:1-16; 21:28-45

• *'I am the true vine'*: John 15/p.638. *Pictures* pp.40, 42, 43, 293, 427, 638.

VIRGIN BIRTH OF JESUS Matthew 1; Luke 1 – 2/ pp.550-552 and article p.596.

VISIONS *Of Isaiah*: Isaiah 6/pp.421-422

• *of Ezekiel*: Ezekiel 1; 8 – 11; 37:40 – 48/pp.462ff.

• *of Daniel*: Daniel 7 - 12/ pp.476ff.

• *of Zechariah*, pp.507ff.

• *of Peter at Joppa*: Acts 10:3/ pp.649-650

• *of John*: Revelation/pp.766ff.

VOYAGE TO ROME, PAUL'S Acts 27 – 28/pp.668-669 *Map* p.667.

W

WAR, WEAPONS *Pictures* pp.262-263 (sling, bow, helmet), 301, 302 ('The siege of Lachish'), 375, 431, 432 (Assyrians), 455, 500-501, 522 (archers, helmet).

WATCHTOWER, WATCHMAN Isaiah 21; Ezekiel 3; 33; Habakkuk 2/pp.462, 469, 503 (with picture p.502). *Pictures* pp.408-409, 412.

WELL *Pictures* pp.35, 137, 625.

WISDOM The expression of an attitude to life which is centred on God and his laws (see 'Wisdom in Proverbs and Job', p.395): Exodus 28:3; Deuteronomy 34:9; 1 Kings 3:5-14; Job 12:13; 28; Psalms 37:30; 104:24; Proverbs 1; 8; 9; Ecclesiastes 1:13-18; 2:12-26; Isaiah 11:2; Daniel 2:20-23; Matthew 13:54; Luke 2:52; 21:15; Acts 6:3; 1 Corinthians 1:17 – 2:16; 3:18ff.; Colossians 3:16; 2 Timothy 3:15; James 1:5; 3:13-18.

WISDOM LITERATURE *In the Old Testament*: Job, Proverbs, Ecclesiastes/'Poetry and Wisdom': introduction, pp.346-347

• *in the deuterocanonical books*: pp.517-518.

WISDOM OF AMENEMOPE pp.157, 393 (with picture).

WISE MEN Matthew 2/p.552.

WITCHCRAFT See Magic and witchcraft.

WOMAN AT THE WELL John 4/pp.625-626.

WORDS FROM THE CROSS, JESUS' p.590.

WORK *Pictures* pp.42, 43, 253, 312-313, 376, 396, 484-485, 494 (farming), 396 (spinning), 111, 246, 730 (weaving), 419 (dyeing), 449, 517 (the potter), 31, 488 (olive oil production), 292 (baking bread), 106, 163 (brick-making). See also Farmer, farming, Fish, fishing, Scribe, Shepherd.

WORLD See 'God and the universe', p.379.

• *The created universe; the earth*: 2 Samuel 22:16; Job 34:13; Psalms 24:1; 50:12; 90:2; Matthew 4:8; 16:26; John 1:9; Romans 5:12

• *people*: Psalm 9:8; Isaiah 13:11; Luke 2:1; John 3:16-17; 8:26; 14:31; 1 Corinthians 1:21 *the present age*: Matthew 24:3; 28:20; Luke 18:30; Ephesians 1:21.

• *the world in rebellion against God*: John 7:7; 8:23; 14:17; 15:18-19; James 4:4; 1 John 2:15-17; 4:4-5; 5:4-5.

WORSHIP *In Israel*: p.223 and see 'The Psalms in their setting', pp.363-364; see also under Levites, Music, Tabernacle, Temple

• *in Egypt*, p.154. *Picture* p.315.

WRITING *Pictures* pp.31 (Egyptian demotic and hieroglyph), 32, 43, 64, 65, 98, 304 (Hebrew), 71, 72, 73, 546 (Greek), 74 (Coptic), 525 (pens, etc.), 761 (woman with writing-tablet). See also Cuneiform, Hieroglyph, Inscriptions.

YEMENITE BRIDE *Picture* p.406; Yemenite jewellery, see under Gold and jewellery.

ZACCHAEUS Tax collector who climbed a tree at Jericho to get a glimpse of Jesus: Luke 19:1-10/ p.614.

ZACHARIAH/ZACHARIAS See Zechariah.

ZADOK Priest at David's court with Abiathar; founder of the line of Israel's high priests: 2 Samuel 15; 17:15; 19:11; 1 Kings 1; 2:25; 1 Chronicles 6:1, etc./p.277.

ZAREPHATH Town belonging to Sidon, where Elijah stayed; here he restored the widow's son to life: 1 Kings 17:8ff./ *Map* p.290.

ZEALOTS First-century Jewish freedom fighters: pp.530-531.

ZEBOIIM Town at the south of the Dead Sea, destroyed with Sodom and Gomorrah: Genesis 10:19; 14; Deuteronomy 29:23/*Map* p.127.

ZEBULUN 1. One of Jacob's 12 sons; ancestor of one of the tribes of Israel: Genesis 30:20; 49:13/p.152. Family tree p.147.
2. Territory of the tribe of Zebulun: Joshua 19:10-16/ *Map* p.235.

ZECHARIAH/ZECHARIAS The name of a great number of people, notably the following:
1. Zechariah son of Jeroboam II, king of Israel 753-752 BC; assassinated by Shallum: 2 Kings 15:8-12/p.299.
2. The prophet who, with Haggai, spurred the people on to rebuild the Temple, and whose prophecies are recorded in the book of Zechariah/pp.507ff.
3. The father of John the Baptist: Luke 1/pp.597-599.

ZECHARIAH, BOOK OF pp.507ff.

ZEDEKIAH 1. Last king of Judah, whose rebellion brought Nebuchadnezzar's army and destruction on Jerusalem: 2 Kings 24 – 25; 2 Chronicles 36; Jeremiah 21; 32; 34; 37 – 39, etc./ pp.304-305, 327, 450-451.
2. A false prophet of Ahab's day: 1 Kings 22; 2 Chronicles 18.

ZEPHANIAH The prophet whose prophecies are recorded in the book of Zephaniah/p.504.

ZEPHANIAH, BOOK OF p.504.

ZERAH The 'Ethiopian' who invaded Judah and was routed by Asa: 2 Chronicles 14:9-14/p.320.

ZERUBBABEL Leader in the return from exile and rebuilding of the Temple: Ezra 2:2; 3 – 5; Haggai; Zechariah 4/ pp.328, 330, 505-506.

ZIBA Saul's servant who told David of Mephibosheth: 2 Samuel 9; 16/p.273.

ZIKLAG Town taken by the Philistines and given to David by Achish; raided by the Amalekites: 1 Samuel 27:6; 30/*Map* p.264.

ZILPAH Leah's servant who bore Jacob two sons: Genesis 29:24; 30:9–10. Family tree p.147.

ZIMRI Ruler of Israel for one week, 885 BC: 1 Kings 16/ p.290.

ZIN Area of desert near Kadesh-barnea where the Israelites wandered after the exodus: Numbers 13:21; 20:1; 27:14, etc./see *Map* p.166.

ZION One of the hills of Jerusalem; David's city; also stands for Jerusalem as the city of God's Temple/pp.362, 373, 380, 388.

ZIPH Area to which David fled from Saul; but the men of the town betrayed him: 1 Samuel 23:14ff./*Map* p.264.

ZIPPORAH Jethro's daughter; wife of Moses: Exodus 2:21; 4:24ff.; 18/p.166.

ZOAN/TANIS Ancient town in the Egyptian Nile delta: Numbers 13:22; Isaiah 19:11, etc./*Map* p.154.

ZOAR Town near Sodom to which Lot fled escaping destruction: Genesis 13:10; 14:2, 8; 19:18ff./ *Map* p.127.

ZOBAH Somewhere in the region of Damascus; Aramaean kingdom defeated by David: 2 Samuel 8:3; 10:6; 1 Kings 11:23.

ZOPHAR One of Job's three friends: Job 2:11, etc./ pp.351, 355.

ZORAH Birthplace of Samson: Judges 13:2; 16:31/ *Map* p.246.

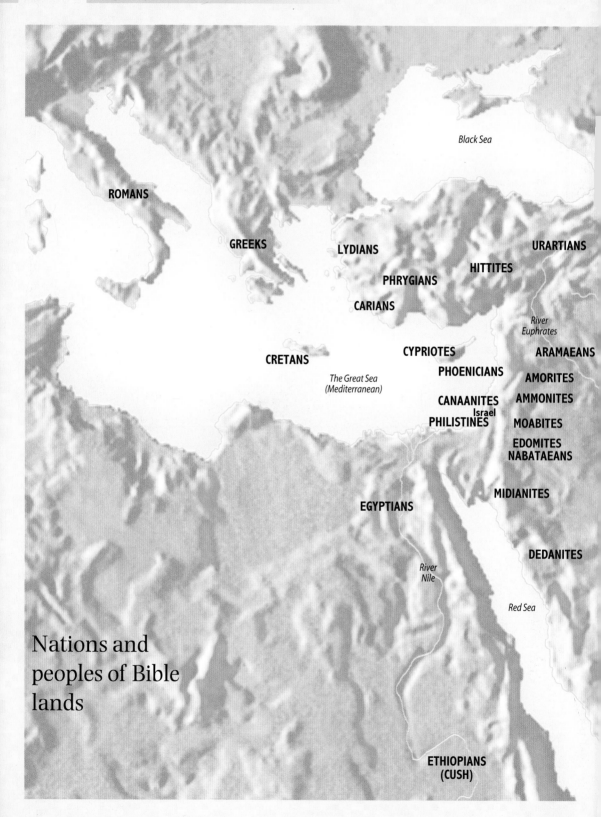

Black Sea

ROMANS

GREEKS

LYDIANS

URARTIANS

HITTITES

PHRYGIANS

CARIANS

River
Euphrates

CYPRIOTES

ARAMAEANS

CRETANS

AMORITES

PHOENICIANS

The Great Sea
(Mediterranean)

CANAANITES

AMMONITES

Israel

PHILISTINES

MOABITES

EDOMITES
NABATAEANS

MIDIANITES

EGYPTIANS

DEDANITES

River
Nile

Red Sea

Nations and peoples of Bible lands

ETHIOPIANS
(CUSH)